VW Golf & Jetta

Owners Workshop Manual

A K Legg AAE MIMI

Models covered

(4610 - 3AS3 - 416)

Golf / Golf Plus ('Mk V') Hatchback & Estate and Jetta Saloon

Petrol: 1.4 litre (1390cc), 1.6 litre (1595cc & 1598cc) & 2.0 litre (1984cc), inc. turbo
Diesel: 1.9 litre (1896cc) & 2.0 litre (1968cc) inc. turbo-diesel

Does NOT cover models with 1.4 litre TSi supercharged/turbo ('Twincharger') petrol engine, 2.0 litre chain drive petrol engine, 1.6 litre 'Fuelflex' engine, or 1.6 litre TDi diesel engine
Does NOT cover GTi 30, GTi Pirelli, R32 or 4-Motion models

ABCDE
FGHIJ
K

A book in the **Haynes Owners Workshop Manual Series**

ISBN **978 0 85733 976 8**

British Library Cataloguing in Publication Data
A catalogue record for this book is available from the British Library.

Printed in the USA

Haynes Publishing
Sparkford, Yeovil, Somerset BA22 7JJ, England

Haynes North America, Inc
861 Lawrence Drive, Newbury Park, California 91320, USA

Haynes Publishing Nordiska AB
Box 1504, 751 45 UPPSALA, Sverige

Printed using 33-lb Resolute Book 65 4.0 from Resolute Forest Products Calhoun, TN mill. Resolute is a member of World Wildlife Fund's Climate Savers programme committed to significantly reducing GHG emissions. This paper uses 50% less wood fibre than traditional offset. The Calhoun Mill is certified to the following sustainable forest management and chain of custody standards: SFI, PEFC and FSC Controlled Wood.

Contents

LIVING WITH YOUR VW GOLF/JETTA

Contents

The Mk 5 Golf and Jetta models covered by this manual date from early 2004 to 2009.

Models have been produced with a wide range of engines, including 1.4, 1.6 and 2.0 litre petrol turbo and non-turbo versions, as well as normally-aspirated and turbocharged 1.9 and 2.0 litre diesel engines. All engines use either 'indirect' or 'direct' fuel injection, and are fitted with a wide range of emission control systems. All the engines are of a well-proven design and, provided regular maintenance is carried out, are unlikely to give trouble.

Golf models are available in 3- and 5-door Hatchback bodystyles, 5-door estate, whilst Jetta models are available in 4-door Saloon form. Golf Plus models use the same engines, suspension and braking systems, but have a higher roof line to give an MPV 'feel'.

Fully-independent front and rear suspension is fitted, with the components attached to a subframe assembly; the rear suspension uses trailing arms together with multi-link transverse arms.

A five- or six-speed manual gearbox is fitted, with a six-speed automatic gearbox or 6/7 speed DSG semi-automatic transmission available as an option for some petrol and diesel models.

A wide range of standard and optional equipment is available within the model range to suit most tastes, including an anti-lock braking system and air conditioning.

For the home mechanic, Golf and Jetta models are straightforward vehicles to maintain, and most of the items requiring frequent attention are easily accessible.

Your Golf and Jetta Manual

The aim of this manual is to help you get the best value from your vehicle. It can do so in several ways. It can help you decide what work must be done (even should you choose to get it done by a garage). It will also provide information on routine maintenance and servicing, and give a logical course of action and diagnosis when random faults occur. However, it is hoped that you will use the manual by tackling the work yourself. On simpler jobs it may even be quicker than booking the car into a garage and going there twice, to leave and collect it. Perhaps most important, a lot of money can be saved by avoiding the costs a garage must charge to cover its labour and overheads.

The manual has drawings and descriptions to show the function of the various components so that their layout can be understood. Tasks are described and photographed in a clear step-by-step sequence.

References to the 'left' and 'right' of the vehicle are in the sense of a person in the driver's seat facing forward.

Acknowledgements

Thanks are due to Draper Tools Limited, who provided some of the workshop tools, and to all those people at Sparkford who helped in the production of this manual.

This manual is not a direct reproduction of the vehicle manufacturer's data, and its publication should not be taken as implying any technical approval by the vehicle manufacturers or importers.

We take great pride in the accuracy of information given in this manual, but vehicle manufacturers make alterations and design changes during the production run of a particular vehicle of which they do not inform us. No liability can be accepted by the authors or publishers for loss, damage or injury caused by any errors in, or omissions from, the information given.

Working on your car can be dangerous. This page shows just some of the potential risks and hazards, with the aim of creating a safety-conscious attitude.

General hazards

Scalding

• Don't remove the radiator or expansion tank cap while the engine is hot.

• Engine oil, transmission fluid or power steering fluid may also be dangerously hot if the engine has recently been running.

Burning

• Beware of burns from the exhaust system and from any part of the engine. Brake discs and drums can also be extremely hot immediately after use.

Crushing

• When working under or near a raised vehicle, always supplement the jack with axle stands, or use drive-on ramps.
Never venture under a car which is only supported by a jack.

• Take care if loosening or tightening high-torque nuts when the vehicle is on stands. Initial loosening and final tightening should be done with the wheels on the ground.

Fire

• Fuel is highly flammable; fuel vapour is explosive.

• Don't let fuel spill onto a hot engine.

• Do not smoke or allow naked lights (including pilot lights) anywhere near a vehicle being worked on. Also beware of creating sparks (electrically or by use of tools).

• Fuel vapour is heavier than air, so don't work on the fuel system with the vehicle over an inspection pit.

• Another cause of fire is an electrical overload or short-circuit. Take care when repairing or modifying the vehicle wiring.

• Keep a fire extinguisher handy, of a type suitable for use on fuel and electrical fires.

Electric shock

• Ignition HT and Xenon headlight voltages can be dangerous, especially to people with heart problems or a pacemaker. Don't work on or near these systems with the engine running or the ignition switched on.

• Mains voltage is also dangerous. Make sure that any mains-operated equipment is correctly earthed. Mains power points should be protected by a residual current device (RCD) circuit breaker.

Fume or gas intoxication

• Exhaust fumes are poisonous; they can contain carbon monoxide, which is rapidly fatal if inhaled. Never run the engine in a confined space such as a garage with the doors shut.

• Fuel vapour is also poisonous, as are the vapours from some cleaning solvents and paint thinners.

Poisonous or irritant substances

• Avoid skin contact with battery acid and with any fuel, fluid or lubricant, especially antifreeze, brake hydraulic fluid and Diesel fuel. Don't syphon them by mouth. If such a substance is swallowed or gets into the eyes, seek medical advice.

• Prolonged contact with used engine oil can cause skin cancer. Wear gloves or use a barrier cream if necessary. Change out of oil-soaked clothes and do not keep oily rags in your pocket.

• Air conditioning refrigerant forms a poisonous gas if exposed to a naked flame (including a cigarette). It can also cause skin burns on contact.

Asbestos

• Asbestos dust can cause cancer if inhaled or swallowed. Asbestos may be found in gaskets and in brake and clutch linings. When dealing with such components it is safest to assume that they contain asbestos.

Special hazards

Hydrofluoric acid

• This extremely corrosive acid is formed when certain types of synthetic rubber, found in some O-rings, oil seals, fuel hoses etc, are exposed to temperatures above 4000C. The rubber changes into a charred or sticky substance containing the acid. *Once formed, the acid remains dangerous for years. If it gets onto the skin, it may be necessary to amputate the limb concerned.*

• When dealing with a vehicle which has suffered a fire, or with components salvaged from such a vehicle, wear protective gloves and discard them after use.

The battery

• Batteries contain sulphuric acid, which attacks clothing, eyes and skin. Take care when topping-up or carrying the battery.

• The hydrogen gas given off by the battery is highly explosive. Never cause a spark or allow a naked light nearby. Be careful when connecting and disconnecting battery chargers or jump leads.

Air bags

• Air bags can cause injury if they go off accidentally. Take care when removing the steering wheel and trim panels. Special storage instructions may apply.

Diesel injection equipment

• Diesel injection pumps supply fuel at very high pressure. Take care when working on the fuel injectors and fuel pipes.

Warning: Never expose the hands, face or any other part of the body to injector spray; the fuel can penetrate the skin with potentially fatal results.

Remember...

DO

• Do use eye protection when using power tools, and when working under the vehicle.

• Do wear gloves or use barrier cream to protect your hands when necessary.

• Do get someone to check periodically that all is well when working alone on the vehicle.

• Do keep loose clothing and long hair well out of the way of moving mechanical parts.

• Do remove rings, wristwatch etc, before working on the vehicle – especially the electrical system.

• Do ensure that any lifting or jacking equipment has a safe working load rating adequate for the job.

DON'T

• Don't attempt to lift a heavy component which may be beyond your capability – get assistance.

• Don't rush to finish a job, or take unverified short cuts.

• Don't use ill-fitting tools which may slip and cause injury.

• Don't leave tools or parts lying around where someone can trip over them. Mop up oil and fuel spills at once.

• Don't allow children or pets to play in or near a vehicle being worked on.

The following pages are intended to help in dealing with common roadside emergencies and breakdowns. You will find more detailed fault finding information at the back of the manual, and repair information in the main chapters.

If your car won't start and the starter motor doesn't turn

- ☐ If it's a model with automatic transmission, make sure the selector is in P or N.
- ☐ Open the bonnet and make sure that the battery terminals are clean and tight.
- ☐ Switch on the headlights and try to start the engine. If the headlights go very dim when you're trying to start, the battery is probably flat. Get out of trouble by jump starting (see next page) using a friend's car.

If your car won't start even though the starter motor turns as normal

- ☐ Is there fuel in the tank?
- ☐ Is there moisture on electrical components under the bonnet? Switch off the ignition, then wipe off any obvious dampness with a dry cloth. Spray a water-repellent aerosol product (WD-40 or equivalent) on ignition and fuel system electrical connectors like those shown in the photos. (Note that diesel engines don't usually suffer from damp).

A Check the condition and security of the battery connections.

B Check the fuses in the fusebox located on the left-hand side of the engine compartment

Check that electrical connections are secure (with the ignition switched off) and spray them with a water-dispersant spray like WD-40 if you suspect a problem due to damp.

C Check the wiring to the ignition coils beneath the engine top cover (petrol models only)

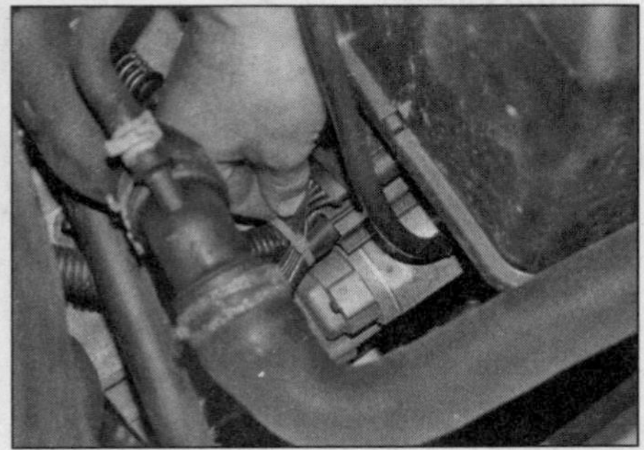

D Check that the starter motor wiring is secure

Jump starting

HAYNES HiNT *Jump starting will get you out of trouble, but you must correct whatever made the battery go flat in the first place. There are three possibilities:*

***1** The battery has been drained by repeated attempts to start, or by leaving the lights on.*

***2** The charging system is not working properly (alternator drivebelt slack or broken, alternator wiring fault or alternator itself faulty).*

***3** The battery itself is at fault (electrolyte low, or battery worn out).*

When jump-starting a car, observe the following precautions:

✓ Before connecting the booster battery, make sure that the ignition is switched off.

Caution: Remove the key in case the central locking engages when the jump leads are connected

✓ Ensure that all electrical equipment (lights, heater, wipers, etc) is switched off.

✓ Take note of any special precautions printed on the battery case.

✓ Make sure that the booster battery is the same voltage as the discharged one in the vehicle.

✓ If the battery is being jump-started from the battery in another vehicle, the two vehicles MUST NOT TOUCH each other.

✓ Make sure that the transmission is in neutral (or PARK, in the case of automatic transmission).

Budget jump leads can be a false economy, as they often do not pass enough current to start large capacity or diesel engines. They can also get hot.

1 Connect one end of the red jump lead to the positive (+) terminal of the flat battery

2 Connect the other end of the red lead to the positive (+) terminal of the booster battery.

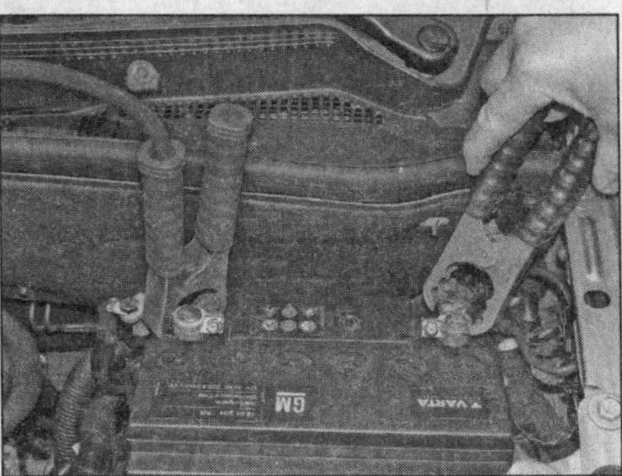

3 Connect one end of the black jump lead to the negative (-) terminal of the booster battery

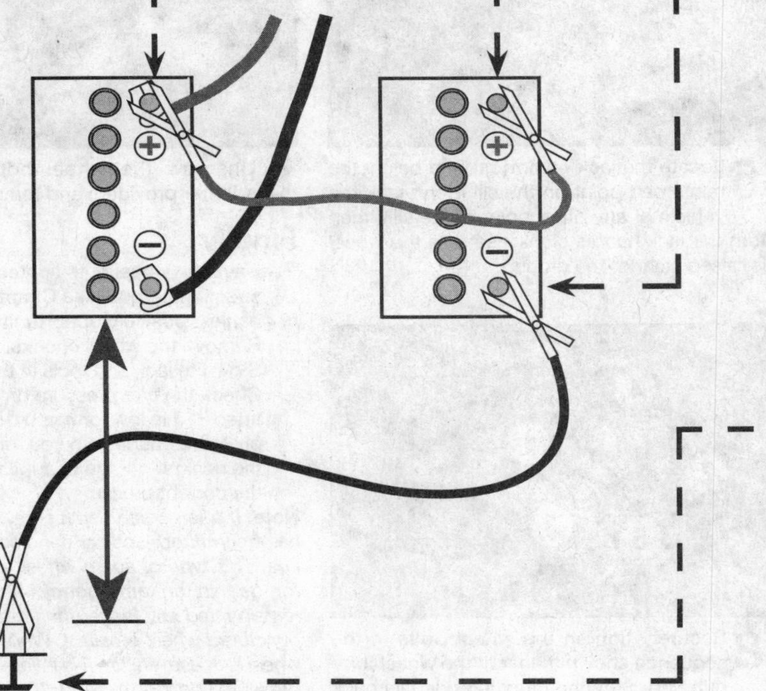

4 Connect the other end of the black jump lead to a bolt or bracket on the engine block, well away from the battery, on the vehicle to be started.

5 Make sure that the jump leads will not come into contact with the fan, drive-belts or other moving parts of the engine.

6 Start the engine using the booster battery and run it at idle speed. Switch on the lights, rear window demister and heater blower motor, then disconnect the jump leads in the reverse order of connection. Turn off the lights etc.

Wheel changing

Some of the details shown here will vary according to model

Warning: ***Do not change a wheel in a situation where you risk being hit by other traffic. On busy roads, try to stop in a lay-by or a gateway. Be wary of passing traffic while changing the wheel – it is easy to become distracted by the job in hand.***

Preparation

- ☐ When a puncture occurs, stop as soon as it is safe to do so.
- ☐ Park on firm level ground, if possible, and well out of the way of other traffic.
- ☐ Use hazard warning lights if necessary.
- ☐ If you have one, use a warning triangle to alert other drivers of your presence.
- ☐ Apply the handbrake and engage first or reverse gear (or P on models with automatic transmission).
- ☐ Chock the wheel diagonally opposite the one being removed – a couple of large stones will do for this.
- ☐ If the ground is soft, use a flat piece of wood to spread the load under the jack.

Changing the wheel

1 The spare wheel and tools are stored in the luggage compartment. Raise the floor covering, and lift out the jack and wheel changing tools from the centre of the wheel.

2 Use the wire hook to remove the wheel bolt caps.

3 Use the wheel brace to slacken each wheel bolt by half a turn.

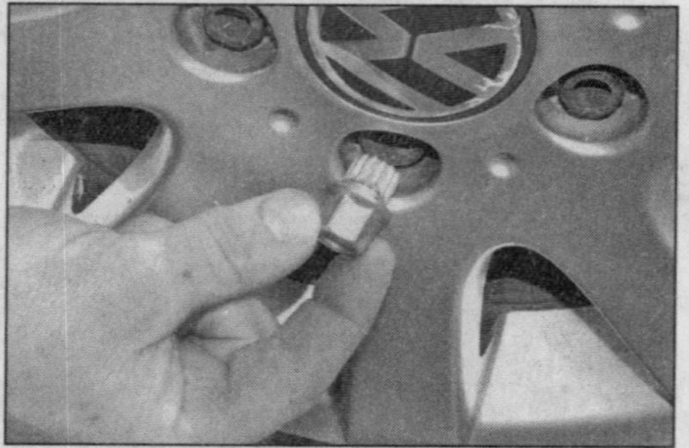

4 Use the special adapter when slackening the locking wheel bolt.

5 Locate the jack on firm ground below the reinforced point on the sill (don't jack the vehicle at any other point of the sill), then turn the jack handle clockwise until the wheel is raised clear of the ground.

6 Unscrew the wheel bolts (using the adapter provided) and remove the wheel.

7 Fit the spare wheel, and screw in the bolts. Lightly tighten the bolts with the wheelbrace then lower the vehicle to the ground.

8 Securely tighten the wheel bolts in the sequence shown then refit the wheel trim/hub cap. Stow the punctured wheel back in the spare wheel well.

Finally . . .

- ☐ Have the wheel nuts tightened to the specified torque (see Chapter 10) at the earliest possible opportunity.
- ☐ Remove the wheel chocks.
- ☐ Stow the jack and tools in the spare wheel.
- ☐ Check the tyre pressure on the wheel just fitted. If it is low, or if you don't have a pressure gauge with you, drive slowly to the nearest garage and inflate the tyre to the correct pressure.

Note: *If a temporary 'space-saver' spare wheel has been fitted, special conditions apply to its use. This type of spare wheel is only intended for use in an emergency, and should not remain fitted any longer than it takes to get the punctured wheel repaired. While the temporary wheel is in use, ensure it is inflated to the correct pressure, do not exceed 50 mph, and avoid harsh acceleration, braking or cornering.*

Identifying leaks

Puddles on the garage floor or drive, or obvious wetness under the bonnet or underneath the car, suggest a leak that needs investigating. It can sometimes be difficult to decide where the leak is coming from, especially if an engine undershield is fitted. Leaking oil or fluid can also be blown rearwards by the passage of air under the car, giving a false impression of where the problem lies.

Warning: Most automotive oils and fluids are poisonous. Wash them off skin, and change out of contaminated clothing, without delay.

The smell of a fluid leaking from the car may provide a clue to what's leaking. Some fluids are distinctively coloured. It may help to remove the engine undershield, clean the car carefully and to park it over some clean paper overnight as an aid to locating the source of the leak. Remember that some leaks may only occur while the engine is running.

Sump oil

Engine oil may leak from the drain plug...

Oil from filter

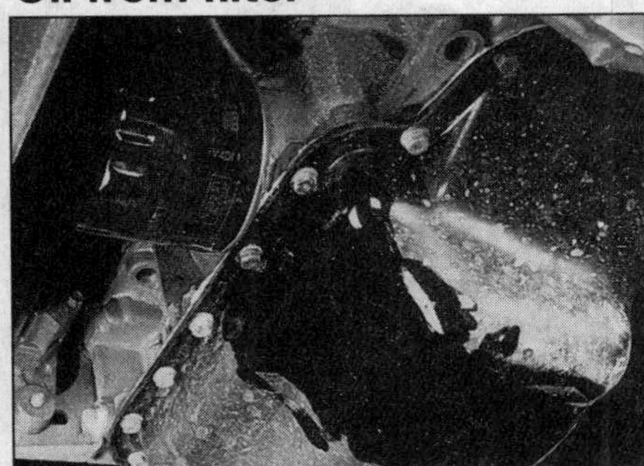

...or from the base of the oil filter.

Gearbox oil

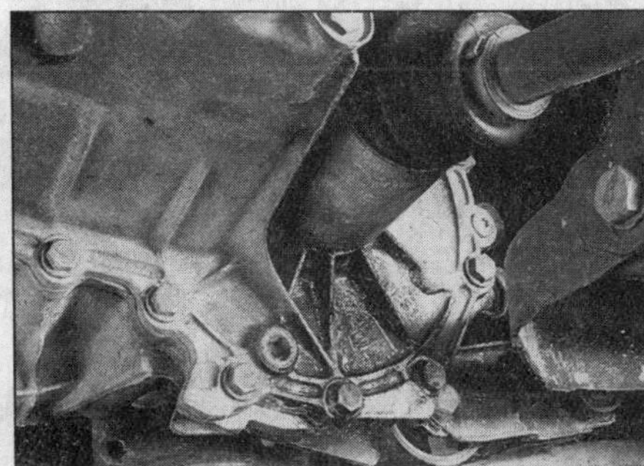

Gearbox oil can leak from the seals at the inboard ends of the driveshafts.

Antifreeze

Leaking antifreeze often leaves a crystalline deposit like this.

Brake fluid

A leak occurring at a wheel is almost certainly brake fluid.

Power steering fluid

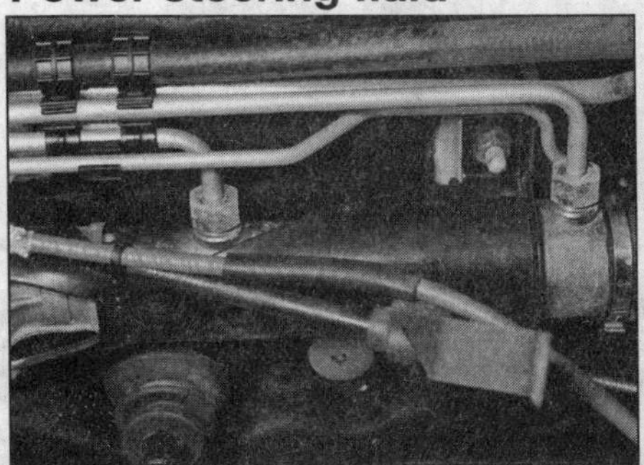

Power steering fluid may leak from the pipe connectors on the steering rack.

Towing

When all else fails, you may find yourself having to get a tow home – or of course you may be helping somebody else. Long-distance recovery should only be done by a garage or breakdown service. For shorter distances, DIY towing using another car is easy enough, but observe the following points:

☐ Use a proper tow-rope – they are not expensive. The vehicle being towed must display an ON TOW sign in its rear window.

☐ Always turn the ignition key to the 'On' position when the vehicle is being towed, so that the steering lock is released, and the direction indicator and brake lights work.

☐ Only attach the tow-rope to the towing eyes provided. The front towing eye is supplied as part of the toolkit stored in the luggage compartment. To fit the eye, remove the vent/cover from the front bumper. Screw the eye into position anti-clockwise (it has a **left-handed** thread), and tighten using the wheelbrace handle. The rear towing eye is located beneath the right-hand side of the rear bumper.

☐ Before being towed, release the handbrake and select neutral on the transmission. On models with automatic transmission, do not exceed 30 mph and do not tow for more than 30 miles. If in doubt, do not tow, or transmission damage may result.

☐ Note that greater-than-usual pedal pressure will be required to operate the brakes, since the vacuum servo unit is only operational with the engine running.

☐ Greater-than-usual steering effort will also be required.

☐ The driver of the car being towed must keep the tow-rope taut at all times to avoid snatching.

☐ Make sure that both drivers know the route before setting off.

☐ Only drive at moderate speeds and keep the distance towed to a minimum. Drive smoothly and allow plenty of time for slowing down at junctions.

Introduction

There are some very simple checks which need only take a few minutes to carry out, but which could save you a lot of inconvenience and expense.

These *Weekly checks* require no great skill or special tools, and the small amount of time they take to perform could prove to be very well spent, for example:

☐ Keeping an eye on tyre condition and pressures, will not only help to stop them wearing out prematurely, but could also save your life.

☐ Many breakdowns are caused by electrical problems. Battery-related faults are particularly common, and a quick check on a regular basis will often prevent the majority of these.

☐ If your car develops a brake fluid leak, the first time you might know about it is when your brakes don't work properly. Checking the level regularly will give advance warning of this kind of problem.

☐ If the oil or coolant levels run low, the cost of repairing any engine damage will be far greater than fixing the leak, for example.

Underbonnet check points

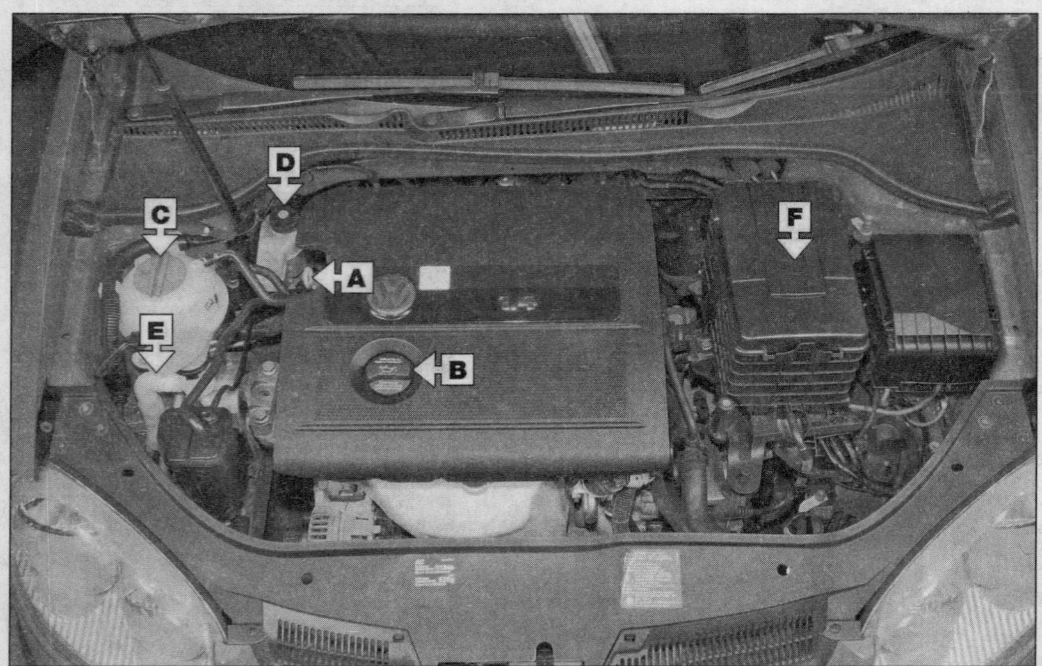

◀ **1.4 litre 16-valve petrol**

A *Engine oil level dipstick*
B *Engine oil filler cap*
C *Coolant expansion tank*
D *Brake (and clutch) fluid reservoir*
E *Screen washer fluid reservoir*
F *Battery*

◀ **1.6 litre FSi 16-valve petrol**

A *Engine oil level dipstick*
B *Engine oil filler cap*
C *Coolant expansion tank*
D *Brake (and clutch) fluid reservoir*
E *Screen washer fluid reservoir*
F *Battery*

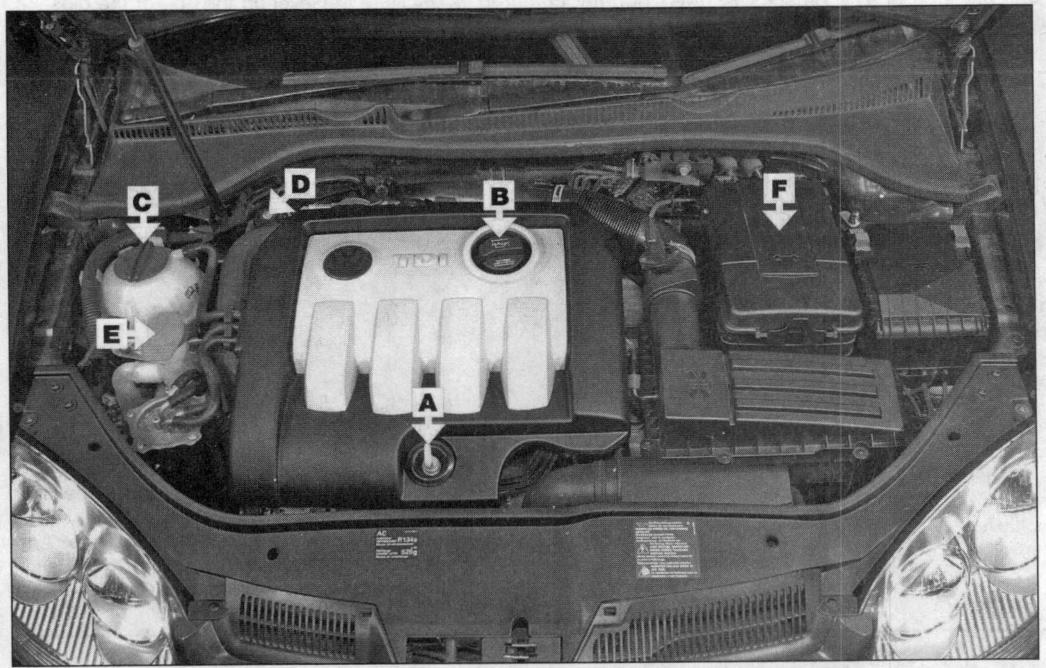

◀ **1.9 litre TDi diesel**

A *Engine oil level dipstick*
B *Engine oil filler cap*
C *Coolant expansion tank*
D *Brake (and clutch) fluid reservoir*
E *Screen washer fluid reservoir*
F *Battery*

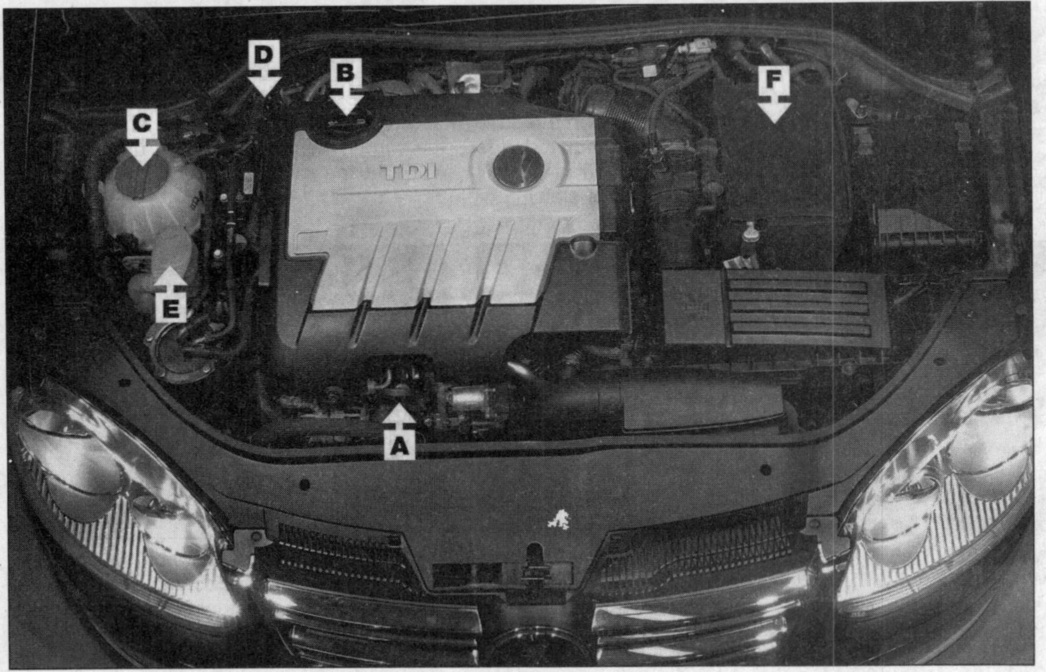

◀ **2.0 litre Common rail diesel**

A *Engine oil level dipstick*
B *Engine oil filler cap*
C *Coolant expansion tank*
D *Brake (and clutch) fluid reservoir*
E *Screen washer fluid reservoir*
F *Battery*

Engine oil level

Before you start

✔ Make sure that the car is on level ground.
✔ Check the oil level before the car is driven, or at least 5 minutes after the engine has been switched off.

If the oil is checked immediately after driving the vehicle, some of the oil will remain in the upper engine components, resulting in an inaccurate reading on the dipstick.

The correct oil

Modern engines place great demands on their oil. It is very important that the correct oil for your car is used (see *Lubricants and fluids*).

Car care

● If you have to add oil frequently, you should check whether you have any oil leaks. Place some clean paper under the car overnight, and check for stains in the morning. If there are no leaks, then the engine may be burning oil.

● Always maintain the level between the upper and lower dipstick marks (see photo 3). If the level is too low, severe engine damage may occur. Oil seal failure may result if the engine is overfilled by adding too much oil.

1 The dipstick is often brightly coloured for easy identification (see *Underbonnet check points* for exact location). Withdraw the dipstick, then use a clean rag or paper towel to wipe the oil from it. Insert the clean dipstick into the tube as far as it will go, then withdraw it again.

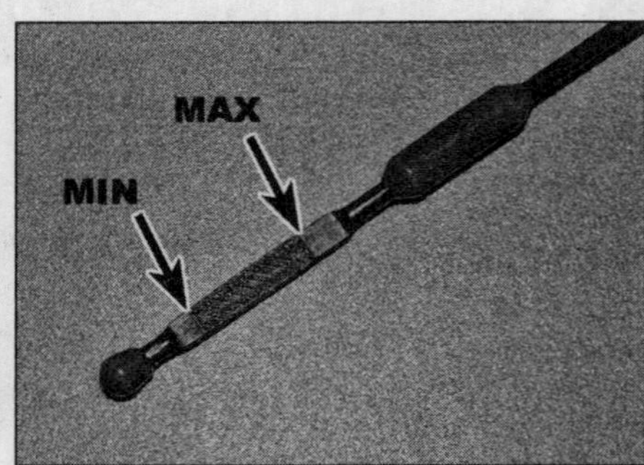

2 Note the level on the end of the dipstick, which should be between the upper (MAX) and lower (MIN) mark.

3 Oil is added through the filler cap aperture. Unscrew the cap.

4 Place some cloth rags around the filler cap aperture, then top-up the level. A funnel may help to reduce spillage. Add the oil slowly, checking the level on the dipstick frequently. Avoid overfilling (see *Car care*).

Coolant level

Warning: Do not attempt to remove the expansion tank pressure cap when the engine is hot, as there is a very great risk of scalding. Do not leave open containers of coolant about, as it is poisonous.

Car care

● With a sealed-type cooling system, adding coolant should not be necessary on a regular basis. If frequent topping-up is required, it is likely there is a leak. Check the radiator, all hoses and joint faces for signs of staining or wetness, and rectify as necessary.

● It is important that antifreeze is used in the cooling system all year round, not just during the winter months. Don't top up with water alone, as the antifreeze will become diluted.

1 The coolant level varies with the temperature of the engine. When the engine is cold, the coolant level should be between the MIN and MAX marks.

2 If topping-up is necessary, wait until the engine is cold. Slowly unscrew the cap to release any pressure present in the cooling system, and remove the cap.

3 Add a mixture of water and the specified antifreeze (see Lubricants and fluids) to the expansion tank until the coolant level is halfway between the level marks. Refit the cap and tighten it securely.

Brake (and clutch) fluid level

Note: *On manual transmission models, the fluid reservoir also supplies the clutch master cylinder with fluid*

Before you start

✔ Make sure that the car is on level ground.

✔ Cleanliness is of great importance when dealing with the braking system, so take care to clean around the reservoir cap before topping-up. Use only clean brake fluid.

Safety first!

● If the reservoir requires repeated topping-up, this is an indication of a fluid leak somewhere in the system, which should be investigated immediately. Note that the level will drop naturally as the brake pad linings wear, but must never be allowed to fall below the MIN mark.

● If a leak is suspected, the car should not be driven until the braking system has been checked. Never take any risks where brakes are concerned.

Warning: Brake fluid can harm your eyes and damage painted surfaces, so use extreme caution when handling and pouring it. Do not use fluid which has been standing open for some time, as it absorbs moisture from the air, which can cause a dangerous loss of braking effectiveness.

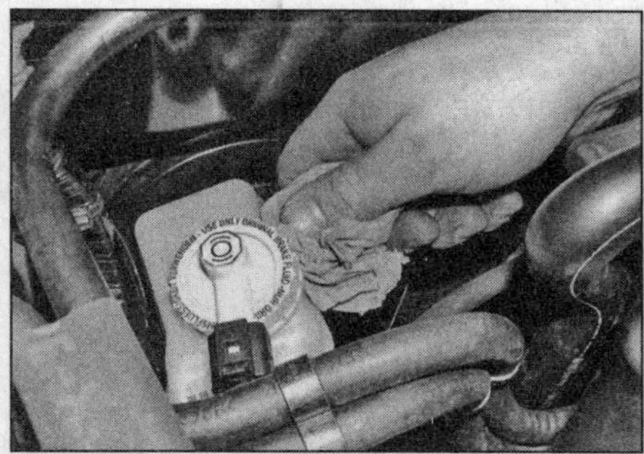

1 The MIN and MAX marks are indicated on the reservoir. The fluid level must be kept between the marks at all times. If topping-up is necessary, first wipe clean the area around the filler cap to prevent dirt entering the hydraulic system.

2 Unscrew and remove the reservoir cap.

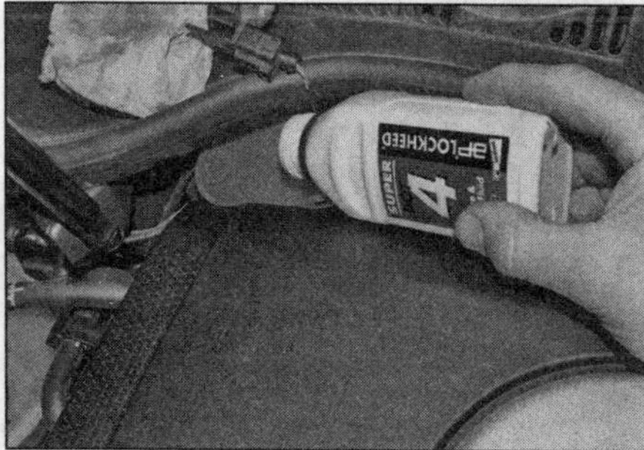

3 Carefully add fluid, taking care not to spill it onto the surrounding components (use a funnel). Use only the specified fluid (see Lubricants and fluids); mixing different types can cause damage to the system. On completion, securely refit the cap and wipe away any spilt fluid.

Washer fluid level

● Screenwash additives not only keep the windscreen clean during bad weather, they also prevent the washer system freezing in cold weather – which is when you are likely to need it most. Don't top-up using plain water, as the screenwash will become diluted, and will freeze in cold weather.

Warning: On no account use engine coolant antifreeze in the screen washer system – this may damage the paintwork.

1 The screenwash fluid reservoir is located on the right-hand side of the engine compartment, behind the headlight. Pull up the filler cap to release it from the reservoir.

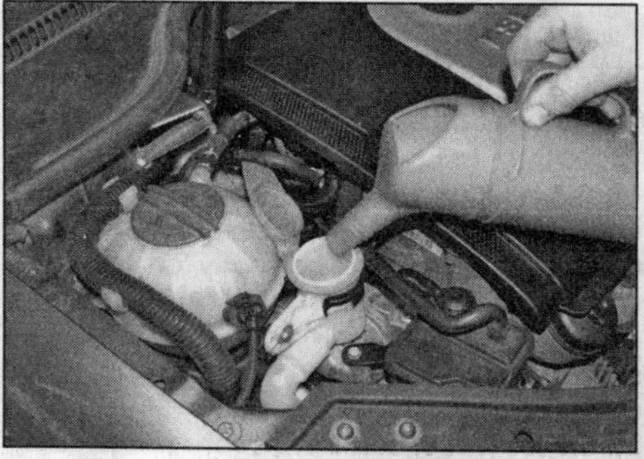

2 When topping-up the reservoir, a screen-wash additive should be added in the quantities recommended on the bottle.

Tyre condition and pressure

It is very important that tyres are in good condition, and at the correct pressure - having a tyre failure at any speed is highly dangerous.

Tyre wear is influenced by driving style - harsh braking and acceleration, or fast cornering, will all produce more rapid tyre wear. As a general rule, the front tyres wear out faster than the rears. Interchanging the tyres from front to rear ("rotating" the tyres) may result in more even wear. However, if this is completely effective, you may have the expense of replacing all four tyres at once!

Remove any nails or stones embedded in the tread before they penetrate the tyre to cause deflation. If removal of a nail does reveal that the tyre has been punctured, refit the nail so that its point of penetration is marked. Then immediately change the wheel, and have the tyre repaired by a tyre dealer.

Regularly check the tyres for damage in the form of cuts or bulges, especially in the sidewalls. Periodically remove the wheels, and clean any dirt or mud from the inside and outside surfaces. Examine the wheel rims for signs of rusting, corrosion or other damage. Light alloy wheels are easily damaged by "kerbing" whilst parking; steel wheels may also become dented or buckled. A new wheel is very often the only way to overcome severe damage.

New tyres should be balanced when they are fitted, but it may become necessary to re-balance them as they wear, or if the balance weights fitted to the wheel rim should fall off. Unbalanced tyres will wear more quickly, as will the steering and suspension components. Wheel imbalance is normally signified by vibration, particularly at a certain speed (typically around 50 mph). If this vibration is felt only through the steering, then it is likely that just the front wheels need balancing. If, however, the vibration is felt through the whole car, the rear wheels could be out of balance. Wheel balancing should be carried out by a tyre dealer or garage.

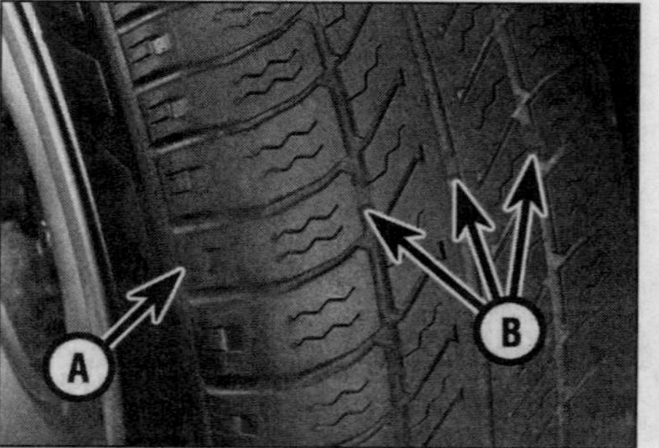

1 ***Tread Depth - visual check***
The original tyres have tread wear safety bands (B), which will appear when the tread depth reaches approximately 1.6 mm. The band positions are indicated by a triangular mark on the tyre sidewall (A).

2 ***Tread Depth - manual check***
Alternatively, tread wear can be monitored with a simple, inexpensive device known as a tread depth indicator gauge.

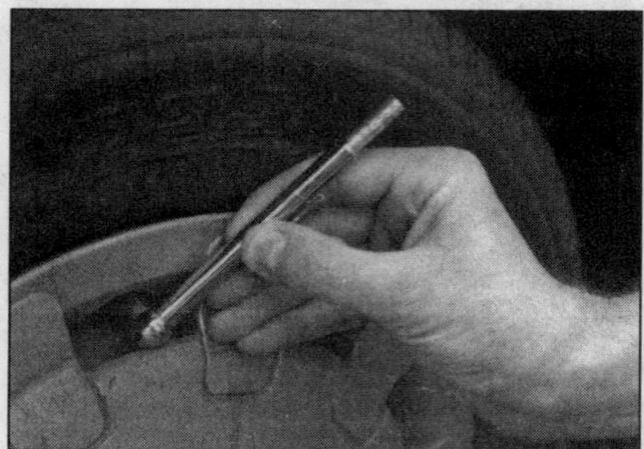

3 ***Tyre Pressure Check***
Check the tyre pressures regularly with the tyres cold. Do not adjust the tyre pressures immediately after the vehicle has been used, or an inaccurate setting will result.

Tyre tread wear patterns

Shoulder Wear

Underinflation (wear on both sides)
Under-inflation will cause overheating of the tyre, because the tyre will flex too much, and the tread will not sit correctly on the road surface. This will cause a loss of grip and excessive wear, not to mention the danger of sudden tyre failure due to heat build-up.
Check and adjust pressures
Incorrect wheel camber (wear on one side)
Repair or renew suspension parts
Hard cornering
Reduce speed!

Centre Wear

Overinflation
Over-inflation will cause rapid wear of the centre part of the tyre tread, coupled with reduced grip, harsher ride, and the danger of shock damage occurring in the tyre casing.
Check and adjust pressures

If you sometimes have to inflate your car's tyres to the higher pressures specified for maximum load or sustained high speed, don't forget to reduce the pressures to normal afterwards.

Uneven Wear

Front tyres may wear unevenly as a result of wheel misalignment. Most tyre dealers and garages can check and adjust the wheel alignment (or "tracking") for a modest charge.
Incorrect camber or castor
Repair or renew suspension parts
Malfunctioning suspension
Repair or renew suspension parts
Unbalanced wheel
Balance tyres
Incorrect toe setting
Adjust front wheel alignment
Note: *The feathered edge of the tread which typifies toe wear is best checked by feel.*

Battery

Caution: Before carrying out any work on the vehicle battery, read the precautions given in 'Safety first!' at the start of this manual.

✔ Make sure that the battery tray is in good condition, and that the clamp is tight. Corrosion on the tray, retaining clamp and the battery itself can be removed with a solution of water and baking soda. Thoroughly rinse all cleaned areas with water. Any metal parts damaged by corrosion should be covered with a zinc-based primer, then painted.

✔ Periodically (approximately every three months), check the charge condition of the battery as described in Chapter 5A. A 'magic eye' charge indicator is fitted to the standard battery – if the indicator is green in colour, the battery is fully-charged, however, if it is colourless, it should be recharged. If it is yellow in colour, the battery should be renewed.

✔ If the battery is flat, and you need to jump start your vehicle, see *Jump starting*.

1 The battery is located on the left-hand side of the engine compartment, next to the fuse and relay box. Lift the cover from the insulation box to gain access to the battery terminals. The exterior of the battery should be inspected periodically for damage such as a cracked case or cover.

2 Check the security and condition of all the battery and fuse connections. The exterior of the battery should be inspected periodically for damage such as a cracked case or cover.

3 If corrosion (white, fluffy deposits) is evident, remove the cables from the battery terminals (refer to *Disconnecting the battery* in Reference), clean them with a small wire brush, then refit them. Automotive stores sell a tool for cleaning the battery post . . .

4 . . . as well as the battery cable clamps. **Note:** *VW specifically prohibit the use of grease on the battery terminals*.

Electrical systems

✔ Check all external lights and the horn. Refer to the appropriate Sections of Chapter 12 for details if any of the circuits are found to be inoperative.

✔ Visually check all accessible wiring connectors, harnesses and retaining clips for security, and for signs of chafing or damage.

If you need to check your brake lights and indicators unaided, back up to a wall or garage door and operate the lights. The reflected light should show if they are working properly.

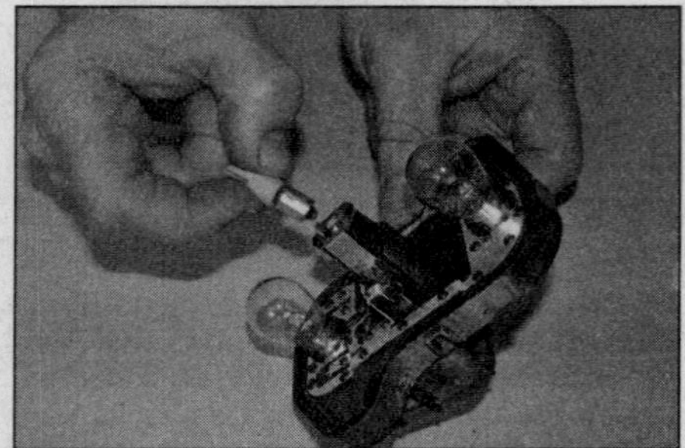

1 If a single indicator light, brake light or headlight has failed, it is likely that a bulb has blown and will need to be renewed. Refer to Chapter 12 for details. If both brake lights have failed, it is possible that the brake light switch operated by the brake pedal has failed. Refer to Chapter 9 for details.

2 If more than one indicator light or headlight has failed, it is likely that either a fuse has blown or that there is a fault in the circuit (see *Electrical fault finding* in Chapter 12). The main fuses are in the fusebox beneath a cover on the right-hand end of the facia panel. Use a small screwdriver to prise off the cover. The circuits protected by the fuses are shown on the inside of the cover. Additional fuses and fusible links are in the fusebox located on the left-hand side of the engine compartment.

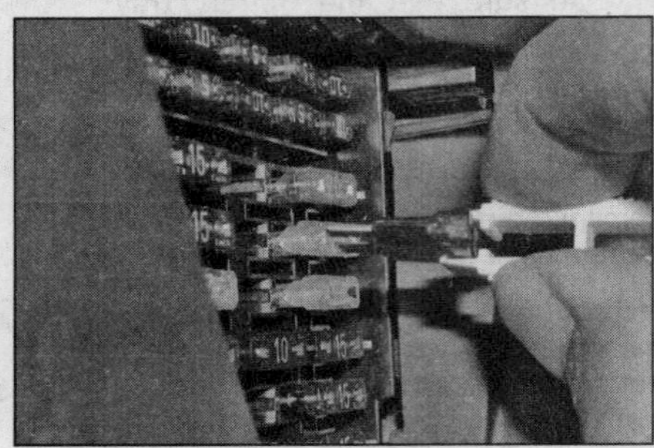

3 To renew a blown fuse, pull it from its location in the fusebox, using the plastic pliers provided. Fit a new fuse of the same rating, available from car accessory shops. It is important that you find the reason that the fuse blew (see *Electrical fault finding* in Chapter 12).

Wiper blades

Note: *It is possible to park the wipers in a Service/Winter position with both wipers pointing upwards to allow unrestricted removal of the blades. To do this, operate the wipers within 10 seconds of switching off the ignition. The wiper arms can now be lifted away from the windscreen.*

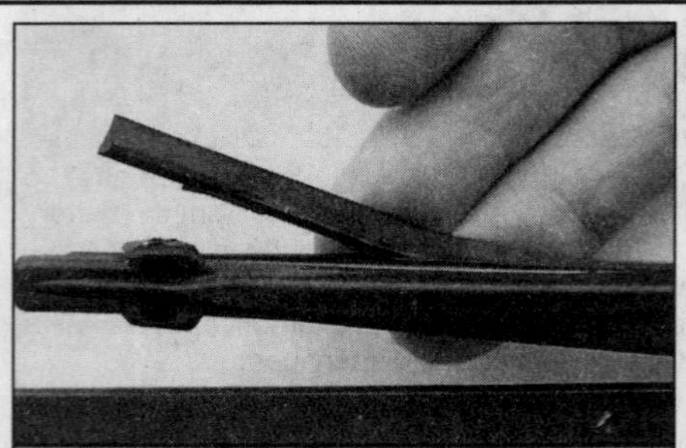

1 Check the condition of the wiper blades; if they are cracked or show any signs of deterioration, or if the glass swept area is smeared, renew them. For maximum clarity of vision, wiper blades should be renewed annually, as a matter of course.

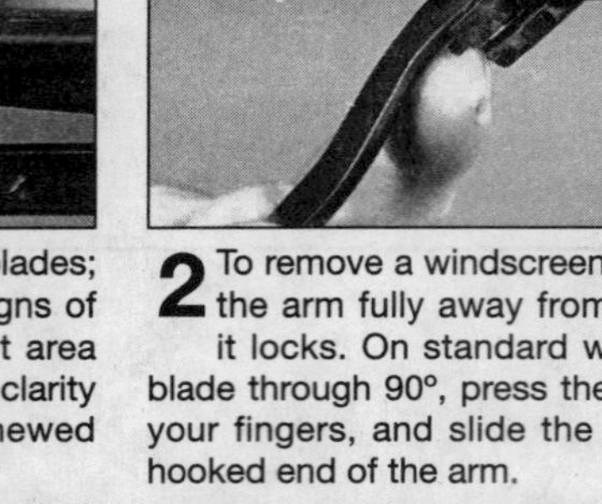

2 To remove a windscreen wiper blade, pull the arm fully away from the screen until it locks. On standard wipers, swivel the blade through 90°, press the locking tab with your fingers, and slide the blade out of the hooked end of the arm.

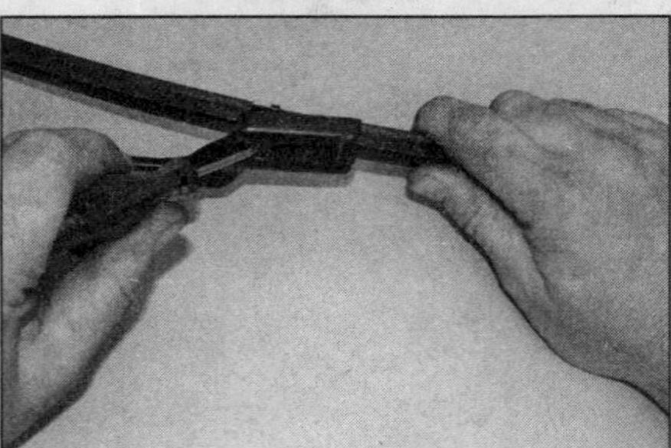

3 On aerodynamic wipers, depress the catch with a screwdriver, and pull the blade from the arm.

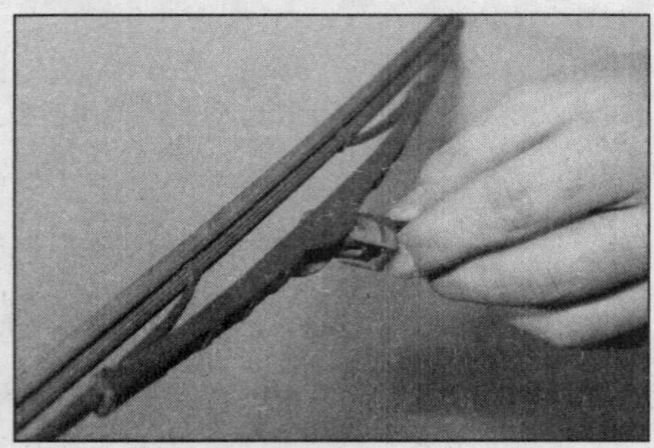

4 Where applicable, don't forget to check the tailgate wiper blade as well. To remove the blade, depress the retaining tab and slide the blade out of the hooked end of the arm.

Lubricants and fluids

Note: *Using lubricants and fluids which do not meet the VW standard may invalidate the warranty*

Engine (petrol)	
Standard (distance/time) service interval	Multigrade engine oil, viscosity SAE 5W/40 to 20W/50 VW engine oil VW 501 01, 502 00, 504 00 or better
LongLife (variable) service interval	VW LongLife engine oil VW 503 00, 504 00 or better
Engine (diesel)	
Standard (distance/time) service interval	Multigrade engine oil, viscosity SAE 5W/40 to 20W/50
Engines without particulate filter	VW 505 01 or better
Engines with particulate filter	VW 507 00 or better
LongLife (variable) service interval	VW LongLife engine oil
Engines without particulate filter	VW 506 01, 507 00 or better
Engines with particulate filter	VW 507 00 or better
Cooling system	VW additive G13 only (antifreeze and corrosion protection)
Manual transmission	Synthetic gear oil, viscosity SAE 75W/90 VW G50
Automatic transmission	VW ATF
DSG semi-automatic transmissions	G05 217 1A2
Braking system	Hydraulic fluid to SAE J1703F or DOT 4

Tyre pressures

Note: *The recommended tyre pressures for each vehicle are given on a sticker attached to the inside of the fuel filler flap. The pressures given are for the original equipment tyres – the recommended pressures may vary if any other make or type of tyre is fitted; check with the tyre manufacturer or supplier for latest recommendations. The following pressures are typical.*

	Front	Rear
Golf models		
Normal load	1.9 bars (28 psi)	1.9 bars (28 psi)
Full load:		
175/80R14 tyres	2.2 bars (32 psi)	3.0 bars (44 psi)
All other tyres	2.1 bars (30 psi)	2.6 bars (38 psi)
Jetta models		
Normal load	1.9 bars (28 psi)	1.9 bars (28 psi)
Full load	2.1 bars (30 psi)	2.8 bars (41 psi)

Notes

Chapter 1 Part A:
Routine maintenance and servicing – petrol models

Contents

Degrees of difficulty

Easy, suitable for novice with little experience 

Fairly easy, suitable for beginner with some experience

Fairly difficult, suitable for competent DIY mechanic

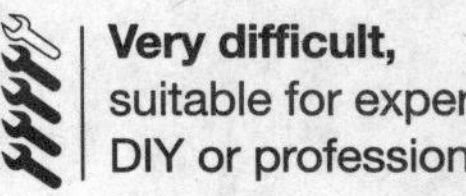

Difficult, suitable for experienced DIY mechanic

Very difficult, suitable for expert DIY or professional 

Lubricants and fluids

Refer to end of *Weekly checks* on page 0•17

Engine codes*

1.4 litre:	
Indirect injection petrol engine	BCA and BUD
Direct injection petrol engine (FSi)	BKG and BLN
Direct injection turbocharged engine (TSi)	CAXA
1.6 litre:	
SOHC petrol engine	BGU, BSE and BSF
DOHC direct injection petrol engine (FSi)	BAG, BLP and BLF
2.0 litre petrol engine:	
Non-turbo	AXW, BLX, BLY, BLR, BVX, BVY and BVZ
Turbo	AXX, BPY and BWA

**See 'Vehicle identification' at the end of this manual for the location of engine code markings.*

Capacities

Engine oil – including filter (approximate)

1.4 litre engines:	
Except engine code CAXA	3.2 litres
Engine code CAXA	3.6 litres
1.6 litre SOHC engines	4.5 litres
1.6 litre FSi engines	3.6 litres
2.0 litre engines	4.6 litres

Cooling system (approximate)

1.4 litre engines	5.6 litres
1.6 litre SOHC engines	8.0 litres
1.6 litre FSi engines	5.6 litres
2.0 litre engines	8.0 litres

Transmission

Manual transmission*:	
Type 0AF	2.0 litres
Type 0AG	2.1 litres
Type 0A4	1.9 litres
Type 02S	1.9 litres
Type 02Q	2.3 litres
Automatic transmission (Type 09G):	
Main transmission unit including final drive	7.0 litres
** See Chapter 7A for application details*	
DSG transmission:	
Type 02E (6-speed)	5.2 litres
Type 0AM (7-speed)	Not available

Fuel tank (approximate)

All models	55 litres

Washer reservoirs

Models with headlight washers	5.5 litres
Models without headlight washers	3.0 litres

Cooling system

Antifreeze mixture:

40% antifreeze	Protection down to -25°C
50% antifreeze	Protection down to -35°C

Note: *Refer to antifreeze manufacturer for latest recommendations.*

Ignition system

Spark plugs:	Type	Electrode gap
1.4 litre engine codes:		
BCA	VW 101000033	0.9 to 1.1 mm
BUD	VW 101905617C	1.0 to 1.1 mm
BKG and BLN	VW 101000068AA	0.9 to 1.1 mm
CAXA	Not available	
1.6 litre engine codes:		
BGU, BSE and BSF	VW 101000033AA	0.9 to 1.1 mm
BAG, BLP and BLF	VW 101000068AA	0.9 to 1.1 mm
2.0 litre engine codes:		
AXW, BLX, BLR, BVX and BVY	VW 101905620	1.0 to 1.1 mm
BLY and BVZ	VW 101905610A	0.8 to 0.9 mm
AXX, BPY and BWA	VW 101905631B	0.7 to 0.8 mm

Brakes

Brake pad lining minimum thickness:

Front	2.0 mm
Rear	2.0 mm

Torque wrench settings

	Nm	lbf ft
Automatic transmission level plug	27	20
Manual gearbox drain plug (02S transmission only)	35	25
Manual gearbox filler/level plug	30	22
Oil filter cap (as applicable)	25	18
Pivot pin bolt (02S transmission only)	25	18
Reversing light switch	20	15
Roadwheel bolts	120	89
Spark plugs	30	22
Sump drain plug*	30	22

**Do not re-use*

Maintenance schedule – petrol models

The maintenance intervals in this manual are provided with the assumption that you, not the dealer, will be carrying out the work. These are the minimum intervals recommended by us for vehicles driven daily. If you wish to keep your vehicle in peak condition at all times, you may wish to perform some of these procedures more often. We encourage frequent maintenance, since it enhances the efficiency, performance and resale value of your vehicle.

When the vehicle is new, it should be serviced by a dealer service department (or other workshop recognised by the vehicle manufacturer as providing the same standard of service) in order to preserve the warranty. The vehicle manufacturer may reject warranty claims if you are unable to prove that servicing has been carried out as and when specified, using only original equipment parts or parts certified to be of equivalent quality.

All VW Golf/Jetta models are equipped with a service interval display indicator in the instrument panel. Every time the engine is started the panel will illuminate for approximately 20 seconds with service information. With the standard non-variable display, the service intervals are in accordance with specific distances and time periods. With the LongLife display, the service interval is variable according to the number of starts, length of journeys, vehicle speeds, brake pad wear, bonnet opening frequency, fuel consumption, oil level and oil temperature, however the vehicle **must** be serviced at least every two years. At a distance of 2000 miles before the next service is due, 'Service in 2000 miles' will appear at the bottom of the speedometer, and this figure will reduce in steps of 100 units as the vehicle is used. Once the service interval has been reached, the display will flash 'Service' or 'Service Now'. Note that if the variable (LongLife) service interval is being used, the engine must **only** be filled with the recommended **long-life** engine oil (see *Lubricants and fluids*).

After completing a service, VW technicians use a special instrument to reset the service display to the next service interval, and a print-out is put in the vehicle service record. The display can be reset by the owner as described in Section 5, but note that for models using the 'LongLife' interval, the procedure will automatically reset the display to the 10 000 miles 'distance' interval. To have the display reset to the 'variable' (LongLife) interval, it is necessary to take the vehicle to a VW dealer who will use a special instrument to encode the on-board computer.

Every 250 miles or weekly

☐ Refer to Weekly checks

'Oil' on display

☐ Renew the engine oil and filter (Section 3)

Note: *Frequent oil and filter changes are good for the engine. We recommend changing the oil at least once a year.*

☐ Check the front and rear brake pad thickness (Section 4)

☐ Reset the service interval display (Section 5)

'01' on display

In addition to the items listed above, carry out the following:

☐ Check the condition of the exhaust system and its mountings (Section 6)

☐ Check all underbonnet components and hoses for fluid and oil leaks (Section 7)

☐ Check the condition of the auxiliary drivebelt (Section 8)

☐ Check the coolant antifreeze concentration (Section 9)

☐ Check the brake hydraulic circuit for leaks and damage (Section 10)

☐ Check the headlight beam adjustment (Section 11)

☐ Renew the pollen filter element (Section 12)

☐ Check the manual transmission oil level (Section 13)

☐ Check the underbody protection for damage (Section 14)

☐ Check the condition of the driveshaft gaiters (Section 15)

☐ Check the steering and suspension components for condition and security (Section 16)

☐ Check the battery condition, security and electrolyte level (Section 17)

☐ Lubricate all hinges and locks (Section 18)

☐ Check the condition of the airbag unit(s) (Section 19)

'01' on display (continued)

☐ Check the operation of the windscreen/tailgate/head-light washer system(s) (as applicable) (Section 20)

☐ Check the engine management self-diagnosis memory for faults (Section 21)

☐ Check the operation of the sunroof and lubricate the guide rails (Section 22)

☐ Carry out a road test and check exhaust emissions (Section 23)

Every 40 000 miles or 4 years, whichever comes first

Note: *Many dealers perform these tasks at every second 01 service.*

☐ Renew the air filter element (Section 24)

☐ Renew the spark plugs (Section 25)

☐ Check the condition of the auxiliary drivebelt (Section 26)

☐ Check the automatic transmission fluid level (Section 27)

Every 60 000 miles

☐ Renew the timing belt (Section 28)

Note: *VW specify timing belt inspection after the first 60 000 miles and then every 20 000 miles until the renewal interval of 120 000 miles, however, if the vehicle is used mainly for short journeys, we recommend that this shorter renewal interval is adhered to. The belt renewal interval is very much up to the individual owner but, bearing in mind that severe engine damage will result if the belt breaks in use, we recommend the shorter interval.*

Every 2 years

☐ Renew the brake (and clutch) fluid (Section 29)

☐ Renew the coolant (Section 30)*

*** Note:** *This work is not included in the VW schedule and should not be required if the recommended VW G12 LongLife coolant antifreeze/inhibitor is used.*

Underbonnet view of a 1.4 litre model (engine code BCA)

1. *Engine oil filler cap*
2. *Engine oil dipstick*
3. *Coolant expansion tank*
4. *Windscreen/headlight washer fluid reservoir*
5. *Ignition coils and spark plugs*
6. *Brake master cylinder fluid reservoir*
7. *Inlet manifold*
8. *Throttle module*
9. *Battery*
10. *Fusebox*
11. *EGR valve*
12. *Alternator*
13. *Evaporative emission charcoal canister*

Underbonnet view of a 1.6 litre FSi model

1. *Engine oil filler cap*
2. *Engine oil dipstick hole*
3. *Coolant expansion tank*
4. *Windscreen/headlight washer fluid reservoir*
5. *Ignition coils and spark plugs*
6. *Brake master cylinder fluid reservoir*
7. *Inlet manifold*
8. *Throttle module*
9. *Battery*
10. *Fusebox*
11. *EGR valve*
12. *Oil filter cap*
13. *Evaporative emission charcoal canister*
14. *High-pressure fuel pump*

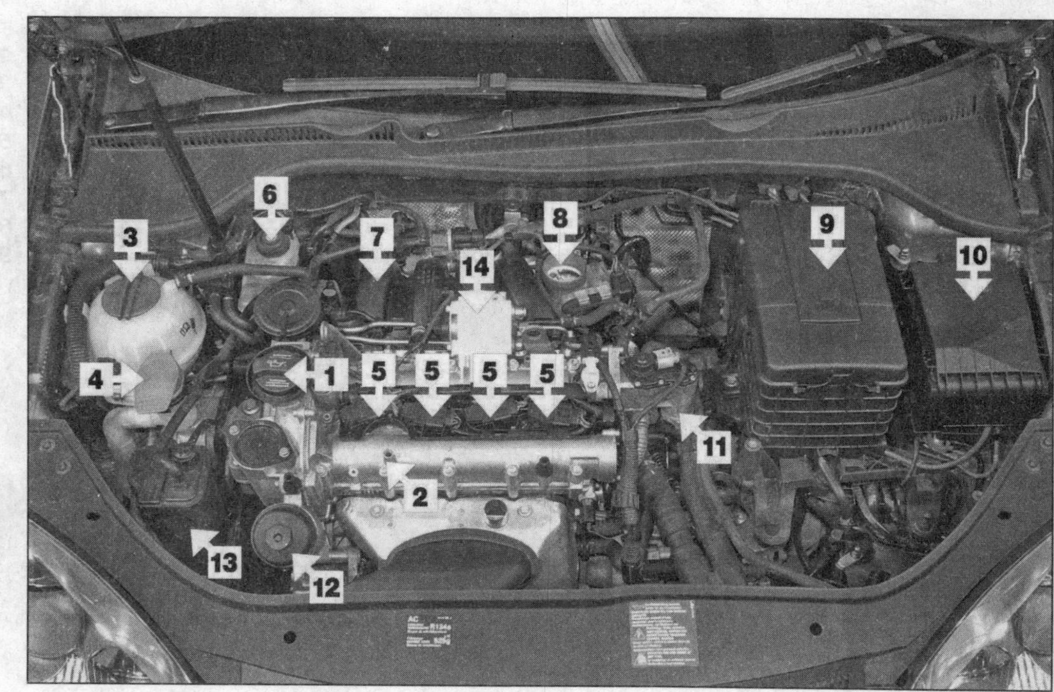

Front underbody view of a 1.6 litre FSi model

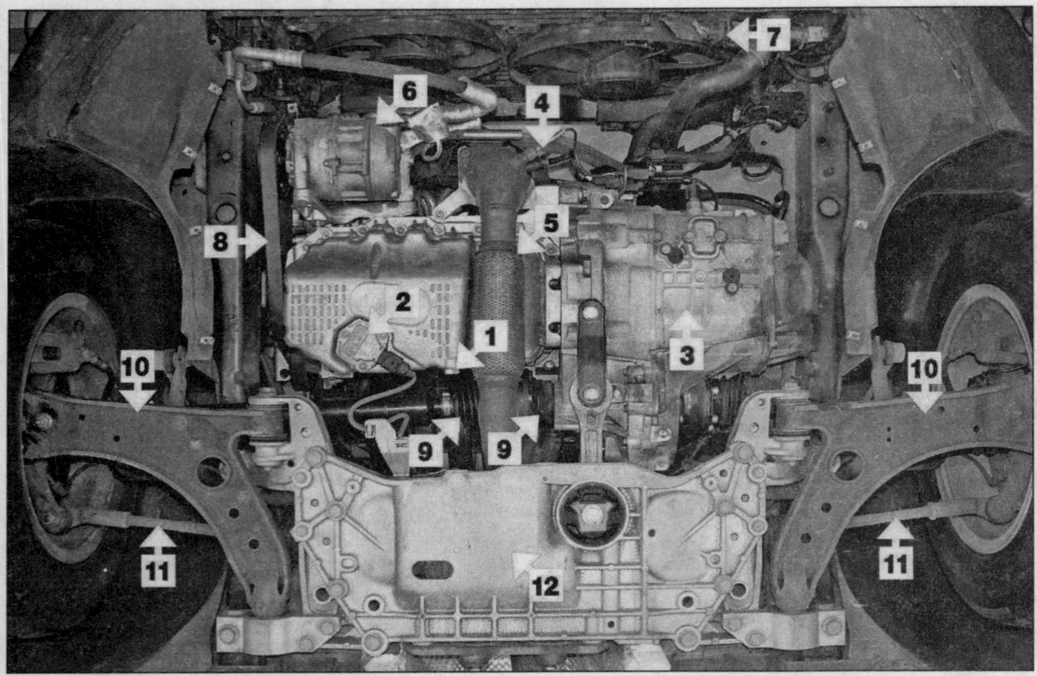

1 Sump drain plug
2 Oil level/temperature sensor
3 Manual transmission
4 Oxygen sensor
5 Exhaust front pipe
6 Air conditioning compressor
7 Radiator and electric cooling fans
8 Auxiliary drivebelt
9 Driveshafts
10 Front suspension lower arms
11 Steering track rods
12 Crossmember

Rear underbody view of a 1.6 litre FSi model

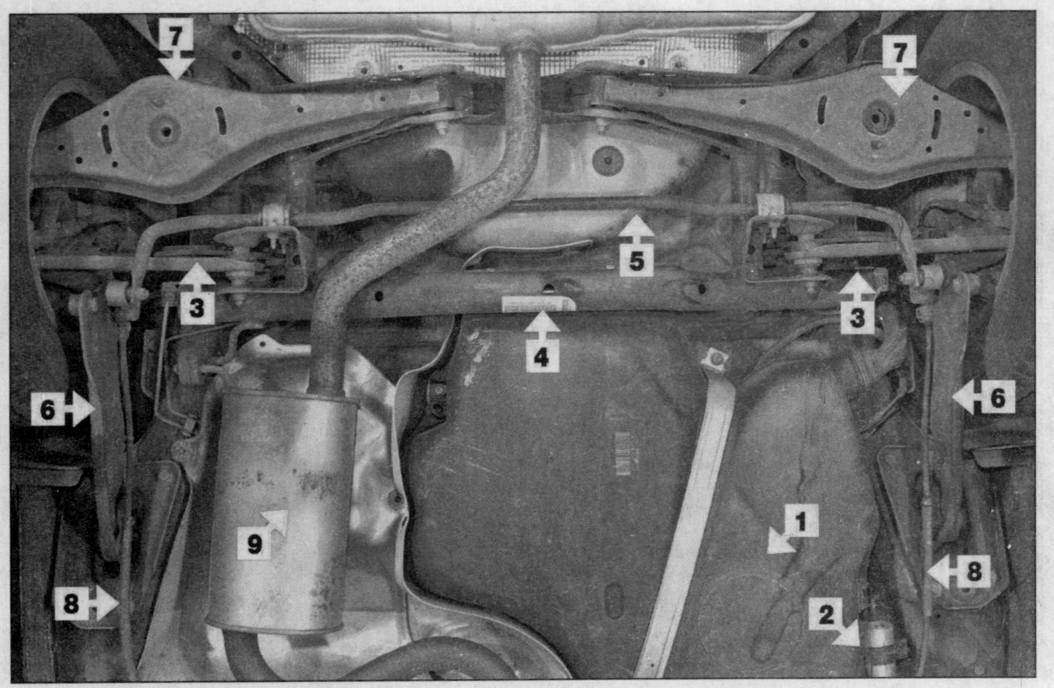

1 Fuel tank
2 Fuel filter
3 Track control rods
4 Rear subframe
5 Rear anti-roll bar
6 Trailing arms
7 Lower transverse links
8 Handbrake cables
9 Exhaust rear silencers and tail pipe

1 Introduction

This Chapter is designed to help the home mechanic maintain his/her vehicle for safety, economy, long life and peak performance.

The Chapter contains a master maintenance schedule, followed by Sections dealing specifically with each task in the schedule. Visual checks, adjustments, component renewal and other helpful items are included. Refer to the accompanying illustrations of the engine compartment and the underside of the vehicle for the locations of the various components.

Servicing your vehicle will provide a planned maintenance programme, which should result in a long and reliable service life. This is a comprehensive plan, so maintaining some items but not others will not produce the same results.

As you service your vehicle, you will discover that many of the procedures can – and should – be grouped together, because of the particular procedure being performed, or because of the proximity of two otherwise unrelated components to one another. For example, if the vehicle is raised for any reason, the exhaust can be inspected at the same time as the suspension and steering components.

The first step in this maintenance programme is to prepare yourself before the actual work begins. Read through all the Sections relevant to the work to be carried out, then make a list and gather all the parts and tools required. If a problem is encountered, seek advice from a parts specialist, or a dealer service department.

2 Regular maintenance

1 If, from the time the vehicle is new, the routine maintenance schedule is followed closely, and frequent checks are made of fluid levels and high-wear items, as suggested throughout this manual, the engine will be kept in relatively good running condition, and the need for additional work will be minimised.

2 It is possible that there will be times when the engine is running poorly due to the lack of regular maintenance. This is even more likely if a used vehicle, which has not received regular and frequent maintenance checks, is purchased. In such cases, additional work may need to be carried out, outside of the regular maintenance intervals.

3 If engine wear is suspected, a compression test (refer to the relevant Part of Chapter 2) will provide valuable information regarding the overall performance of the main internal components. Such a test can be used as a basis to decide on the extent of the work to be carried out. If, for example, a compression test indicates serious internal engine wear, conventional maintenance as described in this Chapter will not greatly improve the performance of the engine, and may prove a waste of time and money, unless extensive overhaul work is carried out first.

4 The following series of operations are those most often required to improve the performance of a generally poor-running engine:

Primary operations

a) Clean, inspect and test the battery (See 'Weekly checks').
b) Check all the engine-related fluids (See 'Weekly checks').
c) Check the condition and tension of the auxiliary drivebelt (Section 8).
d) Renew the spark plugs (Section 25).
e) Check the condition of the air filter, and renew if necessary (Section 24).
f) Check the condition of all hoses, and check for fluid leaks (Section 7).

5 If the above operations do not prove fully effective, carry out the following secondary operations:

Secondary operations

All items listed under *Primary operations*, plus the following:

a) Check the charging system (see Chapter 5A).
b) Check the ignition system (see Chapter 5B).
c) Check the fuel system (see Chapter 4A).
d) Renew the ignition HT leads (where applicable).

'Oil' on display

3 Engine oil and filter renewal

1 Frequent oil and filter changes are the most important maintenance procedures which can be undertaken by the DIY owner. As engine oil ages, it becomes diluted and contaminated, which leads to premature engine wear.

2 Before starting this procedure, gather all the necessary tools and materials. Also make sure that you have plenty of clean rags and newspapers handy, to mop-up any spills. Ideally, the engine oil should be warm, as it will drain better, and more built-up sludge will be removed with it. Take care, however, not to touch the exhaust or any other hot parts of the engine when working under the vehicle. To avoid any possibility of scalding, and to protect yourself from possible skin irritants and other harmful contaminants in used engine oils, it is advisable to wear gloves when carrying out this work. Access to the underside of the vehicle will be greatly improved if it can be raised on a lift, driven onto ramps, or jacked up and supported on axle stands (see *Jacking and vehicle support*). Whichever method is chosen, make sure that the vehicle remains level, or if it is at an angle, that the drain plug is at the lowest point. Undo the retaining screws and remove the engine undertray(s), then also remove the engine top cover where applicable **(see illustration)**.

3 Using a socket and wrench or a ring spanner, slacken the drain plug about half a turn **(see illustrations)**. Position the draining container

3.2 Engine top cover retaining bolts (arrowed)

3.3a The engine oil drain plug location on the sump

3.3b The seal is integral with the plug

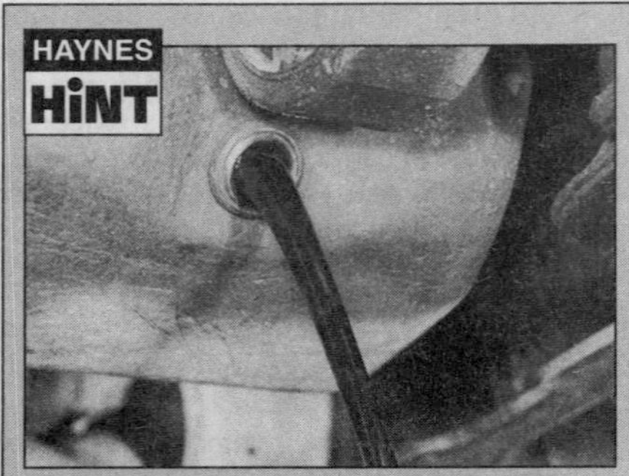

Keep the drain plug pressed into the sump while unscrewing it by hand the last couple of turns. As the plug releases, move it away sharply so the stream of oil issuing from the sump runs into the container, not up your sleeve.

under the drain plug, then remove the plug completely **(see Haynes Hint)**. The seal is integral with the drain plug. Consequently, the drain plug must be renewed.

4 Allow some time for the old oil to drain, noting that it may be necessary to reposition the container as the oil flow slows to a trickle.

5 After all the oil has drained, clean the area around the drain plug opening, and fit the new plug. Tighten the plug to the specified torque.

6 If the filter is also to be renewed, move the container into position under the oil filter **(see illustrations)**.

On 1.4 litre engine codes BCA and BUD a canister-type filter is located from below on the front, right-hand side of the cylinder block.

On 1.6 litre engine codes BGU, BSE and BSF, a canister-type filter is located from below on the front of the cylinder block.

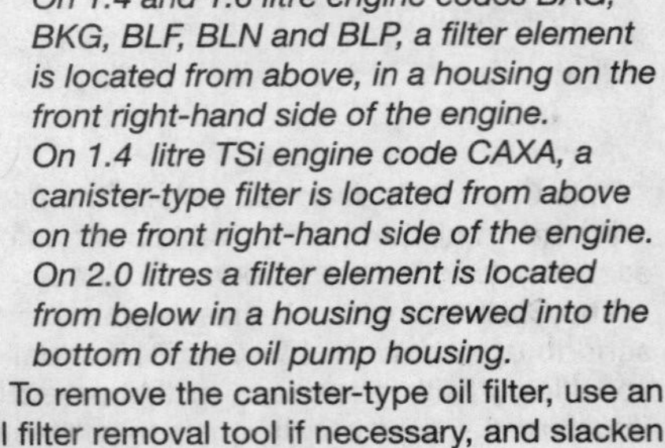

On 1.4 and 1.6 litre engine codes BAG, BKG, BLF, BLN and BLP, a filter element is located from above, in a housing on the front right-hand side of the engine.

On 1.4 litre TSi engine code CAXA, a canister-type filter is located from above on the front right-hand side of the engine.

On 2.0 litres a filter element is located from below in a housing screwed into the bottom of the oil pump housing.

7 To remove the canister-type oil filter, use an oil filter removal tool if necessary, and slacken the filter initially, then unscrew it by hand the rest of the way **(see illustration)**. Empty the oil in the filter into the container. To remove the renewable element type oil filter, unscrew and remove the cap and remove the element and sealing ring **(see illustrations)**. On 2.0 litre engines place a suitable container beneath the filter, and drain the filter housing first by unscrewing the drain plug.

8 Clean the filter housing and cap as necessary, and, on canister-type filters, check the old filter to make sure that the rubber sealing ring has not stuck to the engine. If it has, carefully remove it.

9 To fit the canister-type oil filter, apply a light coating of clean engine oil to the sealing ring on the new filter, then screw it into position on the engine **(see illustration)**. Tighten the filter firmly by hand only – **do not** use any tools.

10 To fit the element-type oil filter, locate it in its housing and refit the cap together with a new sealing ring. Tighten the cap to the specified torque. On 2.0 litre engines, refit and tighten the filter housing drain plug.

3.6a Engine oil filter location on FSi models

3.6b Oil filter location on 1.6 litre engine codes BGU, BSE and BSF

3.6c Oil filter location on TSi models

3.7a Using a canister-type filter removal tool

3.7b Unscrew and remove the cap...

3.7c ...separate the element...

3.7d ...and remove the sealing ring – renewable filter element type

3.9 Apply a thin film of oil to the canister-type filter sealing ring – CAXA engine code filter shown

11 Remove the old oil and all tools from under the car. Refit the engine undertray(s), tighten the retaining screws securely, then lower the car to the ground. Also refit the engine top cover where applicable.

12 Remove the dipstick, then unscrew the oil filler cap from the cylinder head cover. Fill the engine, using the correct grade and type of oil (see *Lubricants and fluids*). An oil can spout or funnel may help to reduce spillage. Pour in half the specified quantity of oil first, then wait a few minutes for the oil to run to the sump. Continue adding oil a small quantity at a time until the level is up to the maximum mark on the dipstick. Refit the filler cap.

13 Start the engine and run it for a few minutes; check for leaks around the oil filter seal and the sump drain plug. Note that there may be a few seconds delay before the oil pressure warning light goes out when the engine is started, as the oil circulates through the engine oil galleries and the new oil filter (where fitted) before the pressure builds-up.

Warning: On turbocharged engines, do not increase the engine speed above idling while the oil pressure light is illuminated, as considerable damage can be caused to the turbocharger.

14 Switch off the engine, and wait a few minutes for the oil to settle in the sump once more. With the new oil circulated and the filter completely full, recheck the level on the dipstick, and add more oil as necessary.

15 Dispose of the used engine oil safely, with reference to *General repair procedures* in the *Reference* section of this manual.

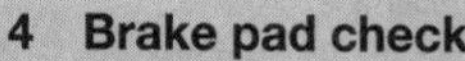

4 Brake pad check

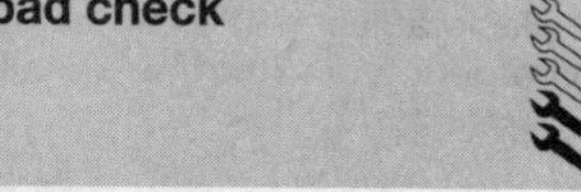

1 The outer brake pads can be checked without removing the wheels, by observing the brake pads through the holes in the wheels **(see illustration)**. If necessary, remove the wheel trim. The thickness of the pad lining must not be less than the dimension given in the Specifications.

2 If the outer pads are worn near their limits, it is worthwhile checking the inner pads as well. Apply the handbrake then jack up vehicle and support it on axle stands (see *Jacking and vehicle support*). Remove the roadwheels.

4.1 The outer brake pads can be observed through the holes in the wheels

3 Use a steel rule to check the thickness of the brake pads, and compare with the minimum thickness given in the Specifications **(see illustration)**.

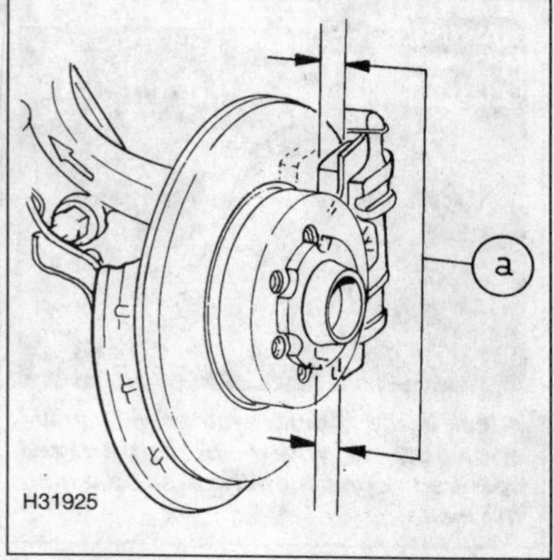

4.3 The thickness (a) of the brake pad linings must not be less than the specified amount

4 For a comprehensive check, the brake pads should be removed and cleaned. The operation of the caliper can then also be checked, and the condition of the brake disc itself can be fully examined on both sides. Refer to Chapter 9.

5 If any pad's friction material is worn to the specified minimum thickness or less, *all four pads at the front or rear, as applicable, must be renewed as a set.*

6 On completion of the check, refit the road-wheels and lower the vehicle to the ground.

5 Resetting the service interval display

1 After all necessary maintenance work has been completed, the service interval display must be reset. VW technicians use a special dedicated instrument to do this, and a print-out is then put in the vehicle service record. It is possible for the owner to reset the display as described in the following paragraphs, but note that the procedure will automatically reset the display to a 10 000 mile interval. To continue with the 'variable' intervals which take into consideration the number of starts, length of journeys, vehicle speeds, brake pad wear, bonnet opening frequency, fuel consumption, oil level and oil temperature, the display must be reset by a VW dealership using the special dedicated instrument.

2 To reset the standard display manually, switch off the ignition, then press and hold down the trip reset button beneath the speedometer. Turn the digital clock reset knob clockwise, and the trip display will now show 'service - - -'. Depress the clock reset knob as required to alternate between individual services, however, do not zero the display otherwise incorrect readings will be shown.

3 To reset the LongLife display manually, switch off the ignition, then press and hold down the trip reset button beneath the speedometer. Switch on the ignition and release the reset button, and note that the relevant service will appear in the display. Turn the digital clock reset knob clockwise, and the display will now return to normal. Switch off the ignition to complete the resetting procedure. Do not zero the display otherwise incorrect readings will be shown.

'01' on display

6 Exhaust system check

1 With the engine cold (at least an hour after the vehicle has been driven), check the complete exhaust system from the engine to the end of the tailpipe. The exhaust system is most easily checked with the vehicle raised on a hoist, or supported on axle stands, so that the exhaust components are readily visible and accessible (see *Jacking and vehicle support*).

2 Check the exhaust pipes and connections for evidence of leaks, severe corrosion and damage. Make sure that all brackets and mountings are in good condition, and that all relevant nuts and bolts are tight. Leakage at any of the joints or in other parts of the system will usually show up as a black sooty stain in the vicinity of the leak.

3 Rattles and other noises can often be traced to the exhaust system, especially the brackets and mountings. Try to move the pipes and silencers. If the components are able to come into contact with the body or suspension parts, secure the system with new mountings. Otherwise separate the joints (if possible) and twist the pipes as necessary to provide additional clearance.

7 Hose and fluid leak check

1 Visually inspect the engine joint faces, gaskets and seals for any signs of water or oil leaks. Pay particular attention to the areas around the camshaft cover, cylinder head, oil filter and sump joint faces. Bear in mind that, over a period of time, some very slight seepage

A leak in the cooling system will usually show up as white- or antifreeze-coloured deposits on the area adjoining the leak.

from these areas is to be expected – what you are really looking for is any indication of a serious leak. Should a leak be found, renew the offending gasket or oil seal by referring to the appropriate Chapters in this manual.

2 Also check the security and condition of all the engine-related pipes and hoses. Ensure that all cable-ties or securing clips are in place and in good condition. Clips which are broken or missing can lead to chafing of the hoses, pipes or wiring, which could cause more serious problems in the future.

3 Carefully check the radiator hoses and heater hoses along their entire length. Renew any hose which is cracked, swollen or deteriorated. Cracks will show up better if the hose is squeezed. Pay close attention to the hose clips that secure the hoses to the cooling system components. Hose clips can pinch and puncture hoses, resulting in cooling system leaks.

4 Inspect all the cooling system components (hoses, joint faces, etc) for leaks **(see Haynes Hint)**. Where any problems of this nature are found on system components, renew the component or gasket with reference to Chapter 3.

5 Where applicable, inspect the automatic transmission fluid cooler hoses for leaks or deterioration.

6 With the vehicle raised, inspect the petrol tank and filler neck for punctures, cracks and other damage. The connection between the filler neck and tank is especially critical. Sometimes a rubber filler neck or connecting hose will leak due to loose retaining clamps or deteriorated rubber.

8.2 Checking the underside of the auxiliary drivebelt with a mirror

7 Carefully check all rubber hoses and metal fuel lines leading away from the petrol tank. Check for loose connections, deteriorated hoses, crimped lines, and other damage. Pay particular attention to the vent pipes and hoses, which often loop up around the filler neck and can become blocked or crimped. Follow the lines to the front of the vehicle, carefully inspecting them all the way. Renew damaged sections as necessary.

8 From within the engine compartment, check the security of all fuel hose attachments and pipe unions, and inspect the fuel hoses and vacuum hoses for kinks, chafing and deterioration.

9 Where applicable, check the condition of the power steering fluid hoses and pipes.

8 Auxiliary drivebelt check

1 Apply the handbrake, then jack up the front of the vehicle and support it on axle stands (see *Jacking and vehicle support*).

2 Using a socket on the crankshaft pulley bolt, turn the engine slowly clockwise so that the full length of the auxiliary drivebelt can be examined. Look for cracks, splitting and fraying on the surface of the belt; check also for signs of glazing (shiny patches) and separation of the belt plies. Use a mirror to check the underside of the drivebelt **(see illustration)**. If damage or wear is visible, or if there are traces of oil or grease on it, the belt should be renewed (see Section 26).

9 Antifreeze check

1 The cooling system should be filled with the recommended G12 antifreeze and corrosion protection fluid – **do not** mix this antifreeze with any other type. Over a period of time, the concentration of fluid may be reduced due to topping-up (this can be avoided by topping-up with the correct antifreeze mixture – see Specifications) or fluid loss. If loss of coolant has been evident, it is important to make the necessary repair before adding fresh fluid.

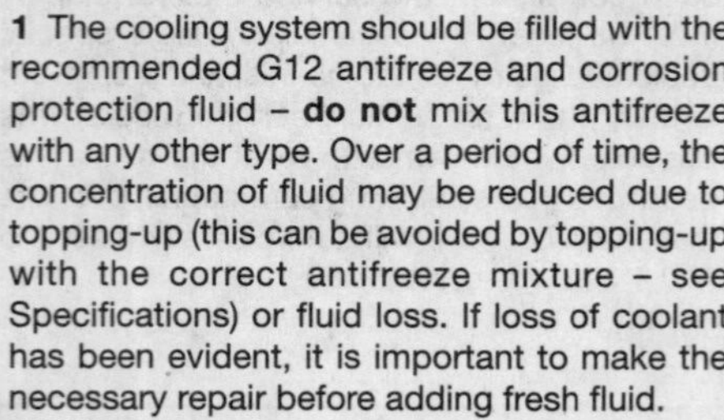

2 With the engine **cold**, carefully remove the cap from the expansion tank. If the engine is not completely cold, place a cloth rag over the cap before removing it, and remove it slowly to allow any pressure to escape.

3 Antifreeze checkers are available from car accessory shops. Draw some coolant from the expansion tank and observe how many plastic balls are floating in the checker. Usually, 2 or 3 balls must be floating for the correct concentration of antifreeze, but follow the manufacturer's instructions.

4 If the concentration is incorrect, it will be necessary to either withdraw some coolant and add antifreeze, or alternatively drain the old coolant and add fresh coolant of the correct concentration (see Section 30).

10 Brake hydraulic circuit check

1 Check the entire brake hydraulic circuit for leaks and damage. Start by checking the master cylinder in the engine compartment. At the same time, check the vacuum servo unit and ABS units for signs of fluid leakage.

2 Raise the front and rear of the vehicle and support it on axle stands (see *Jacking and vehicle support*). Check the rigid hydraulic brake lines for corrosion and damage. Also check the brake pressure regulator in the same manner.

3 At the front of the vehicle, check that the flexible hydraulic hoses to the calipers are not twisted or chafing on any of the surrounding suspension components. Turn the steering on full lock to make this check. Also check that the hoses are not brittle or cracked.

4 Lower the vehicle to the ground after making the checks.

11 Headlight beam adjustment

1 Accurate adjustment of the headlight beam is only possible using optical beam-setting equipment, and this work should therefore be carried out by a VW dealer or service station with the necessary facilities.

2 Basic adjustments can be carried out in an emergency, and further details are given in Chapter 12.

12 Pollen filter element renewal

1 The pollen filter is located in the heater unit and is accessed from inside the car, on the passenger's side.

2 Remove the clips and withdraw the facia lower trim from beneath the glovebox **(see illustration)**.

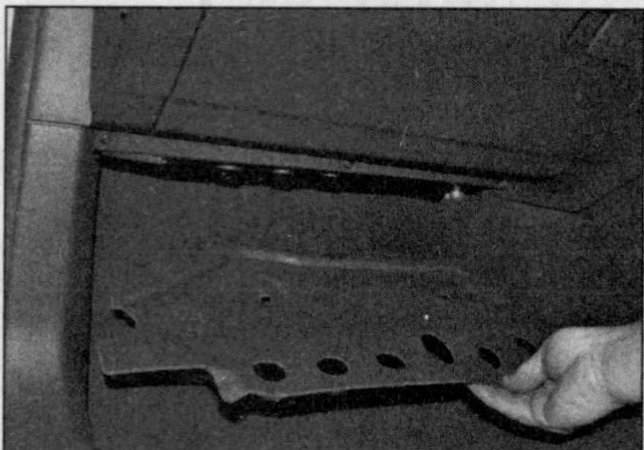

12.2 Remove the facia lower trim from beneath the glovebox

3 Undo the screws and remove the access cover **(see illustration)**.
4 Slide out the pollen filter element downwards from the heater unit **(see illustration)**.
5 Fit the new element then refit the access cover.
6 Refit the glovebox with reference to Chapter 11.

13 Manual transmission oil level check

1 Park the car on a level surface. For improved access to the filler/level plug, apply the handbrake, then jack up the front of the vehicle and support it on axle stands (see *Jacking and vehicle support*), but note that the rear of the vehicle should also be raised to ensure an accurate level check. The oil level must be checked before the car is driven, or at least 5 minutes after the engine has been switched off. If the oil is checked immediately after driving the car, some of the oil will remain distributed around the transmission components, resulting in an inaccurate level reading.

All except engine code CAXA (1.4 litre TSi with 02S transmission)

2 Undo the retaining screws and remove the engine undertray. Wipe clean the area around the transmission filler/level plug which is situated in the following location:

a) *1.4 and 1.6 litre engines – the filler/level plug is situated on the rear right-hand side of the final drive casing **(see illustration)**.*
b) *2.0 litre engines – the filler/level plug is situated on the front of the transmission casing **(see illustration)**.*

3 The oil level should reach the lower edge of the filler/level hole. A certain amount of oil will have gathered behind the filler/level plug, and will trickle out when it is removed; this does **not** necessarily indicate that the level is correct. To ensure that a true level is established, wait until the initial trickle has stopped, then add oil as necessary until a trickle of new oil can be seen emerging. The level will be correct when the flow ceases; use only good-quality oil of the specified type.
4 If the transmission has been overfilled so that oil flows out when the filler/level plug is removed, check that the car is completely level (front-to-rear and side-to-side), and allow the surplus to drain off into a suitable container.
5 When the oil level is correct, refit the filler/level plug and tighten it to the specified torque. Wipe off any spilt oil then refit the engine undertray(s), tighten the retaining screws securely, and lower the car to the ground.

Engine code CAXA

7 Undo the fasteners and remove the engine undertray.
8 On these transmissions, it's impossible to check the level of the oil through the 'filler' plug, due to the angle of the engine/transmission installation angle; the level of the fluid is above the lower edge of the filler hole. The only method of ensuring the correct fluid level, is to completely drain and refill the transmission.
9 Remove the air cleaner housing as described in Chapter 4A.
10 In order to drain the transmission, the pivot pin must be removed from the underside of the transmission casing. However, to prevent the position of the selector forks being altered, press the selector shaft down, then turn the angled locking rod upwards, and lock the shaft in position **(see illustration)**.
11 Place a container under the transmission casing.
12 Undo the retaining bolt, pull out the pivot pin nearest the passengers roadwheel and allow the oil to drain **(see illustration)**. The pivot pin O-ring seal must be renewed.
13 When the oil has finished draining clean the surrounding area, then refit the pivot pin (with a new O-ring seal), and tighten the retaining bolt to the specified torque.
14 Unscrew the drain plug from the base of the differential housing, and allow the oil to drain **(see illustration 13.12)**.
15 When the oil has finished draining, clean the surrounding area, refit the drain plug and tighten it to the specified torque.
16 Rotate the selector shaft locking rod to its original position.
17 Unscrew the reversing light switch from the top of the transmission casing.
18 Using a 600 mm length of 10 mm (external) diameter hose, and funnel, add 1.9 litres of new oil to the transmission.
19 Refit the reversing light switch, and tighten it to the specified torque.
20 The remainder of refitting is a reversal of removal.

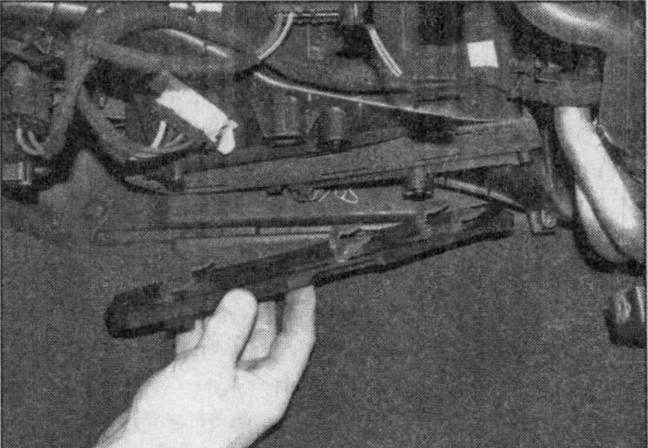

12.3 Remove the access cover...

12.4 ...and slide out the pollen filter element

13.2a Transmission filler/level plug location on 1.4 and 1.6 litre engines

13.2b Transmission filler/level plug location on 2.0 litre engines

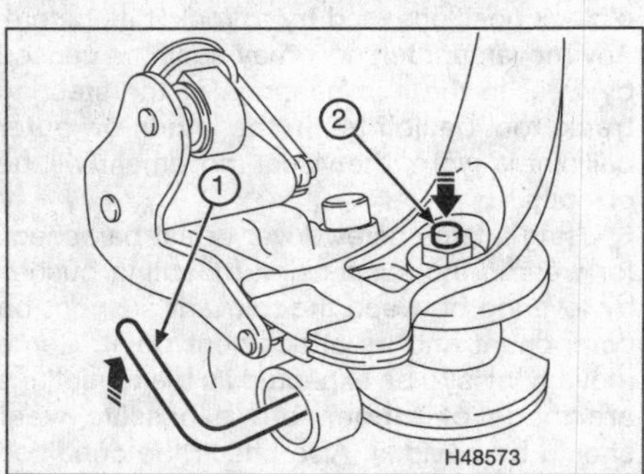

13.10 Press-down the selector shaft (2), and rotate the locking rod (1) upwards

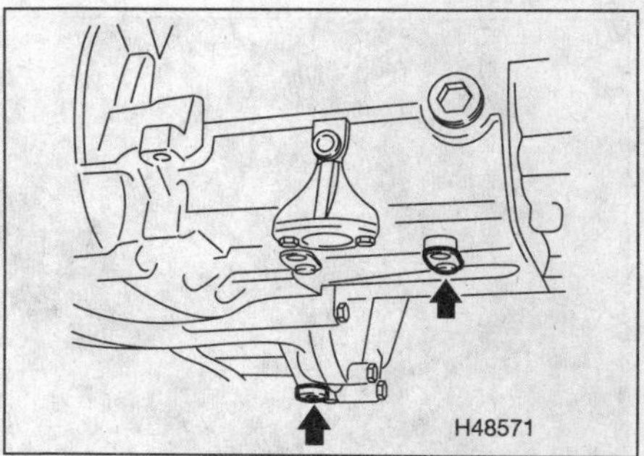

13.12 Transmission pivot pin, and drain plug (arrowed)

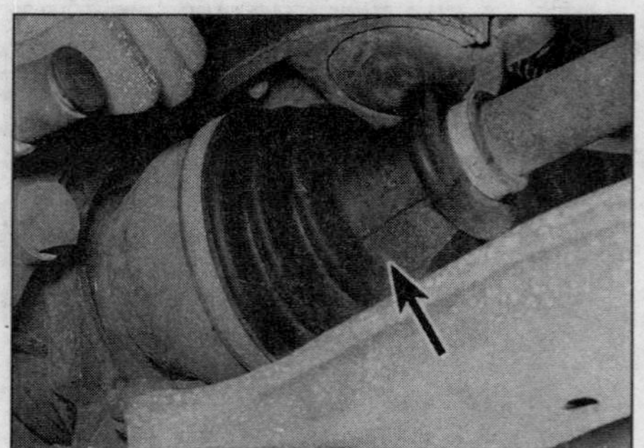

15.1 Check the condition of the driveshaft gaiters (arrowed)

14 Underbody protection check

Raise and support the vehicle on axle stands (see *Jacking and vehicle support*). Using an electric torch or lead light, inspect the entire underside of the vehicle, paying particular attention to the wheel arches. Look for any damage to the flexible underbody coating, which may crack or flake off with age, leading to corrosion. Also check that the wheel arch liners are securely attached with any clips provided – if they come loose, dirt may get in behind the liners and defeat their purpose. If there is any damage to the underseal, or any corrosion, it should be repaired before the damage gets too serious.

15 Driveshaft gaiter check

1 With the vehicle raised and securely supported on stands, slowly rotate the roadwheel. Inspect the condition of the outer constant velocity (CV) joint rubber gaiters, squeezing the gaiters to open out the folds. Check for signs of cracking, splits or deterioration of the rubber, which may allow the grease to escape, and lead to water and grit entry into the joint. Also check the security and condition of the retaining clips. Repeat these checks on the inner joints **(see illustration)**. If any damage or deterioration is found, the gaiters should be renewed (see Chapter 8).

16.4 Check for wear in the hub bearings by grasping the wheel and trying to rock it

2 At the same time, check the general condition of the CV joints themselves by first holding the driveshaft and attempting to rotate the wheel. Repeat this check by holding the inner joint and attempting to rotate the driveshaft. Any appreciable movement indicates wear in the joints, wear in the driveshaft splines, or a loose driveshaft retaining nut.

16 Steering and suspension check

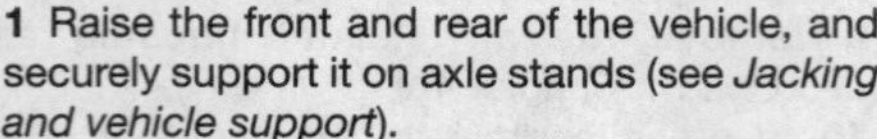

1 Raise the front and rear of the vehicle, and securely support it on axle stands (see *Jacking and vehicle support*).

2 Visually inspect the track rod end balljoint dust cover, the lower front suspension balljoint dust cover, and the steering rack-and-pinion gaiters for splits, chafing or deterioration. Any wear of these components will cause loss of lubricant, together with dirt and water entry, resulting in rapid deterioration of the balljoints or steering gear.

3 Check the power steering fluid hoses for chafing or deterioration, and the pipe and hose unions for fluid leaks. Also check for signs of fluid leakage under pressure from the steering gear rubber gaiters, which would indicate failed fluid seals within the steering gear.

4 Grasp the roadwheel at the 12 o'clock and 6 o'clock positions, and try to rock it **(see illustration)**. Very slight free play may be felt, but if the movement is appreciable, further investigation is necessary to determine the source. Continue rocking the wheel while an assistant depresses the footbrake. If the movement is now eliminated or significantly reduced, it is likely that the hub bearings are at fault. If the free play is still evident with the footbrake depressed, then there is wear in the suspension joints or mountings.

5 Now grasp the wheel at the 9 o'clock and 3 o'clock positions, and try to rock it as before. Any movement felt now may again be caused by wear in the hub bearings or the steering track rod balljoints. If the inner or outer balljoint is worn, the visual movement will be obvious.

6 Using a large screwdriver or flat bar, check for wear in the suspension mounting bushes by levering between the relevant suspension component and its attachment point. Some movement is to be expected as the mountings are made of rubber, but excessive wear should be obvious. Also check the condition of any visible rubber bushes, looking for splits, cracks or contamination of the rubber.

7 With the car standing on its wheels, have an assistant turn the steering wheel back-and-forth about an eighth of a turn each way. There should be very little, if any, lost movement between the steering wheel and roadwheels. If this is not the case, closely observe the joints and mountings previously described, but in addition, check the steering column universal joints for wear, and the rack-and-pinion steering gear itself.

8 Check for any signs of fluid leakage around the front suspension struts and rear shock absorber. Should any fluid be noticed, the suspension strut or shock absorber is defective internally, and should be renewed. **Note:** *Suspension struts/shock absorbers should always be renewed in pairs on the same axle to ensure correct vehicle handling.*

9 The efficiency of the suspension strut/shock absorber may be checked by bouncing the vehicle at each corner. Generally speaking, the body will return to its normal position and stop after being depressed. If it rises and returns on a rebound, the suspension strut/shock absorber is probably suspect. Examine also the suspension strut/shock absorber upper and lower mountings for any signs of wear.

17 Battery check

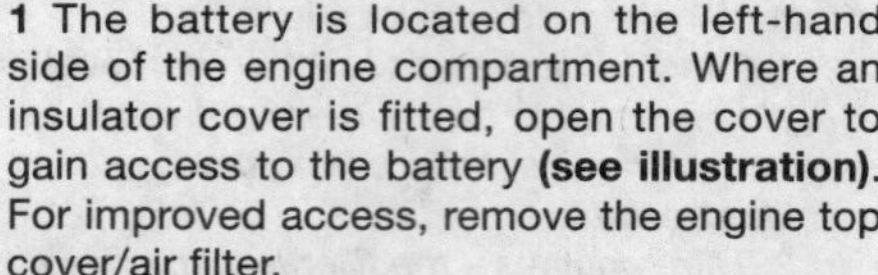

1 The battery is located on the left-hand side of the engine compartment. Where an insulator cover is fitted, open the cover to gain access to the battery **(see illustration)**. For improved access, remove the engine top cover/air filter.

2 Where necessary, open the fuse holder plastic cover (squeeze together the locking lugs to release the cover) to gain access to the battery positive (+) terminal and fuse holder connections.

3 Check that both battery terminals and all the fuse holder connections are securely attached and are free from corrosion. **Note:** *Before disconnecting the terminals from the battery, refer to 'Disconnecting the battery' in the Reference Chapter at the end of this manual.*

17.1 Battery location

4 Check the battery casing for signs of damage or cracking and check the battery retaining clamp bolt is securely tightened. If the battery casing is damaged in any way the battery must be renewed (see Chapter 5A).

5 If the vehicle is not fitted with a sealed-for-life maintenance-free battery, check the electrolyte level is between the MAX and MIN level markings on the battery casing. If topping-up is necessary, remove the battery (see Chapter 5A) from the vehicle then remove the cell caps/cover (as applicable). Using distilled water, top the electrolyte level of each cell up to the MAX level mark then securely refit the cell caps/cover. Ensure the battery has not been overfilled then refit the battery to the vehicle (see Chapter 5A).

6 On completion of the check, clip the cover securely back onto the fuse holder and close up the insulator cover (where fitted).

18 Hinge and lock lubrication

1 Lubricate the hinges of the bonnet, doors and tailgate with a light general-purpose oil. Similarly, lubricate all latches, locks and lock strikers. At the same time, check the security and operation of all the locks, adjusting them if necessary (see Chapter 11).

2 Lightly lubricate the bonnet release mechanism and cable with a suitable grease.

19 Airbag unit check

Inspect the exterior condition of the airbag(s) for signs of damage or deterioration. If an airbag shows signs of damage, it must be renewed (see Chapter 12). Note that it is not permissible to attach any stickers to the surface of the airbag, as this may affect the deployment of the unit.

20 Windscreen/tailgate/ headlight washer system check

1 Check that each of the washer jet nozzles are clear and that each nozzle provides a strong jet of washer fluid.

2 The tailgate jet should be aimed to spray at the centre of the screen, using a pin.

3 The windscreen washer nozzles should be aimed slightly above the centre of the screen using a small screwdriver to turn the jet eccentric.

4 The headlight inner jet should be aimed slightly above the horizontal centreline of the headlight, and the outer jet should be aimed slightly below the centreline. VW technicians use a special tool to adjust the headlight jet after pulling the jet out onto its stop.

5 Especially during the winter months, make sure that the washer fluid frost concentration is sufficient.

21 Engine management self-diagnosis memory fault check

This work should be carried out by a VW dealer or diagnostic specialist using special equipment. The diagnostic socket is located behind a cover beneath the central part of the facia. The cover is clipped in position.

22 Sunroof check and lubrication

1 Check the operation of the sunroof, and leave it in the fully open position.

2 Wipe clean the guide rails on each side of the sunroof opening, then apply lubricant to them. VW recommend lubricant spray G 052 778.

23 Road test and exhaust emissions check

Instruments and electrical equipment

1 Check the operation of all instruments and electrical equipment including the air conditioning system.

2 Make sure that all instruments read correctly, and switch on all electrical equipment in turn, to check that it functions properly.

Steering and suspension

3 Check for any abnormalities in the steering, suspension, handling or road 'feel'.

4 Drive the vehicle, and check that there are no unusual vibrations or noises which may indicate wear in the driveshafts, wheel bearings, etc.

5 Check that the steering feels positive, with no excessive 'sloppiness', or roughness, and check for any suspension noises when cornering and driving over bumps.

Drivetrain

6 Check the performance of the engine, clutch (where applicable), gearbox/transmission and driveshafts.

7 Listen for any unusual noises from the engine, clutch and gearbox/transmission.

8 Make sure the engine runs smoothly at idle, and there is no hesitation on accelerating.

9 Check that, where applicable, the clutch action is smooth and progressive, that the drive is taken up smoothly, and that the pedal travel is not excessive. Also listen for any noises when the clutch pedal is depressed.

10 On manual gearbox models, check that all gears can be engaged smoothly without noise, and that the gear lever action is smooth and not abnormally vague or 'notchy'.

11 On automatic transmission models, make sure that all gearchanges occur smoothly, without snatching, and without an increase in engine speed between changes. Check that all the gear positions can be selected with the vehicle at rest. If any problems are found, they should be referred to a VW dealer.

12 Listen for a metallic clicking sound from the front of the vehicle, as the vehicle is driven slowly in a circle with the steering on full-lock. Carry out this check in both directions. If a clicking noise is heard, this indicates wear in a driveshaft joint, in which case renew the joint if necessary.

Braking system

13 Make sure that the vehicle does not pull to one side when braking, and that the wheels do not lock when braking hard.

14 Check that there is no vibration through the steering when braking.

15 Check that the handbrake operates correctly without excessive movement of the lever, and that it holds the vehicle stationary on a slope.

16 Test the operation of the brake servo unit as follows. With the engine off, depress the footbrake four or five times to exhaust the vacuum. Hold the brake pedal depressed, then start the engine. As the engine starts, there should be a noticeable 'give' in the brake pedal as vacuum builds-up. Allow the engine to run for at least two minutes, and then switch it off. If the brake pedal is depressed now, it should be possible to detect a hiss from the servo as the pedal is depressed. After about four or five applications, no further hissing should be heard, and the pedal should feel considerably harder.

17 Under controlled emergency braking, the pulsing of the ABS unit must be felt at the footbrake pedal.

Exhaust emissions check

18 Although not part of the manufacturer's maintenance schedule, this check will normally be carried out on a regular basis according to the country the vehicle is operated in. Currently in the UK, exhaust emissions testing is included as part of the annual MOT test after the vehicle is 3 years old. In Germany the test is made when the vehicle is 3 years old, then repeated every 2 years.

24.1 Remove the engine oil dipstick...

24.2 ...lift the engine top cover/air cleaner...

24.3 ...then disconnect the wiring from the inlet air temperature sensor...

Every 40 000 miles or 4 years

24 Air filter element renewal

Engine codes BCA, BAG, BKG, BLF, BLN, BLP, AXX, BPY and BWA

1 The air filter element is located in the engine top cover. First, remove the engine oil dipstick **(see illustration)**.

2 Release each corner of the engine top cover by pulling sharply upwards. This will also release the air cleaner housing from the throttle valve module/housing **(see illustration)**.

3 Disconnect the wiring from the inlet air temperature sensor **(see illustration)**.

4 Disconnect the crankcase ventilation hose from the air cleaner housing or camshaft housing, and lift the assembly from the engine **(see illustration)**.

5 With the assembly inverted on the bench, if necessary remove the rubber grommet, then undo the screw and remove the air temperature sensor **(see illustrations)**.

6 Undo the screws and separate the air cleaner housing from the top cover, then remove the filter element **(see illustrations)**.

7 Fit the new filter element using a reversal of the removal procedure.

Engine code BUD

8 The air cleaner is located on the inlet manifold at the rear of the engine. First, press down the clips and release the air inlet duct from the engine compartment front crossmember.

9 At the front left-hand corner, disconnect the hose from the non-return valve.

10 Release the right-hand rear and left-hand front corners by pulling sharply upwards.

11 With the assembly on the bench, undo the screws and remove the cover, then remove the air filter element.

12 Fit the new filter element using a reversal of the removal procedure.

Engine codes BGU, BSE, BSF, AXW, BLX, BLY, BLR, BVX, BVY, BVZ and CAXA

13 The air cleaner is located in front of the battery on the left-hand side of the engine compartment. First, remove the engine top cover.

24.4 ...and disconnect the crankcase ventilation hose from the camshaft housing

24.5a Remove the rubber grommet...

24.5b ...and air temperature sensor

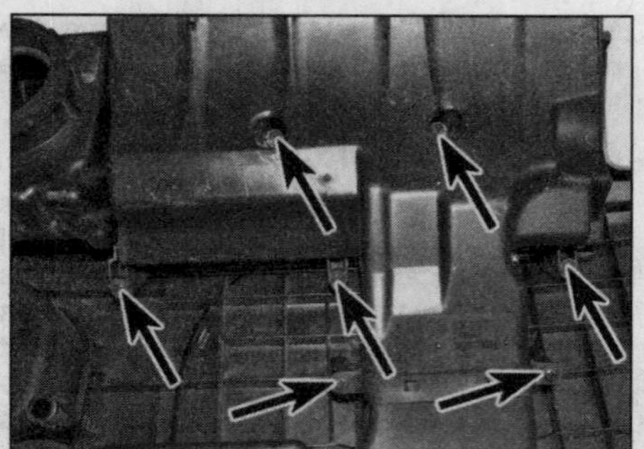
24.6a Undo the screws...

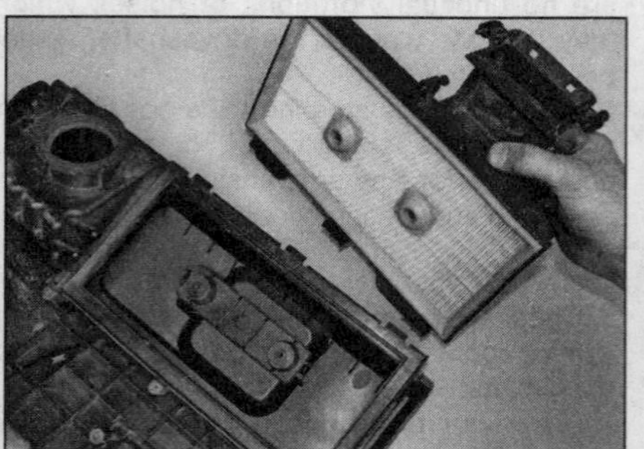
24.6b ...separate the air cleaner housing...

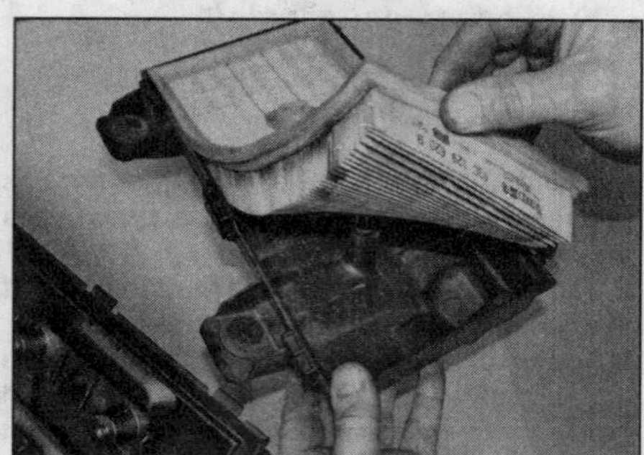
24.6c ...then remove the filter element

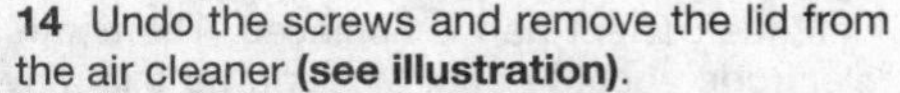

24.14 Undo the air filter cover screws (arrowed)

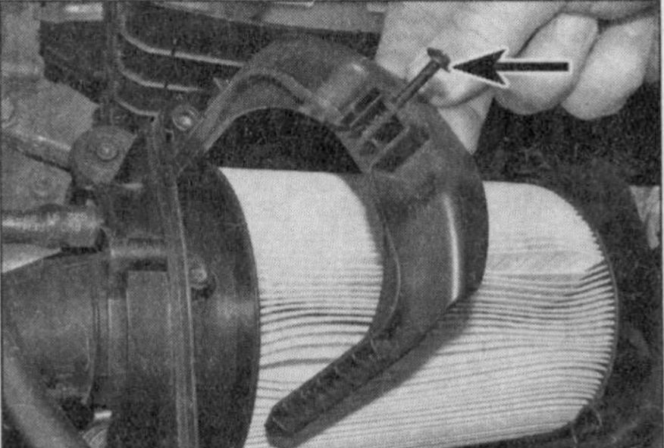

24.15a Undo the screw (arrowed), and lift out the clamp...

24.15b ...followed by the air filter element

14 Undo the screws and remove the lid from the air cleaner **(see illustration)**.

15 Undo the screw and slide out the clamp, then remove the filter element from the housing **(see illustrations)**.

16 Fit the new filter element using a reversal of the removal procedure.

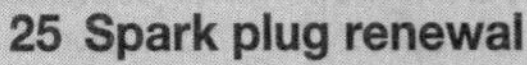

25 Spark plug renewal

1 The correct functioning of the spark plugs is vital for the correct running and efficiency of the engine. It is essential that the plugs fitted are appropriate for the engine (a suitable type is specified at the beginning of this Chapter). If this type is used and the engine is in good condition, the spark plugs should not need attention between scheduled renewal intervals. Spark plug cleaning is rarely necessary, and should not be attempted unless specialised equipment is available, as damage can easily be caused to the firing ends.

Engine codes BCA and BUD

2 Remove the engine top cover.

3 Remove the ignition HT coils and wiring from the tops of the spark plugs. VW technicians use special tool T10094 to pull out the coils, however, a length of welding rod bent to hook under the connectors may be used instead. If necessary, the wiring can be disconnected before removing the coils.

Engine codes BAG, BKG, BLF, BLN and BLP

4 Remove the engine top cover.

5 Remove the ignition HT coils and wiring from the tops of the spark plugs. VW technicians use special tools T10094 and T10118 to pull out the coils, however, a length of welding rod bent to hook under the connectors may be used instead. Working on each coil separately, slightly pull out the coil, then disconnect the wiring by inserting a screwdriver to release the locking device **(see illustrations)**.

Engine codes BGU, BSE and BSF

Note: *The spark plugs are located beneath the inlet manifold upper section, and are very difficult to access. VW technicians use a special tool to disconnect the HT leads, together with a universally-jointed spark plug socket to unscrew the spark plugs. If these tools are not available, the alternative method is to remove the inlet manifold upper section (see Chapter 4A).*

6 Remove the engine top cover.

7 Disconnect the HT lead connectors from the spark plugs. To do this, VW technicians use special tool T10112 to disconnect Nos 1 and 4 leads, and ordinary spark plug lead pliers to disconnect Nos 2 and 3. The special tool is approximately 30 cm in length with a bayonet-type claw at the bottom, which engages the HT lead connectors. If this tool is not available, or if an alternative tool cannot be fabricated, the upper inlet manifold section must be removed to improve access.

Engine code CAXA

8 Unclip the hose (where fitted), undo the retaining bolts, and remove the plastic cover from the top of the engine **(see illustration 3.2)**.

9 Release the clamps, undo the retaining bolts, and move the breather hose on the top of the engine, to one side **(see illustration)**.

10 Release the clips to allow the wiring to move from the wiring harness guide **(see illustration)**.

11 Remove the ignition HT coils and wiring from the tops of the spark plugs. VW technicians use special tool T10094 to pull out the coils, however, a length of welding rod (or similar) bent to hook under the connectors may be used instead **(see illustrations)**.

25.5a A length of welding rod bent as shown, can be used to pull out the ignition HT coils...

25.5b ...and disconnect the wiring

25.9 Engine breather pipe retaining bolts (arrowed)

25.10 Release the clips securing the wiring in the harness guide

25.11a Use a hooked tool to pull up the ignition coil...

25.11b ...and disconnect the wiring plug

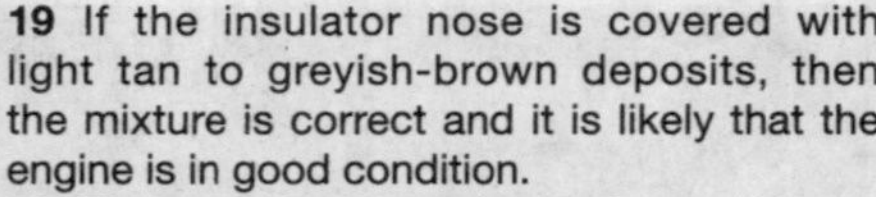

2.0 litre engine

12 Remove the engine top cover.

13 Unscrew the two bolts securing the HT wiring loom to the camshaft cover.

14 Remove the ignition HT coils and wiring from the tops of the spark plugs. VW technicians use special tool T40039 to pull out the coils, however, a length of welding rod bent to hook under the connectors may be used instead. Pull out the coils approximately 30.0 mm, then disconnect the wiring by pressing connectors toward the coils, and lifting at the same time.

All engines

15 It is advisable to remove the dirt from the spark plug recesses using a clean brush, vacuum cleaner or compressed air before removing the plugs, to prevent dirt dropping into the cylinders.

16 Unscrew the plugs using a spark plug spanner, suitable box spanner or a deep socket and extension bar. Keep the socket aligned with the spark plug – if it is forcibly moved to one side, the ceramic insulator may be broken off. The use of a universal joint socket will be helpful. As each plug is removed, examine it as follows.

17 Examination of the spark plugs will give a good indication of the condition of the engine. If the insulator nose of the spark plug is clean and white, with no deposits, this is indicative of a weak mixture or too hot a plug (a hot plug transfers heat away from the electrode slowly, a cold plug transfers heat away quickly).

18 If the tip and insulator nose are covered with hard black-looking deposits, then this is indicative that the mixture is too rich. Should the plug be black and oily, then it is likely that the engine is fairly worn, as well as the mixture being too rich.

19 If the insulator nose is covered with light tan to greyish-brown deposits, then the mixture is correct and it is likely that the engine is in good condition.

20 The spark plug electrode gap is of considerable importance as, if it is too large or too small, the size of the spark and its efficiency will be seriously impaired. On engines fitted with multi-electrode spark plugs, it is recommended that the plugs are renewed rather than attempting to adjust the gaps. On other spark plugs, the gap should be set to the value given by the manufacturer.

21 To set the gap on single electrode plugs, measure it with a feeler blade and then bend open, or closed, the outer plug electrode until the correct gap is achieved. The centre electrode should never be bent, as this may crack the insulator and cause plug failure, if nothing worse. If using feeler blades, the gap is correct when the appropriate-size blade is a firm sliding fit **(see illustrations)**.

22 Special spark plug electrode gap adjusting tools are available from most motor accessory shops, or from some spark plug manufacturers **(see illustration)**.

23 Before fitting the spark plugs, check that the threaded connector sleeves are tight, and that the plug exterior surfaces and threads are clean. It's often difficult to screw in new spark plugs without cross-threading them – this can be avoided using a piece of rubber hose **(see illustration and Haynes Hint)**.

24 Remove the rubber hose (if used), and tighten the plug to the specified torque using the spark plug socket and a torque wrench. Refit the remaining spark plugs in the same manner.

25 Reconnect and refit the HT leads/ ignition coils using a reversal of the removal procedure.

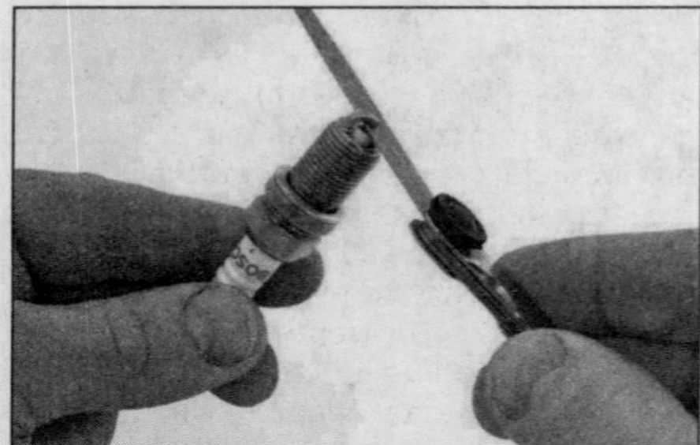

25.21a If single electrode plugs are being fitted, check the electrode gap using a feeler gauge...

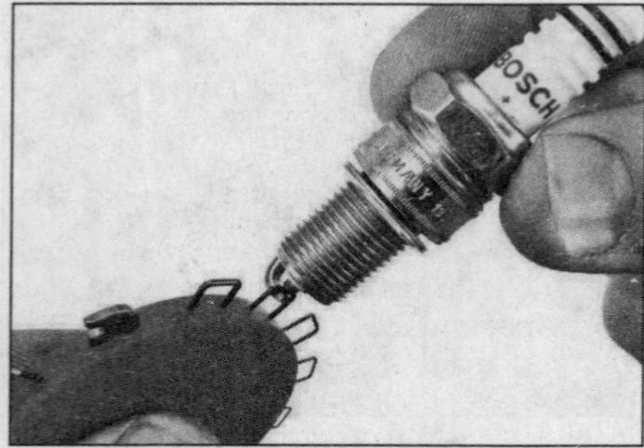

25.21b ...or a wire gauge...

25.22 ...and if necessary adjust the gap by bending the electrode

25.23 Use a rubber hose to avoid cross-threading the spark plugs

HAYNES HiNT

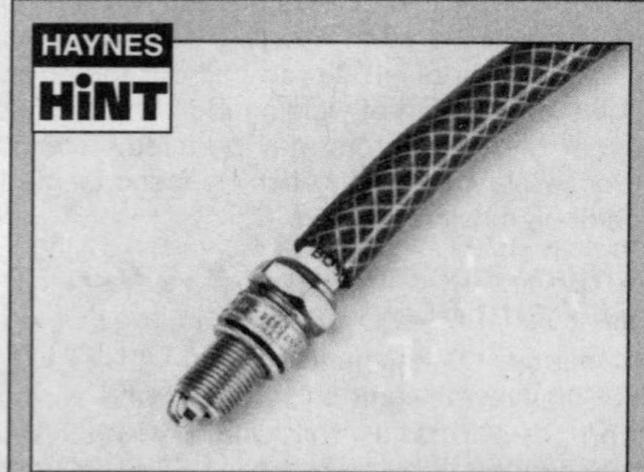

It is very often difficult to insert spark plugs into their holes without cross-threading them. To avoid this possibility, fit a short length of rubber hose over the end of the spark plug. The flexible hose acts as a universal joint to help align the plug with the plug thread, the hose will slip on the spark plug, preventing thread damage to the aluminium cylinder head.

26.7 Removing the auxiliary drivebelt on 1.4 litre non-FSi engines

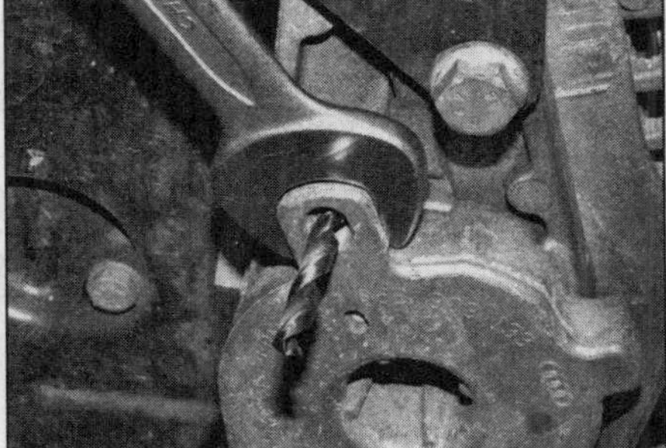
26.8a Locking the auxiliary drivebelt tensioner on 2.0 litre . . .

26.8b . . . and SOHC 1.6 litre engines

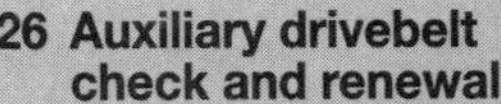

26 Auxiliary drivebelt check and renewal

1 The poly-vee drivebelt drives the alternator and where fitted, the air conditioning compressor.

2 On all engines, the drivebelt tension is adjusted automatically by a spring-tensioned idler.

Checking

3 See Section 8.

Renewal

4 Remove the engine top cover.

5 For improved access, apply the handbrake, then jack up the front of the vehicle and support it on axle stands (see *Jacking and vehicle support*). Remove the right-hand front roadwheel, then remove the access panel from the inner wheel arch.

6 If the drivebelt is to be re-used, mark it for clockwise direction to ensure it is refitted the same way round.

7 On 1.4 litre non-FSi engines (BCA and BUD), use a spanner to turn the tensioner central bolt clockwise to release the tension on the drivebelt, then insert a suitable drill bit or metal rod (approximately 5.5 mm diameter) through the hole in front of the pulley wheel to hold the tensioner **(see illustration)**.

8 On all 2.0 litre engines, and 1.6 litre SOHC engines (BGU, BSE and BSF), use a spanner on the lug provided and turn the tensioner clockwise. Lock the tensioner in its released position by inserting a drill through the lug into the tensioner body **(see illustrations)**.

9 On 1.4 and 1.6 litre FSi/TSi engines (BAG, BKG, BLF, BLN, BLP and CAXA), use a spanner to turn the tensioner central bolt anti-clockwise to release the tension on the drivebelt, then insert a suitable drill bit or metal rod (approximately 4.0 mm diameter) through the hole beneath the pulley wheel to hold the tensioner **(see illustrations)**.

10 Note how the drivebelt is routed, then remove it from the crankshaft pulley, alternator pulley and air conditioning compressor pulley.

11 Locate the new drivebelt on the pulleys,

26.9a On 1.4 and 1.6 litre FSi/ engines, turn the tensioner central bolt clockwise to release the tension on the drivebelt . . .

then release the tensioner. Check that the belt is located correctly in the multi-grooves in the pulleys.

12 Refit the access panel and roadwheel, and lower the vehicle to the ground. Refit the engine top cover.

27 Automatic transmission fluid level check

Note: *An accurate fluid level check can only be made with the transmission fluid at a temperature of between 35 and 45°C, and if it is not possible to ascertain this temperature, it is strongly recommended that the check be made by a VW dealer who will have the instrumentation to check the temperature and to check the transmission electronics for fault codes. Overfilling or underfilling adversely affects the function of the transmission.*

1 Take the vehicle on a short journey to warm the transmission slightly (see Note at the start of this Section), then park the vehicle on level ground and engage P with the selector lever. Raise the front and rear of the vehicle and support it on axle stands (see *Jacking and vehicle support*), ensuring the vehicle is kept level. Undo the retaining screws and remove the engine undertray to gain access to the base of the transmission unit.

2 Start the engine and run it at idle speed until the transmission fluid temperature reaches 35°C.

26.9b . . . then insert a drill bit or metal rod to lock the tensioner

3 Unscrew the fluid level plug from the bottom of the transmission sump **(see illustration)**.

4 If fluid **continually** drips from the level tube as the fluid temperature increases, the fluid level is correct and does not need to be topped-up. Note that there will be some fluid already present in the level tube, and it will be necessary to observe when this amount has drained before making the level check. Make sure that the check is made before the fluid temperature reaches 45°C.

5 If no fluid drips from the level tube, even when the fluid temperature has reached 45°C, it will be necessary to add fluid. VW technicians use an adapter which screws

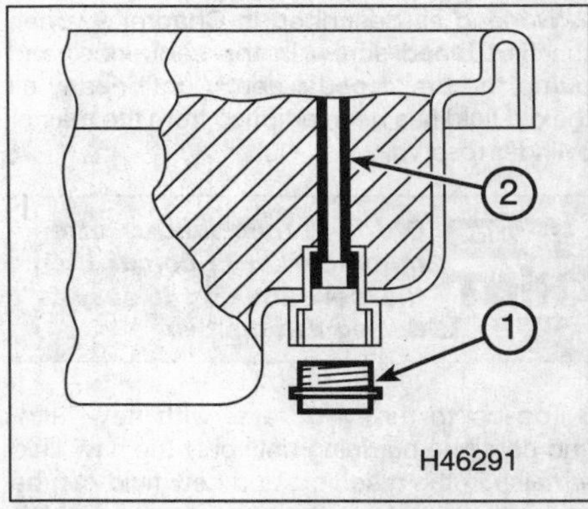

27.3 Automatic transmission fluid level check

1 Level plug 2 Level tube

into the bottom of the transmission sump, however, a tube inserted up through the drain plug (into the space above the fluid), will allow fluid to be added. Ideally, the fluid should be allowed to cool before adding the fluid.

6 Check the condition of the seal on the level plug and renew it if necessary by cutting off the old seal and fitting a new one. Refit the plug and tighten to the specified torque.

7 Refit the engine undertray, tighten the retaining screws securely, and lower the vehicle to the ground.

8 Frequent need for topping-up indicates that there is a leak, which should be corrected as soon as possible.

Every 60 000 miles

28 Timing belt renewal

Note: *This Section only applies to engine codes BCA, BUD, BGU, BSE, BSF, AXW, BLX, BLY, AXX, BLR, BPY, BWA, BVX, BVY and BVZ.*

Note: *VW say that 1.4 and 1.6 litre models only require a* ***check*** *at this interval, however, we recommend that the timing belt is renewed as is required for all 2.0 litre models.*

Inspection

1 Release the clips and remove the upper timing belt cover (refer to Chapter 2A, 2B or 2D).

2 Using a spanner or socket on the crankshaft pulley bolt, turn the engine slowly in a clockwise direction. **Do not** turn the engine on the camshaft bolt.

3 Check the complete length of the timing belt for signs of cracking, tooth separation, fraying, side glazing, and oil or grease contamination. Use a torch and mirror to check the underside of the belt.

4 If there is any evidence of wear or damage as described in the last paragraph, the timing belt **must** be renewed. A broken belt will cause major damage to the engine.

5 After making the check, refit the upper timing belt cover and remove the spanner/socket from the crankshaft pulley bolt.

Renewal

6 Refer to Chapter 2A, 2B or 2D for details.

Every 2 years

29 Brake (and clutch) fluid renewal

Warning: Brake hydraulic fluid can harm your eyes and damage painted surfaces, so use extreme caution when handling and pouring it. Do not use fluid that has been standing open for some time, as it absorbs moisture from the air. Excess moisture can cause a dangerous loss of braking effectiveness.

1 The procedure is similar to that for the bleeding of the hydraulic system as described in Chapter 9, except that the brake fluid reservoir should be emptied by syphoning, using a clean poultry baster or similar before starting, and allowance should be made for the old fluid to be expelled when bleeding a section of the circuit. Since the clutch hydraulic system also uses fluid from the brake system reservoir, it should also be bled at the same time by referring to Chapter 6.

2 Working as described in Chapter 9, open the first bleed screw in the sequence, and pump the brake pedal gently until nearly all the old fluid has been emptied from the master cylinder reservoir.

Old hydraulic fluid is often much darker in colour than the new, making it easy to distinguish the two.

3 Top-up to the MAX level with new fluid, and continue pumping until only the new fluid remains in the reservoir, and new fluid can be seen emerging from the bleed screw. Tighten the screw, and top the reservoir level up to the MAX level line.

4 Work through all the remaining bleed screws in the sequence until new fluid can be seen at all of them. Be careful to keep the master cylinder reservoir topped-up to above the MIN level at all times, or air may enter the system and greatly increase the length of the task.

5 When the operation is complete, check that all bleed screws are securely tightened, and that their dust caps are refitted. Wash off all traces of spilt fluid, and recheck the master cylinder reservoir fluid level.

6 On models with manual transmission, once the brake fluid has been changed the clutch fluid should also be renewed. Referring to Chapter 6, bleed the clutch until new fluid is seen to be emerging from the slave cylinder bleed screw, keeping the master cylinder fluid level above the MIN level line at all times to prevent air entering the system. Once the new fluid emerges, securely tighten the bleed screw then disconnect and remove the bleeding equipment. Securely refit the dust cap then wash off all traces of spilt fluid.

7 On all models, ensure the master cylinder fluid level is correct (see *Weekly checks*) and thoroughly check the operation of the brakes and (where necessary) clutch before taking the car on the road.

30 Coolant renewal

Warning: Wait until the engine is cold before starting this procedure. Do not allow antifreeze to come in contact with your skin, or with the painted surfaces of the vehicle. Rinse off spills immediately with plenty of water. Never leave antifreeze lying around in an open container, or in a puddle in the driveway or on the garage floor. Children and pets are attracted by its sweet smell, but antifreeze can be fatal if ingested.

Note: *This work is not included in the VW schedule and should not be required if the recommended VW G12 LongLife coolant antifreeze/inhibitor is used. However, if standard antifreeze/inhibitor is used, the work should be carried out at the recommended interval.*

Cooling system draining

1 With the engine completely cold, unscrew the expansion tank cap.

2 Firmly apply the handbrake then jack up the front of the vehicle and support it on axle stands (see *Jacking and vehicle support*). Undo the retaining screws and remove the engine undertray to gain access to the base of the radiator.

3 Position a suitable container beneath the coolant drain outlet which is fitted to the coolant bottom hose end fitting. Loosen the drain plug (there is no need to remove it completely) and allow the coolant to drain into the container. If desired, a length of tubing can be fitted to the drain outlet to direct the flow of coolant during draining. Where no drain outlet is fitted to the hose end fitting, remove the retaining clip and disconnect the bottom hose from the radiator to drain the coolant (see Chapter 3).

4 On engines with an oil cooler, to fully drain the system also disconnect one of the coolant hoses from the oil cooler which is located at the front of the cylinder block.

5 If the coolant has been drained for a reason other than renewal, then provided it is clean, it can be re-used.

6 Once all the coolant has drained, securely tighten the radiator drain plug or reconnect the bottom hose to the radiator (as applicable). Where necessary, also reconnect the coolant hose to the oil cooler and secure it in position with the retaining clip. Refit the undertray, and tighten the retaining screws securely.

7 On 1.4 litre TSi engines (code CAXA), release the clamps and disconnect the intercooler coolant hoses from the auxiliary radiator, and allow the coolant to drain **(see illustrations)**.
8 Reconnect the auxiliary radiator coolant hoses, when draining has ceased.

Cooling system flushing

9 If the recommended VW coolant has not been used and coolant renewal has been neglected, or if the antifreeze mixture has become diluted, the cooling system may gradually lose efficiency, as the coolant passages become restricted due to rust, scale deposits, and other sediment. The cooling system efficiency can be restored by flushing the system clean.
10 The radiator should be flushed separately from the engine, to avoid excess contamination.

Radiator flushing

11 To flush the radiator, first tighten the radiator drain plug.
12 Disconnect the top and bottom hoses and any other relevant hoses from the radiator (see Chapter 3).
13 Insert a garden hose into the radiator top inlet. Direct a flow of clean water through the radiator, and continue flushing until clean water emerges from the radiator bottom outlet.
14 If after a reasonable period, the water still does not run clear, the radiator can be flushed with a good proprietary cleaning agent. It is important that their manufacturer's instructions are followed carefully. If the contamination is particularly bad, insert the hose in the radiator bottom outlet, and reverse-flush the radiator.

Engine flushing

15 To flush the engine, remove the thermostat (see Chapter 3).
16 With the bottom hose disconnected from the radiator, insert a garden hose into the coolant housing. Direct a clean flow of water through the engine, and continue flushing until clean water emerges from the radiator bottom hose.

30.7a Prise out the wire clip a little, and disconnect the auxiliary radiator lower hose (arrowed)...

30.7b ...and upper hose

17 When flushing is complete, refit the thermostat and reconnect the hoses (see Chapter 3).

Cooling system filling

18 Before attempting to fill the cooling system, ensure the drain plug is securely closed and make sure that all hoses are securely connected and their retaining clips are in good condition. If the recommended VW coolant is not being used, ensure that a suitable antifreeze mixture is used all year round, to prevent corrosion of the engine components (see following sub-Section). **Note:** *VW recommend that only distilled water should be used.*
19 Remove the expansion tank filler cap and slowly fill the system with the coolant. Continue to fill the cooling system until bubbles stop appearing in the expansion tank. Help to bleed the air from the system by repeatedly squeezing the radiator bottom hose.
20 When no more bubbles appear, top the coolant level up to the MAX level mark then securely refit the cap to the expansion tank.
21 Run the engine at a fast idle speed until the cooling fan cuts in. Wait for the fan to stop then switch the engine off and allow the engine to cool.
22 When the engine has cooled, check the coolant level with reference to *Weekly checks*. Top-up the level if necessary, and refit the expansion tank cap.

Antifreeze mixture

23 If the recommended VW coolant is not being used, the antifreeze should always be renewed at the specified intervals. This is necessary not only to maintain the antifreeze properties, but also to prevent corrosion which would otherwise occur as the corrosion inhibitors become progressively less effective.
24 Always use an ethylene-glycol based antifreeze which is suitable for use in mixed-metal cooling systems. The quantity of antifreeze and levels of protection are indicated in the Specifications.
25 Before adding antifreeze, the cooling system should be completely drained, preferably flushed, and all hoses checked for condition and security.
26 After filling with antifreeze, a label should be attached to the expansion tank, stating the type and concentration of antifreeze used, and the date installed. Any subsequent topping-up should be made with the same type and concentration of antifreeze.
Caution: Do not use engine antifreeze in the windscreen/tailgate washer system, as it will damage the vehicle paintwork. A screenwash additive should be added to the washer system in the quantities stated on the bottle.

Chapter 1 Part B:
Routine maintenance and servicing – diesel models

Contents

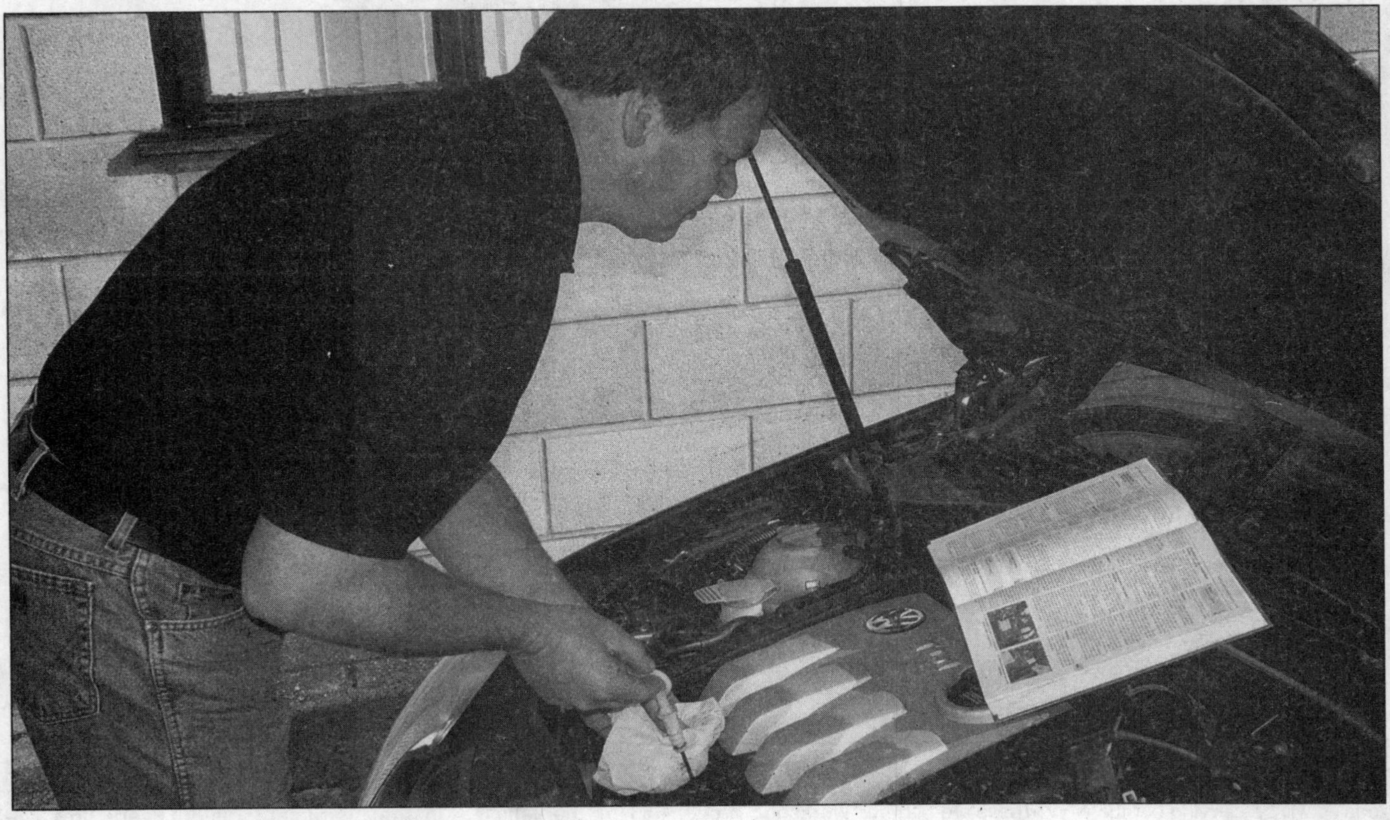

Degrees of difficulty

Easy, suitable for novice with little experience 	**Fairly easy,** suitable for beginner with some experience	**Fairly difficult,** suitable for competent DIY mechanic	**Difficult,** suitable for experienced DIY mechanic 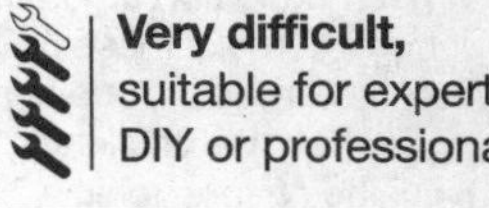	**Very difficult,** suitable for expert DIY or professional 

Lubricants and fluids

Refer to the end of *Weekly checks*

Engine codes*

PD unit injector engine:	
1.9 litre, 8-valve, turbo, SOHC	BJB, BKC, BRU, BLS, BXE and BXF
2.0 litre:	
8-valve, non-turbo, SOHC	BDK
8-valve, turbo, SOHC	BMM
16-valve, turbo, DOHC	AZV, BKD and BMN
Common rail injection engine	CBDA and CBDB

**See 'Vehicle identification' at the end of this manual for the location of engine code markings.*

Capacities

Engine oil (including filter)

All engines:	
PD injection engines	4.5 litres
Common rail injection engines	4.3 litres

Cooling system

All engines	6.2 litres

Transmission*

Manual transmission:	
Type 0AF	2.0 litres
Type 0A4	1.9 litres
* *See Chapter 7A for application details*	
DSG transmission (02E)	1.9 litres

Fuel tank (approximate)

All models	55 litres

Washer reservoirs

Models with headlight washers	5.5 litres
Models without headlight washers	3.0 litres

Engine

Timing belt wear limit (PD injection engines only)	22.0 mm wide

Cooling system

Antifreeze mixture:	
40% antifreeze	Protection down to -25°C
50% antifreeze	Protection down to -35°C

Note: *Refer to antifreeze manufacturer for latest recommendations.*

Brakes

Brake pad lining minimum thickness:	
Front	2.0 mm
Rear	2.0 mm

Torque wrench settings

	Nm	lbf ft
Manual gearbox filler/level plug:		
Multi-point socket head	30	22
Hexagon socket head	45	31
Oil filter cap	25	18
Roadwheel bolts	120	89
Sump drain plug	30	22

Maintenance schedule

The maintenance intervals in this manual are provided with the assumption that you, not the dealer, will be carrying out the work. These are the minimum intervals recommended by us for vehicles driven daily. If you wish to keep your vehicle in peak condition at all times, you may wish to perform some of these procedures more often. We encourage frequent maintenance, since it enhances the efficiency, performance and resale value of your vehicle.

When the vehicle is new, it should be serviced by a dealer service department (or other workshop recognised by the vehicle manufacturer as providing the same standard of service) in order to preserve the warranty. The vehicle manufacturer may reject warranty claims if you are unable to prove that servicing has been carried out as and when specified, using only original equipment parts or parts certified to be of equivalent quality.

All VW Golf/Jetta models are equipped with a service interval display indicator in the instrument panel. Every time the engine is started the panel will illuminate for approximately 20 seconds with service information. With the standard non-variable display, the service intervals are in accordance with specific distances and time periods. With the LongLife display, the service interval is variable according to the number of starts, length of journeys, vehicle speeds, brake pad wear, bonnet opening frequency, fuel consumption, oil level and oil temperature, however the vehicle **must** be serviced at least every two years. At a distance of 2000 miles before the next service is due, 'Service in 2000 miles' will appear at the bottom of the speedometer, and this figure will reduce in steps of 100 units as the vehicle is used. Once the service interval has been reached, the display will flash 'Service' or 'Service Now'. Note that if the variable (LongLife) service interval is being used, the engine must **only** be filled with the recommended **long-life** engine oil (see *Lubricants and fluids*).

After completing a service, VW technicians use a special instrument to reset the service display to the next service interval, and a print-out is put in the vehicle service record. The display can be reset by the owner as described in Section 5, but note that for models using the 'LongLife' interval, the procedure will automatically reset the display to the 10 000 miles 'distance' interval. To have the display reset to the 'variable' (LongLife) interval, it is necessary to take the vehicle to a VW dealer who will use a special instrument to encode the on-board computer.

Every 250 miles

- ☐ Refer to *Weekly checks*

'Oil' on display

- ☐ Renew the engine oil and filter (Section 3)

Note: *Frequent oil and filter changes are good for the engine. We recommend changing the oil at least once a year.*

- ☐ Check the front and rear brake pad thickness (Section 4)
- ☐ Reset the service interval display (Section 5)

'01' on display

In addition to the items listed above, carry out the following:

- ☐ Check the condition of the exhaust system and its mountings (Section 6)
- ☐ Check all underbonnet components and hoses for fluid and oil leaks (Section 7)
- ☐ Renew the fuel filter* (Section 8)
- ☐ Check the condition of the auxiliary drivebelt (Section 9)
- ☐ Check the coolant antifreeze concentration (Section 10)
- ☐ Check the brake hydraulic circuit for leaks and damage (Section 11)
- ☐ Check the headlight beam adjustment (Section 12)
- ☐ Renew the pollen filter element (Section 13)
- ☐ Check the manual transmission oil level (Section 14)
- ☐ Check the underbody protection for damage (Section 15)
- ☐ Check the condition of the driveshaft gaiters (Section 16)
- ☐ Check the steering and suspension components for condition and security (Section 17)
- ☐ Check the battery condition, security and electrolyte level (Section 18)
- ☐ Lubricate all hinges and locks (Section 19)
- ☐ Check the condition of the airbag unit(s) (Section 20)
- ☐ Check the operation of the windscreen/tailgate/headlight washer system(s) (as applicable) (Section 21)
- ☐ Check the engine management self-diagnosis memory for faults (Section 22)
- ☐ Check the operation of the sunroof and lubricate the guide rails (Section 23)
- ☐ Carry out a road test and check exhaust emissions (Section 24)

** Only when using diesel fuel not conforming to DIN EN 590 or when using RME fuel (diester)*

Every 35 000 miles

- ☐ Renew DSG transmission oil and filter (Section 25)

Every 40 000 miles or 4 years, whichever comes first

Note: *Many dealers perform these tasks at every second 01 service.*

- ☐ Renew the air filter element (Section 26)
- ☐ Renew the fuel filter* (Section 27)
- ☐ Check the condition of the auxiliary drivebelt (Section 28)

** Only when using diesel fuel conforming to DIN EN 590*

Every 60 000 miles

- ☐ Renew the timing belt and tensioner roller (Section 29)

Note: *VW specify a timing belt renewal interval of 75 000 miles for models manufactured up to MY 2006, and 95 000 miles for models manufactured from MY 2007-on. They specify a tensioner roller renewal interval of 150 000 miles for models manufactured up to MY 2006, and 190 000 miles for models manufactured from MY 2007-on. However, if the vehicle is used mainly for short journeys, we recommend that this shorter renewal interval is adhered to. The belt and tensioner renewal interval is very much up to the individual owner but, bearing in mind that severe engine damage will result if the belt breaks in use, we recommend the shorter interval.*

Every 95 000 miles, then every 19 000 miles

- ☐ Check the particulate filter ash deposit mass (Section 32)

Every 2 years

- ☐ Renew the brake (and clutch) fluid (Section 30)
- ☐ Renew the coolant* (Section 31)

*** Note:** *This work is not included in the VW schedule and should not be required if the recommended VW G12 LongLife coolant antifreeze/inhibitor is used.*

Component location – diesel models

Underbonnet view of a 1.9 litre model

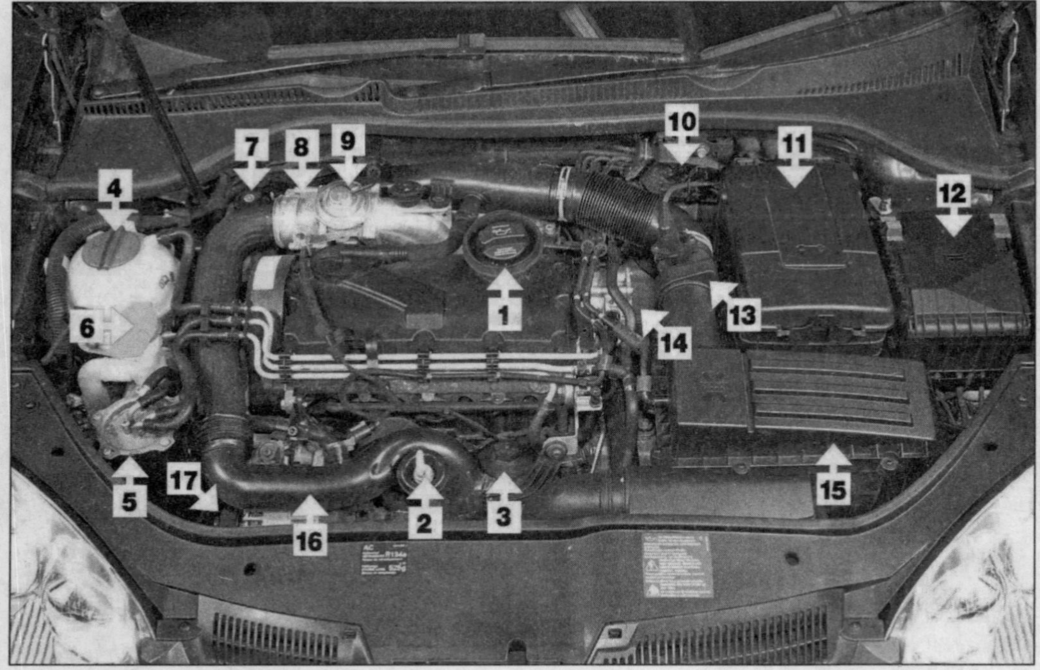

1 *Engine oil filler cap*
2 *Engine oil dipstick*
3 *Oil filter*
4 *Coolant expansion tank*
5 *Fuel filter*
6 *Windscreen/headlight washer fluid reservoir*
7 *Master cylinder brake fluid reservoir*
8 *Inlet manifold flap motor*
9 *EGR valve*
10 *EGR vacuum-solenoid valve*
11 *Battery*
12 *Fusebox*
13 *Air mass meter*
14 *Combined fuel lift pump and brake vacuum pump*
15 *Air cleaner housing*
16 *Air duct from intercooler to inlet manifold*
17 *Alternator*

Underbonnet view of a 2.0 litre SDi model

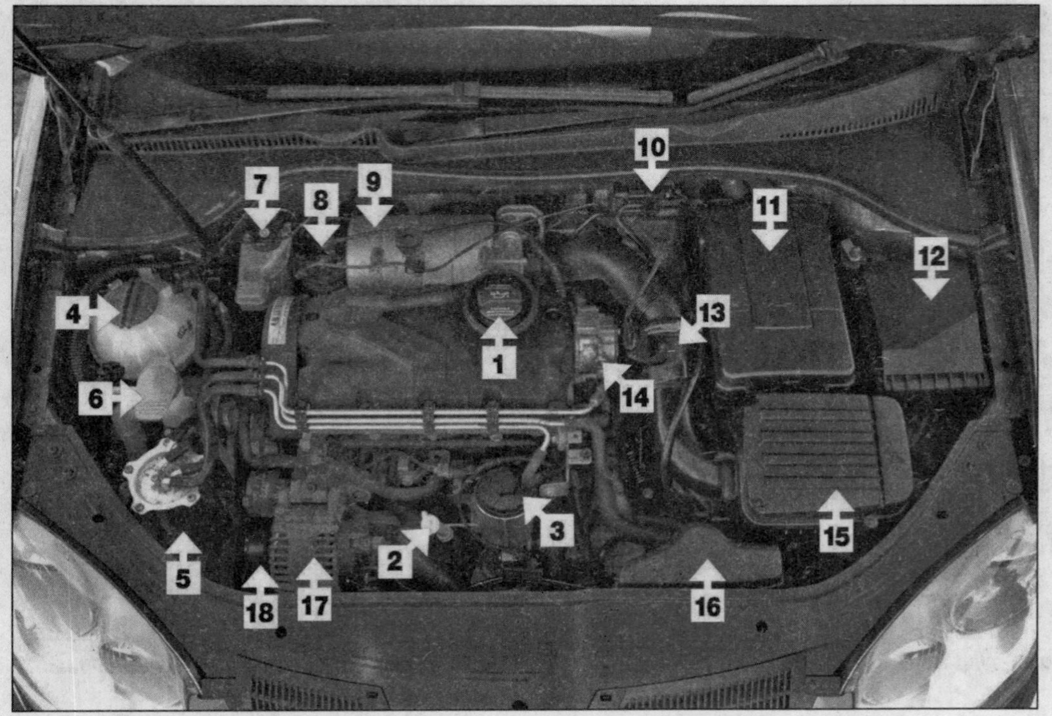

1 *Engine oil filler cap*
2 *Engine oil dipstick*
3 *Oil filter*
4 *Coolant expansion tank*
5 *Fuel filter*
6 *Windscreen/headlight/ rear window washer fluid reservoir*
7 *Master cylinder brake fluid reservoir*
8 *EGR valve*
9 *Inlet manifold (with exhaust manifold beneath)*
10 *EGR vacuum-solenoid valve*
11 *Battery*
12 *Fusebox*
13 *Air mass meter*
14 *Combined fuel lift pump and brake vacuum pump*
15 *Air cleaner housing*
16 *Inlet air duct*
17 *Alternator*
18 *Auxiliary drivebelt and tensioner*

Underbonnet view of a 2.0 litre TDi Unit injection model

1 *Engine oil filler cap*
2 *Engine oil dipstick*
3 *Oil filter*
4 *Coolant expansion tank*
5 *Fuel filter*
6 *Windscreen/headlight/ rear window washer fluid reservoir*
7 *Vacuum reservoir*
8 *Master cylinder brake fluid reservoir*
9 *Air duct from air cleaner to turbocharger*
10 *Vacuum solenoid valve*
11 *Air mass meter*
12 *Battery*
13 *Fusebox*
14 *Air cleaner housing*
15 *Inlet air duct*
16 *Combined fuel lift pump and brake vacuum pump*
17 *EGR valve*
18 *Inlet manifold flap motor*

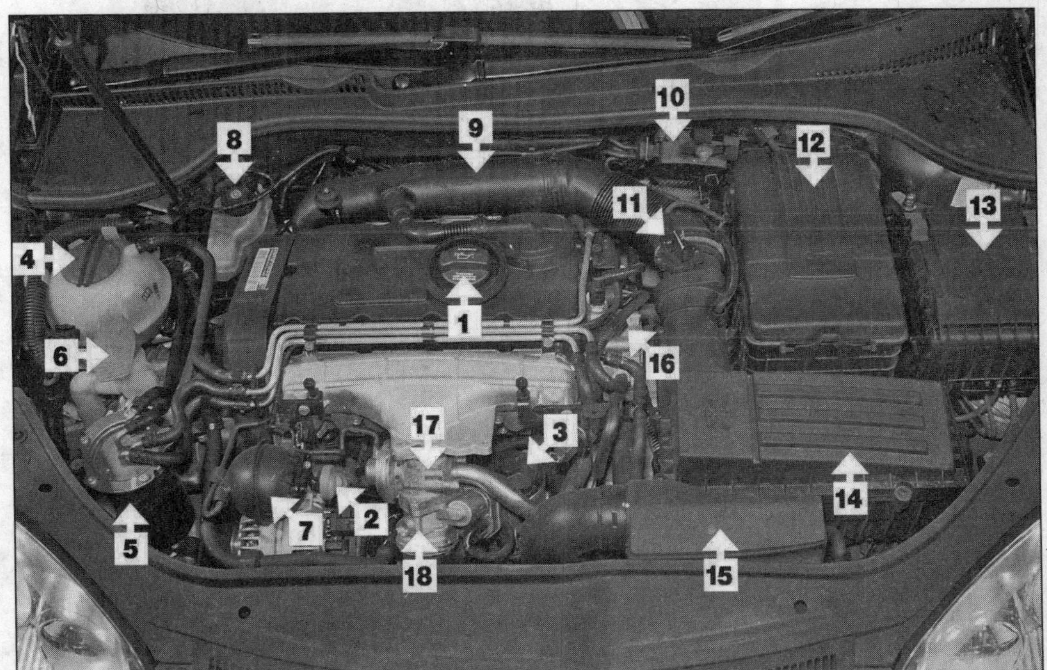

Underbonnet view of a 2.0 litre TDi Common rail injection model

1 *Engine oil filler cap*
2 *Engine oil dipstick*
3 *Oil filter*
4 *Coolant expansion tank*
5 *Fuel filter*
6 *Windscreen/headlight/ rear window washer fluid reservoir*
7 *Common fuel rail*
8 *Particulate filter*
9 *High-pressure fuel pump*
10 *Battery*
11 *Fusebox*
12 *Air cleaner housing*

Front underbody view of a 1.9 litre TDi model

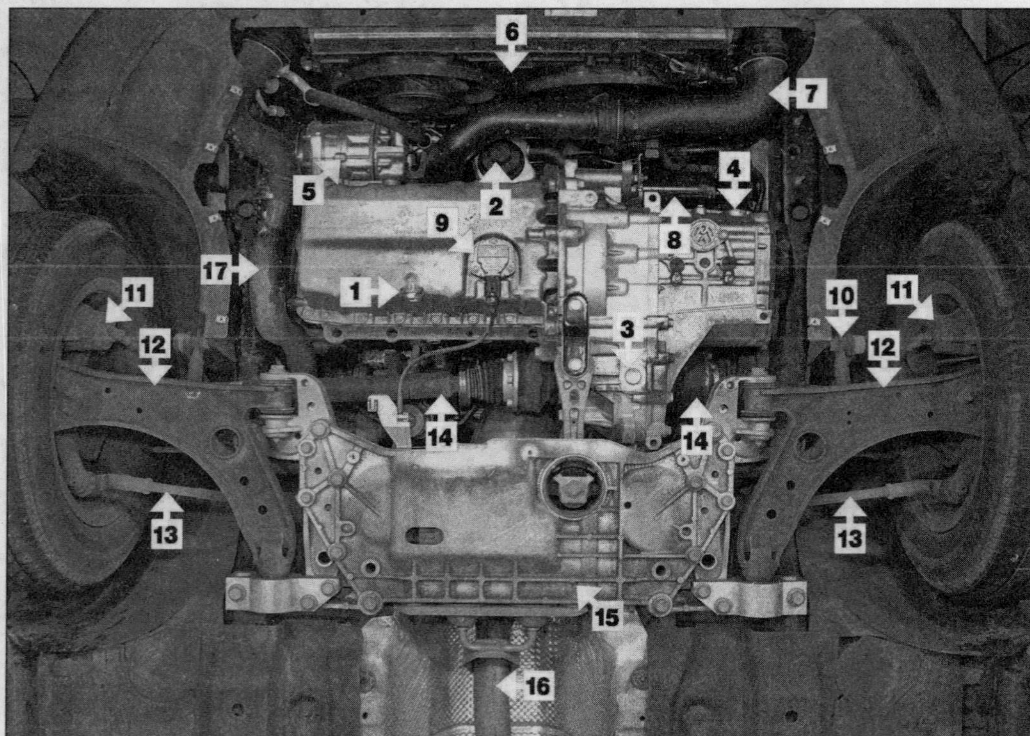

1 *Sump drain plug*
2 *Oil cooler/filter base cap*
3 *Manual transmission drain plug*
4 *Manual transmission filler/ level plug*
5 *Air conditioning compressor*
6 *Radiator and electric cooling fans*
7 *Air duct to intercooler*
8 *Starter motor*
9 *Engine oil level/ temperature sensor*
10 *Front anti-roll bar*
11 *Front brake calipers*
12 *Front suspension lower arms*
13 *Steering track rod arms*
14 *Driveshafts*
15 *Front suspension subframe*
16 *Exhaust pipe*

Rear underbody view of a 1.9 litre TDi model

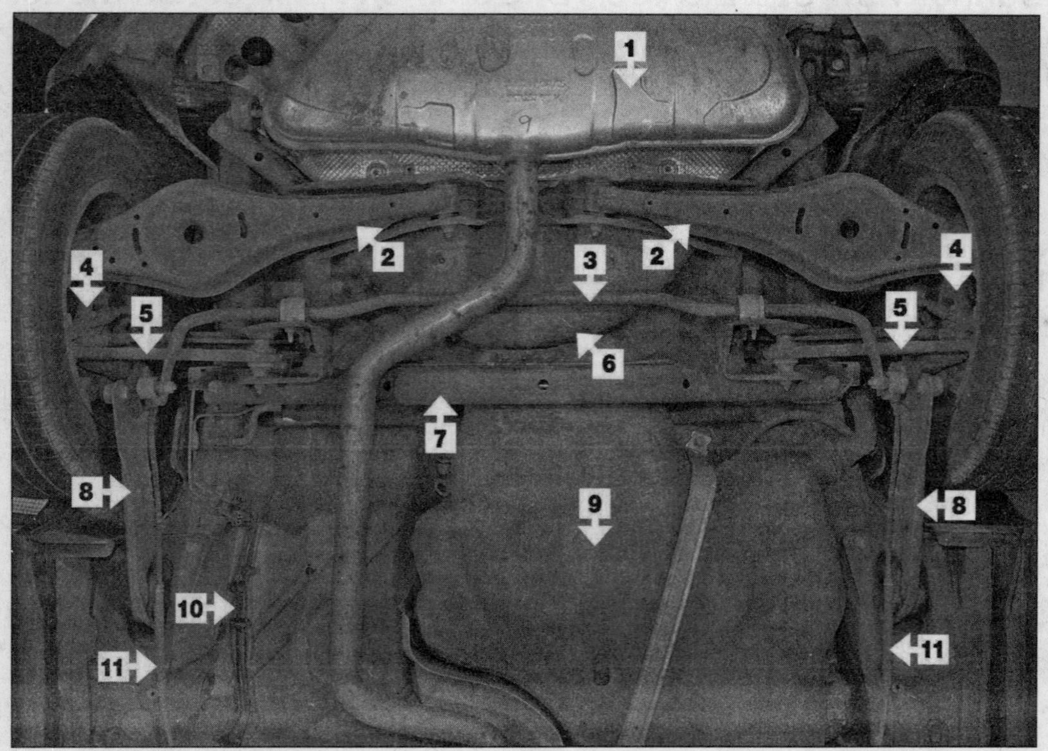

1 *Exhaust rear silencer*
2 *Rear track control rod*
3 *Rear anti-roll bar*
4 *Rear wheel bearing housing*
5 *Rear suspension transverse links*
6 *Spare wheel well*
7 *Rear suspension subframe*
8 *Rear trailing arm and bracket*
9 *Fuel tank*
10 *Hydraulic brake lines*
11 *Handbrake cables*

1 Introduction

This Chapter is designed to help the home mechanic maintain his/her vehicle for safety, economy, long life and peak performance.

The Chapter contains a master maintenance schedule, followed by Sections dealing specifically with each task in the schedule. Visual checks, adjustments, component renewal and other helpful items are included. Refer to the accompanying illustrations of the engine compartment and the underside of the vehicle for the locations of the various components.

Servicing your vehicle will provide a planned maintenance programme, which should result in a long and reliable service life. This is a comprehensive plan, so maintaining some items but not others will not produce the same results.

As you service your vehicle, you will discover that many of the procedures can – and should – be grouped together, because of the particular procedure being performed, or because of the proximity of two otherwise unrelated components to one another. For example, if the vehicle is raised for any reason, the exhaust can be inspected at the same time as the suspension and steering components.

The first step in this maintenance programme is to prepare yourself before the actual work begins. Read through all the Sections relevant to the work to be carried out, then make a list and gather all the parts and tools required. If a problem is encountered, seek advice from a parts specialist, or a dealer service department.

2 Regular maintenance

1 If, from the time the vehicle is new, the routine maintenance schedule is followed closely, and frequent checks are made of fluid levels and high-wear items, as suggested throughout this manual, the engine will be kept in relatively good running condition, and the need for additional work will be minimised.

2 It is possible that there will be times when the engine is running poorly due to the lack of regular maintenance. This is even more likely if a used vehicle, which has not received regular and frequent maintenance checks, is purchased. In such cases, additional work may need to be carried out, outside of the regular maintenance intervals.

3 If engine wear is suspected, a compression test (refer to Chapter 2E or 2F) will provide valuable information regarding the overall performance of the main internal components. Such a test can be used as a basis to decide on the extent of the work to be carried out. If, for example, a compression test indicates serious internal engine wear, conventional maintenance as described in this Chapter will not greatly improve the performance of the engine, and may prove a waste of time and money, unless extensive overhaul work is carried out first.

4 The following series of operations are those most often required to improve the performance of a generally poor-running engine:

Primary operations

a) Clean, inspect and test the battery (See 'Weekly checks').
b) Check all the engine-related fluids (See 'Weekly checks').
c) Drain the water from the fuel filter.
d) Check the condition and tension of the auxiliary drivebelt (Section 9).
e) Check the condition of the air filter, and renew if necessary (Section 26).
f) Check the condition of all hoses, and check for fluid leaks (Section 7).

5 If the above operations do not prove fully effective, carry out the following secondary operations:

Secondary operations

All items listed under *Primary operations*, plus the following:

a) Check the charging system (see Chapter 5A).
b) Check the preheating system (see Chapter 5C).
c) Renew the fuel filter (Section 8) and check the fuel system (see Chapter 4B).

'Oil' on display

3 Engine oil and filter renewal

1 Frequent oil and filter changes are the most important preventative maintenance procedures which can be undertaken by the DIY owner. As engine oil ages, it becomes diluted and contaminated, which leads to premature engine wear.

2 Before starting this procedure, gather all the necessary tools and materials. Also make sure that you have plenty of clean rags and newspapers handy, to mop-up any spills. Ideally, the engine oil should be warm, as it will drain better, and more built-up sludge will be removed with it. Take care, however, not to touch the exhaust or any other hot parts of the engine when working under the vehicle. To avoid any possibility of scalding, and to protect yourself from possible skin irritants and other harmful contaminants in used engine oils, it is advisable to wear gloves when carrying out this work. Access to the underside of the vehicle will be greatly improved if it can be raised on a lift, driven onto ramps, or jacked up and supported on axle stands (see *Jacking and vehicle support*). Whichever method is chosen, make sure that the vehicle remains level, or if it is at an angle, that the drain plug is at the lowest point. Undo the retaining screws and remove the engine undertray, then also remove the engine top cover **(see illustrations)**.

3 Slacken the sump drain plug about half a turn. Position the draining container under the drain plug, then remove the plug completely **(see illustration and Haynes Hint)**. To drain

3.2a Pull the plastic cover upwards – common rail injection models

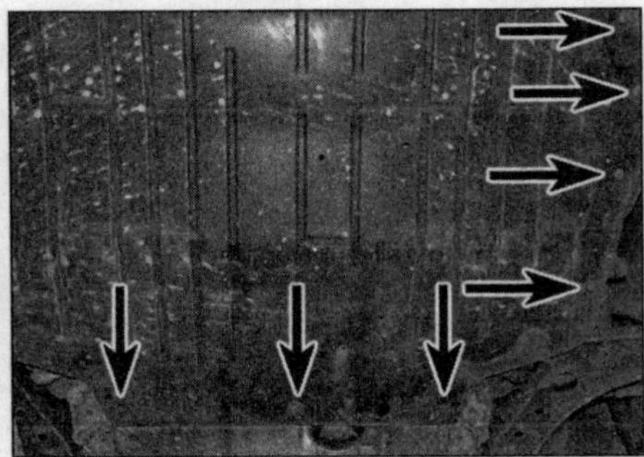

3.2b The engine undertray is secured by various screws along the rear, and side edges

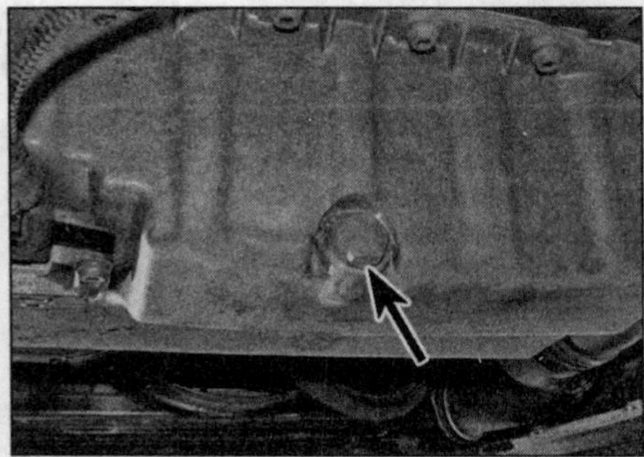

3.3 Sump drain plug

HAYNES HiNT

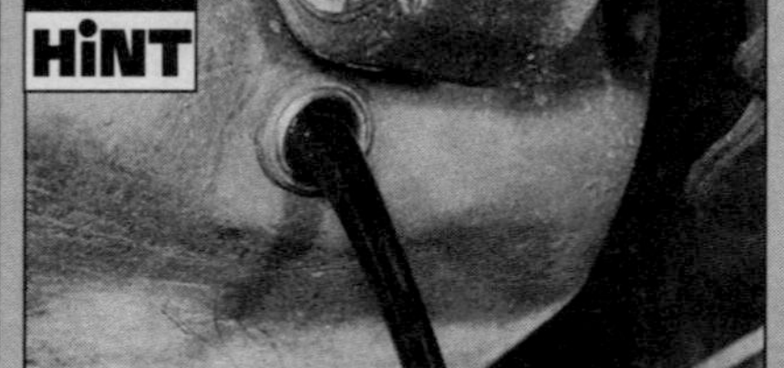

Keep the drain plug pressed into the sump while unscrewing it by hand the last couple of turns. As the plug releases, move it away sharply so the stream of oil issuing from the sump runs into the container, not up your sleeve.

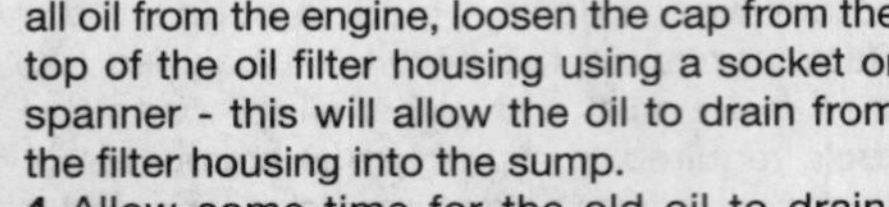

all oil from the engine, loosen the cap from the top of the oil filter housing using a socket or spanner - this will allow the oil to drain from the filter housing into the sump.

4 Allow some time for the old oil to drain, noting that it may be necessary to reposition the container as the oil flow slows to a trickle.

5 After all the oil has drained, wipe off the drain plug with a clean rag, and fit a new sealing washer. Clean the area around the drain plug opening, and refit the plug. Tighten the plug securely. **Note:** *On some engines, the sealing washer is integral with the drain plug. On these engines, the drain plug must be renewed.*

6 Place absorbent cloths around the oil filter housing to catch any spilt oil. Where necessary, unbolt the bracket and unclip the wiring loom from over the oil filter.

7 Fully unscrew the cap from the top of the oil filter and remove it together with the filter element. Recover the large sealing ring from the cap, and the small sealing ring from the centre rod. Unclip the filter element from the cap and dispose of it **(see illustrations)**.

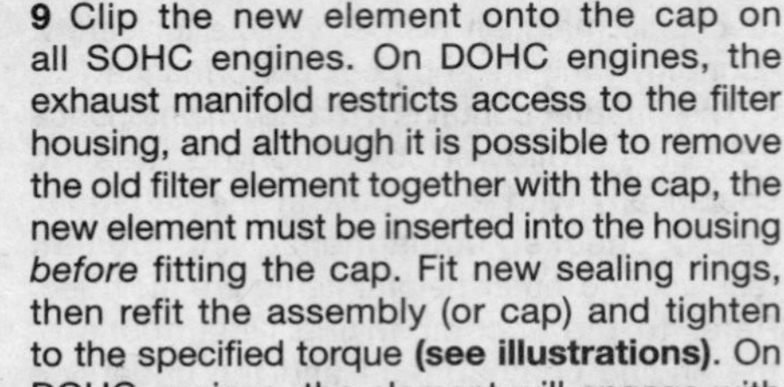

8 Using a clean rag, wipe all oil and sludge from the inside of the filter housing and cap.

9 Clip the new element onto the cap on all SOHC engines. On DOHC engines, the exhaust manifold restricts access to the filter housing, and although it is possible to remove the old filter element together with the cap, the new element must be inserted into the housing *before* fitting the cap. Fit new sealing rings, then refit the assembly (or cap) and tighten to the specified torque **(see illustrations)**. On DOHC engines, the element will engage with the cap as the cap is tightened. Wipe up any spilt oil before refitting the engine top cover.

10 Remove the old oil and all tools from under the car then refit the undertray and lower the car to the ground. Also refit the engine top cover.

11 Remove the dipstick, then unscrew the oil filler cap from the cylinder head cover. Fill the engine, using the correct grade and type of oil (see *Lubricants and fluids*). An oil can spout or funnel may help to reduce spillage. Pour in half the specified quantity of oil first **(see illustration)**, then wait a few minutes for the oil to run to the sump (see *Weekly checks*). Continue adding oil a small quantity at a time until the level is up to the maximum mark on the dipstick. Refit the filler cap.

12 Start the engine and run it for a few minutes; check for leaks around the oil filter cap and the sump drain plug. Note that there

3.7a Use a 32 mm socket to unscrew the filter cap

3.7b On common rail engines, undo the bolt (arrowed) and move the vacuum valve to one side

3.7c Remove the large sealing ring

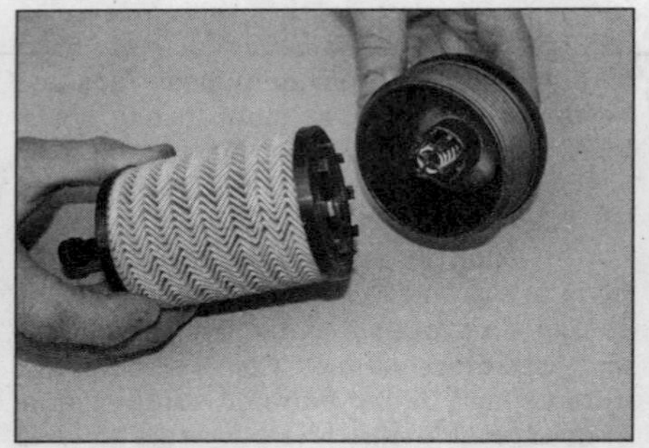

3.9a On SOHC engines, clip the new element onto the cap...

3.9b ...then refit to the oil filter housing

3.9c On DOHC engines, locate the element in the filter housing first...

3.9d ...then tighten the cap

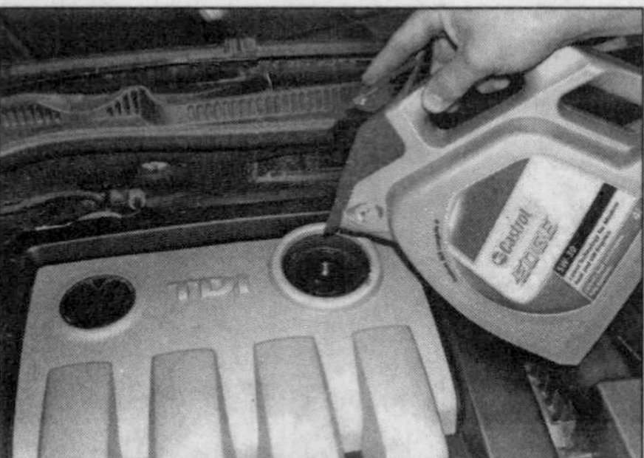

3.11 Pour in half the specified quantity of oil first, wait, then add the rest

may be a few seconds delay before the oil pressure warning light goes out when the engine is started, as the oil circulates through the engine oil galleries and the new oil filter before the pressure builds-up.

Warning: Do not increase the engine speed above idling while the oil pressure light is illuminated, as considerable damage can be caused to the turbocharger.

13 Switch off the engine, and wait a few minutes for the oil to settle in the sump once more. With the new oil circulated and the filter completely full, recheck the level on the dipstick, and add more oil as necessary.

14 Dispose of the used engine oil safely, with reference to *General repair procedures* in the *Reference* section of this manual.

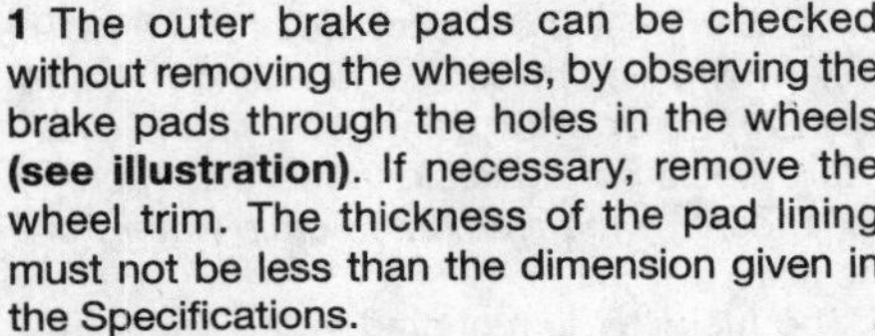

4 Brake pad check

1 The outer brake pads can be checked without removing the wheels, by observing the brake pads through the holes in the wheels **(see illustration)**. If necessary, remove the wheel trim. The thickness of the pad lining must not be less than the dimension given in the Specifications.

2 If the outer pads are worn near their limits, it is worthwhile checking the inner pads as well. Apply the handbrake then jack up vehicle and support it on axle stands (see *Jacking and vehicle support*). Remove the roadwheels.

3 Use a steel rule to check the thickness of the brake pads, and compare with the minimum thickness given in the Specifications **(see illustration)**.

4 For a comprehensive check, the brake pads should be removed and cleaned. The operation of the caliper can then also be checked, and the condition of the brake disc itself can be fully examined on both sides. Refer to Chapter 9.

4.1 The outer brake pads can be observed through the holes in the wheels

5 If any pad's friction material is worn to the specified minimum thickness or less, *all four pads at the front or rear, as applicable, must be renewed as a set.*

6 On completion of the check, refit the wheels and lower the vehicle to the ground.

5 Resetting the service interval display

1 After all necessary maintenance work has been completed, the service interval display must be reset. VW technicians use a special dedicated instrument to do this, and a print-out is then put in the vehicle service record. It is possible for the owner to reset the display as described in the following paragraphs, but note that the procedure will automatically reset the display to a 10 000 mile interval. To continue with the 'variable' intervals which take into consideration the number of starts, length of journeys, vehicle speeds, brake pad wear, bonnet opening frequency, fuel consumption, oil level and oil temperature, the display must be reset by a VW dealership using the special dedicated instrument.

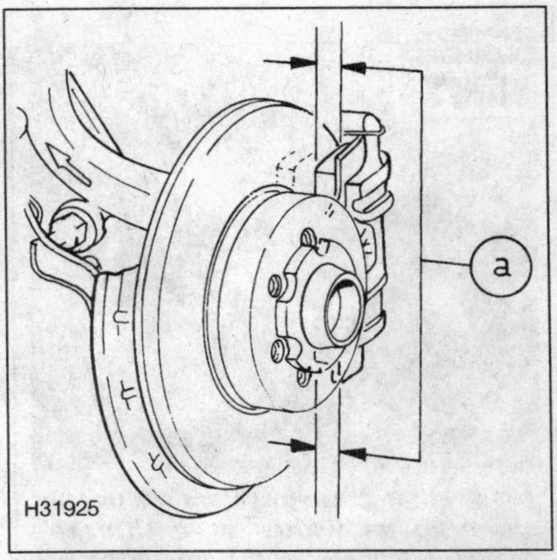

4.3 The thickness (a) of the brake pad linings must not be less than the specified amount

2 To reset the standard display manually, switch off the ignition, then press and hold down the trip reset button beneath the speedometer. Turn the digital clock reset knob clockwise, and the trip display will now show 'service - - -'. Depress the clock reset knob as required to alternate between individual services, however, do not zero the display otherwise incorrect readings will be shown.

3 To reset the LongLife display manually, switch off the ignition, then press and hold down the trip reset button beneath the speedometer. Switch on the ignition and release the reset button, and note that the relevant service will appear in the display. Turn the digital clock reset knob clockwise, and the display will now return to normal. Switch off the ignition to complete the resetting procedure. Do not zero the display otherwise incorrect readings will be shown.

'01' on display

6 Exhaust system check

1 With the engine cold (at least an hour after the vehicle has been driven), check the complete exhaust system from the engine to the end of the tailpipe. The exhaust system is most easily checked with the vehicle raised on a hoist, or suitably supported on axle stands, so that the exhaust components are readily visible and accessible (see *Jacking and vehicle support*).

2 Check the exhaust pipes and connections for evidence of leaks, severe corrosion and damage. Make sure that all brackets and mountings are in good condition, and that all relevant nuts and bolts are tight. Leakage at any of the joints or in other parts of the system will usually show up as a black sooty stain in the vicinity of the leak.

3 Rattles and other noises can often be traced to the exhaust system, especially the brackets and mountings. Try to move the pipes and silencers. If the components are able to come into contact with the body or suspension parts, secure the system with new mountings. Otherwise separate the joints (if possible) and twist the pipes as necessary to provide additional clearance.

7 Hose and fluid leak check

1 Visually inspect the engine joint faces, gaskets and seals for any signs of water or oil leaks. Pay particular attention to the areas around the camshaft cover, cylinder head, oil filter and sump joint faces. Bear in mind that, over a period of time, some very slight seepage from these areas is to be expected – what you are really looking for is any indication of a serious leak. Should a leak be found, renew the offending gasket or oil seal by referring to the appropriate Chapters in this manual.

2 Also check the security and condition of all the engine-related pipes and hoses. Ensure that all cable-ties or securing clips are in place and in good condition. Clips which are broken or missing can lead to chafing of the hoses, pipes or wiring, which could cause more serious problems in the future.

3 Carefully check the radiator hoses and heater hoses along their entire length. Renew any hose which is cracked, swollen or deteriorated. Cracks will show up better if

A leak in the cooling system will usually show up as white- or antifreeze-coloured deposits on the area adjoining the leak.

the hose is squeezed. Pay close attention to the hose clips that secure the hoses to the cooling system components. Hose clips can pinch and puncture hoses, resulting in cooling system leaks.

4 Inspect all the cooling system components (hoses, joint faces, etc) for leaks **(see Haynes Hint)**. Where any problems of this nature are found on system components, renew the component or gasket with reference to Chapter 3.

5 Where applicable, inspect the automatic transmission fluid cooler hoses for leaks or deterioration.

6 With the vehicle raised, inspect the fuel tank and filler neck for punctures, cracks and other damage. The connection between the filler neck and tank is especially critical. Sometimes a rubber filler neck or connecting hose will leak due to loose retaining clamps or deteriorated rubber.

7 Carefully check all rubber hoses and metal fuel lines leading away from the tank. Check for loose connections, deteriorated hoses, crimped lines, and other damage. Pay particular attention to the vent pipes and hoses, which often loop up around the filler neck and can become blocked or crimped. Follow the lines to the front of the vehicle, carefully inspecting them all the way. Renew damaged sections as necessary.

8 From within the engine compartment, check the security of all fuel hose attachments and pipe unions, and inspect the fuel hoses and vacuum hoses for kinks, chafing and deterioration.

9 Check the condition of the power steering fluid hoses and pipes.

8 Fuel filter renewal (vehicles using high sulphur diesel fuel)

Note: *Carry out this procedure at this interval only when using diesel fuel not conforming to DIN EN 590 or when using RME fuel (diester) – this fuel is not available in the UK. There is no longer any requirement to drain water from the filter.*

1 The fuel filter is mounted in the right-hand front corner of the engine compartment **(see illustration)**. Place rags around the filter to absorb any fuel that may be spilt.

2 Early models are fitted with a water-extraction plug in the filter cover, however this was discontinued on later models. Where fitted, unscrew the plug and use a pipette to draw out approximately 100 ml of fuel **(see illustrations)**. Have a container handy to deposit the fuel.

3 Undo the screws and lift the cover from the top of the filter housing. Remove the seal and discard, as a new one must be used on refitting. Also, remove the inner seal from the top of the filter element centre pillar **(see illustrations)**.

4 Using a screwdriver, prise the old filter element from the housing and discard **(see illustration)**.

5 Insert the new filter element, and press down fully onto the centre pillar **(see illustration)**.

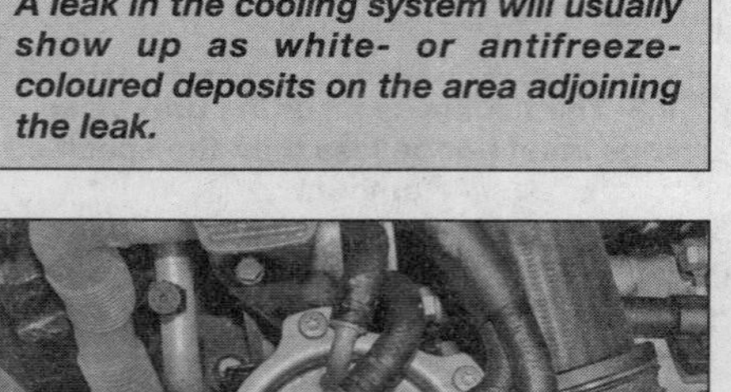

8.1 The fuel filter is mounted in the right-hand front corner of the engine compartment

8.2a Unscrew the plug...

8.2b ...and use a pipette to draw out approximately 100 ml of fuel

8.3a Lift the cover from the housing...

8.3b ...then remove the cover seal...

8.3c ...and the centre seal

8.4 Remove the old filter element

6 Locate a new inner seal on the centre pillar.

7 Fit a new seal to the cover, then refit to the housing. Insert the screws and tighten securely.

8 On early models, refit and tighten the water-extraction plug.

9 Start and run the engine at idle, then check around the fuel filter for fuel leaks. **Note:** *It may take a few seconds of cranking before the engine starts.*

9 Auxiliary drivebelt check

1 Apply the handbrake, then jack up the front of the vehicle and support it on axle stands (see *Jacking and vehicle support*).

2 Using a socket on the crankshaft pulley bolt, turn the engine slowly clockwise so that the full length of the auxiliary drivebelt can be examined. Look for cracks, splitting and fraying on the surface of the belt; check also for signs of glazing (shiny patches) and separation of the belt plies. If damage or wear is visible, or if there are traces of oil or grease on it, the belt should be renewed (see Section 27).

10 Antifreeze check

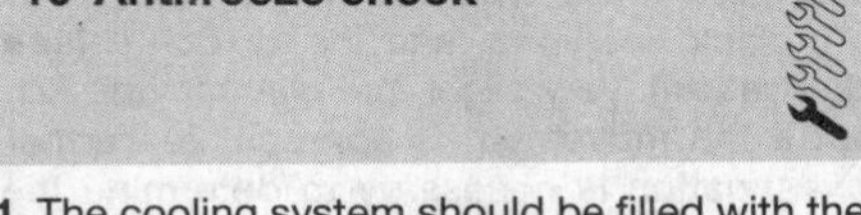

1 The cooling system should be filled with the recommended G12 antifreeze and corrosion protection fluid – **do not** mix this antifreeze with any other type. Over a period of time, the concentration of fluid may be reduced due to topping-up (this can be avoided by topping-up with the correct antifreeze mixture – see Specifications) or fluid loss. If loss of coolant has been evident, it is important to make the necessary repair before adding fresh fluid.

2 With the engine **cold**, carefully remove the cap from the expansion tank. If the engine is not completely cold, place a cloth rag over the cap before removing it, and remove it slowly to allow any pressure to escape.

3 Antifreeze checkers are available from car accessory shops. Draw some coolant from the expansion tank and observe how many plastic balls are floating in the checker. Usually, 2 or 3 balls must be floating for the correct concentration of antifreeze, but follow the manufacturer's instructions.

4 If the concentration is incorrect, it will be necessary to either withdraw some coolant and add antifreeze, or alternatively drain the old coolant and add fresh coolant of the correct concentration (see Section 30).

11 Brake hydraulic circuit check

1 Check the entire brake hydraulic circuit for leaks and damage. Start by checking the master cylinder in the engine compartment. At the same time, check the vacuum servo unit and ABS units for signs of fluid leakage.

2 Raise the front and rear of the vehicle and support it on axle stands (see *Jacking and vehicle support*). Check the rigid hydraulic brake lines for corrosion and damage.

3 At the front of the vehicle, check that the flexible hydraulic hoses to the calipers are not twisted or chafing on any of the surrounding suspension components. Turn the steering on full lock to make this check. Also check that the hoses are not brittle or cracked.

4 Lower the vehicle to the ground after making the checks.

12 Headlight beam adjustment

1 Accurate adjustment of the headlight beam is only possible using optical beam-setting equipment, and this work should therefore be carried out by a VW dealer or service station with the necessary facilities.

2 Basic adjustments can be carried out in an emergency, and further details are given in Chapter 12.

13 Pollen filter element renewal

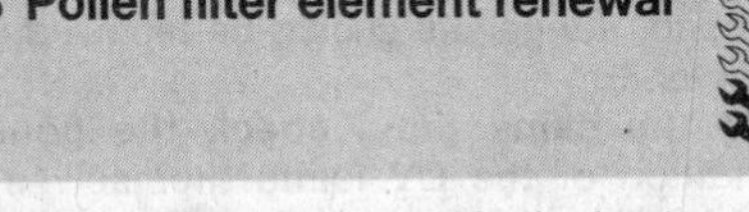

1 The pollen filter is located in the heater unit and is accessed from inside the car, on the passenger's side.

8.5 Insert the new filter element

2 Remove the clips and withdraw the facia lower trim from beneath the glovebox **(see illustration)**.

3 Undo the screws and remove the access cover **(see illustration)**.

4 Slide out the pollen filter element downwards from the heater unit **(see illustration)**.

5 Fit the new element then refit the access cover.

6 Refit the glovebox with reference to Chapter 11.

14 Manual transmission oil level check

1 Park the car on a level surface. For improved access to the filler/level plug, apply the handbrake, then jack up the front of the vehicle and support it on axle stands (see *Jacking and vehicle support*), but note that the rear of the vehicle should also be raised to ensure an accurate level check. The oil level must be checked before the car is driven, or at least 5 minutes after the engine has been switched off. If the oil is checked immediately after driving the car, some of the oil will remain distributed around the transmission components, resulting in an inaccurate level reading.

2 Undo the retaining screws and remove the engine undertray(s). Wipe clean the area around the transmission filler/level plug which is situated in the following location:

a) 1.9 litre engines – the filler/level plug is

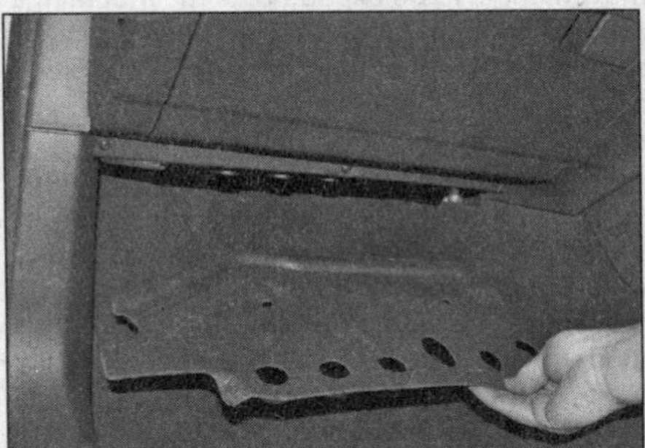

13.2 Remove the facia lower trim from beneath the glovebox

13.3 Remove the access cover...

13.4 ...and slide out the pollen filter element

14.2a Transmission filler/level plug location on 1.9 litre engines

*situated on the front of the transmission casing **(see illustration).***

b) *2.0 litre engines with 5-speed transmissions – the filler/level plug is situated on the rear right-hand side of the final drive casing **(see illustration).***

c) *2.0 litre engines with 6-speed transmissions – the filler/level plug is located on the front side of the transmission.*

3 The oil level should reach the lower edge of the filler/level hole. A certain amount of oil will have gathered behind the filler/level plug, and will trickle out when it is removed; this does **not** necessarily indicate that the level is correct. To ensure that a true level is established, wait until the initial trickle has stopped, then add oil as necessary until a trickle of new oil can be seen emerging. The level will be correct when the flow ceases; use only good-quality oil of the specified type.

4 If the transmission has been overfilled so that oil flows out when the filler/level plug is removed, check that the car is completely level (front-to-rear and side-to-side), and allow the surplus to drain off into a suitable container.

5 When the oil level is correct, refit the filler/level plug and tighten it to the specified torque. Wipe off any spilt oil then refit the engine undertray(s), tighten the retaining screws securely, and lower the car to the ground.

15 Underbody protection check

Raise and support the vehicle on axle stands

14.2b Transmission filler/level plug location on 2.0 litre engines

(see *Jacking and vehicle support*). Using an electric torch or lead light, inspect the entire underside of the vehicle, paying particular attention to the wheel arches. Look for any damage to the flexible underbody coating, which may crack or flake off with age, leading to corrosion. Also check that the wheel arch liners are securely attached with any clips provided – if they come loose, dirt may get in behind the liners and defeat their purpose. If there is any damage to the underseal, or any corrosion, it should be repaired before the damage gets too serious.

16 Driveshaft gaiter check

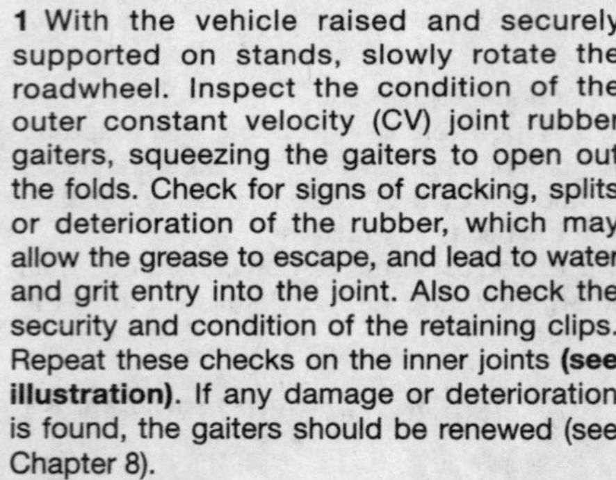

1 With the vehicle raised and securely supported on stands, slowly rotate the roadwheel. Inspect the condition of the outer constant velocity (CV) joint rubber gaiters, squeezing the gaiters to open out the folds. Check for signs of cracking, splits or deterioration of the rubber, which may allow the grease to escape, and lead to water and grit entry into the joint. Also check the security and condition of the retaining clips. Repeat these checks on the inner joints **(see illustration)**. If any damage or deterioration is found, the gaiters should be renewed (see Chapter 8).

2 At the same time, check the general condition of the CV joints themselves by first holding the driveshaft and attempting to rotate the wheel. Repeat this check by holding the inner joint and attempting to rotate the driveshaft. Any appreciable movement indicates wear in the joints, wear in the driveshaft splines, or a loose driveshaft retaining nut.

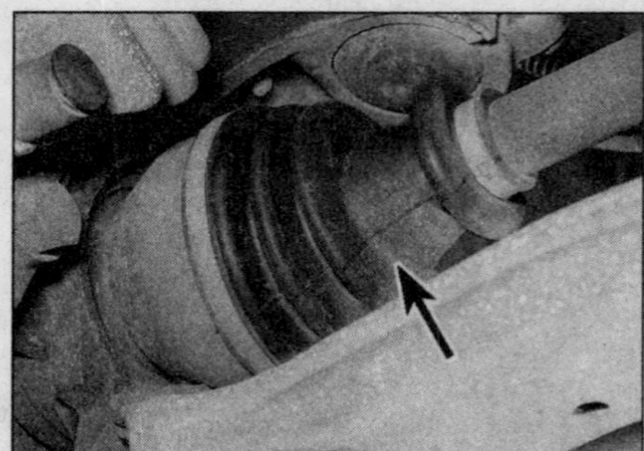

16.1 Check the condition of the driveshaft gaiters (arrowed)

17.4 Check for wear in the hub bearings by grasping the wheel and trying to rock it

17 Steering and suspension check

1 Raise the front and rear of the vehicle, and securely support it on axle stands (see *Jacking and vehicle support*).

2 Visually inspect the track rod end balljoint dust cover, the lower front suspension balljoint dust cover, and the steering rack-and-pinion gaiters for splits, chafing or deterioration. Any wear of these components will cause loss of lubricant, together with dirt and water entry, resulting in rapid deterioration of the balljoints or steering gear.

3 Check the power steering fluid hoses for chafing or deterioration, and the pipe and hose unions for fluid leaks. Also check for signs of fluid leakage under pressure from the steering gear rubber gaiters, which would indicate failed fluid seals within the steering gear.

4 Grasp the roadwheel at the 12 o'clock and 6 o'clock positions, and try to rock it **(see illustration)**. Very slight free play may be felt, but if the movement is appreciable, further investigation is necessary to determine the source. Continue rocking the wheel while an assistant depresses the footbrake. If the movement is now eliminated or significantly reduced, it is likely that the hub bearings are at fault. If the free play is still evident with the footbrake depressed, then there is wear in the suspension joints or mountings.

5 Now grasp the wheel at the 9 o'clock and 3 o'clock positions, and try to rock it as before. Any movement felt now may again be caused by wear in the hub bearings or the steering track rod balljoints. If the inner or outer balljoint is worn, the visual movement will be obvious.

6 Using a large screwdriver or flat bar, check for wear in the suspension mounting bushes by levering between the relevant suspension component and its attachment point. Some movement is to be expected as the mountings are made of rubber, but excessive wear should be obvious. Also check the condition of any visible rubber bushes, looking for splits, cracks or contamination of the rubber.

7 With the car standing on its wheels, have an assistant turn the steering wheel back-and-forth about an eighth of a turn each way. There should be very little, if any, lost movement between the steering wheel and roadwheels. If this is not the case, closely observe the joints and mountings previously described, but in addition, check the steering column universal joints for wear, and the rack-and-pinion steering gear itself.

8 Check for any signs of fluid leakage

around the front suspension struts and rear shock absorber. Should any fluid be noticed, the suspension strut or shock absorber is defective internally, and should be renewed. **Note:** *Suspension struts/shock absorbers should always be renewed in pairs on the same axle to ensure correct vehicle handling.*

9 The efficiency of the suspension strut/shock absorber may be checked by bouncing the vehicle at each corner. Generally speaking, the body will return to its normal position and stop after being depressed. If it rises and returns on a rebound, the suspension strut/shock absorber is probably suspect. Examine also the suspension strut/shock absorber upper and lower mountings for any signs of wear.

18 Battery check

1 The battery is located on the left-hand side of the engine compartment. Where an insulator cover is fitted, open the cover to gain access to the battery **(see illustration)**. For improved access, remove the engine top cover/air filter.

2 Where necessary, open the fuse holder plastic cover (squeeze together the locking lugs to release the cover) to gain access to the battery positive (+) terminal and fuse holder connections.

3 Check that both battery terminals and all the fuse holder connections are securely attached and are free from corrosion. **Note:** *Before disconnecting the terminals from the battery, refer to 'Disconnecting the battery' in the Reference Chapter at the end of this manual.*

4 Check the battery casing for signs of damage or cracking and check the battery retaining clamp bolt is securely tightened. If the battery casing is damaged in any way the battery must be renewed (see Chapter 5A).

5 If the vehicle is not fitted with a sealed-for-life maintenance-free battery, check the electrolyte level is between the MAX and MIN level markings on the battery casing. If topping-up is necessary, remove the battery (see Chapter 5A) from the vehicle then remove the cell caps/cover (as applicable). Using distilled water, top the electrolyte level of each cell up to the MAX level mark then securely refit the cell caps/cover. Ensure the battery has not been overfilled then refit the battery to the vehicle (see Chapter 5A).

6 On completion of the check, clip the cover securely back onto the fuse holder and close up the insulator cover (where fitted).

19 Hinge and lock lubrication

1 Lubricate the hinges of the bonnet, doors and tailgate with a light general-purpose oil. Similarly, lubricate all latches, locks and lock

18.1 Battery location beneath the insulation cover

strikers. At the same time, check the security and operation of all the locks, adjusting them if necessary (see Chapter 11).

2 Lightly lubricate the bonnet release mechanism and cable with a suitable grease.

20 Airbag unit check

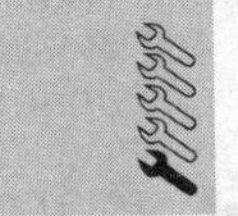

Inspect the exterior condition of the airbag(s) for signs of damage or deterioration. If an airbag shows signs of damage, it must be renewed (see Chapter 12). Note that it is not permissible to attach any stickers to the surface of the airbag, as this may affect the deployment of the unit.

21 Windscreen/tailgate/ headlight washer system check

1 Check that each of the washer jet nozzles are clear and that each nozzle provides a strong jet of washer fluid.

2 The tailgate jet should be aimed to spray at the centre of the screen, using a pin.

3 The windscreen washer nozzles should be aimed slightly above the centre of the screen using a small screwdriver to turn the jet eccentric.

4 On Golf models, the headlight inner jet should be aimed slightly above the horizontal centreline of the headlight, and the outer jet should be aimed slightly below the centreline. On Jetta models, the headlight jet should be aimed slightly below the horizontal centreline of the headlight. VW technicians use a special tool to adjust the headlight jet after pulling the jet out onto its stop.

5 Especially during the winter months, make sure that the washer fluid frost concentration is sufficient.

22 Engine management self-diagnosis memory fault check

This work should be carried out by a VW dealer or diagnostic specialist using special equipment. The diagnostic socket is located behind a cover beneath the central part of the facia. The cover is clipped in position.

23 Sunroof check and lubrication

1 Check the operation of the sunroof, and leave it in the fully open position.

2 Wipe clean the guide rails on each side of the sunroof opening, then apply lubricant to them. VW recommend lubricant spray G 052 778.

24 Road test and exhaust emissions check

Instruments and electrical equipment

1 Check the operation of all instruments and electrical equipment including the air conditioning system.

2 Make sure that all instruments read correctly, and switch on all electrical equipment in turn, to check that it functions properly.

Steering and suspension

3 Check for any abnormalities in the steering, suspension, handling or road 'feel'.

4 Drive the vehicle, and check that there are no unusual vibrations or noises which may indicate wear in the driveshafts, wheel bearings, etc.

5 Check that the steering feels positive, with no excessive 'sloppiness', or roughness, and check for any suspension noises when cornering and driving over bumps.

Drivetrain

6 Check the performance of the engine, clutch (where applicable), gearbox/transmission and driveshafts.

7 Listen for any unusual noises from the engine, clutch and gearbox/transmission.

8 Make sure the engine runs smoothly at idle, and there is no hesitation on accelerating.

9 Check that, where applicable, the clutch action is smooth and progressive, that the drive is taken up smoothly, and that the pedal travel is not excessive. Also listen for any noises when the clutch pedal is depressed.

10 On manual gearbox models, check that all gears can be engaged smoothly without noise, and that the gear lever action is smooth and not abnormally vague or 'notchy'.

11 On automatic transmission models, make sure that all gearchanges occur smoothly, without snatching, and without an increase in engine speed between changes. Check that all the gear positions can be selected with the vehicle at rest. If any problems are found, they should be referred to a VW dealer.

12 Listen for a metallic clicking sound from the front of the vehicle, as the vehicle is driven slowly in a circle with the steering on full-lock.

Carry out this check in both directions. If a clicking noise is heard, this indicates wear in a driveshaft joint, in which case renew the joint if necessary.

Braking system

13 Make sure that the vehicle does not pull to one side when braking, and that the wheels do not lock when braking hard.

14 Check that there is no vibration through the steering when braking.

15 Check that the handbrake operates correctly without excessive movement of the lever, and that it holds the vehicle stationary on a slope.

16 Test the operation of the brake servo unit as follows. With the engine off, depress the footbrake four or five times to exhaust the vacuum. Hold the brake pedal depressed, then start the engine. As the engine starts, there should be a noticeable 'give' in the brake pedal as vacuum builds-up. Allow the engine to run for at least two minutes, and then switch it off. If the brake pedal is depressed now, it should be possible to detect a hiss from the servo as the pedal is depressed. After about four or five applications, no further hissing should be heard, and the pedal should feel considerably harder.

17 Under controlled emergency braking, the pulsing of the ABS unit must be felt at the footbrake pedal.

Exhaust emissions check

18 Although not part of the manufacturer's maintenance schedule, this check will normally be carried out on a regular basis according to the country the vehicle is operated in. Currently in the UK, exhaust emissions testing is included as part of the annual MOT test after the vehicle is 3 years old. In Germany the test is made when the vehicle is 3 years old, then repeated every 2 years.

Every 35 000 miles

25 DSG transmission oil and filter renewal

Renewal of the transmission fluid and filter requires access to VW diagnostic equipment to establish the correct temperature of the fluid, and special VW tools/adapters to replenish the fluid. Therefore we recommend this task is entrusted to a VW dealer or suitably equipped specialist.

Every 40 000 miles or 4 years

26 Air filter element renewal

Non-turbo models

1 The air cleaner is located in front of the battery in the left-hand front corner of the engine compartment. First, remove the engine top cover **(see illustration)**.

2 Undo the screws and remove the lid from the air cleaner **(see illustration)**.

3 Undo the screw and slide out the clamp, then remove the filter element from the housing **(see illustrations)**.

4 Remove any debris that may have collected inside the air cleaner.

5 Fit a new air filter element in position, ensuring that the edges are securely seated.

6 Refit the clamp and lid, tightening the screws securely, then refit the engine top cover.

Turbo models

7 The air cleaner is located in front of the battery in the left-hand front corner of the engine compartment **(see illustration)**.

26.1 Air cleaner location on the 2.0 litre engine

26.2 Remove the lid...

26.3a ...undo the screw...

26.3b ...slide out the clamp...

26.3c ...and remove the filter element

26.7 The air cleaner is located in the left-hand front corner of the engine compartment

8 First, remove the engine top cover. Undo the screws and lift the air cleaner lid complete with air mass meter 10 to 15 cm from the base **(see illustration)**. Take care not to strain the air mass meter wiring and air duct.

9 Lift out the air filter element, noting how it is fitted **(see illustration)**.

10 Remove any debris that may have collected inside the air cleaner.

11 Fit a new air filter element in position, ensuring that the edges are securely seated.

12 Refit the lid and tighten the screws, then refit the engine top cover.

26.8 Undo the screws and lift the cover from the air cleaner body...

26.9 ...then lift out the air filter element

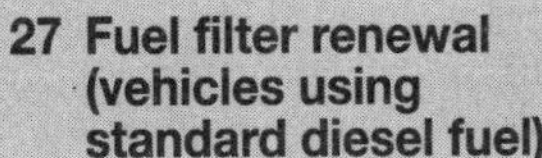

27 Fuel filter renewal (vehicles using standard diesel fuel)

Note: *Carry out this procedure at this interval only when using diesel fuel conforming to DIN EN 590 (standard fuel in the UK).*

Refer to Section 8.

28 Auxiliary drivebelt check and renewal

Check

1 See Section 9.

Renewal

2 For improved access, apply the handbrake, then jack up the front of the vehicle and support it on axle stands (see *Jacking and vehicle support*).

3 Remove the right-hand front roadwheel, then remove the access panel from the inner wheel arch.

4 Use a spanner on the lug provided and turn the tensioner clockwise. Lock the tensioner in its released position by inserting a drill bit through the lug into the tensioner body **(see illustrations)**.

5 Note how the drivebelt is routed, then remove it from the crankshaft pulley, alternator pulley, and air conditioning compressor pulley (as applicable).

6 Locate the new drivebelt on the pulleys, then remove the drill bit and release the tensioner. Check that the belt is located correctly in the multi-grooves in the pulleys.

7 Refit the access panel and roadwheel, and lower the vehicle to the ground.

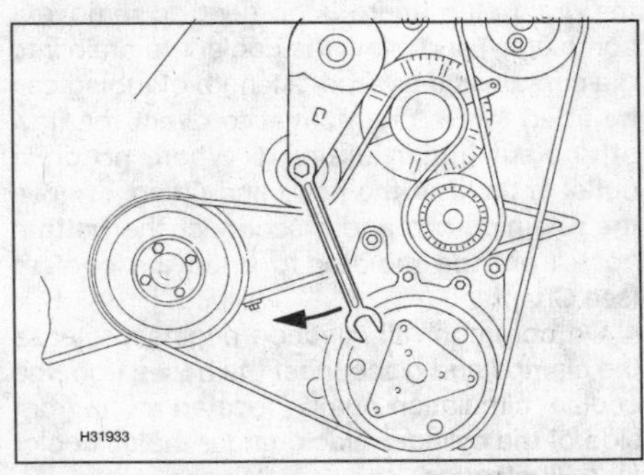

28.4a Release the tensioner and insert a drill bit to hold it in place – PD unit injector engines

28.4b Insert a 4 mm drill bit (arrowed) to lock the tensioner in place – Common rail injection engines

Every 60 000 miles

29 Timing belt and tensioner roller renewal

Refer to Chapter 2E or 2F for details of renewing the timing belt and tensioner roller.

Every 2 years

30 Brake (and clutch) fluid renewal

Warning: Brake hydraulic fluid can harm your eyes and damage painted surfaces, so use extreme caution when handling and pouring it. Do not use fluid that has been standing open for some time, as it absorbs moisture from the air. Excess moisture can cause a dangerous loss of braking effectiveness.

1 The procedure is similar to that for the bleeding of the hydraulic system as described in Chapter 9, except that the brake fluid reservoir should be emptied by syphoning, using a clean poultry baster or similar before starting, and allowance should be made for the old fluid to be expelled when bleeding a section of the circuit. Since the clutch hydraulic system also uses fluid from the brake system reservoir, it should also be bled at the same time by referring to Chapter 6.

2 Working as described in Chapter 9, open the first bleed screw in the sequence, and pump the brake pedal gently until nearly all the old fluid has been emptied from the master cylinder reservoir.

Old hydraulic fluid is often much darker in colour than the new, making it easy to distinguish the two.

3 Top-up to the MAX level with new fluid, and continue pumping until only the new fluid remains in the reservoir, and new fluid can be

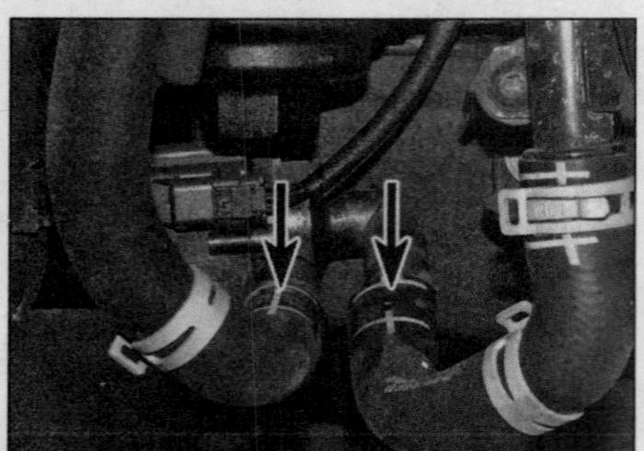

31.4 Disconnect the hoses from the circulation pump (arrowed)

seen emerging from the bleed screw. Tighten the screw, and top the reservoir level up to the MAX level line.

4 Work through all the remaining bleed screws in the sequence until new fluid can be seen at all of them. Be careful to keep the master cylinder reservoir topped-up to above the MIN level at all times, or air may enter the system and greatly increase the length of the task.

5 When the operation is complete, check that all bleed screws are securely tightened, and that their dust caps are refitted. Wash off all traces of spilt fluid, and recheck the master cylinder reservoir fluid level.

6 On models with a manual transmission unit, once the brake fluid has been changed the clutch fluid should also be renewed. Referring to Chapter 6, bleed the clutch until new fluid is seen to be emerging from the slave cylinder bleed screw, keeping the master cylinder fluid level above the MIN level line at all times to prevent air entering the system. Once the new fluid emerges, securely tighten the bleed screw then disconnect and remove the bleeding equipment. Securely refit the dust cap then wash off all traces of spilt fluid.

7 On all models, ensure the master cylinder fluid level is correct (see *Weekly checks*) and thoroughly check the operation of the brakes and (where necessary) clutch before taking the car on the road.

31 Coolant renewal

Note: *This work is not included in the VW schedule and should not be required if the recommended VW G12 LongLife coolant antifreeze/inhibitor is used. However, if standard antifreeze/inhibitor is used, the work should be carried out at the recommended interval.*

Warning: Wait until the engine is cold before starting this procedure. Do not allow antifreeze to come in contact with your skin, or with the painted surfaces of the vehicle. Rinse off spills immediately with plenty of water. Never leave antifreeze lying around in an open container, or in a puddle in the driveway or on the garage floor. Children and pets are attracted by its sweet smell, but antifreeze can be fatal if ingested.

Cooling system draining

1 With the engine completely cold, unscrew the expansion tank cap.

2 Firmly apply the handbrake then jack up the front of the vehicle and support it on axle stands (see *Jacking and vehicle support*). Undo the retaining screws and remove the engine undertray(s) to gain access to the base of the radiator.

3 Position a suitable container beneath the coolant drain outlet which is fitted to the coolant bottom hose end fitting. Loosen the drain plug (there is no need to remove it completely) and allow the coolant to drain into the container. If desired, a length of tubing can be fitted to the drain outlet to direct the flow of coolant during draining. Where no drain outlet is fitted to the hose end fitting, remove the retaining clip and disconnect the bottom hose from the radiator to drain the coolant (see Chapter 3).

4 On common rail injection engines, release the clamps and disconnect the hoses from the coolant circulation pump , located at the front side of the cylinder block, under the oil cooler **(see illustration)**.

5 To fully drain the system also disconnect one of the coolant hoses from the oil cooler which is located at the front of the cylinder block (see Chapter 2E or 2F).

6 If the coolant has been drained for a reason other than renewal, then provided it is clean, it can be re-used, though this is not recommended.

7 Once all the coolant has drained, securely tighten the radiator drain plug or reconnect the bottom hose to the radiator (as applicable). Also reconnect the coolant hose to the oil cooler and secure it in position with the retaining clip. Refit the undertray(s), tighten the retaining screws securely.

Cooling system flushing

8 If the recommended VW coolant has not been used and coolant renewal has been neglected, or if the antifreeze mixture has become diluted, the cooling system may gradually lose efficiency, as the coolant passages become restricted due to rust, scale deposits, and other sediment. The cooling system efficiency can be restored by flushing the system clean.

9 The radiator should be flushed separately from the engine, to avoid excess contamination.

Radiator flushing

10 To flush the radiator, first tighten the radiator drain plug.

11 Disconnect the top and bottom hoses and any other relevant hoses from the radiator (see Chapter 3).

12 Insert a garden hose into the radiator top inlet. Direct a flow of clean water through the radiator, and continue flushing until clean water emerges from the radiator bottom outlet.

13 If after a reasonable period, the water still does not run clear, the radiator can be flushed with a good proprietary cleaning agent. It is important that their manufacturer's instructions are followed carefully. If the contamination is particularly bad, insert the hose in the radiator bottom outlet, and reverse-flush the radiator.

Engine flushing

14 To flush the engine, remove the thermostat (see Chapter 3).

15 With the bottom hose disconnected from the radiator, insert a garden hose into the coolant housing. Direct a clean flow of water through the engine, and continue flushing until clean water emerges from the radiator bottom hose.

16 When flushing is complete, refit the thermo-stat and reconnect the hoses (see Chapter 3).

Cooling system filling

17 Before attempting to fill the cooling system, ensure the drain plug is securely closed and make sure that all hoses are connected and are securely retained by their clips. If the recommended VW coolant is not being used, ensure that a suitable antifreeze mixture is used all year round, to prevent corrosion of the engine components (see following sub-Section).

18 Remove the expansion tank filler cap and slowly fill the system with the coolant. Continue to fill the cooling system until bubbles stop appearing in the expansion tank. Help to bleed the air from the system by repeatedly squeezing the radiator bottom hose.

19 When no more bubbles appear, top the coolant level up to the MAX level mark then securely refit the cap to the expansion tank.

20 Run the engine at a fast idle speed until the cooling fan cuts in. Wait for the fan to stop then switch the engine off and allow the engine to cool.

21 When the engine has cooled, check the coolant level with reference to *Weekly checks*. Top-up the level if necessary, and refit the expansion tank cap.

Antifreeze mixture

22 If the recommended VW coolant is not being used, the antifreeze should always be renewed at the specified intervals. This is necessary not only to maintain the antifreeze properties, but also to prevent corrosion which would otherwise occur as the corrosion inhibitors become progressively less effective.

23 Always use an ethylene-glycol based antifreeze which is suitable for use in mixed-metal cooling systems. The quantity of antifreeze and levels of protection are indicated in the Specifications.

24 Before adding antifreeze, the cooling system should be completely drained, preferably flushed, and all hoses checked for condition and security.

25 After filling with antifreeze, a label should be attached to the expansion tank, stating the type and concentration of antifreeze used, and the date installed. Any subsequent topping-up should be made with the same type and concentration of antifreeze.

Caution: Do not use engine antifreeze in the windscreen/tailgate washer system, as it will damage the vehicle paintwork. A screenwash additive should be added to the washer system in the quantities stated on the bottle.

Every 95 000 miles, then every 19 000 miles

32 Particulate filter ash deposit mass check

Eventually, the amount of ash deposited in the particle filter by the filtration process will cause a blockage, and engine running problems. VW state that the maximum amount of ash is 60g. At this point, the particle filter must be renewed. Unfortunately, the mass of the ash can only be established using dedicated VW diagnostic equipment, connected to the vehicle through the diagnostic plug under the drivers side of the facia. Consequently, we recommend this task is entrusted to a VW dealer or suitably equipped specialist.

Particle filters are fitted to the following engine codes (see Chapter 2):

BLS, BMM, BMN, CBDA and CBDB

Chapter 2 Part A:
1.6 litre SOHC petrol engine in-car repair procedures

Contents

Degrees of difficulty

Easy, suitable for novice with little experience 

Fairly easy, suitable for beginner with some experience

Fairly difficult, suitable for competent DIY mechanic

Difficult, suitable for experienced DIY mechanic

Very difficult, suitable for expert DIY or professional 

Specifications

General

Manufacturer's engine codes*:	
1595 cc (with roller rocker fingers)	BGU, BSE and BSF
Maximum power output	75 kW at 5600 rpm
Maximum torque output	148 Nm at 3800 rpm
Bore	81.0 mm
Stroke	77.4 mm
Compression ratio	10.5 : 1
Compression pressures:	
Minimum compression pressure	Approximately 7.0 bar
Maximum difference between cylinders	Approximately 3.0 bar
Firing order	1 – 3 – 4 – 2
No 1 cylinder location	Timing belt end

*** Note:** *See 'Vehicle identification' at the end of this manual for the location of engine code markings.*

Lubrication system

Oil pump type	Gear type, chain-driven from crankshaft
Oil pressure (oil temperature 80°C):	
At 2000 rpm	2.7 to 4.5 bar

Camshaft

Camshaft endfloat (maximum)	0.17 mm
Camshaft bearing running clearance (maximum)	0.1 mm
Camshaft run-out (maximum)	0.04 mm

Torque wrench settings

	Nm	lbf ft
Ancillary (alternator, etc) bracket mounting bolts	45	33
Auxiliary drivebelt tensioner securing bolt	23	17
Big-end bearing cap bolts*:		
Stage 1	30	22
Stage 2	Angle-tighten a further 90°	
Camshaft bearing retaining frame nuts	23	17
Camshaft cover bolts	9	7
Camshaft sprocket bolt	100	74
Coolant outlet elbow bolts	10	7
Coolant pump bolts	15	11
Crankshaft oil seal housing bolts	15	11
Crankshaft position sensor wheel-to-crankshaft bolts*:		
Stage 1	10	7
Stage 2	Angle-tighten a further 90°	
Crankshaft pulley bolts	25	18
Crankshaft sprocket bolt*:		
Stage 1	90	66
Stage 2	Angle-tighten a further 90°	
Cylinder block oil gallery plug	100	74
Cylinder head bolts*:		
Stage 1	40	30
Stage 2	Angle-tighten a further 90°	
Stage 3	Angle-tighten a further 90°	
Driveplate mounting bolts*:		
Stage 1	60	44
Stage 2	Angle-tighten a further 90°	
Engine mountings:		
RH engine mounting:		
Limiter:		
Stage 1	20	15
Stage 2	Angle-tighten a further 90°	
Mounting to engine:		
Stage 1	60	44
Stage 2	Angle-tighten a further 90°	
Mounting to body:		
Stage 1	40	30
Stage 2	Angle-tighten a further 90°	
LH engine mounting:		
Mounting to body:		
Stage 1	60	44
Stage 2	Angle-tighten a further 90°	
Mounting to transmission:		
Stage 1	40	30
Stage 2	Angle-tighten a further 90°	
Rear mounting link:		
To transmission:		
Stage 1	40	30
Stage 2	Angle-tighten a further 90°	
To subframe:		
Stage 1	100	74
Stage 2	Angle-tighten a further 90°	
Exhaust manifold to head nuts	25	18
Exhaust pipe to manifold nuts	25	18
Flywheel*:		
Stage 1	60	44
Stage 2	Angle-tighten a further 90°	
Inlet manifold to head	25	18
Inlet manifold upper section to lower section	3	2
Main bearing cap bolts*:		
Stage 1	40	30
Stage 2	Angle-tighten a further 90°	
Oil baffle plate securing bolts	15	11
Oil cooler securing nut	25	18
Oil drain plug	30	22
Oil filter housing-to-cylinder block bolts*:		
Stage 1	15	11
Stage 2	Angle-tighten a further 90°	

Torque wrench settings (continued)	Nm	lbf ft
Oil level/temperature sender bolts	10	7
Oil pick-up pipe-to-oil pump bolts	15	11
Oil pressure relief valve plug	40	30
Oil pressure warning light switch	25	18
Oil pump	15	11
Oil pump chain tensioner bolt	15	11
Oil pump sprocket bolt:		
Stage 1	20	15
Stage 2	Angle-tighten a further 90°	
Oil spray jet/pressure relief valve bolts	27	20
Roadwheel bolts	120	89
Sump:		
Sump-to-cylinder block bolts	15	11
Sump-to-transmission bolts	25	18
Thermostat cover bolts	15	11
Timing belt outer cover bolts	10	7
Timing belt rear cover bolts:		
Small bolts	10	7
Large bolt	23	17
Timing belt tensioner nut	23	17

**Do not re-use*

1 General information

How to use this Chapter

This Part of Chapter 2 describes those repair procedures that can reasonably be carried out on the engine while it remains in the vehicle. If the engine has been removed from the vehicle and is being dismantled as described in Part G, any preliminary dismantling procedures can be ignored.

Note that while it may be possible physically to overhaul certain items while the engine is in the vehicle, such tasks are not usually carried out as separate operations, and usually require the execution of several additional procedures (not to mention the cleaning of components and of oilways); for this reason, all such tasks are classed as major overhaul procedures, and are described in Part G of this Chapter.

Engine description

Throughout this Chapter, engines are identified by the manufacturer's code letters. A listing of all engines covered, together with their code letters, is given in the Specifications.

The engine covered in this Part of the Chapter is of water-cooled, single-overhead camshaft (SOHC), in-line four-cylinder design. The 1595 cc engine has an aluminium alloy cylinder block fitted with cast-iron cylinder liners, and an aluminium alloy cylinder head. The engine is transversely mounted at the front of the vehicle, with the transmission unit on its left-hand end.

The crankshaft is of five-bearing type, and thrustwashers are fitted to the centre main bearing to control crankshaft endfloat.

The camshaft is mounted at the top of the cylinder head and is driven by a toothed timing belt from the crankshaft sprocket. It is secured to the cylinder head by a retaining frame.

The valves are closed by coil springs, and the valves run in guides pressed into the cylinder head. The camshafts actuate the valves by roller rocker fingers supported by hydraulic tappets.

The oil pump is driven via a chain from a sprocket on the crankshaft. Oil is drawn from the sump through a strainer, and then forced through an externally-mounted, renewable filter. From there, it is distributed to the cylinder head, where it lubricates the camshaft journals and hydraulic tappets, and also to the crankcase, where it lubricates the main bearings, connecting rod big-ends, gudgeon pins and cylinder bores. A coolant-fed oil cooler is fitted to all engines.

Engine coolant is circulated by a pump, driven by the timing belt. For details of the cooling system, refer to Chapter 3.

Operations with engine in car

The following operations can be performed without removing the engine:

a) Compression pressure – testing.
b) Camshaft cover – removal and refitting.
c) Crankshaft pulley – removal and refitting.
d) Timing belt covers – removal and refitting.
e) Timing belt – removal, refitting and adjustment.
f) Timing belt tensioner and sprockets – removal and refitting.
g) Camshaft oil seal – renewal.
h) Camshaft and hydraulic tappets – removal, inspection and refitting.
i) Cylinder head – removal and refitting.
j) Cylinder head and pistons – decarbonising.
k) Sump – removal and refitting.
l) Oil pump – removal, overhaul and refitting.
m) Crankshaft oil seals – renewal.
n) Engine/transmission mountings – inspection and renewal.
o) Flywheel/driveplate – removal, inspection and refitting.

Note: *It is possible to remove the pistons and connecting rods (after removing the cylinder head and sump) without removing the engine. However, this is not recommended. Work of this nature is more easily and thoroughly completed with the engine on the bench, as described in Chapter 2G.*

2 Compression test – description and interpretation

Caution: The following work may insert fault codes in the engine management ECU. These fault codes must be cleared by a VW dealer.

Note: *A suitable compression tester will be required for this test.*

1 When engine performance is down, or if misfiring occurs which cannot be attributed to the ignition or fuel systems, a compression test can provide diagnostic clues as to the engine's condition. If the test is performed regularly it can give warning of trouble before any other symptoms become apparent.

2 The engine must be fully warmed-up to normal operating temperature, the battery must be fully-charged and the spark plugs must be removed. The aid of an assistant will be required.

3 Disable the ignition system by disconnecting the wiring plug from the DIS unit (see Chapter 5B).

4 Referring to Chapter 4A, disconnect the wiring from the outer injectors.

5 Fit a compression tester to the No 1 cylinder spark plug hole. The type of tester which screws into the plug thread is preferred.

6 Have the assistant hold the throttle wide

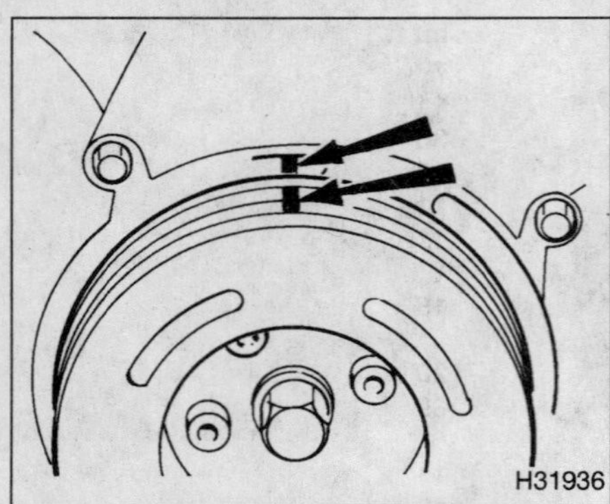

3.4 Crankshaft pulley TDC mark aligned with mark on timing belt lower cover

open and crank the engine for several seconds on the starter motor. Note: The throttle will not operate until the ignition is switched on. After one or two revolutions, the compression pressure should build-up to a maximum figure and then stabilise. Record the highest reading obtained.

7 Repeat the test on the remaining cylinders, recording the pressure in each.

8 All cylinders should produce very similar pressures. Any difference greater than that specified indicates the existence of a fault. Note that the compression should build-up quickly in a healthy engine. Low compression on the first stroke, followed by gradually increasing pressure on successive strokes, indicates worn piston rings. A low compression reading on the first stroke, which does not build-up during successive strokes, indicates leaking valves or a blown head gasket (a cracked head could also be the cause). Deposits on the undersides of the valve heads can also cause low compression.

9 If the pressure in any cylinder is reduced to the specified minimum or less, carry out the following test to isolate the cause. Introduce a teaspoonful of clean oil into that cylinder through its spark plug hole and repeat the test.

10 If the addition of oil temporarily improves the compression pressure, this indicates that bore or piston wear is responsible for the pressure loss. No improvement suggests that leaking or burnt valves, or a blown head gasket, may be to blame.

11 A low reading from two adjacent cylinders is almost certainly due to the head gasket having blown between them and the presence of coolant in the engine oil will confirm this.

12 If one cylinder is about 20 percent lower than the others and the engine has a slightly rough idle, a worn camshaft lobe could be the cause.

13 If the compression reading is unusually high, the combustion chambers are probably coated with carbon deposits. If this is the case, the cylinder head should be removed and decarbonised.

14 On completion of the test, refit the spark plugs, and reconnect the DIS unit.

15 Have any fault codes cleared by a VW dealer.

3.5a Camshaft sprocket TDC mark aligned with timing mark on timing belt rear cover

3.5b Engine set to TDC as seen in-car

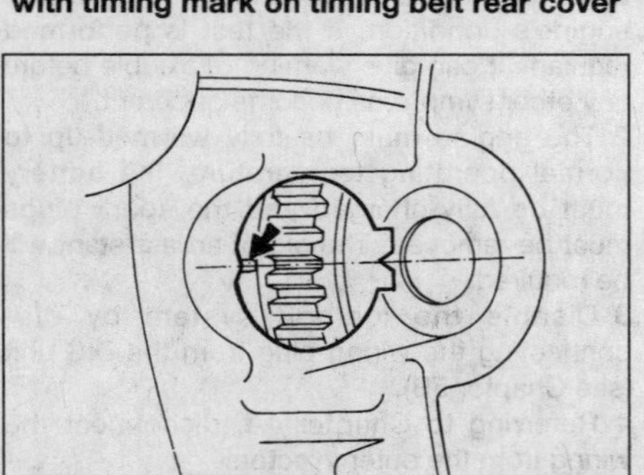

3.6a Flywheel TDC marking aligned with pointer on transmission casing – manual transmission model

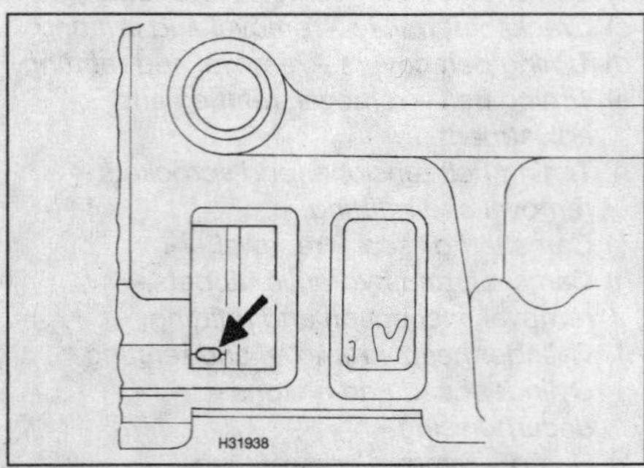

3.6b Driveplate TDC marking aligned with window in transmission casing – automatic transmission model

3 Engine assembly and valve timing marks – general information and usage

General information

1 TDC is the highest point in the cylinder that each piston reaches as it travels up and down when the crankshaft turns. Each piston reaches TDC at the end of the compression stroke and again at the end of the exhaust stroke, but TDC generally refers to piston position on the compression stroke. No 1 piston is at the timing belt end of the engine.

2 Positioning No 1 piston at TDC is an essential part of many procedures, such as timing belt removal and camshaft removal.

3 The design of the engines covered in this Chapter is such that piston-to-valve contact may occur if the camshaft or crankshaft is turned with the timing belt removed. For this reason, it is important to ensure that the camshaft and crankshaft do not move in relation to each other once the timing belt has been removed from the engine.

4 On most models, the crankshaft pulley has a mark which, when aligned with a corresponding reference mark on the timing belt cover, indicates that No 1 piston (and hence also No 4 piston) is at TDC **(see illustration)**.

5 The camshaft sprocket is also equipped with a timing mark. When this mark is aligned with the OT mark on the rear timing belt cover, No 1 piston is at TDC on the compression stroke **(see illustrations)**.

6 Additionally, the flywheel/driveplate has a TDC marking, which can be observed by removing a protective cover from the transmission bellhousing. The mark take the form of a notch in the edge of the flywheel on manual transmission models, or an O marking on automatic transmission models **(see illustrations)**.

Setting No 1 cylinder to TDC

7 Before starting work, make sure that the ignition is switched off.

8 Remove the engine top cover.

9 If desired, the make the engine easier to turn, remove all of the spark plugs as described in Chapter 1A.

10 Remove the upper timing belt cover as described in Section 6.

11 Turn the engine clockwise, using a spanner on the crankshaft sprocket bolt, until the TDC mark on the crankshaft pulley or flywheel/driveplate is aligned with the corresponding mark on the timing belt cover or transmission casing (as applicable), and the mark on the camshaft sprocket is aligned with the corresponding mark on the rear timing belt cover.

4 Camshaft cover – removal and refitting

Removal

1 Remove the upper part of the inlet manifold as described in Chapter 4A.

2 Loosen the clip and disconnect the breather hose from the rear of the camshaft cover.

3 To improve access, remove the upper timing belt cover with reference to Section 6.

4 Unscrew the bolts securing the camshaft cover to the cylinder head, starting from the outside and working inwards. Note the location of any support brackets. Examine the special bolts and renew them if there is any indication of leaking.

5 Lift the camshaft cover from the cylinder head, and recover the gasket.

6 Where fitted, lift the oil deflector from the camshaft cover or the top of the cylinder head.

Refitting

7 Inspect the camshaft cover gasket, and renew if necessary.

8 Thoroughly clean the mating surfaces of the camshaft cover and the camshaft retaining frame, then locate it in position.

9 Tighten the bolts progressively to the specified torque, starting from the inside and working outwards.

10 Where removed, refit the upper timing cover, with reference to Section 6.

11 Reconnect the breather hose.

12 Refit the upper part of the inlet manifold as described in Chapter 4A.

5 Crankshaft pulley – removal and refitting

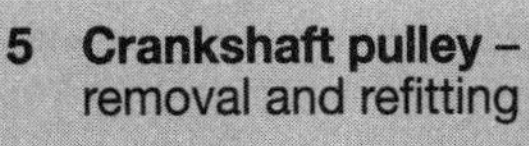

Removal

1 Check the ignition and all electrical consumers are switched off.

2 For improved access, raise the front right-hand side of the vehicle, and support securely on axle stands (see *Jacking and vehicle support*). Remove the roadwheel.

3 Remove the securing screws and withdraw the engine undertray(s) and wheel arch liner access panel **(see illustration)**.

4 If necessary (for any later work to be carried out), turn the crankshaft using a socket or spanner on the crankshaft sprocket bolt until the relevant timing marks align (see Section 3).

5 Loosen only the bolts securing the crankshaft pulley to the sprocket **(see illustration)**. If necessary, the pulley can be prevented from turning by counterholding with a spanner or socket on the crankshaft sprocket bolt.

6 Remove the auxiliary drivebelt, as described in Chapter 1A.

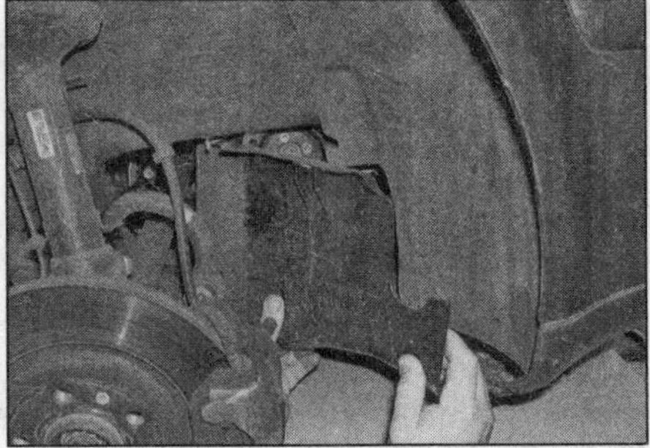

5.3 Removing the wheel arch liner access panel

7 Make a note of the fitted position of the pulley, then unscrew the bolts securing the pulley to the sprocket, and remove the pulley.

Refitting

8 Refit the pulley to the sprocket, locating the small offset hole over the sprocket peg as noted on removal, then refit the pulley securing bolts.

9 Refit and tension the auxiliary drivebelt as described in Chapter 1A.

10 Prevent the crankshaft from turning then tighten the pulley securing bolts to the specified torque.

11 Refit the engine undertray and wheel arch liner as applicable.

12 Refit the roadwheel and lower the vehicle to the ground.

6 Timing belt covers – removal and refitting

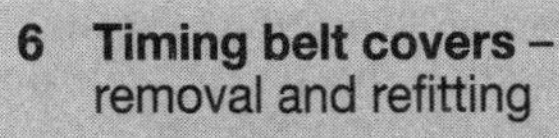

Upper outer cover

Removal

1 Release the securing clip at the front and rear of the cover, and lift the cover out of the section below it, noting how it fits **(see illustrations)**.

Refitting

2 Refitting is a reversal of removal. Engage the base of the cover correctly (this is a fiddly operation) before trying to secure the upper clips, or they will not engage.

5.5 View of the crankshaft pulley, showing the four securing bolts

Centre outer cover

Removal

3 Remove the upper outer cover as described previously in this Section.

4 Remove the two bolts and nut securing the right-angled bracket fitted above the auxiliary drivebelt tensioner, and remove the bracket to improve access.

5 Unscrew the securing bolts, and withdraw the cover from the engine.

Refitting

6 Refitting is a reversal of removal.

Lower outer cover

Removal

7 Remove the upper and centre covers as described previously in this Section.

8 Remove the crankshaft pulley as described in Section 5.

9 Unscrew the securing bolts, and withdraw the cover from the front of the engine.

Refitting

10 Refitting is a reversal of removal.

Upper inner cover

Removal

11 Remove the upper outer cover as described previously in this Section, then remove the camshaft sprocket (see Section 8).

12 Unbolt and remove the timing belt inner cover and remove from the engine.

Refitting

13 Refitting is a reversal of removal.

6.1a Release the clip at the front and rear of the cover...

6.1b ...and lift off the upper cover

Lower inner cover

Removal

14 Remove the timing belt as described in Section 7.
15 Unscrew the securing bolts and remove the timing belt lower inner cover.

Refitting

16 Refitting is a reversal of removal, but refit and tension the timing belt as described in Section 7.

7 Timing belt – removal and refitting

Removal

1 Remove the engine top cover.
2 Remove the auxiliary drivebelt as described in Chapter 1A.
3 Unscrew the securing nut and bolts, and remove the right-angled bracket over the auxiliary drivebelt tensioner; the tensioner is now held by one further bolt at the top – remove the bolt and withdraw the tensioner from the engine.
4 Unbolt the coolant expansion tank, and move it clear of the working area, leaving the hoses connected.
5 Remove the timing belt upper outer cover, with reference to Section 6.
6 Turn the crankshaft to position No 1 piston at TDC, as described in Section 3.
7 Attach a hoist and lifting tackle to the engine lifting brackets on the cylinder head, and raise the hoist to just take the weight of the engine.
8 Unscrew the securing bolts and remove the right-hand engine mounting assembly, with reference to Section 17.
9 Remove the crankshaft pulley, with reference to Section 5. Before finally removing the pulley, check that No 1 piston is still positioned at TDC (Section 3).
10 Unbolt the right-hand engine mounting bracket from the engine. Note that it may be necessary to raise the engine slightly, using the hoist, to allow access to unscrew the engine mounting securing bolts (once the bolts have been unscrewed, it will probably be necessary to leave the bolts in position in the bracket until the bracket has been removed) **(see illustration)**.
11 Remove the timing belt centre and lower outer covers, with reference to Section 6.
12 If the timing belt is to be refitted, mark its running direction.
13 Loosen the timing belt tensioner securing nut to release the tensioner, then withdraw the timing belt from the sprockets.
14 Turn the crankshaft a quarter-turn (90°) anti-clockwise to position Nos 1 and 4 pistons slightly down their bores from the TDC position. This will eliminate any risk of piston-to-valve contact if the crankshaft or camshaft is turned whilst the timing belt is removed.

Refitting

15 Check that the camshaft sprocket timing mark is aligned with the corresponding mark on the rear timing belt cover (Section 3), then turn the crankshaft a quarter-turn (90°) clockwise to reposition Nos 1 and 4 pistons at TDC. Ensure that the appropriate crankshaft timing marks are aligned. If it is not possible to view the flywheel/driveplate timing marks, temporarily refit the crankshaft pulley and timing belt cover, and turn the crankshaft to align the mark on the pulley with the corresponding mark on the belt cover.
16 Fit the timing belt around the crankshaft sprocket, coolant pump sprocket, tensioner, and camshaft sprocket. Where applicable, observe the running direction markings.
17 The timing belt must now be tensioned as follows.
18 Engage a pair of angled circlip pliers, or a similar tool, with the two holes in the centre of the tensioner pulley, then turn the pulley back-and-forth from the clockwise stop to the anti-clockwise stop, five times.
19 Turn the tensioner pulley anti-clockwise to its stop, then slowly release the tension on the pulley until the tension indicator pointer is aligned with the centre of the indicator notch **(see illustration).** It may be necessary to use a mirror to view the tension indicator alignment.
20 Hold the tensioner pulley in position, with the pointer and notch aligned, and tighten the tensioner nut to the specified torque.
21 Turn the crankshaft through two complete revolutions clockwise until the No 1 piston is positioned at TDC again, with the timing marks aligned (Section 3). It is important to ensure that the last one-eighth of a turn of rotation is completed without stopping.
22 Check that the tension indicator pointer is still aligned with the centre of the indicator notch. If the pointer is not aligned with the centre of the notch, repeat the tensioning procedure given in paragraphs 18 to 22. If the pointer and notch are correctly aligned, proceed as follows.
23 Refit the timing belt lower and centre covers, with reference to Section 6.
24 Refit the crankshaft pulley, with reference to Section 5, and tighten the securing bolts to the specified torque.
25 Refit the right-hand engine mounting bracket, and tighten the securing bolts to the specified torque (slide the securing bolts into position in the bracket before offering the bracket up to the engine).
26 Refit the right-hand engine mounting assembly, and check the mounting alignment as described in Section 17. Once the mounting alignment is correct, tighten the securing bolts to the specified torque.

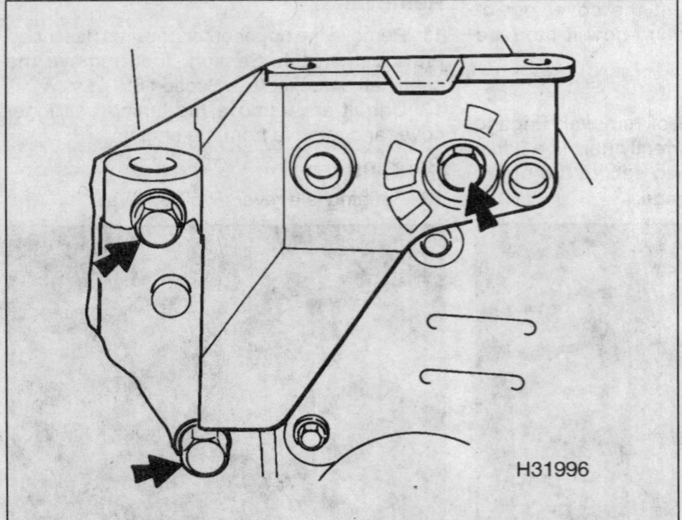

7.10 Right-hand engine mounting bracket-to-engine bolts

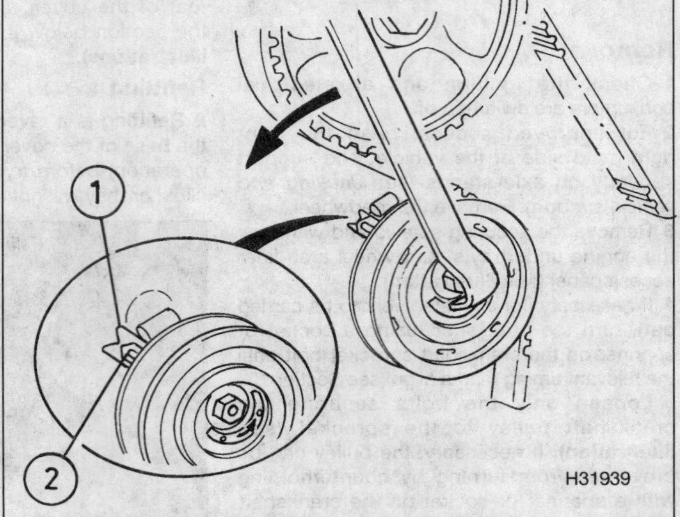

7.19 Tension the timing belt so that the tension indicator pointer (2) is aligned with the centre of the indicator notch (1)

27 Disconnect the hoist and lifting tackle from the engine.

28 Refit the timing belt upper outer cover.

29 Refit the auxiliary drivebelt tensioner, and tighten the securing bolts to the specified torque, then refit the auxiliary drivebelt as described in Chapter 1A.

30 Refit the engine top cover.

8 Timing belt tensioner and sprockets – removal and refitting

Camshaft sprocket

Removal

1 Remove the timing belt as described in Section 7.

2 The camshaft must be held stationary as the sprocket bolt is slackened, and this can be achieved by making up a tool, and using it to hold the sprocket stationary by means of the holes in the sprocket face **(see illustration)**.

3 Unscrew the sprocket bolt and withdraw it, then withdraw the sprocket from the end of the camshaft. Recover the Woodruff key if it is loose.

4 Where necessary, remove the timing belt upper inner cover.

Refitting

5 Prior to refitting, check the camshaft oil seal for signs of leakage, and if necessary renew the seal as described in Section 11.

6 Where removed, refit the timing belt upper inner cover.

7 Refit the Woodruff key to the end of the camshaft, then refit the sprocket.

8 Tighten the sprocket bolt to the specified torque, preventing the sprocket from turning using the method used on removal.

9 Refit the timing belt as described in Section 7.

Crankshaft sprocket

Removal

10 Remove the timing belt as described in Section 7.

11 The crankshaft must be held stationary as the sprocket bolt is slackened. On manual transmission models, engage top gear and apply the footbrake pedal firmly. On automatic transmission models, unbolt the starter motor and use a wide-bladed screwdriver engaged with the driveplate ring gear to hold the crankshaft stationary.

12 Unscrew the sprocket bolt (note that the bolt is very tight), and withdraw the sprocket from the crankshaft **(see illustrations)**.

Refitting

13 Locate the sprocket on the crankshaft, with the flange against the oil seal housing, then tighten the new securing bolt to the specified torque, whilst holding the crankshaft stationary using the method employed during removal.

Warning: Do not turn the crankshaft, as the pistons may hit the valves.

14 Refit the timing belt as described in Section 7.

Coolant pump sprocket

15 The coolant pump sprocket is integral with the coolant pump, and cannot be removed separately. Refer to Chapter 3 for details of coolant pump removal.

Tensioner assembly

Removal

16 Remove the timing belt as described in Section 7.

17 Unscrew the securing nut and recover the washer, then withdraw the tensioner assembly from the stud on the engine.

Refitting

18 Offer the tensioner assembly into position over the mounting stud, ensuring that the lug on the tensioner backplate engages with the corresponding cut-out in the cylinder head.

19 Refit the securing nut, ensuring that the washer is in place, but do not fully tighten the nut at this stage.

20 Refit and tension the timing belt as described in Section 7.

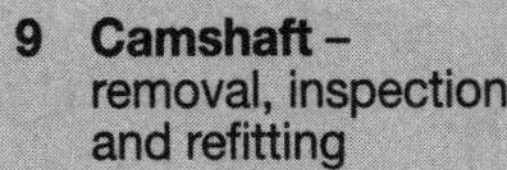

9 Camshaft – removal, inspection and refitting

Note: *New camshaft seal(s) should be used on refitting. VW sealant (D 188 800 A1 or equivalent) will be required to seal the joints between the camshaft retaining frame and the cylinder head on refitting.*

Removal

1 Remove the camshaft cover as described in Section 4.

2 Remove the timing belt as described in Section 7.

3 Remove the camshaft sprocket as described in Section 8, then unbolt the inner belt cover.

4 Progressively loosen the nuts securing numbers 5, 1 and 3 bearing caps, then 2 and 4, using an alternating diagonal sequence (No 1 bearing cap is at the timing belt end of the engine). Note that as the nuts are slackened, the valve springs will push the camshaft up **(see illustration)**.

8.2 Using a home-made tool to hold the camshaft sprocket (tool shown being used when tightening bolt)

5 Lift the camshaft retaining frame from the cylinder head.

6 Lift the camshaft from the cylinder head, then remove the oil seal and the sealing cap from the ends of the camshaft and discard them. New seals will be required for refitting.

7 To remove the hydraulic tappets and roller rocker fingers, see Section 10.

Inspection

8 With the camshaft removed, examine the bearing caps/retaining frame and the bearing locations in the cylinder head for signs of obvious wear or pitting. If evident, a new cylinder head will probably be required. Also check that the oil supply holes in the cylinder head are free from obstructions.

9 Visually inspect the camshaft for evidence of wear on the surfaces of the lobes and journals. Normally their surfaces should be smooth and have a dull shine; look for scoring, erosion or pitting and areas that appear highly polished, indicating excessive wear. Accelerated wear will occur once the hardened exterior of the camshaft has been damaged, so always renew worn items. **Note:** *If these symptoms are visible on the tips of the camshaft lobes, check the corresponding tappet/rocker finger, as it may probably be worn as well.*

10 If the machined surfaces of the camshaft appear discoloured or blued, it is likely that it has been overheated at some point, probably due to inadequate lubrication.

8.12a Unscrew the securing bolt...

8.12b ...and withdraw the sprocket from the crankshaft

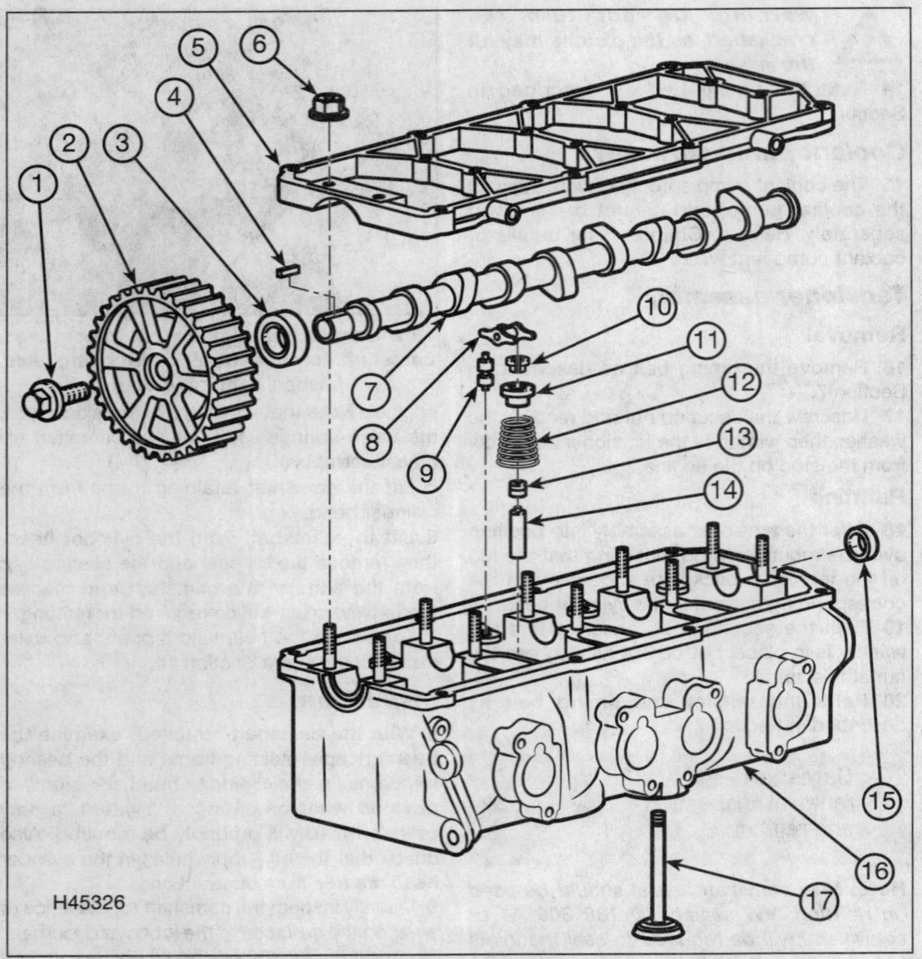

9.4 Layout of the camshaft and roller rocker fingers

1 Bolt
2 Camshaft sprocket
3 Oil seal
4 Parallel key
5 Retaining ladder frame
6 Retaining nut
7 Camshaft
8 Roller rocker finger
9 Support
10 Collets
11 Upper valve spring washer
12 Valve spring
13 Valve stem seal
14 Valve guide
15 Camshaft end sealing cap
16 Cylinder head
17 Valve

11 To measure the camshaft endfloat, temporarily refit the camshaft to the cylinder head, then fit the frame and tighten the retaining nuts to the specified torque setting. Anchor a DTI gauge to the timing belt end of the cylinder head. Push the camshaft to one end of the cylinder head as far as it will travel, then rest the DTI gauge probe on the end face of the camshaft, and zero the gauge. Push the camshaft as far as it will go to the other end of the cylinder head, and record the gauge reading. Verify the reading by pushing the camshaft back to its original position and checking that the gauge indicates zero again **(see illustration)**. **Note:** *The hydraulic tappets must* ***not*** *be fitted whilst this measurement is being taken.*

Refitting

12 Ensure that the crankshaft has been turned to position Number 1 and 4 pistons slightly down their bores from the TDC position (Section 7). This will eliminate any risk of piston-to-valve contact.

13 Refit the hydraulic tappets/roller rocker fingers as described in Section 10.

14 Lubricate the camshaft and cylinder head bearing journals with clean engine oil **(see illustration)**.

15 Carefully lower the camshaft into position in the cylinder head making sure that the cam lobes for No 1 cylinder are pointing upwards.

16 Fit a new oil seal to the camshaft. Make sure that the closed end of the seal faces the camshaft sprocket end of the camshaft, and take care not to damage the seal lip. Locate the seal against the seat in the cylinder head.

17 Oil the upper surfaces of the camshaft bearing journals in the retaining frame, without getting oil onto the sealing surface, where it meets the cylinder head.

18 Ensure that the mating faces/groove of the cylinder head and retaining frame are clean and free from traces of old sealant, then apply an even bead of sealant (VW sealant – D 188 800 A1 or equivalent) to the groove in the lower surface of the retaining frame. **Note:** *The frame must be ready to tighten down without delay, as soon as it comes into contact with the cylinder head surface the sealant begins to harden immediately.*

19 Before the frame is tightened down, fit a new sealing cap to the transmission end of the camshaft, fitting it flush to the end of the cylinder head.

20 With the frame in position, tighten the retaining nuts for bearing caps 2 and 4, using an alternating diagonal sequence. Then fit and tighten the nuts for 1, 3 and 5 progressively in a diagonal sequence. Note that as the nuts are tightened, the camshaft will be forced down against the pressure of the valve springs.

21 Tighten the retaining nuts to the specified torque in sequence **(see illustration)**.

9.11 Checking the camshaft endfloat using a DTI gauge

9.14 Lubricate the camshaft bearings with clean engine oil

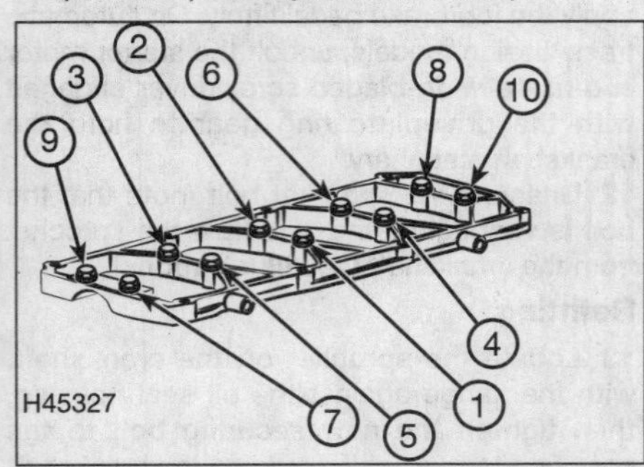

9.21 Tightening sequence for camshaft retaining frame

22 Refit the camshaft sprocket as described in Section 8.
23 Refit and tension the timing belt as described in Section 7.
24 Refit the camshaft cover as described in Section 4.

10 Hydraulic tappets/roller rocker fingers – removal, inspection and refitting

Removal

1 Remove the camshaft, as described in Section 9.
2 As the components are removed, keep them in strict order, so that they can be refitted in their original locations. Accelerated wear leading to early failure will result if the tappets and rocker fingers are interchanged.
3 Note the fitted position, then unclip the rocker fingers from the hydraulic tappets and lift them from the cylinder head.
4 Carefully lift the tappets from their bores in the cylinder head. It is advisable to store the tappets (in the correct order) upright in an oil bath whilst they are removed from the engine. Make a note of the position of each tappet, as they must be refitted in their original locations on reassembly.

Inspection

5 Check the cylinder head bore contact surfaces and the hydraulic tappets for signs of scoring or damage. Also, check that the oil holes in the tappets are free from obstructions. If significant scoring or damage is found, it may be necessary to renew the cylinder head and the complete set of tappets.
6 Check the valve, tappet and camshaft contact faces of the rockers for wear or damage, and also check the rockers for any signs of cracking. Renew any worn or damaged rockers.
7 Inspect the camshaft, as described in Section 9.

Refitting

8 Smear some clean engine oil onto the sides of the hydraulic tappets, and offer them into position in their original bores in the cylinder head. Push them down until they are seated correctly and lubricate the upper surface of the tappet.
9 Oil the rocker contact faces of the tappets, and the tops of the valve stems, then refit the rockers to their original locations, ensuring that the rockers are securely clipped onto the tappets.
10 Lubricate the camshaft lobe contact surfaces and refit the camshaft as described in Section 9.

11 Camshaft oil seal – renewal

Note: *The oil seals are a PTFE (Teflon) type and are fitted dry, without using any grease or oil. These have a wider sealing lip and have been introduced instead of the coil spring type oil seal.*
1 Remove the timing belt as described in Section 7.
2 Remove the camshaft sprocket as described in Section 8.
3 Drill two small holes into the existing oil seal, diagonally opposite each other. Take great care to avoid drilling through into the seal housing or camshaft sealing surface. Thread two self-tapping screws into the holes and, using a pair of pliers, pull on the heads of the screws to extract the oil seal.
4 Clean out the seal housing and the sealing surface of the camshaft by wiping it with a lint-free cloth. Remove any swarf or burrs that may cause the seal to leak.
5 Carefully push the seal over the camshaft until it is positioned above its housing. To prevent damage to the sealing lips, wrap some adhesive tape around the end of the camshaft.
6 Using a hammer and a socket of suitable diameter, drive the seal squarely into its housing. **Note:** *Select a socket that bears only on the hard outer surface of the seal, not the inner lip which can easily be damaged.* Remove the adhesive tape from the end of the camshaft after the seal has been located correctly.
7 Refit the camshaft sprocket with reference to Section 8.
8 Refit and tension the timing belt as described in Section 7.

12 Cylinder head – removal, inspection and refitting

Note: *The cylinder head must be removed with the engine cold. New cylinder head bolts and a new cylinder head gasket will be required on refitting.*

Removal

1 Switch off the ignition and all electrical consumers, and remove the ignition key.
2 Remove the engine top cover.
3 Drain the cooling system as described in Chapter 1A.
4 Remove the upper inlet manifold as described in Chapter 4A. Insert clean cloth in the lower manifold ports to prevent entry of dust and dirt.

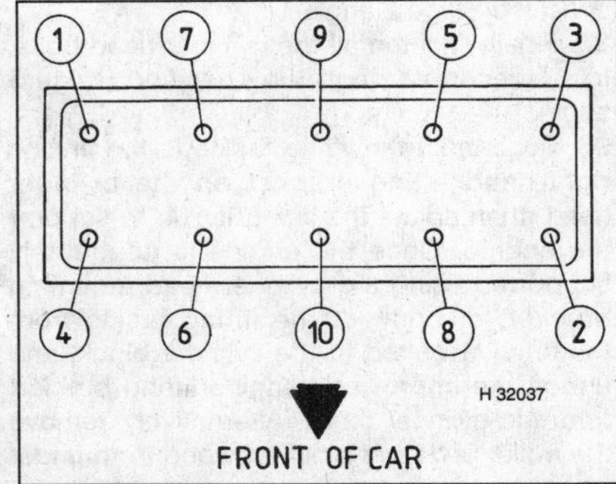

12.19 Cylinder head bolt slackening sequence

5 Unbolt the coolant distributor housing from the left-hand end of the cylinder head, and recover the O-ring. There is no need to disconnect the hoses.
6 Loosen the clip and disconnect the breather hose from the outlet on the rear of the cylinder head.
7 Disconnect all wiring from the cylinder head, noting their locations for refitting.
8 Remove the exhaust front section, complete with the catalytic converter and the manifold support bracket, as described in Chapter 4C. Support the exhaust to one side.
9 Remove the auxiliary drivebelt as described in Chapter 1A.
10 Remove the timing belt as described in Section 7.
11 Remove the camshaft sprocket as described in Section 8, then unbolt and remove the timing belt inner cover.
12 On models with secondary air injection, disconnect and remove the secondary air injection system pipes, and remove the pressure pipe bracket. Remove the secondary air injection pump and mounting bracket, with reference to Chapter 4C.
13 Disconnect the hose from the charcoal canister solenoid valve at the right-hand side of the engine compartment.
14 Remove the following components:
a) *Spark plug HT leads.*
b) *Camshaft position sensor wiring connector.*
c) *Unscrew the securing nut and bolts, and remove the right-angled bracket and auxiliary drivebelt tensioner from the engine.*

15 As the engine is currently supported using a hoist and lifting tackle attached to the right-hand engine lifting bracket on the cylinder head, it is now necessary to attach a suitable bracket to the cylinder block, so that the engine can still be supported as the cylinder head is removed. Alternatively, the engine can be supported using a trolley jack and a block of wood positioned under the engine sump.
16 If the engine is to be supported using a hoist, bolt a suitable bracket to the cylinder block. Attach a second set of lifting tackle to the hoist, and adjust the lifting tackle to support the engine using the bracket attached to the cylinder block. Once the engine is supported using the bracket attached to the cylinder block, disconnect the lifting tackle from the lifting bracket on the cylinder head.
17 Remove the camshaft cover as described in Section 4.
18 Make a final check to ensure that all relevant wiring, pipes and hoses have been disconnected to facilitate cylinder head removal.
19 Progressively slacken the cylinder head bolts, by one turn at a time, in order **(see illustration)**. Remove the cylinder head bolts.

12.32 Typical cylinder head gasket markings

20 With all the bolts removed, lift the cylinder head from the block, together with the exhaust manifold, and the lower section of the inlet manifold. If the cylinder head is stuck, tap it with a soft-faced mallet to break the joint. **Do not** insert a lever into the gasket joint.
21 Lift the cylinder head gasket from the block.
22 If desired, the exhaust manifold and the lower section of the inlet manifold can be removed from the cylinder head with reference to Chapters 4C and 4A respectively.

Inspection

23 Dismantling and inspection of the cylinder head is covered in Part G of this Chapter.

Refitting

24 The mating faces of the cylinder head and block must be perfectly clean before refitting the head.
25 Use a scraper to remove all traces of gasket and carbon, also clean the tops of the pistons. Take particular care with the aluminium surfaces, as the soft metal is easily damaged.
26 Make sure that debris is not allowed to enter the oil and water passages – this is particularly important for the oil circuit, as carbon could block the oil supply to the camshaft and crankshaft bearings. Using adhesive tape and paper, seal the water, oil and bolt holes in the cylinder block. To prevent carbon entering the gap between the pistons and bores, smear a little grease in the gap.

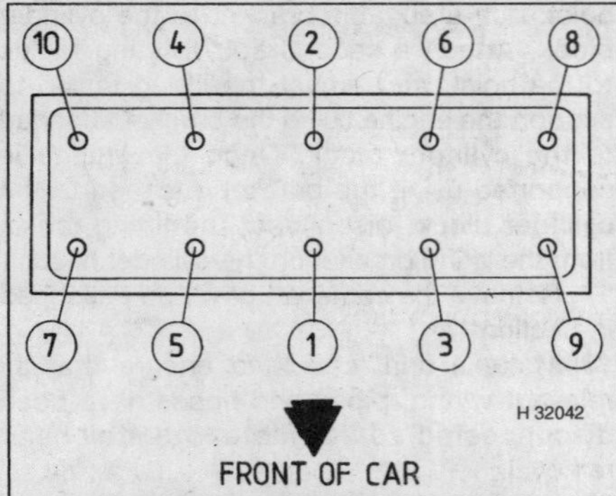

12.35 Cylinder head bolt tightening sequence

After cleaning a piston, rotate the crankshaft so that the piston moves down the bore, then wipe out the grease and carbon with a cloth rag. Clean the other piston crowns in the same way.
27 Check the head and block for nicks, deep scratches and other damage. If slight, they may be removed carefully with a file. More serious damage may be repaired by machining, but this is a specialist job.
28 If warpage of the cylinder head is suspected, use a straight-edge to check it for distortion, as described in Part G of this Chapter.
29 Ensure that the cylinder head bolt holes in the crankcase are clean and free of oil. Syringe or soak up any oil left in the bolt holes. This is most important in order that the correct bolt tightening torque can be applied, and to prevent the possibility of the block being cracked by hydraulic pressure when the bolts are tightened.
30 Ensure that the crankshaft has been turned to position Nos 1 and 4 pistons slightly down their bores from the TDC position (refer to timing belt refitting in Section 7). This will eliminate any risk of piston-to-valve contact as the cylinder head is refitted.
31 Where applicable, refit the exhaust manifold and the lower section of the inlet manifold to the cylinder head with reference to Chapters 4A and 4C.
32 Ensure that the cylinder head locating dowels are in place in the cylinder block, then fit a new cylinder head gasket over the dowels, ensuring that the part number is uppermost. Where applicable, the OBEN/TOP marking should also be uppermost **(see illustration)**. Note that VW recommend that the gasket is only removed from its packaging immediately prior to fitting.
33 Lower the cylinder head into position on the gasket, ensuring that it engages correctly over the dowels.
34 Fit the new cylinder head bolts, and screw them in as far as possible by hand.
35 Working progressively, in sequence, tighten all the cylinder head bolts to the specified Stage 1 torque **(see illustration)**.
36 Again working progressively, in sequence, tighten all the cylinder head bolts through the specified Stage 2 angle.
37 Finally, tighten all the cylinder head bolts, in sequence, through the specified Stage 3 angle.
38 Reconnect the lifting tackle to the engine right-hand lifting bracket on the cylinder head, then adjust the lifting tackle to support the engine. Once the engine is adequately supported using the cylinder head mounting bracket, disconnect the lifting tackle from the bracket bolted to the cylinder block, and unbolt the improvised engine lifting bracket from the cylinder block. Alternatively, remove the trolley jack and block of wood from under the sump.
39 Refit the camshaft cover as described in Section 4.
40 Refit the timing belt inner cover, then refer to Section 8 and refit the camshaft sprocket.
41 Refit and tension the timing belt as described in Section 7.
42 Refit the exhaust front section as described in Chapter 4C.
43 Where applicable, refit the secondary air injection pump and pipes, with reference to Chapter 4C.
44 Refit the coolant distribution housing, and reconnect the coolant hoses.
45 Reconnect the charcoal canister solenoid valve hose.
46 Refit the auxiliary drivebelt as described in Chapter 1A.
47 Refit the following components:
a) Spark plug HT leads.
b) Camshaft position sensor wiring connector.
c) Refit the right-angled bracket and auxiliary drivebelt tensioner to the engine.
48 Reconnect all wiring.
49 Refit the upper part of the inlet manifold, as described in Chapter 4A.
50 Refill the cooling system as described in Chapter 1A.
51 Refit the engine top cover.

13 Sump – removal and refitting

Note: *VW sealant (D 176 404 A2 or equivalent) will be required to seal the sump on refitting.*

Removal

1 Apply the handbrake, then jack up the front of the vehicle and support securely on axle stands (see *Jacking and vehicle support*).
2 Remove the securing screws and withdraw the engine undertray(s).
3 Drain the engine oil as described in Chapter 1A.
4 Where fitted, disconnect the wiring connector from the oil level/temperature sender in the sump **(see illustration)**.
5 Unscrew and remove the bolts securing the sump to the cylinder block, and the bolts securing the sump to the transmission casing, then withdraw the sump. If necessary, release the sump by tapping with a soft-faced hammer.
6 If desired, unbolt the oil baffle plate from the cylinder block.

13.4 Disconnect the wiring connector from the oil level/temperature sender

Refitting

7 Begin refitting by thoroughly cleaning the mating faces of the sump and cylinder block. Ensure that all traces of old sealant are removed.

8 Where applicable, refit the oil baffle plate, and tighten the securing bolts.

9 Ensure that the cylinder block mating face of the sump is free from all traces of old sealant, oil and grease, and then apply a 2.0 to 3.0 mm thick bead of silicone sealant (VW D 176 404 A2 or equivalent) to the sump **(see illustration)**. Note that the sealant should be run around the inside of the bolt holes in the sump. The sump must be fitted within 5 minutes of applying the sealant.

10 Offer the sump up to the cylinder block, then refit the sump-to-cylinder block bolts, and lightly tighten them by hand, working progressively in a diagonal sequence. **Note:** *If the sump is being refitted with the engine and transmission separated, make sure that the sump is flush with the flywheel/driveplate end of the cylinder block.*

11 Refit the sump-to-transmission casing bolts, and tighten them lightly, using a socket.

12 Again working in a diagonal sequence, *lightly* tighten the sump-to-cylinder block bolts, using a socket.

13 Tighten the sump-to-transmission casing bolts to the specified torque.

14 Working in a diagonal sequence, progressively tighten the sump-to-cylinder block bolts to the specified torque.

15 Refit the wiring connector to the oil level/temperature sender (where fitted), then refit the engine undertray(s), and lower the vehicle to the ground.

16 Allow at least 30 minutes from the time of refitting the sump for the sealant to dry, then refill the engine with oil, with reference to Chapter 1A.

14 Oil pump, drive chain and sprockets – removal, inspection and refitting

Oil pump removal

1 Remove the sump as described in Section 13.

2 Unscrew the securing bolts, and remove the oil baffle from the cylinder block.

3 Unscrew and remove the three mounting bolts, and release the oil pump from the dowels in the crankcase **(see illustration)**. Unhook the oil pump drive sprocket from the chain and withdraw the oil pump and oil pick-up pipe from the engine. Note that the tensioner will attempt to tighten the chain, and it may be necessary to use a screwdriver to hold it in its released position before releasing the oil pump sprocket from the chain.

4 If desired, unscrew the flange bolts and remove the suction pipe from the oil pump. Recover the O-ring seal. Unscrew the bolts and remove the cover from the oil pump. **Note:** *If the oil pick-up pipe is removed from the oil pump, a new O-ring will be required on refitting.*

Oil pump inspection

5 Clean the pump thoroughly, and inspect the gear teeth/rotors for signs of damage or wear. If evident, renew the oil pump.

6 To remove the sprocket from the oil pump, unscrew the retaining bolt and slide off the sprocket (note that the sprocket can only be fitted in one position).

Oil pump refitting

7 Prime the pump with oil by pouring oil into the pick-up pipe aperture while turning the driveshaft.

8 Refit the cover to the oil pump and tighten the bolts securely. Where applicable, refit the pick-up pipe to the oil pump, using a new O-ring seal, and tighten the securing bolts.

9 If the drive chain, crankshaft sprocket and tensioner have been removed, delay refitting them until after the oil pump has been mounted on the cylinder block. If they have not been removed, use a screwdriver to press the tensioner against its spring to provide sufficient slack in the chain to refit the oil pump.

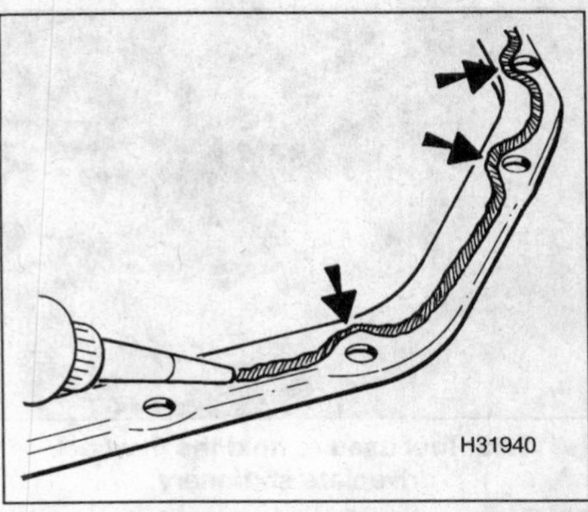

13.9 Apply the sealant around the inside of the bolt holes

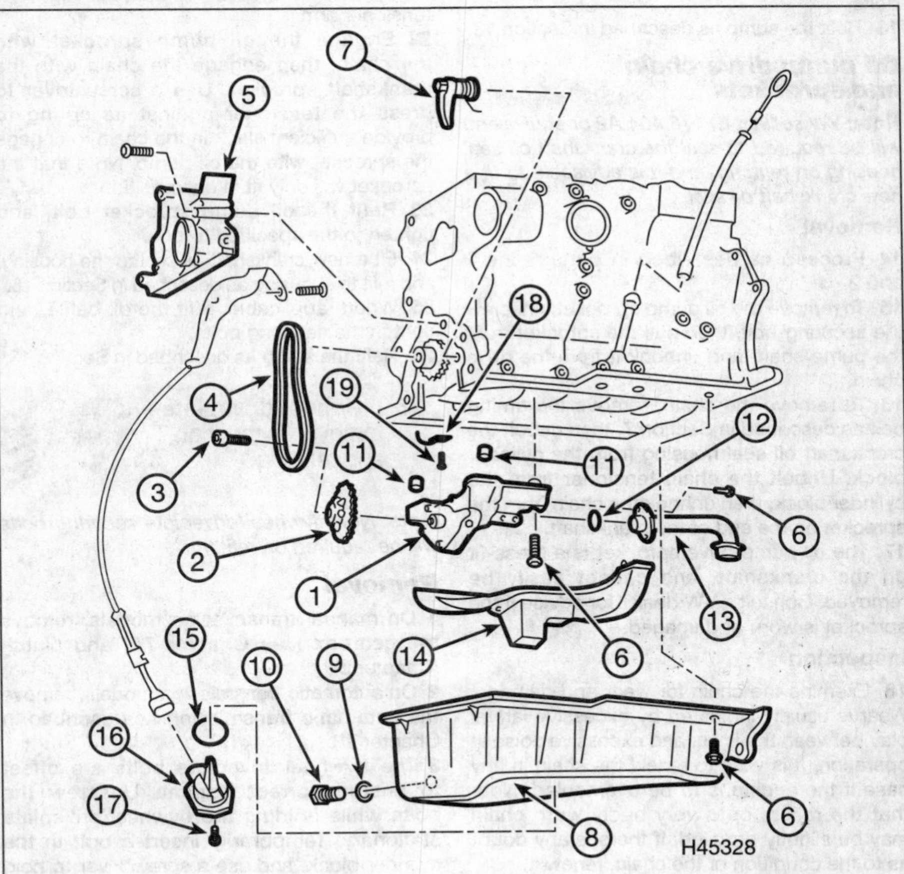

14.3 Sump and oil pump components

1 Oil pump
2 Oil pump sprocket
3 Bolt
4 Oil pump drive chain
5 Crankshaft oil seal housing
6 Bolt
7 Drive chain tensioner
8 Sump
9 Seal
10 Sump drain plug
11 Dowels
12 O-ring
13 Oil pick-up pipe
14 Oil baffle
15 Seal
16 Oil level/temperature sender
17 Bolt
18 Oil spray jet
19 bolt

15.3a Tool used to hold the flywheel/driveplate stationary

15.3b Unscrew the securing bolts...

15.4 ...and remove the flywheel

10 Engage the oil pump sprocket with the drive chain, then locate the oil pump on the dowels. Refit and tighten the three mounting bolts to the specified torque.

11 Where applicable, refit the drive chain, tensioner and crankshaft sprocket using a reversal of the removal procedure.

12 Refit the oil baffle, and tighten the securing bolts.

13 Refit the sump as described in Section 13.

Oil pump drive chain and sprockets

Note: *VW sealant (D 176 404 A2 or equivalent) will be required to seal the crankshaft oil seal housing on refitting, and it is advisable to fit a new crankshaft oil seal.*

Removal

14 Proceed as described in paragraphs 1 and 2.

15 To remove the oil pump sprocket, unscrew the securing bolt, then pull the sprocket from the pump shaft, and unhook it from the drive chain.

16 To remove the chain, remove the timing belt as described in Section 7, then unbolt the crankshaft oil seal housing from the cylinder block. Unbolt the chain tensioner from the cylinder block, then unhook the chain from the sprocket on the end of the crankshaft.

17 The oil pump drive sprocket is a press-fit on the crankshaft, and cannot easily be removed. Consult a VW dealer for advice if the sprocket is worn or damaged.

Inspection

18 Examine the chain for wear and damage. Wear is usually indicated by excessive lateral play between the links, and excessive noise in operation. It is wise to renew the chain in any case if the engine is to be overhauled. Note that the rollers on a very badly worn chain may be slightly grooved. If there is any doubt as to the condition of the chain, renew it.

19 Examine the teeth on the sprockets for wear. Each tooth forms an inverted V. If worn, the side of each tooth under tension will be slightly concave in shape when compared with the other side of the tooth (ie, the teeth will have a hooked appearance). If the teeth appear worn, the sprocket should be renewed (consult a VW dealer for advice if the crankshaft sprocket is worn or damaged).

Refitting

20 If the oil pump has been removed, refit the oil pump as described previously in this Section before refitting the chain and sprocket.

21 Refit the chain tensioner to the cylinder block, and tighten the securing bolt to the specified torque. Make sure that the tensioner spring is correctly positioned to pretension the tensioner arm.

22 Engage the oil pump sprocket with the chain, then engage the chain with the crankshaft sprocket. Use a screwdriver to press the tensioner against its spring to provide sufficient slack in the chain to engage the sprocket with the oil pump. Note that the sprocket will only fit in one position.

23 Refit the oil pump sprocket bolt, and tighten to the specified torque.

24 Fit a new crankshaft oil seal to the housing, and refit the housing as described in Section 16.

25 Where applicable, refit the oil baffle, and tighten the securing bolts.

26 Refit the sump as described in Section 13.

15 Flywheel/driveplate – removal, inspection and refitting

Note: *New flywheel/driveplate securing bolts will be required on refitting.*

Removal

1 On manual transmission models, remove the gearbox (see Chapter 7A) and clutch (Chapter 6).

2 On automatic transmission models, remove the automatic transmission as described in Chapter 7B.

3 The flywheel/driveplate bolts are offset to ensure correct fitment. Unscrew the bolts while holding the flywheel/driveplate stationary. Temporarily insert a bolt in the cylinder block, and use a screwdriver to hold the flywheel/driveplate, or make up a holding tool **(see illustrations)**.

4 Lift the flywheel/driveplate from the crankshaft **(see illustration)**. If removing a driveplate, note the location of the shim (where applicable – between the driveplate and the crankshaft), and the spacer under the securing bolts. Recover the engine-to-transmission plate if it is loose.

Inspection

5 Check the flywheel/driveplate for wear and damage. Examine the starter ring gear for excessive wear to the teeth. If the driveplate or its ring gear are damaged, the complete driveplate must be renewed. The flywheel ring gear, however, may be renewed separately from the flywheel, but the work should be entrusted to a VW dealer. If the clutch friction face is discoloured or scored excessively, it may be possible to regrind it, but this work should also be entrusted to a VW dealer.

Refitting

6 Refitting is a reversal of removal, bearing in mind the following points.

a) *Ensure that the engine-to-transmission plate is in place before fitting the flywheel/driveplate.*

b) *On automatic transmission models temporarily refit the driveplate using the old bolts tightened to 30 Nm (22 lbf ft), and check that the distance from the rear machined face of the cylinder block to the torque converter mounting face on the driveplate is between 19.5 and 21.1 mm. The measurement is most easily made through one of the holes in the driveplate, using vernier calipers. If necessary, remove the driveplate, and fit a shim between the driveplate and the crankshaft to achieve the correct dimension.*

c) *On automatic transmission models, the raised pip on the spacer under the securing bolts must face the torque converter.*

d) *Use new bolts when refitting the flywheel or driveplate, and coat the threads of the bolts with locking fluid before inserting them. Tighten the securing bolts to the specified torque.*

16 Crankshaft oil seals – renewal

Note: *The oil seals are a PTFE (Teflon) type and are fitted dry, without using any grease or oil. These have a wider sealing lip and have been introduced instead of the coil spring type oil seal.*

Timing belt end oil seal

Note: *If the oil seal housing is removed, VW sealant (D 176 404 A2, or equivalent) will be required to seal the housing on refitting.*

1 Remove the timing belt as described in Section 7, and the crankshaft sprocket with reference to Section 8.

2 To remove the seal without removing the housing, drill two small holes diagonally opposite each other, insert self-tapping screws, and pull on the heads of the screws with pliers.

3 Alternatively, to remove the oil seal complete with its housing, proceed as follows.

a) *Remove the sump as described in Section 13. This is necessary to ensure a satisfactory seal between the sump and oil seal housing on refitting.*
b) *Unbolt and remove the oil seal housing.*
c) *Working on the bench, lever the oil seal from the housing using a suitable screwdriver. Take care not to damage the seal seating in the housing.*

4 Thoroughly clean the oil seal seating in the housing.

5 Wind a length of tape around the end of the crankshaft to protect the oil seal lips as the seal (and housing, where applicable) is fitted.

6 Fit a new oil seal to the housing, pressing or driving it into position using a socket or tube of suitable diameter. Ensure that the socket or tube bears only on the hard outer ring of the seal, and take care not to damage the seal lips. Press or drive the seal into position until it is seated on the shoulder in the housing. Make sure that the closed end of the seal is facing outwards.

7 If the oil seal housing has been removed, proceed as follows, otherwise proceed to paragraph 9.

8 Clean all traces of old sealant from the crankshaft oil seal housing and the cylinder block. Apply a bead of VW sealant (D 176 404 A2, or equivalent), 2.0 to 3.0 mm thick along the cylinder block mating face of the oil seal housing **(see illustration)**. Note that the seal housing must be refitted within 5 minutes of applying the sealant.

Caution: DO NOT put excessive amounts of sealant onto the housing as it may get into the sump and block the oil pick-up pipe.

9 Refit the oil seal housing, taking care not to damage the seal (see paragraph 5), then tighten the bolts progressively to the specified torque.

10 Refit the sump as described in Section 13.

11 Refit the crankshaft sprocket with reference to Section 8, and the timing belt as described in Section 7.

Flywheel/driveplate end oil seal

Note: *If the original seal housing was fitted using sealant, VW sealant (D 176 404 A2, or equivalent) will be required to seal the housing on refitting.*

12 Remove the clutch pressure plate/flywheel/driveplate as described in Section 15.

13 Remove the sump as described in

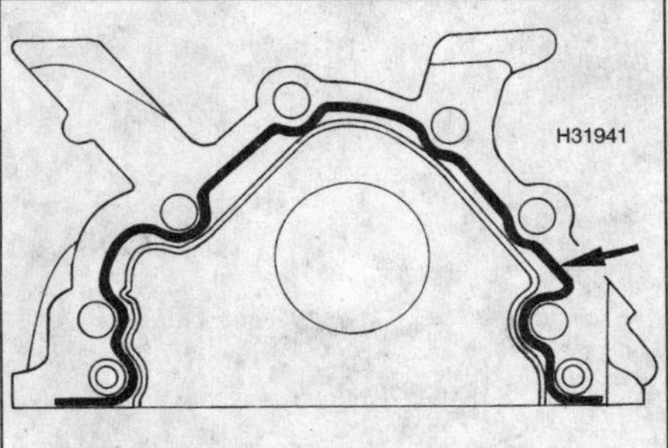

16.8 Apply sealant to the cylinder block mating face of the crankshaft oil seal housing

Section 13. This is necessary to ensure a satisfactory seal between the sump and oil seal housing on refitting.

14 Unbolt and remove the oil seal housing, complete with the oil seal.

15 The new oil seal will be supplied ready-fitted to a new oil seal housing.

16 Thoroughly clean the oil seal housing mating face on the cylinder block.

17 New oil seal/housing assemblies are supplied with a fitting tool to prevent damage to the oil seal as it is being fitted. Locate the tool over the end of the crankshaft.

18 If the original oil seal housing was fitted using sealant, apply a thin bead of VW sealant (D 176 404 A2, or equivalent) to the cylinder block mating face of the oil seal housing. Note that the seal housing must be refitted within 5 minutes of applying the sealant.

Caution: DO NOT put excessive amounts of sealant onto the housing as it may get into the sump and block the oil pick-up pipe.

19 Carefully fit the oil seal/housing assembly over the rear of the crankshaft, and tighten the bolts progressively, in a diagonal sequence, to the specified torque.

20 Remove the oil seal protector tool from the end of the crankshaft.

21 Refit the sump as described in Section 13.

22 Refit the clutch pressure plate/flywheel/driveplate as described in Section 15.

17 Engine/transmission mountings – inspection and renewal

Inspection

1 If improved access is required, jack up the front of the vehicle, and support it securely on axle stands (see *Jacking and vehicle support*). Remove the engine top cover which also incorporates the air filter, then remove the engine undertray(s).

2 Check the mounting rubbers to see if they are cracked, hardened or separated from the metal at any point; renew the mounting if any such damage or deterioration is evident.

3 Check that all the mountings are securely tightened; use a torque wrench to check if possible.

4 Using a large screwdriver or a crowbar, check for wear in the mounting by carefully levering against it to check for free play. Where this is not possible, enlist the aid of an assistant to move the engine/transmission back-and-forth, or from side-to-side, whilst you observe the mounting. While some free play is to be expected, even from new components, excessive wear should be obvious. If excessive free play is found, check first that the fasteners are correctly secured, then renew any worn components as described in the following paragraphs.

Renewal

Right-hand mounting

Note: *New mounting securing bolts will be required on refitting.*

5 Attach a hoist and lifting tackle to the engine lifting brackets on the cylinder head, and raise the hoist to just take the weight of the engine. Alternatively the engine can be supported on a trolley jack under the engine. Use a block of wood between the sump and the head of the jack, to prevent any damage to the sump.

6 For improved access, unbolt the coolant reservoir and move it to one side, leaving the coolant hoses connected.

7 Where applicable, move any wiring harnesses, pipes or hoses to one side to enable removal of the engine mounting.

8 Unscrew the bolts securing the mounting to the engine, then unscrew the bolts securing it to the body. Also, unbolt the movement limiter. Withdraw the mounting from the engine compartment.

9 Refitting is a reversal of removal, bearing in mind the following points.

a) *Use new securing bolts.*
b) *Tighten all fixings to the specified torque.*

Left-hand mounting

Note: *New mounting bolts will be required on refitting (there is no need to renew the smaller mounting-to-body bolts).*

10 Remove the engine top cover which also incorporates the air filter.

11 Attach a hoist and lifting tackle to the engine lifting brackets on the cylinder head, and raise the hoist to just take the weight of the engine and transmission. Alternatively the engine can be supported on a trolley jack under the transmission. Use a block of wood between the transmission and the head of the jack, to prevent any damage to the transmission.

12 Remove the battery, as described in Chapter 5A, then disconnect the main starter motor feed cable from the positive battery terminal box.

13 Release any relevant wiring or hoses from the clips on the battery tray, then unscrew the four securing bolts and remove the battery tray.

14 Unscrew the bolts securing the mounting to the transmission, and the remaining bolts securing the mounting to the body, then lift the mounting from the engine compartment.

17.19 Engine/transmission rear mounting seen from underneath

15 Refitting is a reversal of removal, bearing in mind the following points:
a) *Use new mounting bolts.*
b) *Tighten all fixings to the specified torque.*

Rear mounting (torque arm)

Note: *New mounting bolts will be required on refitting.*

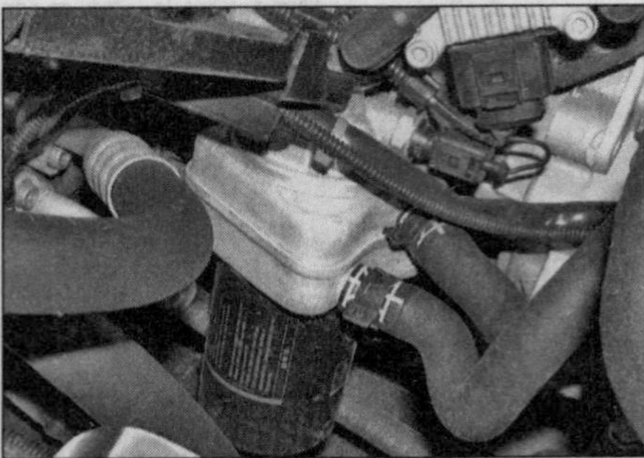

18.1a Oil cooler

16 Apply the handbrake, then jack up the front of the vehicle and support securely on axle stands (see *Jacking and vehicle support*). Remove the engine undertray(s) for access to the rear mounting (torque arm).

17 Support the rear of the transmission beneath the final drive housing. To do this, use a trolley jack and block of wood, or alternatively wedge a block of wood between the transmission and the subframe.

18 Working under the vehicle, unscrew and remove the bolt securing the mounting to the subframe.

19 Unscrew the two bolts securing the mounting to the transmission, then withdraw the mounting from under the vehicle **(see illustration).**

20 Refitting is a reversal of removal, but use new mounting securing bolts, and tighten all fixings to the specified torque.

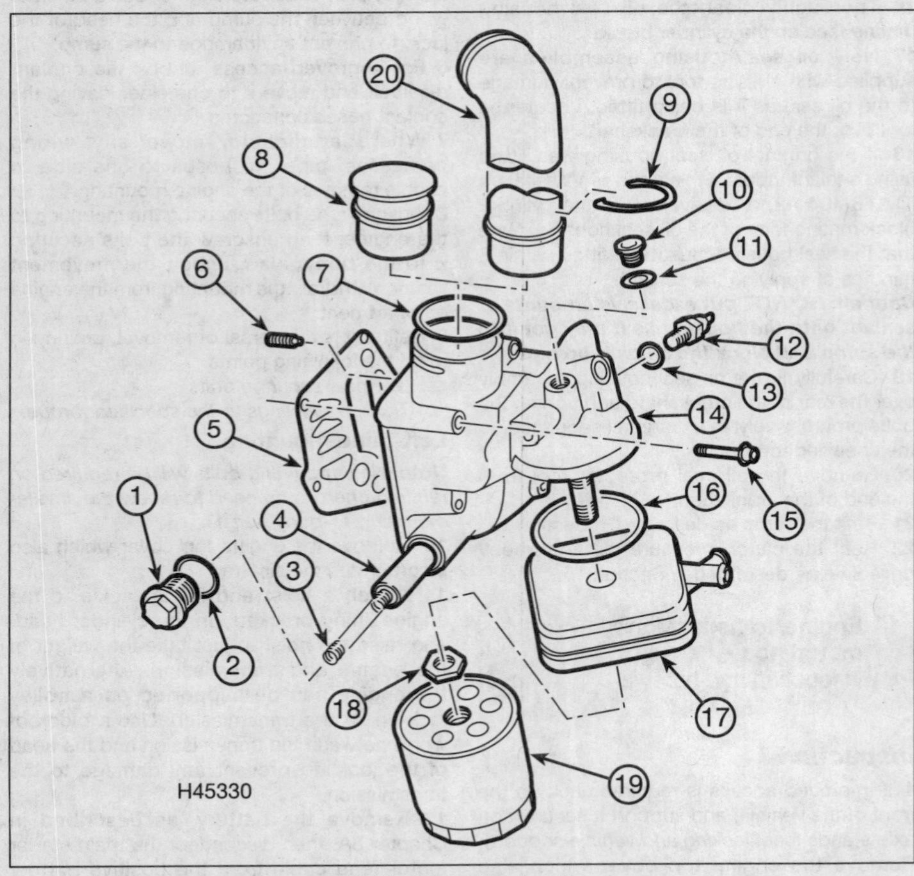

18.1b Oil cooler details

1 *Sealing plug*
2 *Seal*
3 *Oil pressure relief valve spring*
4 *Oil pressure relief valve piston*
5 *Gasket*
6 *Non-return valve*
7 *Seal*
8 *Sealing cap (not fitted)*
9 *Retaining clip*
10 *Sealing plug*
11 *Seal*
12 *Oil pressure warning light switch*
13 *Seal*
14 *Oil filter housing*
15 *Bolt*
16 *Seal*
17 *Oil cooler*
18 *Nut*
19 *Oil filter*
20 *Connecting pipe*

18 Engine oil cooler – removal and refitting

Note: *The oil cooler is only fitted to engine code BGU. A new oil filter and a new oil cooler O-ring will be required on refitting.*

Removal

1 The oil cooler is mounted above the oil filter, at the front of the cylinder block **(see illustrations).**

2 Position a container beneath the oil filter to catch escaping oil and coolant, then remove the oil filter, with reference to Chapter 1A if necessary.

3 Clamp the oil cooler coolant hoses to minimise coolant spillage, then remove the clips, and disconnect the hoses from the oil cooler. Be prepared for coolant spillage.

4 Where applicable, release the oil cooler pipes from any retaining brackets or clips.

5 Unscrew the oil cooler securing nut from the oil filter mounting threads, then slide off the oil cooler. Recover the O-ring from the top of the oil cooler.

Refitting

6 Refitting is a reversal of removal, bearing in mind the following points.
a) *Use a new oil cooler O-ring.*
b) *Fit a new oil filter.*
c) *On completion, check and if necessary top-up the oil and coolant levels.*

19 Oil pressure relief valve – removal, inspection and refitting

Removal

1 The oil pressure relief valve is fitted to the right-hand side of the oil filter housing.

2 Wipe clean the area around the relief valve plug then slacken and remove the plug and sealing ring from the filter housing. Withdraw the valve spring and piston, noting their correct fitted positions. If the valve is to be left removed from the engine for any length of time, plug the hole in the oil filter housing.

Inspection

3 Examine the relief valve piston and spring for signs of wear or damage. At the time of writing

it appears that the relief valve spring and piston were not available separately; check with your VW dealer for the latest parts availability. If the spring and piston are worn it will be necessary to renew the complete oil filter housing assembly. The valve plug and sealing ring are listed as separate components.

Refitting

4 Fit the piston to the inner end of the spring then insert the assembly into the oil filter housing. Ensure the sealing ring is correctly fitted to the valve plug then fit the plug to the housing, tightening it to the specified torque.
5 On completion, check and, if necessary, top-up the engine oil as described in *Weekly checks*.

20 Oil pressure warning light switch – removal and refitting

Removal

1 The oil pressure warning light switch is fitted to the left-hand side of the oil filter housing.
2 Disconnect the wiring connector and wipe clean the area around the switch.
3 Unscrew the switch from the filter housing and remove it, along with its sealing washer. If the switch is to be left removed from the engine for any length of time, plug the oil filter housing aperture.

Refitting

4 Examine the sealing washer for signs of damage or deterioration and if necessary renew.
5 Refit the switch, complete with washer, and tighten it to the specified torque.
6 Securely reconnect the wiring connector then check and, if necessary, top-up the engine oil as described in *Weekly checks*.

21 Oil level/temperature sender – removal and refitting

Removal

1 The oil level/temperature sender is fitted to bottom of the sump **(see illustration)**.
2 Drain the engine oil as described in Chapter 1A.
3 Disconnect the wiring connector and wipe clean the area around the sender.

21.1 Oil level/temperature sender – located in the base of the sump

4 Undo the three retaining bolts and remove the sender.

Refitting

5 Examine the sealing washer for signs of damage or deterioration and if necessary renew.
6 Refit the sender and tighten the retaining bolts to the specified torque.
7 Securely reconnect the wiring connector then refill the engine with oil, with reference to Chapter 1A.
8 On completion, check and, if necessary, top-up the engine oil as described in *Weekly checks*.

Chapter 2 Part B:
1.4 litre DOHC petrol engine in-car repair procedures

Contents

Degrees of difficulty

Easy, suitable for novice with little experience 	**Fairly easy,** suitable for beginner with some experience	**Fairly difficult,** suitable for competent DIY mechanic	**Difficult,** suitable for experienced DIY mechanic	**Very difficult,** suitable for expert DIY or professional 

Specifications

General

Manufacturer's engine codes*:	
1390 cc	BCA and BUD
Maximum power output:	
Engine code BCA	55 kW at 5000 rpm
Engine code BUD	59 kW at 5000 rpm
Maximum torque output:	
Engine code BCA	126 Nm at 3300 rpm
Engine code BUD	130 Nm at 4200 rpm
Bore	76.5 mm
Stroke	75.6 mm
Compression ratio	10.5 : 1
Compression pressures:	
Minimum compression pressure	Approximately 7.0 bar
Maximum difference between cylinders	Approximately 3.0 bar
Firing order	1 – 3 – 4 – 2
No 1 cylinder location	Timing belt end

* **Note:** *See 'Vehicle identification' at the end of this manual for the location of engine code markings.*

Camshafts

Camshaft endfloat	0.40 mm
Camshaft bearing running clearance	N/A
Camshaft run-out	N/A

Lubrication system

Oil pump type	Rotor type, driven directly from crankshaft
Oil pressure (oil temperature 80°C):	
At idling	No figure specified
At 2000 rpm	2.0 bar
In excess of 2000 rpm	7.0 bar maximum

Torque wrench settings	Nm	lbf ft
Ancillary (alternator, etc) bracket mounting bolts	50	37
Auxiliary drivebelt tensioner securing bolt:		
M8 bolt:		
Stage 1	20	15
Stage 2	Angle-tighten a further 90°	
M10 bolt	45	33
Big-end bearing caps bolt/nuts*:		
Stage 1	30	22
Stage 2	Angle-tighten a further 90°	
Camshaft carrier bolts*:		
Stage 1	10	7
Stage 2	Angle-tighten a further 90°	
Camshaft sealing cap bolts	10	7
Camshaft sprocket bolts*:		
Stage 1	20	15
Stage 2	Angle-tighten a further 90°	
Coolant pump bolts	20	15
Crankcase breather/oil separator bolts	10	7
Crankshaft oil seal housing bolts	10	7
Crankshaft pulley/sprocket bolt*:		
Old type (without drilled head):		
Stage 1	90	66
Stage 2	Angle-tighten a further 90°	
New type (with drilled head):		
Stage 1	150	111
Stage 2	Angle-tighten a further 180°	
Cylinder head bolts*:		
Stage 1	30	22
Stage 2	Angle-tighten a further 90°	
Stage 3	Angle-tighten a further 90°	
Driveplate mounting bolts*:		
Stage 1	60	44
Stage 2	Angle-tighten a further 90°	
Engine mountings:		
Left-hand mounting-to-body bolts:		
Large bolts*:		
Stage 1	40	30
Stage 2	Angle-tighten a further 90°	
Small bolts	25	18
Left-hand mounting-to-engine bracket bolts	100	74
Right-hand mounting-to-body bolts*:		
Stage 1	40	30
Stage 2	Angle-tighten a further 90°	
Right-hand mounting plate bolts (small bolts)	25	18
Right-hand mounting-to-engine bracket bolts	100	74
Right-hand mounting bracket-to-engine bolts	50	37
Rear engine/transmission mounting:		
Bracket-to-subframe bolts*:		
Stage 1	20	15
Stage 2	Angle-tighten a further 90°	
Bracket-to-transmission bolts*:		
Stage 1	40	30
Stage 2	Angle-tighten a further 90°	
Engine-to-automatic transmission bolts:		
M12 bolts	80	59
M10 cylinder block-to-transmission bolts	60	44
M10 sump-to-transmission bolts	25	18
Engine-to-manual transmission bolts:		
M10 bolts	40	30
M12 bolts	80	59
Engine-to-manual transmission cover plate bolts	10	7
Exhaust manifold nuts	25	18
Exhaust pipe-to-manifold nuts	40	30
Flywheel mounting bolts*:		
Stage 1	60	44
Stage 2	Angle-tighten a further 90°	
Oil cooler securing nut	25	18

Torque wrench settings (continued)	Nm	lbf ft
Oil drain plug	30	22
Oil level/temperature sender-to-sump bolts	10	7
Oil pick-up pipe securing bolts	10	7
Oil pressure warning light switch	25	18
Oil pump securing bolts*	12	9
Sump:		
Sump-to-cylinder block bolts	13	10
Sump-to-transmission bolts	45	33
Timing belt idler pulley bolt	50	37
Timing belt outer cover bolts:		
Small bolts	10	7
Large bolts	20	15
Timing belt rear cover bolts:		
Small bolts	10	7
Large bolt (coolant pump bolts)	20	15
Timing belt tensioner:		
Main timing belt tensioner bolt	20	15
Secondary timing belt tensioner bolt	20	15

** Do not re-use*

1 General information

How to use this Chapter

This Part of Chapter 2 describes those repair procedures that can reasonably be carried out on the engine while it remains in the vehicle. If the engine has been removed from the vehicle and is being dismantled as described in Part G, any preliminary dismantling procedures can be ignored.

Note that while it may be possible physically to overhaul certain items while the engine is in the vehicle, such tasks are not usually carried out as separate operations, and usually require the execution of several additional procedures (not to mention the cleaning of components and of oilways); for this reason, all such tasks are classed as major overhaul procedures, and are described in Part G of this Chapter.

Caution: The crankshaft must not be removed on these engines – just loosening and retightening the main bearing bolts will render the cylinder block unserviceable. If the crankshaft or bearings are excessively worn or damaged, the complete cylinder block must be renewed.

Engine description

Throughout this Chapter, engines are identified by the manufacturer's code letters. A listing of all engines covered, together with their code letters, is given in the Specifications.

The engines are water-cooled, double overhead camshaft, in-line four-cylinder units. All engines have an aluminium-alloy cylinder head and block. All engines are mounted transversely at the front of the vehicle, with the transmission bolted to the left-hand end of the engine.

The crankshaft is of five-bearing type, and thrustwashers are fitted to the centre main bearing to control crankshaft endfloat.

The crankshaft and main bearings are matched to the alloy cylinder block, and it is not possible to reassemble the crankshaft and cylinder block once the components have been separated. If the crankshaft or bearings are worn, the complete cylinder block/crankshaft assembly must be renewed.

The inlet camshaft is driven by a toothed belt from the crankshaft sprocket, and the exhaust camshaft is driven from the inlet camshaft by a second toothed belt. The camshafts are located in a camshaft carrier, which is bolted to the top of the cylinder head.

The valves are closed by coil springs, and run in guides pressed into the cylinder head. The camshafts actuate the valves by roller rockers and hydraulic tappets. There are four valves per cylinder; two inlet valves and two exhaust valves.

The oil pump is driven directly from the front of the crankshaft. Oil is drawn from the sump through a strainer, and then forced through an externally-mounted, renewable filter. From there, it is distributed to the cylinder head, where it lubricates the camshaft journals and hydraulic tappets, and also to the crankcase, where it lubricates the main bearings, connecting rod big-ends, gudgeon pins and cylinder bores. A coolant-fed oil cooler is fitted to most engines.

On all engines, engine coolant is circulated by a pump, driven by the main timing belt. For details of the cooling system, refer to Chapter 3.

Operations with engine in car

The following operations can be performed without removing the engine:

a) Compression pressure – testing.
b) Camshaft carrier – removal and refitting.
c) Crankshaft pulley – removal and refitting.
d) Timing belt covers – removal and refitting.
e) Timing belt – removal, refitting and adjustment.
f) Timing belt tensioner and sprockets – removal and refitting.
g) Inlet camshaft timing belt, sprockets and tensioner – removal and refitting.
h) Inlet camshaft adjuster mechanism – removal and refitting.
i) Camshaft oil seals – renewal.
j) Camshafts and hydraulic tappets – removal, inspection and refitting.
k) Cylinder head – removal and refitting.
l) Cylinder head and pistons – decarbonising.
m) Sump – removal and refitting.
n) Oil pump – removal, overhaul and refitting.
o) Crankshaft oil seals – renewal.
p) Engine/transmission mountings – inspection and renewal.
q) Flywheel/driveplate – removal, inspection and refitting.

Note: *It is possible to remove the pistons and connecting rods (after removing the cylinder head and sump) without removing the engine. However, this is not recommended. Work of this nature is more easily and thoroughly completed with the engine on the bench, as described in Chapter 2G.*

2 Compression test – description and interpretation

Caution: The following work may insert fault codes in the engine management ECU. These fault codes must be cleared by a VW dealer.

Note: *A suitable compression tester will be required for this test.*

1 When engine performance is down, or if misfiring occurs which cannot be attributed to the ignition or fuel systems, a compression test can provide diagnostic clues as to the engine's condition. If the test is performed regularly, it can give warning of trouble before any other symptoms become apparent.

2 The engine must be fully warmed-up to normal operating temperature, the battery must be fully-charged and the spark plugs must be removed. The aid of an assistant will be required.

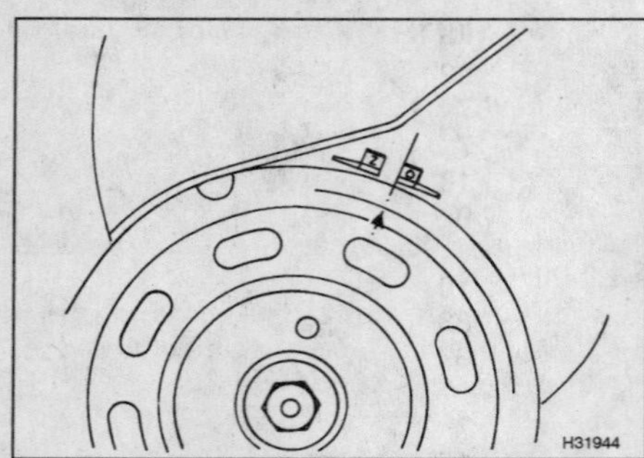

3.4a Crankshaft pulley timing mark aligned with TDC mark on timing belt cover

3.4b Timing mark scribed on inner flange of pulley aligned with TDC mark on timing belt cover

3 Disable the ignition and fuel injectors by removing fuses SB6 and SB29 from the fusebox.

4 Fit a compression tester to the No 1 cylinder spark plug hole. The type of tester that screws into the plug thread is preferred.

5 Have the assistant hold the throttle wide open and crank the engine for several seconds on the starter motor. **Note:** *The throttle will not operate until the ignition is switched on*. After one or two revolutions, the compression pressure should build-up to a maximum figure and then stabilise. Record the highest reading obtained.

6 Repeat the test on the remaining cylinders, recording the pressure in each.

7 All cylinders should produce very similar pressures. Any difference greater than that specified indicates the existence of a fault. Note that the compression should build-up quickly in a healthy engine. Low compression on the first stroke, followed by gradually increasing pressure on successive strokes, indicates worn piston rings. A low compression reading on the first stroke, which does not build-up during successive strokes, indicates leaking valves or a blown head gasket (a cracked head could also be the cause). Deposits on the undersides of the valve heads can also cause low compression.

8 If the pressure in any cylinder is reduced to the specified minimum or less, carry out the following test to isolate the cause. Introduce a teaspoonful of clean oil into that cylinder through its spark plug hole and repeat the test.

9 If the addition of oil temporarily improves the compression pressure, this indicates that bore or piston wear is responsible for the pressure loss. No improvement suggests that leaking or burnt valves, or a blown head gasket, may be to blame.

10 A low reading from two adjacent cylinders is almost certainly due to the head gasket having blown between them and the presence of coolant in the engine oil will confirm this.

11 If one cylinder is about 20 percent lower than the others and the engine has a slightly rough idle, a worn camshaft lobe could be the cause.

12 If the compression reading is unusually high, the combustion chambers are probably coated with carbon deposits. If this is the case, the cylinder head should be removed and decarbonised.

13 On completion of the test, refit the spark plugs and the fuses.

14 Have any fault codes cleared by a VW dealer.

3 Engine assembly and valve timing marks – general information and usage

General information

1 TDC is the highest point in the cylinder that each piston reaches as it travels up-and-down when the crankshaft turns. Each piston reaches TDC at the end of the compression stroke and again at the end of the exhaust stroke, but TDC generally refers to piston position on the compression stroke. No 1 piston is at the timing belt end of the engine.

2 Positioning No 1 piston at TDC is an essential part of many procedures, such as timing belt removal and camshaft removal.

3 The design of the engines covered in this Chapter is such that piston-to-valve contact may occur if the camshaft or crankshaft is turned with the timing belt removed. For this reason, it is important to ensure that the camshaft and crankshaft do not move in relation to each other once the timing belt has been removed from the engine.

4 The crankshaft pulley has a mark which, when aligned with a corresponding reference mark on the timing belt cover, indicates that No 1 piston (and hence also No 4 piston) is at TDC. Note that on some models, the crankshaft pulley timing mark is located on the outer flange of the pulley. In order to make alignment of the timing marks easier, it is advisable to remove the pulley (see Section 5) and, using a set-square, scribe a corresponding mark on the inner flange of the pulley **(see illustrations)**.

5 There is also a timing mark which can be used with the crankshaft sprocket – this is useful if the crankshaft pulley and timing belt have been removed. When No 1 piston is at TDC, the crankshaft sprocket tooth with the chamfered inner edge aligns with a cast arrow on the oil pump **(see illustration)**.

6 The camshaft sprockets are equipped with

3.5 Crankshaft sprocket tooth with chamfered edge aligns with cast arrow on oil pump

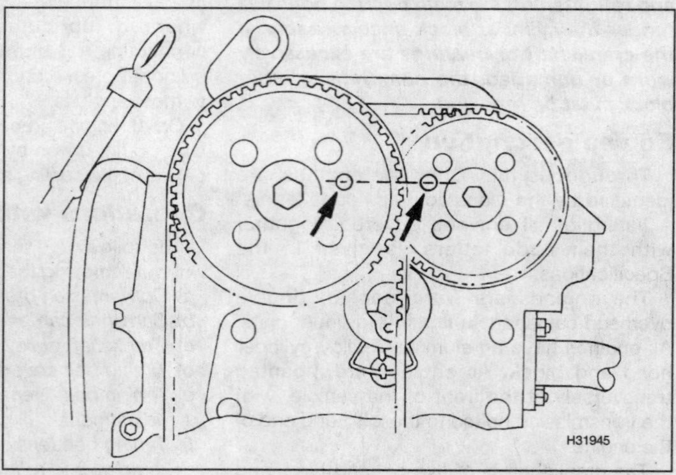

3.6 Camshaft sprocket positioning holes aligned with holes in camshaft carrier (No 1 piston at TDC)

TDC positioning holes. When the positioning holes are aligned with the corresponding holes in the camshaft carrier, No 1 piston is at TDC on the compression stroke **(see illustration)**.

7 Additionally, the flywheel/driveplate has a TDC marking, which can be observed by unscrewing a protective plastic cover from the transmission bellhousing. The mark takes the form of a notch in the edge of the flywheel on manual transmission models, or an O marking on automatic transmission models. Note that it is not possible to use these marks on all models due to the limited access available to view the marks.

Setting No 1 cylinder to TDC

Note: *Suitable locking pins will be required to lock the camshaft sprockets in position during this procedure. On some engines, it may be necessary to use a small mirror to view the timing marks from under the wheel arch.*

8 Before starting work, make sure that the ignition and all electrical consumers are switched off.

9 Remove the engine top cover, and remove the air cleaner assembly as described in Chapter 4A.

10 If desired, to make the engine easier to turn, remove all of the spark plugs as described in Chapter 1A.

11 Apply the handbrake, then jack up the front of the vehicle and support on axle stands (see *Jacking and vehicle support*). Remove the right-hand front roadwheel, then remove the securing screws and/or clips, and remove the appropriate engine undertrays and wheel arch liner to enable access to the crankshaft pulley.

12 Remove the upper timing belt cover as described in Section 6.

13 Turn the engine clockwise, using a spanner on the crankshaft pulley bolt, until the TDC mark on the crankshaft pulley or flywheel/driveplate is aligned with the corresponding mark on the timing belt cover or transmission casing, and the locking pin holes in the camshaft sprockets are aligned with the corresponding holes in the camshaft carrier.

14 If necessary, to give sufficient clearance for the camshaft locking tool to be engaged with the camshaft sprockets, unbolt the air cleaner support bracket from the engine mounting.

3.16 Improvised tool used to lock camshaft sprockets in position at TDC (viewed with engine removed, and timing belt removed from engine)

15 A suitable tool will now be required to lock the camshaft sprockets in the TDC position. A special VW tool is available for this purpose, but a suitable tool can be improvised using two M8 bolts and nuts, and a short length of steel bar. With the camshaft sprocket positioned as described in paragraph 13, measure the distance between the locking pin hole centres, and drill two corresponding 8 mm clearance holes in the length of steel bar. Slide the M8 bolts through the holes in the bar, and secure them using the nuts.

16 Slide the tool into position in the holes in the camshaft sprockets, ensuring that the pins (or bolts) engage with the holes in the camshaft carrier **(see illustration)**. The engine is now locked in position, with No 1 piston at TDC on the firing stroke.

4 Crankshaft pulley – removal and refitting

Removal

1 Switch off the ignition and all electrical consumers and remove the ignition key.

2 For improved access, jack up the front of the vehicle, and support securely on axle stands (see *Jacking and vehicle support*). Remove the right-hand front roadwheel.

3 Remove the securing screws and/or release the clips, and withdraw the relevant engine undertray and wheel arch liner to enable access to the crankshaft pulley.

4 If necessary (for any later work to be carried out), turn the crankshaft using a socket or spanner on the crankshaft pulley bolt, until the relevant timing marks align (see Section 3).

5 Remove the auxiliary drivebelt, as described in Chapter 1A.

6 To prevent the crankshaft from turning as the pulley bolt is slackened, a suitable tool can be used. Engage the tool with two of the slots in the pulley **(see illustration)**.

7 Counterhold the pulley, and slacken the pulley bolt (take care – the bolt is very tight) using a socket and a suitable extension.

8 Unscrew the bolt, and remove the pulley **(see illustration)**.

9 Refit the crankshaft pulley securing bolt, with a spacer washer positioned under its head, to retain the crankshaft sprocket.

Refitting

10 Unscrew the crankshaft pulley/sprocket bolt used to retain the sprocket, and remove the spacer washer, then refit the pulley to the sprocket. Ensure that the locating pin on the sprocket engages with the corresponding hole in the pulley.

11 Oil the threads of the new crankshaft pulley bolt. Prevent the crankshaft from turning as during removal, then fit the new pulley securing bolt, and tighten it to the specified torque, in the two stages given in the Specifications.

12 Refit and tension the auxiliary drivebelt as described in Chapter 1A.

13 Refit the engine undertray and wheel arch liner.

14 Refit the roadwheel and lower the vehicle to the ground.

5 Timing belt covers – removal and refitting

Upper outer cover

1 Remove the air cleaner assembly as described in Chapter 4A.

2 Release the two securing clips, and lift the cover from the engine **(see illustration)**.

3 Refitting is a reversal of removal.

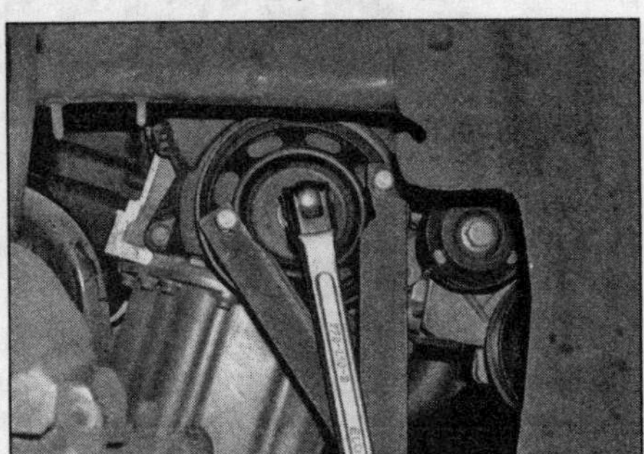

4.6 Counterhold the crankshaft pulley using a tool similar to that shown

4.8 Removing the crankshaft pulley

5.2 Removing the upper outer timing belt cover

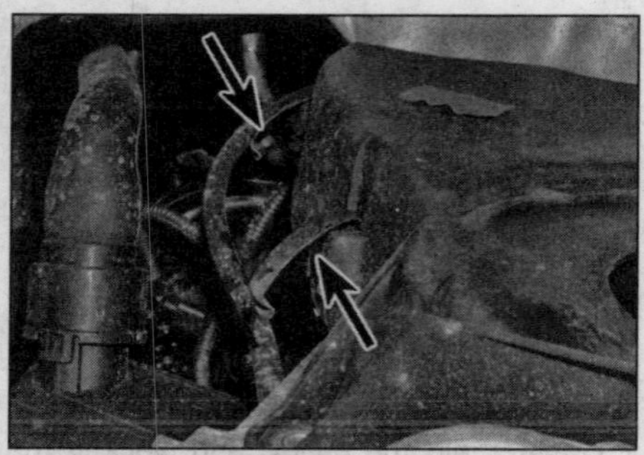
5.5a Release the two securing clips...

5.5b ...then unscrew the two lower securing bolts...

5.5c ...and the single bolt securing the cover to the engine mounting bracket...

5.5d ...and withdraw the lower timing belt cover

Lower outer cover

4 Remove the crankshaft pulley, as described in Section 5.

5 Release the two cover securing clips, located at the rear of the engine, then unscrew the two lower securing bolts, and the single bolt securing the cover to the engine mounting bracket. Withdraw the cover downwards from the engine **(see illustrations).**

6 Refitting is a reversal of removal, but refit the crankshaft pulley with reference to Section 5.

Rear timing belt cover

Note: *As the rear timing belt cover securing bolts also secure the coolant pump, it is advisable to drain the cooling system (see Chapter 1A) before starting this procedure, and to renew the coolant pump seal/gasket (Chapter 3) before refitting the cover. Refill the cooling system with reference to Chapter 1A.*

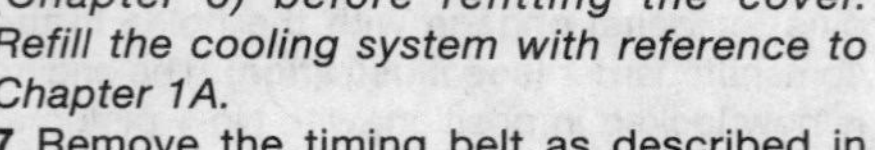

7 Remove the timing belt as described in Section 7.

8 Unbolt the timing belt idler pulley/bracket assembly **(see illustration).**

9 Unscrew the rear timing belt cover securing bolt located next to the right-hand engine lifting eye **(see illustration).**

10 Unscrew the two securing bolts, and remove the rear timing belt cover. Note that the bolts also secure the coolant pump **(see illustration).**

11 Refitting is a reversal of removal, but tighten the timing belt idler pulley/bracket bolt to the specified torque, and refit the timing belt as described in Section 7.

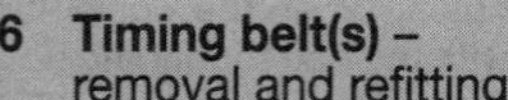

6 Timing belt(s) – removal and refitting

Main timing belt

Removal

1 The engines in this Chapter have two timing belts; the main timing belt drives the inlet camshaft from the crankshaft, and the secondary timing belt drives the exhaust camshaft from the inlet camshaft.

2 Switch off the ignition and all electrical consumers and remove the ignition key.

3 Remove the air cleaner assembly as described in Chapter 4A.

4 Release the two securing clips and remove the upper outer timing belt cover.

5 Turn the crankshaft to position No 1 piston at TDC on the firing stroke, and lock the camshaft sprockets in position, as described in Section 3.

6 Remove the crankshaft pulley as described in Section 4. Refit the crankshaft pulley securing bolt, with a spacer washer positioned under its head, to retain the crankshaft sprocket.

7 Remove the lower outer timing belt cover, as described in Section 5.

8 Where applicable, on models with air conditioning, unscrew the securing bolt, and remove the auxiliary drivebelt idler pulley.

9 Similarly, unscrew the two securing screws, and move the coolant expansion tank clear of the working area **(see illustrations).**

10 Attach a hoist and lifting tackle to the right-hand (timing belt end) engine lifting bracket, and raise the hoist to just take the weight of the engine.

11 Remove the complete right-hand engine mounting assembly, as described in Section 17.

12 Unscrew the four securing bolts, and remove the right-hand engine mounting bracket from the engine.

13 If either of the timing belts are to be refitted, mark their running directions to ensure correct refitting.

14 Engage a suitable Allen key with the hole in the main timing belt tensioner plate, then

5.8 Removing the idler pulley/bracket assembly (viewed with engine removed)

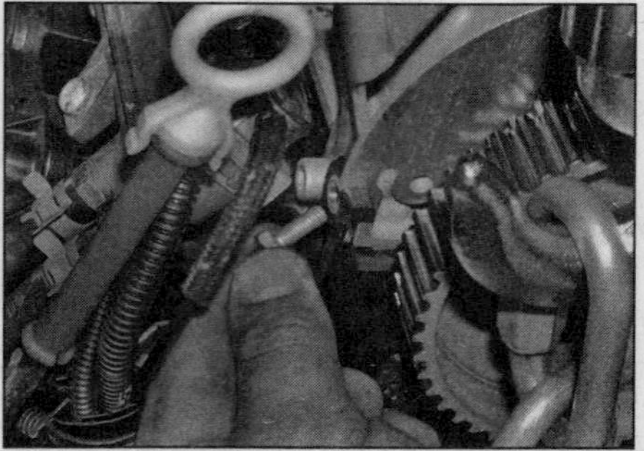
5.9 Unscrew the rear timing belt cover securing bolt located next to the right-hand engine lifting eye

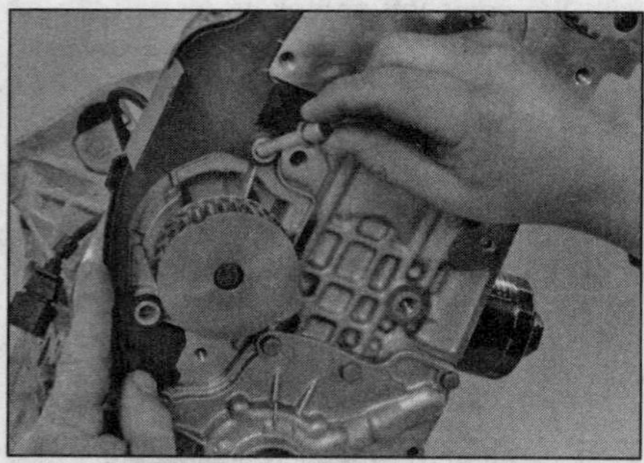
5.10 Removing the rear timing belt cover (viewed with engine removed)

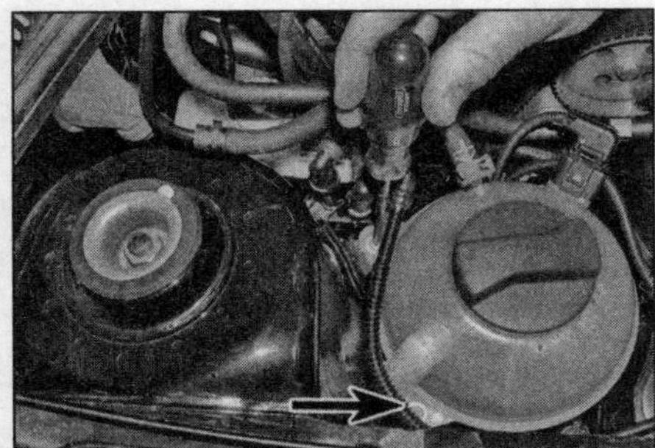

6.9a Unscrew the securing screws...

slacken the tensioner bolt, lever the tensioner anti-clockwise using the Allen key (to release the tension on the belt), and retighten the tensioner bolt **(see illustration)**.

15 Temporarily remove the camshaft sprocket locking tool, then slide the main timing belt from the sprockets, noting its routing **(see illustration)**. Refit the camshaft sprocket locking tool once the timing belt has been removed.

16 Turn the crankshaft a quarter-turn (90°) anti-clockwise to position Nos 1 and 4 pistons slightly down their bores from the TDC position. This will eliminate any risk of piston-to-valve contact if a camshaft is turned whilst the timing belt is removed.

Refitting

17 Where applicable, reposition the crankshaft at TDC (see paragraph 20) and ensure that the secondary drivebelt has been refitted and tensioned. Temporarily remove the camshaft sprocket locking tool, and fit the main timing belt around the sprockets. Work in an anti-clockwise direction, starting at the coolant pump, followed by the tensioner roller, crankshaft sprocket, idler roller, inlet camshaft sprocket and the second idler roller. If the original belt is being refitted, observe the running direction markings. Once the belt has been refitted, refit the camshaft sprocket locking tool.

18 Ensure that the tensioner bolt is slack, then engage an Allen key with the hole in the tensioner plate, and turn the plate clockwise until the tension indicator pointer is aligned with the centre of the cut-out in the backplate **(see illustration)**. Tighten the tensioner securing bolt to the specified torque.

19 Remove the camshaft sprocket locking tool.

20 Using a spanner or socket on the crankshaft pulley bolt, turn the engine through two complete turns in the normal direction of rotation, until the crankshaft sprocket tooth with the chamfered inner edge is aligned with the corresponding mark on the oil pump housing. Check that the locking tool can again be fitted to lock the camshaft sprockets in position – if not, one or both of the timing belts may have been incorrectly fitted.

21 With the crankshaft timing marks aligned, and the camshaft sprockets locked in position, check the tension of the timing belts. The secondary and main tension indicators should be positioned as described in paragraphs 38 and 18 respectively – if not, repeat the appropriate tensioning procedure, then recheck the tension.

6.9b ...and move the coolant expansion tank clear of the working area

22 When the belt tension is correct, refit the right-hand engine mounting bracket, and tighten the securing bolts to the specified torque.

23 Refit the complete right-hand engine mounting assembly, as described in Section 17.

24 Disconnect the hoist and lifting tackle from the engine lifting bracket.

25 Refit the coolant reservoir.

26 Where applicable, refit the auxiliary drivebelt idler pulley.

27 Refit the lower outer timing belt cover, with reference to Section 5 if necessary.

6.15 Removing the main timing belt

6.32a Slacken the secondary timing belt tensioner bolt, and lever the tensioner clockwise using an Allen key...

6.14 Slacken the tensioner bolt and lever the tensioner anti-clockwise using an Allen key, then retighten the tensioner bolt

28 Refit the crankshaft pulley as described in Section 4.

29 Refit the upper outer timing belt cover.

30 Refit the air cleaner assembly then refit the engine top cover.

Inlet camshaft timing belt

Removal

31 Once the main timing belt has been removed, to remove the secondary timing belt, proceed as follows.

32 Engage a suitable Allen key with the hole in the secondary timing belt tensioner plate, then slacken the tensioner bolt, and lever the tensioner clockwise using the Allen key (to release the tension on the belt). Unscrew the securing bolt, and remove the secondary timing belt tensioner **(see illustrations)**.

33 Temporarily remove the camshaft sprocket

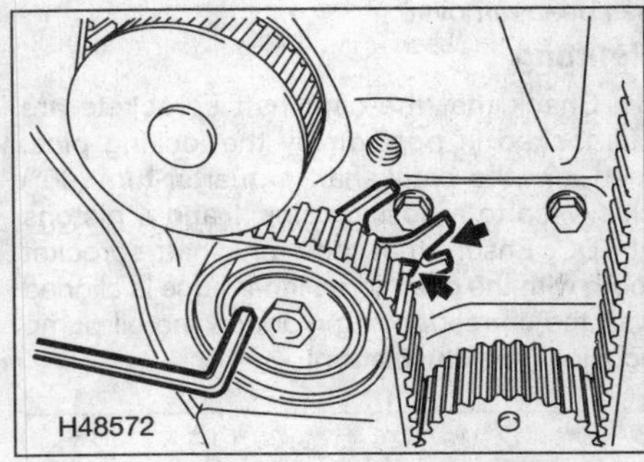

6.18 The pointer must align with the centre of the cut-out (arrowed)

6.32b ...then unscrew the securing bolt and remove the tensioner

6.33 Removing the secondary timing belt

6.34 Crankshaft sprocket tooth with chamfered edge aligned with cast arrow on oil pump

6.37 The secondary timing belt tensioner pointer should be positioned on the far right of the tensioner backplate, and the lug on the backplate should be engaged with the core plug hole

6.38 Turn the tensioner anti-clockwise until the tensioner pointer aligns with the lug on the tensioner backplate, with the lug positioned against the left-hand stop in the core plug hole

locking tool, and slide the secondary timing belt from the sprockets **(see illustration).** Refit the sprocket locking tool once the belt has been removed.

Refitting

34 Check that the camshaft sprockets are still locked in position by the locking pins, then turn the crankshaft a quarter-turn (90°) clockwise to reposition Nos 1 and 4 pistons at TDC. Ensure that the crankshaft sprocket tooth with the chamfered inner edge is aligned with the corresponding mark on the oil pump housing **(see illustration).**

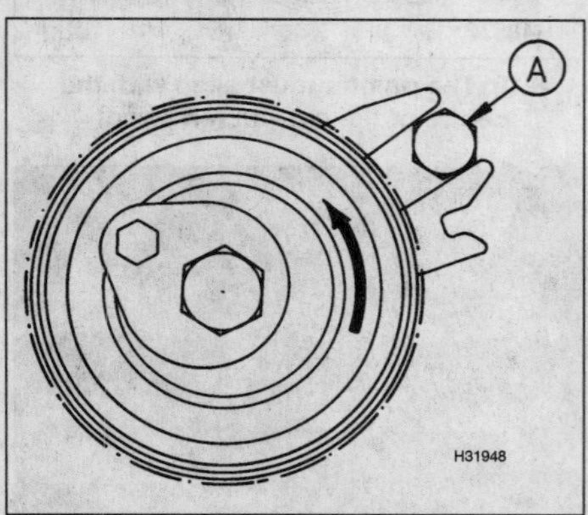

7.3 Turn the tensioner anti-clockwise to the position shown before fitting. Note that the cut-out engages with the bolt (A) on the cylinder block when fitting

35 Temporarily remove the camshaft sprocket locking tool, and fit the secondary timing belt around the camshaft sprockets. Make sure that the belt is as tight as possible on its top run between the sprockets (but note that there will be some slack in the belt). If the original belt is being refitted, observe the running direction markings. Refit the camshaft sprocket locking tool once the belt has been fitted to the sprockets.

36 Check that the secondary timing belt tensioner pointer is positioned on the far right of the tensioner backplate.

37 Press the secondary timing belt up using the tensioner, and fit the tensioner securing bolt (if necessary turn the tensioner with an Allen key until the bolt hole in the tensioner aligns with the bolt hole in the cylinder head). Make sure that the lug on the tensioner backplate engages with the core plug hole in the cylinder head **(see illustration).**

38 Use the Allen key to turn the tensioner anti-clockwise until the tensioner pointer aligns with the lug on the tensioner backplate, with the lug positioned against the left-hand stop in the core plug hole **(see illustration).** Tighten the tensioner bolt to the specified torque.

7 Timing belt tensioner and sprockets – removal and refitting

Main timing belt tensioner

Removal

1 Remove the main timing belt as described in Section 6.

2 Unscrew the main timing belt tensioner bolt, and remove the tensioner from the engine.

3 Engage an Allen key with the hole in the tensioner plate, and turn the tensioner anti-clockwise **(see illustration).**

Refitting

4 Refit the tensioner to the engine, ensuring that the cut-out in the tensioner backplate engages with the bolt on the cylinder block. Refit the tensioner securing bolt, and tighten by hand.

5 Refit and tension the main timing belt as described in Section 6.

Inlet camshaft timing belt tensioner

6 Removal and refitting of the tensioner is described as part of the timing belt removal procedure in Section 6.

Main timing belt idler pulleys

Removal

7 Remove the timing belt as described in Section 6.

8 Unscrew the securing bolt and remove the relevant idler pulley. Note that the smaller pulley (the idler pulley nearest the inlet manifold side of the engine) can be removed complete with its mounting bracket (unbolt the mounting bracket bolt, leaving the pulley attached to the bracket) **(see illustrations).**

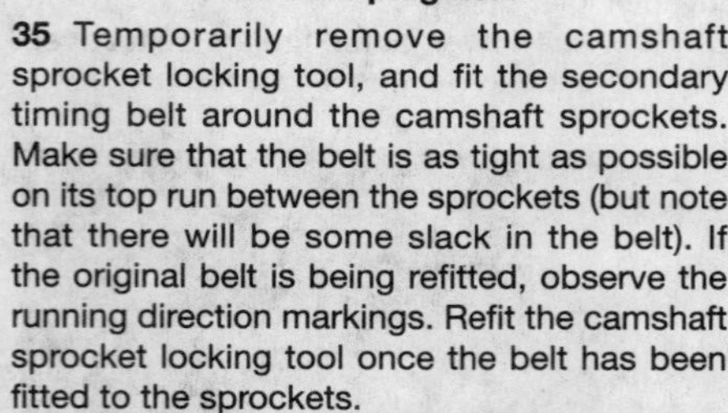

7.8a Removing the smaller...

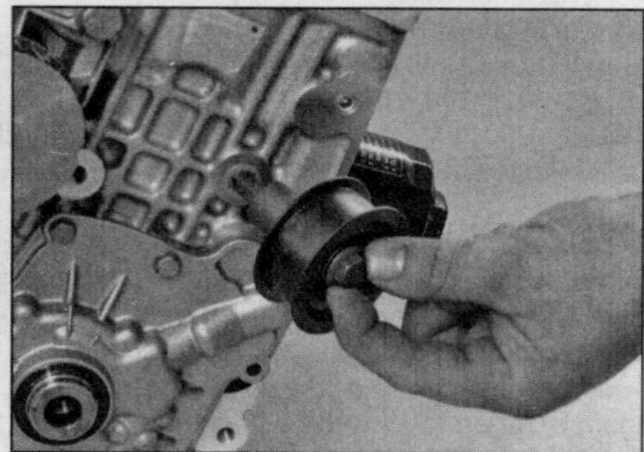
7.8b ...and larger timing belt idler pulleys

7.13 Refitting the crankshaft sprocket. Pulley locating pin (arrowed) must be outermost

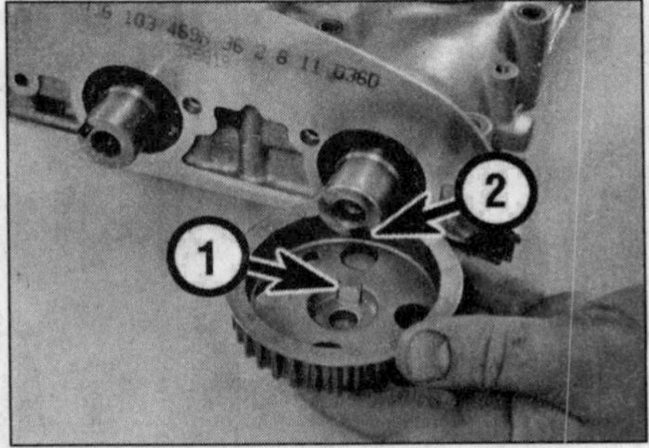

7.18 Refit the sprocket, ensuring that the lug (1) on the sprocket engages with the notch (2) in the end of the camshaft

7.19 Tighten the sprocket securing bolt using a suitable tool to hold the sprocket stationary

Refitting

9 Refit the relevant idler pulley and tighten the securing bolt to the specified torque. Note that if the smaller idler pulley has been removed complete with its bracket, ensure that the bracket locates over the rear timing belt cover bolt on refitting.

10 Refit and tension the main timing belt as described in Section 6.

Crankshaft sprocket

Removal

11 Remove the main timing belt as described in Section 6.

12 Unscrew the crankshaft pulley bolt, and the washer used to retain the sprocket, and withdraw the sprocket from the crankshaft.

Refitting

13 Commence refitting by positioning the sprocket on the end of the crankshaft, noting that the pulley locating pin must be outermost **(see illustration)**. Temporarily refit the pulley securing bolt and washer to retain the sprocket.

14 Refit the main timing belt as described in Section 6.

Camshaft sprockets

Removal

15 Remove the main and secondary timing belts as described in Section 6. Ensure that the crankshaft has been turned a quarter-turn (90°) anti-clockwise to position Nos 1 and 4 pistons slightly down their bores from the TDC position. This will eliminate any risk of piston-to-valve contact if a camshaft is turned whilst the timing belt is removed.

16 The relevant camshaft sprocket bolt must now be slackened. The camshaft must be prevented from turning as the sprocket bolt is unscrewed – **do not** rely solely on the sprocket locking tool for this. To hold the sprocket, make up a tool and use it to hold the sprocket stationary by means of the holes in the sprocket.

17 Unscrew the camshaft sprocket bolt, and withdraw the sprocket from the end of the camshaft, noting which way round it is fitted.

Refitting

18 Commence refitting by offering the sprocket up to the camshaft, ensuring that lug on the sprocket engages with the notch in the end of the camshaft. If both camshaft sprockets have been removed, note that the double sprocket (for the main and secondary timing belts) should be fitted to the inlet camshaft, and note that the exhaust camshaft sprocket must be fitted first **(see illustration)**.

19 Fit a new sprocket securing bolt, then use the tool to hold the sprocket stationary, as during removal, and tighten the bolt to the specified torque, in the two stages given in the Specifications **(see illustration)**.

20 Refit the secondary and main timing belts as described in Section 6.

Coolant pump sprocket

21 The coolant pump sprocket is integral with the coolant pump. Refer to Chapter 3 for details of coolant pump removal.

8 Camshaft carrier – removal and refitting

Note: *New camshaft carrier securing bolts must be used on refitting. Suitable sealant (VW AMV 188 003, or equivalent) will be required, and two M6 studs (approximately 70 mm long) will be required ñ see text.*

Removal

1 Switch off the ignition and all electrical consumers and remove the ignition key.

2 On engine code BUD, unbolt the cover from the camshaft carrier.

3 Remove the main and secondary timing belts, as described in Section 6.

4 Remove the ignition HT coils as described in Chapter 5B. Unbolt the coil wiring earth lead from the top of the camshaft cover, then release the coil wiring from the clips on the camshaft cover, and move the wiring clear of the camshaft cover.

5 Disconnect the breather hose from the rear of the cylinder head.

6 Disconnect the inlet camshaft position sensor wiring connector **(see illustration)**.

7 Disconnect the wiring plug from the oil pressure warning light switch, located at the front left-hand corner of the camshaft carrier. Release the wiring harness from the clip on the end of the camshaft carrier, and move the wiring to one side **(see illustrations)**.

8 Remove the rear timing belt cover securing

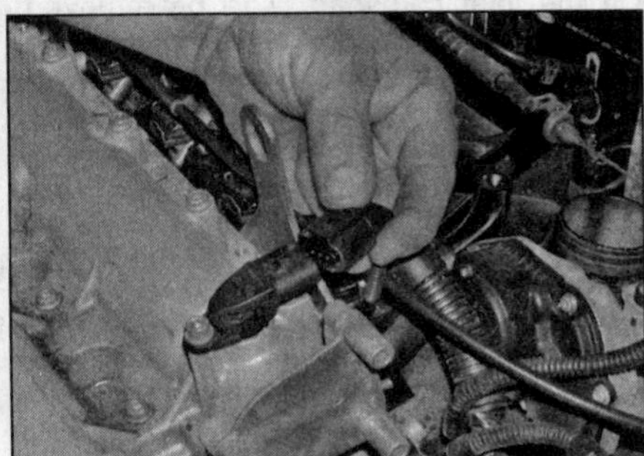

8.6 Disconnect the wiring connector from the inlet camshaft position sensor

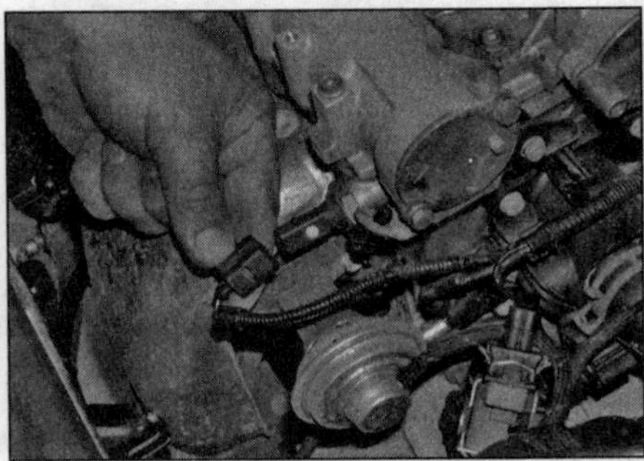

8.7a Disconnect the oil pressure warning light switch wiring plug...

8.7b ...then release the wiring from the clip on the end of the camshaft carrier

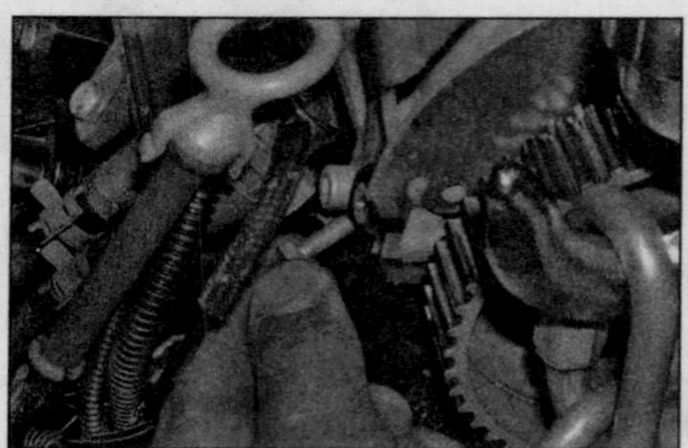
8.8 Remove the rear timing belt cover securing bolt located next to the right-hand engine lifting eye

8.9 Remove the camshaft carrier securing bolts...

8.10 ...then lift the camshaft carrier from the cylinder head

8.14 Apply a thin, even coat of sealant to the cylinder head mating face of the camshaft carrier

8.17 Tightening a camshaft carrier bolt through the specified Stage 2 angle

bolt, located next to the right-hand engine lifting eye **(see illustration)**.

9 Working progressively from the centre out, in a diagonal sequence, slacken and remove the camshaft carrier securing bolts **(see illustration)**.

10 Carefully lift the camshaft carrier from the cylinder head **(see illustration)**. The camshafts can be removed from the carrier, as described in Section 9.

Refitting

11 Commence refitting by thoroughly cleaning all traces of old sealant, and all traces of oil and grease, from the mating faces of the cylinder head and camshaft carrier. Ensure that no debris enters the cylinder head or camshaft carrier.

12 Ensure that the crankshaft is still positioned a quarter-turn (90°) anti-clockwise from the TDC position, and that the camshafts are locked in position with the locking tool, as described in Section 3.

13 Check that the valve rockers are correctly located on the valves, and securely clipped into position on the hydraulic tappets.

14 Apply a thin, even coat of sealant (VW AMV 188 003, or equivalent) to the cylinder head mating face of the camshaft carrier **(see illustration)**. Do not apply the sealant too thickly, as excess sealant may enter and block the oilways, causing engine damage.

15 Carefully lower the camshaft carrier onto the cylinder head, until the camshafts rest on the rockers. Note that the camshaft carrier locates on dowels in the cylinder head; if desired, to make fitting easier, two guide studs can be made up as follows:

a) Cut the heads off two M6 bolts, then cut slots in the top of each bolt to enable the bolt to be unscrewed using a flat-bladed screwdriver.

b) Screw one bolt into each of the camshaft carrier bolt locations at opposite corners of the cylinder head.

c) Lower the camshaft carrier over the bolts to guide it into position on the cylinder head.

16 Fit new camshaft carrier securing bolts, and tighten them progressively, working from the centre out, in a diagonal sequence (ie, tighten all bolts through one turn, then tighten all bolts through a further turn, and so on). Ensure that the camshaft carrier sits squarely on the cylinder head as the bolts are tightened, and make sure that the carrier engages with the cylinder head dowels. Where applicable, once the camshaft carrier contacts the surface of the cylinder head, unscrew the two guide studs, and fit the two remaining new camshaft carrier securing bolts in their place.

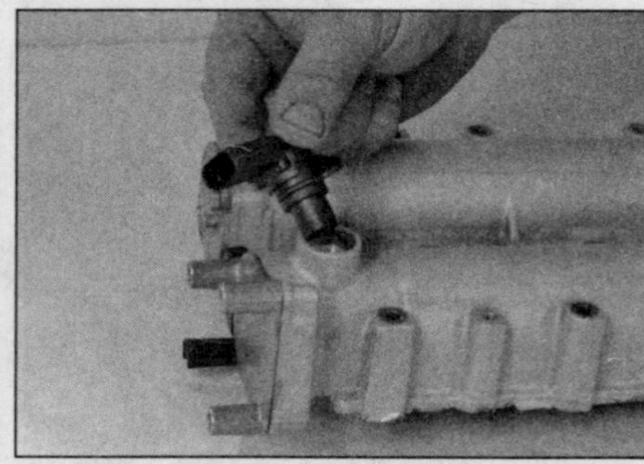
9.3 Remove the inlet camshaft position sensor

17 Tighten the camshaft carrier securing bolts to the specified torque, in the two stages given in the Specifications **(see illustration)**.

18 Leave the camshaft carrier sealant to dry for approximately 30 minutes before carrying out any further work on the cylinder head or camshaft carrier.

19 Once the sealant has been allowed to dry, refit the rear timing belt cover bolt.

20 Reconnect the oil pressure warning light switch wiring plug, and clip the wiring into position on the end of the camshaft carrier.

21 Reconnect the camshaft position sensor wiring connector.

22 Refit the ignition coils with reference to Chapter 5B.

23 Refit the secondary and main timing belts, as described in Section 6.

24 On engine code BUD, refit the cover to the camshaft carrier and tighten the bolts securely.

9 Camshafts – removal, inspection and refitting

Removal

1 Remove the camshaft carrier as described in Section 8.

2 Remove the camshaft sprockets, with reference to Section 7.

3 If the inlet camshaft is to be removed, unscrew the securing bolt, and remove the inlet camshaft position sensor **(see illustration)**.

4 Remove the relevant camshaft carrier endplate **(see illustration)**.

5 Carefully withdraw the relevant camshaft from the endplate end of the camshaft carrier, taking care not to damage the bearing surfaces of the camshaft and housing as the camshaft is withdrawn **(see illustration)**.

Inspection

6 Visually inspect the camshafts for evidence of wear on the surfaces of the lobes and journals. Normally their surfaces should be smooth and have a dull shine; look for

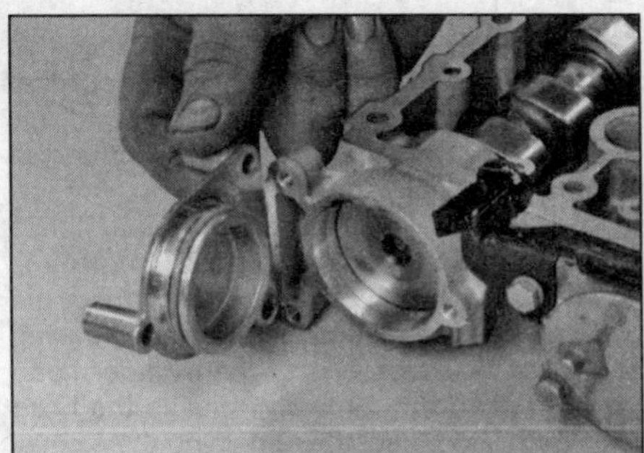

9.4 Remove the camshaft carrier endplate

9.5 Withdraw the camshaft from the endplate end of the camshaft carrier

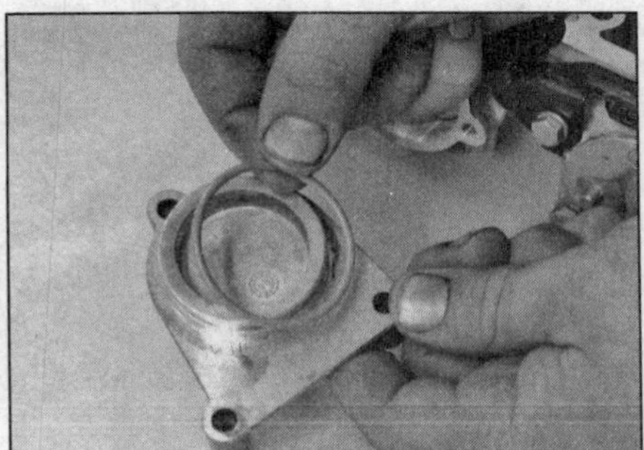

9.10 Renew the camshaft carrier endplate O-ring

scoring, erosion or pitting and areas that appear highly polished, indicating excessive wear. Accelerated wear will occur once the hardened exterior of the camshaft has been damaged, so always renew worn items. **Note:** *If these symptoms are visible on the tips of the camshaft lobes, check the corresponding rocker, as it will probably be worn as well.*

7 If the machined surfaces of the camshaft appear discoloured or blued, it is likely that it has been overheated at some point, probably due to inadequate lubrication. This may have distorted the shaft, so check the run-out as follows: place the camshaft between two V-blocks and, using a DTI gauge, measure the run-out at the centre journal. No maximum run-out figure is quoted by the manufacturers, but it should be obvious if the camshaft is excessively distorted.

8 To measure camshaft endfloat, temporarily refit the relevant camshaft to the camshaft carrier, and refit the endplate to the rear of the camshaft carrier. Anchor a DTI gauge to the timing belt end of the camshaft carrier and align the gauge probe with the camshaft axis. Push the camshaft to one end of the camshaft carrier as far as it will travel, then rest the DTI gauge probe on the end of the camshaft, and zero the gauge display. Push the camshaft as far as it will go to the other end of the camshaft carrier, and record the gauge reading. Verify the reading by pushing the camshaft back to its original position and checking that the gauge indicates zero again.

9 Check that the camshaft endfloat measurement is within the limit listed in the Specifications. Wear outside of this limit may be cured by renewing the relevant camshaft carrier endplate, although wear is unlikely to be confined to any one component, so renewal of the camshafts and camshaft carrier must be considered.

Refitting

10 Refitting is a reversal of removal, bearing in mind the following points.

a) *Before refitting the camshaft, renew the camshaft oil seal, with reference to Section 11.*
b) *Lubricate the bearing surfaces in the camshaft carrier, and the camshaft lobes before refitting the camshaft(s).*
c) *Renew the sealing O-ring on each camshaft carrier endplate **(see illustration)**.*
d) *Refit the camshaft sprocket(s) with reference to Section 7, noting that if both sprockets have been removed, the exhaust camshaft sprocket must be fitted first.*
e) *Refit the camshaft carrier as described in Section 8.*

10 Rockers and tappets – removal, inspection and refitting

Removal

1 Remove the camshaft carrier, as described in Section 8.

2 As the components are removed, keep them in strict order, so that they can be refitted in their original locations.

3 Unclip the rockers from the hydraulic tappets, and lift them from the cylinder head **(see illustration)**.

4 Carefully lift the tappets from their bores in the cylinder head. It is advisable to store the tappets (in order) upright in an oil bath whilst they are removed from the engine.

Inspection

5 Check the cylinder head bore contact surfaces of the tappets for signs of scoring or damage. Similarly, check the tappet bores in the cylinder head for signs of scoring or damage. If significant scoring or damage is found, it may be necessary to renew the cylinder head and the complete set of tappets.

10.3 Removing a rocker (hydraulic tappets arrowed)

6 Inspect the hydraulic tappets for obvious signs of wear or damage, and renew if necessary. Check that the oil holes in the tappets are free from obstructions.

7 Check the valve, tappet, and camshaft contact faces of the rockers for wear or damage, and also check the rockers for any signs of cracking. Renew any worn or damaged rockers.

8 Inspect the camshaft lobes, as described in Section 11.

Refitting

9 Oil the tappet bores in the cylinder head, and the tappets themselves, then carefully slide the tappets into their original bores **(see illustration)**.

10 Oil the rocker contact faces of the tappets, and the tops of the valve stems, then refit the rockers to their original locations, ensuring that the rockers are securely clipped onto the tappets.

11 Check the endfloat of each camshaft, as described in Section 9, then refit the camshaft carrier as described in Section 8.

11 Camshaft oil seals – renewal

Right-hand oil seals

1 Remove the main and secondary timing belts as described in Section 7.

10.9 Oil the tappets before fitting

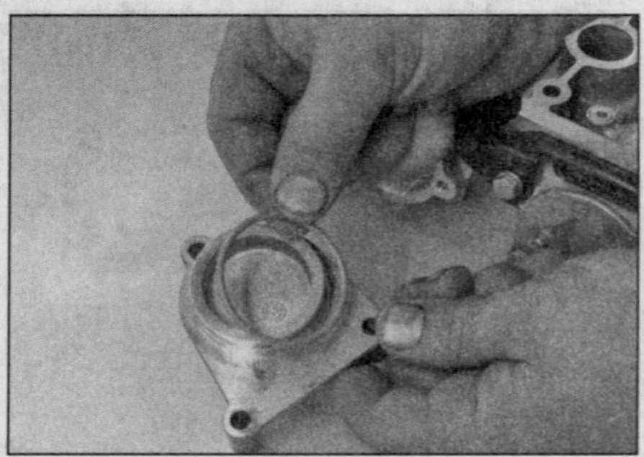

11.12 Locate the new O-ring in the groove in the endplate

2 Remove the relevant camshaft sprocket as described in Section 8.

3 Drill two small holes into the existing oil seal, diagonally opposite each other. Take great care to avoid drilling through into the seal housing or camshaft sealing surface. Thread two self-tapping screws into the holes and, using a pair of pliers, pull on the heads of the screws to extract the oil seal.

4 Clean out the seal housing and the sealing surface of the camshaft by wiping it with a lint-free cloth. Remove any swarf or burrs that may cause the seal to leak.

5 Lubricate the lip and outer edge of the new oil seal with clean engine oil, and push it over the camshaft until it is positioned above its housing. To prevent damage to the sealing lips, wrap some adhesive tape around the end of the camshaft.

6 Using a hammer and a socket of suitable diameter, drive the seal squarely into its housing. **Note:** *Select a socket that bears only on the hard outer surface of the seal, not the inner lip which can easily be damaged.*

7 Refit the relevant camshaft sprocket with reference to Section 8.

8 Refit and tension the secondary and main timing belts as described in Section 7.

Left-hand oil seals

9 The camshaft oil seals take the form of O-rings located in the grooves in the camshaft carrier endplates.

10 Unscrew the securing bolts, and remove the relevant camshaft endplate.

11 Prise the old O-ring from the groove in the endplate.

12 Lightly oil the new O-ring, and carefully locate it in the groove in the endplate **(see illustration)**.

13 Refit the endplate and tighten the bolts securely.

12 Cylinder head – removal, inspection and refitting

Note: *The cylinder head must be removed with the engine cold. New cylinder head bolts, a new cylinder head gasket, new inlet manifold O-rings, and a new exhaust manifold gasket will be required on refitting.*

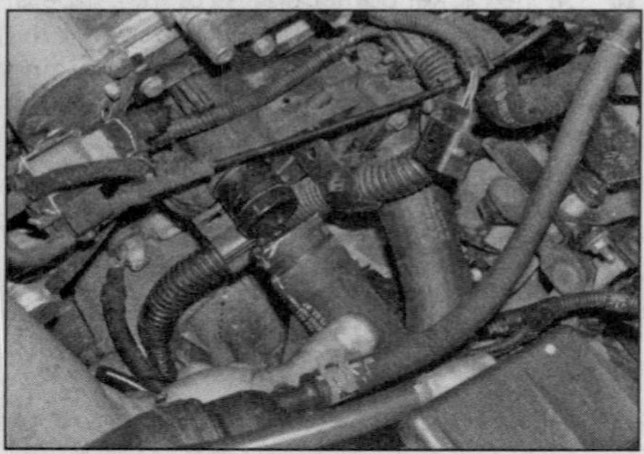

12.4 Disconnect the radiator hoses from the coolant housing

12.7 A lifting bracket can be bolted to the cylinder block using a long bolt screwed into the hole next to the coolant pump

12.9 Unscrew the bolt securing the oil level dipstick tube bracket to the cylinder head

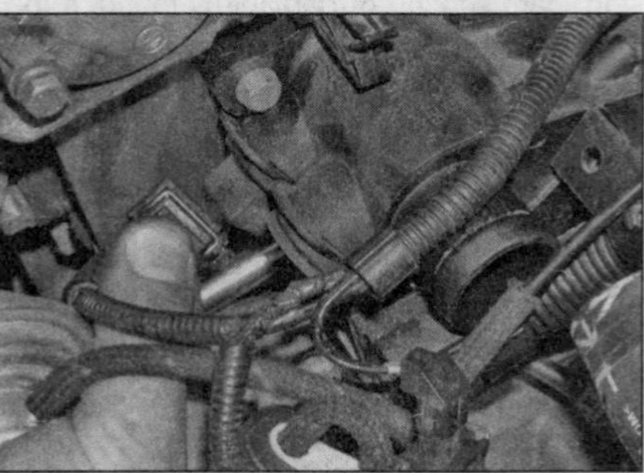

12.13 Disconnect the coolant temperature sensor wiring plug

Removal

1 Switch off the ignition and all electrical consumers, and remove the ignition key.

2 Drain the cooling system as described in Chapter 1A.

3 Remove the air cleaner assembly, complete with the air trunking, as described in Chapter 4A.

4 Release the hose clips, and disconnect the two radiator hoses from the coolant housing at the transmission end of the cylinder head **(see illustration)**. Similarly, release the hose clips and disconnect the remaining three small coolant hoses from the rear of the coolant housing.

5 Remove the main and secondary timing belts as described in Section 6.

6 As the engine is currently supported using a hoist attached to the engine lifting brackets bolted to the cylinder head, it is now necessary to attach a suitable bracket to the cylinder block, so that the engine can still be supported as the cylinder head is removed.

7 A suitable engine lifting bracket can be bolted to the cylinder block using spacers, and a long bolt screwed into the hole located next to the coolant pump **(see illustration)**. Ideally, attach a second set of lifting tackle to the hoist, adjust the lifting tackle to support the engine using the bracket attached to the cylinder block, then disconnect the lifting tackle attached to the bracket on the cylinder head. Alternatively, temporarily support the engine under the sump using a jack and a block of wood, then transfer the lifting tackle from the bracket on the cylinder head to the bracket bolted to the cylinder block.

8 Remove the camshaft carrier, rockers and tappets, with reference to Sections 8 and 10.

9 Unscrew the bolt securing the oil level dipstick tube bracket to the cylinder head, then lift the dipstick tube, and turn it to one side, to clear the working area **(see illustration)**. Release the wiring harnesses from the clip on the dipstick tube bracket. Note that the dipstick tube bracket bolt also secures the inlet manifold.

10 Disconnect the fuel supply line located next to the coolant expansion tank. Squeeze the button to do this.

11 Disconnect the hose from the charcoal canister to the inlet manifold.

12 Disconnect the hose from the brake servo to the inlet manifold.

13 Disconnect the wiring from the following:

a) Knock sensor on the rear of the engine.
b) Inlet manifold pressure sender and air temperature sender.
c) Engine speed sender.
d) Coolant temperature sender ***(see illustration)****.*
e) Oil pressure switch.
f) Throttle valve control module.
g) Injectors.
h) Heated vacuum valve on oil separator.
i) Crankcase breather on inlet manifold.

14 Unclip the wiring from the bracket attached to the exhaust heat shield, then

12.14a Unclip the wiring from the bracket on the exhaust heat shield...

12.14b ...then remove the heat shield

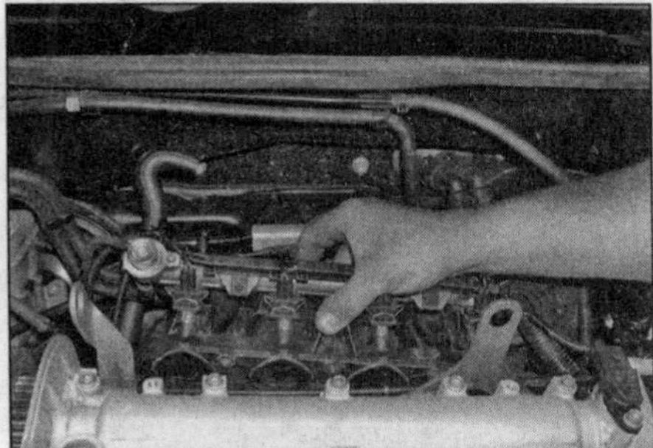
12.18 Lift the inlet manifold back from the engine

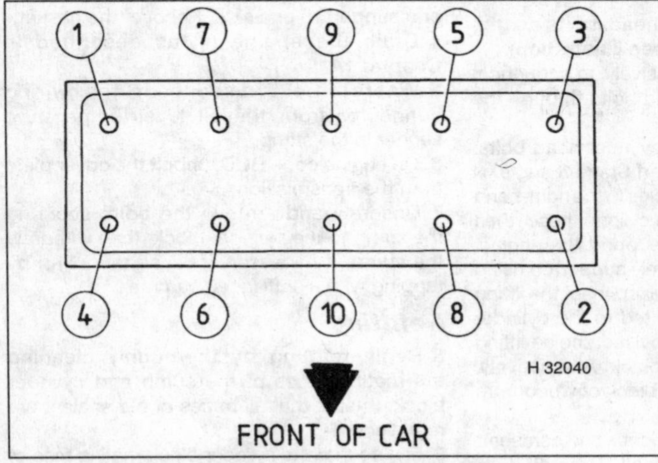

12.19a Cylinder head bolt slackening sequence

12.19b Slackening the cylinder head bolts

unscrew the securing bolts (two upper bolts and one lower bolt), and remove the heat shield **(see illustrations)**.

15 Disconnect the exhaust front section from the manifold with reference to Chapter 4C. If desired, the exhaust manifold can be removed completely.

16 Unscrew and remove the bolt securing the timing belt inner cover to the cylinder head (located near the right-hand engine lifting eye).

17 Unbolt and remove the timing belt idler bracket.

18 Unscrew the six securing bolts (three upper and three lower) and lift the inlet manifold back from the engine **(see illustration)**. Ensure that the inlet manifold is adequately supported in the engine compartment, and take care not to strain any wires, cables or hoses. Recover the O-rings if they are loose. **Note:** *On engine code BUD, remove the EGR pipe from the inlet manifold.*

19 Progressively slacken the cylinder head bolts in order, then unscrew and remove the bolts **(see illustrations)**.

20 With all the bolts removed, lift the cylinder head from the block **(see illustration)**. If the cylinder head is stuck, tap it with a soft-faced mallet to break the joint. **Do not** insert a lever into the gasket joint. As the cylinder head is lifted off, release the coolant pump pipe from the thermostat housing on the cylinder head.

21 Lift the cylinder head gasket from the block.

Inspection

22 Dismantling and inspection of the cylinder head is covered in Part F of this Chapter. Additionally, check the condition of the coolant pump pipe-to-thermostat housing O-ring, and renew if necessary.

Refitting

23 The mating faces of the cylinder head and block must be perfectly clean before refitting the head. Use a scraper to remove all traces of gasket and carbon, also clean the tops of the pistons. Take particular care with the aluminium surfaces, as the soft metal is easily damaged. Make sure that debris is not allowed to enter the oil and water passages – this is particularly important for the oil circuit, as carbon could block the oil supply to the camshaft and crankshaft bearings. Using adhesive tape and paper, seal the water, oil and bolt holes in the cylinder block. To prevent carbon entering the gap between the pistons and bores, smear a little grease in the gap. After cleaning a piston, rotate the crankshaft to that the piston moves down the bore, then wipe out the grease and carbon with a cloth rag. Clean the other piston crowns in the same way.

12.20 Removing the cylinder head

24 Check the head and block for nicks, deep scratches and other damage. If slight, they may be removed carefully with a file. More serious damage may be repaired by machining, but this is a specialist job.

25 If warpage of the cylinder head is suspected, use a straight-edge to check it for distortion, as described in Part F of this Chapter.

26 Ensure that the cylinder head bolt holes in the crankcase are clean and free of oil. Syringe or soak up any oil left in the bolt holes. This is most important in order that the correct bolt tightening torque can be applied, and

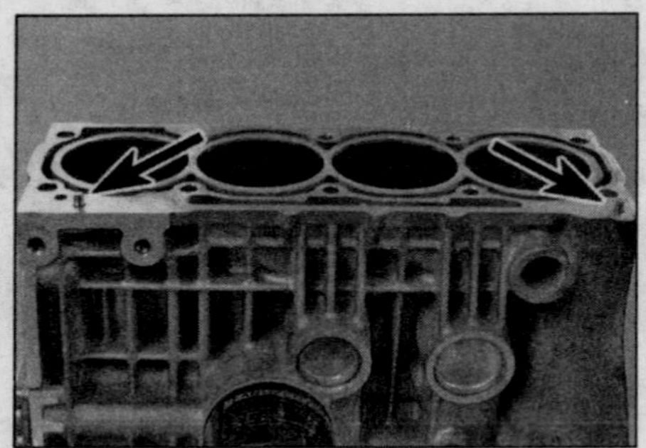

12.28a Ensure that the dowels are in place in the cylinder block

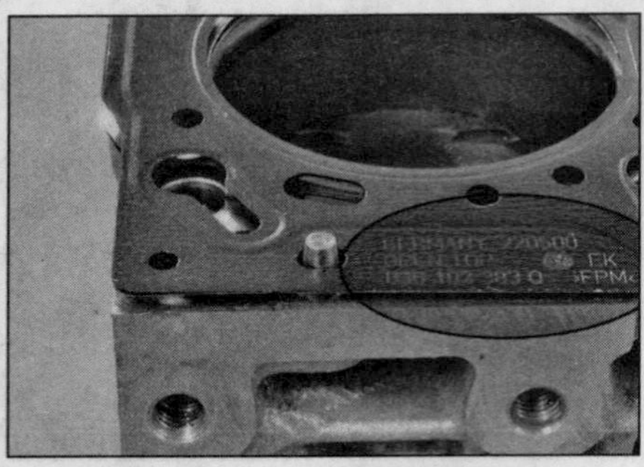

12.28b Ensure that the part number and OBEN/TOP markings on the cylinder head gasket are uppermost

to prevent the possibility of the block being cracked by hydraulic pressure when the bolts are tightened.

27 Ensure that the crankshaft has been turned to position Nos 1 and 4 pistons slightly down their bores from the TDC position (see Sec-tion 6). This will eliminate any risk of piston-to-valve contact as the cylinder head is refitted. Also ensure that the camshaft sprockets are locked in the TDC position using the locking tool, as described in Section 3.

28 Ensure that the cylinder head locating dowels are in place in the cylinder block, then fit a new cylinder head gasket over the dowels, ensuring that the part number is uppermost. Where applicable, the OBEN/TOP marking should also be uppermost **(see illustrations)**. Note that VW recommend that the gasket is only removed from its packaging immediately prior to fitting.

29 Lower the cylinder head into position on the gasket, ensuring that it engages correctly over the dowels. As the cylinder head is lowered into position, ensure that the coolant pump pipe engages with the thermostat housing (use a new O-ring if necessary).

30 Fit the new cylinder head bolts, and screw them in as far as possible by hand.

31 Working progressively, in sequence, tighten all the cylinder head bolts to the specified Stage 1 torque **(see illustration)**.

32 Again working progressively, in sequence, tighten all the cylinder head bolts through the specified Stage 2 angle.

33 Finally, tighten all the cylinder head bolts, in sequence, to the specified Stage 3 angle.

34 Reconnect the lifting tackle to the right-hand engine lifting bracket on the cylinder head, then adjust the lifting tackle to support the engine. Once the engine is adequately supported using the cylinder head bracket, disconnect the lifting tackle from the bracket bolted to the cylinder block, and unbolt the improvised engine lifting bracket from the cylinder block. Alternatively, remove the trolley jack and block of wood from under the sump.

35 Refit the rockers and tappets, and camshaft carrier as described in Sections 10 and 8.

36 Further refitting is a reversal of removal, bearing in mind the following points.

a) Renew gaskets and O-rings as required.
b) Ensure that all wires, pipes and hoses are correctly reconnected and routed, as noted before removal.
c) Tighten all fixings to the specified torque, where given.
d) On completion, refill the cooling system as described in Chapter 1A.

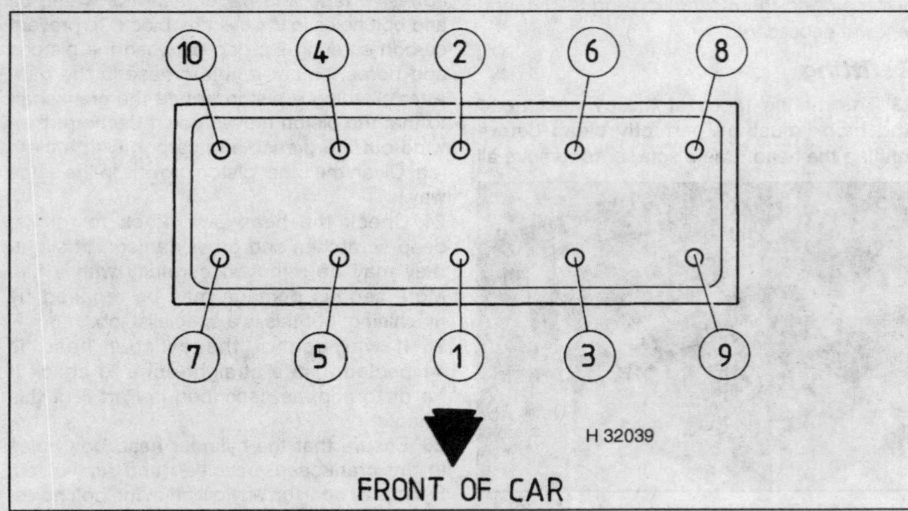

12.31 Cylinder head bolt tightening sequence

13 Sump – removal and refitting

Note: *VW sealant (D 176 404 A2 or equivalent) will be required to seal the sump on refitting.*

Removal

1 Apply the handbrake, then jack up the front of the vehicle and support securely on axle stands (see *Jacking and vehicle support*).

2 Remove the securing screws and withdraw the engine undertray(s).

3 Detach the exhaust front pipe from the exhaust manifold with reference to Chapter 4C and support to one side. Recover the gasket.

4 Drain the engine oil as described in Chapter 1A.

5 Where fitted, disconnect the wiring connector from the oil level/temperature sender in the sump.

6 On engine code BUD, unbolt the cover plate from the transmission.

7 Unscrew and remove the bolts securing the sump to the cylinder block, then withdraw the sump. If necessary, release the sump by tapping with a soft-faced hammer.

Refitting

8 Begin refitting by thoroughly cleaning the mating faces of the sump and cylinder block. Ensure that all traces of old sealant are removed.

9 Ensure that the cylinder block mating face of the sump is free from all traces of old sealant, oil and grease, and then apply a 2.0 to 3.0 mm thick bead of silicone sealant (VW D 176 404 A2 or equivalent) to the sump. Note that the sealant should be run around the inside of the bolt holes in the sump. The sump must be fitted within 5 minutes of applying the sealant.

10 Offer the sump up to the cylinder block, then refit the sump-to-cylinder block bolts, and lightly tighten them by hand, working progressively in a diagonal sequence. **Note:** *If the sump is being refitted with the engine and transmission separated, make sure that the sump is flush with the flywheel/driveplate end of the cylinder block. If necessary, temporarily screw two M6 studs into the block to act as guides.*

11 Refit the sump-to-block bolts, and tighten them lightly, using a socket.

12 Working in a diagonal sequence, progressively tighten the sump-to-cylinder block bolts to the specified torque.

13 On engine code BUD, refit the cover plate to the transmission and tighten the bolts.

14 Refit the exhaust front pipe together with a new gasket with reference to Chapter 4C.

15 Refit the wiring connector to the oil level/temperature sender (where fitted), then refit the engine undertray(s), and lower the vehicle to the ground.

16 Allow at least 30 minutes from the time of refitting the sump for the sealant to dry, then refill the engine with oil, with reference to Chapter 1A.

14.7 Removing the oil pick-up pipe

14.9 Removing the oil pump

14.11 Lifting off the oil pump rear cover

14 Oil pump – removal, inspection and refitting

Removal

1 Remove the main timing belt, as described in Section 6.

2 Refit the crankshaft pulley securing bolt, with a spacer washer positioned under its head, to retain the crankshaft sprocket.

3 Turn the crankshaft a quarter-turn (90°) clockwise to reposition Nos 1 and 4 pistons at TDC. Ensure that the crankshaft sprocket tooth with the chamfered inner edge is aligned with the corresponding mark on the oil pump housing (see Section 3).

4 Turn the crankshaft to move the crankshaft sprocket three teeth anti-clockwise away from the TDC position. The third tooth to the right of the tooth with the ground down outer edge must align with the corresponding mark on the oil pump housing. This procedure positions the crankshaft with one of the polygon cams pointing upwards to enable correct oil pump refitting.

5 Remove the main timing belt tensioner, as described in Section 7.

6 Remove the sump as described in Section 13.

7 Unscrew the securing bolts and remove the oil pick-up pipe from the oil pump and cylinder block **(see illustration)**. Recover the gasket.

8 Remove the crankshaft sprocket, noting which way round it is fitted.

9 Unscrew the securing bolts, noting their locations to ensure correct refitting, and remove the oil pump **(see illustration)**. Recover the gasket.

Inspection

10 No spare parts are available for the oil pump, and if worn or faulty, the complete pump must be renewed.

11 To inspect the oil pump rotors, remove the securing screws, and lift off the oil pump rear cover **(see illustration)**.

12 Note that the rotors fit with the punched dots on the edges of the rotors facing the oil pump cover **(see illustration)**.

13 Lift out the rotors, and inspect them for wear and damage. If there are any signs of wear or damage, the complete oil pump assembly must be renewed.

14 Lubricate the contact faces of the rotors with clean engine oil, then refit the rotors to the pump, ensuring that the punched dots on the edges of the rotors face the pump cover.

15 Refit the pump cover, and tighten the screws securely.

16 Using a flat-bladed screwdriver, prise the crankshaft oil seal from the oil pump, and discard it **(see illustration)**.

17 Thoroughly clean the oil seal seat in the oil pump.

18 Press or drive a new oil seal into position in the oil pump, using a socket or tube of suitable diameter **(see illustration)**. Ensure that the seal seats squarely in the oil pump. Ensure that the socket or tube bears only on the hard outer ring of the seal, and take care not to damage the seal lips. Press or drive the seal into position until it is seated on the shoulder in the housing. Make sure that the closed end of the seal is facing outwards.

Refitting

19 Commence refitting by cleaning all traces of old gasket and sealant from the mating faces of the cylinder block and oil pump.

20 Wind a length of tape around the front of the crankshaft to protect the oil seal lips as the oil pump is slid into position.

21 Fit a new oil pump gasket over the dowels in the cylinder block **(see illustration)**.

22 Turn the inner oil pump rotor to align one of the drive cut-outs in the edge of the inner rotor with the line on the oil pump rear cover **(see illustration)**.

23 Lightly oil the four tips of the oil pump drive cam on the end of the crankshaft.

24 Coat the lips of the crankshaft oil seal with a thin film of clean engine oil.

14.12 Note that the rotors fit with the punched dots facing the oil pump cover

14.16 Prise the crankshaft oil seal from the oil pump

14.18 Driving a new oil seal into the oil pump using a socket

14.21 Fit a new gasket over the dowels in the cylinder block

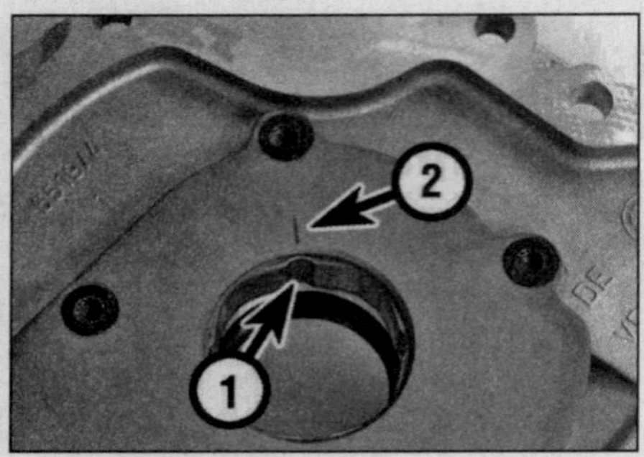

14.22 Align one of the drive cut-outs (1) in the edge of the rotor with the line (2) on the oil pump rear cover

25 Slide the oil pump into position over the end of the crankshaft until it engages with the dowels, taking care not to damage the oil seal, and ensuring that the inner rotor engages with the drive cam on the crankshaft **(see illustration)**.

26 Fit new oil pump securing bolts, to the locations noted before removal, and tighten them to the specified torque **(see illustration)**.

27 Remove the tape from the end of the crankshaft, then refit the crankshaft sprocket, noting that the pulley locating pin must be outermost. Temporarily refit the securing bolt and washer to retain the sprocket.

28 Refit the oil pick-up pipe, using a new gasket, and tighten the securing bolts to the specified torque **(see illustration)**.

29 Refit the sump as described in Section 13.

30 Refit the main timing belt tensioner as described in Section 7.

31 Refit the main timing belt as described in Section 6.

15 Flywheel/driveplate – removal, inspection and refitting

Removal

1 On manual transmission models, remove the gearbox (Chapter 7A) and clutch (Chapter 6).

2 On automatic transmission models, remove the automatic transmission as described in Chapter 7B.

14.26 Fit the new oil pump securing bolts to the locations noted before removal

14.25 Slide the oil pump over the end of the crankshaft. Note the tape used to protect the oil seal

3 The flywheel/driveplate bolts are offset to ensure correct fitment. Unscrew the bolts while holding the flywheel/driveplate stationary. Temporarily insert a bolt in the cylinder block, and use a screwdriver to hold the flywheel/driveplate, or make up a holding tool.

4 Lift the flywheel/driveplate from the crankshaft. If removing a driveplate, note the location of the shim (where applicable – between the driveplate and the crankshaft), and the spacer under the securing bolts. Recover the engine-to-transmission plate if it is loose.

Inspection

5 Check the flywheel/driveplate for wear and damage. Examine the starter ring gear for excessive wear to the teeth. If the driveplate or its ring gear are damaged, the complete driveplate must be renewed. The flywheel ring gear, however, may be renewed separately from the flywheel, but the work should be entrusted to a VW dealer. If the clutch friction face is discoloured or scored excessively, it may be possible to regrind it, but this work should also be entrusted to a VW dealer.

Refitting

6 Refitting is a reversal of removal, bearing in mind the following points.

a) *Ensure that the engine-to-transmission plate is in place before fitting the flywheel/driveplate.*
b) *On automatic transmission models temporarily refit the driveplate using the old bolts tightened to 30 Nm (22 lbf ft), and check that the distance from the rear machined face of the cylinder block to the torque converter mounting face on the driveplate is between 19.5 and 21.1 mm. The measurement is most easily made through one of the holes in the driveplate, using vernier calipers. If necessary, remove the driveplate, and fit a shim between the driveplate and the crankshaft to achieve the correct dimension.*
c) *On automatic transmission models, the raised pip on the spacer under the securing bolts must face the torque converter.*
d) *Use new bolts when refitting the flywheel or driveplate, and coat the threads of the bolts with locking fluid before inserting them. Tighten the securing bolts to the specified torque.*

14.28 Fit a new oil pick-up pipe gasket

16 Crankshaft oil seals – renewal

Timing belt end oil seal

1 Remove the main timing belt as described in Section 6, and the crankshaft sprocket with reference to Section 7.

2 To remove the seal without removing the oil pump, drill two small holes diagonally opposite each other, insert self-tapping screws, and pull on the heads of the screws with pliers.

3 Alternatively, the oil seal can be removed with the oil pump, as described in Section 14.

4 Thoroughly clean the oil seal seating in the oil pump.

5 Wind a length of tape around the end of the crankshaft to protect the oil seal lips as the seal is fitted.

6 Fit a new oil seal to the oil pump, pressing or driving it into position using a socket or tube of suitable diameter. Ensure that the socket or tube bears only on the hard outer ring of the seal, and take care not to damage the seal lips. Press or drive the seal into position until it is seated on the shoulder in the oil pump. Make sure that the closed end of the seal is facing outwards.

7 Refit the crankshaft sprocket with reference to Section 8, and the main timing belt as described in Section 7.

Flywheel/driveplate end oil seal

8 The crankshaft left-hand oil seal is integral with the housing, and must be renewed as an assembly, complete with the crankshaft speed/position sensor wheel. The sensor wheel is attached to the oil seal/housing assembly, and is a press-fit on the crankshaft flange. VW special tool T10134 is required to fit this assembly and, in the workshop, we found that there is no means of accurately aligning the sensor wheel on the crankshaft without the tool (there is no locating key, and there are no alignment marks). If the sensor wheel is not precisely aligned on the crankshaft, the crankshaft speed/position sensor will send incorrect TDC signals to the engine management ECU, and the engine will not run correctly (the engine may not run at all). As the appropriate special tool is only available to VW dealers, there is no alternative but to have the new assembly fitted by a VW dealer.

17 Engine/transmission mountings – inspection and renewal

Inspection

1 If improved access is required, jack up the front of the vehicle, and support it securely on axle stands (see *Jacking and vehicle support*). Remove the engine top cover which also incorporates the air filter, then remove the engine undertray(s).

2 Check the mounting rubbers to see if they are cracked, hardened or separated from the metal at any point; renew the mounting if any such damage or deterioration is evident.

3 Check that all the mountings are securely tightened; use a torque wrench to check if possible.

4 Using a large screwdriver or a crowbar, check for wear in the mounting by carefully levering against it to check for free play. Where this is not possible, enlist the aid of an assistant to move the engine/transmission back-and-forth, or from side-to-side, whilst you observe the mounting. While some free play is to be expected, even from new components, excessive wear should be obvious. If excessive free play is found, check first that the fasteners are correctly secured, then renew any worn components as described in the following paragraphs.

Renewal

Right-hand mounting

5 Attach a hoist and lifting tackle to the engine lifting brackets on the cylinder head, and raise the hoist to just take the weight of the engine. Alternatively the engine can be supported on a trolley jack under the engine. Use a block of wood between the sump and the head of the jack, to prevent any damage to the sump.

6 For improved access, unbolt the coolant reservoir and move it to one side, leaving the coolant hoses connected.

7 Where applicable, move any wiring harnesses, pipes or hoses to one side to enable removal of the engine mounting **(see illustration)**.

8 Unbolt the bracket for the charcoal canister from the mounting.

9 Unscrew the bolts securing the mounting to the engine, then unscrew the bolts securing it to the body. Also, unbolt the movement limiter. Withdraw the mounting from the engine compartment.

10 Refitting is a reversal of removal, bearing in mind the following points:

a) *Use new securing bolts.*
b) *Tighten all fixings to the specified torque.*

17.7 Right-hand engine mounting

Left-hand mounting

Note: *New mounting bolts will be required on refitting (there is no need to renew the smaller mounting-to-body bolts).*

11 Remove the engine top cover which also incorporates the air filter.

12 Attach a hoist and lifting tackle to the engine lifting brackets on the cylinder head, and raise the hoist to just take the weight of the engine and transmission. Alternatively the engine can be supported on a trolley jack under the transmission. Use a block of wood between the transmission and the head of the jack, to prevent any damage to the transmission.

13 Remove the battery, as described in Chapter 5A, then disconnect the main starter motor feed cable from the positive battery terminal box.

14 Release any relevant wiring or hoses from the clips on the battery tray, then unscrew the four securing bolts and remove the battery tray.

15 Unscrew the bolts securing the mounting to the transmission, and the remaining bolts securing the mounting to the body, then lift the mounting from the engine compartment.

16 Refitting is a reversal of removal, bearing in mind the following points:

a) *Use new mounting bolts.*
b) *Tighten all fixings to the specified torque.*

Rear mounting (torque arm)

17 Apply the handbrake, then jack up the front of the vehicle and support securely on axle stands (see *Jacking and vehicle support*). Remove the engine undertray(s) for access to the rear mounting (torque arm).

18 Support the rear of the transmission beneath the final drive housing. To do this, use a trolley jack and block of wood, or alternatively wedge a block of wood between the transmission and the subframe.

19 Working under the vehicle, unscrew and remove the bolt securing the mounting to the subframe.

20 Unscrew the two bolts securing the mounting to the transmission, then withdraw the mounting from under the vehicle **(see illustration)**.

21 Refitting is a reversal of removal, but use new mounting securing bolts, and tighten all fixings to the specified torque.

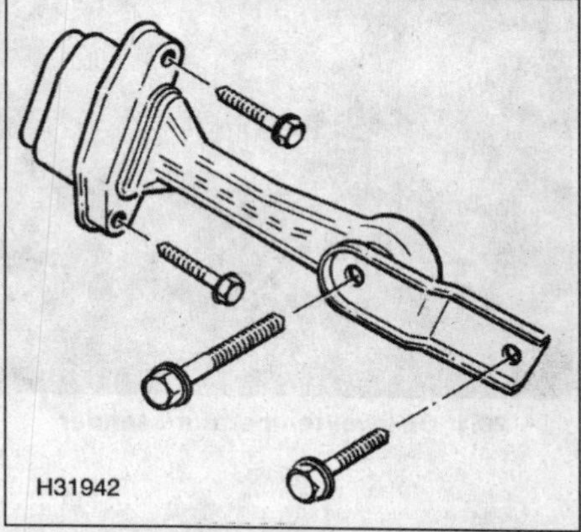

17.20 Engine/transmission rear mounting components

18 Oil pressure relief valve – removal, inspection and refitting

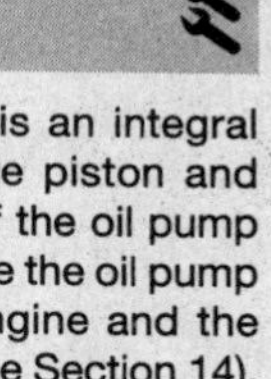

1 The oil pressure relief valve is an integral part of the oil pump. The valve piston and spring are located to the side of the oil pump rotors and can be inspected once the oil pump has been removed from the engine and the rear cover has been removed (see Section 14). If any sign of wear or damage is found the oil pump assembly will have to be renewed; the relief valve piston and spring are not available separately.

19 Oil pressure warning light switch – removal and refitting

Removal

1 The oil pressure warning light switch is fitted to the front of the cylinder head, on its left-hand end. To gain access to the switch, remove the engine top cover.

2 Disconnect the wiring connector and wipe clean the area around the switch **(see illustration)**.

3 Unscrew the switch from the cylinder head and remove it along with its sealing washer. If the switch is to be left removed from the

19.2 Disconnect the oil pressure switch wiring connector

20.1 Oil level/temperature sender

engine for any length of time, plug the hole in the cylinder head.

Refitting

4 Examine the sealing washer for signs of damage or deterioration and if necessary renew.
5 Refit the switch, complete with washer, and tighten it to the specified torque.
6 Securely reconnect the wiring connector then refit the engine cover. Check and, if necessary, top-up the engine oil as described in *Weekly checks*.

20 Oil level/temperature sender – removal and refitting

Removal

1 The oil level/temperature sender is fitted to bottom of the sump **(see illustration)**.
2 Drain the engine oil as described in Chapter 1A.
3 Disconnect the wiring connector and wipe clean the area around the sender.
4 Undo the three retaining bolts and remove the sender.

Refitting

5 Examine the sealing washer for signs of damage or deterioration and if necessary renew.
6 Refit the switch and tighten the retaining bolts to the specified torque.
7 Securely reconnect the wiring connector then refill the engine with oil, with reference to Chapter 1A.
8 On completion, check and, if necessary, top-up the engine oil as described in *Weekly checks*.

Chapter 2 Part C:
1.4 & 1.6 litre direct injection petrol engine in-car repair procedures

Contents

Degrees of difficulty

Easy, suitable for novice with little experience	**Fairly easy,** suitable for beginner with some experience	**Fairly difficult,** suitable for competent DIY mechanic	**Difficult,** suitable for experienced DIY mechanic	**Very difficult,** suitable for expert DIY or professional

Specifications

General

Type	Four-cylinder in-line, chain-driven double (DOHC) overhead camshaft, four stroke, liquid-cooled
Manufacturer's engine codes*:	
1390 cc	BKG, BLN and CAXA
1598 cc	BAG, BLP and BLF
Maximum power output:	
1390 cc:	
Engine codes BKG and BLN	66 kW at 5000 rpm
Engine code CAXA (turbocharged)	90 kW at 5000 rpm
1598 cc	85 kW at 6000 rpm
Maximum torque output:	
1390 cc:	
Engine codes BKG and BLN	130 Nm at 3750 rpm
Engine code CAXA	200 Nm at 1500 – 4000 rpm
1598 cc	155 Nm at 4000 rpm
Bore	76.5 mm
Stroke:	
1390 cc	75.6 mm
1598 cc	86.9 mm
Compression ratio:	
All except engine code CAXA	12.0 : 1
Engine code CAXA	10.0 : 1
Compression pressures:	
Minimum compression pressure	Approximately 11.0 bars
Maximum difference between cylinders	Approximately 3.0 bars
Firing order	1 – 3 – 4 – 2
No 1 cylinder location	Crankshaft pulley end
Direction of crankshaft rotation	Clockwise (when viewed from right-hand side of vehicle)

* **Note:** *See 'Vehicle identification' at the end of this manual for the location of engine code markings.*

Lubrication system

Oil pump type	Chain-driven from crankshaft
Minimum oil pressure (oil temperature 80°C):	
At 2000 rpm	2.0 bar

Camshaft

Camshaft endfloat (maximum)	0.40 mm

Torque wrench settings

	Nm	lbf ft
Auxiliary drivebelt idler pulley bolt	40	30
Auxiliary drivebelt tensioner:		
Stage 1:		
Non-turbo engines	20	15
Turbo engines	40	30
Stage 2	Angle-tighten a further 90°	
Camshaft housing:		
Stage 1	10	7
Stage 2	Angle-tighten a further 90°	
Camshaft position sensor	10	7
Camshaft sprocket bolt**:		
Exhaust (1.6 litre) Note: Left-hand thread:		
Stage 1	40	30
Stage 2	Angle-tighten a further 90°	
Exhaust (1.4 litre):		
Stage 1	50	37
Stage 2	Angle-tighten a further 90°	
Inlet:		
Stage 1	50	37
Stage 2	Angle-tighten a further 90°	
Coolant pump pulley	20	15
Crankshaft oil seal housing**	12	9
Crankshaft pulley bolt (old):		
Stage 1	90	66
Stage 2	Angle-tighten a further 90°	
Crankshaft pulley bolt (modified, with drilling in bolt head)**:		
Stage 1	150	111
Stage 2	Angle-tighten a further 180°	
Cylinder head bolts**:		
Stage 1	30	22
Stage 2	Angle-tighten a further 90°	
Stage 3	Angle-tighten a further 90°	
Crankshaft speed sender	5	4
Driveplate bolts* **:		
Stage 1	60	44
Stage 2	Angle-tighten a further 90°	
Engine mountings**:		
RH engine mounting:		
Limiter:		
Stage 1	20	15
Stage 2	Angle-tighten a further 90°	
Mounting to engine:		
Stage 1	60	44
Stage 2	Angle-tighten a further 90°	
Mounting to body:		
Stage 1	40	30
Stage 2	Angle-tighten a further 90°	
LH engine mounting*:		
Mounting to body:		
Stage 1	60	44
Stage 2	Angle-tighten a further 90°	
Mounting to transmission:		
Stage 1	40	30
Stage 2	Angle-tighten a further 90°	
Rear mounting (torque arm)*:		
To transmission:		
Stage 1:		
Grade 8.8	40	30
Grade 10.9	50	37
Stage 2	Angle-tighten a further 90°	
To subframe:		
Stage 1	100	74
Stage 2	Angle-tighten a further 90°	
Flywheel bolts* **:		
Stage 1	60	44
Stage 2	Angle-tighten a further 90°	

Torque wrench settings (continued)

	Nm	lbf ft
Fuel line:		
Banjo bolt	15	11
Union nut	15	11
Oil filter cap	25	18
Oil level and temperature sender	10	7
Oil pressure switch	25	18
Oil pump	25	18
Oil pump sprocket**:		
Stage 1	20	15
Stage 2	Angle-tighten a further 90°	
Oil pump chain tensioner	15	11
Sump	13	10
Sump oil drain plug	30	22
Thermostat housing	10	7
Timing chain tensioner	9	7
Timing cover:		
M6 bolt	10	7
M10 bolt	50	37

** Use thread-locking compound.*
***Do not re-use*

1 General information

How to use this Chapter

This Part of Chapter 2 describes those repair procedures that can reasonably be carried out on the engine while it remains in the vehicle. If the engine has been removed from the vehicle and is being dismantled as described in Part G, any preliminary dismantling procedures can be ignored.

Note that while it may be possible physically to overhaul certain items while the engine is in the vehicle, such tasks are not usually carried out as separate operations, and usually require the execution of several additional procedures (not to mention the cleaning of components and of oilways); for this reason, all such tasks are classed as major overhaul procedures, and are described in Part G of this Chapter.

Caution: The crankshaft must not be removed on these engines – just loosening and retightening the main bearing bolts will render the cylinder block unserviceable. If the crankshaft or bearings are excessively worn or damaged, the complete cylinder block must be renewed.

Engine description

The engine is a double overhead camshaft (DOHC), in-line four-cylinder unit, which is mounted transversely at the front of the vehicle, with the transmission bolted to the left-hand end of the engine. It has a direct injection fuel system, referred to as FSi (Fuel Stratified Injection) – turbocharged versions are referred to as TSi (Turbocharged Stratified Injection).

The cylinder block, cylinder head and camshaft housing are all cast in aluminium alloy. The cylinder bores are machined in the cylinder block. The crankshaft has five main bearings, and thrustwashers are fitted to number 3 main bearing to control crankshaft endfloat.

Camshaft drive is by chain from the crankshaft, and the chain is tensioned by a hydraulic tensioner. The valves are closed by coil springs and the camshafts actuate the valves by roller rockers and hydraulic tappets. There are 4 valves per cylinder.

The flywheel is located on a flange at the left-hand end of the crankshaft. The main bearings and the big-end bearings are of shell type, whilst the connecting rod small-end bearings are of the bronze bush type, being pressed into the connecting rod and reamed to suit.

The oil pump is chain-driven from the front of the crankshaft. Oil is drawn from the sump through a strainer and circulated through an externally-mounted filter to the various engine components.

Operations with engine in car

The following work can be carried out with the engine in the vehicle:

a) Compression pressure – testing.
b) Crankshaft pulley – removal and refitting.
c) Timing cover – removal and refitting.
d) Timing chain – renewal.
e) Timing chain tensioner and sprockets – removal and refitting.
f) Camshaft(s) and hydraulic tappets – removal and refitting.
g) Cylinder head – removal and refitting.*
h) Cylinder head – decarbonising.
i) Sump – removal and refitting.
j) Oil pump – removal, overhaul and refitting.
k) Crankshaft oil seals – renewal.
l) Engine/transmission mountings – inspection and renewal.
m) Flywheel/driveplate – removal, inspection and refitting.

** Cylinder head dismantling procedures are detailed in Chapter 2G.*

Note: *It is possible to remove the pistons and connecting rods (after removing the cylinder head and sump) without removing the engine from the car, however this is not recommended. Work of this nature is more easily and thoroughly completed with the engine on the bench, as described in Chapter 2G.*

2 Compression test – description and interpretation

1 When engine performance is down, or if misfiring occurs which cannot be attributed to the ignition or fuel systems, a compression test can provide diagnostic clues as to the engine's condition. If the test is performed regularly, it can give warning of trouble before any other symptoms become apparent.

2 The engine must be fully warmed-up to normal operating temperature, the battery must be fully-charged, and the spark plugs together with their ignition coils must be removed (Chapter 1A). The aid of an assistant will also be required.

3 Remove the fuel pump fuse 6 from the fusebox on the driver's end of the facia.

4 Fit a compression tester to the No 1 cylinder spark plug hole – the type of tester which screws into the plug thread is to be preferred.

5 Have the assistant hold the throttle wide open and crank the engine on the starter motor; after one or two revolutions, the compression pressure should build-up to a maximum figure and then stabilise. Record the highest reading obtained.

6 Repeat the test on the remaining cylinders, recording the pressure in each.

7 All cylinders should produce very similar pressures, of the order of 10 to 15 bars. Any one cylinder reading below 7 bars, or a difference of more than 3 bars between cylinders, suggests a fault.

8 Note that the compression should build-up quickly in a healthy engine; low compression on the first stroke, followed by gradually increasing pressure on successive strokes, indicates worn piston rings.

3.5 Remove the cover from the inlet camshaft

3.6a Remove the cover from the exhaust camshaft...

3.6b ...and remove the O-ring seal

9 A low compression reading on the first stroke, which does not build-up during successive strokes, indicates leaking valves or a blown head gasket (a cracked head could also be the cause).

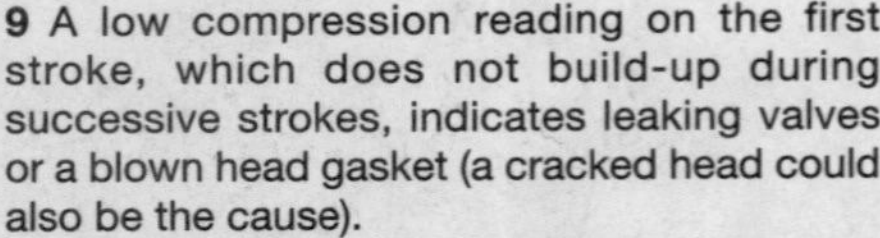

10 If the pressure in any cylinder is reduced to 10 bars or less, carry out the following test to isolate the cause. Introduce a teaspoonful of clean oil into that cylinder through its spark plug hole and repeat the test.

11 If the addition of oil temporarily improves the compression pressure, this indicates that bore or piston wear is responsible for the pressure loss. No improvement suggests that leaking or burnt valves, or a blown head gasket, may be to blame.

12 A low reading from two adjacent cylinders is almost certainly due to the head gasket having blown between them; the presence of coolant in the engine oil will confirm this.

13 If one cylinder is about 20 percent lower than the others and the engine has a slightly rough idle, a worn camshaft lobe could be the cause.

14 On completion of the test, refit the spark plugs and ignition coils. Refit the fuel pump fuse 6.

3 Engine assembly and valve timing marks - general information and usage

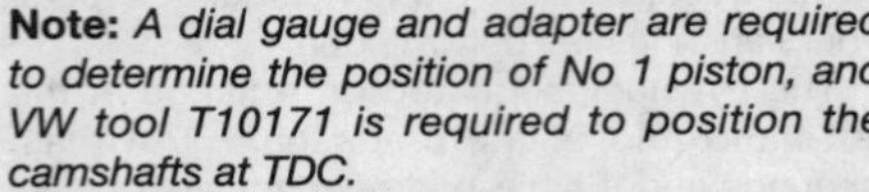

Note: *A dial gauge and adapter are required to determine the position of No 1 piston, and VW tool T10171 is required to position the camshafts at TDC.*

1 Top dead centre (TDC) is the highest point in its travel up-and-down its cylinder bore that each piston reaches as the crankshaft rotates. While each piston reaches TDC both at the top of the compression stroke and again at the top of the exhaust stroke, for the purpose of timing the engine, TDC refers to the No 1 piston position at the top of its compression stroke.

2 No 1 piston and cylinder are at the right-hand (timing chain) end of the engine. Note that the crankshaft rotates clockwise when viewed from the right-hand side of the vehicle.

3 Switch off the ignition and all electrical consumers, and remove the ignition key. Remove all the spark plugs as described in Chapter 1A.

All except engine code CAXA

4 Remove the engine top cover/air filter as follows:

a) *Disconnect the crankcase ventilation hose from the engine top cover/air filter.*
b) *Disconnect the wiring from the air temperature sensor.*
c) *Pull out the dipstick from the centre of the engine top cover/air filter.*
d) *Release the four corners and withdraw the top cover/air filter.*

5 Remove the EGR (exhaust gas recirculation) valve as described in Chapter 4C, then remove the cover for access to the inlet camshaft **(see illustration)**. Discard the O-ring seal and obtain a new seal.

6 Unbolt the cover from the left-hand end of the cylinder head for access to the exhaust camshaft. Discard the O-ring seal and obtain a new seal **(see illustrations)**.

Engine code CAXA

7 Drain the coolant as described in Chapter 1A.

8 Undo the bolts securing the engine top cover, unclip the coolant hoses from the right-hand end, and pull the cover upwards **(see illustration)**.

9 Disconnect the hoses, then undo the bolt and remove the coolant pipe from the camshaft housing/cylinder block **(see illustration)**.

10 Unclip the wiring harness, and pull the coolant pipe away from the cylinder head **(see illustration)**.

11 Disconnect the wiring plug, and unscrew the oil pressure switch **(see illustration)**.

12 Undo the bolts and remove the covers for access to the camshafts **(see illustration)**.

3.8 Engine top cover retaining bolts (arrowed)

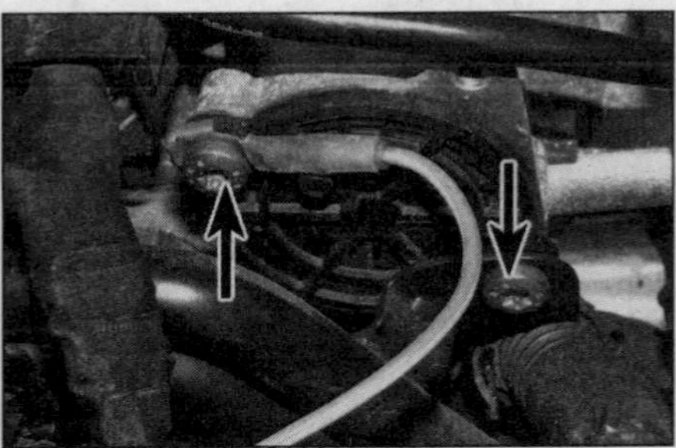

3.9 Coolant pipe retaining bolt and harness earth connection at the left-hand end of the cylinder head (arrowed)

3.10 Unclip the wiring harness (arrowed)

3.11 Unscrew the oil pressure switch (arrowed)

Discard the O-ring seals – new ones must be fitted.

All engines

13 Turn the engine with a socket on the crankshaft pulley bolt until the TDC timing holes in the ends of the exhaust and inlet camshafts are at the 4 o'clock and 8 o'clock positions respectively. The engine is now at TDC on No 1 piston **(see illustration)**.

14 Screw the dial gauge and adapter into No 1 spark plug hole, then determine TDC position by rotating the crankshaft back-and-forth so that the gauge can be zeroed. Now turn the crankshaft anti-clockwise 45°, then turn it slowly to the TDC position **(see illustration)**. If the crankshaft is turned more than 0.01 mm past TDC, repeat the procedure.

15 With No 1 piston finally at TDC, mark the left-hand ends of the camshafts accurately in relation to the camshaft housing with a felt-tipped pen. Note that VW technicians use tool number T10171 to verify this position **(see illustration)**, however, although the preferable method, the tool is unlikely to be available to the home mechanic.

16 Remove the dial gauge and adapter.

17 The remainder of refitting is a reversal of removal.

4 Crankshaft pulley – removal and refitting

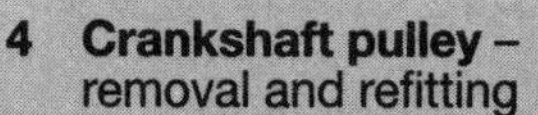

Note: *The crankshaft pulley bolt must be renewed whenever removed, however, on non-turbo engines, a modified bearing sleeve repair set was introduced consisting of the sleeve and two diamond-coated discs* ***(see illustration)****. The new discs prevent the crankshaft turning when the bolt is being tightened.*

Removal

1 Apply the handbrake, then jack up the front of the vehicle and support it on axle stands (see *Jacking and vehicle support*). Remove the right-hand front roadwheel.

2 Remove the wheel arch liner with reference to Chapter 11.

3 Mark the auxiliary drivebelt for normal rotation to ensure correct refitting, and note its routing for ease of refitting. Remove the drivebelt as described in Chapter 1A.

4 Set the engine to its TDC position as described in Section 3.

Caution: Do not turn the engine during the following procedure.

5 The crankshaft pulley must now be held stationary while the bolt is loosened **(see illustration)**. VW technicians use a tool which locates in the pulley cut-outs, and a similar tool can be fabricated out of a length of metal bar with two long bolts attached to one end. If a tool is not available, have an assistant engage 4th gear and apply firm pressure to the footbrake pedal, then loosen the crankshaft pulley bolt.

6 Unscrew and remove the bolt and withdraw the pulley from the nose of the crankshaft **(see illustrations)**. The bolt must be renewed whenever removed, however, on non-turbo engines, it is recommended that the modified sleeve and discs (see Note) are also renewed together with a new oil seal at the same time. Check with your VW dealer to confirm which sleeve is fitted, and if necessary remove them from the nose of the crankshaft. Remove the oil seal with reference to Section 12.

3.12 Undo the bolts (arrowed) and remove the covers

3.13 Exhaust and inlet camshafts set at TDC

3.14 Determining the exact TDC position with a dial gauge

3.15 Using VW tool T10171 to set the camshafts at TDC

4.0 Modified crankshaft bearing sleeve repair kit

4.5 Crankshaft pulley and bolt

4.6a Unscrew the bolt...

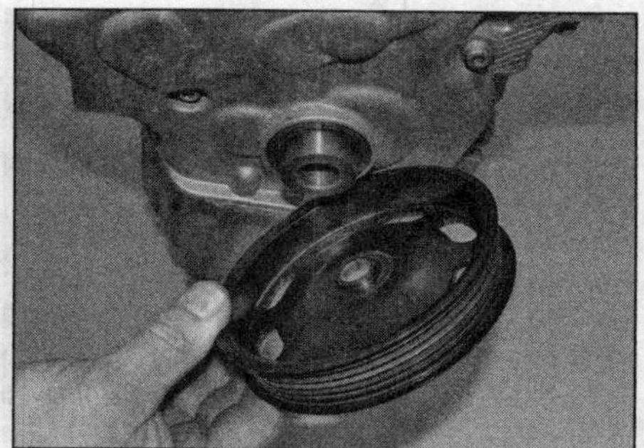

4.6b ...and remove the crankshaft pulley

4.8a Fit the O-ring seal...

4.8b ...then assemble the inner disc (23 mm diameter) to the sleeve...

4.8c ...and fit to the crankshaft

4.10 Fitting the crankshaft pulley and outer disc (19 mm diameter)

Refitting

7 Thoroughly clean the nose of the crankshaft and timing cover.

Non-turbo engines

8 Fit the O-ring seal, then assemble the bearing sleeve and inner disc (23 mm diameter) on the new bolt, and fit the bolt to the crankshaft, turning it approximately two full turns into the crankshaft. Push the sleeve and disc fully onto the crankshaft and unscrew the bolt **(see illustrations)**.

9 Fit the new oil seal as described in Section 12.

10 Assemble the pulley and outer disc (19 mm diameter) on the bolt and screw the bolt onto the crankshaft **(see illustration)**. The tightening procedure varies according to the old or modified parts as follows:

a) *For the old version, hold the pulley as for removal, and tighten the bolt in the two stages given in Specifications.*

b) *The modified version requires a greater tightening torque and angle, and it is important to check that the crankshaft does not turn, especially during the angle-tightening. Hold the pulley as for removal and note the TDC markings made in paragraph 4. After fully tightening the bolt in the two stages given in Specifications, the marks must remain aligned with each other. If not, a new bolt must be obtained and the procedure repeated.*

Turbo engines

11 Fit the new bolt. It is important to check that the crankshaft does not turn, especially during the angle-tightening. Hold the pulley as for removal and note the TDC markings made in paragraph 4. After fully tightening the bolt in the two stages given in Specifications, the marks must remain aligned with each other. If not, a new bolt must be obtained and the procedure repeated.

All engines

12 Refit the auxiliary drivebelt as described in Chapter 1A.

13 Refit the wheel arch liner (Chapter 11), then refit the roadwheel and lower the vehicle to the ground.

5.2 Loosen the coolant pump pulley retaining bolts

5.4 Remove the coolant pump pulley

5.6a Remove the compressor/tensioner mounting bracket...

5.6b ...and the auxiliary drivebelt idler pulley

5 Timing cover – removal and refitting

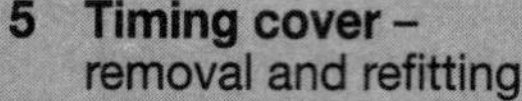

Removal

1 Apply the handbrake, then jack up the front of the vehicle and support it on axle stands (see *Jacking and vehicle support*). Remove the right-hand front roadwheel and the splash guard from beneath the engine. For improved access, also remove the right-hand front wheel arch liner.

2 Mark the auxiliary drivebelt for normal rotation to ensure correct refitting, and note its routing for ease of refitting. Loosen the coolant pump pulley retaining bolts **(see illustration)**, then remove the drivebelt as described in Chapter 1A.

3 Set the engine to its TDC position as described in Section 3.

4 Fully unscrew the retaining bolts and remove the coolant pump pulley from the drive flange **(see illustration)**.

5 Refer to Chapter 3 and unbolt the air conditioning compressor from its mounting bracket and suspend to one side. **Do not** disconnect the refrigerant lines.

6 Unbolt the compressor/tensioner mounting bracket and the auxiliary drivebelt idler pulley **(see illustrations)**.

7 Remove the alternator as described in Chapter 5A.
8 Remove the crankshaft pulley as described in Section 4.
9 Remove the sump as described in Section 9.
10 The right-hand end of the engine must now be supported while the engine mounting is removed, and the engine then held in a safe position in order to carry out the remaining work. To do this, use a hoist or support bar attached to the engine lifting eyes – this is preferable to using a trolley jack beneath the engine. With the engine supported, remove the right-hand engine mounting with reference to Section 14.
11 Progressively unscrew and remove all of the retaining bolts, noting their locations as they are of different lengths, then remove the timing cover from the engine. Note that most of the bolts require an Allen key to remove them. If necessary, tap the cover lightly to release it, then withdraw the cover from the location dowels. Remove the gasket and the O-ring seal and discard them as new ones must be used on refitting **(see illustration)**.
12 As the cover is removed, the bearing sleeve may remain in the oil seal. Leave the sleeve in position if the oil seal is not to be renewed. Alternatively, renew the oil seal with reference to Section 12 **(see illustration)**.

Refitting

13 Thoroughly clean the cover and block/head contact surfaces, then locate a new gasket on the engine **(see illustration)**.
14 To aid refitting, temporarily fit two studs to the block/head to act as guides. Locate the cover together with the bearing sleeve onto the engine **(see illustration)**, then insert the bolts and tighten them progressively to the specified torques.
15 The remainder of refitting is a reversal of removal.

6 Timing chain, tensioner and sprockets – removal, inspection and refitting

Removal

1 Remove the timing cover as described in Section 5.
2 The timing chain tensioner rail must now be released from the chain and the hydraulic tensioner locked. To do this, press the lower end of the rail rearwards so that it forces the piston into the hydraulic tensioner, then insert a suitable 3.0 mm diameter tool through the holes provided to retain the piston **(see illustration)**.
3 Unbolt the tensioner from the cylinder block **(see illustration)**.
4 Mark the timing chain for direction of rotation so that it is refitted the same way round **(see illustration)**.
5 While holding the inlet camshaft sprocket stationary, loosen both sprocket retaining bolts, noting that on 1.6 litre and 1.4 litre turbocharged engines, the inlet camshaft adjuster sprocket bolt has a **left-hand thread**. On 1.4 litre non-turbo engines, the inlet camshaft sprocket is the same as the exhaust one, and the bolt has a right-hand thread. Use a holding tool made from two lengths of bar, with two bolts located to engage with the sprocket.
6 Unscrew and remove the bolts and remove the timing chain, camshaft sprockets and exhaust camshaft sprocket shaft. Unhook the chain from the crankshaft sprocket **(see illustrations)**.

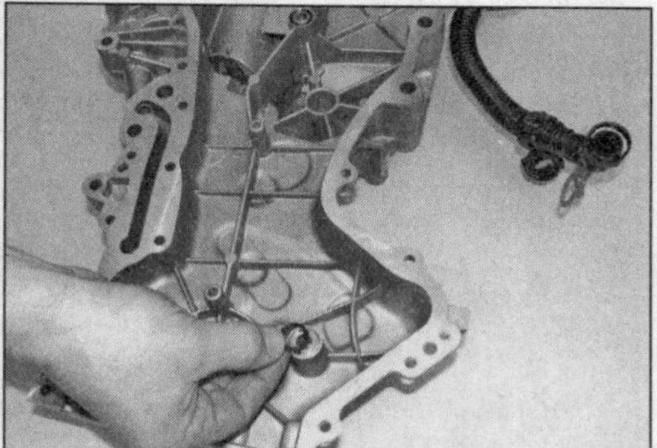

5.11 Remove the O-ring seal from the inside of the timing cover

5.12 Remove the bearing sleeve from the timing cover

5.13 Fit a new timing cover gasket

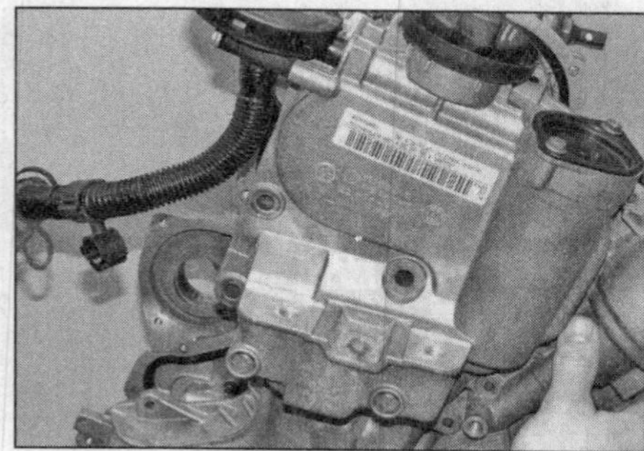

5.14 Locate the timing cover on the engine

6.2 Press the timing chain tensioner and insert a 3.0 mm diameter drill bit or rod to lock the tensioner

6.3 Remove the timing chain tensioner

6.4 If the timing chain is to be refitted, mark it with a dab of paint

6.6a Unscrew the bolt...

6.6b ...remove the exhaust camshaft sprocket...

6.6c ...and shaft...

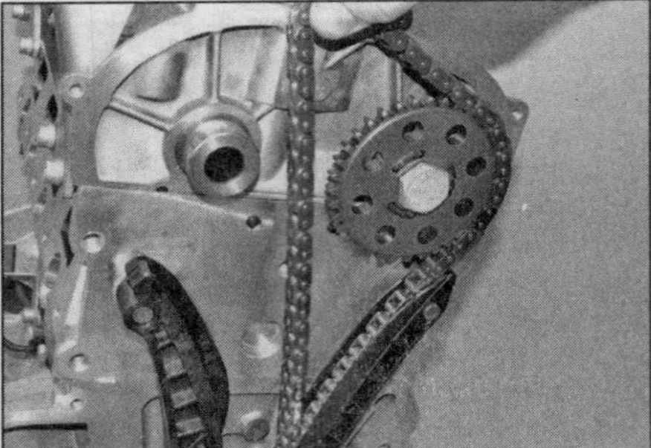
6.6d ...then unhook the timing chain from the inlet camshaft sprocket...

6.6e ...and remove the inlet camshaft sprocket

6.7 Remove the plastic cover...

6.9 ...unbolt the chain tensioner...

7 To remove the oil pump sprocket, first remove the plastic cover **(see illustration)**.

8 Hold the sprocket stationary and loosen the retaining bolt.

9 Using a screwdriver, unhook the chain tensioner spring and remove it. Unscrew the mounting bolt and remove the chain tensioner **(see illustration)**.

10 Mark the oil pump chain for direction of rotation so that it can be refitted the same way round. Remove the retaining bolt and remove the sprocket and chain from the crankshaft sprocket **(see illustration)**. Discard the oil pump sprocket bolt as a new one must be used on refitting.

6.10 ...and remove the sprocket and chain from the crankshaft sprocket

6.11 Remove the crankshaft sprocket

11 Pull the sprocket from the crankshaft, noting that it has a lug which locates in a groove in the crankshaft journal **(see illustration)**.

12 Remove the timing chain guides from the engine **(see illustration)**.

Inspection

13 Thoroughly clean all components, then examine the timing chain and oil pump drive chain for excessive wear. Also check the sprocket teeth for wear. If the engine has covered a high mileage, the chain and sprockets should be renewed as a matter of course.

14 The crankshaft pulley bolt must be renewed whenever removed.

Refitting

15 Check that the crankshaft is still at TDC, then refit the sprocket and engage the lug with the groove. As a precaution against the sprocket moving out of the groove, mark it in relation to the cylinder block so that its position can be easily checked **(see illustration)**.

16 Engage the oil pump sprocket in the chain, making sure the chain is the correct way round, then locate the chain on the crankshaft sprocket. Locate the sprocket on the oil pump (it will only go in one position), insert the new bolt and tighten to the specified torque and angle while holding it as for removal **(see illustration)**.

17 Refit the oil pump chain tensioner and

6.12 Remove the timing chain guides

6.15 Mark the crankshaft sprocket in relation to the cylinder block so that its position can be easily checked

tighten the mounting bolt to the specified torque. Refit the tensioner spring and the plastic cover.

18 Check that the crankshaft sprocket is still aligned with the TDC mark made on the cylinder block.

19 Refit the sprocket to the exhaust camshaft using a new bolt, and hand-tighten it.

20 With the timing chain the correct way round as previously noted, engage it with the crankshaft sprocket, then locate the chain on the front guide and exhaust sprocket. Engage the inlet camshaft sprocket in the chain and refit to the camshaft with a new bolt. Hand-tighten the bolt at this stage.

21 Refit the timing tensioner and tighten the bolts to the specified torque.

22 Remove the locking tool to release the tensioner.

23 Check that the TDC marks on the crankshaft sprocket and cylinder block, and the marks on the ends of the camshafts are still aligned correctly.

24 Tighten the camshaft sprocket bolts to the specified torque and angle while holding them stationary as for removal.

25 Check the TDC timing marks on the crankshaft sprocket and ends of the camshafts for correct alignment.

26 Refit the timing cover with reference to Section 3.

7 Camshaft housing, camshafts and hydraulic tappets – removal, inspection and refitting

Removal

1 On 1.4 litre turbocharged engines, remove the turbocharger as described in Chapter 4C.

2 Remove the timing cover as described in Section 5.

3 Remove the timing chain and camshaft sprockets as described in Section 6.

4 For the remaining removal procedure the pistons must be positioned half-way down their bores as a precaution against the valves touching them. Temporarily refit the crankshaft pulley, insert and tighten the pulley bolt, then turn the crankshaft 45° anti-clockwise so that all of the pistons are half-way down their bores.

5 Disconnect the wiring from the fuel low-pressure sender, and from the high-pressure pump.

6 Unbolt the earth cable from the camshaft housing.

7 Remove the ignition coils with reference to Chapter 5B, then remove the wiring harness and cable guide. Note that VW technicians use a special tool (T10094) to remove the coils, however, a length of bent welding rod or similar hooked under the wiring plugs may be used to extract them.

8 Cover the fuel line to the high-pressure pump with cloth then unscrew the banjo and union nut and disconnect it.

6.16 Tighten the oil pump sprocket bolt

Warning: The fuel system is under pressure – wear gloves and eye protection to prevent injuries.

9 Unscrew the bolts and move the fuel lines to one side.

10 Disconnect the wiring from the camshaft position sensor **(see illustration)**.

11 Remove the engine oil dipstick.

12 Remove the inlet manifold lower part with reference to Chapter 4A.

13 Unbolt the left-hand engine lifting eye.

14 Progressively unscrew the mounting bolts and remove the camshaft housing complete with camshafts from the top of the cylinder head. If it is tight, use a mallet or rubber hammer to tap the housing in several places in order to release it from the locating dowels and studs.

15 With the camshaft housing on the bench, clean away the sealant from the cylinder head and cover. Remove the small filter and O-ring from the cylinder head **(see illustration)**.

16 Obtain a suitable box with compartments for each of the roller/rocker arms and hydraulic tappets, so that they can be identified for their correct position. Remove the arms and hydraulic tappets from the cylinder head and place them in the box, making sure they are identified for location to ensure correct refitting **(see illustration)**.

17 Identify each camshaft for location and position, then lift them out from the camshaft housing **(see illustration)**. **Note:** *The inlet camshaft has an additional cam to operate the high-pressure pump.*

Inspection

18 Thoroughly clean the camshafts and housing, making sure that all of the sealant is removed from the mating surfaces. Also, clean the cylinder head upper mating surface.

Caution: Make sure that the TDC alignment marks are not removed from the ends of the camshaft and the housing.

19 Visually inspect each camshaft for evidence of wear on the surfaces of the lobes and journals **(see illustration)**. Normally their surfaces should be smooth and have a dull shine; look for scoring, erosion or pitting and areas that appear highly polished, indicating excessive wear. Accelerated wear will occur once the hardened exterior of the camshaft has been damaged, so always renew worn items.

20 If the machined surfaces of the camshaft

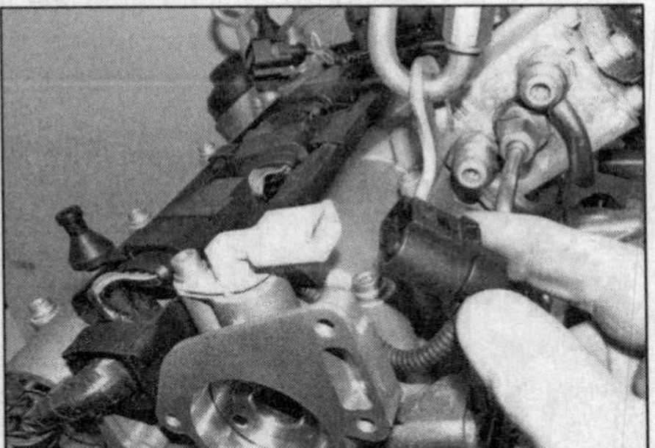

7.10 Disconnect the wiring from the camshaft position sensor

7.15 Remove the small filter from the cylinder head

7.16 Place the roller/rocker arms and hydraulic tappets in a box with compartments to keep them identified for position

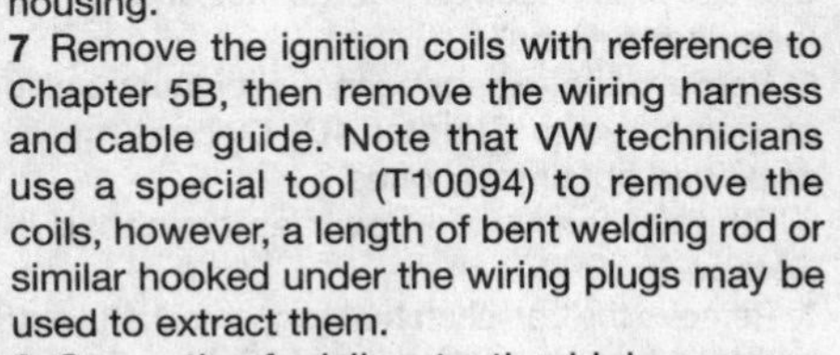

7.17 Remove the camshafts from the housing

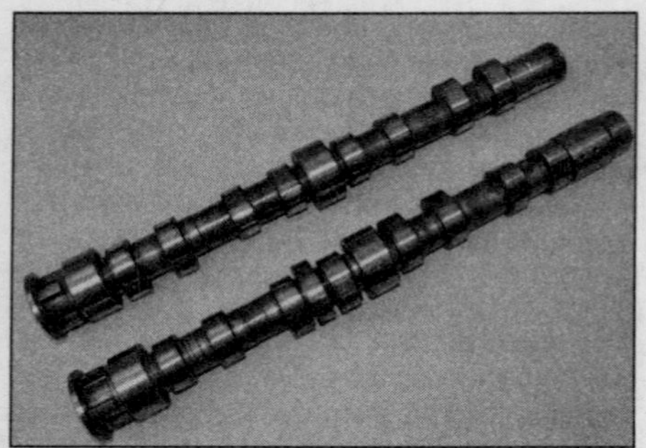
7.19 Clean the camshafts and inspect them for wear and damage

7.23a Detach the hydraulic tappets from the roller/rockers to inspect them...

7.23b ...then reassemble them

appear discoloured or blued, it is likely that it has been overheated at some point, probably due to inadequate lubrication.

21 To measure the camshaft endfloat, temporarily locate them in the housing and refit the EGR valve and end cover. Anchor a DTI gauge to the end of the housing and align the gauge probe with the camshaft axis. Push one of the camshafts to one end of the housing as far as it will travel, then rest the DTI gauge probe on the end of the camshaft, and zero the gauge display. Push the camshaft as far as it will go to the other end of the housing, and record the gauge reading. Verify the reading by pushing the camshaft back to its original position and checking that the gauge indicates zero again. Repeat the checking procedure for the remaining camshaft.

22 Check that the camshaft endfloat measurement is within the limit given in the Specifications. Wear outside of this limit is unlikely to be confined to any one component, so renewal of the camshafts and housing must be considered.

23 Inspect the hydraulic tappets and roller/rockers for obvious signs of wear or damage, and renew if necessary **(see illustrations)**. Check that the oil holes in the tappets are free from obstructions.

Refitting

24 Lubricate the camshaft journals and bearing surfaces in the camshaft housing, then locate the camshafts in their respective bores.

25 Set the camshafts to their TDC position. If the VW tool is available, fit the special tool to hold the camshafts **(see illustration)**.

26 With the camshaft housing inverted on the bench, apply a thin film of sealant to the mating surfaces **(see illustration)**. Do not apply the sealant too thick otherwise it may enter the lubrication system and cause expensive damage to the engine.

27 Lubricate the roller/rocker arms and hydraulic tappets, and refit them to their correct positions in the cylinder head **(see illustration)**, then refit the small O-ring to the cylinder head. Make sure each arm is correctly clipped to the tappets.

28 As an aid to refitting the camshaft housing, fit two temporary studs to two opposite corners of the cylinder head **(see illustration)**. Taking care not to allow any oil to drop onto the sealant, carefully lower the housing onto the cylinder head.

29 Remove the temporary studs and insert the retaining bolts hand-tight. Now progressively tighten the bolts to the Stage 1 specified torque, starting in the centre and working outwards in a spiral fashion.

30 Angle-tighten the bolts by the specified amount.

31 The remainder of refitting is a reversal of removal.

7.25 Fit the VW tool to hold the camshafts in their TDC position

7.26 Apply a thin film of sealant to the camshaft housing mating surface

7.27 Lubricate the roller/rocker arms and hydraulic tappets before refitting them

7.28 Fit two temporary studs as shown to act as guides for the camshaft housing

8 Cylinder head – removal, inspection and refitting

Removal

1 Remove the engine and transmission from the vehicle, and remove the transmission from the engine as described in Part G of this Chapter.

2 Remove the upper and lower inlet manifolds as described in Chapter 4A.

3 Remove the exhaust manifold as described in Chapter 4C.

4 Unbolt the thermostat housing from the left-hand end of the cylinder head, and at the same time release it from the rear engine coolant pipe. Recover the gasket and O-ring **(see illustrations)**.

5 Remove the exhaust gas recirculation valve as described in Chapter 4C. Discard the oil seals and obtain new ones.

6 Remove the timing cover as described in Section 5.

7 Remove the camshaft housing, camshafts and hydraulic tappets as described in Section 7.

8 Progressively slacken the cylinder head bolts in the reverse order to that given for tightening in paragraph 21. Remove the cylinder head bolts **(see illustration)**. **Note:** *The bolts must not be re-used ñ obtain new ones.*

9 With all the bolts removed, lift the cylinder head from the block (together with the inlet and exhaust manifolds, if not removed). If the cylinder head is stuck, tap it with a soft-faced mallet to break the joint. **Do not** insert a lever into the gasket joint.

10 Lift the cylinder head gasket from the block.

Inspection

11 Dismantling and inspection of the cylinder head is covered in Part F of this Chapter.

12 The mating faces of the cylinder head and block must be perfectly clean before refitting the head.

13 Use a scraper to remove all traces of gasket and carbon, also clean the tops of the pistons. Take particular care with the aluminium surfaces, as the soft metal is easily damaged.

14 Make sure that debris is not allowed to enter the oil and water passages – this is particularly important for the oil circuit, as carbon could block the oil supply to the camshaft and crankshaft bearings. Using adhesive tape and paper, seal the water, oil and bolt holes in the cylinder block. To prevent carbon entering the gap between the pistons and bores, smear a little grease in the gap. After cleaning a piston, rotate the crankshaft so that the piston moves down the bore, then wipe out the grease and carbon with a cloth rag. Clean the other piston crowns in the same way.

15 Check the head and block for nicks, deep scratches and other damage. If slight, they may be removed carefully with a file. More serious damage may be repaired by machining, but this is a specialist job. If warpage of the cylinder head is suspected, use a straight-edge to check it for distortion, as described in Part G of this Chapter.

Refitting

16 Before refitting the cylinder head, the

8.4a Remove the thermostat housing from the cylinder head and release it from the rear engine coolant pipe...

8.4b ...then recover the gasket...

8.4c ...and O-ring seal from the coolant pipe

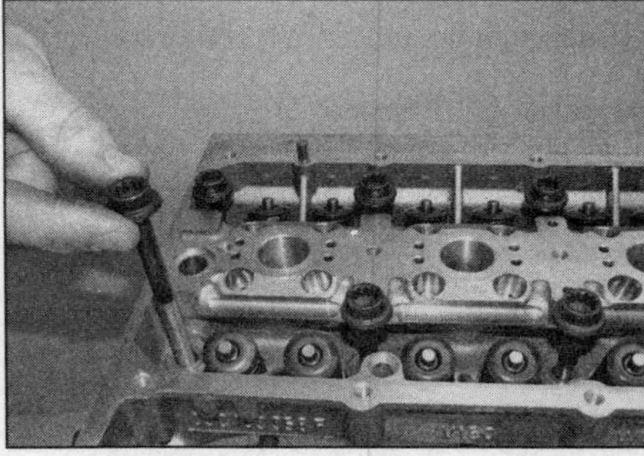

8.8 Remove the cylinder head bolts

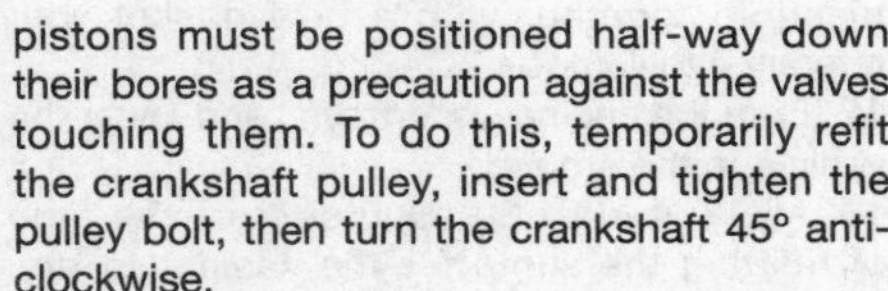

pistons must be positioned half-way down their bores as a precaution against the valves touching them. To do this, temporarily refit the crankshaft pulley, insert and tighten the pulley bolt, then turn the crankshaft 45° anti-clockwise.

17 Ensure that the cylinder head bolt holes in the cylinder block are clean and free of oil. Syringe or soak up any oil left in the bolt holes. This is most important in order that the correct bolt tightening torque can be applied, and to prevent the possibility of the block being cracked by hydraulic pressure when the bolts are tightened.

18 Ensure that the cylinder head locating dowels are in place in the cylinder block, then fit a new cylinder head gasket over the dowels, ensuring that the part number is uppermost **(see illustration)**. Where applicable, the OBEN/TOP marking should also be uppermost. Note that VW recommend that the gasket is only removed from its packaging immediately prior to fitting.

19 Lower the cylinder head into position on the gasket, ensuring that it engages correctly over the dowels.

20 Insert the new cylinder bolts and tighten them as far as possible by hand.

21 Working in sequence, tighten all the cylinder head bolts to the specified Stage 1 torque **(see illustration)**.

22 Again working in sequence, tighten all

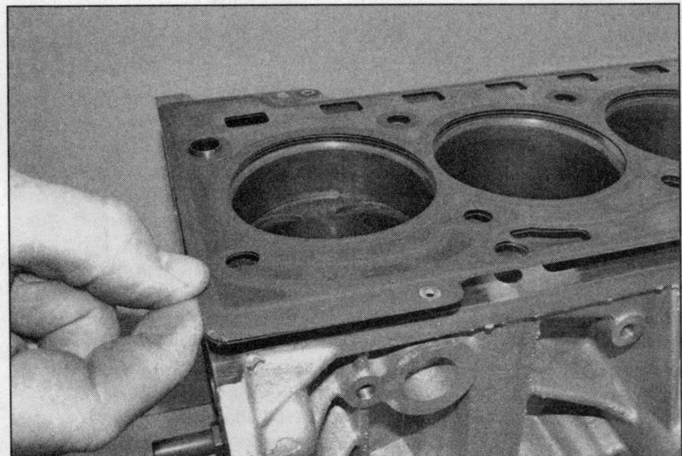

8.18 Fit the new cylinder head gasket

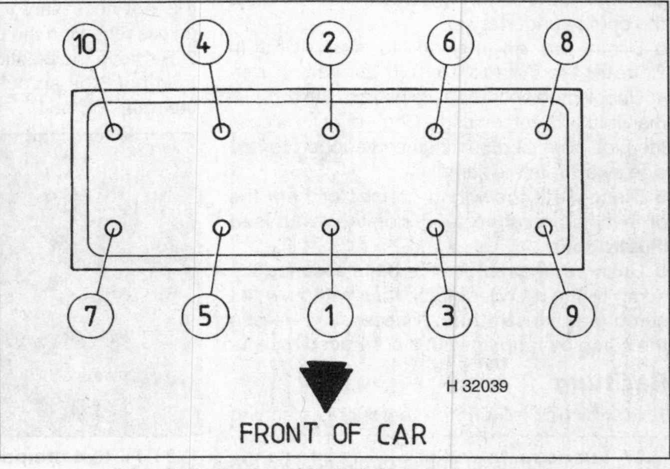

8.21 Cylinder head bolt tightening sequence

9.5 Oil level/temperature sender

the cylinder head bolts through the specified Stage 2 angle.

23 Finally, tighten all the cylinder head bolts, in sequence, through the specified Stage 3 angle.

24 Refit the hydraulic tappets, camshafts and camshaft housing as described in Section 7.

25 Refit the timing cover as described in Section 5.

26 Refit the exhaust gas recirculation valve together with new oil seals as described in Chapter 4C.

27 Clean the contact surfaces then refit the thermostat housing to the cylinder head and rear engine coolant pipe, using a new gasket and O-ring. Tighten the bolts to the specified torque.

28 Refit the exhaust manifold (Chapter 4C) and inlet manifolds (Chapter 4A).

29 Refit the transmission to the engine, and refit the assembly to the vehicle as described in Part F of this Chapter.

9 Sump – removal and refitting

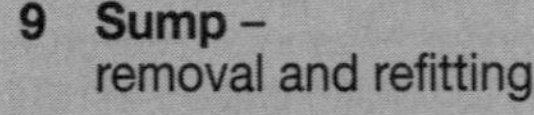

Removal

1 Apply the handbrake, then jack up the front of the vehicle and support securely on axle stands (see *Jacking and vehicle support*).

2 Remove the securing screws and withdraw the engine undertray(s).

3 Drain the engine oil as described in Chapter 1A.

4 Unbolt the front exhaust pipe from the exhaust manifold with reference to Chapter 4C. Release the pipe from its mountings and support to one side away from the sump.

5 Disconnect the wiring connector from the oil level/temperature sender on the sump **(see illustration)**.

6 Unscrew and remove the bolts securing the sump to the cylinder block, then withdraw the sump **(see illustration)**. If necessary, release the sump by tapping with a soft-faced mallet.

Refitting

7 Commence refitting by thoroughly cleaning the mating faces of the sump and cylinder block. Ensure that all traces of old sealant are removed.

9.6 Remove the sump

8 Ensure that the cylinder block mating face of the sump is free from all traces of old sealant, oil and grease, and then apply a 2.0 to 3.0 mm thick bead of silicone sealant (D 176404 A2 or equivalent) to the sump **(see illustration)**. Note that the sealant should be run around the inside of the bolt holes in the sump. The sump must be fitted within 5 minutes of applying the sealant.

9 Offer the sump up to the cylinder block, then refit the retaining bolts, and progressively tighten them in diagonal sequence to the specified torque **(see Haynes Hint)**.

10 Reconnect the wiring to the oil level/ temperature sender on the sump.

11 Refit the front exhaust pipe to the exhaust manifold together with a new gasket with reference to Chapter 4C.

12 Refit the engine undertray(s) and lower the vehicle to the ground.

13 Allow at least 30 minutes from the time of refitting the sump for the sealant to dry, then refill the engine with oil, with reference to Chapter 1A.

10 Oil pump, drive chain and sprockets – removal, inspection and refitting

Removal

1 Remove the sump as described in Section 9. It is not necessary to remove the timing cover unless renewing the timing chain.

2 Remove the plastic cover from the oil pump, then hold the sprocket stationary and loosen the retaining bolt.

10.4 Remove the oil pump

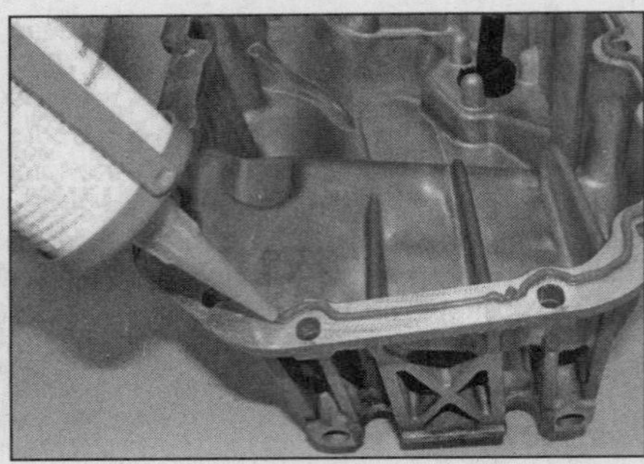

9.8 Apply sealant to the sump mating surface

3 Press the chain tensioner outwards with a screwdriver, then unscrew the bolt and remove the sprocket from the oil pump and chain. Note that the sprocket will only fit in one position on the oil pump.

4 Unscrew the mounting bolts and withdraw the oil pump from the dowels in the cylinder block **(see illustration)**.

5 If it is required to remove the oil pump chain and tensioner, refer to Section 6 for the removal of the timing cover.

Inspection

6 Thoroughly clean all components, then examine the oil pump drive chain for excessive wear. Also check the sprocket teeth for wear. If the engine has covered a high mileage, the chain and sprockets should be renewed as a matter of course. **Note:** *The crankshaft pulley bolt must be renewed whenever removed.*

Refitting

7 If removed, refit the oil pump drive chain and tensioner with reference to Section 6.

8 Locate the oil pump on the cylinder block dowels, insert the mounting bolts and tighten them to the specified torque.

9 Engage the sprocket with the chain, then press the tensioner outwards with a screwdriver, locate the sprocket on the oil pump, and tighten the retaining bolt to the specified torque and angle while holding the sprocket stationary as for removal.

10 Refit the plastic cover.

11 Refit the sump with reference to Section 9.

11 Oil pressure warning light switch – removal and refitting

Removal

1 The oil pressure warning light switch is located on the left-hand end of the cylinder head.

2 On 1.4 litre turbocharged engines, undo the bolt and pull the coolant pipe away from the cylinder head **(see illustration 3.9)**.

3 Disconnect the wiring connector and wipe clean the area around the switch.

4 Unscrew the switch from the cylinder head and remove it, along with its sealing washer

(see illustration 3.11). If the switch is to be left removed from the engine for any length of time, plug the cylinder head aperture.

Refitting

5 Examine the sealing washer for signs of damage or deterioration and if necessary renew.

6 Refit the switch, complete with washer, and tighten it to the specified torque.

7 Securely reconnect the wiring connector then check and, if necessary, top-up the engine oil as described in *Weekly checks*.

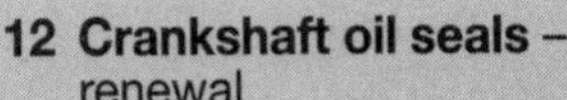

12 Crankshaft oil seals – renewal

Timing chain end oil seal

1 Remove the crankshaft pulley as described in Section 4, then note the fitted depth of the oil seal in the timing cover.

2 Carefully lever the old seal out of the timing cover using a suitable flat-bladed screwdriver, taking care not to damage the cover or crankshaft intermediate sleeve. Alternatively, punch or drill two small holes opposite each other in the seal, then screw a self-tapping screw into each and pull on the screws with pliers to extract the seal **(see illustration)**.

3 Clean the cover recess and sleeve. Note that the new oil seal **must not** be oiled or greased, and the contact surfaces of the timing cover and sleeve must be completely dry.

4 New oil seals are provided with a fitting adapter incorporating an oil seal expander. First, make sure the intermediate sleeve is located fully on the crankshaft, then hold the expander on the crankshaft nose and press the oil seal over it onto the sleeve. Using the adapter, drive the oil seal fully into the timing cover **(see illustrations)**. Alternatively, the seal can be tapped into position using a suitable tubular drift, such as a socket, which bears only on the hard outer edge of the seal. Note that the sealing lips must face inwards.

5 Refit the crankshaft pulley as described in Section 4.

Flywheel/driveplate end oil seal

Note: *The flywheel end oil seal is integral with the oil seal housing and speed sender, and is supplied with a new timing ring. If the oil seal is faulty, the housing must be renewed, however, a special VW tool (T10134) is required to press the new housing into position. Note that removing the oil seal will also remove the serrated timing ring from the end of the crankshaft, and a special VW tool is required to fit the ring in its exact position.*

6 Remove the flywheel/driveplate as described in Section 13. Also, remove the intermediate plate.

7 Set the engine to TDC as described in Section 3.

12.2 Prise out the crankshaft timing chain end oil seal

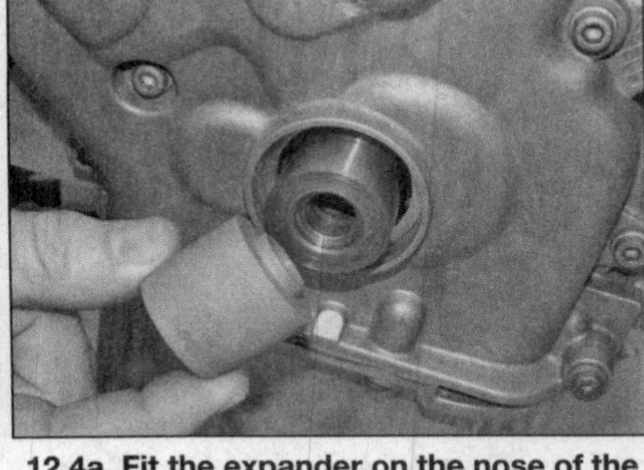

12.4a Fit the expander on the nose of the crankshaft...

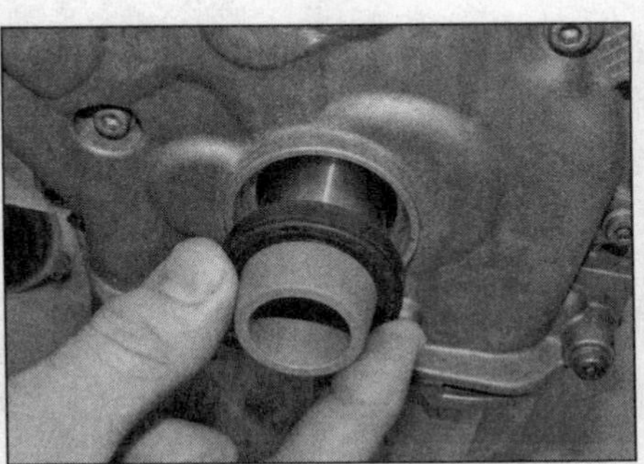

12.4b ...then press the oil seal over it onto the crankshaft sleeve...

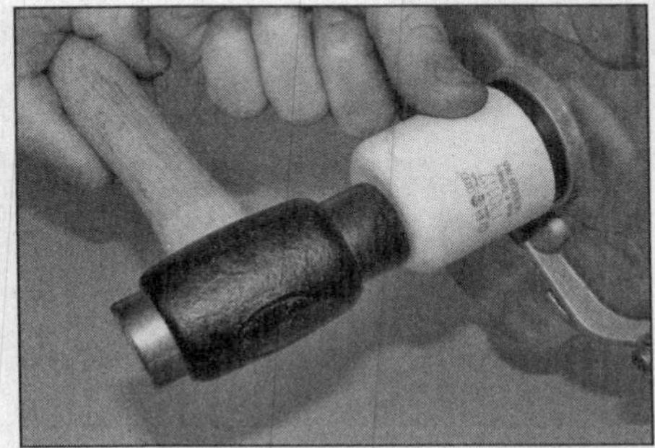

12.4c ...and drive it fully into the timing cover

8 Remove the sump as described in Section 9.

9 Disconnect the wiring from the engine speed sender on the oil seal housing, then unbolt and remove the sender and recover the rubber grommet **(see illustrations)**.

10 Unscrew and remove the housing securing bolts **(see illustration)**. Discard the bolts as new ones must used on refitting.

11 The housing must be pressed off using three M6 bolts screwed into the threaded holes provided. Tighten the bolts progressively until the housing is released **(see illustrations)**,

12.9a Remove the engine speed sender...

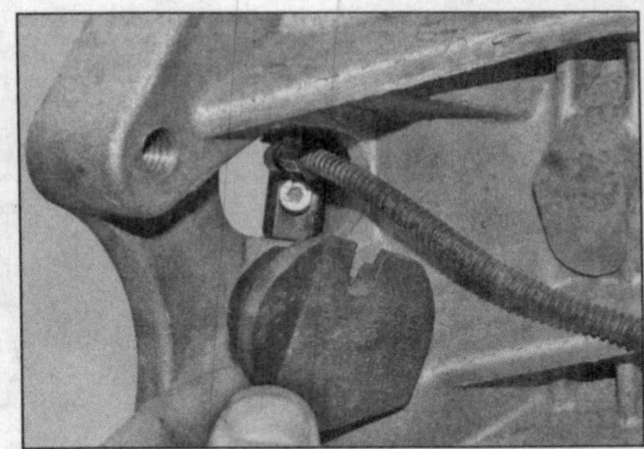

12.9b ...and recover the rubber grommet

12.10 Unscrew the housing securing bolts...

12.11a ...then use three M6 bolts to force the housing from the cylinder block

12.11b Flywheel end oil seal and housing together with the timing ring

12.13a Assemble the new housing to the VW tool...

then remove the bolts. As the housing is removed, the timing ring will be forced from the end of the crankshaft. If the housing is to be re-used, do not move the timing ring from its TDC position.

12.15a Fit the housing and tool to the end of the crankshaft...

12.15c Check the clearance between the timing ring and the outer surface of the crankshaft

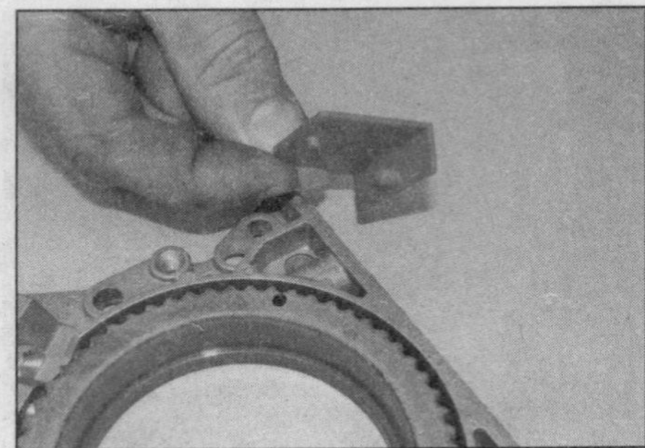
12.12a Remove the plastic clip...

12.13b ...making sure that the pin and hole are aligned with each other

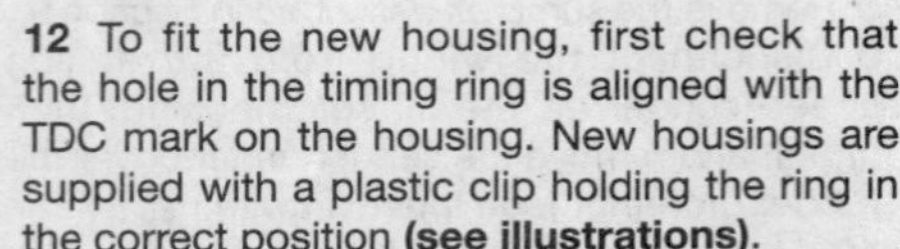
12 To fit the new housing, first check that the hole in the timing ring is aligned with the TDC mark on the housing. New housings are supplied with a plastic clip holding the ring in the correct position **(see illustrations)**.

12.15b ...then tighten the centre nut to force the timing ring onto the crankshaft

13.3 Unscrew the flywheel bolts using a home-made holding tool

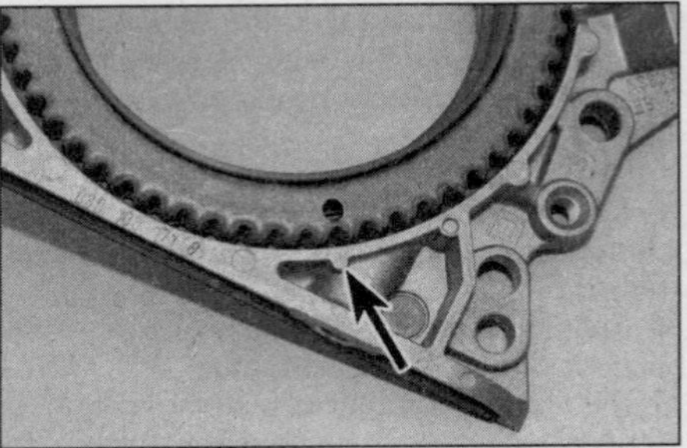
12.12b ...and check that the hole in the timing ring is aligned with the TDC mark on the housing

13 Assemble the new housing to the special VW tool, making sure that the TDC pin and hole are aligned and the lip support ring is located in the oil seal **(see illustrations)**.

14 Wipe clean the crankshaft and check that the engine is still at TDC.

15 Fit the tool and new housing over the crankshaft and onto the cylinder block, using two M6 bolts to guide the housing. By tightening the tool nut to 35 Nm (26 lbf ft), the timing ring is forced onto the end of the crankshaft. The timing ring is in its fully-fitted position if there is a distance of 0.5 mm between its outer edges and the outer surface of the crankshaft. After tightening the nut, there must also be a small air gap between the housing and the cylinder block **(see illustrations)**.

16 Remove the guide bolts and fit the new housing securing bolts, tightening them to the specified torque.

17 Insert the crankshaft speed sender mounting bolt and tighten to the specified torque.

18 Refit the sump as described in Section 9.

19 Refit the intermediate plate and flywheel with reference to Section 13.

13 Flywheel/driveplate – removal, inspection and refitting

Removal

1 On manual transmission models, remove the gearbox (see Chapter 7A) and clutch (see Chapter 6).

2 On automatic transmission models, remove the automatic transmission as described in Chapter 7B.

3 The flywheel/driveplate bolts are offset to ensure correct fitment. Unscrew the bolts while holding the flywheel/driveplate stationary. Temporarily insert a bolt in the cylinder block, and use a screwdriver to hold the flywheel/driveplate, or make up a holding tool **(see illustration)**. Discard the bolts as new ones must be used on refitting.

4 Lift the flywheel/driveplate from the crankshaft. Recover the engine-to-transmission intermediate plate if it is loose **(see illustrations)**.

Inspection

5 Check the flywheel/driveplate for wear and damage. Examine the starter ring gear for excessive wear to the teeth; if evident, the flywheel/driveplate must be renewed complete as the ring gear is not supplied separately. If the clutch contact surface is worn excessively, it may be possible to have it reground by a specialist.

Refitting

6 Refitting is a reversal of removal, bearing in mind the following points.

a) Ensure that the engine-to-transmission intermediate plate is in place before fitting the flywheel/driveplate.

b) Use new bolts when refitting the flywheel or driveplate, and coat the threads of the bolts with locking fluid before inserting them. Tighten the securing bolts to the specified torque.

13.4a Remove the flywheel from the crankshaft...

13.4b ...and remove the intermediate plate

14 Engine/transmission mountings – inspection and renewal

Inspection

1 If improved access is required, jack up the front of the vehicle, and support it securely on axle stands (see *Jacking and vehicle support*). Remove the engine undertray(s).

2 Check the mounting rubbers to see if they are cracked, hardened or separated from the metal at any point; renew the mounting if any such damage or deterioration is evident.

3 Check that all the mountings are securely tightened; use a torque wrench to check if possible.

4 Using a large screwdriver or a crowbar, check for wear in the mounting by carefully levering against it to check for free play. Where this is not possible, enlist the aid of an assistant to move the engine/transmission back-and-forth, or from side-to-side, whilst you observe the mounting. While some free play is to be expected, even from new components, excessive wear should be obvious. If excessive free play is found, check first that the fasteners are correctly secured, then renew any worn components as described in the following paragraphs.

Renewal

Right-hand mounting

5 Attach a hoist and lifting tackle to the engine lifting brackets on the cylinder head, and raise the hoist to just take the weight of the engine. Alternatively the engine can be supported on a trolley jack under the engine. Use a block of wood between the sump and the head of the jack, to prevent any damage to the sump.

6 For improved access, unbolt the coolant reservoir and move it to one side, leaving the coolant hoses connected.

7 Where applicable, move any wiring harnesses, pipes or hoses to one side to enable removal of the engine mounting.

8 Unscrew the bolts securing the mounting to the engine **(see illustration)**, then unscrew the bolts securing it to the body. Also, unbolt the movement limiter. Withdraw the mounting from the engine compartment.

9 Refitting is a reversal of removal, bearing in mind the following points.

a) Use new securing bolts.

b) Tighten all fixings to the specified torque.

Left-hand mounting

10 Remove the engine top cover which also incorporates the air filter.

11 Attach a hoist and lifting tackle to the engine lifting brackets on the cylinder head, and raise the hoist to just take the weight of the engine and transmission. Alternatively the engine can be supported on a trolley jack under the transmission. Use a block of wood between the transmission and the head of the jack, to prevent any damage to the transmission.

12 Remove the battery, as described in Chapter 5A, then disconnect the main starter motor feed cable from the positive battery terminal box.

13 Release any relevant wiring or hoses from the clips on the battery tray, then unscrew the four securing bolts and remove the battery tray.

14 Unscrew the bolts securing the mounting to the transmission, and the remaining bolts securing the mounting to the body, then lift the mounting from the engine compartment. Note that on some models, the earth cable is located on the mounting **(see illustrations)**.

14.8 Right-hand engine mounting

14.14a Left-hand engine mounting

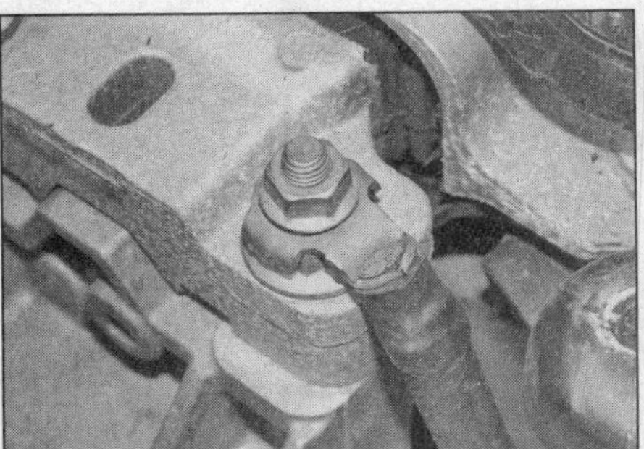

14.14b Earth cable located on the left-hand engine mounting

14.14c Remove the left-hand engine mounting

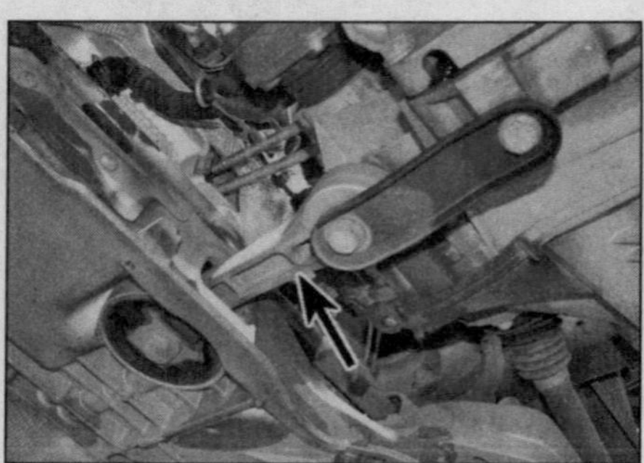

14.16 Rear engine mounting/torque arm

15 Refitting is a reversal of removal, bearing in mind the following points:

a) Use new mounting bolts.

b) Tighten all fixings to the specified torque.

Rear mounting (torque arm)

16 Apply the handbrake, then jack up the front of the vehicle and support securely on axle stands (see *Jacking and vehicle support*). Remove the engine undertray(s) for access to the rear mounting (torque arm) **(see illustration)**.

17 Support the rear of the transmission beneath the final drive housing. To do this, use a trolley jack and block of wood, or alternatively wedge a block of wood between the transmission and the subframe.

18 Working under the vehicle, unscrew and remove the bolt securing the mounting to the subframe.

19 Unscrew the two bolts securing the mounting to the transmission, then withdraw the mounting from under the vehicle.

20 Refitting is a reversal of removal, but use new mounting securing bolts, and tighten all fixings to the specified torque.

Chapter 2 Part D:
2.0 litre direct injection petrol engine in-car repair procedures

Contents

Degrees of difficulty

Easy, suitable for novice with little experience	**Fairly easy,** suitable for beginner with some experience	**Fairly difficult,** suitable for competent DIY mechanic	**Difficult,** suitable for experienced DIY mechanic	**Very difficult,** suitable for expert DIY or professional

Specifications

General

Manufacturer's engine codes*:	
1984 cc non-turbo	AXW, BLX, BLY, BLR, BVX, BVY and BVZ
1984 cc turbo	AXX, BPY and BWA
Maximum power output:	
Non-turbo	110 kW at 6000 rpm
Turbo	147 kW at 5700 rpm
Maximum torque output:	
Non-turbo	200 Nm at 3500 rpm
Turbo	280 Nm at 2000 rpm
Bore	82.5 mm
Stroke	92.8 mm
Compression ratio:	
Engine code BWA	10.3 : 1
Engine codes BLY, BVZ, AXX and BPY	10.5 : 1
Engine codes AXW, BLX, BLR, BVX and BVY	11.5 : 1
Compression pressures:	
Minimum compression pressure:	
Engine codes BLY, BVZ, AXX, BPY and BWA	Approximately 7.0 bar
Engine codes AXW, BLX, BLR, BVX and BVY	Approximately 8.0 bar
Maximum difference between cylinders	Approximately 3.0 bar
Firing order	1 – 3 – 4 – 2
No 1 cylinder location	Timing belt end

* **Note:** *See 'Vehicle identification' at the end of this manual for the location of engine code markings.*

Camshafts

Camshaft endfloat	0.17 mm
Camshaft bearing running clearance	0.10 mm
Camshaft run-out	0.035 mm

Lubrication system

Oil pump type	Gear type, chain-driven from crankshaft
Oil pressure (oil temperature 80°C):	
At idling	1.2 to 1.6 bar
At 2000 rpm	2.7 to 4.5 bar

Torque wrench settings	Nm	lbf ft
Ancillaries bracket to engine block	45	33
Auxiliary drivebelt idler pulley	40	30
Auxiliary drivebelt tensioner bolts	23	17
Balancer shaft housing bolts*:		
Stage 1	15	11
Stage 2	Angle-tighten a further 90°	
Balancer shaft/oil pump drive chain tensioner bolts	15	11
Big-end bearing caps bolts*:		
Stage 1	30	22
Stage 2	Angle-tighten a further 90°	
Camshaft adjuster chain tensioner	10	7
Camshaft adjuster rear cover	10	7
Camshaft adjuster-to-exhaust camshaft bolt:		
Stage 1	20	15
Stage 2	Angle-tighten a further 45°	
Camshaft bearing ladder*:		
Stage 1	8	6
Stage 2	Angle-tighten a further 90°	
Camshaft cover	10	7
Camshaft position sensor	10	7
Camshaft sprocket:		
Stage 1	50	37
Stage 2	Angle-tighten a further 180°	
Coolant elbow	15	11
Crankshaft timing belt end oil seal housing	35	26
Crankshaft pulley bolts*:		
Stage 1	10	7
Stage 2	Angle-tighten a further 90°	
Crankshaft sprocket centre bolt*:		
Stage 1	90	66
Stage 2	Angle-tighten a further 90°	
Crankshaft flywheel end oil seal housing	15	11
Cylinder head bolts*:		
Stage 1	40	30
Stage 2	Angle-tighten a further 90°	
Stage 3	Angle-tighten a further 90°	
Driveplate mounting bolts*:		
Stage 1	60	44
Stage 2	Angle-tighten a further 90°	
Engine mountings:		
RH engine mounting:		
Limiter:		
Stage 1	20	15
Stage 2	Angle-tighten a further 90°	
Mounting to engine:		
Stage 1	60	44
Stage 2	Angle-tighten a further 90°	
Mounting to body:		
Stage 1	40	30
Stage 2	Angle-tighten a further 90°	
LH engine mounting:		
Mounting to body:		
Stage 1	60	44
Stage 2	Angle-tighten a further 90°	
Mounting to transmission:		
Stage 1	40	30
Stage 2	Angle-tighten a further 90°	
Rear mounting link:		
To transmission:		
Stage 1	40	30
Stage 2	Angle-tighten a further 90°	
To subframe:		
Stage 1	100	74
Stage 2	Angle-tighten a further 90°	
Engine speed sender	10	7
Flywheel mounting bolts*:		
Stage 1	60	44
Stage 2	Angle-tighten a further 90°	

Torque wrench settings (continued)	Nm	lbf ft
Intake manifold support	40	30
Knock sensor	20	15
Main bearing cap bolts*:		
Stage 1	65	48
Stage 2	Angle-tighten a further 90°	
Oil filter housing	15	11
Oil jets	27	20
Oil pressure relief valve plug	15	11
Oil pump cover-to-balancer shaft housing	8	6
Oil pump sprocket bolt*:		
Stage 1	20	15
Stage 2	Angle-tighten a further 90°	
Roadwheel bolts	120	89
Sump:		
Sump-to-block bolts	15	11
Sump-to-transmission bolts	40	30
Timing belt covers	10	7
Timing belt inner cover	10	7
Timing belt idler roller:		
Large	40	30
Small	25	18
Timing belt tensioner roller:		
Engine code AXW and turbo without a split cover	23	17
Engine codes BLR, BLX, BLY, BVX, BVY and BVZ and turbo with a split cover	25	18

** Do not re-use*

1 General information

How to use this Chapter

This Part of Chapter 2 describes those repair procedures that can reasonably be carried out on the engine while it remains in the vehicle. If the engine has been removed from the vehicle and is being dismantled as described in Part G, any preliminary dismantling procedures can be ignored.

Note that while it may be possible physically to overhaul certain items while the engine is in the vehicle, such tasks are not usually carried out as separate operations, and usually require the execution of several additional procedures (not to mention the cleaning of components and of oilways); for this reason, all such tasks are classed as major overhaul procedures, and are described in Part G of this Chapter.

Engine description

Throughout this Chapter, engines are identified by the manufacturer's code letters. A listing of all engines covered, together with their code letters, is given in the Specifications.

The engines are water-cooled, double overhead camshaft (DOHC), in-line four-cylinder direct injection units, with aluminium cylinder blocks and cylinder heads. All are mounted transversely at the front of the vehicle, with the transmission bolted to the left-hand end of the engine.

The crankshaft is of five-bearing type, and thrust washers are fitted to the centre main bearing to control crankshaft endfloat.

The cylinder head carries the double camshafts. It also houses the intake and exhaust valves, which are closed by single coil springs, and which run in guides pressed into the cylinder head. The camshaft actuates the valves by cam followers and hydraulic tappets mounted in the cylinder head. The cylinder head contains integral oilways which supply and lubricate the tappets.

The timing belt drives the exhaust camshaft, and the intake camshaft is driven from the exhaust camshaft by chain at the left-hand end of the camshafts. A hydraulic tensioner is fitted to the chain, to automatically vary the intake camshaft valve timing.

The valves are operated from the camshafts through rocker arms and hydraulic adjusters - the valve clearances are adjusted automatically.

The engine coolant pump is driven by the toothed timing belt.

Lubricant is circulated under pressure by a pump, driven by a chain from the crankshaft. Oil is drawn from the sump through a strainer, and then forced through an externally-mounted, renewable screw-on filter. From there, it is distributed to the cylinder head, where it lubricates the camshaft journals and hydraulic tappets, and also to the crankcase, where it lubricates the main bearings, connecting rod big-ends, gudgeon pins and cylinder bores. An oil pressure switch is located on the oil filter housing, operating at 1.4 bars. An oil cooler mounted above the oil filter is supplied with coolant from the cooling system to reduce the temperature of the oil before it re-enters the engine.

A balancer shaft housing is fitted below the cylinder block. The two contra-rotating shafts are driven by the same chain that drives the oil pump. The shafts have integral weights fitted along their length, and as they spin, the forces created cancel out almost all of the vibration generated by the engine.

Operations with engine in car

The following operations can be performed without removing the engine:

a) Compression pressure – testing.
b) Auxiliary drivebelt – removal and refitting.
c) Camshafts – removal and refitting.
d) Camshaft oil seals – renewal.
e) Camshaft sprocket – removal and refitting.
f) Coolant pump – removal and refitting (refer to Chapter 3).
g) Crankshaft oil seals – renewal.
h) Crankshaft sprocket – removal and refitting.
i) Cylinder head – removal and refitting.*
j) Engine mountings – inspection and renewal.
k) Balancer shaft housing – renewal.
l) Oil pump and pick-up assembly – removal and refitting.
m) Sump – removal and refitting.
n) Timing belt, sprockets and cover – removal, inspection and refitting.
o) Flywheel/driveplate – removal and refitting

** Cylinder head dismantling procedures are detailed in Chapter 2F.*

Note: *It is possible to remove the pistons and connecting rods (after removing the cylinder head and sump) without removing the engine. However, this is not recommended. Work of this nature is more easily and thoroughly completed with the engine on the bench, as described in Chapter 2G.*

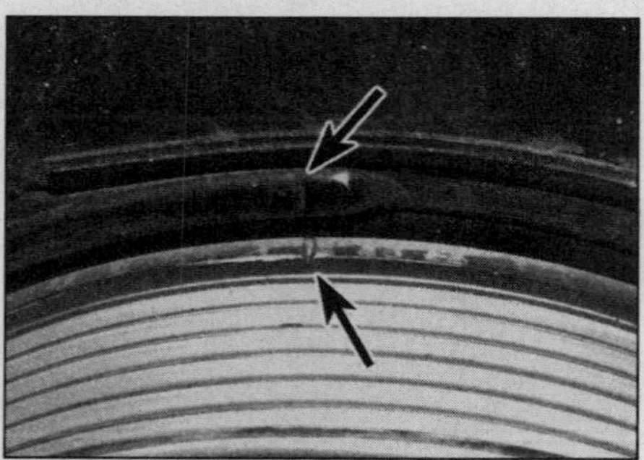

2.4 Crankshaft pulley TDC marks

2 Engine valve timing marks – general information and usage

General information

1 The crankshaft and camshaft sprockets are driven by the timing belt, and rotate in phase with each other. When the timing belt is removed during servicing or repair, it is possible for the shafts to rotate independently of each other, and the correct phasing is then lost.

2 The design of the engines covered in this Chapter is such that piston-to-valve contact will occur if the crankshaft is turned with the timing belt removed. For this reason, it is important that the correct phasing between the camshaft and crankshaft is preserved whilst the timing belt is off the engine. This is achieved by setting the engine in a reference condition (known as Top Dead Centre or TDC) before the timing belt is removed, and then preventing the shafts from rotating until the belt is refitted. Similarly, if the engine has been dismantled for overhaul, the engine can be set to TDC during reassembly to ensure that the correct shaft phasing is restored. **Note:** *The coolant pump is also driven by the timing belt, but the pump alignment is not critical.*

3 TDC is the highest position a piston reaches within its respective cylinder – in a four-stroke engine, each piston reaches TDC twice per cycle; once on the compression stroke, and once on the exhaust stroke. In general, TDC normally refers to No 1 cylinder on the compression stroke. Note that the cylinders are numbered one to four, starting from the timing belt end of the engine.

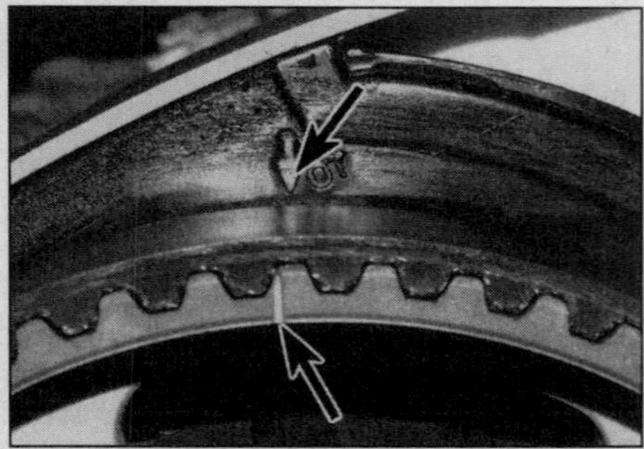

2 5 Exhaust camshaft TDC marks

4 The crankshaft pulley has a mark which, when aligned with a reference mark on the timing belt cover, indicates that No 1 cylinder (and hence also No 4 cylinder) is at TDC **(see illustration)**.

5 The exhaust camshaft sprocket is also equipped with a timing mark **(see illustration)** – when this is aligned with a mark on the small upper timing belt cover or camshaft cover, No 1 cylinder is at TDC compression.

Setting TDC on No 1 cylinder

6 Before starting work, make sure that the ignition is switched off.

7 Pull the engine top cover upwards from its fasteners.

8 Remove all of the spark plugs as described in Chapter 1A.

9 Remove the timing belt upper, outer cover as described in Section 4.

10 Turn the engine clockwise with a spanner on the crankshaft pulley until the timing mark on the outer circumference of the camshaft sprocket aligns with the mark on the timing belt cover. With this aligned, the timing mark on the crankshaft pulley should align with the mark on the lower timing belt cover.

3 Cylinder compression test

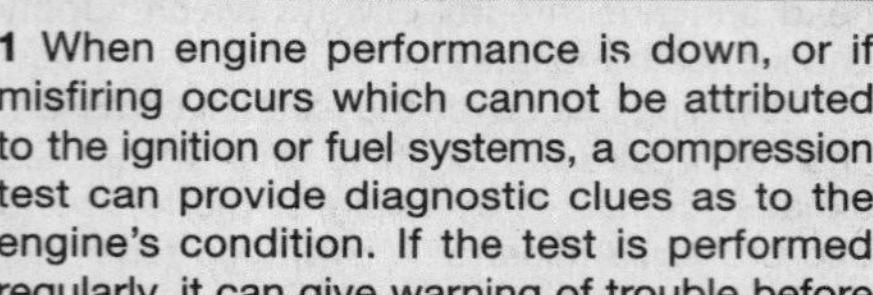

1 When engine performance is down, or if misfiring occurs which cannot be attributed to the ignition or fuel systems, a compression test can provide diagnostic clues as to the engine's condition. If the test is performed regularly, it can give warning of trouble before any other symptoms become apparent.

2 The engine must be fully warmed-up to normal operating temperature, the battery must be fully charged, and all the spark plugs must be removed (refer to Chapter 1A). The aid of an assistant will also be required. Pull the plastic cover on the top of the engine upwards from its fasteners.

3 Remove the spark plugs as described in Chapter 1A.

4 Disable the injectors by disconnecting the wiring plug under the intake manifold.

5 Fit a compression tester to the No 1 cylinder spark plug hole – the type of tester which screws into the plug thread is preferable.

6 Have an assistant hold the throttle wide open. Crank the engine on the starter motor several seconds. After one or two revolutions, the compression pressure should build-up to a maximum figure, and then stabilise. Record the highest reading obtained.

7 Repeat the test on the remaining cylinders, recording the pressure in each. Keep the throttle wide open.

8 All cylinders should produce very similar pressures; a difference of more than 3 bars between any two cylinders indicates a fault. Note that the compression should build-up quickly in a healthy engine. Low compression on the first stroke, followed by gradually-increasing pressure on successive strokes, indicates worn piston rings. A low compression reading on the first stroke, which does not build-up during successive strokes, indicates leaking valves or a blown head gasket (a cracked head could also be the cause).

9 Refer to the Specifications section of this Chapter, and compare the recorded compression figures with those stated by the manufacturer.

10 On completion of the test, refit the spark plugs, injector wiring plug and top cover. Note that in some cases, disconnecting the wiring plugs from the coils and injectors then cranking the engine may cause fault codes to be stored by the engine management ECM – have these codes erased by means of a suitable diagnostic tool/fault code reader. See your VW dealer or specialist.

4 Timing belt – removal, inspection and refitting

General information

1 The primary function of the toothed timing belt is to drive the camshafts. Should the belt slip or break in service, the valve timing will be disturbed and piston-to-valve contact will occur, resulting in serious engine damage. For this reason, it is important that the timing belt is tensioned correctly, and inspected regularly for signs of wear or deterioration.

Removal

2 Before starting work, remove the fuel pump fuse with reference to Chapter 12. **Note:** *The fuel pump will be activated by the driverís side door contact switch, if the battery remains connected.* Alternatively, disconnect the battery negative lead (refer to *Disconnecting the battery* in the *Reference* Chapter at the end of this manual).

3 Apply the handbrake, then jack up the front of the vehicle and support it on axle stands (see *Jacking and vehicle support*). Undo the fasteners and remove the engine undertray, then remove the right-hand front roadwheel and the wheel arch liner. On turbo models, also remove the charge air hose.

4 Pull the plastic cover/air filter (as applicable) on the top of the engine upwards to release it from the fasteners.

5 Remove the auxiliary drivebelt with reference to Section 6. Also unbolt the tensioner from the front of the engine **(see illustration)**.

6 Disconnect the fuel supply and breather line located next to the coolant expansion tank. On engine codes AXW and BPY, also disconnect the vacuum line.

7 Remove the activated charcoal filter and hoses (Chapter 4C).

4.5 Remove the auxiliary drivebelt tensioner

4.9 Timing belt upper cover screws

4.11a Crankshaft pulley bolts...

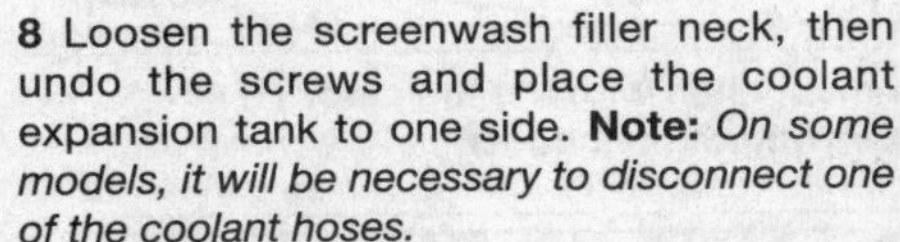

8 Loosen the screenwash filler neck, then undo the screws and place the coolant expansion tank to one side. **Note:** *On some models, it will be necessary to disconnect one of the coolant hoses.*

9 On engine codes BVX, BVY, BVZ and turbo engines with a split cover, remove the timing belt upper cover, and unbolt the auxiliary drivebelt tensioner. On engine code AXW, remove the timing belt upper cover **(see illustration).**

10 Set the engine to TDC as described in Section 2.

11 Hold the crankshaft stationary with a spanner on the centre bolt, then unscrew the pulley bolts and remove the pulley from the crankshaft sprocket **(see illustrations).**

12 Remove the lower timing belt cover, then check that the engine is still at TDC, and mark the crankshaft sprocket in relation to the cylinder block to indicate its TDC position **(see illustration).**

13 On engine codes BLR, BLX, BLY, BVX, BVY, BVZ and turbo engines with a split cover, carry out the following:

a) *Refer to Chapter 4C and disconnect the exhaust front pipe from the exhaust manifold/turbocharger. Unbolt the exhaust mounting bracket from the underbody, and support the exhaust pipe on an axle stand.*

b) *Disconnect the driveshafts from the transmission with reference to Chapter 7A or 7B, and tie them to the underbody.*

c) *Release the air conditioning pipes from the supports on the right-hand side of the engine compartment.* ***Do not*** *open the air conditioning refrigerant lines.*

14 Support the right-hand end of the engine with a hoist.

15 Beneath the vehicle, unbolt the rear engine torque arm from the bottom of the transmission.

16 Unbolt the right-hand engine mounting and bracket from the engine and body (see Section 16), and raise the engine as far as possible to provide access to the timing belt.

17 On engine code AXW, unbolt and remove the timing belt centre cover. On engine codes BLR, BLX, BLY, BVX, BVY and BVZ, unbolt and remove the single timing belt cover. On engine codes BVX, BVY and BVZ and turbo

4.11b ...and pulley location hole

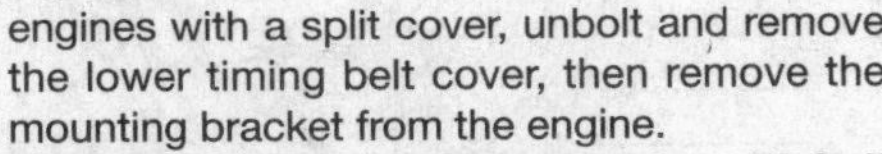

engines with a split cover, unbolt and remove the lower timing belt cover, then remove the mounting bracket from the engine.

18 Check again that the engine is at TDC. If the timing belt is to be refitted, mark its normal direction of travel with chalk or a marker pen.

Engine code AXW and turbo engines without a split cover

19 Insert VW special tool T10020 into the holes in the tensioner hub arm, then slacken the tensioner nut and rotate the hub clockwise to relieve the tension **(see illustration).** Temporarily tighten the nut to retain the tensioner in the released position. In the absence of the special tool, a sturdy pair of right-angle circlip pliers will suffice.

Engine codes BLR, BLX, BLY, BVX, BVY, BVZ and turbo engines with a split cover

20 Slacken the nut in the centre of the tensioner pulley to relieve the tension in the belt.

All engines

21 Slip the timing belt off of the crankshaft, camshaft, and coolant pump sprockets, and remove it from the engine. **Do not** bend the timing belt sharply if it is to be re-used.

Inspection

22 Examine the belt for evidence of contamination by coolant or lubricant. If this is the case, find the source of the contamination before progressing any further. Check the belt for signs of wear or damage, particularly around the leading edges of the belt teeth. Renew the

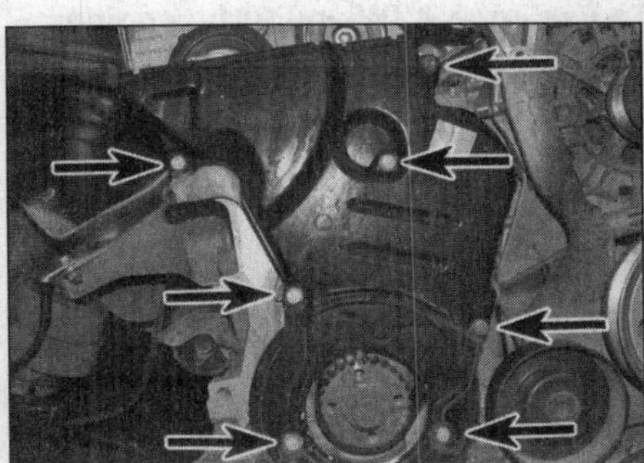

4.12 Timing belt cover retaining bolts

belt if its condition is in doubt; the cost of belt renewal is negligible compared with potential cost of the engine repairs, should the belt fail in service. The belt must be renewed if it has covered the mileage stated by the manufacturer (see Chapter 1A), however, even if it has covered less, it is recommended to renew it regardless of condition as a precautionary measure. **Note:** *If the timing belt is not going to be refitted for some time, it is a wise precaution to hang a warning label on the steering wheel, to remind yourself (and others) not to turn the engine.*

Refitting

23 Ensure that the timing mark on the camshaft and crankshaft sprockets are correctly aligned with the corresponding TDC reference marks on the timing belt cover; refer to Section 2 for details.

4.19 Remove the timing belt tensioner

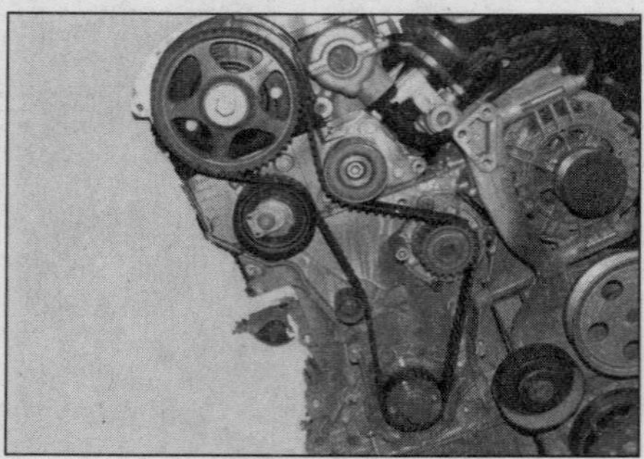

4.24 Timing belt routing

Engine code AXW and turbo engines without a split cover

24 Loop the timing belt under the crankshaft sprocket loosely, observing the direction of rotation markings if the old timing belt is being refitted. Engage the timing belt teeth with the crankshaft sprocket, then manoeuvre it into position over the coolant pump and camshaft sprockets, tensioner pulley and finally the idler pulleys **(see illustration)**.

25 Refit the lower timing cover and tighten the bolts, then locate the pulley for the auxiliary drivebelt on the crankshaft sprocket, and tighten the new bolts to the specified torque and angle. Note that the pulley will only fit in one fitting position – with the hole in the pulley over the projection on the crankshaft sprocket. Make sure that the TDC marks are correctly aligned.

26 Check the tensioner roller locating arm is correctly located in the backplate, then insert the VW special tool T10020 (or circlip pliers) into the holes in the tensioner hub arm.

27 Slacken the retaining nut, and rotate the tensioner hub anti-clockwise until the notch in the hub is past the indicator (over-tensioned), then slowly release the tension until the notch aligns with the indicator **(see illustration)**. Tighten the tensioner nut to the specified torque.

4.27 The notch (2) in the tensioner hub must align with the indicator (1) – engine code AXW and turbo without split cover

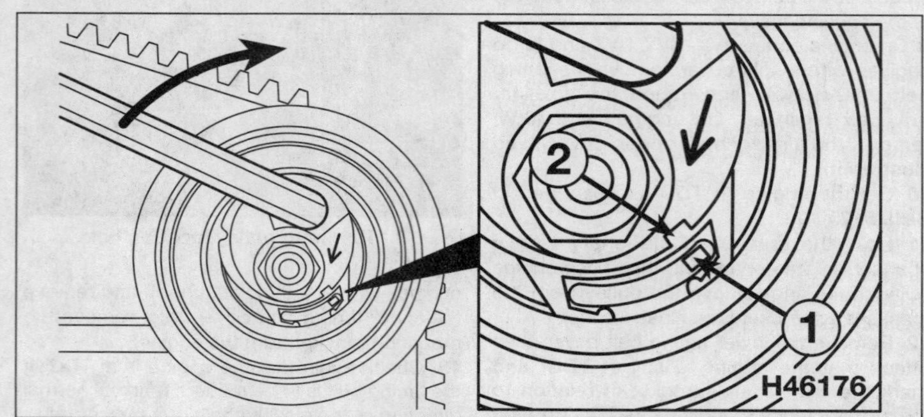

4.29 Align the notch (2) with the indicator (1) – engine codes BLR, BLX, BLY, BVX, BVY, BVZ and turbo with split cover

Engine codes BLR, BLX, BLY, BVX, BVY, BVZ and turbo engines with a split cover

28 Loop the timing belt under the crankshaft sprocket loosely, observing the direction of rotation markings if the old timing belt is being refitted. Engage the timing belt teeth with the crankshaft sprocket, then manoeuvre it into position over the coolant pump and camshaft sprockets, tensioner pulley and finally the idler pulleys.

29 With the tensioner centre nut loose, insert an 8 mm Allen key into the tensioner arm in the centre of the pulley, and rotate the arm clockwise until the notch in the arm is past the indicator (over-tensioned), then slowly release the tensioner until the notch is aligned with the indicator **(see illustration)**. Tighten the tensioner nut to the specified torque.

All engines

30 Using a spanner or wrench and socket on the crankshaft pulley centre bolt, rotate the crankshaft through two complete revolutions. Reset the engine to TDC on No 1 cylinder with reference to Section 2, and check that the crankshaft pulley and camshaft sprocket timing marks are correctly aligned. Recheck the timing belt tension and adjust it, if necessary.

31 The remaining procedure is a reversal of removal.

5.2a Tensioner hub and nut

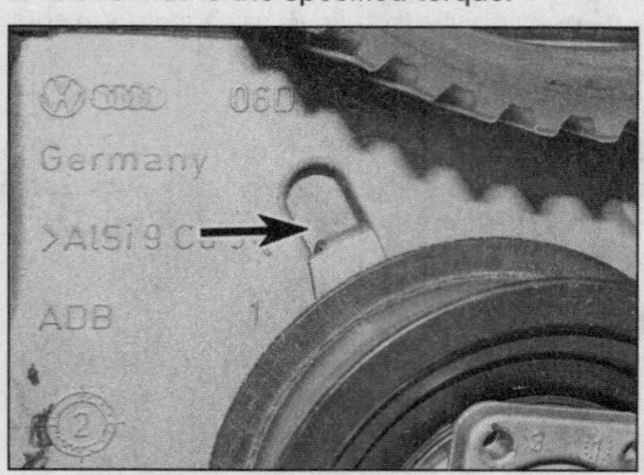

5.2b Tensioner hub location recess in the cylinder head

5 Timing belt tensioner and sprockets – removal, inspection and refitting

Removal

1 Remove the timing belt as described in Section 4.

Tensioner/roller

2 Undo the tensioner hub nut and withdraw the assembly from position. Note that on later engines from 06/2004, the tensioner hub locates in a recess in the cylinder head **(see illustrations)**.

Camshaft sprocket

3 To prevent any accidental piston-to-valve contact, rotate the crankshaft 90° anti-clockwise.

4 Unscrew the camshaft sprocket bolt, while holding the sprocket stationary using a tool as shown. Remove the bolt, washer (where fitted), sprocket, and the key **(see illustrations)**. If necessary, use a 2-legged puller to remove the sprocket. If necessary, a VW special puller (T40001) is available.

Crankshaft sprocket

5 To prevent any accidental piston-to-valve contact, rotate the crankshaft 90° anti-clockwise.

6 Unscrew and discard the crankshaft sprocket bolt, and remove the sprocket **(see illustrations)**. The bolt is very tight, and the crankshaft must be held stationary. On manual gearbox models, engage top gear and apply the footbrake pedal firmly. On automatic transmission models, remove the starter motor (Chapter 5A) and use a wide-bladed screwdriver in the ring gear to hold the crankshaft stationary.

Inspection

7 Clean all the sprockets and examine them for wear and damage. Spin the tensioner roller, and check that it runs smoothly.

8 Check the tensioner for signs of wear and/or damage and renew if necessary.

Refitting

Tensioner/roller

9 Refit the tensioner roller and spring assembly using a reversal of the removal procedure.

10 Refit the timing belt as described in Section 4.

Camshaft sprocket

11 Locate the key on the camshaft and refit the sprocket, and bolt. Tighten the bolt to the specified torque while holding the sprocket using the method employed on removal. Note the sprocket must be refitted with the narrow web facing forwards.

12 Carefully turn the crankshaft 90° clockwise, back to the TDC position.

13 Refit the timing belt as described in Section 4.

Crankshaft sprocket

14 Locate the sprocket on the crankshaft, then install the new bolt (do not oil the threads), and tighten the bolt to the specified torque while holding the crankshaft stationary using the method employed on removal. **Note:** *Do not allow the crankshaft to rotate.*

15 Carefully turn the crankshaft 90° clockwise, back to the TDC position.

16 Refit the timing belt as described in Section 4.

5.4a Unscrew the camshaft sprocket bolt

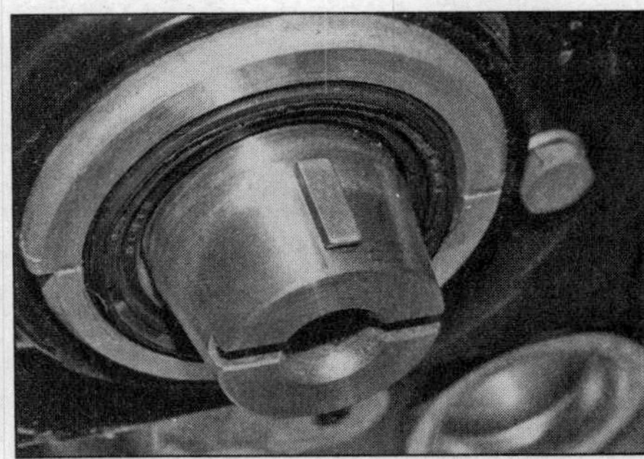

5.4b Camshaft sprocket location key

5.6a Unscrew the bolt…

5.6b …and remove the crankshaft sprocket

6 Auxiliary drivebelt – removal and refitting

Refer to Chapter 1A.

7 Camshaft cover – removal and refitting

Removal

1 Remove the engine top cover.

2 Remove the ignition coils as described in Chapter 5B.

3 Undo the 2 bolts securing the timing belt upper cover to the camshaft cover.

4 Disconnect the engine breather hose(s) from the camshaft cover **(see illustration)**.

7.4 Disconnect the engine breather hoses from the camshaft cover

5 Progressively and evenly unscrew the bolts securing the camshaft cover to the cylinder head.

6 Lift the camshaft cover from the cylinder head and recover the gasket. On turbo models, unbolt the valve body from the camshaft cover and recover the gasket.

Refitting

7 Clean the surfaces of the camshaft cover and cylinder head. On turbo models, refit the valve body to the camshaft cover together with a new gasket, and tighten the bolts securely.

8 Check the condition of the camshaft cover gasket and renew if necessary.

9 Carefully fit the gasket to the camshaft cover, ensuring the bolts locate correctly in the gasket, and position the assembly on the cylinder head. Progressively and evenly tighten the bolts to the specified torque.

10 Reconnect the breather hoses to the camshaft cover.

11 Apply a little thread-locking compound, then refit the timing belt cover bolts and tighten them to the specified torque.

12 Refit the ignition coils (Chapter 5B) then refit the engine top cover.

8 Camshaft oil seals – renewal

Exhaust camshaft

1 Remove the camshaft sprocket as described in Section 5. Recover the key from the camshaft.

8.4 Wrap adhesive tape around the camshaft to protect the oil seal when fitting

8.5 Fit the exhaust camshaft oil seal

8.8 Remove the rubber cap from the intake camshaft

8.9 The new rubber cap in position

2 Drill two small holes into the existing oil seal, diagonally opposite each other. Thread two self-tapping screws into the holes, and using two pairs of pliers, pull on the heads of the screws to extract the oil seal. Take great care to avoid drilling through into the seal housing or camshaft sealing surface.

3 Clean out the seal housing and sealing surface of the camshaft by wiping it with a lint-free cloth. Remove any swarf or burrs that may cause the seal to leak.

4 Carefully wrap adhesive tape around the end of the camshaft, to protect the seal lip from the edges of the shaft and keyway **(see illustration)**.

5 Do not lubricate the lip of the new oil seal – it must be fitted dry. Push the new seal over the end of the camshaft, ensuring the lip of the seal is not damaged by the sharp edges of the camshaft and keyway. Use a suitable tubular spacer (socket or similar) that bears only on the hard outer edge of the seal, and a hammer to gently and gradually/evenly push the seal into place. Try to install the seal as squarely as possible **(see illustration)**.

6 Refit the camshaft sprocket with reference to Section 5.

Intake camshaft

7 Remove the upper section of the timing belt cover as described in Section 4.

8 Using a screwdriver or pry bar, pierce the centre of the rubber cap, and lever it from place **(see illustration)**.

9 Ensure the bore of the cylinder head/bearing ladder is clean, then drive the new cap into place, until it's flush with the casing **(see illustration)**. Note that the rubber cap should be fitted dry, no oil, grease or sealant is to be used.

10 Refit the timing belt cover as described in Section 4.

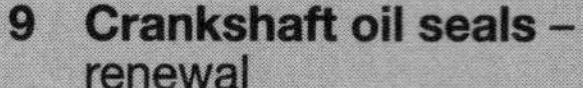

9 Crankshaft oil seals – renewal

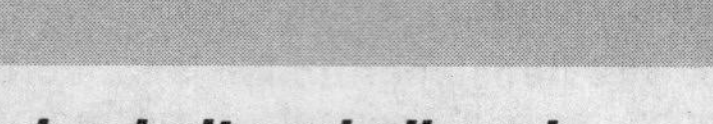

Timing belt end oil seal

1 Remove the timing belt and crankshaft sprocket, with reference to Section 5.

2 The seal may be renewed without removing the housing by drilling two small holes diagonally opposite each other, inserting self-tapping screws, and pulling on the heads of the screws with pliers. Alternatively, remove the auxiliary belt idler pulley (where applicable) unbolt and remove the housing (including the relevant sump bolts) and remove the gasket then lever out the oil seal on the bench **(see illustrations)**.

9.2a Drill two small holes and fit self-tapping screws in the oil seal...

9.2b ...then pull out the oil seal

9.2c Remove the auxiliary drivebelt idler pulley

9.2d Unbolt the housing...

9.2e ...and drive out the oil seal

9.4a Use a socket to drive in the new oil seal

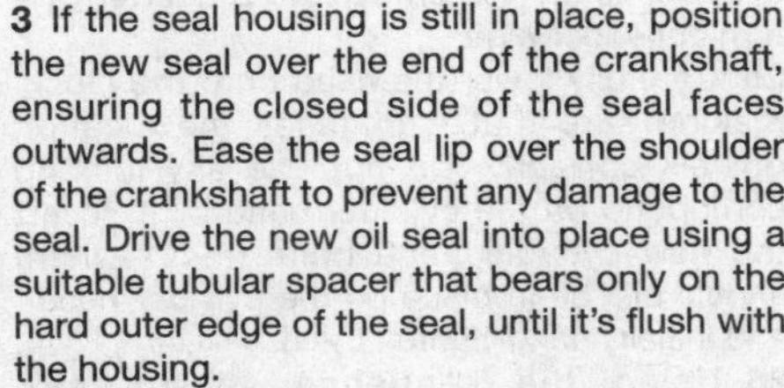

9.4b Fitted oil seal

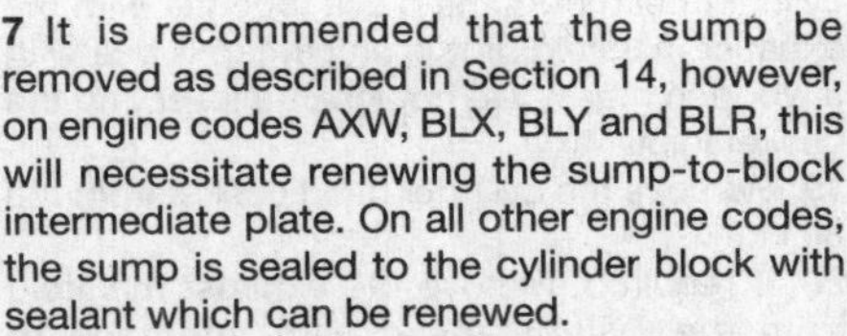

9.4c Apply sealant 'inside' the bolt holes as shown

3 If the seal housing is still in place, position the new seal over the end of the crankshaft, ensuring the closed side of the seal faces outwards. Ease the seal lip over the shoulder of the crankshaft to prevent any damage to the seal. Drive the new oil seal into place using a suitable tubular spacer that bears only on the hard outer edge of the seal, until it's flush with the housing.

4 If the housing has been removed, remove all traces of the sealant from the mating faces of the housing, cylinder block and sump. Use a socket (or similar) to drive the new seal into place (flush with the housing), then apply a thin bead (2.0 mm) of suitable sealant (available from VW dealers/parts specialists) to the housing mating faces. Ensure the bead of sealant is routed 'inside' the bolts holes. Do not apply too much sealant, as any excess may find its way into the oil system. Apply a bead of sealant to the joint between the sump and cylinder block. Refit the housing, easing the seal over the end of the crankshaft, and tighten the bolts to the specified torque. Tighten the bolts securing the housing to the cylinder block first, followed by the sump bolts **(see illustrations)**. *Note that the housing must be in position with the bolts tightened within 5 minutes of applying the sealant.*

5 Refit the timing belt and crankshaft sprocket, with reference to Section 5.

Flywheel/driveplate end oil seal

6 Remove the flywheel/driveplate, with reference to Section 13.

7 It is recommended that the sump be removed as described in Section 14, however, on engine codes AXW, BLX, BLY and BLR, this will necessitate renewing the sump-to-block intermediate plate. On all other engine codes, the sump is sealed to the cylinder block with sealant which can be renewed.

8 Pull the adapter plate from the locating dowels on the rear of the cylinder block, and remove it from the engine.

9 Unbolt and remove the housing (including the relevant sump bolts, where applicable). The seal is only available complete with the housing.

10 Carefully remove any sealant residue from the cylinder block and sump mating surfaces.

11 Where applicable, apply a little sealant to the joint between the sump and cylinder block, then apply a thin layer of sealant to the base of the new housing. The new seal is supplied with a guide sleeve fitted to the centre of the seal. Position the housing and seal over the end of the crankshaft and gently, evenly, push it into position, and tighten the bolts evenly in diagonal sequence to the specified torque, then remove the tool **(see illustrations)**.

12 Refit the adapter plate, locating it over the oil seal housing, and onto the 2 dowels at the back of the cylinder head **(see illustration)**.

13 Where applicable, refit the sump with reference to Section 12.

14 Refit the flywheel/driveplate, with reference to Section 12.

10 Cylinder head – removal and refitting

Note: *Cylinder head dismantling and overhaul is covered in Chapter 2G.*

Removal

1 Before starting work, switch off the ignition and all electrical consumers and remove the ignition key.

2 Apply the handbrake, then jack up the front of the vehicle and support it on axle stands (see *Jacking and vehicle support*).

3 Remove the engine top cover by pulling it upwards from its fasteners.

4 On Golf Plus models, remove the plenum chamber bulkhead at the rear of the engine compartment.

5 Drain the cooling system as described in Chapter 1A.

6 Working beneath the vehicle, unscrew the nuts securing the front exhaust pipe to the exhaust manifold, then unbolt the exhaust mounting from the crossmember and support the exhaust on an axle stand. **Note:** *Do not bend the exhaust pipe flexible joint more than 10°.*

7 Unbolt and remove the exhaust manifold supports.

8 Remove the air filter housing and intake hoses.

9 Disconnect the coolant elbow from the left-hand end of the cylinder head.

9.11a Position the housing and seal over the crankshaft...

9.11b ...and use the guide sleeve to fit the oil seal

9.12 Refit the adapter plate, locating it as shown

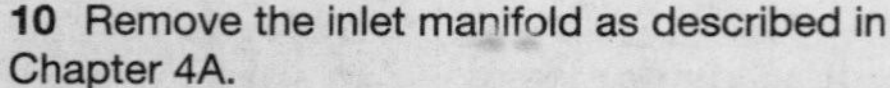
10.17 Remove the cylinder head bolts

10.23a Fit the new cylinder head gasket with the part number facing upwards

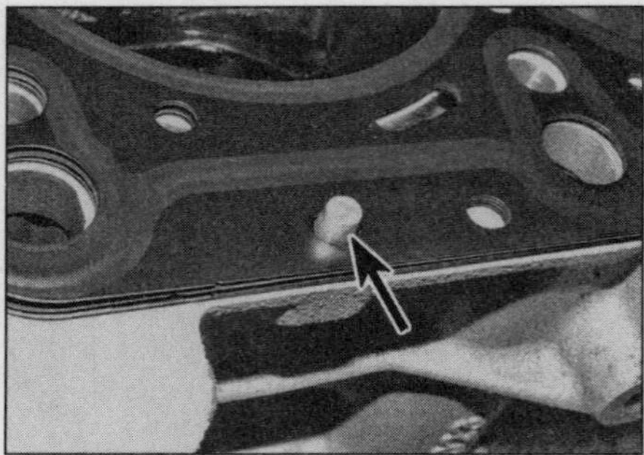
10.23b Head gasket location dowel

10 Remove the inlet manifold as described in Chapter 4A.

11 Note their fitted positions, then disconnect all electrical connectors from the cylinder head, including the injector loom connectors, oil pressure switch plug and the electrically-controlled thermostat plug. Release the wiring harness from the small coolant pipe on the left-hand side of the engine.

12 On engine codes AXW, BLX, BLY and BLR, disconnect the coolant hoses from the throttle valve control module. Also, where applicable, remove the EGR pipe between the inlet manifold and the EGR valve, and disconnect the coolant hoses.

13 Remove the auxiliary drivebelt as described in Chapter 1A.

14 Remove the timing belt as described in Section 4.

15 Remove the camshaft cover as described in Section 7.

16 Make a final check to ensure all relevant electrical connectors and coolant hoses have been disconnected. Plug or cover any openings to prevent fluid spillage and contamination.

17 Unscrew the M10 Ribe cylinder head bolts a turn at a time, in **reverse** order to the tightening sequence and remove them **(see illustration)**. Discard the bolts, new ones must be fitted.

18 With the help of an assistant, lift the cylinder head from the block together with the exhaust manifold. If it is stuck, tap it free with a wooden mallet. Do not insert a lever into the gasket joint.

19 Remove the cylinder head gasket from the block.

20 If required, remove the exhaust manifold from the cylinder head with reference to Chapter 4C.

Refitting

21 Thoroughly clean the contact faces of the cylinder head and block. Also clean any oil or coolant from the bolt holes in the block – if this precaution is not taken, not only will the tightening torque be incorrect but there is the possibility of damaging the block.

22 If removed, refit the exhaust manifold to the cylinder head together with a new gasket with reference to Chapter 4C.

23 Locate a new gasket on the block, with the part number facing upwards, and readable from the intake side of the engine. Make sure that the location dowels are in position **(see illustrations)**. VW recommend that the gasket is removed from its packaging just prior to fitting it. Handle the gasket with great care – damage to the silicone or indented areas will lead to leaks.

24 At this point the crankshaft should still be set at TDC on cylinders 1 and 4. In order to prevent any accidental piston-to-valve contact, rotate the crankshaft a quarter of a turn anti-clockwise.

25 Carefully lower the head onto the block, making sure that it engages the location dowels correctly. Do not use any jointing compound on the cylinder head joint. Insert the new cylinder head bolts (the washers should still be in place on the cylinder head), and initially hand-tighten them.

26 Using the sequence shown **(see illustration)** tighten all the bolts to the Stage 1 torque given in the Specifications.

27 Angle-tighten the bolts in the same sequence to the Stage 2 and Stage 3 angles given in the Specifications **(see illustration)**.

28 Rotate the crankshaft a quarter of a turn clockwise, back to TDC on cylinders 1 and 4.

29 Refit the camshaft cover with reference to Section 7.

30 The remainder of refitting is a reversal of removal, noting the following points:

a) Ensure all electrical connectors are securing reconnected, and the harnesses are correctly routed – refit any cable clips removed during dismantling.

b) Ensure all coolant hoses are reconnected, and all retaining clips are refitted in their original positions.

c) Apply a little thread-locking compound to the tensioner roller mounting plate bolts.

d) If any of the coolant hose clips appear weak or corroded – renew them.

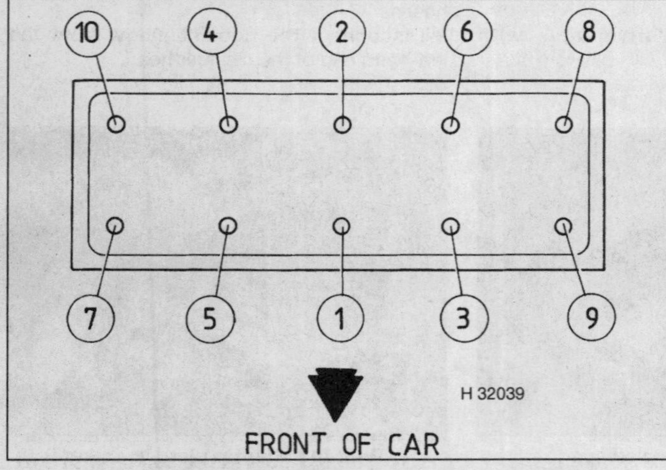

10.26 Cylinder head bolt tightening sequence

10.27 Angle-tightening the cylinder head bolts

e) On completion, refill the cooling system with new antifreeze mixture (see Chapter 1A).

f) If you suspect the engine oil has been contaminated with coolant, change the oil and filter as described in Chapter 1A.

11 Camshafts – removal, inspection and refitting

Removal

1 Remove the inlet manifold and high-pressure fuel pump as described in Chapter 4A.

2 Remove the camshaft cover (Section 7) then undo the retaining bolts and remove the cover from the chain adjuster at the left-hand end of the cylinder head.

3 Using VW tool T10092 and an M5 nut, lock the tensioner in place, then undo the tensioner retaining Torx bolts. In the absence of the VW tool, use a 5 mm bolt and locknut **(see illustration)**.

4 Paint alignment marks between the chain links, the adjuster, and the intake sprocket **(see illustration)**. Count the number of links between the alignment marks and make a note in case the chain needs to be renewed, in which case the alignment marks can be transferred to the new chain.

5 Remove the camshaft sprocket as described in Section 5.

6 Working gradually and evenly, from the outside-in, slacken and remove the camshaft bearing ladder Torx bolts. Remove the bearing ladder.

7 Lift the camshafts together with the tensioner and chain from the cylinder head. Disengage the camshafts from the chain and discard the oil seal.

8 Lift the rocker arms and hydraulic tappets from their bores and store them with the valve contact surface facing downwards, to prevent the oil from draining out. It is recommended that the tappets are kept immersed in oil for the period they are removed from the cylinder head. Make a note of the position of each tappet and rocker arm, as they must be fitted to the same valves on reassembly – accelerated wear leading to early failure will result if they are interchanged.

Inspection

9 Visually inspect each camshaft for evidence of wear on the surfaces of the lobes and journals. Normally their surfaces should be smooth and have a dull shine; look for scoring, erosion or pitting and areas that appear highly polished, indicating excessive wear. Accelerated wear will occur once the hardened exterior of the camshaft has been damaged, so always renew worn items. **Note:** *If these symptoms are visible on the tips of the camshaft lobes, check the corresponding tappet, as it will probably be worn as well.*

10 If the machined surfaces of the camshaft appear discoloured or blued, it is likely that it has been overheated at some point, probably due to inadequate lubrication. This may have distorted the shaft, so have it checked by an VW dealer or engine reconditioning specialist.

11.3 Lock the tensioner in place using a 5 mm bolt and locknut

11 To measure the camshaft endfloat, temporarily refit the relevant camshaft to the cylinder head, then fit the bearing ladder, and tighten the retaining nuts to the specified first stage torque setting. Anchor a DTI gauge to the timing belt end of the cylinder head and align the gauge probe with the camshaft axis. Push the camshaft to one end of the cylinder head as far as it will travel, then rest the DTI gauge probe on the end of the camshaft, and zero the gauge display. Push the camshaft as far as it will go to the other end of the cylinder head, and record the gauge reading. Verify the reading by pushing the camshaft back to its original position and checking that the gauge indicates zero again. Repeat the check on the remaining camshaft. **Note:** *The hydraulic tappets must not be fitted whilst this measurement is being taken.*

12 Check that the camshaft endfloat measurement is within the limit listed in the Specifications. Wear outside of this limit is unlikely to be confined to any one component, so renewal of the camshaft, cylinder head and bearing ladder must be considered.

Refitting

13 Smear some clean engine oil onto the sides of the hydraulic tappets/rocker arms, and fit them into position in their bores in the cylinder head. Push them down until they contact the valves, then lubricate the camshaft lobe contact surfaces **(see illustration)**.

11.4 Paint alignment marks as shown to ensure correct refitting

14 Refit the chain onto the camshaft sprockets, aligning the previously-made marks, and position the tensioner in the chain. Ensure the cylinder head bolt cut-outs in the camshafts face each other **(see illustration)**. Note that the side surfaces of the cut-outs should be exactly vertical.

15 Lubricate the running surfaces of the cylinder head and camshafts with clean engine oil, then lay the camshafts in position in the cylinder head.

16 Apply a 2.0 mm wide bead of sealant (available from VW dealers/parts specialists) to the grooves on the underside of the bearing ladder. As the sealant starts to harden immediately, no time should be allowed to elapse before fitting the bearing ladder.

17 Refit the bearing ladder to the cylinder head, then fit the new bolts and working from the inside-out tighten the bolts in several stages until the bearing ladder make contact the with cylinder head over the complete area of the mating surface. Now tighten the bolts to the specified torque.

18 Fit VW special tool T10252 over the camshafts to check the alignment. It may be necessary to rotate the camshafts slightly to fit the tool. In the absence of the tool, have an assistant hold the exhaust camshaft stationary, and rotate the intake camshaft so the chain free play is equal on the top and lower run of the chain. The sides of the cut-outs in the camshafts must be vertical.

19 Fit new camshaft seal(s) as described in Section 8.

20 Refit the camshaft sprocket with reference to Section 5.

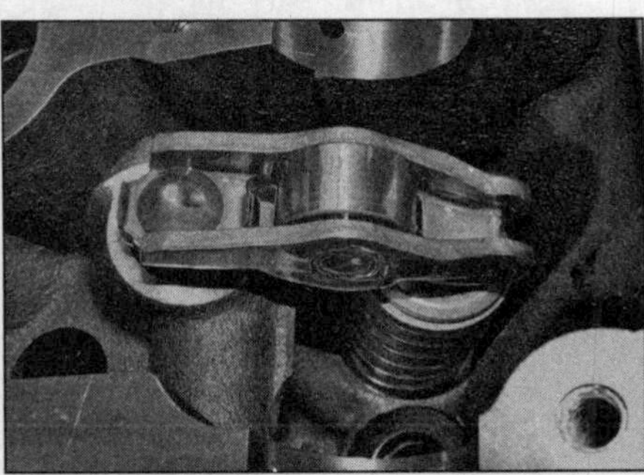

11.13 Refit the hydraulic tappets and rockers

11.14 The cut-outs in the camshafts must face inwards

11.22 Refit the camshaft adjuster rear cover together with a new gasket

21 Remove the VW tool (where applicable), then apply a little thread-locking compound and tighten the tensioner retaining bolts. Remove the bolt used to lock the tensioner.

22 Refit the camshaft adjuster rear cover with a new gasket, then apply a little thread-locking compound and tighten the retaining bolts to the specified torque **(see illustration)**.

23 Refit the camshaft cover (Section 7).

24 Refit the high-pressure fuel pump and the inlet manifold as described in Chapter 4A.

12 Hydraulic tappets – operational check

Warning: After fitting hydraulic tappets, wait a minimum of 30 minutes (or preferably, leave

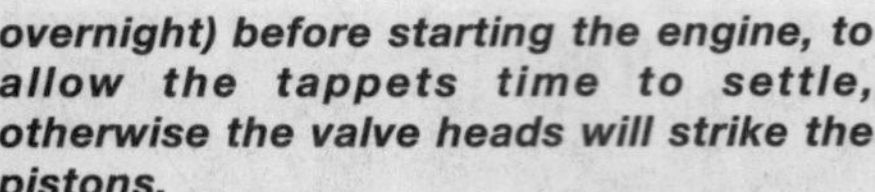

overnight) before starting the engine, to allow the tappets time to settle, otherwise the valve heads will strike the pistons.

1 The hydraulic tappets are self-adjusting, and require no attention whilst in service.

2 If the hydraulic tappets become excessively noisy, their operation can be checked as described below.

3 Run the engine until it reaches its normal operating temperature. Switch off the engine, then refer to Section 7 and remove the camshaft cover.

4 Rotate the camshaft by turning the crankshaft with a socket and wrench, until the first cam lobe over No 1 cylinder is pointing upwards.

5 Using a non-metallic tool, press the tappet downwards then use a feeler blade to check the free travel. If this is more than 0.2 mm before the valve starts to open, the tappet should be renewed.

6 Hydraulic tappet removal and refitting is described as part of the cylinder head overhaul sequence – see Chapter 2G for details.

7 If hydraulic tappet noise occurs repeatedly when travelling short distances, renew the oil retention valve located in the rear of the oil filter mounting housing. It will be necessary to remove the oil filter, then unbolt the housing from the cylinder block and recover the gasket. Use a suitable key to unscrew the valve, and tighten the new valve securely. Refit the housing together with a new gasket.

13 Flywheel/driveplate – removal, inspection and refitting

Removal

1 On manual gearbox models, remove the gearbox (see Chapter 7A) and clutch (Chapter 6).

2 On automatic transmission models, remove the automatic transmission as described in Chapter 7B.

Manual transmission

3 These models are fitted with a dual-mass flywheel. Begin by making alignment marks between the flywheel and the crankshaft.

4 Rotate the outside of the dual-mass flywheel so that the bolts align with the holes **(see illustration)**.

5 Unscrew the bolts and remove the flywheel. Use a locking tool to counterhold the flywheel **(see illustration)**. Discard the bolts, new ones must be fitted. **Note:** *In order not to damage the flywheel, do not use a pneumatic or impact driver to unscrew the bolts ñ only use hand tools.*

Automatic transmission

6 Make alignment marks between the driveplate and crankshaft.

7 Unscrew the bolts and remove the driveplate. Use a locking tool to counterhold the driveplate. Discard the bolts, new ones must be fitted.

8 Remove the shim from behind the driveplate.

Inspection

9 Check the flywheel/driveplate for wear and damage. Examine the starter ring gear for excessive wear to the teeth; if evident, the flywheel/driveplate must be renewed complete as the ring gear is not supplied separately. If the clutch contact surface is worn excessively, it may be possible to have it reground by a specialist.

10 The following are *guidelines* only, but should indicate whether professional inspection is necessary. There should be no cracks in the drive surface of the flywheel. If cracks are evident, the flywheel may need renewing.The dual-mass flywheel should be checked as follows.

Warpage: Place a straight-edge across the face of the drive surface, and check by trying to insert a feeler gauge between the straight-edge and the drive surface **(see illustration)**. The flywheel will normally warp like a bowl – ie, higher on the outer edge. If the warpage is more than 0.40 mm, the flywheel may need renewing.

Free rotational movement: This is the distance the drive surface of the flywheel can be turned independently of the flywheel primary element, using finger effort alone. Move the drive surface in one direction and make a mark where the locating pin aligns with the flywheel edge. Move the drive surface in the other direction (finger pressure only) and make another mark **(see illustration)**.

13.4 Align the bolts with the holes

13.5 Using a locking tool to hold the flywheel

13.10a Check the dual mass flywheel for warpage

13.10b Check the free rotational movement of the dual mass flywheel

The total of free movement should not exceed 10.0 mm. If it's more, the flywheel may need renewing.

Total rotational movement: This is the total distance the drive surface can be turned independently of the flywheel primary element. Insert two bolts into the clutch pressure plate/ damper unit mounting holes, and with the crankshaft/flywheel held stationary, use a lever/ pry bar between the bolts and use some effort to move the drive surface fully in one direction – make a mark where the locating pin aligns with the flywheel edge. Now force the drive surface fully in the opposite direction, and make another mark. The total rotational movement should not exceed 44.00 mm. If it does, have the flywheel professionally inspected.

Lateral movement: The lateral movement (up and down) of the drive surface in relation to the primary element of the flywheel, should not exceed 2.0 mm. If it does, the flywheel may need renewing. This can be checked by pressing the drive surface down on one side into the flywheel (flywheel horizontal) and making an alignment mark between the drive surface and the inner edge of the primary element. Now press down on the opposite side of the drive surface, and make another mark above the original one. The difference between the two marks is the lateral movement **(see illustration)**.

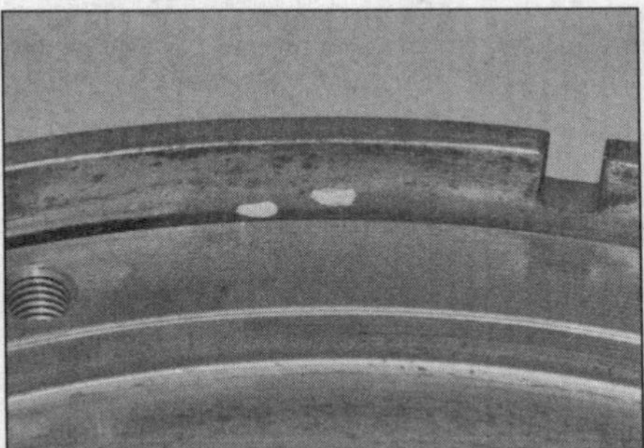

13.10c Check the lateral movement of the dual mass flywheel

Refitting

11 Refitting is a reversal of removal, but use new bolts and tighten them to the specified torque.

14 Sump – removal and refitting

Note: *VW insist that on engine codes AXW, BLX, BLY, and BLR, the intermediate plate between the oil pump/balancer shaft housing and the engine block must be renewed when the sump is removed. Oil pump/balancer shaft renewal is described in Section 15.*

Removal

1 Apply the handbrake, then jack up the front of the vehicle and support it on axle stands (see *Jacking and vehicle support*).

2 Release the fasteners, remove the engine undertray, then undo the bolts and detach the undertray bracket.

3 Position a container beneath the sump, then unscrew the drain plug and drain the engine oil. Clean the plug and if necessary renew the washer, then refit and tighten the plug after all the oil has drained. Remove the dipstick from the engine.

4 Remove the auxiliary drivebelt as described in Chapter 1A.

5 Disconnect the oil temperature sensor wiring plug from the base of the sump.

6 Undo the bolt and detach the refrigerant support pipe from the sump.

7 Disconnect the wiring plug, then undo the bolts and position the air conditioning compressor to one side (where applicable). Support the compressor by suspending it from the vehicle body with wire/string – there is no need to disconnect the refrigerant pipes, but ensure they are not damaged or kinked during the process.

8 Unbolt the stop bracket/torque arm bracket from the front of the engine.

9 On vehicles with gas discharge headlights, unclip the vehicle height sensor actuator rod from the front-left lower transverse link arm.

10 Undo the bolts and detach the inboard clamps from the front-anti roll bar.

11 Detach the starter motor cables from under the engine mounting by cutting the plastic cable ties and easing them from the plastic ducting.

12 Unscrew and remove the nuts from the bottom of each engine mounting.

13 Remove the engine top cover, then release the clips and remove the intake ducting form the air cleaner to the throttle body.

14 Connect a suitable hoist to the engine, then raise it as far as possible without damaging or stretching the coolant hoses and wiring.

15 Mark the fitted position of the subframe, then position a workshop trolley jack to take the weight, then undo the bolts and lower the front subframe.

16 Gradually unscrew and remove the sump bolts working in a diagonal pattern. Note that on manual transmission models, the two rear sump bolts are accessed through a cut-out in the flywheel – turn the flywheel as necessary to align the cut-out **(see illustration)**.

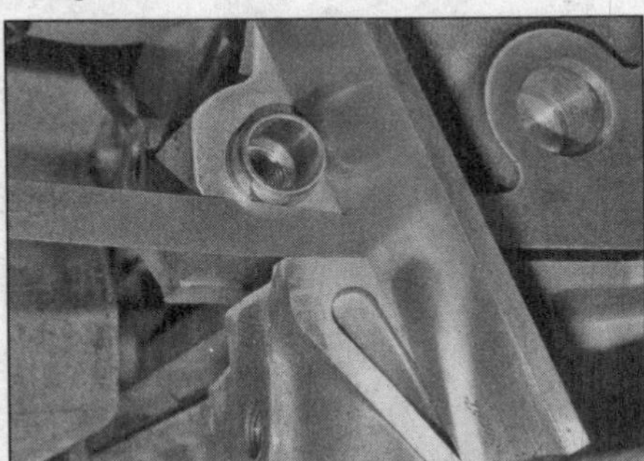

14.19 Position the sump in relation to the cylinder block

14.16 Rear sump bolts

17 Remove the sump. If it is stuck, tap it gently with a mallet to free it.

Refitting

18 Thoroughly clean the contact faces of the sump. It is recommended that a rotary wire brush is used to clean away the sealant.

19 Refit the sump and tighten the retaining bolts hand-tight initially. If the engine is out of the car, make sure that the rear edge of the sump overhangs the rear edge of the cylinder block by 0.8 mm, so that it is flush when the adapter plate is fitted **(see illustration)**. Progressively tighten the sump bolts in a diagonal pattern to the specified torque. It is advisable to wait at least 30 minutes for the intermediate plate sealant to set before filling the engine with oil.

20 The remaining refitting procedure is a reversal removal, but tighten the nuts and bolts to the specified torque where given in the Specifications. On completion, fill the engine with the correct quantity of oil as described in Chapter 1A.

15 Oil pump and balancer shaft housing – removal, inspection and refitting

Removal

1 Set the engine to TDC on No 1 cylinder as described in Section 2.

2 Remove the sump as described in Section 14.

3 Undo the 2 bolts securing the oil pipe at the rear of the engine block **(see illustration)**.

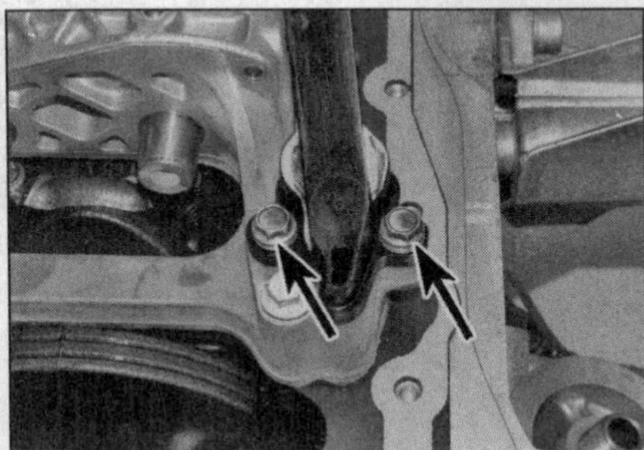

15.3 Oil pipe on the rear of the block

15.4a Depress the tabs...

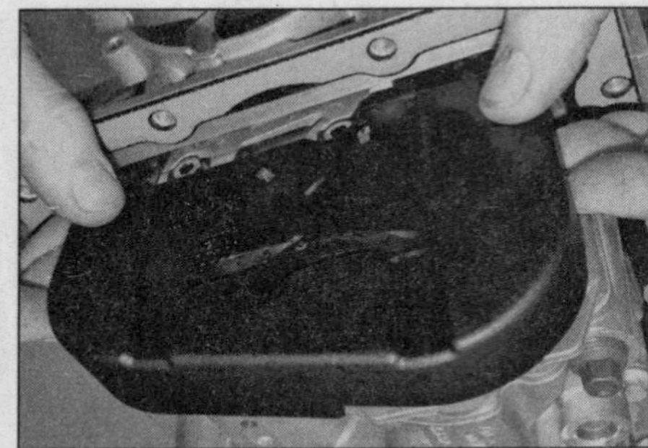

15.4b ...and remove the chain/sprocket cover

15.5 Loosen the oil pump drive sprocket retaining bolt

15.6 Lock the drive chain tensioner with a drill bit

15.9 Unbolt the drive chain tensioner

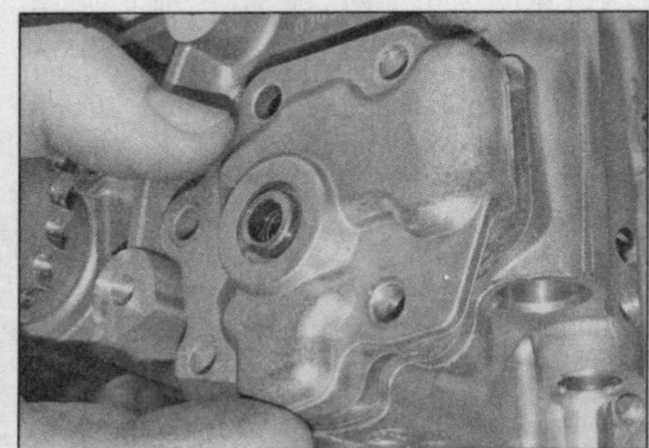

15.10 Remove the cover from the oil pump

4 Using a small screwdriver, depress the tabs to release the retaining clips, and remove the chain/sprocket cover horizontally **(see illustrations)**.

5 Use a Torx bit to slacken the oil pump drive sprocket retaining bolt approximately 1 turn **(see illustration)**.

6 Using a screwdriver, push the drive chain tensioner blade to relieve the tension on the chain. Insert a 3 mm drill bit into the hole in the tensioner assembly to lock the blade in this position **(see illustration)**

7 Remove the Torx bolt and pull the sprocket from the oil pump shaft. Disengage the sprockets from the chain.

8 Working from the outside-in, gradually and evenly slacken and remove the bolts securing the balance shaft housing and intermediate plate. Note the fitted positions of the bolts – some are longer than others. Remove the balancer shaft housing and plate from the engine block, noting that the housing locates on dowels. Discard the retaining bolts, new ones must be fitted. VW insist that the intermediate plate is renewed.

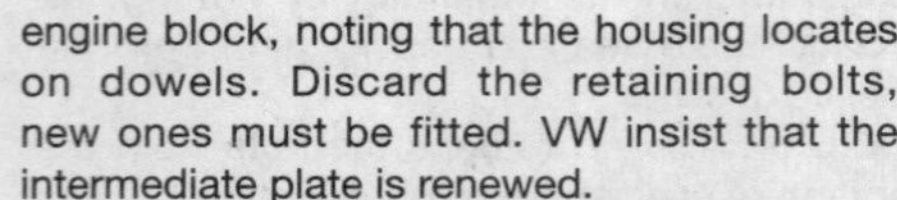

9 Undo the retaining bolts and remove the drive chain tensioner from the balance shaft housing **(see illustration)**.

10 If required, undo the 5 bolts and remove the oil pump cover. Pull the inner and outer rotors from the pump **(see illustration)**

Inspection

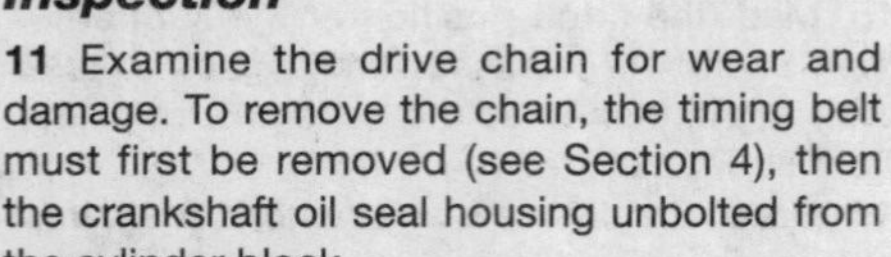

11 Examine the drive chain for wear and damage. To remove the chain, the timing belt must first be removed (see Section 4), then the crankshaft oil seal housing unbolted from the cylinder block.

12 It is not advisable to dismantle the balancer shafts and housing. No separate parts are available. If faulty, the complete assembly must be renewed.

13 If the oil pump has been dismantled, clean the components and check them for wear and damage. Examine the inner and outer rotors for scoring or any signs of wear/damage. If evident, renew the oil pump.

14 If the oil pump components are re-usable, fit the outer, and inner rotors to the pump body, with the marks on the ends of the inner rotor facing inwards and the one on the outer rotor facing outwards **(see illustrations)**. Refit the pump cover and tighten the retaining bolts to the specified torque.

Refitting

15 Prime the pump with oil by pouring oil into the suction pipe aperture while turning the driveshaft.

16 Refit the chain tensioner assembly to the balancer shaft housing, and tighten the retaining bolts to the specified torque. Ensure the tensioner blade is in the locked position, as described in paragraph 6.

17 Apply a bead of suitable sealant, approximately 2.0 mm thick, to the cylinder block side of the intermediate plate **(see illustration)**. Take great care not to apply the sealant too thickly, as any excess may find its way in the oil galleries.

18 Position the intermediate plate over the locating dowels on the cylinder block sealing surface. Feed the drive chain through the intermediate plate.

19 Position the balancer shaft housing on the base of the cylinder block/intermediate plate, then insert the new bolts (ensure the new O-ring is fitted to the appropriate bolt). Working from the inside tighten the new bolts

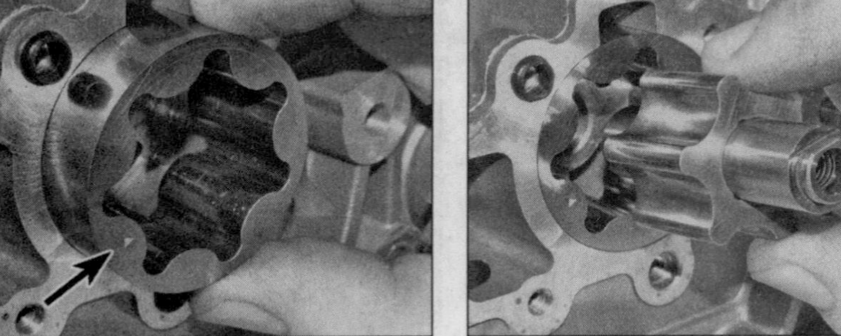

15.14a Outer rotor alignment mark

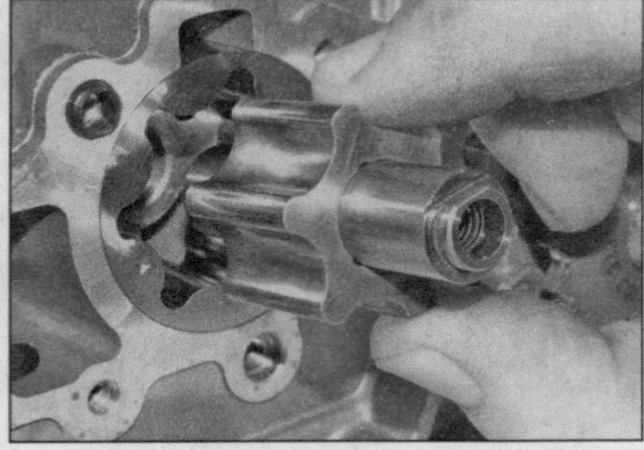

15.14b Remove the inner rotor

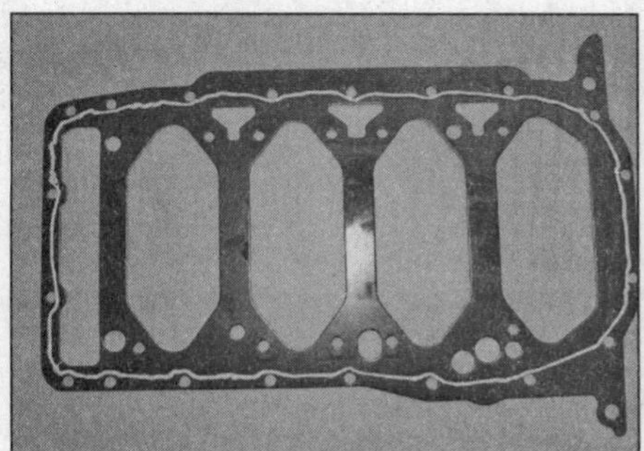
15.17 Apply sealant to the intermediate plate as shown

15.20 Lock the balancer shaft sprocket in its TDC position

15.21 Oil pump sprocket locating flat

to the Stage one torque setting, then in the same order, tighten them to the Stage two setting. Ensure the correct length bolt is fitted to the correct positions.

20 Ensure the crankshaft pulley is still in the TDC, then rotate the balancer shaft sprocket until the mark on the sprocket face is aligned with the locating hole, Insert an 5.0 mm drill bit into the hole to lock the sprocket in this position **(see illustration)**.

21 Engage the drive chain with the balancer shaft sprocket, then fit the oil pump sprocket into the chain. Fit the sprocket on to the oil pump shaft, noting that the sprocket will only fit in one position – if necessary, rotate the oil pump shaft to enable the fitment of the sprocket **(see illustration)**. Fit the new sprocket retaining bolt and tighten it to the specified torque.

22 Remove the balancer shaft sprocket locking tool (drill bit), and the Allen key locking the tensioner blade.

23 Refit the cover over the drive sprockets, and secure it with the retaining clips.

24 On non-turbocharged models, refit the oil pipe to the housing, and tighten the bolts securely.

25 Refit the sump with reference to Section 14.

16 Engine mountings – inspection and renewal

Inspection

1 If improved access is required, jack up the front of the vehicle, and support it securely on axle stands (see *Jacking and vehicle support*). Remove the engine top cover which also incorporates the air filter, then remove the engine undertray(s).

2 Check the mounting rubbers to see if they are cracked, hardened or separated from the metal at any point; renew the mounting if any such damage or deterioration is evident.

3 Check that all the mountings are securely tightened; use a torque wrench to check if possible.

4 Using a large screwdriver or a crowbar, check for wear in the mounting by carefully levering against it to check for free play. Where this is not possible, enlist the aid of an assistant to move the engine/transmission back-and-forth, or from side-to-side, whilst you observe the mounting. While some free play is to be expected, even from new components, excessive wear should be obvious. If excessive free play is found, check first that the fasteners are correctly secured, then renew any worn components as described in the following paragraphs.

Renewal

Right-hand mounting

5 Attach a hoist and lifting tackle to the engine lifting brackets on the cylinder head, and raise the hoist to just take the weight of the engine. Alternatively the engine can be supported on a trolley jack under the engine. Use a block of wood between the sump and the head of the jack, to prevent any damage to the sump.

6 For improved access, unbolt the coolant reservoir and move it to one side, leaving the coolant hoses connected.

7 Where applicable, move any wiring harnesses, pipes or hoses to one side to enable removal of the engine mounting.

8 Unscrew the bolts securing the mounting to the engine, then unscrew the bolts securing it to the body. Also, unbolt the movement limiter. Withdraw the mounting from the engine compartment.

9 Refitting is a reversal of removal, bearing in mind the following points.

a) Use new securing bolts.
b) Tighten all fixings to the specified torque.

Left-hand mounting

Note: *New mounting bolts will be required on refitting (there is no need to renew the smaller mounting-to-body bolts).*

10 Remove the engine top cover which also incorporates the air filter.

11 Attach a hoist and lifting tackle to the engine lifting brackets on the cylinder head, and raise the hoist to just take the weight of the engine and transmission. Alternatively the engine can be supported on a trolley jack under the transmission. Use a block of wood between the transmission and the head of the jack, to prevent any damage to the transmission.

12 Remove the battery, as described in Chapter 5A, then disconnect the main starter motor feed cable from the positive battery terminal box.

13 Release any relevant wiring or hoses from the clips on the battery tray, then unscrew the four securing bolts and remove the battery tray.

14 Unscrew the bolts securing the mounting to the transmission, and the remaining bolts securing the mounting to the body, then lift the mounting from the engine compartment.

15 Refitting is a reversal of removal, bearing in mind the following points:

a) Use new mounting bolts.
b) Tighten all fixings to the specified torque.

Rear mounting (torque arm)

16 Apply the handbrake, then jack up the front of the vehicle and support securely on axle stands (see *Jacking and vehicle support*). Remove the engine undertray(s) for access to the rear mounting (torque arm).

17 Support the rear of the transmission beneath the final drive housing. To do this, use a trolley jack and block of wood, or alternatively wedge a block of wood between the transmission and the subframe.

18 Working under the vehicle, unscrew and remove the bolt securing the mounting to the subframe.

19 Unscrew the two bolts securing the mounting to the transmission, then withdraw the mounting from under the vehicle.

20 Refitting is a reversal of removal, but use new mounting securing bolts, and tighten all fixings to the specified torque.

Chapter 2 Part E:
Diesel engine in-car repair procedures – PD unit injector engines

Contents

Degrees of difficulty

Easy, suitable for novice with little experience

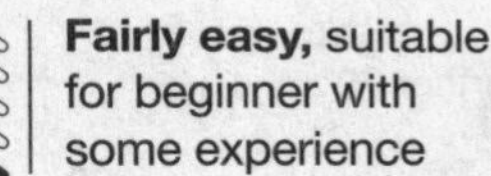

Fairly easy, suitable for beginner with some experience

Fairly difficult, suitable for competent DIY mechanic

Difficult, suitable for experienced DIY mechanic

Very difficult, suitable for expert DIY or professional

Specifications

General

Manufacturer's engine codes*:		
1896 cc (1.9 litre), 8-valve, turbo, SOHC	BJB, BKC, BRU, BLS, BXE and BXF	
1968 cc (2.0 litre), 8-valve, non-turbo, SOHC	BDK	
1968 cc (2.0 litre), 8-valve, turbo, SOHC	BMM	
1968 cc (2.0 litre), 16-valve, turbo, DOHC	AZV, BKD and BMN	
Maximum outputs:	**Power**	**Torque**
Engine code BJB	77 kW at 4000 rpm	250 Nm at 1900 rpm
Engine code BKC	77 kW at 4000 rpm	250 Nm at 1900 rpm
Engine code BRU	66 kW at 4000 rpm	210 Nm at 1800 to 2500 rpm
Engine code BLS	77 kW at 4000 rpm	250 Nm at 1900 rpm
Engine code BXE	77 kW at 4000 rpm	250 Nm at 1900 rpm
Engine code BXF	66 kW at 4000 rpm	210 Nm at 1800 rpm
Engine code AZV	100 kW at 4000 rpm	320 Nm at 1750 rpm
Engine code BKD	103 kW at 4000 rpm	320 Nm at 1750 rpm
Engine code BDK	55 kW at 4200 rpm	140 Nm at 2200 to 2400 rpm
Engine code BMM	103 kW at 4000 rpm	320 Nm at 1750 to 2500 rpm
Engine code BMN	125 kW at 4200 rpm	350 Nm at 1800 rpm
Bore:		
1896 cc engines	79.5 mm	
1968 cc engines	81.0 mm	
Stroke	95.5 mm	
Compression ratio:		
Engine code BJB, BKC, BRU, BXF, BDK, BMM	19.0 : 1	
Engine code BLS, BXE, AZV, BKD, BMN	18.5 : 1	
Compression pressures:		
Minimum compression pressure	Approximately 19.0 bar	
Maximum difference between cylinders	Approximately 5.0 bar	
Firing order	1 – 3 – 4 – 2	
No 1 cylinder location	Timing belt end	

* **Note:** *See 'Vehicle identification' at the end of this manual for the location of engine code markings.*

Camshaft

Camshaft endfloat (maximum)	0.15 mm
Camshaft bearing running clearance (maximum)	0.11 mm
Camshaft run-out (maximum)	0.01 mm

Lubrication system

Oil pump type	Gear type, chain-driven from crankshaft
Oil pressure (oil temperature 80°C, at 2000 rpm)	2.0 bar

Torque wrench settings

	Nm	lbf ft
Ancillary (alternator, etc) bracket mounting bolts	45	33
Air conditioning compressor	45	33
Alternator and tensioner	25	18
Auxiliary drivebelt tensioner securing bolt	25	18
Big-end bearing caps bolts*:		
Stage 1	30	22
Stage 2	Angle-tighten a further 90°	
Camshaft bearing cap bolts*:		
SOHC engines:		
Stage 1	8	6
Stage 2	Angle-tighten a further 90°	
Camshaft bearing frame bolts*:		
DOHC engines	20	15
Camshaft cover nuts/bolts	10	7
Camshaft sprocket hub centre bolt	100	74
Camshaft sprocket-to-hub bolts	25	18
Coolant pump bolts	15	11
Crankshaft oil seal housing bolts	15	11
Crankshaft pulley-to-sprocket bolts:		
Stage 1	10	7
Stage 2	Angle-tighten a further 90°	
Crankshaft sprocket bolt*:		
Stage 1	120	89
Stage 2	Angle-tighten a further 90°	
Cylinder head bolts*:		
Stage 1	35	26
Stage 2	60	44
Stage 3	Angle-tighten a further 90°	
Stage 4	Angle-tighten a further 90°	
Driveplate:		
Stage 1	60	44
Stage 2	Angle-tighten a further 90°	
Engine mountings:		
RH engine mounting:		
Limiter:		
Stage 1	20	15
Stage 2	Angle-tighten a further 90°	
Mounting to engine:		
Stage 1	60	44
Stage 2	Angle-tighten a further 90°	
Mounting to body:		
Stage 1	40	30
Stage 2	Angle-tighten a further 90°	
LH engine mounting:		
Mounting to body:		
Stage 1	60	44
Stage 2	Angle-tighten a further 90°	
Mounting to transmission:		
Stage 1	40	30
Stage 2	Angle-tighten a further 90°	
Rear mounting link:		
To transmission:		
Stage 1	40	30
Stage 2	Angle-tighten a further 90°	
To subframe:		
Stage 1	100	74
Stage 2	Angle-tighten a further 90°	

Torque wrench settings (continued)	Nm	lbf ft
Flywheel:		
Stage 1	60	44
Stage 2	Angle-tighten a further 90°	
Glow plugs:		
SOHC engines	15	11
DOHC engines	10	7
Injector rocker arm shafts*:		
Stage 1	20	15
Stage 2	Angle-tighten a further 90°	
Main bearing cap bolts*:		
Stage 1	65	48
Stage 2	Angle-tighten a further 90°	
Oil drain plug	30	22
Oil filter housing-to-cylinder block bolts*:		
Stage 1	15	11
Stage 2	Angle-tighten a further 90°	
Oil filter cover	25	18
Oil level/temperature sensor-to-sump bolts	10	7
Oil pick-up pipe securing bolts	15	11
Oil pressure relief valve plug	40	30
Oil pressure warning light switch	20	15
Oil pump chain tensioner bolt	15	11
Oil pump securing bolts	15	11
Oil pump sprocket securing bolt:		
Stage 1	20	15
Stage 2	Angle-tighten a further 90°	
Piston oil spray jet bolt	25	18
Sump:		
Sump-to-cylinder block bolts	15	11
Sump-to-transmission bolts	45	33
Tandem pump	20	15
Thermostat housing	15	11
Timing belt idler pulley bolt	20	15
Timing belt outer cover bolts	10	7
Timing belt rear cover-to-cylinder head bolt	10	7
Timing belt tensioner roller securing nut:		
Stage 1	20	15
Stage 2	Angle-tighten a further 45°	
Timing belt idler pulleys:		
Lower right-hand idler roller (below coolant pump sprocket) bolt*:		
Stage 1	40	30
Stage 2	Angle-tighten a further 90°	
Upper idler roller bolt	20	15
Turbocharger/exhaust manifold	20	15
Turbocharger oil supply line union nut	22	16

**Do not re-use*

1 General information

How to use this Chapter

This Part of Chapter 2 describes those repair procedures that can reasonably be carried out on the engine while it remains in the vehicle. If the engine has been removed from the vehicle and is being dismantled as described in Part G, any preliminary dismantling procedures can be ignored.

Note that while it may be possible physically to overhaul certain items while the engine is in the vehicle, such tasks are not usually carried out as separate operations, and usually require the execution of several additional procedures (not to mention the cleaning of components and of oilways); for this reason, all such tasks are classed as major overhaul procedures, and are described in Part G of this Chapter.

Engine description

Throughout this Chapter, engines are referred to by type, and are identified and referred to by the manufacturer's code letters. A listing of all engines covered, together with their code letters, is given in the Specifications at the start of this Chapter.

The engines are water-cooled, single (1896 cc) or double (1968 cc) overhead camshaft(s), in-line four-cylinder units, with cast-iron cylinder blocks and aluminium-alloy cylinder heads. All are mounted transversely at the front of the vehicle, with the transmission bolted to the left-hand end of the engine.

The crankshaft is of five-bearing type, and thrustwashers are fitted to the centre main bearing to control crankshaft endfloat.

Drive for the single (1896 cc) or double (1968 cc) camshafts is by a toothed timing belt from the crankshaft. Each camshaft is mounted at the top of the cylinder head, and is secured by bearing caps (1896 cc) or a bearing frame/ladder (1968 cc).

The valves are closed by coil springs, and run in guides pressed into the cylinder head. On 1896cc engines, the camshaft actuates the valves directly, through hydraulic tappets; on 1968 cc engines, the valves are operated by roller rocker arms incorporating hydraulic tappets.

The gear-type oil pump is driven by a chain from a sprocket on the crankshaft. Oil is drawn from the sump through a strainer,

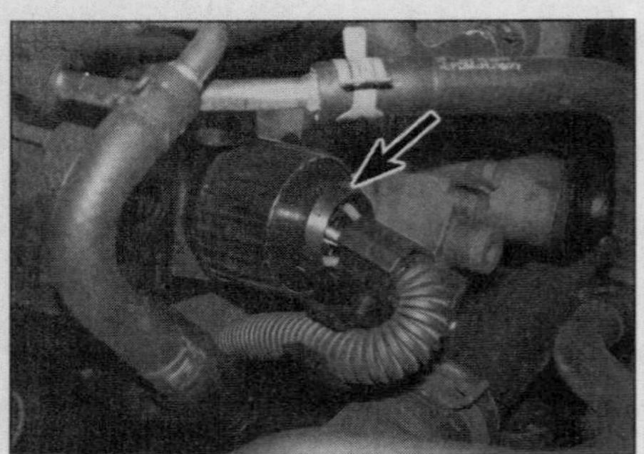

2.3 Disconnect the injector solenoids wiring plug connector (arrowed)

and then forced through an externally-mounted, renewable filter. From there, it is distributed to the cylinder head, where it lubricates the camshaft journals and hydraulic tappets, and also to the crankcase, where it lubricates the main bearings, connecting rod big-ends, gudgeon pins and cylinder bores. A coolant-fed oil cooler is fitted to the oil filter housing on all engines. Oil jets are fitted to the base of each cylinder – these spray oil onto the underside of the pistons, to improve cooling.

All engines are fitted with a combined brake servo vacuum pump and fuel lift pump (tandem pump), driven by the camshaft on the transmission end of the cylinder head.

On all engines, engine coolant is circulated by a pump, driven by the timing belt. For details of the cooling system, refer to Chapter 3.

Operations with engine in car

The following operations can be performed without removing the engine:

a) Compression pressure – testing.
b) Camshaft cover – removal and refitting.
c) Crankshaft pulley – removal and refitting.
d) Timing belt covers – removal and refitting.
e) Timing belt – removal, refitting and adjustment.
f) Timing belt tensioner and sprockets – removal and refitting.
g) Camshaft oil seals – renewal.
h) Camshaft(s) and hydraulic tappets – removal, inspection and refitting.
i) Cylinder head – removal and refitting.
j) Cylinder head and pistons – decarbonising.
k) Sump – removal and refitting.
l) Oil pump – removal, overhaul and refitting.
m) Crankshaft oil seals – renewal.
n) Engine/transmission mountings – inspection and renewal.
o) Flywheel/driveplate – removal, inspection and refitting.

Note: *It is possible to remove the pistons and connecting rods (after removing the cylinder head and sump) without removing the engine. However, this is not recommended. Work of this nature is more easily and thoroughly completed with the engine on the bench, as described in Chapter 2G.*

2 Compression and leakdown tests – description and interpretation

Compression test

Note: *A compression tester suitable for use with diesel engines will be required for this test.*

1 When engine performance is down, or if misfiring occurs which cannot be attributed to the ignition or fuel systems, a compression test can provide diagnostic clues as to the engine's condition. If the test is performed regularly, it can give warning of trouble before any other symptoms become apparent.

2 The engine must be fully warmed-up to normal operating temperature, the battery must be fully-charged, and you will require the aid of an assistant.

3 Disconnect the injector solenoids by disconnecting the connector at the end of the cylinder head **(see illustration)**. **Note:** *As a result of the wiring being disconnected, faults may be stored in the ECU memory. These must be erased after the compression test.*

4 Remove the glow plugs as described in Chapter 5C, then fit a compression tester to the No 1 cylinder glow plug hole. The type of tester which screws into the plug thread is preferred.

5 Have your assistant crank the engine for several seconds on the starter motor. After one or two revolutions, the compression pressure should build-up to a maximum figure and then stabilise. Record the highest reading obtained.

6 Repeat the test on the remaining cylinders, recording the pressure in each.

7 The cause of poor compression is less easy to establish on a diesel engine than on a petrol engine. The effect of introducing oil into the cylinders (wet testing) is not conclusive, because there is a risk that the oil will sit in the recess on the piston crown, instead of passing to the rings. However, the following can be used as a rough guide to diagnosis.

8 All cylinders should produce very similar pressures. Any difference greater than that specified indicates the existence of a fault. Note that the compression should build-up quickly in a healthy engine. Low compression on the first stroke, followed by gradually increasing pressure on successive strokes, indicates worn piston rings. A low compression reading on the first stroke, which does not build-up during successive strokes, indicates leaking valves or a blown head gasket (a cracked head could also be the cause).

9 A low reading from two adjacent cylinders is almost certainly due to the head gasket having blown between them and the presence of coolant in the engine oil will confirm this.

10 On completion, remove the compression tester, and refit the glow plugs, with reference to Chapter 5C.

11 Reconnect the wiring to the injector solenoids. Finally, have a VW dealer erase any fault codes from the ECU memory.

Leakdown test

12 A leakdown test measures the rate at which compressed air fed into the cylinder is lost. It is an alternative to a compression test, and in many ways it is better, since the escaping air provides easy identification of where pressure loss is occurring (piston rings, valves or head gasket).

13 The equipment required for leakdown testing is unlikely to be available to the home mechanic. If poor compression is suspected, have the test performed by a suitably-equipped garage.

3 Engine assembly and valve timing marks – general information and usage

General information

1 TDC is the highest point in the cylinder that each piston reaches as it travels up-and-down when the crankshaft turns. Each piston reaches TDC at the end of the compression stroke and again at the end of the exhaust stroke, but TDC generally refers to piston position on the compression stroke. No 1 piston is at the timing belt end of the engine.

2 Positioning No 1 piston at TDC is an essential part of many procedures, such as timing belt removal and camshaft removal.

3 The design of the engines covered in this Chapter is such that piston-to-valve contact may occur if the camshaft or crankshaft is turned with the timing belt removed. For this reason, it is important to ensure that the camshaft and crankshaft do not move in relation to each other once the timing belt has been removed from the engine.

Setting TDC on No 1 cylinder

Note: *VAG special tool T10050 (early) or T10100 (late) is required to lock the crankshaft sprocket in the TDC position. The early type tool locates directly onto the sprocket teeth, but, the contour of the teeth on the later type means that the tool must be pushed onto the sprocket teeth from the right-hand end of the engine.*

4 Remove the auxiliary drivebelt(s) as described in Chapter 1B.

5 Remove the crankshaft pulley/vibration damper as described in Section 5.

6 Remove the timing belt covers as described in Section 6.

7 Remove the glow plugs, as described in Chapter 5C, to allow the engine to turn more easily. **Note:** *On DOHC engines the glow plugs are accessed by removing the camshaft cover, so this may not be considered an option.*

8 Using a spanner or socket on the crankshaft sprocket bolt, turn the crankshaft in the normal direction of rotation (clockwise) until the

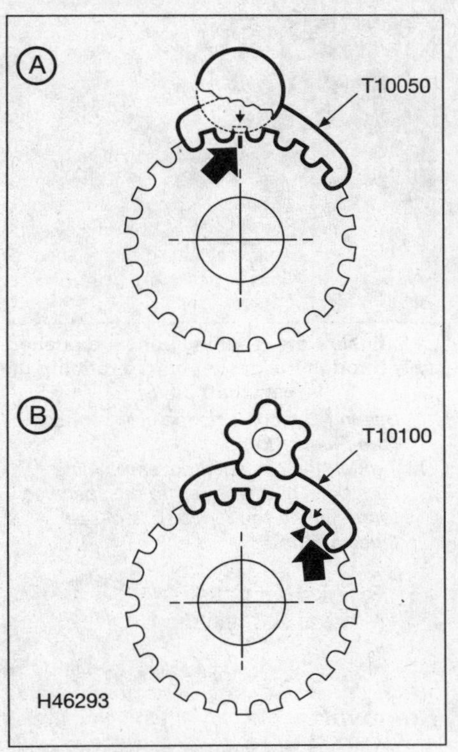

3.8a TDC setting tools

3.8b Position the crankshaft so that the mark on the sprocket is almost vertical (arrowed)...

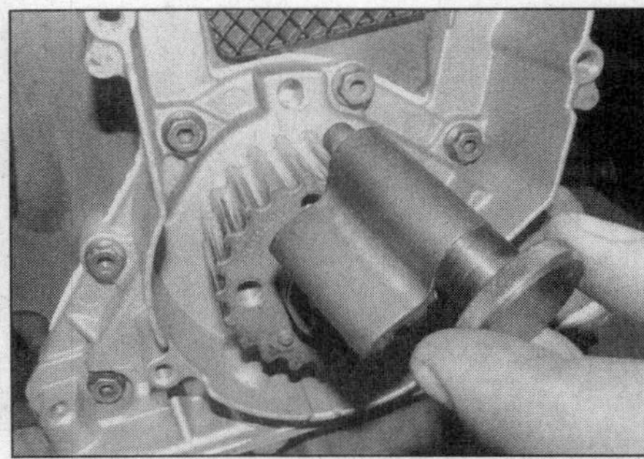
3.8c ...then insert the VW tool T10050...

3.8d ...and align the marks (arrowed) on the tool and sprocket

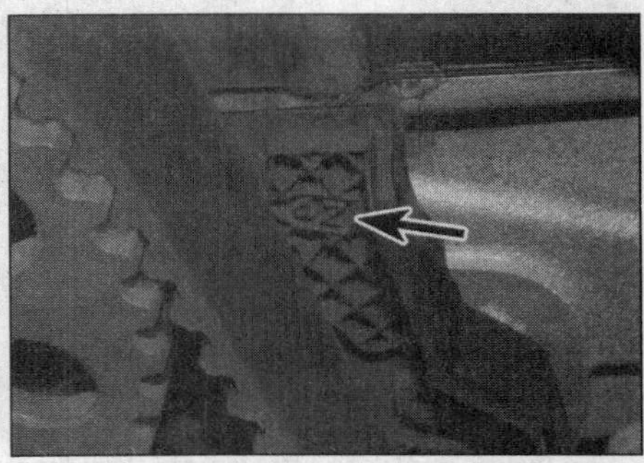
3.9 Align the arrow on the rear of the cover (arrowed) between the lugs on the rear of the camshaft hub sender wheel

alignment mark on the face of the sprocket is almost vertical for tool T10050, or at 2 o'clock for tool T10100 **(see illustrations)**.

9 On engine codes BJB, BKC, BDK, BMM, BRU, BLS, BXE and BXF, the arrow (marked 4Z) on the rear section of the upper timing belt upper cover aligns between the two lugs on the rear of the camshaft hub sender wheel **(see illustration)**.

10 On engine codes AZV, BKD and BMN, the pointer on the rear section of the timing belt inner cover aligns with the camshaft hub sender wheel, and the marks on the camshaft toothed segments and sprockets must be vertical.

11 While in this position it should be possible to insert the VAG tool to lock the crankshaft, and a 6 mm diameter rod to lock the camshaft(s) **(see illustrations)**. **Note:** *The mark on the crankshaft sprocket and the mark on the VAG tool must align, whilst at the same time the shaft of tool must engage in the drilling in the crankshaft oil seal housing.*

12 The engine is now set to TDC on No 1 cylinder.

4 Camshaft cover – removal and refitting

Removal

1 Remove the dipstick and prise off and remove the engine top cover, then disconnect the breather hose from the camshaft cover **(see illustration)**.

2 Unscrew the camshaft cover retaining bolts and lift the cover away. If it sticks, do not attempt to lever it off – instead free it by working around the cover and tapping it lightly with a soft-faced mallet. Note on DOHC engines, it will be necessary to unbolt the air

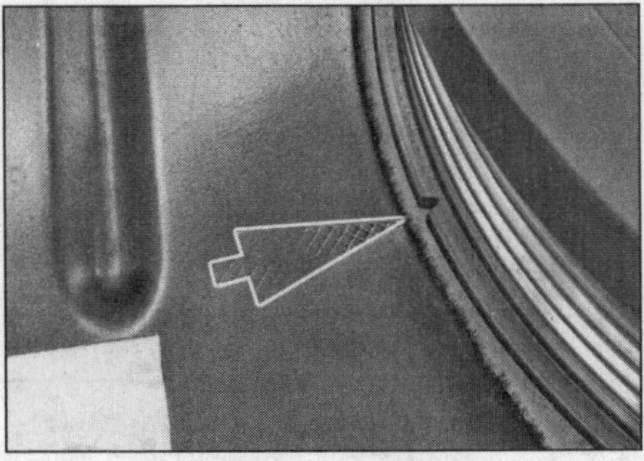
3.10 TDC mark and notch (2.0 litre DOHC engine)

3.11a Using the VAG tool to lock the crankshaft at TDC

3.11b Insert a 6 mm drill bit through the camshaft hub into the cylinder head to lock the camshaft

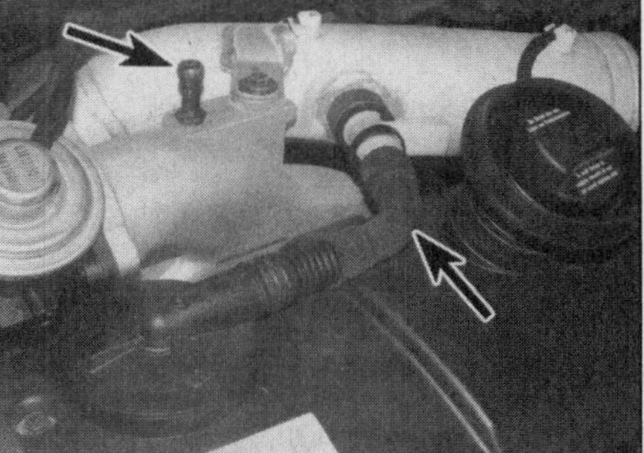
4.1 One of the cover locating pegs (arrowed) and also breather pipe (arrowed)

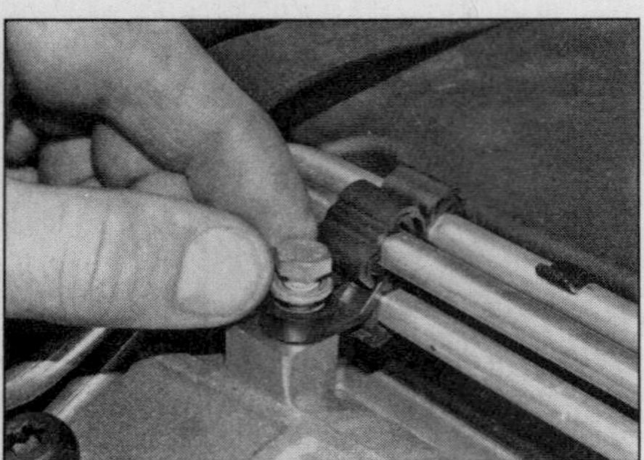

4.2a Unbolt the fuel lines to provide additional clearance...

4.2b ...when removing the camshaft cover on 2.0 litre DOHC engines

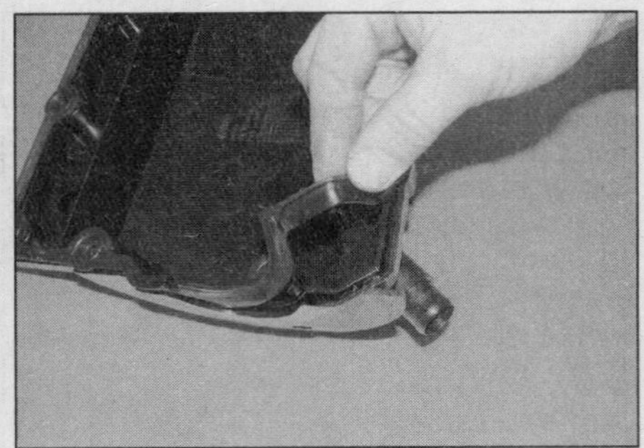

4.3 Ensure the retaining bolts are pushed fully through the gasket before refitting the camshaft cover

4.5a Apply sealant to the points (arrowed) on the cylinder head

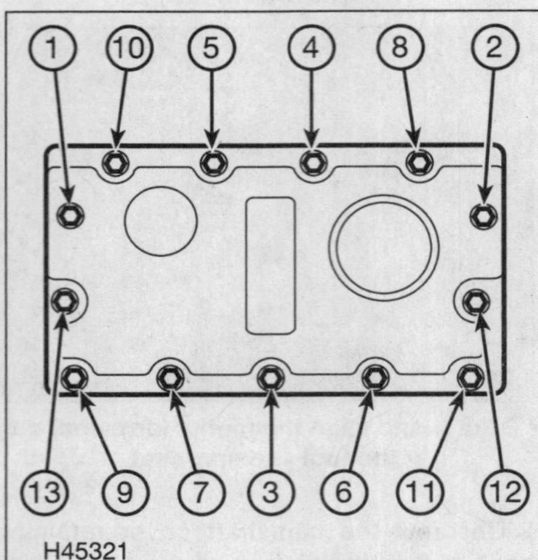

4.5b Camshaft cover tightening sequence (SOHC engines)

ducting from the rear of the cylinder head, and unbolt the fuel lines from the front of the cylinder head to provide additional clearance **(see illustrations)**.

3 Recover the camshaft cover gasket. Inspect the gasket carefully, and renew it if damage or deterioration is evident – note that the retaining bolts must be pushed fully through the gasket *before* refitting the cover **(see illustration)**.

4 Clean the mating surfaces of the cylinder head and camshaft cover thoroughly, removing all traces of oil and old gasket – take care to avoid damaging the surfaces as you do this.

Refitting

5 Refit the camshaft cover by following the removal procedure in reverse, noting the following points:

*a) On engine codes BJB, BKC, BRU, BLS, BXE, BXF, BDK and BMM, apply suitable sealant to the points where the camshaft bearing cap contacts the cylinder head **(see illustration)**.*

*b) Tighten the camshaft cover retaining nuts/bolts progressively to the specified torque in the sequence shown **(see illustrations)**.*

5 Crankshaft pulley – removal and refitting

Removal

1 Switch off the ignition and all electrical consumers and remove the ignition key.

2 For improved access, raise the front right-hand side of the vehicle, and support securely on axle stands (see *Jacking and vehicle support*). Remove the roadwheel.

3 Remove the securing screws and withdraw the engine undertray(s) and/or wheel arch liner panels. On turbo models, unscrew the nut at the rear, and the washer-type fasteners further forward, then release the air hose clip and manipulate out the plastic air duct for the intercooler **(see illustration)**.

4 Where applicable, prise the cover from the centre of the pulley to expose the securing bolts **(see illustration)**.

5 Slacken the bolts securing the crankshaft pulley to the sprocket **(see illustration)**. If necessary, the pulley can be prevented from turning by counterholding with a spanner or socket on the crankshaft sprocket bolt.

6 Remove the auxiliary drivebelt, as described in Chapter 1B.

5.3 Remove the intercooler air duct for access to the crankshaft pulley

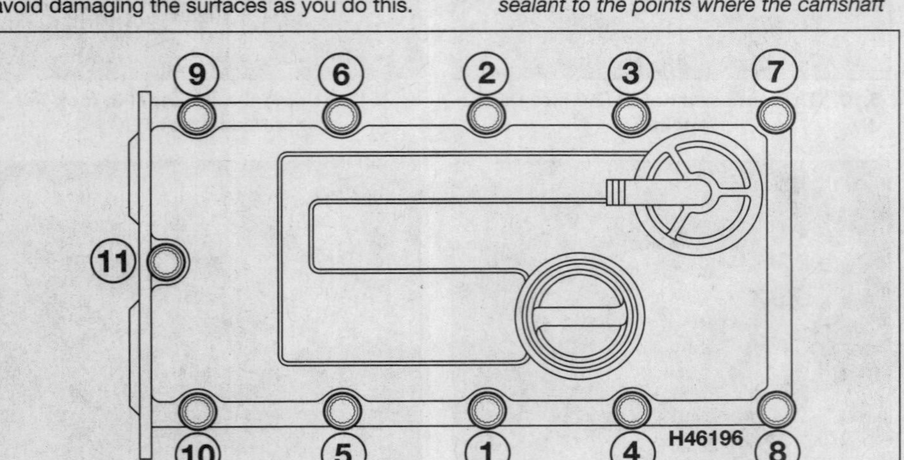

4.5c Camshaft cover tightening sequence (DOHC engine)

7 Unscrew the bolts securing the pulley to the sprocket, and remove the pulley **(see illustration)**.

Refitting

8 Refit the pulley over the locating peg on the crankshaft sprocket, then refit the pulley securing bolts.
9 Refit and tension the auxiliary drivebelt as described in Chapter 1B.
10 Prevent the crankshaft from turning as during removal, then fit the pulley securing bolts, and tighten to the specified torque.
11 Refit the engine undertray(s), wheel arch liners and the intercooler air duct, as applicable.
12 Refit the roadwheel and lower the vehicle to the ground.

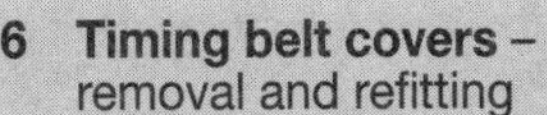

6 Timing belt covers – removal and refitting

Upper outer cover

1 Where applicable, release the retaining clips and remove the air intake hose from across the top of the timing belt cover **(see illustration)**.
2 Release the uppermost part of the timing belt outer cover by prising open the metal spring clips, then withdraw the cover away from the engine. On DOHC engines there are three clips, two at the front and a single one at the rear of the cover **(see illustrations)**.
3 Refitting is a reversal of removal, noting that the lower edge of the upper cover engages with the centre cover.

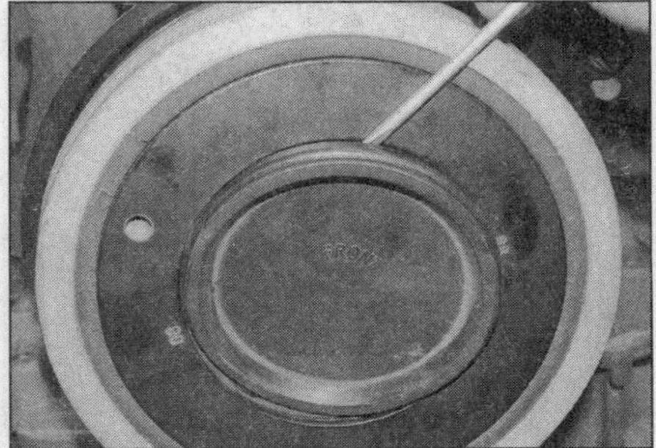

5.4 Prise out the crankshaft pulley centre cap

Centre outer cover

4 Remove the auxiliary drivebelt as described in Chapter 1B.
5 Remove the crankshaft pulley as described in Section 5. It is assumed that, if the centre cover is being removed, the lower cover will be also – if not, simply remove the components described in Section 5 for access to the crankshaft pulley, and leave the pulley in position.
6 With the upper cover removed (paragraphs 1 to 3), unscrew and remove the retaining bolts from the centre cover. Withdraw the centre cover from the engine, noting how it fits over the lower cover **(see illustration)**.
7 Refitting is a reversal of the removal procedure.

Lower outer cover

8 Remove the upper and centre covers as described previously.

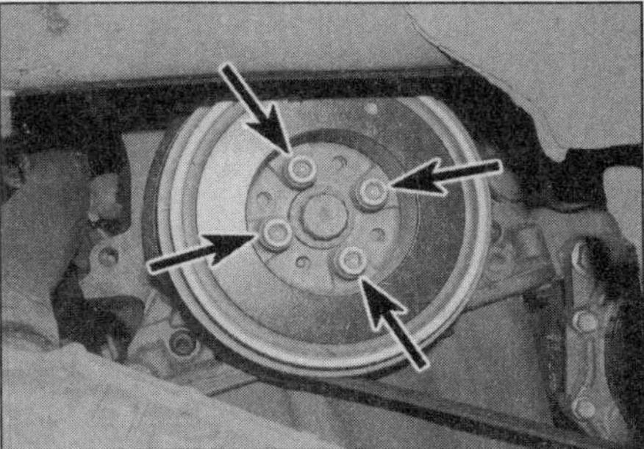

5.5 Showing the four crankshaft pulley bolts (arrowed)

5.7 Removing the crankshaft pulley

9 If not already done, remove the crankshaft pulley as described in Section 5.
10 Unscrew the remaining bolt(s) securing the lower cover, and lift it out **(see illustration)**.
11 Refitting is a reversal of removal; locate

6.1 Remove the air intake hose from across the top of the timing belt cover

6.2a Release the retaining clips (one arrowed)...

6.2b ...and withdraw the upper cover

6.2c Remove the upper timing cover (2.0 litre DOHC engine)

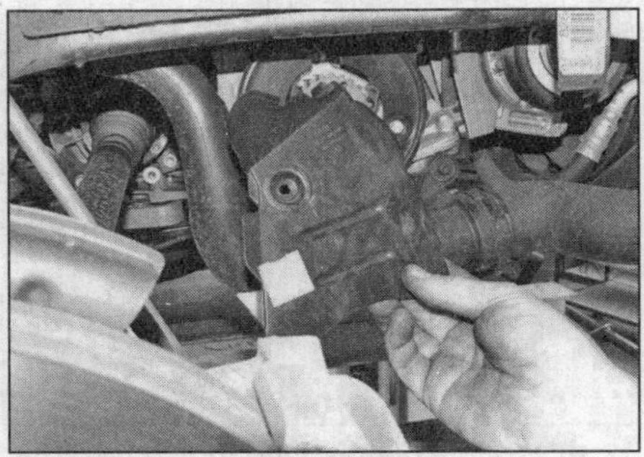

6.6 Remove the centre outer timing cover (2.0 litre DOHC engine)

6.10 Remove the lower outer timing cover (2.0 litre DOHC engine)

7.4 Remove the front section of the wheel arch liner

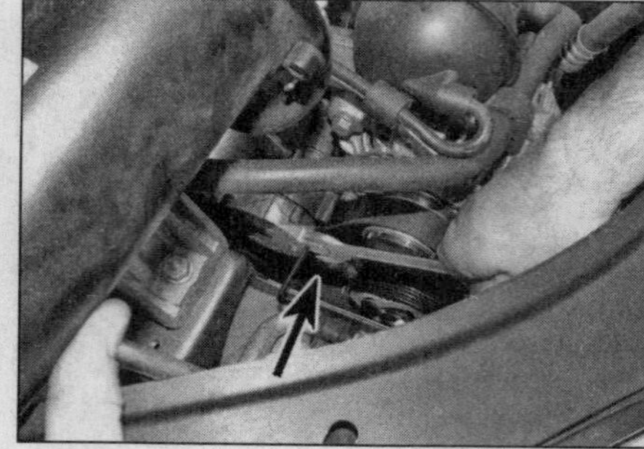

7.5a Use a spanner to turn the tensioner clockwise...

7.5b ...then lock with a suitable metal rod...

7.5c ...remove the auxiliary drivebelt...

7.5d ...and unbolt the tensioner (2.0 litre DOHC engine)

the centre cover in place before fitting the top two bolts.

Rear cover

12 Remove the upper, centre and lower covers as described previously.

13 Remove the timing belt, tensioner and sprockets as described in Sections 7 and 8.

14 Slacken and withdraw the retaining bolts and lift the timing belt inner cover from the studs on the end of the engine, and remove it from the engine compartment.

15 Refitting is a reversal of removal.

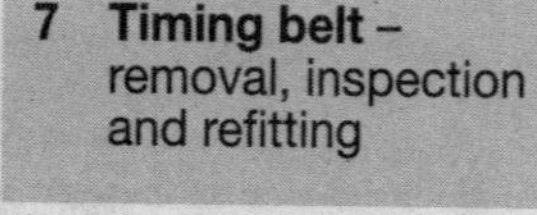

7 Timing belt – removal, inspection and refitting

Note: *A modified right-hand engine mounting was introduced in 05/2005 (SOHC engines) and 06/2006 (DOHC engines), making it unnecessary to remove the mounting for timing belt removal.*

Removal

1 The primary function of the toothed timing belt is to drive the camshaft, but it also drives the coolant pump. Should the belt slip or break in service, the valve timing will be disturbed and piston-to-valve contact may occur, resulting in serious engine damage. For this reason, it is important that the timing belt is tensioned correctly, and inspected regularly for signs of wear or deterioration.

2 Switch off the ignition and all electrical consumers and remove the ignition key.

3 Apply the handbrake, then jack up the front of the vehicle and support securely on axle stands (see *Jacking and vehicle support*).

4 Remove the securing screws and withdraw the engine undertray(s), and the front section of the right-hand wheel arch liner **(see illustration)**. Also, remove the engine top cover.

5 Remove the auxiliary drivebelt as described in Chapter 1B, then unbolt and remove the drivebelt tensioner **(see illustrations)**.

6 Remove the crankshaft pulley/vibration damper as described in Section 5.

7 Remove the timing belt covers as described in Section 6.

8 On SOHC engines manufactured up to 04/2005, and 2.0 litre DOHC engines manufactured up to 05/2006, support the engine and remove the right-hand engine mounting as described in Section 18. Note that on DOHC engines, the mounting bracket on the engine can only be removed with the timing belt loose.

7.16 Using a home-made tool to hold the camshaft sprocket while loosening the bolts

9 Remove the fuel filter from its bracket and place to one side.

10 On 06/2006-on 2.0 litre DOHC engines, disconnect the fuel supply and return lines. Also, where necessary on all engines, remove the intercooler charge air pipe.

11 Unbolt the filler neck from the screen washer reservoir.

12 Where applicable, unbolt the fuel filter bracket from the engine mounting.

13 Unbolt the coolant expansion tank and position it to one side. **Note:** *Do not disconnect the hoses.*

14 Set the engine to TDC on No 1 cylinder as described in Section 3.

15 If the original timing belt is to be refitted, mark the running direction of the belt, to ensure correct refitting.

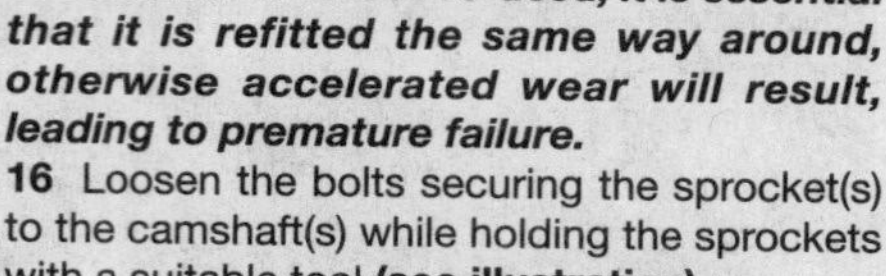

Caution: If the belt appears to be in good condition and can be re-used, it is essential that it is refitted the same way around, otherwise accelerated wear will result, leading to premature failure.

16 Loosen the bolts securing the sprocket(s) to the camshaft(s) while holding the sprockets with a suitable tool **(see illustration)**.

17 Loosen the timing belt tensioner securing nut, then use circlip pliers or an Allen key (as applicable) to turn the tensioner anti-clockwise until a suitable pin or drill bit can be inserted through the locking holes. Now, turn the tensioner clockwise to the stop and tighten the securing nut.

18 Slide the belt from the sprockets, taking care not to twist or kink the belt excessively if it is to be re-used.

Inspection

19 Examine the belt for evidence of contamination by coolant or lubricant. If this is the case, find the source of the contamination before progressing any further. Check the belt for signs of wear or damage, particularly around the leading edges of the belt teeth. Renew the belt if its condition is in doubt; the cost of belt renewal is negligible compared with potential cost of the engine repairs, should the belt fail in service. The belt must be renewed if it has covered the mileage given in Chapter 1B, however, if it has covered less, it is prudent to renew it regardless of condition, as a precautionary measure.

20 If the timing belt is not going to be refitted for some time, it is a wise precaution to hang a warning label on the steering wheel, to remind yourself (and others) not to attempt to start the engine.

Refitting

21 Ensure that the crankshaft and camshaft are still set to TDC on No 1 cylinder, as described in Section 3.

22 Position the camshaft sprocket(s) so that the securing bolts are in the centre part of the elongated holes **(see illustration)**.

23 Loop the timing belt loosely under the crankshaft sprocket. **Note:** *Observe any direction of rotation markings on the belt.*

24 Engage the timing belt teeth with the camshaft sprocket(s), then manoeuvre it into position around the tensioning roller, crankshaft sprocket, and finally around the coolant pump sprocket. Make sure that the belt teeth seat correctly on the sprockets. **Note:** *Slight adjustment to the position of the camshaft sprocket may be necessary to achieve this.* Avoid bending the belt back on itself or twisting it excessively as you do this. Ensure that any slack in the belt is in the section of belt that passes over the tensioner roller.

25 Loosen the timing belt tensioner securing nut, and turn the tensioner anti-clockwise with the circlip pliers or an Allen key (as applicable) until the locking pin can be removed. Now, turn the tensioner clockwise until the pointer is in the middle of the gap in the tensioner base plate. With the tensioner held in this position, tighten the securing nut to the specified torque and angle.

26 Tighten the camshaft sprocket bolts to the specified torque, remove the sprocket locking pin(s) and the crankshaft locking tool.

27 Using a spanner or wrench and socket on the crankshaft pulley centre bolt, rotate the crankshaft through two complete revolutions. Reset the engine to TDC on No 1 cylinder, with reference to Section 3 and check that the crankshaft and camshaft sprocket locking pins can still be inserted. If the camshaft sprocket locking pin(s) cannot be inserted, slacken the retaining bolts, turn the **hub(s)** until the pin(s) fit, and tighten the sprocket retaining bolts to the specified torque.

7.22 Position the camshaft sprocket so that the securing bolts are in the centre part of the elongated holes

28 Refit the coolant expansion tank.

29 Where applicable, refit the fuel filter bracket to the engine mounting.

30 Refit the screen washer reservoir filler neck.

31 Refit the fuel filter to its bracket, and where necessary reconnect the fuel lines and intercooler charge air pipe.

32 Where applicable, refit the right-hand engine mounting as described in Section 18.

33 Refit the timing belt covers as described in Section 6.

34 Refit the crankshaft pulley/vibration damper as described in Section 5.

35 Refit the auxiliary drivebelt and tensioner with reference to Chapter 1B.

36 Refit the engine undertray(s), right-hand wheel arch liner and engine top cover, and lower the vehicle to the ground.

8 Timing belt tensioner and sprockets – removal and refitting

Timing belt tensioner

Removal

1 Remove the timing belt as described in Section 7.

2 Unscrew the timing belt tensioner nut, and remove the tensioner from the engine **(see illustration)**.

3 When refitting the tensioner to the engine, ensure that the lug on the tensioner backplate engages with the corresponding cut-out in the rear timing belt cover, then refit the tensioner nut **(see illustration)**.

Refitting

4 Refit and tension the timing belt as described in Section 7, making sure that the tensioner backplate is correctly engaged with the hole in the cylinder head.

Idler pulleys

Removal

5 Remove the timing belt as described in Section 7.

6 Unscrew the relevant idler pulley securing bolt/nut, then withdraw the pulley.

Refitting

7 Refit the pulley and tighten the securing bolt or nut to the specified torque. **Note:** *Renew the bolt (where applicable).*

8 Refit and tension the timing belt as described in Section 7.

Crankshaft sprocket

Removal

9 Remove the timing belt as described in Section 7.

10 The sprocket securing bolt must now be slackened, and the crankshaft must be prevented from turning as the sprocket bolt is unscrewed. To hold the sprocket, make up a suitable tool, and screw it to the sprocket using a two bolts screwed into two of the crankshaft pulley bolt holes.

11 Hold the sprocket using the tool, then slacken the sprocket securing bolt. Take care, as the bolt is very tight. **Do not** allow the crankshaft to turn as the bolt is slackened.

12 Unscrew the bolt, and slide the sprocket from the end of the crankshaft, noting which way round the sprocket's raised boss is fitted.

Refitting

13 Commence refitting by positioning the sprocket on the end of the crankshaft, with the raised boss fitted as noted on removal.

14 Fit a new sprocket securing bolt, then counterhold the sprocket using the method employed on removal, and tighten the bolt to the specified torque in the two stages given in the Specifications **(see illustration)**.

15 Refit the timing belt as described in Section 7.

8.2 Timing belt tensioner nut

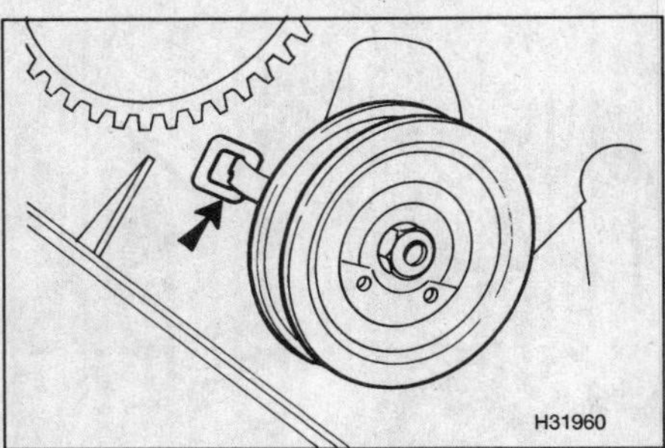

8.3 Ensure that the lug on the tensioner backplate engages with the cut-out in the rear timing belt cover

8.14 Fit a new crankshaft sprocket securing bolt

8.22 Using a fabricated tool to counterhold the camshaft hub

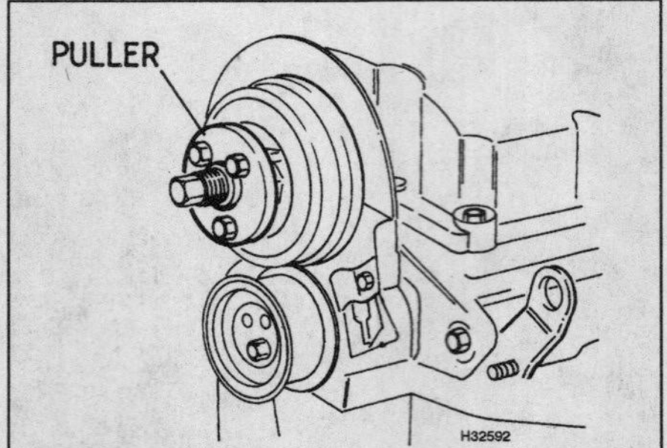

8.23 Attach a three-legged puller to the hub, and evenly tighten the puller until the hub is free of the camshaft taper

8.24 The built in key in the hub taper must align with the keyway in the camshaft taper (arrowed)

Camshaft sprocket

Removal

16 Remove the timing belt as described in Section 7.

17 Unscrew and remove the three retaining bolts and remove the camshaft sprocket from the camshaft hub.

Refitting

18 Refit the sprocket ensuring that it is fitted the correct way round, as noted before removal, then insert the sprocket bolts, and tighten by hand only at this stage.

19 If the crankshaft has been turned, turn the crankshaft clockwise 90° back to TDC.

20 Refit and tension the timing belt as described in Section 7.

Camshaft hub

Note: *VAG technicians use special tool T10051 to counterhold the hub, however it is possible to fabricate a suitable alternative ñ see below.*

Removal

21 Remove the camshaft sprocket as described previously in this Section.

22 Engage special tool T10051 with the three locating holes in the face of the hub to prevent the hub from turning. If this tool is not available, fabricate a suitable alternative. Whilst holding the tool, undo the central hub retaining bolt about two turns **(see illustration)**.

23 Leaving the central hub retaining bolt in place, attach VW tool T10052 (or a similar three-legged puller) to the hub, and evenly tighten the puller until the hub is free of the camshaft taper **(see illustration)**.

Refitting

24 Ensure that the camshaft taper and the hub centre is clean and dry, locate the hub on the taper, noting that the built-in key in the hub taper must align with the keyway in the camshaft taper **(see illustration)**.

25 Hold the hub in this position with tool T10051 (or similar home-made tool), and tighten the central bolt to the specified torque.

26 Refit the camshaft sprocket as described previously in this Section.

Coolant pump sprocket

27 The coolant pump sprocket is integral with the coolant pump. Refer to Chapter 3 for details of coolant pump removal.

9 Pump injector rocker shaft assembly – removal and refitting

Removal

1 Remove the camshaft cover as described in Section 4. In order to ensure that the rocker arms are refitted to their original locations, use a marker pen or paint and number the arms 1 to 4, with No 1 nearest the timing belt end of the engine. If the arms are not fitted to their original locations the injector basic clearance setting procedure must be carried out as described in Chapter 4B.

2 Slacken the locknut of the adjustment screw on the end of the rocker arm above the respective injector, and undo the adjustment screw until the rocker arm lies against the plunger pin of the injector. Starting at the outside and working in, gradually and evenly slacken and remove the rocker shaft retaining bolts. Lift off the rocker shaft. Discard the rocker shaft bolts, new ones must be fitted **(see illustrations)**.

Refitting

3 Thoroughly check the rocker shaft, rocker arms and camshaft bearing cap seating surface for any signs of excessive wear or damage.

4 Smear some grease (VW No G000 100) onto the contact face of each rocker arm adjustment screw, and refit the rocker shaft assembly, tightening the new retaining bolts as follows. Starting from the inside out, hand-tighten the bolts. Again, from the inside out, tighten the bolts to the Stage one torque setting. Finally, from the inside out, tighten the bolts to the Stage two angle tightening setting.

5 Attach a DTI (Dial Test Indicator) gauge to the cylinder head upper surface, and position the DTI probe against the top of the adjustment screw. Turn the crankshaft until the rocker arm roller is on the highest point of its corresponding camshaft lobe, and the adjustment screw is at its lowest. Once this position has been established, remove the DTI gauge, screw the adjustment screw in until firm resistance is felt, and the injector

9.2a Slacken the rocker shaft adjustment screws

9.2b Starting with the outer bolts first, carefully and evenly slacken the rocker shaft retaining bolts (SOHC engine)

9.2c Rocker shaft retaining bolts – 3 of 4 shown (DOHC engine)

10.4 Tandem fuel/brake vacuum pump (DOHC engine)

10.6 Check the camshaft bearing caps (arrowed) for markings

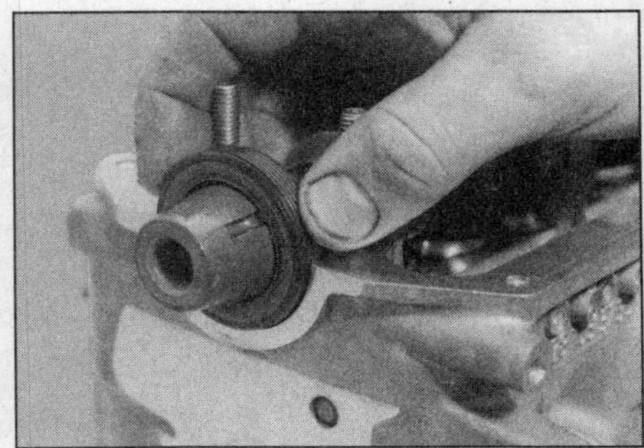

10.11 Remove the camshaft oil seal

spring cannot be compressed further. Turn the adjustment screw **anti-clockwise** 180°, and tighten the locknut to the specified torque. Repeat this procedure for any other injectors that have been refitted.

6 Refit the camshaft cover and upper timing belt cover, as described in Section 4.

7 Start the engine and check that it runs correctly.

10 Camshaft and hydraulic tappets – removal, inspection and refitting

Note: *New camshaft oil seal(s) will be required on refitting. On engine codes AZV, BKD, and BMN (DOHC), VW removal tool T10262 (or similar tool) will be required to remove the camshaft retaining frame – this is necessary to prevent distortion and damage to the camshaft retaining frame as it is being removed.*

Removal

1 Turn the crankshaft to position No 1 piston at TDC on the firing stroke, and lock the camshaft and the fuel injection sprocket in position, as described in Section 3.

2 Remove the timing belt as described in Section 7.

3 Remove the camshaft sprocket(s) and hubs as described in Section 8.

4 Remove the tandem fuel/brake vacuum pump (where fitted) as described in Chapter 9 **(see illustration)**.

5 Remove the injector rocker arms and shaft as described in Section 9.

Engine codes BJB, BDK, BMM, BKC, BRU, BLS, BXE and BXF

6 Check the camshaft bearing caps for identification markings **(see illustration)**. The bearing caps are normally stamped with their respective cylinder numbers. If no marks are present, make suitable marks using a scriber or punch. The caps should be numbered from 1 to 5, with No 1 at the timing belt end of the engine. Note on which side of the bearing caps the marks are made to ensure that they are refitted the correct way round.

7 The camshaft rotates in shell bearings. As the camshaft bearing caps are removed, recover the shell bearing halves from the camshaft. Number the back of the bearings with a felt pen to ensure that, if re-used, the bearings are fitted to their original locations. **Note:** *Fitted into the cylinder head, under each camshaft bearing cap, is a washer for each cylinder head bolt.*

8 Unscrew the securing nuts, and remove Nos 1, 3 and 5 bearing caps.

9 Working progressively, in a diagonal sequence, slacken the nuts securing Nos 2 and 4 bearing caps. Note that as the nuts are slackened, the valve springs will push the camshaft up.

10 Once the nuts securing Nos 2 and 4 bearing caps have been fully slackened lift off the bearing caps.

11 Carefully lift the camshaft from the cylinder head, keeping it level and supported at both ends as it is removed so that the journals and lobes are not damaged. Remove the oil seal from the end of the camshaft and discard it – a new one will be required for refitting **(see illustration)**.

12 Lift the hydraulic tappets from their bores in the cylinder head, and store them with the valve contact surfaces facing downwards, to prevent the oil from draining out. It is recommended that the tappets are kept immersed in oil for the period they are removed from the cylinder head. Make a note of the position of each tappet, as they must be refitted in their original locations on reassembly – accelerated wear leading to early failure will result if the tappets are interchanged.

13 Recover the lower shell bearing halves from the cylinder head; number the back of the shells with a felt pen to ensure that, if re-used, the bearings are fitted to their original locations.

Engine codes AZV, BKD and BMN

14 Unscrew the upper bolt securing the EGR cooler bracket.

15 Disconnect the wiring from the unit injectors and glow plugs. To disconnect the wiring connector from the left-hand end of the cylinder head, use a screwdriver to pull out the plastic red lock, then unscrew the collar and pull the connector from the pins. To remove the wiring conduit, first undo the screws retaining it to the cylinder head, then release the multi-pin plug by raising the clip and unscrewing the outer threaded collar, ideally using the special VW tool T10310 which engages the three slots **(see illustrations)**.

16 Progressively unscrew the camshaft retaining frame bolts starting from the outside to inside.

10.15a Disconnect the wiring from the unit injectors

10.15b Wiring loom connector, showing the three pins in the outer collar

10.15c Retaining clip on the inside of the wiring loom connector

10.24 Check camshaft endfloat using a DTI gauge

17 The VW tool is now used to remove the retaining bearing frame. First, fully unscrew the ejector bolts, then fit the tool to the frame and tighten the bolts. Screw in the ejector bolts until they contact the cylinder head bolt(s), then progressively tighten them so that the bearing frame is released from the cylinder head.

18 Carefully lift the camshafts from the cylinder head, keeping them identified for location. Remove the oil seals from the ends of the camshafts and discard them – new ones will be required for refitting.

19 To remove the exhaust roller rocker fingers and hydraulic tappets, carry out the following:

a) Drain the coolant as described in Chapter 1B.

b) Remove the connecting pipe between the EGR valve and bypass flap.

c) Remove the thermostat housing as described in Chapter 3.

d) Unscrew the plug from the end of the exhaust roller rocker shaft. Note: If the plug is very tight, the shaft may be deformed while unscrewing it, making the oil supply hole alignment incorrect. If this happens, renew the shaft.

e) Undo the screw securing the roller rocker shaft to the cylinder head.

20 To remove either exhaust or inlet roller rocker fingers and hydraulic tappets, use VW slide hammer/puller tool T10055 to pull the shaft from the cylinder head while removing the roller rockers. Store the rockers in a container with numbered compartments to ensure they are refitted to their correct locations. It is recommended that the tappets are kept immersed in oil for the period they are removed from the cylinder head.

Inspection – all engines

21 With the camshaft(s) removed, examine the bearing caps/frame and the bearing locations in the cylinder head for signs of obvious wear or pitting. If evident, a new cylinder head will probably be required. Also check that the oil supply holes in the cylinder head are free from obstructions.

22 Visually inspect the camshaft for evidence of wear on the surfaces of the lobes and journals. Normally their surfaces should be smooth and have a dull shine; look for scoring, erosion or pitting and areas that appear highly polished, indicating excessive wear. Accelerated wear will occur once the hardened exterior of the camshaft has been damaged, so always renew worn items. **Note:** *If these symptoms are visible on the tips of the camshaft lobes, check the corresponding tappet, as it will probably be worn as well.*

23 If the machined surfaces of the camshaft appear discoloured or blued, it is likely that it has been overheated at some point, probably due to inadequate lubrication. This may have distorted the shaft, so check the run-out as follows: place the camshaft between two V-blocks and using a DTI gauge, measure the run-out at the centre journal. If it exceeds the figure quoted in the Specifications at the start of this Chapter, renew the camshaft.

24 To measure the camshaft endfloat, temporarily refit the camshaft to the cylinder head, then fit Nos 1 and 5 bearing caps and tighten the retaining nuts to the specified torque setting. Anchor a DTI gauge to the timing belt end of the cylinder head **(see illustration)**. Push the camshaft to one end of the cylinder head as far as it will travel, then rest the DTI gauge probe on the end face of the camshaft, and zero the gauge. Push the camshaft as far as it will go to the other end of the cylinder head, and record the gauge reading. Verify the reading by pushing the camshaft back to its original position and checking that the gauge indicates zero again. **Note:** *The hydraulic tappets must* ***not*** *be fitted whilst this measurement is being taken.*

25 Check that the camshaft endfloat measurement is within the limit listed in the Specifications. If the measurement is outside the specified limit, wear is unlikely to be confined to any one component, so renewal of the camshaft, cylinder head and bearing caps must be considered.

26 The camshaft bearing running clearance should now be measured. This will be difficult to achieve without a range of micrometers or internal/external expanding calipers, measure the outside diameters of the camshaft bearing surfaces and the internal diameters formed by the bearing caps/frame (and shell bearings where applicable) and the bearing locations in the cylinder head. The difference between these two measurements is the running clearance.

27 Compare the camshaft running clearance measurements with the figure given in the Specifications; if any are outside the specified tolerance, the camshaft, cylinder head and bearing caps/frame (and shell bearings where applicable) should be renewed.

28 Inspect the hydraulic tappets for obvious signs of wear or damage, and renew if necessary. Check that the oil holes in the tappets are free from obstructions.

Refitting

Engine codes BJB, BDK, BMM, BKC, BRU, BLS, BXE and BXF

29 Smear some clean engine oil onto the sides of the hydraulic tappets, and offer them into position in their original bores in the cylinder head. Push them down until they contact the valves, then lubricate the camshaft lobe contact surfaces.

30 Lubricate the camshaft and cylinder head bearing journals and shell bearings with clean engine oil.

31 Carefully lower the camshaft into position in the cylinder head making sure that the cam lobes for No 1 cylinder are pointing upwards.

32 Refit a new camshaft oil seal on the end of the camshaft. Make sure that the closed end of the seal faces the camshaft sprocket end of the camshaft, and take care not to damage the seal lip. Locate the seal against the seat in the cylinder head.

33 Oil the upper surfaces of the camshaft bearing journals and shell bearings, then fit Nos 2 and 4 bearing caps. Ensure that they are fitted the right way round and in the correct locations, then progressively tighten the retaining nuts in a diagonal sequence to the specified torque. Note that as the nuts are tightened, the camshaft will be forced down against the pressure of the valve springs.

34 Fit bearing caps 1, 3 and 5 over the camshaft and progressively tighten the nuts to the specified torque. Note that it may be necessary to locate No 5 bearing cap by tapping lightly on the end of the camshaft.

35 Refit the injector rocker arms as described in Section 9.

Engine codes AZV, BKD and BMN

36 Oil the roller rocker fingers and hydraulic tappets together with the shafts, then insert each shaft into the cylinder head while at the same time fitting the roller rockers in their correct order. The inlet shaft must be inserted until flush with the cylinder head. The exhaust shaft must be correctly aligned with the retaining bolt hole. Insert and tighten the bolt securely.

37 Reverse the procedures listed in paragraph 19.

38 Lubricate the camshaft and cylinder head bearing journals with clean engine oil.

39 Carefully lower the camshafts into position in the cylinder head making sure that the cam lobes for No 1 cylinder are pointing upwards.

40 Fit new camshaft oil seals on the end of the camshafts. Make sure that the closed end of the seal faces the camshaft sprocket end of the camshaft, and take care not to damage the seal lip. Locate the seal against the seat in the cylinder head.

41 Oil the upper surfaces of the camshaft bearing frame journals, then apply sealant to the mating surfaces of the bearing frame and cylinder head.

42 Refit the bearing frame together with the rocker arms and shaft, using the VW tool, ensuring the frame is the correct way round. Progressively tighten the retaining bolts to

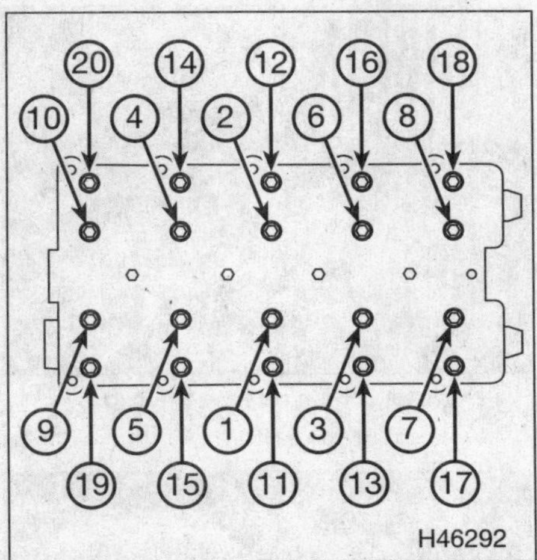

10.42 Camshaft bearing frame bolt tightening sequence

the specified torque in the order shown **(see illustration)**, then remove the tool. Note that as the bolts are tightened, the camshafts will be forced down against the pressure of the valve springs.

43 Tighten the rocker arm shaft bolts to the specified angle. Refit the wiring conduit and secure the connectors.

All engines

44 Renew the camshaft oil seal(s) as applicable with reference to Section 12.

45 Refit the tandem fuel/brake vacuum pump (where fitted) as described in Chapter 9.

46 Refit the camshaft sprocket(s) and hubs as described in Section 8.

47 Refit the timing belt as described in Section 7.

11 Hydraulic tappets – testing

Warning: After fitting hydraulic tappets, wait a minimum of 30 minutes (or preferably, leave overnight) before starting the engine, to allow the tappets time to settle, otherwise the valve heads will strike the pistons.

1 The hydraulic tappets are self-adjusting, and require no attention whilst in service.

2 If the hydraulic tappets become excessively noisy, their operation can be checked as described below.

3 Start the engine, and run it until it reaches normal operating temperature, increase the engine speed to approximately 2500 rpm for 2 minutes.

4 If any hydraulic tappets are heard to be noisy, carry out the following checks.

5 Remove the camshaft cover as described in Section 4.

6 Using a socket or spanner on the crankshaft sprocket bolt, turn the crankshaft until the tip of the camshaft lobe above the tappet to be checked is pointing vertically upwards.

7 Using feeler blades, check the clearance between the top of the tappet, and the cam lobe. If the play is in excess of 0.1 mm, renew the relevant tappet. If the play is less than 0.1 mm, or there is no play, proceed as follows.

8 Press down on the tappet using a wooden or plastic instrument **(see illustration)**. If free play in excess of 1.0 mm is present before the tappet contacts the valve stem, renew the relevant tappet.

9 On completion, refit the camshaft cover as described in Section 4.

12 Camshaft oil seals – renewal

Right-hand oil seal(s)

1 Remove the timing belt as described in Section 7.

2 Remove the camshaft sprocket and hub, as described in Section 8.

3 Drill two small holes into the existing oil seal, diagonally opposite each other. Take great care to avoid drilling through into the seal housing or camshaft sealing surface. Thread two self-tapping screws into the holes, and using a pair of pliers, pull on the heads of the screws to extract the oil seal.

4 Clean out the seal housing and the sealing surface of the camshaft by wiping it with a lint-free cloth. Remove any swarf or burrs that may cause the seal to leak.

5 Do **not** lubricate the lip and outer edge of the new oil seal, push it over the camshaft until it is positioned in place above its housing. To prevent damage to the sealing lips, wrap some adhesive tape around the end of the camshaft.

6 Using a hammer and a socket of suitable diameter, drive the seal squarely into its housing. **Note:** *Select a socket that bears only on the hard outer surface of the seal, not the inner lip which can easily be damaged.*

7 Refit the camshaft sprocket and its hub, as described in Section 8.

8 Refit and tension the timing belt as described in Section 7.

Left-hand oil seal

9 The left-hand camshaft oil seal is formed by the brake vacuum pump seal. Refer to Chapter 9 for details of brake vacuum pump removal and refitting.

13.1 Remove the battery

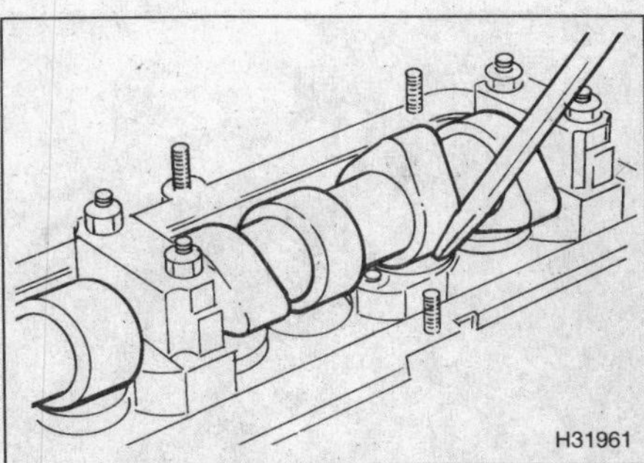

11.8 Press down on the tappet using a wooden or plastic instrument

13 Cylinder head – removal, inspection and refitting

Note: *The cylinder head must be removed with the engine cold. New cylinder head bolts and a new cylinder head gasket will be required on refitting, and suitable studs will be required to guide the cylinder head into position ñ see text.*

Removal

1 Switch off the ignition and all electrical consumers, and remove the ignition key. For improved access on DOHC engines, remove the battery as described in Chapter 5A **(see illustration)**.

2 Drain the cooling system and engine oil as described in Chapter 1B.

3 Remove the cover from the plenum chamber located just in front of the windscreen. Also, unbolt and remove the panel from the rear of the engine compartment **(see illustration)**.

4 Remove the air filter complete with the air mass meter and air ducts. Also, where applicable, unbolt and remove the duct from the turbocharger **(see illustrations)**.

5 Disconnect the fuel supply and return lines, and also the coolant hoses from the cylinder head. In the interests of safety, it is recommended that the fuel is syphoned from the tandem pump on the left-hand end of the

13.3 Remove the panel from the rear of the engine compartment

13.4a Disconnect the wiring...

13.4b ...and vacuum hose...

13.4c ...then release the clip...

13.4d ...undo the screw...

13.4e ...remove the upper...

13.4f ...and lower covers...

13.4g ...and remove the air cleaner and ducting

13.4h Remove the duct from the turbocharger

13.5 Undo the four tandem pump retaining bolts (arrowed)

cylinder head. If necessary, the pump may be unbolted and removed **(see illustration)**.

6 Remove the fuel filter from its mounting bracket and position to one side.

7 Remove the front exhaust pipe as described in Chapter 4D.

8 Remove the turbocharger support and oil return line from the turbocharger. Also, remove the oil supply pipe and place to one side.

9 Remove the camshaft cover as described in Section 4.

10 Remove the timing belt as described in Section 7. Where the right-hand engine mounting has been removed, ensure the engine is supported adequately on a trolley jack and block of wood.

11 Remove the camshaft sprocket and timing belt tensioner as described in Section 8.

12 Where applicable, unscrew the bolt(s) securing the rear timing belt cover to the cylinder head **(see illustrations)**.

13 Remove the camshaft position sensor from the right-hand end of the cylinder head **(see illustration)**. Note that on DOHC engines, the idler roller must be loosened to release the sensor wiring.

14 Remove the exhaust gas recirculation connecting pipe **(see illustration)**.

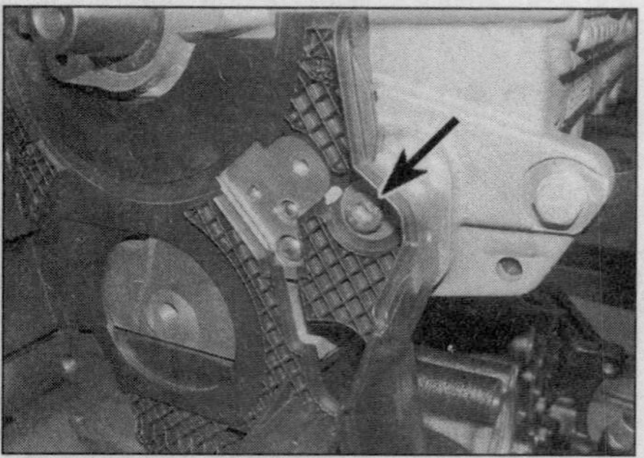
13.12a Where applicable, undo the bolt (arrowed) from the inner cover...

13.12b ...and the one (arrowed) on the side of the cover

13.13 Unscrew the bolt and remove the camshaft position sensor

13.14 EGR connecting pipe at the flap housing

13.15 Disconnect the central connector for the injectors

13.16a Disconnect the coolant hose from the end of the cylinder head

13.16b Disconnect the vacuum pipes (arrowed)

13.17 The camshaft retaining frame inner row bolts are tightened into the tops of the front cylinder head bolts

15 Note the locations of all the electrical wiring, then disconnect them methodically **(see illustration)**.

16 Disconnect all vacuum and coolant hoses **(see illustrations)**.

17 On DOHC engines, unbolt and remove the injector rocker arm shaft as follows. Slacken the locknut of the adjustment screw on the end of the rocker arm above each of the injectors, and undo the adjustment screw until the rocker arm lies against the plunger pin of the injector. Starting at the outside and working in, gradually and evenly slacken and remove the rocker shaft retaining bolts. Lift off the rocker shaft – this will allow access to the rear cylinder head bolts. Now unscrew the row of inner bolts securing the camshaft retaining frame – the bolts screw into the tops of the front cylinder head bolts, and are located behind the exhaust camshaft **(see illustration)**. As the bolts are removed, recover the large washers.

18 Using a multi-splined tool, undo the cylinder head bolts, working from the outside-in, evenly and gradually **(see illustration)**. Check that nothing remains connected, and lift the cylinder head from the engine block. Seek assistance if possible, as it is a heavy assembly, especially as it is being removed complete with the manifolds.

19 Remove the gasket from the top of the block, noting the locating dowels. If the dowels are a loose fit, remove them and store them with the head for safe-keeping. Do not discard the gasket yet – it will be needed for identification purposes. If desired, the manifolds can be removed from the cylinder head with reference to Chapter 4B (inlet manifold) or 4D (exhaust manifold).

Inspection

20 Dismantling and inspection of the cylinder head is covered in Part Chapter 2D.

Cylinder head gasket selection

Note: *A dial test indicator (DTI) will be required for this operation.*

21 Examine the old cylinder head gasket for manufacturer's identification markings **(see illustration)**. These will be in the form of holes or notches, and a part number on the edge of the gasket. Unless new pistons have been fitted, the new cylinder head gasket must be of the same type as the old one.

22 If new piston assemblies have been fitted as part of an engine overhaul, or if a new short engine is to be fitted, the projection of the piston crowns above the cylinder head mating face of the cylinder block at TDC must be measured. This measurement is used to determine the thickness of the new cylinder head gasket required.

23 Anchor a dial test indicator (DTI) to the top face (cylinder head gasket mating face) of the cylinder block, and zero the gauge on the gasket mating face.

24 Rest the gauge probe on No 1 piston crown, and turn the crankshaft slowly by hand until the piston reaches TDC. Measure and record the maximum piston projection at TDC **(see illustration)**.

25 Repeat the measurement for the remaining pistons, and record the results.

26 If the measurements differ from piston-to-

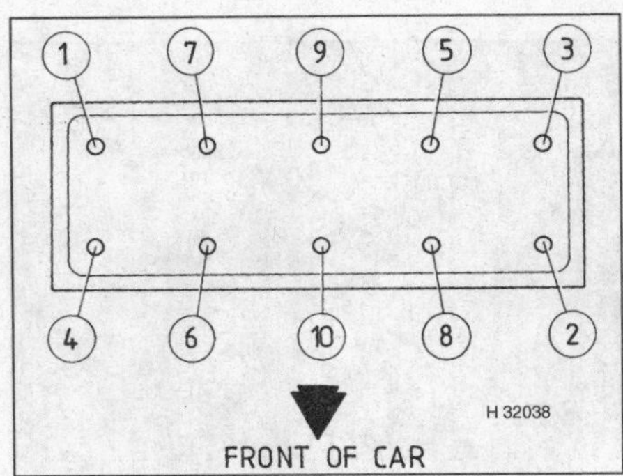

13.18 Cylinder head bolt slackening sequence

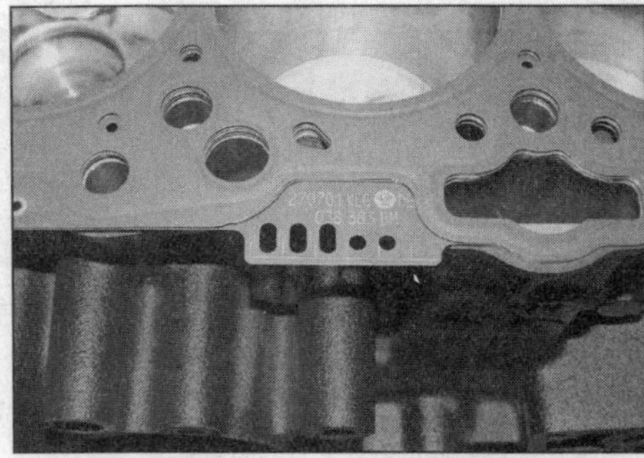

13.21 The thickness of the cylinder head gasket can be identified by notches or holes

13.24 Measuring the piston projection at TDC using a dial gauge

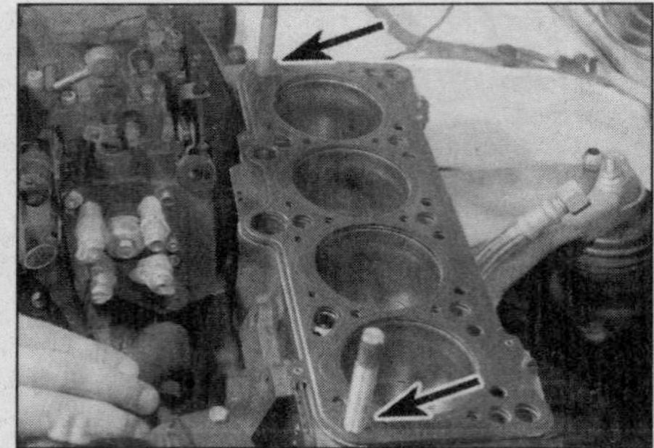

13.36 Two of the old head bolts (arrowed) can be used as cylinder head alignment guides

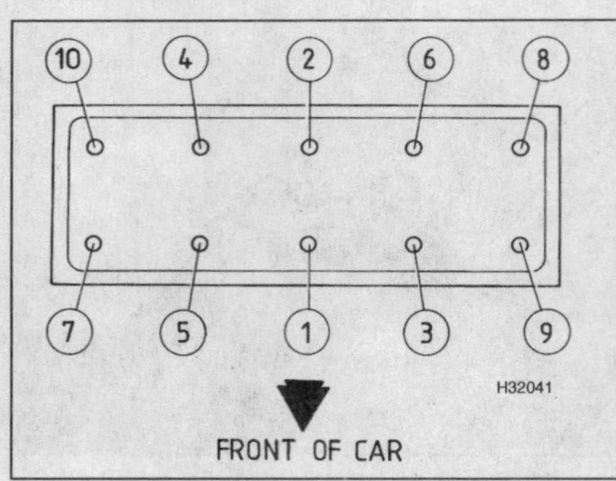

13.41a Cylinder head bolt tightening sequence

piston, take the highest figure, and use this to determine the thickness of the head gasket required as follows.

Piston projection	Gasket identification (number of holes/ notches)
0.91 to 1.00 mm	1
0.01 to 1.10 mm	2
1.11 to 1.20 mm	3

27 Purchase a new gasket according to the results of the measurements.

Refitting

Note: *If a VW exchange cylinder head, complete with camshaft(s), is to be fitted, the manufacturers recommend the following:*

a) Lubricate the contact surfaces between the tappets and the cam lobes before fitting the camshaft cover.

b) Do not remove the plastic protectors from the open valves until immediately before fitting the cylinder head.

c) Additionally, if a new cylinder head is fitted, VW recommend that the coolant is renewed.

28 The mating faces of the cylinder head and block must be perfectly clean before refitting the head. Use a scraper to remove all traces of gasket and carbon, also clean the tops of the pistons. Take particular care with the aluminium surfaces, as the soft metal is easily damaged.

29 Make sure that debris is not allowed to enter the oil and water passages – this is particularly important for the oil circuit, as carbon could block the oil supply to the camshaft and crankshaft bearings. Using adhesive tape and paper, seal the water, oil and bolt holes in the cylinder block.

30 To prevent carbon entering the gap between the pistons and bores, smear a little grease in the gap. After cleaning a piston, rotate the crankshaft to that the piston moves down the bore, then wipe out the grease and carbon with a cloth rag. Clean the other piston crowns in the same way.

31 Check the head and block for nicks, deep scratches and other damage. If slight, they may be removed carefully with a file. More serious damage may be repaired by machining, but this is a specialist job.

32 If warpage of the cylinder head is suspected, use a straight-edge to check it for distortion, as described in Chapter 2G.

33 Ensure that the cylinder head bolt holes in the crankcase are clean and free of oil. Syringe or soak up any oil left in the bolt holes. This is most important in order that the correct bolt tightening torque can be applied, and to prevent the possibility of the block being cracked by hydraulic pressure when the bolts are tightened.

34 Turn the crankshaft anti-clockwise all the pistons at an equal height, approximately half-way down their bores from the TDC position (see Section 3). This will eliminate any risk of piston-to-valve contact as the cylinder head is refitted.

35 Where applicable, refit the manifolds with reference to Chapters 4B and/or 4D.

13.41b Use a torque wrench to tighten the cylinder head bolts

13.43 Angle-tighten the cylinder head bolts

36 To guide the cylinder head into position, screw two long studs (or old cylinder head bolts with the heads cut off, and slots cut in the ends to enable the bolts to be unscrewed) into the cylinder block **(see illustration)**.

37 Ensure that the cylinder head locating dowels are in place in the cylinder block, then fit the new cylinder head gasket over the dowels, ensuring that the part number is uppermost. Where applicable, the OBEN/ TOP marking should also be uppermost. Note that VW recommend that the gasket is only removed from its packaging immediately prior to fitting.

38 Lower the cylinder head into position on the gasket, ensuring that it engages correctly over the guide studs and dowels.

39 Fit the new cylinder head bolts to the eight remaining bolt locations, and screw them in as far as possible by hand.

40 Unscrew the two guide studs from the exhaust side of the cylinder block, then screw in the two remaining new cylinder head bolts as far as possible by hand.

41 Working progressively, in sequence, tighten all the cylinder head bolts to the specified Stage 1 torque **(see illustrations)**.

42 Again working progressively, in sequence, tighten all the cylinder head bolts to the specified Stage 2 torque.

43 Tighten all the cylinder head bolts, in sequence, through the specified Stage 3 angle **(see illustration)**.

44 Finally, tighten all the cylinder head bolts, in sequence, through the specified Stage 4 angle.

45 After finally tightening the cylinder head bolts, turn the camshaft so that the cam lobes for No 1 cylinder are pointing upwards.

46 Where applicable, reconnect the lifting tackle to the engine lifting brackets on the cylinder head, then adjust the lifting tackle to support the engine. Once the engine is adequately supported using the cylinder head brackets, disconnect the lifting tackle from the bracket bolted to the cylinder block, and unbolt the improvised engine lifting bracket from the cylinder block. Alternatively, remove the trolley jack and block of wood from under the sump.

47 The remainder of the refitting procedure is

17.2 Remove the crankshaft oil seal using self-tapping screws

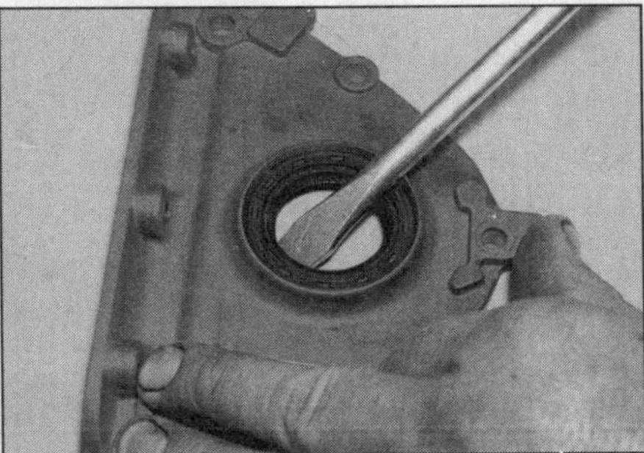

17.3 Prise the oil seal from the crankshaft oil seal housing

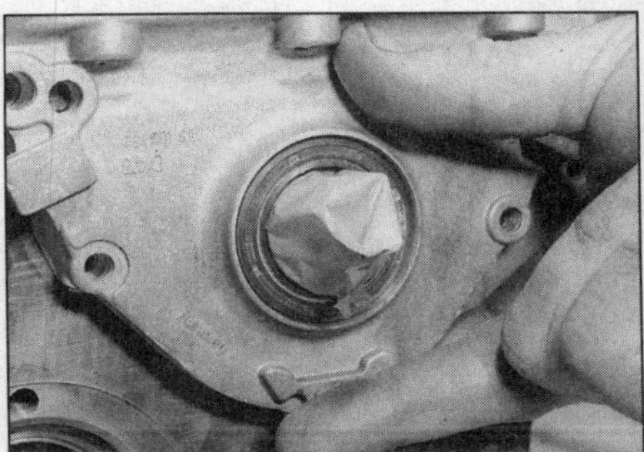

17.9 Slide the oil seal housing over the end of the crankshaft

a reversal of the removal procedure, bearing in mind the following points.

a) *Refit the injector rocker shaft with reference to Chapter 4B.*
b) *Refit the camshaft cover with reference to Section 4.*
c) *On turbo models, use new sealing rings when reconnecting the turbocharger oil return pipe to the cylinder block.*
d) *Reconnect the exhaust front section to the exhaust manifold or turbocharger, as applicable, with reference to Chapter 4D.*
e) *Refit the timing belt tensioner with reference to Section 8.*
f) *Refit the camshaft sprocket as described in Section 8, and refit the timing belt as described in Section 7.*
g) *On non-turbo engines, refit the upper section of the inlet manifold as described in Chapter 4B.*
h) *Refill the cooling system and engine oil as described in Chapter 1B.*

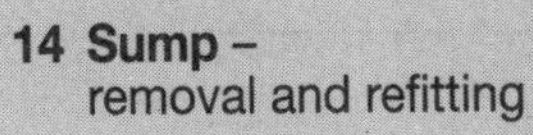

14 Sump – removal and refitting

Proceed as described in Chapter 2A.

15 Oil pump and drive chain – removal, inspection and refitting

Proceed as described in Chapter 2A.

16 Flywheel/driveplate – removal, inspection and refitting

Proceed as described in Chapter 2A.

17 Crankshaft oil seals – renewal

Note 1: *The oil seals are a PTFE (Teflon) type and are fitted dry, without using any grease or oil. These have a wider sealing lip and have been introduced instead of the coil spring type oil seal.*

Note 2: *If the oil seal housing is removed, suitable sealant (VW D 176 404 A2, or equivalent) will be required to seal the housing on refitting.*

Timing belt end oil seal

1 Remove the timing belt as described in Section 7, and the crankshaft sprocket with reference to Section 8.

2 To remove the seal without removing the housing, drill two small holes diagonally opposite each other, insert self-tapping screws, and pull on the heads of the screws with pliers **(see illustration)**.

3 Alternatively, to remove the oil seal complete with its housing, proceed as follows.

a) *Remove the sump as described in Section 14. This is necessary to ensure a satisfactory seal between the sump and oil seal housing on refitting.*
b) *Unbolt and remove the oil seal housing.*
c) *Working on the bench, lever the oil seal from the housing using a suitable screwdriver. Take care not to damage the seal seating in the housing* ***(see illustration)****.*

4 Thoroughly clean the oil seal seating in the housing.

5 Wind a length of tape around the end of the crankshaft to protect the oil seal lips as the seal (and housing, where applicable) is fitted.

6 Fit a new oil seal to the housing, pressing or driving it into position using a socket or tube of suitable diameter. Ensure that the socket or tube bears only on the hard outer ring of the seal, and take care not to damage the seal lips. Press or drive the seal into position until it is seated on the shoulder in the housing. Make sure that the closed end of the seal is facing outwards.

17.17 Locate the crankshaft oil seal fitting tool over the end of the crankshaft

7 If the oil seal housing has been removed, proceed as follows, otherwise proceed to paragraph 11.

8 Clean all traces of old sealant from the crankshaft oil seal housing and the cylinder block, then coat the cylinder block mating faces of the oil seal housing with a 2.0 to 3.0 mm thick bead of sealant (VW D 176 404 A2, or equivalent). Note that the seal housing must be refitted within 5 minutes of applying the sealant.

Caution: DO NOT put excessive amounts of sealant onto the housing as it may get into the sump and block the oil pick-up pipe.

9 Refit the oil seal housing, and tighten the bolts progressively to the specified torque **(see illustration)**.

10 Refit the sump as described in Section 14.

11 Refit the crankshaft sprocket with reference to Section 8, and the timing belt as described in Section 7.

Flywheel/driveplate end oil seal

Note: *The seal housing and crank sensor must be correctly positioned, and this requires a special tool.*

12 Remove the flywheel/driveplate as described in Section 16.

13 Remove the sump as described in Section 14. This is necessary to ensure a satisfactory seal between the sump and oil seal housing on refitting.

14 Unbolt and remove the oil seal housing, complete with the oil seal.

15 The new oil seal will be supplied ready-fitted to a new oil seal housing.

16 Thoroughly clean the oil seal housing mating face on the cylinder block.

17 New oil seal/housing assemblies are supplied with a fitting tool to prevent damage to the oil seal as it is being fitted. Locate the tool over the end of the crankshaft **(see illustration)**.

18 If the original oil seal housing was fitted using sealant, apply a thin bead of suitable sealant (VW D 176 404 A2, or equivalent) to the cylinder block mating face of the oil seal housing. Note that the seal housing must

17.19a Fit the oil seal/housing assembly over the end of the crankshaft...

17.19b ...then tighten the securing bolts to the specified torque

be refitted within 5 minutes of applying the sealant.

Caution: DO NOT put excessive amounts of sealant onto the housing as it may get into the sump and block the oil pick-up pipe.

19 Carefully fit the oil seal/housing assembly over the end of the crankshaft, then refit the securing bolts and tighten the bolts progressively, in a diagonal sequence, to the specified torque **(see illustrations)**.

20 Remove the oil seal protector tool from the end of the crankshaft.

21 Refit the sump as described in Section 14.

22 Refit the flywheel/driveplate as described in Section 16.

18 Engine/transmission mountings – inspection and renewal

Refer to Chapter 2A for the basic procedure, however, note that the right-hand engine mounting is different.

19 Engine oil cooler – removal and refitting

Note: *New sealing rings will be required on refitting.*

Removal

1 The oil cooler is mounted under the oil filter housing on the front of the cylinder block **(see illustration)**.

2 Position a container beneath the oil filter to catch escaping oil and coolant.

3 Clamp the oil cooler coolant hoses to minimise coolant spillage, then remove the clips, and disconnect the hoses from the oil cooler. Be prepared for coolant spillage.

4 Unscrew the oil cooler securing plate from the bottom of the oil filter housing, then slide off the oil cooler. Recover the O-rings from the top and bottom of the oil cooler.

Refitting

5 Refitting is a reversal of removal, bearing in mind the following points:

a) *Use new oil cooler O-rings.*

b) *Tighten the oil cooler securing plate securely.*

c) *On completion, check and if necessary top-up the oil and coolant levels.*

20 Oil pressure warning light switch – removal and refitting

Removal

1 The oil pressure warning light switch is fitted to the oil filter housing. Remove the engine top cover to gain access to the switch (see Section 4).

2 Disconnect the wiring connector and wipe clean the area around the switch.

3 Unscrew the switch from the filter housing and remove it, along with its sealing washer. If the switch is to be left removed from the engine for any length of time, plug the oil filter housing aperture.

Refitting

4 Examine the sealing washer for signs of damage or deterioration and if necessary renew.

5 Refit the switch, complete with washer, and tighten it to the specified torque.

6 Securely reconnect the wiring connector then check and, if necessary, top-up the engine oil as described in *Weekly checks*. On completion, refit the engine top cover(s).

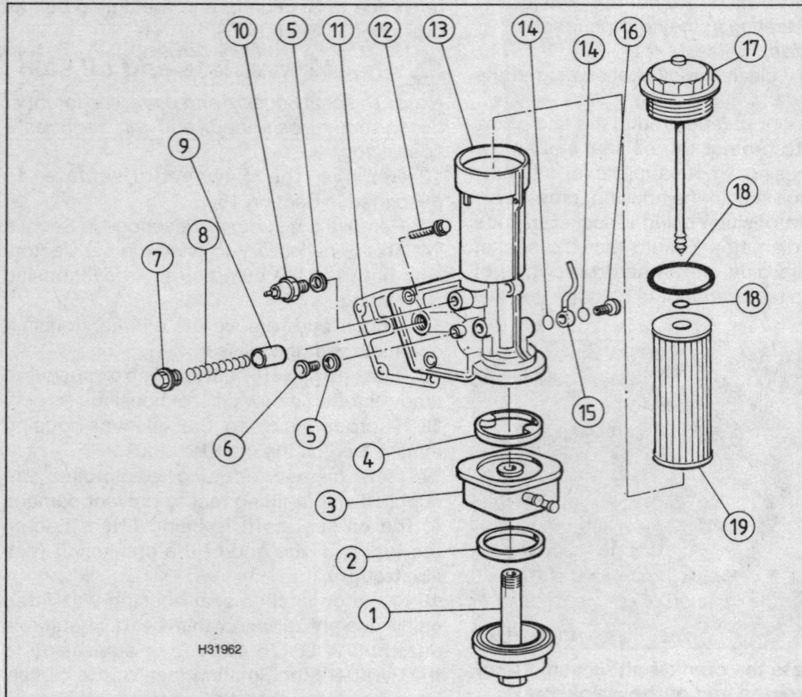

19.1 Oil filter and oil cooler mounting details

1 *Oil cooler securing plate*
2 *O-ring*
3 *Oil cooler*
4 *O-ring*
5 *Washer*
6 *Sealing plug*
7 *Sealing plug*
8 *Oil pressure relief valve spring (not fitted to all models)*
9 *Oil pressure relief valve piston (not fitted to all models)*
10 *Oil pressure warning light switch*
11 *Gasket*
12 *Mounting bolt*
13 *Oil filter housing*
14 *Seal*
15 *Oil supply pipe to turbo*
16 *Banjo bolt – turbo (or sealing plug – non-turbo models)*
17 *Oil filter cover*
18 *O-ring*
19 *Oil filter*

Chapter 2 Part F:
Diesel engine in-car repair procedures – Common rail injector engines

Contents

Degrees of difficulty

Easy, suitable for novice with little experience 

Fairly easy, suitable for beginner with some experience

Fairly difficult, suitable for competent DIY mechanic

Difficult, suitable for experienced DIY mechanic

Very difficult, suitable for expert DIY or professional 

Specifications

General

Manufacturer's engine codes*:		
1968 cc (2.0 litre), 16-valve, DOHC	CBDA, CBDB	
Maximum outputs:	**Power**	**Torque**
Engine code CBDA	100 kW at 4200 rpm	320 Nm at 1750 to 2500 rpm
Engine code CBDB	103 kW at 4200 rpm	320 Nm at 1750 to 2500 rpm
Bore	81.0 mm	
Stroke	95.5 mm	
Compression ratio	16.5 :1	
Compression pressures:		
Minimum compression pressure	Approximately 19.0 bar	
Maximum difference between cylinders	Approximately 5.0 bar	
Firing order	1 – 3 – 4 – 2	
No 1 cylinder location	Timing belt end	

* **Note:** *See 'Vehicle identification' at the end of this manual for the location of engine code markings.*

Lubrication system

Oil pump type	Gear type, chain-driven from crankshaft
Oil pressure (oil temperature 80°C, at 2000 rpm)	2.0 bar

Torque wrench settings

	Nm	lbf ft
Ancillary (alternator, etc) bracket mounting bolts*:		
Stage 1	40	30
Stage 2	Angle-tighten a further 45°	
Auxiliary drivebelt tensioner securing bolt:		
Stage 1	20	15
Stage 2	Angle-tighten a further 180°	
Big-end bearing caps bolts*:		
Stage 1	30	22
Stage 2	Angle-tighten a further 90°	
Camshaft bearing frame bolts/nut	10	7
Camshaft cover bolts	10	7
Camshaft sprocket hub centre bolt	100	74
Camshaft sprocket-to-hub bolts*:		
Stage 1	20	15
Stage 2	Angle-tighten a further 45°	
Common rail bolts	22	16
Coolant pump bolts	15	11
Crankshaft oil seal housing bolts	15	11
Crankshaft pulley-to-sprocket bolts*:		
Stage 1	10	7
Stage 2	Angle-tighten a further 90°	
Crankshaft sprocket bolt*:		
Stage 1	120	89
Stage 2	Angle-tighten a further 90°	
Cylinder head bolts*:		
Stage 1	30	22
Stage 2	60	44
Stage 3	Angle-tighten a further 90°	
Stage 4	Angle-tighten a further 90°	
Engine mountings:		
RH engine mounting*:		
Mounting bracket to engine:		
Stage 1	40	30
Stage 2	Angle-tighten a further 180°	
Mounting to body:		
Stage 1	40	30
Stage 2	Angle-tighten a further 90°	
Mounting to bracket:		
Stage 1	60	44
Stage 2	Angle-tighten a further 90°	
LH engine/transmission mounting*:		
Mounting to body:		
Stage 1	40	30
Stage 2	Angle-tighten a further 90°	
Mounting to bracket on transmission:		
Stage 1	60	44
Stage 2	Angle-tighten a further 90°	
Rear mounting link*:		
Link-to-transmission:		
Stage 1	50	37
Stage 2	Angle-tighten a further 90°	
Link-to-subframe:		
Stage 1	100	74
Stage 2	Angle-tighten a further 90°	
Flywheel*:		
Stage 1	60	44
Stage 2	Angle-tighten a further 90°	
Fuel injector:		
Retaining nuts	10	7
Cover bolts	5	3
Fuel pump hub nut	95	70
Fuel pump sprocket bolts*:		
Stage 1	20	15
Stage 2	Angle-tighten a further 90°	
Main bearing cap bolts*:		
Stage 1	65	48
Stage 2	Angle-tighten a further 90°	

Torque wrench settings (continued)

	Nm	lbf ft
Oil cooler bolt	25	18
Oil drain plug*	30	22
Oil filter housing-to-cylinder block bolts*:		
Stage 1	15	11
Stage 2	Angle-tighten a further 90°	
Oil filter cover	25	18
Oil level/temperature sensor-to-sump bolts	10	7
Oil pick-up pipe securing bolts	10	7
Oil pressure warning light switch	22	16
Oil pump securing bolts	15	11
Piston oil spray jet bolt	25	18
Sump:		
Sump-to-cylinder block bolts	15	11
Sump-to-transmission bolts	45	33
Tandem pump	10	7
Thermostat housing	15	11
Timing belt outer cover bolts	10	7
Timing belt tensioner roller securing nut:		
Stage 1	20	30
Stage 2	Angle-tighten a further 45°	
Timing belt idler pulleys:		
Lower idler roller nut	20	15
Upper idler roller (small) bolt	20	15
Upper idler roller (large) bolt*:		
Stage 1	50	37
Stage 2	Angle-tighten a further 90°	

Do not re-use fasteners

1 General information

How to use this Chapter

This Part of Chapter 2 describes those repair procedures that can reasonably be carried out on the engine while it remains in the vehicle. If the engine has been removed from the vehicle and is being dismantled as described in Part G, any preliminary dismantling procedures can be ignored.

Note that while it may be possible physically to overhaul certain items while the engine is in the vehicle, such tasks are not usually carried out as separate operations, and usually require the execution of several additional procedures (not to mention the cleaning of components and of oilways); for this reason, all such tasks are classed as major overhaul procedures, and are described in Part G of this Chapter.

Engine description

Throughout this Chapter, engines are referred to by type, and are identified and referred to by the manufacturer's code letters. A listing of all engines covered, together with their code letters, is given in the Specifications at the start of this Chapter.

The engines are water-cooled, double overhead camshafts (DOHC), in-line four-cylinder units, with cast-iron cylinder blocks and aluminium-silicone alloy cylinder heads. All are mounted transversely at the front of the vehicle, with the transmission bolted to the left-hand end of the engine.

The crankshaft is of five-bearing type, and thrustwashers are fitted to the centre main bearing to control crankshaft endfloat.

Drive for the exhaust camshaft is by a toothed timing belt from the crankshaft, with the intake camshaft driven by interlocking gears at the left-hand end of both camshafts. The gears incorporate a toothed backlash compensator element. Each camshaft is mounted at the top of the cylinder head, and is secured by a bearing frame/ladder.

The valves are closed by coil springs, and run in guides pressed into the cylinder head. The valves are operated by roller rocker arms incorporating hydraulic tappets.

A twin, counter-rotating balance shaft assembly is fitted to the base of the cylinder block. The rear-most balance shaft is driven by a gear on the crankshaft, via an intermediate gear bolted to the balance shaft housing. The two balance shafts are geared together.

The gear-type oil pump is driven by the front balance shaft. Oil is drawn from the sump through a strainer, and then forced through an externally-mounted, renewable filter. From there, it is distributed to the cylinder head, where it lubricates the camshaft journals and hydraulic tappets, and also to the crankcase, where it lubricates the main bearings, connecting rod big-ends, gudgeon pins and cylinder bores. A coolant-fed oil cooler is fitted to the oil filter housing on all engines. Oil jets are fitted to the base of each cylinder – these spray oil onto the underside of the pistons, to improve cooling.

All engines are fitted with a combined brake servo vacuum pump and fuel lift pump (tandem pump), driven by the camshaft on the transmission end of the cylinder head.

On all engines, engine coolant is circulated by a pump, driven by the timing belt. For details of the cooling system, refer to Chapter 3.

Operations with engine in car

The following operations can be performed without removing the engine:

a) Compression pressure – testing.
b) Camshaft cover – removal and refitting.
c) Crankshaft pulley – removal and refitting.
d) Timing belt covers – removal and refitting.
e) Timing belt – removal, refitting and adjustment.
f) Timing belt tensioner and sprockets – removal and refitting.
g) Camshaft oil seals – renewal.
h) Camshafts and hydraulic tappets – removal, inspection and refitting.
i) Cylinder head – removal and refitting.
j) Cylinder head and pistons – decarbonising.
k) Sump – removal and refitting.
l) Oil pump – removal, overhaul and refitting.
m) Crankshaft oil seals – renewal.
n) Engine/transmission mountings – inspection and renewal.
o) Flywheel/driveplate – removal, inspection and refitting.

Note: *It is possible to remove the pistons and connecting rods (after removing the cylinder head and sump) without removing the engine. However, this is not recommended. Work of this nature is more easily and thoroughly completed with the engine on the bench, as described in Chapter 2G.*

3.8 The alignment mark (arrowed) on the crankshaft sprocket should be almost vertical

3.9a Fit the tool to the hole in the oil seal housing (arrowed)...

2 Compression and leakdown tests – description and interpretation

Compression test

Note: *A compression tester suitable for use with diesel engines will be required for this test.*

1 When engine performance is down, or if misfiring occurs which cannot be attributed to the ignition or fuel systems, a compression test can provide diagnostic clues as to the engine's condition. If the test is performed regularly, it can give warning of trouble before any other symptoms become apparent.

2 The engine must be fully warmed-up to normal operating temperature, the battery must be fully-charged, and you will require the aid of an assistant.

3 Remove the glow plugs as described in Chapter 5, then fit a compression tester to the No 1 cylinder glow plug hole. The type of tester which screws into the plug thread is preferred. **Note:** *Part of the glow plug removal procedure is to disconnect the fuel injector wiring plugs. As a result of the plugs being disconnected and the engine cranked, faults may be stored in the ECU memory. These must be erased after the compression test.*

4 Have your assistant crank the engine for several seconds on the starter motor. After one or two revolutions, the compression pressure should build-up to a maximum figure and then stabilise. Record the highest reading obtained.

3.9b ...so the marks on the tool and sprocket align (arrowed)

5 Repeat the test on the remaining cylinders, recording the pressure in each.

6 The cause of poor compression is less easy to establish on a diesel engine than on a petrol engine. The effect of introducing oil into the cylinders (wet testing) is not conclusive, because there is a risk that the oil will sit in the recess on the piston crown, instead of passing to the rings. However, the following can be used as a rough guide to diagnosis.

7 All cylinders should produce very similar pressures. Any difference greater than that specified indicates the existence of a fault. Note that the compression should build-up quickly in a healthy engine. Low compression on the first stroke, followed by gradually increasing pressure on successive strokes, indicates worn piston rings. A low compression reading on the first stroke, which does not build-up during successive strokes, indicates leaking valves or a blown head gasket (a cracked head could also be the cause).

8 A low reading from two adjacent cylinders is almost certainly due to the head gasket having blown between them and the presence of coolant in the engine oil will confirm this.

9 On completion, remove the compression tester, and refit the glow plugs, with reference to Chapter 5.

10 Reconnect the wiring to the injector solenoids. Finally, have a VW dealer or suitably equipped specialist erase any fault codes from the ECU memory.

Leakdown test

11 A leakdown test measures the rate at which compressed air fed into the cylinder is lost. It is an alternative to a compression test, and in many ways it is better, since the escaping air provides easy identification of where pressure loss is occurring (piston rings, valves or head gasket).

12 The equipment required for leakdown testing is unlikely to be available to the home mechanic. If poor compression is suspected, have the test performed by a suitably-equipped garage.

3.9c Insert a 6 mm drill bit/rod to lock the camshaft hub (arrowed)

3 Engine assembly and valve timing marks – general information and usage

General information

1 TDC is the highest point in the cylinder that each piston reaches as it travels up-and-down when the crankshaft turns. Each piston reaches TDC at the end of the compression stroke and again at the end of the exhaust stroke, but TDC generally refers to piston position on the compression stroke. No 1 piston is at the timing belt end of the engine.

2 Positioning No 1 piston at TDC is an essential part of many procedures, such as timing belt removal and camshaft removal.

3 The design of the engines covered in this Chapter is such that piston-to-valve contact may occur if the camshaft or crankshaft is turned with the timing belt removed. For this reason, it is important to ensure that the camshaft and crankshaft do not move in relation to each other once the timing belt has been removed from the engine.

Setting TDC on No 1 cylinder

Note: *VAG special tool T10050 is required to lock the crankshaft sprocket in the TDC position. Alternatively obtain a tool from automotive tool specialists. Try asttools.co.uk.*

4 Raise the front of the vehicle and support it securely on axle stands (see *Vehicle jacking and support*). Remove the front right-hand road wheel, then release the fasteners and remove the lower section of the wheelarch liner.

5 Remove the auxiliary drivebelt as described in Chapter 1.

6 Remove the crankshaft pulley/vibration damper as described in Section 5.

7 Remove the timing belt outer covers as described in Section 6.

8 Using a spanner or socket on the crankshaft sprocket bolt, turn the crankshaft in the normal direction of rotation (clockwise) until the alignment mark on the face of the sprocket is almost vertical, and the hole in the camshaft sprocket hub aligns with the hole in the cylinder head **(see illustration)**.

9 While in this position it should be possible to insert the VAG tool T10050 to lock the crankshaft, and a 6 mm diameter rod/drill bit to lock the camshafts **(see illustrations)**. **Note:** *The mark on the crankshaft sprocket*

and the mark on the VAG tool must align, whilst at the same time the shaft of tool must engage in the drilling in the crankshaft oil seal housing.
11 The engine is now set to TDC on No 1 cylinder.

4 Camshaft cover – removal and refitting

Removal

1 Remove the fuel injectors and common rail as described in Chapter 4A.
2 Remove the timing belt upper cover as described in Section 6.
3 Note their fitted positions, then disconnect the vacuum hoses from the camshaft cover, and release them, and the wiring loom from the retaining clips at the left-hand end of the cover.
4 Squeeze together the sides of the collar, and disconnect the breather hose from the camshaft cover **(see illustration)**.
5 Release the wiring from the clips at the rear of the cover, then unscrew the camshaft cover retaining bolts and lift the cover away. If the cover sticks, do not attempt to lever it off – instead free it by working around the cover and tapping it lightly with a soft-faced mallet **(see illustration)**.
6 Recover the camshaft cover gasket. Inspect the gasket carefully, and renew it if damage or deterioration is evident – note that the retaining bolts and seals must be pushed fully through the cover **(see illustrations)**.
7 Clean the mating surfaces of the cylinder head and camshaft cover thoroughly, removing all traces of oil – take care to avoid damaging the surfaces as you do this.

Refitting

8 Refit the camshaft cover by following the removal procedure in reverse, tightening the cover retaining bolts to the specified torque in the sequence shown **(see illustration)**.

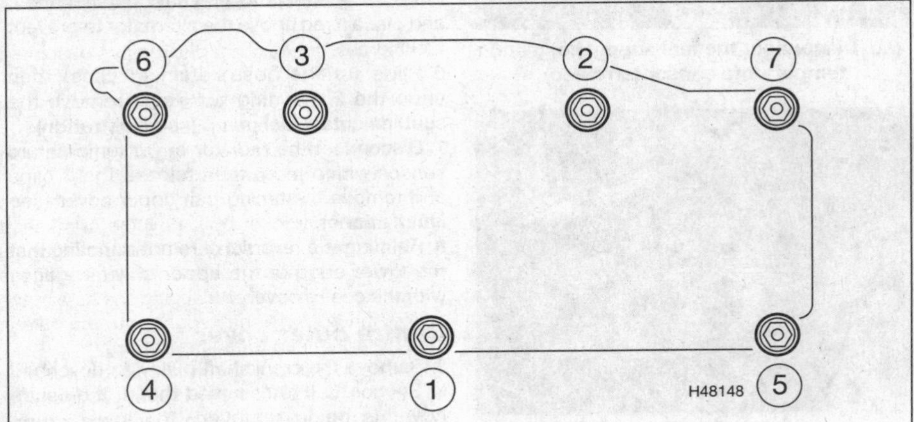

4.8 Cylinder head cover bolt tightening sequence

4.4 Squeeze together the sides of the collar (arrowed) and disconnect the breather hose

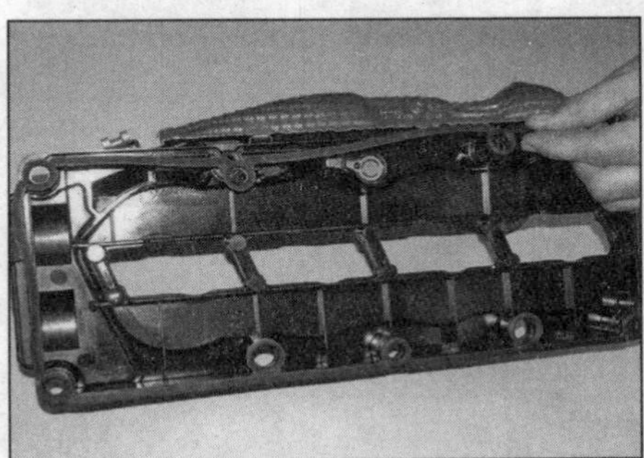
4.6a Renew the cover seal if necessary

5 Crankshaft pulley – removal and refitting

Removal

1 Switch off the ignition and all electrical consumers and remove the ignition key.
2 Raise the front right-hand side of the vehicle, and support securely on axle stands (see *Jacking and vehicle support*). Remove the roadwheel.
3 Remove the securing fasteners and withdraw the lower section of the front wheel arch liner.
4 Slacken the bolts securing the crankshaft pulley to the sprocket **(see illustration)**. If necessary, the pulley can be prevented from turning by counterholding with a spanner or socket on the crankshaft sprocket bolt.
5 Remove the auxiliary drivebelt, as described in Chapter 1.
6 Unscrew the bolts securing the pulley to the sprocket, and remove the pulley. Discard the bolts – new ones must be fitted.

Refitting

7 Refit the pulley over the locating peg on the crankshaft sprocket, then fit the new pulley securing bolts.
8 Refit and tension the auxiliary drivebelt as described in Chapter 1.
9 Prevent the crankshaft from turning as during removal, then fit the pulley securing bolts, and tighten to the specified torque.
10 Refit the wheel arch liner.
11 Refit the roadwheel and lower the vehicle to the ground.

4.5 Undo the bolts and lift away the camshaft cover

4.6b Bolts and seals must be pushed fully through the cover before fitting the gasket

5.4 Undo the pulley bolts, counterholding it with a socket on the centre sprocket bolt

6.1 Pull the plastic cover upwards from the mountings

6.2 Disconnect the wiring plug and undo the retaining bolt (arrowed)

6.3a Note their positions, then disconnect the hoses from the fuel filter

6.3b Plug the openings to prevent contamination

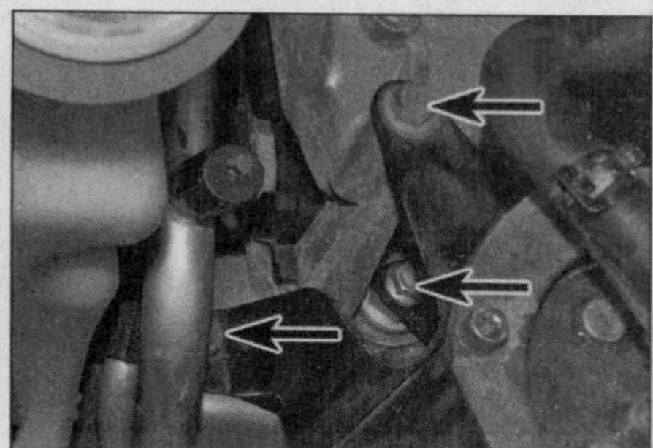
6.4 Undo the nut/bolts (arrowed) and remove the fuel filter

6.5 Disconnect the fuel supply hose and temperature sensor (arrowed)

6.6 Supplementary fuel pump retaining bolts (arrowed)

6.7a Disconnect the temperature sensor wiring plug (arrowed)

6 Timing belt covers – removal and refitting

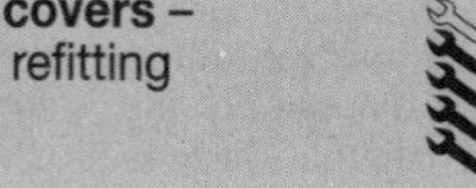

Upper outer cover

1 Pull the engine top cover upwards to release the mountings **(see illustration)**.

2 Disconnect the wiring plug, undo the retaining bolt, and remove the exhaust gas pressure sensor bracket by pushing it forwards **(see illustration)**.

3 Disconnect the wiring plug, unclip the fuel hoses, then release the clamps and disconnect the hoses from the filter **(see illustrations)**. Note the fitted locations of the hoses to aid refitting. Plug the openings to prevent contamination.

4 Undo the bolts/nut and remove the fuel filter assembly **(see illustration)**. Release the hose clamp as the filter assembly is withdrawn.

5 Disconnect the fuel temperature sensor wiring plug, then release the clamp and disconnect the fuel supply pipe from the high-pressure fuel pump **(see illustration)**. Plug the openings to prevent contamination, and place a rag above the alternator to prevent fuel ingress.

6 Slide up the hose retaining clips, then undo the 2 retaining bolts and remove the supplementary fuel pump **(see illustration)**.

7 Disconnect the radiator outlet temperature sensor wiring plug, then release the 3 clips and remove the timing belt upper cover **(see illustrations)**.

8 Refitting is a reversal of removal, noting that the lower edge of the upper cover engages with the centre cover.

Centre outer cover

9 Remove the crankshaft pulley as described in Section 5. It is assumed that, if the centre cover is being removed, the lower cover will be also – if not, simply remove the components described in Section 5 for access to the crankshaft pulley, and leave the pulley in position.

10 Undo the retaining nuts/bolts and move the coolant pipe that lies across the centre cover, away towards the inner wing.

11 With the upper cover removed (paragraphs 1 to 8), unscrew and remove the 3 retaining bolts from the centre cover. Withdraw the centre cover from the engine, noting how it fits over the lower cover **(see illustration)**. Note if the auxiliary belt tensioner is in the 'locked' position as described in the belt removal procedure, the locking drill bit/rod must be removed for access to the cover retaining bolt.

12 Refitting is a reversal of the removal procedure, using a little thread-locking compound on the retaining bolts.

Lower outer cover

13 Remove the upper and centre covers as described previously.

14 If not already done, remove the crankshaft pulley as described in Section 5.

15 Unscrew the remaining bolts securing the lower cover, and remove it **(see illustration)**.

16 Refitting is a reversal of removal; locate the centre cover in place before fitting the top two bolts.

Rear cover

16 Remove the timing belt, tensioner and sprockets as described in Sections 7 and 8.

17 Slacken and withdraw the retaining bolts and lift the timing belt inner cover from the studs on the end of the engine, and remove it from the engine compartment.

18 Refitting is a reversal of removal.

7 Timing belt – removal, inspection and refitting

Removal

1 The primary function of the toothed timing belt is to drive the camshaft, but it also drives the coolant pump and high-pressure fuel pump. Should the belt slip or break in service, the valve timing will be disturbed and piston-to-valve contact may occur, resulting in serious engine damage. For this reason, it is important that the timing belt is tensioned correctly, and inspected regularly for signs of wear or deterioration.

2 Switch off the ignition and all electrical consumers and remove the ignition key.

3 Set the engine to TDC on No. 1 cylinder as described in Section 3.

4 Slacken the 3 bolts securing the sprocket to the camshaft hub **(see illustration)**.

5 Slacken the 3 bolts securing the sprocket to the high-pressure fuel pump **(see illustration)**.

6 Insert a suitable Allen key into the tensioner hub, then slacken the retaining nut and rotate the tensioner hub anti-clockwise until it can be locked in place using a 2.0 m pin/drill bit **(see illustration)**.

7 Now rotate the tensioner hub clockwise to the stop, and hand-tighten the retaining nut.

8 If the original timing belt is to be refitted, mark the running direction of the belt, to ensure correct refitting.

Caution: If the belt appears to be in good condition and can be re-used, it is essential that it is refitted the same way around, otherwise accelerated wear will result, leading to premature failure.

9 Slide the belt from the sprockets, taking care not to twist or kink the belt excessively if it is to be re-used.

Inspection

10 Examine the belt for evidence of contamination by coolant or lubricant. If this is the case, find the source of the contamination before progressing any further. Check the belt for signs of wear or damage, particularly around the leading edges of the belt teeth. Renew the belt if its condition is in doubt; the

6.7b Release the clips (arrowed)...

6.7c ...and manoeuvre the timing belt upper cover from place

6.11 Centre timing belt cover bolts (arrowed)

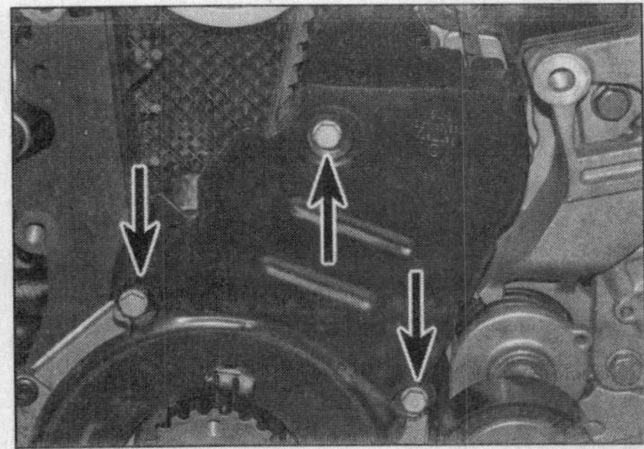

6.15 Lower cover retaining bolts (arrowed)

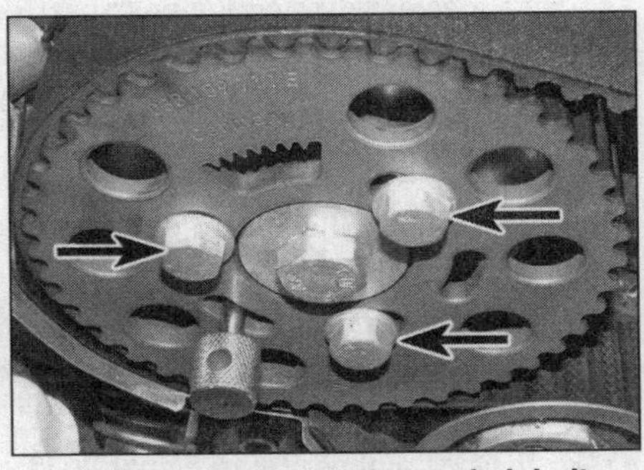

7.4 Slacken the sprocket-to-hub bolts (arrowed)

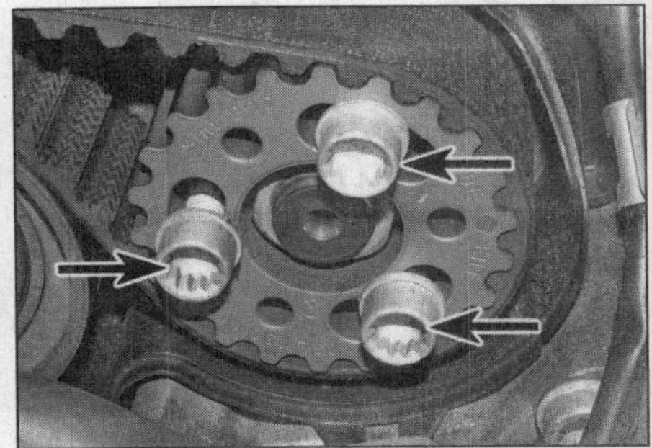

7.5 Slacken the high-pressure fuel pump sprocket bolts (arrowed)

7.6 Insert an Allen key, slacken the nut, and rotate the hub anti-clockwise until a 2 mm rod/drill bit (arrowed) can be inserted to lock the hub to the pulley

7.14 Rotate the high-pressure fuel pump clockwise until a 6 mm drill bit/rod can be inserted into the housing and hub (arrowed)

7.15a Rotate the sprockets fully clockwise until the fuel pump sprocket...

7.15b ...and camshaft sprocket bolts are at the end of the elongated holes

7.18 Timing belt routing

cost of belt renewal is negligible compared with potential cost of the engine repairs, should the belt fail in service. The belt must be renewed if it has covered the mileage given in Chapter 1B, however, if it has covered less, it is prudent to renew it regardless of condition, as a precautionary measure.

11 If the timing belt is not going to be refitted for some time, it is a wise precaution to hang a warning label on the steering wheel, to remind yourself (and others) not to attempt to start the engine.

Refitting

12 Ensure that the crankshaft and camshaft are still set to TDC on No 1 cylinder, as described in Section 3. The camshaft sprocket bolts should be renewed, and slackened at this point.

13 Renew the high-pressure fuel pump sprocket bolts one at a time. They should also be slackened.

14 Using a screwdriver on the bolts heads, rotate the high-pressure fuel pump clockwise until a 6.0 mm locking pin/drill bit can be inserted into the housing adjacent to the sprocket, locking the pump in place **(see illustration)**.

15 Rotate the camshaft sprocket and high-pressure fuel pump sprocket fully clockwise so that the securing bolts are at the end of the elongated holes **(see illustrations)**.

16 Loop the timing belt loosely under the crankshaft sprocket. **Note:** *Observe any direction of rotation markings on the belt.*

17 Fit the belt around the tensioner pulley, engage the timing belt teeth with the camshaft sprockets, then manoeuvre it into position around the coolant pump sprocket and the fuel pump sprocket. Make sure that the belt teeth seat correctly on the sprockets. **Note:** *Slight adjustment to the position of the camshaft sprocket may be necessary to achieve this. Avoid bending the belt back on itself or twisting it excessively as you do this.*

18 Finally, fit the belt around the idler roller **(see illustration)**. Ensure that any slack in the belt is in the section of belt that passes over the tensioner roller.

19 Loosen the timing belt tensioner securing nut, and pull out the tensioner locking pin. Turn the tensioner clockwise with an Allen key until the pointer is just past the middle of the gap in the tensioner base plate **(see illustration)**. With the tensioner held in this position, tighten the securing nut to the specified torque and angle.

20 Counterhold the camshaft sprocket with a home made tool to prevent any rotation, then tighten the camshaft sprocket and fuel pump sprocket bolts to 20 Nm. Remove the sprockets' locking tools and the crankshaft locking tool.

21 Using a spanner or wrench and socket on the crankshaft pulley centre bolt, rotate the crankshaft clockwise through two complete revolutions. Reset the engine to TDC on No 1 cylinder, with reference to Section 3 and refit the crankshaft locking tool.

22 Check that the tensioner roller indicator arm is centred, or within a maximum of 5 mm to the right of the notch in the base plate **(see illustration)**. If not, hold the tensioner hub stationary with an Allen key, slacken the retaining nut and position the arm in the centre of the notch. Tighten the retaining nut to the specified torque. Remove the Allen key.

23 Check that the camshaft sprocket locking pin can still be inserted. **Note:** *It's very difficult to align the locking point of the fuel pump hub again. However, a misalignment of holes will not affect engine performance.*

24 If the camshaft sprocket locking pin cannot be inserted, pull the crankshaft locking tool slight away from the engine, and rotate the crankshaft *anti-clockwise* slightly past TDC. Now slowly rotate the crankshaft clockwise until the camshaft sprocket locking tool can be inserted.

25 If the locating pin of the crankshaft locking tool is to the left of the corresponding hole, slacken the camshaft sprocket bolts, slowly rotate the crankshaft clockwise until the locking tool can be fully inserted. Tighten the camshaft sprocket bolts to 20 Nm.

26 If the locating pin of the crankshaft locking tool is to the right of the corresponding hole, slacken the camshaft sprocket bolts, rotate the crankshaft anti-clockwise slightly until the pin is to the left of the hole, then slowly rotate it clockwise until the lock tool can be fully inserted. Tighten the camshaft sprocket bolts to 20 Nm.

27 Remove the crankshaft and camshaft locking tools, then rotate the crankshaft 2 complete revolutions clockwise and check the locking tools can be reinserted. If necessary, repeat the adjustment procedure described previously.

28 Tighten the camshaft and fuel pump sprocket bolts to the specified torque.

29 The remainder of refitting is a reversal of removal.

7.19 Rotate the tensioner clockwise until the pointer (arrowed) is just past the gap in the base plate

7.22 The pointer should be centred in, or within 5 mm to the right of, the gap in the base plate

8.4 Coolant pipe upper mounting bolt and lower mounting nut (arrowed)

8.6 Engine mounting bracket bolts (arrowed)

8.8 Ensure the lug on the backplate engages with the cut-out in the timing belt cover (arrowed)

8 Timing belt tensioner and sprockets – removal and refitting

Timing belt tensioner

Removal

1 In order to remove the timing belt tensioner, then engine mounting bracket must first be removed. Either support the engine from above using a crossbeam or an engine hoist or support if from underneath with a trolley jack and block of wood.

2 Remove the timing belt as described in Section 7.

3 Undo the bolts and remove the right-hand engine mounting.

4 Undo the bolt securing the coolant pipe to the mounting bracket **(see illustration)**.

5 Working in the wheelarch area, undo the nut securing the lower end of the coolant pipe.

6 Undo the 3 retaining bolts and remove the engine mounting bracket **(see illustration)**.

7 Unscrew the timing belt tensioner nut, and remove the tensioner from the engine.

Refitting

8 When refitting the tensioner to the engine, ensure that the lug on the tensioner backplate engages with the corresponding cut-out in the rear timing belt cover, then refit the tensioner nut **(see illustration)**.

9 The remainder of refitting is a reversal of removal.

Idler pulleys

Removal

10 Remove the timing belt as described in Section 7.

11 Unscrew the relevant idler pulley/roller securing bolt/nut, then withdraw the pulley.

Refitting

12 Refit the pulley and tighten the securing bolt or nut to the specified torque. **Note:** *Renew the large roller/pulley retaining bolt (where applicable).*

13 Refit and tension the timing belt as described in Section 7.

Crankshaft sprocket

Note: *A new crankshaft sprocket securing bolt must be used on refitting.*

Removal

14 Remove the timing belt as described in Section 7.

15 The sprocket securing bolt must now be slackened, and the crankshaft must be prevented from turning as the sprocket bolt is unscrewed. To hold the sprocket, make up a suitable tool, and screw it to the sprocket using a two bolts screwed into two of the crankshaft pulley bolt holes.

16 Hold the sprocket using the tool, then slacken the sprocket securing bolt. Take care, as the bolt is very tight. Do not allow the crankshaft to turn as the bolt is slackened.

17 Unscrew the bolt, and slide the sprocket from the end of the crankshaft, noting which way round the sprocket's raised boss is fitted.

Refitting

18 Commence refitting by positioning the sprocket on the end of the crankshaft.

19 Fit a new sprocket securing bolt, then counterhold the sprocket using the method employed on removal, and tighten the bolt to the specified torque in the two stages given in the Specifications.

20 Refit the timing belt as described in Section 7.

Camshaft sprocket

Removal

21 Remove the timing belt as described in Section 7, then rotate the crankshaft 90° anti-clockwise to prevent any accidental piston-to-valve contact.

22 Unscrew and remove the three retaining bolts and remove the camshaft sprocket from the camshaft hub.

Refitting

23 Refit the sprocket ensuring that it is fitted the correct way round, as noted before removal, then insert the new sprocket bolts, and tighten by hand only at this stage.

24 If the crankshaft has been turned, turn the crankshaft clockwise 90° back to TDC.

25 Refit and tension the timing belt as described in Section 7.

Camshaft hub

Note: *VAG technicians use special tool T10051 to counterhold the hub, however it is possible to fabricate a suitable alternative.*

Removal

26 Remove the camshaft sprocket as described previously in this Section.

27 Engage special tool T10051 with the three locating holes in the face of the hub to prevent the hub from turning. If this tool is not available, fabricate a suitable alternative. Whilst holding the tool, undo the central hub retaining bolt about two turns **(see illustration)**.

28 Slide the hub from the camshaft. If necessary, attach VW tool T10052 (or a similar three-legged puller) to the hub, and evenly tighten the puller until the hub is free of the camshaft taper **(see illustration)**.

8.27 Fabricate a home made tool to counterhold the hub. Undo the bolt...

8.28 ...and slide the hub from the camshaft

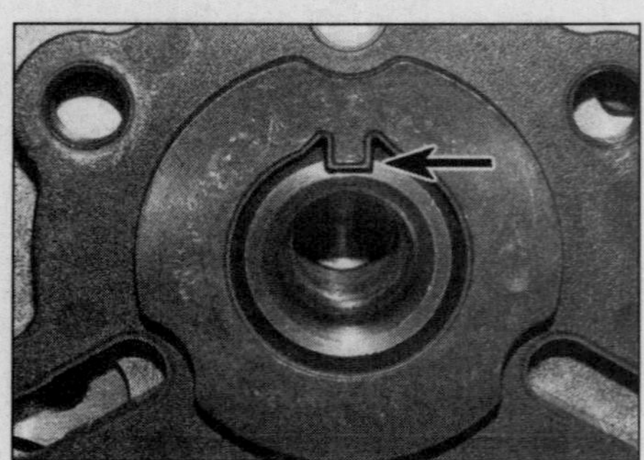

8.29 Ensure the integral key aligns with the keyway in the camshaft (arrowed)

Refitting

29 Ensure that the camshaft taper and the hub centre is clean and dry, locate the hub on the taper, noting that the built-in key in the hub taper must align with the keyway in the camshaft taper **(see illustration)**.

30 Hold the hub in this position with tool T10051 (or similar home-made tool), and tighten the central bolt to the specified torque.

31 Refit the camshaft sprocket as described previously in this Section.

Coolant pump sprocket

32 The coolant pump sprocket is integral with the coolant pump. Refer to Chapter 3 for details of coolant pump removal.

9 Camshaft and hydraulic tappets – removal, inspection and refitting

Note: *A new camshaft oil seal(s) will be required on refitting. VW removal tool T40094 (or similar tool) will be required to refit the camshafts – this is necessary to prevent damage to the retaining frame and cylinder head as the camshafts are refitted.*

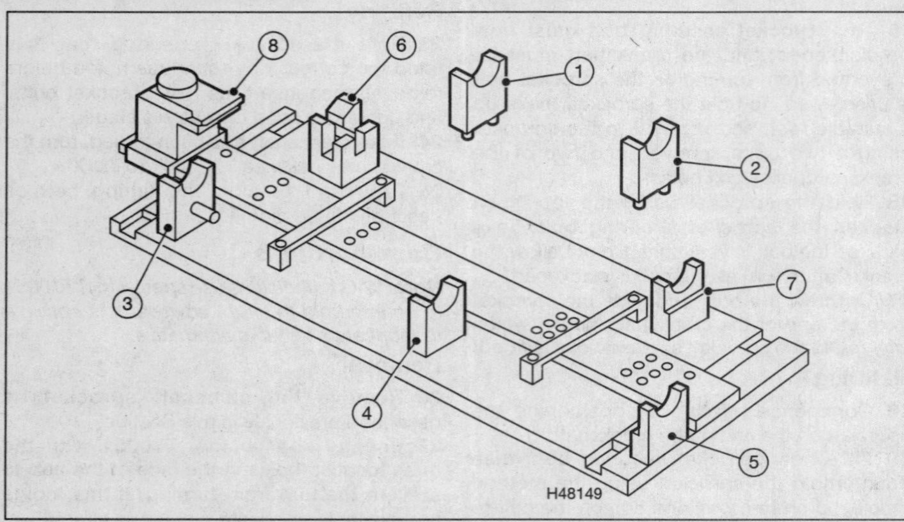

9.12a The different elements of tool no. T40094

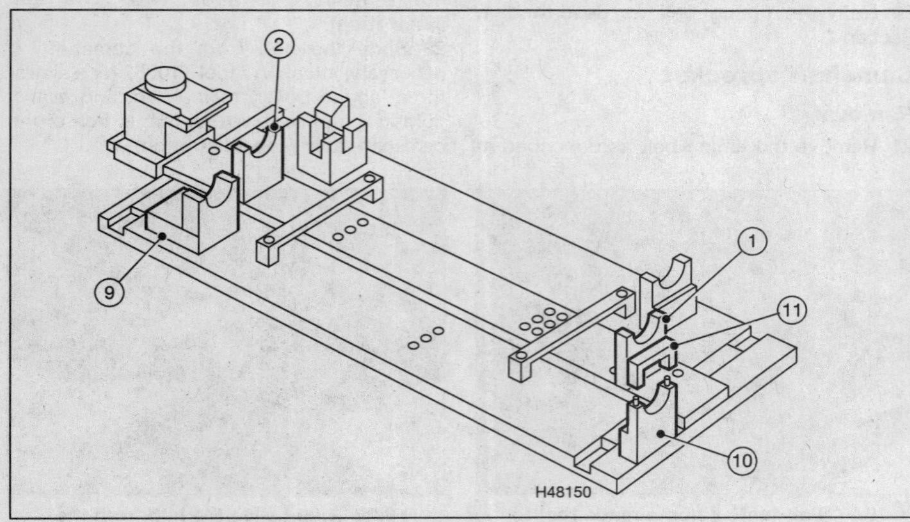

9.12b Position tools no. 1, 2, 9 and 10 as shown

Removal

1 Remove the camshaft hub (see Section 8).

2 Remove the camshaft cover (see Section 4).

3 Remove the brake vacuum pump as described in Chapter 9.

4 Progressively unscrew the camshaft retaining frame bolts in the reverse of the sequence shown in illustration 9.20, and carefully remove the retaining frame.

5 Carefully lift the camshafts from the cylinder head, keeping them identified for location. Remove the oil seal from the end of the camshaft and discard it – a new one will be required for refitting.

6 Lift the rocker arms and hydraulic tappets from place. Store the rockers and tappets in a container with numbered compartments to ensure they are refitted to their correct locations. It is recommended that the tappets are kept immersed in oil for the period they are removed from the cylinder head.

Inspection

7 With the camshafts removed, examine the retaining frame and the bearing locations in the cylinder head for signs of obvious wear or pitting. If evident, a new cylinder head will probably be required. Also check that the oil supply holes in the cylinder head are free from obstructions.

8 Visually inspect the camshafts for evidence of wear on the surfaces of the lobes and journals. Normally their surfaces should be smooth and have a dull shine; look for scoring, erosion or pitting and areas that appear highly polished, indicating excessive wear. Accelerated wear will occur once the hardened exterior of the camshaft has been damaged, so always renew worn items. **Note:** *If these symptoms are visible on the tips of the camshaft lobes, check the corresponding rocker arm, as it will probably be worn as well.*

9 If the machined surfaces of the camshaft appear discoloured or blued, it is likely that it has been overheated at some point, probably due to inadequate lubrication. This may have distorted the shaft, so have the camshaft runout and endfloat checked by an automotive engine reconditioning specialist.

10 Inspect the hydraulic tappets for obvious signs of wear or damage, and renew if necessary. Check that the oil holes in the tappets are free from obstructions.

Refitting

11 Oil the rocker arms and hydraulic tappets, then refit them to their original positions.

Warning: After fitting hydraulic tappets, wait a minimum of 30 minutes (or preferably, leave overnight) before starting the engine, to allow the tappets time to settle, otherwise the valve heads will strike the pistons.

12 To set up the tool, remove the supports number 3, 4 and 5, then install the supports number 9 and 10 at the vacant outer places, support number 2 at position 'A' and number 1 at position 'F' **(see illustrations)**.

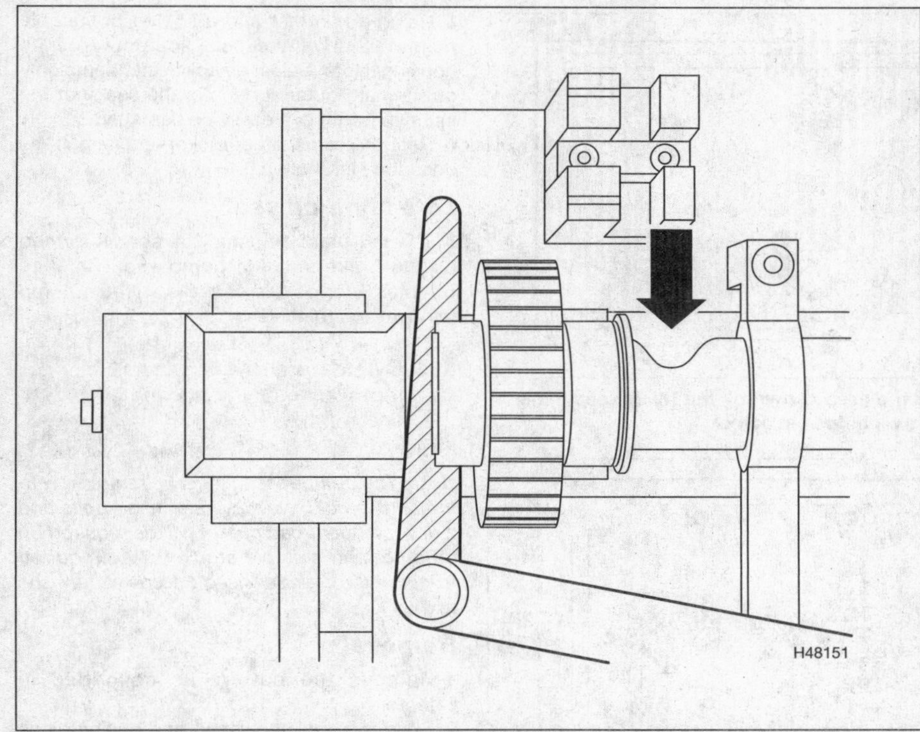

9.13 Position the inlet camshaft on the tool with the bolt indent (arrowed) facing outwards, then slide tool no 8 in to the slot in the end of the camshaft and use a 0.50 mm feeler gauge to remove any free play

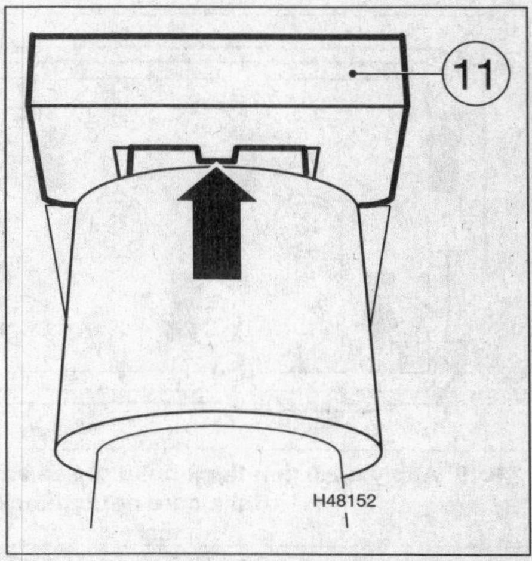

9.14 Fit tool no. 11 into the slot (arrowed) in the end of the exhaust camshaft

13 Position the inlet camshaft as shown with the cylinder head bolt indent facing outwards, then slide the support number 8 into the slot in the end of the camshaft and remove any free play with a 0.50 mm feeler gauge **(see illustration)**.

14 Position the exhaust camshaft on supports numbers 9 and 10, and fit the tool no. 11 into the slot in the end of the camshaft **(see illustration)**.

15 Fit the clamping tool no. T40096 to the gear on the exhaust camshaft, tightening the knurled thumb wheel until the faces of the gear teeth are in alignment. If necessary, use a 13 mm spanner **(see illustration)**.

16 Slide the exhaust camshaft towards the inlet camshaft until the gear teeth engage.

17 Ensure the gasket faces of the retaining frame are clean, then apply a smear of clean engine oil to the bearing surfaces and lower the frame into position over the camshafts. Ensure the bearing surfaces locate correctly on the camshafts.

18 Fit the clamping tool no. T40095 over the camshafts and frame, and tighten the thumbwheels to hold the camshafts in position in the frame **(see illustration)**.

19 Ensure the sealing surfaces of the cylinder head are clean, then apply a 2.0 mm wide bead of sealant (D 176 501 A1 or equivalent) as shown. Take care not to apply too much sealant, ensuring the oil holes supply holes are not blocked **(see illustration)**.

20 Slide out tool nos. 8 and 11, then lift the camshafts, retaining frame and clamping tool from the tool no. 40094. Place the camshafts, frame and tool in place on the cylinder head. Progressively, carefully, hand tighten the frame retaining bolts in the sequence shown, until the retaining frame makes contact with the cylinder head over the complete surface, then

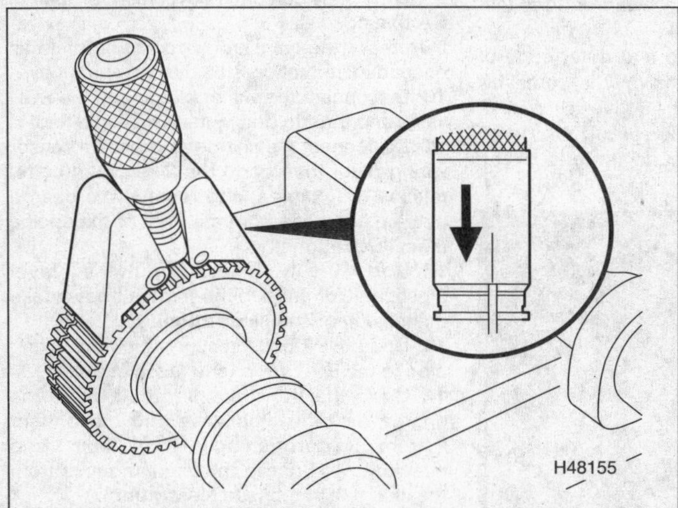

9.15 Tighten the thumbwheel to align the gear teeth. Ensure the clamping jaw with the arrow in seated on the wider gear

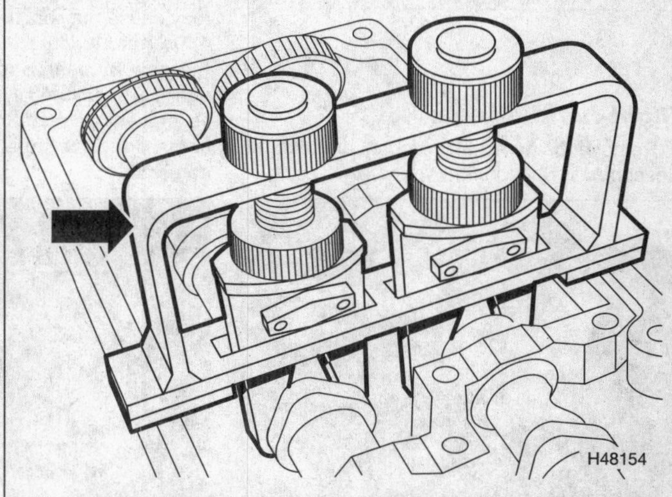

9.18 Secure the camshafts in place in the frame using tool No. T40095 (arrowed)

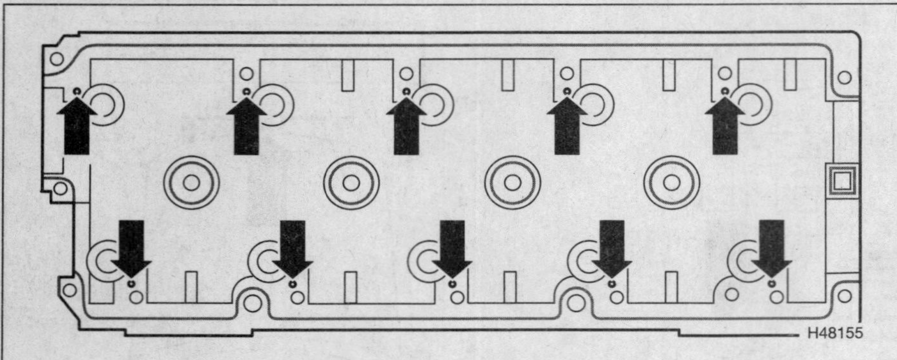

9.19 Apply a 2.0 mm thick bead of sealant to the area shown by the thick, black line. Take care not to block the oil holes (arrowed)

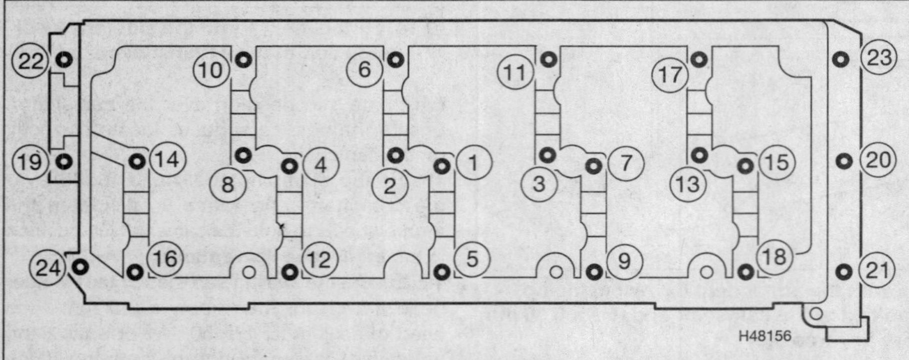

9.20 Camshaft retaining frame bolt tightening sequence

tighten the bolts to the specified torque, again in the correct sequence **(see illustration)**.

21 Remove the gear aligning tool (T40096) and the clamping tool (T40095).

22 Renew the camshaft oil seal (Section 11), then drive in a new sealing cap.

23 The remainder of refitting is a reversal of removal.

10 Camshaft oil seals – renewal

Right-hand oil seal

1 Remove the camshaft sprocket and hub, as described in Section 8.

2 Drill two small holes into the existing oil seal, diagonally opposite each other. Take great care to avoid drilling through into the seal housing or camshaft sealing surface. Thread two self-tapping screws into the holes, and using a pair of pliers, pull on the heads of the screws to extract the oil seal **(see illustration)**.

3 Clean out the seal housing and the sealing surface of the camshaft by wiping it with a lint-free cloth. Remove any swarf or burrs that may cause the seal to leak.

4 Do not lubricate the lip and outer edge of the new oil seal, push it over the camshaft until it is positioned in place above its housing. To prevent damage to the sealing lips, wrap some adhesive tape around the end of the camshaft.

10.2 Screw-in a self-tapping screw, then pull the screw and seal from place

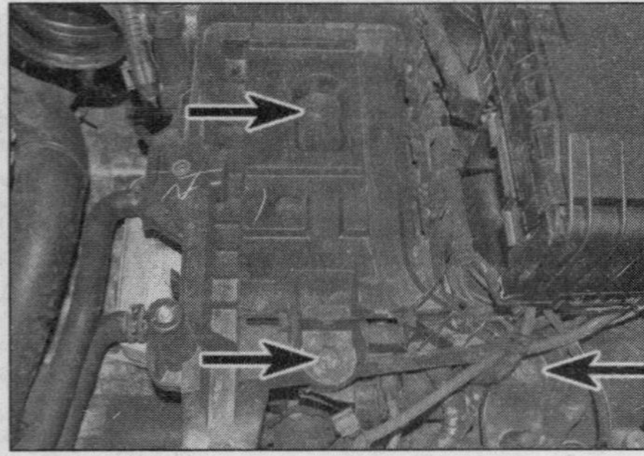

11.5 Battery tray bolts (arrowed)

5 Using a hammer and a socket of suitable diameter, drive the seal squarely into its housing. Note: Select a socket that bears only on the hard outer surface of the seal, not the inner lip which can easily be damaged.

6 Refit the camshaft sprocket and its hub, as described in Section 8.

Left-hand oil seal

7 The left-hand camshaft oil seal is formed by the brake vacuum pump seal. Refer to Chapter 9 for details of brake vacuum pump removal and refitting.

11 Cylinder head – removal, inspection and refitting

Note: *The cylinder head must be removed with the engine cold. New cylinder head bolts and a new cylinder head gasket will be required on refitting, and suitable studs will be required to guide the cylinder head into position – see text.*

Removal

1 Remove the battery as described in Chapter 5.

2 Drain the cooling system and engine oil as described in Chapter 1.

3 Pull the plastic cover on the top of the engine upwards from its mountings.

4 Remove the air filter housing as described in Chapter 4A.

5 Undo the bolts and remove the battery tray **(see illustration)**.

6 Remove the radiator cooling fan(s) and shroud as described in Chapter 3.

7 Undo the bolts and remove the air hose/duct from the intercooler to the turbocharger. Release the wiring looms from the clips as necessary to enable the duct to be manoeuvred from place.

8 Remove the camshaft cover as described in Section 4.

9 Remove the camshaft sprocket and hub as described in Section 8.

10 Disconnect the wiring plugs from the EGR valve and throttle body/intake manifold flap.

11 Disconnect the charge air pressure sensor wiring plug, then undo the 2 retaining bolts, release the clamps, and remove the charge air pipe and hose from the front of the engine **(see illustrations)**.

12 Undo the bolt securing the oil level dipstick guide tube to the throttle body/intake manifold flap **(see illustration)**.

13 Undo the 2 bolts securing the connecting pipe to the EGR valve **(see illustration)**.

14 Undo the front retaining bolt, twist the charge air pipe clockwise and disconnect it from the turbocharger. Note their fitted positions, and unclip the vacuum pipes from the charge air pipe **(see illustration)**.

15 Apply a little lubrication spray to the rubber sleeve, pull up the pipe from the vacuum pump, then undo the 4 retaining bolts and

11.11a Disconnect the pressure sensor wiring plug (arrowed)...

11.11b ...then remove the charge air pipe and hose (arrowed)

11.12 Oil level dipstick guide tube bolt (arrowed)

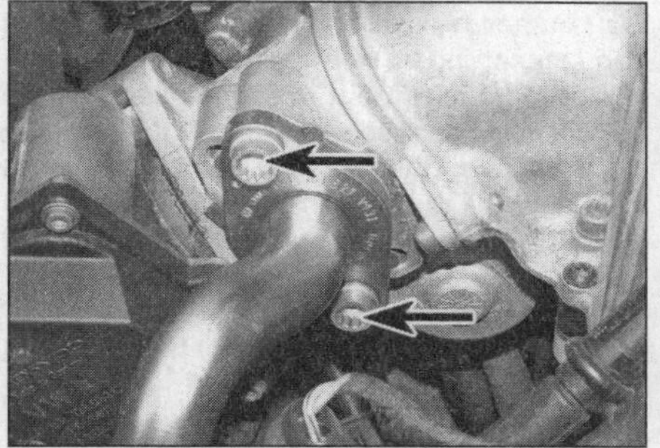
11.13 EGR pipe-to-valve bolts (arrowed)

11.14 Charge air pipe retaining bolt (arrowed). Note the position of the vacuum hoses

11.15 With some lubrication, the hose connection pulls up from the vacuum pump

remove the vacuum pump from the left-hand end of the cylinder head **(see illustration)**. Renew the pump-to-cylinder head seal.

16 Disconnect the coolant temperature sensor wiring plug at the left-hand end of the cylinder head, and release the wiring loom from any retaining clips.

17 Disconnect the gearchange cables from the levers on the transmission as described in Chapter 7.

18 Undo the bolts/nut, securing the gearchange bracket to the top of the transmission. Move the bracket and cables to one side.

19 Undo the bolts securing the EGR pipe to the cooler at the left-hand end of the engine, and the nut securing the bracket to the cylinder head, then remove the pipe **(see illustration)**. Recover the gasket at each end.

20 Working underneath the vehicle, slacken the Allen bolt and release the clamp securing the diesel particulate filter/catalytic converter to the turbocharger, then undo the bolts/nuts securing the brackets to the cylinder block/head and lay the filter/converter to one side.

21 Undo the nuts and multi-spline bolts securing the EGR pipe to the right-hand end of the exhaust manifold and EGR cooler **(see illustration)**. Remove the pipe and recover the gaskets.

22 Trace the exhaust manifold gas temperature sensor wiring back, releasing it from any retaining clips, disconnect its wiring plug at the bulkhead, and slide it from the retaining bracket. Unclip the wiring loom from the top of the turbocharger heatshield.

23 Undo the bolt securing the support bracket/oil return pipe to the underside of the turbocharger, then undo the bolt securing the top of the support bracket to the underside of the turbocharger. Now pull and twist the support bracket to disconnect it from the oil return pipe at the top. Remove the pipe/bracket **(see illustrations)**. Note the O-ring and copper sealing washer on the lower banjo bolt, and the 2 O-rings fitted to the base of the oil return pipe still fitted to the turbocharger.

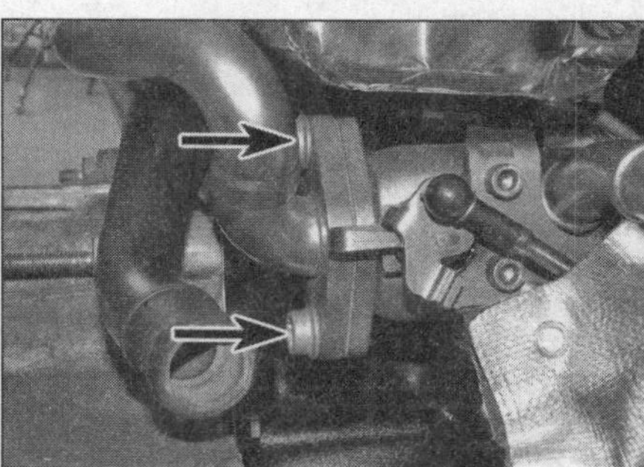
11.19 EGR pipe-to-cooler bolts (arrowed)

11.21 Remove the EGR pipe between the manifold and cooler

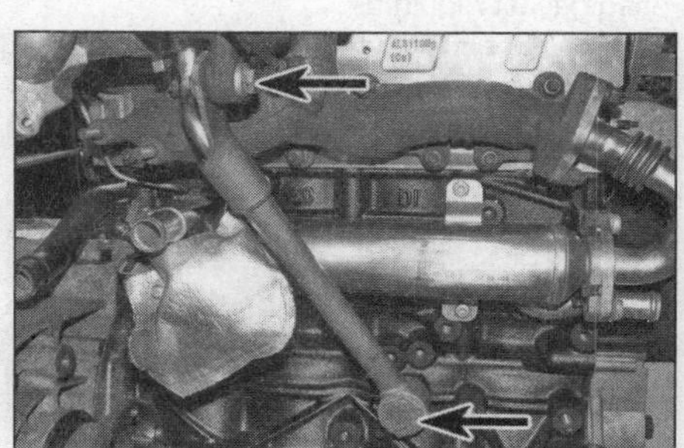
11.23a Undo the banjo bolt at the base of the turbocharger support bracket/oil return pipe and the bolt at the top

11.23b Note the 2 O-ring seals (arrowed) at the base of the oil return pipe

11.26 Undo the bolt (arrowed) securing the timing belt guard

11.27 Undo the boost pressure solenoid valve nuts (arrowed)

11.28 Undo the cylinder head bolts using a M12 multi-splined (12 pointed star) tool

24 Note their fitted locations, then release the clamps and disconnect the various coolant hoses from the cylinder head.

25 Undo the bolt securing the turbocharger oil supply pipe bracket at the left-hand end of the cylinder head, the nut securing the bracket on the rear of the head, then undo the union bolts and remove the pipe. Renew any seals.

26 Undo the bolt securing the timing belt guard adjacent to the timing belt tensioner, and the bolt securing the camshaft position sensor, then remove the tensioner retaining nut **(see illustration)**.

27 Disconnect the turbocharger wastegate position sensor wiring plug, and the intake manifold change-over valve wiring plug. Note their fitted positions and disconnect the vacuum hoses from the EGR cooler (where the plastic pipe joins the metal pipe at the back of the cylinder head) and the turbocharger wastegate actuator. Undo the nuts securing the boost pressure solenoid valve to the bulkhead. Release the loom wiring plug, lay the wiring loom and vacuum hoses over the front of the engine, clear of the cylinder head **(see illustration)**. Make a final check to ensure all relevant wiring and vacuum hoses have been disconnected. Note the loom/hose routing to aid refitting.

28 Using an M12 multi-splined tool (12 pointed star), undo the cylinder head bolts, working from the outside-in, evenly and gradually **(see illustration)**. Remove the bolts and recover the washers. Check that nothing remains connected, and starting at the gearbox side, lift the cylinder head from the engine block, sliding the belt tensioner from the mounting stud as the cylinder head is removed. Seek assistance if possible, as it is a heavy assembly, especially as it is being removed complete with the manifolds.

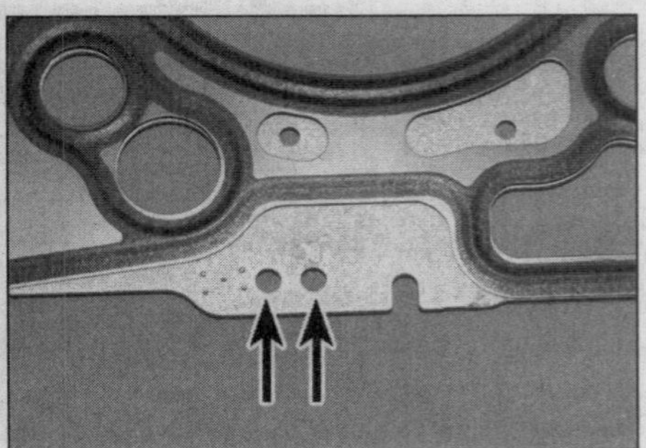
11.31 The holes (arrowed) identify the thickness of the cylinder head gasket

29 Remove the gasket from the top of the block, noting the locating dowels. If the dowels are a loose fit, remove them and store them with the head for safe-keeping. Do not discard the gasket yet – it will be needed for identification purposes. If desired, the manifolds can be removed from the cylinder head with reference to Chapter 4B (inlet manifold) or 4D (exhaust manifold).

Inspection

30 Dismantling and inspection of the cylinder head is covered in Part Chapter 2G.

Cylinder head gasket selection

Note: *A dial test indicator (DTI) will be required for this operation.*

31 Examine the old cylinder head gasket for manufacturer's identification markings **(see illustration)**. These will be in the form of holes, and a part number on the edge of the gasket. Unless new pistons have been fitted, the new cylinder head gasket must be of the same type as the old one.

32 If new piston assemblies have been fitted as part of an engine overhaul, or if a new short engine is to be fitted, the projection of the piston crowns above the cylinder head mating face of the cylinder block at TDC must be measured. This measurement is used to determine the thickness of the new cylinder head gasket required.

11.34 Measure the piston protrusion using a DTI gauge

33 Anchor a dial test indicator (DTI) to the top face (cylinder head gasket mating face) of the cylinder block, and zero the gauge on the gasket mating face.

34 Rest the gauge probe on No 1 piston crown, and turn the crankshaft slowly by hand until the piston reaches TDC. Measure and record the maximum piston projection at TDC **(see illustration)**.

35 Repeat the measurement for the remaining pistons, and record the results.

36 If the measurements differ from piston-to-piston, take the highest figure, and use this to determine the thickness of the head gasket required as follows.

Piston projection	Gasket identification (number of holes)
0.91 to 1.00 mm	1
1.01 to 1.10 mm	2
1.11 to 1.20 mm	3

37 Purchase a new gasket according to the results of the measurements.

Refitting

38 The mating faces of the cylinder head and block must be perfectly clean before refitting the head. Use a scraper to remove all traces of gasket and carbon, also clean the tops of the pistons. Take particular care with the aluminium surfaces, as the soft metal is easily damaged.

39 Make sure that debris is not allowed to enter the oil and water passages – this is particularly important for the oil circuit, as carbon could block the oil supply to the camshaft and crankshaft bearings. Using adhesive tape and paper, seal the water, oil and bolt holes in the cylinder block.

40 To prevent carbon entering the gap between the pistons and bores, smear a little grease in the gap. After cleaning a piston, rotate the crankshaft to that the piston moves down the bore, then wipe out the grease and carbon with a cloth rag. Clean the other piston crowns in the same way.

41 Check the head and block for nicks, deep scratches and other damage. If slight, they may be removed carefully with a file. More serious damage may be repaired by machining, but this is a specialist job.

42 If warpage of the cylinder head is suspected, use a straight-edge to check it for distortion, as described in Chapter 2C.

43 Ensure that the cylinder head bolt holes in the crankcase are clean and free of oil. Syringe or soak up any oil left in the bolt holes. This is most important in order that the correct bolt tightening torque can be applied, and to prevent the possibility of the block being cracked by hydraulic pressure when the bolts are tightened.

44 Turn the crankshaft anti-clockwise all the pistons at an equal height, approximately half-way down their bores from the TDC position (see Section 3). This will eliminate any risk of piston-to-valve contact as the cylinder head is refitted.

45 Where applicable, refit the manifolds with reference to Chapters 4A and/or 4B.

46 Ensure that the cylinder head locating dowels are in place in the cylinder block, then fit the new cylinder head gasket over the dowels, ensuring that the part number is uppermost **(see illustration)**. Note that VW recommend that the gasket is only removed from its packaging immediately prior to fitting.

47 Lower the cylinder head into position on the gasket, ensuring that it engages correctly over the dowels. Refit the timing belt tensioner as the cylinder head is refitted.

48 Fit the washers in place then fit the new cylinder head bolts to the locations, and screw them in as far as possible by hand. Do not oil the bolt threads.

49 Working progressively, in sequence, tighten all the cylinder head bolts to the specified Stage 1 torque **(see illustrations)**.

50 Again working progressively, in sequence, tighten all the cylinder head bolts to the specified Stage 2 torque.

51 Tighten all the cylinder head bolts, in sequence, through the specified Stage 3 angle **(see illustration)**.

52 Finally, tighten all the cylinder head bolts, in sequence, through the specified Stage 4 angle.

53 The remainder of the refitting procedure is a reversal of the removal procedure, noting the following points:

a) Tighten all fasteners to their specified torque where given.
b) Renew all seals and gaskets.
c) Refill the cooling system as described in Chapter 1.
d) Ensure all wiring is correctly routed.

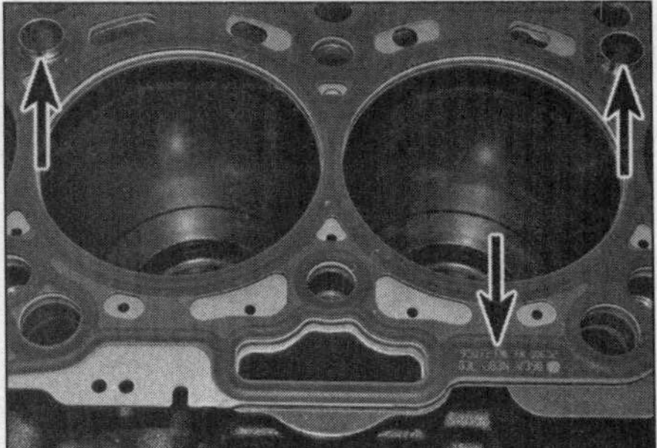

11.46 Ensure the dowels are in place, then fit the new gasket with the part number uppermost (arrowed)

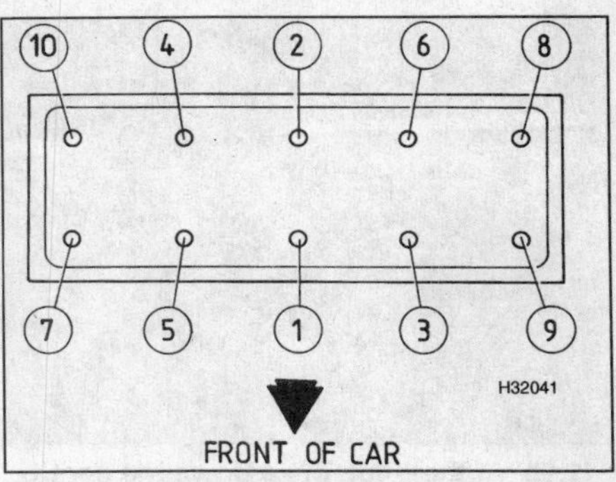

11.49a Cylinder head bolt tightening sequence

11.49b Tighten the cylinder head bolts to the Stage 1 torque

11.51 Use an angle-tightening gauge

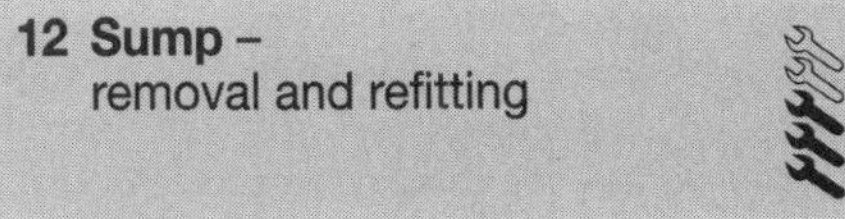

12 Sump – removal and refitting

Removal

1 Apply the handbrake, then jack up the front of the vehicle and support securely on axle stands (see *Jacking and vehicle support*).

2 Remove the securing screws and withdraw the engine undershield(s).

3 Drain the engine oil as described in Chapter 1B.

4 Release the clamp, raise the retaining clip and remove the air duct from the intercooler outlet **(see illustration)**.

5 Undo the retaining bolts, release the clamp and remove the charger air pipe from the front of the cylinder block **(see illustration 11.11a and 11.11b)**. Disconnect the charger air pressure sensor wiring plug as the pipe is withdrawn.

6 Undo the retaining bolt and move the electric coolant circulation pump to one side **(see illustration)**.

7 Undo the bolt securing the turbo-to-intercooler air pipe to the sump.

8 Disconnect the wiring connector from the oil level/temperature sender in the sump.

9 Pull the sump insulation cover downwards at the rear to release the retaining clips, then prise down the centre clip and pull the clip on the front side of the cover downwards (where fitted) **(see illustrations)**.

10 Unscrew and remove the bolts securing the sump to the cylinder block, and the bolts securing the sump to the transmission casing, then withdraw the sump. If necessary, release the sump by tapping with a soft-faced hammer.

12.4 Raise the clip (arrowed) and disconnect the air duct from the intercooler

12.6 Electric coolant circulation pump retaining bolt (arrowed)

12.9a Pull the insulation down at the rear to release the clips (arrowed)

12.9b At the front, prise down the centre pin and pull the clip downwards (arrowed)

Refitting

11 Begin refitting by thoroughly cleaning the mating faces of the sump and cylinder block. Ensure that all traces of old sealant are removed.

12 Ensure that the cylinder block mating face of the sump is free from all traces of old sealant, oil and grease, and then apply a 2.0 to 3.0 mm thick bead of silicone sealant (VW D 176 404 A2 or equivalent) to the sump **(see illustration)**. Note that the sealant should be run around the inside of the bolt holes in the sump. The sump must be fitted within 5 minutes of applying the sealant.

13 Offer the sump up to the cylinder block, then refit the sump-to-cylinder block bolts, and lightly tighten them by hand, working progressively in a diagonal sequence. **Note:** *If the sump is being refitted with the engine and transmission separated, make sure that the sump is flush with the flywheel end of the cylinder block.*

14 Refit the sump-to-transmission casing bolts, and tighten them lightly, using a socket.

15 Again working in a diagonal sequence, lightly tighten the sump-to-cylinder block bolts, using a socket.

16 Tighten the sump-to-transmission casing bolts to the specified torque.

17 Working in a diagonal sequence, progressively tighten the sump-to-cylinder block bolts to the specified torque.

18 The remainder of refitting is a reversal of removal, noting to allow at least 30 minutes from the time of refitting the sump for the sealant to dry, then refill the engine with oil, with reference to Chapter 1.

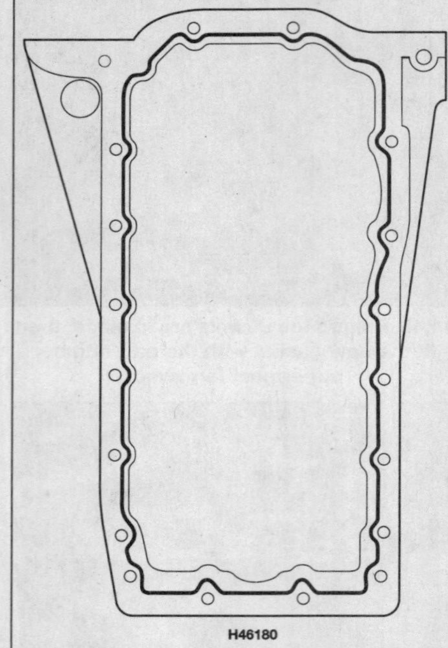

12.12 Apply a bead of sealant to the around the inside of the bolt holes

13 Oil pump and drive chain – removal, inspection and refitting

Proceed as described in Chapter 2A.

14 Flywheel – removal, inspection and refitting

Removal

1 On manual gearbox models, remove the gearbox (see Chapter 7A) and clutch (see Chapter 6).

2 On automatic transmission models, remove the automatic transmission as described in Chapter 7B.

3 These models are fitted with a dual-mass flywheel. The flywheel can only be fitted in one position due to the offset of the flywheel mounting holes in the end of the crankshaft.

4 Rotate the outside of the dual-mass flywheel so that the bolts align with the holes (if necessary).

5 Unscrew the bolts and remove the flywheel. Use a locking tool to counter hold the flywheel **(see illustration)**. Discard the bolts, new ones must be fitted. **Note:** *In order not to damage the flywheel, do not allow the bolt heads to make contact with the flywheel during the unscrewing procedure.*

Inspection

6 Check the flywheel for wear and damage. Examine the starter ring gear for excessive wear to the teeth. If the driveplate or its ring gear are damaged, the complete driveplate must be renewed. The flywheel ring gear, however, may be renewed separately from the flywheel, but the work should be entrusted to a VW dealer. If the clutch friction face is discoloured or scored excessively, it may be possible to regrind it, but this work should also be entrusted to a VW dealer.

7 The following are guidelines only, but should indicate whether professional inspection is necessary. The dual-mass flywheel should be checked as follows:

Warpage: Place a straight edge across the face of the drive surface, and check by trying to insert a feeler gauge between the straight edge and the drive surface **(see illustration)**. The flywheel will normally warp like a bowl – ie. Higher on the outer edge. If the warpage is more than 0.40 mm, the flywheel may need replacing.

Free rotational movement: This is the distance the drive surface of the flywheel can be turned independently of the flywheel primary element, using finger effort alone. Move the drive surface in one direction and make a mark where the locating pin aligns with the flywheel edge. Move the drive surface in the other direction (finger pressure only) and make another mark **(see illustration)**. The total of free movement should not exceed 20.0 mm. If it's more, the flywheel may need replacing.

Total rotational movement: This is the total distance the drive surface can be turned independently of the flywheel primary element.

14.5 Use a locking tool to counterhold the flywheel

14.7a Flywheel warpage check – see text

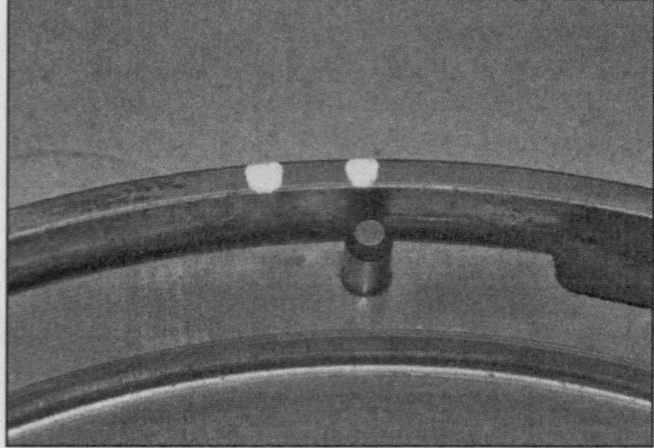

14.7b Flywheel free rotational movement check alignment marks – see text

Insert two bolts into the clutch pressure plate/damper unit mounting holes, and with the crankshaft/flywheel held stationary, use a lever/pry bar between the bolts and use some effort to move the drive surface fully in one direction – make a mark where the locating pin aligns with the flywheel edge. Now force the drive surface fully in the opposite direction, and make another mark. The total rotational movement should not exceed 44.00 mm. If it does, have the flywheel professionally inspected.

Lateral movement: The lateral movement (up and down) of the drive surface in relation to the primary element of the flywheel, should not exceed 2.0 mm. If it does, the flywheel may need replacing. This can be checked by pressing the drive surface down on one side into the flywheel (flywheel horizontal) and making an alignment mark between the drive surface and the inner edge of the primary element. Now press down on the opposite side of the drive surface, and make another mark above the original one. The difference between the two marks is the lateral movement **(see illustration).**

There should be no cracks in the drive surface of the flywheel. If cracks are evident, the flywheel may need replacing.

Refitting

8 Refitting is a reversal of removal. Use new bolts when refitting the flywheel or driveplate, and coat the threads of the bolts with locking fluid before inserting them. Tighten them to the specified torque.

15 Crankshaft oil seals – renewal

Note: *The oil seals are a PTFE (Teflon) type and are fitted dry, without using any grease or oil. These have a wider sealing lip and have been introduced instead of the coil spring type oil seal.*

Timing belt end oil seal

1 Remove the timing belt as described in Section 7, and the crankshaft sprocket with reference to Section 8.

2 To remove the seal without removing the housing, drill two small holes diagonally opposite each other, insert self-tapping screws, and pull on the heads of the screws with pliers **(see illustration).**

3 Alternatively, to remove the oil seal complete with its housing, proceed as follows.

a) Remove the sump as described in Section 12. This is necessary to ensure a satisfactory seal between the sump and oil seal housing on refitting.

b) Unbolt and remove the oil seal housing.

c) Working on the bench, lever the oil seal from the housing using a suitable screwdriver. Take care not to damage the seal seating in the housing **(see illustration).**

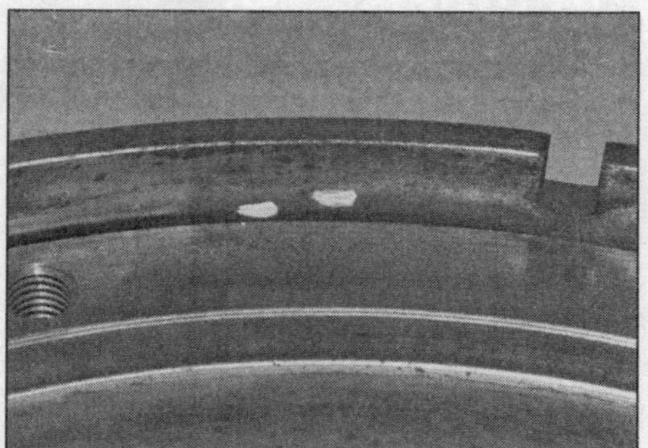

14.7c Flywheel lateral movement check marks – see text

4 Thoroughly clean the oil seal seating in the housing.

5 Wind a length of tape around the end of the crankshaft to protect the oil seal lips as the seal (and housing, where applicable) is fitted.

6 Fit a new oil seal to the housing, pressing or driving it into position using a socket or tube of suitable diameter. Ensure that the socket or tube bears only on the hard outer ring of the seal, and take care not to damage the seal lips. Press or drive the seal into position until it is seated on the shoulder in the housing. Make sure that the closed end of the seal is facing outwards.

7 If the oil seal housing has been removed, proceed as follows, otherwise proceed to paragraph 11.

8 Clean all traces of old sealant from the crankshaft oil seal housing and the cylinder block, then coat the cylinder block mating faces of the oil seal housing with a 2.0 to 3.0 mm thick bead of silicone sealant (VW D 176 404 A2, or equivalent). Note that the seal housing must be refitted within 5 minutes of applying the sealant.

Caution: DO NOT put excessive amounts of sealant onto the housing as it may get into the sump and block the oil pick-up pipe.

9 Refit the oil seal housing, and tighten the bolts progressively to the specified torque **(see illustration).**

10 Refit the sump as described in Section 12.

11 Refit the crankshaft sprocket with reference to Section 8, and the timing belt as described in Section 7.

Flywheel end oil seal

Note: *In these engines, the seal, sealing flange and sender wheel are a complete unit. Special tools are required to refit the sealing flange, and press the sender wheel onto the end of the crankshaft. It is not possible to accurately fit these parts without the tools, which may be available from VW (part no. T10134) and are available from aftermarket automotive tool specialists. Eg. Laser tools).*

12 Remove the flywheel as described in Section 14, then prise the intermediate plate from the locating dowels on the cylinder block.

13 Undo the bolts securing the sealing flange to the cylinder block **(see illustration).**

14 Insert three 6 x 35 mm bolts into the threaded holes in the sealing flange. Tighten the bolts gradually and evenly, and press the

15.2 Pull the screw and seal from place using pliers

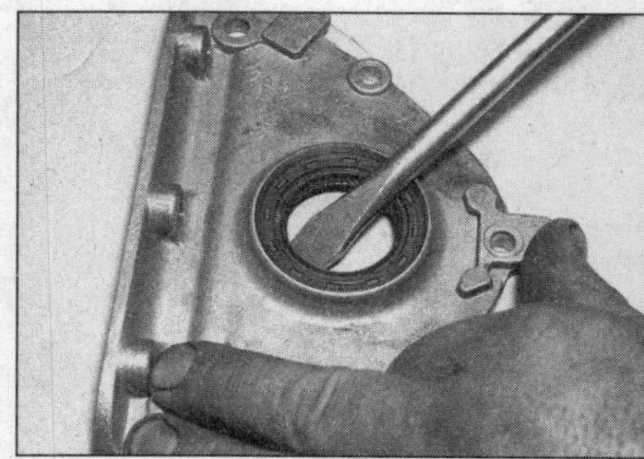

15.3 Prise the oil seal form the crankshaft oil seal housing

15.9 Slide the oil seal housing over the end of the crankshaft

15.13 Sealing flange bolts (arrowed)

15.14 Screw in 6 x 35 mm bolts (arrowed) and draw the sealing flange and sender wheel from place

15.16a Rotate the nut until its level with the end of the clamping surface (arrowed)...

15.16b ...then clamp it in a vice

sealing flange, and sender wheel from the crankshaft/cylinder block **(see illustration)**. The seal, sender wheel and sealing flange are supplied as a complete unit.

15 Ensure the mating face of the cylinder block is clean and free from debris. The new sealing flange/seal/sender wheel assembly is supplied with a sealing lip support ring, which serves as a fitting sleeve, and must not be removed prior to installation. Equally, the sender wheel must not be separated from the assembly.

16 If using the VW tool, proceed as follows. If using an aftermarket tool specialists product, follow the instructions supplied with the tool. Rotate the large spindle nut until it's level with the end of the clamping surface of the spindle, then clamp the spindle in a vice **(see illustrations)**.

17 Press the tool housing downwards until it rests on the nut and washer. Rotate the nut until the inner part of the tool is at the same height as the housing **(see illustration)**.

18 Remove the seal securing clip. The hole on the sender wheel must align with the marking on the sealing flange **(see illustrations)**.

19 Place the flange outer side down on a clean, flat surface, then press the seal guide fitting sleeve (supplied ready fitted), housing, and sender wheel downwards until all the components are flat on the surface. In this position the upper edge of the sender wheel should be level with the edge of the sealing flange **(see illustrations)**.

20 Place the sealing flange on the assembly tool, so the pin locates in the hole in the sender wheel **(see illustration)**.

21 Push the sealing flange and guide fitting sleeve against the tool whilst tightening the 3 knurled screws. Ensure the pin is still located in the sender wheel **(see illustration)**.

22 Ensure the end of the crankshaft is clean, and is locked at TDC on No. 1 cylinder as described in Section 3.

23 Unscrew the large nut to the end of the spindle threads, then press the spindle inwards as far as possible **(see illustration)**.

24 Align the flat side of the assembly with the sump flange, then secure the tool to the crankshaft using the integral Allen bolts **(see illustration)**. Only hand tighten the bolts.

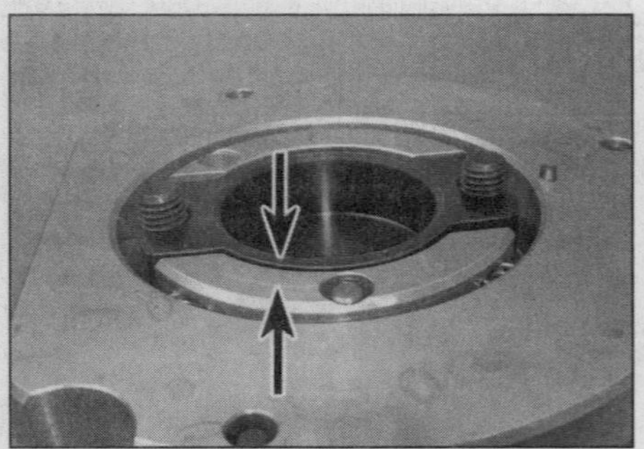
15.17 Rotate the nut until the inner part of the tool is flush with the housing (arrowed)

15.18a Remove the securing clip ...

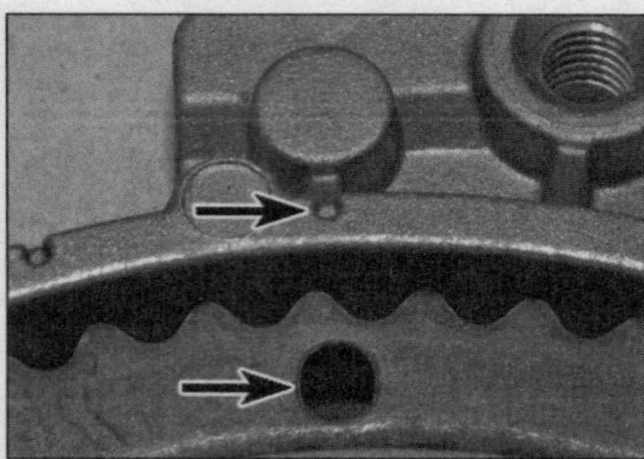
15.18b ...the hole in the sender wheel should align with the marking on the flange (arrowed)

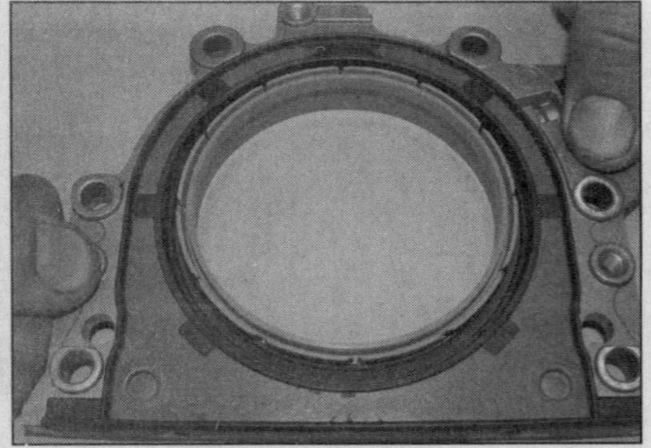
15.19a Press the assembly downwards on a clean, flat surface...

15.19b ...so the upper edge of the sender wheel is level with the edge of the flange (arrowed)

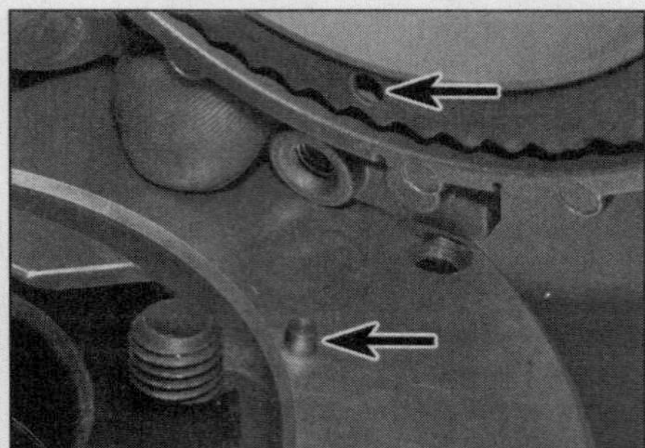
15.20 Fit the flange to the tool, ensuring the pin locates in the hole (arrowed)

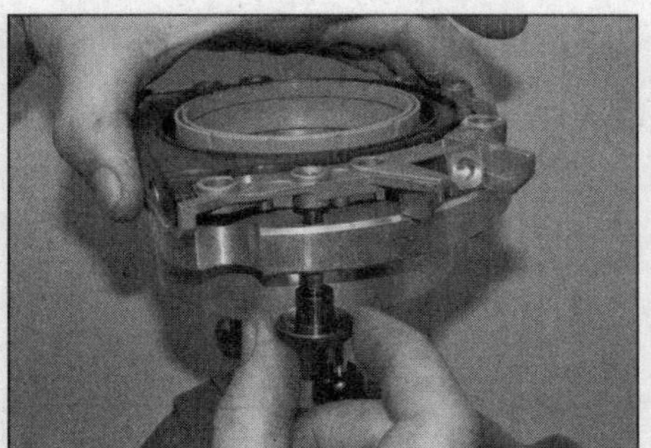

15.21 With the pin engaged in the hole, tighten the 3 knurled screws to secure the flange to the tool

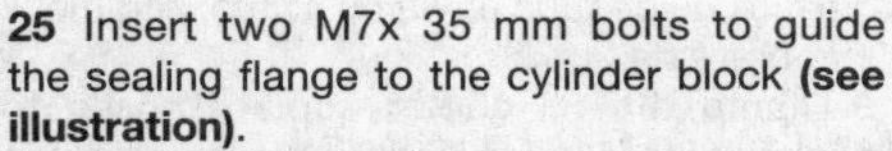

15.23 Unscrew the nut to the end of the thread, and push the spindle in as far as possible

15.24 Hand-tighten the Allen bolts to secure the tool to the crankshaft (arrowed)

25 Insert two M7x 35 mm bolts to guide the sealing flange to the cylinder block **(see illustration)**.

26 Using hand pressure alone, push the tool assembly onto the crankshaft until the seal guide fitting sleeve contacts the crankshaft flange, then push the guide pin (black knob) into the hole in the crankshaft. This is to ensure the sender wheel reaches its correct installation position **(see illustration)**.

27 Rotate the large nut until it makes contact with the tool housing, then tighten it to 35 Nm. After tightening this nut, a small air gap must still be present between the sealing flange and cylinder block **(see illustration)**.

28 Unscrew the large nut, the two M7 x 35 Nm screws, the three knurled screws and the Allen bolts securing the tool to the crankshaft. Remove the tool, and pull the seal guide fitting sleeve from place (if it didn't come out with the tool).

29 Use a vernier caliper or feeler gauge to measure the fitted depth of the sender wheel in relation to the crankshaft flange **(see illustration)**. The correct depth is 0.5 mm.

30 If the gap is correct, fit the sealing flange bolts and tighten them to the specified torque.

31 If the gap is too small, re-attach the tool to the sealing flange and crankshaft, then refit the two M7 x 35 mm guide bolts to the flange. Tighten the large spindle nut to 40 Nm, remove the tool and re-measure the air gap. If the gap is still too small, re-attach the tool and tighten the spindle nut to 45 Nm. Re-measure the gap. When the gap is correct, refit the flange retaining bolts, and tighten them to the specified torque.

32 The remainder of refitting is a reversal of removal.

16 Engine/transmission mountings – inspection and renewal

Inspection

1 If improved access is required, jack up the front of the vehicle, and support it securely on axle stands (see *Jacking and vehicle support*). Remove the engine top cover which also incorporates the air filter, then remove the engine undershield(s).

2 Check the mounting rubbers to see if they are cracked, hardened or separated from the metal at any point; renew the mounting if any such damage or deterioration is evident.

3 Check that all the mountings are securely tightened; use a torque wrench to check if possible.

4 Using a large screwdriver or a crowbar, check for wear in the mounting by carefully levering against it to check for free play. Where this is not possible, enlist the aid of an assistant to move the engine/transmission back-and-forth, or from side-to-side, whilst you observe the mounting. While some free play is to be expected, even from new components, excessive wear should be obvious. If excessive free play is found, check first that the fasteners are correctly secured, then renew any worn components as described in the following paragraphs.

Renewal

Right-hand mounting

Note: *New mounting securing bolts will be required on refitting.*

5 Attach a hoist and lifting tackle to the engine lifting brackets on the cylinder head, and raise the hoist to just take the weight of the engine. Alternatively the engine can be supported on a trolley jack under the engine. Use a block of wood between the sump and the head of the jack, to prevent any damage to the sump.

15.25 Use 2 M7 x 35 mm screws (arrowed) to guide the sealing flange

15.26 Push the black knob (arrowed) into the hole in the crankshaft

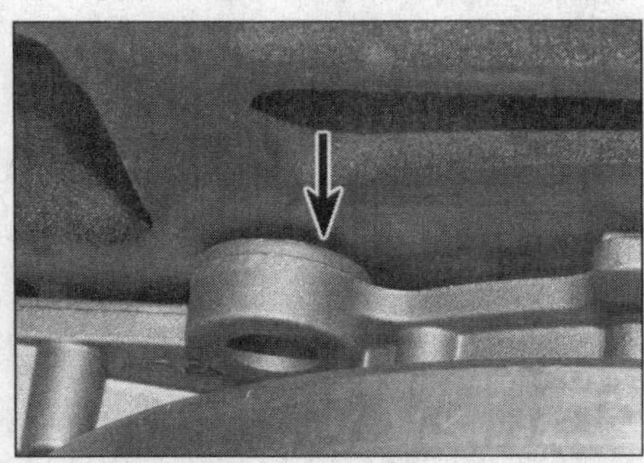

15.27 After tightening the spindle nut (35 Nm) then should be an air gap between the sealing flange and the cylinder block (arrowed)

15.29 Measure the fitted depth of the sender wheel in relation to the end of the crankshaft

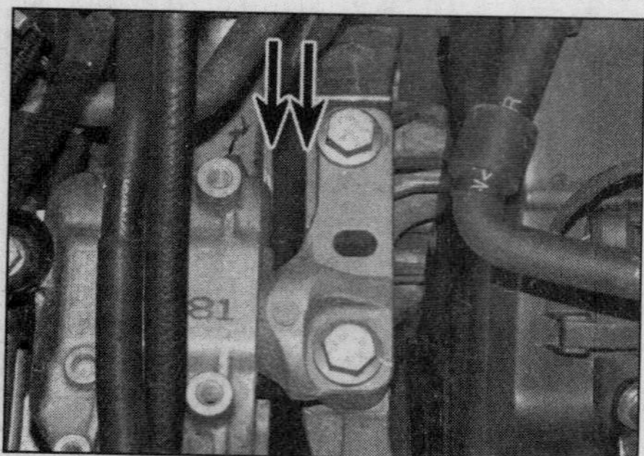
16.9 There must be at least 10 mm between the bracket and the chassis member (arrowed)

16.18 Rear mounting arm-to-transmission bolts (arrowed)

18.1 Oil pressure warning light switch

6 For improved access, unbolt the coolant reservoir and move it to one side, leaving the coolant hoses connected.
7 Where applicable, move any wiring harnesses, pipes or hoses to one side to enable removal of the engine mounting.
8 Unscrew the bolts securing the mounting to the engine bracket, then unscrew the bolts securing it to the body. Also, unbolt the movement limiter. Withdraw the mounting from the engine compartment.
9 Refitting is a reversal of removal, bearing in mind the following points.

a) *Use new securing bolts.*
b) *There must be at least 10 mm between the engine mounting bracket and the right-hand side chassis member* ***(see illustration)****.*
c) *The side of the mounting support arm must be parallel to the side of the engine mounting bracket.*
d) *Tighten all fixings to the specified torque.*

Left-hand mounting

Note: *New mounting bolts will be required on refitting***.**
10 Remove the engine top cover.
11 Attach a hoist and lifting tackle to the engine lifting brackets on the cylinder head, and raise the hoist to just take the weight of the engine and transmission. Alternatively the engine can be supported on a trolley jack under the transmission. Use a block of wood between the transmission and the head of the jack, to prevent any damage to the transmission.
12 Remove the battery and battery tray, as described in Chapter 5.
13 Unscrew the bolts securing the mounting to the transmission, and the remaining bolts securing the mounting to the body, then lift the mounting from the engine compartment.
14 Refitting is a reversal of removal, bearing in mind the following points:

a) *Use new mounting bolts.*
b) *The edges of the mounting support arm must be parallel to the edge of the mounting .*
c) *Tighten all fixings to the specified torque.*

Rear mounting (torque arm)

Note: *New mounting bolts will be required on refitting***.**
15 Apply the handbrake, then jack up the front of the vehicle and support securely on axle stands (see *Jacking and vehicle support*). Remove the engine undershield(s) for access to the rear mounting (torque arm).
16 Support the rear of the transmission beneath the final drive housing. To do this, use a trolley jack and block of wood, or alternatively wedge a block of wood between the transmission and the subframe.
17 Working under the vehicle, unscrew and remove the bolt securing the mounting to the subframe.
18 Unscrew the two bolts securing the mounting to the transmission, then withdraw the mounting from under the vehicle **(see illustration)**.
19 Refitting is a reversal of removal, but use new mounting securing bolts, and tighten all fixings to the specified torque.

17 Engine oil cooler – removal and refitting

Removal

1 The oil cooler is mounted under the oil filter housing on the front of the cylinder block.
2 Position a container beneath the oil filter to catch escaping oil and coolant.
3 Remove the air filter housing as described in Chapter 4B.
4 Remove the radiator cooling fan and shroud as described in Chapter 3.
5 Unclip the wiring harness, then undo the bolt and remove the bracket from the front of the oil filter housing.
6 Undo the bolt(s), release the clamps and move the charge air pipe to one side.
7 Undo the bolt and move the electric coolant pump to one side.
8 Undo the bolts and pull the engine oil dipstick guide tube upwards a little, and move it to one side.
9 Clamp the oil cooler coolant hoses to minimise coolant spillage, then remove the clips, and disconnect the hoses from the oil cooler. Be prepared for coolant spillage.
10 Unscrew the oil cooler securing plate from the bottom of the oil filter housing, then slide off the oil cooler. Recover the O-rings from the top and bottom of the oil cooler.

Refitting

1 Refitting is a reversal of removal, bearing in mind the following points:

a) *Use new oil cooler O-rings.*
b) *Tighten the oil cooler securing plate securely.*
c) *On completion, check and if necessary top-up the oil and coolant levels.*

18 Oil pressure warning light switch – removal and refitting

Removal

1 The oil pressure warning light switch is fitted to the oil filter housing **(see illustration)**. Remove the engine top cover to gain access to the switch (see Section 4).
2 Disconnect the wiring connector and wipe clean the area around the switch.
3 Unscrew the switch from the filter housing and remove it, along with its sealing washer. If the switch is to be left removed from the engine for any length of time, plug the oil filter housing aperture.

Refitting

4 Examine the sealing washer for signs of damage or deterioration and if necessary renew.
5 Refit the switch, complete with washer, and tighten it to the specified torque.
6 Securely reconnect the wiring connector then check and, if necessary, top-up the engine oil as described in *Weekly checks*. On completion, refit the engine top cover(s).

Chapter 2 Part G:
Engine removal and overhaul procedures

Contents

Degrees of difficulty

Easy, suitable for novice with little experience 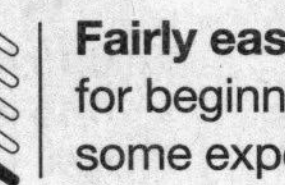

Fairly easy, suitable for beginner with some experience

Fairly difficult, suitable for competent DIY mechanic

Difficult, suitable for experienced DIY mechanic

Very difficult, suitable for expert DIY or professional

Specifications

Engine codes*

1.4 litre:	
Indirect injection petrol engine	BCA and BUD
Direct injection petrol engine (FSi)	BKG and BLN
Direct injection turbocharged engine (TSi)	CAXA
1.6 litre:	
SOHC petrol engine	BGU, BSE and BSF
DOHC direct injection petrol engine (FSi)	BAG, BLP and BLF
2.0 litre petrol engine:	
Non-turbo	AXW, BLX, BLY, BLR, BVX, BVY and BVZ
Turbo	AXX, BPY and BWA
Diesel engine:	
PD unit injector engine:	
1.9 litre, 8-valve, turbo, SOHC	BJB, BKC, BRU, BLS, BXE and BXF
2.0 litre:	
8-valve, non-turbo, SOHC	BDK
8-valve, turbo, SOHC	BMM
16-valve, turbo, DOHC	AZV, BKD and BMN
Common rail injection engine	CBDA and CBDB

* **Note:** *See 'Vehicle identification' at the end of this manual for the location of engine code markings.*

Piston rings

	New	Wear limit
End gaps:		
Petrol engines:		
1.4 litre BCA and BUD:		
Top compression ring	0.20 to 0.50 mm	1.0 mm
Lower compression ring	0.40 to 0.70 mm	1.0 mm
Oil scraper ring	0.40 to 1.40 mm	N/A
1.4 litre BKG and BLN:		
Top compression ring	0.20 to 0.50 mm	1.0 mm
Lower compression ring	0.40 to 0.60 mm	1.0 mm
Oil scraper ring	0.20 to 1.10 mm	N/A
1.4 litre CAXA:		
Top compression ring	0.20 to 0.40 mm	1.0 mm
Lower compression ring	0.40 to 0.60 mm	1.0 mm
Oil scraper ring	0.20 to 0.80 mm	N/A
1.6 litre BGU, BSE and BSF:		
Compression rings	0.20 to 0.40 mm	0.80 mm
Oil scraper ring	0.25 to 0.50 mm	0.80 mm
1.6 litre BAG, BLF and BLP:		
Top compression ring	0.20 to 0.50 mm	1.0 mm
Lower compression ring	0.40 to 0.60 mm	1.0 mm
Oil scraper ring	0.20 to 1.10 mm	N/A
2.0 litre:		
Compression rings	0.20 to 0.40 mm	0.80 mm
Oil scraper ring	0.25 to 0.50 mm	0.80 mm
Diesel engines:		
1.9 litre:		
Compression rings	0.20 to 0.40 mm	1.0 mm
Oil scraper ring	0.25 to 0.50 mm	1.0 mm
2.0 litre:		
Compression rings	0.25 to 0.50 mm	1.0 mm
Oil scraper ring	0.25 to 0.50 mm	1.0 mm
Ring-to-groove clearance:		
Petrol engines:		
1.4 litre BCA and BUD:		
Top compression ring	0.04 to 0.08 mm	0.15 mm
Lower compression ring	0.04 to 0.08 mm	0.15 mm
Oil scraper ring	N/A	N/A
1.4 litre BKG, BLN and CAXA:		
Top compression ring	0.04 to 0.08 mm	0.15 mm
Lower compression ring	0.02 to 0.06 mm	0.15 mm
Oil scraper ring	N/A	N/A
1.6 litre BGU, BSE and BSF:		
Compression rings	0.20 to 0.40 mm	0.80 mm
Oil scraper ring	0.25 to 0.50 mm	0.80 mm
1.6 litre BAG, BLF and BLP:		
Top compression ring	0.04 to 0.08 mm	0.15 mm
Lower compression ring	0.02 to 0.06 mm	0.15 mm
Oil scraper ring	N/A	N/A
2.0 litre:		
Compression rings	0.06 to 0.09 mm	0.20 mm
Oil scraper ring	0.03 to 0.06 mm	0.15 mm
Diesel engines		
1st compression ring	0.06 to 0.09 mm	0.25 mm
2nd compression ring	0.05 to 0.08 mm	0.25 mm
Oil scraper ring	0.03 to 0.06 mm	0.15 mm

Crankshaft endfloat

	New	Wear limit
Petrol engines:		
1.4 litre	See Note in Section 2	
1.6 litre BGU, BSE and BSF	0.07 to 0.23 mm	0.30 mm
1.6 litre BAG, BLF and BLP	See Note in Section 2	
2.0 litre	0.07 to 0.23 mm	0.30 mm
Diesel engines	0.07 to 0.23 mm	0.30 mm

Cylinder head

Minimum permissible dimension between top of valve stem and top surface of cylinder head:

Petrol engines:	
1.4 litre:	
Inlet valves	7.6 mm
Exhaust valves	7.6 mm
1.6 litre BGU, BSE and BSF:	
Inlet valves	31.7 mm
Exhaust valves	31.7 mm
1.6 litre BAG, BLF and BLP:	
Inlet valves	7.6 mm
Exhaust valves	7.6 mm
2.0 litre	No reworking permitted
Diesel engines	No reworking permitted

Minimum cylinder head height:

Petrol engines:	
1.4 litre	No reworking permitted
1.6 litre BGU, BSE and BSF	132.9 mm
1.6 litre BAG, BLF and BLP	No reworking permitted
2.0 litre	No reworking permitted
Diesel engines	No reworking permitted

Maximum cylinder head gasket face distortion:

Petrol engines:	
1.4 litre	0.05 mm
1.6 litre BGU, BSE and BSF	0.1 mm
1.6 litre BAG, BLF and BLP	0.05 mm
2.0 litre	0.1 mm
Diesel engines	0.1 mm

Valves

Valve stem diameter:	Inlet valves	Exhaust valves
Petrol engines:		
1.4 litre	5.973 mm	5.953 mm
1.6 litre BGU, BSE and BSF	5.980 ± 0.007 mm	5.965 ± 0.007 mm
1.6 litre BAG, BLF and BLP	5.973 mm	5.953 mm
2.0 litre AXX, BPY and BWA	5.98 mm	5.95 mm
2.0 litre AXW, BLX, BLY, BLR, BVX, BVY and BVZ	5.980 mm	5.965 mm
Diesel engines:		
1.9 litre	6.980 mm	6.956 mm
2.0 litre BDK and BMM	6.980 mm	6.956 mm
2.0 litre AZV, BKD and BMN	5.980 mm	5.965 mm
2.0 litre CBDA and CBDB	5.980	5.965 mm
Valve seat angle (all engines)	45°	45°

Torque wrench settings

Refer to Chapter 2A, 2B, 2C, 2D, 2E or 2F as applicable.

1 General information

How to use this Chapter

Included in this Part of Chapter 2 are details of removing the engine from the car and general overhaul procedures for the cylinder head, cylinder block and all other engine internal components.

The information given ranges from advice concerning preparation for an overhaul and the purchase of new parts, to detailed step-by-step procedures covering removal, inspection, renovation and refitting of engine internal components.

After Section 8, all instructions are based on the assumption that the engine has been removed from the car. For information concerning in-car engine repair, as well as the removal and refitting of those external components necessary for full overhaul, refer to the relevant in-car repair procedure section (Chapters 2A, 2B, 2C, 2D, 2E or 2F) and to Section 5 of this Chapter. Ignore any preliminary dismantling operations described in the relevant in-car repair sections that are no longer relevant once the engine has been removed from the car.

Apart from torque wrench settings, which are given at the beginning of the relevant in-car repair procedure in Chapters 2A, 2B, 2C, 2D, 2E or 2F, all specifications relating to engine overhaul are given at the beginning of this Part of Chapter 2.

2 Engine overhaul – general information

Note: *On all 1.4 litre, and 1.6 litre DOHC engines, the crankshaft must not be removed. Just loosening the main bearing cap bolts will cause deformation of the cylinder block. On these engines, if the crankshaft or main bearing surfaces are worn or damaged, the complete crankshaft/cylinder block assembly must be renewed.*

1 It is not always easy to determine when, or if, an engine should be completely overhauled, as a number of factors must be considered.

2 High mileage is not necessarily an

indication that an overhaul is needed, while low mileage does not preclude the need for an overhaul. Frequency of servicing is probably the most important consideration. An engine which has had regular and frequent oil and filter changes, as well as other required maintenance, should give many thousands of miles of reliable service. Conversely, a neglected engine may require an overhaul very early in its life.

3 Excessive oil consumption is an indication that piston rings, valve seals and/or valve guides are in need of attention. Make sure that oil leaks are not responsible before deciding that the rings and/or guides are worn. Perform a compression (or leakdown) test, as described in Part A, B, C, D, E or F of this Chapter (as applicable), to determine the likely cause of the problem.

4 Check the oil pressure with a gauge fitted in place of the oil pressure switch, and compare it with that specified (see Specifications in Part A, B, C, D, E or F of this Chapter). If it is extremely low, the main and big-end bearings, and/or the oil pump, are probably worn.

5 Loss of power, rough running, knocking or metallic engine noises, excessive valve gear noise, and high fuel consumption may also point to the need for an overhaul, especially if they are all present at the same time. If a complete service does not remedy the situation, major mechanical work is the only solution.

6 An engine overhaul involves restoring all internal parts to the specification of a new engine. During an overhaul, the pistons and the piston rings are renewed. New main and big-end bearings are generally fitted (where possible); if necessary, the crankshaft may be renewed to restore the journals. The valves are also serviced as well, since they are usually in less-than-perfect condition at this point. While the engine is being overhauled, other components, such as the starter and alternator, can be overhauled as well. The end result should be an as-new engine that will give many trouble-free miles. **Note:** *Critical cooling system components such as the hoses, thermostat and coolant pump should be renewed when an engine is overhauled. The radiator should be checked carefully, to ensure that it is not clogged or leaking. Also, it is a good idea to renew the oil pump whenever the engine is overhauled.*

7 Before beginning the engine overhaul, read through the entire procedure, to familiarise yourself with the scope and requirements of the job. Overhauling an engine is not difficult if you follow carefully all of the instructions, have the necessary tools and equipment, and pay close attention to all specifications. It can, however, be time-consuming. Plan on the car being off the road for a minimum of two weeks, especially if parts must be taken to an engineering works for repair or reconditioning. Check on the availability of parts and make sure that any necessary special tools and equipment are obtained in advance. Most work can be done with typical hand tools, although a number of precision measuring tools are required for inspecting parts to determine if they must be renewed. Often the engineering works will handle the inspection of parts and offer advice concerning reconditioning and renewal. **Note:** *Always wait until the engine has been completely dismantled, and until all components (especially the cylinder block and the crankshaft) have been inspected, before deciding what service and repair operations must be performed by an engineering works. The condition of these components will be the major factor to consider when determining whether to overhaul the original engine, or to buy a reconditioned unit. Do not, therefore, purchase parts or have overhaul work done on other components until they have been thoroughly inspected.* As a general rule, time is the primary cost of an overhaul, so it does not pay to fit worn or sub-standard parts.

8 As a final note, to ensure maximum life and minimum trouble from a reconditioned engine, everything must be assembled with care, in a spotlessly-clean environment.

3 Engine/transmission removal – preparation and precautions

If you have decided that the engine must be removed for overhaul or major repair work, several preliminary steps should be taken.

Locating a suitable place to work is extremely important. Adequate work space, along with storage space for the vehicle, will be needed. If a workshop or garage is not available, at the very least a solid, level, clean work surface is required.

If possible, clear some shelving close to the work area and use it to store the engine components and ancillaries as they are removed and dismantled. In this manner, the components stand a better chance of staying clean and undamaged during the overhaul. Laying out components in groups together with their fixings bolts, screws, etc, will save time and avoid confusion when the engine is refitted.

Clean the engine compartment and engine before beginning the removal procedure; this will help visibility and help to keep tools clean.

The help of an assistant is essential; there are certain instances when one person cannot safely perform all of the operations required to remove the engine from the vehicle. Safety is of primary importance, considering the potential hazards involved in this kind of operation. A second person should always be in attendance to offer help in an emergency. If this is the first time you have removed an engine, advice and aid from someone more experienced would also be beneficial.

Plan the operation ahead of time. Before starting work, obtain (or arrange for the hire of) all of the tools and equipment you will need. Access to the following items will allow the task of removing and refitting the engine to be completed safely and with relative ease: a hoist and lifting tackle – rated in excess of the weight of the engine, complete sets of spanners and sockets as described at the rear of this manual, wooden blocks, and plenty of rags and cleaning solvent for mopping-up spilled oil, coolant and fuel. A selection of different-sized plastic storage bins will also prove useful for keeping dismantled components grouped together. If any of the equipment must be hired, make sure that you arrange for it in advance, and perform all of the operations possible without it beforehand; this may save you time and money.

Plan on the vehicle being out of use for quite a while, especially if you intend to carry out an engine overhaul. Read through the whole of this Section and work out a strategy based on your own experience, and the tools, time and workspace available to you. Some of the overhaul processes may have to be carried out by a VW dealer or an engineering works – these establishments often have busy schedules, so it would be prudent to consult them before removing or dismantling the engine, to get an idea of the amount of time required to carry out the work.

When removing the engine from the vehicle, be methodical about the disconnection of external components. Labelling cables and hoses as they are removed will greatly assist the refitting process.

Always be extremely careful when lifting the engine from the engine compartment. Serious injury can result from careless actions. If help is required, it is better to wait until it is available rather than risk personal injury and/or damage components by continuing alone. By planning ahead and taking your time, a job of this nature, although major, can be accomplished successfully and without incident.

4 Engine and transmission – removal and refitting

Removal

1 Except on 1.4 litre engine codes BCA and BUD, the engine and transmission assembly is lowered from the engine compartment, and withdrawn from under the car. On engine codes BCA and BUD, the engine and transmission are lifted from the engine compartment. On all models, access to the front of the engine is gained by moving the lock carrier assembly to its Service position, or alternatively removing it completely after evacuating the air conditioning system (by an air conditioning specialist).

2 Switch off the ignition and all electrical consumers, and remove the ignition key.

4.3 Remove the air inlet ducting from the engine compartment front crossmember

4.4a Remove the battery box...

4.4b ...and tray

4.6a Disconnect the bonnet release cable...

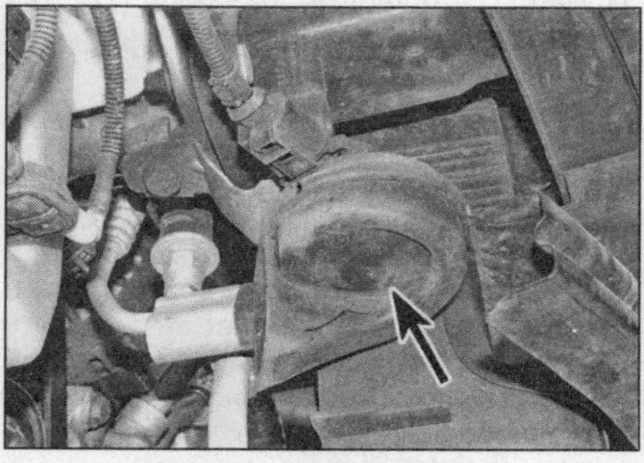
4.6b ...remove the horn...

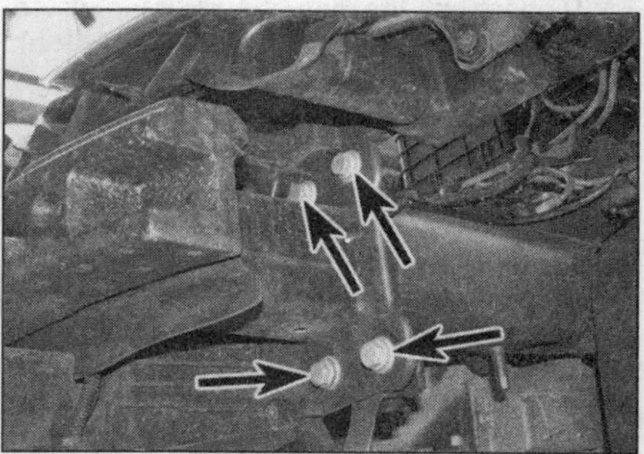
4.6c ...unscrew the mounting bolts and fit the threaded rods

3 Remove the engine top cover and air filter (Chapter 4) and all associated air ducting **(see illustration)**.

4 Remove the battery as described in Chapter 5A, then remove the battery tray **(see illustrations)**.

5 Apply the handbrake, then jack up the front of the vehicle and support it on axle stands (see *Jacking and vehicle support*). Remove both front roadwheels.

6 Move the lock carrier, located at the front of the engine compartment, to its Service position as follows.

a) *Remove the front bumper (Chapter 11).*
b) *Disconnect the bonnet release cable over the right-hand headlight* ***(see illustration).***
c) *On models with a turbocharger, remove the air ducts.*
d) *Remove the horn (Chapter 12)* ***(see illustration).***
e) *Support the lock carrier, then unscrew the mounting bolts and substitute them with one threaded rod on each side of the car* ***(see illustration).***
f) *Carefully pull the lock carrier forwards approximately 10 cm to provide access to the front of the engine.*

Alternatively, the air conditioning system may be evacuated by a specialist, and the lock carrier removed completely from the front of the car to provide additional working space.

Warning: Have the air conditioning system discharged by a suitably-qualified specialist before attempting to remove the compressor.

7 Drain the cooling system as described in Chapter 1A or 1B. If preferred, the electric cooling fan temperature sensor may be removed from the bottom hose to drain the system **(see illustration)**.

8 Noting their locations, disconnect all wiring, coolant hoses, vacuum hoses and fuel lines from the engine/transmission, with reference to the relevant Chapters of this Manual. Alternatively, the engine wiring loom may remain on the engine by disconnecting it from the left-hand side of the engine compartment, and removing the engine management ECU (Chapter 4) located on the bulkhead **(see illustrations)**. Tape over or plug fuel lines to prevent entry of dust and dirt.

9 Remove the front exhaust pipe with reference to Chapter 4C or 4D.

10 Unbolt the rear engine support/torque arm from the transmission **(see illustration)**.

4.7 Remove the electric cooling fan switch from the bottom hose to drain the cooling system

4.8a Remove the wiring from the supports on the front of the engine

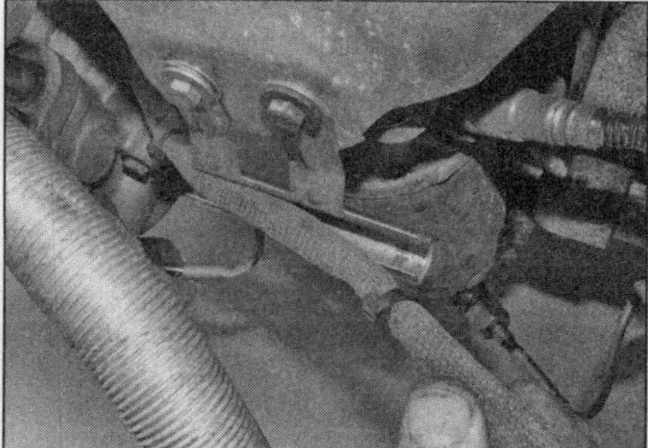
4.8b Engine wiring loom support on exhaust manifold

4.10 Remove the rear engine support/ torque arm

4.11 Disconnect the gearchange cables

11 Disconnect the gearchange mechanism with reference to Chapter 7 **(see illustration)**.

12 On manual transmission models, remove the clutch slave cylinder. **Note:** *Do not depress the clutch pedal once the slave cylinder has been removed.*

13 Refer to Chapter 3 and unbolt the air conditioning compressor from the front of the engine, without disconnecting the refrigerant lines. Suspend the compressor to one side of the engine compartment.

14 Refer to Chapter 8 and disconnect the driveshafts from the transmission drive flanges. Suspend them from the underbody **(see illustration)**.

15 Unbolt the washer fluid reservoir for access to the right-engine mounting. Also unbolt the coolant expansion tank and place to one side.

16 Connect a hoist and lifting tackle to the engine lifting brackets on the cylinder head, and raise the hoist to just take the weight of the engine/transmission **(see illustration)**.

17 Unbolt the right- and left-hand engine mountings with reference to Chapter 2A, 2B, 2C, 2D, 2E or 2F.

18 Make a final check to ensure that all relevant wiring, hoses and pipes have been disconnected, then carefully swivel the engine/ transmission assembly away from the sides of the engine compartment, lift it upwards or lower it (see paragraph 1), and withdraw forwards from the front of the car **(see illustration)**.

Separation

Engine and manual transmission

19 Remove the starter motor (Chapter 5A).

20 Where applicable, unscrew the bolt securing the small engine-to-transmission plate to the transmission.

21 Ensure that both engine and transmission are adequately supported, then unscrew the remaining engine-to-transmission bolts, noting the location of each bolt, and the locations of any brackets secured by the bolts.

22 Carefully withdraw the transmission from the engine, ensuring that the weight of the transmission is not allowed to hang on the input shaft while it is engaged with the clutch friction disc. Recover the engine-to-transmission plate.

Engine and automatic transmission

23 Remove the starter motor (Chapter 5A).

09G transmissions

24 Prise out the torque converter nuts cover from the transmission casing. The cover is located behind the left-hand driveshaft flange. Turn the crankshaft to position one of the torque converter-to-driveplate nuts in the access aperture. Unscrew and remove the nut whilst preventing the engine from turning using a wide-bladed screwdriver engaged with the ring gear teeth on the driveplate.

25 Using the same method described in the previous paragraph, unscrew the remaining two torque converter-to-driveplate nuts, turning the crankshaft a third-of-a-turn at a time to locate them.

26 Ensure that both engine and transmission are adequately supported, then unscrew the engine-to-transmission bolts, noting the location of each bolt, and the locations of any brackets secured by the bolts.

27 Carefully withdraw the transmission from the engine (take care – the transmission is heavy), making sure that the torque converter remains fully engaged with the transmission input shaft. If necessary, use a lever to release the torque converter from the driveplate. Recover the engine-to-transmission plate.

28 Once the transmission has been separated from the engine, strap a restraining bar across the front of the bellhousing to keep the torque converter in position.

DSG (Dual clutch) transmissions

29 Disconnect the coolant hoses from the gearbox oil cooler. Plug the openings to prevent contamination.

30 Disconnect the wiring harness between the engine and gearbox, and move to one side.

31 Ensure that both engine and transmission are adequately supported, then unscrew the engine-to-transmission bolts, noting the location of each bolt, and the locations of any brackets secured by the bolts.

32 Carefully withdraw the transmission from the engine (take care – the transmission is heavy).

Reconnection and refitting

Engine and manual transmission

33 Reconnection and refitting are a reversal of removal, bearing in mind the following points:

a) *Smear the splines of the transmission input shaft with a little high melting-point grease.*
b) *Ensure that any brackets noted before removal are in place on the engine-to-transmission bolts.*
c) *Tighten all fixings to the specified torque, where given.*
d) *Where applicable, have the air conditioning system recharged with refrigerant by a suitably-qualified professional.*
e) *Ensure that all wiring, hoses and pipes are correctly reconnected and routed as noted before removal.*
f) *Ensure that the fuel lines are correctly reconnected.*
g) *On completion, refill the cooling system as described in Chapter 1A or 1B.*

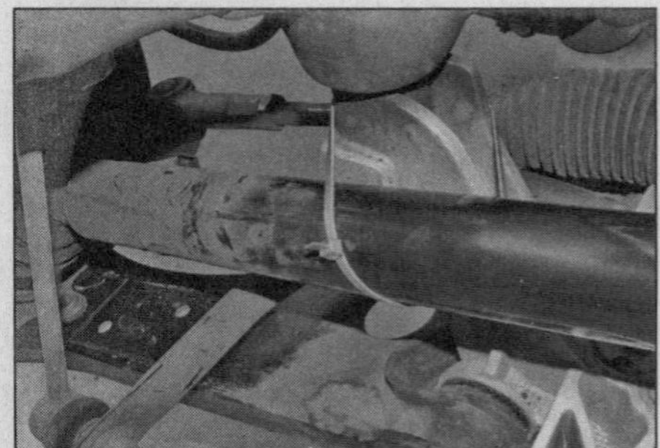
4.14 Use plastic cable ties to suspend the driveshafts from the underbody

4.16 Lift the engine/transmission with a hoist

4.18 Engine/transmission assembly removed from the car and on a workbench

Engine and automatic transmission

34 Reconnection and refitting are a reversal of removal, bearing in mind the following points:

a) *When fitting the torque converter (where applicable), make sure that both the drive pins engage with the transmission fluid pump.*
b) *On completion, check and if necessary top-up the automatic transmission fluid level as described in Chapter 1A or 1B.*

5 Engine overhaul – preliminary information

1 It is much easier to dismantle and work on the engine if it is mounted on a portable engine stand. These stands can often be hired from a tool hire shop. Before the engine is mounted on a stand, the flywheel should be removed, so that the stand bolts can be tightened into the end of the cylinder block/crankcase. **Note:** *Do not measure cylinder bore dimensions with the engine mounted on this type of stand.*

2 If a stand is not available, it is possible to dismantle the engine with it blocked up on a sturdy workbench, or on the floor. Be very careful not to tip or drop the engine when working without a stand.

3 If you intend to obtain a reconditioned engine, all ancillaries must be removed first, to be transferred to the new engine (just as they will if you are doing a complete engine overhaul yourself). These components include the following (it may be necessary to transfer additional components, such as the oil level dipstick/tube assembly, oil filter housing, etc, depending on which components are supplied with the reconditioned engine:

Petrol engines

a) *Alternator (including mounting brackets) and starter motor (Chapter 5A).*
b) *The ignition system components including all sensors and spark plugs (Chapters 1A and 5B).*
c) *The fuel injection system components (Chapter 4A).*
d) *All electrical switches, actuators and sensors, and the engine wiring harness (Chapters 3, 4A and 5B).*
e) *Inlet and exhaust manifolds, and turbocharger (where applicable) (Chapters 4A and 4C).*
f) *Engine mountings (see the relevant part of Chapter 2).*
g) *Clutch components (Chapter 6).*
h) *Oil separator (where applicable).*

Diesel engines

a) *Alternator (including mounting brackets) and starter motor (Chapter 5A).*
b) *The glow plug/preheating system components (Chapter 5C).*
c) *All fuel system components, including fuel injectors, all sensors and actuators (Chapter 4B).*
d) *The brake vacuum pump (Chapter 9).*
e) *All electrical switches, actuators and sensors, and the engine wiring harness (Chapter 3, 4B and 5C).*
f) *Inlet and exhaust manifolds/turbocharger (where applicable) (Chapters 4B and 4D).*
g) *Engine mountings (see Chapter 2E or 2F).*
h) *Clutch components (Chapter 6).*

All engines

Note: *When removing the external components from the engine, pay close attention to details that may be helpful or important during refitting. Note the fitted position of gaskets, seals, spacers, pins, washers, bolts, and other small components.*

4 If you are obtaining a short engine (the engine cylinder block/crankcase, crankshaft, pistons and connecting rods, all fully assembled), then the cylinder head, sump, oil pump, timing belt(s) and chain (as applicable – together with tensioner(s) and covers), auxiliary drivebelt (together with its tensioner), coolant pump, thermostat housing, coolant outlet elbows, oil filter housing and where applicable oil cooler will also have to be removed.

5 If you are planning a full overhaul, the engine can be dismantled in the order given below:

a) *Inlet and exhaust manifolds (see the relevant part of Chapter 4).*
b) *Timing belt or timing chain (as applicable), sprockets and tensioner (see the relevant part of Chapter 2).*
c) *Cylinder head (see the relevant part of Chapter 2).*
d) *Flywheel/driveplate (see the relevant part of Chapter 2).*
e) *Sump (see the relevant part of Chapter 2).*
f) *Oil pump (see the relevant part of Chapter 2).*
g) *Piston/connecting rod assemblies (see Section 9).*
h) *Crankshaft (see Section 10).*

6 Cylinder head – dismantling

Note: *A valve spring compressor tool will be required for this operation.*

SOHC petrol engines

1 With the cylinder head removed (see relevant part of Chapter 2), proceed as follows.

2 Remove the inlet and exhaust manifolds as described in Chapter 4A and 4C respectively.

3 Remove the camshaft and hydraulic tappets/roller rocker fingers, as described in the relevant part of Chapter 2A.

4 If desired, unbolt the coolant housing from the rear of the cylinder head, and recover the seal.

5 If not already done, remove the camshaft position sensor, with reference to Chapter 4A.

6 Unscrew the securing nut, and recover the washer, and remove the timing belt tensioner pulley from the stud on the cylinder head.

7 Unbolt any remaining auxiliary brackets and/or engine lifting brackets from the cylinder head as necessary, noting their locations to aid refitting.

8 Turn the cylinder head over, and rest it on one side.

9 Using a valve spring compressor, compress each valve spring in turn until the split collets can be removed. Release the compressor, and lift off the spring cap and spring. If, when the valve spring compressor is screwed down, the spring cap refuses to free and expose the split collets, gently tap the top of the tool, directly over the spring cap, with a light hammer. This will free the retainer **(see illustrations)**.

10 Using a pair of pliers, or a removal tool,

6.9a Compress a valve spring with a compressor tool

6.9b Remove the spring cap...

6.9c ...and valve spring

6.10a Use a removal tool...

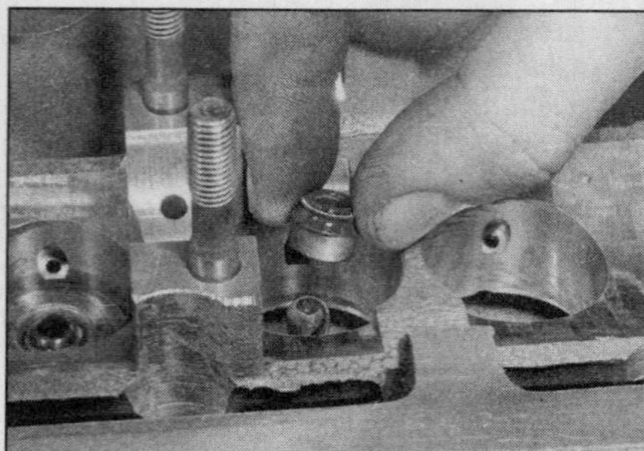
6.10b ...to remove the valve stem oil seals

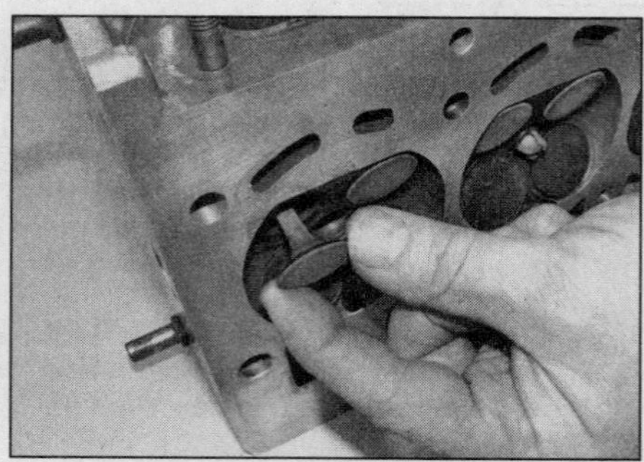
6.11 Removing a valve

carefully extract the valve stem oil seal from the top of the valve guide **(see illustrations)**.

11 Withdraw the valve from the gasket side of the cylinder head **(see illustration)**.

12 It is essential that each valve is stored together with its collets, cap, spring and spring seat. The valves should be kept in their correct sequences, unless they are so badly worn that they are to be renewed.

DOHC petrol engines

13 With the cylinder head removed, proceed as follows.

14 Remove the inlet and exhaust manifolds as described in Chapter 4A and 4C respectively.

15 On 1.4 litre BCA and BUD engines, unscrew the securing bolt and remove the secondary timing belt tensioner from the timing belt end of the cylinder head.

16 Unbolt any remaining auxiliary brackets and/or engine lifting brackets from the cylinder head as necessary, noting their locations to aid refitting.

17 Proceed as described in paragraphs 8 to 12, but when labelling the valve components, make sure that the valves are identified as inlet and exhaust, as well as numbered.

Diesel engines

18 With the cylinder head removed, proceed as follows.

19 Remove the inlet and exhaust manifolds (and turbocharger, where applicable) as described in Chapters 4B and 4D.

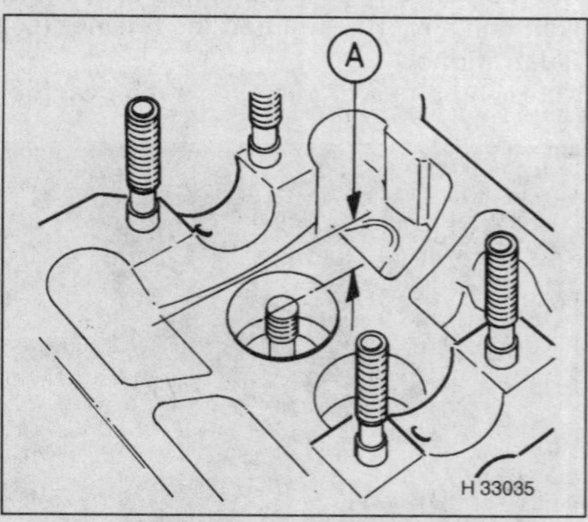

7.6 Measure the distance (A) between the top face of the valve stem and the top surface of the cylinder head

20 Remove the camshaft and hydraulic tappets, as described in Chapter 2E or 2F.

21 Remove the glow plugs, with reference to Chapter 5C.

22 Remove the fuel injectors, with reference to Chapter 4B.

23 Unscrew the nut and remove the timing belt tensioner pulley from the stud on the timing belt end of the cylinder head.

24 Unbolt any remaining auxiliary brackets and/or engine lifting brackets from the cylinder head as necessary, noting their locations to aid refitting.

25 Proceed as described in paragraphs 8 to 12.

7 Cylinder head and valves – cleaning and inspection

1 Thorough cleaning of the cylinder head and valve components, followed by a detailed inspection, will enable you to decide how much valve service work must be carried out during engine overhaul. **Note:** *If the engine has been severely overheated, it is best to assume that the cylinder head is warped ñ check carefully for signs of this.*

Cleaning

2 Using a suitable degreasing agent, remove all traces of oil deposits from the cylinder head, paying particular attention to the camshaft bearing surfaces, hydraulic tappet bores, valve guides and oilways. Scrape off any traces of old gasket from the mating surfaces, taking care not to score or gouge them. If using emery paper, do not use a grade of less than 100. Turn the head over and, using a blunt blade, scrape any carbon deposits from the combustion chambers and ports. Finally, wash the entire head casting with a suitable solvent to remove the remaining debris.

3 Clean the valve heads and stems using a fine wire brush (or a power-operated wire brush). If the valve is covered with heavy carbon deposits, scrape off the majority of the deposits with a blunt blade first, then use the wire brush.

4 Thoroughly clean the remainder of the components using solvent and allow them to dry completely. Discard the oil seals, as new ones must be fitted when the cylinder head is reassembled.

Inspection

Cylinder head

Note: *If the valve seats are to be recut, ensure that the maximum permissible reworking dimension (where applicable) is not exceeded (the maximum dimension will only allow minimal reworking to produce a perfect seal between valve and seat). If the maximum dimension is exceeded, the function of the hydraulic tappets cannot be guaranteed, and the cylinder head must be renewed. Refer to paragraph 6 for details of how to calculate the maximum permissible reworking dimension. Reworking is* **not** *permitted on 2.0 litre petrol engines and all diesel engines.*

5 Examine the head casting closely to identify any damage or cracks that may have developed. Cracks can often be identified from evidence of coolant or oil leakage. Pay particular attention to the areas around the valve seats and spark plug/fuel injector holes. If cracking is discovered in this area, VW state that on diesel engines and SOHC petrol engines, the cylinder head may be re-used, provided the cracks are no larger than 0.5 mm wide on diesel engines, or 0.3 mm wide on SOHC petrol engines. More serious damage will mean the renewal of the cylinder head casting.

6 Moderately pitted and scorched valve seats can be repaired by lapping the valves in during reassembly, as described later in this Chapter. Badly worn or damaged valve seats may be restored by recutting where permitted, however, the maximum permissible reworking dimension **must** not be exceeded, only minimal reworking being possible (see note at beginning of paragraph 5). To calculate the maximum permissible reworking dimension, proceed as follows **(see illustration)**:

a) If a new valve is to be fitted, use the new valve for the following calculation.

b) Insert the valve into its guide in the cylinder head, and push the valve firmly on to its seat.

c) Using a flat edge placed across the top surface of the cylinder head, measure the distance between the top face of the valve stem, and the top surface of the cylinder head. Record the measurement obtained.

d) Consult the Specifications, and look up

7.7 Measure the distortion of the cylinder head gasket surface

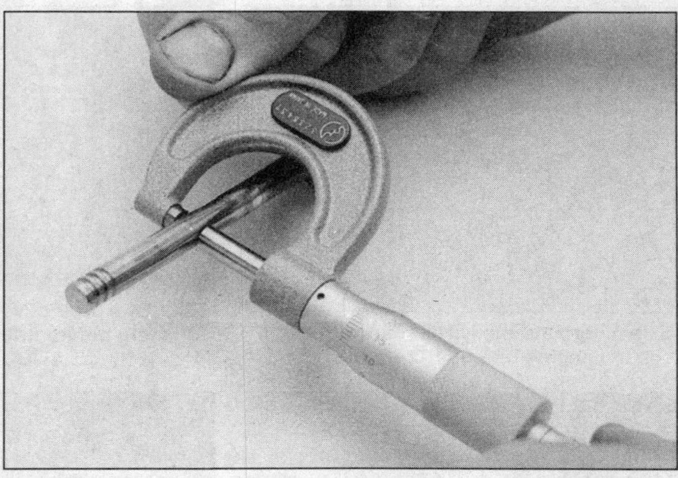
7.11 Measure the diameter of the valve stems using a micrometer

the value for the minimum permissible dimension between the top face of the valve stem and the top surface of the cylinder head.

e) Now take the measured distance and subtract the minimum permissible dimension, to give the maximum permissible reworking dimension; eg,
Measured distance (34.4 mm)
Minus Minimum permissible dimension (34.0 mm)
= Maximum permissible reworking dimension (0.4 mm).

7 Measure any distortion of the gasket surfaces using a straight-edge and a set of feeler blades. Take one measurement longitudinally on the manifold mating surface(s). Take several measurements across the head gasket surface, to assess the level of distortion in all planes **(see illustration)**. Compare the measurements with the figures in the Specifications.

8 On 1.6 litre SOHC petrol engines, if the head is distorted beyond the specified limit, it may be possible to have it machined by an engineering works, provided that the minimum permissible cylinder head height is maintained.

9 On all other engines, if the head is distorted beyond the specified limit, the head must be renewed.

Camshaft

10 Inspection of the camshaft is covered in Parts A to F of this Chapter, as applicable.

Valves and associated components

11 Examine each valve closely for signs of wear. Inspect the valve stems for wear ridges, scoring or variations in diameter; measure their diameters at several points along their lengths with a micrometer, and compare with the figures given in the Specifications **(see illustration)**.

12 The valve heads should not be cracked, badly pitted or charred. Note that light pitting of the valve head can be rectified by lapping-in the valves during reassembly, as described in Section 8.

13 Check that the valve stem end face is free from excessive pitting or indentation; this could be caused by defective hydraulic tappets.

14 Using vernier calipers, measure the free length of each of the valve springs. As a manufacturer's figure is not quoted, the only way to check the length of the springs is by comparison with a new component. Note that valve springs are usually renewed during a major engine overhaul **(see illustration)**.

15 Stand each spring on its end on a flat surface, against an engineer's square **(see illustration)**. Check the squareness of the spring visually, and renew it if it appears distorted.

16 Renew the valve stem oil seals regardless of their apparent condition.

8 Cylinder head – reassembly

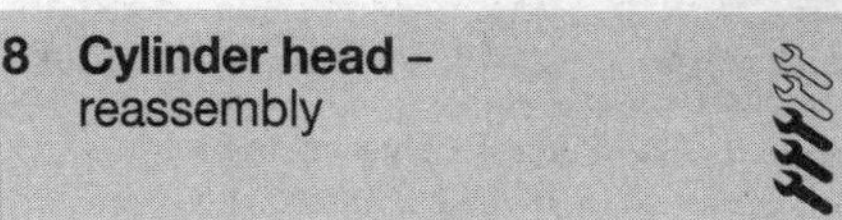

Note: *A valve spring compressor tool will be required for this operation.*

SOHC petrol engines

1 To achieve a gas-tight seal between the valves and their seats, it will be necessary to lap-in (or grind-in) the valves. To complete this process you will need a quantity of fine/coarse grinding paste and a grinding tool – this can either be of the rubber sucker type, or the automatic type which is driven by a rotary power tool.

2 Smear a small quantity of *fine* grinding paste on the sealing face of the valve head. Turn the cylinder head over so that the combustion chambers are facing upwards and insert the valve into the correct guide. Attach the grinding tool to the valve head and using a backward/forward rotary action, grind the valve head into its seat. Periodically lift the valve and rotate it to redistribute the grinding paste **(see illustration)**.

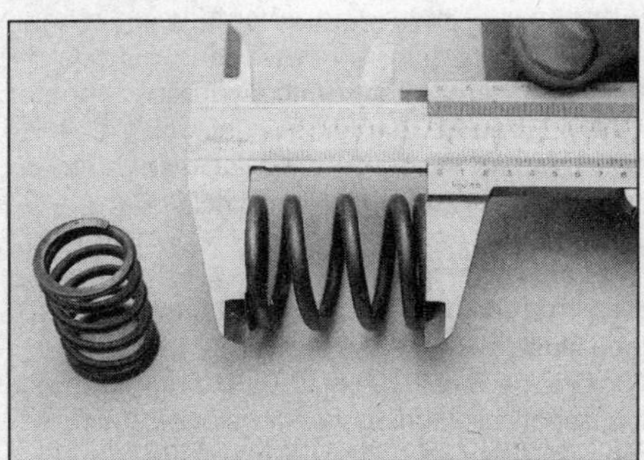
7.14 Measure the free length of each valve spring

7.15 Check the squareness of a valve spring

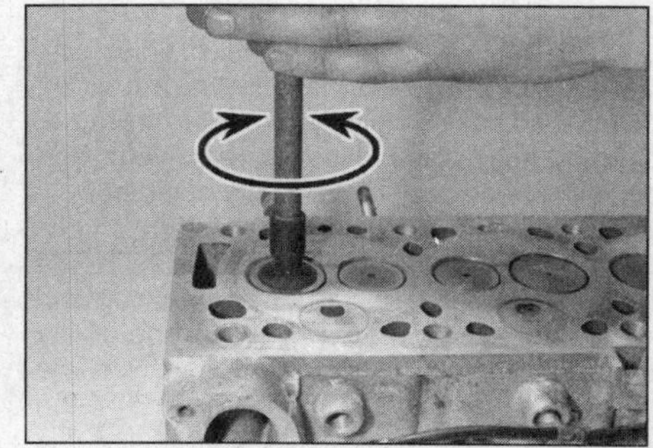
8.2 Grinding-in a valve

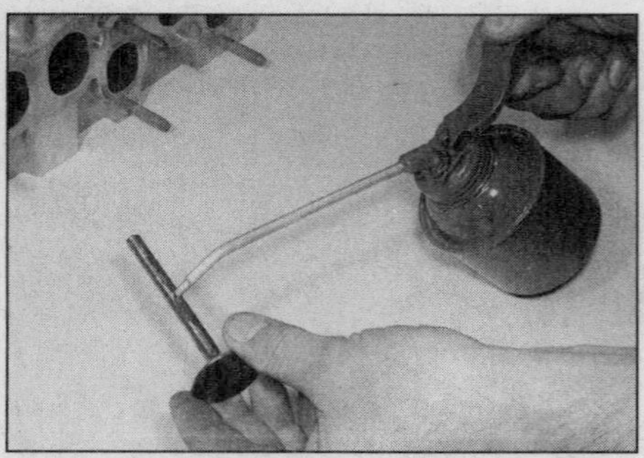
8.8a Lubricate the valve stem with clean engine oil – SOHC engine

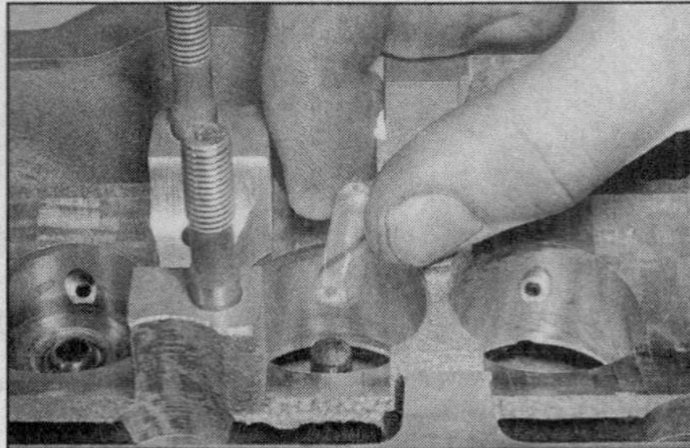
8.8b Fit a protective sleeve over the valve stem before fitting the stem seal – SOHC engine

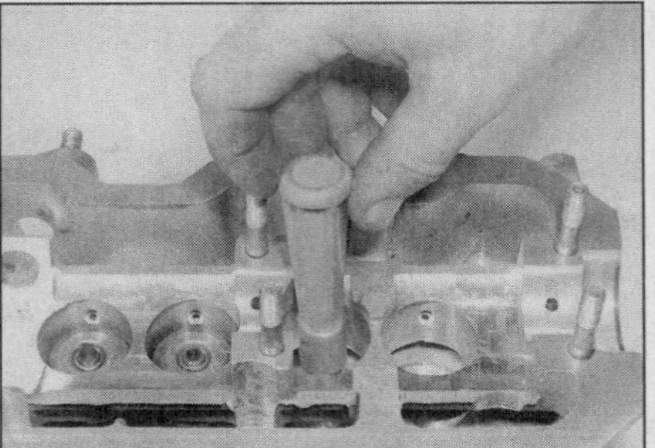
8.9 Use a special installer to fit a valve stem oil seal – SOHC engine

8.10 Fit a valve spring – SOHC engine

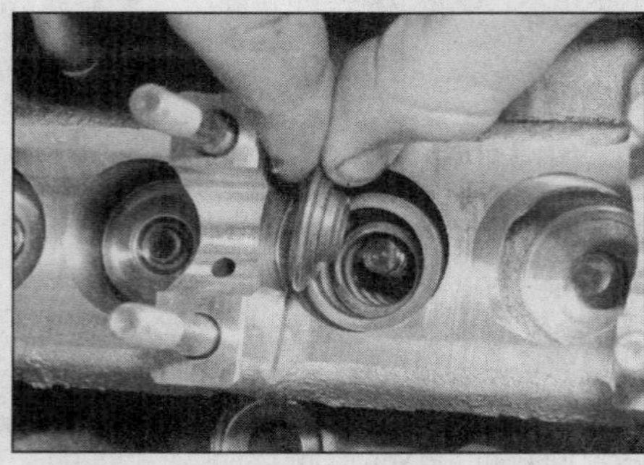
8.11a Fit the upper spring seat – SOHC engine

8.11b Use grease to hold the split collets in the groove

3 Continue this process until the contact between valve and seat produces an unbroken, matt grey ring of uniform width, on both faces. Repeat the operation on the remaining valves.

4 If the valves and seats are so badly pitted that coarse grinding paste must be used, bear in that there is a maximum permissible reworking dimension for the valves and seats. Refer to the Specifications at the beginning of this Chapter for the minimum dimension from the end of the valve stem to the top face of the cylinder head (see Section 7, paragraph 6). If this minimum dimension is exceeded due to excessive lapping-in, the hydraulic tappets may not operate correctly, and the cylinder head must be renewed.

5 Assuming the repair is feasible, work as described previously, but use coarse grinding paste initially, to achieve a dull finish on the valve face and seat. Wash off the coarse paste with solvent and repeat the process using fine grinding paste to obtain the correct finish.

6 When all the valves have been ground in, remove all traces of grinding paste from the cylinder head and valves using solvent, and allow the head and valves to dry completely.

7 Turn the cylinder head on its side.

8 Working on one valve at a time, lubricate the valve stem with clean engine oil, and insert the valve into its guide. Fit one of the protective plastic sleeves supplied with the new valve stem oil seals over the end of the valve stem – this will protect the oil seal as it is being fitted **(see illustrations)**.

9 Dip a new valve stem seal in clean engine oil, and carefully push it over the valve stem and onto the top of the valve guide – take care not to damage the stem seal as it is fitted. Use a suitable long-reach socket or a valve stem seal fitting tool to press the seal firmly into position **(see illustration)**. Remove the protective sleeve from the valve stem.

10 Locate the valve spring over the valve stem, ensuring that the lower end of the spring seats correctly on the cylinder head **(see illustration)**.

11 Fit the upper spring seat over the top of the spring, then using a valve spring compressor, compress the spring until the upper seat is pushed beyond the collet grooves in the valve stem. Refit the split collets. Gradually release the spring compressor, checking that the collets remain correctly seated as the spring extends. When correctly seated, the upper spring seat should force the collets securely into the grooves in the end of the valve stem **(see illustrations)**.

8.19a Use a long-reach socket to fit a valve stem oil seal

12 Repeat this process for the remaining sets of valve components, ensuring that all components are refitted to their original locations. To settle the components after installation, strike the end of each valve stem with a mallet, using a block of wood to protect the stem from damage. Check before progressing any further that the split collets remain firmly seated in the grooves in the end of the valve stem.

13 Refit any auxiliary brackets and/or engine lifting brackets to their original locations, as noted before removal.

14 Refit the timing belt tensioner pulley, and secure with the nut and washer.

15 Where applicable, refit the camshaft position sensor, with reference to Chapter 4A.

16 Where applicable, refit the coolant housing to the rear of the cylinder head, using a new seal.

17 Refit the camshaft and hydraulic tappets as described in Chapter 2A.

18 Refit the inlet and exhaust manifolds as described in Chapters 4A and 4C.

DOHC petrol engines

19 Proceed as described in paragraphs 1 to 13 **(see illustrations)**.

20 On 1.4 litre BCA and BUD engines, refit the secondary timing belt tensioner, then refit the securing bolt.

21 Refit the inlet and exhaust manifolds as described in Chapter 4A and 4C.

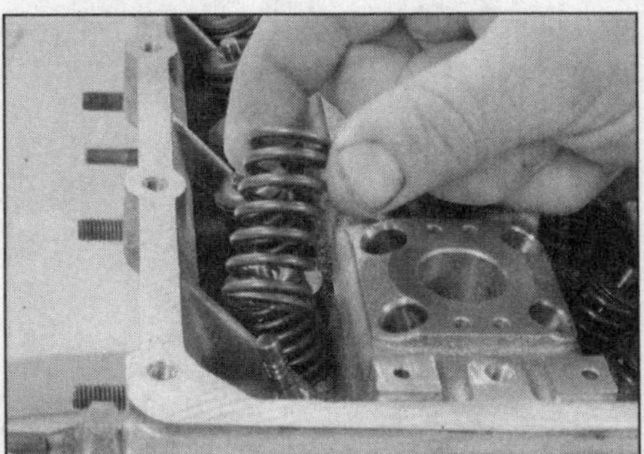

8.19b Fit a valve spring...

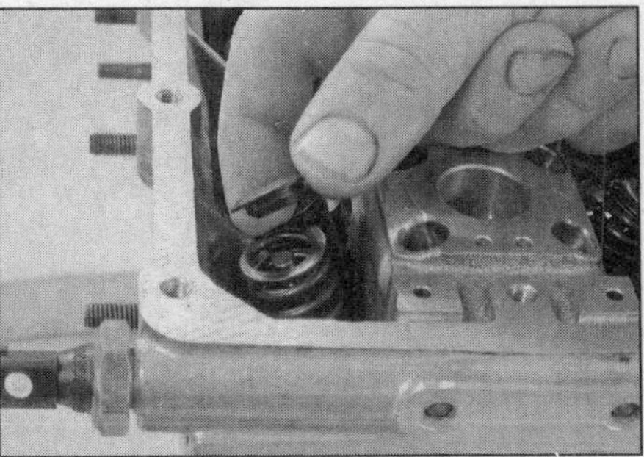

8.19c ...and upper spring seat – 1.4 litre DOHC engine

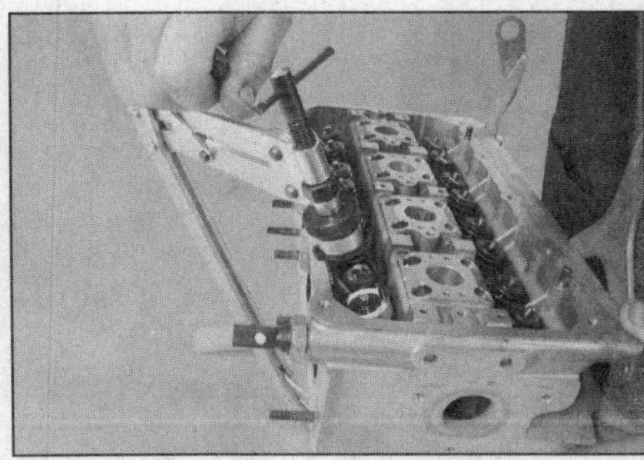

8.19d Compress a valve spring using a compressor tool – 1.4 litre DOHC engine

Diesel engines

22 Proceed as described in paragraphs 1 to 13.
23 Refit the timing belt tensioner pulley to the stud on the cylinder head, and refit the securing nut.
24 Refit the fuel injectors, with reference to Chapter 4B.
25 Refit the glow plugs, with reference to Chapter 5C.
26 Refit the hydraulic tappets and camshaft, as described in Chapter 2E or 2F.
27 Refit the inlet and exhaust manifolds (and turbocharger, where applicable), as described in Chapters 4B and 4D.

9 Piston/connecting rod assemblies – removal

1 Proceed as follows according to engine type:

a) On SOHC petrol engines, remove the cylinder head, sump and oil baffle plate, and oil pump and pick-up pipe, as described in Chapter 2A.
b) On 1.4 and 1.6 litre DOHC petrol engines, remove the cylinder head, sump, and oil pick-up pipe, as described in Chapter 2B or 2C.
c) On 2.0 litre DOHC engines, remove the cylinder head, sump and oil baffle plate, oil pump and pick-up pipe, and the balancer shaft assembly as described in Chapter 2D.
d) On diesel engines, remove the cylinder head, sump and oil baffle plate, and oil pump and pick-up pipe, as described in Chapter 2E or 2F.

2 Inspect the tops of the cylinder bores for ridges at the point where the pistons reach top dead centre. These must be removed otherwise the pistons may be damaged when they are pushed out of their bores. Use a scraper or ridge reamer to remove the ridges. Such a ridge indicates excessive wear of the cylinder bore.
3 Check the connecting rods and big-end caps for identification markings. Both connecting rods and caps should be marked with the cylinder number on one side of each assembly. Note that No 1 cylinder is at the timing belt end of the engine. If no marks are present, using a hammer and centre-punch, paint or similar, mark each connecting rod and big-end bearing cap with its respective cylinder number – note on which side of the connecting rods and caps the marks are made **(see illustration)**.
4 Similarly, check the piston crowns for direction markings. An arrow on each piston crown should point towards the timing belt end of the engine. On some engines, this mark may be obscured by carbon build-up, in which case the piston crown should be cleaned to check for a mark. In some cases, the direction arrow may have worn off, in which case a suitable mark should be made on the piston crown using a scriber – do not deeply score the piston crown, but ensure that the mark is easily visible.
5 Turn the crankshaft to bring Nos 1 and 4 pistons to bottom dead centre.
6 Unscrew the bolts or nuts, as applicable, from No 1 piston big-end bearing cap. Lift off the cap, and recover the bottom half bearing shell. If the bearing shells are to be re-used, tape the cap and bearing shell together. Note that if the bearing shells are to be re-used, they must be fitted to the original connecting rod and cap **(see illustrations)**.
7 Where the bearing caps are secured with nuts, wrap the threaded ends of the bolts with insulating tape to prevent them scratching the crankpins and bores when the pistons are removed **(see illustration)**.
8 Using a hammer handle, push the piston up through the bore, and remove it from the top of the cylinder block. Where applicable, take care not to damage the piston cooling oil spray jets in the cylinder block as the piston/connecting rod assembly is removed. Recover the upper bearing shell, and tape it to the connecting rod for safe-keeping.

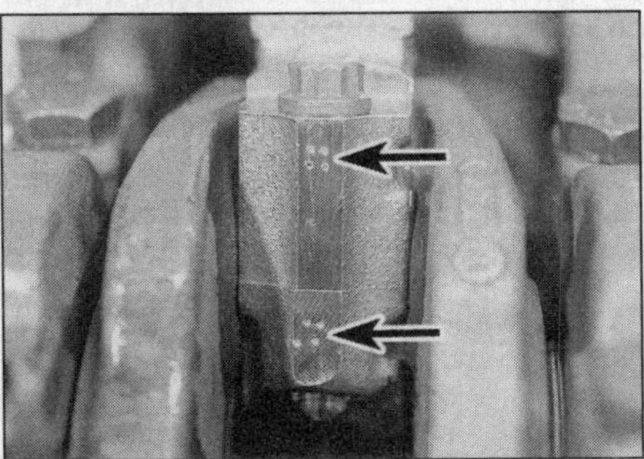

9.3 Mark the big-end caps and connecting rods with their cylinder numbers (arrowed)

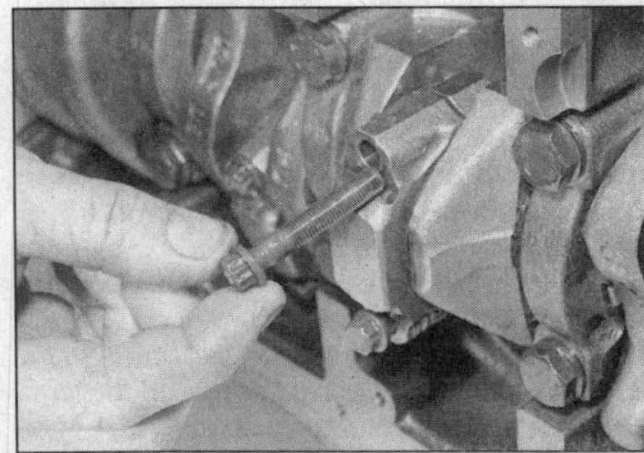

9.6a Unscrew the big-end bearing cap bolts...

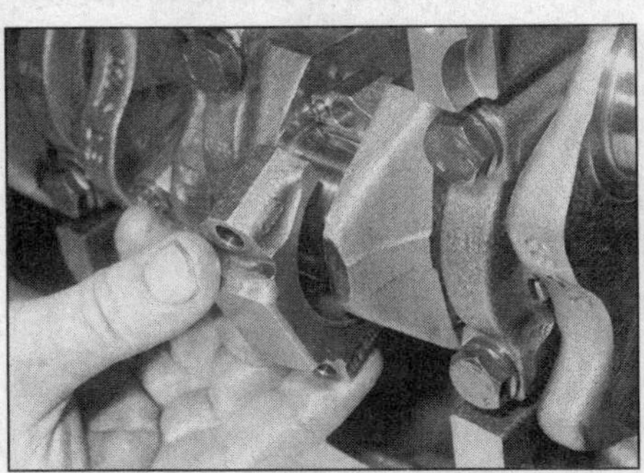

9.6b ...and remove the cap

9.7 Wrap the threaded ends of the bolts with tape

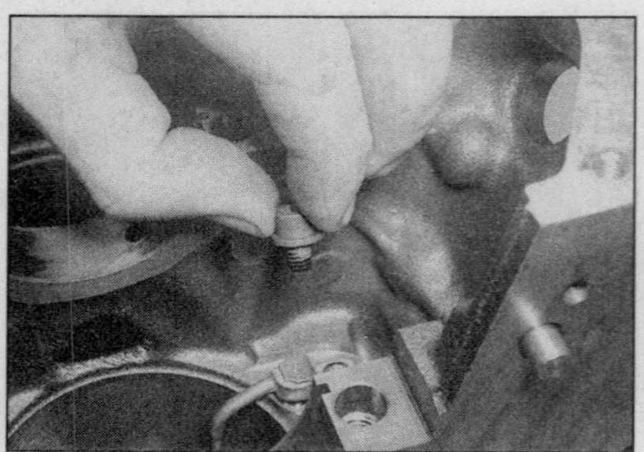
9.12a Remove the securing bolts...

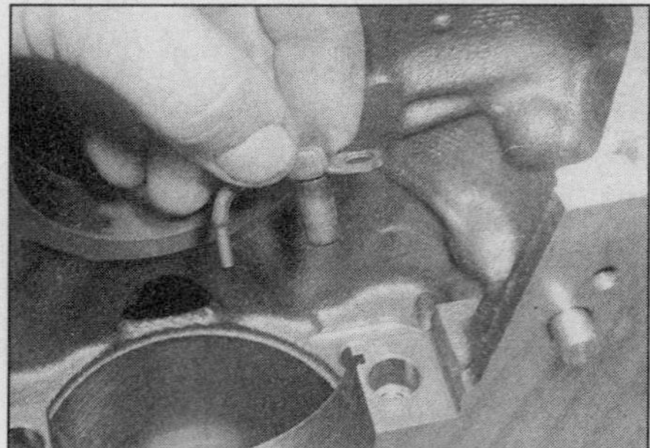
9.12b ...and withdraw the piston cooling oil spray jets

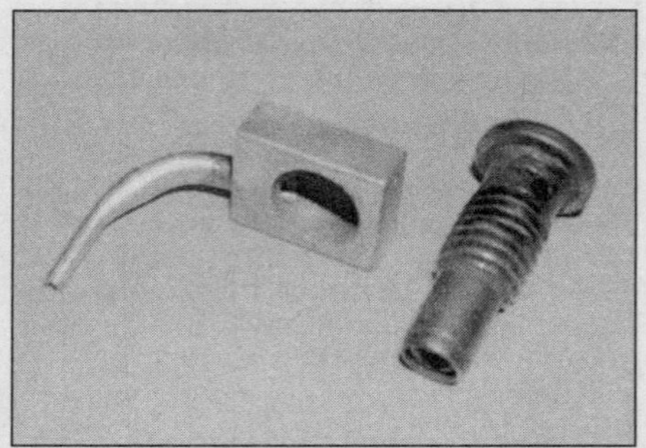
9.12c Piston cooling spray jet and retainer

9 Loosely refit the big-end cap to the connecting rod, and secure with the bolts or nuts, as applicable – this will help to keep the components in their correct order.
10 Remove No 4 piston assembly in the same way.
11 Turn the crankshaft as necessary to bring Nos 2 and 3 pistons to bottom dead centre, and remove them in the same way.
12 Where applicable, remove the securing bolts, and withdraw the piston cooling oil spray jets from the bottom of the cylinder block **(see illustrations)**.

10 Crankshaft – removal

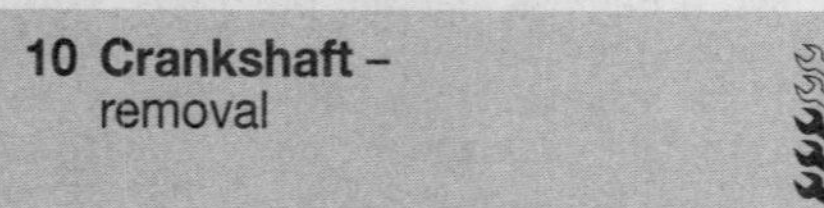

Warning: On all 1.4 litre, and 1.6 litre DOHC engines, the crankshaft must not be removed. Just loosening the main bearing cap bolts on these engines will cause deformation of the cylinder block. If the crankshaft or main bearing surfaces are worn or damaged, the complete crankshaft/cylinder block assembly must be renewed. The following procedure applies to all other engines.
Note: *If no work is to be done on the pistons and connecting rods, there is no need to push the pistons out of the cylinder bores. The pistons should just be pushed far enough up the bores so that they are positioned clear of the crankshaft journals.*
1 Proceed as follows according to engine type:

a) On SOHC petrol engines, remove the timing belt and crankshaft sprocket, sump and oil baffle plate, oil pump and pick-up pipe, flywheel/driveplate, and the crankshaft oil seal housings, as described in Chapter 2A.
b) On DOHC petrol engines, remove the timing belt/chain, sump, oil pump and pick-up pipe, flywheel/driveplate, and the crankshaft oil seal housing, as described in Chapter 2B, 2C or 2D. ***Note:*** *On 2.0 litre engines, it will necessary to remove the balancer shaft assembly.*
c) On diesel engines, remove the timing belt and crankshaft sprocket, sump and oil baffle plate, oil pump and pick-up pipe, flywheel/driveplate, and the crankshaft oil seal housings, as described in Chapter 2E or 2F.

2 Remove the pistons and connecting rods, or disconnect them from the crankshaft, as described in Section 9 (see Note at the beginning of this Section).
3 Check the crankshaft endfloat as described in Section 13, then proceed as follows.
4 The main bearing caps should be numbered 1 to 5 from the timing belt end of the engine. If the bearing caps are not marked, mark them accordingly using a centre-punch. Note the orientation of the markings to ensure correct refitting.
5 Slacken and remove the main bearing cap bolts, and lift off each cap. If the caps appear to be stuck, tap them with a soft-faced mallet to free them from the cylinder block **(see illustration)**. Recover the lower bearing shells, and tape them to their caps for safe-keeping.
6 Recover the lower crankshaft endfloat control thrustwasher halves from either side of the No 3 main bearing cap, noting their orientation.
7 Lift the crankshaft from the cylinder block **(see illustration)**. Take care, as the crankshaft is heavy. On engines with a crankshaft speed/position sensor fitted, lay the crankshaft on wooden blocks – **do not** rest the crankshaft on the sensor wheel.
8 Recover the upper bearing shells from the cylinder block, and tape them to their respective caps for safe-keeping. Similarly, recover the upper crankshaft endfloat control thrustwasher halves, noting their orientation.
9 On engines with a crankshaft speed/position sensor wheel, unscrew the securing bolts, and remove the sensor wheel, noting which way round it is fitted.

11 Cylinder block/crankcase – cleaning and inspection

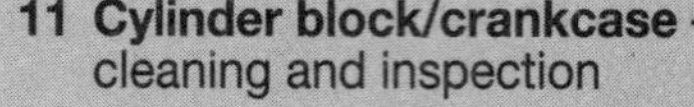

Cleaning

1 Remove all external components and electrical switches/sensors from the block, including mounting brackets, the coolant pump, the oil filter, and oil cooler **(see illustration)**, etc. For complete cleaning, the core plugs should ideally be removed. Drill a small hole in the plugs, then insert a self-tapping screw into the hole. Extract the plugs by pulling on the screw with a pair of grips, or by using a slide hammer.

10.5 Slacken and remove the main bearing cap bolts

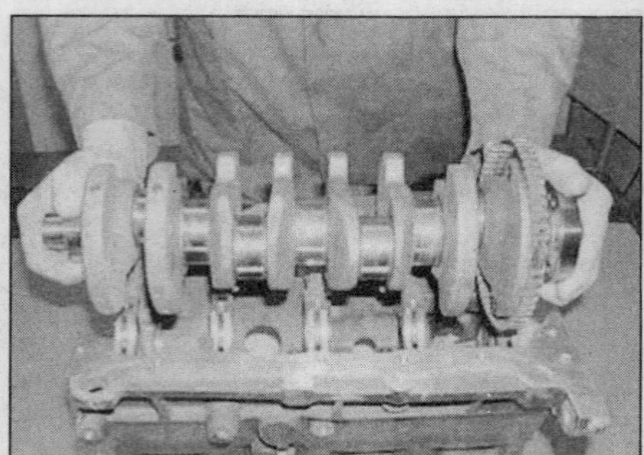
10.7 Lift the crankshaft from the cylinder block

11.1 Oil cooler located on the front of the engine

2 Scrape all traces of gasket and sealant from the cylinder block/crankcase, taking care not to damage the sealing surfaces.

3 Remove all oil gallery plugs (where fitted). The plugs are usually very tight – they may have to be drilled out, and the holes retapped. Use new plugs when the engine is reassembled.

4 If the casting is extremely dirty, it should be steam-cleaned. After this, clean all oil holes and galleries one more time. Flush all internal passages with warm water until the water runs clear. Dry thoroughly, and apply a light film of oil to all mating surfaces and cylinder bores, to prevent rusting. If you have access to compressed air, use it to speed up the drying process, and to blow out all the oil holes and galleries.

Warning: Wear eye protection when using compressed air.

5 If the castings are not very dirty, you can do an adequate cleaning job with hot, soapy water and a stiff brush. Take plenty of time, and do a thorough job. Regardless of the cleaning method used, be sure to clean all oil holes and galleries very thoroughly, and to dry all components well. Protect the cylinder bores as described above, to prevent rusting.

6 Where applicable, check the piston cooling oil spray jets for damage, and renew if necessary. Check the oil spray hole and the oil passages for blockage.

7 All threaded holes must be clean, to ensure accurate torque readings during reassembly. To clean the threads, run the correct-size tap into each of the holes to remove rust, corrosion, thread sealant or sludge, and to restore damaged threads **(see illustration)**. If possible, use compressed air to clear the holes free of debris produced by this operation. **Note:** *Take extra care to exclude all cleaning liquid from blind tapped holes, as the casting may be cracked by hydraulic action if a bolt is threaded into a hole containing liquid.*

8 After coating the mating surfaces of the new core plugs with suitable sealant, fit them to the cylinder block. Make sure that they are driven in straight and seated correctly, or leakage could result.

9 Apply suitable sealant to the new oil gallery plugs, and insert them into the holes in the block. Tighten them securely.

10 If the engine is not going to be reassembled immediately, cover it with a large plastic bag to keep it clean; protect all mating surfaces and the cylinder bores, to prevent rusting.

Inspection

11 Visually check the castings for cracks and corrosion. Look for stripped threads in the threaded holes. If there has been any history of internal coolant leakage, it may be worthwhile having an engine overhaul specialist check the cylinder block/crankcase for cracks with special equipment. If defects are found, have them repaired, if possible, or renew the assembly.

12 Check each cylinder bore for scuffing and scoring.

13 If in any doubt as the condition of the cylinder block have the block/bores inspected and measured by an engine reconditioning specialist. They will be able to advise on whether the block is serviceable, whether a rebore is necessary, and supply the appropriate pistons and rings.

14 If the bores are in reasonably good condition and not excessively worn, then it may only be necessary to renew the piston rings.

15 If this is the case, the bores should be honed, to allow the new rings to bed-in correctly and provide the best possible seal. Consult an engine reconditioning specialist

16 On diesel engines, if the oil/water pump housing was removed, it can be refitted at this stage if wished. Use a new gasket, and before fully tightening the bolts, align the housing faces with those of the engine block.

17 The cylinder block/crankcase should now be completely clean and dry, with all components checked for wear or damage, and repaired or overhauled as necessary.

18 Apply a light coating of engine oil to the mating surfaces and cylinder bores to prevent rust forming.

19 Refit as many ancillary components as possible, for safe-keeping. If reassembly is not to start immediately, cover the block with a large plastic bag to keep it clean, and protect the machined surfaces as described above to prevent rusting.

11.7 To clean the cylinder block threads, run a correct-size tap into the holes

12 Piston/connecting rod assemblies – cleaning and inspection

Cleaning

1 Before the inspection process can begin, the piston/connecting rod assemblies must be cleaned, and the original piston rings removed from the pistons.

2 The rings should have smooth, polished working surfaces, with no dull or carbon-coated sections (showing that the ring is not sealing correctly against the bore wall, so allowing combustion gases to blow by) and no traces of wear on their top and bottom surfaces. The end gaps should be clear of carbon, but not polished (indicating a too-small end gap), and all the rings (including the elements of the oil control ring) should be free to rotate in their grooves, but without excessive up-and-down movement. If the rings appear to be in good condition, they are probably fit for further use; check the end gaps (in an unworn part of the bore) as described in Section 16.

3 If any of the rings appears to be worn or damaged, or has an end gap significantly different from the specified value, the usual course of action is to renew all of them as a set. **Note:** *While it is usual to renew piston rings when an engine is overhauled, they may be re-used if in acceptable condition. If re-using the rings, make sure that each ring is marked during removal to ensure that it is refitted correctly.*

4 Carefully expand the old rings over the top of the pistons. The use of two or three old feeler blades will be helpful in preventing the rings dropping into empty grooves **(see illustration)**. Be careful not to scratch the piston with the ends of the ring. The rings are brittle, and will snap if they are spread too far. They are also very sharp – protect your hands and fingers. Note that the third ring incorporates an expander. Keep each set of rings with its piston if the old rings are to be re-used. Note which way up each ring is fitted to ensure correct refitting.

5 Scrape away all traces of carbon from the top of the piston. A hand-held wire brush (or a piece of fine emery cloth) can be used, once the majority of the deposits have been scraped away.

6 Remove the carbon from the ring grooves in the piston, using an old ring. Break the ring in half to do this (be careful not to cut your fingers – piston rings are sharp). Be careful to remove only the carbon deposits – do not remove any metal, and do not nick or scratch the sides of the ring grooves.

7 Once the deposits have been removed, clean the piston/connecting rod assembly with paraffin or a suitable solvent, and dry thoroughly. Make sure that the oil return holes in the ring grooves are clear.

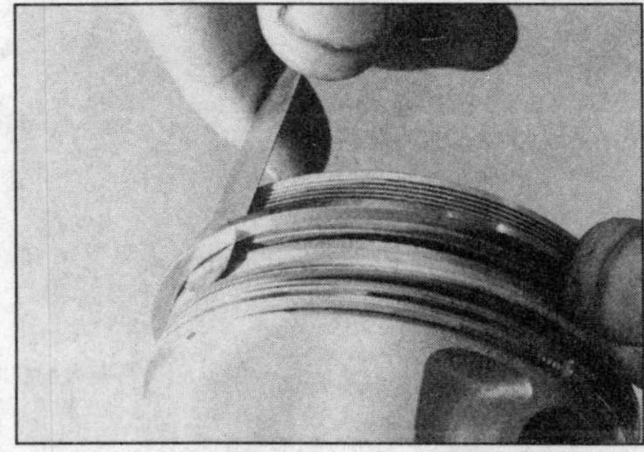

12.4 Old feeler blades can be used to prevent piston rings from dropping into empty grooves

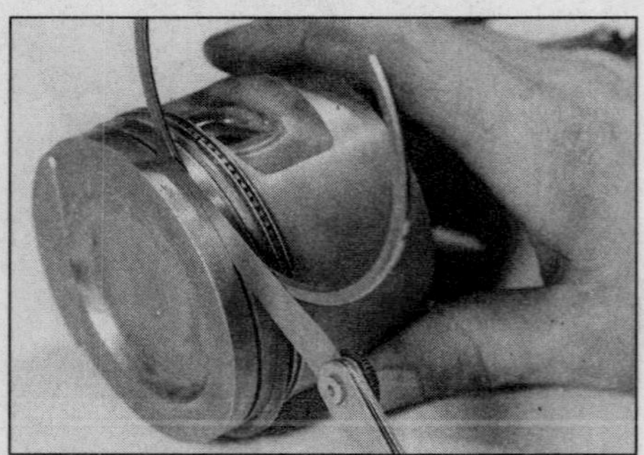
12.17 Measure the piston ring-to-groove clearance using a feeler blade

12.20a Use a small flat-bladed screwdriver to prise out the circlip...

12.20b ...then push out the gudgeon pin and separate the piston and connecting rod

Inspection

8 If the pistons and cylinder bores are not damaged or worn excessively, and if the cylinder block does not need to be rebored, the original pistons can be refitted.

9 Have the pistons and cylinder bore measure by an engine reconditioning specialist. They will be able to advise on possible repairs, and supply the correct replacement parts. **Note:** *If the cylinder block was rebored during a previous overhaul, oversize pistons may already have been fitted.*

10 Normal piston wear shows up as even vertical wear on the piston thrust surfaces, and slight looseness of the top ring in its groove. New piston rings should always be used when the engine is reassembled.

11 Carefully inspect each piston for cracks around the skirt, around the gudgeon pin holes, and at the piston ring 'lands' (between the ring grooves).

12 Look for scoring and scuffing on the piston skirt, holes in the piston crown, and burned areas at the edge of the crown. If the skirt is scored or scuffed, the engine may have been suffering from overheating, and/or abnormal combustion which caused excessively high operating temperatures. The cooling and lubrication systems should be checked thoroughly.

13 Scorch marks on the sides of the pistons show that blow-by has occurred.

14 A hole in the piston crown, or burned areas at the edge of the piston crown, indicates that abnormal combustion (pre-ignition, knocking, or detonation) has been occurring.

15 If any of the above problems exist, the causes must be investigated and corrected, or the damage will occur again. The causes may include incorrect ignition/injection pump timing, inlet air leaks or incorrect air/fuel mixture (petrol engines), or a faulty fuel injector (diesel engines).

16 Corrosion of the piston, in the form of pitting, indicates that coolant has been leaking into the combustion chamber and/or the crankcase. Again, the cause must be corrected, or the problem may persist in the rebuilt engine.

17 Locate a new piston ring in the appropriate groove and measure the ring-to-groove clearance using a feeler blade **(see illustration)**. Note that the rings are of different widths, so use the correct ring for the groove. Compare the measurements with those listed; if the clearances are outside of the tolerance band, then the piston must be renewed. Confirm this by checking the width of the piston ring with a micrometer.

18 Examine each connecting rod carefully for signs of damage, such as cracks around the big-end and small-end bearings. Check that the rod is not bent or distorted. Damage is highly unlikely, unless the engine has been seized or badly overheated. Detailed checking of the connecting rod assembly can only be carried out by a VW dealer or engine repair specialist with the necessary equipment.

19 The gudgeon pins are of the floating type, secured in position by two circlips. The pistons and connecting rods can be separated as follows.

20 Using a small flat-bladed screwdriver, prise out the circlips, and push out the gudgeon pin **(see illustrations)**. Hand pressure should be sufficient to remove the pin. Identify the piston and rod to ensure correct reassembly. Discard the circlips – new ones *must* be used on refitting. If the gudgeon pin proves difficult to remove, heat the piston to 60°C with hot water – the resulting expansion will then allow the two components to be separated.

21 Examine the gudgeon pin and connecting rod small-end bearing for signs of wear or damage. It should be possible to push the gudgeon pin through the connecting rod bush by hand, without noticeable play. Wear can be cured by renewing both the pin and bush. Bush renewal, however, is a specialist job – press facilities are required, and the new bush must be reamed accurately.

22 Examine all components, and obtain any new parts from your VW dealer or engine reconditioning specialist. If new pistons are purchased, they will be supplied complete with gudgeon pins and circlips. Circlips can also be purchased individually.

23 The orientation of the piston with respect to the connecting rod must be correct when the two are reassembled. The piston crown is marked with an arrow (which may be obscured by carbon deposits); this must point towards the timing belt/chain end of the engine when the piston is installed. The connecting rod and its bearing cap both have recesses machined into them on one side, close to their mating surfaces – these recesses must both face the same way as the arrow on the piston crown (ie, towards the timing belt/chain end of the engine) when correctly installed. Reassemble the two components to satisfy this requirement **(see illustrations)**.

24 Apply a smear of clean engine oil to the gudgeon pin. Slide it into the piston and through the connecting rod small-end. Check that the piston pivots freely on the rod, then secure the gudgeon pin in position with two new circlips. Ensure that each circlip is correctly located in its groove in the piston.

25 Repeat the cleaning and inspection process for the remaining pistons and connecting rods.

12.23a The piston crown is marked with an arrow which must point towards the timing belt/chain end of the engine

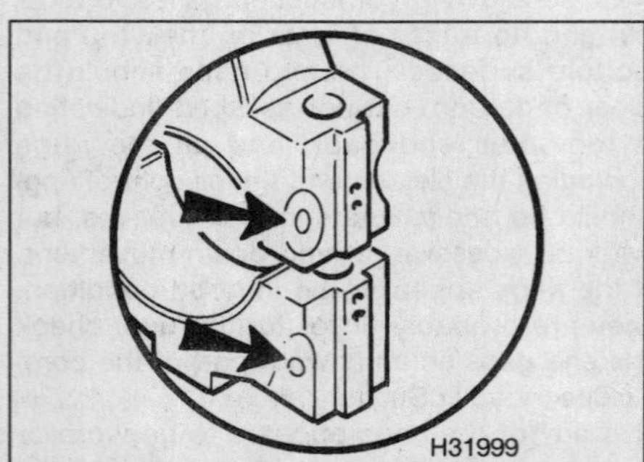

12.23b The recesses (arrowed) in the connecting rod and bearing cap must face the timing belt/chain end of the engine

13 Crankshaft – checking endfloat and inspection

Checking endfloat

1 If the crankshaft endfloat is to be checked, this must be done when the crankshaft is still installed in the cylinder block/crankcase, but is free to move (see Section 10).

2 Check the endfloat using a dial gauge in contact with the end of the crankshaft. Push the crankshaft fully one way, and then zero the gauge. Push the crankshaft fully the other way, and check the endfloat. The result can be compared with the specified amount, and will give an indication as to whether new thrustwasher halves are required **(see illustration)**. Note that all thrustwashers must be of the same thickness.

3 If a dial gauge is not available, feeler blades can be used. First push the crankshaft fully towards the flywheel end of the engine, then use feeler blades to measure the gap between the web of No 3 crankpin and the thrustwasher halves **(see illustration)**.

Inspection

4 Clean the crankshaft using paraffin or a suitable solvent, and dry it, preferably with compressed air if available. Be sure to clean the oil holes with a pipe cleaner or similar probe, to ensure that they are not obstructed.

Warning: Wear eye protection when using compressed air.

5 Check the main and big-end bearing journals for uneven wear, scoring, pitting and cracking.

6 Big-end bearing wear is accompanied by distinct metallic knocking when the engine is running (particularly noticeable when the engine is pulling from low speed) and some loss of oil pressure.

7 Main bearing wear is accompanied by severe engine vibration and rumble – getting progressively worse as engine speed increases – and again by loss of oil pressure.

8 Check the bearing journal for roughness by running a finger lightly over the bearing surface. Any roughness (which will be accompanied by obvious bearing wear) indicates that the crankshaft requires regrinding (where possible) or renewal.

9 If the crankshaft has been reground, check for burrs around the crankshaft oil holes (the holes are usually chamfered, so burrs should not be a problem unless regrinding has been carried out carelessly). Remove any burrs with a fine file or scraper, and thoroughly clean the oil holes as described previously.

10 Have the crankshaft measured and inspected by an engine reconditioning specialist. They will be able to advise any possible repairs and supply the correct parts.

11 Check the oil seal contact surfaces at each end of the crankshaft for wear and damage. If the seal has worn a deep groove in the surface of the crankshaft, consult an engine overhaul specialist; repair may be possible, but otherwise a new crankshaft will be required.

13.2 Measure crankshaft endfloat using a dial gauge

13.3 Measure crankshaft endfloat using feeler blades

12 If the crankshaft journals have not already been reground, it may be possible to have the crankshaft reconditioned, and to fit undersize shells (see Section 17). If no undersize shells are available and the crankshaft has worn beyond the specified limits, it will have to be renewed. Consult your VW dealer or engine specialist for further information on parts availability.

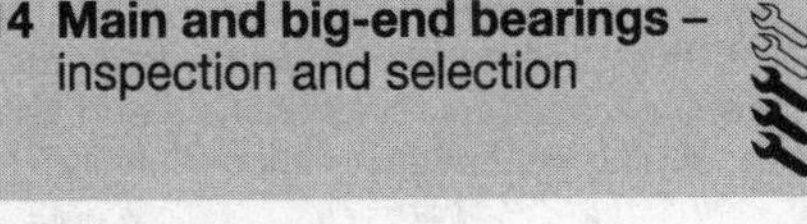

14 Main and big-end bearings – inspection and selection

Inspection

1 Even though the main and big-end bearings should be renewed during the engine overhaul, the old bearings should be retained for close examination, as they may reveal valuable information about the condition of the engine **(see illustration)**.

2 Bearing failure can occur due to lack of lubrication, the presence of dirt or other foreign particles, overloading the engine, or corrosion. Regardless of the cause of bearing failure, the cause must be corrected before the engine is reassembled, to prevent it from happening again.

3 When examining the bearing shells, remove them from the cylinder block/crankcase, the main bearing caps, the connecting rods and the connecting rod big-end bearing caps. Lay them out on a clean surface in the same general position as their location in the engine. This will enable you to match any bearing problems with the corresponding crankshaft journal. Do not touch any shell's internal bearing surface with your fingers while checking it, or the delicate surface may be scratched.

4 Dirt and other foreign matter gets into the engine in a variety of ways. It may be left in the engine during assembly, or it may pass through filters or the crankcase ventilation system. It may get into the oil, and from there into the bearings. Metal chips from machining operations and normal engine wear are often present. Abrasives are sometimes left in engine components after reconditioning, especially when parts are not thoroughly cleaned using the proper cleaning methods. Whatever the source, these foreign objects often end up embedded in the soft bearing material, and are easily recognised. Large particles will not embed in the bearing, but will score or gouge the bearing and journal. The best prevention for this cause of bearing failure is to clean all parts thoroughly, and keep everything spotlessly-clean during engine assembly. Frequent and regular engine oil and filter changes are also recommended.

5 Lack of lubrication (or lubrication breakdown) has a number of interrelated causes. Excessive heat (which thins the oil), overloading (which squeezes the oil from the bearing face) and oil leakage (from excessive bearing clearances, worn oil pump or high engine speeds) all contribute to lubrication breakdown. Blocked oil passages, which usually are the result of misaligned oil holes in a bearing shell, will also oil-starve a bearing, and destroy it. When lack of lubrication is the cause of bearing failure, the bearing material is wiped or extruded from the steel backing of

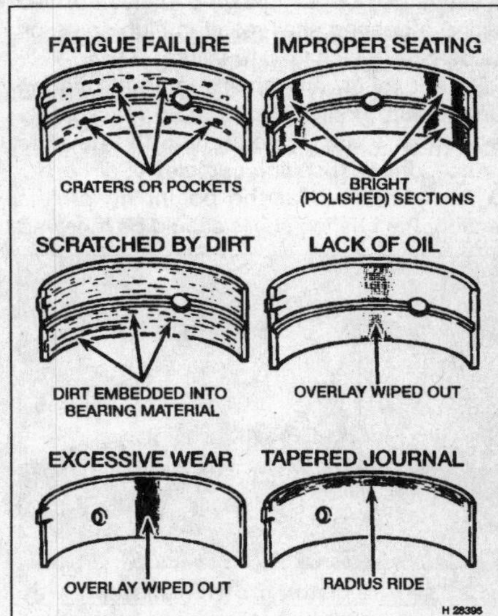

14.1 Typical bearing failures

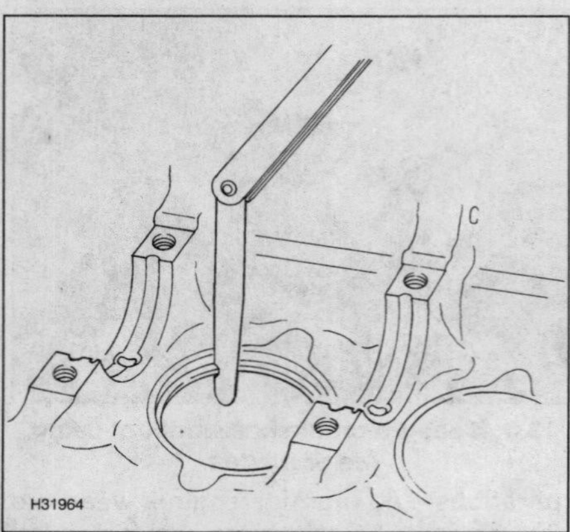

16.4 Check a piston ring end gap using a feeler blade

the bearing. Temperatures may increase to the point where the steel backing turns blue from overheating.

6 Driving habits can have a definite effect on bearing life. Full-throttle, low-speed operation (labouring the engine) puts very high loads on bearings, tending to squeeze out the oil film. These loads cause the bearings to flex, which produces fine cracks in the bearing face (fatigue failure). Eventually, the bearing material will loosen in pieces, and tear away from the steel backing.

7 Short-distance driving leads to corrosion of bearings, because insufficient engine heat is produced to drive off the condensed water and corrosive gases. These products collect in the engine oil, forming acid and sludge. As the oil is carried to the engine bearings, the acid attacks and corrodes the bearing material.

8 Incorrect bearing installation during engine assembly will lead to bearing failure as well. Tight-fitting bearings leave insufficient bearing running clearance, and will result in oil starvation. Dirt or foreign particles trapped behind a bearing shell result in high spots on the bearing, which lead to failure.

9 *Do not* touch any shell's internal bearing surface with your fingers during reassembly as there is a risk of scratching the delicate surface, or of depositing particles of dirt on it.

10 As mentioned at the beginning of this Section, the bearing shells should be renewed as a matter of course during engine overhaul. To do otherwise is false economy.

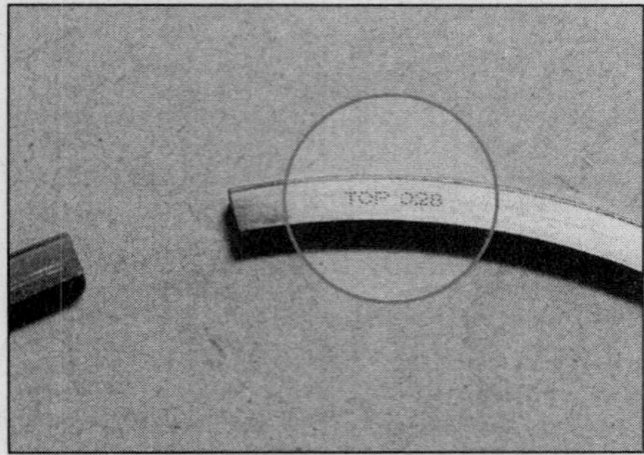

16.9 Piston ring TOP marking

Selection

11 Main and big-end bearings for the engines described in this Chapter are available in standard sizes and a range of undersizes to suit reground crankshafts.

12 Have the crankshaft measured by an engine reconditioning specialist. They will be able to supply the correctly sized bearings.

15 Engine overhaul – reassembly sequence

1 Before reassembly begins, ensure that all new parts have been obtained, and that all necessary tools are available. Read through the entire procedure to familiarise yourself with the work involved, and to ensure that all items necessary for reassembly of the engine are at hand. In addition to all normal tools and materials, thread-locking compound will be needed. A suitable tube of liquid sealant will also be required for the joint faces that are fitted without gaskets.

2 In order to save time and avoid problems, engine reassembly can be carried out in the following order, referring to Part A, B, C, D, E or F of this Chapter unless otherwise stated. Where applicable, use new gaskets and seals when refitting the various components.

a) Crankshaft (Section 17).
b) Piston/connecting rod assemblies (Section 18).
c) Oil pump.
d) Sump.
e) Flywheel/driveplate.
f) Cylinder head.
g) Timing belt/chain, tensioner and sprockets.
h) Engine external components.

3 At this stage, all engine components should be absolutely clean and dry, with all faults repaired. The components should be laid out (or in individual containers) on a completely clean work surface.

16 Piston rings – refitting

1 Before fitting new piston rings, the ring end gaps must be checked as follows.

2 Lay out the piston/connecting rod assemblies and the new piston ring sets, so that the ring sets will be matched with the same piston and cylinder during the end gap measurement and subsequent engine reassembly.

3 Insert the top ring into the first cylinder, and push it down the bore using the top of the piston. This will ensure that the ring remains square with the cylinder walls. Position the ring approximately 15.0 mm the bottom of the cylinder bore, at the lower limit of ring travel. Note that the top and second compression rings are different.

4 Measure the end gap using feeler blades, and compare the measurements with the figures given in the Specifications **(see illustration)**.

5 If the gap is too small (unlikely if genuine VW parts are used), it must be enlarged, or the ring ends may contact each other during engine operation, causing serious damage. Ideally, new piston rings providing the correct end gap should be fitted. As a last resort, the end gap can be increased by filing the ring ends very carefully with a fine file. Mount the file in a vice equipped with soft jaws, slip the ring over the file with the ends contacting the file face, and slowly move the ring to remove material from the ends. Take care, as piston rings are sharp, and are easily broken.

6 With new piston rings, it is unlikely that the end gap will be too large. If the gaps are too large, check that you have the correct rings for your engine and for the particular cylinder bore size.

7 Repeat the checking procedure for each ring in the first cylinder, and then for the rings in the remaining cylinders. Remember to keep rings, pistons and cylinders matched up.

8 Once the ring end gaps have been checked and if necessary corrected, the rings can be fitted to the pistons.

9 Fit the piston rings using the same technique as for removal. Fit the bottom (oil control) ring first, and work up. Note that a two- or three-section oil control ring may be fitted; where a two-section ring is fitted, first insert the wire expander, then fit the ring. Ensure that the rings are fitted the correct way up – the top surface of the rings is normally marked TOP **(see illustration)**. Offset the piston ring gaps by 120° from each other. **Note:** *Always follow any instructions supplied with the new piston ring sets ñ different manufacturers may specify different procedures. Do not mix up the top and second compression rings, as they have different cross-sections.*

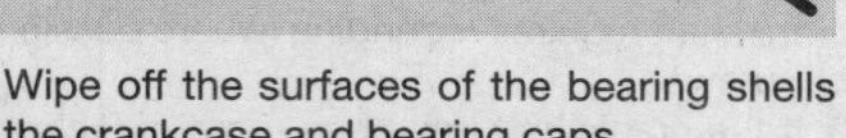

17 Crankshaft – refitting

1 Wipe off the surfaces of the bearing shells in the crankcase and bearing caps.

2 Press the bearing shells into their locations, ensuring that the tab on each shell engages In the notch in the cylinder block or bearing cap, and that the oil holes In the cylinder block and bearing shell are aligned **(see illustration)**. Take care not to touch any shells bearing surface with your fingers.

3 Where applicable, refit the crankshaft speed/position sensor wheel, and tighten the securing bolts to the specified torque. Make sure that the sensor wheel is correctly orientated as noted before removal.

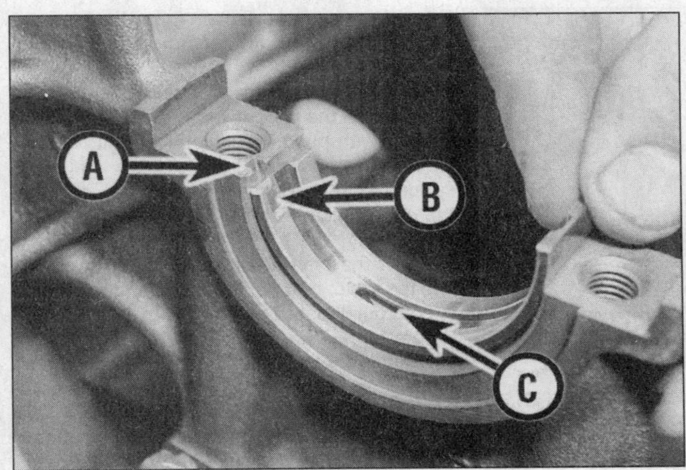

17.2 Bearing shell correctly refitted

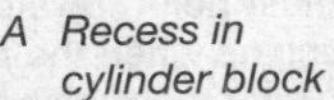
A Recess in cylinder block
B Lug on bearing shell
C Oil hole

17.4 Lubricate the upper bearing shells

4 Liberally coat the bearing shells in the crankcase with clean engine oil of the appropriate grade **(see illustration)**. Make sure that the bearing shells are still correctly seated in their locations.

5 Lower the crankshaft into position so that No 1 cylinder crankpin is at BDC, ready for fitting No 1 piston. Ensure that the crankshaft endfloat control thrustwasher halves, either side of the No 3 main bearing location, remain in position. Where applicable, take care not to damage the crankshaft speed/position sensor wheel as the crankshaft is lowered into position.

6 Lubricate the lower bearing shells in the main bearing caps with clean engine oil. Make sure that the crankshaft endfloat control thrustwasher halves are still correctly seated either side of No 3 bearing cap **(see illustrations)**.

7 Fit the main bearing caps in the correct order and orientation – No 1 bearing cap must be at the timing belt end of the engine and the bearing shell tab locating recesses in the crankcase and bearing caps must be adjacent to each other **(see illustration)**. Insert the bearing cap bolts (using new bolts where necessary), and hand-tighten them only.

8 Working from the centre bearing cap outwards, tighten the bearing cap bolts to their specified torque. On engines where two Stages are given for the torque, tighten all bolts to the Stage 1 torque, then go round again, and tighten all bolts through the Stage 2 angle **(see illustrations)**.

9 Check that the crankshaft rotates freely by turning it by hand. If resistance is felt, recheck the bearing running clearances, as described previously.

10 Check the crankshaft endfloat as described at the beginning of Section 13. If the thrust surfaces of the crankshaft have been checked and new thrustwashers have been fitted, then the endfloat should be within specification.

11 Refit the pistons and connecting rods or reconnect them to the crankshaft as described in Section 20.

12 Proceed as follows according to engine type:

a) On SOHC petrol engines, refit the crankshaft oil seal housings, flywheel/driveplate, oil pump and pick-up pipe, sump and oil baffle plate, and the crankshaft sprocket and timing belt, as described in Chapter 2A.

b) On DOHC petrol engines, refit the

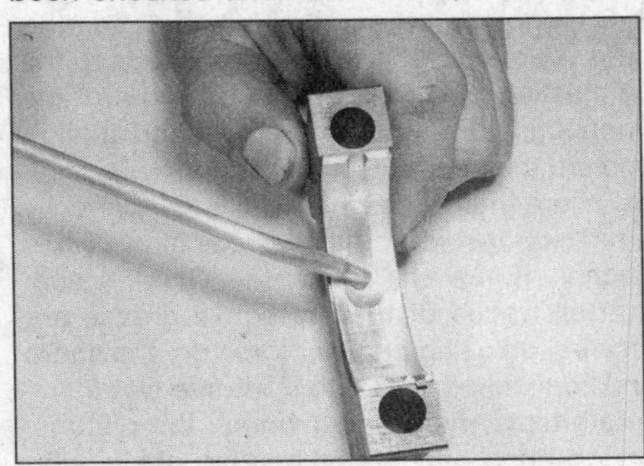
17.6a Lubricate the lower bearing shells...

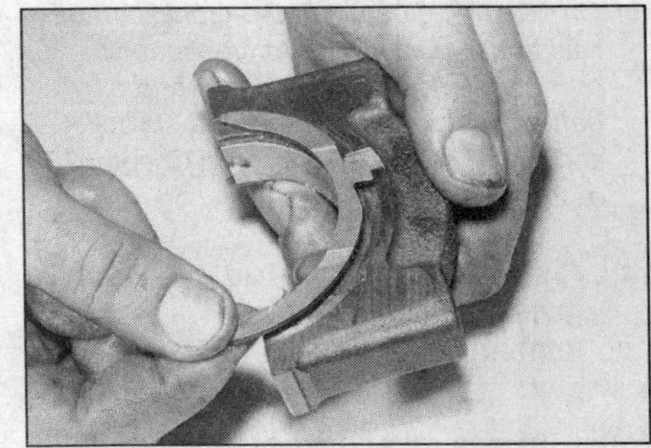
17.6b ...and make sure that the thrustwashers are correctly seated

17.7 Fitting No 1 main bearing cap

17.8a Tighten the main bearing cap bolts to the specified torque...

17.8b ...then through the specified angle

18.5a Lubricate the pistons...

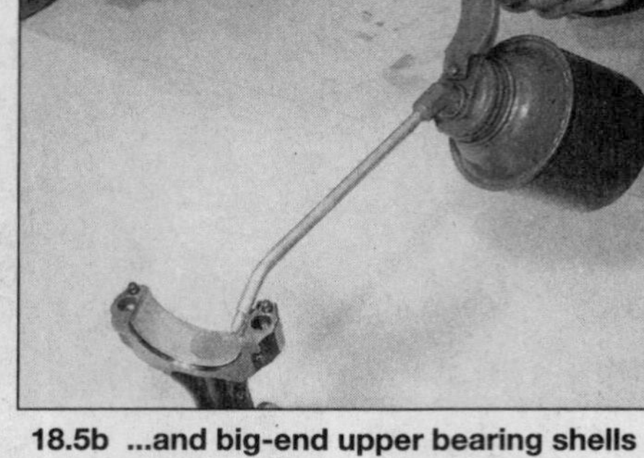

18.5b ...and big-end upper bearing shells with clean engine oil

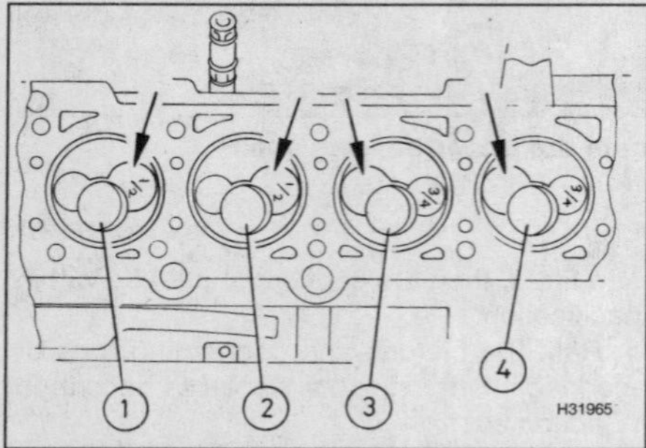

18.8a Piston orientation and coding on SOHC diesel engines ...

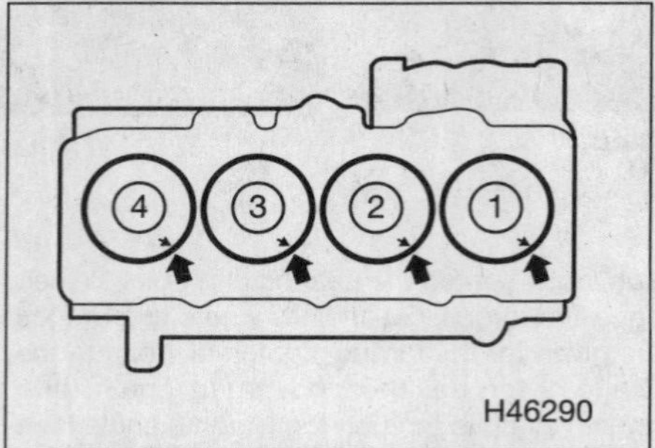

18.8b ...and on DOHC diesel engines

crankshaft oil seal housing, flywheel/ driveplate, oil pump and pick-up pipe, sump, and main timing belt, as described in Chapter 2B, 2C or 2D. ***Note:*** *On 2.0 litre engines, it will necessary to refit the balancer shaft assembly.*

c) On diesel engines, refit the crankshaft oil seal housings, flywheel/driveplate, oil pump and pick-up pipe, sump and oil baffle plate, and the crankshaft sprocket and timing belt, as described in Chapter 2E or 2F.

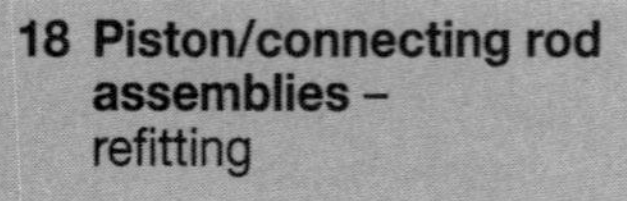

18 Piston/connecting rod assemblies – refitting

Note: *A piston ring compressor tool will be required for this operation.*

1 Note that the following procedure assumes that the crankshaft main bearing caps are in place.

2 Where applicable, refit the piston cooling oil spray jets to the bottom of the cylinder block, and tighten the securing bolts to the specified torque.

3 On engines where the big-end bearing caps are secured by nuts, fit new bolts to the connecting rods. Tap the old bolts out of the connecting rods using a soft-faced mallet, and tap the new bolts into position.

4 Ensure that the bearing shells are correctly fitted, as described at the beginning of this Section. If new shells are being fitted, ensure that all traces of the protective grease are cleaned off using paraffin. Wipe dry the shells and connecting rods with a lint-free cloth.

5 Lubricate the cylinder bores, the pistons, piston rings and upper bearing shells with clean engine oil **(see illustrations)**. Lay out each piston/connecting rod assembly in order on a clean work surface. Where the bearing caps are secured with nuts, pad the threaded ends of the bolts with insulating tape to prevent them scratching the crankpins and bores when the pistons are refitted.

6 Start with piston/connecting rod assembly No 1. Make sure that the piston rings are still spaced as described in Section 16, then clamp them in position with a piston ring compressor tool.

7 Insert the piston/connecting rod assembly into the top of cylinder No 1. Lower the big-end in first, guiding it to protect the cylinder bores. Where oil jets are located at the bottoms of the bores, take particular care not to damage them when guiding the connecting rods onto the crankpins.

8 Ensure that the orientation of the piston in its cylinder is correct – the piston crown, connecting rod and big-end bearing cap have markings, which must point towards the timing belt end of the engine when the piston is installed in the bore – refer to Section 12 for details. On SOHC diesel engines, the piston crowns are specially shaped to improve the engine's combustion characteristics. Because of this, pistons 1 and 2 are different to pistons 3 and 4. When correctly fitted, the larger inlet valve chambers on pistons 1 and 2 must face the flywheel/driveplate end of the engine, and the larger inlet valve chambers on the remaining pistons must face the timing belt end of the engine. New pistons have number markings on their crowns to indicate their type – 1/2 denotes piston 1 or 2, 3/4 indicates piston 3 or 4. On DOHC diesel engines, make sure the arrows on the piston crowns point towards the timing belt end of the engine **(see illustrations)**.

9 Using a block of wood or hammer handle against the piston crown, tap the assembly into the cylinder until the piston crown is flush with the top of the cylinder **(see illustration)**.

10 Ensure that the bearing shell is still correctly installed in the connecting rod, then liberally lubricate the crankpin and both bearing shells with clean engine oil.

11 Taking care not to mark the cylinder bores, tap the piston/connecting rod assembly down the bore and onto the crankpin. On engines where the big-end caps are secured by nuts, remove the insulating tape from the threaded ends of the connecting rod bolts. Oil the bolt threads, and on engines where the big-end caps are secured by bolts, oil the undersides of the bolt heads.

12 Fit the big-end bearing cap, tightening its retaining nuts or bolts (as applicable) finger-tight at first. The connecting rod and its bearing cap both have recesses machined into them on one side, close to their mating surfaces – these recesses must both face the same way as the arrow on the piston crown (ie, towards the timing end of the engine) when correctly installed. Reassemble the two components to satisfy this requirement.

13 Tighten the retaining bolts or nuts (as applicable) to the specified torque and angle,

18.9 Using a hammer handle to tap the piston into its bore

18.13a Tighten the big-end bearing cap bolts/nuts to the specified torque...

in the two stages given in the Specifications **(see illustrations)**.

14 Refit the remaining three piston/connecting rod assemblies in the same way.

15 Rotate the crankshaft by hand. Check that it turns freely; some stiffness is to be expected if new parts have been fitted, but there should be no binding or tight spots.

16 On diesel engines, if new pistons have been fitted, or if a new short engine has been fitted, the projection of the piston crowns above the cylinder head mating face of the cylinder block at TDC must be measured. This measurement is used to determine the thickness of the new cylinder head gasket required. This procedure is described as part of the Cylinder head – removal, inspection and refitting procedure in Chapter 2E or 2F.

17 Proceed as follows according to engine type:

a) *On SOHC petrol engines, refit the oil pump and pick-up pipe, sump and oil baffle plate, and cylinder head, as described in Chapter 2A.*
b) *On 1.4 and 1.6 litre DOHC petrol engines, refit the oil pick-up pipe, sump, and cylinder head, as described in Chapter 2B or 2C.*
c) *On 2.0 litre DOHC engines, refit the oil pump and pick-up pipe, sump and oil baffle plate, cylinder head, and the balancer shaft assembly as described in Chapter 2D.*
d) *On diesel engines, refit the oil pump and pick-up pipe, sump and oil baffle plate, and cylinder head, as described in Chapter 2E or 2F.*

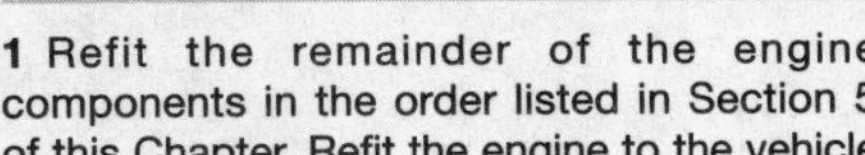

19 Engine – initial start-up after overhaul and reassembly

1 Refit the remainder of the engine components in the order listed in Section 5 of this Chapter. Refit the engine to the vehicle as described in the relevant Section of this Chapter. Double-check the engine oil and coolant levels, and make a final check that everything has been reconnected. Make sure that there are no tools or rags left in the engine compartment.

18.13b ...then through the specified angle

2 Where necessary, reconnect the battery leads with reference to *Disconnecting the battery* at the rear of this manual.

Petrol models

3 Remove the spark plugs, referring to Chapter 1A for details.

4 The engine must be immobilised such that it can be turned over using the starter motor without starting – disable the fuel pump by unplugging the fuel pump power relay from the relay board with reference to Chapter 12, and also disable the ignition system by disconnecting the wiring from the DIS module or coils, as applicable.

Caution: To prevent damage to the catalytic converter, it is important to disable the fuel system.

5 Turn the engine using the starter motor until the oil pressure warning lamp goes out. If the lamp fails to extinguish after several seconds of cranking, check the engine oil level and oil filter security. Assuming these are correct, check the security of the oil pressure switch wiring – do not progress any further until you are satisfied that oil is being pumped around the engine at sufficient pressure.

6 Refit the spark plugs, and reconnect the wiring to the fuel pump relay and DIS module or coils, as applicable.

Diesel models

7 Disconnect the injector harness wiring plug at the end of the cylinder head – refer to Chapter 4B for details.

8 Turn the engine using the starter motor until the oil pressure warning lamp goes out.

9 If the lamp fails to extinguish after several seconds of cranking, check the engine oil level and oil filter security. Assuming these are correct, check the security of the oil pressure switch cabling – do not progress any further until you are satisfied that oil is being pumped around the engine at sufficient pressure.

10 Reconnect the injector wiring plug.

All models

11 Start the engine, but be aware that as fuel system components have been disturbed, the cranking time may be a little longer than usual.

12 While the engine is idling, check for fuel, water and oil leaks. Don't be alarmed if there are some odd smells and the occasional plume of smoke as components heat up and burn off oil deposits.

13 Assuming all is well, keep the engine idling until hot water is felt circulating through the top hose.

14 After a few minutes, recheck the oil and coolant levels, and top-up as necessary.

15 There is no need to retighten the cylinder head bolts once the engine has been run following reassembly.

16 If new pistons, rings or crankshaft bearings have been fitted, the engine must be treated as new, and run-in for the first 600 miles. *Do not* operate the engine at full-throttle, or allow it to labour at low engine speeds in any gear. It is recommended that the engine oil and filter are changed at the end of this period.

Notes

Chapter 3
Cooling, heating and air conditioning systems

Contents

Degrees of difficulty

Easy, suitable for novice with little experience 	**Fairly easy,** suitable for beginner with some experience	**Fairly difficult,** suitable for competent DIY mechanic	**Difficult,** suitable for experienced DIY mechanic	**Very difficult,** suitable for expert DIY or professional 

Specifications

Engine codes*

1.4 litre:	
Indirect injection petrol engine	BCA and BUD
Direct injection petrol engine (FSi)	BKG and BLN
Direct injection turbocharged engine (TSi)	CAXA
1.6 litre:	
SOHC petrol engine	BGU, BSE and BSF
DOHC direct injection petrol engine (FSi)	BAG, BLP and BLF
2.0 litre petrol engine:	
Non-turbo	AXW, BLX, BLY, BLR, BVX, BVY and BVZ
Turbo	AXX, BPY and BWA
Diesel engine:	
PD unit injector engine:	
1.9 litre, 8-valve, turbo, SOHC	BJB, BKC, BRU, BLS, BXE and BXF
2.0 litre:	
8-valve, non-turbo, SOHC	BDK
8-valve, turbo, SOHC	BMM
16-valve, turbo, DOHC	AZV, BKD and BMN
Common rail injection engine	CBDA and CBDB

* **Note:** *See 'Vehicle identification' at the end of this manual for the location of engine code markings.*

Cooling system pressure cap

Opening pressure	1.4 to 1.6 bar

Thermostat

	Begins to open	Fully open
By-pass thermostat only, fitted to auto models	75°C	85°C
Petrol engines:		
1.4 litre engine codes BCA and BUD	84°C	98°C
1.4 litre engine codes BKG and BLN:		
Thermostat 1 (long element)	87°C	102°C
Thermostat 2 (short element)	103°C	120°C
1.4 litre engine code CAXA:		
Thermostat 1 (long element)	83°C	97°C
Thermostat 2 (short element)	105°C	121°C
1.6 litre engine codes BGU, BSE and BSF	87°C	102°C
1.6 litre engine codes BAG, BLF and BLP:		
Thermostat 1 (long element)	87°C	102°C
Thermostat 2 (short element)	103°C	120°C
2.0 litre	105°C	Map-controlled
Diesel engines	85°C	105°C

Torque wrench settings

	Nm	lbf ft
Coolant pipe to map-controlled thermostat housing:		
2.0 litre non-turbo engine	10	7
2.0 litre turbo engine	5	4
Coolant pump:		
1.4 litre petrol engine codes BCA and BUD	20	15
1.4 litre petrol engine codes BKG and BLN	25	18
1.6 litre petrol engine codes BGU, BSE and BSF	15	11
1.6 litre petrol engine codes BAG, BLF and BLP	25	18
2.0 litre petrol engine	15	11
Diesel engines:		
PD unit injector engines	15	11
Common rail engines	9	6
Coolant pump pulley	20	15
Radiator	5	4
Radiator cooling fan shroud bolts	5	4
Thermostat cover bolts:		
1.4 litre petrol engine codes BCA and BUD	7	5
1.4 litre petrol engine codes BKG, BLN and CAXA	5	4
1.6 litre petrol engine codes BGU, BSE and BSF	15	11
1.6 litre petrol engine codes BAG, BLF and BLP	5	4
2.0 litre petrol engine	Not applicable	
All diesel engines	15	11
Thermostat housing bolts:		
1.4 litre petrol engine	10	7
1.6 litre petrol engine codes BGU, BSE and BSF	Not applicable	
1.6 litre petrol engine codes BAG, BLF and BLP	10	7
2.0 litre petrol engine	15	11
All diesel engines	Not applicable	

1 General information and precautions

A pressurised cooling system is used, with a pump, an aluminium crossflow radiator, two electric cooling fans, a thermostat and a heater matrix, as well as the interconnecting hoses. On automatic transmission models, a temperature-sensitive by-pass thermostat is fitted on the coolant return from the transmission oil cooler. A temperature-sensitive by-pass thermostat is also fitted in the coolant return from the turbocharger on engine codes AXX and BWA. On 1.4 and 1.6 litre DOHC petrol engines, the thermostat is located on the top left-hand end of the cylinder head, in the coolant supply to the top of the radiator – on engine codes BAG, BKG, BLF, BLN, BLP and CAXA, there are two thermostats located in the same housing, each having a different temperature control range. On all other engines (1.6 litre SOHC and 2.0 litre petrol engines, and all diesel engines), the thermostat is located in the front, right-hand side of the cylinder block, in the coolant return from the radiator.

The system functions as follows. Coolant is circulated through the cylinder block and head passages by the coolant pump which is driven by the auxiliary drivebelt on petrol engine codes BKG, BLN, BAG, BLP, BLF and CAXA, or by the timing belt on all other petrol and diesel engines. On common rail diesel engines, an electrically operated coolant pump is also fitted. The coolant cools the cylinder bores, combustion surfaces and valve seats of the engine.

When the engine is cold, the thermostat is closed and the coolant only circulates around the engine and the heater matrix in the passenger compartment, however, when the engine reaches a predetermined temperature, the thermostat opens and the coolant passes through the radiator for additional cooling. The coolant enters the top of the radiator and is cooled, as it circulates down through the cooling tubes, by the inrush of air when the car is in forward motion. Airflow is supplemented by the action of the electric cooling fans when necessary. Upon leaving the bottom of the radiator, the coolant returns to the engine and the cycle is repeated. As described earlier, the thermostat is located according to engine type, either in the coolant supply to the top of the radiator, or in the coolant return from the bottom of the radiator. The effect is identical in both cases – when it is closed, there is no circulation through the radiator, and when it is open, there is circulation. On some engines, the action of the thermostat is determined in conjunction with the engine management ECU.

Refer to Section 11 for information on the air conditioning system.

Precautions

Warning: Do not attempt to remove the expansion tank filler cap or disturb any part of the cooling system while the engine is hot, as there is a high risk of scalding. If the expansion tank filler cap must be removed before the engine and radiator have fully cooled (even though this is not recommended) the pressure in the cooling system must first be relieved. Cover the cap with a thick layer of cloth, to avoid scalding, and slowly unscrew the filler cap until a hissing sound can be heard. When the hissing has stopped, indicating that the pressure has reduced, slowly unscrew the filler cap until it can be removed; if more hissing sounds are heard, wait until they have stopped before unscrewing the cap completely. At all times keep well away from the filler cap opening.

- ***Do not allow antifreeze to come into contact with skin or painted surfaces of the vehicle. Rinse off spills immediately with plenty of water. Never leave antifreeze lying around in an open container or in a puddle in the driveway or on the garage floor. Children and pets are attracted by its sweet smell. Antifreeze can be fatal if ingested.***
- ***If the engine is hot, the electric cooling fan may start rotating even if the engine is not running, so be careful to keep hands, hair and loose clothing well clear when working in the engine compartment.***
- ***Refer to Section 11 for additional precautions to be observed when working on models with air conditioning.***

2 Cooling system hoses – disconnection and renewal

Note: *Refer to the warnings given in Section 1 of this Chapter before proceeding.*

1 If the checks described in the relevant part

of Chapter 1 reveal a faulty hose, it must be renewed as follows.
2 First drain the cooling system as described in Chapter 1A or 1B. If the coolant is not due for renewal, it may be re-used if it is collected in a clean container.
3 To disconnect a hose, release its retaining clips, then move them along the hose, clear of the relevant inlet/outlet union. Carefully work the hose free.
4 In order to disconnect the radiator inlet and outlet hoses, apply pressure to hold the hose on to the relevant union, pull out the spring clip and pull the hose from the union **(see illustration)**. Note that the radiator inlet and outlet unions are fragile; do not use excessive force when attempting to remove the hoses. If a hose proves to be difficult to remove, try to release it by rotating the hose ends before attempting to free it.
5 When fitting a hose, first slide the clips onto the hose, then work the hose into position. If clamp type clips were originally fitted, it is a good idea to use screw type clips when refitting the hose. If the hose is stiff, use a little soapy water as a lubricant, or soften the hose by soaking it in hot water.
6 Work the hose into position, checking that it is correctly routed, then slide each clip along the hose until it passes over the flared end of the relevant union, before securing it in position with the retaining clip.
7 Prior to refitting a radiator inlet or outlet hose, renew the connection O-ring regardless of condition. The connections are a push-fit over the radiator unions.

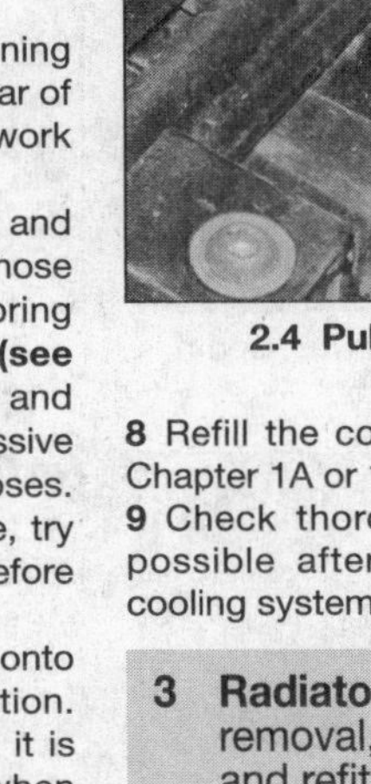

2.4 Pull out the retaining clip

8 Refill the cooling system as described in Chapter 1A or 1B.
9 Check thoroughly for leaks as soon as possible after disturbing any part of the cooling system.

3 Radiator – removal, inspection and refitting

Removal

1 Switch off the ignition and all electrical consumers.
2 Except on engine codes BGU, BSE and BSF, move the lock carrier, located at the front of the engine compartment, to its Service position as follows. On engine codes BGU, BSE and BSF, it is sufficient to remove the front bumper only.

a) Remove the front bumper (Chapter 11).
*b) Disconnect the bonnet release cable over the right-hand headlight **(see illustration)**.*
c) On models with a turbocharger, remove the air ducts.
*d) Remove the horn (Chapter 12) **(see illustration)**.*
*e) Support the lock carrier, then unscrew the mounting bolts and substitute them with one threaded rod on each side of the car **(see illustration)**.*
f) Carefully pull the lock carrier forwards approximately 10 cm to provide access to the front of the engine.

3 Drain the cooling system as described in Chapter 1A or 1B. If preferred, the electric cooling fan temperature sensor may be removed from the bottom hose to drain the system **(see illustration)**.
4 Disconnect the wiring from the cooling fan connector at the bottom left-hand side of the radiator.
5 On all non-turbo engines except petrol engine codes BAG, BKG, BLF, BLN and BLP, unscrew the mounting bolts and remove the fans together with the cowling from the rear of the radiator. On petrol models, lift the fans upwards, and on diesel models lower the fans and remove from beneath the car. On diesel models, also remove the noise insulation tray and air cleaner inlet duct. **Note:** *On turbo engines, the fans can remain with the radiator, then be separated on the bench.*
6 Disconnect the coolant hoses from the radiator by pulling out the clips and easing off the hoses **(see illustrations)**.

3.2a Disconnect the bonnet release cable...

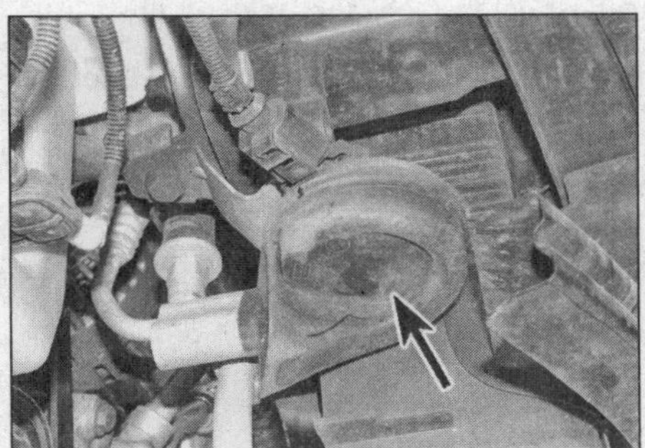

3.2b ...remove the horn...

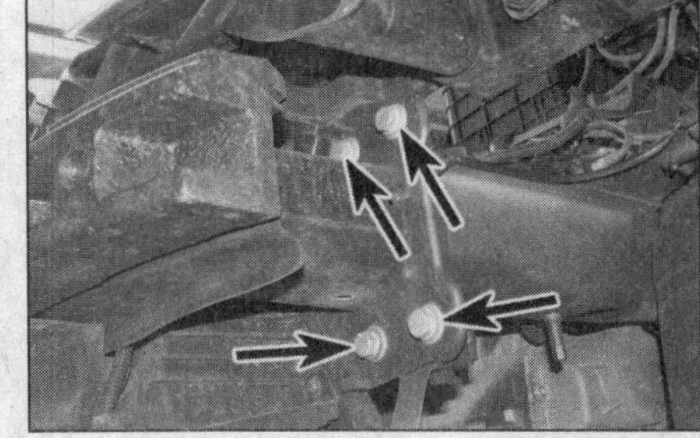

3.2c ...and substitute the lock carrier mounting bolts with one threaded rod each side

3.3 Removing the cooling fan temperature sensor to drain the cooling system

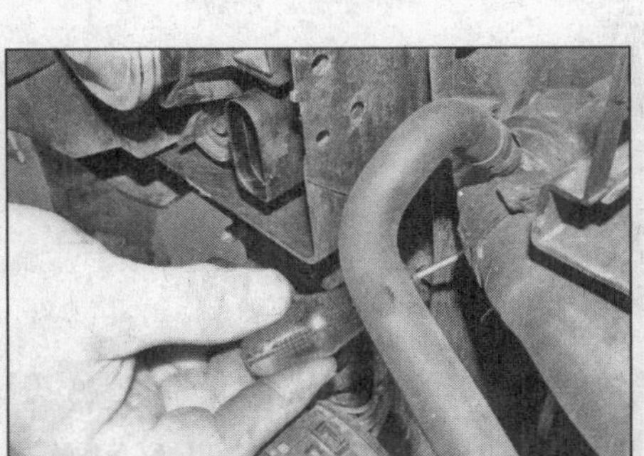

3.6a Pull out the clips with a screwdriver...

3.6b ...and disconnect the hoses from the radiator

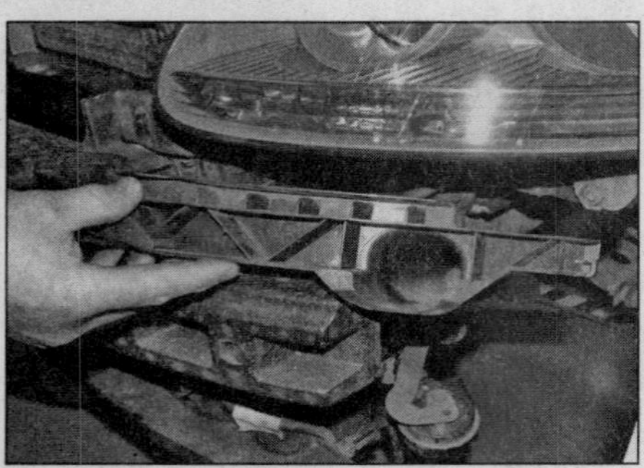
3.8a Where necessary, remove the plastic bracket...

3.14a Radiator lower mounting rubber grommets on the lock carrier...

7 From the rear of the lock carrier, undo the screws securing the air conditioning condenser to the radiator, and also remove the support clamps for the refrigerant lines. Note that may be necessary to delay removing the left-hand screw until the radiator mounting have been released. **Do not** disconnect the refrigerant lines.

8 On all non-turbo engines, undo the screws securing the radiator upper mounting rubber bushes to the front crossmember – access is from the front of the car. Where necessary, remove the plastic bracket for access to the screws. Move the top of the radiator slightly to the rear, and withdraw it upwards from the lower mounting rubber grommets in the lock carrier **(see illustrations)**.

9 On turbo engines, support the radiator then undo the screws securing it to the lock carrier. Lower the radiator and remove from under the

3.8b ... for access to the radiator upper mountings

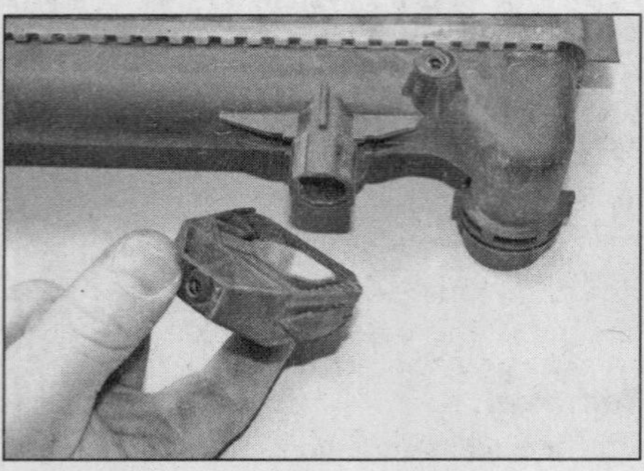
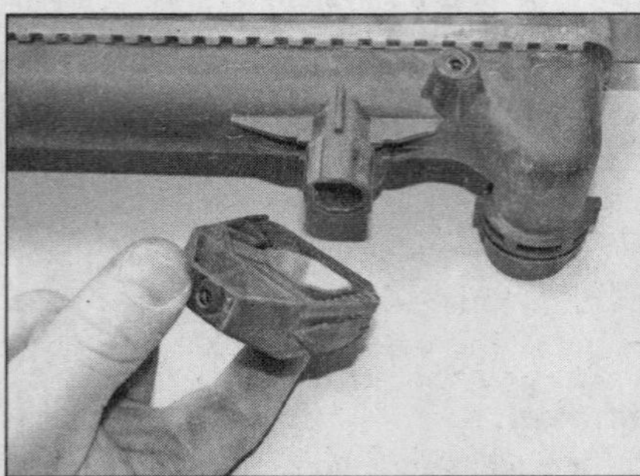
3.14b ...and upper mounting rubbers on the radiator

car. If necessary, unbolt the fans and cowling with the radiator on the bench.

Inspection

10 If the radiator has been removed due to suspected blockage, reverse flush it as described in the relevant part of Chapter 1.

11 Clean dirt and debris from the radiator fins, using an airline (in which case, wear eye protection) or a soft brush. Be careful, as the fins are sharp and easily damaged.

12 If necessary, a radiator specialist can perform a 'flow test' on the radiator, to establish whether an internal blockage exists.

13 A leaking radiator must be referred to a specialist for permanent repair. Do not attempt to weld or solder a leaking radiator, as damage may result.

14 Check the radiator mounting rubbers, and renew if necessary **(see illustrations)**.

3.8c Radiator removed from the lock carrier

Refitting

15 Refitting is a reversal of removal. On completion, refill the cooling system using the correct type of antifreeze as described in the relevant part of Chapter 1.

4 Thermostat – removal, testing and refitting

1.4 and 1.6 litre DOHC petrol engines

Removal

1 The thermostat is located in a housing at the left-hand end of the cylinder head. First, remove the engine top cover.

2 Drain the cooling system as described in Chapter 1A.

3 Disconnect the coolant hose(s) from the thermostat cover.

4 Undo the retaining screws, and remove the thermostat cover, noting the locations of any brackets secured by the screws, then lift out the thermostat. Recover the O-ring if it is loose. On engine codes BAG, BKG, BLF, BLN and BLP, remove the spring and plunger for access to the thermostat element **(see illustrations)**.

Testing

Note: *If there is any question about the operation of the thermostat, it's best to renew it – they are not usually expensive items.*

4.4a Undo the screws...

4.4b ...remove the thermostat cover...

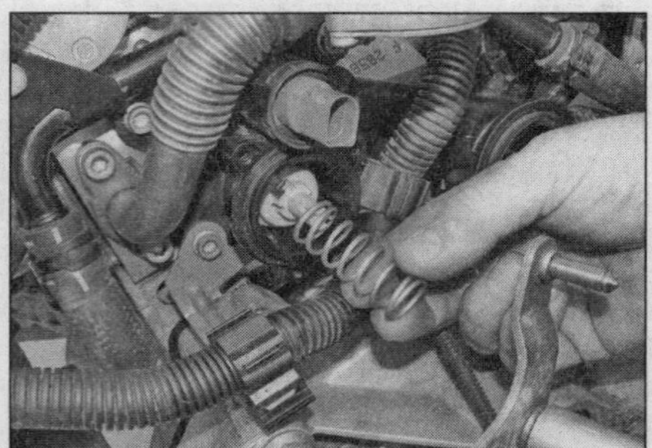
4.4c ...followed by the spring...

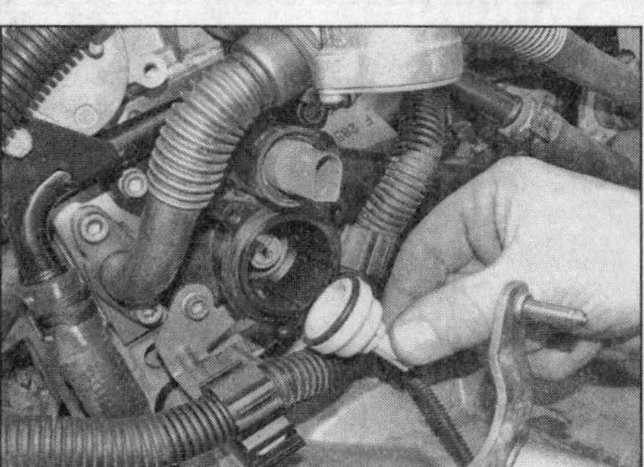
4.4d ...and plunger...

4.4e ...for access to the thermostat element

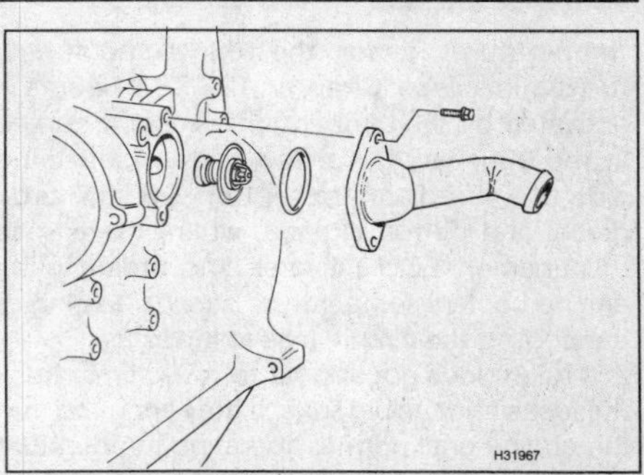
4.11 Thermostat components on 1.6 litre SOHC and 2.0 litre petrol engines

Testing involves heating in, or over, an open pan of boiling water, which carries with it the risk of scalding. A thermostat which has seen more than five years' service may well be past its best already.

5 A rough test of the thermostat may be made by suspending it with a piece of string in a container full of water, but not touching the container. Heat the water to bring it to the boil – the thermostat must open by the time the water boils. If not, renew it.

6 If a thermometer is available, the precise opening temperature of the thermostat may be determined, and compared with the figures given in the Specifications. The opening temperature is also marked on the thermostat. On engine codes BAG, BKG, BLF, BLN, BLP and CAXA, accurate testing will be difficult with the elements removed, and some indication may be obtained by testing with the thermostat assembled inside the housing.

7 A thermostat which fails to close as the water cools must also be renewed.

Refitting

8 Refitting is a reversal of removal, bearing in mind the following points.

a) Refit the thermostat using a new O-ring.
b) Refill the cooling system with the correct type and quantity of coolant as described in Chapter 1A.

1.6 litre SOHC and 2.0 litre petrol engines

Removal

9 The thermostat is located behind a connection flange in the front right-hand side of the engine block. Remove the engine top cover.

10 Drain the cooling system as described in Chapter 1A.

11 Disconnect the coolant hose from the thermostat cover/connection flange **(see illustration)**.

12 Unscrew the two securing bolts, and remove the thermostat cover/connection flange, noting the locations of any brackets secured by the bolts, then lift out the thermostat. Recover the O-ring if it is loose.

Testing

13 Proceed as described in paragraphs 5 to 7.

On 2.0 litre engines, additional testing is possible for the map-controlled thermostat – connect a 12 volt supply to the two terminals, and check that the minimum lift of the thermostat is 7.0 mm after 10 minutes, proving that the heating resistor is functioning correctly.

Refitting

14 Refitting is a reversal of removal, bearing in mind the following points.

a) Refit the thermostat using a new O-ring.
b) Where applicable, the thermostat should be fitted with the brace almost vertical.
c) Ensure that any brackets are in place on the thermostat cover bolts as noted before removal.
d) Refill the cooling system with the correct type and quantity of coolant as described in Chapter 1A.

Diesel engines

Removal

15 The thermostat is located behind a connection flange in the front side of the engine block, at the timing belt end.

16 Drain the cooling system as described in Chapter 1B. Prise out the sealing caps, undo the retaining nuts and remove the engine covers.

17 On common rail engines (codes CBDA and CBDB), remove the throttle valve assembly as described in Chapter 4B.

18 Release the securing clip and disconnect the coolant hose from the thermostat cover/connection flange.

4.19a Thermostat cover screws

19 Unscrew the two securing bolts, and remove the thermostat cover/connection flange complete with the thermostat. Note the locations of any brackets secured by the bolts. Recover the O-ring if it is loose **(see illustrations)**.

20 To remove the thermostat from the cover, twist the thermostat 90° anti-clockwise, and pull it from the cover.

Testing

21 Proceed as described in paragraphs 5 to 7.

Refitting

22 Refitting is a reversal of removal, bearing in mind the following points.

a) Refit the thermostat using a new O-ring.
b) Insert the thermostat into the cover and twist 90° clockwise.
c) The thermostat should be fitted with the brace almost vertical.
d) Ensure that any brackets are in place on the thermostat cover bolts as noted before removal.
e) Refill the cooling system with the correct type and quantity of coolant as described in Chapter 1B.

5 Electric cooling fans – testing, removal and refitting

Testing

1 Two electric cooling fans are fitted to all models. The cooling fans are supplied with current through the ignition switch, cooling fan control unit (located on the motor),

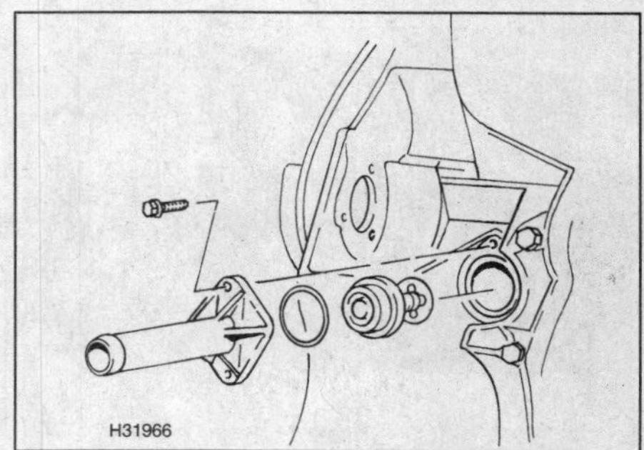
4.19b Thermostat assembly – diesel engines

temperature sensor, the relays and fuses/ fusible link (see Chapter 12). The circuit is activated by the temperature sensor mounted in the outlet elbow at the bottom, left-hand side of the radiator, except on 2.0 litre turbo diesel and petrol engines, where the engine management ECU activates it according to the engine coolant temperature sensor. Testing of the cooling fan circuit is as follows.

2 If a fan does not appear to work, first check the fuses and fusible links. If they are good, run the engine until normal operating temperature is reached, then allow it to idle. If the fan does not cut-in within a few minutes, the cause may be the temperature sender (where applicable) which can be checked by a VW dealer using specialist diagnostic equipment.

3 The motors can be checked by disconnecting the motor wiring connector and connecting a 12 volt supply directly to the motor terminals. If the motor is faulty, it must be renewed, as no spares are available.

4 If the fan still fails to operate, check the cooling fan circuit wiring (Chapter 12). Check each wire for continuity and ensure that all connections are clean and free of corrosion.

5 On models with a cooling fan control unit, if no fault can be found, then it is likely that the cooling fan control unit is faulty. Testing of the unit should be entrusted to a VW dealer or specialist; if the unit is faulty it must be renewed.

Removal

6 Switch off the ignition and all electrical consumers. Remove the engine top cover.

7 On engine codes BCA, BUD, BAG, BKG, BLF, BLN and BLP, move the lock carrier (located at the front of the engine compartment) to its Service position as follows.

a) Remove the front bumper (Chapter 11).
b) Disconnect the bonnet release cable over the right-hand headlight.
c) On models with a turbocharger, remove the air ducts.
d) Remove the horn (Chapter 12).
e) Support the lock carrier, then unscrew the mounting bolts and substitute them with one threaded rod on each side of the car.
f) Carefully pull the lock carrier forwards approximately 10 cm to provide access to the front of the engine.

8 On petrol engine codes BGU, BSE, BSF, AXW, BLX, BLY, BLR, BVX, BVY and BVZ, undo the screws and remove the air duct from the top of the lock carrier. Also, on engine codes BGU, BSE and BSF, remove the air inlet duct from the bottom of the damping chamber.

9 Disconnect the wiring plug for the cooling fan motors **(see illustration)**.

10 Unscrew the bolts securing the cooling fan shroud to the radiator, and withdraw either upwards or downwards according to model **(see illustrations)**. Note that the engine undertray must be removed before lowering the cooling fan shroud.

11 To remove the fans and motors from the shroud, first disconnect and release the wiring plugs, then unscrew the nuts and remove the units **(see illustrations)**.

Refitting

12 Refitting is a reversal of removal.

6 Cooling system electrical sensors – testing, removal and refitting

Cooling fan temperature sensor

Testing

1 Where fitted, the sensor is located in the outlet elbow at the bottom left-hand side of the radiator (see Section 5).

2 The sensor contains a thermistor, which consists of an electronic component whose electrical resistance decreases at a predetermined rate as its temperature rises. When the coolant is cold, the sensor resistance is high, current flow through the gauge is reduced, and the gauge needle points towards the 'cold' end of the scale. No resistance-to-temperature values are available. Therefore the only method of accurately checking the sensor is with dedicated diagnostic equipment, and should be entrusted to a VW dealer or specialist. If the sensor is faulty, it must be renewed.

Removal and refitting

3 The engine and radiator should be cold before removing the sensor. Switch off the ignition and all electrical consumers.

4 Either drain the cooling system (as described in Chapter 1A or 1B), or have ready a suitable plug which can be used to plug the sensor aperture whilst it is removed.

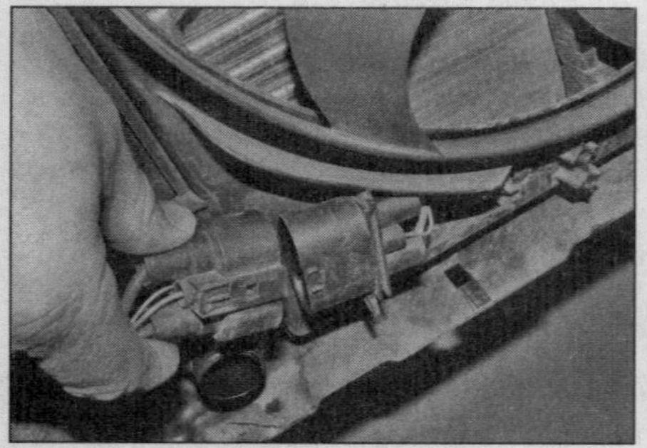

5.9 Disconnect the wiring...

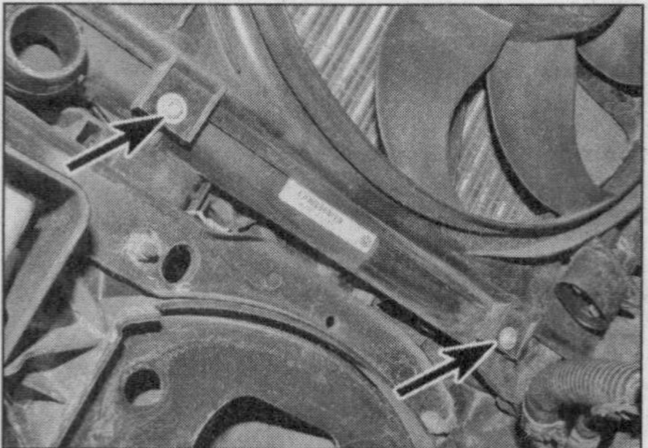

5.10a ...unscrew the bolts...

5.10b ...and remove the cooling fan shroud and motors

5.10c Cooling fan shroud and motors removed from the radiator

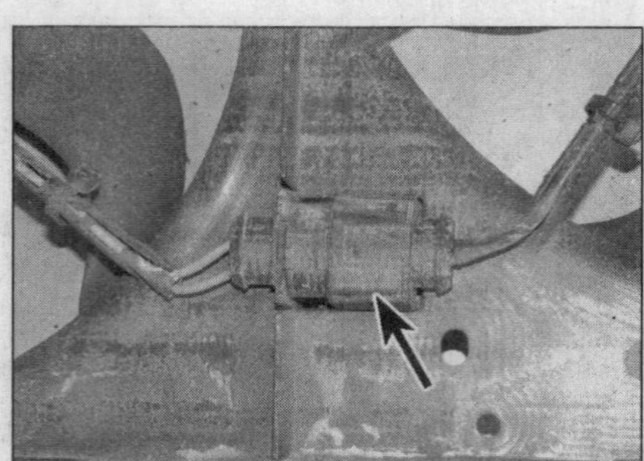

5.11a Disconnect and release the wiring plugs...

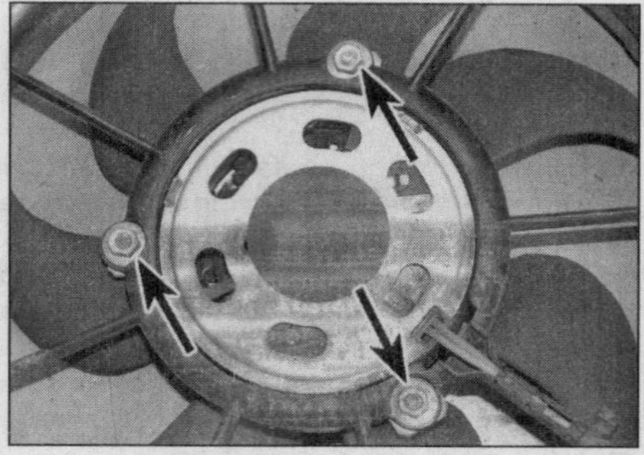

5.11b ...and unscrew the motor retaining nuts

6.6a Pull out the clip...

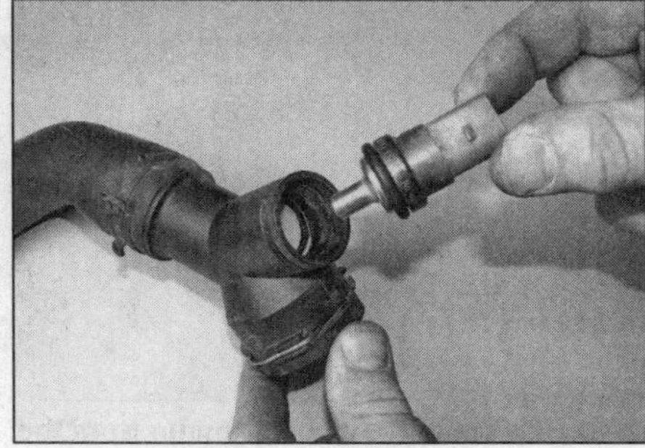
6.6b ...remove the sensor...

6.6c ...and recover the O-ring seals from the elbow and sensor

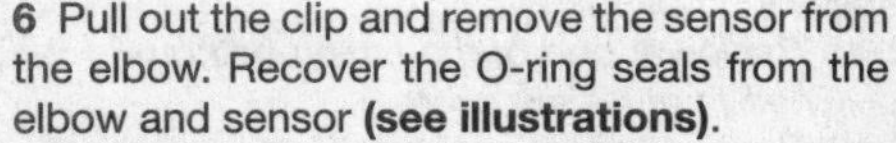

5 Disconnect the wiring plug from the sensor.

6 Pull out the clip and remove the sensor from the elbow. Recover the O-ring seals from the elbow and sensor **(see illustrations)**.

7 Refitting is a reversal of removal, but tighten the sensor securely. On completion, refill the cooling system with the correct type and quantity of coolant as described in Chapter 1A or 1B, or top-up as described in *Weekly checks*.

8 Start the engine and run it until it reaches normal operating temperature, then continue to run the engine and check that the cooling fan cuts in and functions correctly.

Coolant temperature sensor

Testing

9 The sensor is located at the left-hand end of the cylinder head **(see illustration)**.

10 The sensor contains a thermistor, which consists of an electronic component whose electrical resistance decreases at a predetermined rate as its temperature rises. When the coolant is cold, the sensor resistance is high, current flow through the gauge is reduced, and the gauge needle points towards the 'cold' end of the scale. No resistance-to-temperature values are available. Therefore the only method of accurately checking the sensor is with dedicated diagnostic equipment, and should be entrusted to a VW dealer or specialist. If the sensor is faulty, it must be renewed.

6.9 Engine coolant temperature sensor on diesel engines

Removal and refitting

11 Remove the engine top cover.

12 Disconnect the wiring from the sensor **(see illustration)**, located on the thermostat housing at the left-hand end of the cylinder head. Partially drain the cooling system to below the level of the sensor (as described in Chapter 1A or 1B).

13 Pull out the retaining clip and withdraw the sensor from the housing. Recover the O-ring **(see illustrations)**.

14 Refitting is a reversal of removal. Bearing in mind the following points.

a) Refit the sensor with a new O-ring.

b) Refill the cooling system as described in Chapter 1A or 1B, or top-up as described in 'Weekly checks'.

6.12 Disconnect the wiring...

7 Coolant pump – removal and refitting

1.4 and 1.6 litre engine codes BKG, BLN, BAG, BLP, BLF and CAXA

Note: *New coolant pumps are supplied with an integrated seal.*

Belt-driven pump

Removal

1 Drain the cooling system as described in Chapter 1A.

2 Before removing the auxiliary drivebelt, loosen the coolant pump pulley bolts **(see illustration)**, then remove the drivebelt as described in Chapter 1A.

6.13a ... then pull out the retaining clip...

6.13b ...and withdraw the coolant temperature sensor and O-ring seal from the thermostat housing

7.2 Loosen the coolant pump pulley bolts before removing the auxiliary drivebelt

7.3 Removing the pulley from the coolant pump

7.4a Removing the coolant pump from the cylinder block – engine codes BKG, BLN, BAG, BLP, BLF and CAXA

7.4b Coolant pump removed from the engine

3 Unscrew the bolts and remove the pulley from the coolant pump **(see illustration)**.

4 Unscrew the mounting bolts and remove the coolant pump from the cylinder block **(see illustrations)**.

Refitting

5 Refitting is a reversal of removal, bearing in mind the following points.

a) *Clean the mating surfaces thoroughly before fitting the pump. If the original pump is being refitted, use a suitable sealant.*
b) *Refill the cooling system as described in Chapter 1A.*

Electric circulation pump

Note: *Only fitted to 1.4 litre turbocharged engines (code CAXA)*

6 On these models, the intercooler and turbocharger are cooled by a separate system, incorporating an auxiliary radiator, and an electrically operated coolant circulation pump. Begin by raising the front of the vehicle (see *Vehicle jacking and support*), then remove the engine undershield. The pump is located under the inlet manifold. Access is limited. To improve access, remove the inlet manifold as described in Chapter 3.

7 Disconnect the wiring plug from the pump.

8 Clamp the coolant hoses to prevent loss, then release the clamps and disconnect the hoses from the pump **(see illustration)**.

9 Undo the retaining bolt and remove the pump.

10 Refitting is a reversal of removal. Top up the coolant as described in Chapter 1A.

7.8 The electric circulation pump is located above the right-hand driveshaft (arrowed)

1.4 litre engine code BCA and BUD

Note: *New coolant pumps are supplied with an integrated seal.*

Removal

11 Drain the cooling system as described in Chapter 1A.

12 Remove the camshaft timing belt as described in Chapter 2B. If the belt is to be re-used, note the direction of rotation.

13 Remove the camshaft timing belt idler roller, and the upper bolt from the rear timing belt cover.

14 Unscrew the coolant pump retaining bolts, and withdraw the pump from the engine block together with the rear timing belt cover. Recover the O-ring seal from the groove in the pump. If faulty, the pump must be renewed **(see illustration)**.

Refitting

15 Refitting is a reversal of removal, bearing in mind the following points.

a) *Clean the mating surfaces thoroughly before fitting the pump. If the original pump is being refitted, use a suitable sealant.*
b) *Refill the cooling system as described in Chapter 1A.*

1.6 litre SOHC and 2.0 litre engine

Removal

16 Drain the cooling system as described in Chapter 1A.

7.14 Coolant pump removal – engine codes BCA and BUD

17 Remove the camshaft timing belt as described in Chapter 2A or 2D, noting the following points.

a) *The lower part of the timing belt guard need not be removed.*
b) *The timing belt should be left in position on the crankshaft sprocket.*
c) *Cover the timing belt with a cloth to protect it from coolant.*

18 Remove the two securing bolts, and remove the rear timing belt guard.

19 Remove the remaining retaining bolts, and withdraw the coolant pump from the engine block. Recover the O-ring seal from the groove in the pump. If the pump is faulty, it must be renewed.

Refitting

20 Refitting is a reversal of removal, bearing in mind the following points.

a) *Fit the coolant pump with a new O-ring.*
b) *Lubricate the O-ring with coolant.*
c) *Install the pump with the cast lug facing down.*
d) *Refill the cooling system as described in Chapter 1A.*

Diesel engines

Primary coolant pump

Removal

21 Drain the cooling system as described in Chapter 1B.

22 Remove the camshaft timing belt as described in Chapter 2E or 2F, noting the following points.

a) *The lower part of the timing belt guard need not be removed.*
b) *The timing belt should be left in position on the crankshaft sprocket.*
c) *Cover the timing belt with a cloth to protect it from coolant.*

23 Unscrew the timing belt idler pulley, and push the pulley downwards approximately 30 mm.

24 Unscrew the coolant pump retaining bolts, and remove the pump from the engine block. Recover the O-ring seal from the groove in the pump. If the pump is faulty, it must be renewed **(see illustration)**.

Refitting

25 Refitting is a reversal of removal, bearing in mind the following points.

a) *Fit the coolant pump with a new O-ring.*

b) Lubricate the O-ring with coolant.
c) Install the pump with the cast lug facing down.
d) Refill the cooling system as described in Chapter 1B.

Electric circulation pump

Note: *This pump is only fitted to common rail engines (codes CBDA and CBDB)*

26 Raise the front of the vehicle and support is securely on axle stands (see *Vehicle jacking and support*).

27 Undo the fasteners and remove the engine undertray **(see illustration)**.

28 Fit hose clamps to the coolants hoses connected to the pump, and release the clips and disconnect the hoses from the pump **(see illustration)**.

29 Disconnect the pump wiring plug.

30 Undo the retaining bolt and remove the pump **(see illustration)**.

31 Refitting is a reversal of removal. Top up the coolant, and bleed the system as described in Chapter 1.

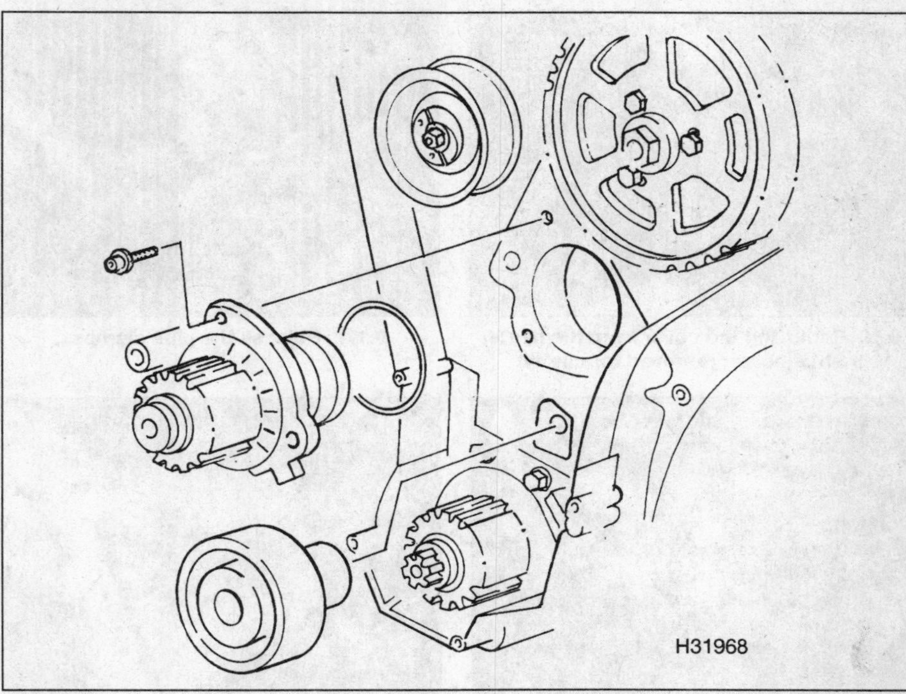

7.24 Coolant pump removal – diesel engines

8 Heating and ventilation system – general information

1 The heating/ventilation system consists of a four-speed blower motor (housed in the passenger compartment), face-level vents in the centre and at each end of the facia, and air ducts to the front and rear footwells.

2 The control unit is located in the facia, and the controls operate flap valves to deflect and mix the air flowing through the various parts of the heating/ventilation system. The flap valves are contained in the air distribution housing, which acts as a central distribution unit, passing air to the various ducts and vents.

3 Cold air enters the system through the grille at the rear of the engine compartment. A pollen filter is fitted to filter out dust, soot, pollen and spores from the air entering the vehicle.

4 The airflow, which can be boosted by the blower, flows through the various ducts, according to the settings of the controls. Stale air is expelled through ducts beneath the rear bumper. If warm air is required, the cold air is passed through the heater matrix, which is heated by the engine coolant.

5 If necessary, the outside air supply can be closed off, allowing the air inside the vehicle to be recirculated. This can be useful to prevent unpleasant odours entering from outside the vehicle, but should only be used briefly, as the recirculated air quality inside the vehicle will soon deteriorate.

9 Heating and ventilation system components – removal and refitting

Models without air conditioning

Heater/ventilation control unit

1 Switch off the ignition and all electrical consumers, then set the heater controls to 'cold', blower to '0', and vent to 'footwell'.

2 Remove the radio as described in Chapter 12. If a radio is not fitted, remove the centre dash panel trim as described in Chapter 11.

3 Unscrew the bolts and remove the control unit from the facia.

4 Disconnect the wiring by releasing the catch.

5 Refitting is a reversal of removal, but ensure the control knobs are positioned as previously noted. Check the operation of the controls.

Temperature flap control cable

6 Remove the heater/ventilation control unit from the facia as described previously.

7 Reach into the facia and disconnect the inner cable and release the cable outer.

8 Remove the trim from the left-hand side of the heater.

9 Disconnect the inner and outer cables from the temperature flap and heater. Note that the cable is located under the support hook on the heater.

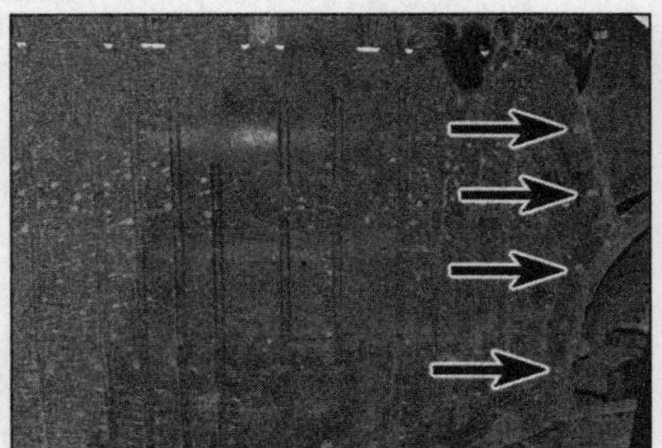

7.27 The engine undertray is secured by numerous screw along the rear, and side edges (arrowed)

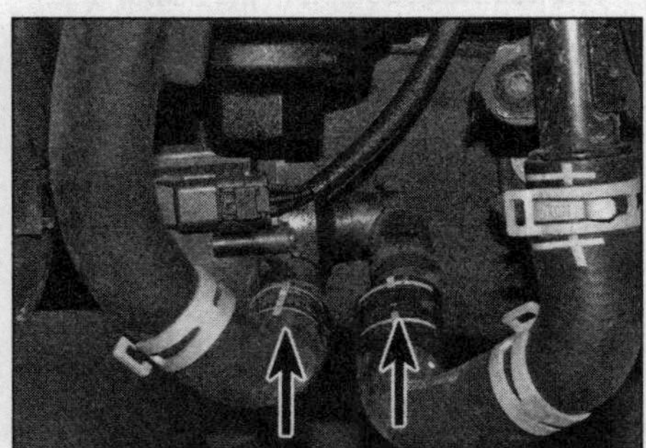

7.28 Disconnect the hoses from the circulation pump

7.30 Circulation pump bracket retaining bolt (arrowed – shown with the charge air pipe removed for clarity)

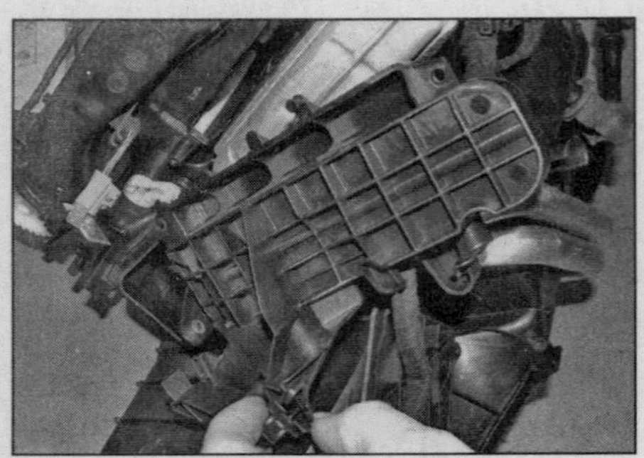
9.16 Removing the cover from the heater matrix (heater removed for clarity)

9.17a Release the pipe clamps...

9.17b ...and pull the coolant pipes from the matrix

9.18 Removing the matrix from the heater unit

10 Refitting is a reversal of removal, but check that the temperature control knob can be turned easily.

Heater matrix

11 At the rear of the engine compartment, remove the bulkhead trim from the plenum chamber.

12 Using hose clamps, clamp the heater matrix inlet and return hoses located on the bulkhead at the rear of the engine compartment. Place a container beneath the hoses, then loosen the clips and disconnect them. Note the location of the hoses for correct refitting.

13 With the hoses disconnected, remove the coolant from the matrix by blowing air into the upper tube, preferably using an airline.

14 Loosen (but do not remove) the bolt located between the matrix upper and lower tubes. This will make removal of the matrix easier.

15 Remove the driver's side footwell trim from the heater. Also, unbolt and remove the footwell vent.

16 Undo the screws and remove the cover from the heater matrix **(see illustration)**. If the upper screw is not accessible, turn the temperature flap control as necessary.

17 Place cloth rags or similar on the floor beneath the heater matrix, then release the pipe clamps and pull the coolant pipes from the matrix **(see illustrations)**.

18 Remove the heater matrix from the heater unit **(see illustration)**.

19 Refitting is a reversal of removal, noting the following.

a) Make sure the seal is fitted correctly around the perimeter of the matrix.

b) When reconnecting the coolant pipes, moisten the seals with coolant and make sure the conical ends locate in the matrix. After reconnecting the pipes, the clamps must turn easily before tightening them securely.

c) Check that the rubber grommet in the bulkhead is correctly located in its hole.

d) Top-up the coolant level with reference to 'Weekly Checks' at the beginning of this Manual.

Heater unit

20 Remove the facia panel as described in Chapter 11.

21 At the rear of the engine compartment, remove the bulkhead trim from the plenum chamber.

22 Remove the right- and left-hand rear footwell ducts from the heater unit. It is recommended that the complete floor carpet is removed first, as the ducts are located below the carpets **(see illustrations)**. Also remove the centre console air duct.

23 Using hose clamps, clamp the heater matrix inlet and return hoses located on the bulkhead at the rear of the engine compartment. Place a container beneath the hoses, then pull out the clips and disconnect them **(see illustrations)**. Note the location of the hoses for correct refitting.

24 With the hoses disconnected, remove the coolant from the matrix by blowing air into the upper tube, preferably using an airline.

25 Inside the car, place cloth rags or similar on the floor beneath the heater unit.

26 Unbolt the wiring retainer from the passenger side of the heater unit **(see illustration)**.

27 Note the location and routing of all wiring, then disconnect it from the heater unit. Also

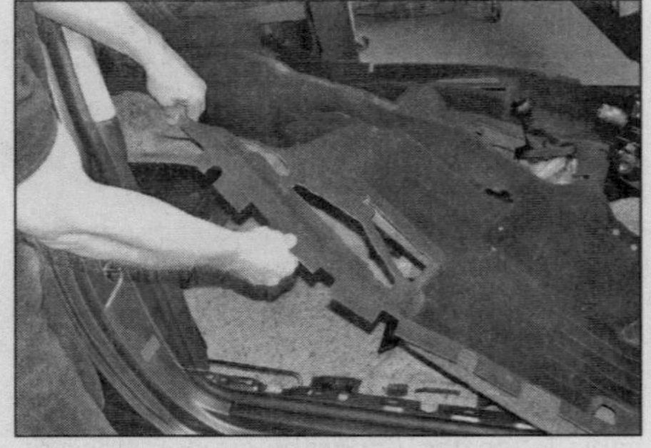
9.22a Remove the complete carpet...

9.22b ...then remove the right- and left-hand rear footwell ducts from the heater unit

9.23a Pull out the clips...

9.23b ...and disconnect the hoses from the heater matrix

note the location of plastic cable ties to ensure correct refitting.

28 Unbolt and remove the two central support legs located over the rear of the heater unit **(see illustration)**.

29 Remove the air inlet duct from the top of the heater, then undo the screws and remove the remaining support bracket from the centre of the heater unit **(see illustrations)**.

30 Unscrew the remaining heater unit mounting bolts.

31 Carefully pull the heater unit from the bulkhead, taking care not to damage or bend the matrix tubes on the bulkhead. The help of an assistant may be required. Be prepared for coolant spillage as the assembly is removed from inside the car.

32 If necessary, the heater may be further dismantled on the bench.

33 Refitting is a reversal of removal, but top-up the coolant with reference to *Weekly Checks* at the beginning of this Manual.

Heater blower motor

34 Switch off the ignition and all electrical consumers.

35 Remove the passenger side glovebox as described in Chapter 11.

36 Undo the screws and remove the cover from under the heater blower motor. Disconnect the wiring from the blower motor.

37 Unscrew the single mounting bolt, then release the catch and turn the blower motor anti-clockwise to remove it from the heater housing.

38 Refitting is a reversal of removal.

Heater blower motor series resistor

39 Switch off the ignition and all electrical consumers.

40 Remove the passenger side glovebox as described in Chapter 11.

41 Undo the screws and remove the cover from under the heater blower motor.

42 Disconnect the wiring from the blower series resistor, then remove the resistor by pressing the catch towards the motor.

Caution: The resistor may be very hot if the heater has recently been in use.

43 Refitting is the reverse of removal.

Fresh/recirculating air flap positioning motor

44 Remove the passenger side glovebox as described in Chapter 11.

45 Unclip the cover retaining the motor to the heater housing.

46 Disconnect the wiring, then remove the motor from its mountings and separate it from the air flap lever.

47 Refitting is a reversal of removal. Note that if the motor is renewed, its basic settings must be reprogrammed by a VW dealer using specialist equipment.

Models with air conditioning

Heater/ventilation control unit

48 On models with 'Climatic' air conditioning, the procedure is as described previously in this Section for models without air conditioning. On models with 'Climatronic' air conditioning, the procedure is as described in the following paragraphs.

49 Switch off the ignition and all electrical consumers.

50 Carefully lever the solar sensor from the top of the facia, and disconnect the wiring.

51 Undo the screw and remove the cover from the vent, then unclip the centre vent from the facia.

52 Disconnect the wiring.

53 Undo the screws and carefully lever out the centre surround.

54 Undo the screws and remove the control unit, then disconnect the wiring.

Heater matrix

55 The procedure is as described previously in this Section for models without air conditioning.

9.26 Unscrew the bolts and remove the wiring retainer from the heater unit

9.28 Removing the two central support legs from the rear of the heater unit

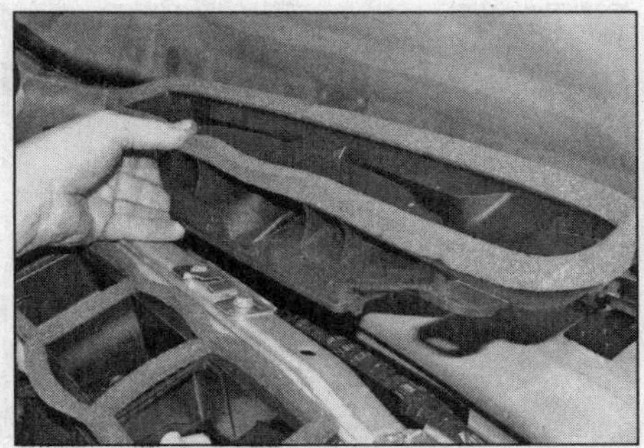

9.29a Remove the air inlet duct...

9.29b ...and support bracket

9.56a Unscrew the bolts and remove the refrigerant lines from the evaporator

Heater/air conditioning unit

Warning: Refer to the precautions given in Section 11.

56 It is not possible to remove the unit without opening the refrigerant circuit to the evaporator, therefore this task must be entrusted to a VW dealer or an air conditioning specialist. With the refrigerant evacuated, the procedure is as described for models without air conditioning, except for the following.

Caution: The air conditioning compressor is driven permanently by the auxiliary drivebelt, and is not fitted with a magnetic clutch. It is not recommended that the engine is started without refrigerant being present in the system, as the compressor may overheat causing internal damage. Note also that if the refrigerant circuit is not opened within 10 minutes of evacuation, slight pressure may develop due to re-evaporation.

a) Where fitted, remove the cover from the expansion valve by unscrewing the nut and releasing the clips.

*b) Unscrew the bolts securing the refrigerant lines to the evaporator on the bulkhead at the rear of the engine compartment, and detach them. Recover the seals and plug the lines and evaporator openings to prevent entry of foreign matter and water vapour. Discard the seals as new ones must be used on refitting **(see illustrations)**.*

c) Remove the footrest and condensation

9.56b Plug the lines and evaporator while they are disconnected

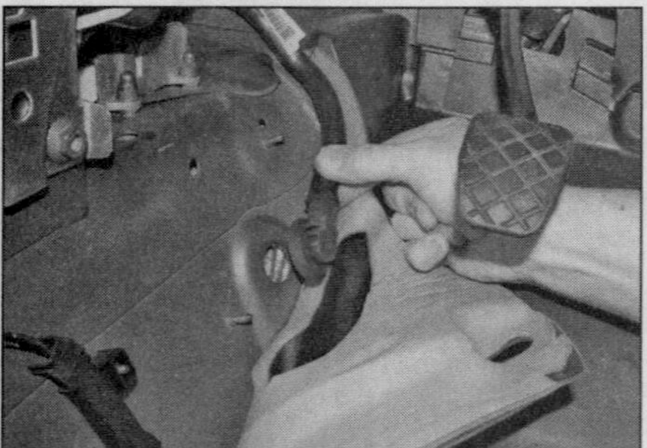

9.56d ...and condensation water drainage hose from the heater unit

*water drainage hose from the driver's side of the heater unit **(see illustrations)**.*

d) Top-up the coolant level with reference to 'Weekly Checks' at the beginning of this Manual.

9.56c Remove the footrest...

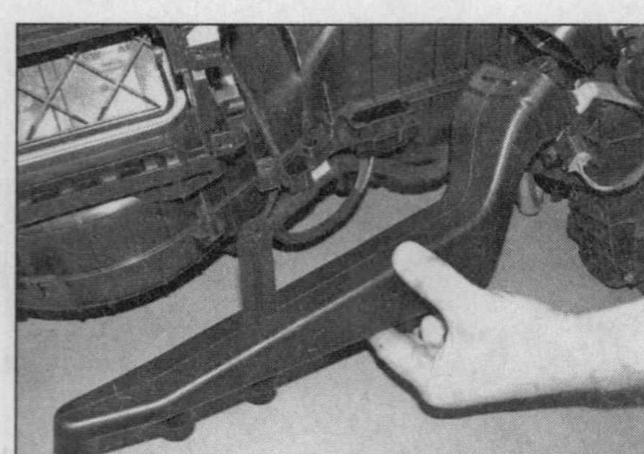

9.61a Remove the air duct...

Heater blower motor

57 The procedure is as described previously in this Section for models without air conditioning.

Heater blower motor series resistor

58 The procedure is as described previously in this Section for models without air conditioning.

Air conditioning evaporator

Warning: Refer to the precautions given in Section 11.

59 Have the refrigerant evacuated from the air conditioning system by a VW dealer or refrigeration specialist.

Caution: The air conditioning compressor is driven permanently by the auxiliary drivebelt, and is not fitted with a magnetic clutch. It is not recommended that the engine is started without refrigerant being present in the system, as the compressor may overheat causing internal damage. Note also that if the refrigerant circuit is not opened within 10 minutes of evacuation, slight pressure may develop due to re-evaporation.

60 Remove the heater/air conditioning unit as described earlier in this Section.

61 Dismantle the unit as shown in the accompanying illustrations **(see illustrations)**. Remove the heater matrix as described earlier in this Section.

62 Remove the evaporator from the housing together with the refrigerant lines and rubber grommet **(see illustration)**.

63 Refitting is a reversal of removal, but fit new seals and have the system recharged by a VW dealer or refrigeration specialist.

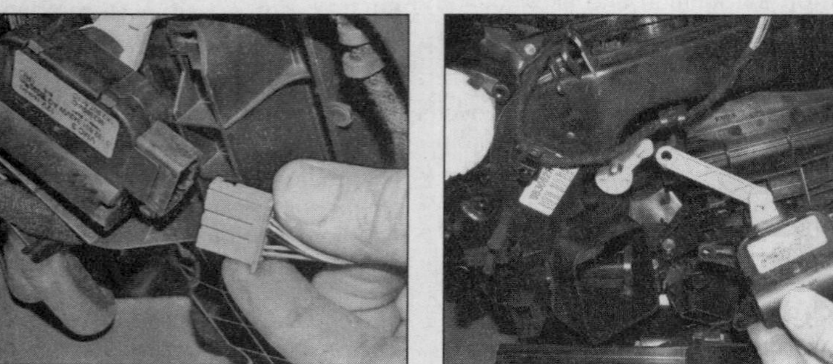

9.61b ...and wiring, noting the loom routing...

9.61c ...then remove the actuator...

9.61d ...unscrew the bolts securing the two section of the heater housing...

9.61e ...unscrew the bolts and separate the evaporator housing from the heater motor housing...

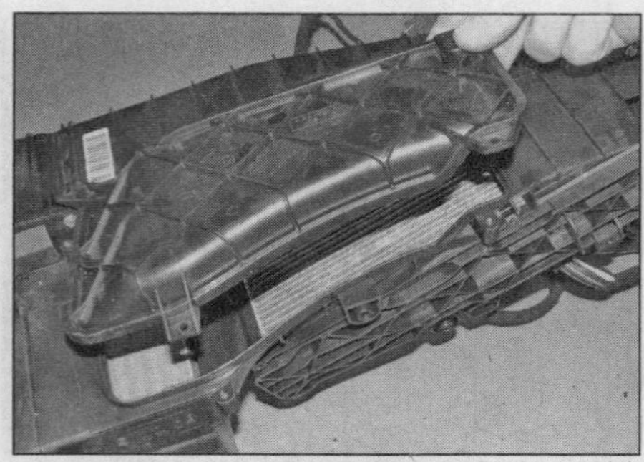

9.61f ...remove the cover...

9.62 ...and remove the evaporator together with refrigerant lines and rubber grommet from the housing

Air conditioning condenser

Warning: Refer to the precautions given in Section 11.

64 The condenser is attached to the front of the radiator. Have the refrigerant evacuated from the air conditioning system by a VW dealer or refrigeration specialist.

Caution: The air conditioning compressor is driven permanently by the auxiliary drivebelt, and is not fitted with a magnetic clutch. It is not recommended that the engine is started without refrigerant being present in the system, as the compressor may overheat causing internal damage. Note also that if the refrigerant circuit is not opened within 10 minutes of evacuation, slight pressure may develop due to re-evaporation.

65 Remove the radiator as described in Section 3 of this Chapter.

66 Undo the screws and disconnect the refrigerant lines from the condenser. Recover the seals and plug the lines and condenser openings to prevent entry of foreign matter and water vapour.

67 Carefully remove the condenser from the lock carrier, taking care not to damage its fins.

68 Refitting is a reversal of removal, but fit new seals and have the system recharged by a VW dealer or refrigeration specialist.

Auxiliary heater

69 Some diesel models are equipped with an auxiliary electrically powered heating element within the heating unit. In order to remove the element, the facia must first be removed as described in Chapter 11.

70 Undo the screws and remove the cover from the heater matrix **(see illustration 9.16)**. If the upper screw is not accessible, turn the temperature flap control as necessary.

71 Note their fitted positions, then disconnect the wiring plugs from the element.

72 Pull the heating element from place .

73 Refitting is a reversal of removal.

10 Heating/ventilation system vents – removal and refitting

Side vents

1 To remove a vent, carefully prise it from the housing using a small flat-bladed screwdriver **(see illustration)**. Take care not to damage the surrounding trim.

2 To refit, carefully push the vent into position until the locating clips engage.

Central facia vents

3 On models with 'Climatronic' air conditioning, carefully lever the solar sensor from the top of the facia, and disconnect the wiring.

4 Remove the mat where fitted, then undo the screw and remove the cover from the vent.

5 Undo the screws, then unclip the centre vent from the facia and disconnect the wiring from the hazard warning switch and passenger airbag warning light.

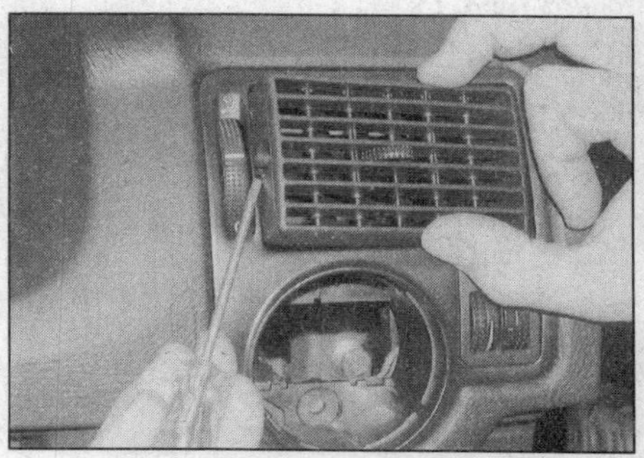

10.1 Carefully prise out the vent

11 Air conditioning system – general information and precautions

General information

Air conditioning is fitted as standard to most models, and is available as manually-operated (Climatic) or automatically-operated (Climatronic). The Climatronic system works in conjunction with the heating and air conditioning systems to maintain a selected vehicle interior temperature fully automatically.

The air conditioning system enables the temperature of incoming air to be lowered, and dehumidifies the air, which makes for rapid demisting and increased comfort. The cooling side of the system works in the same way as a domestic refrigerator. Refrigerant gas is drawn into a belt-driven compressor and passes into a condenser mounted in front of the radiator, where it loses heat and becomes liquid. The liquid passes through an expansion valve to an evaporator, where it changes from liquid under high pressure to gas under low pressure. This change is accompanied by a drop in temperature, which cools the evaporator. The refrigerant returns to the compressor and the cycle begins again.

Air blown through the evaporator passes to the air distribution unit, where it is mixed with hot air blown through the heater matrix to achieve the desired temperature in the passenger compartment.

The heating side of the system works in the same way as on models without air conditioning.

The operation of the system is controlled electronically by coolant temperature switches, and pressure switches which are screwed into the compressor high-pressure line. Any problems with the system should be referred to a VW dealer or an air conditioning specialist.

The only operation which can be carried out easily without discharging the refrigerant is the renewal of the compressor drivebelt, which is covered in the relevant part of Chapter 1. Removal of the evaporator and condenser requires the evacuation of the refrigerant. If necessary the compressor can be unbolted and moved aside, without disconnecting its flexible hoses, after removing the drivebelt **(see illustration)**.

Precautions

- ***When an air conditioning system is fitted, it is necessary to observe special precautions whenever dealing with any part of the system, its associated components and any items which require disconnection of the system. If for any reason the system must be disconnected, entrust this task to your VW dealer or an air conditioning specialist.***

Warning: The refrigeration circuit contains a refrigerant and it is therefore dangerous to disconnect any part of the system without specialised knowledge and equipment. The refrigerant is potentially dangerous and should only be handled by qualified persons. If it is splashed onto the skin it can cause frostbite. It is not itself poisonous, but in the presence of a naked flame (including a cigarette) it forms a poisonous gas. Uncontrolled discharging of the refrigerant is dangerous and potentially damaging to the environment.

- ***Do not operate the air conditioning system if it is known to be short of refrigerant, as this may damage the compressor.***

12 Climatronic system components – removal and refitting

Sunlight penetration sensor

1 Switch off the ignition and all electrical consumers.

2 Using a small screwdriver, gently prise the sensor from the centre top of the facia.

3 Disconnect the wiring plug and withdraw the sensor.

4 Refitting is a reversal of removal.

11.6 Air conditioning compressor bolted to the front of the cylinder block

12.11 Ambient temperature sender location at the front of the radiator/ condenser

Side vent temperature sender

5 Switch off the ignition and all electrical consumers.
6 Unclip the trim panel from the relevant end of the facia.
7 Disconnect the wiring plug from the sender.
8 Turn the sender through 90°, and withdraw it from the housing.
9 Refitting is a reversal of removal.

Ambient temperature sender

10 Pull the centre grille from the fasteners in the front bumper.
11 Unclip the sender from its retainer and disconnect the wiring **(see illustration)**.
12 Refitting is a reversal of removal. Make sure the wiring is fully connected to prevent entry of water.

Chapter 4 Part A: Petrol engine fuel systems

Contents

Degrees of difficulty

Easy, suitable for novice with little experience	**Fairly easy,** suitable for beginner with some experience	**Fairly difficult,** suitable for competent DIY mechanic	**Difficult,** suitable for experienced DIY mechanic	**Very difficult,** suitable for expert DIY or professional

Specifications

Engine codes*

1.4 litre:	
Indirect injection petrol engine	BCA and BUD
Direct injection petrol engine (FSi)	BKG and BLN
Direct injection turbocharged engine (TSi)	CAXA
1.6 litre:	
SOHC petrol engine	BGU, BSE and BSF
DOHC direct injection petrol engine (FSi)	BAG, BLP and BLF
2.0 litre petrol engine:	
Non-turbo	AXW, BLX, BLY, BLR, BVX, BVY and BVZ
Turbo	AXX, BPY and BWA

* **Note:** *See 'Vehicle identification' at the end of this manual for the location of engine code markings.*

System type

1.4 litre engines:	
Engine code BCA	Bosch Motronic ME7.5.10 (indirect injection)
Engine codes BKG and BLN	Bosch Motronic MED9.5.10 (direct injection)
Engine codes BUD	Magneti-Marelli 4HV (indirect injection)
Engine code CAXA	Bosch Motronic MED17 (direct injection)
1.6 litre engines:	
Engine codes BGU, BSE and BSF	Siemens Simos 7 (indirect injection)
Engine codes BAG, BLP and BLF	Bosch Motronic MED9.5.10 (direct injection)
2.0 litre engines:	
Engine code AXW, BLX, BVX, BVY and BVZ	Bosch Motronic MED9.5.10 (direct injection)
Engine code BLY and BLR	Bosch Motronic MED9.5 (direct injection)
Engine code AXX, BPY and BWA	Bosch Motronic MED9.1 (direct injection)

* **Note:** *See 'Vehicle identification' at the end of this manual for the location of engine code markings.*

Fuel system data

Fuel pump type	Electric, immersed in fuel tank
Fuel pump delivery rate:	
All except engine code CAXA	400 cc/min (battery voltage of 12.5 V)
Engine code CAXA	1450 cc/min (battery voltage of 12.5 V)
Regulated fuel pressure:	
All except engine code CAXA	2.5 bar
Engine code CAXA	4.0 to 7.0 bar
Engine idle speed	non-adjustable, electronically controlled
Idle CO content (non-adjustable, electronically-controlled)	0.5% max
Injector electrical resistance (typical)	12 to 17 ohms

Torque wrench settings

	Nm	lbf ft
All models		
Accelerator pedal to bulkhead	10	7
Fuel lift pump/gauge sender retaining ring	110	81
Fuel tank strap retaining bolt	25	18
Knock sensor(s)	20	15
Oxygen sensor(s)	50	37
1.4 and 1.6 litre DOHC engines		
Camshaft position sensor	10	7
Fuel pressure sensor	20	15
High-pressure fuel line to pump:		
Engine codes BAG, BKG and CAXA	15	11
Engine codes BLN, BLP and BLF:		
Upper	30	22
Lower	25	18
High-pressure fuel pump:		
Engine codes BAG and BKG	8	6
Engine codes BLN, BLP and BLF	10	7
Engine code CAXA	20	15
Inlet manifold to cylinder head	20	15
Throttle housing/module mounting bolts	10	7
1.6 litre SOHC engine		
Fuel rail to inlet manifold	8	6
Inlet manifold support:		
To cylinder head	15	11
To inlet manifold	8	6
Inlet manifold to cylinder head	25	18
Inlet manifold upper part-to-lower part screws	3	2
Throttle housing/module mounting bolts	8	6
2.0 litre engines		
Fuel pressure sensor	20	15
Fuel rail mounting bolts	10	7
High-pressure fuel line to pump:		
Engine codes AXX, BPY and BWA:		
Union nut	25	19
Banjo bolt	17	13
Engine code AXW:		
Low-pressure union bolt	15	11
High-pressure union bolt	25	19
Engine codes BLX, BVX, BVY, BVZ, BLY and BLR:		
Low-pressure union bolt	15	11
High-pressure union bolt	15	11
High-pressure fuel pump	10	7
Inlet manifold-to-cylinder head nuts/bolts	10	7
Inlet manifold upper part to lower part	10	7
Throttle housing mounting bolts	8	6

1 General information and precautions

General information

The systems described in this Chapter are all self-contained engine management systems, which control both the fuel injection and ignition. This Chapter deals with the fuel system components only – see Chapter 4C for information on the turbocharger, exhaust and emission control systems, and to Chapter 5B for details of the ignition system.

The fuel injection system consists of a fuel tank, an electric fuel lift pump/level sender unit, a fuel filter, fuel supply and return lines, a throttle housing/module, four electronic fuel injectors, and an Electronic Control Unit (ECU) together with its associated sensors, actuators and wiring. Two basic fuel injection systems are fitted – an indirect (low pressure) injection system where the injectors inject fuel into the inlet manifold upstream of the inlet valves, and a direct (high pressure) injection system where the injectors inject fuel directly into the combustion chambers.

The indirect injection system uses a low pressure fuel rail and injectors fitted to the inlet manifold.

The direct injection system (fitted to FSi (Fuel Stratified injection) and TSi (Turbocharged Stratified injection) engines) uses a high-pressure fuel pump mounted on top of the camshaft housing, actuated by a plunger in contact with the inlet camshaft. Fuel under high pressure is fed into a fuel rail incorporated into the lower inlet manifold. The injectors are located between the lower inlet manifold and cylinder head, and inject fuel directly into the combustion chambers.

The two basic fuel systems function in a very similar way, but there are significant detail differences, particularly in the sensors used and in the inlet manifold arrangements.

The fuel lift pump is immersed in the fuel inside the tank, and delivers a constant supply of fuel through a cartridge filter to the fuel rail or high-pressure fuel pump (according to engine). The fuel pressure regulator maintains a constant fuel pressure to the fuel injectors, and returns excess fuel to the tank through the return line. This constant flow system also helps to reduce fuel temperature, and prevents vaporisation. On 1.4 and 1.6 litre engines, the pressure regulator is located on the fuel rail or high-pressure pump, however, on 2.0 litre engines it is located on the rear of the fuel filter beneath the rear of the car.

The fuel injectors are opened and closed by an Electronic Control Unit (ECU), which calculates the injection timing and duration according to engine speed, crankshaft/ camshaft position, throttle position and rate of opening, inlet manifold depression, inlet air temperature, coolant temperature, roadspeed and exhaust gas oxygen content information, received from sensors mounted on and around the engine.

Inlet air is drawn into the engine through the air cleaner, which contains a renewable paper filter element. On some non-turbo models, the inlet air temperature is regulated by a valve mounted in the air cleaner inlet trunking, which blends air at ambient temperature with hot air, drawn from over the exhaust manifold.

The temperature and pressure of the air entering the throttle housing is measured by a sensor mounted on the inlet manifold. This information is used by the ECU to fine-tune the fuelling requirements for different operating conditions. Turbocharged engines have an additional air temperature sensor mounted downstream of the throttle housing, which monitors the (compressed) air temperature after it has been through the turbocharger and intercooler.

1.4 and 1.6 litre engine with codes BAG, BKG, BLF, BLN and BLP have a variable-length inlet manifold. A vacuum-controlled flap is used to divert the inlet air into one of two paths through the manifold, the paths being of different lengths. Controlling the inlet air in this way has the effect of altering the engine's torque characteristics at different engine speeds and loads.

Idle speed control is achieved partly by an electronic throttle valve positioning module, which is part of the throttle housing, and partly by the ignition system, which gives fine control of the idle speed by altering the ignition timing. As a result, manual adjustment of the engine idle speed is not necessary or possible.

The exhaust gas oxygen content is constantly monitored by the ECU by oxygen sensors (also known as lambda sensors), one before the catalytic converter, and one after – this improves sensor response time and accuracy, and the ECU compares the signals from each sensor to confirm that the converter is working correctly. The ECU uses the information from the sensors to modify the injection timing and duration to maintain the optimum air/fuel ratio. All models are fitted with one, two or three catalytic converters according to engine type – see Chapter 4C.

The ECU also controls the operation of the activated charcoal filter evaporative loss system – refer to Chapter 4C for further details.

It should be noted that fault diagnosis of all the engine management systems described in this Chapter is only possible with dedicated electronic test equipment. Problems with the systems operation should therefore be referred to a VW dealer for assessment. Once the fault has been identified, the removal/refitting sequences detailed in the following Sections will then allow the appropriate component(s) to be renewed as required.

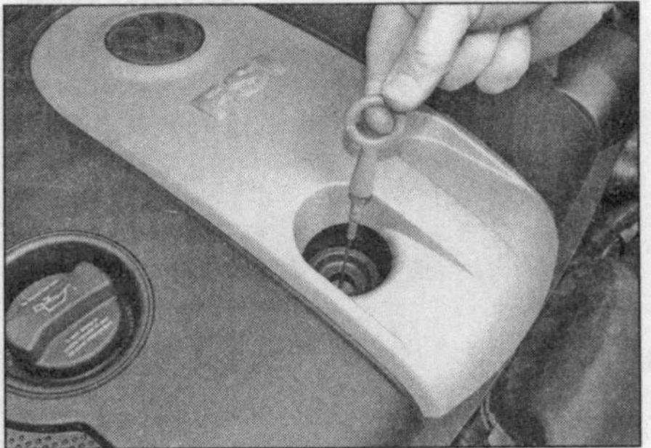
2.1 Remove the engine oil dipstick...

Precautions

Warning: Petrol is extremely flammable – great care must be taken when working on any part of the fuel system.

- ***Do not smoke, or allow any naked flames or uncovered light bulbs near the work area. Note that gas-powered domestic appliances with pilot flames, such as heaters boilers and tumble-dryers, also present a fire hazard – bear this in mind if you are working in an area where such appliances are present. Always keep a suitable fire extinguisher close to the work area, and familiarise yourself with its operation before starting work. Wear eye protection when working on fuel systems, and wash off any fuel spilt on bare skin immediately with soap and water. Note that fuel vapour is just as dangerous as liquid fuel – possibly more so; a vessel that has been emptied of liquid fuel will still contain vapour, and can be potentially explosive.***
- ***Many of the operations described in this Chapter involve the disconnection of fuel lines, which may cause an amount of fuel spillage. Before commencing work, refer to the above 'Warning' and the information in 'Safety first!' at the beginning of this manual.***
- ***Residual fuel pressure always remains in the fuel system, long after the engine has been switched off. This pressure must be relieved in a controlled manner before work can commence on any component in the fuel system – refer to Section 9 for details.***
- ***When working with fuel system components, pay particular attention to cleanliness – dirt entering the fuel system may cause blockages, which will lead to poor running.***
- ***In the interests of personal safety and equipment protection, many of the procedures in this Chapter suggest that the negative lead be removed from the battery terminal. This firstly eliminates the possibility of accidental short-circuits being caused as the vehicle is being worked upon, and secondly prevents damage to electronic components (eg, sensors, actuators, ECUs) which are particularly sensitive to the power surges caused by disconnection or reconnection of the wiring harness whilst they are still 'live'. Refer to 'Disconnecting the battery' at the rear of this manual.***

2 Air cleaner and inlet system – removal and refitting

Removal

Engine codes BCA, BAG, BKG, BLF, BLN, BLP, AXX, BPY and BWA

1 The air cleaner is incorporated in the engine top cover. First, remove the engine oil dipstick **(see illustration)**.

2 Release each corner of the engine top cover by pulling sharply upwards. This will also release the air cleaner housing from the throttle valve module/housing **(see illustration)**.

3 Disconnect the wiring from the inlet air temperature sensor **(see illustration)**.

4 Disconnect the crankshaft ventilation hose from the air cleaner housing or camshaft

2.2 ...lift the engine top cover/air cleaner...

2.3 ...then disconnect the wiring from the inlet air temperature sensor...

2.4 ...and disconnect the crankcase ventilation hose from the camshaft housing

2.5a Remove the rubber grommet...

2.5b ...and air temperature sensor

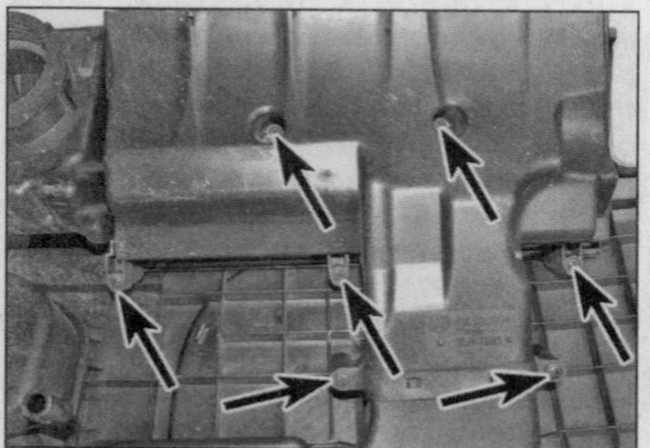
2.6a Undo the screws...

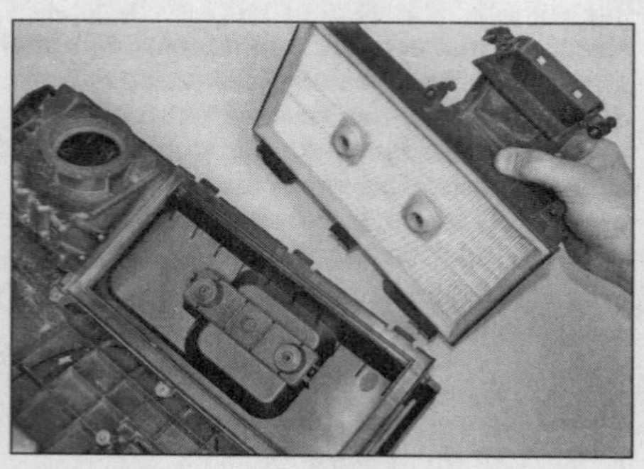
2.6b ...separate the air cleaner housing...

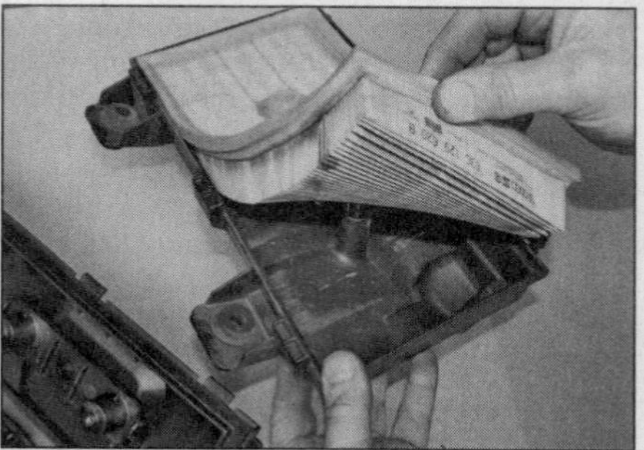
2.6c ...then remove the filter element

housing, and lift the assembly from the engine **(see illustration)**.

5 With the assembly inverted on the bench, if necessary remove the rubber grommet, then undo the screw and remove the air temperature sensor **(see illustrations)**.

6 Undo the screws and separate the air cleaner housing from the top cover, then remove the filter element **(see illustrations)**.

Engine code BUD

7 The air cleaner is located on the inlet manifold at the rear of the engine. First, press down the clips and release the air inlet duct from the engine compartment front crossmember.

8 At the front left-hand corner, disconnect the hose from the non-return valve.

9 Release the right-hand rear and left-hand front corners by pulling sharply upwards.

10 With the assembly on the bench, if necessary, undo the screws and remove the cover, then remove the air filter element.

Engine codes BGU, BSE, BSF, AXW, BLX, BLY, BLR, BVX, BVY, BVZ and CAXA

11 The air cleaner is located in front of the battery on the left-hand side of the engine compartment. First, remove the engine top cover.

12 Undo the screws and remove the lid from the air cleaner.

13 Undo the screw and slide out the clamp, then remove the filter element from the housing.

All except engine code CAXA

14 To remove the housing, unbolt the intake hose elbow then unclip the housing while disconnecting it from the damping chamber air duct.

15 To remove the damping chamber, disconnect the intake air duct, then unscrew the mounting nuts and withdraw from the engine compartment.

16 If necessary, the engine intake air duct may be removed after disconnecting the crankcase ventilation hose and unbolting the duct from the throttle housing/module.

Engine code CAXA

17 Undo the screw each side securing the intake duct to the front panel **(see illustration)**.

18 Release the clamp and disconnect the air intake hose from the turbocharger **(see illustration)**.

19 Disconnect the vacuum hose from the filter housing **(see illustration)**.

20 Undo the retaining bolt and pull the air cleaner housing upwards from the rubber mountings **(see illustrations)**.

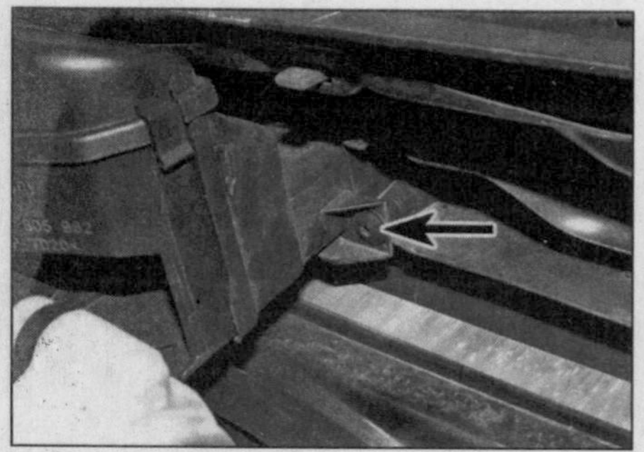
2.17 Undo the screw (arrowed) each side of the intake duct

2.18 Release the clamp (arrowed) and disconnect the hose from the turbocharger

2.19 Disconnect the vacuum hose (arrowed)

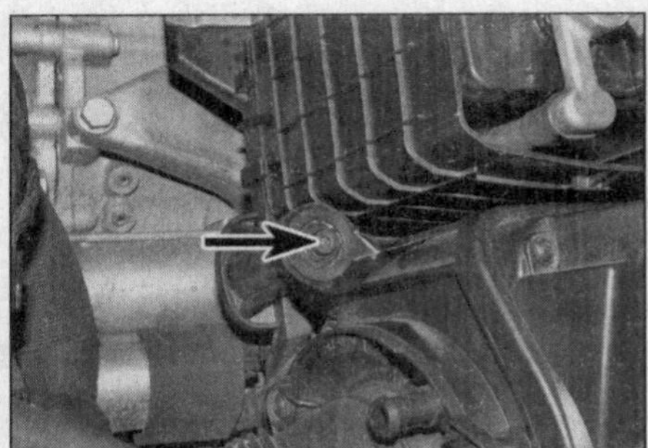

2.20a Undo the retaining bolt (arrowed)...

Refitting

21 Refitting is a reversal of removal, noting the following points:

a) Where applicable, ensure that the air filter element is correctly refitted, referring to Chapter 1A if necessary.

b) It is most important that an airtight seal is made between the air cleaner and the throttle housing/module.

3 Inlet air temperature control system – general information

Note: *This system is not fitted to all models.*

1 Where fitted, the inlet air temperature control system consists of a temperature-controlled flap valve, mounted in its own housing in the air cleaner inlet trunking or in the air cleaner lid, and a duct to the warm-air collector plate over the exhaust manifold.

2 The temperature sensor in the flap valve housing senses the temperature of the inlet air, and opens the valve when a preset lower limit is reached. As the flap valve opens, warm air drawn from around the exhaust manifold blends with the inlet air.

3 As the temperature of the inlet air rises, the sensor closes the flap progressively, until the warm-air supply from the exhaust manifold is completely closed off, and only air at ambient temperature is admitted to the air cleaner.

4 With the ducting removed from the valve housing, the sensor is visible. If a hairdryer and suitable freeze spray is available, the action of the sensor can be tested.

4.6b ...and recover the O-ring seal

2.20b ...and manoeuvre the air cleaner housing from place

4 Fuel system components – removal and refitting

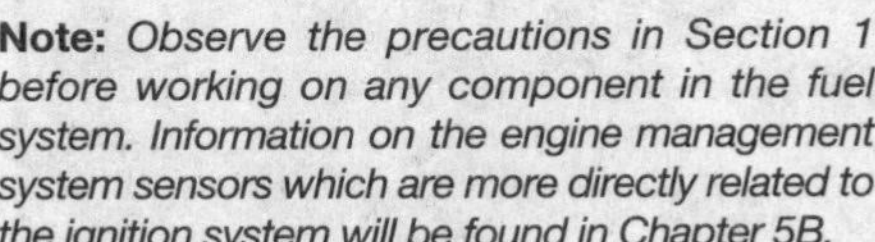

Note: *Observe the precautions in Section 1 before working on any component in the fuel system. Information on the engine management system sensors which are more directly related to the ignition system will be found in Chapter 5B.*

Throttle housing/module

All except engine code CAXA

1 On some models, the throttle housing is coolant-heated, so removing it entails disconnecting two coolant pipes. Even if the cooling system is drained as described in Chapter 1A, it is likely that the throttle housing supply pipes will not be drained, and spillage will result. If the coolant is not due for renewal, it may be preferable not to drain the system, but be prepared to plug the pipes once they have been disconnected.

2 As required, remove the air cleaner/air ducting as described in Section 2.

3 Disconnect the hose for the charcoal canister from the port on the throttle housing. Also disconnect the brake servo vacuum supply hose, where applicable.

4 Disconnect the wiring from the throttle housing/module **(see illustration)**.

5 Where applicable, disconnect the coolant pipes from the throttle housing/module, noting their positions for refitting. Be prepared for coolant spillage, and plug the pipe ends to prevent too much coolant loss.

6 Unscrew and remove the through-bolts, then lift the throttle housing/module away from the inlet manifold. Recover the O-ring seal **(see illustrations)**.

7 Refitting is a reversal of removal, noting the following:

a) Use a new throttle housing-to-inlet manifold seal.

b) Tighten the throttle housing through-bolts evenly to the specified torque.

c) Ensure that all hoses and electrical connectors are refitted securely.

Engine code CAXA

8 Undo the retaining bolts and pull the engine cover upwards **(see illustration)**. Pull out the engine oil level dipstick, and unclip the coolant hoses as the cover is withdrawn.

9 Unclip the pressure/vacuum hoses from the charge air pipe, and disconnect the charge pressure sensor and intake air temperature sensor wiring plugs **(see illustration)**.

4.4 Throttle housing/module – 1.6 litre FSi

4.8 Undo the bolts (arrowed) and remove the engine top cover

4.6a Remove the throttle housing/ module...

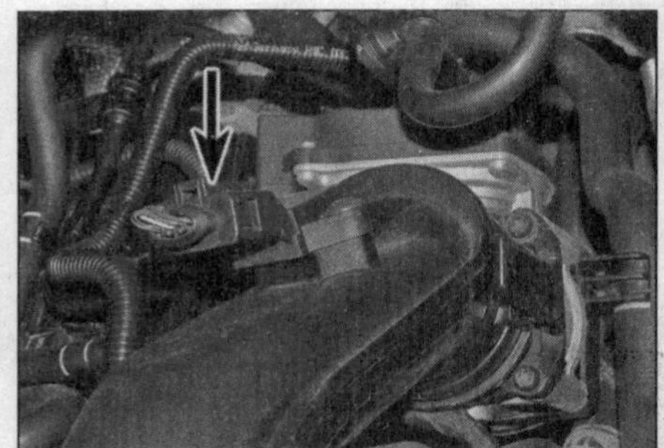

4.9 Disconnect the charge pressure sensor (arrowed)

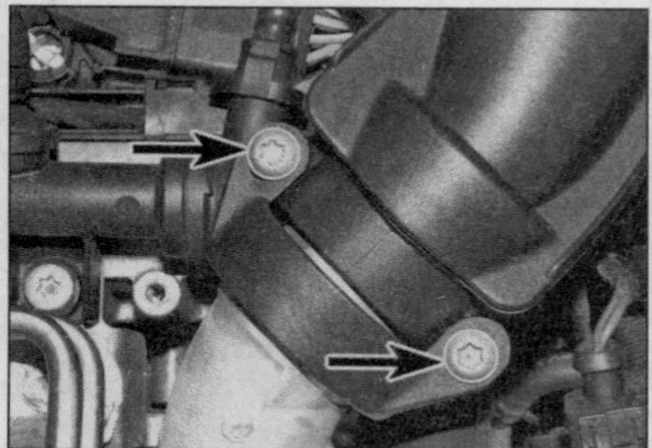
4.10a Undo the screws (arrowed)...

4.10b ...recover the collar...

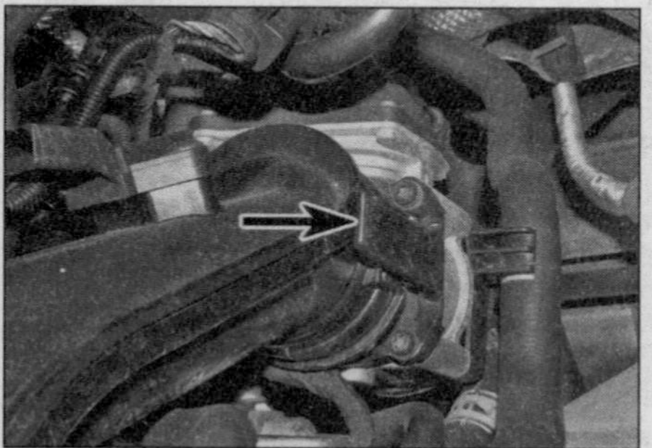
4.10c ...press-out the clip each side (arrowed)...

4.10d ...and remove the charge air pipe

10 The charge air pipe from the turbocharger to the throttle valve is secured by screws at the turbo end, and clips at the valve end. Undo the screws, spread the retaining clips outwards slightly, and remove the charge air pipe **(see illustrations)**.

11 Disconnect the wiring plug, then undo the retaining bolts and remove the throttle housing/module.

12 Refitting is a reversal of removal, noting the following:

a) *Use a new throttle housing-to-inlet manifold seal.*
b) *Tighten the throttle housing through-bolts evenly to the specified torque.*
c) *Ensure that all hoses and electrical connectors are refitted securely.*
d) *Apply a light coat of engine oil to the O-ring seal on the turbocharger prior to refitting the charge air pipe.*

Fuel injectors (and fuel rail where applicable)

Note: *Observe the precautions in Section 1 before working on any component in the fuel system. If a faulty injector is suspected, before removing the injectors, it is worth trying the effect of one of the proprietary injector-cleaning treatments. These can be added to the petrol in the tank, and are intended to clean the injectors as you drive. Note that VW technicians use tool T10133 to remove the injectors and fit the new injector seals – although the tool may not be required to remove the injectors, it will be required to fit the new seals.*

1.4 litre engine codes BCA and BUD

13 Remove fuse 27 from the fusebox to ensure the fuel pump is switched off. This is necessary as opening the driver's door would otherwise start the pump.

14 On the right-hand side of the engine compartment, near the coolant expansion tank, disconnect the fuel supply line. Plug the end of the line to prevent entry of dust and dirt.

15 Disconnect the wiring from the injectors located on the inlet manifold. Also, release the wiring loom.

16 Remove the fuel rail complete with injectors from the inlet manifold.

17 Pull out the clips and remove the injectors from the fuel rail.

1.4 and 1.6 litre engine codes BAG, BKG, BLF, BLN, BLP and CAXA

18 Remove fuse 27 from the fusebox to ensure the fuel pump is switched off. This is necessary as opening the driver's door would otherwise start the pump.

19 On the right-hand side of the engine compartment, near the coolant expansion tank, disconnect the fuel supply line and, where applicable, the return line. Plug the ends of the lines to prevent entry of dust and dirt.

20 Disconnect the wiring from the charcoal canister solenoid valve.

21 Remove the upper and lower parts of the inlet manifold as described in Section 9.

22 On all except engine code CAXA, pull the retaining clip/spacer from the injector **(see illustration)**.

23 On engine code CAXA, remove the spring element and O-ring seal from the top of the injector **(see illustration)**. **Note:** *Both the spring element and O-ring seal must be renewed.*

24 On all engines: At this stage VW technicians use the special slide-hammer tool to remove the injectors, however, if the injectors are not tight, they may have remained with the inlet manifold lower part when it was removed in paragraph 20 **(see illustration)**.

1.6 litre engine codes BGU, BSE and BSF

25 On the right-hand side of the engine compartment, near the coolant expansion tank, disconnect the fuel supply line. Plug the end of the line to prevent entry of dust and dirt.

26 Disconnect the wiring from the injectors.

27 Remove the lower part of the inlet manifold complete with fuel rail, as described in Section 9.

4.22 Pull the retaining clip/spacer from the injector

4.23 Renew the O-ring seal and spring element (arrowed)

4.24 Removing the fuel injectors from the cylinder head

28 Pull out the clips and remove the injectors from the fuel rail.

2.0 litre engine codes AXX, BPY and BWA

29 Remove the inlet manifold complete with fuel rail as described in Section 9, then disconnect all hoses and fuel lines, and unbolt the fuel rail from the inlet manifold. Tape over or seal the intake ports in the cylinder head to prevent entry of dust and dirt.
30 Using a screwdriver, bend the lugs on the injector support rings to one side, then remove the rings. Note that the lugs will most likely break, and new rings will be required for refitting.
31 At this stage VW technicians use the special slide-hammer tool to remove the injectors, however, the injectors may not be tight.

2.0 litre engine codes AXW, BLX, BVX, BVY, BVZ, BLY, BLR

32 Remove the inlet manifold upper part as described in Section 9.
33 On the right-hand side of the engine compartment, near the coolant expansion tank, disconnect the fuel supply line and, where applicable, the return line. Plug the ends of the lines to prevent entry of dust and dirt.
34 Disconnect the wiring from the injectors.
35 Disconnect the crankcase ventilation hose, and pull off the engine oil dipstick together with the guide tube.
36 Unbolt the fuel pipes.
37 Unbolt and remove the fuel rail together with the manifold flaps from the injectors.
38 Tape over or seal the intake ports in the cylinder head to prevent entry of dust and dirt.
39 Using a screwdriver, bend the lugs on the injector support rings to one side, then remove the rings. Note that the lugs will most likely break, and new rings will be required for refitting.
40 At this stage VW technicians use the special slide-hammer tool to remove the injectors, however, the injectors may not be tight.

All engine codes

41 Refitting is a reversal of removal, but thoroughly clean the cylinder head seatings, and fit new injector seals **(see illustrations)**. On all engine codes except BCA, BUD, BGU, BSE and BSF, the seals are made of Teflon, and the special VW tool will be required to compress the seals before fitting the injectors to the cylinder head. **Do not** grease or oil the seals on these engines. On engine codes BCA, BUD, BGU, BSE and BSF (ie, low-pressure injection system), lightly moisten the O-ring seals with clean engine oil.

Fuel pressure regulator (2.0 litre engines)

Note: *Observe the precautions in Section 1 before working on any component in the fuel system.*

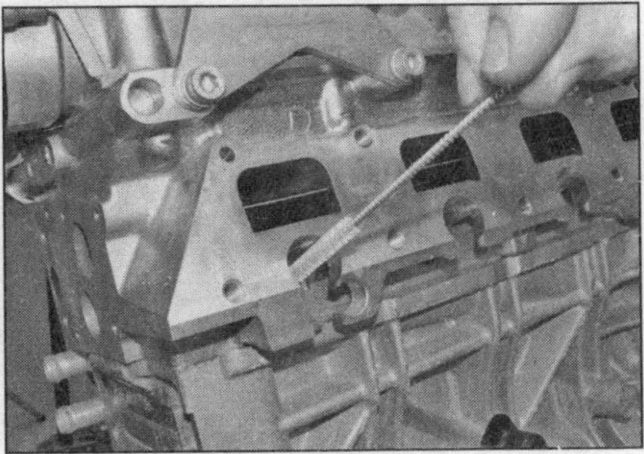

4.41a Thoroughly clean the injector seatings in the cylinder head

42 The fuel pressure regulator is located on the fuel filter beneath the rear of the car. First, chock the front wheels, then jack up the rear of the car and support on axle stands (*see Jacking and vehicle support)*.
43 Fit hose clamps to the filter inlet and outlet hoses.
44 Place a suitable container beneath the filter, then disconnect the hoses.
45 Unscrew the clamp bolt and remove the filter from its mounting.
46 Pull out the clip and remove the pressure regulator from the rear of the filter. Recover the seal and O-ring and discard them as new ones must be used on refitting.
47 Refitting is a reversal of removal, but use a new seal and O-ring.

Throttle valve positioner

48 The positioner is matched to the throttle housing/module during manufacture, and

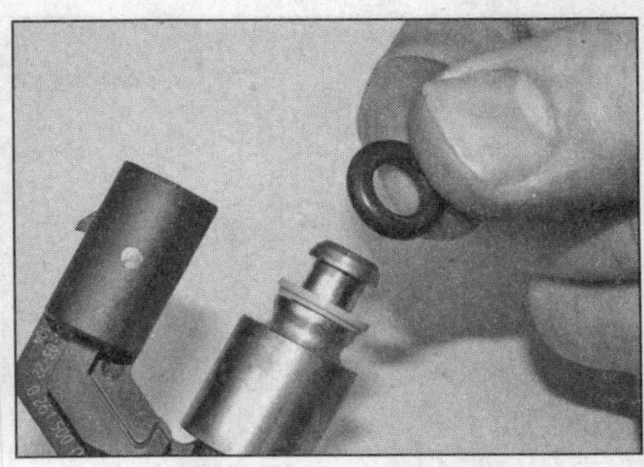

4.41b Fitting new injector seals

is not available separately – if defective, a complete throttle housing/module will be required.

Throttle pedal/position sensor

49 All models are fitted with a 'fly-by-wire' throttle where the position sensor is integral with the accelerator pedal. Working inside the car, remove the plastic cover (where fitted) from below the accelerator and brake pedals **(see illustration).**
50 Prise off the cap, and undo the screw securing the throttle pedal to the bulkhead **(see illustration).**
51 The throttle pedal is clipped to the floor. Insert two feeler blades or insert a screwdriver through the holes provided to release the clips **(see illustration).**
52 Withdraw the throttle pedal and disconnect the wiring and support **(see illustration).**
53 Refitting is a reversal of removal.

4.49 Remove the plastic cover from below the pedals...

4.50 ...prise off the cap and undo the screw...

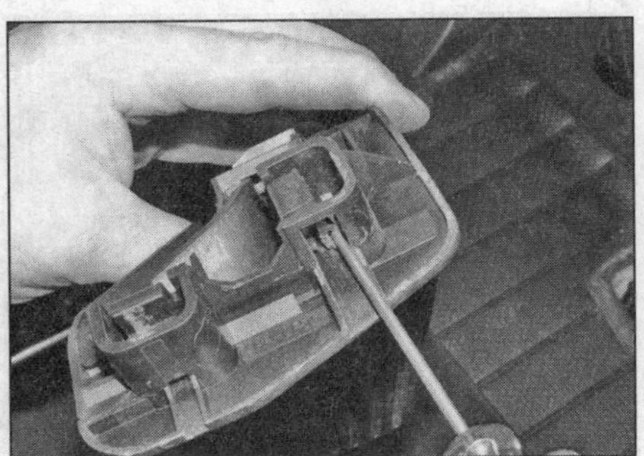

4.51 ...release the clips (sensor removed for clarity)...

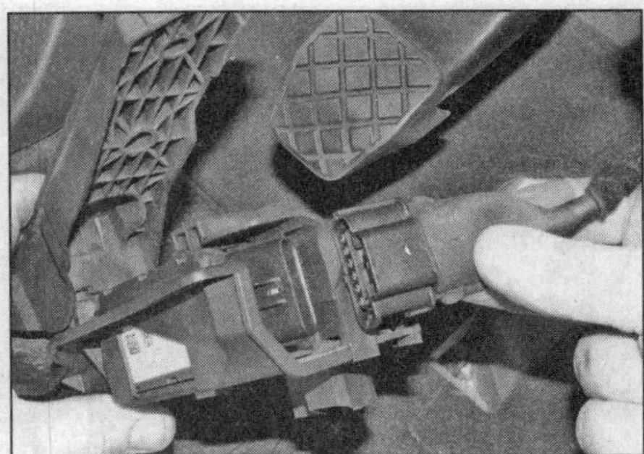

4.52 ...then remove the throttle pedal/ sensor and disconnect the wiring

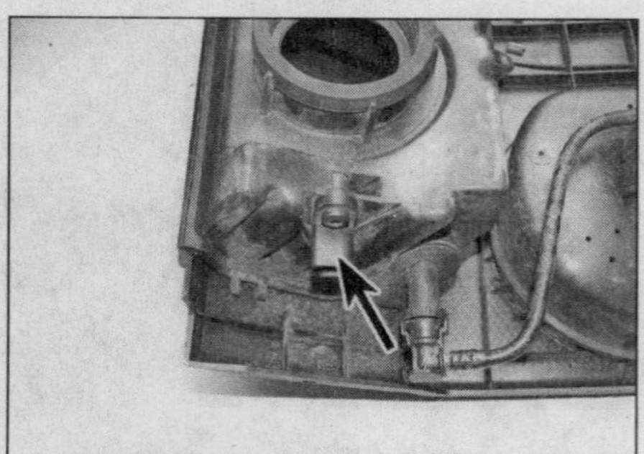

4.58 Inlet air temperature sender – 1.6 litre FSi

Inlet air temperature/ pressure sender

1.4 litre engine codes BCA and BUD

54 The air temperature and pressure sender is located on the right-hand side of the inlet manifold. Note that access is limited.

55 Disconnect the wiring from the sender.

56 Undo the two screws and remove the sender from the inlet manifold. Recover the seal and discard, as a new one must be used on refitting.

57 Refitting is a reversal of removal, but fit a new seal.

1.4 and 1.6 litre engine codes BAG, BKG, BLF, BLN and BLP

58 The air temperature sender is located on the side of the engine top cover/air filter **(see illustration)** – if necessary, remove the cover as described in Section 2. First, disconnect the wiring.

59 Undo the screw and remove the sender. Recover the seal and discard, as a new one must be used on refitting.

60 Refitting is a reversal of removal, but fit a new seal.

1.4 litre engine code CAXA

61 The air temperature/charge air pressure sensor is located on charge air pipe **(see illustration 4.9)**. Undo the screws and remove the sensor. Renew the O-ring seal.

62 The inlet manifold pressure sensor is located on the top of the inlet manifold **(see illustration)**. Undo the screw and remove the sensor. Renew the O-ring seal.

63 Refitting is a reversal of removal.

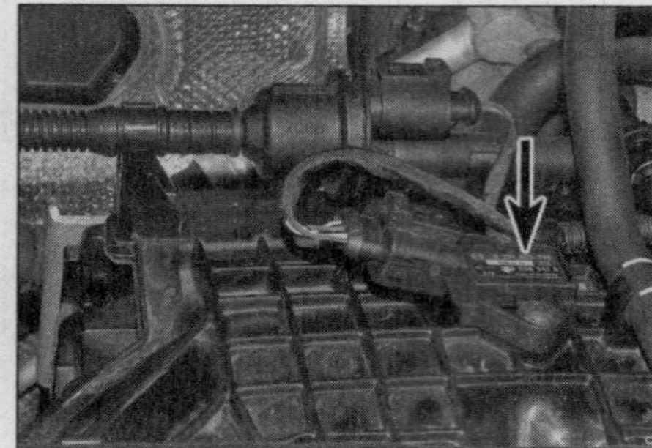

4.62 Inlet manifold presser sensor (arrowed) – engine code CAXA

1.6 litre engine codes BGU, BSE and BSF

64 The air temperature and pressure sender is located on the top of the upper inlet manifold. First, disconnect the wiring.

65 Undo the two screws and remove the sender from the inlet manifold. Recover the seal and discard, as a new one must be used on refitting.

66 Refitting is a reversal of removal, but fit a new seal.

2.0 litre engine codes AXX, BPY and BWA

67 The air temperature sender is located on the rear of the inlet manifold. First, disconnect the wiring.

68 Undo the screw and remove the sender. Recover the seal and discard, as a new one must be used on refitting.

69 Refitting is a reversal of removal, but fit a new seal.

2.0 litre engine codes AXW, BLX, BVX, BVY, BVZ, BLY and BLR

70 The air temperature and pressure sender is located on the bottom right-hand of the inlet manifold. Note that access is limited.

71 Disconnect the wiring from the sender.

72 Undo the two screws and remove the sender from the inlet manifold. Recover the seal and discard, as a new one must be used on refitting.

73 Refitting is a reversal of removal, but fit a new seal.

Coolant temperature sensor

74 Refer to Chapter 3.

Oxygen (lambda) sensors

Warning: Working on the sensors is only advisable with the engine (and therefore the exhaust system) completely cold. The catalytic converter in particular will be very hot for some time after the engine has been switched off.

75 All models have one sensor threaded into the exhaust manifold or at the top of the exhaust downpipe, ahead of the catalytic converter, and a second sensor mounted in the exhaust front pipe or intermediate pipe, downstream of the converter. Refer to Chapter 4C for more details **(see illustration)**.

76 Working from the sensor, trace the wiring harness from the oxygen sensor back to the connector, and disconnect it. Typically, the wiring plug is coloured black for the upstream sensor, and brown for the downstream sensor – **do not** confuse exhaust gas temperature senders fitted to the exhaust system. Unclip the sensor wiring from any retaining clips, noting how it is routed.

77 Access to the upstream sensor is possible on some models from above, while the downstream sensor (where fitted) is only accessible from below **(see illustration)**.

78 Unscrew and remove the sensor, taking care to avoid damaging the sensor probe as it is removed. **Note:** *As a flying lead remains connected to the sensor after it has been disconnected, if the correct-size spanner is not available, a slotted socket will be required to remove the sensor.*

79 Apply a little high-temperature anti-seize grease to the sensor threads – avoid contaminating the probe tip.

80 Refit the sensor, tightening it to the correct torque. Reconnect the wiring.

Engine speed sensor

81 On 1.4 and 1.6 litre engines, the engine speed sensor is mounted at the left-hand rear of the cylinder block, next to the transmission bellhousing, and access is very difficult. Prise out the rubber bung for access to the sensor **(see illustration)**.

82 On all other engines, the engine speed sensor is mounted on the front, left-hand side of the cylinder block, adjacent to the mating surface of the block and transmission bellhousing, next to the oil filter. If necessary, drain the engine oil

4.75 Oxygen sensor (upper) location on 1.6 litre FSi – note location of exhaust gas temperature sensor (lower)

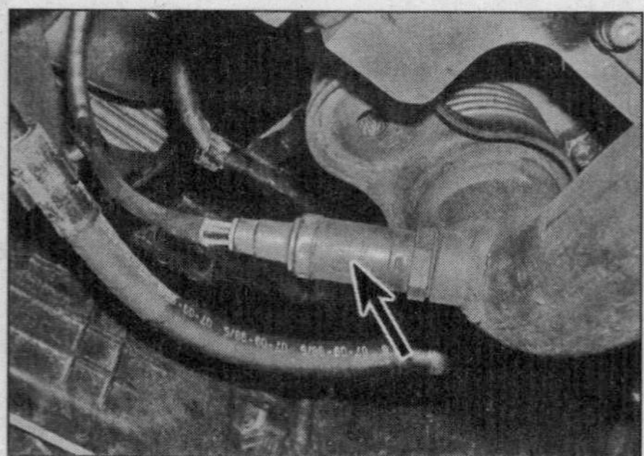

4.77 Oxygen sensor location on the exhaust downpipe

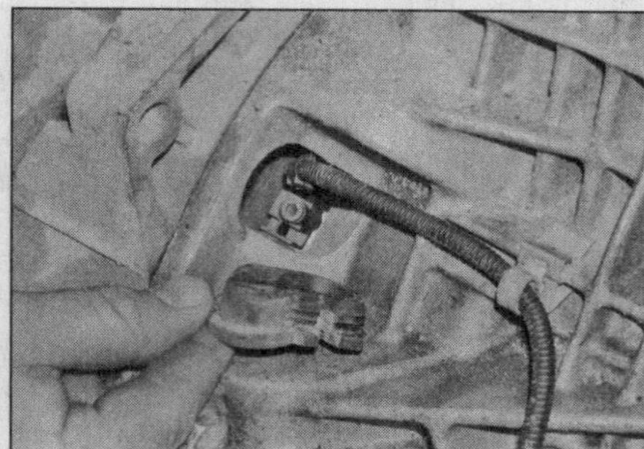

4.81 Prise out the rubber bung for access to the speed sensor

and remove the oil filter and cooler to improve access, with reference to Chapter 1A.

83 Trace the wiring back from the sensor, and unplug the harness connector.

84 Unscrew the retaining bolt and withdraw the sensor from the cylinder block.

85 Refitting is a reversal of removal.

Camshaft position sensor

1.4 litre engine codes BCA and BUD

86 The camshaft position sensor is located on the top, left-hand rear of the camshaft housing. First, remove the engine top cover.

87 Disconnect the wiring **(see illustration)**.

88 Undo the screw and remove the sensor. Recover the O-ring seal.

89 Refitting is a reversal of removal, but fit a new O-ring seal.

1.4 and 1.6 litre engine codes BAG, BKG, BLF, BLN, BLP and CAXA

90 The camshaft position sensor is located on the left-hand rear of the cylinder head cover. Undo the bolts (where applicable) and remove the engine top cover.

91 Undo the bolt and withdraw the sensor. If the O-ring seal is damaged, renew it.

92 Refitting is a reversal of removal, tightening the retaining bolt to the specified torque.

1.6 litre engine codes BGU, BSE and BSF

93 The camshaft position sensor is located on the left-hand rear face of the cylinder head. First, remove the engine top cover.

94 Disconnect the wiring **(see illustration)**.

95 Undo the screw and remove the sensor. Recover the O-ring seal.

96 Refitting is a reversal of removal, but fit a new O-ring seal.

2.0 litre engine

97 The camshaft position sensor is located on the right-hand end of the cylinder head, near the front.

98 Disconnect the wiring.

99 Undo the screw and remove the sensor. Recover the O-ring seal.

100 Refitting is a reversal of removal, but fit a new O-ring seal.

Clutch pedal switch

101 The clutch pedal switch is clipped to the clutch master cylinder on the pedal bracket. Remove the master cylinder as described in Chapter 6.

102 Unclip the pedal switch from the bottom of the master cylinder.

103 Refitting is a reversal of removal.

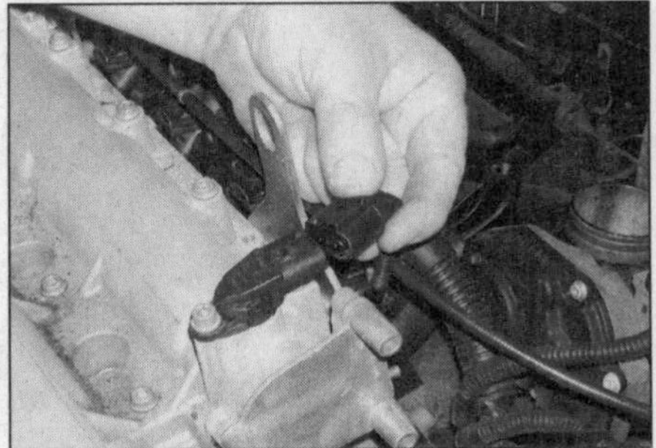

4.87 Disconnecting the camshaft position sensor wiring – 1.4 litre engine

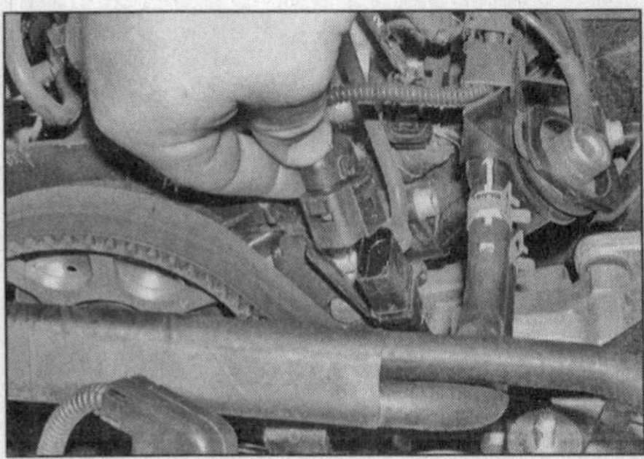

4.94 Disconnecting the camshaft position sensor – 1.6 litre SOHC engine

Electronic control unit (ECU)

Caution: Always wait at least 30 seconds after switching off the ignition before disconnecting the wiring from the ECU. When the wiring is disconnected, all the learned values are erased, although any contents of the fault memory are retained. After reconnecting the wiring, the basic settings must be reinstated by a VW dealer using a special test instrument. Note also that if the ECU is renewed, the identification of the new ECU must be transferred to the immobiliser control unit by a VW dealer.

104 The ECU is located centrally behind the engine compartment bulkhead, under one of the windscreen cowl panels. Remove the wiper arms and cowl panel as for windscreen wiper motor removal and refitting, described in Chapter 12.

105 Where the security cover is secured with pop-rivets, drill them off **(see illustration)**. Where it is secured with bolts, unscrew and remove them.

106 Remove the security cover then disconnect the wiring plugs. To disconnect the front plug, use a screwdriver to lever up the catch **(see illustrations)**.

107 Withdraw the electronic control unit from its location and disconnect the rear plug **(see illustrations)**.

108 Refitting is a reversal of removal. Bear in mind the comments made in the Caution above – the ECU will not work correctly until it has been electronically coded.

4.105 Drill off the pop rivets...

4.106a ...then remove the security cover...

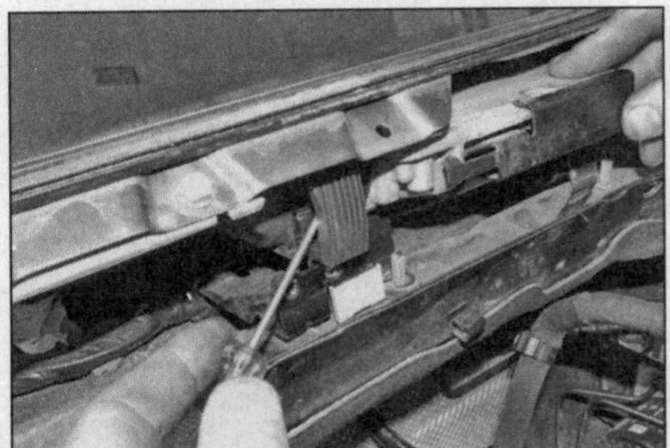

4.106b ...and disconnect the front wiring plug by levering up the catch

4.107a Withdraw the electronic control unit...

4.107b ...and disconnect the rear wiring plug

4.109 High-pressure fuel pump – 1.6 litre FSi

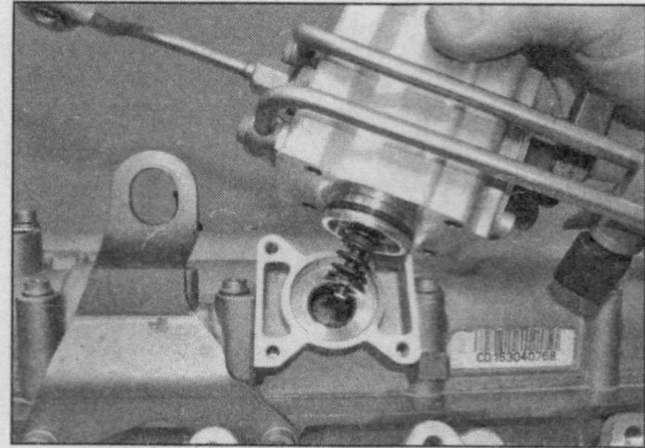

4.114a Remove the high-pressure fuel pump...

4.114b ...and recover the O-ring seal

4.114c High-pressure fuel pump – engine code CAXA

4.115 Removing the bucket tappet

High-pressure fuel pump

109 The high-pressure fuel pump is located on top of the camshaft housing **(see illustration)**. First, remove the engine top cover/air cleaner.
110 On engine codes BAG and BKG, remove the EGR connecting pipe with reference to Part 4C of this Chapter.
111 On 2.0 litre engines, set the engine to TDC as described in Chapter 2D.
112 Position cloth rags around the high-pressure fuel pump, then disconnect the fuel lines as follows:

- *a) On 1.4 and 1.6 litre engine codes BAG and BKG, unscrew the union nut and banjo bolts and disconnect the fuel lines.*
- *b) On 1.4 and 1.6 litre engine codes BLN, BLP, BLF and CAXA, release the clips and disconnect the low-pressure fuel line near the coolant expansion tank, and from the high-pressure pump. Unscrew the union nuts and disconnect the high-pressure fuel lines.*
- *c) On 2.0 litre engines, unscrew the union nut and banjo bolt and disconnect the fuel lines.*

113 Disconnect the wiring, and remove the wiring guide where fitted.
114 Unscrew the mounting bolts, then remove the high-pressure fuel pump from the top of the camshaft housing. Recover the O-ring seal and discard it, as a new one must used on refitting **(see illustrations)**.
115 Extract the bucket tappet **(see illustration)**.
116 Clean the mating faces of the pump and camshaft housing.
117 Lubricate the bucket tappet with clean engine oil, then insert it in the camshaft housing.
118 Smear clean engine oil on the new O-ring seal, then refit the fuel pump together with the O-ring seal. Insert the mounting bolts and tighten to the specified torque.
119 Reconnect the wiring, then reconnect the fuel lines and tighten the union nut(s) and banjo bolts to the specified torque. To ensure correct seating, the nut(s) and bolts must be progressively tightened to their specified torque.
120 On engine codes BAG and BKG, refit the EGR connecting pipe with reference to Part 4C of this Chapter.
121 Refit the engine top cover/air cleaner.

Fuel pressure sensor

122 The fuel pressure sensor is only fitted to FSi/TSi engines. On 1.4 and 1.6 litre engines, it is located on the lower inlet manifold. On 2.0 litre engines, it is located on the fuel rail. Access is restricted, and may be improved by jacking up and supporting the front of the vehicle on axle stands (see *Jacking and vehicle support*). Remove the engine undertray as necessary.
123 Depressurise the fuel injection system as described in Section 8.
124 Disconnect the wiring from the sensor, then unscrew and remove it. Be prepared for some loss of fuel by positioning a suitable container beneath the sensor.
125 Refitting is a reversal of removal, but tighten the sensor to the specified torque.

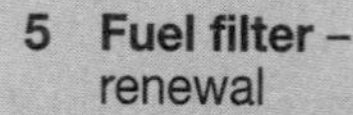

5 Fuel filter – renewal

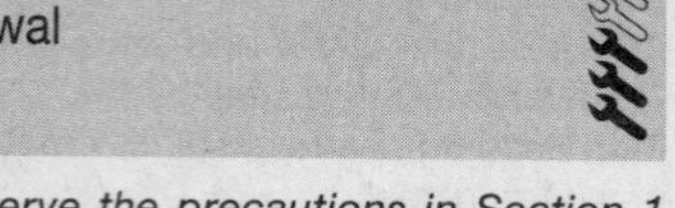

Note: *Observe the precautions in Section 1 before working on any component in the fuel system.*

1 The fuel filter is located in front of the fuel tank, on the right-hand underside of the car **(see illustration)**.
2 Jack up the right-hand rear of the car, and support it on an axle stand (see *Jacking and vehicle support*). When positioning the axle stand, ensure that it will not inhibit access to the filter.
3 To further improve access, unhook the handbrake cable from the adjacent wire clip.
4 Disconnect the fuel hoses at each end of the filter, noting their locations for refitting. The connections are of quick-release type, disconnected by squeezing the catch on each **(see illustration)**. It may be necessary to release the hoses from the clips on the underside of the car, to allow greater

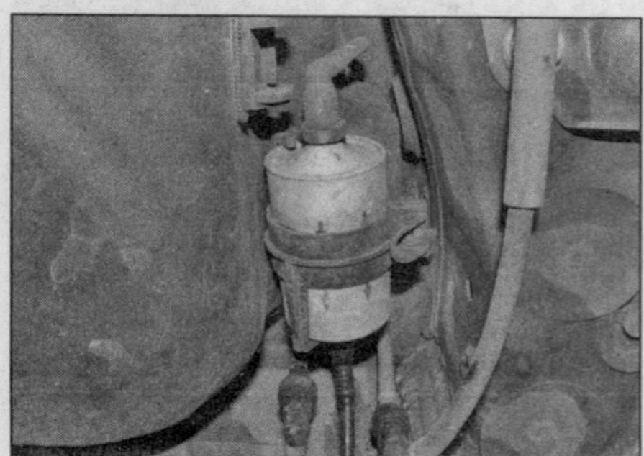

5.1 Fuel filter location

5.4 Disconnect the fuel hoses...

5.6a ...then loosen the clip...

5.6b ...and remove the fuel filter

movement. Both filter hoses should be black.

5 The filter is held in position by a large-diameter worm-drive clip. Before removing the filter, look for an arrow marking, which points in the direction of fuel flow – in this case, towards the front of the car. The new filter must be fitted the same way round.

6 Loosen the worm-drive clip, and slide the filter out of position **(see illustrations)**. Try to keep it as level as possible, to reduce fuel spillage. Dispose of the old filter carefully – even if the fuel inside is tipped out, the filter element will still be soaked in fuel, and will be highly flammable.

7 Offer the new filter into position, ensuring that the direction-of-flow arrow is pointing towards the front of the car. Tighten the worm-drive clip securely, but without risking crushing the filter body.

8 Connect the fuel hoses to each end of the filter, in the same positions as noted on removal. Push the hoses fully onto the filter stubs, and if necessary, clip them back to the underside of the car. Hook the handbrake cable back in place, if it was disturbed.

9 Lower the car to the ground, then start the engine and check for signs of fuel leakage at both ends of the filter.

6 Fuel lift pump and gauge sender unit – removal and refitting

Note: *Observe the precautions in Section 1 before working on any component in the fuel system.*

Warning: Avoid direct skin contact with fuel – wear protective clothing and gloves when handling fuel system components. Ensure that the work area is well-ventilated to prevent the build-up of fuel vapour.

General information

1 The fuel lift pump and gauge sender unit are combined in one assembly, which is mounted in the top of the fuel tank. Access is beneath a cover in the load space floor. The unit protrudes into the fuel tank, and its removal involves exposing the contents of the tank to the atmosphere.

Removal

2 Ensure that the vehicle is parked on a level surface, then disconnect the battery negative lead and position it away from the terminal. **Note:** *Refer to 'Disconnecting the battery' at the rear of this manual first.*

3 Remove the rear seat cushion (Chapter 11), and lift the carpet from the load space floor.

4 Unclip and disconnect the wiring connector block, then prise up the cover and disconnect the wiring from the top of the lift pump/gauge sender unit **(see illustrations)**.

5 Pad the area around the supply and return fuel hoses with rags to absorb any spilt fuel from the fuel lines, then squeeze the catches to release the hose clips and disconnect them **(see illustration)**. Observe the supply and return arrow markings on the ports – label the fuel hoses accordingly to ensure correct refitting later. The supply pipe is black, and may have white markings, while the return pipe is blue, or has blue markings.

6 Note the position of the alignment marks, then unscrew and remove the securing ring. Use a pair of water pump pliers (or home-made tool) to grip and rotate the securing ring **(see illustrations)**.

6.4a Disconnect the wiring connector block...

6.4b ...then prise up the cover and disconnect the wiring from the pump/gauge unit

6.5 Fuel supply and return hoses

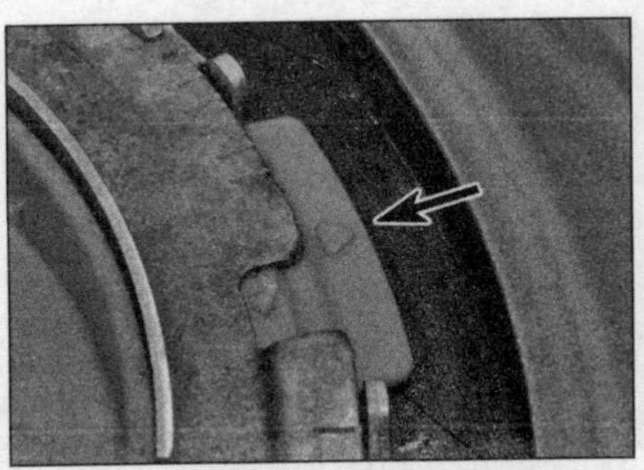
6.6a Note the alignment marks...

6.6b ...then use a suitable tool to unscrew...

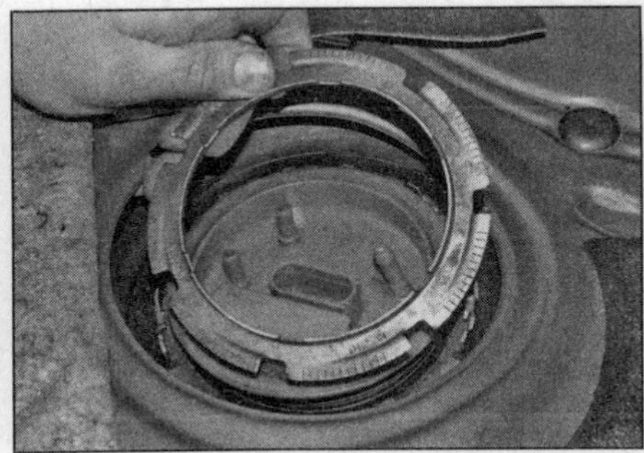
6.6c ...and remove the securing ring

6.7 Removing the lift pump/gauge sender unit from the fuel tank

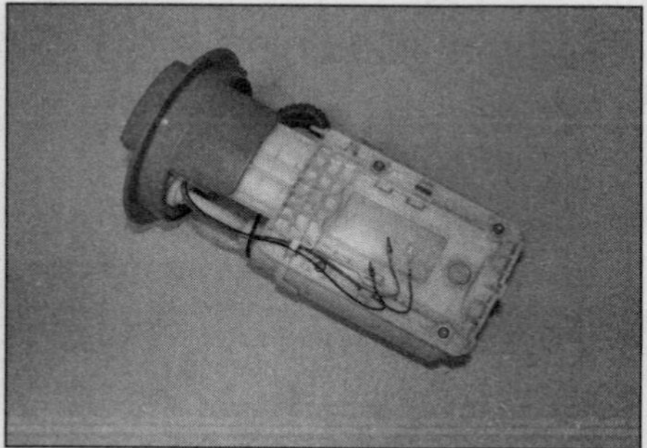
6.8 Lift pump/gauge sender unit removed from the car

6.10 If not removed with the unit, recover the rubber seal and check its condition

7 Lift out the lift pump/gauge sender unit, holding it above the level of the fuel in the tank until the excess fuel has drained out. Recover the flange and seal **(see illustration)**.

8 With the pump/sender unit removed from the car, lay it on an absorbent card or rag **(see illustration)**. Inspect the float at the end of the sender unit swinging arm for punctures and fuel ingress – renew the unit if it appears damaged.

9 The fuel pick-up incorporated in the assembly is spring-loaded to ensure that it always draws fuel from the lowest part of the tank. Check that the pick-up is free to move under spring tension with respect to the sender unit body.

10 Inspect the rubber seal from the fuel tank aperture for signs of fatigue – renew it if necessary **(see illustration)**.

11 Inspect the sender unit wiper and track; clean off any dirt and debris that may have accumulated, and look for breaks in the track.

All except engine code CAXA

12 If required, the sender unit can be separated from the assembly, as follows. Disconnect the two small wires (note their positions), then remove the four screws and slide the unit downwards to remove **(see illustrations)**.

13 The unit top plate can be removed by releasing the plastic tags at either side; recover the large spring which fits onto a peg on the plate underside **(see illustrations)**.

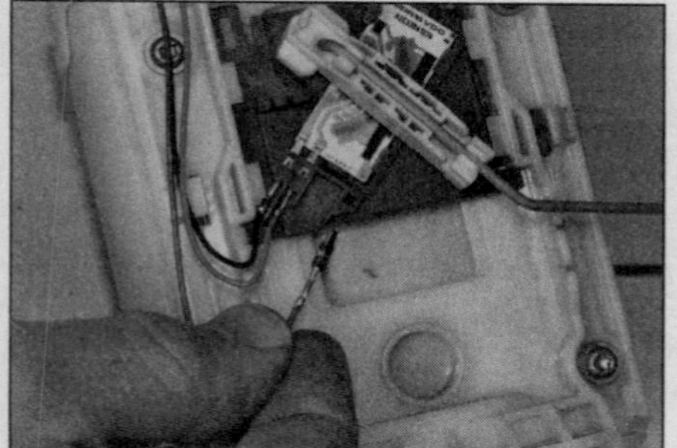
6.12a Disconnect the small wires...

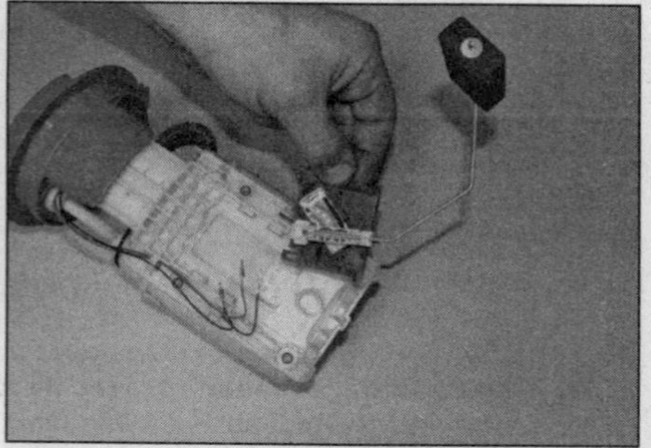
6.12b ...then undo the screws and slide out the sender unit

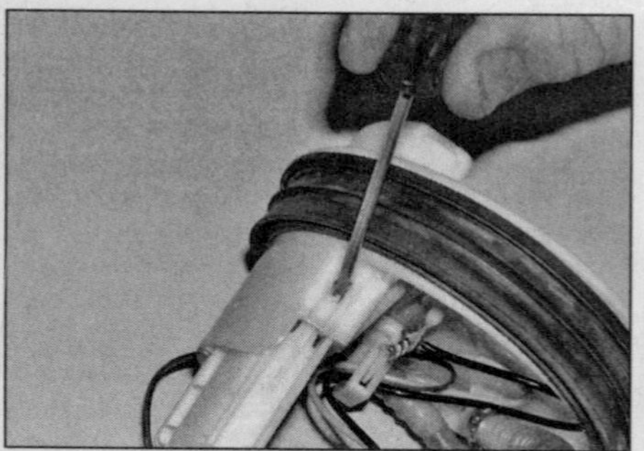
6.13a Prise up the retaining tags . . .

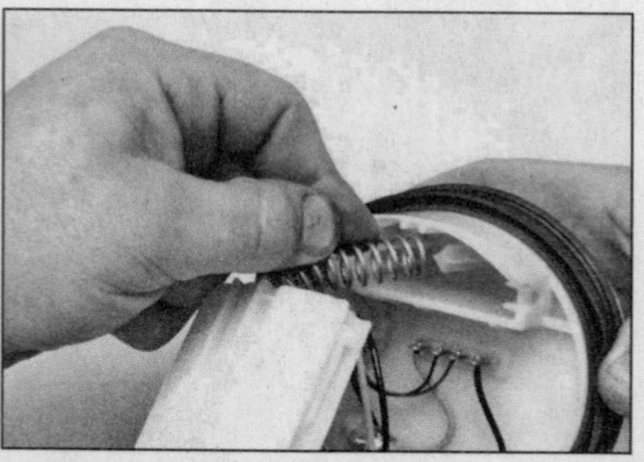
6.13b ...and recover the spring fitted under the top plate

Engine code CAXA

14 Gently pull the sender unit to the side and upwards at the same time. If the sender unit is reluctant to release, gently push the retaining tabs outwards at the same time as pull the sender unit upwards **(see illustrations)**.

15 Note their fitted positions, release the clips and disconnect the sender unit wiring plugs **(see illustration)**. **Note:** *On later sender units, the plugs are release by depressing the clips on the front and rear of the plastic housing.*

Refitting

16 Refit the lift pump/sender unit by following the removal procedure in reverse, noting the following points:

a) *Take care not to bend the float arm as the unit is refitted.*

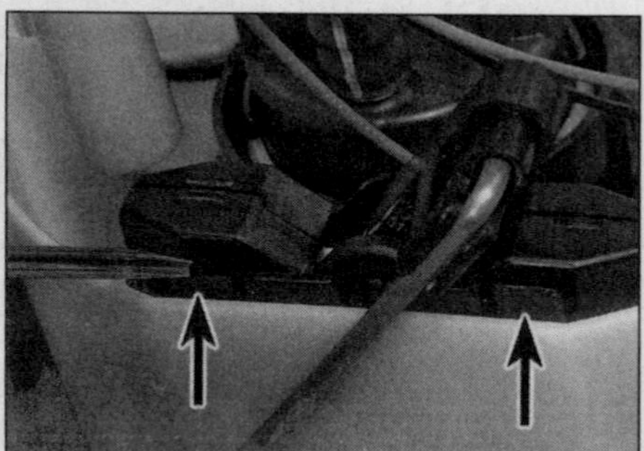
6.14a Press the clips (arrowed) to the outside...

6.14b ...and slide the sender unit upwards

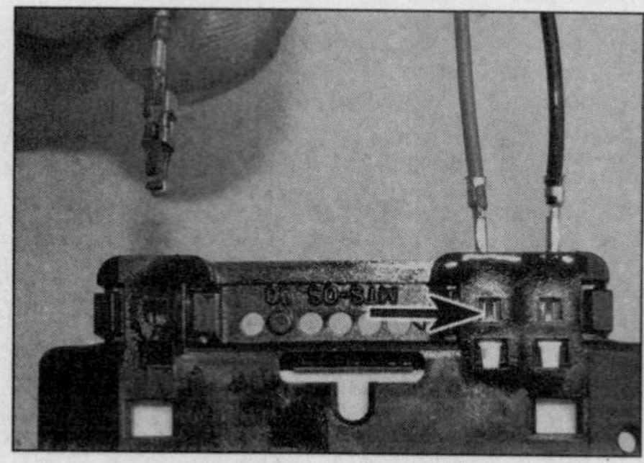
6.15 Depress the clips (arrowed) and pull the wiring plugs from the sender

b) Smear the outside of tank aperture rubber seal with clean fuel or lubricating spray, to ease fitting. Locate the seal in the tank aperture before fitting the lift pump/ sender unit ***(see illustrations)****.*
c) The arrow markings on the sender unit body and the access aperture must be aligned.
d) Reconnect the fuel hoses to the correct ports – observe the direction-of-flow arrow markings, and refer to paragraph 5. Ensure that the fuel hose fittings click fully into place.
e) On completion, check that all associated pipes are securely clipped to the tank, then run the engine and check for fuel leaks.

6.16a Locate the seal in the tank aperture...

6.16b ...then fit the lift pump/sender unit

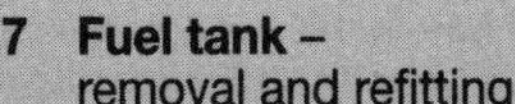

7 Fuel tank – removal and refitting

Note: *Observe the precautions in Section 1 before working on any component in the fuel system.*

Removal

1 Before the tank can be removed, it must be drained of as much fuel as possible. As no drain plug is provided, it is preferable to carry out this operation with the tank almost empty.
2 Open the fuel filler flap, and unscrew the fuel filler cap – leave the cap loosely in place.
3 Disconnect the battery negative lead and position it away from the terminal. **Note:** *Refer to 'Disconnecting the battery' at the rear of this manual first.* Using a hand pump or syphon, remove any remaining fuel from the bottom of the tank.
4 Loosen the right-hand rear wheel bolts, then jack up the rear of the car and remove the right-hand rear wheel.
5 Remove the right-hand rear wheel arch liner as described in Chapter 11.
6 Gain access to the top of the fuel pump/ sender unit as described in Section 6, and disconnect the wiring harness from the top of the pump/sender unit at the multiway connector.
7 Unscrew the fuel filler flap unit retaining screw (on the side opposite the flap hinge), and ease the flap unit out of position. Recover the rubber seal which fits around the filler neck.
8 Unbolt the filler pipe from the body.
9 Release the mounting rubbers and support the rear of the exhaust system to allow removal of the fuel tank.
10 Disconnect the fuel and charcoal canister breather lines as necessary.
11 Position a trolley jack under the centre of the tank. Insert a block of wood between the jack head and the tank to prevent damage to the tank surface. Raise the jack until it just takes the weight of the tank.
12 Unscrew the mounting bolt and detach the tank strap.
13 Lower the jack and tank away from the underside of the vehicle. If necessary, unscrew the nuts and remove the heat shield from the tank.
14 If the tank is contaminated with sediment or water, remove the fuel pump/sender unit (see Section 6) and swill the tank out with clean fuel. The tank is injection-moulded from a synthetic material, and if damaged, it should be renewed. However, in certain cases it may be possible to have small leaks or minor damage repaired. Seek the advice of a suitable specialist before attempting to repair the fuel tank.

Refitting

15 Refitting is the reverse of the removal procedure, noting the following points:
a) When lifting the tank back into position, make sure the mounting rubbers are correctly positioned, and take care to ensure none of the hoses get trapped between the tank and vehicle body.
b) Ensure that all pipes and hoses are correctly routed, are not kinked, and are securely held in position with their retaining clips.
c) Tighten the tank strap retaining bolt to the specified torque.
d) On completion, refill the tank with fuel, and exhaustively check for signs of leakage prior to taking the vehicle out on the road.

8 Fuel injection system – depressurisation

Note: *Observe the precautions in Section 1 before working on any component in the fuel system.*

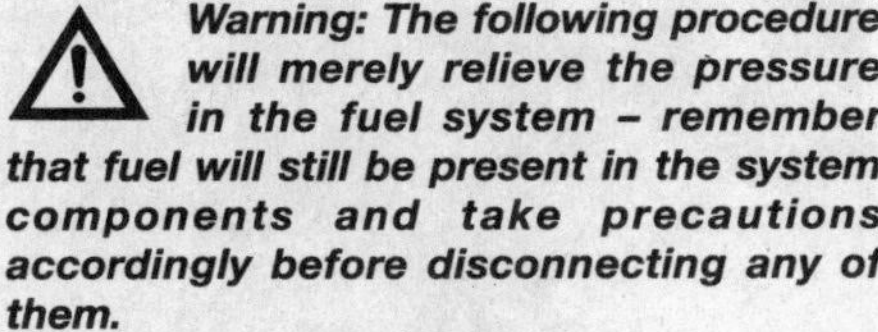

Warning: The following procedure will merely relieve the pressure in the fuel system – remember that fuel will still be present in the system components and take precautions accordingly before disconnecting any of them.

1 The fuel system referred to in this Section is defined as the tank-mounted fuel pump, the fuel filter, the fuel injectors, the fuel pressure regulator, and the metal pipes and flexible hoses of the fuel lines between these components. All these contain fuel, which will be under pressure while the engine is running and/or while the ignition is switched on. The pressure will remain for some time after the ignition has been switched off, and must be relieved before any of these components are disturbed for servicing work. Ideally, the engine should be allowed to cool completely before work commences.
2 On all engines with the Bosch high-pressure system (ie, not engine codes BCA, BUD, BGU, BSE and BSF), disconnect the wiring from the fuel pressure regulating valve on the high-pressure pump, then run the engine at idling speed for 10 seconds. **Note:** *With the engine switched off, disconnect the fuel lines as quickly as possible, as the internal fuel pressure will rise due to heat from the engine.*
3 On engine codes BCA, BUD, BGU, BSE and BSF, refer to Chapter 12 and remove the fuel pump relay. Alternatively, identify and remove the fuel pump fuse from the fusebox. With the fuel pump disabled, crank the engine for about ten seconds. The engine may fire and run for a while, but let it continue running until it stops. The fuel injectors should have opened enough times during cranking to considerably reduce the line fuel pressure, and reduce the risk of fuel spraying out when a fuel line is disturbed.
4 Disconnect the battery negative lead and position it away from the terminal. **Note:** *Refer to 'Disconnecting the battery' at the rear of this manual first.*
5 Place a suitable container beneath the relevant connection/union to be disconnected, and have a large rag ready to soak up any escaping fuel not being caught by the container.
6 Slowly open the connection to avoid a sudden release of pressure, and position the rag around the connection to catch any fuel spray which may be expelled. Once the pressure has been released, disconnect the fuel line. Insert plugs to minimise fuel loss and prevent the entry of dirt into the fuel system.
7 After working on the fuel system, reconnect the wiring/fuse/relay as applicable. Have the engine management fault code memory checked by a VW dealer for codes inserted when disconnecting the wiring.

9.8a Loosening the inlet manifold mounting bolts

9.8b Removing the inlet manifold from the cylinder head – 1.4 litre DOHC engine

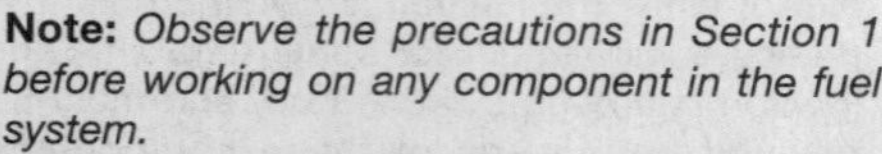

9 Inlet manifold and associated components – removal and refitting

Note: *Observe the precautions in Section 1 before working on any component in the fuel system.*

1 The design of the inlet manifold varies considerably depending on engine type. The following engines are fitted with a one-piece inlet manifold:

1.4 litre engine codes BCA and BUD
On these engines, the fuel rail is attached to and injects into the inlet manifold.

2.0 litre engine codes AXX, BPY and BWA
On these engines, the fuel rail is bolted to the bottom of the inlet manifold, but connects to the tops of the injectors located on the front of the cylinder head.

The following engines are fitted with a two-piece inlet manifold – the upper part has to be removed for various routine servicing tasks:

1.4 and 1.6 litre engine codes BAG, BKG, BLF, BLN, BLP and CAXA
On these engines, the lower manifold is effectively the fuel rail, and the upper manifold is bolted to it.

1.6 litre engine codes BGU, BSE and BSF
On these engines, the fuel rail is attached to and injects into the lower inlet manifold.

2.0 litre engine codes AXW, BLX, BLY, BLR, BVX, BVY and BVZ
On these engines, the lower manifold on the front of the cylinder head is effectively the fuel rail, and the upper manifold is attached to it with plastic ducts.

One-piece manifold

Removal

2 Disconnect the battery negative lead and position it away from the terminal. **Note:** *Refer to 'Disconnecting the battery' at the rear of this manual first.*

3 With reference to Section 4, remove the throttle housing/module from the inlet manifold.

4 Disconnect the vacuum hoses for the fuel pressure regulator, and (if not already removed) for the brake servo. Note how the hoses are routed, for use when refitting.

5 On low-pressure injection systems only, remove the fuel rail and injectors as described in Section 4. However, if the manifold is being removed as part of another procedure (such as cylinder head or engine removal), the fuel rail can be left in place.

6 Disconnect the wiring plug from the inlet air temperature/pressure sensor, referring if necessary to Section 4 for more details.

7 Where fitted, unbolt and remove the manifold support bracket from the engine block, then unbolt the mounting bracket for the secondary air inlet valve from the front of the manifold.

8 Progressively loosen the bolts/nuts and withdraw the manifold from the cylinder head **(see illustrations)**. Recover the gasket or the four seals as applicable – all should be renewed when refitting the manifold. On 2.0 litre engine codes AXX, BPY and BWA, unbolt the intake manifold flap motor and disconnect the coupling rod from the flap lever, and if necessary unbolt the fuel rail.

Refitting

9 Refitting is a reversal of removal. Use a new gasket or seals, as applicable, and tighten the retaining bolts/nuts to the specified torque. It is most important that there are no air leaks at the joint.

Two-piece manifold – upper part

Removal

10 Disconnect the battery negative lead and position it away from the terminal. **Note:** *Refer to 'Disconnecting the battery' at the rear of this manual first.*

11 With reference to Section 4, remove the throttle housing/module from the inlet manifold. If preferred, the housing need not be unbolted from the manifold, and can be removed with it, but all the services to the housing must be disconnected.

12 Release the hose clip and disconnect the brake servo vacuum hose from the manifold **(see illustration)**.

13 Disconnect and unclip all wiring, coolant and vacuum hoses from the manifold (as applicable), noting their location for correct refitting **(see illustrations)**. Use clamps on the coolant hoses to minimise spillage.

14 As applicable, unbolt the support brackets from the manifold.

15 Remove the screws securing the upper part of the manifold to the lower part **(see illustration)**. Where necessary, prise out the plastic flanges.

16 Lift the upper part of the manifold off the

9.12 Disconnecting the brake servo vacuum hose – 1.6 litre SOHC engine

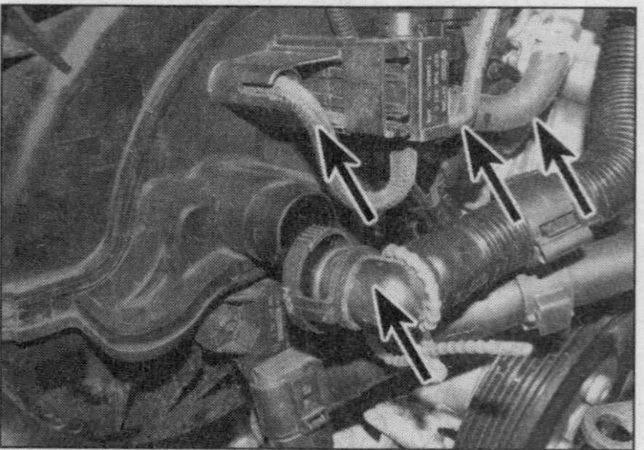

9.13a Disconnecting the hoses from the inlet manifold

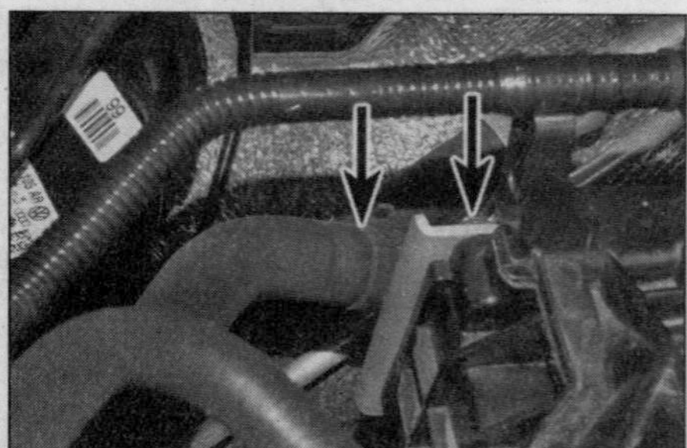

9.13b On engine code CAXA, 2 coolant hoses are attached to the intercooler at the rear of the manifold (arrowed)

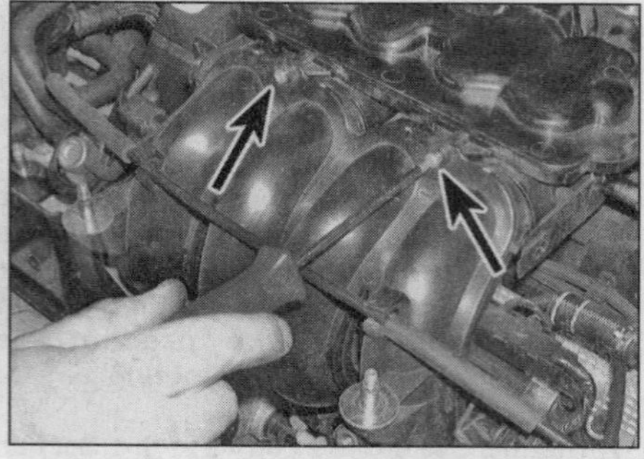

9.15 Unscrew the two screws (arrowed) securing the two manifold sections

9.16a Removing the upper part of the inlet manifold – 1.6 litre SOHC

9.16b Removing the upper part of the inlet manifold – 1.6 litre FSi

9.16c Recover the four seals – 1.6 litre FSi

lower part, and remove it from the engine compartment. Recover the four seals, single gasket or plastic air ducts **(see illustrations)**.

Refitting

17 Refitting is a reversal of removal. Use new seals, gaskets or ducts as necessary, and tighten the upper-to-lower part bolts to the specified torque. It is most important that there are no air leaks at the joint.

Two-piece manifold – lower part

Removal

18 Remove the upper part of the manifold as described previously in this Section.

19 On 1.6 litre engine codes BGU, BSE and BSF, to improve access to the manifold mounting bolts, remove the fuel rail and injectors with reference to Section 4. If the lower part is to be removed with the fuel rail, at least the fuel lines and injector wiring must be disconnected.

20 As applicable, disconnect the wiring plug from the camshaft position sensor on the right-hand side of the engine.

21 As applicable, the secondary air injection pump must be removed from the front of the manifold – refer to Chapter 4C.

22 On 1.4 and 1.6 litre engine codes BAG, BKG, BLF, BLN and BLP, use a 2.5 mm diameter drill bit to lock the vacuum actuator in order to prevent damage to the flaps. Also, on all engines, disconnect the wiring from the fuel pressure sensor and unscrew the fuel supply union nut and return line **(see illustrations)**.

23 Check around the manifold, and unclip any hoses or wiring which may still be attached.

24 Progressively loosen the nuts and bolts and withdraw the manifold from the cylinder head. Recover the seals/gasket(s) – all should be renewed when refitting the manifold. On 1.4 and 1.6 litre engine codes BAG, BKG, BLF, BLN and BLP, the injectors may remain in the lower manifold – remove them and refer to Section 4 when refitting them **(see illustrations)**.

9.22a Use a drill bit to lock the flap actuator vacuum unit before removing the inlet manifold lower part

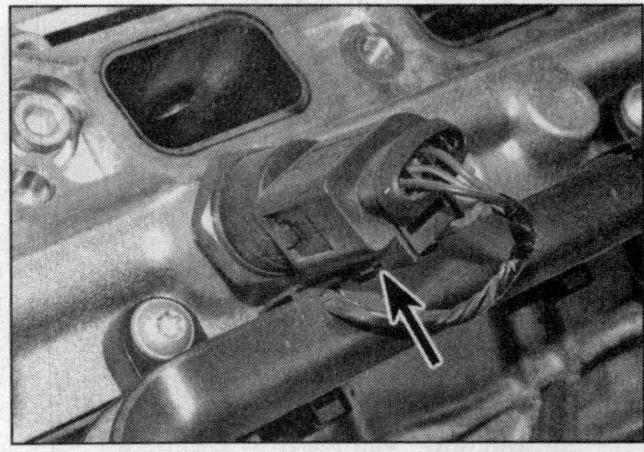
9.22b Fuel pressure sensor location on the inlet manifold lower part – 1.6 litre FSi

9.22c Fuel supply line union nut...

9.22d ...and return line – 1.6 litre FSi

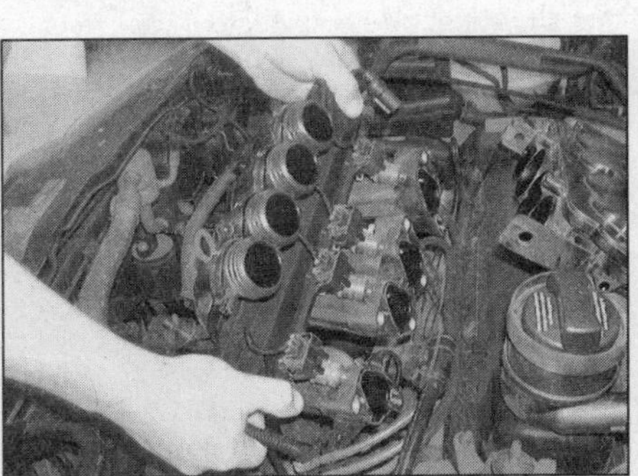
9.24a Removing the lower part of inlet manifold – 1.6 litre SOHC

9.24b Remove the lower part of the inlet manifold (complete with injectors)...

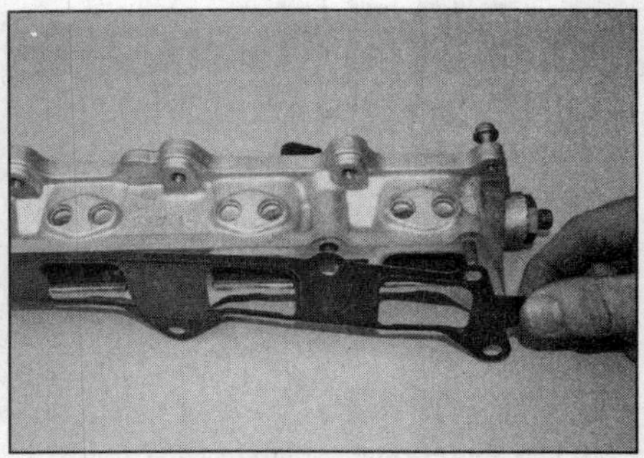
9.24c ...and recover the gasket – 1.6 litre FSi

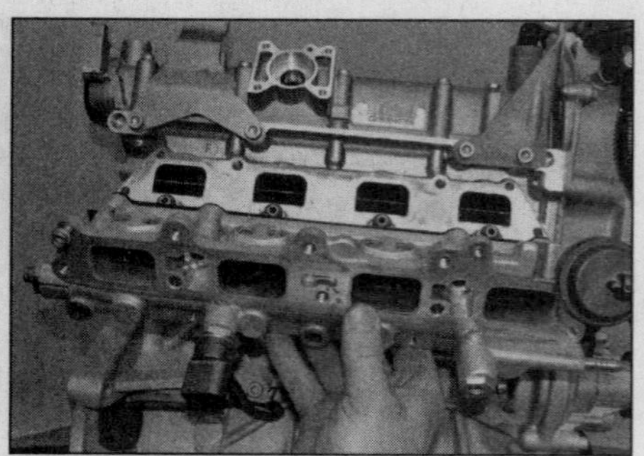

9.25 Fitting the lower part of the inlet manifold (injectors fitted to cylinder head)

Refitting

25 Refitting is a reversal of removal **(see illustration)**. Use new seals or gaskets as necessary, and tighten the manifold-to-head nuts and bolts to the specified torque. It is most important that there are no air leaks at the joint.

10 Fuel injection system – testing and adjustment

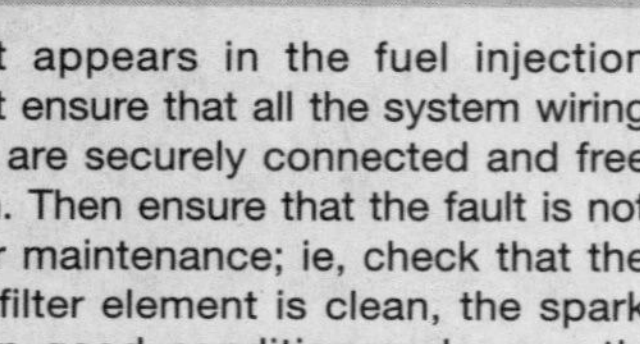

1 If a fault appears in the fuel injection system, first ensure that all the system wiring connectors are securely connected and free of corrosion. Then ensure that the fault is not due to poor maintenance; ie, check that the air cleaner filter element is clean, the spark plugs are in good condition and correctly gapped, the cylinder compression pressures are correct, the ignition system wiring is in good condition and securely connected, and the engine breather hoses are clear and undamaged, referring to Chapter 1A, Chapter 2A, 2B, 2D or 2D and Chapter 5B.

2 If these checks fail to reveal the cause of the problem, the vehicle should be taken to a suitably-equipped VW dealer for testing. A diagnostic connector is incorporated in the engine management system wiring harness, into which dedicated electronic test equipment can be plugged (the connector is located behind a trim panel above the front ashtray – unclip and remove the panel for access). The test equipment is capable of 'interrogating' the engine management system ECU electronically and accessing its internal fault log (reading fault codes).

3 Fault codes can only be extracted from the ECU using a dedicated fault code reader. A VW dealer will obviously have such a reader, but they are also available from other suppliers. It is unlikely to be cost-effective for the private owner to purchase a fault code reader, but a well-equipped local garage or auto-electrical specialist will have one.

4 Using this equipment, faults can be pin-pointed quickly and simply, even if their occurrence is intermittent. Testing all the system components individually in an attempt to locate the fault by elimination is a time-consuming operation that is unlikely to be fruitful (particularly if the fault occurs dynamically), and carries a high risk of damage to the ECU's internal components.

5 Experienced home mechanics equipped with an accurate tachometer and a carefully-calibrated exhaust gas analyser may be able to check the exhaust gas CO content and the engine idle speed; if these are found to be out of specification, then the vehicle must be taken to a suitably-equipped VW dealer for assessment. Neither the air/fuel mixture (exhaust gas CO content) nor the engine idle speed are manually adjustable; incorrect test results indicate the need for maintenance (possibly, injector cleaning) or a fault within the fuel injection system.

11 Cruise control system – general information

1 Certain models may be equipped with a cruise control system, in which the driver can set a chosen speed, which the system will then try to maintain regardless of gradients, etc.

2 Once the desired speed has been set, the system is entirely under the control of the engine management ECU, which regulates the speed with the throttle housing.

3 The system is deactivated if the clutch or brake pedals are pressed, signalled by the clutch pedal switch (Section 4) or the brake stop-light switch (Chapter 9).

4 The cruise control switch is part of the steering column turn signal combination switch, which can be removed as described in Chapter 12.

5 Any problems with the system which are not caused by wiring faults or failure of the components mentioned in this Section should be referred to a VW dealer. In the event of a problem occurring, it is advisable to first take the car to a suitably-equipped dealer for electronic fault diagnosis, using a fault code reader – refer to Section 10.

Chapter 4 Part B:
Diesel engine fuel systems

Contents

Degrees of difficulty

Easy, suitable for novice with little experience 

Fairly easy, suitable for beginner with some experience

Fairly difficult, suitable for competent DIY mechanic

Difficult, suitable for experienced DIY mechanic

Very difficult, suitable for expert DIY or professional 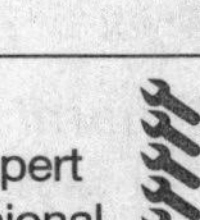

Specifications

Engine codes*

1.9 litre, 8-valve, turbo, SOHC	BJB, BKC, BRU, BLS, BXE and BXF
2.0 litre PD unit injection:	
8-valve, non-turbo, SOHC	BDK
8-valve, turbo, SOHC	BMM
16-valve, turbo, DOHC	AZV, BKD and BMN
2.0 litre common rail injection	CBDA, CBDB

* **Note:** *See 'Vehicle identification' at the end of this manual for the location of engine code markings.*

General

Fuel injection system	Electronic, direct, unit injectors or common rail injection
Firing order	1-3-4-2
Maximum engine speed	N/A (ECU controlled)
Engine fast idle speed	N/A (ECU controlled)

Tandem pump (PD Unit injector engines only)

Fuel pressure at 1500 rpm	3.5 bar

Turbocharger

Type	Garrett or KKK

Torque wrench settings

	Nm	lbf ft
Camshaft position sensor	10	7
Common fuel rail	15	11
EGR pipe flange bolts	25	18
EGR valve mounting bolt:		
Except engine code BDK	10	7
Engine code BDK	20	15
Engine speed/TDC sender	5	4
Flap motor housing	10	7
Injector clamp/mounting:		
1.9 litre PD unit injector engines*:		
Stage 1	12	9
Stage 2	Angle-tighten a further 270°	
2.0 litre PD unit injector engines*:		
Stage 1	3	2
Stage 2	Angle-tighten a further 90°	
Stage 3	Angle-tighten a further 180°	
Common rail injector engines:		
Clamp nut	10	7
Cover bolt	5	4
Inlet manifold to cylinder head:		
Engine codes BJB, BKC, BDK, BMM, BRU, BLS, BXE and BXF*	22	16
Engine codes AZV, BKD and BMN*	20	15
Engine codes CBDA and CBDB	10	7
Pump injector rocker shaft bolts*:		
Stage 1	20	15
Stage 2	Angle-tighten a further 90°	
Tandem pump bolts:		
Engine codes BJB, BKC, BDK, BMM, BRU, BLS, BXE and BXF:		
Upper	20	15
Lower	10	7
Engine codes AZV, BKD and BMN	20	15

* *Do not re-use*

1 General information and precautions

General information

All engines covered by this Manual are fitted with a direct-injection fuelling system, incorporating a fuel tank, an engine-bay mounted fuel filter with an integral water separator, fuel supply and return lines and four fuel injectors. Models with the 1.9 or 2.0 litre PD Unit injector engines, also have a fuel cooler mounted beneath the right-hand side of the car, on the underbody.

However, two different types of fuel injection system are fitted. The first is first is known as the 'PD' (Pumpe Duese) or Unit injector system, where fuel is delivered by a camshaft driven 'tandem pump' at low pressure to the injectors (known as 'Unit injectors'). A 'roller rocker' assembly, mounted above the camshaft bearing caps, uses an extra set of camshaft lobes to compress the top of each injector once per firing cycle. This arrangement creates high injection pressures. The precise timing of the pre-injection and main injection is controlled by the engine management ECM and a solenoid on each injector.

The second type is the familiar Common Rail system, where fuel is supplied from a timing belt-driven high-pressure pump to a common fuel rail (or reservoir). The four injectors are fitted into the cylinder head and are connected to the fuel rail by rigid metal pipes. The precise timing of the pre-, main, and post-injections are controlled by the engine management ECM and an electrically operated Piezo crystal incorporated into the injector design. All engines are fitted with a turbocharger.

The direct-injection fuelling system is controlled electronically by a diesel engine management system, comprising an Electronic Control Module (ECM) and its associated sensors, actuators and wiring. In addition, the ECM manages the operation of the Exhaust Gas Recirculation (EGR) emission control system (Chapter 4D), the turbocharger boost pressure control system and the glow plug control system (Chapter 5).

1.1 The EOBD diagnostic connector (arrowed) is located under the drivers side of the facia

A flap valve/throttle valve module fitted to the intake manifold is closed by the ECM for 3 seconds as the engine is switched off, to minimise the air intake as the engine shuts down. This minimises the vibration felt as the pistons come up against the volume of highly compressed air present in the combustion chambers.

It should be noted that fault diagnosis of the diesel engine management system is only possible with dedicated electronic test equipment. Problems with the system's operation should therefore be referred to a VW dealer or suitably-equipped specialist for assessment. Once the fault has been identified, the removal/refitting sequences detailed in the following Sections will then allow the appropriate component(s) to be renewed as required.

The EOBD diagnostic connector is located under the drivers side of the facia **(see illustration)**.

Precautions

Many of the operations described in this Chapter involve the disconnection of fuel lines, which may cause an amount of fuel spillage. Before commencing work, refer to the warnings below and the information in *Safety first!* at the beginning of this manual.

Warning: When working on any part of the fuel system, avoid direct contact skin contact with diesel fuel – wear protective clothing

and gloves when handling fuel system components. Ensure that the work area is well-ventilated to prevent the build-up of diesel fuel vapour.

- ***Fuel injectors operate at extremely high pressures and the jet of fuel produced at the nozzle is capable of piercing skin, with potentially fatal results. When working with pressurised injectors, take care to avoid exposing any part of the body to the fuel spray. It is recommended that a diesel fuel systems specialist should carry out any pressure testing of the fuel system components.***
- ***Under no circumstances should diesel fuel be allowed to come into contact with coolant hoses – wipe off accidental spillage immediately. Hoses that have been contaminated with fuel for an extended period should be renewed.***
- ***Diesel fuel systems are particularly sensitive to contamination from dirt, air and water. Pay particular attention to cleanliness when working on any part of the fuel system, to prevent the ingress of dirt. Thoroughly clean the area around fuel unions before disconnecting them. Only use lint-free cloths and clean fuel for component cleansing.***
- ***Store dismantled components in sealed containers to prevent contamination and the formation of condensation.***

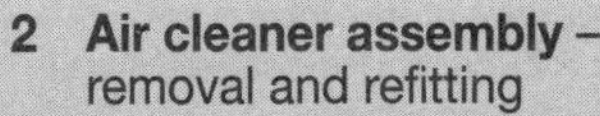

2 Air cleaner assembly – removal and refitting

Removal

Non-turbo PD injection models

1 The air cleaner is located in front of the battery in the left-hand front corner of the engine compartment. First, remove the engine top cover.

2 Undo the screws and remove the lid from the air cleaner.

3 Undo the screw and slide out the clamp, then remove the filter element from the housing.

4 To remove the housing, unbolt the intake hose elbow then unclip the housing while disconnecting it from the damping chamber air duct.

2.8a Disconnect the air mass meter wiring plug...

2.8b ...and the vacuum hose below it

2.13 Unclip the cover from the air intake

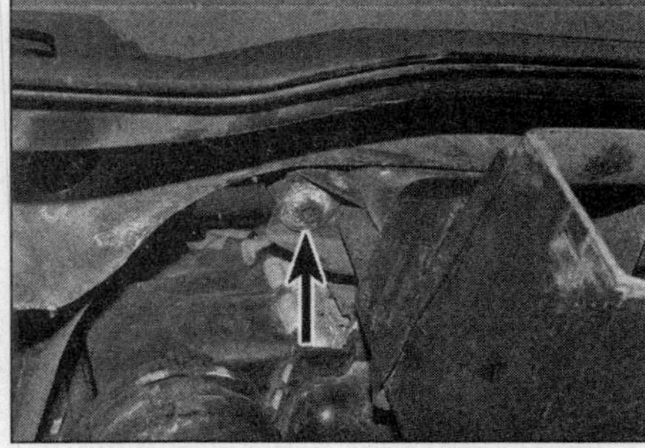

2.14 Undo the screw (arrowed) each side of the intake

5 To remove the damping chamber, disconnect the intake air duct, then unscrew the mounting nuts and withdraw from the engine compartment.

6 If necessary, the engine intake air duct may be removed after disconnecting the crankcase ventilation hose and unbolting the duct from the throttle housing/module.

Turbo PD injection models

7 Loosen the clip and disconnect the air duct from the air mass meter.

8 Disconnect the wiring from the air mass meter. Also disconnect the vacuum hose below the air mass meter wiring connector **(see illustrations)**.

9 On engine code BMM, disconnect the crankcase ventilation hose from the base.

10 Undo the screws and lift the air cleaner lid complete with air mass meter from the base.

11 Lift out the air filter element, noting how it is fitted.

12 Disconnect the air duct from the front of the base, then unscrew the mounting nuts and withdraw the base from the engine compartment.

Common rail models

13 Release the fasteners and remove the cover from the air intake at the bonnet slam panel **(see illustration)**.

14 Undo the screws securing the intake, then lift the ducting out of the intake **(see illustration)**.

15 Depress the clips and disconnect the intake ducting from the air cleaner assembly **(see illustration)**.

16 Disconnect the wiring plug from the air mass meter.

17 Disconnect the vacuum pipe from the air cleaner assembly **(see illustration)**.

18 Loosen the clip and disconnect the air duct from the air mass meter.

19 Undo the retaining bolt and lift the air cleaner assembly from place **(see illustration)**.

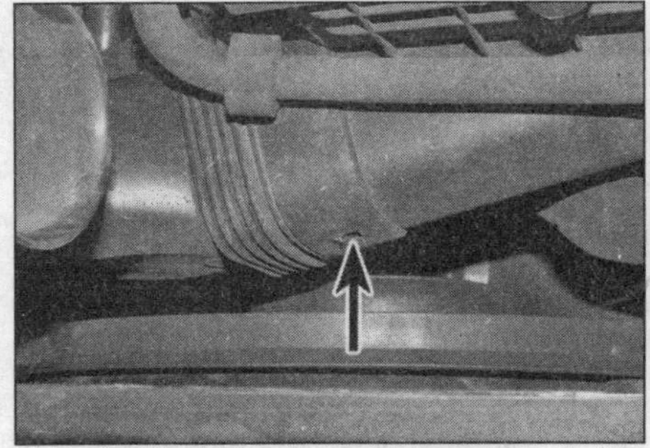

2.15 Depress the clip (arrowed) each side and disconnect the intake ducting

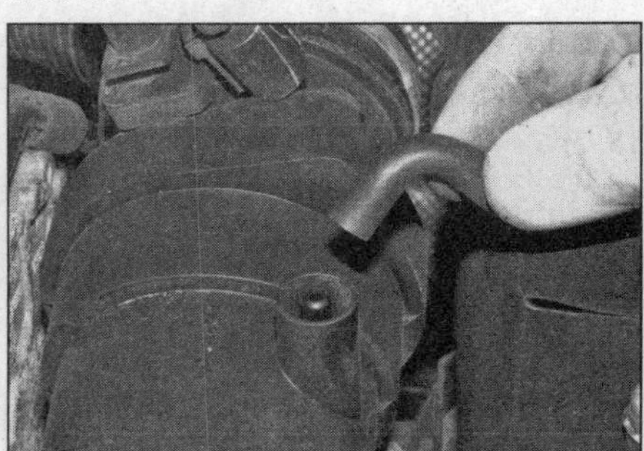

2.17 Disconnect the vacuum pipe

2.19 Air cleaner assembly retaining bolt (arrowed)

3.9 Fuel temperature sensor (arrowed) – common rail engines

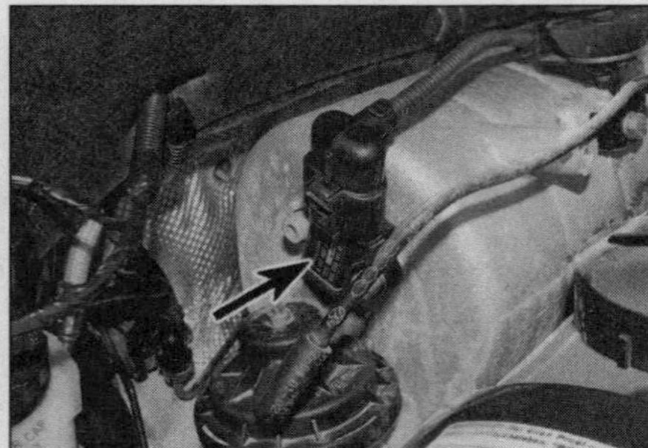

3.11 Inlet air temperature sensor on non-turbo models

3.21 Air mass meter location on engine code BKC

Refitting

20 Refit the air cleaner by following the removal procedure in reverse.

3 Diesel engine management system – component removal and refitting

Throttle pedal/position sensor

Removal

1 All models are fitted with a 'fly-by-wire' throttle where the position sensor is integral with the accelerator pedal. Working inside the car, remove the plastic cover (where fitted) from below the accelerator and brake pedals.

2 Prise off the cover, and undo the screw securing the throttle pedal to the bulkhead.

3 The throttle pedal is clipped to the floor. Insert two feeler blades or similar through the holes provided to release the clips.

4 Withdraw the throttle pedal and disconnect the wiring and support.

Refitting

5 Refitting is a reversal of removal.

Coolant temperature sensors

6 Refer to Chapter 3.

Fuel temperature sensor

Removal

7 The fuel temperature sensor is located in the fuel return line to the fuel filter in the engine compartment on PD unit injection engines or in the fuel supply line at the top of the high-pressure fuel pump on common rail injection engines. First, disconnect the wiring.

8 On PD unit injection engines, remove the securing clip, then extract the sensor from the fuel line housing and recover the O-ring seal.

9 On common rail injection engines, release the clamps and disconnect the hoses from the sensor assembly **(see illustration)**.

Refitting

10 Refit the fuel temperature sensor by reversing the removal procedure, using a new O-ring seal (where applicable).

Inlet air temperature sensor

PD unit injection engines only

11 All turbo models have an air temperature sensor built into the air mass meter – this sensor is an integral part of the air mass meter, and cannot be renewed separately. On non-turbo models, the air temperature sensor is located on the right-hand side of the inlet manifold, and is removed after disconnecting the wiring and unscrewing the retaining screws. Check and if necessary renew the gasket before refitting and tightening the screws **(see illustration)**.

Charge air pressure/ temperature sensor

Removal

12 The charge air pressure and temperature sensor is fitted either on the intercooler inlet elbow (engine code BMM), or on the air hose from the intercooler to the inlet manifold (engine codes BJB, BKC, BRU, BLS, BXE, BXF, AZV, BKD, BMN, CBDA and CBDB). Except for engine code BMM, jack up the front of the vehicle and support it on axle stands (see *Jacking and vehicle support*), then remove the engine undertray. For engine code BMM, remove the right-hand headlight as described in Chapter 12.

13 Disconnect the wiring then undo the screw and remove the sensor from its location.

Refitting

14 Refit the sensor by reversing the removal procedure, using a new O-ring seal.

Engine speed/TDC sensor

Removal

15 The engine speed/TDC sensor is mounted on the front cylinder block, adjacent to the mating surface of the block and transmission bellhousing.

16 Access is from beneath the engine compartment. Apply the handbrake, then jack up the front of the vehicle and support it on axle stands (see *Jacking and vehicle support*). Remove the engine undertray.

17 Fit hose clamps to the hoses attached to the oil cooler, then disconnect them. Be prepared for some loss of coolant.

18 Unbolt and remove the oil filter bracket.

19 Remove the retaining screw and withdraw the sensor from the cylinder block.

Refitting

20 Refit the sensor by reversing the removal procedure.

Air mass meter

Removal

21 The air mass meter is located in the outlet from the air cleaner assembly on the left-hand side of the engine compartment **(see illustration)**. On turbo models, it is attached to the air cleaner lid with screws, but on non-turbo models, it is located between the air cleaner outlet elbow inlet manifold.

22 Loosen the clips and disconnect the air ducting from the air mass meter.

23 Disconnect the wiring and the vacuum hose. On turbo models, undo the retaining screws securing the meter to the air cleaner. Withdraw the meter and recover the O-ring seal.

Caution: Handle the air mass meter carefully – its internal components are easily damaged.

Refitting

24 Refitting is a reversal of removal. Renew the O-ring seal if it appears damaged.

Absolute pressure (altitude) sensor

25 The absolute pressure sensor is an integral part of the ECU, and hence cannot be renewed separately.

Inlet manifold flap motor/housing

Note: *On engine code BJB, the inlet manifold flap housing is vacuum-operated and is incorporated into the EGR valve, whereas all other engine codes have a separate electrically-operated flap motor.*

Removal

26 Remove the engine top cover.

27 Loosen the clip (or release the spring clip) and disconnect the air trunking from the flap housing.

28 Except for engine code BJB, disconnect the flap control motor wiring plug from the housing.

3.29a EGR solenoid valve location on engine compartment bulkhead

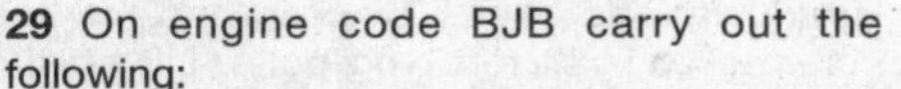

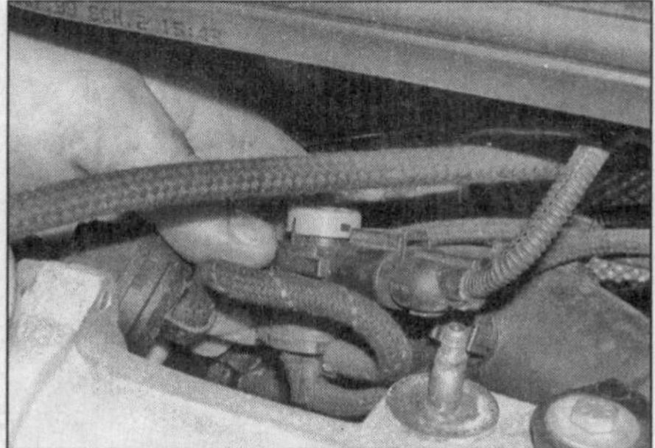

3.29b Unclip the inlet manifold flap solenoid valve...

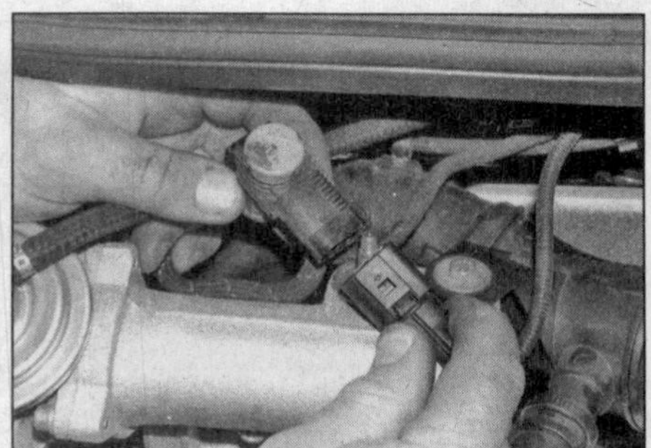

3.29c ...and disconnect the wiring plug

29 On engine code BJB carry out the following:

a) *Disconnect the EGR vacuum hose from the top of the housing.*

b) *Unbolt the EGR valve pipe and recover the gasket.*

c) *Trace the hose back from the flap vacuum unit to the solenoid valve, and disconnect the pipe from the valve **(see illustration)**.*

d) *Unclip the solenoid valve for the inlet manifold flap operating vacuum capsule; disconnect the wiring plug and vacuum hose from the solenoid, and remove it **(see illustrations)**.*

30 On non-turbo models, unscrew the four housing retaining bolts, and withdraw the housing from the inlet manifold. Recover the O-ring seal.

31 On turbo models, unscrew the bolts securing the flap housing to the EGR valve/housing/manifold, remove the flap housing and recover the O-ring seal. Note that except on engine code BJB, the bolts also secure the EGR valve to the exhaust manifold, so temporarily refit them to hold the EGR valve in position.

Refitting

32 Refitting is a reversal of removal. Renew the O-ring seal if it appears damaged.

Clutch pedal switch

Removal

33 The clutch pedal switch is clipped to the clutch master cylinder on the pedal bracket. Remove the master cylinder as described in Chapter 6.

34 Unclip the pedal switch from the bottom of the master cylinder.

Refitting

35 Refitting is a reversal of removal.

Electronic control unit (ECU)

Caution: Always wait at least 30 seconds after switching off the ignition before disconnecting the wiring from the ECU. When the wiring is disconnected, all the learned values are erased, however any contents of the fault memory are retained. After reconnecting the wiring, the basic settings must be reinstated by a VW dealer using a special test instrument. Note also that if the ECU is renewed, the identification of the new ECU must be transferred to the immobiliser control unit by a VW dealer.

Removal

36 The ECU is located centrally behind the engine compartment bulkhead, under one of the windscreen cowl panels. Remove the wiper arms and cowl panel as for windscreen wiper motor removal and refitting, described in Chapter 12.

37 Where the security cover is secured with pop-rivets or shear bolts, drill them out **(see illustration)**. Where it is secured with bolts, unscrew and remove them.

38 Remove the security cover then disconnect the wiring plugs **(see illustrations)**.

Refitting

39 Refitting is a reversal of removal. Bear in mind the comments made in the Caution above – the ECU will not work correctly until it has been electronically-coded.

3.37 Drill off the pop rivets...

3.38a ...then remove the security cover...

3.38b ...and disconnect the front wiring plug by levering up the catch

3.38c Withdraw the electronic control unit...

3.38d ...and disconnect the rear wiring plug

4.4 Undo the adjustment screw until the rocker arm lies against the plunger pin of the injector

4.6 Remove the clamping block securing bolt (arrowed)

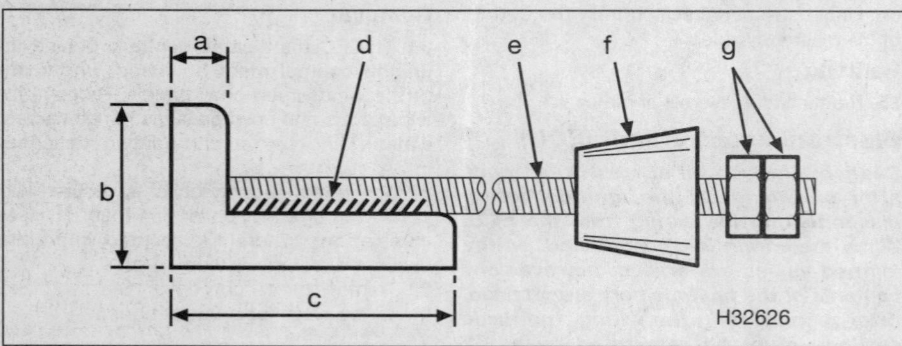

4.8a Unit injector removal tool

a 5 mm
b 15 mm
c 25 mm
d Weld/braze the rod to the angle-iron
e Threaded rod
f Cylindrical weight
g Locknut

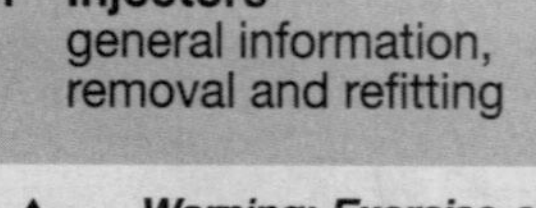

4 Injectors – general information, removal and refitting

Warning: Exercise extreme caution when working on the fuel injectors. Never expose the hands or any part of the body to injector spray, as the high pressure can cause the fuel to penetrate the skin, with possibly fatal results. You are strongly advised to have any work which involves testing the injectors under pressure carried out by a dealer or fuel injection specialist. Refer to the precautions given in Section 1 of this Chapter before proceeding.

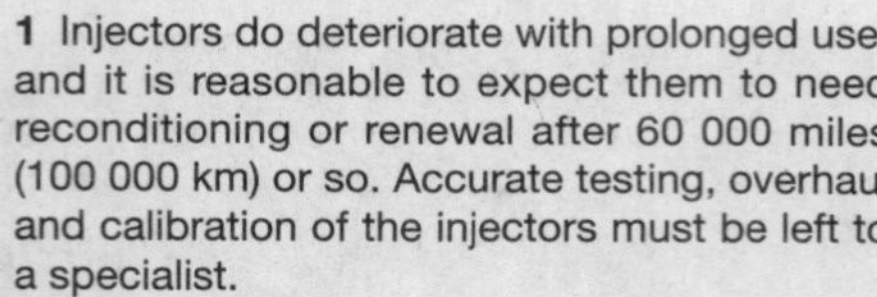

General information

1 Injectors do deteriorate with prolonged use, and it is reasonable to expect them to need reconditioning or renewal after 60 000 miles (100 000 km) or so. Accurate testing, overhaul and calibration of the injectors must be left to a specialist.

Removal

Note: *Take care not to allow dirt into the injectors or fuel pipes during this procedure. Do not drop the injectors or allow the needles at their tips to become damaged. The injectors are precision-made to fine limits, and must not be handled roughly. Keep the injectors identified for position to ensure correct refitting.*

Engine codes BDK, BJB, BKC, BRU, BLS, BXE, BXF, BMM

2 With reference to Chapter 2E, remove the upper timing belt cover and camshaft cover.

3 Using a spanner or socket, turn the crankshaft pulley until the rocker arm for the injector which is to be removed, is at its highest, ie, the injector plunger spring is under the least amount of tension.

4 Slacken the locknut of the adjustment screw on the end of the rocker arm above the injector, and undo the adjustment screw until the rocker arm lies against the plunger pin of the injector **(see illustration)**.

5 Starting at the outside and working in, gradually and evenly slacken and remove the rocker shaft retaining bolts. Lift off the rocker shaft. Check the contact face of each adjustment screw, and renew any that show signs of wear.

6 Undo the clamping block securing bolt and remove the block from the side of the injector **(see illustration)**.

7 Using a small screwdriver, carefully prise the wiring connector from the injector.

8 VW technicians use a slide hammer (tool T10055) to pull the injector from the cylinder head. This is a slide hammer which engages in the side of the injector. If this tool is not available, it is possible to fabricate an equivalent using a short section of angle-iron, a length of threaded rod, a cylindrical weight, and two locknuts. Weld/braze the rod to the angle-iron, slide the weight over the rod, and lock the two nuts together at the end of the rod to provide the stop for the weight **(see illustration)**. Seat the slide hammer/tool in the slot on the side on the injector, and pull the injector out using a few gently taps. Recover circlip, the heat shield and O-rings and discard. New ones must be used for refitting **(see illustration)**.

9 If required, the injector wiring loom/rail can be removed from the cylinder head by undoing the two retaining nuts/bolts at the back of the head. To prevent the wiring connectors fouling the cylinder head casting as the assembly is withdrawn, insert the connectors into the storage slots in the plastic wiring rail. Carefully push the assembly to the rear, and out of the casting **(see illustrations)**.

4.8b Seat the slide hammer/tool in the slot on the side on the injector, and pull the injector out

4.9a Undo the two nuts at the back of the head and slide the injector loom/rail out

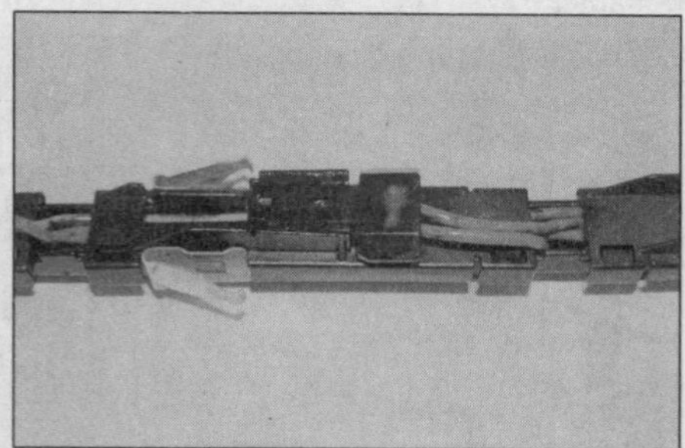

4.9b The injector connectors will slide into the loom/rail to prevent them from being damaged as the assembly is withdrawn/inserted into the cylinder head

4.16a Pull the engine cover upwards

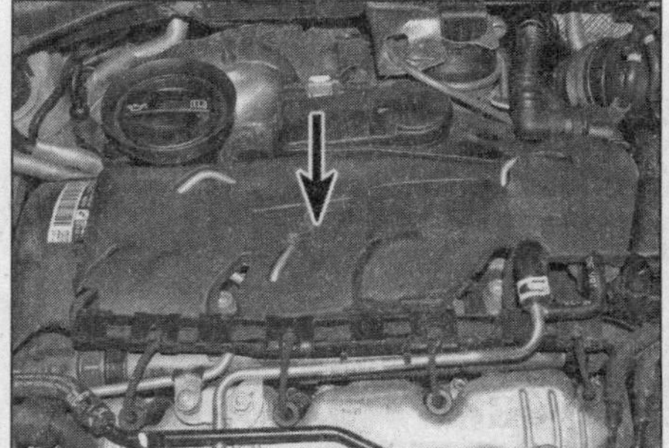
4.16b Lift the foam insulation (arrowed) from place

4.17 Lever up the clip (arrowed) and disconnect the injector wiring plugs

4.18a Hold down the outer tabs, and prise up the centre piece (arrowed)...

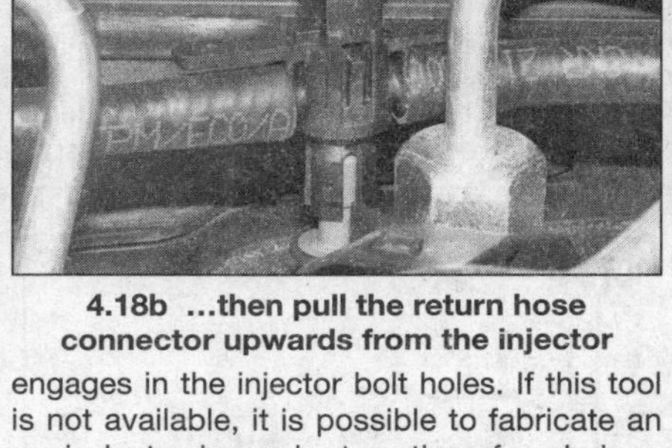
4.18b ...then pull the return hose connector upwards from the injector

4.19 Undo the unions and remove the high-pressure pipes between the common rail and the injectors

Engine codes AZV, BKD, BMN

10 With reference to Chapter 2E, remove the upper timing belt cover and camshaft cover.

11 Slacken the locknut of the adjustment screw on the end of the rocker arm above the respective injector, and undo the adjustment screw until the rocker arm lies against the plunger pin of the injector.

12 Starting at the outside and working in, gradually and evenly slacken and remove the rocker shaft retaining bolts. Lift off the rocker shaft. Check the contact face of each adjustment screw, and renew any that show signs of wear.

13 Using a pair of pliers, carefully pull the wiring connector from the injector.

14 The unit injectors have two mounting bolts each. Unscrew and remove the two bolts.

15 VW technicians use a slide hammer (tool T10133) to pull the injector from the cylinder head. This is a slide hammer which engages in the injector bolt holes. If this tool is not available, it is possible to fabricate an equivalent using a short section of angle-iron, a length of threaded rod, a cylindrical weight, and two locknuts. Weld/braze the rod to the angle-iron, slide the weight over the rod, and lock the two nuts together at the end of the rod to provide the stop for the weight **(see illustration 4.8a)**. Pull the injector out of the cylinder head. Recover the heat shield and O-rings and discard. New ones must be used for refitting.

Engine codes CBDA and CBDB

16 Pull the plastic cover over the engine upwards from its' mountings. Where fitted, remove the foam insulation over the injectors **(see illustrations)**.

17 Disconnect the injector wiring plugs **(see illustration)**.

18 Ensure the area around the injectors and the pipes/return hoses is clean and free from debris. The use of a vacuum cleaner is recommended. Push the return hose connector downwards at its tabs, then pull up the centre piece and disconnect them from the injectors **(see illustrations)**. Plug the openings to prevent contamination.

19 Undo the unions remove the high-pressure pipes between the common fuel rail and the injectors **(see illustration)**. Plug the openings to prevent contamination.

20 Undo the bolts securing the injector clamp cover, the slightly lift the cover and rotate it 90° for access to the injector retaining nuts **(see illustrations)**.

21 Unscrew the injector retaining nuts.

22 VW technicians use a slide hammer (tool T10055) and adapter (T10055/1) to pull the injector from the cylinder head. This is a slide hammer with an adapter which screws onto the top of the. If this tool is not available, it is possible to fabricate an equivalent using slide

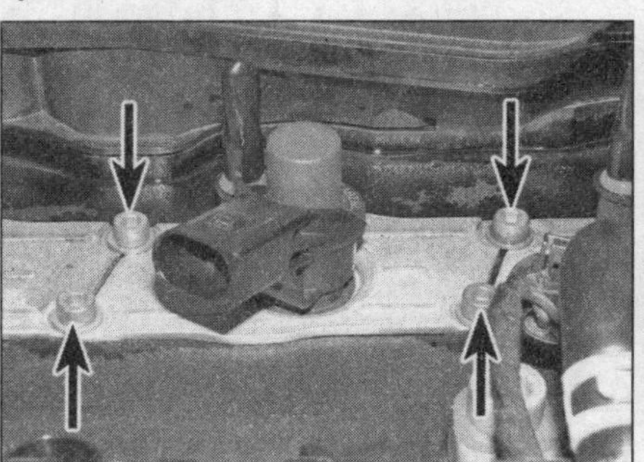
4.20a Undo the injector clamp cover bolts (arrowed)...

4.20b ...then lift and rotate it 90°

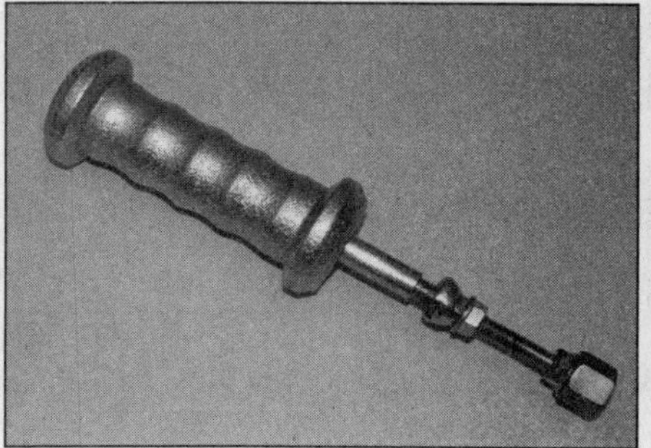
4.22a We attached an old injector pipe union onto the end of the slide hammer...

4.22b ...screwed it onto the top of the injector...

4.22c ...and pulled it from the cylinder head

4.23 Care must be used to ensure that the injector O-rings are fitted without being twisted

hammer with the union from an old injector pipe brazed/welded onto the end. Screw the tool onto the top of the injector, and pull the injector out using a few gently taps. Recover the clamping piece, copper seal and O-rings and discard. New ones must be used for refitting **(see illustrations)**. **Note:** *The injectors can only be refitted to their original positions. Make the injectors to avoid confusion if refitting the original injectors.*

Refitting

Engine codes BDK, BJB, BKC, BRU, BLS, BXE, BXF, BMM

23 Prior to refitting the injectors, the three O-rings, heat insulation washer and clip must be renewed. Due to the high injection pressures, it is essential that the O-rings are fitted without being twisted. VW recommend the use of three special assembly sleeves to install the O-rings squarely. It may be prudent to entrust O-ring renewal to a VW dealer or suitably-equipped injection specialist, rather than risk subsequent leaks **(see illustration)**.

24 After renewing the O-rings, fit the heat shield and secure it in place with the circlip **(see illustration)**.

25 Smear clean engine oil onto the O-rings, and push the injector evenly down into the cylinder head onto its stop.

26 Fit the clamping block alongside the injector, but only hand-tighten the new retaining bolt at this stage.

27 It is essential that the injectors are fitted at right-angles to the clamping block. In order to achieve this, measure the distance from the rear face of the cylinder head to the rounded section of the injector **(see illustrations)**. The dimensions (a) are as follows:

Cylinder 1 = 333.0 ± 0.8 mm
Cylinder 2 = 245.0 ± 0.8 mm
Cylinder 3 = 153.6 ± 0.8 mm
Cylinder 4 = 65.6 ± 0.8 mm

28 Once the injector(s) are aligned correctly, tighten the clamping bolt to the specified Stage 1 torque setting, and the Stage 2 angle tightening setting. **Note:** *If an injector has been renewed, it is essential that the adjustment screw, locknut of the corresponding rocker and ball-pin are renewed at the same time. The ball-pins simply pull out of the injector spring cap. There is an O-ring in each spring cap to stop the ball-pins from falling out.*

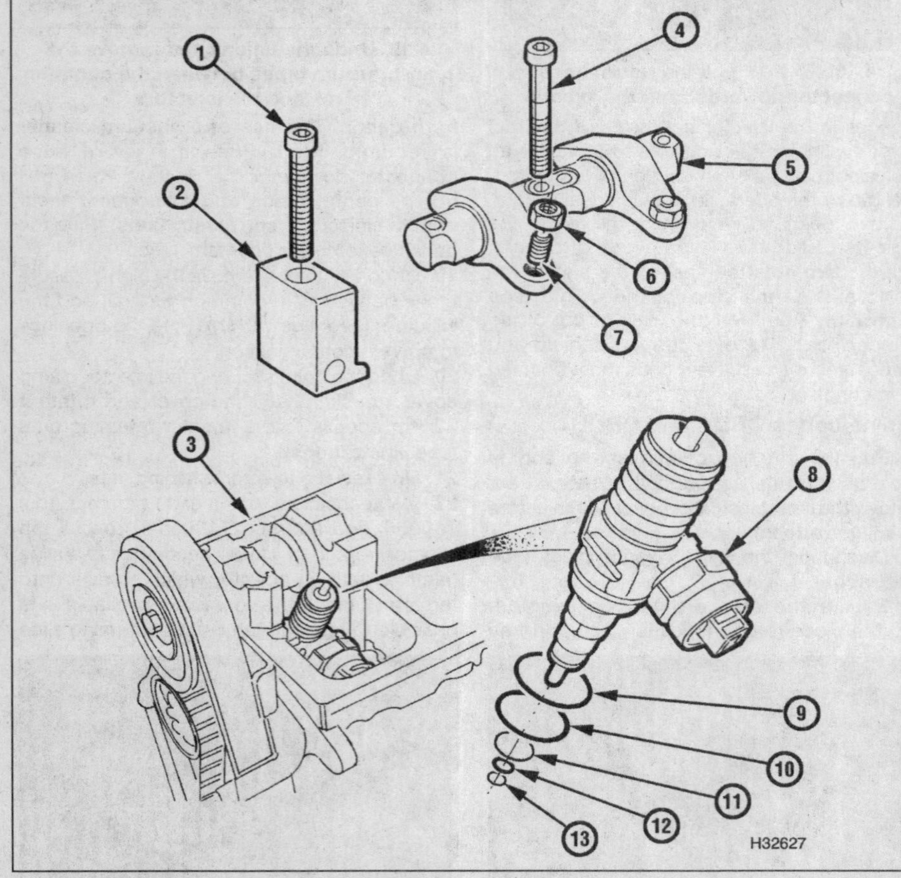

4.24 Unit injector – engine codes BDK, BJB, BKC, BRU, BLS, BXE, BXF and BMM

1 *Bolt*
2 *Clamping block*
3 *Cylinder head*
4 *Bolt*
5 *Rocker arm*
6 *Nut*
7 *Adjuster*
8 *Unit injector*
9 *O-ring*
10 *O-ring*
11 *O-ring*
12 *Heat shield*
13 *Circlip*

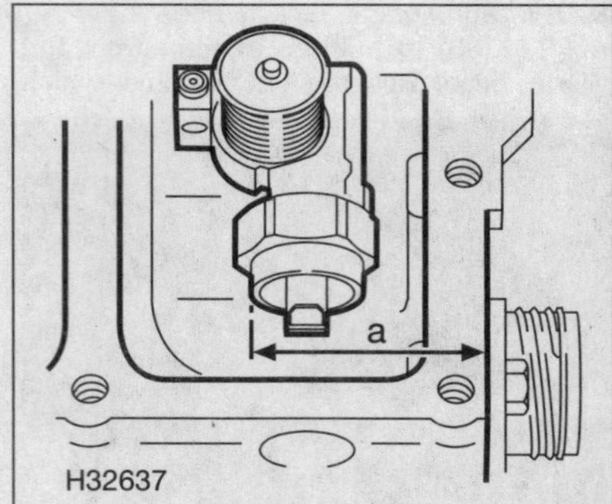

4.27a Measure the distance (a) from the rear of the cylinder head to the rounded section of the injector (see text)

4.27b Use a set square against the edge of the injector...

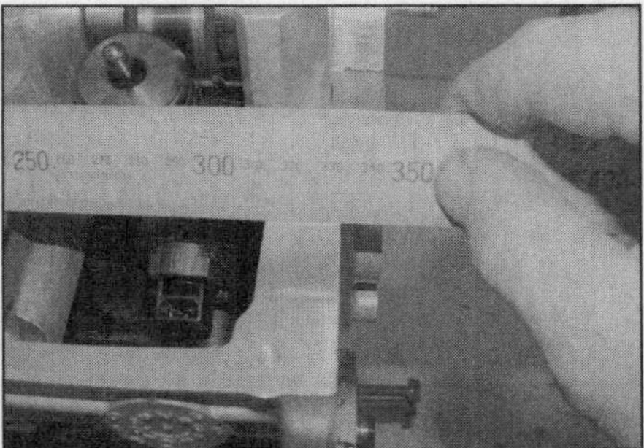

4.27c ...and measure the distance to the rear of the cylinder head

4.30 Attach a DTI (Dial Test Indicator) gauge to the cylinder head upper surface, and position the DTI probe against the top of the adjustment screw

29 Smear some grease (VW No G000 100) onto the contact face of each rocker arm adjustment screw, and refit the rocker shaft assembly to the camshaft bearing caps, tightening the retaining bolts as follows. Starting from the inside out, hand-tighten the bolts. Again, from the inside out, tighten the bolts to the Stage 1 torque setting. Finally, from the inside out, tighten the bolts to the Stage 2 angle tightening setting.

30 The following procedure is only necessary if an injector has been removed and refitted/ renewed. Attach a DTI (Dial Test Indicator) gauge to the cylinder head upper surface, and position the DTI probe against the top of the adjustment screw **(see illustration)**. Turn the crankshaft until the rocker arm roller is on the highest point of its corresponding camshaft lobe, and the adjustment screw is at its lowest. Once this position has been established, remove the DTI gauge, screw the adjustment screw in until firm resistance is felt, and the injector spring cannot be compressed further. Turn the adjustment screw **anti-clockwise** 180°, and tighten the locknut to the specified torque. Repeat this procedure for any other injectors that have been refitted.

31 Reconnect the wiring plug to the injector.

32 Refit the camshaft cover and upper timing belt cover, as described in Chapter 2E.

33 Bleed the fuel system as described in Section 10.

Engine codes (16-valve) AZV, BKD, BMN

34 Prior to refitting the injectors, the O-ring and heat insulation washer must be renewed. Due to the high injection pressures, it is essential that the O-ring is fitted without being twisted. VW recommend the use of a special assembly sleeve to install the O-ring squarely. It may be prudent to entrust O-ring renewal to a VW dealer or suitably-equipped injection specialist, rather than risk subsequent leaks. In addition, VW recommend that the adjustment screws, and the ball-pins (located on the tops of the injectors) are renewed.

35 Smear clean engine oil onto the O-ring, and push the injector together with the heat shield evenly down into the cylinder head onto its stop. It is absolutely important that the injector is inserted fully at this stage, as subsequent tightening of the mounting bolts may otherwise cause damage. VW technicians use a special lever to press the injectors fully into the head.

36 Insert the mounting bolts and tighten in the three stages given in the Specifications.

37 Smear some grease (VW No G000 100) onto the contact face of each rocker arm adjustment screw, and refit the rocker shaft assembly, tightening the retaining bolts as follows. Starting from the inside out, hand-tighten the bolts. Again, from the inside out, tighten the bolts to the Stage 1 torque setting. Finally, from the inside out, tighten the bolts to the Stage 2 angle tightening setting.

38 The following procedure is only necessary if an injector has been removed and refitted/ renewed. Attach a DTI (Dial Test Indicator) gauge to the cylinder head upper surface, and position the DTI probe against the top of the adjustment screw. Turn the crankshaft until the rocker arm roller is on the highest point of its corresponding camshaft lobe, and the adjustment screw is at its lowest. Once this position has been established, remove the DTI gauge, screw the adjustment screw in until firm resistance is felt, and the injector spring cannot be compressed further. Turn the adjustment screw **anti-clockwise** 180°, and tighten the locknut to the specified torque. Repeat this procedure for any other injectors that have been refitted.

39 Reconnect the wiring plug to the injector.

40 Refit the camshaft cover and upper timing belt cover, as described in Chapter 2E.

41 Bleed the fuel system as described in Section 10.

Engine codes CBDA and CBDB

42 Ensure the area around the injector locations in the cylinder head are clean and free from debris. Use a vacuum cleaner if available. Clean any carbon deposits from the injector and sealing surfaces with a cloth soaked in clean engine oil or rust-releasing spray.

43 If new cover plates are to be fitted, slide them on now **(see illustration)**.

44 To remove the copper seal, spray rust-releasing spray around the injector nozzle, then clamp the seal in a vice, and use a twisting motion to pull the injector from the seal. Push the new copper seal into place **(see illustration)**.

45 Apply a little clean engine oil to the return pipe connection on the injector, and fit the new O-ring **(see illustration)**.

46 To renew the main injector O-ring seal, VW specify the use of tool no. T10377. This

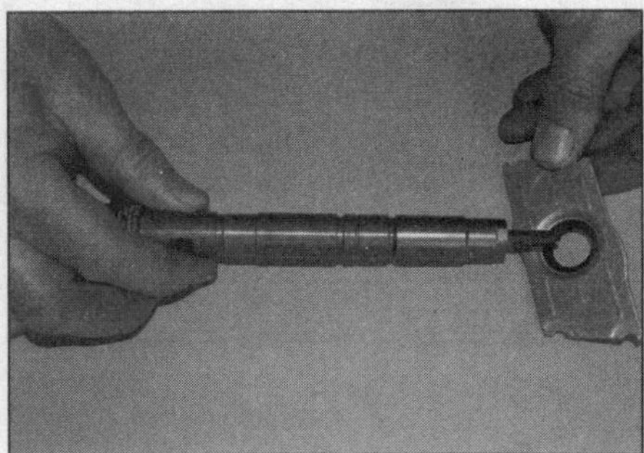

4.43 Slide the new cover plate onto the injector

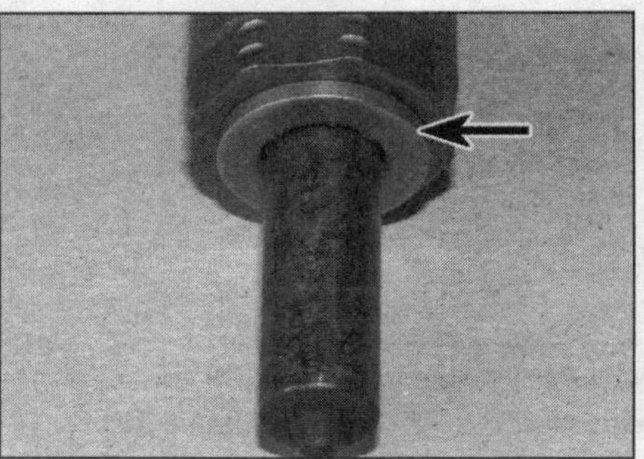

4.44 Push the new copper seal (arrowed) into place

4.45 Fit the new return pipe O-ring (arrowed) to the top of the injector

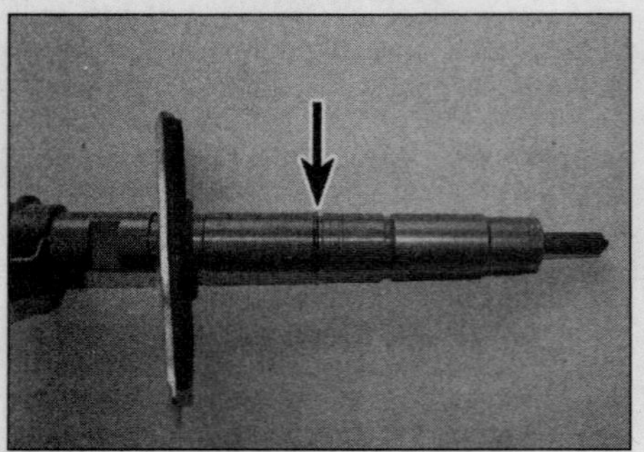
4.46 Fit a new main O-ring (arrowed) without twisting it

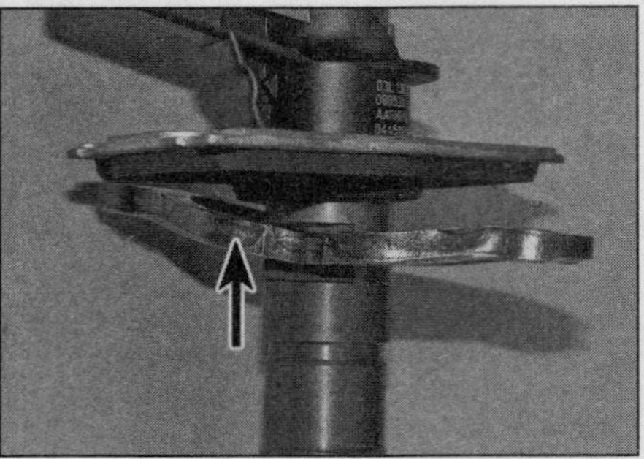
4.47 Slide the new clamping piece (arrowed) onto the injector

tool allows the O-ring to slide over the end of the injector without twisting. With care, the seals can be fitted without the tool **(see illustration)**.

47 Slide the new clamping piece onto injector as shown **(see illustration)**.

48 Apply a smear of clean engine oil to the main O-ring seal, and insert the injector into place in the cylinder head. Note that if the original injectors are being refitted, they must go into their original positions. Tighten the injector clamping piece retaining nuts to the specified torque.

49 Rotate the cover back to position and tighten the retaining bolt to the specified torque.

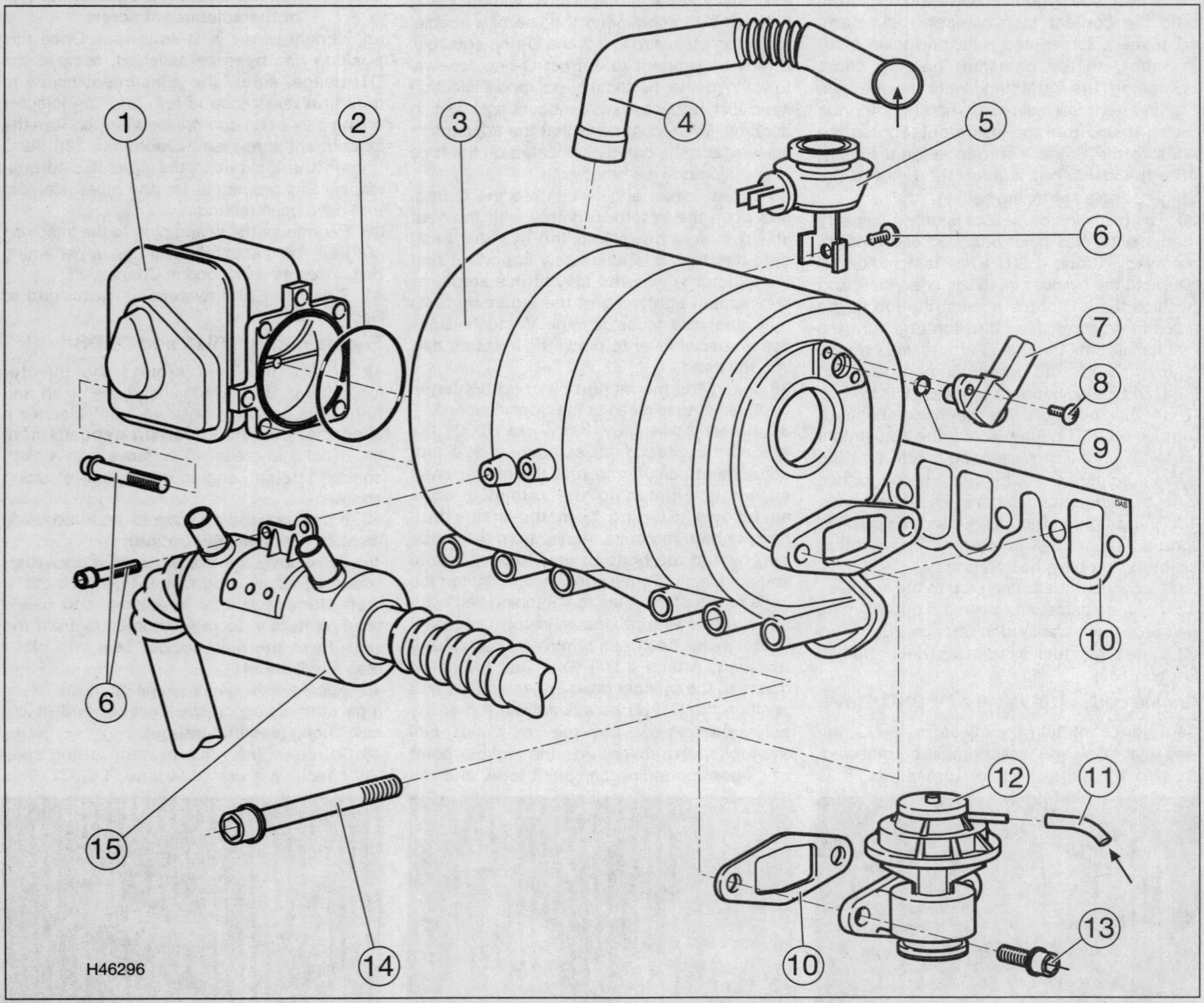

5.1a Inlet manifold details – non-turbo engine code BDK

1 Inlet manifold flap motor
2 O-ring seal
3 Inlet manifold
4 Crankcase ventilation hose
5 Bracket
6 Bolt
7 Inlet air temperature sensor
8 Screw
9 O-ring seal
10 Gasket
11 Vacuum hose
12 EGR valve
13 Bolt
14 Bolt
15 EGR gas cooler

50 Refit the high-pressure fuel pipes and tighten the unions to the specified torque. Note that the pipes may be re-used providing the tapered seats are undamaged, the pipes are not deformed, constricted or corroded.

51 The remainder of refitting is a reversal of removal, noting the following:

a) If one or more injectors have been renewed, the 'injector delivery calibration values' and 'injector voltage calibration values' must be entered into the ECM using VW diagnostic equipment (VAS 5051). Entrust this task to a VW dealer or suitably equipped specialist.

b) After completion of the work, the fuel system must be bled as described in Section 10.

5 Inlet manifold – removal and refitting

Engine codes BDK, BJB, BKC, BRU, BLS, BXE, BXF and BMM

Removal

1 With the exception of engine code BDK, a conventional inlet manifold is fitted to the rear of the cylinder head. Engine code BDK has a cylindrical-type inlet manifold, with a manifold flap motor bolted to its left-hand end, and an EGR valve bolted to its right-hand end. First, remove the engine top cover **(see illustrations)**.

2 Where not integral with the inlet manifold, remove the flap motor and EGR valve with reference to Section 3 of this Chapter, and to Chapter 4D.

3 On engine code BDK, disconnect the crankcase breather pipe, and also unbolt the EGR cooler from the rear of the manifold.

4 Where applicable, remove the heat shield from the manifold, then unscrew the mounting bolts and remove the inlet manifold from the cylinder head. Recover the gasket and discard, as a new one must be used on refitting **(see illustration)**.

Refitting

5 Refitting is a reversal of removal, using new manifold, EGR pipe and manifold flap assembly gaskets/O-rings. Tighten the mounting bolts to the specified torque.

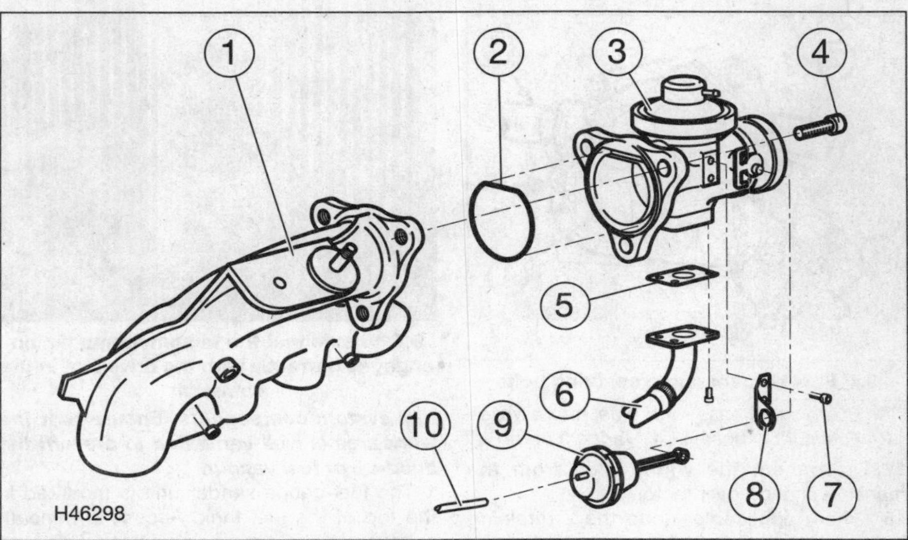

5.1b Inlet manifold details – turbo engines

1 *Inlet manifold*
2 *O-ring seal*
3 *Combined EGR valve and flap housing*
4 *Screw*
5 *Gasket*
6 *EGR pipe*
7 *Screw*
8 *Bracket*
9 *Vacuum actuator (engine code BJB) – electric on other engines*
10 *Vacuum hose to solenoid (engine code BJB)*

Engine codes AZV, BKD and BMN

Removal

6 A conventional inlet manifold is fitted to the rear of the cylinder head, however, on engine code BMN, a vacuum-operated valve controls two interior channels, one of which has an optimised routing for improved air swirl (this manifold has 8 ports). First, remove the engine top cover.

7 Remove the flap motor/housing and EGR valve with reference to Section 3 of this Chapter, and to Chapter 4D.

8 On engine code BMN, disconnect and unbolt the swirl control vacuum unit from the left-hand end of the inlet manifold.

9 Unbolt the support bracket(s) and cable holder.

10 Unscrew the mounting bolts and remove the inlet manifold from the cylinder head. Recover the gasket and discard, as a new one must be used on refitting.

Refitting

11 Refitting is a reversal of removal, using new manifold, EGR pipe and manifold flap assembly gaskets/O-rings. Tighten the mounting bolts to the specified torque.

Engine codes CBDA and CBDB

Removal

12 Remove the intake manifold flap housing and motor as described in Section 3 of this Chapter.

13 Using thin, long-nosed pliers, carefully pull the wiring plugs from the top of the glow plugs **(see illustration)**.

14 With reference to Section 4, disconnect the fuel return pipes from the injectors, fuel rail, and high-pressure pump.

15 Undo the retaining nut and remove the fuel return pipe **(see illustration)**.

16 Undo the unions and disconnect the high-pressure fuel pipe between the pump and fuel rail.

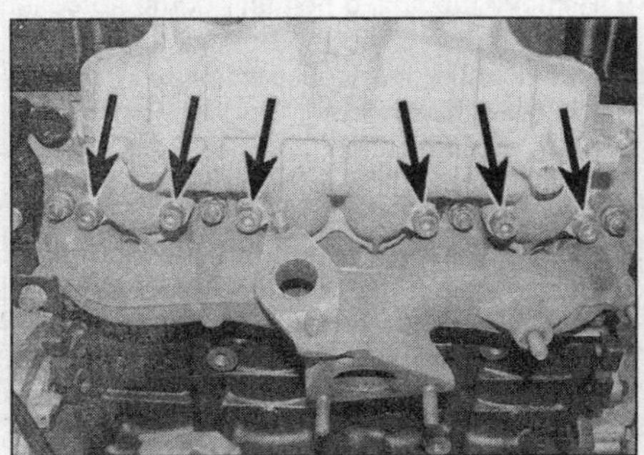

5.4 Unscrew the inlet manifold mounting bolts – engine code BJB

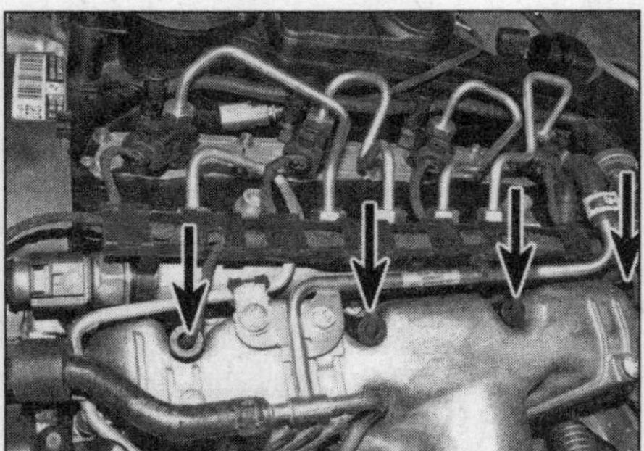

5.13 Pull the wiring plugs from the glow plugs

5.15 Fuel return pipe nut (arrowed)

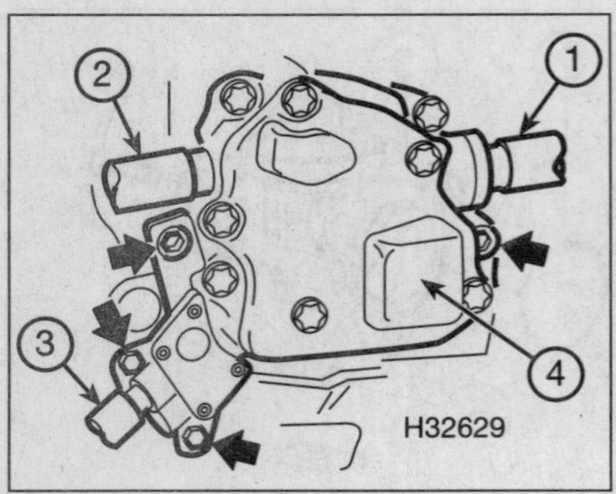

9.4 Fuel tandem pump securing bolts

1 Brake servo hose
2 Fuel supply hose
3 Fuel return hose
4 Tandem pump

17 Disconnect the wiring plug from the manifold change-over motor.

18 Where applicable, undo the 2 retaining bolts and pull the engine oil level dipstick guide tube upwards from place.

19 Undo the retaining bolts and manoeuvre the manifold from position.

Refitting

20 Refitting is a reversal of removal, using new manifold bolts, seals, EGR pipe and manifold flap assembly gaskets. Remember to renew any self-locking nuts.

6 Fuel filter – renewal

Note: *Observe the precautions in Section 1 before working on any component in the fuel system.*

Refer to Chapter 1B.

7 Fuel gauge sender unit – removal and refitting

Note: *Observe the precautions in Section 1 before working on any component in the fuel system.*

Warning: Avoid direct skin contact with fuel – wear protective clothing and gloves when handling fuel system components. Ensure that the work area is well-ventilated to prevent the build-up of fuel vapour.

9.7 Ensure that the tandem pump pinion engages correctly with the drive slot in the camshaft

1 The fuel gauge sender unit is mounted in the top of the fuel tank. Access is beneath a cover in the load space floor. The unit protrudes into the fuel tank, and its removal involves exposing the contents of the tank to the atmosphere.

2 Refer to the procedures in Chapter 4A for removal and refitting procedures.

8 Fuel tank – removal and refitting

Note: *Observe the precautions in Section 1 before working on any component in the fuel system.*

1 Refer to the procedures in Chapter 4A. There is no breather pipe to disconnect at the front of the tank – instead, the fuel supply pipe (coloured black) should be disconnected, along with the return pipe (coloured blue).

9 Fuel pump – removal and refitting

Tandem fuel pump (PD unit injection engines only)

Note: *Disconnecting the central connector for the unit injectors may cause a fault code to be logged by the engine management ECU. This code can only be erased by a VW dealer or suitably-equipped specialist.*

Removal

1 The tandem fuel pump is located on the left-hand end of the cylinder head. It is effectively a vacuum pump (for the braking system) and a fuel lift pump (for the fuel injection system). First, remove the engine top cover.

2 Disconnect the fuel supply hose (marked white) and the return hose (marked blue) from the fuel filter and drain all fuel from the hoses into a suitable container.

3 Remove the air cleaner assembly together with the air mass meter and air ducting, with reference to Section 2.

4 Release the retaining clip (where fitted) and disconnect the brake servo pipe from the tandem pump **(see illustration)**.

5 Disconnect the fuel supply hose (marked white) and the return hose (marked blue) from the tandem pump.

6 Unscrew the four retaining bolts and remove the tandem pump from the cylinder head. Recover the gasket and discard, as a new one must be used on refitting. There are no serviceable parts within the tandem pump. If the pump is faulty, it must be renewed.

Refitting

7 Refitting is a reversal of removal, but use a new gasket and tighten the mounting bolts to the specified torque. Ensure the pump pinion engages correctly with the drive slot in the camshaft **(see illustration)**. It is recommended that the tandem pump is primed with fuel as follows. Disconnect the fuel filter return hose (marked blue), and connect the hose to a hand vacuum pump. Operate the vacuum pump until fuel comes out of the return hose. Take care not to suck any fuel into the vacuum pump. Reconnect the return hose to the fuel filter.

8 Have the engine management ECU's fault memory interrogated and erased by a VW dealer or suitably-equipped specialist.

High-pressure fuel pump (common rail injection engines only)

Removal

9 Remove the timing belt and pump sprocket as described in Chapter 2B.

10 Disconnect the fuel supply hose from the pump **(see illustration)**. Plug all openings to prevent contamination.

11 Disconnect the wiring plug from the sensor on the pump.

12 Undo the bolts securing the pump-to-common rail high-pressure pipe support brackets **(see illustration)**.

13 Pulling only under the ridge at the top of the connectors, disconnect the glow plug wiring connectors. **Note:** *Take care not to damage the connectors or wiring, as the glow plug wiring loom/connectors are only available as a complete assembly.*

9.10 Release the clip (arrowed) and disconnect the fuel supply hose

9.12 High-pressure pipe support bracket bolts (arrowed)

14 Undo the bolts securing the coolant pipe to the intake manifold, and position the pipe to one side.

15 Disconnect the fuel return pipes from the pump and the common fuel rail **(see illustration)**.

16 Undo the unions and disconnect the high-pressure fuel pipe between the pump and common fuel rail.

17 Counterhold the pump hub using VW tool No. T10051, and undo the pump hub nut. In the absence of this special tool, counterhold the hub using a suitable C-spanner **(see illustration)**.

18 Using a suitable two-legged puller and two 8 mm bolts, remove the hub from the pump shaft **(see illustrations)**.

19 Undo the 3 retaining bolts and remove the pump.

Refitting

20 Refitting is a reversal of removal, noting the following points:

a) *Ensure all fuel pipes/hose connections are clean and free from debris.*
b) *The high-pressure fuel pipe from the pump to the common rail maybe re-used providing it's not been damaged.*
c) *Tighten all fasteners to their specified torque where given.*
d) *Fill the pump with clean fuel through the fuel supply pipe aperture prior to starting* **(see illustration)**.
e) *Bleed the fuel system as described in Section 10.*

Supplementary fuel pump (common rail injection engines only)

Removal

21 Disconnect the wiring plug from the exhaust gas pressure sensor, then undo the retaining bolt and move the sensor and bracket to one side **(see illustration)**.

22 Undo the retaining bolts and lift the supplementary fuel pump upwards to access the fuel pipes and wiring plug.

23 Release the fuel hoses from the retaining clips, and disconnect the fuel pump wiring plug.

24 Release the clamps and disconnect the fuel supply pipe from the fuel filter. Plug/cover the openings to prevent contamination.

25 Disconnect the fuel temperature sensor wiring plug, release the clamp and disconnect the fuel supply pipe from the high-pressure fuel pump. Plug/cover the openings to prevent contamination.

Refitting

26 Refitting is a reversal of removal, noting the following points:

a) *Ensure the hoses are not kinked.*
b) *Ensure all connections are clean and free from debris.*
c) *Note the hose connections: The return hose is blue (or blue markings), and the supply hose is white.*
d) *Bleed the system as described in Section 10.*

9.15 Fuel pump return hose (arrowed)

9.17 Counterhold the pump hub with a C-spanner, and undo the nut

9.18a Use a two-legged puller and 8 mm bolts to pull the hub from the pump shaft

9.18b Note the locating peg (arrowed) in the pump shaft

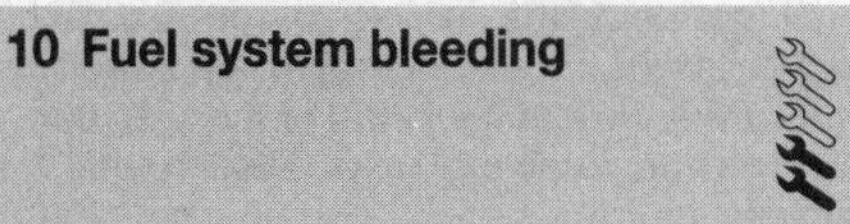

10 Fuel system bleeding

1.9 and 2.0 litre PD Unit injector engines

1 Attach a hand-held vacuum pump to the return outlet (coloured blue) from the tandem fuel pump, and operate the pump until a steady stream of fuel appears from the outlet. Start the engine and check for leaks.

2.0 litre Common rail engines

2 Prime the high pressure fuel pump by filling it with clean diesel through the fuel supply aperture **(see illustration 9.20)**, then operate the starter for shorts bursts (no more than 10 seconds at a time) until the engine starts. Operate the engine at a fast idle (approx 2000 rpm) for several minutes before allowing it to return to its normal idle speed.

3 If the engine fails to start, it must be filled/bled using VW diagnostic equipment (VAS5051 etc.). Using this equipment operates the electric fuel pumps for 3 minutes.

4 Once the engine has been started, test drive the vehicle over a distance of at least 15 miles with at least one period of full acceleration. If there is any air left in the fuel system, the engine management ECM may switch to 'limp home' mode, and store a fault code. Have the fault code cleared and road test the vehicle again.

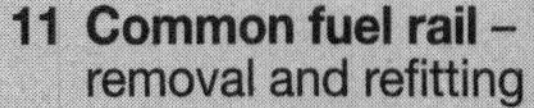

11 Common fuel rail – removal and refitting

Note: *Observe the precautions in Section 1 before working on any component in the fuel system.*

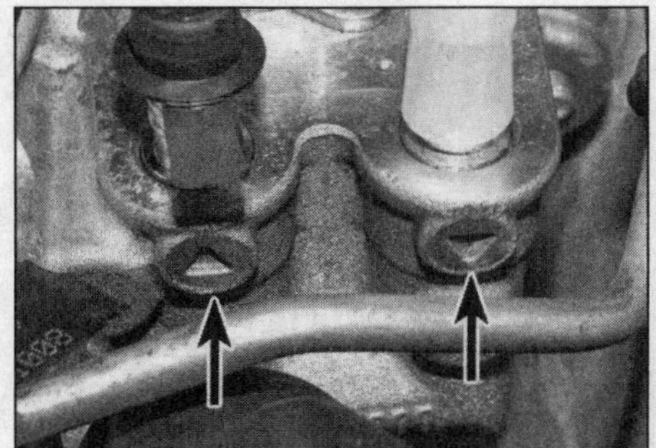

9.20 The triangles adjacent to the pump apertures indicate fuel flow (arrowed)

9.21 Undo the bolt (arrowed) and slide the bracket/sensor forwards

11.6 Remove the high-pressure pipe between the pump and common rail (arrowed)

11.7a Undo the bolts (arrowed) securing the common rail

11.7b Unscrew the pressure sensor...

11.7c ...and pressure regulator

Removal

1 Pull the plastic cover on the top of the engine upwards from its' mountings and remove the foam insulation (where fitted) **(see illustrations 4.16a and 4.16b)** Ensure the area around the fuel rail and pipes is clean and free from debris. If available, use a vacuum cleaner.

2 Disconnect the wiring plugs from the fuel pressure regulating valve, and the fuel pressure sensor at each end of the fuel rail.

3 Undo the retaining bolts, disconnect the coolant return hose from the expansion tank, and move the coolant pipe/hose to one side.

4 Unplug the centre 2 glow plugs, disconnect the fuel return hoses from the high-pressure pump and common fuel rail, then undo the retaining bolts and remove the return fuel manifold from the intake manifold. Plug the openings to prevent contamination.

5 Unclip the wiring loom guide from the common fuel rail, pull the wiring plugs from the top of the remaining glow plugs, and move the wiring guide to one.

6 Undo the unions and remove the high-pressure pipes from the common fuel rail to the injectors and the high-pressure pump **(see illustration)**. Release the pipe from the retaining clips. Plug the openings to prevent contamination.

7 Undo the multi-spline retaining bolts and remove the common rail **(see illustration)**. If required, note their fitted positions, then unscrew the fuel pressure sensor and pressure regulating valve from the common rail **(see illustrations)**. Plug the openings to prevent contamination. **Note:** *VW insist that once removed, the pressure regulating valve cannot be re-used.*

Refitting

8 Where applicable, refit the fuel pressure sensor and the new regulating valve to the common rail, and tighten them to the specified torque. Note that the threads of the sensors must be clean and free from oil and grease.

9 The remainder of refitting is a reversal of removal, noting the following points:

a) *Refit the high-pressure fuel pipes and tighten the unions to the specified torque. Note that the high-pressure fuel pipes may be re-used providing the tapered seats are undamaged, the pipes are not deformed, constricted or corroded.*

b) *After completion of the work, the fuel system must be bled as described in Section 10.*

Chapter 4 Part C: Emission control and exhaust systems – petrol engines

Contents

Degrees of difficulty

Easy, suitable for novice with little experience	**Fairly easy,** suitable for beginner with some experience	**Fairly difficult,** suitable for competent DIY mechanic	**Difficult,** suitable for experienced DIY mechanic	**Very difficult,** suitable for expert DIY or professional

Specifications

Engine codes*

1.4 litre:	
Indirect injection petrol engine	BCA and BUD
Direct injection petrol engine (FSi)	BKG and BLN
Direct injection turbocharged engine (TSi)	CAXA
1.6 litre:	
SOHC petrol engine	BGU, BSE and BSF
DOHC direct injection petrol engine (FSi)	BAG, BLP and BLF
2.0 litre petrol engine:	
Non-turbo	AXW, BLX, BLY, BLR, BVX, BVY and BVZ
Turbo	AXX, BPY and BWA

* **Note:** *See 'Vehicle identification' at the end of this manual for the location of engine code markings.*

Emission control applications

Engine	Application
1.4 litre engine code BCA	One cat in downpipe, one in intermediate pipe, pre-cat oxygen sensor in top of downpipe, after-cat sensor behind cat in intermediate pipe, EGR system with potentiometer control. No EGR system from 2006-on
1.4 litre engine code BUD	One cat in exhaust manifold, one in intermediate pipe, pre-cat oxygen sensor in exhaust manifold, after-cat sensor behind cat in intermediate pipe, no EGR system
1.4 litre engine code BLN	One cat in downpipe, one in intermediate pipe. Pre-cat oxygen sensor in top of downpipe, NOx sensor behind cat in intermediate pipe, gas temperature sensor in front of cat in intermediate pipe, EGR system with potentiometer control
1.4 litre engine code BKG	One cat in downpipe, one in intermediate pipe. Pre-cat oxygen sensor in top of downpipe, after-cat sensor behind cat in intermediate pipe, gas temperature sensor after primary cat, EGR system with potentiometer control
1.4 litre engine code CAXA	One cat in exhaust manifold, one in intermediate pipe. Pre-cat oxygen sensor in exhaust manifold, after-cat sensor in intermediate pipe. No EGR system.
1.6 litre engine codes BGU, BSE and BSF	One cat in intermediate pipe. Pre-cat oxygen sensor in exhaust manifold, after-cat sensor behind cat in intermediate pipe, EGR system with potentiometer control on engine code BGU, secondary air injection on engine codes BGU and BSE
1.6 litre engine code BAG	One cat in downpipe, one in intermediate pipe. Pre-cat oxygen sensor in top of downpipe, after-cat sensor behind cat in intermediate pipe, gas temperature sensor after primary cat, EGR system with potentiometer control
1.6 litre engine codes BLF and BLP	One cat in downpipe, one in intermediate pipe. Pre-cat oxygen sensor in top of downpipe, NOx sensor behind cat in intermediate pipe, gas temperature sensor in front of cat in intermediate pipe (not BLF), EGR system with potentiometer control
2.0 litre engine codes AXW and BLX	Two cats in double bank exhaust manifold, one NOx storage cat in downpipe, two pre-cat oxygen sensors in double-branch exhaust manifold, two after-cat sensors in double fork downpipe, one NOx sensor behind NOx cat in downpipe, gas temperature sensor in front of cat in downpipe, EGR system with potentiometer control
2.0 litre engine codes BLR, BVX and BVY	Two cats in double bank exhaust manifold, one in downpipe, two pre-cat oxygen sensors in exhaust manifold, two after-cat sensors in double fork downpipe, after-cat sensor behind cat in downpipe, EGR system with potentiometer control
2.0 litre engine codes BLY and BVZ	One cat in downpipe, one pre-cat oxygen sensor in front of cat in downpipe, one after-cat sensor behind cat in downpipe, no EGR system
2.0 litre engine codes AXX, BPY and BWA	One cat in downpipe, one pre-cat oxygen sensor in front of cat in downpipe, one after-cat sensor behind cat in downpipe, no EGR system

Torque wrench settings

	Nm	lbf ft
Coolant pipe banjo bolts	35	26
EGR pipe flange bolts to throttle housing	10	7
EGR pipe flange nuts/bolts:		
1.4 litre engine code BCA (to inlet manifold)	7	5
1.4 litre engine codes BKG and BLN:		
To EGR valve	8	6
To cylinder head	18	13
1.6 litre engine codes BGU, BSE and BSF	25	18
1.6 litre engine codes BAG, BLF and BLP:		
To EGR valve	8	6
To cylinder head	18	13
2.0 litre engine codes AXW, BLX, BLR, BVX and BVY:		
To EGR valve	10	7
To exhaust manifold	15	11
To inlet manifold	10	7
EGR pipe mounting bolts:		
1.6 litre engine codes BGU, BSE and BSF	25	18
All other engines	10	7
EGR pipe union nut:		
1.4 litre engine codes BCA and BUD	35	26
1.6 litre engine codes BGU, BSE and BSF	60	44

Torque wrench settings (continued)

	Nm	lbf ft
EGR valve mounting/through-bolts:		
1.4 litre engine codes BCA and BUD	20	15
1.4 litre engine codes BKG, and BLN	10	7
1.6 litre engine codes BAG, BLF and BLP	10	7
2.0 litre engine codes AXW, BLX, BLR, BVX and BVY	25	18
Exhaust clamp nuts	40	30
Exhaust manifold nuts:		
2.0 litre models*	25	18
1.4 litre models	16	12
Exhaust manifold support bracket to engine	25	18
Exhaust manifold-to-downpipe nuts*	40	30
Exhaust mounting bracket nuts and bolts	25	18
Intercooler mounting bolts:		
All except engine code CAXA	10	7
Engine code CAXA	7	3
Oil supply pipe banjo bolts*	30	22
Oil return pipe bolts	8	6
Oxygen sensor	50	37
Secondary air adapter plate mounting bolts	10	7
Secondary air combi-valve mounting bolts	10	7
Secondary air pipe union nuts	25	18
Turbocharger support bracket to engine	25	18
Turbocharger-to-downpipe nuts**	40	30
Turbocharger-to-manifold bolts**	30	22
Turbocharger-to-support bracket bolt	30	22

** Do not re-use*
*** Use thread-locking compound*

1 General information

Emission control systems

All petrol models are designed to use unleaded petrol, and are controlled by engine management systems that are programmed to give the best compromise between driveability, fuel consumption and exhaust emission production. In addition, a number of systems are fitted that help to minimise other harmful emissions. A crankcase emission control system is fitted, which reduces the release of pollutants from the engine's lubrication system, and a catalytic converter is fitted which reduces exhaust gas pollutant. An evaporative loss emission control system is fitted which reduces the release of gaseous hydrocarbons from the fuel tank.

Crankcase emission control

To reduce the emission of unburned hydrocarbons from the crankcase into the atmosphere, the engine is sealed and the blow-by gases and oil vapour are drawn from inside the crankcase, through a wire-mesh oil separator, into the inlet tract to be burned by the engine during normal combustion.

Under conditions of high manifold depression, the gases will be sucked positively out of the crankcase. Under conditions of low manifold depression, the gases are forced out of the crankcase by the (relatively) higher crankcase pressure. If the engine is worn, the raised crankcase pressure (due to increased blow-by) will cause some of the flow to return under all manifold conditions.

Exhaust emission control

To minimise the amount of pollutants which escape into the atmosphere, all petrol models are fitted with one or two catalytic converters in the exhaust system. The fuelling system is of the closed-loop type, in which an oxygen (lambda) sensor in the exhaust system provides the engine management system ECU with constant feedback, enabling the ECU to adjust the air/fuel mixture to optimise combustion.

The oxygen sensor has a built-in heating element, controlled by the ECU through the oxygen sensor relay, to quickly bring the sensor's tip to its optimum operating temperature. The sensor's tip is sensitive to oxygen, and sends a voltage signal to the ECU that varies according to the amount of oxygen in the exhaust gas. If the inlet air/fuel mixture is too rich, the exhaust gases are low in oxygen so the sensor sends a low-voltage signal, the voltage rising as the mixture weakens and the amount of oxygen rises in the exhaust gases. Peak conversion efficiency of all major pollutants occurs if the inlet air/fuel mixture is maintained at the chemically-correct ratio for the complete combustion of petrol of 14.7 parts (by weight) of air to 1 part of fuel (the stoichiometric ratio). The sensor output voltage alters in a large step at this point, the ECU using the signal change as a reference point and correcting the inlet air/fuel mixture accordingly by altering the fuel injector pulse width.

Most models have two sensors, one before and one after the main catalytic converter, however, some models have four sensors, two before and two after the catalytic converter. This enables more efficient monitoring of the exhaust gas, allowing a faster response time. The overall efficiency of the converter itself can also be checked. Details of the oxygen sensor removal and refitting are given in Chapter 4A.

An Exhaust Gas Recirculation (EGR) system is also fitted to some models. This reduces the level of nitrogen oxides produced during combustion by introducing a proportion of the exhaust gas back into the inlet manifold, under certain engine operating conditions, via a plunger valve. The system is controlled electronically by the engine management ECU.

A secondary air system is fitted to 1.6 litre engine codes BGU and BSE, to reduce cold-start emissions when the catalytic converter is still warming-up. The system is an electric air pump, fed with air from the air cleaner, and a system of valves. When the engine is cold, air is pumped into the exhaust manifold, and mixes with the exhaust gas, in order to prolong combustion of any unburnt exhaust gases. The process also helps to bring the catalytic converter to its working temperature more quickly. When the engine coolant temperature is high enough, and the converter is operating normally, the system is switched off by the engine management ECU.

Evaporative emission control

To minimise the escape of unburned hydrocarbons into the atmosphere, an evaporative loss emission control system is fitted to all petrol models. The fuel tank filler cap is sealed and a charcoal canister is

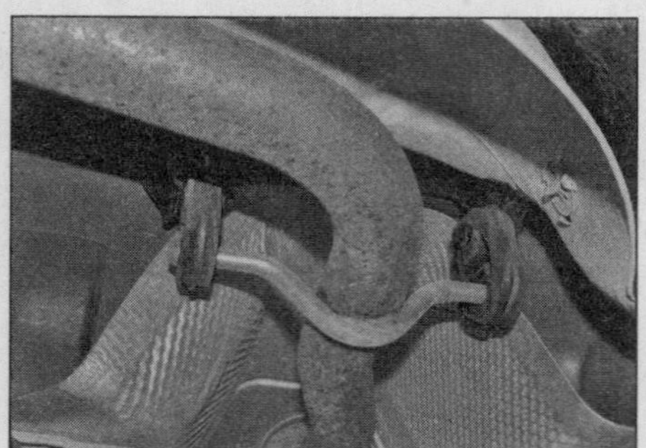

1.12 Rear exhaust pipe mounting on 1.4 litre engine code BCA

mounted underneath the right-hand wing to collect the petrol vapours released from the fuel contained in the fuel tank. It stores them until they can be drawn from the canister (under the control of the fuel injection/ignition system ECU) via the purge valve(s) into the inlet tract, where they are then burned by the engine during normal combustion.

To ensure that the engine runs correctly when it is cold and/or idling and to protect the catalytic converter from the effects of an over-rich mixture, the purge control valve(s) are not opened by the ECU until the engine has warmed-up, and the engine is under load; the valve solenoid is then modulated on and off to allow the stored vapour to pass into the inlet tract.

Exhaust systems

On most models, the exhaust system is the exhaust manifold, front pipe(s), intermediate pipe and silencer, and tailpipe and silencer. The systems fitted differ in detail depending on the engine fitted – for example, in how the catalytic converter is incorporated into the system. On some models the converter is incorporated in the exhaust manifold, while on others it is part of the exhaust front pipe. Where two converters are fitted, an additional exhaust section with catalytic converter is fitted behind the front pipe and catalytic converter. On turbocharged models, the turbocharger is integral with the exhaust manifold, and is driven by the exhaust gases.

The system is supported by various metal brackets screwed to the vehicle floor, with rubber vibration dampers fitted to suppress noise **(see illustration).**

2.2 Charcoal canister location on right-hand inner wing – mounting bolt arrowed

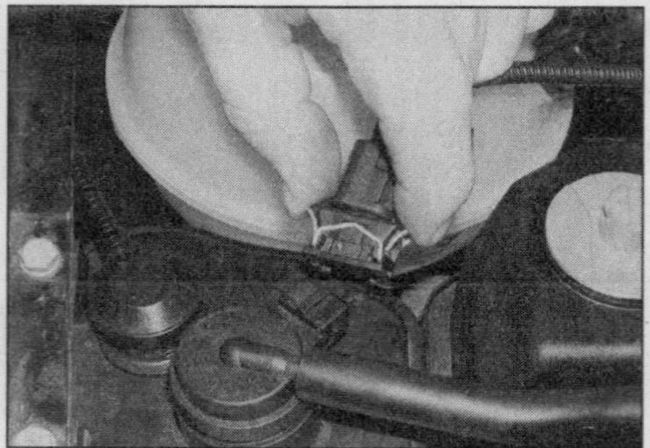

2.3 Disconnect the purge valve wiring connector

2.4a Pull off the larger hose from the purge valve...

2.4b ...if required, the purge valve can be prised out and removed

2 Evaporative loss emission control system – information and component renewal

1 The evaporative loss emission control system consists of the purge valve, the activated charcoal filter canister and a series of connecting vacuum hoses.

2 The purge valve and canister are located on the right-hand side of the engine compartment, in front of the windscreen washer reservoir filler **(see illustration).**

3 Ensure that the ignition is switched off, then unplug the wiring harness from the purge valve at the connector **(see illustration).**

4 Pull off the larger hose (which leads to the throttle housing); if required, the purge valve can now be prised out from the top of the canister. Prise out the round end fitting to which the smaller (tank breather) hose is attached **(see illustrations).**

5 Unscrew the mounting bolt, then lift the charcoal canister out of its lower mounting, noting how it is fitted, and remove it from the engine compartment **(see illustration).**

6 Refitting is a reversal of removal.

3 Crankcase emission system – general information

1 The crankcase emission control system consists of hoses connecting the crankcase to the air cleaner or inlet manifold. Oil separator units are fitted to some petrol engines, usually at the back of the engine **(see illustration).**

2 The system requires no attention other than to check at regular intervals that the hoses, valve and oil separator are free of blockages and in good condition.

2.4c Prise out the tank breather hose end fitting

2.5 Removing the charcoal canister

3.1 Oil separator box on rear of engine (seen with engine removed)

4.2 EGR valve location on engine codes BAG, BKG, BLF, BLN and BLP

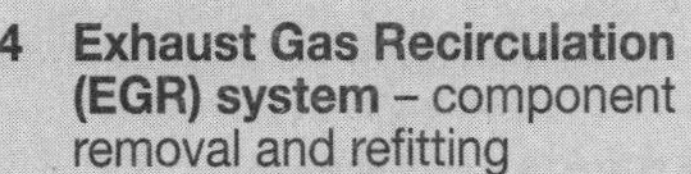

4 Exhaust Gas Recirculation (EGR) system – component removal and refitting

1 The EGR system consists of the EGR valve, the modulator (solenoid) valve and a series of connecting vacuum hoses.

2 The EGR valve is mounted as follows:

a) On engine code BCA, it is located on the left-hand end of the cylinder head with a connecting pipe to the inlet manifold on the rear of the head. Note that engine code BCA is not fitted with an EGR valve from 2006-on.

*b) On engine codes BAG, BKG, BLF, BLN and BLP, it is located on the left-hand end of the cylinder head, on the cover plate for the inlet camshaft **(see illustration)**, with connecting pipes to the inlet manifold on the rear of the head, and to the exhaust ports on the front of the head. The exhaust gases are cooled by coolant from the engine cooling system.*

c) On engine codes BGU, BSE and BSF it is located on the left-hand end of the cylinder head, with connecting hoses from the air cleaner, throttle housing and exhaust manifold.

d) On engine codes AXW, BLX, BLR, BVX and BVY it is located on the right-hand rear of the cylinder head, with connecting pipes to the inlet manifold on the front of the head, and to the exhaust manifold on the rear of the head. The exhaust gases are cooled by coolant from the engine cooling system.

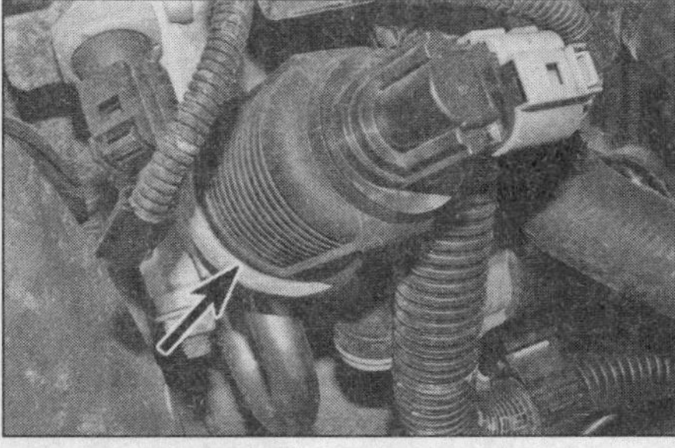

4.5 On engine code BCA, the EGR valve is located on the left-hand end of the cylinder head

3 To improve access, remove the engine top cover. Removal details vary according to model.

EGR valve

1.4 litre engine code BCA (pre-2006)

4 Remove the engine top cover.

5 Disconnect the wiring from the EGR valve located on the left-hand end of the cylinder head **(see illustration)**.

6 Unscrew the two mounting bolts and pull the connecting pipe from the inlet manifold. Recover the O-ring seal.

7 Unscrew the nuts and remove the connecting pipe from the EGR valve. Recover the gasket.

8 Slide the EGR valve from the studs on the cylinder head. Recover the gasket.

9 Refitting is a reversal of removal, but use new gaskets and a new O-ring seal. Tighten the nuts and bolts to the specified torque where given.

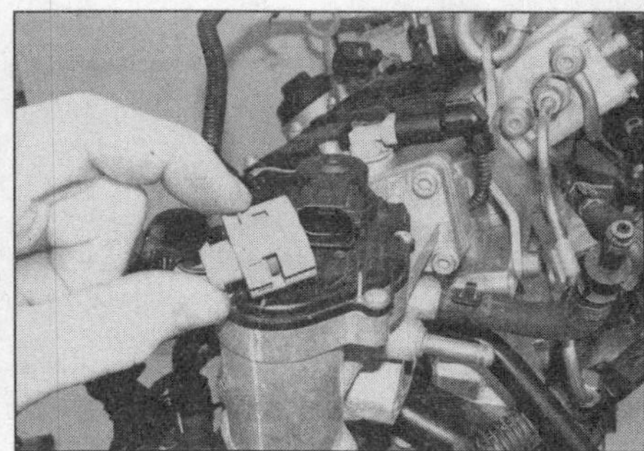

4.11 Disconnect the wiring

1.4 & 1.6 litre engine codes BAG, BKG, BLF, BLN and BLP

10 Remove the engine top cover.

11 Disconnect the wiring from the EGR valve located on the left-hand end of the cylinder head **(see illustration)**.

12 Fit hose clamps to the hoses connected to the EGR valve, then loosen the clips and disconnect them.

13 Unscrew the flange bolts and remove the connecting pipe from the EGR valve and cylinder head. Recover the gaskets **(see illustrations)**.

14 Unscrew the flange bolts and remove the connecting pipe from the EGR valve and inlet manifold. Recover the gasket and O-ring seal **(see illustrations)**.

4.13a Connecting pipe flange on the cylinder head...

4.13b ... and on the EGR valve

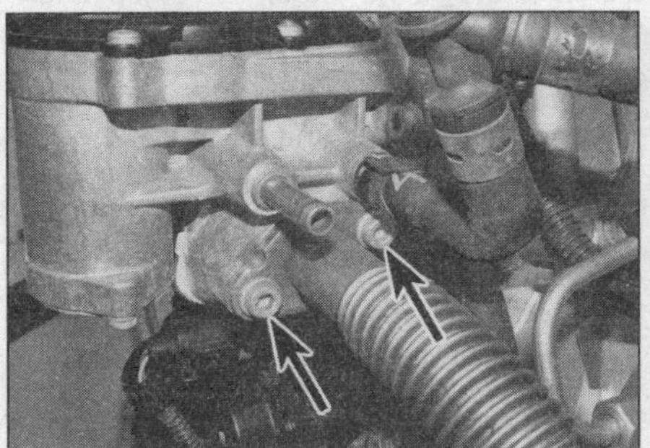

4.14a Unscrew the flange bolts on the EGR valve...

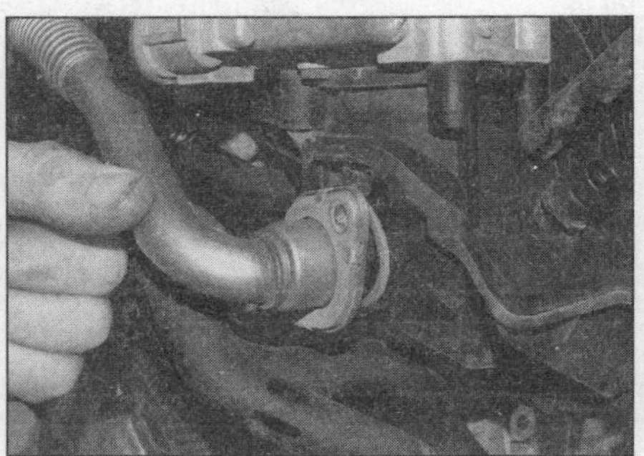

4.14b ... and inlet manifold...

4.14c ... remove the connecting pipe...

4.14d ... and recover the gasket/O-ring seal

15 Unscrew the mounting bolts and remove the EGR valve from the inlet camshaft cover plate on the cylinder head **(see illustration)**. Do not disturb the cover plate.

16 Refitting is a reversal of removal, but use new gaskets and a new O-ring seal. Tighten the bolts to the specified torque where given. Check and if necessary top-up the cooling system.

1.6 litre engine codes BGU, BSE and BSF

17 Remove the engine top cover.

18 Disconnect the air hose and wiring plug from the EGR valve.

19 Unscrew the two nuts from the EGR pipe flange at the EGR valve.

20 Trace the EGR pipework back from the valve, and unscrew the pipe mounting bolt. Unscrew the union nut at the exhaust manifold, and disconnect the EGR pipe from the manifold. Unscrew the two bolts at the throttle housing flange, and separate the joint. Apart from the oxygen sensor wiring harness clipped to it, the EGR pipework is now sufficiently free to move it aside without risking damage.

21 Move the EGR pipe flange at the EGR valve aside, off the two studs; recover the gasket. Slide the EGR valve off the mounting studs, and remove it.

22 Refitting is a reversal of removal. Use new gaskets, and tighten the EGR pipe mountings to the specified torque.

2.0 litre non-turbo

23 Remove the engine top cover.

24 Disconnect the wiring from the EGR valve located on the right-hand rear of the cylinder head.

25 Fit hose clamps to the hoses connected to the EGR valve, then loosen the clips and disconnect them.

26 Unscrew the flange and mounting bolts and disconnect the connecting pipe from the inlet manifold and EGR valve. Recover the O-ring seal and gasket.

27 Unscrew the flange and mounting bolts and disconnect the connecting pipe from the exhaust manifold and EGR valve. Recover the gaskets.

28 Unscrew the mounting bolts and remove the EGR valve from the cylinder head. Note the location of the bracket.

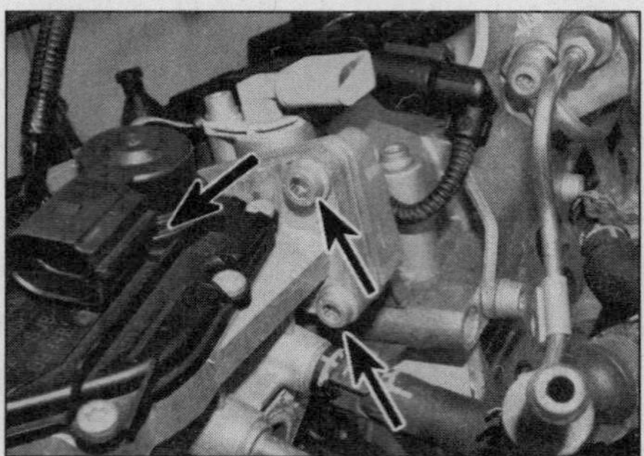

4.15 EGR valve mounting bolts

29 Refitting is a reversal of removal but use new gaskets and a new O-ring seal. Tighten the bolts to the specified torque where given. Check and if necessary top-up the cooling system.

5 Secondary air injection system – information and component renewal

Note: *Secondary air injection is only fitted to 1.6 litre engine codes BGU and BSE.*

1 The secondary air injection system (also known as a 'pulse-air' system) consists of an electrically-operated air pump (fed with air from the air cleaner), a relay for the air pump, a vacuum-operated air supply combi-valve, a solenoid valve to regulate the vacuum supply, and pipework to feed the air into the exhaust manifold. For more information on the principles of operation, refer to Section 1 **(see illustration)**.

Air pump

2 The air pump is mounted on a bracket attached to the lower section of the inlet manifold. To improve access to the pump, remove the engine top cover.

3 Disconnect the air hoses on top of the pump by squeezing together the lugs on the hose end fittings, and pulling the hoses upwards. Recover the O-ring seal from each hose – new seals should be used when refitting. The hoses are of different sizes, and so cannot be refitted incorrectly.

4 Disconnect the wiring plug from the air pump.

5 Unscrew the pump-to-mounting bracket nuts/nuts and bolts (as applicable) and slide the pump out of the mounting bracket.

6 If required, the mounting bracket can be removed from the inlet manifold. The bracket is secured by two bolts and a nut, or by three bolts, depending on model. Where three bolts are used, they are of different lengths, so note their locations.

7 Refitting is a reversal of removal.

Air pump relay

8 The relay is located in the engine compartment fuse and relay box – refer to Chapter 12 for more details.

Air supply combi-valve

9 The combi-valve is mounted on top of the exhaust manifold. To improve access to the valve, remove the engine top cover.

10 Where necessary, loosen and remove the nuts securing the heat shield over the exhaust manifold; this will allow the shield to be moved for access to the combi-valve mounting bolts.

11 Disconnect the vacuum hose and the large-diameter air hose from the valve – the air hose is released by squeezing together the lugs on the hose end fitting.

12 Remove the two valve mounting bolts from below the valve, and lift the valve off its mounting flange. Recover the gasket.

13 Refitting is a reversal of removal. Use a new gasket, and tighten the mounting bolts to the specified torque.

Vacuum solenoid valve

14 The solenoid valve is mounted at the rear of the engine compartment, near the combi-valve.

15 Disconnect the wiring plug and vacuum pipes from the valve – note which ports the pipes are fitted to, to avoid confusion when refitting.

16 Unscrew the bolts, or unclip the valve, and remove it from its mounting bracket.

17 Refitting is a reversal of removal.

Combi-valve adapter elbow

18 The combi-valve is mounted on an adapter elbow, which is screwed onto the exhaust manifold. This elbow can be removed if required (after removing the combi-valve as described above and the EGR valve) by unscrewing the adapter mounting bolts; recover the gasket. When refitting, use a new gasket, and tighten the adapter elbow mounting bolts to the specified torque.

6 Turbocharger – general information, precautions, removal and refitting

Note: *A turbocharger is only fitted to 1.4 litre engine code CAXA, and 2.0 litre engine codes AXX, BPY and BWA.*

General information

1 The turbocharger is integral with the exhaust manifold and cannot be removed separately. Lubrication is provided by an oil supply pipe that runs from the engine oil filter mounting. Oil is returned to the sump through a return pipe that connects to the sump. On 2.0 litre models, the turbocharger unit has a separate wastegate valve and vacuum actuator diaphragm, which is used to control the boost pressure applied to the inlet manifold. On 1.4 litre models, a water-cooled turbocharger is fitted, and the charge pressure is controlled by an electrically operated air recirculation valve.

2 The turbocharger's internal components rotate at a very high speed, and as such are sensitive to contamination; a great deal of damage can be caused by small particles

of dirt, particularly if they strike the delicate turbine blades.

Precautions

The turbocharger operates at extremely high speeds and temperatures. Certain precautions must be observed to avoid premature failure of the turbo, or injury to the operator.

- ***Do not operate the turbo with any parts exposed. Foreign objects falling onto the rotating vanes could cause excessive damage and (if ejected) personal injury.***
- ***Cover the turbocharger air inlet ducts to prevent debris entering, and clean using lint-free cloths only.***
- ***Do not race the engine immediately after start-up, especially if it is cold. Give the oil a few seconds to circulate.***

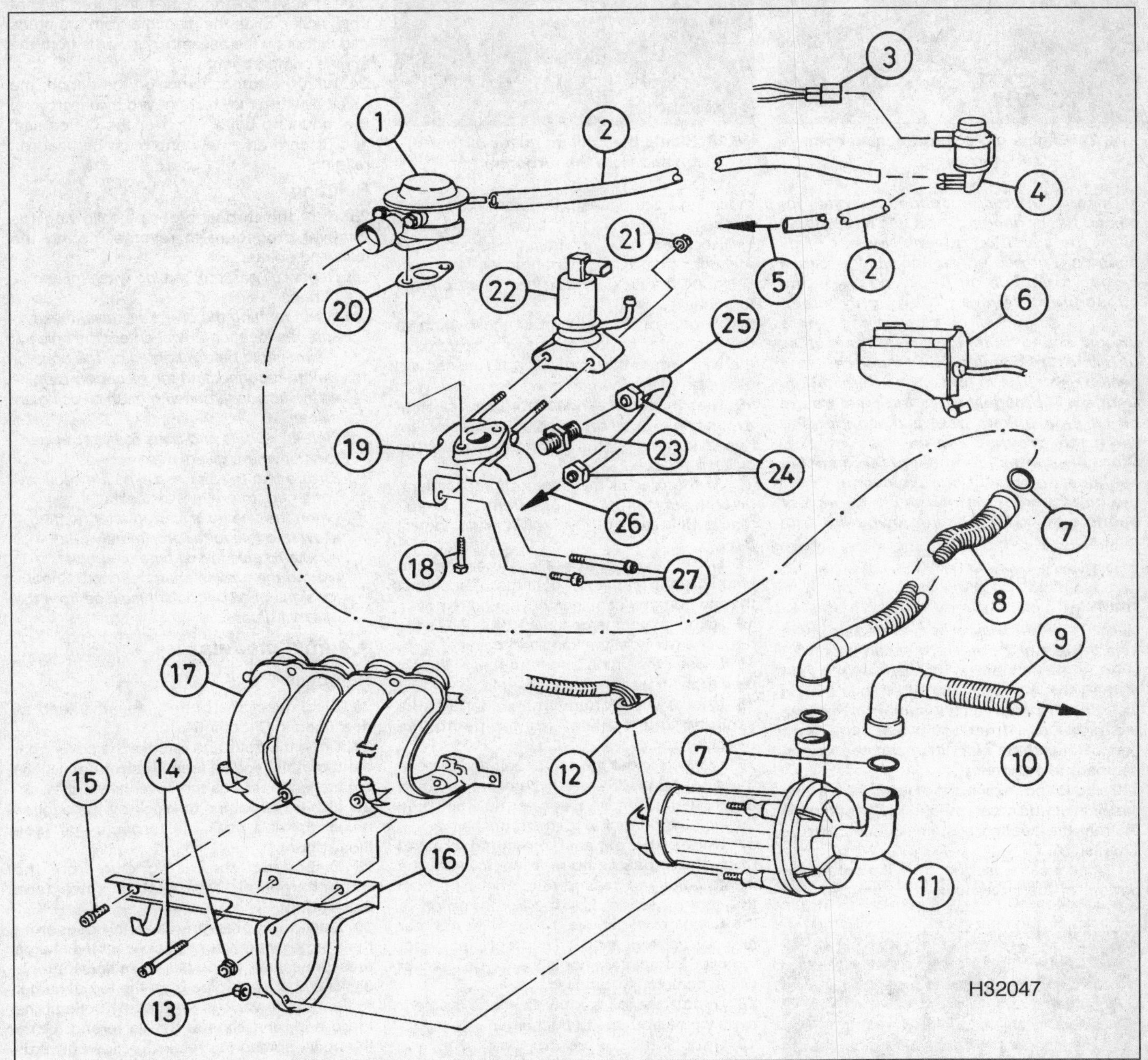

5.1 Secondary air injection system components – 1.6 litre engine codes BGU and BSE

1 Air supply combi-valve
2 Vacuum hose
3 Wiring plug
4 Secondary air inlet valve
5 To connection on brake servo pipe
6 Air pump relay
7 O-ring
8 Pressure hose
9 Inlet hose
10 From air cleaner
11 Secondary air pump
12 Wiring plug
13 Pump mounting nut
14 Mounting bracket bolt
15 Mounting bracket bolt
16 Pump mounting bracket
17 Inlet manifold lower section
18 Adapter plate bolts
19 Adapter plate
20 Gasket
21 Mounting nut
22 EGR valve
23 Union adapter
24 Secondary air pipe union nut
25 Secondary air pipe
26 To union on exhaust manifold
27 Adapter plate bolts

6.27 Engine top cover retaining bolts (arrowed)

6.28 Clamp the coolant hoses (arrowed) to, and from the turbocharger

• *Observe the recommended intervals for oil and filter changing, and use a reputable oil of the specified quality. Neglect of oil changing, or use of inferior oil, can cause carbon formation on the turbo shaft and subsequent failure. Thoroughly clean the area around all oil pipe unions before disconnecting them, to prevent the ingress of dirt. Store dismantled components in a sealed container to prevent contamination.*

Caution: Thoroughly clean the area around all oil pipe unions before disconnecting them, to prevent the ingress of dirt. Store dismantled components in a sealed container to prevent contamination. Cover the turbocharger air inlet ducts to prevent debris entering, and clean using lint-free cloths only.

2.0 litre models

Removal

Note: *The turbocharger is removed upwards from the rear of the engine compartment.*

3 Apply the handbrake, then jack up the front of the vehicle and support it on axle stands (see *Jacking and vehicle support*). Remove the right-hand front roadwheel, the front part of the wheel arch liner, and the engine compartment undertray.

4 Remove the engine top cover/air filter and the air inlet duct as described in Chapter 4A.

5 Drain the cooling system as described in Chapter 1A.

6 Disconnect the air duct from the right-hand bottom of the intercooler, then unscrew the mounting bolts beneath the crankshaft pulley and remove the duct from the turbocharger.

7 Disconnect the wiring from the turbocharger and unbolt the wiring loom bracket.

8 Unbolt the air duct adapter plate from the turbocharger.

9 Disconnect the oxygen sensor wiring at the connector on the bulkhead. Also remove the wiring from the spark plug HT leads, and place the wiring loom to one side.

10 Disconnect the hose from the coolant expansion tank, then disconnect the coolant hoses located at the left-hand end of the cylinder head.

11 At the rear of the engine compartment, disconnect the upper hose from the heater matrix. Unbolt the protective plate and coolant pipe.

12 Unbolt the crankcase breather line and heat shield from the turbocharger, disconnect the line from the camshaft cover and remove.

13 Remove the charcoal canister hose to the turbocharger from the camshaft cover.

14 Loosen the union bolt from the oil supply pipe to the top of the turbocharger.

15 Unscrew and remove the upper nuts securing the exhaust front pipe to the turbocharger.

16 Working under the car, unbolt and remove the right-hand driveshaft heat shield, then unscrew and remove the lower nuts securing the exhaust front pipe to the turbocharger.

17 Unbolt the exhaust mounting bracket from the crossmember, then loosen the clamp bolts and separate the front pipe from the centre section. Pull the front pipe off of the turbocharger, move it slightly to the rear and secure to one side. The front pipe is not removed completely, nor is the oxygen sensor wiring completely removed.

18 Unbolt the oil supply line and coolant supply pipe from the turbocharger.

19 Unbolt the oil return line from the turbocharger.

20 Unbolt the turbocharger support bracket.

21 To provide additional working room, unscrew the bolts securing the rear engine torque arm to the bottom of the transmission, then pull the engine approximately 20 mm to the rear and secure in this position with a ratchet-type strap.

22 As applicable, detach the coolant pipe located on the right-hand side of the engine, near the engine mounting. The retaining nuts only require loosening.

23 Unscrew the nuts securing the turbocharger/exhaust manifold to the cylinder head, noting the location of the coolant pipe bracket on the right-hand stud (where applicable). Slide the manifold from the studs and withdraw the assembly upwards from the engine compartment.

24 With the turbocharger on the bench, the divert air valve may be removed by unscrewing the mounting bolts. Recover the O-ring seal and discard as a new one must be used on refitting.

Refitting

25 Refit the turbocharger by following the removal procedure in reverse, noting the following points:

a) *Renew all gaskets, sealing washers and O-rings.*
b) *When refitting the divert air valve, make sure the location dowel enters the hole in the manifold before tightening the bolts.*
c) *Before reconnecting the oil supply pipe, fill the turbocharger with fresh oil using an oil can.*
d) *Tighten all nuts and bolts to the specified torque, where given.*
e) *Ensure that the air hose clips are securely tightened, to prevent air leaks.*
f) *When the engine is started after refitting, allow it to idle for approximately one minute to give the oil time to circulate around the turbine shaft bearings. Check for signs of oil or coolant leakage from the relevant unions.*

1.4 litre models

Removal

26 Disconnect the battery negative lead as described in Chapter 5A.

27 Undo the bolts and remove the cover from the top of the engine **(see illustration)**. Unclip the coolant hoses as the cover is withdrawn.

28 Use hose clamps to block-off the coolant hoses to, and from the turbocharger **(see illustration)**.

29 Disconnect the wiring plug from the turbocharger air recirculation valve **(see illustration)**.

30 Unclip the pressure/vacuum hoses from the charge air pipe, and disconnect the charge pressure sensor wiring plug **(see illustration)**.

31 The charge air pipe from the turbocharger to the throttle valve is secured by bolts at the turbo end, and clips at the valve end. Undo the bolts, spread the retaining clips outwards slightly, and remove the charge air pipe **(see illustrations)**.

32 Release the clamp and disconnect the air inlet hose from the turbocharger **(see illustration)**.

33 Undo the retaining bolts and remove the turbocharger heat shield **(see illustration)**. Note the bolt on the underside of the heat shield.

6.30 Disconnect the charge air pressure sensor wiring plug (arrowed)

34 Release the clamps and disconnect the turbocharger coolant hoses from the coolant pipes.

35 Undo the retaining bolts and remove the metal coolant pipes from the turbocharger **(see illustration)**.

36 Remove the auxiliary drivebelt as described in Chapter 1A.

37 With reference to Chapter 3, unbolt the air conditioning compressor, and secure it to the lock carrier. **Note:** *There's no need to disconnect the refrigerant pipes.*

38 Undo the nuts securing the catalytic converter to the turbocharger.

39 Unclip the wiring harness, disconnect any wiring plugs from the catalytic converter, then undo the nuts securing it to the exhaust pipe and lower it from place. Renew the seal.

40 Undo the retaining bolts and pull the exhaust manifold heat shield forwards from place.

41 The turbocharger oil supply pipe is secured to the cylinder head by one bolt, the turbocharger by one bolt, and the cylinder block by one banjo bolt. Undo the bolts and remove the oil supply pipe. Discard the seals – new ones must be fitted.

42 Undo the retaining bolt and remove the bracket above the exhaust manifold **(see illustration)**.

43 Undo the bolts securing the oil return pipe to the turbocharger and cylinder block, and remove the pipe. New gaskets will be needed.

44 If the alternator is secured by nuts with inner drive splines, slacken the nuts.

45 Undo the retaining nuts and remove the turbocharger, complete with the exhaust manifold.

Refitting

46 Refit the turbocharger by following the removal procedure in reverse, noting the following points:

a) Renew all gaskets, sealing washers and O-rings.

b) Top up the coolant if necessary.

c) Before reconnecting the oil supply pipe, fill the turbocharger with fresh oil using an oil can.

d) Tighten all nuts and bolts to the specified torque, where given.

e) Ensure that the air hose clips are securely tightened, to prevent air leaks.

f) When the engine is started after refitting, allow it to idle for approximately one minute to give the oil time to circulate around the turbine shaft bearings. Check for signs of oil or coolant leakage from the relevant unions.

7 Intercooler – general information, removal and refitting

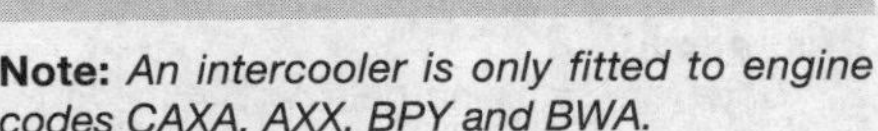

Note: *An intercooler is only fitted to engine codes CAXA, AXX, BPY and BWA.*

1 The intercooler is effectively an 'air radiator', used to cool the pressurised inlet air before it enters the engine.

6.31a Undo the bolts (arrowed)...

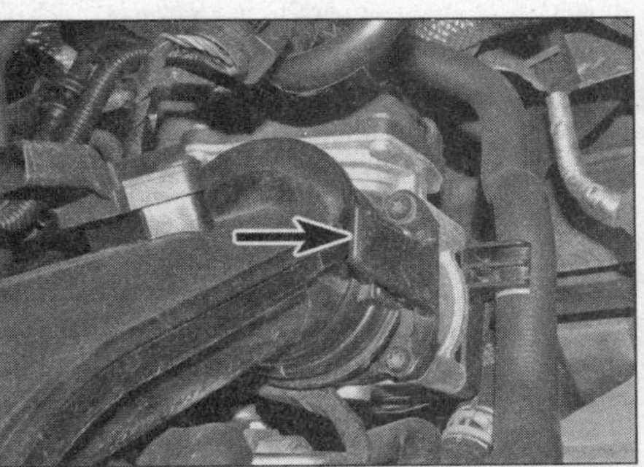

6.31c ...push-out the clip each side (arrowed)...

2 When the turbocharger compresses the inlet air, one side-effect is that the air is heated, causing the air to expand. If the inlet air can be cooled, a greater effective volume of air will be inducted, and the engine will produce more power.

6.32 Release the clamp (arrowed) and disconnect the air inlet hose

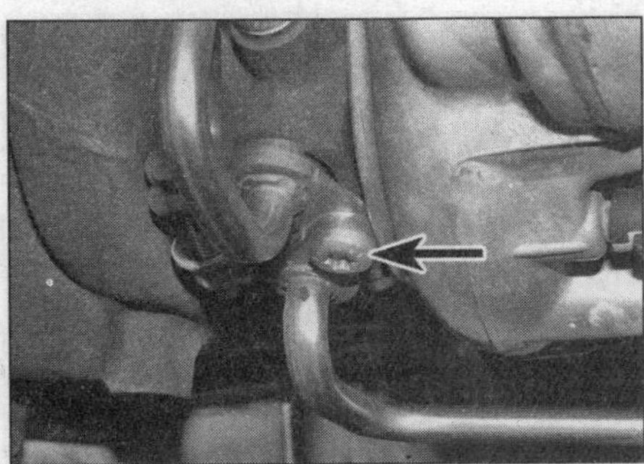

6.35 Coolant pipes retaining bolt (arrowed)

6.31b ...recover the collar...

6.31d ...and remove the charge air pipe

Engine codes AXX, BPY and BWA

3 The compressed air from the turbocharger, which would normally be fed straight into the inlet manifold, is instead ducted around the engine to the base of the intercooler. The

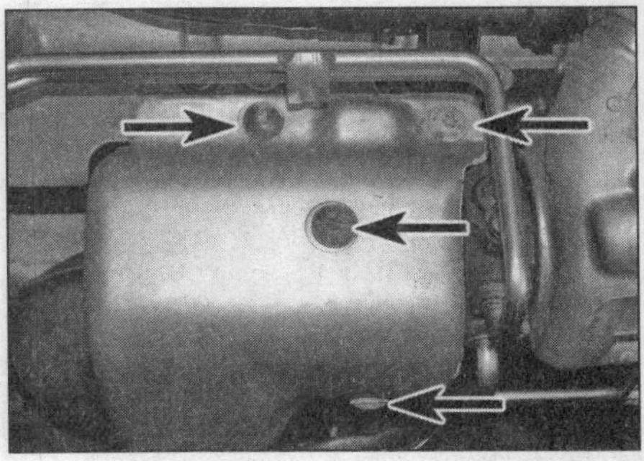

6.33 Turbocharger heat shield bolts (arrowed)

6.42 Undo the bolt (arrowed) and remove the bracket

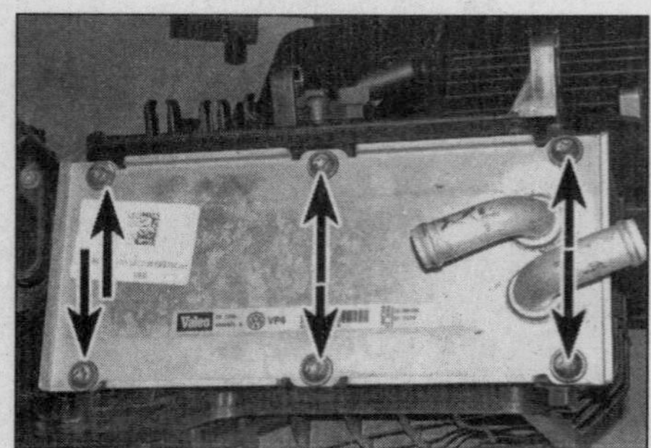

7.9 Intercooler retaining bolts (arrowed) – engine code CAXA

intercooler is mounted at the front of the car, in the airflow. The heated air entering the base of the unit rises upwards, and is cooled by the airflow over the intercooler fins, much as with the radiator. When it reaches the top of the intercooler, the cooled air is then ducted into the throttle housing.

Engine code CAXA

4 On these models, the intercooler is fitted into the inlet manifold, and the temperature of the intake air is controlled by engine coolant flowing through the intercooler galleries.

Removal

Engine codes AXX, BPY and BWA

4 The intercooler is located in front of the radiator on the lock carrier (the crossmember incorporating the headlights and radiator grille). Remove the radiator as described in Chapter 3 for access to the intercooler. This procedure includes moving the lock carrier to its Service position.

5 Release the air ducts from the inlet and outlet elbows at the bottom of the intercooler.

6 Undo the screws securing the upper mounting rubbers to the lock carrier, and lift the intercooler upwards from the lower mountings, taking care not to damage the cooling fins.

7 Examine the mounting rubbers and renew them if necessary. Also, examine the intercooler for any damage, and check the air hoses for splits.

Engine code CAXA

8 Remove the lower part of the inlet manifold as described in Chapter 4A.

9 Working from the ends of the intercooler towards the middle, gradually, evenly, slacken the retaining bolts and pull the intercooler squarely from the manifold **(see illustration)**.

Refitting

Engine codes AXX, BPY and BWA

10 Refitting is a reversal of removal, referring to Chapter 3 when refitting the radiator. Ensure that the air hose clips are securely refitted, to prevent air leaks.

Engine code CAXA

11 Check the condition of the sealing gasket and renew if necessary.

12 Ensure the sealing strip is fitted to the edge of the intercooler, and the sealing gasket is fitted correctly on the inlet manifold.

13 Push the intercooler squarely into the manifold, then gradually and evenly, tighten the retaining bolts to the specified torque.

14 Refit the inlet manifold as described in Chapter 4A.

8 Exhaust manifold – removal and refitting

Note: *This Section only covers removal of the exhaust manifold on non-turbo models. It is integral with the turbocharger on turbo models.*

Removal

1.4 and 1.6 litre engine codes BCA, BUD, BAG, BKG, BLF, BLN and BLP

1 Apply the handbrake, then jack up the front of the vehicle and support it on axle stands (see *Jacking and vehicle support*).

2 The exhaust manifold is located on the front of the cylinder head **(see illustration)**. For access to it, first remove the engine top cover, then move the lock carrier to its Service position as follows, leaving the air conditioning refrigerant lines connected to the compressor:

a) *Remove the front bumper (Chapter 11).*
b) *Disconnect the bonnet release cable over the right-hand headlight (Chapter 11).*
c) *Where necessary, remove the horn (Chapter 12).*
d) *Support the lock carrier, then unscrew the mounting bolts and substitute them with one threaded rod on each side of the car.*
e) *Carefully pull the lock carrier forwards approximately 10 cm to provide access to the front of the engine.*

3 Under the car, unbolt the exhaust front pipe/catalytic converter front mounting from the subframe and from the rear of the engine, then unscrew the nuts securing the front pipe/ catalytic converter flange to the bottom of the exhaust manifold, and lower it until clear of the manifold studs. Recover the gasket **(see illustrations)**. Support the front pipe on an axle stand taking care not to strain the oxygen sensor wiring.

4 Remove the rubber bellows, then unbolt the hot-air shroud from the exhaust manifold, noting the cable guide bracket on the lower bolts **(see illustrations)**.

5 On engine code BUD, disconnect the

8.2 Exhaust manifold location on the front of the engine

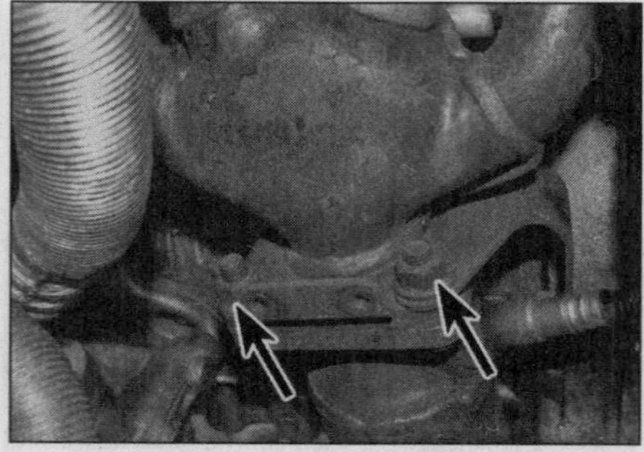

8.3a Catalytic converter-to-manifold mounting nuts

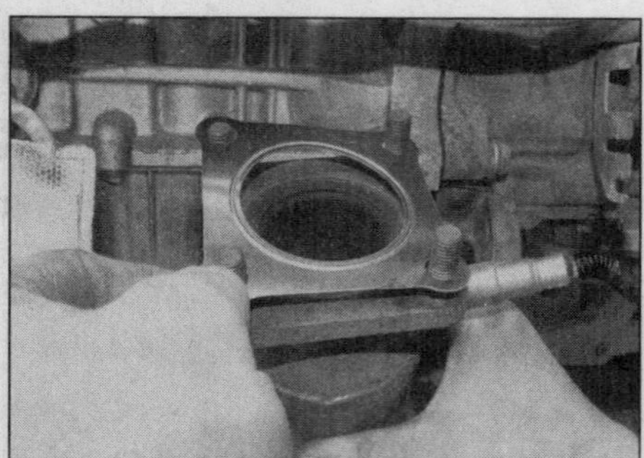

8.3b Recover the gasket located between the exhaust manifold and catalytic converter

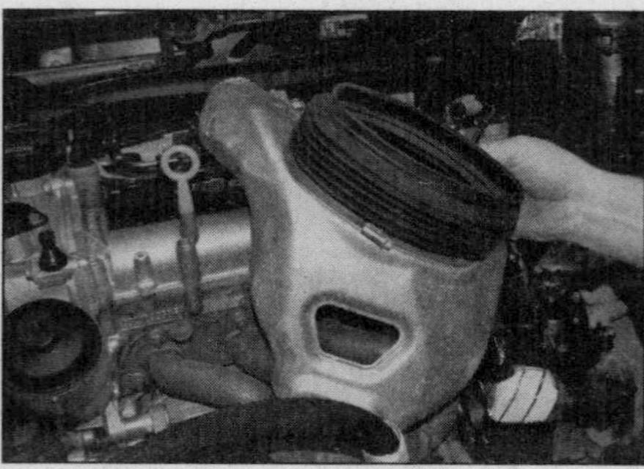

8.4a Removing the hot-air shroud

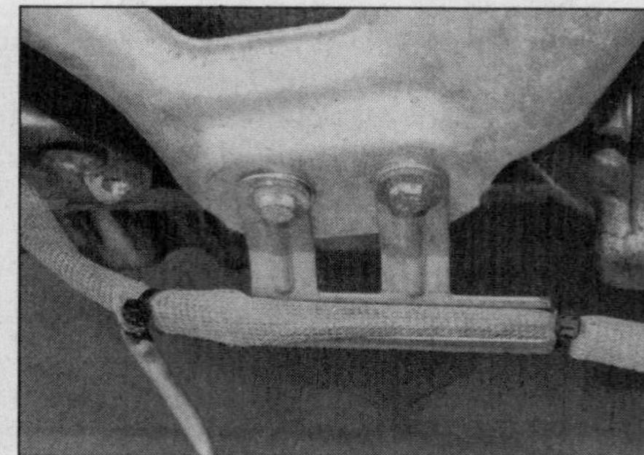

8.4b Cable guide bracket on the shroud lower mounting bolts

wiring from the oxygen sensor located above the catalytic converter on the manifold. Alternatively, remove it completely with reference to Chapter 4A.

6 Unscrew the nuts and withdraw the exhaust manifold from the cylinder head. Discard the nuts as new ones must be used on refitting. Also, recover the gasket and discard **(see illustrations)**.

1.6 litre engine codes BGU, BSE and BSF

7 Remove the engine top cover.

8 Remove the front exhaust pipe together with the catalytic converter as described in Section 9.

9 Remove the inlet manifold as described in Chapter 4A.

10 On the bulkhead at the rear of the engine compartment, disconnect the oxygen sensor wiring at the connector.

11 On engine code BGU, remove the EGR connecting pipe at the rear of the cylinder head.

12 Unscrew the nuts and remove the heat shield from the exhaust manifold, then unscrew the nuts and withdraw the exhaust manifold from the cylinder head. Note the location of the brackets. Recover the gasket and discard, as a new one must be used on refitting.

2.0 litre non-turbo

13 Apply the handbrake, then jack up the front of the vehicle and support it on axle stands (see *Jacking and vehicle support*).

14 Remove the engine top cover.

15 Unscrew the nuts securing the exhaust twin-branch front pipe to the exhaust manifold, then unbolt the exhaust front mounting from the subframe, and the support bracket from the transmission. Lower the front pipe from the manifold and support on an axle stand. Recover the gasket and discard it, as a new one must be used on refitting.

16 At the rear of the engine compartment, disconnect the oxygen sensor wiring on the bulkhead.

17 The EGR valve must now be removed and placed to one side, leaving the coolant hoses still attached. To do this, detach the EGR connecting pipe and release all wiring and hose supports from the valve, then unbolt and remove the valve.

18 Unbolt the heat shield from the exhaust manifold.

19 Unscrew the nuts and withdraw the exhaust manifold from the cylinder head. Discard the nuts as new ones must be used on refitting. Also, recover the gasket and discard.

2.0 litre turbo

20 The exhaust manifold is integral with the turbocharger. Refer to Section 6 for the removal and refitting procedure.

Refitting

21 Refitting is a reversal of the removal procedure, but fit new gaskets and tighten all nuts and bolts to the specified torque where given.

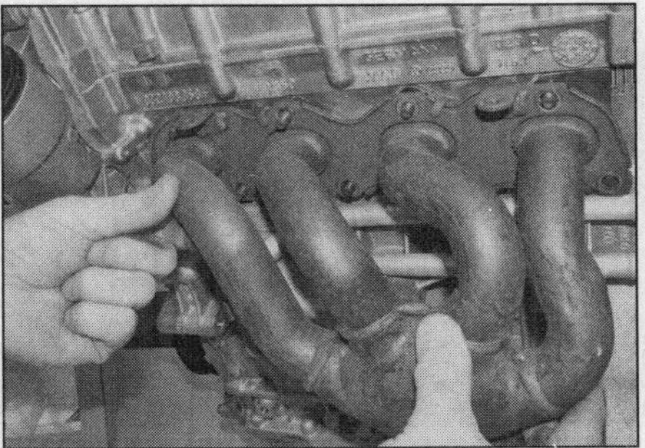

8.6a Unbolt and remove the exhaust manifold...

8.6b ...and recover the gasket

9 Exhaust system – component renewal

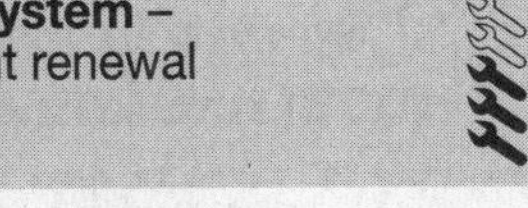

Warning: Allow ample time for the exhaust system to cool before starting work. In particular, note that the catalytic converter runs at very high temperatures. If there is any chance that the system may still be hot, wear suitable gloves. When removing the exhaust sections, take care not to damage the oxygen sensors if they are not removed from their locations.

Removal

1 The original VW system fitted in the factory is in three sections: the front section, the centre section, and the rear section and silencer(s). A catalytic converter is fitted to all models, and is variously located in the exhaust manifold, front pipe, or centre section. Some models have two catalytic converters fitted. On engine codes BCA and BUD, the rear section has a front and rear silencer, however each silencer may be renewed separately by cutting the middle of the pipe and fitting a joining clamp.

2 To remove part of the system, first jack up the front or rear of the car and support it on axle stands (see *Jacking and vehicle support).* Alternatively, position the car over an inspection pit or on car ramps.

Front pipe

Note: *Handle the flexible, braided section of the front pipe carefully, and do not bend it excessively.*

3 Before removing the front section of the exhaust, establish how many oxygen sensors are fitted. Trace the wiring back from each sensor, and disconnect the wiring connector **(see illustration)**.

4 Unclip the oxygen sensor wiring from any clips or brackets, noting how it is routed for refitting.

5 If a new front section is being fitted, unscrew the oxygen sensors from the pipe, as applicable. If two sensors are fitted, note which fits where, as they should not be interchanged.

6 Unscrew the nuts or loosen the clamp at the rear of the pipe **(see illustration)**.

7 Unscrew and remove the nuts securing the front flange to the exhaust manifold or turbocharger. On some models, the shield over the right-hand driveshaft inner CV joint must be removed to improve access. Separate the front joint, and move it down sufficiently to clear the mounting studs.

8 Support the front of the pipe, then detach from the centre section. Where a clamp is fitted, slide the clamp either forwards or backwards to separate the joint. Twist the front pipe slightly from side-to-side, while pulling towards the front to release it from the rear section. When the pipe is free, lower it to the ground and remove it from under the car.

Rear pipe and silencers

9 If the factory-fitted VW rear section is being

9.3 Oxygen sensors and wiring on the catalytic converter

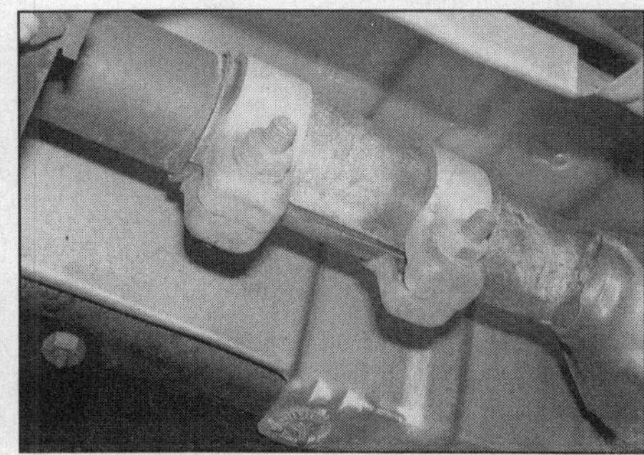

9.6 Exhaust front pipe rear connector (1.6 litre FSi)

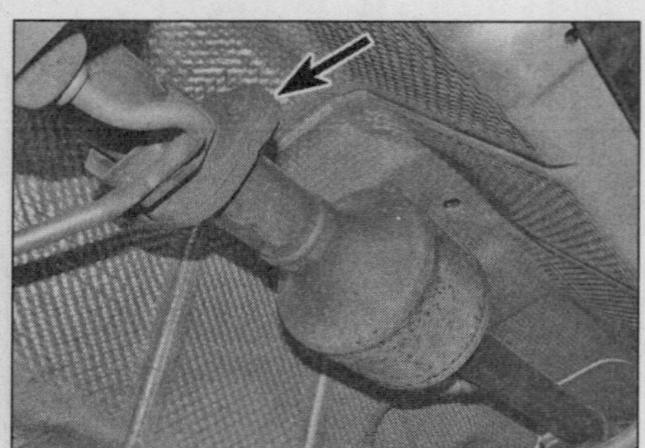

9.11 Front pipe-to-centre pipe flange on 1.4 litre engine code BCA

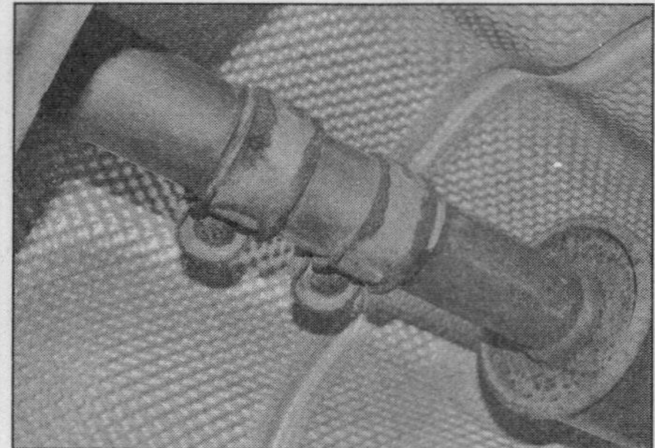

9.12 Clamp between the centre and rear exhaust sections on 1.4 litre engine code BCA

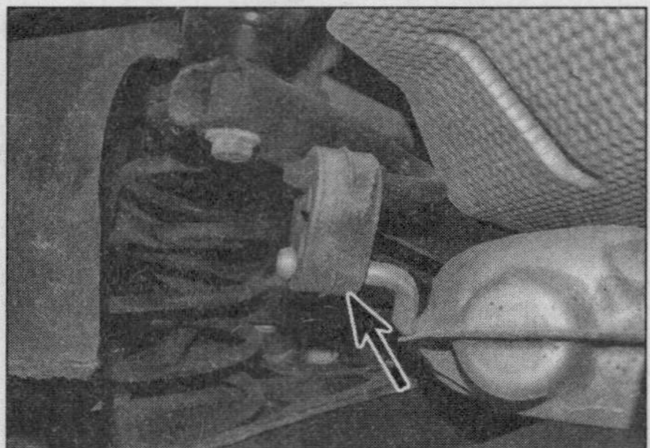

9.13 Exhaust rear silencer mounting rubber (1.6 litre FSi)

worked on, examine the pipe between the two silencers for three pairs of punch marks, or three line markings. The centre marking indicates the point at which to cut the pipe, while the outer marks indicate the position for the ends of the new clamp required when refitting. Cut through the pipe using the centre mark as a guide, making the cut as square to the pipe as possible if either section is to be re-used.

10 If the factory-fitted rear section has already been renewed, loosen the nuts securing the clamp between the silencers so that the clamp can be moved.

Centre silencer

11 To remove the centre silencer, first unbolt the clamp or flange behind the catalyst **(see illustration)**. Where necessary, remove the bolts securing the two mounting brackets to the centre cradle under the car. To improve access, also remove the nuts securing the cradle to the underside of the car, and lower the cradle completely.

12 As necessary, slide the clamps at either end of the silencer section to release the pipe ends, and lower the silencer out of position **(see illustration)**.

Rear silencer

13 Depending on model, the rear silencer is supported either just at the very back, or in front and behind, by a rubber mounting which is bolted to the underside of the car **(see illustration)**. The silencer is attached to these mountings by metal pegs which push into the rubber section of each mounting.

14 Unscrew the bolts, and release the mounting(s) from the underside of the car. On models with two silencer mountings, it may prove sufficient to unbolt only one, and to prise the silencer from the remaining mounting, but for preference, both should be removed.

15 Where applicable, slide the clamp at the front end of the silencer section to release the pipe ends, and lower the silencer out of position.

Refitting

16 Each section is refitted by a reversal of the removal sequence, noting the following points:

a) Ensure that all traces of corrosion have been removed from the flanges or pipe ends, and renew all necessary gaskets.

b) If necessary, renew the clamps, and use the markings on the pipes as a guide to the clamp's correct fitted position.

c) Inspect the mountings for signs of damage or deterioration, and renew as necessary.

d) If using exhaust assembly paste, make sure this is only applied to joints downstream of the catalyst.

e) Prior to tightening the exhaust system mountings and clamps, ensure that all rubber mountings are correctly located and that there is adequate clearance between the exhaust system and vehicle underbody. Try to ensure that no unnecessary twisting stresses are applied to the pipes – move the pipes relative to each other at the clamps to relieve this.

10 Catalytic converter – general information and precautions

1 The catalytic converter is a reliable and simple device which needs no maintenance in itself, but there are some facts of which an owner should be aware if the converter is to function properly for its full service life:

a) DO NOT use leaded or lead-replacement petrol in a car equipped with a catalytic converter – the lead (or other additives) will coat the precious metals, reducing their converting efficiency and will eventually destroy the converter.

b) Always keep the ignition and fuel systems well-maintained in accordance with the manufacturer's schedule (see Chapter 1A).

c) If the engine develops a misfire, do not drive the car at all (or at least as little as possible) until the fault is cured.

d) DO NOT push- or tow-start the car – this will soak the catalytic converter in unburned fuel, causing it to overheat when the engine does start.

e) DO NOT switch off the ignition at high engine speeds – ie, do not 'blip' the throttle immediately before switching off the engine.

f) DO NOT use fuel or engine oil additives – these may contain substances harmful to the catalytic converter.

g) DO NOT continue to use the car if the engine burns oil to the extent of leaving a visible trail of blue smoke.

h) Remember that the catalytic converter operates at very high temperatures. DO NOT, therefore, park the car in dry undergrowth, over long grass or piles of dead leaves after a long run.

i) Remember that the catalytic converter is FRAGILE – do not strike it with tools during servicing work, and take care handling it when removing it from the car for any reason.

j) In some cases, a sulphurous smell (like that of rotten eggs) may be noticed from the exhaust. This is common to many catalytic converter-equipped cars, and has more to do with the sulphur content of the brand of fuel being used than the converter itself.

k) The catalytic converter, used on a well-maintained and well-driven car, should last for between 50 000 and 100 000 miles – if the converter is no longer effective, it must be renewed.

Chapter 4 Part D:
Emission control and exhaust systems – diesel engines

Contents

Degrees of difficulty

Easy, suitable for novice with little experience 	**Fairly easy,** suitable for beginner with some experience	**Fairly difficult,** suitable for competent DIY mechanic	**Difficult,** suitable for experienced DIY mechanic 	**Very difficult,** suitable for expert DIY or professional

Specifications

Engine codes*

1.9 litre, 8-valve, turbo, SOHC	BJB, BKC, BRU, BLS, BXE and BXF
2.0 litre PD unit injection:	
8-valve, non-turbo, SOHC	BDK
8-valve, turbo, SOHC	BMM
16-valve, turbo, DOHC	AZV, BKD and BMN
2.0 litre common rail injection	CBDA, CBDB

* **Note:** *See 'Vehicle identification' at the end of this manual for the location of engine code markings.*

Emission control applications

1.9 litre	One cat in downpipe, EGR system OR Particulate filter/cat in downpipe with oxygen sensor, exhaust gas temperature sensor and exhaust gas pressure sensor, EGR system
2.0 litre:	
Engine code BDK	One cat in exhaust manifold, EGR system
Engine codes AZV, BKD and BMN	One cat in downpipe, EGR system OR Particulate filter/cat in downpipe with oxygen sensor, exhaust gas temperature sensor and exhaust gas pressure sensor, EGR system
Engine codes BMM, CBDA and CBDB	Particulate filter/cat in downpipe with oxygen sensor, exhaust gas temperature sensor and exhaust gas pressure sensor, EGR system

Torque wrench settings

Torque wrench settings	Nm	lbf ft
Cooler to bypass flap housing (2.0 litre)	10	7
EGR pipe nuts/bolts	22	16
EGR valve (non-turbo)	20	15
EGR valve (common rail engines)	8	6
Exhaust clamp nuts	25	18
Exhaust manifold (non-turbo)	25	18
Exhaust manifold-to-downpipe nuts*	25	18
Intercooler mounting bolts	8	6
Turbocharger/exhaust manifold*:		
Engine code BLS	25	18
Except engine code BLS	20	15
Turbocharger oil return pipe flange bolts	17	13
Turbocharger oil return union nut	30	22
Turbocharger oil supply union nut	22	16
Turbocharger-to-downpipe clamp	7	5

* *Do not re-use*

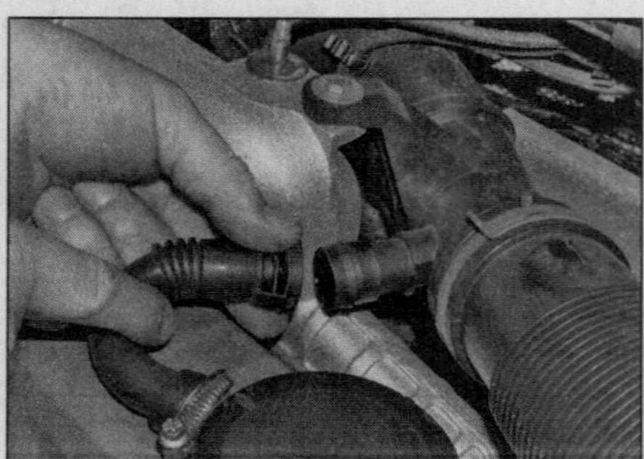

2.1 Disconnecting the pressure-regulating valve breather hose

1 General information

Emission control systems

All diesel-engined models have a crankcase emission control system, and in addition, are fitted with a catalytic converter. All diesel engines are fitted with an Exhaust Gas Recirculation (EGR) system to reduce exhaust emissions.

Crankcase emission control

To reduce the emission of unburned hydrocarbons from the crankcase into the atmosphere, the engine is sealed and the blow-by gases and oil vapour are drawn from inside the crankcase, through a wire mesh oil separator, into the inlet tract to be burned by the engine during normal combustion.

Under conditions of high manifold depression, the gases will be sucked positively out of the crankcase. Under conditions of low manifold depression, the gases are forced out of the crankcase by the (relatively) higher crankcase pressure. If the engine is worn, the raised crankcase pressure (due to increased blow-by) will cause some of the flow to return under all manifold conditions. All diesel engines have a pressure-regulating valve on the camshaft cover, to control the flow of gases from the crankcase.

Exhaust emission control

An oxidation catalyst is fitted in the exhaust system of all diesel-engined models. This has the effect of removing a large proportion of the gaseous hydrocarbons, carbon monoxide and particulates present in the exhaust gas. On some models, a particulate filter is fitted behind the catalytic converter in order to filter out soot particles.

An Exhaust Gas Recirculation (EGR) system is fitted to all diesel-engined models. This reduces the level of nitrogen oxides produced during combustion by introducing a proportion of the exhaust gas back into the inlet manifold under certain engine operating conditions. The system is controlled electronically by the diesel engine management ECU.

Exhaust systems

The exhaust system consists of the exhaust manifold, front pipe with catalytic converter/ particulate filter, intermediate pipe and silencer, and tailpipe and silencer. On turbo models, the turbocharger is integral with the exhaust manifold, and is driven by the exhaust gases.

The system is supported by various metal brackets screwed to the vehicle floor, with rubber vibration dampers fitted to suppress noise.

2 Crankcase emission system – general information

1 The crankcase emission control system consists of hoses connecting the crankcase to the air cleaner or inlet manifold. In addition, on non-turbo engines, a pressure-regulating valve is fitted to the camshaft cover **(see illustration)**.

2 The system requires no attention other than to check at regular intervals that the hoses and pressure-regulating valve are free of blockages and in good condition.

3 Exhaust Gas Recirculation (EGR) system – component removal

1 The EGR system consists of the EGR valve which directs exhaust gas from the exhaust manifold to the inlet manifold, and a control valve which actuates the system according to engine load and speed. On engines with a vacuum-operated EGR system, the control valve is a solenoid valve which opens vacuum from the inlet manifold to the EGR valve actuator when the solenoid is energised by the engine management ECU. Where a recirculation potentiometer is fitted, control of the system is directly from the engine management ECU which activates the control motor.

2 On the non-turbo engine code BDK, the EGR valve is mounted on the right-hand end of the inlet manifold and is connected to the exhaust manifold by a short metal pipe and a gas cooler. The gas cooler uses coolant from the engine cooling system to cool the exhaust gases before passing them to the inlet manifold. The system is activated by a solenoid valve mounted at the rear of the engine compartment.

3 On turbo engines, the EGR valve is located as follows:

a) Engine code BJB – the EGR valve is integral with the inlet manifold flap housing located on the inlet manifold, and is joined to the exhaust manifold by a flanged pipe. A vacuum solenoid control valve is mounted on the engine compartment bulkhead.

*b) Engine codes BKC, BRU, BXE, BXF, AZV, BKD and BMN – the EGR valve is located between the flap housing and inlet manifold, and is joined to the exhaust manifold by a flanged pipe **(see illustration)**. A vacuum solenoid control valve is mounted on the engine compartment bulkhead.*

c) Engine codes BLS and BMM – the EGR valve is integral with a gas recirculation potentiometer located on a housing located between the flap housing and inlet manifold. A flanged pipe connects the housing to the exhaust manifold. A vacuum solenoid control valve is mounted on the engine compartment bulkhead.

d) Engine codes CBDA and CBDB – the EGR valve is integral with a gas recirculation potentiometer located on a housing located between the flap housing and inlet manifold.

3.3 EGR valve location on engine code BKC

3.4a EGR solenoid valve location on non-turbo models ...

3.4b ... and turbo models

EGR vacuum-solenoid valve

Note: *On engine code BDK (non-turbo) the valve has two vacuum hoses attached to it, whereas on all other engines it has six vacuum hoses.*

4 The EGR vacuum-solenoid valve is mounted on the bulkhead at the rear of the engine compartment **(see illustrations)**. Do not confuse the EGR solenoid with the turbo boost pressure solenoid, which is mounted further to the left (left as seen from the driver's seat).

5 Disconnect the wiring plug from the solenoid valve. On some models access can be improved by removing the cover from the engine compartment fusebox.

6 Identify and disconnect the vacuum hoses.

7 Unscrew the solenoid valve mounting bolt, and remove the valve from the bulkhead.

8 Refitting is a reversal of removal. Ensure that the hoses and wiring plug are reconnected securely and correctly.

EGR valve

Engine code BDK

9 Remove the engine top cover.

10 Disconnect the vacuum hose from the port on the EGR valve.

11 Loosen the clamp bolt which secures the valve to the short connecting pipe.

12 Unscrew and remove the two EGR valve mounting bolts.

13 Separate the valve from the inlet manifold, and recover the gasket. Ease the valve upwards out of the clamp and connecting pipe, and remove it.

14 The gas cooler can also be removed if required. Fit hose clamps to the two coolant hoses, then disconnect them from the cooler. Unscrew the clamp on the exhaust manifold, then unbolt the gas cooler from the inlet manifold. Recover the sealing washer.

15 Refitting is a reversal of removal. Use a new gasket and sealing washer, and tighten the bolts to the specified torque.

Engine code BJB

16 The EGR valve is incorporated into the inlet manifold flap motor/housing. Refer to Chapter 4B for the removal and refitting procedures for the combined unit. It is not possible to separate the EGR valve from the flap housing.

Engine codes BKC, BRU, BXE, BXF, AZV, BKD and BMN

17 Remove the inlet manifold flap motor/housing as described in Chapter 4B.

18 Unscrew the bolts and separate the connecting pipe from the bottom of the EGR valve. Recover the gasket and discard it, as a new one must be used on refitting.

19 Remove the EGR valve from the inlet manifold and recover the O-ring seal.

20 Refitting is a reversal of removal, but renew the gasket and O-ring seal.

Engine codes BLS and BMM

21 Remove the engine top cover.

22 Disconnect the wiring from the combined EGR valve and recirculation potentiometer.

23 Unscrew the mounting bolts and remove the EGR valve/potentiometer from the inlet housing. Recover the O-ring seal and discard, as a new one must be used on refitting.

24 To remove the inlet housing, first remove the inlet manifold flap motor/housing as described in Chapter 4B, then remove the EGR valve as described earlier in this sub-Section. Unbolt the connecting pipe and recover the gasket, then unbolt the housing from the inlet manifold. Recover the O-ring seal. Discard the O-ring seal and gasket, as new ones must be used on refitting.

25 Refitting is a reversal of removal, but fit a new gasket and O-ring seals. Note that if the combined EGR valve and potentiometer unit is renewed, after initially switching on the ignition, the ignition must be switched off then on again. Wait one complete minute to allow the control unit to learn the position of the valve, and check that an audible click is heard from the main relay, then switch the ignition off.

Engine codes CBDA and CBDB

26 Remove the inlet manifold throttle valve as described in Chapter 4B.

27 Undo the bolts securing the pipe to the EGR valve **(see illustration)**.

28 Disconnect the EGR valve wiring plug.

29 Undo the bolts and detach the valve from the inlet manifold. Discard the O-ring seal – a new one must be fitted.

30 Refitting is a reversal of removal, using a new EGR valve O-ring seal, and tightening the retaining bolts to the specified torque.

3.27 EGR pipe-to-valve bolts (arrowed)

4 Turbocharger – general information and precautions

General information

A turbocharger is fitted to all engines except engine code BDK, and is integral with the exhaust manifold.

The turbocharger increases engine efficiency by raising the pressure in the inlet manifold above atmospheric pressure. Instead of the air simply being sucked into the cylinders, it is forced in.

Energy for the operation of the turbocharger comes from the exhaust gas. The gas flows through a specially-shaped housing (the turbine housing) and in so doing, spins the turbine wheel. The turbine wheel is attached to a shaft, at the end of which is another vaned wheel, known as the compressor wheel. The compressor wheel spins in its own housing, and compresses the inducted air on the way to the inlet manifold.

Between the turbocharger and the inlet manifold, the compressed air passes through an intercooler (see Section 7 for details). The purpose of the intercooler is to remove from the inducted air some of the heat gained in being compressed. Because cooler air is denser, removal of this heat further increases engine efficiency.

Boost pressure (the pressure in the inlet manifold) is limited by a wastegate, which diverts the exhaust gas away from the turbine wheel in response to a pressure-sensitive actuator.

The turbo shaft is pressure-lubricated by an oil feed pipe from the engine oil filter mounting. The shaft 'floats' on a cushion of oil. Oil is returned to the sump through a return pipe that connects to the sump.

Precautions

The turbocharger operates at extremely high speeds and temperatures. Certain precautions must be observed to avoid premature failure of the turbo, or injury to the operator.

- ***Do not operate the turbo with any parts exposed – foreign objects falling onto the rotating vanes could cause excessive damage and (if ejected) personal injury.***
- ***Cover the turbocharger air inlet ducts to prevent debris entering, and clean using lint-free cloths only.***
- ***Do not race the engine immediately after start-up, especially if it is cold. Give the oil a few seconds to circulate.***
- ***Observe the recommended intervals for oil and filter changing, and use a reputable oil of the specified quality. Neglect of oil changing, or use of inferior oil, can cause carbon formation on the turbo shaft and subsequent failure. Thoroughly clean the area around all oil pipe unions before disconnecting them, to prevent the ingress of dirt. Store dismantled components in a sealed container to prevent contamination.***

5 Turbocharger and exhaust manifold – removal and refitting

Note: *This Section describes removal of the turbocharger together with the exhaust manifold. On all diesel engines covered in this Manual, the turbocharger cannot be removed from the exhaust manifold.*

Removal

1 Apply the handbrake, then jack up the front of the vehicle and support it on axle stands

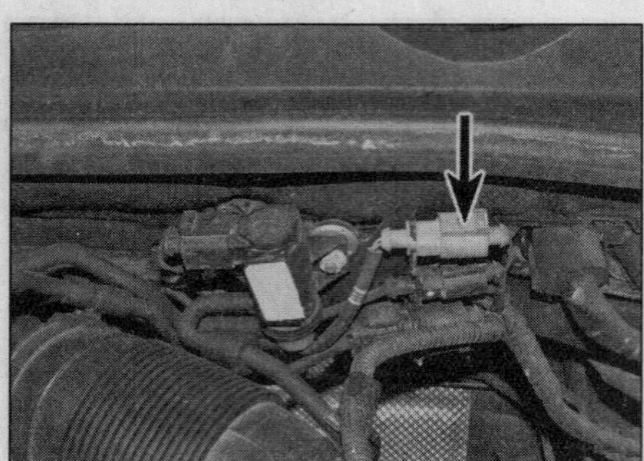

5.13 Exhaust gas temperature sensor wiring plug

(see *Jacking and vehicle support*). Remove the engine compartment undertray and the engine top cover.

2 Remove the right-hand driveshaft as described in Chapter 8.

3 Remove the front suspension subframe as follows:

a) *Unbolt the exhaust system mounting from the subframe.*
b) *Unbolt the heat shield from the subframe.*
c) *Remove the engine rear mounting link from the subframe and transmission with reference to the relevant part of Chapter 2.*
d) *Support the subframe on a trolley jack, then unscrew the bolts securing the steering gear and anti-roll bar to the subframe.*
e) *Unscrew the mounting bolts and lower the subframe to the ground.*

PD unit injection engines

4 On engine code BLS detach the particulate filter from the turbocharger as follows:

a) *Disconnect the wiring from the exhaust gas pressure sensor, then unbolt the sensor.*
b) *Disconnect the wiring from the particulate filter then loosen the clamp and detach the filter from the turbocharger.*

5 Where fitted, unscrew the bolts from the auxiliary heater coolant pipes.

6 Unbolt the turbocharger support bracket then unscrew the union nut from the turbocharger oil return line.

7 Remove the EGR cooler connecting pipe, and disconnect the charge pressure duct from the turbocharger.

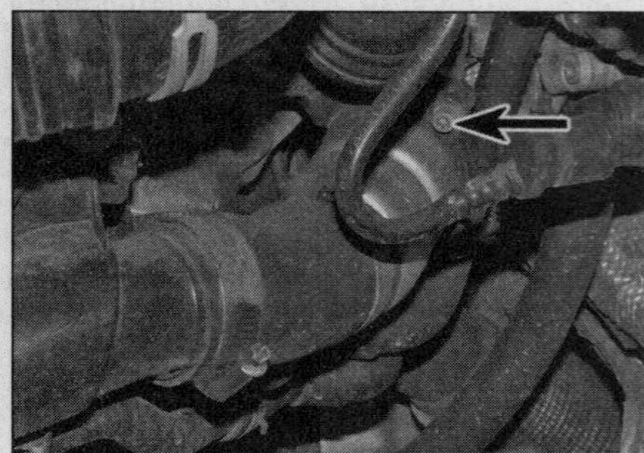

5.15 Turbocharger outlet retaining bolt

8 Disconnect the vacuum hose, then unscrew the oil supply line union nut.

9 Unscrew the exhaust manifold mounting bolts.

10 Push the engine forwards as far as possible, then slide the exhaust manifold off its studs and lower it together with the turbocharger from the engine. Recover the gasket from the cylinder head and discard it as a new one must be used on refitting.

Common rail injection engines

11 Release the clamp and disconnect the air intake hose from the turbocharger.

12 Note their fitted positions, then disconnect the wiring plugs and vacuum hose(s) from the turbocharger vacuum unit/vane position sensor.

13 Located at the engine compartment bulkhead, disconnect the exhaust gas temperature sensor wiring plug, and detach the connector from the bulkhead bracket **(see illustration)**.

14 Undo the oil supply pipe union nut from the top of the turbocharger.

15 Undo the retaining bolt, slacken the clamp and pull the connecting hose from the turbocharger outlet **(see illustration)**.

16 Remove the particulate filter as described in Section 9.

17 Engine codes BLS and BMM – the EGR valve is integral with a gas recirculation potentiometer located on a housing located between the flap housing and inlet manifold.

18 Undo the bolts and remove the EGR pipe between the exhaust manifold and EGR cooler.

19 Unscrew the exhaust gas temperature sensor from the exhaust manifold.

20 Undo the banjo bolt securing the lower end of the turbo oil return pipe/support to the cylinder block. Discard the seals – new ones must be fitted.

21 Remove the bolt securing the upper end of the turbocharger support, then rotate it 90° and pull the support downwards and off the oil return pipe.

22 Remove the exhaust manifold heat shield.

23 Undo the retaining nuts and manoeuvre the exhaust manifold/turbocharger assembly downwards from place.

Refitting

24 Refit the turbocharger by following the removal procedure in reverse, noting the following points:

a) *Renew all gaskets, sealing washers and O-rings.*
b) *Before reconnecting the oil supply pipe, fill the turbocharger with fresh oil using an oil can.*
c) *Tighten all nuts and bolts to the specified torque, where given.*
d) *Ensure that the air hose clips are securely tightened, to prevent air leaks.*
e) *When the engine is started after refitting, allow it to idle for approximately one minute to give the oil time to circulate around the turbine shaft bearings. Check for signs of oil or coolant leakage from the relevant unions.*

6 Turbocharger boost control system components – description, removal and refitting

Description

1 The turbocharger wastgate valve is operated by vacuum supplied by the brake vacuum pump mounted on the left-hand end of the cylinder head. The vacuum supply is controlled by an electrically-operated solenoid valve activated by the engine management ECU. The solenoid valve is mounted on the bulkhead at the rear of the engine compartment. On engines fitted with a particulate filter, the valve has three hoses connecting it to the air cleaner, turbocharger and inlet manifold. On all other engines, the valve has six hoses connecting it to the non-return valve, EGR valve, bypass/intake manifold flap, air filter, vacuum reservoir and turbocharger. It is important that the hoses are connected correctly to the solenoid valve.

Boost pressure solenoid valve

Engines with a particulate filter

2 The boost pressure solenoid valve is mounted at the rear of the engine compartment, on the left-hand side of the bulkhead.

3 Disconnect the wiring from the boost pressure valve.

4 Remove the vacuum hoses from the ports on the boost control valve, noting their order of connection carefully to aid correct refitting.

5 Remove the retaining screw and withdraw the valve.

6 Refitting is a reversal of removal.

Engines without a particulate filter

7 The boost pressure solenoid valve is mounted at the rear of the engine compartment, on the left-hand side of the bulkhead.

8 Remove the lid of the fusebox at the left-hand rear of the engine compartment, then disconnect the wiring from the solenoid valve.

9 Remove the vacuum hoses from the ports on the boost control valve, noting their order of connection carefully to aid correct refitting.

10 Remove the retaining screw and withdraw the valve.

11 Refitting is a reversal of removal.

Boost pressure valve (wastegate)

12 The boost pressure valve is an integral part of the turbocharger, and cannot be renewed separately.

7.2a Air duct connection to the left-hand side of the intercooler ...

7.2b ... and to the right-hand side of the intercooler

7.2c Air duct from the turbocharger to the intercooler

7 Intercooler – general information, removal and refitting

General information

1 The intercooler is mounted in front of the cooling system radiator, and removal and refitting procedures are almost identical for petrol and diesel models. The only difference occurs on diesel engine codes BMM and BLS, where the air inlet is at the right-hand top of the intercooler instead of at the right-hand bottom. On these engines a charge air pressure and temperature sensor is fitted to the air inlet.

Removal and refitting

2 Refer to Chapter 4C, however disconnect the wiring from the sensor **(see illustrations)**.

8 Exhaust manifold and catalytic converter – removal and refitting

Note: *This Section describes removal of the exhaust manifold on non-turbo models fitted with engine code BDK. On turbo models, the exhaust manifold and turbocharger are integral, and removal and refitting procedures are described in Section 5.*

Removal

1 Apply the handbrake, then jack up the front of the vehicle and support it on axle stands (see *Jacking and vehicle support*). Remove the engine compartment undertray and the engine top cover.
2 Remove the right-hand driveshaft as described in Chapter 8.
3 Remove the front suspension subframe as follows:
- a) *Unbolt the exhaust system mounting from the subframe.*
- b) *Unbolt the heat shield from the subframe.*
- c) *Remove the engine rear mounting link from the subframe and transmission with reference to the relevant part of Chapter 2.*
- d) *Support the subframe on a trolley jack, then unscrew the bolts securing the steering gear and anti-roll bar to the subframe.*
- e) *Unscrew the mounting bolts and lower the subframe to the ground.*

4 Where fitted, unscrew the bolts from the auxiliary heater coolant pipes.
5 Remove the EGR connecting pipe from the exhaust manifold and from the inlet manifold.
6 Unscrew the retaining nuts, and separate the exhaust downpipe from the manifold. Also, unbolt the support bracket.
7 Unscrew the exhaust manifold mounting bolts.
8 Push the engine forwards as far as possible, then slide the exhaust manifold off its studs and lower it from the engine. Recover the gasket from the cylinder head and discard it as a new one must be used on refitting.

Refitting

9 Refit the exhaust manifold by following the removal procedure in reverse, but renew all gaskets and tighten all nuts and bolts to the specified torque, where given.

9 Exhaust system – component renewal

Warning: Allow ample time for the exhaust system to cool before starting work. In particular, note that the catalytic converter runs at very high temperatures. If there is any chance that the system may still be hot, wear suitable gloves.

Removal

1 The original VW system fitted in the factory is in two sections. On turbo models, the front section includes the catalytic converter (or 'catalyst'), and can be removed complete. On non-turbo models, the catalytic converter is integral with the exhaust manifold. The original rear section cannot be removed in one piece, as it passes over the rear axle – the pipe must be cut through between the centre and rear silencers, at a point marked on the pipe.
2 To remove part of the system, first jack up the front or rear of the car and support it on axle stands (see *Jacking and vehicle support*). Alternatively, position the car over an inspection pit or on car ramps.

Front pipe and catalytic converter or particulate filter

Caution: Handle the flexible, braided section of the front pipe carefully, and do not bend it excessively.

All engine codes except CBDA and CBDB

3 Unscrew the clamp bolt securing the front exhaust pipe to the turbocharger or exhaust manifold.
4 Unscrew the clamp bolt securing the front pipe to the centre/rear exhaust sections, and free the clamp so that both sections can be moved independently.
5 Release the front pipe from the mounting rubbers, then lower the front pipe, and twist it from the centre section. Lower it to the ground and withdraw from under the car.

Engine code CBDA and CBDB

6 Remove the battery and battery tray as described in Chapter 5A.
7 Remove the air cleaner housing as described in Chapter 4B.
8 Working at the engine compartment bulkhead, disconnect the wiring plugs for the oxygen sensor and exhaust gas temperature sensor **(see illustration 5.13)**. Release the wiring harness from the retaining clips.
9 Disconnect the exhaust gas pressure sensor wiring plug, undo the retaining bolt and slide the bracket forwards. Lay the sensor/bracket on the particulate filter.
10 Remove the particulate filter upper retaining bolt.
11 Apply the handbrake, then jack up the front of the vehicle and support it on axle stands (see *Jacking and vehicle support*). Remove the engine compartment undertray.
13 Lower the front suspension subframe as follows:
- a) *Unbolt the exhaust system mounting from the subframe.*
- b) *Unbolt the heat shield from the subframe.*
- c) *Remove the engine rear mounting link from the subframe and transmission with reference to the relevant part of Chapter 2.*
- d) *Support the subframe on a trolley jack, then unscrew the bolts securing the steering gear and anti-roll bar to the subframe.*

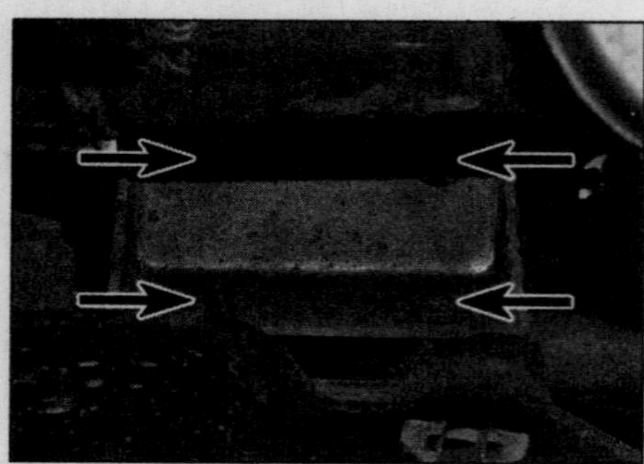

9.15 Particulate filter support bracket bolts/nuts – viewed from beneath

e) Unscrew the mounting bolts and lower the subframe.

14 Slacken the clamp between the turbocharger and the particulate filter.

15 Undo the nuts/bolt securing the particulate filter support brackets **(see illustration)**.

16 Undo the bolts and remove the heat shield above the right-hand driveshaft.

17 Release the clamps and slide the connecting sleeve between the particulate filter and the front exhaust pipe rearwards.

18 Carefully manoeuvre the particulate filter downwards from place. Take care not to damage any wiring, or bend the flexible section of the exhaust pipe at an angle of more than 10°.

Rear pipe and silencers

6 If the factory-fitted VW centre/rear section is being worked on, examine the pipe between the two silencers for three pairs of punch marks, or three line markings. The centre marking indicates the point at which to cut the pipe, while the outer marks indicate the position for the ends of the new clamp required when refitting. Cut through the pipe using the centre mark as a guide, making the cut as square to the pipe as possible if either resulting section is to be re-used.

7 If the factory-fitted rear section has already been renewed, unscrew the clamp bolts between the two sections.

Centre silencer

8 To remove the centre silencer, first loosen the bolts on the clamps at the front and rear of the centre silencer. Release the centre silencer from the rubber mountings, then twist from the front and rear sections, and withdraw from under the car.

Rear silencer

9 The rear silencer is supported by a rubber mounting which is bolted to the underside of the car. Unscrew the clamp bolt securing the rear silencer to the centre silencer.

10 Release the silencer from the rubber mountings, then twist it from the centre section and withdraw from under the car.

Refitting

11 Each section is refitted by a reversal of the removal sequence, noting the following points:

a) Ensure that all traces of corrosion have been removed from the flanges or pipe ends, and renew all necessary gaskets.

b) The design of the clamps used between the exhaust sections means that they play a greater role in ensuring a gas-tight seal – fit new clamps if they are in less than perfect condition.

c) When fitting the clamps, use the markings on the pipes as a guide to the clamp's correct fitted position.

d) Inspect the mountings for signs of damage or deterioration, and renew as necessary.

e) If using exhaust assembly paste, make sure this is only applied to joints downstream of the catalyst.

f) Prior to tightening the exhaust system mountings and clamps, ensure that all rubber mountings are correctly located and that there is adequate clearance between the exhaust system and vehicle underbody.

10 Catalytic converter – general information and precautions

1 The catalytic converter fitted to diesel models is simpler than that fitted to petrol models, but it still needs to be treated with respect to avoid problems. The converter is a reliable and simple device which needs no maintenance in itself, but there are some facts of which an owner should be aware if the converter is to function properly for its full service life:

a) DO NOT use fuel or engine oil additives – these may contain substances harmful to the catalytic converter.

b) DO NOT continue to use the car if the engine burns (engine) oil to the extent of leaving a visible trail of blue smoke.

c) Remember that the catalytic converter is FRAGILE – do not strike it with tools during servicing work, and take care handling it when removing it from the car for any reason.

d) The catalytic converter, used on a well-maintained and well-driven car, should last for between 50 000 and 100 000 miles – if the converter is no longer effective, it must be renewed.

Chapter 5 Part A:
Starting and charging systems

Contents

Degrees of difficulty

Easy, suitable for novice with little experience 	**Fairly easy,** suitable for beginner with some experience	**Fairly difficult,** suitable for competent DIY mechanic	**Difficult,** suitable for experienced DIY mechanic	**Very difficult,** suitable for expert DIY or professional 

Specifications

General

System type	12 volt, negative earth

Starter motor

Rating:	
Petrol engines	12V, 1.1 kW
Diesel engines	12V, 2.0 kW

Battery

Ratings	36 to 72 Ah (depending on model and market)

Alternator

Rating	55, 60, 70 or 90 amp
Minimum brush length	5.0 mm

Torque wrench settings

	Nm	lbf ft
Alternator mounting bolts	25	18
Alternator mounting bracket:		
1.4 litre engines	55	41
1.6, 1.8 and 2.0 litre engines	45	33
Diesel engines	45	33
Auxiliary drivebelt upper tensioner (1.4 TSi models)	22	16
Battery clamping plate bolt	22	16
Starter mounting bolts:		
M10	40	30
M12	80	60

1 General information and precautions

General information

The engine electrical system consists of the charging and starting systems. Because of their engine-related functions, these are covered separately from the body electrical devices such as the lights, instruments, etc (which are covered in Chapter 12). On petrol engine models refer to Part B of this Chapter for information on the ignition system, and on diesel models refer to Part C for the preheating system.

The electrical system is of the 12 volt negative earth type.

The battery is of the low maintenance or maintenance-free (sealed for life) type and is charged by the alternator, which is belt-driven from the crankshaft pulley.

The starter motor is of the pre-engaged type, with an integral solenoid. On starting, the solenoid moves the drive pinion into engagement with the flywheel ring gear before the starter motor is energised. Once the engine has started, a one-way clutch prevents the motor armature being driven by the engine until the pinion disengages from the flywheel.

Further details of the various systems are given in the relevant Sections of this Chapter. While some repair procedures are given, the usual course of action is to renew the component concerned. The owner whose interest extends beyond mere component renewal should obtain a copy of the *Automotive Electrical & Electronic Systems Manual*, available from the publishers of this manual.

Precautions

Warning: It is necessary to take extra care when working on the electrical system to avoid damage to semi-conductor devices (diodes and transistors), and to avoid the risk of personal injury. In addition to the precautions given in 'Safety first!', observe the following when working on the system:

- ***Always remove rings, watches, etc, before working on the electrical system.*** Even with the battery disconnected, capacitive discharge could occur if a component's live terminal is earthed through a metal object. This could cause a shock or nasty burn.
- ***Do not reverse the battery connections.*** Components such as the alternator, electronic control units, or any other components having semi-conductor circuitry could be irreparably damaged.
- ***Never disconnect the battery terminals, the alternator, any electrical wiring or any test instruments when the engine is running.***
- ***Do not allow the engine to turn the alternator when the alternator is not connected.***
- ***Never test for alternator output by flashing the output lead to earth.***
- ***Always ensure that the battery negative lead is disconnected when working on the electrical system.***
- If the engine is being started using jump leads and a slave battery, connect the batteries ***positive-to-positive*** and ***negative-to-negative*** (see *Jump starting* at the beginning of the manual). This also applies when connecting a battery charger.
- Before using electric-arc welding equipment on the car, ***disconnect the battery, alternator and components such as the electronic control units*** (where applicable) to protect them from the risk of damage.

Caution: Certain audio units fitted as standard equipment by VW have a built-in security code to deter thieves. If the power source to the unit is cut, the anti-theft system will activate. Even if the power source is immediately reconnected, the unit will not function until the correct security code has been entered. Therefore, if you do not know the correct security code for the unit do not disconnect the battery negative terminal or remove the radio/cassette unit from the vehicle. Refer to your VW dealer for further information on whether the unit fitted to your car has a security code. Refer to 'Disconnecting the battery' in the Reference section at the rear of this manual.

2 Battery – testing and charging

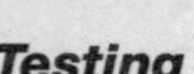

Testing

Standard and low-maintenance battery

1 If the vehicle covers a small annual mileage, it is worthwhile checking the specific gravity of the electrolyte every three months to determine the state of charge of the battery. Remove the battery (see Section 3) then remove the cell caps/cover (as applicable) and use a hydrometer to make the check, comparing the results with the following table. Note that the specific gravity readings assume an electrolyte temperature of 15°C; for every 10°C below 15°C subtract 0.007. For every 10°C above 15°C add 0.007. If the electrolyte level of any cell is low, top it up to the MAX level mark with distilled water.

	Above 25°C	Below 25°C
Fully-charged	*1.210 to 1.230*	*1.270 to 1.290*
70% charged	*1.170 to 1.190*	*1.230 to 1.250*
Discharged	*1.050 to 1.070*	*1.110 to 1.130*

2 If the battery condition is suspect, first check the specific gravity of electrolyte in each cell. A variation of 0.040 or more between any cells indicates loss of electrolyte or deterioration of the internal plates.

3 If the specific gravity variation is 0.040 or more, the battery should be renewed. If the cell variation is satisfactory but the battery is discharged, it should be recharged as described later in this Section.

Maintenance-free battery

4 In cases where a sealed for life maintenance-free battery is fitted, topping-up and testing of the electrolyte in each cell is not possible. The condition of the battery can therefore only be tested using a battery condition indicator or a voltmeter.

5 Certain models may be fitted with a maintenance-free battery with a built-in charge condition indicator. The indicator is located in the top of the battery casing, and indicates the condition of the battery from its colour. If the indicator shows green, then the battery is in a good state of charge. If the indicator turns darker, eventually to black, then the battery requires charging, as described later in this Section. If the indicator shows clear/yellow, then the electrolyte level in the battery is too low to allow further use, and the battery should be renewed. **Do not** attempt to charge, load or jump start a battery when the indicator shows clear/yellow.

All battery types

6 If testing the battery using a voltmeter, connect the voltmeter across the battery and note the voltage. The test is only accurate if the battery has not been subjected to any kind of charge for the previous six hours. If this is not the case, switch on the headlights for 30 seconds, then wait four to five minutes before testing the battery after switching off the headlights. All other electrical circuits must be switched off, so check that the doors and tailgate are fully shut when making the test.

7 If the voltage reading is less than 12.2 volts, then the battery is discharged, whilst a reading of 12.2 to 12.4 volts indicates a partially-discharged condition. The battery should be recharged as described later in this Section.

Charging

Note: *The following is intended as a guide only. Always refer to the manufacturerís recommendations (often printed on a label attached to the battery) before charging a battery.*

8 If the battery is to be recharged, we recommend that you use a low current battery charger. Note that it is not necessary to disconnect the battery leads when using a low current battery charger. If the battery is disconnected (eg, if it is to be removed and recharged on the bench), note that certain 'learned' values will be lost from the engine management ECU memory, requiring the car to be driven over a short distance after refitting the battery. Also, when the battery is reconnected, the warning lights for the ESP and electro-mechanical steering will light up and stay on. They will extinguish if you drive briefly in a straight line at a speed of 9 to 13 mph.

Standard and low maintenance battery

9 Charge the battery at a rate equivalent to

10% of the battery capacity (eg, for a 45 Ah battery charge at 4.5 A) and continue to charge the battery at this rate until no further rise in specific gravity is noted over a four-hour period.

10 Alternatively, a trickle charger charging at the rate of 1.5 amps can safely be used overnight.

11 Specially rapid boost charges which are claimed to restore the power of the battery in 1 to 2 hours are not recommended, as they can cause serious damage to the battery plates through overheating.

12 While charging the battery, note that the temperature of the electrolyte should never exceed 38°C.

Maintenance-free battery

13 This battery type takes considerably longer to fully recharge than the standard type, the time taken being dependent on the extent of discharge, but it can take anything up to three days.

14 The battery should be removed from the car, and a constant voltage type charger is required, to be set, when connected, to 13.9 to 14.9 volts with a charger current below 25 amps. Using this method, the battery should be useable within three hours, giving a voltage reading of 12.5 volts, but this is for a partially-discharged battery and, as mentioned, full charging can take far longer.

15 If the battery is to be charged from a fully-discharged state (condition reading less than 12.2 volts), have it recharged by your local automotive electrician, as the charge rate is higher and constant supervision during charging is necessary.

3 Battery – removal and refitting

Note: *If the vehicle has a security-coded radio, make sure that you have the code number before disconnecting the battery. If necessary, a ëcode-saverí or ëmemory-saverí can be used to preserve the radio code and any other relevant memory values whilst the battery is disconnected (see 'Disconnecting the battery' in the Reference Section).*

Removal

1 The battery is located on the left-hand side of the engine compartment. Where an insulator cover is fitted, open the cover to gain access to the battery. For improved access, remove the engine top cover/air filter.

2 Loosen the clamp nut and disconnect the battery negative (-) then positive (+) leads from the terminals **(see illustration)**.

3 Unscrew the retaining clamp bolt **(see illustration)**, then lift the battery from the plastic insulator box.

4 Unclip and remove the plastic insulator box **(see illustration)**.

5 If necessary, unbolt and remove the battery tray **(see illustration)**.

3.2 Disconnecting the battery positive terminal

Refitting

6 Refit the battery by following the removal procedure in reverse. Tighten the clamp bolt securely.

4 Alternator/charging system – testing in vehicle

Note: *Refer to Section 1 of this Chapter before starting work.*

1 If the charge warning light fails to illuminate when the ignition is switched on, first check the alternator wiring connections for security. If the light still fails to illuminate, check the continuity of the warning light feed wire from the alternator to the bulbholder. If all is satisfactory, the alternator is at fault and should be renewed or taken to an auto-electrician for testing and repair.

2 Similarly, if the charge warning light comes on with the ignition, but is then slow to go out when the engine is started, this may indicate an impending alternator problem. Check all the items listed in the preceding paragraph, and refer to an auto-electrical specialist if no obvious faults are found.

3 If the charge warning light illuminates when the engine is running, stop the engine and check that the auxiliary drivebelt is not broken (see Chapter 1A or 1B) and that the alternator connections are secure. If all is so far satisfactory, check the alternator brushes and slip-rings as described in Section 6. If the fault persists, the alternator should be renewed, or taken to an auto-electrician for testing and repair.

3.4 Unclip and remove the plastic insulator box

3.3 Battery retaining clamp bolt

4 If the alternator output is suspect even though the warning light functions correctly, the regulated voltage may be checked as follows.

5 Connect a voltmeter across the battery terminals, and start the engine.

6 Increase the engine speed until the voltmeter reading remains steady; the reading should be approximately 12 to 13 volts, and no more than 14 volts.

7 Switch on as many electrical accessories (eg, the headlights, heated rear window and heater blower) as possible, and check that the alternator maintains the regulated voltage at around 13 to 14 volts.

8 If the regulated voltage is not as stated, this may be due to worn brushes, weak brush springs, a faulty voltage regulator, a faulty diode, a severed phase winding or worn or damaged slip-rings. The brushes and slip-rings may be checked (see Section 6), but if the fault persists, the alternator should be renewed or taken to an auto-electrician.

5 Alternator – removal and refitting

Removal

1 Disconnect the battery negative lead and position it away from the terminal. **Note:** *Before disconnecting the battery, refer to 'Disconnecting the battery' in the reference section at the rear of this manual.*

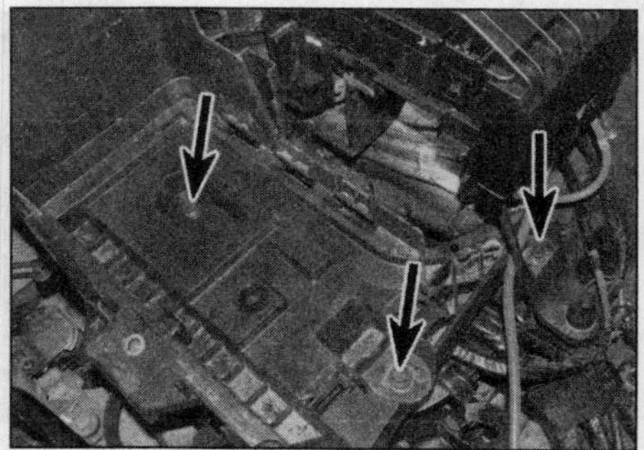

3.5 Battery tray and retaining bolts

5.2 Engine top cover retaining bolts (arrowed)

5.3 Prise out the clip (arrowed) a little, and slide the canister upwards

1.4 litre TSi models

2 Undo the retaining bolts and remove the plastic cover from the top of the engine **(see illustration)**. Unclip the hoses as the cover is withdrawn.

3 Prise out the clip a little, and slide the charcoal canister upwards from its mounting bracket, and place it to one side **(see illustration)**.

4 Remove the auxiliary drivebelt as described in Chapter 1A.

5 Undo the retaining bolts and remove the upper belt idler pulley.

6 Disconnect the wiring plug, remove the mounting bolts and lower the air conditioning compressor. There's no need to disconnect the refrigerant hoses. Suspend it by wire etc. from a suitable position under the vehicle.

7 Pull the 2-pin push-in connector from the alternator.

8 Unscrew the nut and disconnect earth wiring from the alternator.

9 Remove the protective cap (where fitted), unscrew and remove the nut and washers, then disconnect the battery positive cable from the alternator terminal. Where applicable, unscrew the nut and remove the cable guide.

10 Unscrew and remove the lower, then upper bolts, then lower the alternator away from its bracket.

All other models

11 Remove the plastic cover from the top of the engine. Where fitted, disconnect the vacuum hose, undo the retaining bolts and remove the vacuum reservoir **(see illustration)**.

12 Remove the auxiliary drivebelt from the alternator pulley (see Chapter 1A or 1B). Mark the drivebelt for direction to ensure it is refitted in the same position.

Common rail diesel models

13 Move the lock carrier, located at the front of the engine compartment, to its Service position as follows.

a) Remove the front bumper (Chapter 11).

*b) Disconnect the bonnet release cable over the right-hand headlight **(see illustration)**.*

c) On models with a turbocharger, remove the air ducts.

*d) Remove the horn (Chapter 12) **(see illustration)**.*

*e) Support the lock carrier, then unscrew the mounting bolts and substitute them with one threaded rod on each side of the car **(see illustration)**.*

f) Carefully pull the lock carrier forwards approximately 10 cm to provide access to the front of the engine.

All models

14 Pull the 2-pin push-in connector from the alternator **(see illustration)**.

15 Unscrew the nut and disconnect earth wiring from the alternator.

16 Remove the protective cap (where fitted), unscrew and remove the nut and washers, then disconnect the battery positive cable from the alternator terminal. Where applicable, unscrew the nut and remove the cable guide.

17 Unscrew and remove the lower, then upper bolts, then lift the alternator away from its bracket **(see illustration)**.

Refitting

18 Refitting is a reversal of removal. Refer to Chapter 1A or 1B as applicable for details of refitting and tensioning the auxiliary drivebelt. Tighten the alternator mounting bolts to the specified torque.

5.11 Pull the plastic cover upwards – common rail diesel models

5.13a Disconnect the bonnet release cable...

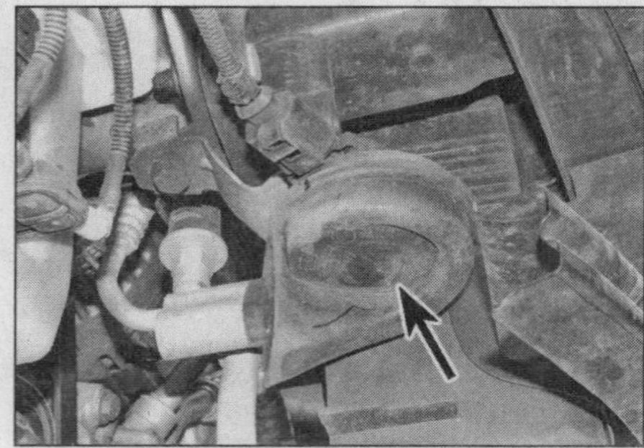
5.13b ...remove the horn...

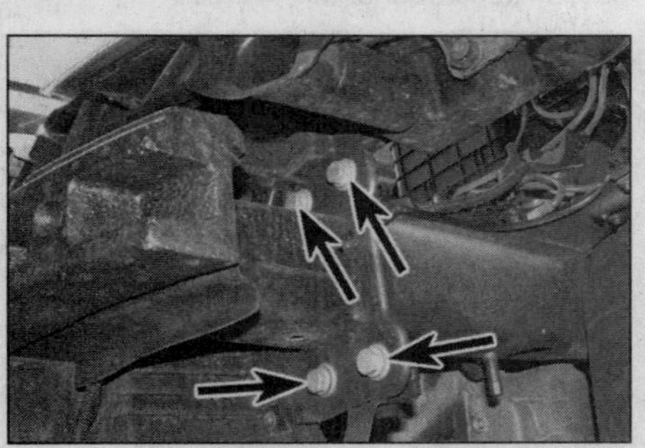
5.13c ...and substitute the lock carrier mounting bolts with one threaded rod each side

5.14 Disconnecting the alternator wiring

5.17 Alternator mounting bolts

6 Alternator – brush holder/regulator module renewal

Removal

1 Remove the alternator, as described in Section 5.
2 Place the alternator on a clean work surface, with the pulley facing down.

Bosch

3 Undo the screw and the two retaining nuts, and lift away the outer plastic cover **(see illustration)**.
4 Unscrew the three securing screws, and remove the voltage regulator **(see illustrations)**.

Valeo

5 Prise off the spring clips, and remove the outer plastic cover **(see illustration)**.
6 Undo the two screws and single nut, and remove the voltage regulator **(see illustrations)**.
7 Slide off the brush cover by depressing the lugs on each side.

Inspection

8 Measure the free length of the brush contacts **(see illustration)**. Check the measurement with the Specifications; renew the module if the brushes are worn below the minimum limit.
9 Clean and inspect the surfaces of the slip-rings **(see illustration)**, at the end of the alternator shaft. If they are excessively worn, or damaged, the alternator must be renewed.

Refitting

Bosch

10 Refit the voltage regulator using a reversal of the removal procedure, tightening the screws securely. On completion, refer to Section 5 and refit the alternator.

Valeo

11 Depress the carbon brushes into the housing, then refit the voltage regulator and tighten the screws and nut securely. Slide on the brush cover until it is heard to engage. On completion, refer to Section 5 and refit the alternator.

7 Starting system – testing

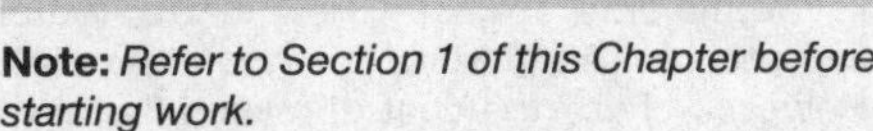

Note: *Refer to Section 1 of this Chapter before starting work.*

1 If the starter motor fails to operate when the ignition key is turned to the appropriate position, the following possible causes may be to blame:

a) *The battery is faulty.*
b) *The electrical connections between the switch, solenoid, battery and starter motor are somewhere failing to pass the necessary current from the battery through the starter to earth.*
c) *The solenoid is faulty.*
d) *The starter motor is mechanically or electrically defective.*

2 To check the battery, switch on the headlights. If they dim after a few seconds, this indicates that the battery is discharged – recharge (see Section 2) or renew the battery. If the headlights glow brightly, operate the ignition switch and observe the lights. If they

6.3 On the Bosch type, remove the outer cover...

6.4a ...undo the screws...

6.4b ...and remove the brush holder/regulator

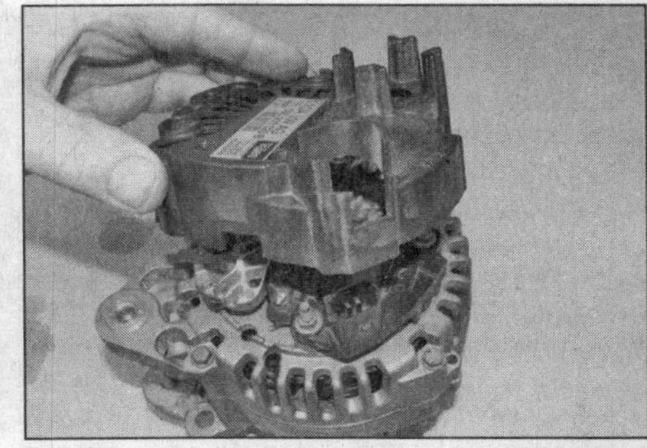

6.5 On the Valeo type, remove the outer plastic cover...

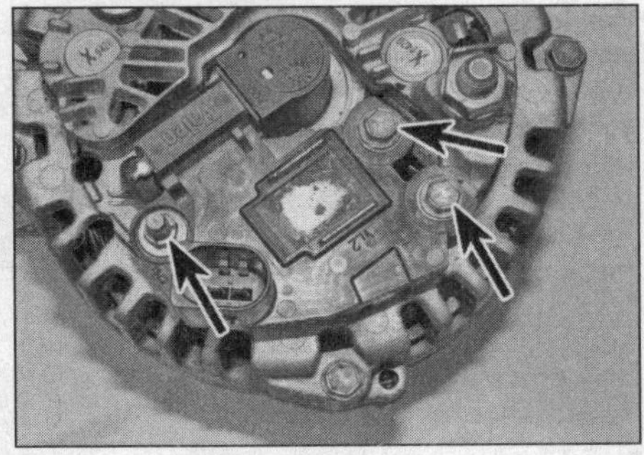

6.6a ...undo the two screws and single nut...

6.6b ...and remove the voltage regulator

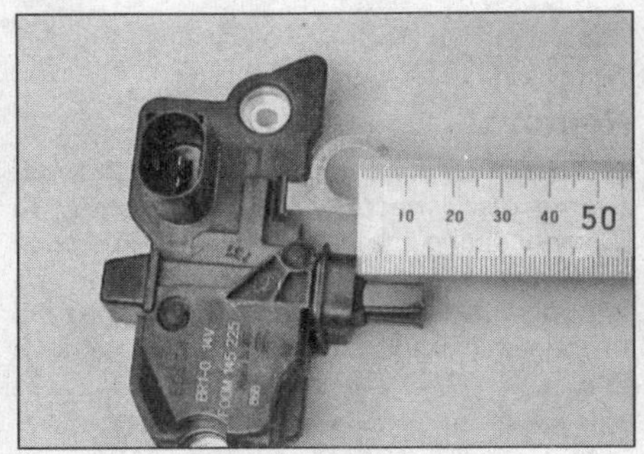

6.8 Measure the brush length

6.9 Clean and inspect the surfaces of the slip-rings

8.6a Remove the plastic cap...

8.6b ...and disconnect the wiring from the starter motor

8.8 Removing the wiring loom support bracket

8.9a Unscrew the upper mounting bolt...

8.9b ...then guide the starter motor out of the bellhousing

dim, then this indicates that current is reaching the starter motor, therefore the fault must lie in the starter motor. If the lights continue to glow brightly (and no clicking sound can be heard from the starter motor solenoid), this indicates that there is a fault in the circuit or solenoid – see following paragraphs. If the starter motor turns slowly when operated, but the battery is in good condition, then this indicates that either the starter motor is faulty, or there is considerable resistance somewhere in the circuit.

3 If a fault in the circuit is suspected, disconnect the battery leads (including the earth connection to the body), the starter/solenoid wiring and the engine/transmission earth strap. **Note:** *Before disconnecting the battery, refer to 'Disconnecting the battery' in the Reference section at the rear of this manual.* Thoroughly clean the connections, and reconnect the leads and wiring, then use a voltmeter or test light to check that full battery voltage is available at the battery positive lead connection to the solenoid, and that the earth is sound.

4 If the battery and all connections are in good condition, check the circuit by disconnecting the wire from the solenoid blade terminal. Connect a voltmeter or test light between the wire end and a good earth (such as the battery negative terminal), and check that the wire is live when the ignition switch is turned to the start position. If it is, then the circuit is sound – if not the circuit wiring can be checked as described in Chapter 12.

5 The solenoid contacts can be checked by connecting a voltmeter or test light between the battery positive feed connection on the starter side of the solenoid, and earth. When the ignition switch is turned to the start position, there should be a reading or lighted bulb, as applicable. If there is no reading or lighted bulb, the solenoid is faulty and should be renewed.

6 If the circuit and solenoid are proved sound, the fault must lie in the starter motor. It may be possible to have the starter motor overhauled by a specialist, but check on the availability and cost of spares before proceeding, as it may prove more economical to obtain a new or exchange motor.

8 Starter motor – removal and refitting

Removal

1 Disconnect the battery negative lead **Note:** *Before disconnecting the battery, refer to 'Disconnecting the battery' in the Reference section at the rear of this manual.*

2 Apply the handbrake, then jack up the front of the vehicle and support it on axle stands (see *Jacking and vehicle support*). Remove the engine undertray.

1.4 litre TSi petrol and 2.0 litre common rail diesel models

3 Disconnect the vacuum hose and pull the plastic cover on the top of the engine from its rubber mountings **(see illustration 5.2 and 5.11).**

4 Remove the air cleaner housing as described in Chapter 4A.

5 On some models it's necessary to remove the charge air pipe from the front of the engine.

All models

6 Remove the plastic cap then unscrew the nut and disconnect the battery positive lead from the starter motor. Also disconnect the wire from the solenoid **(see illustrations).**

7 Unscrew the nut and disconnect the earth cable.

8 Unscrew the nut from the lower starter mounting bolt and remove the wiring loom support bracket **(see illustration).**

9 Unscrew the upper mounting bolt noting the location of the noise insulator, then guide the starter motor out of the bellhousing aperture and downwards out of the engine compartment **(see illustrations).**

Refitting

10 Refit the starter motor by following the removal procedure in reverse. Tighten the mounting bolts to the specified torque.

9 Starter motor – testing and overhaul

If the starter motor is thought to be defective, it should be removed from the vehicle and taken to an auto-electrician for assessment. In the majority of cases, new starter motor brushes can be fitted at a reasonable cost. However, check the cost of repairs first as it may prove more economical to purchase a new or exchange motor.

Chapter 5 Part B:
Ignition system – petrol engines

Contents

Degrees of difficulty

Easy, suitable for novice with little experience 	**Fairly easy,** suitable for beginner with some experience	**Fairly difficult,** suitable for competent DIY mechanic	**Difficult,** suitable for experienced DIY mechanic	**Very difficult,** suitable for expert DIY or professional 

Specifications

System type*

1.4 litre engines:	
Engine code BCA	Bosch Motronic ME7.5.10
Engine codes BKG and BLN	Bosch Motronic MED9.5.10
Engine codes BUD	Magneti-Marelli 4HV
Engine code CAXA	Bosch Motronic MED17
1.6 litre engines:	
Engine codes BGU, BSE and BSF	Siemens Simos 7
Engine codes BAG, BLP and BLF	Bosch Motronic MED9.5.10
2.0 litre engines:	
Engine code AXW, BLX, BVX, BVY and BVZ	Bosch Motronic MED9.5.10
Engine code BLY and BLR	Bosch Motronic MED9.5
Engine code AXX, BPY and BWA	Bosch Motronic MED9.1

** Refer to Chapters 2A to 2D for engine code listings.*

Ignition coil

Type:	
Engine codes BGU, BSE, and BSF	Single DIS coil with four HT lead outputs
All engine codes except BGU, BSE, and BSF	One coil per spark plug
Secondary winding resistance (DIS)	4000 to 6000 ohms

Spark plugs

See Chapter 1A Specifications

Torque wrench settings

Torque wrench settings	Nm	lbf ft
Ignition coil mounting bolts (single DIS coil)	10	7
Knock sensor mounting bolt	20	15
Spark plugs	25	18

1 General information

The Bosch Motronic, Magneti-Marelli, and Simos systems are self-contained engine management systems, which control both the fuel injection and ignition. This Chapter deals with the ignition system components only – refer to Chapter 4A for details of the fuel system components.

The ignition system fitted either of the 'distributorless' (DIS – Distributorless Ignition System) or 'static' type (there are no moving parts). Despite the many different system names and designations, as far as the ignition systems fitted to the Golf and Jetta are concerned, there are essentially only two types of system used – BGU, BSE, and BSF engine codes have a single ignition coil unit with four HT lead terminals, while all other engines have four separate coils, one fitted to each spark plug.

The ignition timing cannot be adjusted by conventional means, and the advance and retard functions are carried out by the Electronic Control Unit (ECU).

The ignition system consists of the spark plugs, HT leads (where applicable), electronic ignition coil unit (or four separate coils), camshaft position sensor (except engine codes BGU, BSE and BSF), and the ECU together with its associated sensors and wiring.

The component layout varies from system to system, but the basic operation is the same for all models: the ECU supplies a voltage to the input stage of the ignition coil, which causes the primary windings in the coil to be energised. The supply voltage is periodically interrupted by the ECU and this results in the collapse of primary magnetic field, which then induces a much larger voltage in the secondary coil, called the HT voltage. This voltage is directed to the spark plug in the cylinder currently on its ignition stroke. The spark plug electrodes form a gap small enough for the HT voltage to arc across, and the resulting spark ignites the fuel/air mixture in the cylinder. The timing of this sequence of events is critical, and is regulated solely by the ECU.

The ECU calculates and controls the ignition timing primarily according to engine speed, crankshaft position, camshaft position, and inlet airflow rate information, received from sensors mounted on and around the engine. Other parameters that affect ignition timing are throttle position and rate of opening, inlet air temperature, coolant temperature and engine knock, monitored by sensors mounted on the engine. Note that most of these sensors have a dual role, in that the information they provide is equally useful in determining the fuelling requirements as in deciding the optimum ignition or firing point – therefore, removal of some of the sensors mentioned below is described in Chapter 4A.

The ECU computes engine speed and crankshaft position from toothed impulse ring attached to the engine crankshaft, with an engine speed sensor whose inductive head runs just above ring. As the crankshaft rotates, the ring 'teeth' pass the engine speed sensor, which transmits a pulse to the ECU every time a tooth passes it. At the top dead centre (TDC) position, there is one missing tooth in the ring periphery, which results in a longer pause between signals from the sensor. The ECU recognises the absence of a pulse from the engine speed sensor at this point, and uses it to establish the TDC position for No 1 piston. The time interval between pulses, and the location of the missing pulse, allow the ECU to accurately determine the position of the crankshaft and its speed. The camshaft position sensor enhances this information by detecting whether a particular piston is on an inlet or an exhaust cycle.

Information on engine load is supplied to the ECU by the inlet manifold pressure sensor, and from the throttle position sensor. The engine load is determined by computation based on the quantity of air being drawn into the engine. Further engine load information is sent to the ECU from the knock sensor(s). These sensors are sensitive to vibration, and detect the knocking which occurs when the engine starts to 'pink' (pre-ignite). If pre-ignition occurs, the ECU retards the ignition timing of the cylinder that is pre-igniting in steps until the pre-ignition ceases. The ECU then advances the ignition timing of that cylinder in steps until it is restored to normal, or until pre-ignition occurs again.

Sensors monitoring coolant temperature, throttle position, camshaft position (except engine codes BGU, BSE and BSF), roadspeed, and (where applicable) automatic transmission gear position and air conditioning system operation, provide additional input signals to the ECU on vehicle operating conditions. From all this constantly-changing data, the ECU selects, and if necessary modifies, a particular ignition advance setting from a map of ignition characteristics stored in its memory.

The ECU also uses the ignition timing to finely adjust the engine idle speed, in response to signals from the air conditioning switch (to prevent stalling), or if the alternator output voltage falls too low.

In the event of a fault in the system due to loss of a signal from one of the sensors, the ECU reverts to an emergency ('limp-home') program. This will allow the car to be driven, although engine operation and performance will be limited. A warning light on the instrument panel will illuminate if the fault is likely to cause an increase in harmful exhaust emissions.

It should be noted that comprehensive fault diagnosis of all the engine management systems described in this Chapter is only possible with dedicated electronic test equipment. In the event of a sensor failing or other fault occurring, a fault code will be stored in the ECU's fault log, which can only be extracted from the ECU using a dedicated fault code reader. A VW dealer will obviously have such a reader, but they are also available from other suppliers. It is unlikely to be cost-effective for the private owner to purchase a fault code reader, but a well-equipped local garage or auto-electrical specialist will have one. Once the fault has been identified, the removal/refitting sequences detailed in the following Sections will then allow the appropriate component(s) to be renewed as required.

Ignition coil(s)

The single coil fitted to BGU, BSE and BSF engine codes operates on the 'wasted spark' principle. The coil unit in fact contains two separate coils – one for cylinders 1 and 4, the other for cylinders 2 and 3. Each of the two coils produces an HT voltage at both outputs every time its primary coil voltage is interrupted – ie, cylinders 1 and 4 always 'fire' together, then 2 and 3 'fire' together. When this happens, one of the two cylinders concerned will be on the compression stroke (and will ignite the fuel/air mixture), while the other one is on the exhaust stroke – because the spark on the exhaust stroke has no effect, it is effectively wasted, hence the term 'wasted spark'.

On engine codes other than BGU, BSE and BSF, each spark plug has its own dedicated 'plug-top' HT coil which fits directly onto the spark plug (no HT leads are therefore needed). Unlike the 'wasted spark' system, on these models a spark is only generated at each plug once every engine cycle.

2 Ignition system – testing

⚠ ***Warning: Extreme care must be taken when working on the system with the ignition switched on; it is possible to get a substantial electric shock from a vehicle's ignition system. Persons with cardiac pacemaker devices should keep well clear of the ignition circuits, components and test equipment. Always switch off the ignition before disconnecting or connecting any component and when using a multimeter to check resistances.***

Engines with one coil per plug

1 If a fault appears in the engine management (fuel injection/ignition) system which is thought to ignition related, first ensure that the fault is not due to a poor electrical connection or poor maintenance; ie, check that the air cleaner filter element is clean, the spark plugs are in good condition and correctly gapped, that the engine breather hoses are clear and undamaged, referring to Chapter 1A for further information. If the engine is running very roughly, check the compression pressures as described in Chapters 2A to 2D (as applicable).

2 If these checks fail to reveal the cause of the problem, the vehicle should be taken to a VW dealer for testing. A diagnostic connector is incorporated in the engine management circuit into which a special electronic diagnostic tester can be plugged (see Chapter 4A). The tester will locate the fault quickly and simply, alleviating the need to test all the system components individually which is a time-consuming operation that carries a high risk of damaging the ECU.

3 The only ignition system checks which can be carried out by the home mechanic are those described in Chapter 1A, relating to the spark plugs. If necessary, the system wiring and wiring connectors can be checked as described in Chapter 12 ensuring that the ECU wiring connector(s) have first been disconnected.

Engines with single DIS coil

4 Refer to the information given in paragraphs 1 to 3. The only other likely cause of ignition trouble is the HT leads, linking the HT coil to the spark plugs. Check the leads as follows. Never disconnect more than one HT lead at a time to avoid possible confusion.

5 Pull the first lead from the plug by gripping the end fitting, not the lead, otherwise the lead connection may be fractured. Check inside the end fitting for signs of corrosion, which will look like a white crusty powder. Push the end fitting back onto the spark plug, ensuring that it is a tight fit on the plug. If not, remove the lead again and use pliers to carefully crimp the metal connector inside the end fitting until it fits securely on the end of the spark plug.

6 Using a clean rag, wipe the entire length of the lead to remove any built-up dirt and grease. Once the lead is clean, check for burns, cracks and other damage. Do not bend the lead excessively, nor pull the lead lengthwise – the conductor inside is quite fragile, and might break.

7 Disconnect the other end of the lead from the HT coil. Again, pull only on the end fitting. Check for corrosion and a tight fit in the same manner as the spark plug end.

8 If an ohmmeter is available, check for continuity between the HT lead terminals. If there is no continuity the lead is faulty and must be renewed (as a guide, the resistance of each lead should be in the region of 4 to 8 k ohms).

9 Refit the lead securely on completion of the check then check the remaining leads one at a time, in the same way. If there is any doubt about the condition of any HT leads, renew them as a complete set.

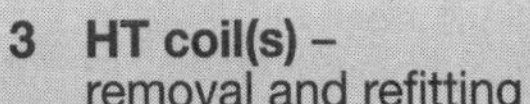

3 HT coil(s) – removal and refitting

Removal

Engines with single DIS coil

1 On all models, the ignition coil unit is mounted on the front of the engine **(see illustration)**.

3.1 The DIS coil is at the front of the engine, above the oil filter housing

2 Make sure the ignition is switched off (take out the key).

3 Where applicable and/or necessary for access, remove the engine top cover(s). Removal details vary according to model, but the cover retaining nuts are concealed under circular covers, which are prised out of the main cover. Where plastic screws or turn-fasteners are used, these can be removed using a wide-bladed screwdriver. Remove the nuts or screws, and lift the cover from the engine, releasing any wiring or hoses attached.

4 Unplug the main wiring plug (LT connector) at the base (or side) of the ignition coil.

5 The original HT leads should be marked from 1 to 4, corresponding to the cylinder/spark plug they serve (No 1 is at the timing belt end of the engine). Some leads are also marked from A to D, and corresponding markings are found on the ignition coil HT terminals – in this case, cylinder A corresponds to No 1, B to No 2, and so on. If there are no markings present, label the HT leads before disconnecting, and either paint a marking on the ignition coil terminals or make a sketch of the lead positions for use when reconnecting.

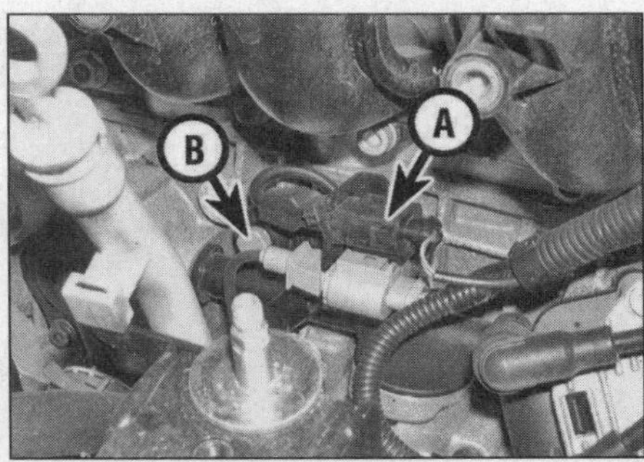

5.3 Knock sensor wiring plug (A) and mounting bolt (B) – 1.6 and 2.0 litre engines

6 Disconnect the HT leads from the ignition coil terminals, then unscrew the three mounting bolts and remove the coil unit from the engine.

Engines with one coil per spark plug

7 Removal of the ignition coils is covered in the spark plug renewal procedure in Chapter 1A, since the coils must be removed for access to the plugs **(see illustration)**.

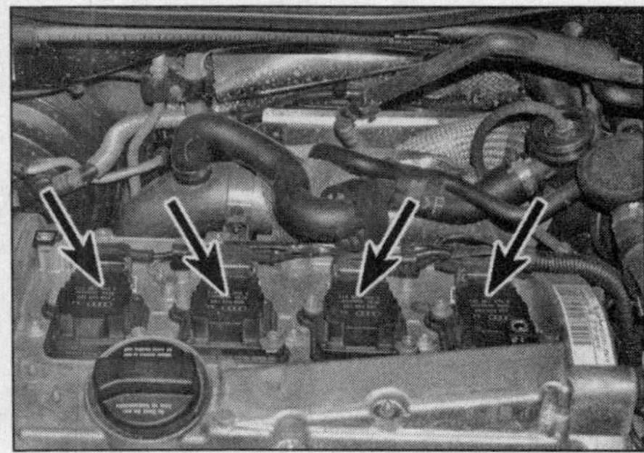

3.7 Ignition coils on engines with one coil per spark plug

Refitting

8 Refitting is a reversal of the relevant removal procedure.

9 Securely tighten the coil mounting bolts. Use the marks noted before disconnecting when refitting the HT leads – if wished, spray a little water-dispersant (such as WD-40) onto each connector as it is refitted (this can also be used on the LT wiring connector).

4 Ignition timing – checking and adjusting

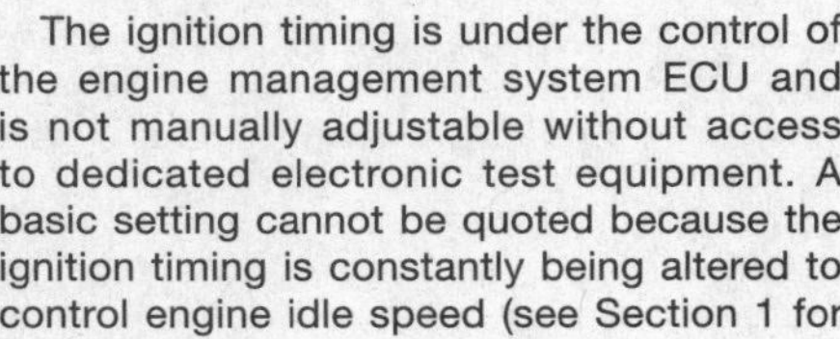

The ignition timing is under the control of the engine management system ECU and is not manually adjustable without access to dedicated electronic test equipment. A basic setting cannot be quoted because the ignition timing is constantly being altered to control engine idle speed (see Section 1 for details).

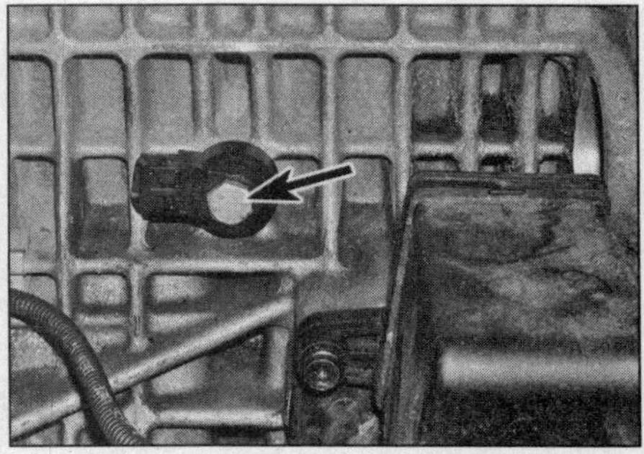

5.4 Knock sensor and mounting bolt – 1.4 litre engine

5 Knock sensor(s) – removal and refitting

Removal

1 The knock sensor(s) is/are located on the inlet manifold side of the cylinder block. **Note:** *Some models, have two knock sensors.*

2 Remove the engine top cover(s) to gain access to the sensor from above. If access from above is not sufficient, firmly apply the handbrake then jack up the front of the vehicle and support it on axle stands (see *Jacking and vehicle support*). Undo the retaining screws and remove the engine undertray(s) so access to the knock sensor can be gained from underneath. Access to the knock sensor(s) is very awkward but it can only be improved by removing the inlet manifold (see Chapter 4A).

3 Disconnect the wiring connector from the sensor or trace the wiring back from the sensor and disconnect its wiring connector (as applicable) **(see illustration)**.

4 Unscrew the mounting bolt and remove the sensor from the cylinder block **(see illustration)**.

Refitting

5 Refitting is the reverse of removal. Ensure the mating surfaces of the sensor and cylinder block are clean and dry and ensure the mounting bolt is tightened to the specified torque to ensure correct operation.

Chapter 5 Part C:
Preheating system – diesel engines

Contents

Degrees of difficulty

Easy, suitable for novice with little experience 	**Fairly easy,** suitable for beginner with some experience	**Fairly difficult,** suitable for competent DIY mechanic	**Difficult,** suitable for experienced DIY mechanic	**Very difficult,** suitable for expert DIY or professional 

Specifications

Glow plugs

Electrical resistance	1.0 ohm
Current consumption (typical – no value quoted by VW)	8 amps (per plug)

Torque wrench setting

	Nm	lbf ft
Glow plug to cylinder head:		
PD Unit injection engines	15	11
Common rail injection engines	18	13

1 General information

To assist cold starting, diesel engined models are fitted with a preheating system, which consists of four glow plugs, a glow plug control unit (incorporated in the ECU), a facia-mounted warning light and the associated electrical wiring.

The glow plugs are miniature electric heating elements, encapsulated in a metal case with a probe at one end and electrical connection at the other. Each inlet tract has a glow plug threaded into it, which is positioned directly in line with the incoming spray of fuel. When the glow plug is energised, the fuel passing over it is heated, allowing its optimum combustion temperature to be achieved more readily in the combustion chamber.

The duration of the preheating period is governed by the ECU, which monitors the temperature of the engine through the coolant temperature sensor and alters the preheating time to suit the conditions.

A facia-mounted warning light informs the driver that preheating is taking place. The light extinguishes when sufficient preheating has taken place to allow the engine to be started, but power will still be supplied to the glow plugs for a further period until the engine is started. If no attempt is made to start the engine, the power supply to the glow plugs is switched off to prevent battery drain and glow plug burn-out. If the warning light flashes, or comes on during normal driving, this indicates a fault with the diesel engine management system, which should be investigated by a VW dealer as soon as possible.

After the engine has been started, the glow plugs continue to operate for a further period of time. This helps to improve fuel combustion whilst the engine is warming-up, resulting in quieter, smoother running and reduced exhaust emissions.

2 Glow plugs – testing, removal and refitting

Warning: Under no circumstances should the glow plugs be tested outside the engine. A correctly-functioning glow plug will become red-hot in a very short time. This fact should also be borne in mind when removing the glow plugs if they have recently been in use.

Caution: DOHC engine codes AZV and BKD are fitted with ceramic glow plugs which are susceptible to internal damage. If a glow plug is dropped from a height of just 2 cm, it may be damaged internally, which could result in ceramic fragments entering the engine causing extensive damage. Do not fit a glow plug that has been dropped.

Testing

1 If the system malfunctions, testing is ultimately by substitution of known good units, but some preliminary checks may be made as described in the following paragraphs.

2 Before testing the system, check that the battery voltage is at least 11.5 volts, using a multimeter. Switch off the ignition.

3 Where necessary for access, remove the engine top cover. **Note:** *On DOHC engines, access to the glowplugs involves removing the camshaft cover. Removal details vary according to model, but the cover retaining nuts are concealed under circular covers, which are prised out of the main cover. Remove the nuts, and lift the cover from the engine, releasing any wiring or hoses attached.*

4 Disconnect the wiring plug from the coolant temperature sender at the left-hand end of the engine (left as seen from the driver's seat) – refer to Chapter 3. Disconnecting the sender in this way simulates a cold engine, which is a requirement for the glow plug system to activate.

5 Disconnect the wiring connector from the most convenient glow plug, and connect a suitable multimeter between the wiring connector and a good earth.

6 Have an assistant switch on the ignition for approximately 20 seconds.

7 Battery voltage should be displayed – note that the voltage will drop to zero when the preheating period ends.

8 If no supply voltage can be detected at the glow plug, then either the glow plug relay (where applicable) or the supply wiring must be faulty. Also check that the glow plug fuse or fusible link (usually located on top of the battery) has not blown – if it has, this may indicate a serious wiring fault; consult a VW dealer for advice.

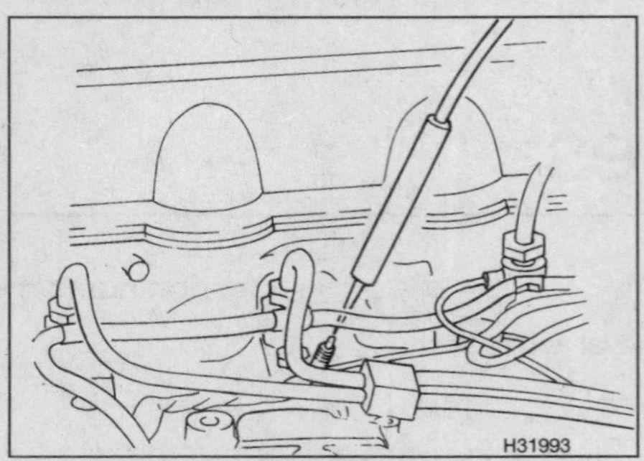

2.10 Testing the glow plugs using a multimeter

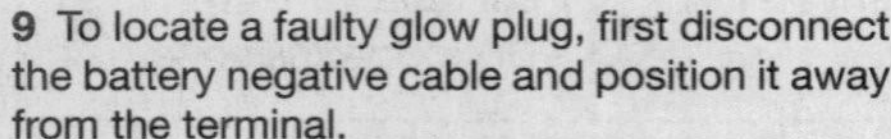

9 To locate a faulty glow plug, first disconnect the battery negative cable and position it away from the terminal.

10 Disconnect the wiring plug from the glow plug terminal. Measure the electrical resistance between the glow plug terminal and the engine earth **(see illustration)**. At the time of writing, this information is not available – as a guide, a resistance of more than a few ohms indicates that the plug is defective.

11 If a suitable ammeter is available, connect it between the glow plug and its wiring connector, and measure the steady-state current consumption (ignore the initial current surge, which will be about 50% higher). As a guide, high current consumption (or no current draw at all) indicates a faulty glow plug.

2.23 Disconnect the wiring plugs from the injectors

2.27a Hold down the tabs...

2.15a Glow plug wiring connector (arrowed) for No 1 injector

12 As a final check, remove the glow plugs and inspect them visually, as described in the next sub-Section.

Removal

Note: *Refer to the Warning at the start of this Section before proceeding.*

PD unit injection engines

13 Disconnect the battery negative (earth) lead (see *Disconnecting the battery*).

14 On the DOHC engine codes AZV and BKD, remove the camshaft cover as described in Chapter 2E.

15 Disconnect the wiring connectors/ rail from the glow plugs, where necessary label the wiring to make refitting easier **(see illustrations)**. On some models, the glow plug wiring is clipped to the injector leak-off hoses – make sure that the clips are not lost as the wiring is pulled away.

2.25 Pull the connectors from the top of the glow plugs

2.27b ...and pull up the centre piece of the fuel return connectors

2.15b Removing the wiring loom/rail from the glow plugs

16 Unscrew and remove the glow plug(s).

17 Inspect the glow plug stems for signs of damage. A badly burned or charred stem may be an indication of a faulty fuel injector.

Common rail injection engines

21 Pull the plastic cover on the top of the engine upwards from its' mountings.

22 Remove the noise insulation from above the injectors.

23 Disconnect the wiring plugs from the injectors, exhaust gas pressure sensor, and fuel rail pressure sensor **(see illustration)**.

24 Undo the retaining bolts and detach the coolant pipe from the intake manifold. Move the pipe to the front of the manifold.

25 Pull the connectors from the top of the glow plugs. Be sure to only pull on the underside of the ridge at the top of the connectors **(see illustration)**.

26 Release the clamp and disconnect the fuel return hose from the fuel rail. Be prepared for fuel spillage.

27 Push down the tabs, pull up the centre piece and disconnect the fuel return connectors from the top of the injectors **(see illustrations)**. Plug the openings to prevent contamination.

28 Move the entire fuel return pipe assembly to the front of the manifold.

29 Lay the glow plug wiring harness to one side.

30 Clean the area around the glow plugs. Use a vacuum cleaner if possible.

31 Using a universal joint, extension and a deep 10 mm socket, unscrew and remove the glow plug(s) from the cylinder head. Note that the plug must be kept 'straight' when being removed – if the ceramic heater tip touches the cylinder head etc. it may easily be damaged.

Refitting

32 Refitting is a reversal of removal, but tighten the glow plugs to the specified torque.

Chapter 6
Clutch

Contents

Degrees of difficulty

Easy, suitable for novice with little experience 	**Fairly easy,** suitable for beginner with some experience	**Fairly difficult,** suitable for competent DIY mechanic	**Difficult,** suitable for experienced DIY mechanic	**Very difficult,** suitable for expert DIY or professional 

Specifications

General

Type:	
Luk clutch	Single dry friction disc, diaphragm spring with spring-loaded hub, self-adjusting pressure plate (SAC)
Sachs clutch	Single dry friction disc, diaphragm spring with spring-loaded hub
Operation	Hydraulic with master and slave cylinders
Application:	
Petrol models:	
1.4 litre engine:	
Non-turbocharged	5-speed transmission 0AF
Turbocharged	6-speed transmission 02S
1.6 litre engine:	
75 kW	5-speed transmission 0AF
85 kW	6-speed transmission 0AG
2.0 litre engine	5-speed transmission 0A4
Diesel models:	
PD Unit injection models:	
1.9 litre engine	5-speed transmission 0A4
2.0 litre engine	5-speed transmission 0AF
Common rail injection models	6-speed transmission 02Q

Torque wrench settings	**Nm**	**lbf ft**
Clutch pedal mounting bracket nuts*	25	18
Clutch pedal pivot nut*	25	18
Clutch pressure plate-to-flywheel bolts*:		
M7 bolt	20	15
M6 bolt	13	10
Clutch release bearing guide sleeve bolts:		
0AF and 0AG transmissions*:		
Stage 1	5	4
Stage 2	Angle-tighten a further 90°	
0A4 and 02S transmissions	20	15
Clutch slave cylinder bolts	20	15

** Use new bolts/nuts.*

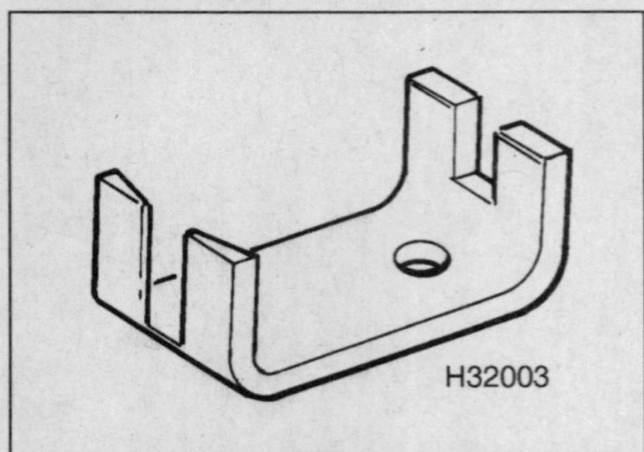

3.4 Over-centre spring retaining tool

1 General information

The clutch is of single dry plate type, incorporating a diaphragm spring pressure plate, and is hydraulically-operated.

The pressure plate is bolted to the rear face of the flywheel, and the friction disc is located between the pressure plate and the flywheel friction surface. The friction disc hub is splined to the transmission input shaft and is free to slide along the splines. Friction lining material is riveted to each side of the disc, and the disc hub incorporates cushioning springs to absorb transmission shocks and ensure a smooth take-up of drive.

On all transmissions except 02Q, when the clutch pedal is depressed, the slave cylinder pushrod moves the release lever forwards. On 02Q transmissions, the slave cylinder is fitted concentrically around the transmission input shaft within the bellhousing. The release bearing is forced onto the pressure plate diaphragm spring fingers. As the centre of the diaphragm spring is pushed in, the outer part of the spring moves out and releases the pressure plate from the friction disc. Drive then ceases to be transmitted to the transmission.

When the clutch pedal is released, the diaphragm spring forces the pressure plate into contact with the linings on the friction disc, and at the same time pushes the disc slightly forward along the input shaft splines into engagement with the flywheel. The friction disc is now firmly sandwiched between the pressure plate and flywheel. This causes drive to be taken up.

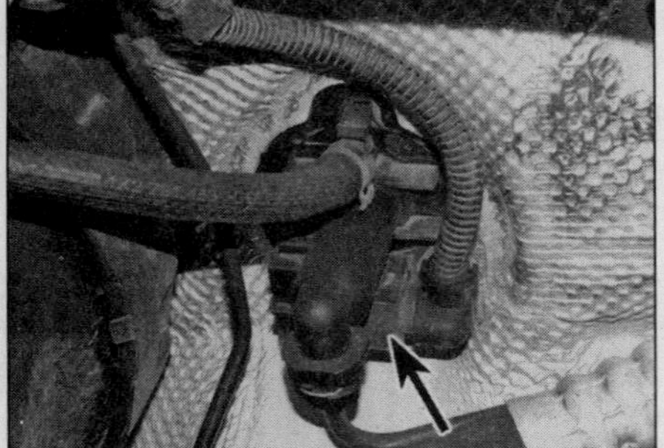

4.3 Clutch master cylinder viewed from the engine compartment

As the linings wear on the friction disc, the pressure plate rest position moves closer to the flywheel resulting in the 'rest' position of the diaphragm spring fingers being raised. The hydraulic system requires no adjustment since the quantity of hydraulic fluid in the circuit automatically compensates for wear every time the clutch pedal is operated.

2 Hydraulic system – bleeding

Warning: Hydraulic fluid is poisonous; thoroughly wash off spills from bare skin without delay. Seek immediate medical advice if any fluid is swallowed or gets into the eyes. Certain types of hydraulic fluid are inflammable and may ignite when brought into contact with hot components. Hydraulic fluid is also an effective paint stripper. If spillage occurs onto painted bodywork or fittings, it should be washed off immediately, using copious quantities of cold water. It is also hygroscopic (ie, it can absorb moisture from the air) which then renders it useless. Old fluid may have suffered contamination, and should never be re-used.

Note: *Suitable pressure-bleeding equipment will be required for this operation.*

1 If any part of the hydraulic system is dismantled, or if air has accidentally entered the system, the system will need to be bled. The presence of air is characterised by the pedal having a spongy feel and it results in difficulty in changing gear.

2 The design of the clutch hydraulic system does not allow bleeding to be carried out using the conventional method of pumping the clutch pedal. In order to remove all air present in the system, it is necessary to use pressure bleeding equipment. This is available from auto accessory shops at relatively low cost.

3 The pressure bleeding equipment should be connected to the brake/clutch hydraulic fluid reservoir in accordance with the manufacturer's instructions. The system is bled through the bleed screw of the clutch slave cylinder, which is located on the top of the transmission housing. Access is best achieved by jacking up the front of the vehicle and supporting it on axle stands (see *Jacking and vehicle support*). Where necessary, remove the undershield for access to the transmission.

4 Bleed the system until the fluid being ejected is free from air bubbles. Close the bleed screw, then disconnect and remove the bleeding equipment.

5 Check the operation of the clutch to see that it is satisfactory. If air still remains in the system, repeat the bleeding operation.

6 Discard any fluid which is bled from the system, even if it looks clean. Hydraulic fluid absorbs water and its re-use can cause internal corrosion of the master and slave cylinders, leading to excessive wear and failure of the seals.

3 Clutch pedal – removal and refitting

Removal

1 Move the driver's seat fully to the rear, and adjust the steering column to its highest position.

2 Remove the driver's side lower facia trim panel, with reference to Chapter 11, then unbolt the crash bar from in front of the clutch pedal.

3 On Golf Plus models, remove the additional trim from beneath the brake and accelerator pedals. Also, remove the clamp bolt and disconnect the steering column universal joint from the steering gear (refer to Chapter 10).

4 Make up a tool similar to that shown, press it into position over the spring to hold the clutch pedal over-centre spring in the compressed position **(see illustration)**.

5 Fully depress the clutch pedal until the tool can be fitted to the over-centre spring to retain it in the compressed position.

6 Release the clutch pedal, and lift out the tool, complete with the over-centre spring.

7 Squeeze together the tabs of the pushrod retaining clip, and separate the pedal from the pushrod.

8 Unscrew the nut from the pedal pivot bolt.

9 Pull out the pivot bolt until the pedal can be removed from the bracket assembly into the driver's footwell.

Refitting

10 Refitting is a reversal of removal, bearing in mind the following points:

a) Press the pushrod retaining clip firmly into the pedal until it is heard to engage.

b) Tighten all fixings to the specified torque, where given.

c) On completion, check the brake/clutch fluid level, and top-up if necessary.

4 Master cylinder – removal, overhaul and refitting

Note: *Refer to the warning at the beginning of Section 2 regarding the hazards of working with hydraulic fluid.*

Removal

1 The clutch master cylinder is located inside the car on the clutch pedal mounting bracket. Hydraulic fluid for the unit is supplied from the brake master cylinder reservoir.

2 Before proceeding, place cloth rags on the carpet inside the car to prevent damage from spilt hydraulic fluid.

3 Working in the engine compartment, clamp the hydraulic fluid hose leading from the brake fluid reservoir to the clutch master cylinder using a brake hose clamp **(see illustration)**.

5.1 Clutch slave cylinder

5.6 Clutch hydraulic fluid line and support bracket

5.7 Removing the clutch slave cylinder

4 Similarly, clamp the rubber section of the hydraulic hose leading from the master cylinder to the slave cylinder using a brake hose clamp, to prevent loss of hydraulic fluid.
5 Remove the engine top cover/air filter assembly. Additionally, on LHD models remove the battery and battery tray with reference to Chapter 5A.
6 Working in the engine compartment, position a suitable container, or a wad of clean cloth, beneath the master cylinder to catch escaping hydraulic fluid. Release the clip and disconnect the fluid supply hose from the master cylinder – be prepared for fluid spillage.
7 Pull the fluid outlet hose retaining clip from the union on the master cylinder, then pull the pipe from the union. Again, be prepared for fluid spillage.
8 Disconnect the wiring from the clutch position sender on the master cylinder.
9 Remove the driver's side lower facia trim panel, with reference to Chapter 11. Additionally, on LHD Golf Plus models, remove the cable guide, footwell vent and fuse/relay box.
10 Unbolt the crash bar from in front of the clutch pedal.
11 Unscrew the securing nuts and remove the clutch pedal mounting bracket from inside the car. Note that the upper nut is difficult to locate.
12 Squeeze together the tabs of the pushrod retaining clip, and separate the pedal from the pushrod. Hold the pedal away from the bracket using a 40 mm wood block or similar.
13 Release the clip and withdraw the master cylinder from the mounting bracket by twisting it anti-clockwise.

Overhaul

14 No spare parts are available from VW for the master cylinder. If the master cylinder is faulty or worn, the complete assembly must be renewed.

Refitting

15 Refitting is a reversal of removal, but bleed the clutch hydraulic system as described in Section 2.

5 Slave cylinder – removal, overhaul and refitting

Note: *Refer to the warning at the beginning of Section 2 regarding the hazards of working with hydraulic fluid.*

Removal

0AF, 0AG, 0A4 transmissions

1 The slave cylinder is located on the top of the transmission casing **(see illustration)**. Access is gained from the engine compartment. The hydraulic components fitted to transmissions 0AF and 0AG are identical, however, those fitted to transmission 0A4 differ slightly.
2 Remove the engine top cover/air filter assembly.
3 Remove the battery and battery tray with reference to Chapter 5A
4 Disconnect the gear selector cables from the gear selector levers, as described in Chapter 7A. Extract the clip and remove the relay lever, then unscrew the nut and remove the selector lever from the top of the transmission. Also, unbolt the cable mounting bracket.
5 Place a wad of clean rag beneath the fluid line connection on the slave cylinder to catch escaping fluid.
6 Pull the fluid pipe retaining clip from the union on the slave cylinder, then pull the pipe from the union. Release the fluid line from the bracket **(see illustration)**, and position it clear of the slave cylinder. Be prepared for fluid spillage.
7 Unscrew the two bolts securing the slave cylinder to the transmission casing, and withdraw the slave cylinder from the transmission **(see illustration)**. Recover the mounting plate on 0AG transmissions.

02S transmission

8 Remove the air cleaner housing as described in Chapter 4A.
9 Remove the battery and battery tray as described in Chapter 5A.
10 Remove the retaining clip and disconnect the gear selector cable from the selector lever.
11 Remove the relay lever from the top of the transmission.
12 Undo the nut and remove the selector lever from the top of the transmission.
13 Undo the retaining nuts and remove the gearchange cables support bracket from the top of the transmission. Move the cable/bracket assembly to one side.
14 Unclip the fluid supply pipe from the bracket.
15 Undo the bolts and remove the gearbox support bracket above the slave cylinder.
16 Place a wad of clean rag beneath the fluid line connection on the slave cylinder to catch escaping fluid.
17 Pull the fluid pipe retaining clip from the union on the slave cylinder, then pull the pipe from the union. Release the fluid line from the bracket, and position it clear of the slave cylinder. Be prepared for fluid spillage.
18 Unscrew the two bolts securing the slave cylinder to the transmission casing, and withdraw the slave cylinder from the transmission.

02Q transmission

19 Remove the transmission as described in Chapter 7A.
20 Release the retaining clip and pull the fluid bleeder connection from the outside of the transmission casing **(see illustration)**.
21 Undo the bolts and remove the slave cylinder/release bearing assembly **(see illustration)**.

5.20 Prise up the clip and pull the bleed screw connection assembly from place

Overhaul

22 No spare parts are available from VW for

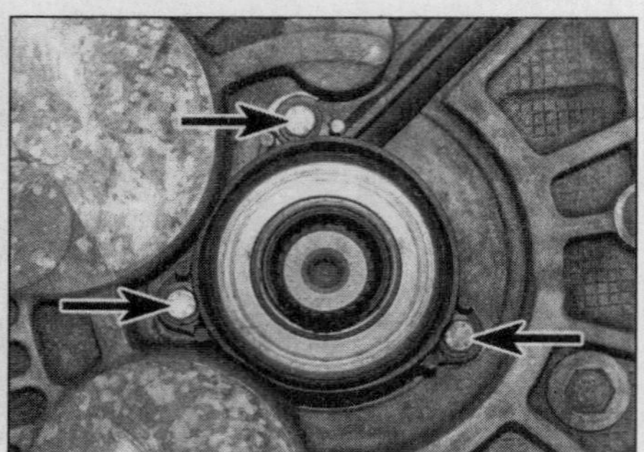

5.21 Slave cylinder/release bearing retaining bolts

the slave cylinder. If the slave cylinder is faulty or worn, the complete assembly must be renewed.

Refitting

23 Refitting is a reversal of removal, bearing in mind the following points:

a) Tighten all fixings to the specified torque where given.

b) On completion, bleed the clutch hydraulic system as described in Section 2.

6 Clutch friction disc and pressure plate – removal, inspection and refitting

Warning: Dust created by clutch wear and deposited on the clutch components may contain asbestos, which is a health hazard. DO NOT blow it out with compressed air or inhale any of it. DO NOT use petrol or petroleum-based solvents to clean off the dust. Brake system cleaner or methylated spirit should be used to flush the dust into a suitable receptacle. After the clutch components are wiped clean with clean rags, dispose of the contaminated rags and cleaner in a sealed container.

Note: *New clutch pressure plate securing bolts will be required on refitting. It is recommended that a friction disc centralising tool is used when refitting the clutch.*

Removal

1 Access to the clutch is obtained by removing the transmission as described in Chapter 7A.

2 Mark the clutch pressure plate and flywheel in relation to each other.

3 Hold the flywheel stationary, then unscrew the clutch pressure plate bolts ¼ of a turn at a time **(see illustration)**. With the bolts unscrewed two or three turns, check that the pressure plate is not binding on the dowel pins. If necessary, use a screwdriver to release the pressure plate. On models with the Sachs clutch, as the bolts are removed the stop pin must slacken. If it doesn't, press the pin towards the flywheel **(see illustration)**.

4 Remove all the bolts, then lift the clutch pressure plate and friction disc from the flywheel.

Inspection

Note: *Due to the amount of work necessary to remove and refit clutch components, it is usually considered good practice to renew the clutch friction disc, pressure plate assembly and release bearing as a matched set, even if only one of these is actually worn enough to require renewal. It is also worth considering the renewal of the clutch components on a preventative basis if the engine and/or transmission have been removed for some other reason.*

5 Clean the pressure plate friction surface, clutch friction disc and flywheel. Do not inhale the dust, as it may contain asbestos which is dangerous to health.

6 Examine the fingers of the diaphragm spring for wear or scoring. If the depth of wear exceeds half the thickness of the fingers, a new pressure plate assembly must be fitted.

7 Examine the pressure plate for scoring, cracking, distortion and discoloration. Light scoring is acceptable, but if excessive, a new pressure plate assembly must be fitted. If the distortion of the friction surface exceeds 1.0 mm, renew it.

8 Examine the friction disc linings for wear and cracking, and for contamination with oil or grease. The linings are worn excessively if they are worn down to, or near, the rivets. Check the disc hub and splines for wear by temporarily fitting it on the transmission input shaft. Renew the friction disc as necessary.

9 Examine the flywheel friction surface for scoring, cracking and discoloration (caused by overheating). If excessive, it may be possible to have the flywheel machined by an engineering works, otherwise it should be renewed.

10 Ensure that all parts are clean, and free of oil or grease, before reassembling. Apply just a small amount of lithium-based grease (VW No. G000100) to the splines of the friction disc hub. **Do not** use copper-based grease. Note that new pressure plates and clutch covers may be coated with protective grease. It is only permissible to clean the grease away from the friction disc lining contact area. Removal of the grease from other areas will shorten the service life of the clutch.

Refitting

11 Commence reassembly by locating the friction disc on the flywheel, with the raised side of the hub facing outwards (normally marked 'Getriebeseite' or 'Gearbox side'). If possible, the centralising tool (see paragraph 20) should be used to hold the disc on the flywheel at this stage **(see illustration)**.

Models with self-adjusting clutch (SAC)

12 On models with a Self-adjusting clutch (SAC), where a new friction disc is fitted,

6.3a Undo the pressure plate retaining screws (arrowed)

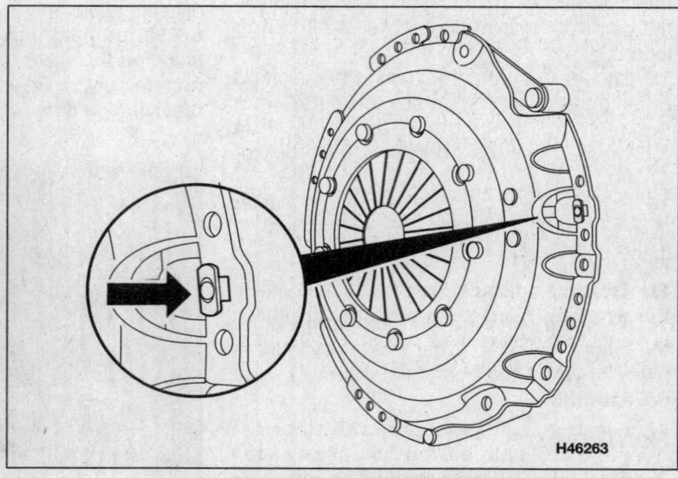

6.3b Ensure the stop pin is free to move

6.11 The friction disc should be marked 'Getriebeseite' or 'Gearbox side'

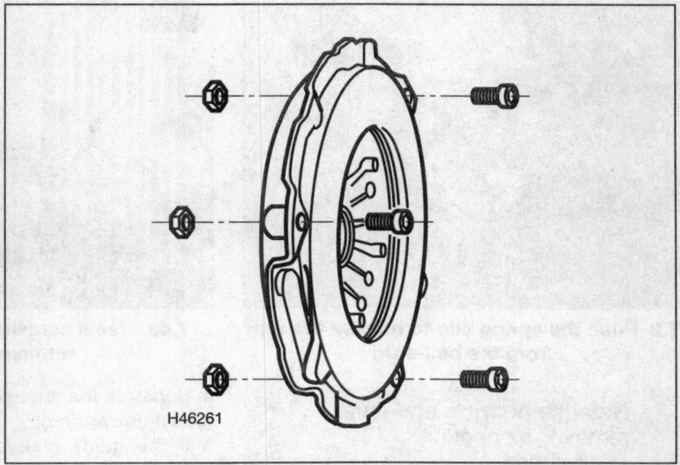

6.13 Insert three 8 mm bolts from the flywheel side, and secure with nuts

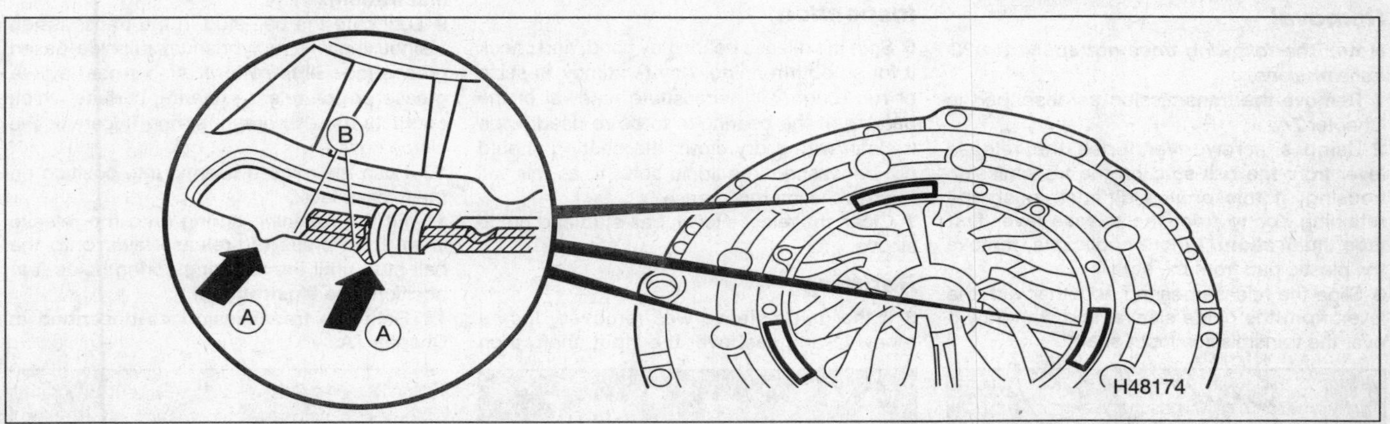

6.15 The edges of the adjuster ring (B) must be between the notches (A)

but the pressure plate is to be re-used, it is necessary to reset the pressure plate adjusting ring prior to assembly as follows.

13 Insert three 8 mm bolts into the pressure plate mounting holes at intervals of 120°. The bolts should be inserted from the flywheel side, and retained by nuts **(see illustration)**.

14 Place the pressure plate face down on the bed of an hydraulic press so that only the heads of the bolts make contact with the press bed, then place a circular spacer over the ends of the diaphragm springs fingers.

15 Use 2 screwdrivers to attempt to rotate the adjuster ring anti-clockwise. Apply just enough pressure with the hydraulic press until it's just possible to move the adjuster ring **(see illustration)**.

16 Once the adjuster ring edges are between the notches, relieve the pressure. The ring is now reset. **Note:** *New pressure plates are supplied in this reset position.*

All models

17 Locate the clutch pressure plate on the disc, and fit it onto the location dowels **(see illustration)**. If refitting the original pressure plate, make sure that the previously-made marks are aligned.

18 Insert the bolts finger-tight to hold the pressure plate in position.

19 The friction disc must now be centralised, to ensure correct alignment of the transmission input shaft with the disc centre. To do this, a proprietary tool may be used, or alternatively, use a wooden mandrel made to fit inside the friction disc and the hole in the centre of the crankshaft. Insert the tool through the friction disc into the crankshaft, and make sure that it is central.

6.17 Fit the pressure plate over the locating dowel pins (arrowed)

20 Tighten the pressure plate bolts progressively and in diagonal sequence, until the specified torque setting is achieved, then remove the centralising tool **(see illustration)**.

21 Check the release bearing in the transmission bellhousing for smooth operation, and if necessary renew it with reference to Section 7.

22 Refit the transmission with reference to Chapter 7A.

6.20 With the pressure plate screws tightened, remove the centralising tool

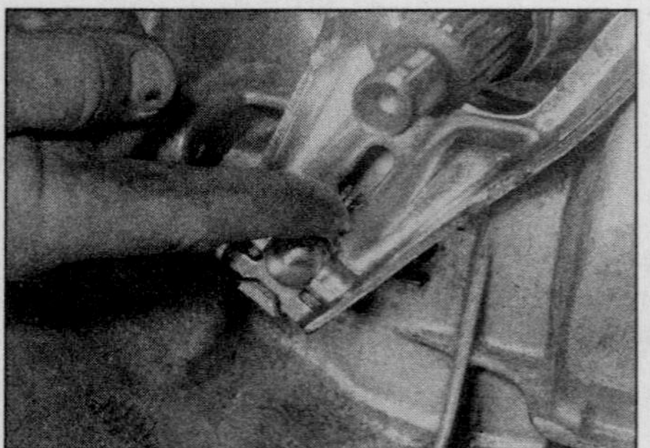

7.2 Push the spring clip to release the arm from the ball-stud

7.4a Use a screwdriver to depress the retaining tags...

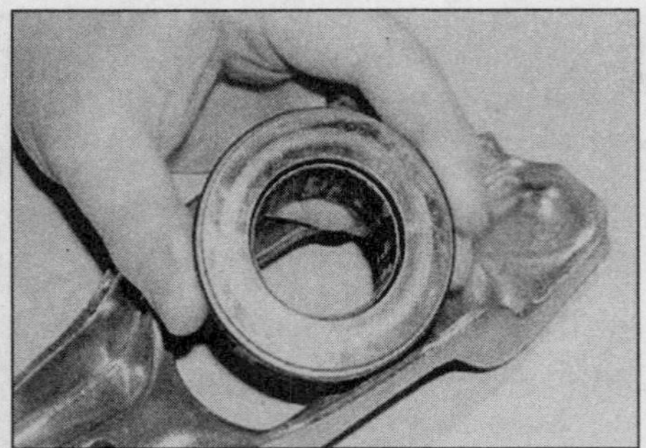

7.4b ...then remove the release bearing from the arm

7 Release bearing and lever – removal, inspection and refitting

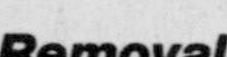

Removal

Note: *The following does not apply to 02Q transmissions.*

1 Remove the transmission as described in Chapter 7A.

2 Using a screwdriver, prise the release lever from the ball-stud on the transmission housing. If this proves difficult, push the retaining spring from the release lever first **(see illustration)**. Where applicable, remove the plastic pad from the stud.

3 Slide the release bearing, together with the lever, from the guide sleeve, and withdraw it over the transmission input shaft.

4 Separate the release bearing from the lever **(see illustrations)**.

5 If the guide sleeve is worn excessively, unbolt it and remove the O-ring seal **(see illustration)**.

Inspection

6 Spin the release bearing by hand, and check it for smooth running. Any tendency to seize or run rough will necessitate renewal of the bearing. If the bearing is to be re-used, wipe it clean with a dry cloth; the bearing should not be washed in a liquid solvent, as this will remove the internal grease.

7 Clean the release lever, ball-stud and guide sleeve.

Refitting

8 If the guide sleeve was removed, locate a new O-ring seal over the input shaft, then fit the guide sleeve and tighten the bolts to the specified torque. If preferred, the guide sleeve may be assembled to the release bearing and lever, and the components fitted over the input shaft as one unit **(see illustration)**.

9 Lubricate the ball-stud in the transmission bellhousing with molybdenum sulphide-based grease **(see illustration)**. Also smear a little grease on the release bearing surface which contacts the diaphragm spring fingers in the clutch cover.

10 Push the release bearing into position on the release lever.

11 Fit the retaining spring onto the release lever, then press the release lever onto the ball-stud until the retaining spring holds it in position **(see illustrations)**.

12 Refit the transmission as described in Chapter 7A.

7.5 Guide sleeve on the transmission

7.8 Fitting the guide sleeve with assembled release bearing and lever

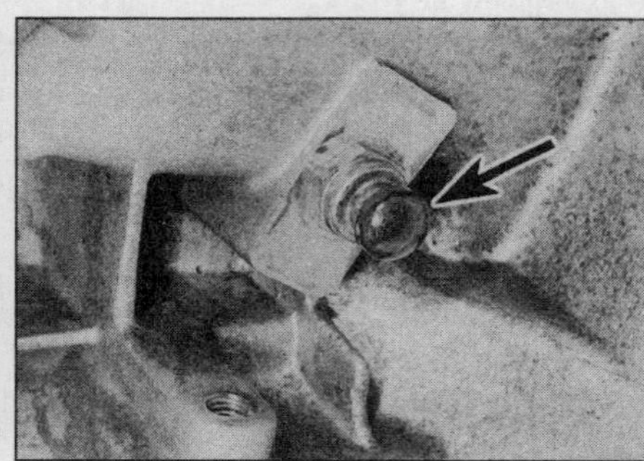

7.9 Lubricate the ball-stud with a little grease

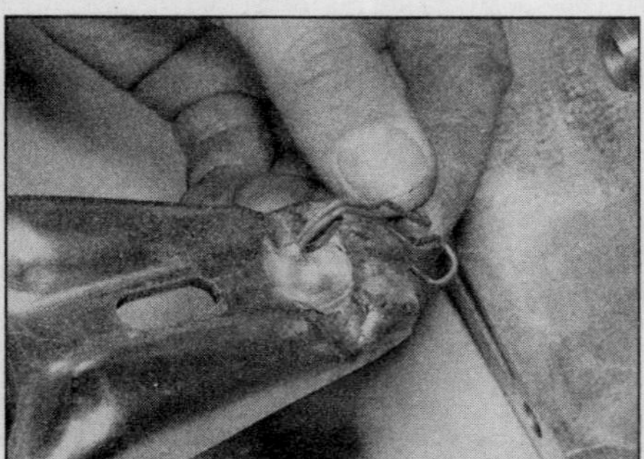

7.11a Locate the spring over the end of the release lever...

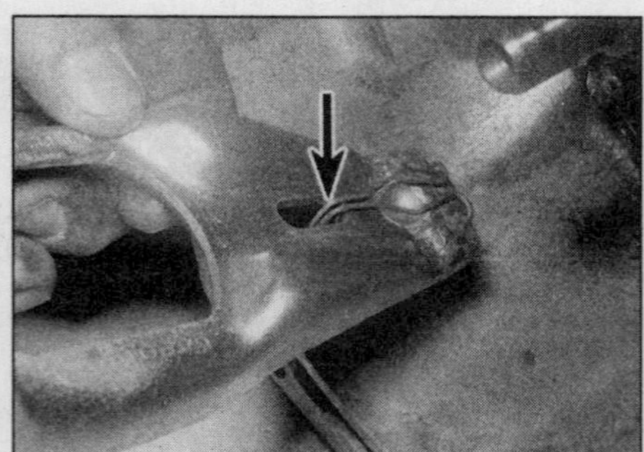

7.11b ...and press the spring into the hole...

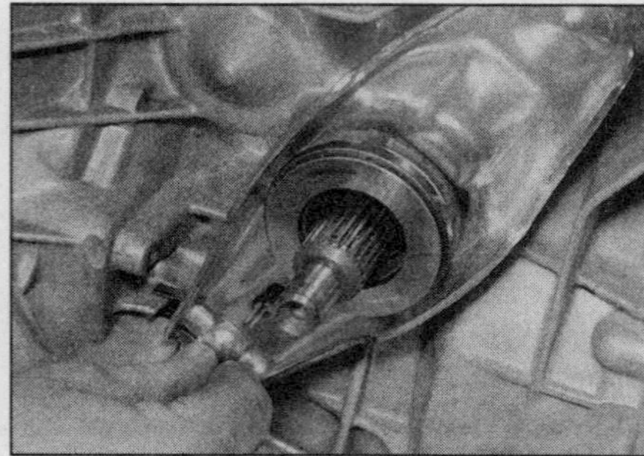

7.11c ...then press the release lever onto the ball-stud until the spring clip holds it in position

Chapter 7 Part A: Manual transmission

Contents

Degrees of difficulty

Easy, suitable for novice with little experience 

Fairly easy, suitable for beginner with some experience

Fairly difficult, suitable for competent DIY mechanic

Difficult, suitable for experienced DIY mechanic

Very difficult, suitable for expert DIY or professional 

Specifications

General

Type	Transversely-mounted, front-wheel-drive layout with integral transaxle differential/final drive, 5 or 6 forward speeds and 1 reverse
Application:	
Petrol models:	
1.4 litre engine:	
Non-turbocharged	5-speed transmission 0AF
Turbocharged	6-speed transmission 02S
1.6 litre engine:	
75 kW	5-speed transmission 0AF
85 kW	6-speed transmission 0AG
2.0 litre engine	5-speed transmission 0A4
Diesel models:	
PD Unit injection models:	
1.9 litre engine	5-speed transmission 0A4
2.0 litre engine	5-speed transmission 0AF
Common rail injection models	6-speed transmission 02Q

Torque wrench settings

Torque wrench settings	Nm	lbf ft
Gearchange bracket	20	15
Reversing light switch	20	15
Selector lever	23	17
Transmission to engine:		
M12 bolts	80	59
M10 bolt	40	30

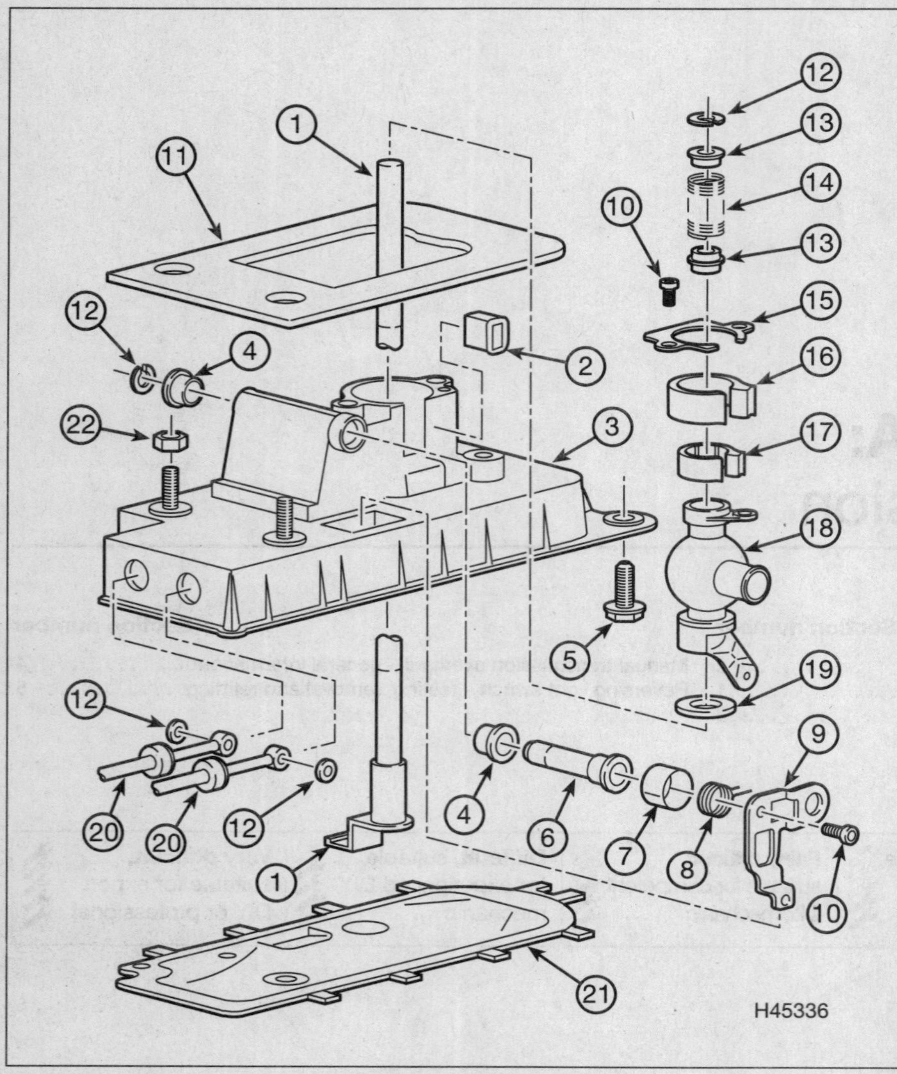

1.3a Gear linkage layout

1 Selector lever
2 Damper
3 Selector lever housing
4 Bush – bearing
5 Bolt
6 Fulcrum pin
7 Bush – guide
8 Spring
9 Selector lever gate
10 Retaining screw
11 Housing seal
12 Securing clip
13 Bush
14 Spring
15 Cover plate
16 Damper collar
17 Bearing
18 Selector lever ball/guide
19 Damping washer
20 Gear selector cable
21 Baseplate
22 Securing nut

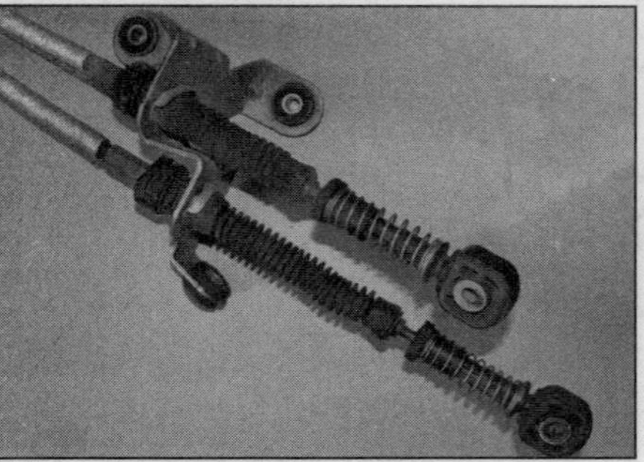

1.3b Transmission end of the gearchange cables

2.2 Push the collar down and lock in position

1 General information

The manual transmission is bolted directly to the left-hand end of the engine. This layout has the advantage of providing the shortest possible drive path to the front wheels, as well as locating the transmission in the airflow through engine bay, optimising cooling. The unit is cased in aluminium alloy.

Drive from the crankshaft is transmitted through the clutch to the gearbox input shaft, which is splined to accept the clutch friction disc.

All forward gears are fitted with synchromesh. The floor-mounted gear lever is connected to the gearbox by shift cables **(see illustrations)**. Levers on the transmission actuate internal selector forks which are connected to the synchromesh sleeves. The sleeves are locked to the gearbox shafts but can slide axially by means of splined hubs, and they press baulk rings into contact with the respective gear/pinion. The coned surfaces between the baulk rings and the pinion/gear act as a friction clutch, that progressively matches the speed of the synchromesh sleeve (and hence the gearbox shaft) with that of the gear/pinion. This allows gearchanges to be carried out smoothly.

Drive is transmitted to the differential crownwheel, which rotates the differential case and planetary gears, thus driving the sun gears and driveshafts. The rotation of the differential planetary gears on their shaft allows the inner roadwheel to rotate at a slower speed than the outer roadwheel during cornering.

2 Gearchange linkage – adjustment

1 Remove the engine top cover, air cleaner housing, and air ducting for access to the top of the transmission.

2 With the gearchange set in the neutral position, push the two locking collars (one on each cable) forwards to compress the springs, turn them clockwise (looking from the driver's seat) to lock into position **(see illustration)**.

3 Press down on the selector shaft on the top of the transmission, and push the locking pin into the transmission while turning it clockwise, until it engages and the selector shaft cannot move **(see illustration)**.

4 Working inside the vehicle, unclip the gear lever gaiter from the centre console. Still in the neutral position, move the gear lever as far to the left as possible and insert the locking pin (or drill bit) through the hole in the base of the gear lever and into the hole in the housing **(see illustration)**.

5 Working back in the engine bay, turn the two locking collars on the cables anti-clockwise so that the springs will release them

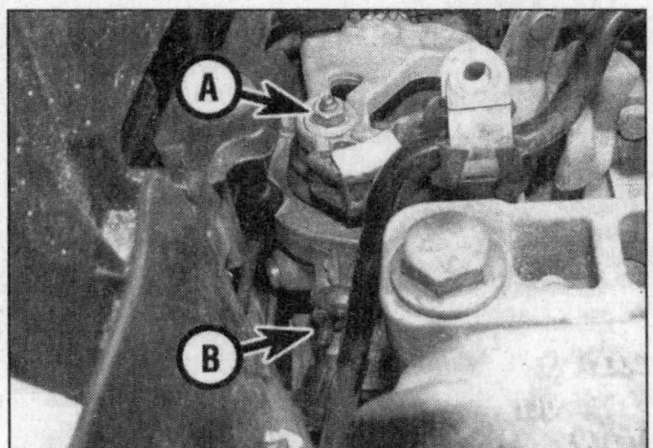

2.3 Press down on (A), then push in locking pin (B)

2.4 Locking the gear lever in position using a drill bit

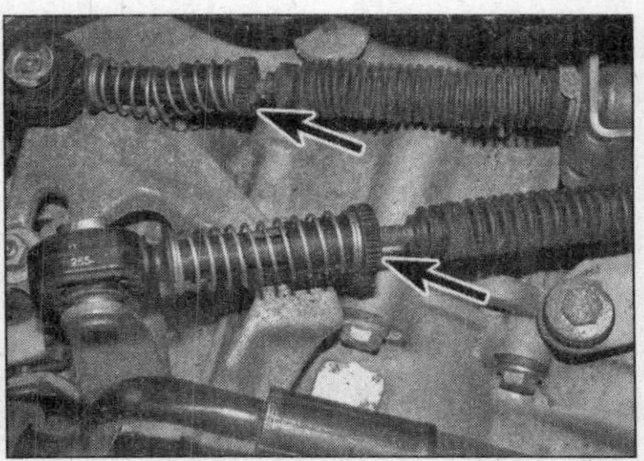

2.5 Release the two locking collars back into position

back into position and lock the cables **(see illustration)**.

6 With the cable adjustment set, the locking pin can now be turned anti-clockwise to its original position pointing upwards.

7 Inside the vehicle, remove the locking pin from the gear lever, then check the operation of the selector mechanism. When the gear lever is at rest in neutral, it should be central, ready to select 3rd or 4th. The gear lever gaiter can now be refitted to the centre console.

8 Refit the air ducting and engine top cover/ air filter.

3 Manual transmission – removal and refitting

Removal

1 Select a solid, level surface to park the vehicle upon. Give yourself enough space to move around it easily. Apply the handbrake and chock the rear wheels.

2 Raise the front of the vehicle and support it securely on axle stands (see *Jacking and vehicle support*). Where fitted, remove the engine/transmission undertray sections. Position a suitable container beneath the transmission, then unscrew the drain plug and drain the transmission oil.

3 Remove the engine top cover/air filter. On 1.4 litre turbocharged models, remove the air cleaner housing as described in Chapter 4A.

4 Remove the battery and battery tray with reference to Chapter 5A.

5 Disconnect the gear selector cables from the gear selector levers. Extract the clip and remove the relay lever, then unscrew the nut and remove the selector lever from the top of the transmission. Also, unbolt and remove the gearchange bracket **(see illustrations)**.

6 On models with the clutch slave cylinder on the top of the transmission, undo the retaining bolts and place the cylinder to one side.

7 On common rail diesel models, seal the slave cylinder flexible hose using a hose clamp, then prise out the clip and pull the fluid pipe from the bleeder connection on the slave cylinder **(see illustration)**.

8 Unbolt the earth cable from the engine or subframe.

9 Unscrew and remove the upper bolts securing the transmission to the engine.

10 With reference to Chapter 5A, remove the starter motor.

11 Remove the lower left-hand wheel arch liner.

12 Disconnect the wiring from the reversing light switch **(see illustration)**.

13 Unbolt the driveshaft protective cover.

14 With reference to the relevant part of Chapter 4, loosen the clamp securing the exhaust intermediate pipe to the rear section. This will allow the engine to be move forwards and backwards during the transmission removal and alignment procedures. Consequently, there is no need to separate the exhaust pipe sections.

15 Using a multispline key, unscrew and remove the bolts securing the driveshafts to the transmission output flanges. Tie the right-hand driveshaft to one side. Tie the left-hand driveshaft to the anti-roll bar, so that the shaft is as high as possible. Alternatively, completely remove the left-hand driveshaft as described in Chapter 8.

16 Unbolt the engine rear mounting torque arm from the bottom of the transmission **(see illustration)**.

3.5a Disconnecting the gearchange cables

3.5b Gearchange bracket

3.7 Prise up the clip a little and pull the hose from the bleeder connection

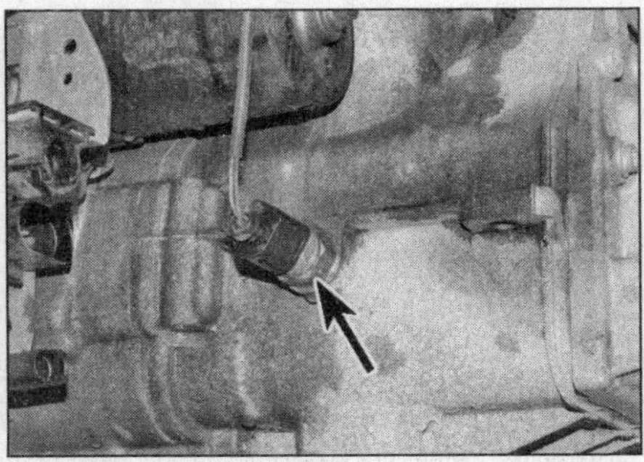

3.12 Reversing light switch on the transmission

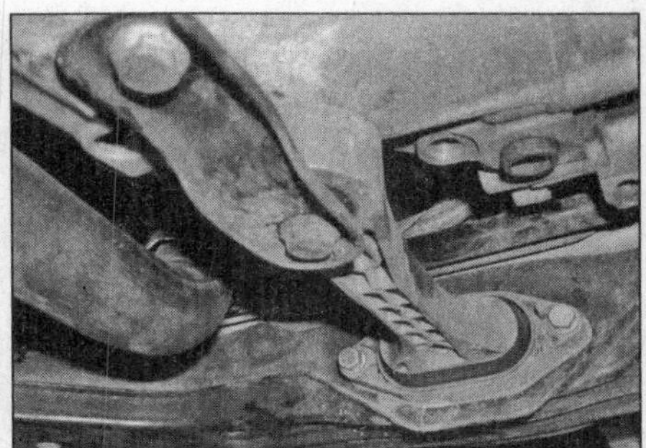

3.16 Unbolt the engine rear mounting torque arm

17 Where applicable, unbolt the cover plate from the transmission bellhousing.
18 Using a suitable hoist, support the weight of the engine.
19 Unscrew the two bolts securing the transmission mounting to the body. Also, unbolt the mounting bracket from the transmission.
20 Lower the engine/transmission assembly slightly and, using a trolley jack, support the transmission. Position the jack so that it can be withdrawn from the left-hand side of the car.
21 Unscrew and remove the remaining lower transmission-to-engine mounting bolts, including the bolt located on the left-hand rear of the engine.
22 Carefully pull the transmission directly away from the engine, taking care not to allow its weight to rest on the clutch friction disc hub. A second person is helpful to pull the engine as far forwards as possible.

Warning: Support the transmission to ensure that it remains steady on the jack head. Keep the transmission level until the input shaft is fully withdrawn from the clutch friction disc.

23 When the transmission is clear of the locating dowels and clutch components, lower the transmission to the ground and withdraw from under the car.

Refitting

24 Refitting the transmission is essentially a reversal of the removal procedure, but note the following points:

a) Apply a smear of high melting-point grease to the clutch friction disc hub splines; take care to avoid contaminating the friction surfaces.
b) In order to align the transmission with the flywheel, gently pull the engine forward as the transmission is manoeuvred into place.
c) Tighten the transmission-to-engine bolts to the specified torque.
d) Refer to the relevant part of Chapter 2 and tighten the engine mounting bolts to the correct torque.
e) Refer to Chapter 8 and tighten the driveshaft bolts to the specified torque.
f) On completion, refer to Section 2 and check the gearchange linkage/cable adjustment.
g) Refill the transmission with the correct grade and quantity of oil. Refer to 'Lubricants and fluids' and Chapter 1A or 1B, as appropriate.

4 Manual transmission overhaul – general information

The overhaul of a manual transmission is a complex (and often expensive) task for the DIY home mechanic to undertake, which requires access to specialist equipment. It involves dismantling and reassembly of many small components, measuring clearances precisely and if necessary, adjusting them by selecting shims and spacers. Internal transmission components are also often difficult to obtain and in many instances, extremely expensive. Because of this, if the transmission develops a fault or becomes noisy, the best course of action is to have the unit overhauled by a specialist repairer or to obtain an exchange reconditioned unit.

Nevertheless, it is not impossible for the more experienced mechanic to overhaul the transmission if the special tools are available and the job is carried out in a deliberate step-by-step manner, to ensure nothing is overlooked.

The tools necessary for an overhaul include internal and external circlip pliers, bearing pullers, a slide hammer, a set of pin punches, a dial test indicator and possibly a hydraulic press. In addition, a large, sturdy workbench and a vice will be required.

During dismantling of the transmission, make careful notes of how each component is fitted to make reassembly easier and accurate.

Before dismantling the transmission, it will help if you have some idea of where the problem lies. Certain problems can be closely related to specific areas in the transmission, which can make component examination and renewal easier. Refer to the *Fault finding* Section in this manual for more information.

5 Reversing light switch – testing, removal and refitting

Testing

1 Ensure that the ignition switch is turned to the OFF position.
2 Unplug the wiring harness from the reversing light switch at the connector. The switch is located on the front or top of the casing **(see illustration 3.12)**.
3 Connect the probes of a continuity tester, or multimeter set to the resistance measurement function, across the terminals of the reversing light switch.
4 The switch contacts are normally open, so with any gear other than reverse selected, the tester/meter should indicate an open circuit or infinite resistance. When reverse gear is selected, the switch contacts should close, causing the tester/meter to indicate continuity or zero resistance.
5 If the switch does not operate correctly, it should be renewed.

Removal

6 Ensure that the ignition switch is turned to the OFF position.
7 Unplug the wiring harness from the reversing light switch at the connector.
8 Unscrew the switch from the transmission casing, and recover the sealing ring.

Refitting

9 Refitting is a reversal of removal.

Chapter 7 Part B: Automatic transmission

Contents

Degrees of difficulty

Easy, suitable for novice with little experience 	**Fairly easy,** suitable for beginner with some experience	**Fairly difficult,** suitable for competent DIY mechanic	**Difficult,** suitable for experienced DIY mechanic	**Very difficult,** suitable for expert DIY or professional 

Specifications

General

Description	Electro-hydraulically controlled planetary gearbox providing six forward speeds and one reverse speed. Drive transmitted through hydrokinetic torque converter. Lock-up clutch on all forward speeds, controlled by electronic control unit (ECU). Shift points controlled by the ECU using 'Fuzzy logic'
Transmission type number	09G

Torque wrench settings

Torque wrench settings	Nm	lbf ft
Multifunction switch:		
Outer spindle nut	13	10
Inner spindle nut	7	5
Mounting bolt	6	4
Selector cable locking bolt	8	6
Torque converter-to-driveplate nuts	60	44
Transmission bellhousing-to-engine bolts:		
M10 bolts	60	44
M12 bolts	80	59
Transmission bellhousing-to-engine sump M10 bolts	25	18
Transmission mounting spacer-to-casing bolts:		
Stage 1	40	30
Stage 2	Angle-tighten a further 90°	

1 General information

The VW type 09G automatic transmission has six forward speeds (and one reverse). The automatic gearchanges are electro-hydraulically controlled and the electronic control unit (ECU) has a 'self diagnosis' facility. The engine control unit gives information to the transmission control unit and exchanges signals with other control units. Some of the signals exchanged are engine speed, engine torque, throttle position, kickdown, ignition timing and cruise control. Any faults are stored in the memory and the transmission will remain in an emergency running mode. If a problem occurs, consult a VW dealer or transmission specialist to test the electrical/electronic controls.

The ECU employs 'Fuzzy logic' to determine the gear up-shift and down-shift points. Instead of having predetermined points for up-shift and down-shift, the ECU takes into account several influencing factors before deciding to shift up or down. These factors include engine speed, driving 'resistance' (engine load), brake pedal position, throttle position, and the rate at which the throttle pedal position is changed. This results in an almost infinite number of shift points, which the ECU can tailor to match the driving style, be that sporty or economic. A kickdown facility is also provided, to enable a faster acceleration response when required.

The transmission consists of three main assemblies, these being the torque converter, which is directly coupled to the engine; the final drive unit, which incorporates the differential unit; and the planetary gearbox, with its multi-disc clutches and brake bands. The transmission is lubricated with automatic transmission fluid (ATF), and is regarded by the manufacturers as being 'filled for life', with no requirement for the fluid to be changed at regular intervals.

The torque converter incorporates an automatic lock-up feature, which eliminates torque converter slip in 2nd, 3rd, 4th, 5th and 6th gears; this aids performance and economy.

The kickdown function of the transmission, which acts to select a lower gear (where possible) on full-throttle acceleration, is operated by the throttle pedal position sensor (see Chapter 4A or 4B for details).

A starter inhibitor relay is fitted, to prevent starter motor operation unless the transmission is in P or N. The relay is located above the main fuse/relay panel (see Chapter 12), and marked 175.

A fault diagnosis system is integrated into the control unit, but analysis can only be undertaken with specialised equipment. It is important that any transmission fault be identified and rectified at the earliest possible opportunity. A VW dealer can 'interrogate' the ECU fault memory for stored fault codes, enabling him to pinpoint the fault quickly. Once the fault has been corrected and any fault codes have been cleared, normal transmission operation is restored.

Because of the need for special test equipment, the complexity of some of the parts, and the need for scrupulous cleanliness when servicing automatic transmissions, the work which the owner can do is limited. Most major repairs and overhaul operations should be left to a VW dealer, who will be equipped with the necessary equipment for fault diagnosis and repair. The information in this Chapter is therefore limited to a description of the removal and refitting of the transmission as a complete unit. The removal, refitting and adjustment of the selector cable is also described.

In the event of a transmission problem occurring, consult a VW dealer or transmission specialist before removing the transmission from the vehicle, since the majority of fault diagnosis is carried out with the transmission *in situ*.

2 Automatic transmission – removal and refitting

Removal

1 The automatic transmission is removed downwards from the engine compartment. First, select a solid, level surface to park the vehicle upon. Give yourself enough space to move around it easily. Select P, apply the handbrake, and chock the rear wheels.

2 Loosen the front wheel bolts, and the left-hand driveshaft hub bolt, then raise the front of the vehicle and rest it securely on axle stands (see *Jacking and vehicle support*). Remove the front wheels. Allow a suitable working clearance underneath for the eventual withdrawal of the transmission.

3 Remove the battery and battery tray as described in Chapter 5A.

4 Remove the engine top cover/air cleaner and relevant air trunking. On models with the air filter housing on the left-hand side of the engine compartment, remove the complete air filter housing and air inlet trunking with reference to the relevant part of Chapter 4.

5 Using a screwdriver, lever off the end of the selector cable from the selector shaft lever, then squeeze together the clip and remove the outer cable from the support bracket. Position the cable to one side.

6 Clamp off the automatic transmission fluid cooler hoses with brake hose type clamps. Release the retaining clips and detach the hoses from the cooler (located on the top of the transmission).

7 Remove the starter motor as described in Chapter 5A.

8 Support the engine with a hoist or support bar located on the front wing inner channels. Depending on the engine, temporarily remove components as necessary to attach the hoist.

9 Remove the upper engine-to-transmission mounting bolts.

10 With reference to Chapter 8, detach the right-hand driveshaft from the transmission, and remove the left-hand driveshaft completely. This procedure will involve detaching the front suspension lower arms from the hub carriers in order to pull out the driveshaft inner joints from the transmission. Tie the RH driveshaft to the underbody.

11 Note their locations, then disconnect all wiring from the transmission.

12 Where applicable, remove the brake vacuum pump and bracket with reference to Chapter 9.

13 Unbolt the engine rear mounting torque arm from the bottom of the transmission.

14 Unclip the blanking cap, located next to the right-hand transmission flange, and turn the engine to locate one of the torque converter-to-driveplate nuts. Unscrew and remove the nut whilst preventing the engine from turning by using a wide-bladed screwdriver engaged with the ring gear teeth on the driveplate visible through the starter aperture. Unscrew the remaining two nuts, turning the engine a third of a turn at a time to locate them.

15 With reference to the relevant part of Chapter 4, separate the exhaust downpipe from the intermediate pipe.

16 Position a trolley jack underneath the transmission, and raise it to just take the weight of the unit.

17 Undo and remove the two bolts securing the left-hand gearbox mounting to the triangular mounting spacer. By controlling both the engine hoist/support bar and the trolley jack, lower the transmission approximately 60 mm. Unscrew the two remaining bolts and one nut, and remove the transmission mounting spacer.

18 Unscrew and remove the lower bolts securing the transmission bellhousing to the engine, noting the bolt locations, as they are of different sizes and lengths.

19 Check that all the fixings and attachments are clear of the transmission. Enlist the aid of an assistant to help in guiding and supporting the transmission during its removal.

20 The transmission is located on engine alignment dowels, and if stuck on them, it may be necessary to carefully tap and prise the transmission free of the dowels to allow separation. Once the transmission is disconnected from the location dowels, swivel the unit out and lower it out of the vehicle.

Warning: Support the transmission to ensure that it remains steady on the jack head. Ensure that the torque converter remains in position on its shaft in the torque converter housing.

21 With the transmission removed, bolt a suitable bar and spacer across the front face of the torque converter housing, to retain the torque converter in position.

Refitting

22 Refitting is a reversal of the removal procedure, but note the following special points:

a) *When reconnecting the transmission to the engine, ensure that the location dowels are in position, and that the transmission is correctly aligned with them before pushing it fully into engagement with the engine. As the torque converter is refitted, ensure that the drive pins at the centre of the torque converter hub engage with the recesses in the automatic transmission fluid pump inner wheel.*

b) *Tighten all retaining bolts to their specified torque wrench settings.*

c) *Reconnect and adjust the selector cable, as described in Section 4.*

d) *On completion, check the transmission fluid level (see Chapter 1A).*

e) *If a new transmission unit has been fitted, it may be necessary to have the transmission ECU 'matched' to the engine management ECU electronically, to ensure correct operation – seek the advice of your VW dealer.*

3 Automatic transmission overhaul – general information

In the event of a fault occurring, it will be necessary to establish whether the fault is electrical, mechanical or hydraulic in nature, before repair work can be contemplated. Diagnosis requires detailed knowledge of the transmission's operation and construction, as well as access to specialised test equipment, and so is deemed to be beyond the scope of this manual. It is therefore essential that problems with the automatic transmission are referred to a VW dealer for assessment.

Note that a faulty transmission should not be removed before the vehicle has been assessed by a dealer, as fault diagnosis is carried out with the transmission *in situ*.

4 Selector cable – removal, refitting and adjustment

Removal

1 Disconnect the battery negative lead and position It away from the terminal. **Note:** *Before disconnecting the battery, refer to 'Disconnecting the battery' in the Reference section at the rear of this manual.*

2 Raise and support the vehicle at the front end on axle stands (see *Jacking and vehicle support*). Allow a suitable working clearance underneath the vehicle.

3 Move the selector lever to the S position.

4 Using a wide-bladed screwdriver, prise

the end of the selector cable from the selector lever on the top of the transmission, then squeeze together the clip and detach the outer cable from the bracket **(see illustration)**. Position the cable to one side.

5 Separate the exhaust downpipe from the intermediate pipe with reference to the relevant part of Chapter 4.

6 Remove the centre tunnel heat shield from the underside of the vehicle to gain access to the selector lever housing.

7 Undo the securing bolts and remove the cover from the selector lever housing.

8 Insert a screwdriver through the housing and push out the pin from the selector cable end fitting.

9 Remove the clip securing the outer cable to the selector lever housing, and withdraw the cable from the housing.

Refitting

10 Refit the selector cable by reversing the removal procedure, noting the following points:

a) ***Do not** grease the cable end fittings. This is stated by VW.*
b) *Ensure that the cable is correctly routed, as noted on removal, and that it is securely held by its retaining clips.*
c) *Take care not to bend or kink the cable.*
d) *Carry out the cable adjustment procedure described below before reconnecting the cable at the transmission end.*
e) *When refitting the outer cable to the selector lever housing and the support bracket, use new clips.*

Adjustment

11 Inside the car, move the selector lever to the P position.

12 At the transmission, slacken the cable locking bolt at the ball socket. Check that both the selector lever inside the car and the lever on the transmission are in their P positions by gently rocking them backwards and forwards to settle the cable. **Do not** move either lever out of the P position.

13 Tighten the cable locking bolt to the specified torque.

14 Verify the operation of the selector lever by shifting through all gear positions and checking that every gear can be selected smoothly and without delay.

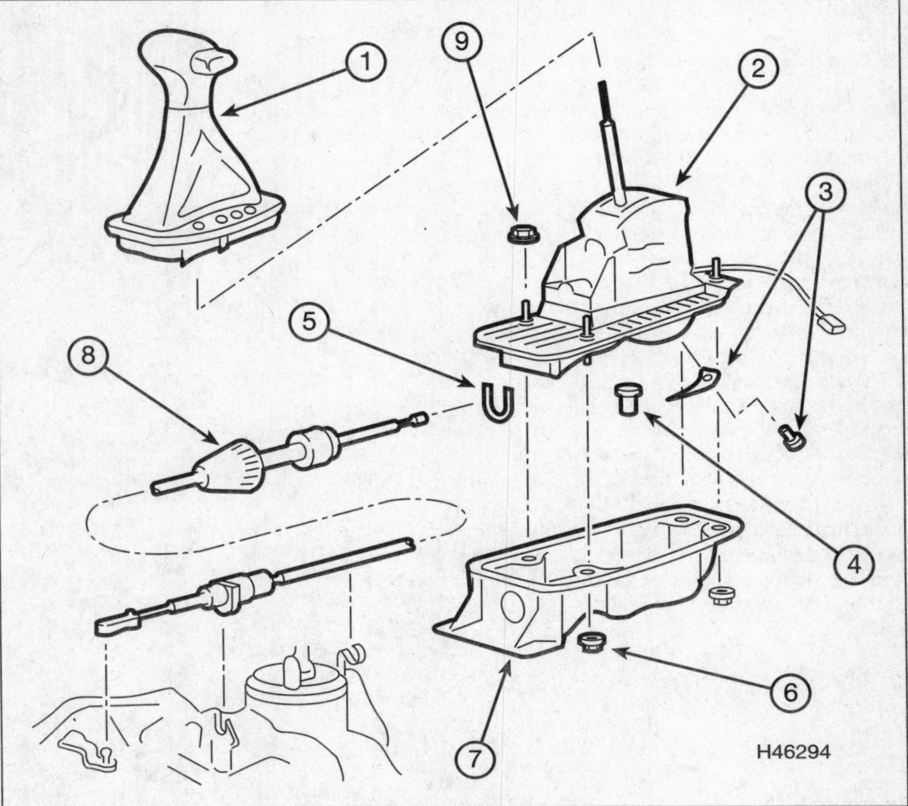

4.4 Selector lever components

1 *Selector knob and gaiter*
2 *Selector lever and mechanism*
3 *Bolt and spring*
4 *Pin*
5 *Locking clip*
6 *Nut*
7 *Cover*
8 *Selector lever cable*
9 *Nut with washer*

5 Multifunction switch – removal and refitting

Removal

1 The multifunction switch is located on the top of the transmission, and its purpose is to prevent inadvertent selection of certain forward and reverse gears while the vehicle is travelling forwards (for example, moving the selector lever into Reverse when moving forwards). First, switch off the ignition and move the selector lever to position N.

2 Using a wide-bladed screwdriver, prise the end of the selector cable from the selector lever on the transmission, then squeeze together the clip and detach the outer cable from the bracket.

3 Disconnect the wiring from the multifunction switch.

4 Unscrew the nut securing the lever to the switch spindle, and remove the lever.

5 Bend back the tabs of the lockwasher, then unscrew the spindle nut **(see illustration)**.

6 Accurately mark the position of the switch in relation to the transmission housing.

7 Unscrew the mounting bolts, then pull the switch from the selector shaft together with the washers.

Refitting

8 Refitting is a reversal of removal, but tighten the spindle nut and switch mounting bolts to the specified torque. Note that VW technicians use a setting gauge to adjust the multifunction switch accurately.

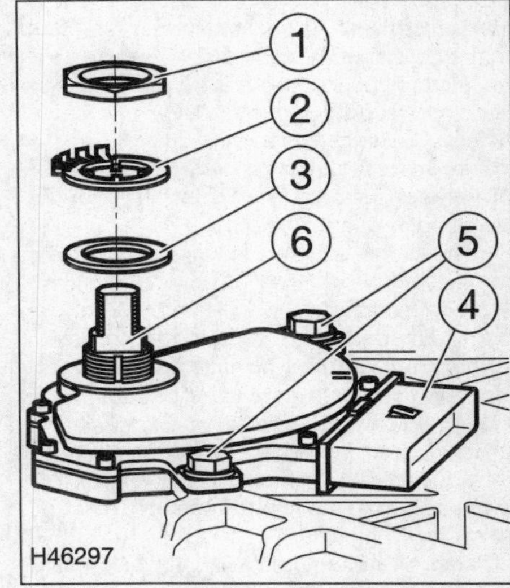

5.5 Multifunction switch spindle nut and washers

1 *Nut*
2 *Lock washer*
3 *Plain washer*
4 *Multifunction switch*
5 *Mounting bolts*
6 *Spindle*

Notes

Chapter 7 Part C:
DSG semi-automatic transmission

Contents

Degrees of difficulty

Easy, suitable for novice with little experience 	**Fairly easy,** suitable for beginner with some experience	**Fairly difficult,** suitable for competent DIY mechanic	**Difficult,** suitable for experienced DIY mechanic	**Very difficult,** suitable for expert DIY or professional 

Specifications

General

Description	DSG (Direct Shift Gearbox) semi-automatic 6- or 7-speed transmission with dual multi-plate clutch, and differential
Transmission type number:	
6-speed	02E
7-speed	0AM

Torque wrench settings

	Nm	lbf ft
Transmission-to-engine bolts:		
M10 bolts	40	30
M12 bolts	80	59
Transmission mounting spacer-to-casing bolts*:		
Stage 1	40	30
Stage 2	Angle-tighten a further 90°	
Transmission mounting spacer-to-bracket bolts*:		
Stage 1	60	44
Stage 2	Angle-tighten a further 90°	

Do not re-use

1 General information

The VW semi-automatic DSG (Direct Shift Gearbox) has six- or seven-forward speeds (and one reverse). In contrast to traditional automatic transmissions where a fluid flywheel (torque converter) transmits the power from the engine to the gearbox, the DSG has two multi-plate clutches. The twin-clutch transmission is essentially two separate gearboxes with a pair of clutches between them. One gearbox provides odd-numbered speeds, the other provides even-numbered speeds. Initially, the "odd" gearbox is in first gear and the "even" gearbox is in second gear. The clutch engages the odd gearbox and the car proceeds in first gear. To change to second gear, the transmission uses the clutches to switch from the odd gearbox to the even gearbox. The odd gearbox immediately pre-selects third gear. At the next change the transmission swaps gearboxes again, engaging third gear, and the even gearbox pre-selects fourth gear. The transmission ECM (Electronic Control Module) calculates the next likely gearchange based on vehicle speed and driver behavior and has the "idle" gearbox pre-select that gear. The main advantages of the DSG is near-instant gear changes, with seamless, highly efficient drive, resulting is less exhaust emissions and fuel consumption.

A fault diagnosis system is integrated into the control unit, but analysis can only be undertaken with specialised equipment. It is important that any transmission fault be identified and rectified at the earliest possible opportunity. A VW dealer or suitable equipped specialist can 'interrogate' the ECM fault memory for stored fault codes, enabling him to pinpoint the fault quickly. Once the fault has been corrected and any fault codes have been cleared, normal transmission operation is restored.

Because of the need for special test equipment, the complexity of some of the parts, and the need for scrupulous cleanliness when these transmissions, the work which the owner can do is limited. Most major repairs and overhaul operations should be left to a VW dealer or specialist, who will be equipped with the necessary equipment for fault diagnosis and repair. The information in this Chapter is therefore limited to a description of the removal and refitting of the transmission as a complete unit. The removal, refitting and adjustment of the selector cable is also described.

In the event of a transmission problem occurring, consult a VW dealer or transmission specialist before removing the transmission from the vehicle, since the majority of fault diagnosis is carried out with the transmission *in situ*.

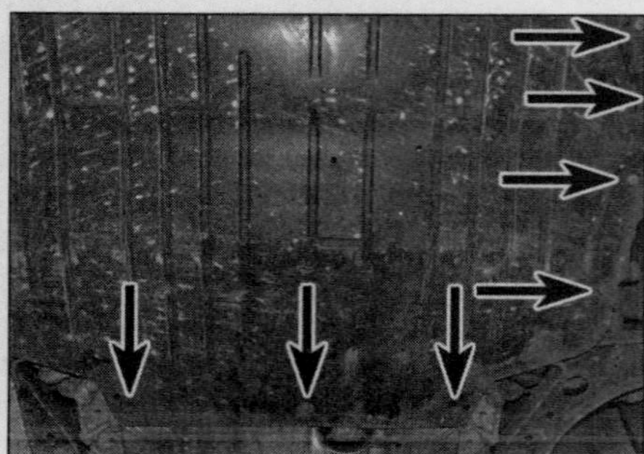

2.2 Undo the fasteners (arrowed) and remove the engine undershield

2.7 Selector cable clip and outer cable circlip (arrowed)

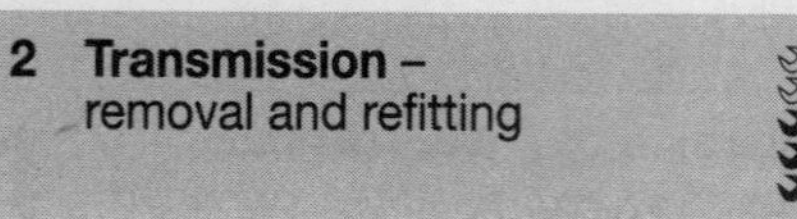

2 Transmission – removal and refitting

Removal

1 The automatic transmission is removed downwards from the engine compartment. First, select a solid, level surface to park the vehicle upon. Give yourself enough space to move around it easily. Select P, apply the handbrake, and chock the rear wheels.

2 Loosen the front wheel bolts, and the driveshaft hub bolts, then raise the front of the vehicle and rest it securely on axle stands (see *Jacking and vehicle support*). Remove the front wheels. Allow a suitable working clearance underneath for the eventual withdrawal of the transmission. Undo the fasteners and remove the engine/transmission undershield **(see illustration)**.

3 Remove the air cleaner housing as described in Chapter 4A.

4 Remove the turbocharger intake hose.

5 Remove the battery and battery tray as described in Chapter 5.

6 Remove the starter motor as described in Chapter 5.

7 Remove the retaining clip, lever off the end of the selector cable from the selector shaft lever, then prise up the circlip and remove the outer cable from the support bracket. Position the cable to one side. Note that both the retaining clip and circlip must be renewed **(see illustration)**.

8 Clamp off the automatic transmission fluid cooler hoses with brake hose type clamps. Release the retaining clips and detach the hoses from the cooler (located on the top of the transmission) **(see illustration)**.

9 Rotate the collar anti-clockwise and disconnect the transmission wiring plug **(see illustration)**. Undo the nuts and detach the wiring loom retainer from the gearbox cover.

10 Remove the upper engine-to-transmission mounting bolts.

11 Release the clips and remove the air hose between the intercooler and the charge air pipe.

12 Remove the radiator cooling fan assembly as described in Chapter 3.

13 Disconnect the wiring plug from the engine oil level/temperature sensor on the sump.

14 Undo the bolts and slide rearwards the tubular exhaust pipe connecting piece between the front and rear sections of the exhaust system.

15 Undo the bolts/nuts and remove the front section of the exhaust pipe.

16 Remove both driveshafts as described in Chapter 8.

17 Undo the bolts and remove the engine rear mounting (torque arm). Position a block of wood between the sump and the subframe to prevent the engine from swinging rearwards.

19 Support the engine with a hoist or support bar located on the front wing inner channels. Depending on the engine, temporarily remove components as necessary to attach the hoist.

20 Position a trolley jack underneath the transmission, and raise it to just take the weight of the unit.

21 Undo and remove the bolts securing the left-hand gearbox mounting to the mounting spacer, and the bolts securing the spacer to the transmission casing. By controlling both the engine hoist/support bar and the trolley jack, lower the transmission approximately 60 mm. Remove the transmission mounting spacer.

22 Remove the transmission-to-engine bolt located in the starter motor aperture.

23 Undo the retaining bolt and remove the small cover plate located above the right-hand driveshaft flange.

24 Lower the engine/transmission until there is sufficient clearance between the upper edge of the transmission and the left-hand chassis member.

25 Unscrew and remove the lower bolts securing the transmission to the engine, noting the bolt locations, as they are of different sizes and lengths.

26 Check that all the fixings and attachments are clear of the transmission. Enlist the aid of an assistant to help in guiding and supporting the transmission during its removal.

27 The transmission is located on engine alignment dowels, and if stuck on them, it may be necessary to carefully tap and prise the transmission free of the dowels to allow separation. Once the transmission is disconnected from the location dowels, swivel the unit out and lower it out of the vehicle.

Warning: Support the transmission to ensure that it remains steady on the jack head.

Refitting

28 Refitting is a reversal of the removal procedure, but note the following special points:

a) Renew the needle bearing in the crankshaft.
b) When reconnecting the transmission to the engine, ensure that the location dowels are in position, and that the transmission is correctly aligned with them before pushing it fully into engagement with the engine.
c) Tighten all retaining bolts to their specified torque wrench settings.
d) Be sure to guide the selector cable into the support bracket as the transmission is refitted – renew the retaining clips.
e) Adjust the selector cable, as described in Section 4.
f) On completion, check the transmission fluid level and coolant level (see Chapter 1).
g) If a new transmission unit has been fitted, it may be necessary to have the transmission ECM 'matched' to the engine management ECM electronically, to ensure correct operation – seek the advice of your VW dealer or suitably equipped specialist.

2.8 Clamp the transmission cooler hoses (arrowed)

2.9 Transmission wiring plug and earth cable (arrowed)

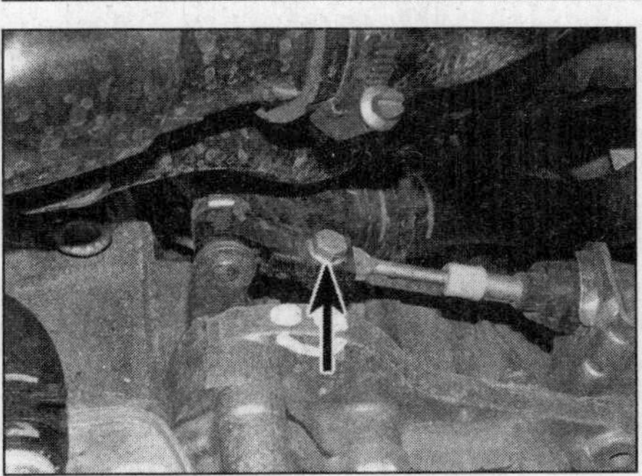

4.2 Slacken the cable adjustment screw (arrowed)

5.2 Prise up the selector lever gaiter surround trim

5.3 Press down the yellow plastic wedge (arrowed)

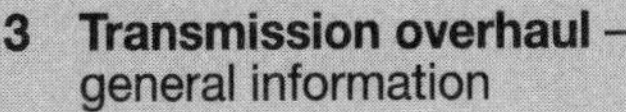

3 Transmission overhaul – general information

In the event of a fault occurring, it will be necessary to establish whether the fault is electrical, mechanical or hydraulic in nature, before repair work can be contemplated. Diagnosis requires detailed knowledge of the transmission's operation and construction, as well as access to specialised test equipment, and so is deemed to be beyond the scope of this manual. It is therefore essential that problems with the automatic transmission are referred to a VW dealer or specialist for assessment.

Note that a faulty transmission should not be removed before the vehicle has been assessed by a dealer or specialist, as fault diagnosis is carried out with the transmission *in situ*.

4 Selector cable – removal, refitting and adjustment

Removal

1 Move the selector lever to the S position, and remove the battery and battery tray as described in Chapter 5.

2 Slacken the adjustment screw on the cable end fitting at the transmission end **(see illustration)**.

3 Prise out the clips securing the cable to the lever on the transmission, and the outer cable to the support bracket **(see illustration 2.7)**. Discard the clips – new ones must be fitted.

4 Pull the cable from the lever and support bracket on the transmission.

5 Raise the front of the vehicle and support it securely on axle stands (see *Vehicle jacking and support*).

6 Separate the exhaust downpipe from the intermediate pipe with reference to the relevant part of Chapter 4.

7 Remove the centre tunnel heat shield from the underside of the vehicle to gain access to the selector lever housing.

8 Undo the securing nuts and remove the cover from the selector lever housing.

9 Remove the clip securing the outer cable to the selector lever housing.

10 Push the retaining tab forwards, the using a screwdriver from beneath, push out the pin from the selector cable end fitting. Remove the cable.

Refitting

11 Refit the selector cable by reversing the removal procedure, noting the following points:

a) ***Do not*** *grease the cable end fittings. This is stated by VW.*

b) *Ensure that the cable is correctly routed, as noted on removal, and that it is securely held by its retaining clips.*

c) *Take care not to bend or kink the cable.*

d) *Carry out the cable adjustment procedure described below before reconnecting the cable at the transmission end.*

e) *When refitting the outer cable to the selector lever housing and the support bracket, use new clips.*

Adjustment

12 Inside the car, move the selector lever to the P position.

13 At the transmission, slacken the cable adjusting bolt at the ball socket. Check that both the selector lever inside the car and the lever on the transmission are in their P positions by gently rocking them backwards and forwards to settle the cable. Do not move either lever out of the P position. The transmission lever is in the P position when it's pushed fully to the right-hand side.

14 Tighten the cable locking bolt.

15 Verify the operation of the selector lever by shifting through all gear positions and checking that every gear can be selected smoothly and without delay.

5 Emergency release of selector lever

1 If the vehicles battery is disconnected or discharged, it is possible to release the selector lever from its locked position. First, ensure the handbrake is fully applied.

2 Carefully prise up the selector lever gaiter surround trim from the console and move it to the left-hand side **(see illustration)**.

3 Press the yellow plastic wedge downwards **(see illustration)**. It should now be possible to move the selector lever to the desired position.

Chapter 8
Driveshafts

Contents

Degrees of difficulty

Easy, suitable for novice with little experience	**Fairly easy,** suitable for beginner with some experience	**Fairly difficult,** suitable for competent DIY mechanic	**Difficult,** suitable for experienced DIY mechanic	**Very difficult,** suitable for expert DIY or professional

Specifications

General

Driveshaft type	Steel shafts with outer constant velocity joints and inner tripod or constant velocity joints (according to type). Some models have an intermediate shaft from the right-hand side of the transmission to the driveshaft
Type code differences:	
VL 90 or VL 100	CV joints each end, inner joint diameter 90 mm or 100 mm bolted to transmission drive flanges on each side
VL 107	CV joints each end, inner joint diameter 107 mm bolted to drive flange on transmission (LH side) or flange on end of intermediate shaft (RH side)
AAR 2600i	CV outer joint, tripod inner joint located in housing splined to sun gear
AAR 3300i	CV outer joint, tripod inner joint housing bolted to transmission drive flange (LH side) or joint located in housing formed on end of intermediate shaft (RH side)

Lubrication

Overhaul and repair	Use only special grease supplied in sachets with gaiter/overhaul kits; joints are otherwise pre-packed with grease and sealed
Joint grease type	
Up to 08/2004	VAG G 000 603 grease
08/2004-on	Refer to VW dealer. **Note:** ***Do not*** *mix with earlier type*
Joint grease quantity	
Outer joint	80 g
Inner joint	130 g

Torque wrench settings

Torque wrench settings	Nm	lbf ft
Driveshaft-to-transmission flange bolts:		
Stage 1	10	7
Stage 2:		
M8	40	30
M10	70	52
Hub bolt*:		
Stage 1	200	148
Stage 2	Angle-tighten a further 180°	
Intermediate shaft bearing to bracket	20	15
Intermediate shaft bracket to block:		
Stage 1	5	4
Stage 2	35	26
Lower arm-to-balljoint nuts*	60	44
Wheel bolts	120	89

** Use new bolt/nuts*

2.3 Remove the heat shield

2.4 Driveshaft/hub bolt

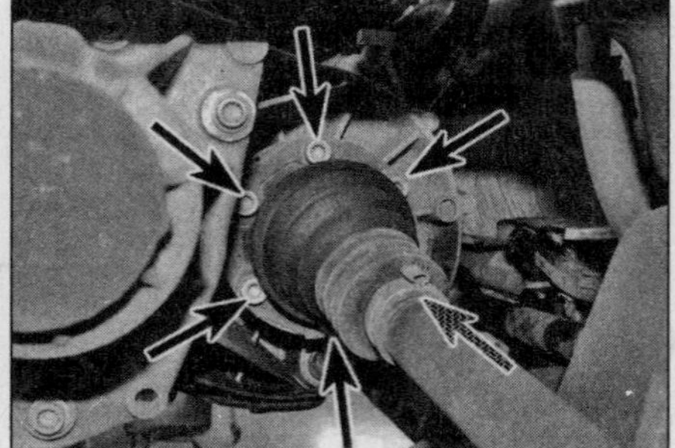

2.8 Driveshaft inner joint and flange bolts

1 General information

Drive is transmitted from the differential to the front wheels by means of two steel driveshafts of either solid or hollow construction (depending on model). Both driveshafts are splined at their outer ends, to accept the wheel hubs, and are secured to the hub by a large bolt. The inner end of each driveshaft is either bolted to a transmission drive flange or splined directly into the differential sun gear. Some models are fitted with an intermediate driveshaft, with its own support bearing, between the transmission and right-hand driveshaft.

Ball-bearing type constant velocity (CV) joints are fitted to the outer ends of each driveshaft, to ensure the smooth and efficient transmission of drive at all the angles possible as the roadwheels move up-and-down with the suspension, and as they turn from side to side under steering.

Plastic gaiters are fitted over both CV joints with steel clips. The gaiters contain the grease which lubricates the joints, and also protect the joints from the entry of dirt and debris.

2 Driveshafts – removal and refitting

Note: *A new hub bolt will be required on refitting. On automatic transmission models, in order to gain the necessary clearance required to withdraw the left-hand driveshaft, it may be necessary to unbolt the rear engine transmission mounting from the subframe, and lift the engine slightly.*

Removal

1 Remove the wheel trim/hub cap (as applicable) then apply the handbrake, and partially unscrew, by a maximum of 90°, the relevant hub bolt with the vehicle resting on its wheels – note that the bolt is very tight, and a suitable extension bar will probably be required to aid unscrewing. Also unscrew the roadwheel securing bolts. **Note:** *Do not loosen the bolt more than 90° with the vehicle standing on the ground, as the wheel bearings may be damaged.*

2 Apply the handbrake, then jack up the front of the vehicle and support it on axle stands (see *Jacking and vehicle support*). Remove the appropriate front roadwheel.

3 Remove the retaining screws and/or clips, and remove the undershields from beneath the engine/transmission unit to gain access to the driveshafts. Where necessary, also unbolt the heat shield from the transmission housing to improve access to the driveshaft inner joint **(see illustration)**.

4 Unscrew and remove the hub bolt **(see illustration). Note:** *Discard the bolt and obtain a new one.*

5 Unscrew the three nuts securing the front suspension lower arm balljoint to the lower arm. Discard the nuts as new ones must be used on refitting.

6 Lever the lower arm downwards to release it from the balljoint studs, then pull the hub carrier outwards, and at the same time withdraw the driveshaft outer constant velocity joint from the hub. If the joint splines are a tight fit in the hub, tap the joint out of the hub using a soft-faced mallet and drift. If this fails to free the driveshaft from the hub, the joint will have to be pressed out using a suitable tool bolted to the hub.

7 Proceed as follows according to type.

Caution: Support the driveshaft by suspending it with wire or string – do not allow it to hang under its own weight, or the joint may be damaged.

Inner joint with drive flange

8 Using a multi-splined tool, unscrew and remove the bolts securing the inner driveshaft joint to the transmission flange and, where applicable, recover the retaining plates from underneath the bolts **(see illustration)**.

Inner joint splined to differential sun gear

9 Position a container beneath the transmission to catch spilt oil, then pull out the driveshaft. The internal driveshaft circlip may be tight in the transmission side gear, in which case careful use of a lever against the transmission casing will be required. Lever against a block of wood to prevent damage to the casing, and take care not to damage the oil seal as the driveshaft is being removed. **Note:** *Pull only on the inner joint housing, not the driveshaft itself, otherwise the gaiter may be damaged.*

Inner joint tripod located in housing on end of intermediate shaft

10 Mark the inner joint housing and driveshaft in relation to each other, then loosen the clip, ease off the rubber gaiter, and pull the tripod out of the housing.

All types

11 Manoeuvre the driveshaft out from underneath the vehicle and (where fitted) recover the gasket from the end of the inner constant velocity joint. **Note:** *Discard the gasket and obtain a new one.*

Caution: Do not allow the vehicle to rest on its wheels with one or both driveshaft(s) removed, as damage to the wheel bearings may result.

12 If moving the vehicle is unavoidable, temporarily insert the outer end of the driveshaft(s) in the hub(s), and tighten the driveshaft retaining bolt(s); in this case, the inner end(s) of the driveshaft(s) must be supported, for example by suspending with string from the vehicle underbody.

Refitting

13 Where applicable, check the condition of the circlip on the inner end of the driveshaft, and if necessary, renew it.

14 As applicable, clean the splines on each end of the driveshaft and in the hub and apply a little oil, and where applicable wipe clean the oil seal in the transmission casing. Check the oil seal and if necessary renew it as described in Chapter 7A or 7B. Smear a little oil on the lips of the oil seal before fitting the driveshaft.

Inner joint with drive flange

15 Ensure that the transmission flange and inner joint mating surfaces are clean and dry. Where necessary, fit a new gasket to the joint by peeling off its backing foil and sticking it in position **(see illustration)**.

16 Manoeuvre the driveshaft into position, and align the inner joint holes with those on the transmission flange. Refit the retaining bolts and where necessary, the plates. Tighten the retaining bolts to the specified torque.

2.15 Locate a new gasket on the inner joint

Inner joint splined to differential sun gear

17 Locate the inner end of the driveshaft into the transmission – turn the driveshaft as necessary to engage the splines. Press in the driveshaft until the internal circlip engages the groove. Check that the circlip is engaged by attempting to pull out the driveshaft with only moderate force.

Inner joint tripod located in housing on end of intermediate shaft

18 Fill the inner joint with the specified quantity of grease, then locate the driveshaft tripod into the housing, aligning the previously-made marks. Ease the gaiter onto the housing, and refit the clip.

All types

19 With the lower arm levered downwards, engage the outer joint with the hub. Fit the new hub bolt and use it to draw the joint fully into position.

20 Align the balljoint studs with the holes in the lower arm, then release the arm and fit the three new nuts. Tighten the nuts to the specified torque.

21 Where applicable (see Note at the beginning of this Section), fit new rear engine/transmission mounting-to-subframe bolts, and tighten the bolts to the specified torque (see relevant part of Chapter 2).

22 Tighten the driveshaft bolt to the Stage 1 torque setting. **Note:** *The bolt must be tightened with the wheel clear of the ground.*

23 Refit the roadwheel and lower the vehicle to the ground, then angle-tighten the driveshaft bolt through the Stage 2 angle (see Specifications).

24 Once the driveshaft bolt is correctly tightened, tighten the wheel bolts to the specified torque and refit the wheel trim/hub cap.

3 Driveshaft rubber gaiters – renewal

1 Remove the driveshaft from the car, as described in Section 2. Continue as described under the relevant sub-heading. Driveshafts with a tripod type inner joint can be identified by the shape of the inner CV joint; the driveshaft retaining bolt holes are in extensions from the joint, giving it a six-pointed star-shaped exterior, in contrast to the smooth, circular shape of the ball-and-cage joint **(see illustrations)**.

3.1a Driveshaft components – models with press-fit metal cover on inner end of inner CV joint

1 *Hub bolt*
2 *Outer joint gaiter*
3 *Gaiter securing clip*
4 *Driveshaft*
5 *Gaiter securing clip*
6 *Inner joint*
7 *Driveshaft-to-transmission flange bolts*
8 *Tripod roller*
9 *Tripod*
10 *Circlip*
11 *Seal (original)*
12 *Seal (repair)*
13 *Metal cover*
14 *Gaiter securing clip*
15 *Inner joint gaiter*
16 *Gaiter securing clip*
17 *Dished washer*
18 *Thrust washer*
19 *Circlip*
20 *Outer joint*

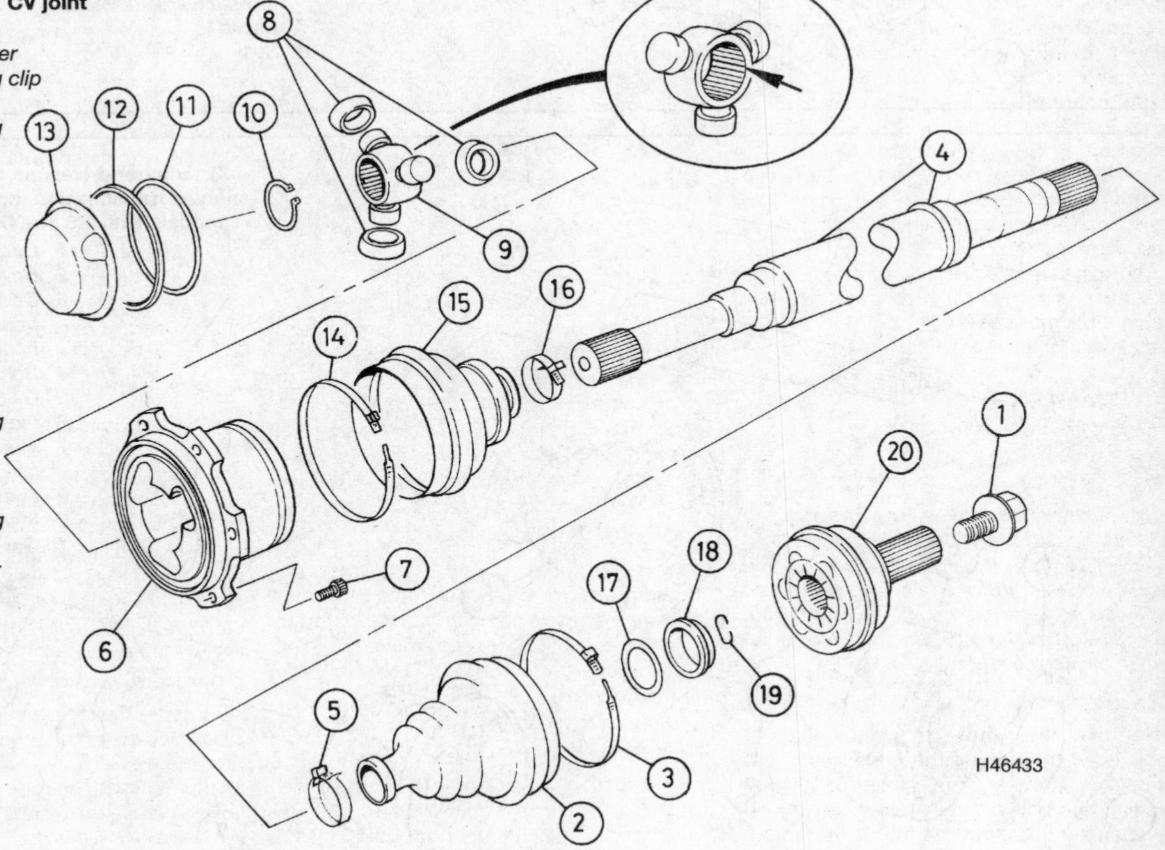

H46433

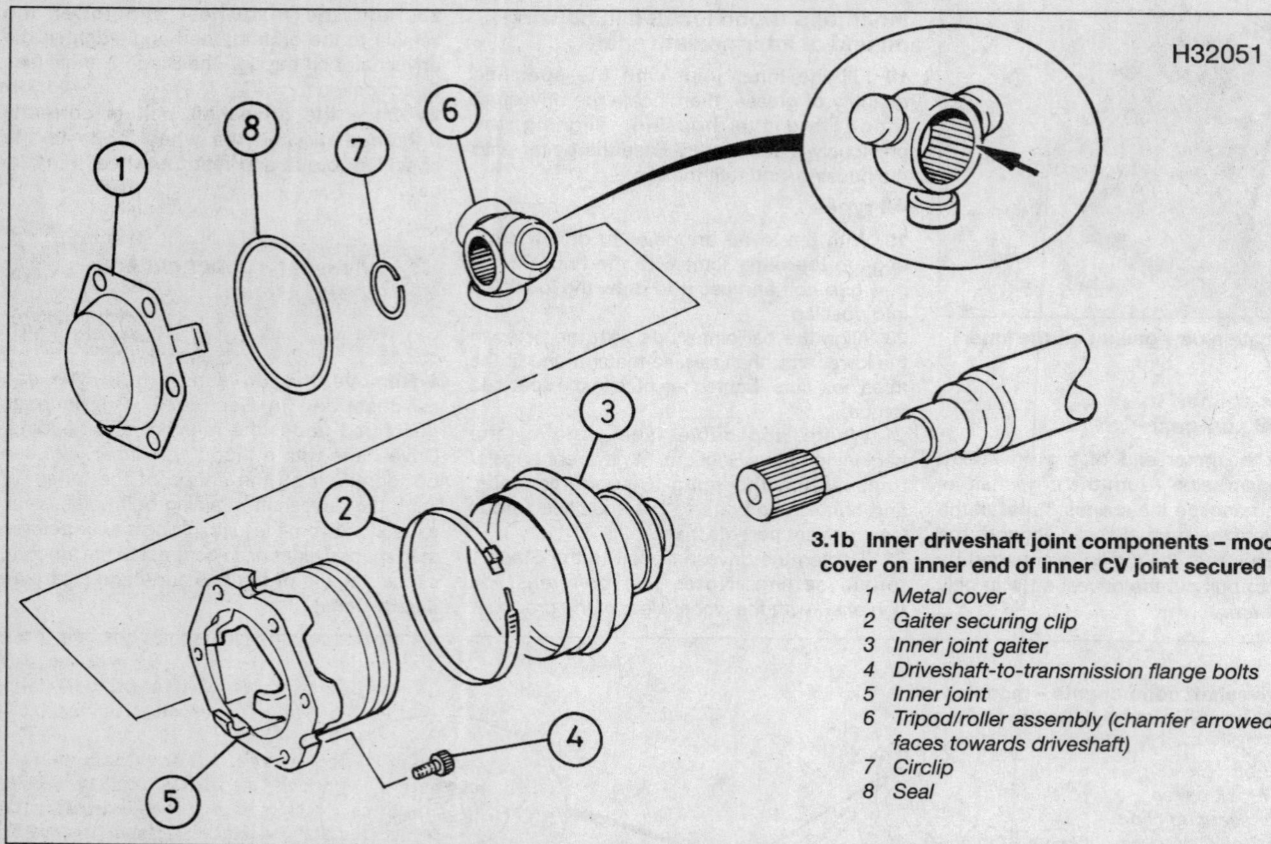

H32051

3.1b Inner driveshaft joint components – models with cover on inner end of inner CV joint secured by tabs

1 *Metal cover*
2 *Gaiter securing clip*
3 *Inner joint gaiter*
4 *Driveshaft-to-transmission flange bolts*
5 *Inner joint*
6 *Tripod/roller assembly (chamfer arrowed faces towards driveshaft)*
7 *Circlip*
8 *Seal*

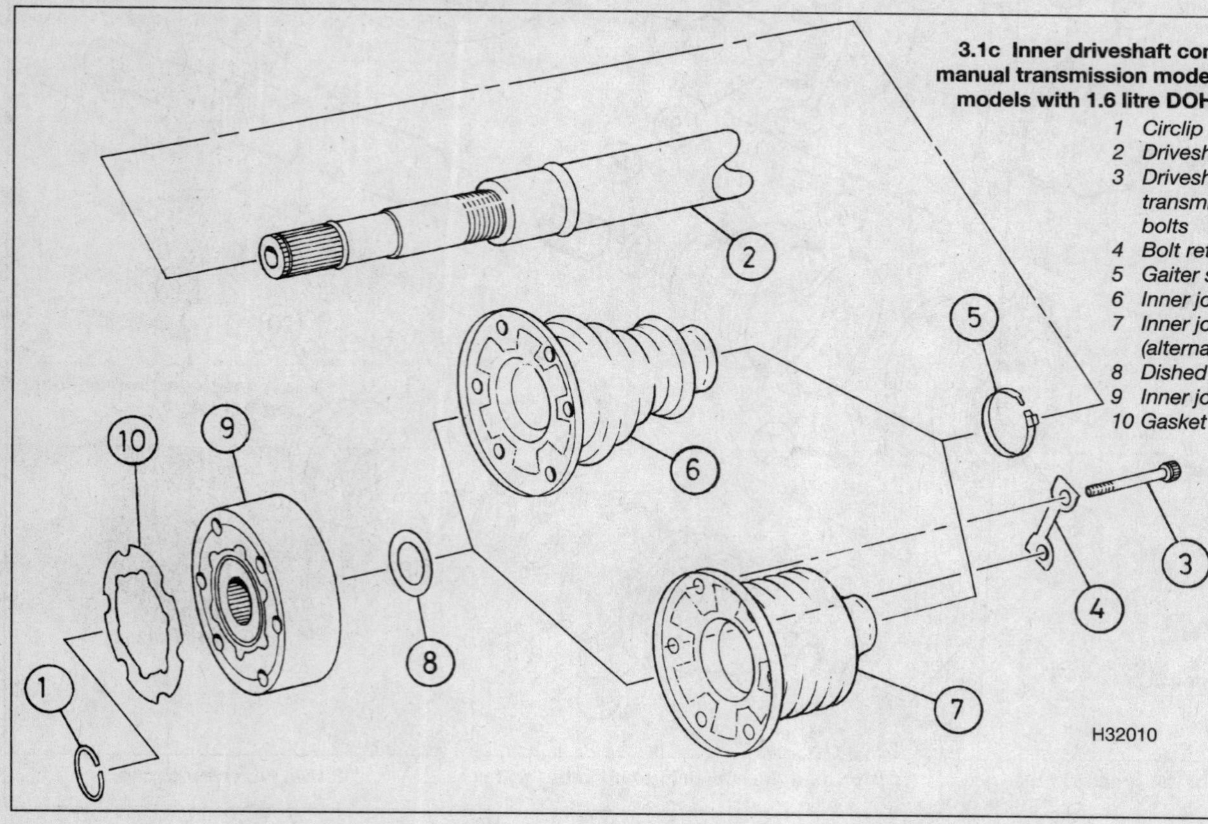

3.1c Inner driveshaft components – manual transmission models (except for models with 1.6 litre DOHC engines)

1 *Circlip*
2 *Driveshaft*
3 *Driveshaft-to-transmission flange bolts*
4 *Bolt retaining plate*
5 *Gaiter securing clip*
6 *Inner joint gaiter*
7 *Inner joint gaiter (alternative type)*
8 *Dished washer*
9 *Inner joint*
10 *Gasket*

H32010

3.2 Release the outer joint gaiter clips...

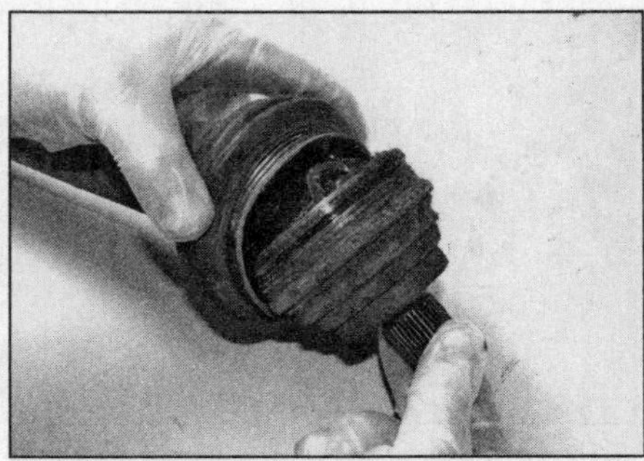
3.3 ...and slide the gaiter away from the joint

3.4 Use a mallet to drive the outer joint from the driveshaft

Outer CV joint gaiter

2 Secure the driveshaft in a vice equipped with soft jaws, and release the two outer joint gaiter retaining clips **(see illustration)**. If necessary, the retaining clips can be cut to release them.

3 Slide the rubber gaiter down the shaft to expose the constant velocity joint, and scoop out excess grease **(see illustration)**.

4 Using a soft-faced mallet, tap the joint off the end of the driveshaft **(see illustration)**.

5 Remove the circlip from the driveshaft groove, and slide off the thrustwasher and dished washer, noting which way around it is fitted **(see illustration)**.

6 Slide the rubber gaiter off the driveshaft and discard it **(see illustration)**.

7 Thoroughly clean the constant velocity joint(s) using paraffin, or a suitable solvent, and dry thoroughly. Carry out a visual inspection as follows.

8 Move the inner splined driving member from side-to-side to expose each ball in turn at the top of its track. Examine the balls for cracks, flat spots or signs of surface pitting.

9 Inspect the ball tracks on the inner and outer members. If the tracks have widened, the balls will no longer be a tight fit. At the same time, check the ball cage windows for wear or cracking between the windows.

10 If on inspection any of the constant velocity joint components are found to be worn or damaged, it will be necessary to renew the complete joint assembly. If the joint is in satisfactory condition, obtain a new gaiter and retaining clips, a constant velocity joint circlip and the correct type of grease. Grease is often supplied with the joint repair kit – if not, use a good-quality molybdenum disulphide grease.

11 Tape over the splines on the end of the driveshaft, to protect the new gaiter as it is slid into place **(see illustration)**.

12 Slide the new gaiter onto the end of the driveshaft, then remove the protective tape from the driveshaft splines.

13 Slide on the dished washer, making sure its convex side is innermost, followed by the thrustwasher.

14 Pack the joint with half the quantity of the specified type of grease. Work the grease well into the bearing tracks whilst twisting the joint, and fill the rubber gaiter with the remaining half **(see illustrations)**.

15 Fit a new circlip to the driveshaft, then tap the joint onto the driveshaft until the circlip engages in its groove **(see illustrations)**. Make sure that the joint is securely retained by the circlip.

16 Ease the gaiter over the joint, and ensure

3.5 Removing the circlip, thrustwasher and dished washer

3.6 Removing the outer gaiter

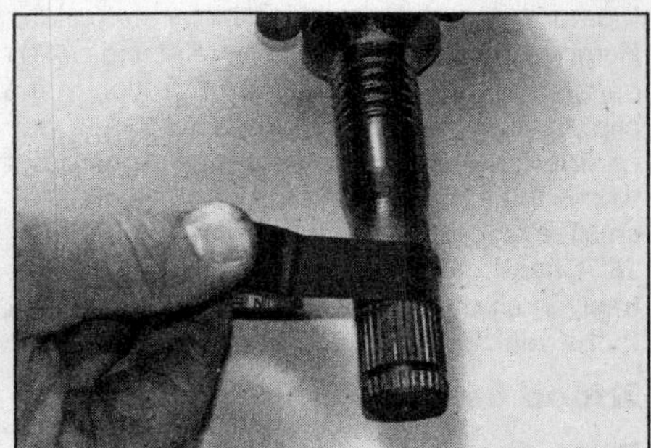
3.11 Temporarily tape over the splines to protect the new gaiter

3.14a Pack half of the grease in the joint...

3.14b ...and the remaining half in the gaiter

3.15a Fit a new circlip...

3.15b ...then refit the outer joint

3.16 Seat the gaiter on the outer joint and driveshaft, then lift its inner lip to equalise the air pressure

3.17a Fit the large metal retaining clip...

3.17b ...and use a suitable tool to tighten it

that the gaiter lips are correctly located on both the driveshaft and constant velocity joint. Lift the outer sealing lip of the gaiter to equalise air pressure within the gaiter **(see illustration)**.

17 Fit the large metal retaining clip to the gaiter. Pull the clip as tight as possible, and locate the hooks on the clip in their slots. Remove any slack in the gaiter retaining clip by carefully compressing the raised section of the clip. In the absence of the special tool, a pair of side-cutters may be used, taking care not to cut the clip **(see illustrations)**. Secure the small retaining clip using the same procedure.

18 Check the constant velocity joint moves freely in all directions, then refit the driveshaft to the vehicle, as described in Section 2.

Tripod inner CV joint gaiter

Press-fit metal cover

19 This type of joint can be recognised from the press-fit metal cover fitted to the end of the CV joint outer member. The cover is round. On models where the inner CV joint gaiter has been renewed previously, a metal cover will not be fitted, in which case this type of joint can be recognised during dismantling by the fact that the tripod rollers are a loose fit on the tripod, and will slide off easily (if the rollers are secured to the tripod, proceed as described in paragraphs 45 to 61).

20 Release the two outer joint gaiter retaining clips. If necessary, the retaining clips can be cut to release them. Slide the rubber gaiter down the shaft, away from the joint outer member.

21 Carefully secure the joint outer member in a vice equipped with soft jaws.

22 Drive a screwdriver through the side of the metal cap over the end of the joint outer member, and use the screwdriver to lever the cap off the outer member. If the cap cannot be levered off, drive a second screwdriver through the opposite side of the cap, and use the two screwdrivers to lever off the cap.

23 Scoop out excess grease from the joint, then remove the O-ring from the groove in the end of the joint outer member.

24 Using a suitable marker pen or a scriber, make alignment marks between the end of the driveshaft, the tripod roller assembly, and the outer member.

25 Support the driveshaft and the joint, and withdraw the outer member from the vice. As the assembly is removed from the vice, make sure that the rollers do not fall off the tripod.

26 Slowly slide the joint outer member down the driveshaft, away from the joint, making sure that the rollers stay on the tripod.

27 Mark the rollers and the arms of the tripod, so that the rollers can be refitted in their original positions, then lift off the rollers and place them to one side on a dry, clean surface.

28 Remove the circlip from the end of the driveshaft.

29 Press or drive the driveshaft from the tripod, taking great care not to damage the surfaces of the roller locating arms.

30 Slide the outer member and the rubber gaiter from the end of the driveshaft.

31 Thoroughly clean the joint components using paraffin, or a suitable solvent, and dry thoroughly. Carry out a visual inspection as follows.

32 Inspect the tripod rollers and the joint outer member for signs of wear, pitting or scuffing on their mating surfaces. Check that the joint rollers rotate smoothly, with no traces of roughness **(see illustration)**.

33 If the rollers or outer member shown signs of wear or damage, it will be necessary to renew the complete driveshaft, since the joint is not available separately. If the joint is in satisfactory condition, obtain a repair kit, consisting of a new gaiter, retaining clips, circlip, and the correct type and quantity of grease.

34 Tape over the splines on the end of the driveshaft, to protect the new gaiter as it is slid into place, then slide the new gaiter and securing clips, and the joint outer member over the end of the driveshaft **(see illustrations)**. Remove the protective tape from the driveshaft splines.

3.32 Check the tripod rollers and outer member for signs of wear

3.34a Tape over the driveshaft splines to protect the new gaiter...

3.34b ...then lever the gaiter carefully over the ridge on the driveshaft

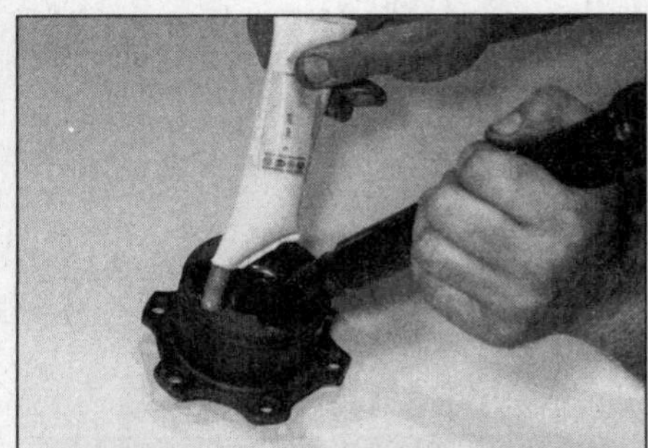
3.39 Work the grease into the joint outer member

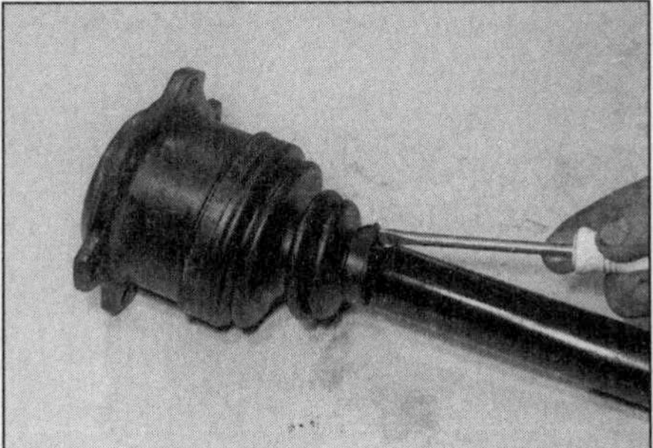
3.41 Lift the gaiter outer end to equalise the air pressure

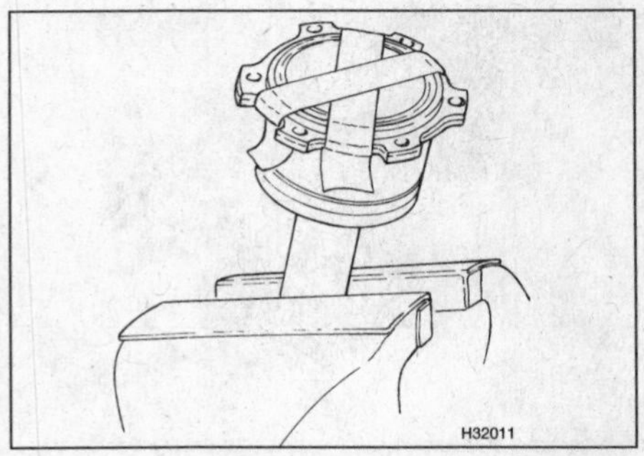

3.44 Tape over the end of the driveshaft joint

35 Press or drive the tripod onto the end of the driveshaft until it contacts the stop, ensuring that the marks made on the end of the driveshaft and the tripod before dismantling are aligned. Note that the chamfered edge of the internal splines on the tripod should face towards the driveshaft.

36 Fit the new circlip to retain the tripod on the end of the driveshaft.

37 Refit the rollers to the tripod, ensuring that they are refitted in their original locations, as noted before removal.

38 Work half of the grease supplied with the repair kit into the inner end of the joint outer member, then slide the outer member over the tripod, ensuring that the marks made during dismantling are aligned, and clamp the outer member in the vice.

39 Work the rest of the grease supplied with the repair kit into the rear of the joint outer member **(see illustration)**.

40 Slide the rubber gaiter up the driveshaft onto the joint outer member, and secure with the large clip, as described in paragraph 17.

41 Lift the gaiter outer end to equalise the air pressure in the gaiter, then secure the outer gaiter securing clip in position using the same method used previously **(see illustration)**.

42 Check that the grease in the joint outer member is evenly distributed around the tripod rollers.

43 Wipe any excess grease from the inner face of the joint outer member, then fit the rectangular profile O-ring provided in the repair kit into the groove in the inner face of the joint outer member. The rectangular profile of the seal acts as a grease seal, and takes the place of the metal cover prised off during dismantling.

44 Check the driveshaft joint moves freely in all directions, then refit the driveshaft to the vehicle, as described in Section 2. To prevent the tripod joint from being pushed back down the driveshaft during refitting, temporarily stick adhesive tape over the open end of the joint outer member **(see illustration)**. Remove the tape just before reconnecting the inner end of the driveshaft to the transmission.

Metal cover secured by tabs

45 This type of joint can be recognised from the metal cover fitted to the end of the CV joint outer member. The cover fits over the end of the outer member flange, and the driveshaft-to-transmission flange bolts pass through the cover. The cover is secured to the outer member flange by three tabs. If the cover is a press-fit, or if no cover is fitted, proceed as described in paragraphs 19 to 44.

46 Proceed as described in paragraphs 20 and 21.

47 Using a screwdriver, prise up the tabs of the metal cap over the end of the joint outer member. Lever the cover from the joint outer member.

48 Proceed as described in paragraphs 23 and 24.

49 Support the driveshaft and the joint, and withdraw the outer member from the vice. Slide the joint outer member down the driveshaft, away from the joint.

50 Remove the circlip from the end of the driveshaft.

51 Press or drive the driveshaft from the tripod, taking great care not to damage the rollers.

52 Proceed as described in paragraphs 30 to 36, taking care not to damage the rollers as the tripod is refitted.

53 Work half of the grease supplied with the repair kit into the inner end of the joint outer member, then slide the outer member over the tripod, ensuring that the marks made during dismantling are aligned, and clamp the outer member in the vice.

54 Work the rest of the grease supplied with the repair kit into the rear of the joint outer member.

55 Slide the rubber gaiter up the driveshaft onto the joint outer member, ensuring that the end of the gaiter seats in the groove in the joint outer member, and secure with the large clip as described in paragraph 17.

56 Lift the gaiter outer end to equalise the air pressure in the gaiter, then secure the outer gaiter securing clip in position using the same method used previously.

57 Check that the grease in the joint outer member is evenly distributed around the tripod rollers.

58 Wipe any excess grease from the inner face of the joint outer member, then fit the O-ring provided in the repair kit into the groove in the inner face of the joint outer member.

59 Fit the new cover supplied in the repair kit to the inner end of the joint outer member, ensuring that the bolt holes in the outer member and cover are aligned.

60 Secure the cover by bending the securing tabs around the edge of the outer member flange.

61 Check the driveshaft joint moves freely in all directions, then refit the driveshaft to the vehicle, as described in Section 2.

Ball-and-cage type inner CV joint

62 Secure the driveshaft in a vice equipped with soft jaws, then release the gaiter small securing clip, securing the gaiter to the driveshaft **(see illustration)**.

63 Using a hammer and a small drift, carefully drive the gaiter metal ring from the joint outer member **(see illustration)**.

3.62 Release the gaiter small securing clip...

3.63 ...drive the metal ring from the joint outer member

3.65 Remove the circlip...

3.66a ...followed by the joint...

3.66b ...dished washer...

3.67 ...and gaiter

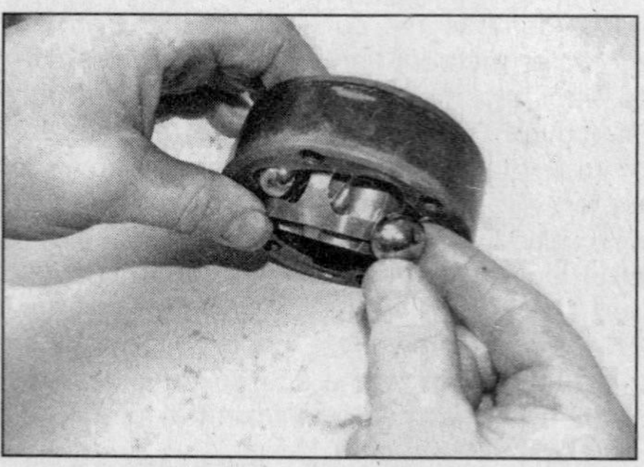

3.68a Tilt the splined hub and cage to remove the ball-bearings...

3.68b ...then separate the hub from the cage

64 Slide the gaiter down the driveshaft to expose the constant velocity joint, and scoop out excess grease.

65 Remove the circlip from the end of the driveshaft using circlip pliers **(see illustration)**.

66 Press or drive the driveshaft from the joint, taking great care not to damage the joint. Recover the dished washer fitted between the constant velocity joint and the gaiter **(see illustrations)**.

67 Slide the gaiter from the end of the driveshaft **(see illustration)**.

68 Proceed as described previously in paragraphs 7 to 12 **(see illustrations)**.

69 Slide the dished washer onto the driveshaft, making sure its convex side is innermost.

70 Fit the joint to the end of the driveshaft, noting that the chamfered edge of the internal splines on the joint should face towards the driveshaft. Drive or press the joint into position until it contacts the shoulder on the driveshaft.

71 Fit a new circlip to retain the joint on the end of the driveshaft.

72 It the left-hand driveshaft is being worked on, mark the final installation position of the gaiter outboard end on the driveshaft using tape or paint – do not scratch the surface of the driveshaft **(see illustration)**.

73 Pack the joint with the half the recommended quantity of grease (see

3.68c Inner CV joint gaiter repair kit

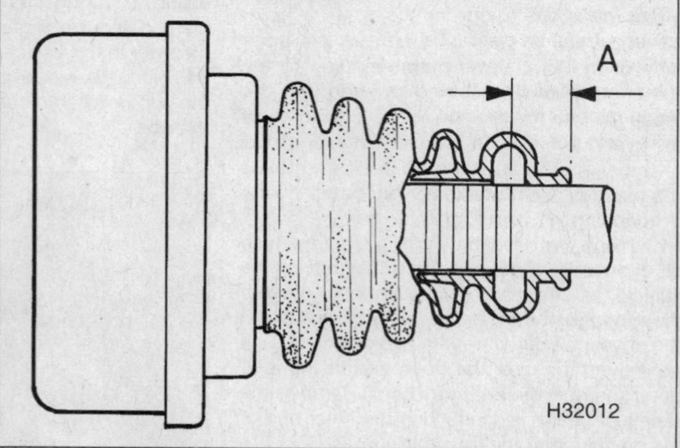

3.72 Installation position of inner joint gaiter on left-hand driveshaft

A = 17.0 mm

Specifications), then pack the gaiter with the remaining half **(see illustrations)**.

74 Slide the gaiter up the driveshaft, and press or drive the gaiter metal ring onto the joint outer member. To ensure the bolt holes are correctly positioned, temporarily fit one of the flange bolts **(see illustrations)**.

75 If the left-hand driveshaft is being worked on, slide the outboard end of the gaiter into position using the mark made previously (see paragraph 72), then secure the outer gaiter securing clip in position as described in paragraph 17.

76 If the right-hand driveshaft is being worked on, slide the outboard end of the gaiter into position on the driveshaft, then secure the outer gaiter securing clip in position as described in paragraph 17 **(see illustration)**.

77 Check the driveshaft joint moves freely in all directions, then refit the driveshaft to the vehicle, as described in Section 2.

4 Driveshaft overhaul – general information

If any of the checks described in Chapter 1A or 1B reveal wear in any driveshaft joint, first remove the roadwheel trim or centre cap (as applicable) and check that the hub bolt is tight. If the bolt is loose, obtain a new one, and tighten it to the specified torque (see Section 2). If the bolt is tight, refit the centre cap/trim, and repeat the check on the other hub bolt.

Road test the vehicle, and listen for a metallic clicking from the front of the vehicle as the vehicle is driven slowly in a circle on full-lock. If a clicking noise is heard, this indicates wear in the outer constant velocity joint; this means that the joint must be renewed.

If vibration consistent with roadspeed is felt through the car when accelerating, there is a possibility of wear in the inner constant velocity joints.

To check the joints for wear, remove the driveshafts, then dismantle them as described in Section 3. If any wear or free play is found, the affected joint must be renewed. Refer to a VW dealer for information on the availability of driveshaft components.

5 Intermediate driveshaft and support bearing assembly – removal, overhaul and refitting

Removal

1 Remove the right-hand driveshaft as described in Section 2.

2 Unscrew the three bolts securing the intermediate driveshaft to the bearing bracket on the rear of the cylinder block.

3 Position a container beneath the transmission to catch spilled oil/fluid when the intermediate shaft is removed.

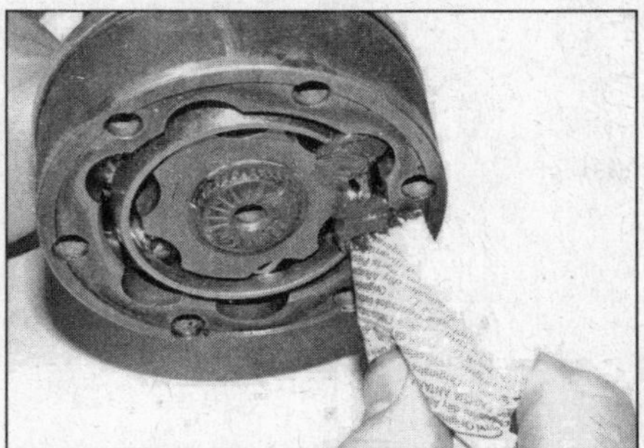

3.73a Pack the inner joint with half of the grease...

3.73b ...then pack the gaiter with the remaining half

3.74a Temporarily fit one of the flange bolts to ensure the bolt holes are correctly aligned...

3.74b ...then drive the metal ring onto the joint outer member

4 Pull the driveshaft from the transmission splined sun gear/input shaft, and withdraw through the bearing bracket.

5 Remove the O-ring seal from the input shaft and discard, as a new one must be used on refitting.

Overhaul

6 Inspect the intermediate driveshaft and bearing for excessive wear and damage, and renew as necessary.

7 Ideally, a hydraulic press will be required to press the driveshaft from the bearing, although it may be possible to drive it out with a soft-faced mallet, while supporting the bearing in a vice.

8 Using a suitable metal tube, press or drive the new bearing fully into position on the driveshaft. Press only on the bearing inner race.

Refitting

9 Refitting is a reversal of removal, but note the following additional points:

a) Fit a new O-ring seal to the input shaft.
b) Tighten all mounting nuts/bolts to the specified torque, where given.
c) Top up the transmission oil/fluid.

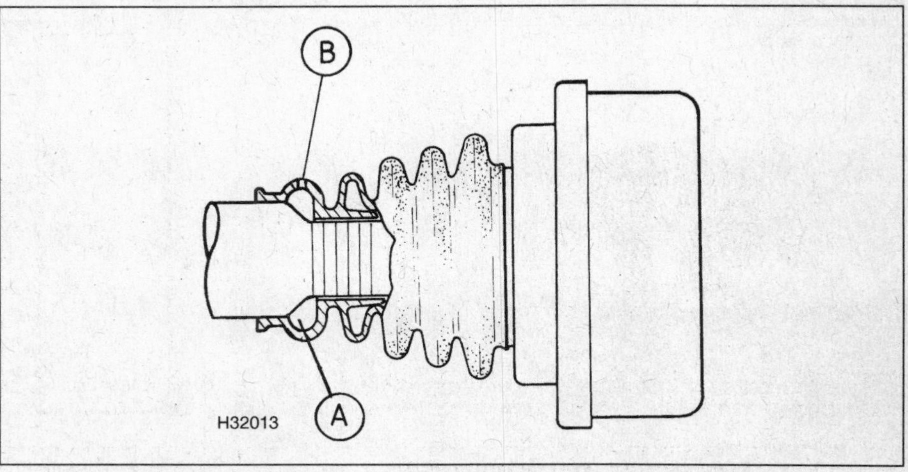

3.76 Installation position of inner joint gaiter on right-hand driveshaft

A Vent chamber in gaiter *B Vent hole*

Chapter 9
Braking system

Contents

Degrees of difficulty

Easy, suitable for novice with little experience 	**Fairly easy,** suitable for beginner with some experience	**Fairly difficult,** suitable for competent DIY mechanic	**Difficult,** suitable for experienced DIY mechanic	**Very difficult,** suitable for expert DIY or professional 

Specifications

Front brakes

Caliper type	FSIII or FN3 (according to model)
Disc diameter:	
FSIII	280 mm
FN3	288 or 312 mm
Disc thickness.	
New:	
FSIII	22.0 mm
FN3	25.0 mm
Minimum permissible thickness:	
FSIII	19.0 mm
FN3	22.0 mm
Maximum disc run-out	0.1 mm
Brake pad lining thickness (all models):	
New	14.0 mm
Minimum	2.0 mm

Rear disc brakes

Caliper type	C38 or CII38 (according to model)
Disc diameter:	
Type C38	255 mm
Type CII38	286 mm
Disc thickness:	
New:	
Type C38	10.0 mm
Type CII38	12.0 mm
Minimum thickness:	
Type C38	8.0 mm
Type CII38	10.0 mm
Maximum disc run-out	0.1 mm
Brake pad lining thickness (all models):	
New	11.0 mm
Minimum	2.0 mm

Torque wrench settings

	Nm	lbf ft
ABS control unit retaining bolts	8	6
ABS wheel sensor retaining bolts	8	6
Brake pedal pivot shaft nut	25	18
Brake light switch (10/05-on models)	5	4
Electric vacuum pump bracket to transmission	25	18
Electric vacuum pump to bracket	8	6
Front brake caliper:		
Guide pins	30	22
Mounting bracket bolts (FN3)	125	92
Front brake disc shield	10	7
Hydraulic brake line union nuts	14	10
Master cylinder mounting nuts	25	18
Rear brake caliper:		
Guide pin bolts*	35	26
Mounting bracket bolts	65	48
Roadwheel bolts	120	89
Servo unit mechanical vacuum pump (diesel models):		
Upper bolts	20	15
Lower bolts	10	7
Servo unit mounting nuts	25	18

** Use new bolts*

1 General information and precautions

General information

The braking system is of servo-assisted, diagonal dual-circuit hydraulic type. The arrangement of the hydraulic system is such that each circuit operates one front and one rear brake from a tandem master cylinder. Under normal circumstances, both circuits operate in unison, but, if there is hydraulic failure in one circuit, full braking force will still be available at two wheels. On petrol engines, vacuum for the servo unit is supplied from the inlet manifold, however, on diesel engines a combined fuel lift pump and vacuum pump is driven off the end of the camshaft.

All models of Golf and Jetta covered by this manual are equipped with disc brakes at the front and rear. ABS is fitted as standard to all models (refer to Section 19 for further information on ABS operation).

The front disc brakes are actuated by single-piston sliding type calipers, which ensure that equal pressure is applied to each disc pad.

The rear brakes are also actuated by single-piston sliding calipers, which incorporate independent mechanical handbrake mechanisms as well.

Precautions

• When servicing any part of the system, work carefully and methodically; also observe scrupulous cleanliness when overhauling any part of the hydraulic system. Always renew components in axle sets (where applicable) if in doubt about their condition, and use only genuine VW parts, or at least those of known good quality. Note the warnings given in *Safety first!* and at relevant points in this Chapter concerning the dangers of asbestos dust and hydraulic fluid.

2 Hydraulic system – bleeding

Warning: Hydraulic fluid is poisonous; wash off immediately and thoroughly in the case of skin contact, and seek immediate medical advice if any fluid is swallowed or gets into the eyes. Certain types of hydraulic fluid are flammable, and may ignite when allowed into contact with hot components; when servicing any hydraulic system, it is safest to assume that the fluid is flammable, and to take precautions against the risk of fire as though it is petrol that is being handled. Hydraulic fluid is also an effective paint stripper, and will attack plastics; if any is spilt, it should be washed off immediately, using copious quantities of fresh water. Finally, it is hygroscopic (it absorbs moisture from the air) – old fluid may be contaminated and unfit for further use. When topping-up or renewing the fluid, always use the recommended type, and ensure that it comes from a freshly-opened sealed container.

Note: *VW specify that at least 0.25 litre of brake fluid should be expelled from each caliper.*

General

1 The correct operation of any hydraulic system is only possible after removing all air from the components and circuit; this is achieved by bleeding the system. Since the clutch hydraulic system also uses fluid from the brake system reservoir, it should also be bled at the same time by referring to Chapter 6, Section 2.

2 During the bleeding procedure, add only clean, unused hydraulic fluid of the recommended type; never re-use fluid that has already been bled from the system. Ensure that sufficient fluid is available before starting work.

3 If there is any possibility of incorrect fluid being already in the system, the brake components and circuit must be flushed completely with uncontaminated, correct fluid, and new seals should be fitted to the various components.

4 If hydraulic fluid has been lost from the system, or air has entered because of a leak, ensure that the fault is cured before continuing further.

5 Park the vehicle on level ground, then chock the wheels and release the handbrake.

6 Check that all pipes and hoses are secure, unions tight and bleed screws closed. Clean any dirt from around the bleed screws.

7 Unscrew the master cylinder reservoir cap, and top the reservoir up to the MAX level line; refit the cap loosely, and remember to maintain the fluid level at least above the MIN level line throughout the procedure, or there is a risk of further air entering the system.

8 There is a number of one-man, do-it-yourself brake bleeding kits currently available from motor accessory shops. It is recommended that one of these kits is used whenever possible, as they greatly simplify the bleeding operation, and reduce the risk of expelled air and fluid being drawn back into the system. If such a kit is not available, the basic (two-man) method must be used, which is described in detail below.

9 If a kit is to be used, prepare the vehicle as described previously, and follow the kit manufacturer's instructions, as the procedure may vary slightly according to the type being used; generally, they are as outlined below in the relevant sub-section.

10 Whichever method is used, the same sequence must be followed (paragraph 12) to ensure the removal of all air from the system.

Bleeding sequence

11 If the system has been only partially

disconnected, and suitable precautions were taken to minimise fluid loss, it should be necessary only to bleed that part of the system.

12 If the complete system is to be bled, then it should be done working in the following sequence:

RHD models

a) Right-hand front brake.
b) Left-hand front brake.
c) Right-hand rear brake.
d) Left-hand rear brake.

LHD models

a) Left-hand front brake.
b) Right-hand front brake.
c) Left-hand rear brake.
d) Right-hand rear brake.

If the hydraulic fluid has run dry in either chamber of the reservoir, the system must be pre-bled as follows, before carrying out the bleeding sequence described above:

a) Bleed the front left and right brakes simultaneously.
b) Bleed the rear left and right brakes simultaneously.

Bleeding

Basic (two-man) method

13 Collect together a clean glass jar of reasonable size, a suitable length of plastic or rubber tubing which is a tight fit over the bleed screw, and a ring spanner to fit the screw. The help of an assistant will also be required.

14 Remove the dust cap from the first screw in the sequence **(see illustration)**. Fit the spanner and tube to the screw, place the other end of the tube in the jar, and pour in sufficient fluid to cover the end of the tube.

15 Ensure that the master cylinder reservoir fluid level is maintained at least above the MIN level line throughout the procedure.

16 Have the assistant fully depress the brake pedal several times to build-up pressure, then maintain it on the final downstroke.

17 While pedal pressure is maintained, unscrew the bleed screw (approximately one turn) and allow the compressed fluid and air to flow into the jar. The assistant should maintain pedal pressure, following it down to the floor if necessary, and should not release it until instructed to do so. When the flow stops, tighten the bleed screw again, have the assistant release the pedal slowly, and recheck the reservoir fluid level.

18 Repeat the steps given in paragraphs 16 and 17 until the fluid emerging from the bleed screw is free from air bubbles. If the master cylinder has been drained and refilled, and air is being bled from the first screw in the sequence, allow approximately five seconds between cycles for the master cylinder passages to refill.

19 When no more air bubbles appear, tighten the bleed screw securely, remove the tube and spanner, and refit the dust cap. Do not overtighten the bleed screw.

20 Repeat the procedure on the remaining screws in the sequence, until all air is removed from the system and the brake pedal feels firm again.

Using a one-way valve kit

21 As their name implies, these kits consist of a length of tubing with a one-way valve fitted, to prevent expelled air and fluid being drawn back into the system; some kits include a translucent container, which can be positioned so that the air bubbles can be more easily seen flowing from the end of the tube.

22 The kit is connected to the bleed screw, which is then opened. The user returns to the driver's seat, depresses the brake pedal with a smooth, steady stroke, and slowly releases it; this is repeated until the expelled fluid is clear of air bubbles **(see illustration)**.

23 Note that these kits simplify work so much that it is easy to forget the master cylinder reservoir fluid level; ensure that this is maintained at least above the MIN level line at all times.

Using a pressure-bleeding kit

24 These kits are usually operated by the reservoir of pressurised air contained in the spare tyre. However, note that it will be probably necessary to reduce the pressure to less than 1.0 bar (14.5 psi); refer to the instructions supplied with the kit.

25 By connecting a pressurised, fluid-filled container to the master cylinder reservoir, bleeding can be carried out simply by opening each screw in turn (in the specified sequence), and allowing the fluid to flow out until no more air bubbles can be seen in the expelled fluid.

26 This method has the advantage that the large reservoir of fluid provides an additional safeguard against air being drawn into the system during bleeding.

27 Pressure-bleeding is particularly effective when bleeding 'difficult' systems, or when bleeding the complete system at the time of routine fluid renewal.

All methods

28 When bleeding is complete, and firm pedal feel is restored, wash off any spilt fluid, tighten the bleed screws securely, and refit their dust caps.

29 Check the hydraulic fluid level in the master cylinder reservoir, and top-up if necessary (see *Weekly checks*).

30 Discard any hydraulic fluid that has been bled from the system; it will not be fit for re-use.

31 Check the feel of the brake pedal. If it feels at all spongy, air must still be present in the system, and further bleeding is required. Failure to bleed satisfactorily after a reasonable repetition of the bleeding procedure may be due to worn master cylinder seals.

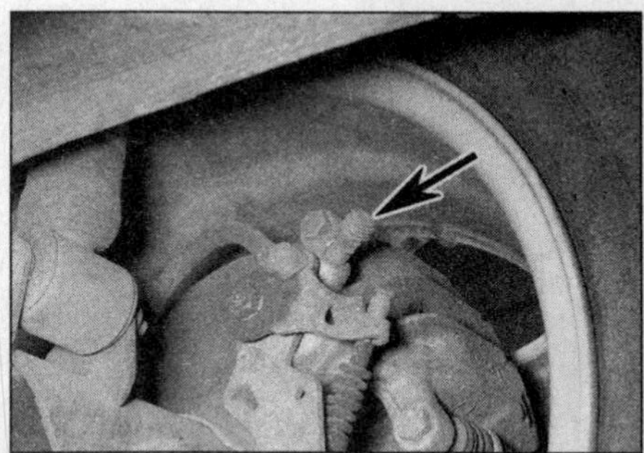

2.14 Remove the dust cap (arrowed) from the first screw in the sequence

3 Hydraulic pipes and hoses – renewal

Note: *Refer to the note in Section 2 concerning the dangers of hydraulic fluid.*

1 If any pipe or hose is to be renewed, minimise fluid loss by first removing the master cylinder reservoir cap, then tightening it down onto a piece of polythene to obtain an airtight seal. Alternatively, flexible hoses can be sealed, if required, using a proprietary brake hose clamp; metal brake pipe unions can be plugged (if care is taken not to allow dirt into the system) or capped immediately they are disconnected. Place a wad of rag under any union that is to be disconnected, to catch any spilt fluid.

2 If a flexible hose is to be disconnected, where applicable unscrew the brake pipe union nut before removing the spring clip which secures the hose to its mounting bracket.

3 To unscrew the union nuts, it is preferable to obtain a brake pipe spanner of the correct size; these are available from most large motor accessory shops. Failing this, a close-fitting open-ended spanner will be required, though if the nuts are tight or corroded, their flats may be rounded-off if the spanner slips. In such a case, a self-locking wrench is often the only way to unscrew a stubborn union, but it follows that the pipe and the damaged nuts must be renewed on reassembly. Always clean a union and surrounding area before disconnecting it. If disconnecting a component with more

2.22 Bleeding a brake using a one-way valve kit

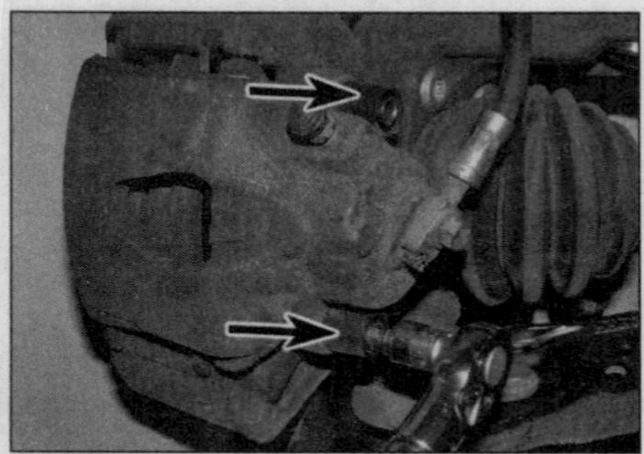
4.4a Unscrew the caliper guide pins...

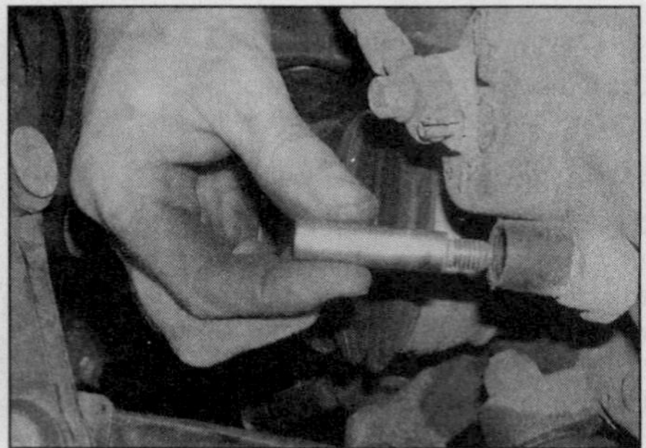
4.4b ...and remove them

4.5a Removing the outer pad...

4.5b ...and inner pad from the caliper

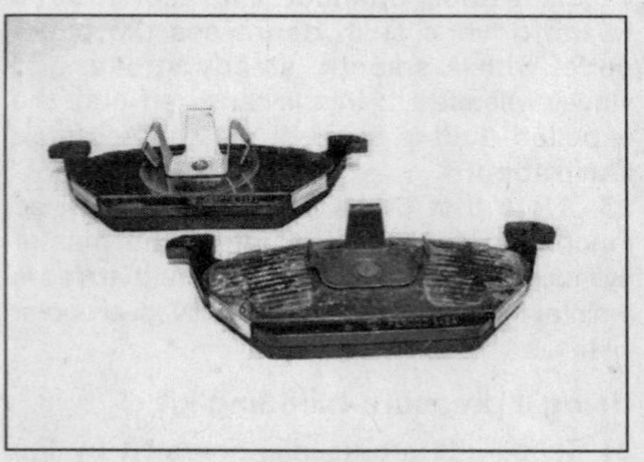
4.5c Front brake pads

than one union, make a careful note of the connections before disturbing any of them.

4 If a brake pipe is to be renewed, it can be obtained, cut to length and with the union nuts and end flares in place, from VW dealers. All that is then necessary is to bend it to shape, following the line of the original, before fitting it to the car. Alternatively, most motor accessory shops can make up brake pipes from kits, but this requires very careful measurement of the original, to ensure that the new pipe is of the correct length. The safest answer is usually to take the original to the shop as a pattern.

5 On refitting, do not overtighten the union nuts. It is not necessary to exercise brute force to obtain a sound joint.

6 Ensure that the pipes and hoses are correctly routed, with no kinks, and that they are secured in the clips or brackets provided. After fitting, remove the polythene from the reservoir, and bleed the hydraulic system as described in Section 2. Wash off any spilt fluid, and check carefully for fluid leaks.

4 Front brake pads – removal, inspection and refitting

Warning: Renew both sets of brake pads at the same time – never renew the pads on only one wheel, as uneven braking may result. Note that the dust created by wear of the pads may contain asbestos, which is a health hazard. Never blow it out with compressed air, and do not inhale any of it. An approved filtering mask should be worn when working on the brakes. DO NOT use petrol or petroleum-based solvents to clean brake parts; use brake cleaner or methylated spirit only.

FSIII calipers

Removal

1 Apply the handbrake, then jack up the front of the vehicle and support it on axle stands (see *Jacking and vehicle support*). Remove the front roadwheels.

2 Trace the brake pad wear sensor wiring (where fitted) back from the pads, and disconnect it from the wiring connector. Note the routing of the wiring, and free it from any relevant retaining clips.

3 Where applicable, to improve access, undo the retaining bolts and remove the air deflector shield from the caliper.

4.9 Open the bleed nipple as the piston is pushed back into the caliper

4 Remove the two protective rubber caps and, using a suitable hexagon key, slacken and remove the two caliper guide pins from the caliper **(see illustrations)**. Then lift the caliper, together with pads, away from the hub carrier, and tie it to the suspension strut using a suitable piece of wire. Do not allow the caliper to hang unsupported on the flexible brake hose.

5 Remove the two brake pads from the caliper, noting that the inner pad is retained in the piston by a spring clip **(see illustrations)**. If the outer pad remains on the carrier, remove it. If the original pads are to be refitted, mark them so that they can be refitted in their original positions.

Inspection

6 First measure the thickness of each brake pad. If either pad is worn at any point to the specified minimum thickness or less, all four pads must be renewed. Also, the pads should be renewed if any are fouled with oil or grease; there is no satisfactory way of degreasing friction material, once contaminated. If any of the brake pads are worn unevenly, or are fouled with oil or grease, trace and rectify the cause before reassembly. New brake pad kits are available from VW dealers.

7 If the brake pads are still serviceable, carefully clean them using a clean, fine wire brush or similar, paying particular attention to the sides and back of the metal backing. Clean out the grooves in the friction material (where applicable), and pick out any large embedded particles of dirt or debris. Carefully clean the pad locations in the caliper body/ mounting bracket.

8 Prior to fitting the pads, check that the guide pins are free to slide easily in the caliper body bushes, and are a reasonably tight fit. Brush the dust and dirt from the caliper and piston, but *do not* inhale it, as it is injurious to health. Inspect the dust seal around the piston for damage, and the piston for evidence of fluid leaks, corrosion or damage. If attention to any of these components is necessary, refer to Section 5.

Refitting

9 If new brake pads are to be fitted, the caliper piston must be pushed back into the cylinder to make room for them. Either use a

4.10 The inboard pad is labelled 'Piston side'

4.11 Ensure the pads and caliper are correctly located on the carrier

4.12 Apply copper grease to the guide pins before inserting them

G-clamp or similar tool, or use suitable pieces of wood as levers. To avoid any dirt entering the ABS solenoid valves, connect a pipe to the bleed nipple and, as the piston is pushed back, open the nipple and allow the displaced fluid to flow through the pipe into a suitable container **(see illustration)**.

10 Fit the new pads into the caliper. The inboard pad (piston side), is marked 'Piston side' **(see illustration)**.

11 Position the caliper and pads over the brake disc ensuring that the lug on the caliper engages correctly with the hub carrier **(see illustration)**. Pass the pad warning sensor wiring (where fitted) through the caliper aperture.

12 Position the caliper until it is possible to install the caliper guide pins. Apply a little copper grease to the pins before refitting them, and tighten them to the specified torque **(see illustration)**. **Note:** *Do not exert excess pressure on the caliper, as this will deform the pad springs, resulting in noisy operation of the brakes.*

13 Where applicable, reconnect the brake pad wear sensor wiring connectors, ensuring that the wiring is correctly routed. Where applicable, refit the air deflector shield to the caliper.

14 Depress the brake pedal repeatedly, until the pads are pressed into firm contact with the brake disc, and normal (non-assisted) pedal pressure is restored.

15 Repeat the above procedure on the remaining front brake caliper.

16 Refit the roadwheels, then lower the vehicle to the ground and tighten the roadwheel bolts to the specified torque.

17 New pads will not give full braking efficiency until they have bedded-in. Be prepared for this, and avoid hard braking as far as possible for the first hundred miles or so after pad renewal.

FN3 calipers

Removal

18 Proceed as described in paragraphs 1 and 2.

19 Using a screwdriver, lever the brake pad retaining spring from the caliper housing **(see illustration)**.

20 Remove the two protective rubber caps and using a suitable hexagon key, slacken and remove the two caliper guide pins from the caliper **(see illustration)**. Then lift the caliper away from the brake pads and hub, and tie it to the suspension strut using a suitable piece of wire. Do not allow the caliper to hang unsupported on the flexible brake hose.

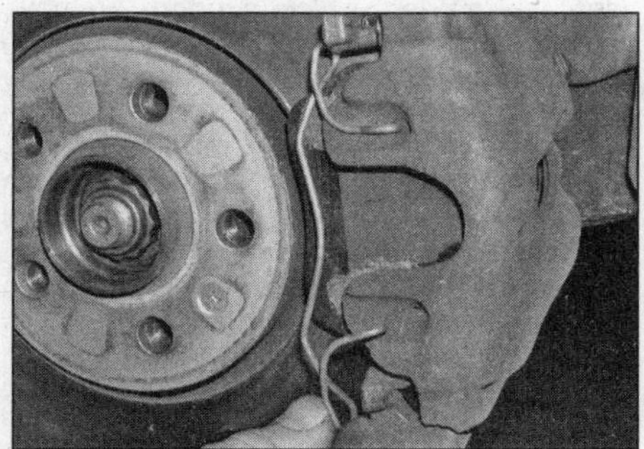

4.19 Lever the spring from the caliper housing

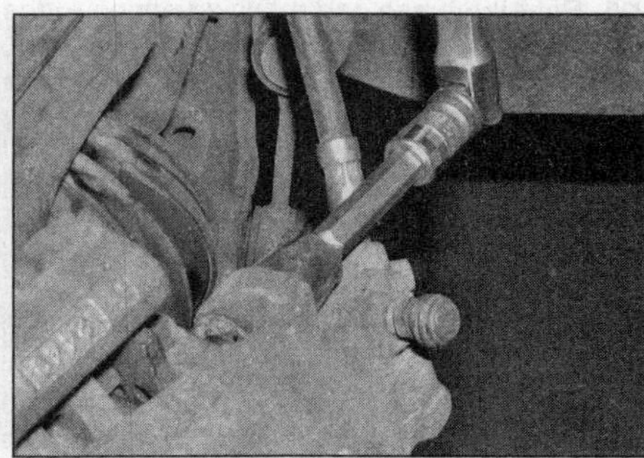

4.20 Undo the caliper guide pins

21 Withdraw the two brake pads from the caliper mounting bracket. If the original pads are to be refitted, identify them so that they can be refitted in their original locations. Where applicable, disconnect the pad wear sensor wiring connector.

Inspection

22 Examine the pads and caliper as described previously in paragraphs 6 to 8. If new pads are to be refitted, refer to paragraph 9 before attempting to push the piston back into the caliper.

Refitting

23 Where applicable, remove the protective foil from the outer pad backplate. Install the outer pad in the caliper mounting bracket, ensuring that the friction material of the pad is against the brake disc. Install the inner (piston side) pad into the caliper. If the original pads are being refitted, ensure that they are refitted to their original locations as noted before removal. The inner pad is fitted with a retaining clip, which engages with the recess in the piston. Where applicable, note that the pad with the wear sensor wiring should be installed as the inner pad. New pads are marked with an arrow on the backing plate, which identifies the direction of rotation. Consequently, the pads should be fitted with the arrows pointing to the ground **(see illustrations)**.

24 Press the caliper into position. Install and tighten the guide pins to the specified torque **(see illustration)**.

4.23a Fit the outer pad to the caliper mounting bracket

4.23b Refit the inner pad

4.24 Install the caliper guide pins

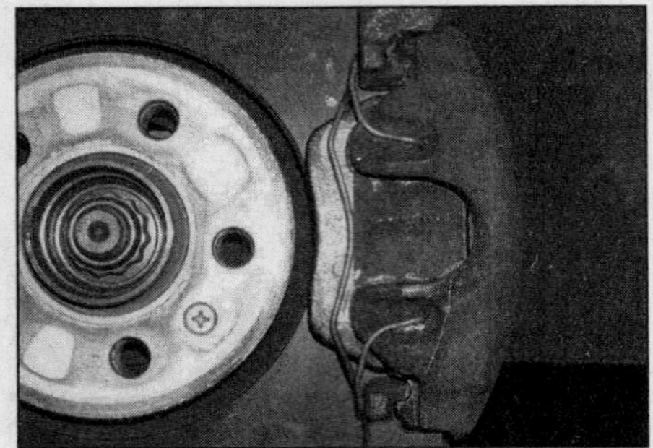

4.25 Refit the retaining spring

25 Refit the brake pad retaining spring to the caliper housing **(see illustration)**.

26 Where applicable, reconnect the brake pad wear sensor wiring connectors, ensuring that the wiring is correctly routed.

27 Depress the brake pedal repeatedly, until the pads are pressed into firm contact with the brake disc, and normal (non-assisted) pedal pressure is restored.

28 Repeat the above procedure on the remaining front brake caliper.

29 Refit the roadwheels, then lower the vehicle to the ground and tighten the roadwheel bolts to the specified torque.

30 Check the hydraulic fluid level as described in *Weekly checks*.

31 New pads will not give full braking efficiency until they have bedded-in. Be prepared for this and avoid hard braking (where possible) in the first hundred miles or so after pad renewal.

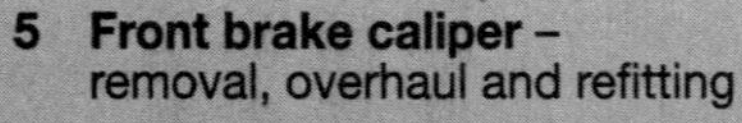

5 Front brake caliper – removal, overhaul and refitting

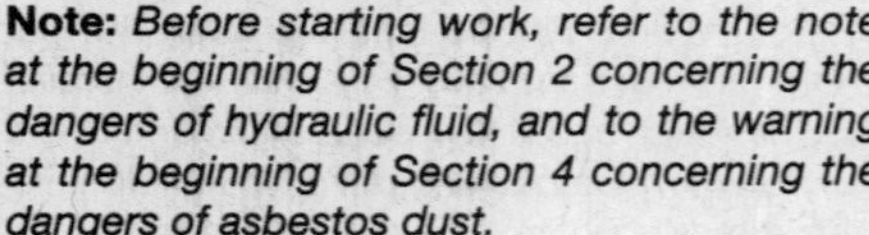

Note: *Before starting work, refer to the note at the beginning of Section 2 concerning the dangers of hydraulic fluid, and to the warning at the beginning of Section 4 concerning the dangers of asbestos dust.*

Removal

1 Apply the handbrake, then jack up the front of the vehicle and support it on axle stands (see *Jacking and vehicle support*). Remove the appropriate roadwheel.

2 Minimise fluid loss by first removing the master cylinder reservoir cap, and then tightening it down onto a piece of polythene, to obtain an airtight seal. Alternatively, use a brake hose clamp, a G-clamp or a similar tool to clamp the flexible hose.

3 Clean the area around the union, then loosen the brake hose union nut.

4 Remove the brake pads as described in Section 4.

5 Unscrew the caliper from the end of the brake hose and remove it from the vehicle.

Overhaul

6 With the caliper on the bench, wipe away all traces of dust and dirt, but *avoid inhaling the dust, as it is injurious to health.*

HAYNES HiNT ***If the piston cannot be withdrawn by hand, it can be pushed out by applying compressed air to the brake hose union hole. Only low pressure should be required, such as is generated by a foot pump. As the piston is expelled, take great care not to trap your fingers between the piston and caliper.***

7 Withdraw the partially-ejected piston from the caliper body, and remove the dust seal.

8 Using a small screwdriver, extract the piston hydraulic seal, taking great care not to damage the caliper bore **(see illustration)**.

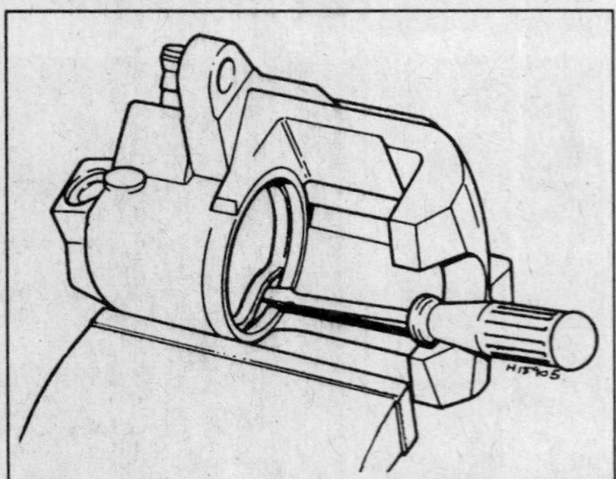

5.8 Use a small screwdriver to extract the caliper piston hydraulic seal

9 Thoroughly clean all components, using only methylated spirit, isopropyl alcohol or clean hydraulic fluid as a cleaning medium. Never use mineral-based solvents such as petrol or paraffin, as they will attack the hydraulic system rubber components. Dry the components immediately, using compressed air or a clean, lint-free cloth. Use compressed air to blow clear the fluid passages.

10 Check all components, and renew any that are worn or damaged. Check particularly the cylinder bore and piston; these should be renewed if they are scratched, worn or corroded in any way (note that this means the renewal of the complete caliper body assembly). Similarly check the condition of the spacers/guide pins and their bushes/bores (as applicable); both spacers/pins should be undamaged and (when cleaned) a reasonably tight sliding fit in their bores. If there is any doubt about the condition of any component, renew it.

11 If the assembly is fit for further use, obtain the appropriate repair kit; the components are available from VW dealers in various combinations.

12 Renew all rubber seals, dust covers and caps disturbed on dismantling as a matter of course; these should never be re-used.

13 On reassembly, ensure that all components are clean and dry.

14 Thinly coat the piston and piston seal with brake fitting paste (VW part no G 052 150 A2). This should be included in the VW caliper overhaul/repair kit.

15 Fit the new piston (fluid) seal, using only your fingers (no tools) to manipulate it into the cylinder bore groove. Fit the new dust seal to the piston, and refit the piston to the cylinder bore using a twisting motion; ensure that the piston enters squarely into the bore. Press the piston fully into the bore, then press the dust seal into the caliper body.

Refitting

16 Screw the caliper fully onto the flexible hose union.

17 Refit the brake pads as described in Section 4.

18 Securely tighten the brake pipe union nut.

19 Remove the brake hose clamp or polythene, as applicable, and bleed the hydraulic system as described in Section 2. Note that, providing the precautions described were taken to minimise brake fluid loss, it should only be necessary to bleed the relevant front brake.

20 Refit the roadwheel, then lower the vehicle to the ground and tighten the roadwheel bolts to the specified torque.

6 Brake disc – inspection, removal and refitting

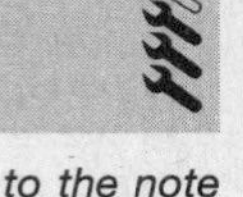

Note: *Before starting work, refer to the note at the beginning of Section 4 concerning the dangers of asbestos dust.*

Note: *If either disc requires renewal, BOTH should be renewed at the same time, to ensure even and consistent braking. New brake pads should also be fitted.*

Front brake disc

Inspection

1 Apply the handbrake, then jack up the front of the car and support it on axle stands (see *Jacking and vehicle support*). Remove the appropriate front roadwheel.

2 Slowly rotate the brake disc so that the full area of both sides can be checked; remove the brake pads if better access is required to the inboard surface. Light scoring is normal in the area swept by the brake pads, but if heavy scoring or cracks are found, the disc must be renewed.

3 It is normal to find a lip of rust and brake dust around the perimeter of the disc; this can be scraped off if required. If, however, a lip has formed due to excessive wear of the brake pad swept area, then the disc thickness must be measured using a micrometer. Take measurements at several places around the disc, at the inside and outside of the pad swept area; if the disc has worn at any point to the specified minimum thickness or less, the disc must be renewed.

4 If the disc is thought to be warped, it can be checked for run-out. Either use a dial gauge mounted on any convenient fixed point, while the disc is slowly rotated, or use feeler blades to measure (at several points all around the disc) the clearance between the disc and a fixed point, such as the caliper mounting bracket. If the measurements obtained are at the specified maximum or beyond, the disc is excessively warped, and must be renewed; however, it is worth checking first that the hub bearing is in good condition (Chapter 1A, Section 16 or Chapter 1B, Section 17, as appropriate). If the run-out is excessive, the disc must be renewed **(see illustration)**.

5 Check the disc for cracks, especially around the wheel bolt holes, and any other wear or damage, and renew if necessary.

Removal

6 Remove the brake pads as described in Section 4.

7 On models with FN3 front brake calipers, unscrew the two bolts securing the brake caliper mounting bracket to the hub carrier, then slide the caliper assembly off the disc. Using a piece of wire or string, tie the caliper to the front suspension coil spring, to avoid placing any strain on the brake hose.

8 Use chalk or paint to mark the relationship of the disc to the hub, then remove the screw securing the brake disc to the hub, and remove the disc **(see illustrations)**. If it is tight, apply penetrating fluid, and tap its rear face gently with a hide or plastic mallet. The use of excessive force could cause the disc to be damaged.

Refitting

9 Refitting is the reverse of the removal procedure, noting the following points:

a) Ensure that the mating surfaces of the disc and hub are clean and flat.

b) Align (if applicable) the marks made on removal, and securely tighten the disc retaining screw.

c) If a new disc has been fitted, use a suitable solvent to wipe any preservative coating from the disc, before refitting the caliper.

d) On models with FN3 brake calipers, slide the caliper into position over the disc, making sure the pads pass either side of the disc. Tighten the caliper bracket mounting bolts to the specified torque.

e) Fit the pads as described in Section 4.

f) Refit the roadwheel, then lower the vehicle to the ground and tighten the roadwheel bolts to the specified torque. On completion, repeatedly depress the brake pedal until normal (non-assisted) pedal pressure returns.

Rear brake disc

Inspection

10 Firmly chock the front wheels, then jack up the rear of the car and support it on axle stands. Remove the appropriate rear road-wheel.

11 Inspect the disc as described in paragraphs 2 to 5.

Removal

12 Unscrew the two bolts securing the brake caliper mounting bracket in position, then slide the caliper assembly off the disc. Using a piece of wire or string, tie the caliper to the rear suspension coil spring, to avoid placing any strain on the hydraulic brake hose.

13 Use chalk or paint to mark the relationship of the disc to the hub, then remove the screw securing the brake disc to the hub, and remove the disc **(see illustration)**. If it is tight, apply penetrating fluid, and tap its rear face gently with a hide or plastic mallet. The use of excessive force could cause the disc to be damaged.

Refitting

14 Refitting is a reversal of the removal procedure, noting the following points:

a) Ensure that the mating surfaces of the disc and hub are clean and flat.

b) Align (if applicable) the marks made on removal, and securely tighten the disc retaining screw.

6.4 Using a DTI gauge to measure disc run-out

c) If a new disc has been fitted, use a suitable solvent to wipe any preservative coating from the disc, before refitting the caliper.

d) Slide the caliper into position over the disc, making sure the pads pass either side of the disc. Tighten the caliper bracket mounting bolts to the specified torque. If new discs have been fitted and there is insufficient clearance between the pads to accommodate the new, thicker disc, it may be necessary to push the piston back into the caliper body as described in Section 8.

e) Refit the roadwheel, then lower the vehicle to the ground and tighten the roadwheel bolts to the specified torque. On completion, repeatedly depress the brake pedal until normal (non-assisted) pedal pressure returns.

7 Front brake disc shield – removal and refitting

Removal

1 Remove the brake disc as described in Section 6.

2 Unscrew the securing bolts, and remove the brake disc shield.

Refitting

3 Refitting is a reversal of removal. Tighten the shield retaining bolts to the specified torque. Refit the brake disc with reference to Section 6.

6.8a Undo the screw...

6.8b ...and remove the front brake disc

6.13 Lift away the disc

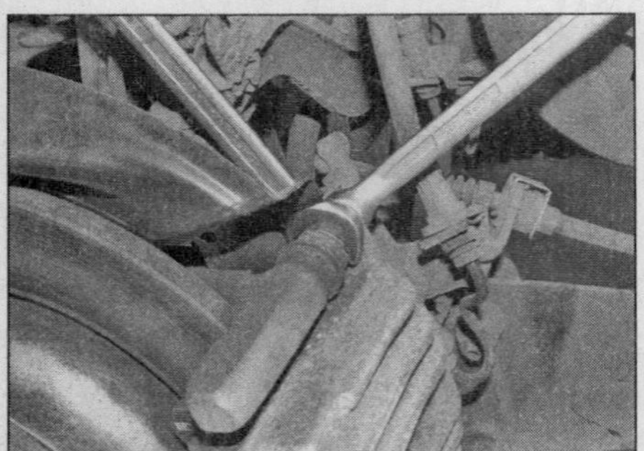
8.3 Counterhold the guide pins

8.4 Remove the caliper

8.5a Remove the outer rear brake pad...

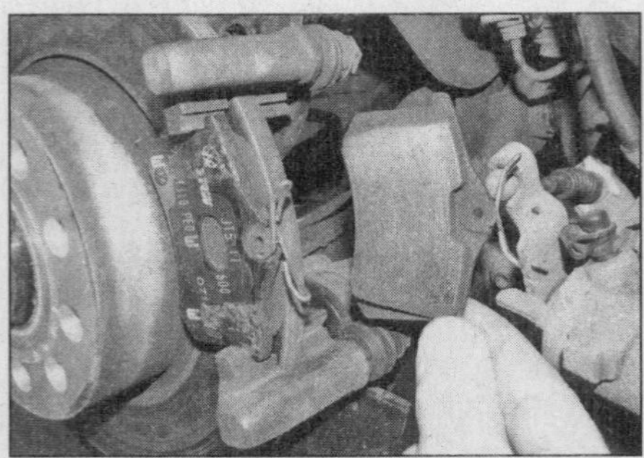
8.5b ...and inner rear brake pad

8 Rear brake pads – removal, inspection and refitting

Note: *Before starting work, refer to the note at the beginning of Section 4 concerning the dangers of asbestos dust. New caliper mounting bolts will be required on refitting.*

Removal

1 Chock the front wheels, then jack up the rear of the vehicle and support it on axle stands (see *Jacking and vehicle support*). Remove the rear wheels.

2 Slacken the handbrake cable and detach it from the caliper as described in Section 16.

3 Slacken and remove the guide pin bolts, using a slim open-ended spanner to prevent the guide pins from rotating **(see illustration)**. Discard the bolts – new ones must be used on refitting.

4 Lift the caliper away from the brake pads, and tie it to the suspension strut using a suitable piece of wire **(see illustration)**. Do not allow the caliper to hang unsupported on the flexible brake hose.

5 Withdraw the two brake pads from the caliper mounting bracket **(see illustrations)**, and on the CII38 type, recover the pad anti-rattle shims from the mounting bracket, noting their correct fitted locations. **Note:** *On the C38 type, the anti-rattle springs are attached to the pads themselves.*

Inspection

6 First measure the thickness of each brake pad. If either pad is worn at any point to the specified minimum thickness or less, **all four** pads must be renewed. Also, the pads should be renewed if any are fouled with oil or grease; there is no satisfactory way of degreasing friction material, once contaminated. If any of the brake pads are worn unevenly, or fouled with oil or grease, trace and rectify the cause before reassembly. New brake pads are available from VW dealers.

7 If the brake pads are still serviceable, carefully clean them using a clean, fine wire brush or similar, paying particular attention to the sides and back of the metal backing. Clean out the grooves in the friction material (where applicable), and pick out any large embedded particles of dirt or debris. Carefully clean the pad locations in the caliper body/ mounting bracket.

8 Prior to fitting the pads, check that the guide pins are free to slide easily in the caliper bracket, and check that the rubber guide pin gaiters are undamaged. Brush the dust and dirt from the caliper and piston, but **do not** inhale it, as it is injurious to health. Inspect the dust seal around the piston for damage, and the piston for evidence of fluid leaks, corrosion or damage. If attention to any of these components is necessary, refer to Section 9.

Refitting

9 If new brake pads are to be fitted, it will be necessary to retract the piston fully, by rotating it in a clockwise direction as it is pushed into the caliper bore **(see Haynes Hint)**. To avoid any dirt entering the ABS solenoid valves, connect a pipe to the bleed nipple, and as the piston is pushed back open the nipple and allow the displaced fluid to flow through the pipe into a suitable container.

10 On the CII38 type, fit the pad anti-rattle shims to the caliper mounting bracket, ensuring that they are correctly located (see note in paragraph 5). Install the pads in the mounting bracket, ensuring that each pad's friction material is against the brake disc. Remove the protective foil from the outer pad backing plate **(see illustrations)**.

11 Slide the caliper back into position over the pads.

12 Press the caliper into position, then install the new guide pin bolts, tightening them to the specified torque setting while retaining the

In the absence of the special tool, the piston can be screwed back into the caliper using a pair of circlip pliers.

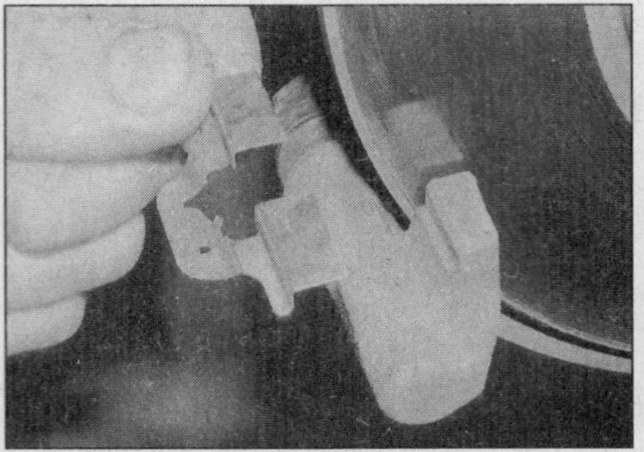
8.10a Refit the anti-rattle shims

8.10b Install the brake pads

guide pin with an open-ended spanner **(see illustration)**.

13 Depress the brake pedal repeatedly, until the pads are pressed into firm contact with the brake disc, and normal (non-assisted) pedal pressure is restored.

14 Repeat the above procedure on the remaining rear brake caliper.

15 Reconnect the handbrake cables to the calipers, and adjust the handbrake as described in Section 14.

16 Refit the roadwheels, then lower the vehicle to the ground and tighten the roadwheel bolts to the specified torque setting.

17 Check the hydraulic fluid level as described in *Weekly checks*.

18 New pads will not give full braking efficiency until they have bedded-in. Be prepared for this, and avoid hard braking as far as possible for the first hundred miles or so after pad renewal.

9 Rear brake caliper – removal, overhaul and refitting

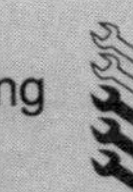

Note: *Before starting work, refer to the note at the beginning of Section 2 concerning the dangers of hydraulic fluid, and to the warning at the beginning of Section 4 concerning the dangers of asbestos dust.*

Removal

1 Chock the front wheels, then jack up the rear of the vehicle and support on axle stands (see *Jacking and vehicle support*). Remove the relevant rear wheel.

2 Minimise fluid loss by first removing the master cylinder reservoir cap, and then tightening it down onto a piece of polythene, to obtain an airtight seal. Alternatively, use a brake hose clamp, a G-clamp or a similar tool to clamp the flexible hose.

3 Clean the area around the union on the caliper, then loosen the brake hose union nut.

4 Lift the caliper from the brake pads as described in Section 8.

5 Unscrew the caliper from the end of the flexible hose and remove it from the vehicle.

Overhaul

Note: *It is not possible to overhaul the brake caliper handbrake mechanism. If the mechanism is faulty, or fluid is leaking from the handbrake lever seal the caliper assembly must be renewed.*

6 With the caliper on the bench, wipe away all traces of dust and dirt, but avoid inhaling the dust, as it is injurious to health.

7 Using a small screwdriver, carefully prise out the dust seal from the caliper, taking care not to damage the piston.

8 Remove the piston from the caliper bore by rotating it in an anti-clockwise direction. This can be achieved using a suitable pair of circlip pliers engaged in the caliper piston slots. Once the piston turns freely but does not come out any further, the piston can be withdrawn by hand.

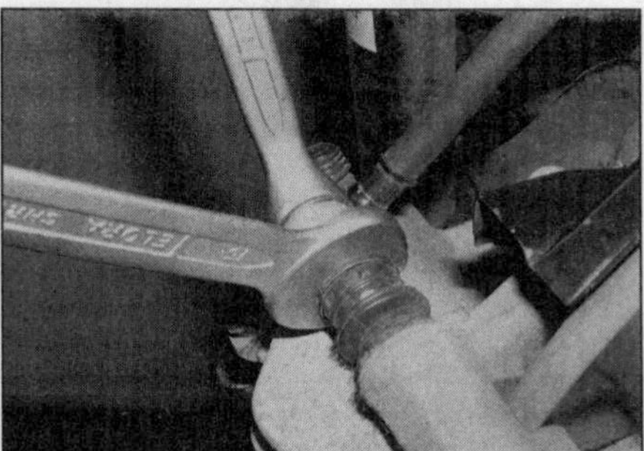

8.12 Hold the guide pin whilst tightening the guide pin bolt

If the piston cannot be withdrawn by hand, it can be pushed out by applying compressed air to the brake hose union hole. Only low pressure should be required, such as is generated by a foot pump. As the piston is expelled, take care not to trap your fingers between the piston and caliper.

9 Using a small screwdriver, extract the piston hydraulic seal(s), taking care not to damage the caliper bore.

10 Withdraw the guide pins from the caliper, and remove the guide sleeve gaiters.

11 Thoroughly clean all components, using only methylated spirit, isopropyl alcohol or clean hydraulic fluid as a cleaning medium. Never use mineral-based solvents such as petrol or paraffin, as they will attack the hydraulic system rubber components. Dry the components immediately, using compressed air or a clean, lint-free cloth. Use compressed air to blow clear the fluid passages.

12 Check all components, and renew any that are worn or damaged. Check particularly the cylinder bore and piston; these should be renewed (note that this means the renewal of the complete caliper body assembly) if they are scratched, worn or corroded in any way. Similarly check the condition of the spacers/guide pins and their bushes/bores (as applicable); both spacers/pins should be undamaged and (when cleaned) a reasonably tight sliding fit in their bores. If there is any doubt about the condition of any component, renew it.

13 If the assembly is fit for further use, obtain the appropriate repair kit; the components are available from VW dealers in various combinations.

14 Renew all rubber seals, dust covers and caps disturbed on dismantling as a matter of course; these should never be re-used.

15 On reassembly, ensure that all components are clean and dry.

16 Smear a thin coat of brake fitting paste (VW part no G 052 150 A2) on the piston, seal and caliper bore. This should be included in the overhaul/repair kit. Fit the new piston (fluid) seal, using only the fingers (no tools) to manipulate into the cylinder bore groove.

17 Fit the new dust seal to the piston groove, then refit the piston assembly. Turn the piston in a clockwise direction, using the method employed on dismantling, until it is fully retracted into the caliper bore.

18 Press the dust seal into position in the caliper housing.

19 Apply the grease supplied in the repair kit, or a copper-based brake grease or anti-seize compound, to the guide pins. Fit the new gaiters to the guide pins and fit the pins to the caliper ensuring that the gaiters are correctly located in the grooves on both the pins and caliper.

20 Prior to refitting, fill the caliper with fresh hydraulic fluid by slackening the bleed screw and pumping the fluid through the caliper until bubble-free fluid is expelled from the union hole.

Refitting

21 Screw the caliper fully onto the flexible hose union.

22 Refit the caliper over the brake pads as described in paragraphs 10 to 12 of Section 8.

23 Securely tighten the brake pipe union nut.

24 Remove the brake hose clamp or remove the polythene from the fluid reservoir, as applicable, and bleed the hydraulic system as described in Section 2. Note that, providing the precautions described were taken to minimise brake fluid loss, it should only be necessary to bleed the relevant rear brake.

25 Connect the handbrake cable to the caliper, and adjust the handbrake as described in Section 14.

26 Refit the roadwheel, then lower the vehicle to the ground and tighten the roadwheel bolts to the specified torque. On completion, check the hydraulic fluid level as described in *Weekly checks*.

10 Brake pedal – removal and refitting

Removal

1 Disconnect the battery negative lead. **Note:** *Before disconnecting the battery, refer to 'Disconnecting the battery' in the reference section at the rear of this manual.*

2 With reference to Chapter 11, remove the driver's side lower facia trim panels, and the trim panel below the dash.

3 Where fitted, unscrew the two retaining screws and remove the connecting plate between the clutch and brake pedals.

4 Where fitted to the pedal bracket, remove the brake light switch as described in Section 18. **Note:** *As from late 2005, the switch is located on the brake master cylinder.*

5 It is now necessary to release the brake pedal from the ball on the vacuum servo pushrod.

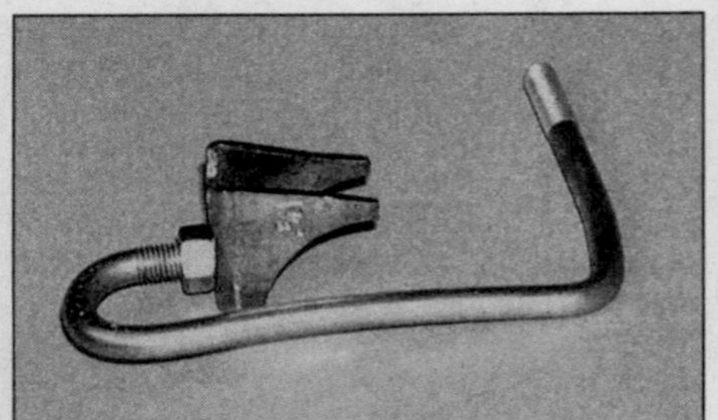
10.5a Improvised special tool constructed from a modified exhaust clamp, used to release the brake pedal from the servo pushrod

10.5b Using the tool to release the brake pedal from the servo pushrod

10.5c Rear view of the brake pedal (pedal removed) showing plastic lugs (arrowed) securing pedal to servo pushrod

To do this, a VW special tool is available, but a suitable alternative can be improvised **(see illustration)**. Note that the plastic lugs in the pedal are very stiff, and it will not be possible to release them by hand. Depress and hold down the pedal, then, using the tool, release the securing lugs, and pull the pedal from the servo pushrod **(see illustrations)**.

6 Undo and remove the pedal bracket support retaining nut **(see illustration)**.

7 Unscrew the five nuts securing the pedal support bracket to the bulkhead/ servo, sufficiently to allow the bracket some movement. Do not remove the nuts completely **(see illustration)**.

8 Undo the pivot shaft nut and slide the pivot shaft to the right, until the pedal is free. Remove the pedal and recover the pivot bush **(see illustration)**.

9 Carefully clean all components, and renew any that are worn or damaged.

Refitting

10 Prior to refitting, apply a smear of multi-purpose grease to the pivot shaft and pedal bearing surfaces.

11 Using a screwdriver, lever the pedal bracket away from the bulkhead **(see illustration)**.

12 Pull the servo unit pushrod down, and at the same time manoeuvre the pedal into position, ensuring that the pivot bush is correctly located.

13 Tighten the five pedal bracket retaining nuts securely, and refit the bracket support retaining nut.

14 Hold the servo unit pushrod, and push the pedal back onto the pushrod ball. Make sure the pedal is securely fastened to the pushrod.

15 Insert the pedal pivot bolt and tighten the retaining nut to the specified torque.

16 Refit the brake light switch, as described in Section 18.

17 Where fitted, refit the connecting plate between the clutch and brake pedals, and tighten the two retaining bolts securely.

18 Refit the facia trim panels as described in Chapter 11.

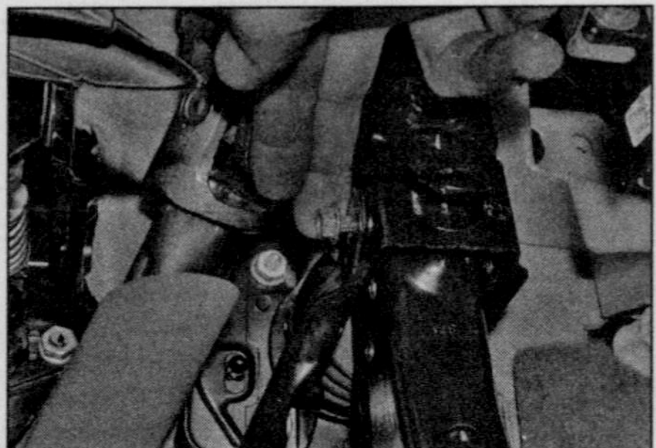
10.6 Undo the support bracket nut

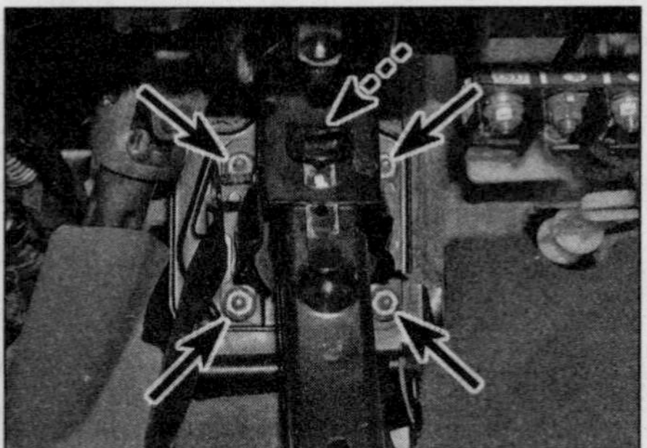
10.7 Slacken the five securing nuts

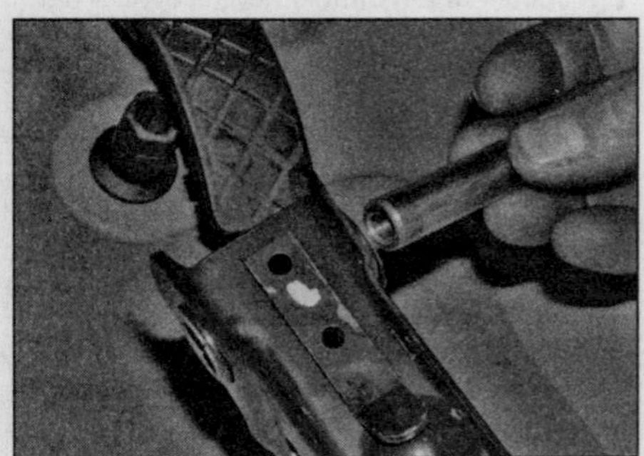
10.8 Recover the pivot bush

10.11 Lever the bracket away from the bulkhead

11 Servo unit – testing, removal and refitting

Testing

1 To test the operation of the servo unit, depress the footbrake several times to exhaust the vacuum, then start the engine whilst keeping the pedal firmly depressed. As the engine starts, there should be a noticeable 'give' in the brake pedal as the vacuum builds-up. Allow the engine to run for at least two minutes, then switch it off. If the brake pedal is now depressed, it should feel normal, but further applications should result in the pedal feeling firmer, with the pedal stroke decreasing with each application.

2 If the servo does not operate as described, first inspect the servo unit non-return valve as described in Section 12. On diesel models, also check the operation of the vacuum pump as described in Section 21 or 22.

3 If the servo unit still fails to operate satisfactorily, the fault lies within the unit itself. Repairs to the unit are not possible – if faulty, the servo unit must be renewed.

Removal

4 Remove the master cylinder as described in Section 13.

5 Where applicable remove the heat shield from the servo, then carefully ease the vacuum hose out from the sealing grommet in the front of the servo. Where applicable, also disconnect the wiring from the servo vacuum sensor, then extract the retaining circlip with a screwdriver, and withdraw the sensor from the servo.

6 On LHD models with manual transmission, refer to Chapter 7A and disconnect the gearchange cables from the levers on the transmission, then unbolt the gearchange support bracket and tie it to one side.

7 With reference to Chapter 11, remove the driver's side lower facia trim panels, and the trim panel below the dash.

8 On models manufactured before late 2005, remove the brake light switch from the pedal bracket as described in Section 18.

9 Where fitted, unscrew the two retaining screws and remove the connecting plate between the clutch and brake pedals (manual transmission models only). Also, where fitted, remove the air duct and cover for access to the servo mounting nuts.

10 It is now necessary to release the brake pedal from the ball on the vacuum servo pushrod. To do this, a VW special tool is available, but a suitable alternative can be improvised. Note that the plastic lugs in the pedal are very stiff, and it will not be possible to release them by hand. Using the tool, release the securing lugs, and pull the pedal from the servo pushrod.

11 Again working in the footwell, undo the nuts securing the servo unit to the bulkhead, then return to the engine compartment and manoeuvre the servo unit out of position, and recover the gasket where fitted. Note that, on some RHD models, it may be necessary to remove the inlet manifold (see Chapter 4A or 4B) to give sufficient clearance to withdraw the servo.

Refitting

12 Check the servo unit vacuum hose sealing grommet for signs of damage or deterioration, and renew if necessary.

13 Where applicable, fit a new gasket to the rear of the servo unit, then reposition the unit in the engine compartment.

14 From inside the vehicle, ensure that the servo unit pushrod is correctly engaged with the brake pedal, and push the pedal onto the pushrod ball. Check the pushrod ball is securely engaged, then refit the servo unit mounting nuts and tighten them to the specified torque.

15 As applicable, refit the connecting plate, air duct and cover.

16 On models manufactured before late 2005, refit the brake light switch.

17 Refit the facia trim panels.

18 On LHD models with manual transmission, refit the gearchange cables and support bracket.

19 Carefully ease the vacuum hose back into position in the servo, taking great care not to displace the sealing grommet. Refit the heat shield to the servo and, where applicable, refit the vacuum sensor and wiring.

20 Refit the master cylinder as described in Section 13 of this Chapter.

21 Where applicable on RHD models, refit the inlet manifold as described in Chapter 4A or 4B.

22 On completion, start the engine and check for air leaks at the vacuum hose-to-servo unit connection; check the operation of the braking system.

13.3a Brake master cylinder and fluid reservoir

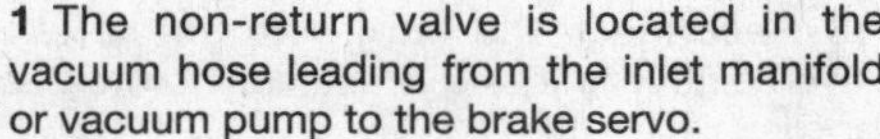

12 Servo non-return valve – testing, removal and refitting

1 The non-return valve is located in the vacuum hose leading from the inlet manifold or vacuum pump to the brake servo.

Removal

2 Ease the vacuum hose out of the servo unit, taking care not to displace the grommet.

3 Note the routing of the hose, then slacken the retaining clip(s) and disconnect the opposite end of the hose assembly from the manifold/pump/ hose, and remove it from the car.

Testing

4 Examine the check valve and vacuum hose for signs of damage, and renew if necessary.

5 The valve may be tested by blowing through it in both directions, air should flow through the valve in one direction only; when blown through from the servo unit end of the valve. Renew the valve if this is not the case.

6 Examine the servo unit rubber sealing grommet for signs of damage or deterioration, and renew as necessary.

Refitting

7 Ensure that the sealing grommet is correctly fitted to the servo unit.

8 Ease the hose union into position in the servo, taking great care not to displace or damage the grommet.

9 Ensure that the hose is correctly routed, and connect it to the inlet manifold/pump/hose, ensuring the hose is secured in the retaining clips.

10 On completion, start the engine and check the valve-to-servo unit connection for signs of air leaks.

13.4 Clutch fluid supply hose and union

13.3b Filler cap incorporating brake fluid level warning switch

13 Master cylinder – removal, overhaul and refitting

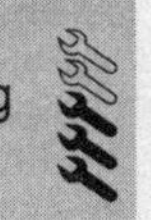

Note: *Before starting work, refer to the warning at the beginning of Section 2 concerning the dangers of hydraulic fluid. A new master cylinder O-ring will be required on refitting.*

Removal

1 Disconnect the battery negative lead. **Note:** *Before disconnecting the battery, refer to 'Disconnecting the battery' in the Reference section at the rear of this manual.* Remove the engine top cover and air inlet trunking.

2 On LHD models, remove the battery and carrier with reference to Chapter 5A.

3 Remove the master cylinder reservoir cap (disconnect the wiring plug from the brake fluid level warning switch), and syphon the hydraulic fluid from the reservoir **(see illustrations)**. **Note:** *Do not syphon the fluid by mouth, as it is poisonous; use a syringe or an old poultry baster.* Also, disconnect the wiring from the brake light switch, where located on the master cylinder.

4 On manual transmission models, disconnect and plug the clutch master cylinder supply hose from the brake reservoir **(see illustration)**.

5 Remove the hydraulic fluid reservoir from the top of the master cylinder. To do this, press the locking tabs outwards, and at the same time, pull the reservoir upwards from the rubber grommets.

6 Wipe clean the area around the brake pipe unions on the side of the master cylinder, and place absorbent rags beneath the pipe unions to catch any leaking fluid. Make a note of the correct fitted positions of the unions, then unscrew the union nuts and carefully withdraw the pipes. Plug or tape over the pipe ends and master cylinder orifices, to minimise the loss of brake fluid, and to prevent the entry of dirt into the system. Wash off any spilt fluid immediately with cold water.

7 Unscrew and remove the two nuts and washers securing the master cylinder to the vacuum servo unit, remove the heat shield (where fitted), then withdraw the unit from the engine compartment **(see illustration)**. Remove the O-ring from the rear of the master cylinder, and discard it.

Overhaul

8 If the master cylinder is faulty, it must be renewed. Repair kits are not available from VW dealer, so the cylinder must be treated as a sealed unit.

9 The only items which can be renewed are the mounting seals for the fluid reservoir; if these show signs of deterioration, prise them out with a screwdriver. Lubricate the new seals with clean brake fluid, and press them into the master cylinder ports.

Refitting

10 Remove all traces of dirt from the master cylinder and servo unit mating surfaces, and fit a new O-ring to the groove on the master cylinder body.

11 Fit the master cylinder to the servo unit, ensuring that the servo unit pushrod enters the master cylinder bore centrally. Refit the heat shield (where applicable), and the master cylinder mounting nuts and washers, and tighten them to the specified torque.

12 Wipe clean the brake pipe unions, then refit them to the master cylinder ports and tighten them securely.

13 Refit the hydraulic fluid reservoir, making sure it is entered correctly in the rubber grommets.

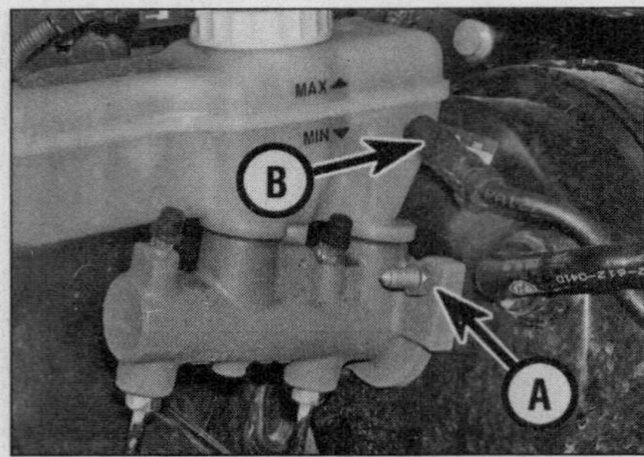

13.7 Brake cylinder nuts (A), and clutch cylinder supply hose (B)

14 On manual transmission models, reconnect the clutch master cylinder supply hose to the reservoir.

15 Refill the master cylinder reservoir with new fluid, and bleed the complete hydraulic system as described in Section 2.

16 Reconnect the wiring to the brake level sender unit and brake light switch as applicable.

17 On LHD models, refit the battery and carrier.

18 Refit the air trunking where necessary, then reconnect the battery negative lead.

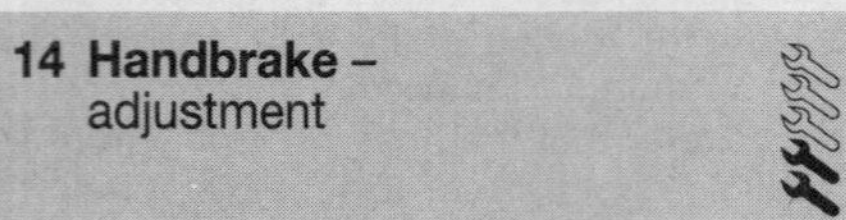

14 Handbrake – adjustment

1 To check the handbrake adjustment, first apply the footbrake firmly several times to establish correct pad-to-disc clearance, then apply and release the handbrake several times.

2 Applying normal moderate pressure, pull the handbrake lever to the fully-applied position, counting the number of clicks from the handbrake ratchet mechanism. If adjustment is correct, there should be approximately 4 to 7 clicks before the handbrake is fully applied. If this is not the case, adjust as follows.

3 Remove the handbrake cover or the centre console (see Chapter 11), as applicable, to gain access to the handbrake lever.

4 Chock the front wheels, then jack up the rear of the vehicle and support it on axle stands.

5 With the handbrake fully released, slacken the handbrake adjuster nut until both the rear caliper handbrake levers are back against their stops **(see illustration)**.

6 From this point, tighten the adjusting nuts until both handbrake levers just move off the caliper stops. Ensure that the gap between each caliper handbrake lever and its stop is between 1.0 and 1.5 mm, and ensure both the right- and left-hand gaps are equal **(see illustration)**. Check that both wheels/discs rotate freely, then check the adjustment by applying the handbrake fully and counting the clicks from the handbrake ratchet (see paragraph 2). If necessary, re-adjust.

7 Once adjustment is correct, refit the handbrake cover or centre console (as applicable).

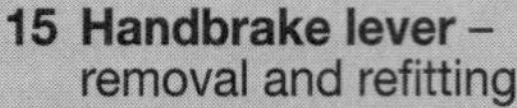

15 Handbrake lever – removal and refitting

Removal

1 Remove the centre console as described in Chapter 11.

2 If desired, remove the handbrake lever cover sleeve by depressing the locating tag with a screwdriver, then sliding the sleeve from the lever.

3 Disconnect the wiring plug from the handbrake 'on' warning light switch.

4 Slacken the handbrake cable adjuster nut sufficiently to allow the ends of the cables to be disengaged from the equaliser plate **(see illustrations)**.

5 Unscrew the retaining nuts, and withdraw the lever and bracket assembly from the floor **(see illustration)**.

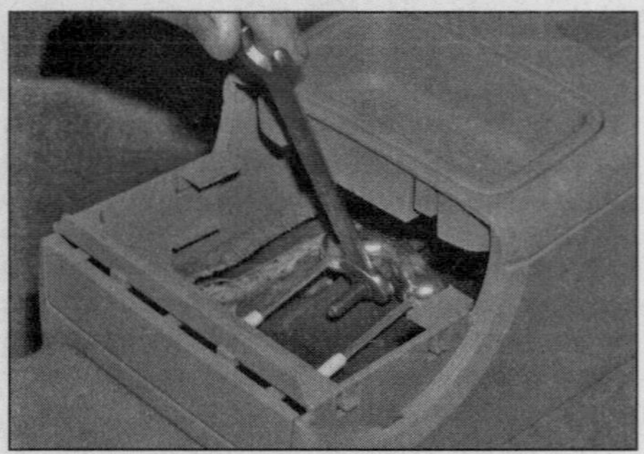

14.5 Slacken the adjuster nut

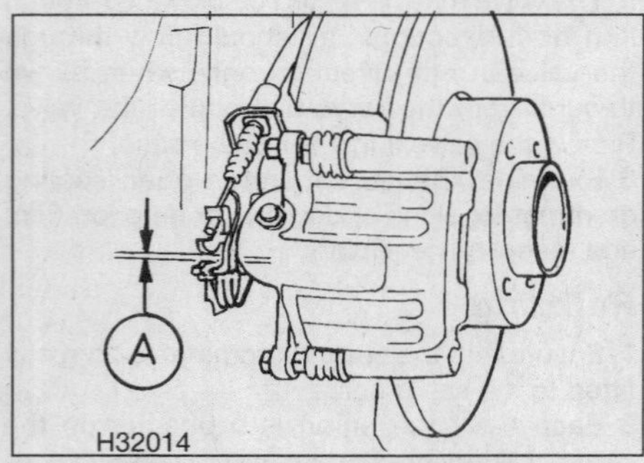

14.6 Turn the nuts until a gap (A) of between 1.0 and 1.5 mm can be seen

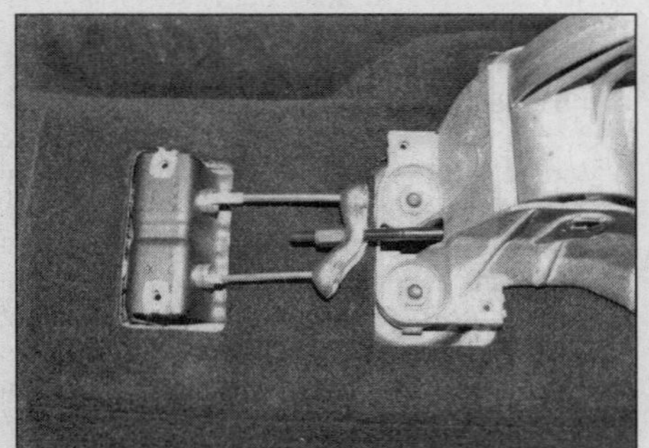

15.4a Handbrake cables and equaliser plate

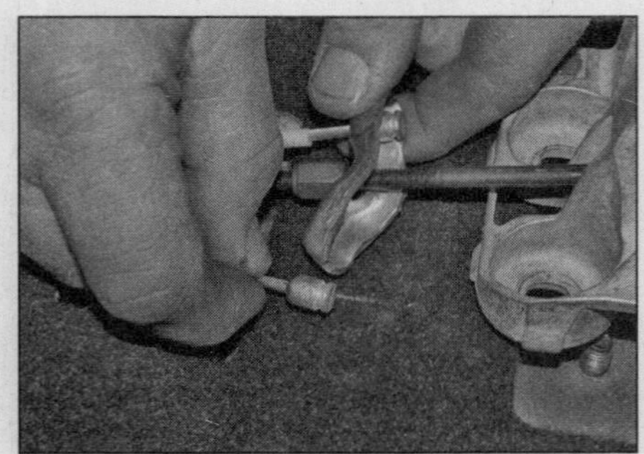

15.4b Disengage the cable

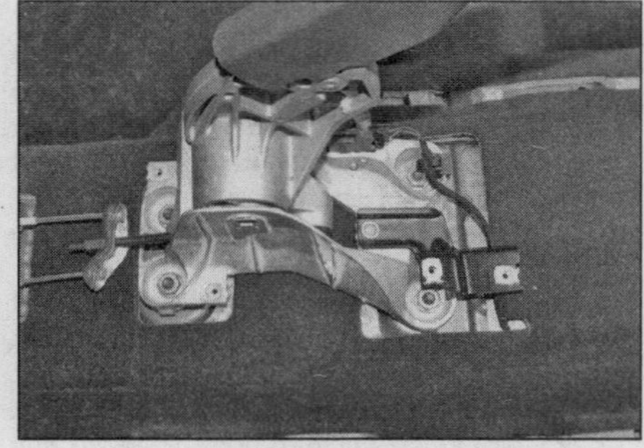

15.5 Handbrake lever and bracket assembly

Refitting

6 Refitting is a reversal of removal, bearing in mind the following points.

a) Prior to refitting the handbrake cover, adjust the handbrake as described in Section 14.

b) Check the operation of the handbrake 'on' warning switch prior to refitting the centre console.

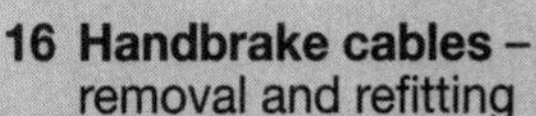

16 Handbrake cables – removal and refitting

Removal

1 Remove the centre console as described in Chapter 11, to gain access to the handbrake lever. The handbrake cable consists of two sections, a right- and a left-hand section, which are linked to the lever by an equaliser plate. Each section can be removed individually.

2 Chock the front wheels, then jack up the rear of the car and support it on axle stands.

3 Slacken the handbrake cable adjuster nut sufficiently to allow the ends of the cables to be disengaged from the equaliser plate.

4 Working back along the length of the cable, note its correct routing, and free it from all the relevant guides and retaining clips.

5 Disengage the inner cable from the caliper handbrake lever, then remove the outer cable retaining clip and detach the cable from the caliper **(see illustration)**. Withdraw the cable from underneath the vehicle.

Refitting

6 Refitting is a reversal of removal, bearing in mind the following points.

a) When locating the handbrake cable sheath in the guide on the rear trailing arm, the cable clamping ring must lie in the middle of the clip.

b) Before refitting the centre console, adjust the handbrake as described in Section 14.

17 Handbrake 'on' warning light switch – removal and refitting

Removal

1 Disconnect the battery negative lead. **Note:** *Before disconnecting the battery, refer to 'Disconnecting the battery' in the reference section at the rear of this manual.*

2 Remove the centre console, with reference to Chapter 11 if necessary.

3 Disconnect the wiring plug from the switch.

4 Squeeze the securing lugs, and withdraw the switch from the handbrake lever assembly **(see illustration)**.

Refitting

5 Refitting is a reversal of removal.

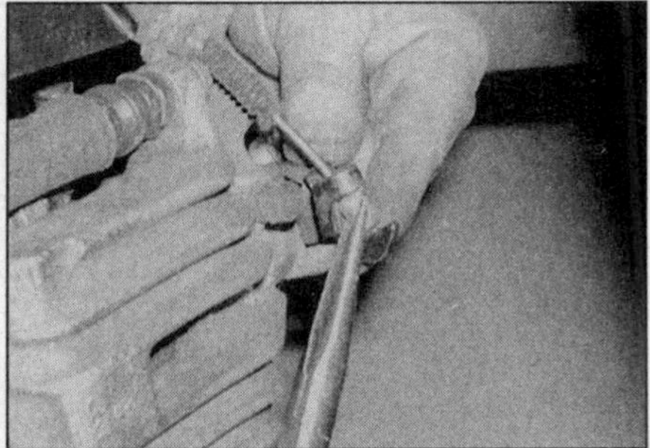

16.5 Release the cable inner from its lever and withdraw the cable from the caliper

18 Brake light switch – removal and refitting

Models up to 10/05

Removal

1 The brake light switch is located on the pedal bracket beneath the facia. Disconnect the battery negative lead. **Note:** *Before disconnecting the battery, refer to 'Disconnecting the battery' in the Reference section at the rear of this manual.*

2 Working in the driver's footwell, remove the lower facia panel, see Chapter 11.

3 Reach up behind the facia and disconnect the wiring connector from the switch **(see illustration)**.

4 Twist the switch through 90° and release it from the mounting bracket.

Refitting

5 Prior to installation, fully extend the brake light switch plunger.

6 Fully depress and hold the brake pedal, then manoeuvre the switch into position. Align the shaped lug of the switch with the corresponding cut-out in the bracket **(see illustration)**. Secure the switch in position it by pushing it into the bracket and twisting it through 90°, then release the brake pedal.

7 Reconnect the wiring connector, and check the operation of the brake lights. The brake lights should illuminate after the brake pedal has travelled approximately 5 mm. If the switch is not functioning correctly, it is faulty and must be renewed; no adjustment is possible.

8 On completion, refit the lower facia panel.

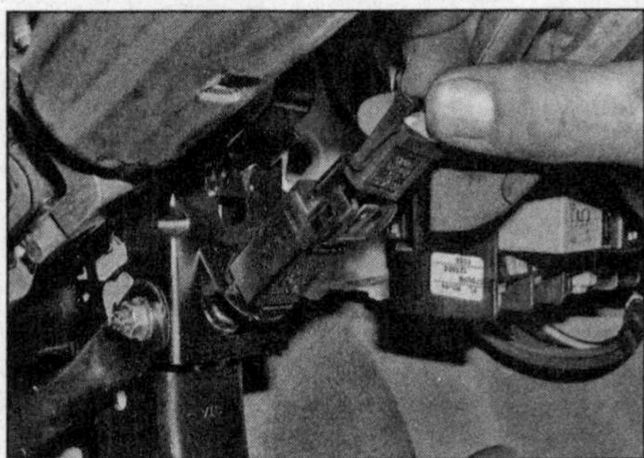

18.3 Disconnect the brake switch

17.4 Removing the handbrake 'on' switch

Models from 10/05

9 The brake light switch is located on the master cylinder. Remove the engine top cover, and where applicable, remove the air inlet trunking to improve access.

10 Disconnect the wiring from the switch.

11 Unscrew the mounting bolt, then pull the switch from the bottom of the master cylinder, and remove it from the locking lug at the top.

Refitting

12 Refitting is a reversal of removal, but tighten the mounting bolt to the specified torque.

19 Anti-lock braking system (ABS) – general information and precautions

The anti-lock braking system (ABS) fitted as standard to all models, prevents wheel lock-up under heavy braking, and not only optimises stopping distances, but also improves steering control. By electronically monitoring the speed of each roadwheel in relation to the other wheels, the system can detect when a wheel is about to lock-up, before control is actually lost. The brake fluid pressure applied to that wheel's brake caliper is then decreased and restored ('modulated') several times a second until control is regained. The system components are: four

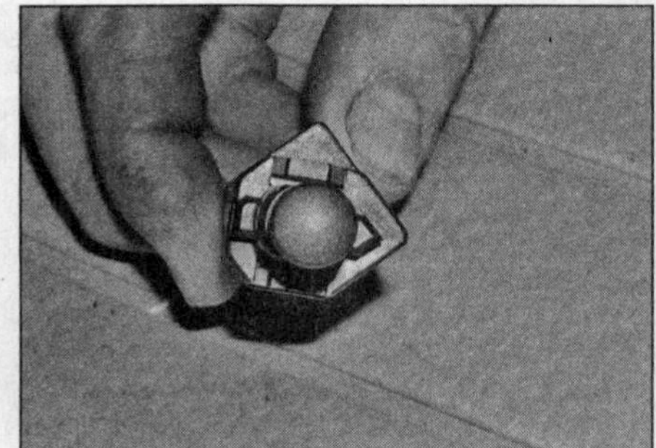

18.6 Align the shaped lug with the corresponding cut-out in the bracket

20.1 ABS hydraulic unit

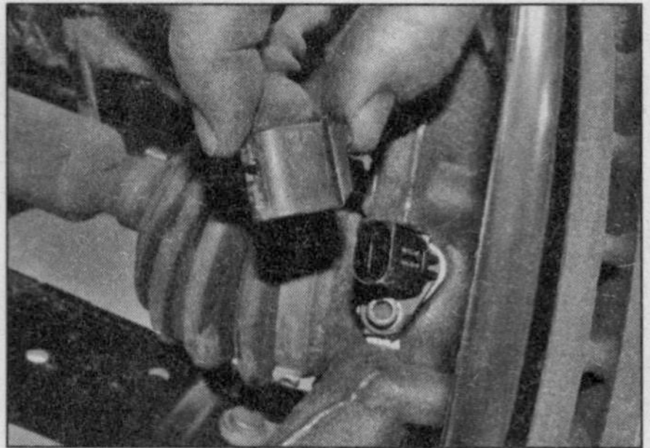
20.4 Disconnect the wiring...

20.5 ...and unbolt the front wheel sensor

wheel speed sensors, a hydraulic unit with integral Electronic Control Unit (ECU), brake lines and a dashboard-mounted warning light. The four wheel sensors are mounted on the wheel hub carriers. Each wheel has a rotating toothed hub mounted on the driveshaft (front) or on the hub (rear). The wheel speed sensors are mounted in close proximity to these hubs. The teeth produce a voltage waveform whose frequency varies with the speed of the hubs. These waveforms are transmitted to the ECU, and used to calculate the rotational speed of each wheel. The ECU has a self-diagnostic facility, to inhibit the operation of the ABS if a fault is detected, lighting the dashboard-mounted warning light. The braking system will then revert to conventional, non-ABS operation. If the nature of the fault is not immediately obvious upon inspection, the vehicle *must* be taken to a VW dealer, who will have the diagnostic equipment required to interrogate the ABS ECU electronically and pin-point the problem.

There are two ABS systems fitted to the models covered in this Manual.

The Mark 70 version includes a traction control system (TCS), which uses the basic ABS system, with an additional pump and valves fitted to the hydraulic actuator. If wheelspin is detected at a speed below 30 mph, one of the valves opens, to allow the pump to pressurise the relevant brake, until the spinning wheel slows to a rotational speed corresponding to the speed of the vehicle. This has the effect of transferring torque to the wheel with most traction. At the same time, the throttle plate is closed slightly, to reduce the torque from the engine.

The Mark 60 version includes electronic differential locking (EDL) and an electronic stability programme (ESP). The EDL system applies the brake of the spinning wheel in order to transfer torque to the wheel with the better grip. On models with ESP, the system recognises critical driving conditions and stabilises the vehicle by individual wheel braking and by intervention in the engine control, which occurs independently of the position of the brake and accelerator pedals.

The operation of the ABS system is entirely dependent on electrical signals. To prevent the system responding to any inaccurate signals, a built-in safety circuit monitors all signals received by the ECU. If an inaccurate signal or low battery voltage is detected, the ABS system is automatically shut down, and the warning light on the instrument panel is illuminated, to inform the driver that the ABS system is not operational. Normal braking will still be available, however.

If a fault does develop in the ABS system, the car must be taken to a VW dealer for fault diagnosis and repair.

20 Anti-lock braking system (ABS) components – removal and refitting

Hydraulic unit

1 Removal and refitting of the hydraulic unit is best entrusted to a VW dealer, as a fault diagnosis check must be performed on completion using specialist equipment **(see illustration)**.

Electronic control module (ECM)

2 The ECM is mounted underneath the hydraulic unit. Although it can be separated from the hydraulic unit, due to the delicacy of the components and the need for absolute cleanliness, it is recommended that the work be entrusted to a VW dealer.

Front wheel sensor

Removal

3 Chock the rear wheels, then firmly apply the handbrake, jack up the front of the car and support on axle stands (see *Jacking and vehicle support*). Remove the appropriate front roadwheel.

4 Disconnect the electrical connector from the sensor by carefully lifting up the retaining tag, and pulling the connector from the sensor **(see illustration)**.

5 Slacken and remove the hexagon socket-head bolt securing the sensor to the hub carrier, and remove the sensor from the car **(see illustration)**.

Refitting

6 Ensure that the sensor and hub carrier sealing faces are clean.

7 Apply a thin coat of multi-purpose grease to the mounting hole inner surface, then fit the sensor to the hub carrier. Refit the retaining bolt and tighten it to the specified torque.

8 Ensure that the sensor wiring is correctly routed and retained by all the necessary clips, and reconnect the wiring connector.

9 Refit the roadwheel, then lower the car to the ground and tighten the roadwheel bolts to the specified torque.

Rear wheel sensor

Removal

10 Chock the front wheels, then jack up the rear of the car and support it on axle stands (see *Jacking and vehicle support*). Remove the appropriate roadwheel.

11 Remove the sensor (paragraphs 4 and 5).

Refitting

12 Refit the sensor as described above in paragraphs 6 to 9.

Front reluctor rings

13 The front reluctor rings are integral with the wheel bearings, and can only be inspected after removal of the driveshafts. If faulty, the bearings must be renewed.

Rear reluctor rings

14 The rear reluctor rings are integral with the rear wheel bearings, and can only be inspected after removal of the rear hubs. If faulty, the rear hub complete with bearing must be renewed as described in Chapter 10.

21 Servo unit mechanical vacuum pump (diesel models) – testing, removal and refitting

Testing

1 The operation of the braking system vacuum pump can be checked using a vacuum gauge. First, remove the engine top cover and the air filter housing. **Note:** *On the diesel models covered in this Manual, the vacuum pump is combined with the fuel lift pump.*

2 Disconnect the vacuum hose from the pump, and connect the gauge to the pump union using a suitable length of hose.

3 Start the engine and allow it to idle, then measure the vacuum created by the pump. As a guide, after one minute, a minimum of approximately 500 mm Hg should be recorded. If the vacuum registered is significantly less than this, it is likely that the pump is faulty. However, seek the advice of a VW dealer before condemning the pump.

4 Reconnect the vacuum hose. Overhaul of the vacuum pump is not possible, since no major components are available separately for it. If faulty, the complete pump assembly must be renewed.

Removal

Note: *A new pump O-ring will be required on refitting.*

5 Release the retaining clip (where fitted), and disconnect the vacuum hose from the top of pump.

6 Note the locations of the fuel supply (white) and return (blue) hoses, then disconnect them.

7 Unscrew the two main upper mounting bolts and the two small lower mounting bolts

8 Withdraw the vacuum pump from the cylinder head, and recover the O-ring seals. Discard them and obtain new ones for using on refitting.

Refitting

9 Fit the new O-ring seals to the vacuum pump, and apply a smear of oil to aid installation.

10 Manoeuvre the vacuum pump into position, making sure that the slot in the pump drive gear aligns with the slot on the pump driveshaft.

11 Refit the pump retaining bolts, and tighten to the specified torque.

12 Reconnect the fuel hoses.

13 Reconnect the vacuum hose and secure with the retaining clip (where fitted).

14 Refit the air filter housing and engine top cover.

22 Servo unit electric vacuum pump (diesel models) – testing, removal and refitting

Note: *The electric vacuum pump is only fitted to models with automatic transmission.*

Testing

1 With the engine stopped, depress the brake pedal several times to exhaust the vacuum in the servo unit. The pedal will become firm.

2 Start the engine, then slowly depress the brake pedal. An audible 'click' must be heard as the electric vacuum pump is activated, and the pedal will be easier to depress. Confirmation that the pump is running can be made by an assistant touching the pump as the pedal is depressed.

3 Overhaul of the electric vacuum pump is not possible, therefore, if faulty, the pump must be renewed.

Removal

4 The electric brake vacuum pump is located on a bracket on the front of the automatic transmission. Apply the handbrake, then jack up the front of the vehicle and support it on axle stands (see *Jacking and vehicle support*). Remove the left-hand front roadwheel.

5 Disconnect the vacuum hose from the pump.

6 Disconnect the wiring from the vacuum pump and release it from the clip.

7 Unscrew the bolts securing the bracket to the transmission and withdraw the assembly from the automatic transmission.

8 Unbolt the bracket from the vacuum pump.

Refitting

9 Refitting is a reversal of removal, but tighten the mounting bolts to the specified torque.

Chapter 10
Suspension and steering systems

Contents

Degrees of difficulty

Easy, suitable for novice with little experience	**Fairly easy,** suitable for beginner with some experience	**Fairly difficult,** suitable for competent DIY mechanic	**Difficult,** suitable for experienced DIY mechanic	**Very difficult,** suitable for expert DIY or professional 

Specifications

Front suspension

Type: Independent, with MacPherson struts incorporating coil springs, telescopic shock absorbers and anti-roll bar

Rear suspension

Type: Trailing arm with Multi-link transverse arms, separate gas-filled telescopic shock absorbers, coil springs and anti-roll bar

Steering

Type: Rack-and-pinion. Electro-mechanical power assistance standard

Wheel alignment and steering angles*

Front wheel:	
Camber angle:	
Standard suspension	-30' ± 30'
Sports suspension:	
Except GTi	-41' ± 30'
GTi	-44' ± 30'
Heavy duty suspension	-14' ± 30'
Maximum difference between sides (all models)	30'
Castor angle:	
Standard suspension	7° 34' ± 30'
Sports suspension	7° 47' ± 30'
Heavy duty suspension	7° 17' ± 30'
Maximum difference between sides (all models)	30'
Toe setting	10' ± 10'
Toe-out on turns (20° left or right):	
Standard suspension	1° 38' ± 20'
Sports suspension:	
Except GTi	1° 40' ± 20'
GTi	1° 22' ± 20'
Heavy duty suspension	1° 38' ± 20'
Rear wheel:	
Camber angle	-1°20' ± 30'
Maximum difference between sides	30'
Toe setting	+10' ± 12.5'

** Refer to a VW dealer for the latest recommendations.*

Roadwheels

Type	Aluminium alloy

Tyres

Size	195/65R15, 205/60R15, 205/55R16, 225/45R17 and 225/40ZR18
Pressures	See *Weekly checks* on page 0•17

Torque wrench settings

	Nm	lbf ft
Front suspension		
Anti-roll bar link	65	48
Anti-roll bar to subframe:		
Stage 1	20	15
Stage 2	Angle-tighten a further 90°	
Hub bolt*	See Chapter 8	
Hub to wheel bearing housing:		
Stage 1	70	52
Stage 2	Angle-tighten a further 90°	
Lower arm:		
To bracket*:		
Stage 1	70	52
Stage 2	Angle-tighten a further 180°	
To front wheel bearing housing (lower balljoint)*	60	44
Mounting bracket to body:		
Stage 1	70	52
Stage 2	Angle-tighten a further 90°	
Mounting bracket to bracket:		
Stage 1	50	37
Stage 2	Angle-tighten a further 90°	
Rear engine mounting:		
To subframe:		
Stage 1	100	74
Stage 2	Angle-tighten a further 90°	
To transmission:		
Stage 1	40	30
Stage 2	Angle-tighten a further 90°	
Subframe-to-underbody/bracket bolts*:		
Stage 1	70	52
Stage 2	Angle-tighten a further 90°	

Torque wrench settings (continued)

	Nm	lbf ft
Front suspension (continued)		
Splash plate to wheel bearing housing	10	7
Suspension strut:		
Bottom clamp*:		
Stage 1	70	52
Stage 2	Angle-tighten a further 90°	
Upper mounting*:		
Stage 1	15	11
Stage 2	Angle-tighten a further 90°	
Upper piston rod	60	44
Vehicle level sender to subframe and lower arm	9	7
Rear suspension		
ABS speed sensor	8	6
Anti-roll bar:		
To subframe*:		
Stage 1	25	18
Stage 2	Angle-tighten a further 45°	
Anti-roll bar link	45	33
Hub to wheel bearing housing:		
Stage 1	180	134
Stage 2	Angle-tighten a further 180°	
Lower transverse link to wheel bearing housing:		
Stage 1	90	66
Stage 2	Angle-tighten a further 90°	
Radius rods:		
To body:		
Stage 1	40	30
Stage 2	Angle-tighten a further 90°	
To subframe:		
Stage 1	90	66
Stage 2	Angle-tighten a further 45°	
Shock absorber:		
To wheel bearing housing	180	134
To shock absorber mounting bracket	25	18
To body*:		
Stage 1	50	37
Stage 2	Angle-tighten a further 45°	
Splash plate to wheel bearing housing	12	9
Stone deflector to transverse link	8	6
Subframe to body:		
Stage 1	90	66
Stage 2	Angle-tighten a further 90°	
Track control rod to subframe:		
Stage 1	90	66
Stage 2	Angle-tighten a further 90°	
Track control rod to wheel bearing housing:		
Stage 1	130	96
Stage 2	Angle-tighten a further 90°	
Trailing arm:		
To wheel bearing housing		
Stage 1	90	66
Stage 2	Angle-tighten a further 90°	
To mounting bracket:		
Stage 1	90	66
Stage 2	Angle-tighten a further 90°	
Mounting bracket to underbody:		
Stage 1	50	37
Stage 2	Angle-tighten a further 45°	
Transverse links to subframe	95	70
Upper transverse link to wheel bearing housing:		
Stage 1	130	96
Stage 2	Angle-tighten a further 90°	
Vehicle level sender	5	4

Torque wrench settings (continued)

	Nm	lbf ft
Steering		
Steering column:		
To mounting bracket*	20	15
Mounting bracket to body	20	15
Strut to mounting bracket/body	20	15
Universal joint to steering gear*:		
Stage 1	20	15
Stage 2	Angle-tighten a further 90°	
Steering gear:		
To subframe*:		
Stage 1	50	37
Stage 2	Angle-tighten a further 90°	
Shield	6	4
Steering wheel to column*:		
Stage 1	30	22
Stage 2	Angle-tighten a further 90°	
Track rod end to track rod	55	41
Track rod end to wheel bearing housing:		
Stage 1	20	15
Stage 2	Angle-tighten a further 90°	
Track rod to steering gear rack	100	74
Roadwheels		
Roadwheel bolts	120	89

** Renew the nut/bolt every time it is removed*

1 General information

The independent front suspension is of the MacPherson strut type, incorporating coil springs and integral telescopic shock absorbers. The struts are located by transverse lower suspension arms, which use rubber inner mounting bushes, and incorporate a balljoint at the outer ends. The front wheel bearing housings, which carry the wheel bearings, brake calipers and the hub/disc assemblies, are attached to the MacPherson struts by clamp bolts, and connected to the lower arms through the balljoints. A front anti-roll bar is fitted to all models. The anti-roll bar is rubber-mounted, and is connected to both lower suspension arms by short links.

The rear suspension consists of a trailing arm, rubber-mounted at its front end to the underbody, a wheel bearing housing, lower main transverse link and coil spring, track control rod, upper transverse link, and separate shock absorber. A rear anti-roll bar is fitted to all models. The anti-roll bar is rubber-mounted on the rear subframe, and is connected to the wheel bearing housings on each side by a short connecting link.

The safety steering column incorporates an intermediate shaft at its lower end. The intermediate shaft is connected to both the steering column and steering gear by universal joints, although the shaft is supplied as part of the column assembly and cannot be separated. Both the inner steering column and intermediate shaft have splined sections which collapse during a major frontal impact. The outer column is also telescopic with two sections, to facilitate reach adjustment.

The steering gear is mounted onto the front subframe, and is connected by two track rods, with balljoints at their inner and outer ends, to the steering arms projecting rearwards from the wheel bearing housings. The track rod ends are threaded to the track rods in order to allow adjustment of the front wheel toe setting. The steering gear has electro-mechanical assistance, and incorporates an integral control unit. It is only functional when the engine is running. There are no hydraulic components, and steering assistance is automatically matched to the vehicle speed, steering wheel torque and steering wheel angle.

All models are fitted with an Anti-lock Brake System (ABS), and can also be fitted with a Traction Control System (TCS), an Electronic Differential Lock (EDL) system and an Electronic Stability Program (ESP). The ABS may also be referred to as including EBD (Electronic Brake Distribution) which means it adjusts the front and rear braking forces according to the weight being carried. The TCS may also be referred to as ASR (Anti Slip Regulation).

The TCS system prevents the front wheels from losing traction during acceleration by reducing the engine output. The system is switched on automatically when the engine is started, and it utilises the ABS system sensors to monitor the rotational speeds of the front wheels.

The ESP system extends the ABS, TCS and EDL functions to reduce wheel spin in difficult driving conditions. It does this by using highly-sensitive sensors which monitor the speed of the vehicle, lateral movement of the vehicle, the brake pressure, and the steering angle of the front wheels. If, for example, the vehicle is tending to oversteer, the brake will be applied to the front outer wheel to correct the situation. If the vehicle is tending to understeer, the brake will be applied to the rear inside wheel. The steering angle of the front wheels is monitored by an angle sensor on the top of the steering column.

The TCS/ESP systems should always be switched on, except when driving with snow chains, driving in snow or driving on loose surfaces, when some wheel spin may be advantageous. The ESP switch is located in the centre of the facia.

Some models are also fitted with an Electronic Differential Lock (EDL) which reduces unequal traction from the front wheels. If one front wheel spins 100 rpm or more faster than the other, the faster wheel is slowed down by applying the brake to that wheel. The system is not the same as the traditional differential lock, where the actual differential gears are locked. Because the system applies a front brake, in the event of a brake disc overheating the system will shut down until the disc has cooled. No warning light is displayed if the system shuts down. As is the case with the TCS system, the EDL system uses the ABS sensors to monitor front wheel speeds.

2 Front wheel bearing housing - removal and refitting

Note: *Renewal of the hub bearings does not require removal of the wheel bearing housing (see Section 3). This Section describes removal of the wheel bearing housing leaving the suspension strut in situ, however, if necessary it can be removed together with the suspension strut, then separated on the bench. All self-locking nuts and bolts disturbed on removal must be renewed as a matter of course.*

Removal

1 Remove the wheel trim/hub cap (as applicable) and loosen the driveshaft retaining bolt (hub bolt) by 90° with the vehicle resting on its wheels. Also loosen the wheel bolts. **Note:** *Do not loosen the hub bolt more than 90° at this stage, or the wheel bearing may be damaged.*

2 Apply the handbrake, then jack up the front of the vehicle and support it on axle stands (see *Jacking and vehicle support*). Remove the front roadwheel.

3 Unscrew and remove the driveshaft retaining bolt.

4 Remove the ABS wheel sensor as described in Chapter 9. Also, unbolt the brake hose/wiring bracket from the strut **(see illustrations)**.

5 Remove the brake disc as described in Chapter 9 **(see illustrations)**. This procedure includes removing the brake caliper, however **do not** disconnect the hydraulic brake hose from the caliper. Using a piece of wire or string, tie the caliper to the front suspension coil spring, to avoid placing any strain on the hydraulic brake hose.

6 Unbolt the splash plate from the wheel bearing housing.

7 Loosen the nut securing the steering track rod balljoint to the wheel bearing housing. To do this, fit a ring spanner to the nut, then hold the balljoint pin stationary using an Allen key. With the nut removed, it may be possible to release the balljoint from the wheel bearing housing by turning the balljoint pin with an Allen key. If not, leave the nut on by a few turns to protect the threads, then use a universal balljoint separator to release the balljoint. Remove the nut completely once the taper has been released.

8 Unscrew the front suspension lower balljoint-to-lower arm retaining nuts **(see illustration)**, then lever the lower arm down to release the balljoint studs from the arm. Now use a soft-faced mallet to tap the driveshaft from the hub splines while pulling out the bottom end of the wheel bearing housing. If the driveshaft is tight on the splines, it may be necessary to use a puller bolted to the hub to remove it. Tie the driveshaft to one side.

2.4a The ABS wheel sensor on the inside of the wheel bearing housing

2.4b Removing the brake hose/wiring bracket

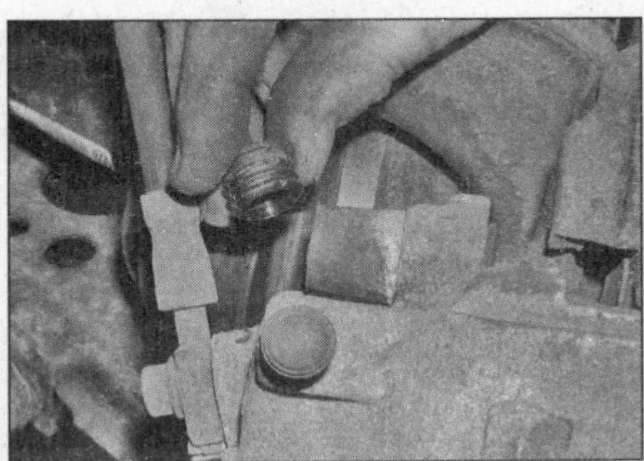

2.5a Remove the caps...

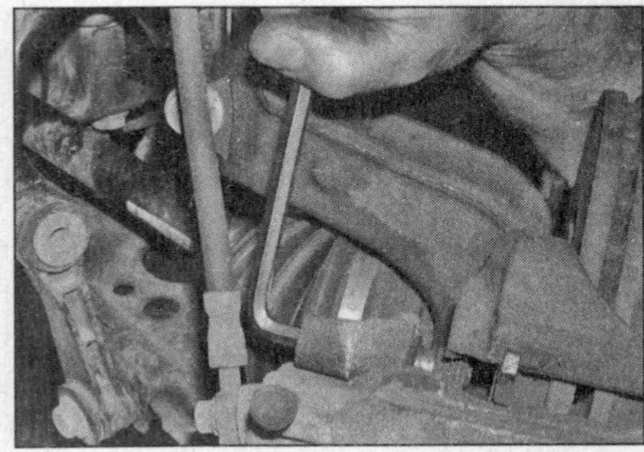

2.5b ...then loosen the guide pins with an Allen key...

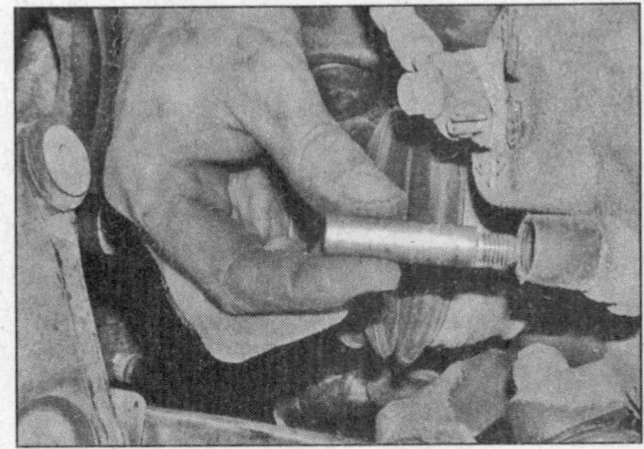

2.5c ...remove the guide pins...

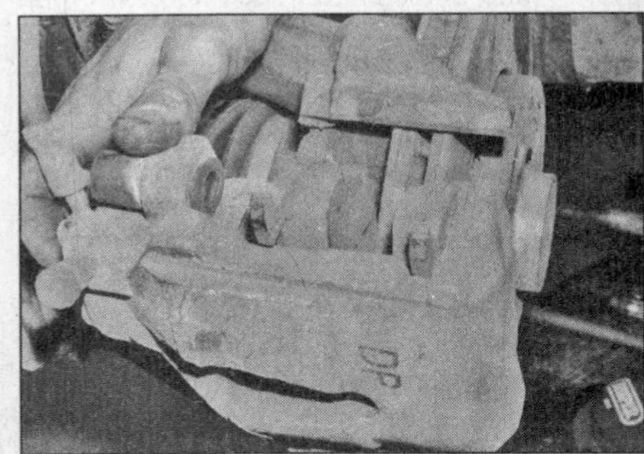

2.5d ...withdraw the brake caliper...

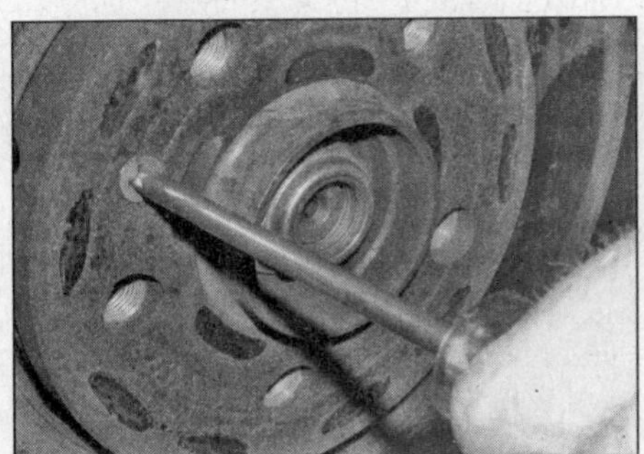

2.5e ...then undo the screws...

2.5f ...and remove the brake disc

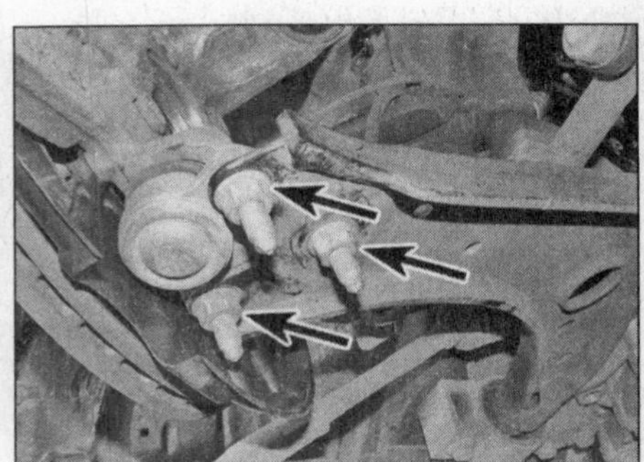

2.8 Lower balljoint-to-arm retaining nuts

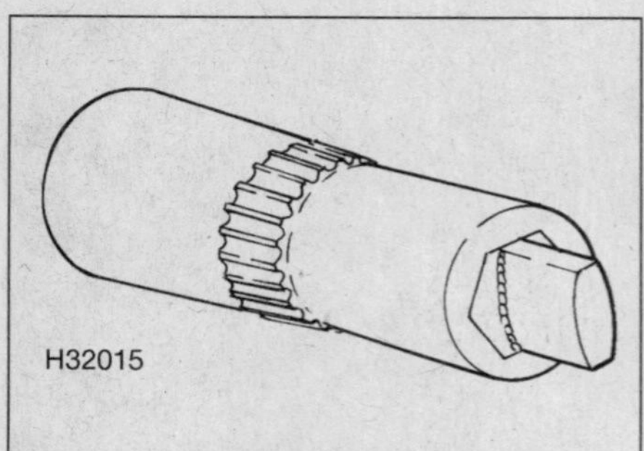

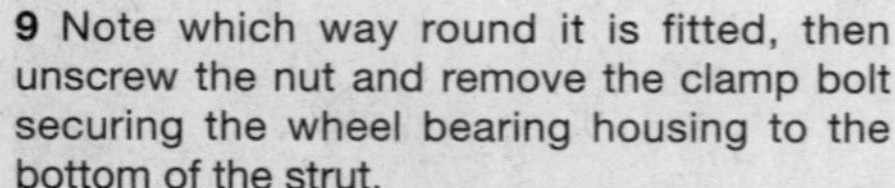

2.10a Tool used by VW technicians to open up the split wheel bearing housing

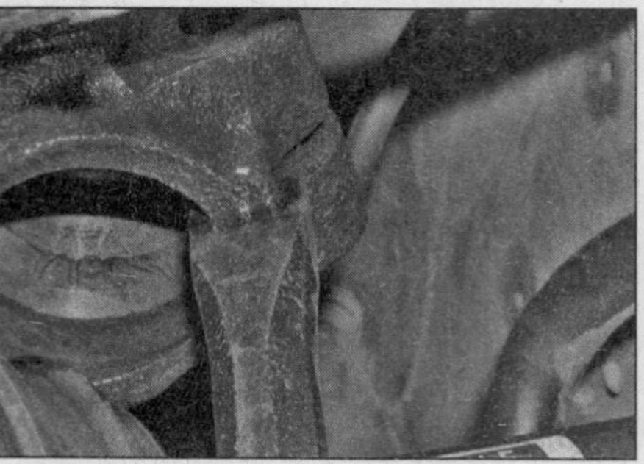

2.10b Using a cold chisel to open up the wheel bearing housing and release the suspension strut

2.10c Withdrawing the wheel bearing housing from the bottom of the suspension strut

9 Note which way round it is fitted, then unscrew the nut and remove the clamp bolt securing the wheel bearing housing to the bottom of the strut.

10 The wheel bearing housing must now be released from the strut. To do this, VW technicians insert a special tool into the split wheel bearing housing, and turn it through 90° to open up the clamp. A similar tool can be made out of an old screwdriver, or alternatively a suitable cold chisel can be driven into the split as a wedge. Slightly press inwards the top of the wheel bearing housing, then push it downwards from the bottom of the strut **(see illustrations)**.

Refitting

11 Ensure that the driveshaft outer joint and hub splines are clean and dry, then lubricate the splines with fresh engine oil. Also lubricate the threads and contact surface of the hub nut/bolt with oil.

12 Lift the wheel bearing assembly into position, and engage the hub with the splines on the outer end of the driveshaft. Fit the new hub bolt, tightening it by hand only at this stage.

13 Engage the wheel bearing housing with the bottom of the suspension strut, making sure that the hole in the side plate aligns with the holes in the split housing. Remove the tool used to open the split.

14 Insert the strut-to-wheel bearing housing clamp bolt from the front, and fit the new retaining nut. Tighten the nut to the specified torque.

15 Refit the lower arm balljoint to the lower arm, and tighten the nuts to the specified torque.

16 Refit the track rod balljoint to the wheel bearing housing, then fit a new retaining nut and tighten it to the specified torque. If necessary, hold the balljoint pin with an Allen key while tightening the nut.

17 Refit the splash plate and tighten the bolts.

18 Refit the brake disc and caliper with reference to Chapter 9.

19 Refit the ABS wheel sensor as described in Chapter 9.

20 Ensure that the outer joint is drawn fully into the hub, then refit the roadwheel.

21 Have an assistant depress the brake pedal, then tighten the driveshaft retaining bolt in the stages given in the Specifications. It is recommended that an angle gauge is used to ensure the correct tightening angle. **Note:** *The car must not be standing on its wheels when tightening the bolt, or the wheel bearing may be damaged.*

22 Lower the vehicle to the ground, tighten the roadwheel bolts, and refit the wheel trim/hub cap.

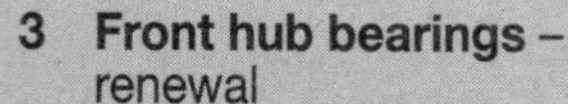

3 Front hub bearings – renewal

Note: *The bearing is a sealed, pre-adjusted and pre-lubricated, double-row roller type, and requires no maintenance. It is bolted to the wheel bearing housing.*

1 Remove the wheel trim/hub cap (as applicable) and loosen the driveshaft retaining bolt (hub bolt) with the vehicle resting on its wheels. **Note:** *Do not loosen the hub bolt more than 90° at this stage, or the wheel bearing may be damaged.* Also loosen the wheel bolts.

2 Apply the handbrake, then jack up the front of the vehicle and support it on axle stands (see *Jacking and vehicle support*). Remove the front roadwheel.

3 Unscrew and remove the driveshaft retaining bolt.

4 Remove the ABS wheel sensor as described in Chapter 9.

5 Remove the brake disc as described in Chapter 9. This procedure includes removing the brake caliper, however **do not** disconnect the hydraulic brake hose from the caliper. Using a piece of wire or string, tie the caliper to the front suspension coil spring, to avoid placing any strain on the hydraulic brake hose.

6 Unbolt the splash plate from the wheel bearing housing **(see illustration)**.

7 Press the driveshaft outer stub towards the transmission as far as possible, then unscrew and remove the wheel bearing retaining bolts from the rear of the housing.

8 Remove the hub/wheel bearing complete with hub from the outside of the housing while sliding it from the driveshaft splines **(see illustrations)**.

9 Fit the new wheel bearing to the housing and engage the hub splines with the driveshaft outer stub.

3.6 Splash plate mounting bolts (wheel bearing housing removed)

3.8a Removing the front hub/wheel bearing from the wheel bearing housing

3.8b Front hub/wheel bearing

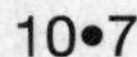

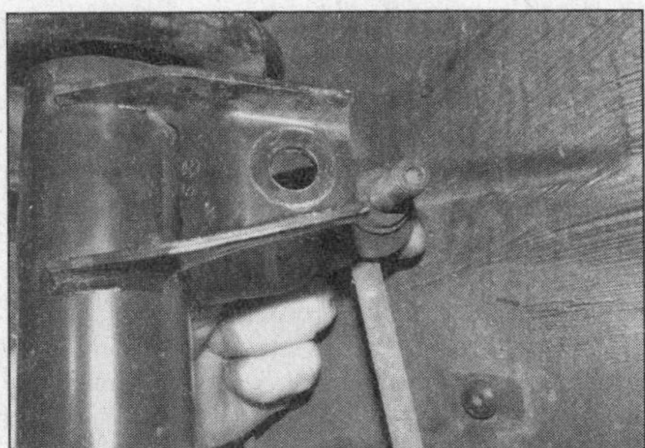

4.3 Disconnect the anti-roll bar from the strut

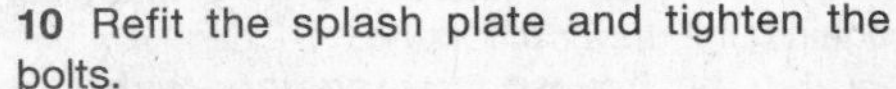

10 Refit the splash plate and tighten the bolts.
11 Refit the brake disc and caliper with reference to Chapter 9.
12 Refit the ABS wheel sensor as described in Chapter 9.
13 Pull the driveshaft outer stub fully into the hub and fit a new hub bolt, hand-tight at this stage.
14 Ensure that the outer joint is drawn fully into the hub, then refit the roadwheel.
15 Tighten the driveshaft retaining bolt in the stages given in the Specifications. It is recommended that an angle gauge is used to ensure the correct tightening angle. **Note:** *The car must not be standing on its wheels when tightening the bolt, or the wheel bearing will be damaged.*
16 Lower the vehicle to the ground, tighten the roadwheel bolts, and refit the wheel trim/hub cap.

4 Front suspension strut – removal, overhaul and refitting

Note: *This section describes removal of the suspension strut leaving the wheel bearing housing in situ, however, if necessary it can be removed together with the wheel bearing housing, then separated on the bench. All self-locking nuts and bolts disturbed on removal must be renewed as a matter of course.*

Removal

1 Remove the wheel trim/hub cap (as applicable) and loosen the driveshaft retaining bolt (hub bolt) with the vehicle resting on its wheels. **Note:** *Do not loosen the hub bolt more than 90° at this stage, or the wheel bearing may be damaged.* Also loosen the wheel bolts.
2 Apply the handbrake, then jack up the front of the vehicle and support it on axle stands (see *Jacking and vehicle support*). Remove the appropriate roadwheel.
3 Unscrew the nut and disconnect the anti-roll bar link from the strut **(see illustration)**.
4 Release the ABS sensor wiring from the strut.

4.5 Unscrew and remove the driveshaft retaining bolt

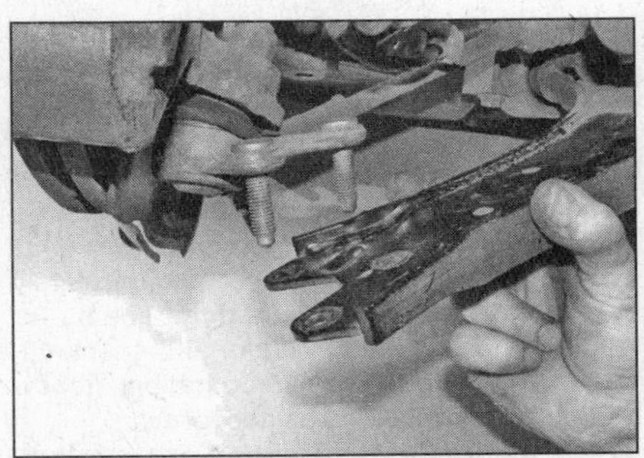

4.6b ...and detach the lower arm from the balljoint studs...

5 Unscrew and remove the driveshaft retaining bolt **(see illustration)**.
6 Unscrew the front suspension lower balljoint-to-lower arm retaining nuts, then lever the lower arm down to release the balljoint studs. Now use a soft-faced mallet to tap the driveshaft from the hub splines while pulling out the bottom end of the wheel bearing housing **(see illustrations)**. If the driveshaft is tight on the splines, it may be necessary to use a puller bolted to the hub to remove it. Tie the driveshaft to one side, then refit the lower balljoint to the lower arm and secure with the nuts, hand-tightened.
7 Note which way round it is fitted, then unscrew the nut and remove the clamp bolt securing the wheel bearing housing to the bottom of the strut **(see illustration)**.
8 The wheel bearing housing must now be released from the strut. To do this, VW technicians insert a special tool into the split wheel bearing housing, and turn it through 90° to open up the clamp. A similar tool such as an Allen key can be used, or alternatively a suitable cold chisel can be driven into the split as a wedge. Slightly press inwards the top of the wheel bearing housing, then push it downwards from the bottom of the strut **(see illustration)**. Support the wheel bearing housing to one side without straining the hydraulic brake hose.
9 Remove the wiper arms (Chapter 12) and the plenum chamber cover (Chapter 11).
10 To ensure correct refitting, mark the strut upper mounting in relation to the body. If the reason for removing the strut is overhaul, loosen the upper mounting centre nut one turn, while holding the piston rod with an Allen key.
11 Support the strut, then unscrew the upper

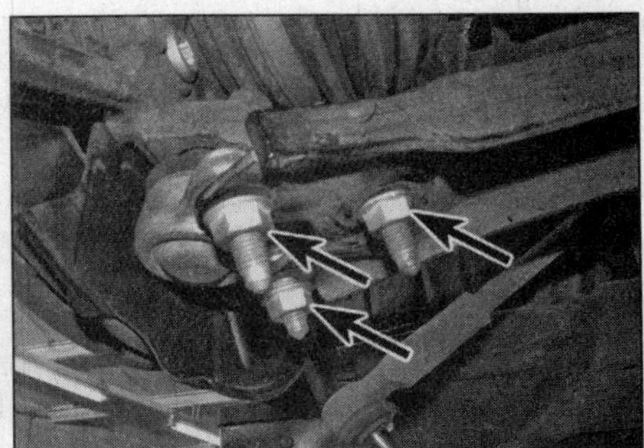

4.6a Unscrew the nuts...

4.6c ...now remove the driveshaft from the hub splines

4.7 Remove the clamp bolt...

4.8 ...then use a suitable tool to expand the split, so that the strut can be pulled from the wheel bearing housing

4.11a Unscrew the upper mounting bolts...

4.11b ...and lower the strut from under the wheel arch

mounting bolts and lower the strut from under the wheel arch **(see illustrations)**.

Overhaul

Warning: Before attempting to dismantle the suspension strut, a suitable tool to hold the coil spring in compression must be obtained. Adjustable coil spring compressors are readily available, and are recommended for this operation. Any attempt to dismantle the strut without such a tool is likely to result in damage or personal injury.

12 With the strut removed from the car, clean away all external dirt. If necessary, mount it upright in a vice during the dismantling procedure.

13 Fit the spring compressor, and compress the coil spring until all tension is relieved from the upper spring seat **(see illustration)**.

14 Unscrew and remove the upper centre retaining nut, whilst retaining the strut piston with a suitable Allen key, then remove the mounting, thrust bearing, and coil spring **(see illustrations)**.

15 Remove the protective sleeve and upper bearing race, then remove the bump stop from the upper mounting **(see illustrations)**.

16 With the strut assembly now completely dismantled, examine all the components for wear, damage or deformation, and check the bearing for smoothness of operation. Renew any of the components as necessary.

17 Examine the strut for signs of fluid leakage. Check the strut piston for signs of pitting along its entire length, and check the strut body for signs of damage. While holding it in an upright position, test the operation of the strut by moving the piston through a full stroke, and then through short strokes of 50 to 100 mm. In both cases, the resistance felt should be smooth and continuous. If the resistance is jerky, or uneven, or if there is any visible sign of wear or damage to the strut, renewal is necessary.

18 If any doubt exists about the condition of the coil spring, carefully remove the spring compressors, and check the spring for distortion and signs of cracking. Renew the spring if it is damaged or distorted, or if there is any doubt as to its condition.

19 Inspect all other components for signs of damage or deterioration, and renew as necessary.

20 Assemble the bump stop to the upper mounting, then refit the upper bearing race and protective sleeve to the mounting. The larger diameter of the bump stop must be against the upper mounting.

21 Fit the coil spring (together with the compressor tool) onto the strut, making sure its lower (larger diameter) end is correctly located against the spring seat stop.

22 Refit the thrust bearing and upper mounting, then screw on a new retaining nut. Tighten the nut to the specified torque while holding the piston rod with an Allen key.

Refitting

23 Manoeuvre the strut into position under the wheel arch, and locate in the suspension strut turret in the previously noted position. If a new strut is being fitted, locate it so that one of the two arrows marked on the upper mounting points forwards, and the bolt holes are aligned. Insert the bolts and tighten to the specified torque.

24 Refit the plenum chamber cover and wiper arms.

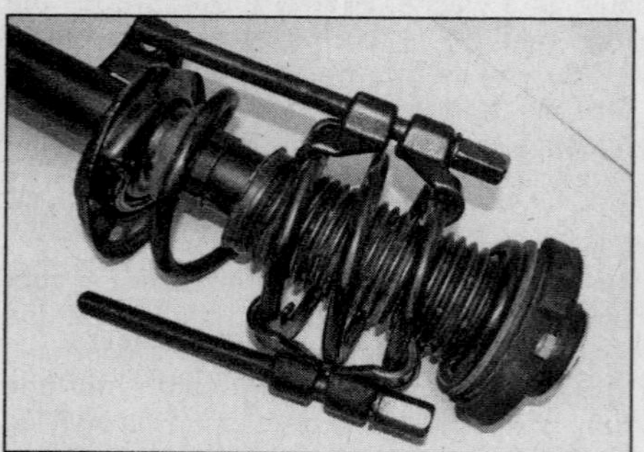

4.13 Compress the coil spring with the compressor tool

4.14a Unscrew the upper centre nut...

4.14b ...then remove the mounting, thrust bearing and coil spring

4.15a Remove the protective sleeve...

4.15b ...and upper bearing race...

4.15c ...then remove the bump stop from the upper mounting

25 Engage the wheel bearing housing with the bottom of the suspension strut, making sure that the hole in the side plate aligns with the holes in the split housing. Raise the housing, while pressing it inwards to assist entry. Use a trolley jack if necessary. When fully entered, remove the tool used to open the split.
26 Insert the new strut-to-wheel bearing housing bolt from the front, and fit the new retaining nut. Tighten the nut to the specified torque.
27 Unscrew the nuts from the lower balljoint and lever down the lower arm to release it from the wheel bearing housing. Insert the outer end of the driveshaft through the hub and engage it with the splines. Fit the new hub bolt, tightening it by hand only at this stage.
28 Refit the lower arm balljoint to the lower arm, and tighten the nuts to the specified torque. Where applicable, refit the headlight range control sensor arm to the lower arm and tighten the nut.
29 Refit the ABS wheel sensor as described in Chapter 9.
30 Ensure that the outer joint is drawn fully into the hub, then refit the roadwheel.
31 Have an assistant depress the brake pedal, then tighten the driveshaft retaining bolt in the stages given in the Specifications. It is recommended that an angle gauge is used to ensure the correct tightening angle. **Note:** *The car must not be standing on its wheels when tightening the bolt, or the wheel bearing may be damaged.*
32 Lower the vehicle to the ground, tighten the roadwheel bolts, and refit the wheel trim/hub cap.

5 Front suspension lower arm – removal, overhaul and refitting

Note: *The lower arm is available in either cast steel or sheet steel ñ when renewing the arm, make sure the correct type is fitted according to model. VW subframe locating pins (T10096) or similar are required for the work in this Section, to ensure correct front wheel alignment. All self-locking nuts and bolts disturbed on removal must be renewed as a matter of course.*

Removal

1 Apply the handbrake, then jack up the front of the vehicle and support it on axle stands (see *Jacking and vehicle support*). Remove the appropriate front roadwheel and the engine compartment undertray.
2 Unscrew the front suspension lower balljoint-to-lower arm retaining nuts, then lever down the lower arm to release the arm from the balljoint studs.
3 At this stage, VW technicians use locating pins T10096 in place of the rear outer subframe mounting bolts to ensure correct front wheel alignment. If these pins are not available, only remove and refit one lower arm at a time, and mark the position of the subframe accurately with dabs of paint.
4 Unscrew and remove the rear outer mounting bolt and, where available, substitute it with a locating pin tightened to 20 Nm (15 lbf ft).
5 Unscrew and remove the front mounting bolt, then support the lower arm and unscrew the two rear inner mounting bolts. Remove the lower arm from beneath the car.

Overhaul

6 Thoroughly clean the lower arm, then check carefully for cracks or any other signs of wear or damage, paying particular attention to the rubber mounting bushes. If either bush requires renewal, take the lower arm to a VW dealer or suitably-equipped garage. Alternatively, a hydraulic press and suitable spacers may be used to press the bushes out of the arm and rear bracket, and to install the new ones. Dip the bushes in a mild solution of washing-up liquid and water. Note the following:

a) *When fitting a new front mounting bush, it must be initially tilted with one lip in the bore. As the bush is inserted, it will straighten up. Make sure the bush is centred in its bore.*
b) *After pressing a new rear mounting bush into the rear mounting bracket, press the bracket and bush fully onto the lower arm rear pivot.*

Refitting

7 Locate the lower arm on the subframe and insert the front mounting bolt loosely.
8 Insert the two rear outer mounting bolts loosely, then position the inner bolt hole in the exact position noted during removal. If a VW location pin was used on removal, the bracket will be correctly positioned on the pin. Tighten the two outer bolts to the specified torque, then remove the pin and refit the inner bolt, and tighten to the specified torque.
9 Tighten the front mounting bolt to the specified torque.
10 Lever down the lower arm and locate the balljoint studs in their holes. Fit the new nuts and tighten to the specified torque.
11 Refit the roadwheel and undertray, and lower the car to the ground.

6 Front suspension lower arm balljoint – removal, inspection and refitting

Note: *All self-locking nuts and bolts disturbed on removal must be renewed as a matter of course.*

Removal

Method 1

1 Remove the wheel bearing housing as described in Section 2.
2 Unscrew and remove the balljoint retaining nut **(see illustration)**, then release the balljoint from the wheel bearing housing using a universal balljoint separator. Withdraw the balljoint.

Method 2

3 Remove the wheel trim/hub cap (as applicable) and loosen the driveshaft retaining bolt (hub bolt) with the vehicle resting on its wheels. **Note:** *Do not loosen the hub bolt more than 90° at this stage, or the wheel bearing may be damaged.* Also loosen the wheel bolts.
4 Apply the handbrake, then jack up the front of the vehicle and support it on axle stands (see *Jacking and vehicle support*). Remove the appropriate roadwheel.
5 Unscrew and remove the driveshaft retaining bolt.
6 Unscrew the front suspension lower balljoint-to-lower arm retaining nuts, then lever the lower arm down to release the balljoint studs. Now use a soft-faced mallet to tap the driveshaft from the hub splines while pulling out the bottom end of the wheel bearing housing. If the driveshaft is tight on the splines, it may be necessary to use a puller bolted to the hub to remove it. It is not necessary to remove the driveshaft completely from the hub. Retain the wheel bearing housing away from the lower arm by inserting a block of wood between the strut and the inner body panel.
7 Unscrew and remove the balljoint retaining nut, then release the balljoint from the wheel bearing housing using a universal balljoint separator. Withdraw the balljoint.

Inspection

8 With the balljoint removed, check that it moves freely, without any sign of roughness. Check also that the balljoint rubber gaiter shows no sign of deterioration, and is free from cracks and splits. Renew as necessary.

Refitting

Method 1

9 Fit the balljoint to the wheel bearing housing and fit the new retaining nut. Tighten the nut to the specified torque setting, noting that the balljoint shank can be retained with an Allen key if necessary to prevent it from rotating.
10 Refit the wheel bearing housing with reference to Section 2.

Method 2

11 Fit the balljoint to the wheel bearing housing and fit the new retaining nut. Tighten the nut

6.2 Front suspension lower arm balljoint retaining nut

to the specified torque setting, noting that the balljoint shank can be retained with an Allen key if necessary to prevent it from rotating.

12 Remove the wooden block and move the strut inwards, then refit the balljoint to the lower arm using new nuts, and tighten them to the specified torque.

13 Refit the driveshaft retaining bolt and tighten it sufficiently to draw the driveshaft fully into the hub, then refit the roadwheel.

14 Have an assistant depress the brake pedal, then tighten the driveshaft retaining bolt in the stages given in the Specifications. It is recommended that an angle gauge is used to ensure the correct tightening angle. **Note:** *The car must not be standing on its wheels when tightening the bolt, or the wheel bearing may be damaged.*

15 Lower the vehicle to the ground, tighten the roadwheel bolts, and refit the wheel trim/hub cap.

7 Front anti-roll bar – removal and refitting

Note: *As the subframe must be lowered during this procedure, VW subframe locating pins (T10096) or similar are required to ensure correct front wheel alignment. All self-locking nuts and bolts disturbed on removal must be renewed as a matter of course.*

Removal

1 Apply the handbrake, then jack up the front of the vehicle and support it on axle stands (see *Jacking and vehicle support*). Remove both front roadwheels and the engine compartment undertray.

2 Inside the car, undo the nuts and remove the trim beneath the foot pedals for access to the steering column universal joint. Unscrew the clamp bolt and pull the universal joint from the steering gear pinion.

3 The anti-roll bar may be removed with or without the side links. Unscrew the nuts securing the links to the struts or anti-roll bar as required.

4 Working on each side in turn, unscrew the front suspension lower balljoint-to-lower arm retaining nuts, then disconnect the track rod ends with reference to Section 25.

5 Unscrew the bolts securing the anti-roll bar clamps to the subframe **(see illustration)**. Mark the anti-roll bar to indicate which way round it is fitted, and the position of the rubber mounting bushes; this will aid refitting.

6 Unscrew and remove the engine/transmission rear mounting bolts from the transmission.

7 Support the subframe with a trolley jack and block of wood. If not using the special VW locating pins T10096, accurately mark the position of the subframe to ensure correct wheel alignment.

8 Unscrew the mounting bolts and slightly lower the subframe, taking care not to damage the electrical wiring. Where available, fit the VW locating pins to facilitate refitting.

9 Lift the anti-roll bar forwards over the bracket, and lower it to the floor.

10 Carefully examine the anti-roll bar components for signs of wear, damage or deterioration, paying particular attention to the rubber mounting bushes. Renew worn components as necessary.

Refitting

11 Refitting is a reversal of removal but tighten all nuts and bolts to the specified torque where given. When refitting the subframe, align it with the marks made on removal, or use the special VW location pins before tightening the mounting bolts. To assist entry of the steering gear gaiter through the bulkhead, apply a soapy solution to it. Have the front wheel alignment checked at the earliest opportunity.

8 Front anti-roll bar connecting link – removal and refitting

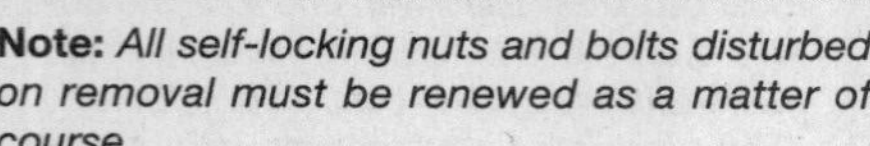

Note: *All self-locking nuts and bolts disturbed on removal must be renewed as a matter of course.*

Removal

1 Apply the handbrake, then jack up the front of the vehicle and support it on axle stands (see *Jacking and vehicle support*). Remove the relevant front roadwheel.

2 Unscrew and remove the nuts securing the link to the strut and anti-roll bar.

3 Inspect the link rubbers for signs of damage or deterioration. If evident, renew the link complete.

Refitting

4 Refitting is a reversal of removal, but tighten the nuts to the specified torque.

9 Rear wheel bearing housing – removal and refitting

Removal

1 Chock the front wheels, then jack up the rear of the vehicle and support it on axle stands (*see Jacking and vehicle support*).

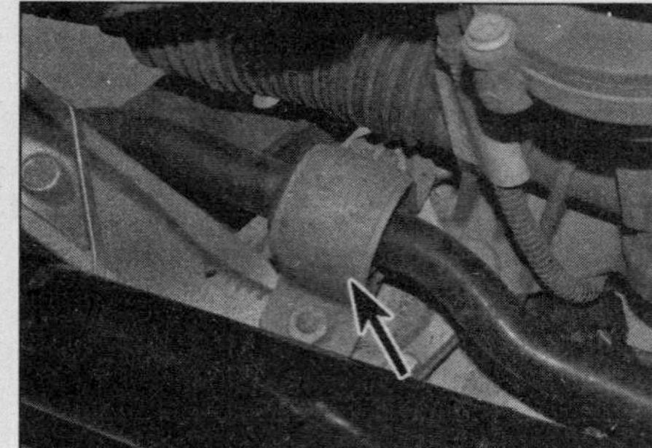

7.5 Front anti-roll bar clamp on the subframe

2 Remove the rear coil spring as described in Section 15.

3 Remove the rear hub as described in Section 10.

4 Unbolt the splash plate from the rear wheel bearing housing.

5 Disconnect the wiring, then unscrew the mounting bolt and remove the ABS sensor from the rear wheel bearing housing.

6 Unscrew the bolt securing the rear shock absorber to the rear wheel bearing housing.

7 Unscrew the bolts securing the upper transverse link and lower transverse links to the rear wheel bearing housing.

8 Unscrew the bolt securing the rear track control rod to the rear wheel bearing housing.

9 Support the rear wheel bearing housing, then unscrew the mounting bolts from the trailing arm. Also, undo the nut and disconnect the anti-roll bar link from the trailing arm.

10 Withdraw the rear wheel bearing housing from the car.

Refitting

Note: *Do not fully tighten the rear wheel bearing housing mounting bolts until the coil spring and shock absorber have been fitted, and the suspension is fully extended.*

11 Attach the rear wheel bearing housing to the rear track control rod, and the upper and lower transverse links, and hand-tighten the bolts.

12 Fit the wheel bearing housing to the trailing arm and insert the rear, upper bolt loosely.

13 Insert the two remaining bolts securing the trailing arm to the rear wheel bearing housing, and tighten them to the specified torque.

14 Refit the splash plate and tighten the bolts to the specified torque.

15 Refit the rear hub with reference to Section 10.

16 Position the centre of the rear hub the following ride-height distance from the centre of the wheel arch, according to model. Use the trolley jack to adjust the position:

Golf models

a) Standard running gear = 380 ± 10 mm
b) Heavy duty running gear = 400 ± 10 mm
c) Sports running gear = 365 ± 10 mm

Golf Estate/Jetta models

a) Standard running gear = 382 ± 10 mm
b) Heavy duty running gear = 402 ± 10 mm
c) Sports running gear = 367 ± 10 mm

Golf Plus models

a) Standard running gear = 378 ± 10 mm
b) Heavy duty running gear = 398 ± 10 mm
c) Sports running gear = 363 ± 10 mm

17 Tighten the following bolts to their specified torque, in the order given:

a) Track control rod.
b) Lower transverse link.
c) Upper transverse link. Position the washer so that it clears the splash plate.

18 Refit the shock absorber lower mounting bolt and tighten to the specified torque.

19 Remove the trolley jack, then refit the rear coil spring with reference to Section 15.

20 Refit the ABS sensor and tighten the mounting bolt. Reconnect the wiring.

21 Refit the roadwheel, then lower the vehicle to the ground, tighten the roadwheel bolts, and refit the wheel trim/hub cap. Have the rear wheel alignment checked and if necessary adjusted by a VW dealer.

10 Rear hub/wheel bearings – checking and renewal

Note: *The rear wheel bearings cannot be renewed independently of the rear hub, because the outer races are formed in the hub itself. If excessive wear is evident, the rear hub must be renewed complete. The rear hub bolt must always be renewed after removal.*

Removal

1 Chock the front roadwheels, then jack up the rear of the vehicle and support on axle stands (see *Jacking and vehicle support*). Release the handbrake and remove the relevant rear roadwheel.

2 Remove the rear brake caliper and mounting bracket with reference to Chapter 9. **Do not** disconnect the hydraulic brake pipe. Move the caliper just clear of the brake disc, without bending the hydraulic pipe excessively, and support it with welding rod or on an axle stand.

3 Undo the crosshead screw then withdraw the brake disc from the hub.

4 Remove the dust cap from the centre of the hub using a screwdriver or cold chisel **(see illustration)**.

10.4 Removing the dust cap

5 Unscrew and remove the hub bolt, using a multi-spline tool. Note that it is tightened to a high torque and a socket extension bar may be required to loosen it. The bolt must be renewed whenever removed.

6 Using a suitable puller, pull the hub and bearings from the stub axle. The bearing inner race will remain on the stub axle, and a puller will be required to remove it; use a sharp cold chisel to move the race away from the stub axle base so that the puller legs can fully engage the race.

7 Examine the hub and bearings for wear, pitting and damage. If any damage is evident, renew the hub complete.

Refitting

8 Wipe clean the stub axle, then check that the bearing races are adequately lubricated with suitable grease. Check that the inner bearing race is located correctly in the hub. Also make sure that the ABS rotor is pressed firmly onto the inner end of the hub.

9 Locate the hub as far as possible on the stub axle.

10 Screw on the new bolt and tighten it to the specified torque.

11 Check the dust cap for damage and renew it if necessary. Use a hammer to carefully tap the cap into the hub. **Note:** *A badly fitting dust cap will allow moisture to enter the bearing, reducing its service life.*

12 Refit the brake disc and tighten the crosshead screw.

13 Refit the rear brake mounting bracket and caliper with reference to Chapter 9.

14 Refit the roadwheel and lower the vehicle to the ground.

11 Rear radius rods – removal and refitting

Removal

1 The rear radius rods (where fitted) extend from the front of the rear subframe to the underbody, just in front of the trailing arms. The bolts on the subframe must only be loosened or tightened with the vehicle resting on its wheels. First, mark the position of the radius rods on the underbody and subframe, using marking pens or dabs of paint, then loosen the bolts securing the radius rod to the subframe.

2 Chock the front roadwheels, then jack up the rear of the vehicle and support on axle stands (see *Jacking and vehicle support*).

3 Unscrew the mounting bolts and remove the radius rod from under the vehicle.

Refitting

4 Locate the radius rod on the underbody and subframe and insert the mounting bolts loosely.

5 Align the radius rod with the marks made on removal, then tighten the two underbody bolts to the specified torque.

6 Lower the vehicle to the ground, then tighten the bolts securing the radius rod to the subframe to the specified torque. Have the rear wheel alignment checked and if necessary adjusted by a VW dealer.

12 Rear track control rod – removal and refitting

Removal

1 Chock the front roadwheels, then jack up the rear of the vehicle and support on axle stands (see *Jacking and vehicle support*). Remove the relevant rear roadwheel.

2 Note the fitted position of the rear track control rod, with the 'closed' side facing forwards. Also, note which way round the mounting bolts are fitted.

3 Unscrew and remove the mounting bolts and nuts, and withdraw the track control rod from under the vehicle. Note the location of the special 'star' washer beneath the head of the bolt securing the outer end of the rod to the wheel bearing housing.

Refitting

4 Refitting is a reversal of removal, but tighten the bolts to the specified torque and position the rod and bolts as previously noted. Check that a clearance exists between the special 'star' washer and the track control rod. Have the rear wheel alignment checked and if necessary adjusted by a VW dealer.

13 Rear transverse links – removal and refitting

Upper link

Removal

1 Chock the front roadwheels, then jack up the rear of the vehicle and support on axle stands (see *Jacking and vehicle support*). Remove the roadwheel.

2 Remove the rear coil spring as described in Section 15.

3 Release the ABS speed sensor wiring from the upper link, then unscrew the bolt securing the link to the wheel bearing housing.

4 At the inner end of the upper link, mark the position of the eccentric bolt and subframe in relation to each other. This alignment determines the camber setting of the rear wheels.

5 Note which way round the eccentric bolt is fitted, then unscrew and remove it and withdraw the upper link.

Refitting

6 Refitting is a reversal of removal, but delay fully-tightening the mounting bolts until the rear suspension is set to the correct ride-height given in Section 9. Make sure the eccentric bolt is correctly aligned as previously noted, and also position the 'star' washer to provide a clearance between one of its points and the splash plate. Have the rear wheel alignment checked and if necessary adjusted by a VW dealer.

Lower transverse link

Removal

7 Chock the front roadwheels, then jack up the rear of the vehicle and support on axle stands (see *Jacking and vehicle support*). Remove the roadwheel.

8 Remove the rear coil spring as described in Section 15.

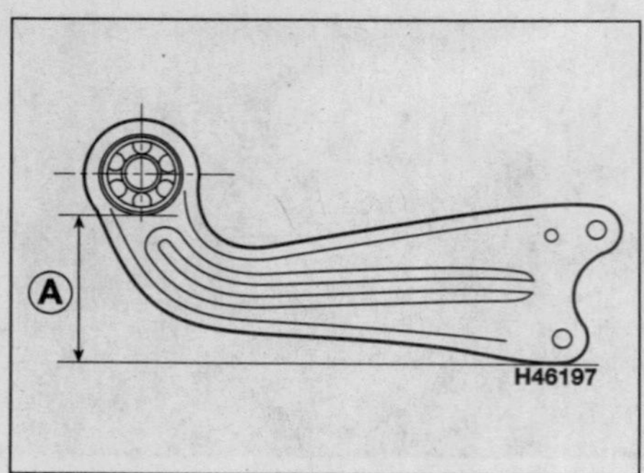

14.9a Make a vertical line on the arm as shown...
A = 114.0 mm

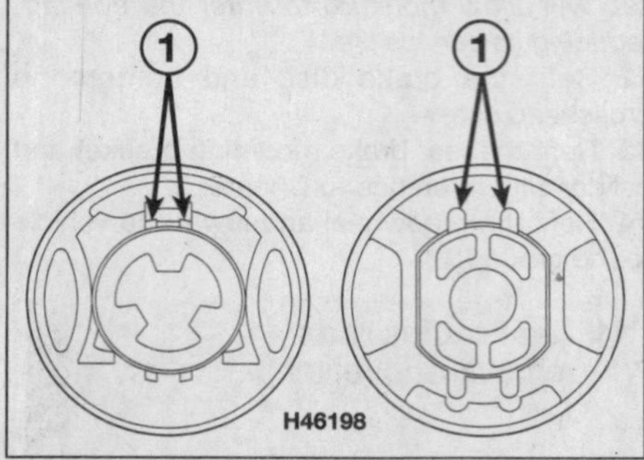

14.9b ...then press in the new bush so that the line is between the two projections (1)

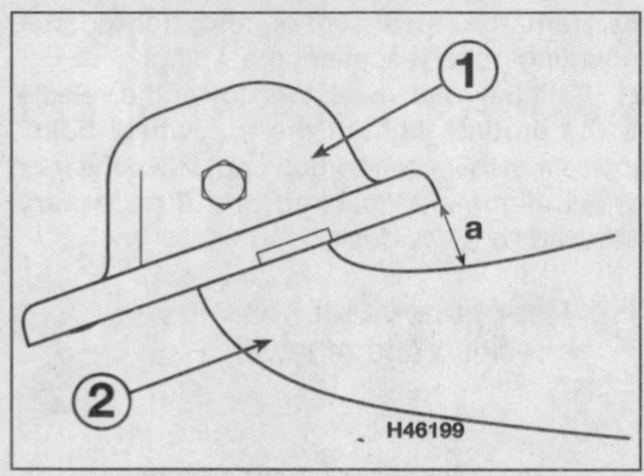

14.10 Mounting bracket assembly to trailing arm
1 Mounting bracket *2 Trailing arm* *a = 34.0 mm*

9 Unscrew the bolt securing the lower transverse link to the wheel bearing housing.
10 On models with headlight range control, unscrew the nut and disconnect the sensor arm from the link.
11 At the inner end of the upper link, mark the position of the eccentric bolt and subframe in relation to each other. This alignment determines the camber setting of the rear wheels.
12 Refer to Chapter 4C or 4D and lower the rear section of the exhaust system for improved access. Support the exhaust on an axle stand.
13 Unscrew and remove the inner bolt and withdraw the lower transverse link from under the car.

Refitting

14 Refitting is a reversal of removal, but delay fully-tightening the mounting bolts until the rear suspension is set to the correct ride-height given in Section 9. Make sure the eccentric bolt is correctly aligned as previously noted, and also position the 'star' washer to provide a clearance between one of its points and the splash plate. Have the rear wheel alignment checked and if necessary adjusted by a VW dealer.

14 Rear trailing arm and bracket – removal, overhaul and refitting

Removal

1 Chock the front roadwheels, then jack up the rear of the vehicle and support on axle stands (see *Jacking and vehicle support*). Remove the roadwheel.
2 Remove the rear coil spring as described in Section 15.
3 Unscrew the bolt securing the handbrake cable support to the trailing arm.
4 Unscrew the nut and detach the anti-roll bar link.
5 Unscrew the bolts securing the trailing arm to the rear wheel bearing housing.
6 Mark the position of the trailing arm front mounting bracket in relation to the underbody.
7 Support the front mounting bracket on a trolley jack, then unscrew the bolts, lower the assembly and withdraw the rear trailing arm and bracket from under the vehicle.

Overhaul

8 Thoroughly clean the trailing arm and bracket, then unscrew the front pivot bolt and separate the arm from the bracket. Check carefully for cracks or any other signs of wear or damage, paying particular attention to the rubber mounting bush.
9 If the bush requires renewal, take the arm to a VW dealer or suitably-equipped garage. Alternatively, a hydraulic press and suitable spacers may be used to press the bush out of the arm, and to install the new one. Dip the bush in a mild solution of washing-up liquid and water. When fitting the new bush to the front of the trailing arm, it is important to position it correctly. Make a vertical line on the arm as shown in the accompanying illustration, then press in the new bush so that the line is between the two projections shown **(see illustrations).**
10 With the new bush in position, locate the front of the arm in the bracket, and insert the bolt. Position the arm in relation to the bracket as shown **(see illustration)** then tighten the bolt/nut to the specified torque. There are two types of bush.

15.2a Rear coil spring

Refitting

11 Fit the trailing arm to the wheel bearing housing and insert the bolts loosely.
12 Fit the anti-roll bar link and screw on the nut loosely.
13 Raise the front mounting bracket and locate it on the underbody in its previously noted position. Insert the new bolts and tighten to the specified torque.
14 Lower the jack then tighten the arm-to-housing bolts to the specified torque.
15 Tighten the anti-roll bar link nut.
16 Refit the handbrake cable support and tighten the bolt.
17 Refit the rear coil spring with reference to Section 15.
18 Refit the roadwheel and lower the vehicle to the ground. Have the rear wheel alignment checked and if necessary adjusted by a VW dealer.

15 Rear coil spring – removal and refitting

Warning: Adjustable coil spring compressors are readily available, and are recommended for this operation. Any attempt to remove the coil spring without such a tool is likely to result in damage or personal injury.

Removal

1 Chock the front roadwheels, then jack up the rear of the vehicle and support on axle stands (see *Jacking and vehicle support*). Remove the relevant rear roadwheel.
2 Fit the tool to the coil spring and compress it until it can be removed from the trailing arm and underbody **(see illustrations)**. With the coil spring on the bench, carefully release the tension of the tool and remove it.
3 With the coil spring removed, recover the upper and lower spring seats and check them for damage. Obtain new ones if necessary, but note that they are different, the lower one having a location pin which enters a hole in the lower transverse link. Also clean thoroughly

the spring locations on the underbody and trailing arm.

Refitting

4 Refitting is a reversal of removal, but make sure that the lower spring seat engages the hole in the lower transverse link, the lower end of the coil spring abuts the stop on the seat, and the upper seat is correctly engaged with the lug on the underbody **(see illustrations)**.

16 Rear shock absorber – removal and refitting

Note: *All self-locking nuts and bolts disturbed on removal must be renewed as a matter of course.*

Removal

1 Before removing the shock absorber, an idea of how effective it is can be gained by depressing the rear corner of the car. If the shock absorber is in good condition, the body should rise then settle in its normal position. If the body oscillates more than this, the shock absorber is defective. **Note:** *To ensure even rear suspension, both rear shock absorbers should be renewed at the same time.*

2 Chock the front roadwheels, then jack up the rear of the vehicle and support on axle stands (see *Jacking and vehicle support*). Remove the relevant rear roadwheel.

3 Remove the wheel arch liner **(see illustration)**.

4 Position a trolley jack and block of wood beneath the coil spring position on the trailing arm, and raise the arm so that the shock absorber is slightly compressed. Note on some models, it may be necessary to remove the stone protection guard first. If preferred, the rear coil spring may be removed completely at this stage.

5 Unscrew the lower mounting bolt, then unscrew the upper mounting bolts and withdraw the shock absorber **(see illustrations)**.

6 With the shock absorber on the bench, remove the cap, then unscrew the nut from the top of the piston rod and remove the upper mounting bracket, followed by the bump stop, and where fitted the support ring, protective tube, and protective cap **(see illustrations)**. **Note:** *Two types of bump stop are supplied; a short version with a support ring, and a long version without a support ring.*

7 If necessary, the action of the shock

15.2b Compress the rear coil spring with the special tool...

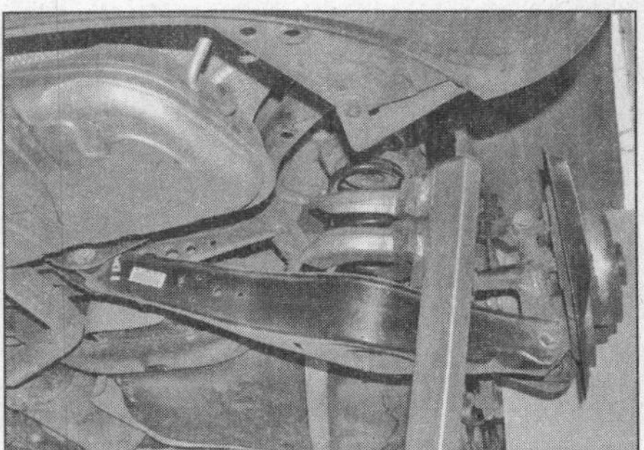

15.2c ...then remove it from the trailing arm and underbody

15.4a Rear coil spring located in the lower transverse link...

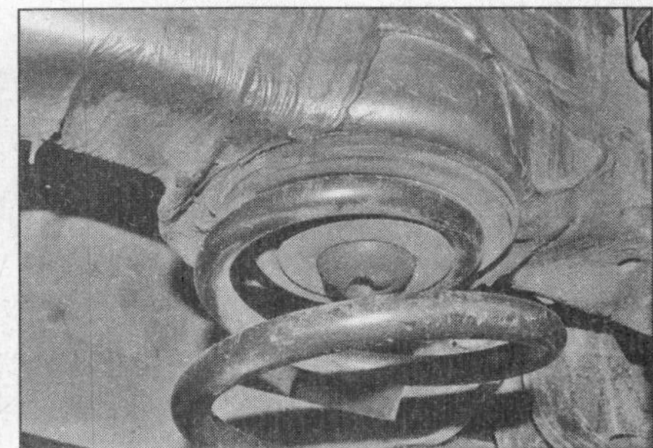

15.4b ...and underbody

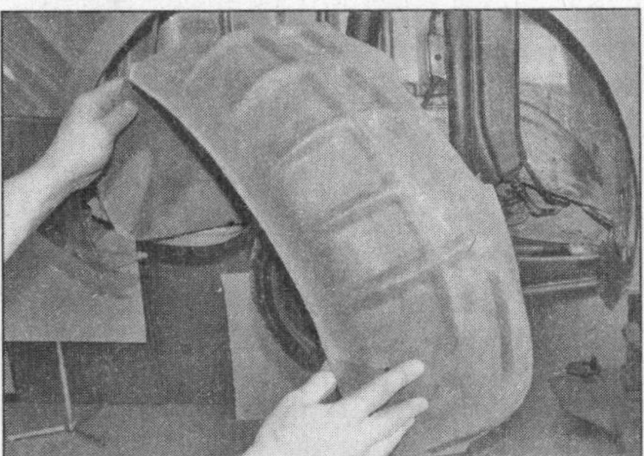

16.3 Removing the rear wheel arch liner

16.5a Unscrew the rear shock absorber lower mounting bolt...

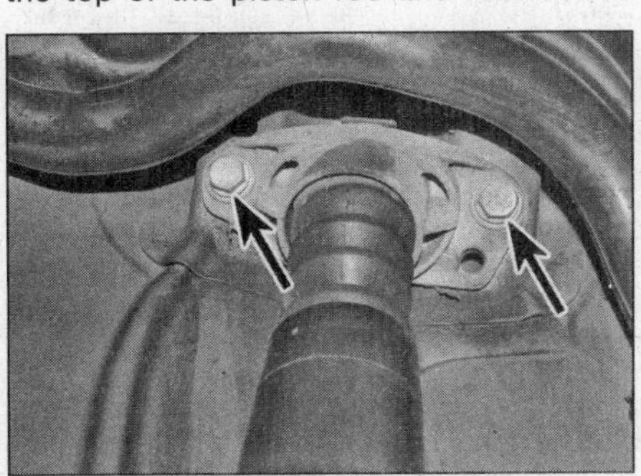

16.5b ...and upper mounting bolts

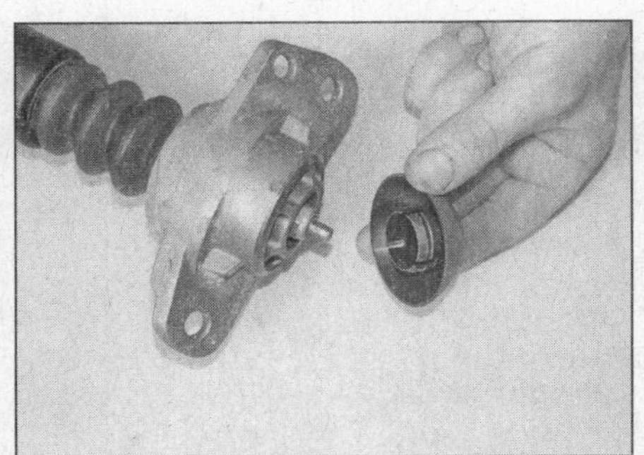

16.6a Remove the cap...

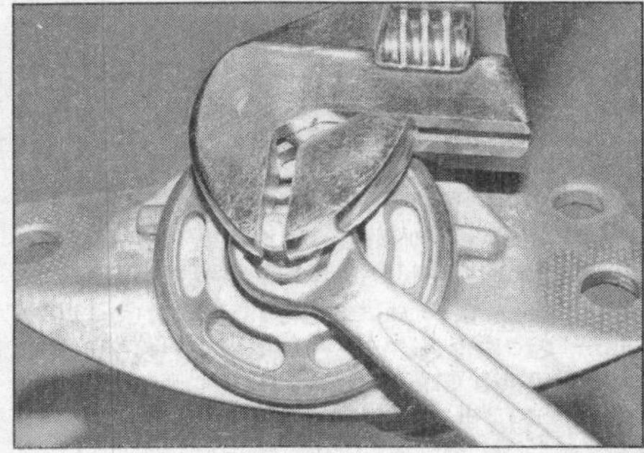

16.6b ...unscrew the nut while holding the piston...

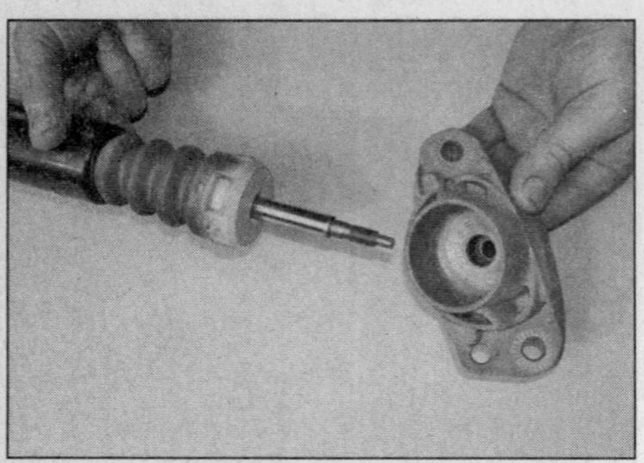

16.6c ...remove the upper mounting bracket...

absorber can be checked by mounting it upright in a vice. Fully depress the rod, then pull it up fully. The piston rod must move smoothly over its complete length.

Refitting

8 Locate the components removed from the top of the shock absorber in their correct order, and screw on a new nut. Tighten the nut and fit the cap.

9 Locate the shock absorber in the rear wheel arch, then insert the upper mounting bolts and tighten to the specified torque.

10 Extend the shock absorber if necessary, and insert the lower mounting bolt loosely.

11 Raise the trailing arm until the rear suspension is set to the correct ride-height given in Section 9, then fully tighten the shock absorber lower mounting bolt.

12 Refit the rear coil spring with reference to Section 15.

13 Refit the wheel arch liner.

14 Refit the roadwheel and lower the vehicle to the ground.

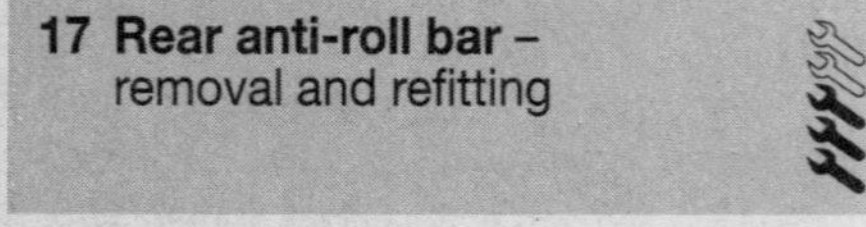

17 Rear anti-roll bar – removal and refitting

Removal

1 Chock the front roadwheels, then jack up the rear of the vehicle and support on axle stands (see *Jacking and vehicle support*). Remove both rear roadwheels.

2 Working on each side in turn, unscrew the nut and detach the side links from the anti-roll bar. Note that on early models with two balljoints, a metal shield is fitted between the link and the anti-roll bar. No shield is fitted to later models with a rubber bush connection to the bar (see Section 18).

3 Mark the anti-roll bar to indicate which way round it is fitted, and the position of the rubber mounting bushes; this will aid refitting.

4 Unscrew the bolts securing the anti-roll bar clamps to the rear subframe, and recover the clamps **(see illustration)**.

Refitting

5 Refitting is a reversal of removal but tighten all nuts and bolts to the specified torque.

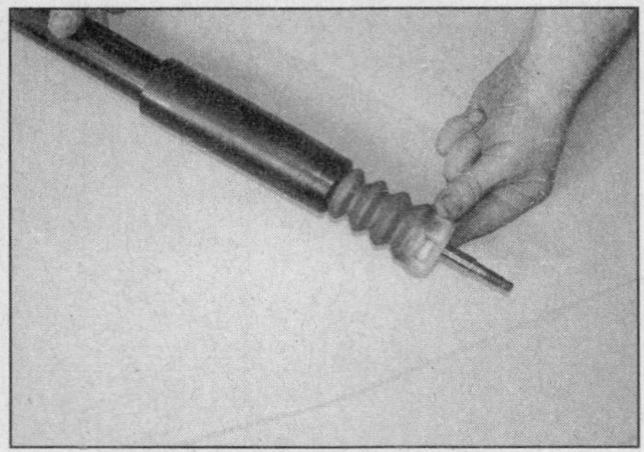

16.6d ...and bump stop

18 Rear anti-roll bar connecting link – removal and refitting

Removal

1 Chock the front roadwheels, then jack up the rear of the vehicle and support on axle stands (see *Jacking and vehicle support*). Remove the relevant rear roadwheel.

2 Note that on early models with two balljoints, a metal shield is fitted between the link and the anti-roll bar. No shield is fitted to later models with a rubber bush connection to the bar – on this type, the link connection to the trailing arm is a balljoint type.

3 Unscrew the nuts securing the link to the anti-roll bar and trailing arm, and withdraw it from under the vehicle. On the early type, recover the metal shield.

4 Inspect the link rubbers/balljoints for signs of damage or deterioration. If evident, renew the link complete.

Refitting

5 Refitting is a reversal of removal, but tighten the nuts to the specified torque.

19 Vehicle level sender – removal and refitting

Removal

1 The front sender for the headlight range control system is located on the left-hand side of the front subframe, and incorporates an arm and link attached to the left-hand front lower suspension arm. The rear sender is bolted to the rear subframe, and an arm and link is attached to a bracket on the lower transverse link. The system is controlled by an ECU located behind a cover on the passenger's side of the instrument panel.

17.4 Rear anti-roll bar mounting clamp

2 To remove the front sender, apply the handbrake then jack up the front of the vehicle and support it on axle stands (see *Jacking and vehicle support*). Remove the front roadwheel, then note the position of the sender on the lower arm. Unscrew the nut and disconnect the link and bracket from the lower arm. Disconnect the wiring then unscrew the bolt and remove the sender from the front subframe.

3 To remove the rear sender, chock the front roadwheels then jack up the rear of the vehicle and support on axle stands (see *Jacking and vehicle support*). Disconnect the wiring from the sender. Unscrew the bolts securing the link and bracket to the lower transverse link, then unscrew the bolts and remove the sender from the rear subframe.

Refitting

4 Refitting is a reversal of removal, but tighten the mounting bolts to the specified torque. If necessary, have the sender outputs checked by a VW dealer. This work requires the use a special equipment not available to the home mechanic.

20 Steering wheel – removal and refitting

Warning: During the airbag removal and refitting procedures, avoid sitting in the front seats.

Removal

1 Set the front wheels in the straight-ahead position, and release the steering lock by inserting the ignition key.

2 Disconnect the battery negative (earth) lead and position it away from the terminal.

3 Adjust the steering column to its highest position, then extend it into the passenger compartment as far as possible, and lock it in this position.

4 Remove the driver's airbag as described in Chapter 12.

Caution: To prevent any discharge of static electricity into the airbag circuit, temporarily touch the vehicle bodywork before disconnecting the wiring.

Warning: Position the airbag in a safe and secure place, away from the work area.

5 Using a multi-spline socket, unscrew and remove the retaining bolt, while holding the steering wheel stationary **(see illustrations)**. Discard the retaining bolt – a new one must be fitted.

6 Check if the steering wheel is marked in relation to the column. If not, use a dab of paint to mark them, then ease the steering wheel from the column splines by firmly rocking it side-to-side **(see illustrations)**.

Refitting

7 Locate the steering wheel on the column splines making sure that the previously-made marks are correctly aligned.
8 Refit the retaining bolt and tighten to the specified torque while holding the steering wheel stationary.
9 Refit the driver's airbag with reference to Chapter 12.
10 Reconnect the battery negative (earth) lead.

21 Steering column – removal, inspection and refitting

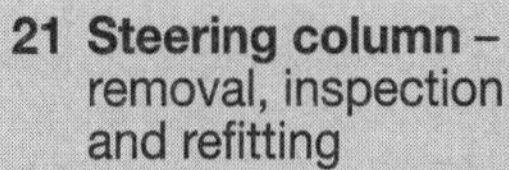

Removal

1 Disconnect the battery negative lead (see *Reference* at end of Manual), and position it away from the terminal.
2 Remove the steering wheel as described in Section 20, and return the steering to the straight-ahead position. Adjust the steering column to its lowest position and extend it into the passenger compartment as far as possible, then lock it in this position.
3 Undo the screws and remove the column height and reach adjustment handle.
4 Release the gap cover, then unclip and remove the upper shroud from the steering column **(see illustrations)**.
5 Undo the two upper screws and single lower screw and remove the lower shroud from the steering column **(see illustrations)**. As the shroud is being removed, release it from the height and reach adjustment handle.
6 Remove the fusebox cover and light switch (see Chapter 12), then undo the screws and remove the lower facia panel located next to the steering column. On models with a storage compartment, remove the compartment first for access to the lower screws.
7 Remove the switch carrier from the top of the steering column as described in Section 22. **Note:** *This work requires fitting new shear-head bolts. If it is not imperative to remove the carrier, leave it in position on the steering column.*
8 Remove the footwell vent from under the steering column.
9 Disconnect the wiring from the ignition switch.
10 Remove the cable guide from below the steering column. To do this, carefully prise up the lugs from the retaining clips.
11 Undo the nuts and remove the trim beneath the foot pedals for access to the steering column universal joint. Unscrew the clamp bolt and pull the universal joint from the steering gear pinion. Note that the pinion shaft has a cut-out to enable fitting of the clamp bolt, and the splined pinion shaft incorporates a flat making it impossible to assemble the joint to the shaft in the wrong position. Discard the clamp bolt; a new one should be used on refitting.
12 Unscrew the bolt and disconnect the earth cable, then remove the wiring harness from the steering column.
13 Note that the inner and outer columns, and the intermediate shaft, are telescopic, to facilitate the reach adjustment. It is important

20.5a Hold the steering wheel stationary while loosening its retaining bolt...

20.5b ...then unscrew and remove the bolt

20.6a The steering wheel should be marked for its central position

20.6b Removing the steering wheel

21.4a Release the gap cover...

21.4b ...then unclip and remove the upper shroud

21.5a Undo the screws...

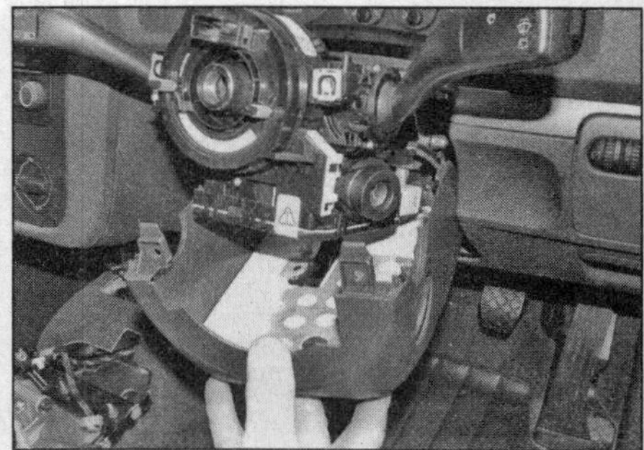

21.5b ...and remove the lower shroud from the steering column

to keep the splined sections of the inner steering column engaged with each other while the steering column is removed. If they become detached due to the outer column sections being separated, especially on a vehicle which has completed a high mileage, it is possible that rattling noises may occur.
14 Unscrew and remove two diagonally-opposite mounting bolts, then support the steering column and unscrew the two remaining bolts **(see illustration)**. Withdraw the steering column from inside the car. Discard the bolts as new ones must be used on refitting. Note that the mounting bracket on the bulkhead has location pins which align the steering column.
Caution: Do not carry the steering column by suspending it from the universal joint or intermediate shaft, as this will damage the universal joint and steering column bushes. Also, do not bend the joints by more than 90°.
15 If necessary, remove the ignition switch/ steering column lock with reference to Section 22.

Inspection

16 The steering column is designed to collapse in the event of a front-end crash, to prevent the steering wheel injuring the driver. Before refitting the steering column, examine the column and mountings for signs of damage and deformation.
17 Check the inner column sections for signs of free play in the column bushes. If any damage or wear is found on the steering column bushes, the column must be renewed as an assembly.
18 The intermediate shaft is permanently attached to the inner column and cannot be renewed separately. Inspect the universal joints for excessive wear. If evident, the complete steering column must be renewed.

Refitting

19 Where removed, refit the ignition switch/ steering column lock/switch carrier with reference to Section 22.
20 Refit the steering column to the bulkhead bracket, insert the new mounting bolts, and tighten to the specified torque.
21 Reconnect the earth cable and tighten the bolt. Refit the wiring harness.
22 Attach the universal joint on the steering

21.14 Steering column mounting bolts

gear pinion splines, insert the new clamp bolt, and tighten to the specified torque.
23 Refit the foot pedal trim and tighten the nuts.
24 Refit the cable guide, making sure that the retaining lugs engage on both sides.
25 Reconnect the wiring to the ignition switch.
26 Refit the footwell vent under the steering column.
27 Refit the light switch with reference to Chapter 12.
28 Refit the facia lower trim panel and tighten the screws, then refit the light switch and fusebox cover.
29 Refit the lower and upper shrouds and tighten the screws. Refit the gap cover.
30 Refit the column height and reach adjustment handle and tighten the screws.
31 Refit the steering wheel with reference to Section 20.
32 Reconnect the battery negative lead.
33 On models with ESP, the steering angle sensor basic settings must be set by a VW dealer using specialist diagnostic equipment.

22 Ignition switch and steering column lock/switch carrier – removal and refitting

Ignition switch

Removal

1 Disconnect the battery negative lead (see *Reference* at end of Manual), and position it away from the terminal.
2 Remove the steering wheel as described in Section 20.
3 Undo the screws and remove the column height and reach adjustment handle.
4 Release the gap cover, then unclip and remove the upper shroud from the steering column.
5 Undo the two upper screws and single lower screw and remove the lower shroud from the steering column. As the shroud is being removed, release it from the height and reach adjustment handle.
6 Carefully pull the wiring plug from the ignition switch.
7 Using a small screwdriver, release the two retaining clips then pull the switch from the steering lock housing.

Refitting

8 Refit the switch to the steering lock housing and press in until the two retaining clips engage.
9 Insert the ignition key and turn it to the Drive position (90°). Also turn the switch in the same position.
10 Reconnect the wiring plug to the ignition switch.
11 Refit the upper and lower shrouds, and tighten the screws. Also, refit the gap cover.
12 Refit the column height and reach adjustment handle, and tighten the screws.
13 Refit the steering wheel with reference to Section 20.
14 Reconnect the battery negative lead.

Steering column lock/ switch carrier

Removal

15 The steering column lock is integral with the wiper and indicator switch carrier, which is secured to the steering column with shear-head bolts.
16 Disconnect the battery negative lead (see *Reference* at end of Manual), and position it away from the terminal.
17 Check that the front wheels are pointing straight-ahead and the steering wheel is in its centre position, then remove the steering wheel as described in Section 20.
18 Undo the screws and remove the column height and reach adjustment handle.
19 Release the gap cover, then unclip and remove the upper shroud from the steering column.
20 Undo the two upper screws and single lower screw and remove the lower shroud from the steering column. As the shroud is being removed, release it from the height and reach adjustment handle.
21 Remove the steering column electronics control unit. To do this, undo the single retaining screw, then insert a 2.5 mm diameter rod or similar through the hole provided, and release the centre clip. Now use a screwdriver to release the rear clip. Pull down the control unit from the column switch carrier and disconnect the wiring **(see illustrations)**.
22 The airbag clock spring/slip-ring must be held in its central position while it is removed,

22.21a Undo the screw...

22.21b ...release the clips...

to ensure correct refitting. Unclip the airbag clock spring/slip-ring from the combination switch carrier by lifting the retaining hooks **(see illustration)**.

23 On models with ESP, pull the steering angle sensor directly away from the combination switch carrier **(see illustration)**.

24 Remove the indicator and windscreen wiper switches by inserting a 1.0 mm feeler gauge through the slot provided to release the switch from the carrier **(see illustrations)**.

25 Disconnect the wiring from the immobiliser coil on the ignition lock housing.

26 The steering column lock/switch carrier is secured by shear-head bolts, and the heads are broken off in the tightening procedure. To remove the old bolts, either drill them out, or use a sharp cold chisel to cut off their heads or turn them anti-clockwise. Withdraw the carrier from the steering column.

27 If necessary, the lock cylinder can be removed from the steering lock housing as follows. **Note:** *The lock cylinder can be removed with the lock in situ by removing the steering wheel and column shrouds.* Insert the ignition key and turn to the Drive position (90°). Insert a piece of wire 1.2 mm in diameter in the drilling next to the ignition key, depress it, then disconnect the wiring and withdraw the lock cylinder from the housing **(see illustrations)**.

Refitting

28 If removed, refit the lock cylinder with the ignition key in the Drive position, then remove the wire. Make sure that the immobiliser coil connection is located correctly in the guide when inserting the lock cylinder.

22.21c ...lower the steering column electronics control unit...

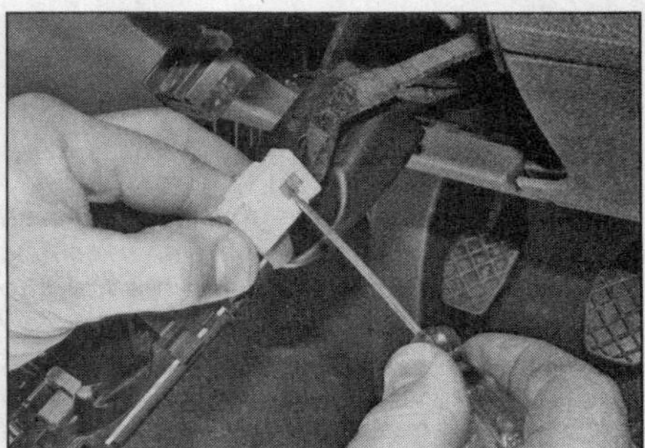

22.21d ...and disconnect the wiring

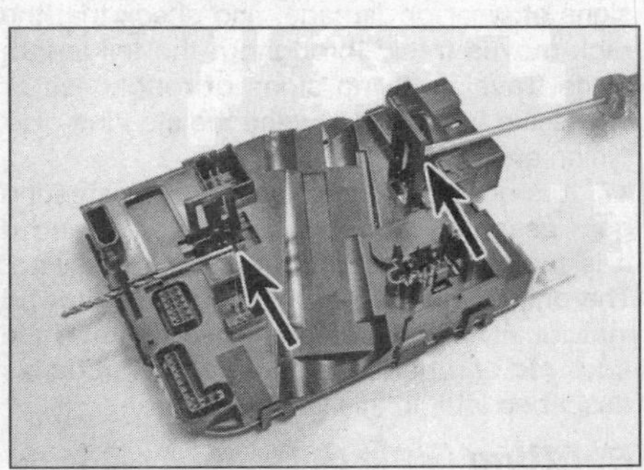

22.21e Showing the position of the retaining clips

22.22 Removing the airbag clock spring/slip-ring from the column

29 Locate the lock/switch carrier on the outer column as far as possible, and insert the new shear-head bolts. Tighten the bolts until their heads break off.

30 The remaining procedure is a reversal of removal, but refer to Chapter 12 when refitting the airbag clock spring/slip-ring to check that it is in its central position.

22.23 Removing the steering angle sensor

22.24a Insert a feeler gauge as shown...

22.24b ...and remove the wiper switch...

22.24c ...and indicator switch

22.27a Disconnect the wiring...

22.27b ...then remove the ignition lock cylinder

23 Steering gear assembly – removal, overhaul and refitting

Note: *As the subframe must be lowered during this procedure, VW subframe locating pins (T10096) or similar are required to ensure correct front wheel alignment. New subframe mounting bolts, track rod balljoint nuts, steering gear retaining bolts, and an intermediate shaft universal joint clamp bolt will be required on refitting.*

Removal

1 Disconnect the battery negative lead (refer to *Disconnecting the battery* in the *Reference* Chapter at the end of this manual).

2 Apply the handbrake, then jack up the front of the vehicle and support it on axle stands positioned on the underbody, leaving the subframe free (see *Jacking and vehicle support*). Position the steering straight-ahead, then remove both front roadwheels. Also remove the engine compartment undertray.

3 Inside the vehicle, undo the screws and remove the plastic cover for access to the universal joint connecting the steering inner column to the steering gear pinion. Unscrew and remove the clamp bolt, and pull the universal joint from the pinion splines. **Note:** *The steering gear pinion incorporates a cut-out for the clamp bolt, and therefore the joint can only be fitted in one position.* Discard the clamp bolt, a new one should be used on refitting.

4 Working on each side in turn, unscrew the nuts from the track rod ends, then use a balljoint separator tool to release the ends from the steering arms on the front wheel bearing housings.

5 Working on each side in turn, unscrew the nuts securing the anti-roll bar links to the struts.

6 Working on each side in turn, unscrew the front suspension lower balljoint-to-lower arm retaining nuts, then lever the lower arms down to release the balljoint studs.

7 Unscrew and remove the engine/transmission rear mounting bolts from the transmission.

8 Unbolt the exhaust system mounting from the subframe.

9 Unbolt the exhaust system heat shield from the subframe.

10 Support the subframe with a trolley jack and block of wood. If not using the special VW locating pins T10096, accurately mark the position of the subframe to ensure correct wheel alignment.

11 Unscrew the mounting bolts and slightly lower the subframe, taking care not to damage the electrical wiring. Where available, fit the VW locating pins to facilitate refitting.

12 Unbolt the heat shield from over the steering gear.

13 Remove the cable guide and disconnect all wiring from the steering gear. Release the wiring from all clips.

Caution: Do not touch the wiring terminals on the electronic control unit, as a static electricity discharge may damage the internal components.

14 Lower the subframe together with the steering gear to the floor.

15 Unbolt the steering gear from the subframe, and carefully place it on the floor taking care not to damage the electronic control unit.

Overhaul

16 Examine the steering gear assembly for signs of wear or damage, and check that the rack moves freely throughout the full length of its travel, with no signs of roughness or excessive free play between the steering gear pinion and rack.

17 It is not possible to overhaul the steering gear assembly housing components, and if it is faulty, the assembly must be renewed. The only components which can be renewed individually are the steering gear gaiters, the track rod end balljoints and the track rods, as described later in this Chapter.

Refitting

18 Locate the steering gear on the subframe, and insert and tighten the bolts for the gear and anti-roll bar before inserting the subframe bolts.

19 Raise the subframe sufficient to refit the cable guide and reconnect all the wiring to the steering gear. Secure the wiring in the clips.

20 Refit the heat shield, then raise the subframe onto the underbody and align it with the marks made on removal, or use the special VW location pins before tightening the mounting bolts. To assist entry of the steering gear gaiter through the bulkhead, apply a soapy solution to it.

21 Refit the exhaust heat shield and mounting, then refit the engine/transmission rear mounting bolts to the transmission and tighten to the specified torque.

22 Locate the front suspension lower balljoints in the lower arms, screw on the new nuts and tighten to the specified torque.

23 Refit the track rod ends with new nuts, and tighten to the specified torque.

24 Inside the car, attach the universal joint on the steering gear pinion splines, insert the new clamp bolt, and tighten to the specified torque.

25 Refit the engine compartment undertray, then refit the wheels and lower the car to the ground.

26 Reconnect the battery negative lead. Have the front wheel alignment checked at the earliest opportunity.

27 On models with ESP, the steering angle sensor basic settings must be set by a VW dealer using specialist diagnostic equipment. If a new steering gear has been fitted, it must also be adapted to the vehicle by a VW dealer.

24 Steering gear rubber gaiters and track rods – renewal

Steering gear rubber gaiters

1 Remove the track rod end balljoint as described in Section 25. Also, unscrew the locking nut after noting its position.

2 Wipe clean the rubber gaiter to prevent entry of dirt or moisture. Note the fitted position of the gaiter on the track rod, then release the retaining clips and slide the gaiter off the steering gear housing and track rod.

3 Wipe clean the track rod and the steering gear housing, then apply a film of suitable grease to the surface of the rack. To do this, turn the steering wheel as necessary to fully extend the rack from the housing, then reposition it in its central position.

4 Carefully slide the new gaiter onto the track rod, and locate it on the steering gear housing. Position the gaiter as previously noted on removal, making sure that it is not twisted, then lift the outer sealing lip of the gaiter to equalise air pressure within the gaiter.

5 Secure the gaiter in position with new retaining clips. Where crimped-type clips are used, pull the clip as tight as possible, and locate the hooks in their slots. Remove any slack in the clip by carefully compressing the raised section. In the absence of the special crimping tool, a pair of side-cutters may be used, taking care not to cut the clip.

6 Screw on the locking nut, then refit the track rod end balljoint as described in Section 25.

Track rods

7 Remove the relevant steering gear rubber gaiter as described earlier. If there is insufficient working room with the steering gear mounted in the car, remove it as described in Section 23 and hold it in a vice while renewing the track rod.

8 Hold the steering rack stationary with one spanner on the flats provided, then loosen the balljoint nut with another spanner. Fully unscrew the nut and remove the track rod from the rack.

9 Locate the new track rod on the end of the steering rack and screw on the nut. Hold the rack stationary with one spanner and tighten the balljoint nut to the specified torque. A crow's foot adapter may be required since the track rod prevents access with a socket, and care must be taken to apply the correct torque in this situation.

10 Refit the steering gear or rubber gaiter with reference to the earlier paragraphs or Section 23. On completion check and, if necessary, adjust the front wheel alignment as described in Section 26.

25.4a Using an Allen key to hold the balljoint shank while loosening the nut

25.4b Using a balljoint separator to release the track rod balljoint from the steering arm on the wheel bearing housing

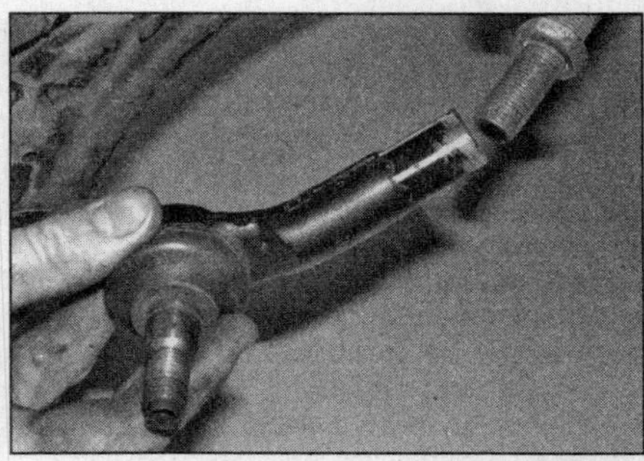

25.5 Unscrewing the track rod end from the track rod

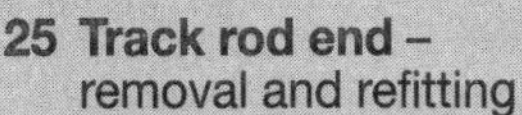

25 Track rod end – removal and refitting

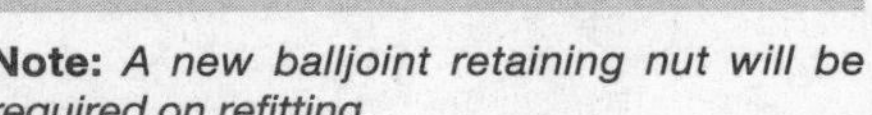

Note: *A new balljoint retaining nut will be required on refitting.*

Removal

1 Apply the handbrake, then jack up the front of the vehicle and support it on axle stands (see *Jacking and vehicle support*). Remove the relevant roadwheel.

2 If the track rod end is to be re-used, mark its position in relation to the track rod to facilitate refitting.

3 Unscrew the track rod end locknut by a quarter of a turn. Do not move the locknut from this position, as it will serve as a handy reference mark on refitting.

4 Loosen and remove the nut securing the track rod end balljoint to the wheel bearing housing, and release the balljoint tapered shank using a universal balljoint separator. Note that the balljoint shank has a hexagon hole – hold the shank with an Allen key while loosening the nut **(see illustrations)**.

5 Counting the exact number of turns necessary to do so, unscrew the track rod end from the track rod **(see illustration)**.

6 Carefully clean the balljoint and the threads. Renew the balljoint if its movement is sloppy or too stiff, if excessively worn, or if damaged in any way; carefully check the stud taper and threads. If the balljoint gaiter is damaged, the complete balljoint assembly must be renewed; it is not possible to obtain the gaiter separately.

Refitting

7 Screw the track rod end onto the track rod by the number of turns noted on removal. This should bring the track rod end to within a quarter of a turn of the locknut, with the alignment marks that were made on removal (if applicable) lined up. Tighten the locknut.

8 Refit the balljoint shank to the steering arm on the wheel bearing housing, then fit a new retaining nut and tighten it to the specified torque. Hold the shank with an Allen key if necessary.

9 Refit the roadwheel, then lower the car to the ground and tighten the roadwheel bolts to the specified torque.

10 Check and, if necessary, adjust the front wheel toe setting as described in Section 26.

26 Wheel alignment and steering angles – general information

Definitions

1 A car's steering and suspension geometry is defined in three basic settings – all angles are expressed in degrees; the steering axis is defined as an imaginary line drawn through the axis of the suspension strut, extended where necessary to contact the ground **(see illustration)**.

2 Camber is the angle between each roadwheel and a vertical line drawn through its centre and tyre contact patch, when viewed from the front or rear of the car. Positive camber is when the roadwheels are tilted outwards from the vertical at the top; negative camber is when they are tilted inwards.

3 Camber angle is only adjustable by loosening the front suspension subframe mounting bolts and moving it slightly to one side. This also alters the Castor angle. The camber angle can be checked using a camber checking gauge.

4 Castor is the angle between the steering axis and a vertical line drawn through each roadwheel's centre and tyre contact patch, when viewed from the side of the car. Positive castor is when the steering axis is tilted so that it contacts the ground ahead of the vertical; negative castor is when it contacts the ground behind the vertical. Slight castor angle adjustment is possible by loosening the front suspension subframe bolts and moving it slightly to one side. This also alters the Camber angle.

5 Castor is not easily adjustable, and is given for reference only; while it can be checked using a castor checking gauge, if the figure obtained is significantly different from that specified, the car must be taken for careful checking by a professional, as the fault can only be caused by wear or damage to the body or suspension components.

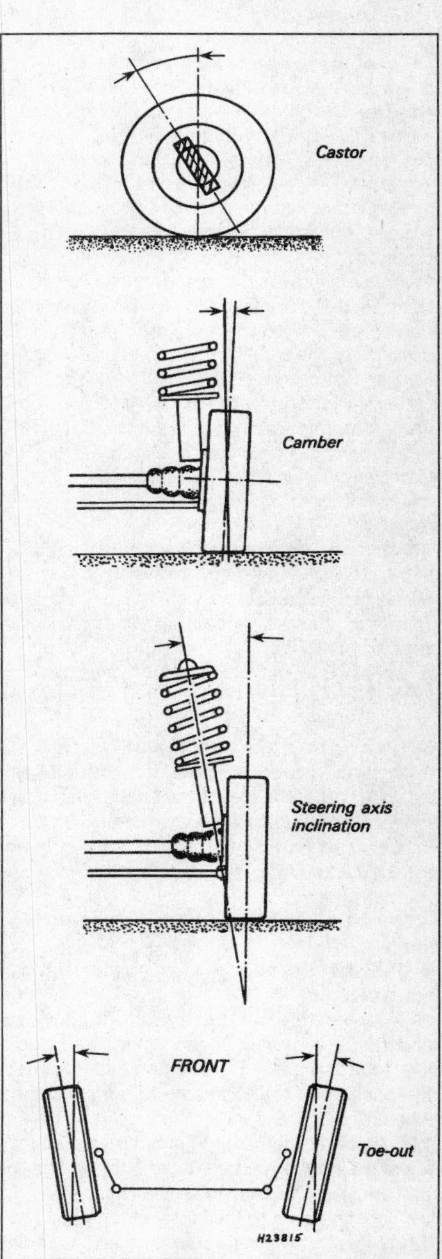

26.1 Front wheel geometry

6 Toe is the difference, viewed from above, between lines drawn through the roadwheel centres and the car's centre-line. Toe-in is when the roadwheels point inwards, towards each other at the front, while toe-out is when they splay outwards from each other at the front.

7 The front wheel toe setting is adjusted by screwing the track rod(s) in/out of the outer balljoint(s) to alter the effective length of the track rod assembly.

8 Rear wheel toe setting is not adjustable, and is given for reference only. While it can be checked, if the figure obtained is significantly different from that specified, the car must be taken for careful checking by a professional, as the fault can only be caused by wear or damage to the body or suspension components.

Checking and adjustment

9 Due to the special measuring equipment necessary to check the wheel alignment, and the skill required to use it properly, the checking and adjustment of these settings is best left to a VW dealer or similar expert. Note that most tyre-fitting centres now possess sophisticated checking equipment.

Chapter 11
Bodywork and fittings

Contents

Degrees of difficulty

Easy, suitable for novice with little experience 	**Fairly easy,** suitable for beginner with some experience	**Fairly difficult,** suitable for competent DIY mechanic	**Difficult,** suitable for experienced DIY mechanic	**Very difficult,** suitable for expert DIY or professional

Specifications

Torque wrench settings	**Nm**	**lbf ft**
Bonnet	22	16
Door hinges:		
To body*:		
Stage 1	20	15
Stage 2	Angle-tighten a further 90°	
To door*	50	37
Eccentric pin	28	21
Guide bolt	10	7
Door lock	18	13
Door skin panel bolts:		
Five front and rear bolts	14	10
Remaining bolts	10	7
Front seat mounting retaining bolts	40	30
Rear seat mounting bolts/nuts (Plus models)	60	44
Seat belt and stalk anchorage bolts*	40	30
Side impact bar	20	15
Tailgate	10	7
Tailgate hinge retaining bolts	24	18

** Renew the bolts*

1 General information

The body shell is made of pressed-steel sections, and is available in both three- and five-door Hatchback, five-door estate, and four-door Saloon versions. Most components are welded together, and some use is made of structural adhesives; the front wings are bolted on.

The bonnet, door, and some other vulnerable panels are made of zinc-coated metal, and are further protected by being coated with an anti-chip primer before being sprayed.

Extensive use is made of plastic materials, mainly in the interior, but also in exterior components. The front and rear bumpers, and front grille, are injection-moulded from a synthetic material that is very strong and yet light. Plastic components such as wheel arch liners are fitted to the underside of the vehicle, to improve the body's resistance to corrosion.

2 Maintenance – bodywork and underframe

The general condition of a vehicle's bodywork is the one thing that significantly affects its value. Maintenance is easy, but needs to be regular. Neglect, particularly after minor damage, can lead quickly to further deterioration and costly repair bills. It is important also to keep watch on those parts of the vehicle not immediately visible, for instance the underside, inside all the wheel arches, and the lower part of the engine compartment.

The basic maintenance routine for the bodywork is washing – preferably with a lot of water, from a hose. This will remove all the loose solids which may have stuck to the vehicle. It is important to flush these off in such a way as to prevent grit from scratching the finish. The wheel arches and underframe need washing in the same way, to remove any accumulated mud, which will retain moisture and tend to encourage rust. Paradoxically enough, the best time to clean the underframe and wheel arches is in wet weather, when the mud is thoroughly wet and soft. In very wet weather, the underframe is usually cleaned of large accumulations automatically, and this is a good time for inspection.

Periodically, except on vehicles with a wax-based underbody protective coating, it is a good idea to have the whole of the underframe of the vehicle steam-cleaned, engine compartment included, so that a thorough inspection can be carried out to see what minor repairs and renovations are necessary. Steam-cleaning is available at many garages, and is necessary for the removal of the accumulation of oily grime, which sometimes is allowed to become thick in certain areas. If steam-cleaning facilities are not available, there are some excellent grease solvents available which can be brush-applied; the dirt can then be simply hosed off. Note that these methods should not be used on vehicles with wax-based underbody protective coating, or the coating will be removed. Such vehicles should be inspected annually, preferably just prior to Winter, when the underbody should be washed down, and any damage to the wax coating repaired. Ideally, a completely fresh coat should be applied. It would also be worth considering the use of such wax-based protection for injection into door panels, sills, box sections, etc, as an additional safeguard against rust damage, where such protection is not provided by the vehicle manufacturer.

After washing paintwork, wipe off with a chamois leather to give an unspotted clear finish. A coat of clear protective wax polish will give added protection against chemical pollutants in the air. If the paintwork sheen has dulled or oxidised, use a cleaner/polisher combination to restore the brilliance of the shine. This requires a little effort, but such dulling is usually caused because regular washing has been neglected. Care needs to be taken with metallic paintwork, as special non-abrasive cleaner/polisher is required to avoid damage to the finish. Always check that the door and ventilator opening drain holes and pipes are completely clear, so that water can be drained out. Brightwork should be treated in the same way as paintwork. Windscreens and windows can be kept clear of the smeary film which often appears, by the use of proprietary glass cleaner. Never use any form of wax or other body or chromium polish on glass.

3 Maintenance – upholstery and carpets

Mats and carpets should be brushed or vacuum-cleaned regularly, to keep them free of grit. If they are badly stained, remove them from the vehicle for scrubbing or sponging, and make quite sure they are dry before refitting. Seats and interior trim panels can be kept clean by wiping with a damp cloth. If they do become stained (which can be more apparent on light-coloured upholstery), use a little liquid detergent and a soft nail brush to scour the grime out of the grain of the material. Do not forget to keep the headlining clean in the same way as the upholstery. When using liquid cleaners inside the vehicle, do not over-wet the surfaces being cleaned. Excessive damp could get into the seams and padded interior, causing stains, offensive odours or even rot.

If the inside of the vehicle gets wet accidentally, it is worthwhile taking some trouble to dry it out properly, particularly where carpets are involved. Do not leave oil or electric heaters inside the vehicle for this purpose.

4 Minor body damage – repair

Scratches

If the scratch is very superficial, and does not penetrate to the metal of the bodywork, repair is very simple. Lightly rub the area of the scratch with a paintwork renovator, or a very fine cutting paste, to remove loose paint from the scratch, and to clear the surrounding bodywork of wax polish. Rinse the area with clean water.

Apply touch-up paint to the scratch using a fine paint brush; continue to apply fine layers of paint until the surface of the paint in the scratch is level with the surrounding paintwork. Allow the new paint at least two weeks to harden, then blend it into the surrounding paintwork by rubbing the scratch area with a paintwork renovator or a very fine cutting paste. Finally, apply wax polish.

Where the scratch has penetrated right through to the metal of the bodywork, causing the metal to rust, a different repair technique is required. Remove any loose rust from the bottom of the scratch with a penknife, then apply rust-inhibiting paint to prevent the formation of rust in the future. Using a rubber or nylon applicator, fill the scratch with bodystopper paste. If required, this paste can be mixed with cellulose thinners to provide a very thin paste which is ideal for filling narrow scratches. Before the stopper-paste in the scratch hardens, wrap a piece of smooth cotton rag around the top of a finger. Dip the finger in cellulose thinners, and quickly sweep it across the surface of the stopper-paste in the scratch; this will ensure that the surface of the stopper-paste is slightly hollowed. The scratch can now be painted over as described earlier in this Section.

Dents

When deep denting of the vehicle's bodywork has taken place, the first task is to pull the dent out, until the affected bodywork almost attains its original shape. There is little point in trying to restore the original shape completely, as the metal in the damaged area will have stretched on impact, and cannot be reshaped fully to its original contour. It is better to bring the level of the dent up to a point which is about 3 mm below the level of the surrounding bodywork. In cases where the dent is very shallow anyway, it is not worth trying to pull it out at all. If the underside of the dent is accessible, it can be hammered out gently from behind, using a mallet with a wooden or plastic head. Whilst doing this, hold a suitable block of wood firmly against the outside of the panel, to absorb the impact from the hammer blows and thus prevent a large area of the bodywork from being 'belled-out'.

Should the dent be in a section of the

bodywork which has a double skin, or some other factor making it inaccessible from behind, a different technique is called for. Drill several small holes through the metal inside the area – particularly in the deeper section. Then screw long self-tapping screws into the holes, just sufficiently for them to gain a good purchase in the metal. Now the dent can be pulled out by pulling on the protruding heads of the screws with a pair of pliers.

The next stage of the repair is the removal of the paint from the damaged area, and from an inch or so of the surrounding 'sound' bodywork. This is accomplished most easily by using a wire brush or abrasive pad on a power drill, although it can be done just as effectively by hand, using sheets of abrasive paper. To complete the preparation for filling, score the surface of the bare metal with a screwdriver or the tang of a file, or alternatively, drill small holes in the affected area. This will provide a really good 'key' for the filler paste.

To complete the repair, see the Section on filling and respraying.

Rust holes or gashes

Remove all paint from the affected area, and from an inch or so of the surrounding 'sound' bodywork, using an abrasive pad or a wire brush on a power drill. If these are not available, a few sheets of abrasive paper will do the job most effectively. With the paint removed, you will be able to judge the severity of the corrosion, and therefore decide whether to renew the whole panel (if this is possible) or to repair the affected area. New body panels are not as expensive as most people think, and it is often quicker and more satisfactory to fit a new panel than to attempt to repair large areas of corrosion.

Remove all fittings from the affected area, except those which will act as a guide to the original shape of the damaged bodywork (eg headlight shells etc). Then, using tin snips or a hacksaw blade, remove all loose metal and any other metal badly affected by corrosion. Hammer the edges of the hole inwards, in order to create a slight depression for the filler paste.

Wire-brush the affected area to remove the powdery rust from the surface of the remaining metal. Paint the affected area with rust-inhibiting paint, if the back of the rusted area is accessible, treat this also.

Before filling can take place, it will be necessary to block the hole in some way. This can be achieved by the use of aluminium or plastic mesh, or aluminium tape.

Aluminium or plastic mesh, or glass-fibre matting, is probably the best material to use for a large hole. Cut a piece to the approximate size and shape of the hole to be filled, then position it in the hole so that its edges are below the level of the surrounding bodywork. It can be retained in position by several blobs of filler paste around its periphery.

Aluminium tape should be used for small or very narrow holes. Pull a piece off the roll, trim it to the approximate size and shape required, then pull off the backing paper (if used) and stick the tape over the hole; it can be overlapped if the thickness of one piece is insufficient. Burnish down the edges of the tape with the handle of a screwdriver or similar, to ensure that the tape is securely attached to the metal underneath.

Filling and respraying

Before using this Section, see the Sections on dent, deep scratch, rust holes and gash repairs.

Many types of bodyfiller are available, but generally speaking, those proprietary kits which contain a tin of filler paste and a tube of resin hardener are best for this type of repair. A wide, flexible plastic or nylon applicator will be found invaluable for imparting a smooth and well-contoured finish to the surface of the filler.

Mix up a little filler on a clean piece of card or board – measure the hardener carefully (follow the maker's instructions on the pack), otherwise the filler will set too rapidly or too slowly. Using the applicator, apply the filler paste to the prepared area; draw the applicator across the surface of the filler to achieve the correct contour and to level the surface. As soon as a contour that approximates to the correct one is achieved, stop working the paste – if you carry on too long, the paste will become sticky and begin to 'pick-up' on the applicator. Continue to add thin layers of filler paste at 20-minute intervals, until the level of the filler is just proud of the surrounding bodywork.

Once the filler has hardened, the excess can be removed using a metal plane or file. From then on, progressively-finer grades of abrasive paper should be used, starting with a 40-grade production paper, and finishing with a 400-grade wet-and-dry paper. Always wrap the abrasive paper around a flat rubber, cork, or wooden block – otherwise the surface of the filler will not be completely flat. During the smoothing of the filler surface, the wet-and-dry paper should be periodically rinsed in water. This will ensure that a very smooth finish is imparted to the filler at the final stage.

At this stage, the dent should be surrounded by a ring of bare metal, which in turn should be encircled by the finely 'feathered' edge of the good paintwork. Rinse the repair area with clean water, until all of the dust produced by the rubbing-down operation has gone.

Spray the whole area with a light coat of primer – this will show up any imperfections in the surface of the filler. Repair these imperfections with fresh filler paste or bodystopper, and once more smooth the surface with abrasive paper. Repeat this spray-and-repair procedure until you are satisfied that the surface of the filler, and the feathered edge of the paintwork, are perfect. Clean the repair area with clean water, and allow to dry fully.

The repair area is now ready for final spraying. Paint spraying must be carried out in a warm, dry, windless and dust-free atmosphere. This condition can be created artificially if you have access to a large indoor working area, but if you are forced to work in the open, you will have to pick your day very carefully. If you are working indoors, dousing the floor in the work area with water will help to settle the dust which would otherwise be in the atmosphere. If the repair area is confined to one body panel, mask off the surrounding panels; this will help to minimise the effects of a slight mis-match in paint colours. Bodywork fittings (eg chrome strips, door handles etc) will also need to be masked off. Use genuine masking tape, and several thicknesses of newspaper, for the masking operations.

Before commencing to spray, agitate the aerosol can thoroughly, then spray a test area (an old tin, or similar) until the technique is mastered. Cover the repair area with a thick coat of primer; the thickness should be built up using several thin layers of paint, rather than one thick one. Using 400-grade wet-and-dry paper, rub down the surface of the primer until it is really smooth. While doing this, the work area should be thoroughly doused with water, and the wet-and-dry paper periodically rinsed in water. Allow to dry before spraying on more paint.

Spray on the top coat, again building up the thickness by using several thin layers of paint. Start spraying at one edge of the repair area, and then, using a side-to-side motion, work until the whole repair area and about 2 inches of the surrounding original paintwork is covered. Remove all masking material 10 to 15 minutes after spraying on the final coat of paint.

Allow the new paint at least two weeks to harden, then, using a paintwork renovator, or a very fine cutting paste, blend the edges of the paint into the existing paintwork. Finally, apply wax polish.

Plastic components

With the use of more and more plastic body components by the vehicle manufacturers (eg bumpers. spoilers, and in some cases major body panels), rectification of more serious damage to such items has become a matter of either entrusting repair work to a specialist in this field, or renewing complete components. Repair of such damage by the DIY owner is not really feasible, owing to the cost of the equipment and materials required for effecting such repairs. The basic technique involves making a groove along the line of the crack in the plastic, using a rotary burr in a power drill. The damaged part is then welded back together, using a hot-air gun to heat up and fuse a plastic filler rod into the groove. Any excess plastic is then removed, and the area rubbed down to a smooth finish. It is important that a filler rod of the correct plastic is used, as body components can be made of a variety of different types (eg polycarbonate, ABS, polypropylene).

6.2a Undo the screws - hatchback/ saloon...

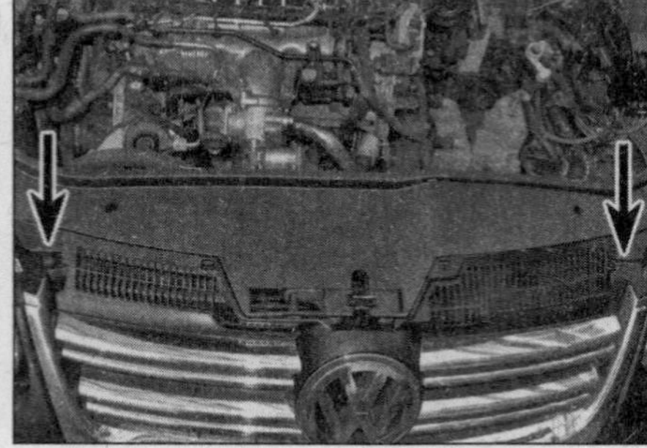

6.2b ...estate...

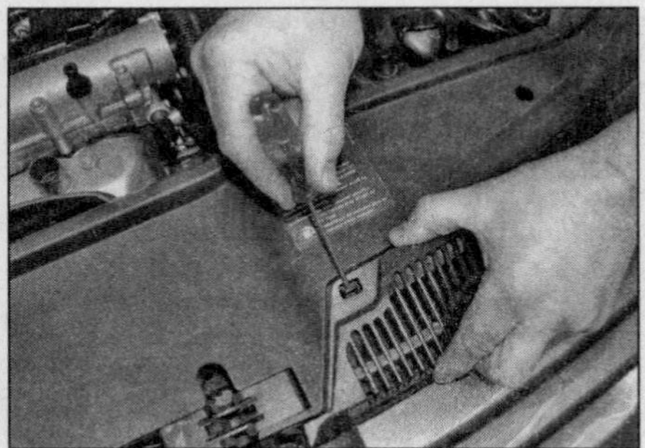

6.3 ...release the clips...

Damage of a less serious nature (abrasions, minor cracks etc) can be repaired by the DIY owner using a two-part epoxy filler repair material. Once mixed in equal proportions, this is used in similar fashion to the bodywork filler used on metal panels. The filler is usually cured in twenty to thirty minutes, ready for sanding and painting.

If the owner is renewing a complete component himself, or if he has repaired it with epoxy filler, he will be left with the problem of finding a suitable paint for finishing which is compatible with the type of plastic used. At one time, the use of a universal paint was not possible, owing to the complex range of plastics encountered in body component applications. Standard paints, generally speaking, will not bond to plastic or rubber satisfactorily. However, it is now possible to obtain a plastic body parts finishing kit which consists of a pre-primer treatment, a primer and coloured top coat. Full instructions are normally supplied with a kit, but basically, the method of use is to first apply the pre-primer to the component concerned, and allow it to dry for up to 30 minutes. Then the primer is applied, and left to dry for about an hour before finally applying the special-coloured top coat. The result is a correctly-coloured component, where the paint will flex with the plastic or rubber, a property that standard paint does not normally possess.

5 Major body damage – repair

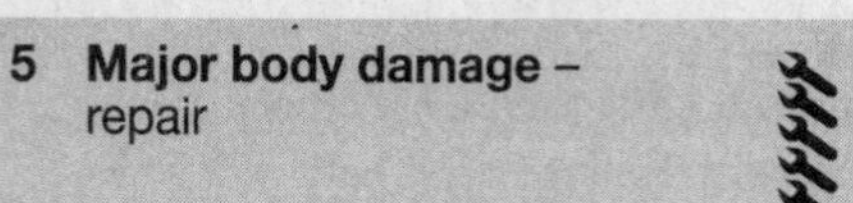

Where serious damage has occurred, or large areas need renewal due to neglect, it means that complete new panels will need welding-in, and this is best left to professionals. If the damage is due to impact, it will also be necessary to check completely the alignment of the body shell, and this can only be carried out accurately by a VW dealer using special jigs. If the body is left misaligned, it is primarily dangerous, as the car will not handle properly, and secondly, uneven stresses will be imposed on the steering, suspension and possibly transmission, causing abnormal wear, or complete failure, particularly to such items as the tyres.

6.4 ...then lift the radiator grille from the locking hooks

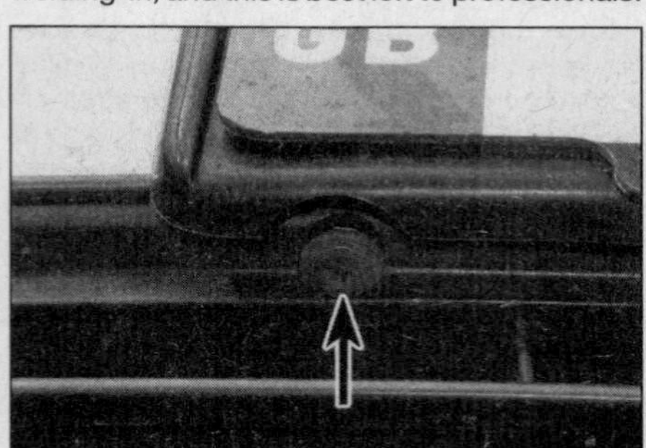

6.5a Undo the screws...

6.5b ...and lift the grille from place

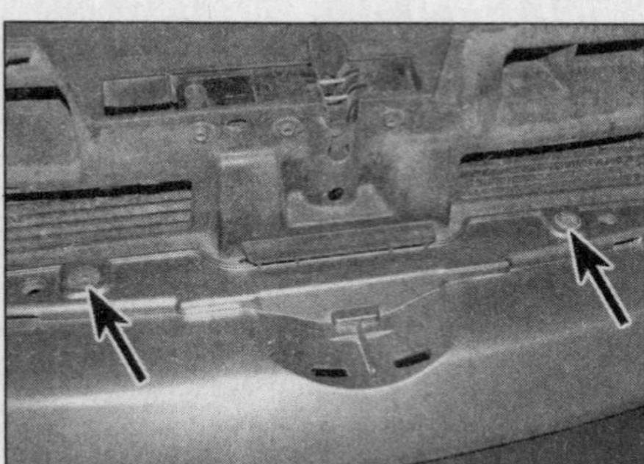

6.6a Unscrew the upper centre...

6 Front bumper – removal and refitting

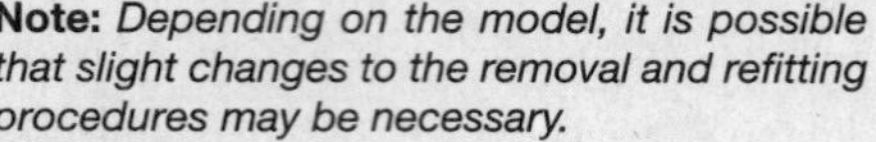

Note: *Depending on the model, it is possible that slight changes to the removal and refitting procedures may be necessary.*

Removal

1 Apply the handbrake, then jack up the front of the vehicle and support it on axle stands (see *Jacking and vehicle support*).

2 Open the bonnet, and undo the screws securing the radiator grille to the engine compartment crossbar **(see illustrations)**.

3 Using a screwdriver, release the clips **(see illustration)**.

Models up to 08/07

4 Tilt the radiator grille backwards and pull it upwards to release the locking hooks from the front bumper **(see illustration)**.

Models from 09/07

5 Undo 2 screws beneath number plate lower edge, and lift the radiator grille from place **(see illustrations)**.

All models

6 Undo the bumper upper mounting screws **(see illustrations)**.

7 Undo the lower screws from the front edge of the bumper **(see illustration)**.

8 Working on each side in turn, undo the screws securing the wheel arch liners to the bumper ends **(see illustrations)**.

9 With the help of an assistant, depress the catches (models upto 08/09) accessed through the bumper grille **(see illustration)**, push the bumper ends forwards, and withdraw the front bumper from the vehicle until it is

6.6b ...and upper side screws (up to 08/07 only)...

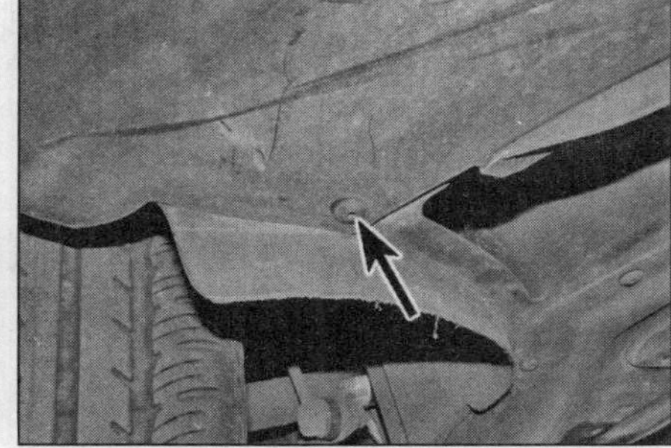

6.7 ...then unscrew the lower screws...

6.8a ...the lower wheel arch screws...

possible to disconnect the wiring from the foglights and ambient temperature sensor. Also, where applicable, release the headlamp washer hoses.

10 On models with headlamp washers, remove the washer jets as described in Chapter 12.

Refitting

11 Refitting is a reverse of the removal procedure, ensuring that the bumper ends engage correctly with the locating guides as the bumper is refitted.

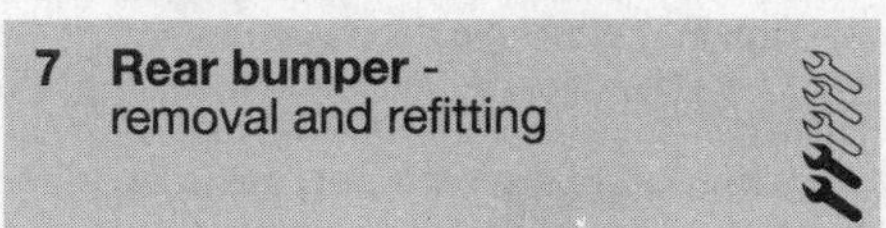

7 Rear bumper - removal and refitting

Note: *Depending on the model, it is possible that slight changes to the removal and refitting procedures may be necessary.*

Removal

1 To improve access, chock the front wheels, then jack up the rear of the vehicle and support it on axle stands (see *Jacking and vehicle support*).

2 Remove the rear light clusters as described in Chapter 12, Section 7.

3 Remove the six screws (three each side) securing the wheel arch liners to the bumper ends **(see illustration)**. Where necessary, push the centre pins out from the plastic rivets on the ends of the bumper and remove the rivets.

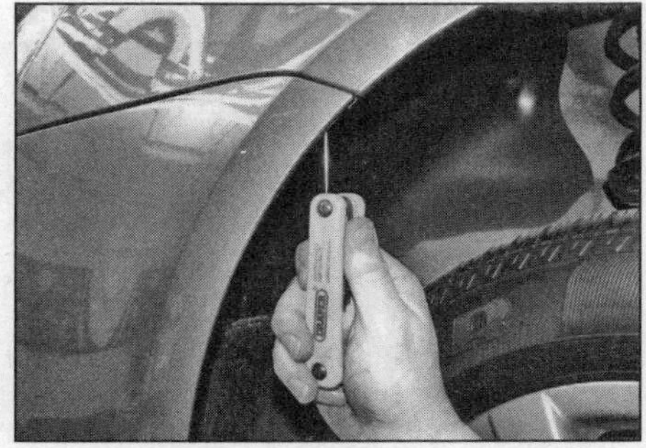

6.8b ...and upper wheel arch screws...

4 On Jetta models, remove the trim from each side of the rear luggage compartment, and unscrew the single mounting bolt **(see illustration)**.

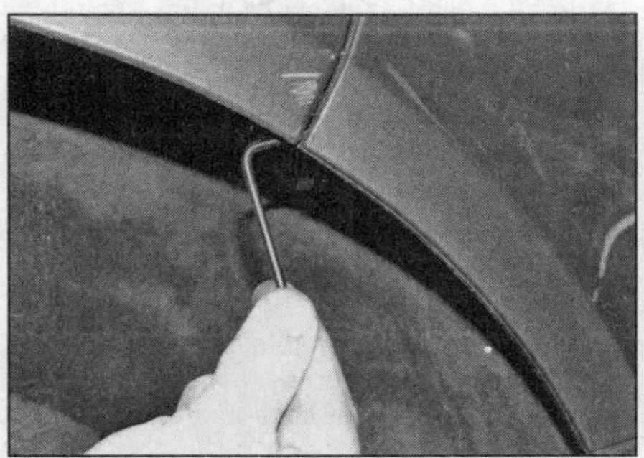

7.3 Removing the rear bumper-to-wheel arch liner screws

6.9 ...then release the catches through the bumper grille, and withdraw the front bumper

5 Undo the screws from the lower edge of the bumper **(see illustrations)**.

6 Undo the upper mounting screws **(see illustrations)**.

7.4 Unscrew the single mounting bolt for the rear bumper on each side

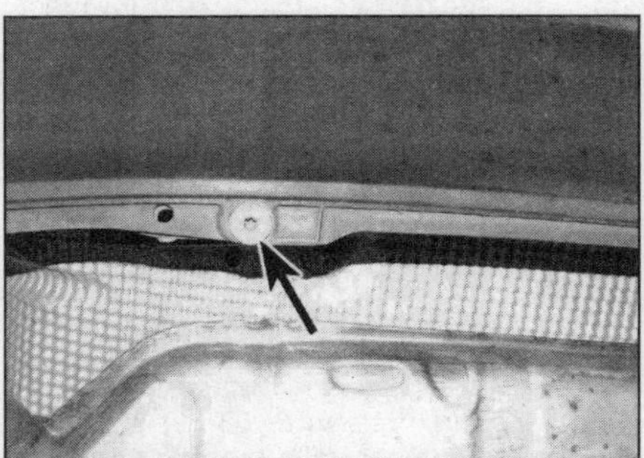

7.5a Rear bumper lower screws (hatchback/saloon)

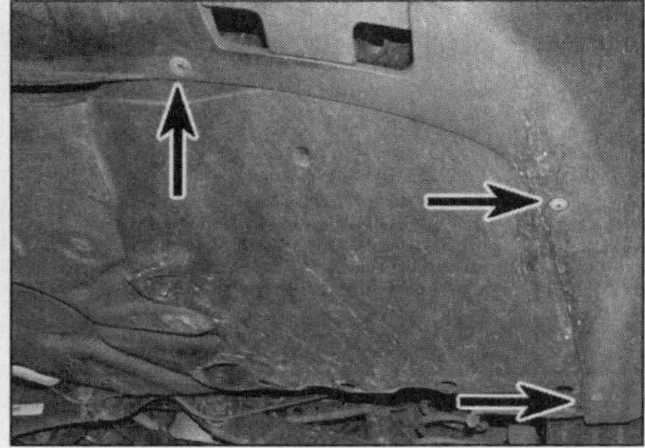

7.5b Rear bumper lower screws (estate)

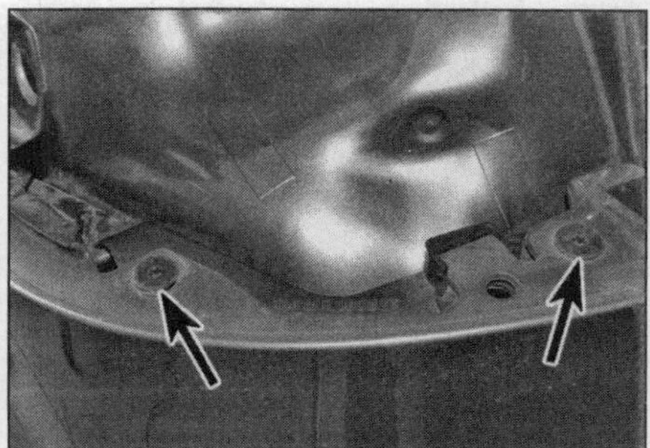

7.6a Rear bumper upper screws (hatchback/saloon)

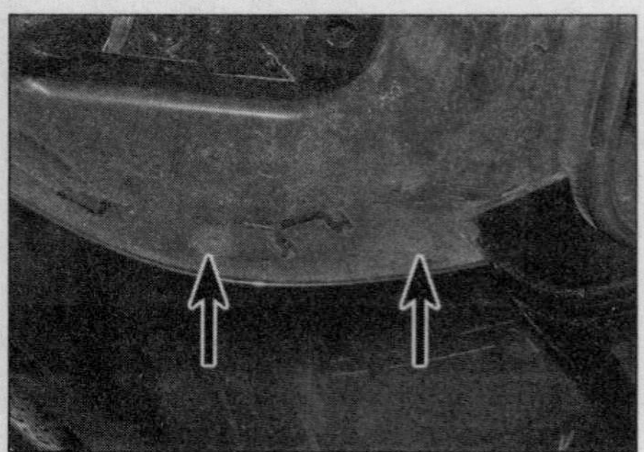

7.6b Rear bumper upper screws (estate)

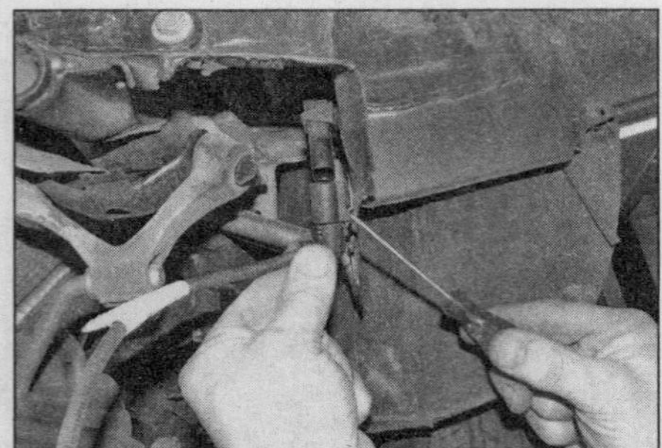

7.7 Disconnecting the number plate wiring

7 With the help of an assistant, release the bumper from the guides at the left- and right-hand ends, then withdraw the bumper from the rear of the vehicle until it is possible to disconnect the wiring from the number plate lights **(see illustration)**.

Refitting

8 Refitting is a reverse of the removal procedure, ensuring that the bumper ends engage correctly with the slides as the bumper is refitted. Retrieve the centre pins for the plastic rivets from the plastic slides before refitting the bumper - renew if necessary.

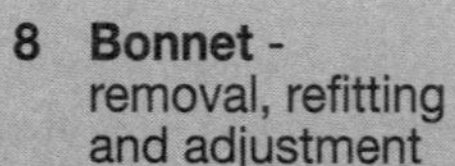

8 Bonnet - removal, refitting and adjustment

Removal

1 Open the bonnet and using a pencil or felt tip pen, mark the outline of each bonnet hinge relative to the bonnet, to use as a guide on refitting **(see illustration)**.

2 Disconnect the washer hose from the windscreen washer jets and, where necessary, disconnect the wiring from the jet heating elements.

3 With the help of an assistant to support the bonnet, disconnect the gas support strut as described in Section 15.

4 Undo the bonnet retaining bolts and carefully lift the bonnet clear. Store the bonnet out of the way in a safe place.

5 Inspect the bonnet hinges for signs of wear and free play at the pivots, and if necessary renew. Each hinge is secured to the body by two bolts, mark the position of the hinge on the body then undo the retaining bolts and remove it from the vehicle. On refitting, align the new hinge with the marks and tighten the retaining bolts.

Refitting and adjustment

6 With the aid of an assistant, offer up the bonnet and loosely fit the retaining bolts. Align the hinges with the marks made on removal, then tighten the retaining bolts securely.

7 Refit the washer hose, wiring and gas strut in the reverse order of removal.

8 Close the bonnet, and check for alignment with the adjacent panels. If necessary, unscrew the hinge bolts and re-align the bonnet. Once the bonnet is correctly aligned, tighten the hinge bolts. Check that the bonnet fastens and releases satisfactorily.

9 Bonnet release cable – removal and refitting

Removal

1 The bonnet release cable is in two sections, with a coupling located over the headlight. To remove the short front section at the lock end, first release the coupling by unhooking the pivoting clamp, then unhook the inner cable end from the coupling. To release the cable at the lock, remove the lock as described in Section 10, then depress the end fitting and pull it out.

2 To remove the rear section, first release the coupling as described in paragraph 1.

3 Working inside the vehicle, locate the release lever and pull it out approximately 2 cm, then insert a small screwdriver into the gap between the release lever and its securing clip. Let the lever return to its original position, then release the clip with a screwdriver (note that the clip falls behind the trim) **(see illustrations)**.

4 Unscrew the accelerator stop nut and plastic screw, then unclip the trim at the centre and at the lower edge from sill trim to remove.

5 Release the outer cable by unclipping forwards from the lever bracket and detach the inner cable from the lever.

6 Release the cable sealing grommet from the bulkhead.

7 Work along the length of the cable, noting its correct routing, and free it from the retaining clips and ties.

8 Disconnect the outer cable from under the crossmember on the lock housing.

9 Tie a length of string to the end of the cable inside the vehicle, then withdraw the cable through into the engine compartment.

10 Once the cable is free, untie the string and leave it in position in the vehicle; the string can then be used to draw the new cable back into position.

Refitting

11 Tie the inner end of the string to the end of the cable, then use the string to draw the bonnet release cable back from the engine compartment. Once the cable is through, untie the string.

12 Refitting is a reversal of the removal. **Note:** *Before refitting the release lever, fit the securing clip into the lever first, then push the lever back into place.*

13 Ensure the rubber grommet in the bulkhead is fitted correctly, and the cable is correctly routed and secured to all the relevant retaining clips.

14 Before closing the bonnet, check the operation of the release lever and cable.

8.1 Bonnet hinge

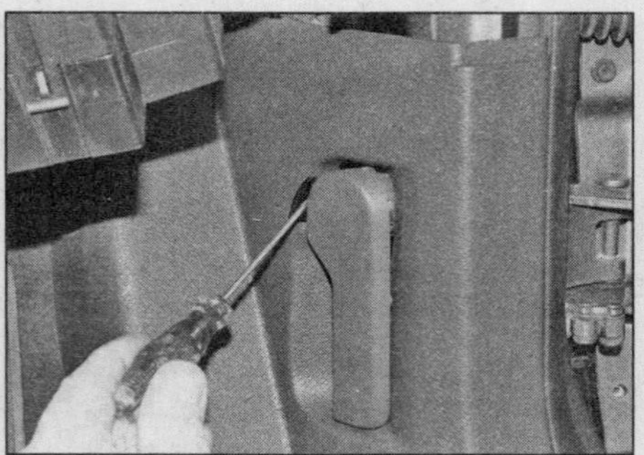

9.3a Insert a screwdriver as shown...

9.3b ...and remove the clip securing the bonnet release handle

10 Bonnet lock – removal and refitting

Removal

1 Open the bonnet then remove the radiator grille, as described in Section 6.

2 Disconnect the wiring for the contact microswitch at the connector located over the headlight **(see illustration)**.

3 Disconnect the bonnet cable at the join adapter located over the headlight, by lifting the cover and releasing the cable end fitting **(see illustrations)**. This will allow the cable to be disconnected from the bonnet lock.

4 Note the location of the three mounting bolts in their slots to ensure correct adjustment on refitting, then unscrew and remove them **(see illustration)**.

5 Prise the lock from the crossmember, then disconnect the cable by lifting the cover and unhooking the cable end fitting from the lock lever **(see illustrations)**.

6 Pull off the wiring support clips beneath the crossmember, then withdraw the lock while at the same time guiding the wiring through the hole in the crossmember **(see illustration)**.

Refitting

7 Refitting is a reversal of removal. Check that the bonnet fastens and releases satisfactorily before refitting the radiator grille. If adjustment is necessary, loosen the bonnet lock retaining bolts, and adjust the position of the lock to suit. Finally, tighten the bolts.

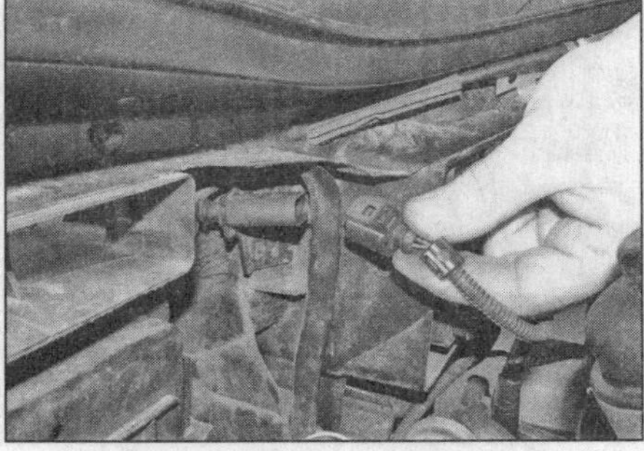

10.2 Disconnecting the bonnet lock microswitch located over the headlight

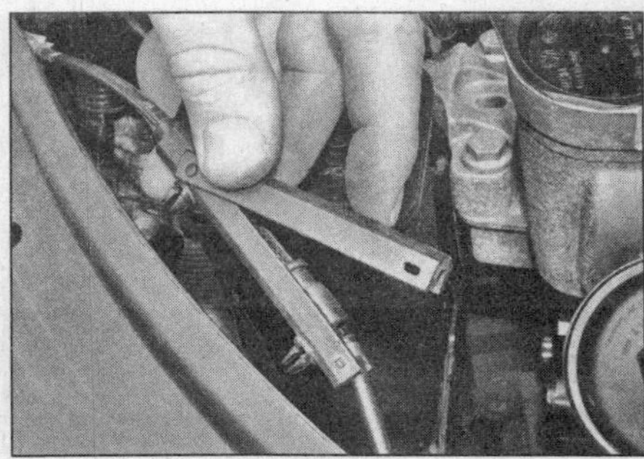

10.3a Lift the cover...

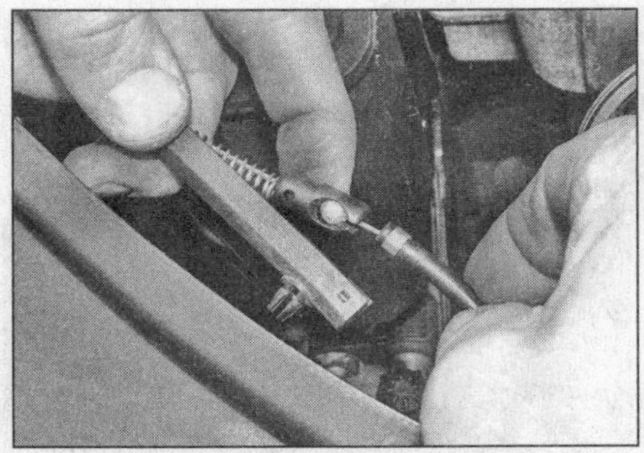

10.3b ...and release the bonnet lock cable at the join adapter

10.4 Unscrew the mounting bolts...

10.5a ...prise the lock from the crossmember...

10.5b ...and disconnect the cable

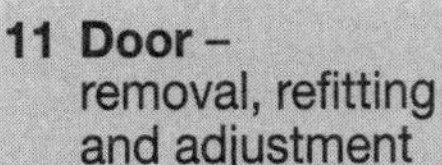

11 Door – removal, refitting and adjustment

Note: *The hinge bolts must always be renewed if loosened.*

Removal

1 Open the door then disconnect the wiring at the A- or B-pillar as applicable. To do this, first release the rubber bellows by pressing the small tab at the top **(see illustration)**. Pull out the locking lever and disconnect the wiring plug.

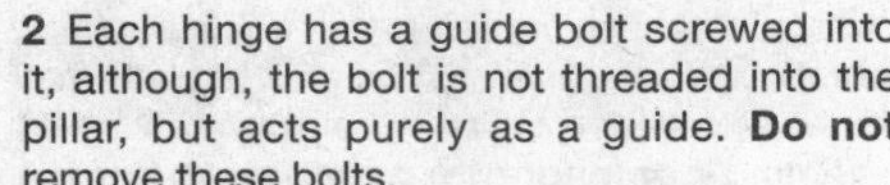

2 Each hinge has a guide bolt screwed into it, although, the bolt is not threaded into the pillar, but acts purely as a guide. **Do not** remove these bolts.

3 Unscrew and remove the upper and lower bolts from the lower hinge, then support the door and unscrew the upper bolt from the upper hinge **(see illustrations)**. Withdraw the door from the A- or B-pillar.

4 Examine the hinges for signs of wear or

10.6 Feed the bonnet lock wiring through the hole in the crossmember

11.1 Rubber bellows for wiring protection

11.3a Front door upper hinge...

11.3b ...and lower hinge

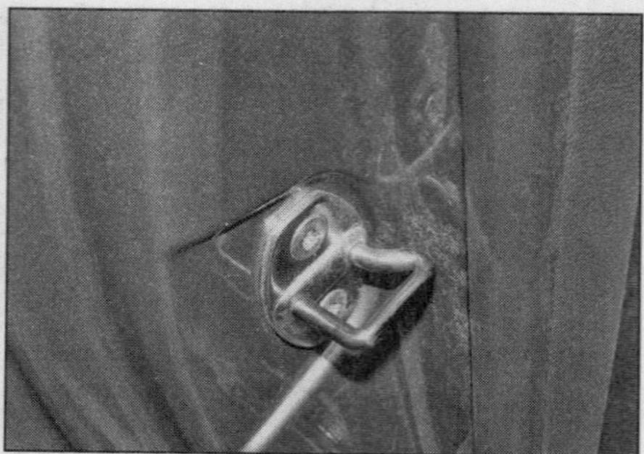
11.9 Door lock striker mounted on the B-pillar

damage. If renewal is necessary, the upper hinge can be unbolted from the A- or B-pillar from the outside, however, the lower hinge retaining bolts are fitted from inside the vehicle making it necessary to remove the A- or B-pillar trim for access to them. Before removing them, accurately mark their position to ensure correct refitting.

12.2a Prise up the grip/switch recess from the door inner trim panel...

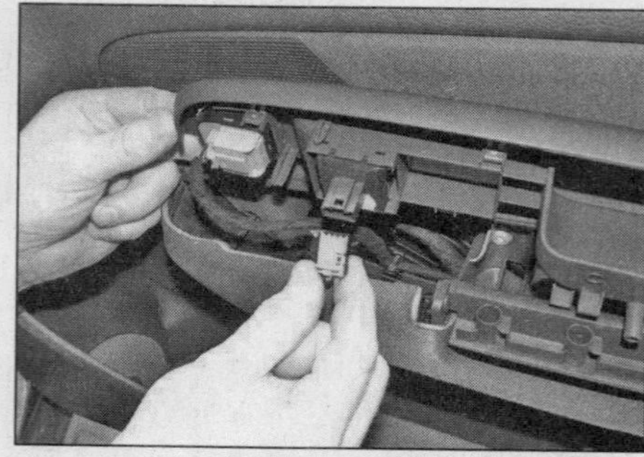
12.2b ...and disconnect the wiring

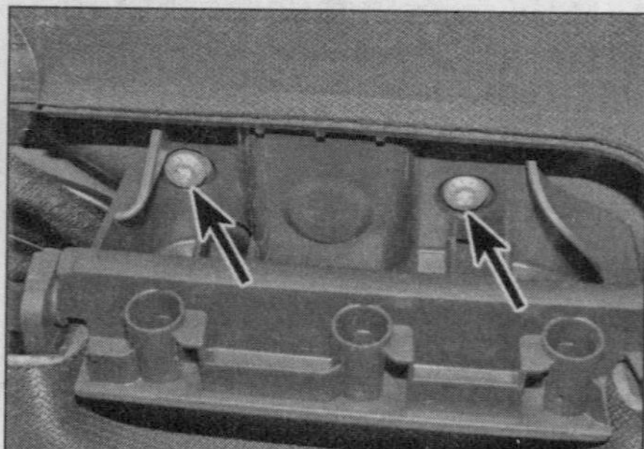
12.3 Undo the screws

12.4a Door inner trim panel upper front...

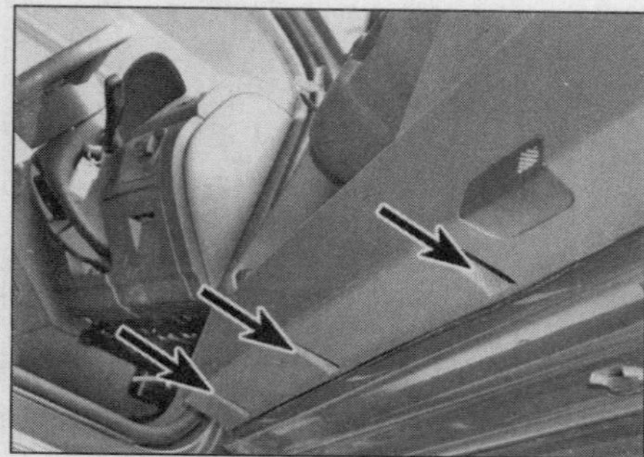
12.4b ...and lower retaining screws

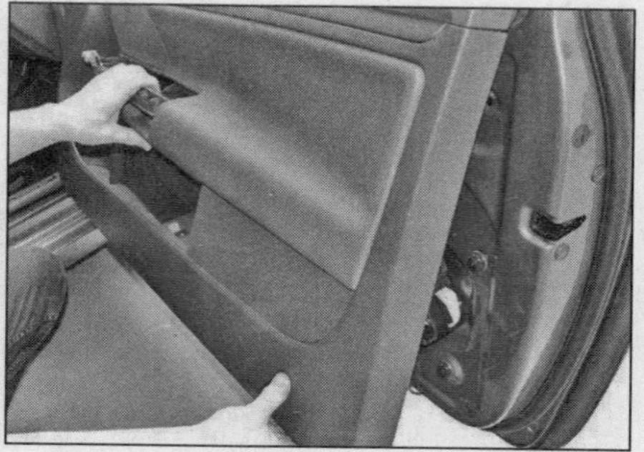
12.5 Release the door panel from the studs...

Refitting

5 Where renewed, fit the hinges and tighten the bolts to the specified torque. Refit the trim.

6 With the aid of an assistant, offer up the door to the vehicle and locate it on the guide bolts. Fit the new hinge bolts and tighten to the specified torque.

7 Reconnect the wiring plug and secure with the locking lever.

8 Refit the rubber bellows.

Adjustment

9 Close the door and check the door alignment with the surrounding body panels. There must be an even gap all around, and the door must be level with the surrounding body panels. Slight adjustment can be made with the eccentric pin of the upper hinge; loosen the lock bolt then turn the pin as necessary and retighten the lock-bolt. If necessary, adjust the door outer skin position by loosening the retaining bolts on the rear edge of the door. Check that the striker enters the door lock centrally as the door is closed, and if necessary adjust the position of the striker by loosening its mounting bolts **(see illustration)**.

12 Door inner trim panel – removal and refitting

Removal

Driver's door

1 Switch off the ignition.

2 Lift the grip/switch recess from the trim panel by carefully inserting a screwdriver or similar tool under its inner, rear lip, and levering upwards. Disconnect the wiring from the switch as applicable **(see illustrations)**.

3 Undo the two trim panel screws located in the grip/switch recess **(see illustration)**.

4 Undo the screws from the upper front corner and lower edge of the trim panel **(see illustrations)**.

5 Release the door trim panel studs, carefully levering between the panel and door with a flat-bladed lever. Work around the outside of the panel, and when all the studs are released, lift the door trim panel upwards and off the window slot. Support the panel away from the door **(see illustration)**.

6 Disconnect the wiring from the loudspeaker and door control unit **(see illustration)**.

7 Unhook the cable from the inner door handle, and remove the trim panel from the vehicle **(see illustration)**.

8 To remove the trim from the inside of the door mirror, undo the screw then lever the trim from the clips. Also disconnect the wiring from the 'tweeter' loudspeaker.

Front passenger's door

9 Using a screwdriver, carefully unclip the upper trim cover from the door grab handle and remove it.

10 Undo the trim retaining screws located inside the grab handle.

11 Undo the screws from the upper front corner and lower edge of the trim panel.

12 Release the door trim panel studs, carefully levering between the panel and door with a flat-bladed lever. Work around the outside of the panel, and when all the studs are released, lift the door trim panel upwards and off the window slot. Support the panel away from the door.

13 Disconnect the wiring from the loudspeaker and door control unit.

14 Unhook the cable from the inner door handle, and remove the trim panel from the vehicle.

15 To remove the trim from the inside of the door mirror, undo the screw then lever the trim from the clips. Also disconnect the wiring from the 'tweeter' loudspeaker.

Rear doors

16 On models with manually-operated windows, note the closed position of the handle, then press the spacer/clip located under the handle towards the front of the car, and slide the handle from the splines **(see illustrations)**.

17 Using a screwdriver, carefully unclip the upper trim cover from the door grab handle and remove it **(see illustrations)**.

18 Undo the trim retaining screws located inside the grab handle **(see illustration)**.

19 Undo the screw from the lower edge of the trim panel **(see illustration)**.

20 Release the door trim panel studs, carefully levering between the panel and door with a flat-bladed lever. Work around the outside of the panel, and when all the studs are released, lift the door trim panel upwards and off the window slot. Support the panel away from the door **(see illustration)**.

21 Where applicable, disconnect the wiring from the trim panel.

22 Unhook the cable from the inner door handle, and remove the trim panel from the vehicle **(see illustration)**.

12.6 ...and disconnect the wiring from the loudspeaker

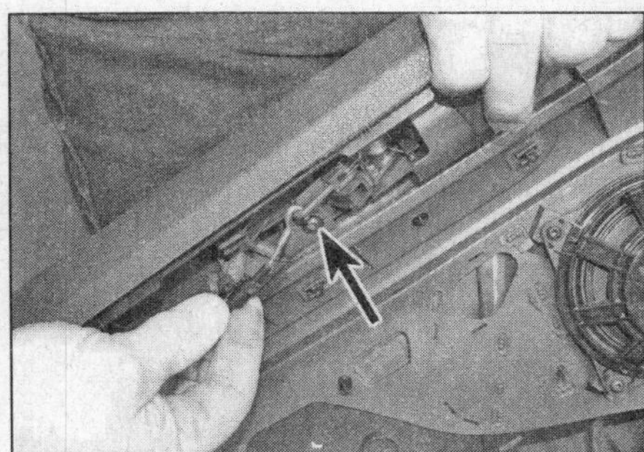

12.7 Unhook the cable from the inner door handle

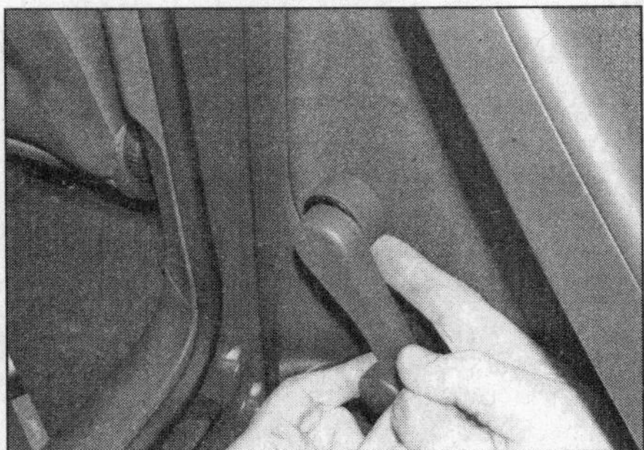

12.16a Press the spacer/clip...

12.16b ...and slide the handle from the splines

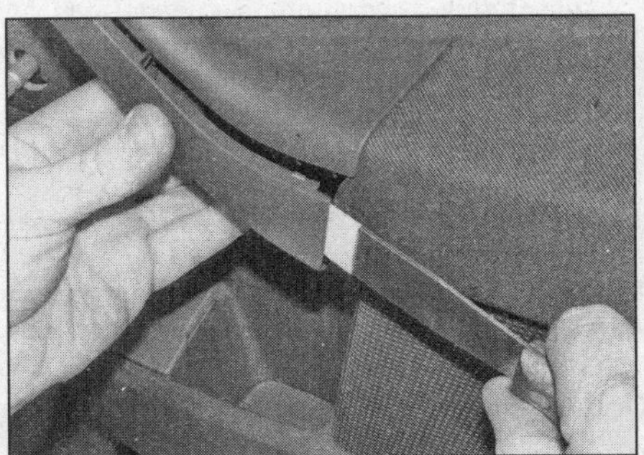

12.17a Unclip the upper trim cover...

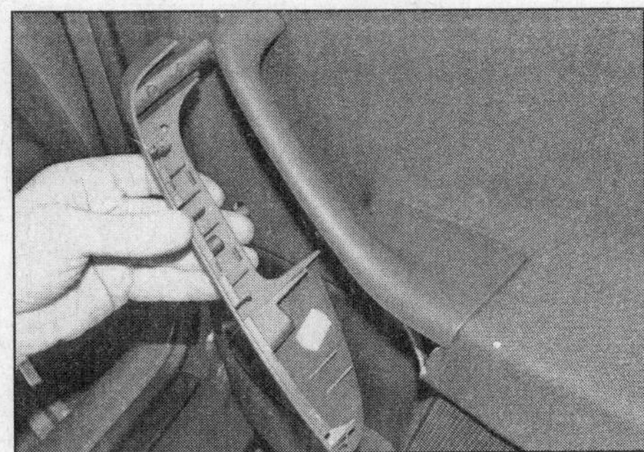

12.17b ...and remove it from the grab handle

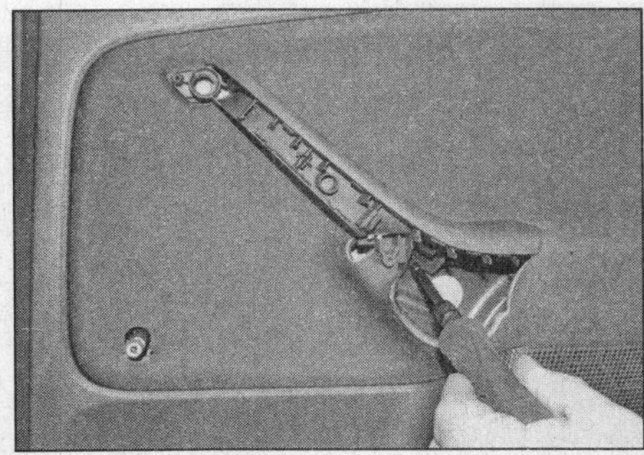

12.18 Undo the upper retaining screws...

12.19 ...and lower retaining screw...

12.20 ...and withdraw the door trim panel...

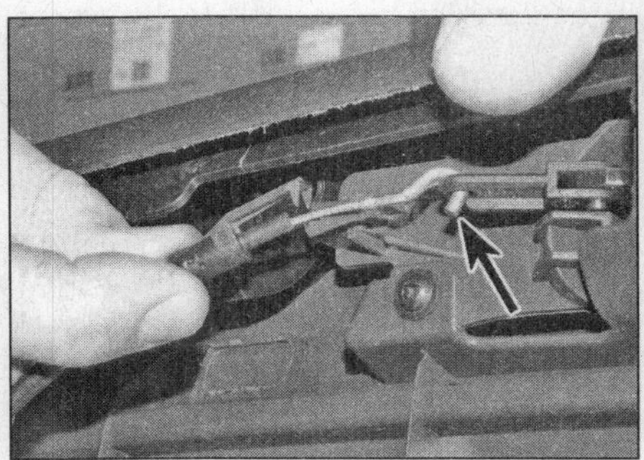

12.22 ...then unhook the cable from the inner door handle

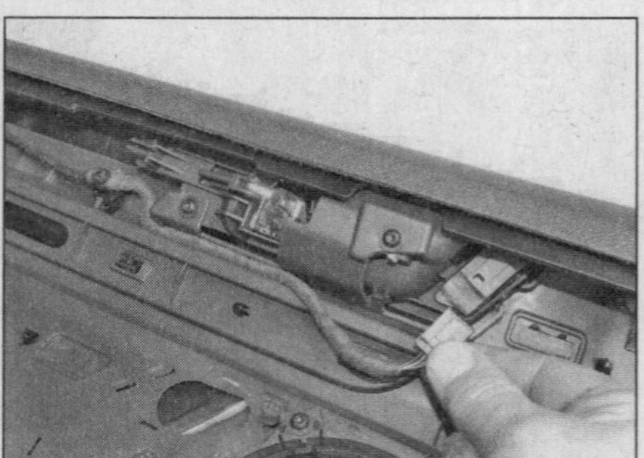
13.2a Disconnect the wiring...

13.2b ...then undo the screw and remove the interior door handle

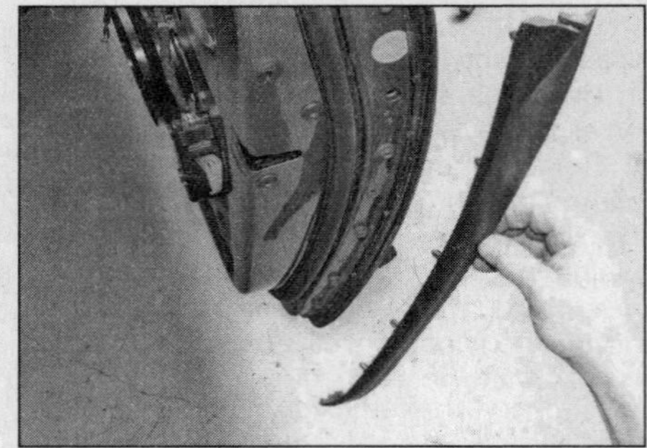
13.3 Remove the plastic cap...

Refitting

23 Before refitting, check whether any of the trim panel retaining studs were broken on removal, and renew them as necessary. Refitting of the trim panel is then a reversal of removal. Check the operation of the door electrical equipment.

13 Door handle and lock components – removal and refitting

Removal

Interior door handle

1 Remove the door inner trim panel as described in Section 12.

2 Undo the screw on the inside of the door trim panel, then disconnect the wiring and unclip the door handle to remove it **(see illustrations)**.

Front door lock cylinder housing or rear door housing and end cap

3 Open the door, then remove the plastic cap in the rear edge of the door to locate the retaining screw **(see illustration)**.

4 Pull out the door handle, and hold it in this position whilst undoing the Torx retaining screw until it comes to its stop. Do not remove the screw too far or the locking ring may fall into the door **(see illustration)**.

5 Pull the lock cylinder housing out of the door handle, and release the handle to the original position **(see illustration)**. On older vehicles, the housing may be corroded into the door aperture making it difficult to remove. **Note:** *Do not drop the locking ring into the door, as it will be necessary to remove the inner trim panel to recover it.*

13.4 ...pull out the door handle, and undo the screw until it comes to the stop

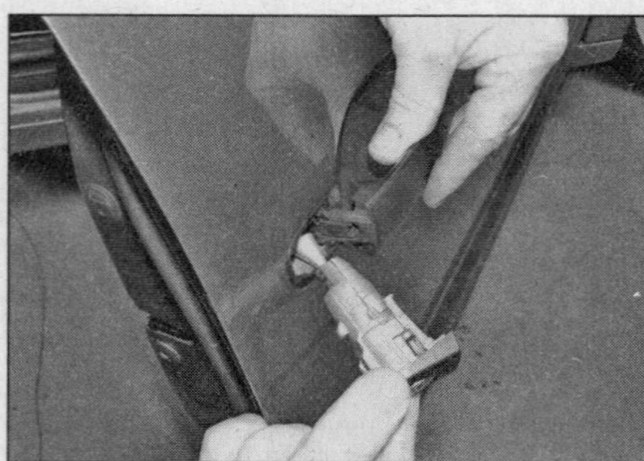
13.5 Removing the door lock cylinder housing

Exterior door handle

6 Remove the door lock cylinder housing as described in paragraphs 3 to 5.

7 Working through the lock cylinder aperture, disconnect the lock release cable from the handle then unhook the handle from the door. Recover the gasket **(see illustrations)**.

Exterior door handle mounting plate

8 Remove the exterior door handle as described in paragraphs 6 and 7.

9 Remove the door outer skin as follows:

a) Lever out the clips and remove the cover from the rear edge of the door – start at the bottom and work upwards.

b) Lever out the clips and remove the cover from the front edge of the door.

c) Remove the bolt securing the mounting plate. The bolt is located through the handle aperture.

d) To ensure refitting in the same position, mark the bolts and outer skin panel in relation to each other.

e) Remove all the perimeter bolts, however, note the location of each bolt as they are of different lengths.

f) Remove the skin from the door.

10 Release the retaining rubbers from the guide pins **(see illustration)**.

11 Slide the mounting plate forwards to release the guide pins, then remove it from the door **(see illustration)**.

Door lock

12 Remove the exterior door handle mounting plate as described in paragraphs 8 to 11.

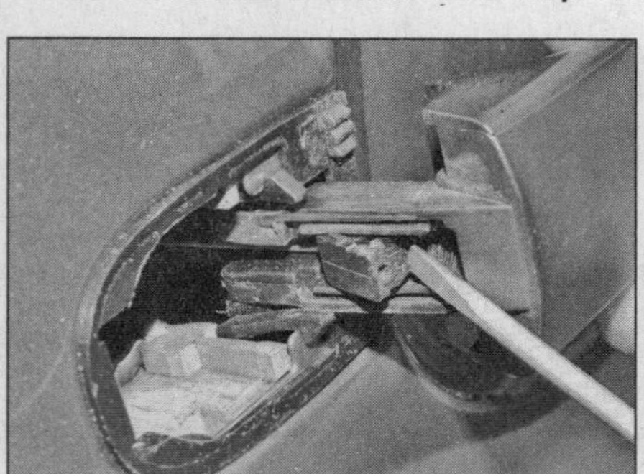
13.7a Disconnect the lock release cable...

13.7b ...then unhook the exterior door handle

13.10 Release the retaining rubbers from the guide pins

13 Unclip the cover from the door lock. **Note:** *The cover is not supplied with new door locks.*
14 Disconnect the wiring for the lock microswitch at the connector.
15 Unscrew the lock mounting bolts, then disconnect the inner handle cable by turning it through 90°, and withdraw the lock from the door **(see illustrations)**.

Refitting

Interior door handle

16 Clip the handle back into position and secure with the screw on the inside of the door trim. Refit the door trim panel as described in Section 12.

Front door lock cylinder housing or rear door housing and end cap

17 Insert the lock cylinder housing in the door. As it is fitted, it should make an audible click as it locates in the mounting plate.
18 Allow the exterior handle to rest lightly against the door panel, then tighten the Torx retaining screw.
19 Refit the plastic cap to cover the screw.
20 Check the operation of the lock before closing the door, by sliding a screwdriver into the lock to operate the mechanism. If it does not function correctly, remove the housing and check that the cable is located correctly in the exterior handle.

Exterior door handle

21 Before refitting the handle, the lock must be 'set' as follows to ensure correct attachment of the cable to the exterior handle. VW technicians use a special 'hooked' tool which is inserted into the door in order to move the internal spring to its 'catch' position. A tool can be fabricated out of welding rod or stout wire **(see illustration)**.
22 Locate the gasket on the door, then insert the handle into the door at the front end, and pivot the handle into position.
23 With the handle pressed against the door, refit the cable into the door handle and clip it firmly into the recess.
24 Refit the lock cylinder housing (front door) or housing and end cap (rear door) as described above and check that it functions correctly. Note that the internal spring (see paragraph 21) will be released automatically when the handle is first operated.

Exterior door handle mounting plate

25 Refitting is a reversal of removal, but position the outer skin panel as previously noted, and tighten all bolts securely.

Door lock

26 Attach the cable to the lock, then refit the lock and secure with the mounting bolts tightened to the specified torque.
27 Reconnect the wiring.
28 Clip the cover onto the lock.
29 Refit the exterior door handle mounting plate with reference to paragraph 25.

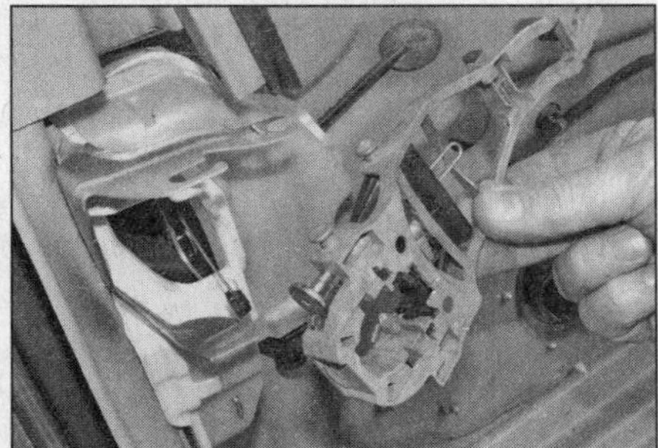

13.11 Slide the mounting plate forwards to release the guide pins

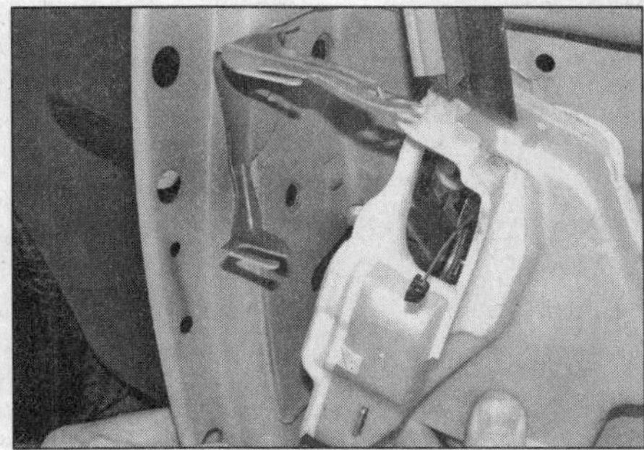

13.15a Remove the door lock from the door...

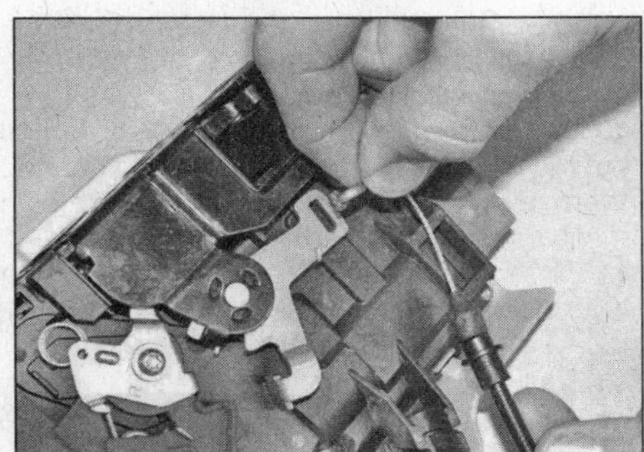

13.15b ...and disconnect the cable

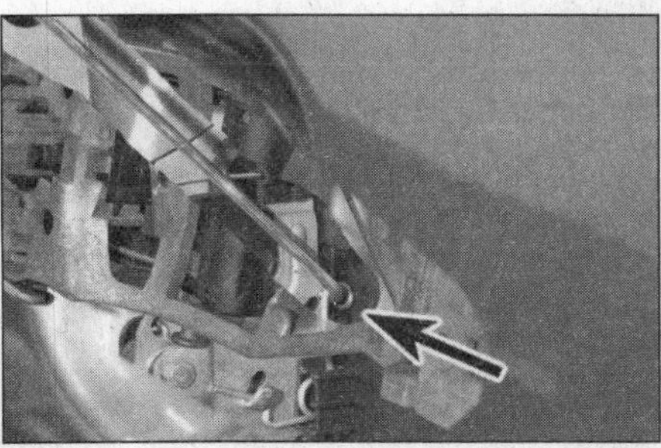

13.21 Tool made from welding rod used to 'set' the door lock before fitting the exterior door handle (cutaway view)

14 Door window glass and regulator – removal and refitting

Removal

Front door window glass

1 Remove the door inner trim panel as described in Section 12.
2 Prise out the access caps from the inner door panel **(see illustration)**.
3 Temporarily connect the wiring to the switches, then switch on the ignition, and lower the window glass until the bolts attaching it to the regulator are visible through the access holes. If there is a fault with the electric motor, remove the motor in order to lower the glass.
4 Loosen the bolts on the regulator to release the window glass clamps **(see illustration)**. Note that the bolts are fitted from the outside, so will have to be turned clockwise to loosen them.
5 Lift the rear of the window glass so that it is tilted, then remove it upwards from the door **(see illustration)**.

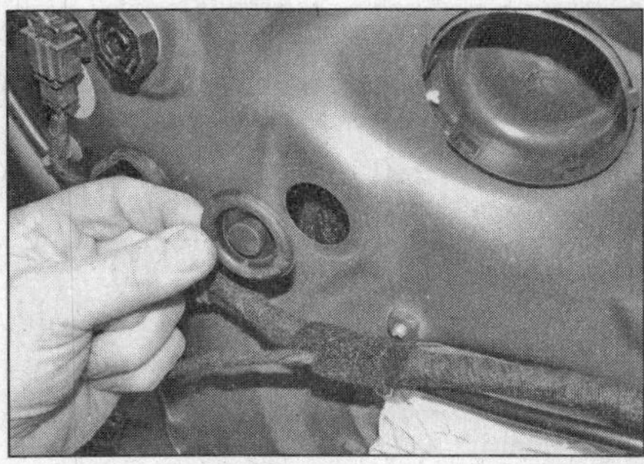

14.2 Prise out the access caps

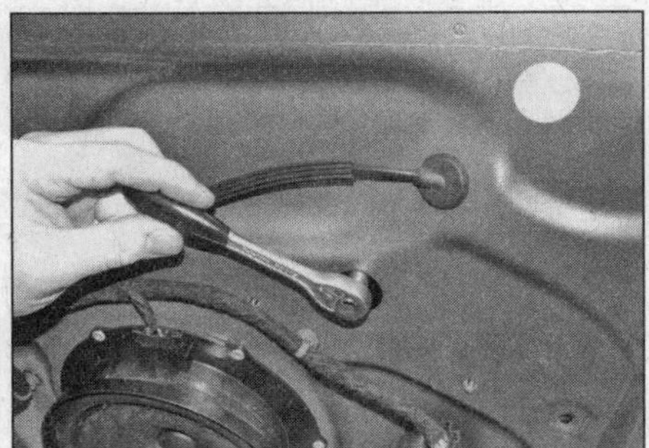

14.4 Loosening the window glass clamps

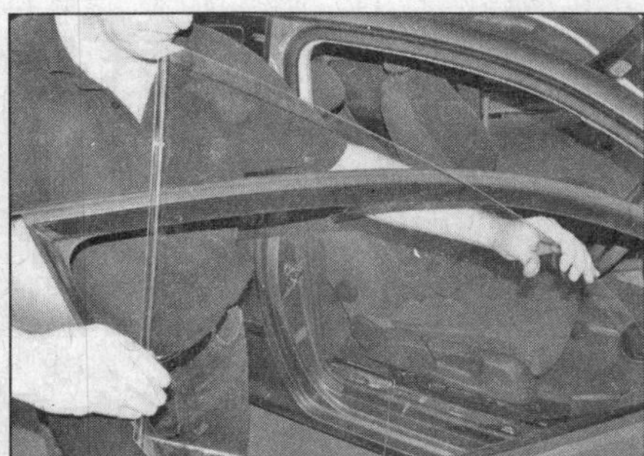

14.5 Lift the window glass from the front door

14.7 Remove the access cap...

14.9 ...then use a 5.0 mm bolt to pull out the plastic centre roll-pin

14.10 Pull out the rubber moulding for access to the glass retaining screws

Rear door window glass

6 Remove the door inner trim panel as described in Section 12.

7 Prise out the access cap from the inner door panel **(see illustration)**.

8 Lower the window glass until the plastic roll-pin is visible through the access hole. On models with electric windows, temporarily reconnect the switch to operate the glass. If there is a fault with the electric motor, remove the motor in order to lower the glass.

9 Screw a 5.0 mm diameter bolt of length approximate 70 mm into the plastic centre roll-pin and pull it out **(see illustration)**. Now, screw an 8.0 mm diameter bolt into the outer part of the roll-pin. Do not drop the roll-pin inside the door, otherwise further dismantling will be required to retrieve it. It is recommended that the roll-pin is renewed whenever removed. On Jetta models, now remove the window regulator motor as described later in this Chapter, and move the window glass fully downwards.

10 At the front of the window aperture, pull out the rubber moulding from the trim upright, then undo the screws and pull the trim forwards **(see illustration)**.

11 Lift the window glass and withdraw it from the outside of the door.

Rear door fixed window

12 Remove the door outer skin as follows:

a) Lever out the clips and remove the cover from the rear edge of the door – start at the bottom and work upwards.

b) Lever out the clips and remove the cover from the front edge of the door.

c) Remove the bolt securing the mounting plate. The bolt is located through the handle aperture.

d) To ensure refitting in the same position, mark the bolts and outer skin panel in relation to each other.

e) Remove all the perimeter bolts, however, note the location of each bolt as they are of different lengths.

f) Remove the skin from the door.

13 Remove the door window glass as described in paragraphs 6 to 11.

14 Pull out the rubber guide channel, then the bolts and remove the centre rib from the channel.

15 Using a screwdriver, separate the guide channel and fixed window from the door frame, and withdraw.

Window regulator

16 Remove the door outer skin as follows:

a) Lever out the clips and remove the cover from the rear edge of the door – start at the bottom and work upwards.

b) Lever out the clips and remove the cover from the front edge of the door.

c) Unscrew the bolt securing the mounting plate. The bolt is located through the handle aperture.

d) To ensure refitting in the same position, mark the bolts and outer skin panel in relation to each other.

*e) Unscrew all the perimeter bolts, however, note the location of each bolt as they are of different lengths **(see illustrations)**.*

*f) Remove the skin from the door **(see illustration)**.*

17 Unscrew the nuts and bolts and remove the side impact protection bar from the door **(see illustration)**. **Note:** *The nuts and bolts are painted at the factory, and may require careful loosening to avoid shearing their threads.*

18 Remove the door window glass as described earlier.

19 Unscrew the bolts from the motor mounting plate.

20 Unscrew the mounting bolts from the regulator brackets, and withdraw the assembly from the door. At the same time, disconnect the wiring from the motor **(see illustrations)**.

Window regulator motor and control unit

21 Remove the door inner trim panel as described in Section 12.

22 With the window fully closed, use adhesive tape to hold the glass in position.

14.16a Unscrew the door skin bolts...

14.16b ...noting their location as they are of different lengths

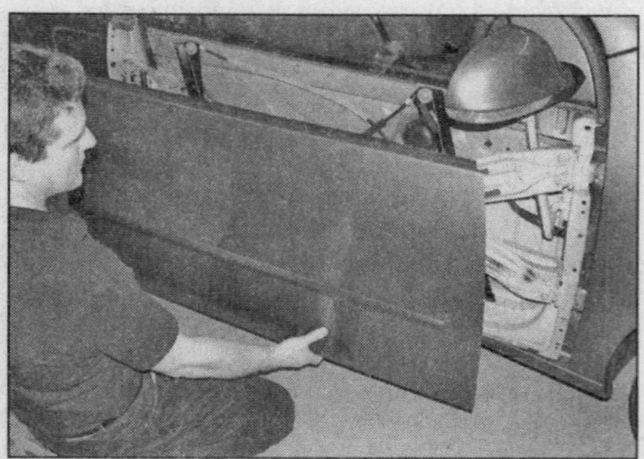
14.16c Removing the door skin

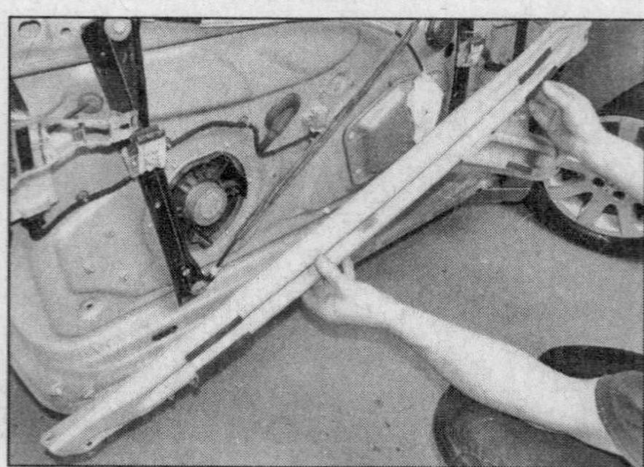
14.17 Removing the side impact protection bar

23 Use a screwdriver to carefully disconnect the wiring plugs from the motor.
24 Unscrew the mounting bolts and remove the motor and control unit from the mounting plate.

Refitting

Front door window glass

25 Carefully lower the tilted window glass into the door and engage it with the regulator clamps. Apply light downwards pressure to the glass to make sure it is correctly located in the channels, then tighten the regulator clamp bolts.
26 If necessary, the window may be checked for correct operation at this stage by connecting the wiring to the switches.
27 Refit the access caps.
28 Refit the door inner trim panel with reference to Section 12.

Rear door window glass

29 Before fitting the window glass to the door, fit the roll-pin so that it extends by equal amounts on each side of the glass. Secure with the inner pin.
30 Lower the window glass into the door and locate the roll-pin on the regulator clip. Press directly downwards until the roll-pin engages with the clip.
31 Reposition the trim and tighten the screws, then refit the rubber moulding. On Jetta models, refit the window regulator motor.
32 If necessary, the window may be checked for correct operation at this stage by connecting the wiring to the switches.
33 Refit the access cap.
34 Refit the door inner trim panel with reference to Section 12.

Rear door fixed window

35 Refitting is a reversal of removal.

Window regulator

36 Refit the regulator brackets and mounting plate and tighten the bolt/nuts securely.
37 Refit the window glass as described earlier.
38 Refit the side impact protection bar and tighten the bolts to the specified torque.
39 Refit the door outer skin
40 Refitting is a reversal of removal, but position the outer skin panel as previously noted, and tighten all bolts securely.

Window regulator motor and control unit

41 Locate the motor and control unit on the mounting plate and insert the mounting bolts hand-tight.
42 Reconnect the wiring plugs, then remove the adhesive tape and operate the window down and up a short distance to allow the splines between the motor and cable drum to engage.
43 Fully tighten the motor mounting bolts.
44 Operate the window twice to its upper and lower stops to normalise the window and activate the pinch/roll-back function.

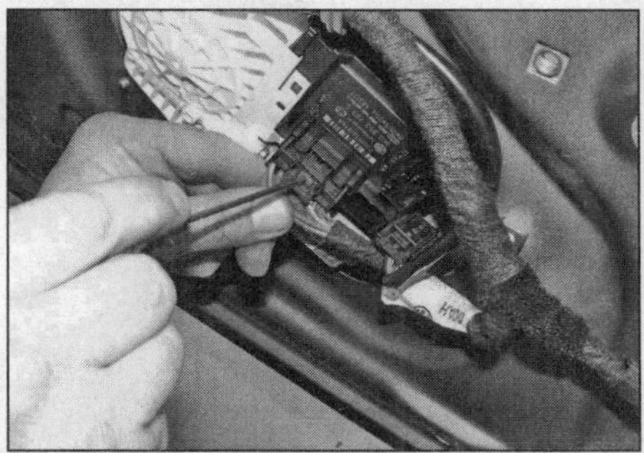

14.20a Disconnecting the window regulator motor wiring

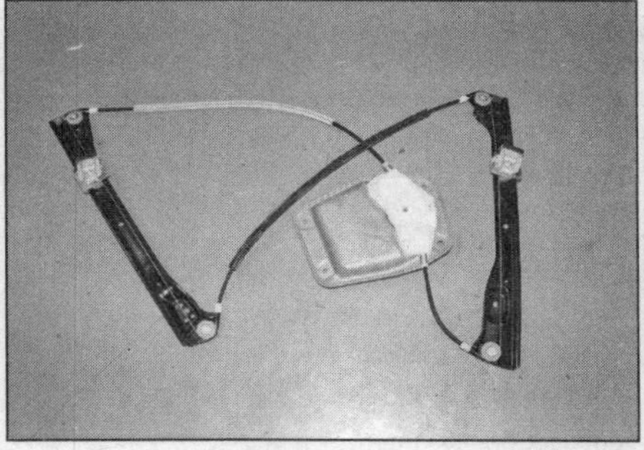

14.20b Window regulator removed from the door

45 Refit the door inner trim panel with reference to Section 12.

15 Tailgate and support struts – removal and refitting

Removal

Tailgate

1 With the tailgate open, prise out the covers (where fitted) and undo the trim panel retaining screws inside the grab handles **(see illustration)**. Release the trim panel clips, carefully levering between the panel and tailgate with a flat-bladed screwdriver. Work around the outside of the panel, and when all the clips are released, unclip from the upper trim and remove the panel.
2 Remove the parcel shelf retainers (where fitted) from the upper trim by pulling out the centre pins, then remove both the retainers. Unclip the upper trim from the tailgate starting from the outer ends and working towards the middle.
3 Disconnect the wiring connectors situated behind the trim panel and free the washer hose from the tailgate wiper motor. Disconnect the wiring connectors from the heated rear screen terminals and free the wiring grommets from the tailgate.
4 Tie a piece of string to each end of the wiring then, noting the correct routing of the wiring harness, release the harness rubber grommets from the tailgate and withdraw the wiring. When the end of the wiring appears, untie the string and leave it in position in the tailgate; it can then be used on refitting to draw the wiring into position.
5 Using a suitable marker pen, draw around the outline of each hinge marking its correct position on the tailgate.
6 With the help of an assistant to support the tailgate, remove the support struts as described below.
7 Unscrew and remove the bolts securing the hinges to the tailgate **(see illustration)**. Where necessary, recover the gaskets which are fitted between the hinge and vehicle body.
8 Inspect the hinges for signs of wear or damage and renew if necessary. The hinges are secured to the vehicle by nuts or bolts (depending on model) which can be accessed once the headlining rear cover strip has been removed.

Support struts

Warning: The support struts are filled with a gas and must be disposed of safely.

9 With the help of an assistant, support the tailgate in the open position.
10 Using a small flat-bladed screwdriver lift the locking clip, and pull the gas support strut off its balljoint mounting on the tailgate **(see illustrations)**. Repeat the procedure on the lower strut mounting and remove the strut from the vehicle body. **Note:** *If the gas strut is to be re-used, the locking clip must not be taken all the way out, or the clip will be damaged.*

15.1 Prise out the covers, and undo the screws in the grab handle recesses

15.7 Tailgate hinges

15.10a Lift locking clip upwards; do not remove clip completely...

15.10b ...then pull strut off balljoint

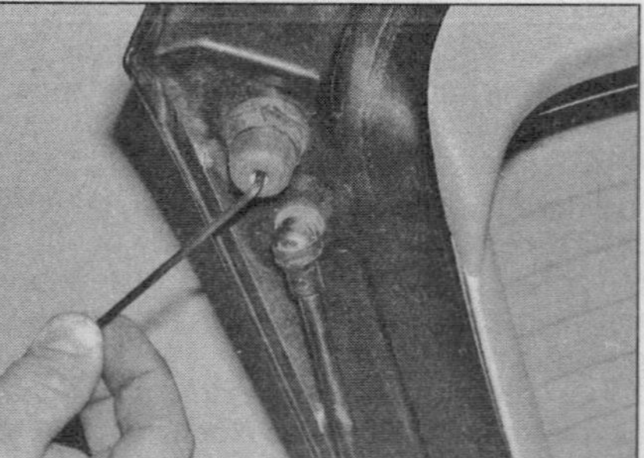
15.13a Slacken the centre screw to adjust the tailgate buffer...

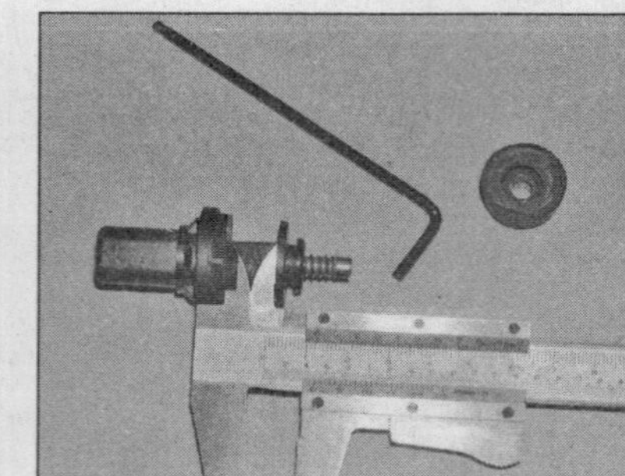
15.13b ...check the setting on each buffer to line up tailgate

Refitting

Tailgate

11 Refitting is the reverse of removal, aligning the hinges with the marks made before removal. Tighten retaining bolts to the specified torque.

12 On completion, close the tailgate and check its alignment with the surrounding panels. If necessary slight adjustment can be made by unscrewing the retaining bolts and repositioning the tailgate on its hinges. If the tailgate buffers are in need of adjustment, continue as follows.

13 Locate the adjustment buffers on the tailgate. Through the hole in the rubber cap, insert an Allen key and undo the screw until the centre notched slide will move freely in or out, in the housing. When the adjustment buffer has been set to the correct position tighten the centre screw. When renewing buffers the notched slide is preset at 12.5 mm from the housing **(see illustrations)**. To remove the adjustment buffer, turn anti-clockwise 90° with a spanner.

Support struts

14 Refitting is a reverse of the removal procedure, ensuring that the strut is securely retained by its retaining clips.

16 Tailgate lock components – removal and refitting

Removal

Tailgate lock

1 Open up the tailgate and remove the trim panel as described in Section 15. **Note:** *If the lock is inoperative, the tailgate can be opened manually by opening the emergency access cover from inside the car **(see illustrations)**.*

2 Disconnect the wiring from the lock **(see illustration)**.

3 Undo the retaining bolts and remove the lock from the tailgate.

Tailgate handle/release unit

4 Open up the tailgate and remove the trim panel as described in Section 15. **Note:** *If the lock is inoperative, the tailgate can be opened manually by opening the emergency access cover from inside the car.*

Hatchback/Plus models

5 Remove the tailgate wiper motor as described in Chapter 12.

6 Disconnect the wiring from the handle/release unit **(see illustration)**.

7 Undo the retaining screws holding the unit to the tailgate and locking brackets, then turn it clockwise and remove **(see illustrations)**.

16.1a Remove the emergency cover...

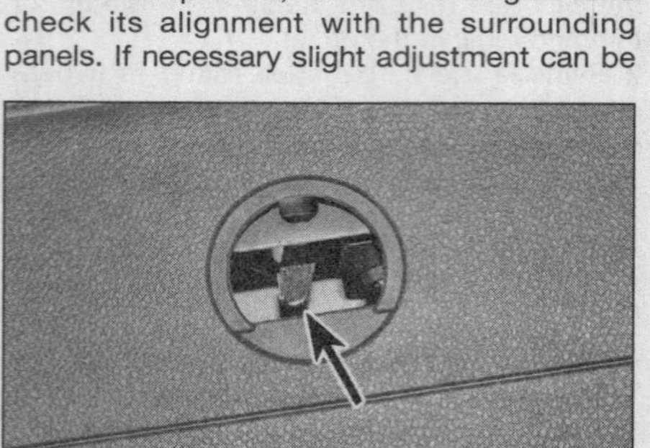
16.1b ...and operate the lever to open the tailgate

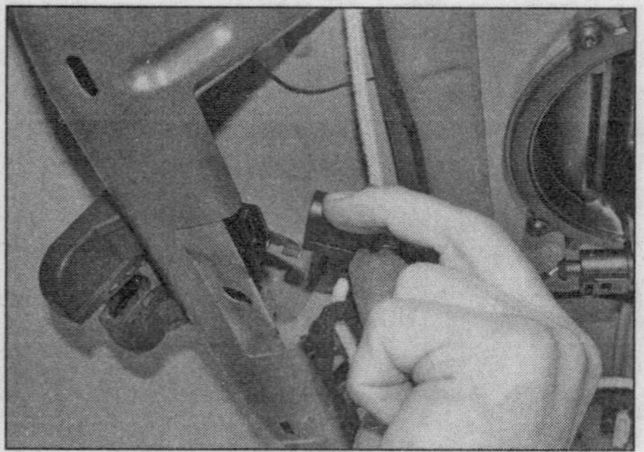
16.2 Disconnect the wiring from the tailgate lock

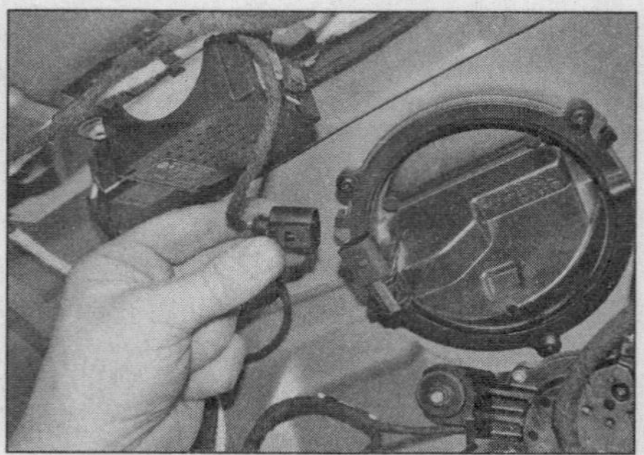
16.6 Disconnect the wiring ...

16.7a Undo the retaining screws...

Estate models

8 Disconnect the wiring plug, then undo the 2 nuts and remove the release unit **(see illustration).**

Refitting

9 Refitting is a reversal of removal, however, before refitting the trim panel, check the operation of the lock components.

17 Boot lid and support struts – removal and refitting

Removal

Boot lid

1 Open up the boot lid then ensure the ignition and all electrical consumers are switched off.

2 Remove the lock cover and emergency release lever cover, then undo the two bolts from the handle recess. Using a wide-blade tool, release the trim retaining clips by prising near each clip. Unhook the emergency release lever cable and remove the trim **(see illustrations).**

3 Disconnect all the wiring connectors from the number plate lights and the boot lock assembly, then tie a piece of string to each end of the wiring **(see illustrations).** Noting the correct routing of the wiring harness, release the harness rubber grommets from the boot lid and withdraw the wiring. When the end of the wiring appears, untie the string and leave it in position in the boot lid; it can then be used on refitting to draw the wiring into position

4 Unclip the plastic wiring cover from the left-hand hinge to release the wiring. Detach the support struts as described below.

5 Draw around the outline of each hinge with a suitable marker pen then unscrew and remove the hinge retaining nuts and remove the boot lid from the vehicle.

6 Inspect the hinges for signs of wear or damage and renew if necessary; the hinges are secured to the vehicle body by bolts.

Support struts

Warning: The support struts are filled with gas and must be disposed of safely.

7 With the help of an assistant, support the boot lid in the open position.

8 Using a small flat-bladed screwdriver lift the locking clip, and pull the gas support strut off its balljoint mounting on the boot lid. Repeat the procedure on the lower strut mounting and remove the strut from the vehicle body **(see illustration). Note:** *If the gas strut is to be re-used, the locking clip must not be taken all the way out, or the clip will be damaged.*

16.7b ...and remove the tailgate handle/ release unit

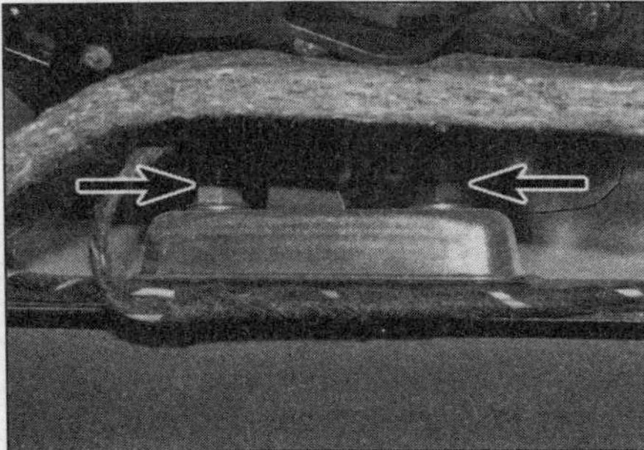

16.8 Release unit retaining nuts (arrowed) - Estate

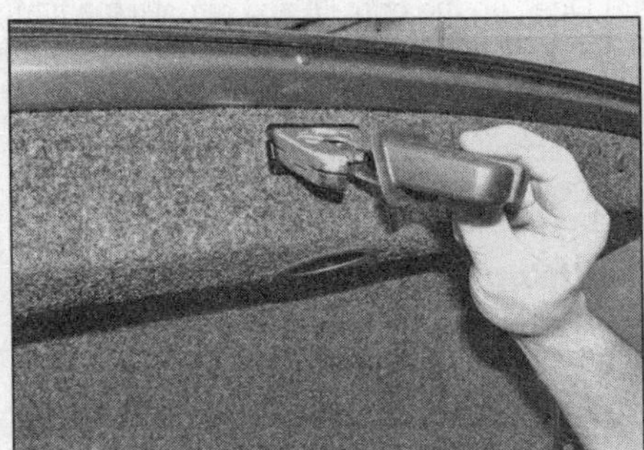

17.2a Remove the lock cover...

17.2b ...and emergency release lever cover...

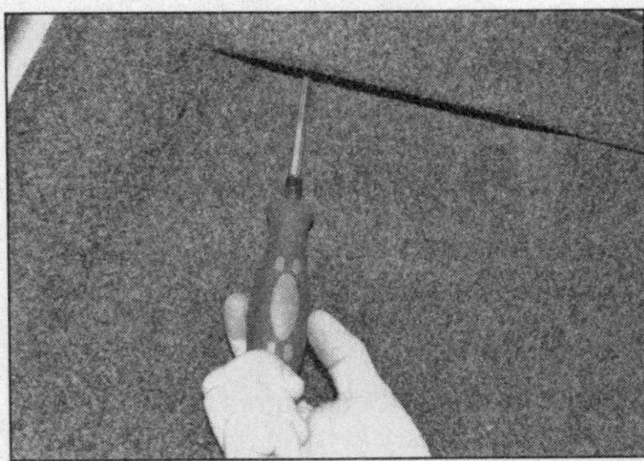

17.2c ...then unscrew the bolts from the handle recess...

17.2d ...and use a wide-blade tool to prise off the trim panel

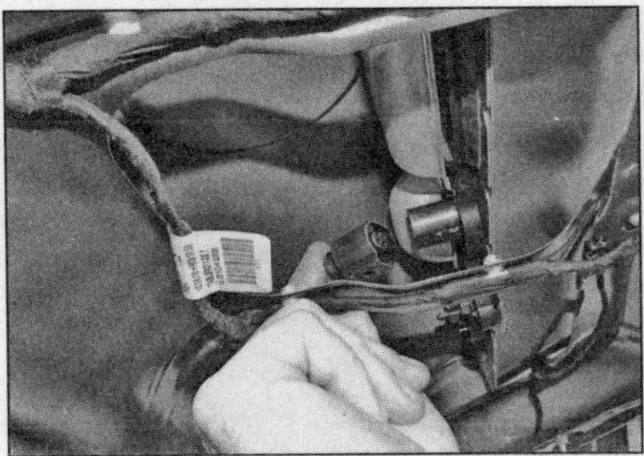

17.3a Rear lighting...

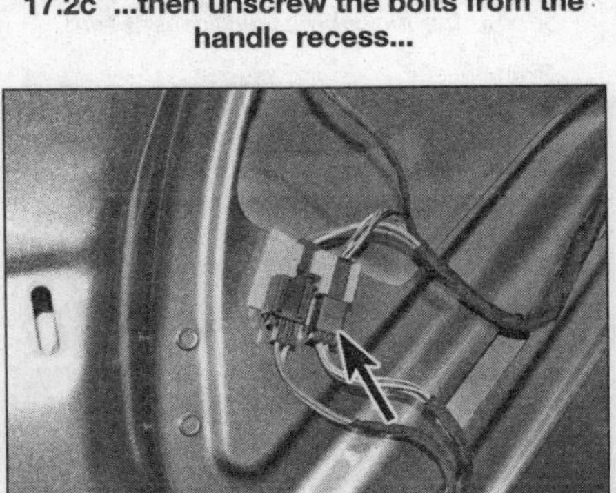

17.3b ...and boot lid wiring

17.8 Boot lid support strut lower balljoint mounting

17.10 Boot lid lock striker located on the rear valance

Refitting

Boot lid

9 Refitting is the reverse of removal, aligning the hinges with the marks made before removal.

10 On completion, close the boot lid and check its alignment with the surrounding panels. If necessary slight adjustment can be made by unscrewing the retaining nuts and repositioning the boot lid on its hinges. If further adjustment is required see the tailgate refitting procedure in Section 15. Slight adjustment is also possible by loosening the striker bolts and repositioning the striker **(see illustration)**.

Support struts

11 Refitting is a reverse of removal, ensuring the strut is securely retained by its clips.

18 Boot lid lock components – removal and refitting

Removal

Boot lid lock

1 Open up the boot lid then unclip and remove the outer cover from the boot lid lock.

2 Remove the trim panel as described in Section 17.

3 Reach into the boot lid and unclip the cover **(see illustration)**.

4 Disconnect the wiring from the lock.

18.3 Unclip the cover from the boot lid lock

5 Unhook the lock cylinder cable from the lock lever.

6 Undo the retaining nuts and withdraw the lock from the boot lid, then unhook the central locking cable.

Boot lid lock cylinder

7 Open up the boot lid and remove the trim panel as described in Section 17.

8 Reach into the boot lid and disconnect the wiring from the lock cylinder.

9 Unhook the cable from the lock cylinder.

10 Undo the retaining nuts and withdraw the lock cylinder.

Boot lid grip strip

11 Open up the boot lid and remove the trim panel as described in Section 17.

12 Remove the lock cylinder as described earlier.

13 Disconnect the wiring, then undo the retaining nuts and withdraw the grip strip from the boot lid **(see illustration)**.

Refitting

14 Refitting is a reversal of removal, but tighten the retaining nuts securely. Check the operation of the lock components on completion.

19 Central locking components – description, removal and refitting

Note: *Before disconnecting the battery, refer to 'Disconnecting the battery' at the rear of this manual.*

Description

1 The central locking system consists of the following main components. Note that the central locking and anti-theft alarm systems share some components (see Chapter 12):

a) Convenience system central control unit located behind the glovebox.
b) Door control units integrated in the window regulator motors.
c) Electric door lock actuators integrated in the door locks.
d) Fuel tank filler cap flap actuator located behind the luggage compartment trim.
e) Tailgate/boot lid lock actuator located in the tailgate/boot lid, together with the release button.
f) Anti-theft alarm horn located beneath the right-hand front wheel arch.
g) Bonnet contact switch located on the bonnet lock.
h) Remote control transmitter on the ignition key fob.

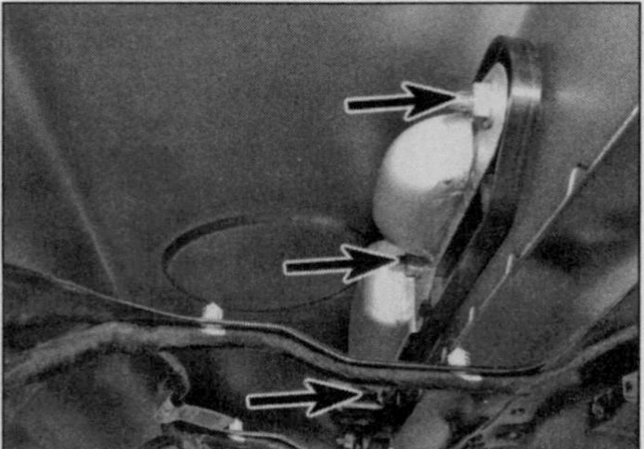

18.13 Boot lid grip strip retaining nuts

Removal

Convenience system control unit

2 Remove the glovebox as described in Section 27.

3 Disconnect the wiring from the control unit and remove it.

Door control unit

4 Remove the window regulator motor as described in Section 14.

Electric door lock actuator

5 Remove the door lock as described in Section 13.

Fuel tank filler cap flap actuator

6 Remove the right-hand trim from the luggage compartment with reference to Section 27.

7 Disconnect the wiring from the actuator.

8 Unscrew the mounting bolt and withdraw the actuator from the inner body panel.

Tailgate/boot lid lock activator

9 Remove the tailgate handle/release unit as described in Section 16.

Anti-theft alarm horn

10 Switch off the ignition.

11 Apply the handbrake, then jack up the front of the vehicle and support it on axle stands (see *Jacking and vehicle support*). Remove the right-hand front roadwheel.

12 Remove the wheel arch liner with reference to Section 23.

13 Use a drill to remove the pop rivets securing the horn to the inner body panel.

14 Withdraw the horn and disconnect the wiring.

Bonnet contact switch

15 Remove the bonnet lock as described in Section 10. If necessary, the operating cable may remain attached to the lock.

16 On the lock, release the tab and push the switch from the slotted holes.

Remote control transmitter battery

17 Using a screwdriver inserted in the slot, separate the transmitter unit from the key.

18 Prise apart the covers, then lever out the battery, noting which way round it is fitted.

Refitting

19 Refitting is a reversal of removal. Use new pop rivets when refitting the anti-theft alarm horn. On completion check the operation of the central locking system.

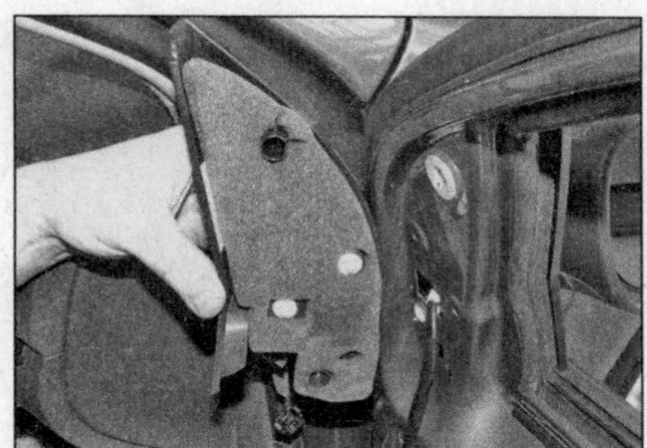

20.3 Removing the small trim panel for access to the exterior mirror mounting bolts

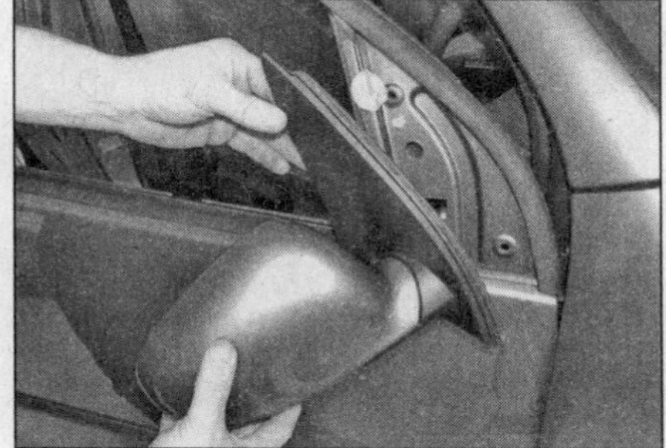

20.4a Removing the exterior mirror...

20.4b ...and gasket

20 Exterior mirrors and associated components – removal and refitting

Removal

Exterior mirror

1 Remove the door inner trim panel as described in Section 12.

2 Disconnect the wiring for the exterior mirror at the window regulator motor/control unit. Also, release the wiring from the support clips.

3 Remove the small trim panel **(see illustration)**, then prise out the cover over the front mounting bolt, and unscrew all the mounting bolts while supporting the exterior mirror.

4 Withdraw the exterior mirror from the door while guiding the wiring through the hole. If necessary, remove the gasket **(see illustrations)**.

Mirror glass

Note: *The mirror glass is clipped into place. Removal of the glass without the VW special forked tool (number 80-200) is likely to result in breakage of the glass. Wear protective gloves and glasses to prevent personal injury.*

5 Press in the bottom of the mirror glass so that the top edge is furthest from the housing. Protect the edge of the housing with masking tape, then insert the special tool and lever the mirror glass from its mounting clips. Take great care when removing the glass; do not use excessive force as the glass is easily broken. If the VW special tool is not available, use a flat-bladed lever with tape around to prevent any damage to the mirror housing **(see illustration)**.

6 Disconnect the wiring connectors from the mirror heating element **(see illustration)**.

Mirror housing

7 Remove the mirror glass as described in paragraphs 5 and 6.

8 The housing latches must now be released from the locking hooks. To do this, insert a screwdriver or similar tool between the front of the housing and the turn signal repeater lens, and slide it from the inside to the outside **(see illustration)**.

9 Pull the housing forwards from its mounting and withdraw it upwards **(see illustration)**.

Mirror switch

10 Refer to Chapter 12.

Refitting

11 Refitting is the reverse of the relevant removal procedure. When refitting the mirror glass, press firmly at the centre taking care not to use excessive force, as the glass is easily broken.

21 Windscreen and rear window glass – general information

These areas of glass are bonded in position with a special adhesive. Renewal of such fixed glass is a difficult, messy and time-consuming task, which is beyond the scope of the home mechanic. It is difficult, unless one has plenty of practice, to obtain a secure, waterproof fit. Furthermore, the task carries a high risk of breakage; this applies especially to the laminated glass windscreen. In view of this, owners are strongly advised to have this sort of work carried out by one of the many specialist windscreen fitters.

22 Sunroof – general information

Due to the complexity of the sunroof mechanism, considerable expertise is needed to repair, renew or adjust the sunroof components successfully. Removal of the roof first requires the headlining to be removed, which is a complex and tedious operation, and not a task to be undertaken lightly.

20.5 Remove the exterior mirror glass...

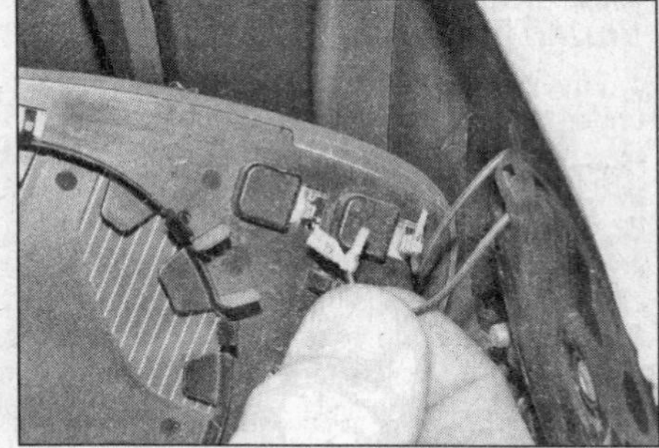

20.6 ...and disconnect the wiring

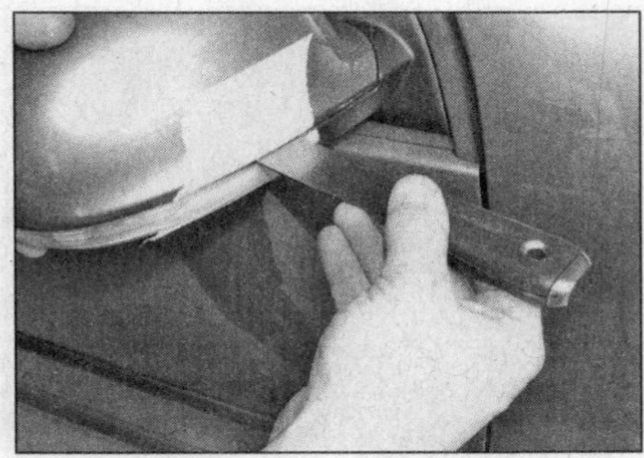

20.8 Releasing the mirror housing latches with a suitable tool

20.9 Removing the mirror housing

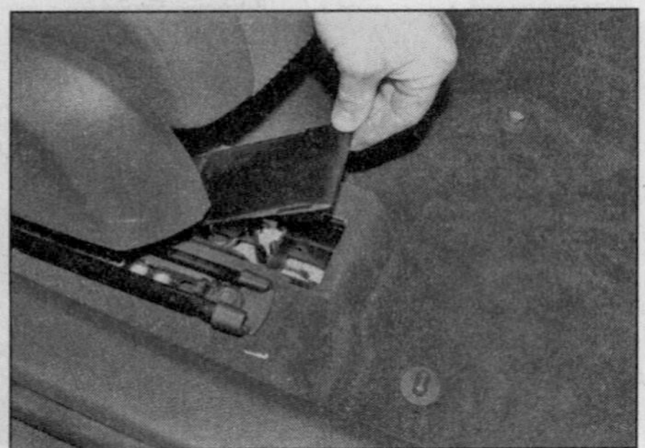

24.4 Remove the front seat wiring cover

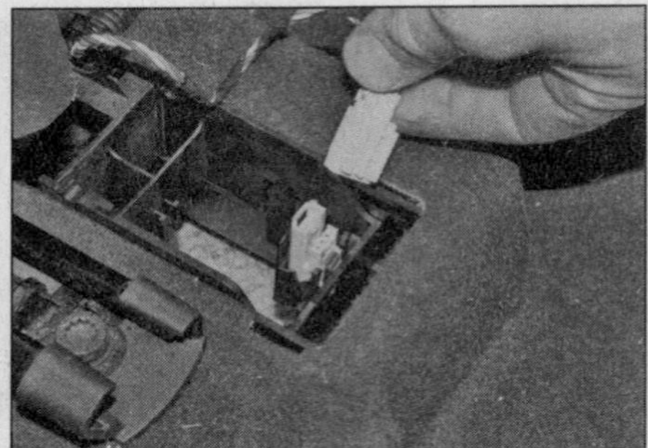

24.5 Disconnect the front seat wiring

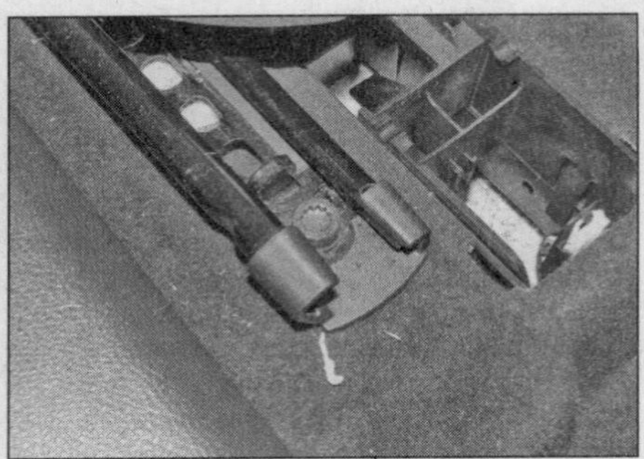

24.6 Front seat mounting bolt

Therefore, any problems with the sunroof should be referred to a VW dealer. On models with an electric sunroof, if the sunroof motor fails to operate, first check the relevant fuse. If the fault cannot be traced and rectified, the sunroof can be opened and closed manually using an Allen key to turn the motor spindle (a suitable key is supplied with the vehicle, and should be clipped onto the inside of the sunroof motor trim). To gain access to the motor, unclip the rear of the trim cover to open. Unclip the Allen key, then insert it fully into the motor opening (against spring pressure). Rotate the key to move the sunroof to the required position.

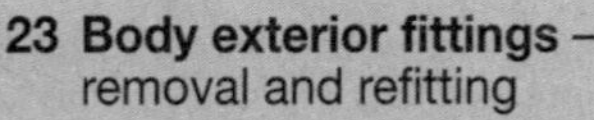

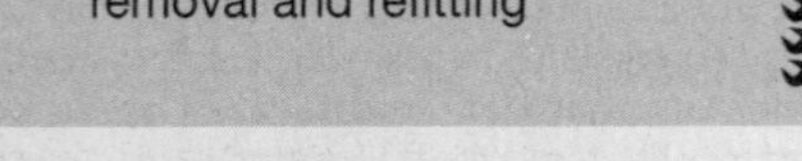

23 Body exterior fittings – removal and refitting

Wheel arch liners and body under-panels

1 The various plastic covers fitted to the underside of the vehicle are secured in position by a mixture of screws, nuts and retaining clips and removal will be fairly obvious on inspection. Work methodically around the panel removing its retaining screws and releasing its retaining clips until the panel is free and can be removed from the underside of the vehicle. Most clips used on the vehicle are simply prised out of position. Remove the wheels to ease the removal of the wheel arch liners.

2 On refitting, renew any retaining clips that may have been broken on removal, and ensure that the panel is securely retained by all the relevant clips and screws.

Body trim strips and badges

3 The various body trim strips and badges are held in position with a special adhesive tape and locating lugs. Removal requires the trim/badge to be heated, to soften the adhesive, and then carefully lifted away from the surface. Due to the high risk of damage to the vehicle's paintwork during this operation, it is recommended that this task should be entrusted to a VW dealer.

24 Seats – removal and refitting

Note: *Refer to the warnings in Chapter 12 on side airbags.*

Removal

Front seats

Note: *The amount of wiring connectors under the seat may, vary depending on the vehicle specification.*

1 Disconnect the battery negative lead (refer to *Disconnecting the battery* in the *Reference* Chapter at the end of this manual).

2 Where fitted, remove the drawer from the seat.

3 Slide the seat forwards as far as possible and unscrew the rear mounting bolts.

4 Slide the seat rearwards as far as possible then remove the wiring connector cover **(see illustration)**.

5 Disconnect the seat wiring **(see illustration)**. VW technicians fit an adapter to the airbag wiring connector as a safety precaution, however, wrap the connector with insulation tape instead.

Warning: As a precaution against unintentional electrostatic discharge into the airbag, briefly touch part of the vehicle body before disconnecting the wiring.

6 Unscrew the front mounting bolts **(see illustration)**.

7 Check that the wiring harness is released from any clips in the floor, then remove the seat from the vehicle. Do not lift the seat by the seat belt stalk or by the seat adjustment levers. If necessary, have an assistant help to remove the seat as it is heavy, and surrounding trim panels may be otherwise damaged.

Rear seat cushion

Hatchback models

8 At the rear of the seat cushion, unclip the four guides from the child seat mountings (where fitted).

9 Lift the front edge of the cushion from the location sockets, then push the cushion to the rear and pull upwards **(see illustrations)**.

Plus models

Note: *On these models, the cushion is removed along with the backrest.*

10 Slide the seat fully forwards, and undo the bolts at the rear end of the rails **(see illustration)**.

11 Prise out the plastic caps, and undo the 2 nuts at the front of the seat rails.

12 Remove the plastic trims, then slide the

24.9a Lift the front of the cushion...

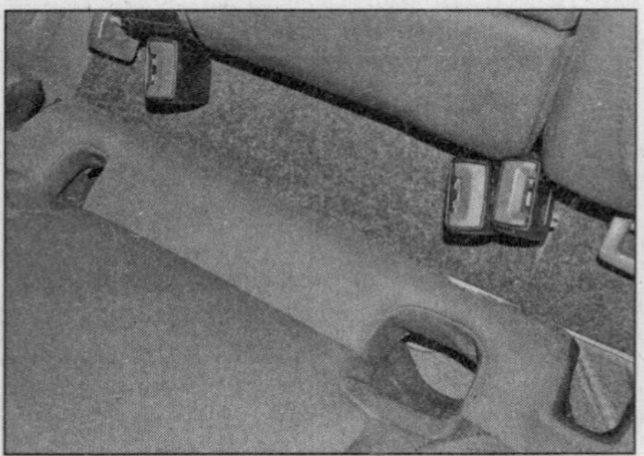

24.9b ...then release its rear edge from the seat belt stalks

24.10 Remove the bolts (arrowed) at the rear of the seat rails

seats forwards and manoeuvre them from the vehicle.

Estate models

13 Fold the seat cushion forwards, then press the hinge rods sideways to detach them from the hinge bracket.

Rear seat backrest

14 Remove the cushion as described in paragraphs 8 and 9.

15 Fold the backrest forwards, then pull back the carpet and remove the trim (where fitted) from the centre mounting **(see illustration)**.

16 Unbolt the clamp, then remove the right backrest by lifting it from the centre mounting and sliding it off the outer mounting pin **(see illustrations)**.

17 Unscrew the bolt and remove the centre stalk from the floor.

18 Remove the left backrest by lifting it from the centre mounting and sliding it off the outer mounting pin.

Refitting

19 Refitting is a reversal of removal, but tighten the mounting bolts to the specified torque where given.

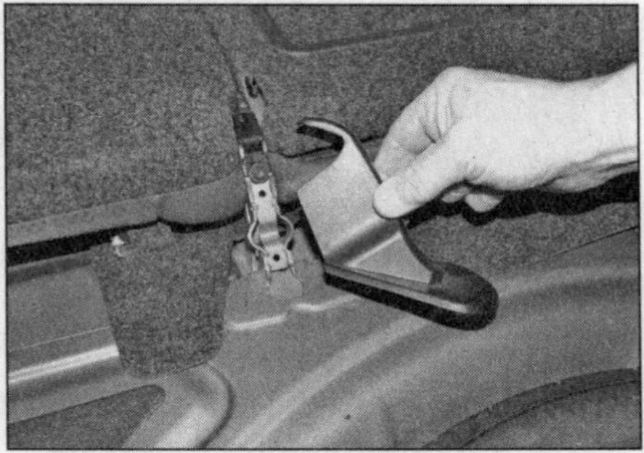

24.15 Remove the trim (where fitted) from the centre mounting...

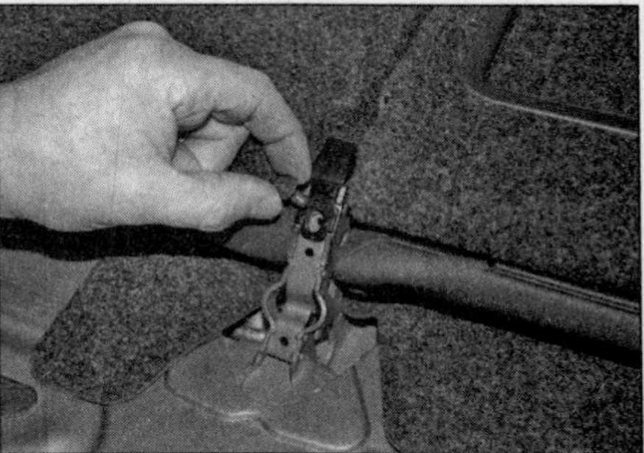

24.16a ...unbolt the clamp...

24.16b ...lift the rear seat backrest from the centre mounting...

24.16c ...and slide it off the outer mounting pin

25 Front seat belt tensioning mechanism – general information

All models covered in this manual are fitted with a front seat belt tensioner system incorporated in each of the inertia reels. Rear seat belt inertia reels with the tensioner system are only fitted to some models, other models having standard inertia reels.

The system is designed to instantaneously take up any slack in the seat belt in the case of a sudden frontal impact, therefore reducing the possibility of injury to the front seat occupants. The seat belt tensioner is triggered by a frontal impact above a predetermined force. Lesser impacts, including impacts from behind, will not trigger the system.

When the system is triggered, the explosive gas in the tensioner mechanism retracts and locks the seat belt. This prevents the seat belt moving and keeps the occupant firmly in position in the seat. Once the tensioner has been triggered, the seat belt will be permanently locked and the assembly must be renewed.

There is a risk of personal injury if the system is triggered inadvertently when working on the vehicle, and it is therefore strongly recommended that any work involving the seat belt inertia reels is entrusted to a VW dealer. Note the following warnings before contemplating any work on the front seat belts.

Warning: Do not expose the tensioner mechanism to temperatures in excess of 100°C.

- ***If the tensioner mechanism is dropped, it must be renewed, even it has suffered no apparent damage.***
- ***Do not allow any solvents to come into contact with the tensioner mechanism.***
- ***Do not attempt to open the tensioner mechanism as it contains explosive gas.***
- ***Tensioners must be discharged before they are disposed of, but this task should be entrusted to a VW dealer.***

26 Seat belt components – removal and refitting

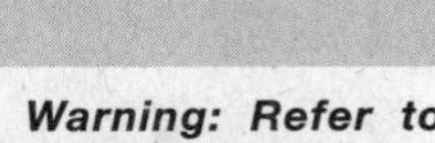

Warning: Refer to Section 25 before proceeding.

Front seat belt removal

4- and 5-door models

1 Disconnect the battery negative lead (refer to *Disconnecting the battery* in the *Reference* Chapter at the end of this manual).

2 Remove the upper and lower trim panels from the B-pillar with reference to Section 27.

3 Unscrew and remove the seat belt lower anchor mounting bolt and remove the belt from the floor. Note that the bolt is micro-encapsulated and must be heated with a hot air blower before being loosened. Protect the seat belt with a dampened cloth while heating the bolt. Discard the bolt and obtain a new one. Also, note that the threads of the corresponding nut must be cleaned with a tap before fitting the new bolt.

4 Unscrew the mounting bolt and remove the inertia reel from the bottom of the B-pillar. Disconnect the wiring from the reel.

Warning: As a precaution against unintentional electrostatic discharge, briefly touch part of the vehicle body before disconnecting the wiring.

5 Undo the screws and remove the belt guide from the B-pillar.

6 Unscrew and remove the bolt securing the seat belt upper anchor to the height adjuster on the B-pillar.

7 Remove the seat belt assembly from the vehicle.

8 To remove the belt height adjustment, remove the securing bolt and lift upwards from the pillar.

3-door models

9 Remove the relevant rear seat and backrest as described in Section 24.

10 Remove the upper trim panel from the B-pillar with reference to Section 27.

11 Remove the sill panel moulding and the side panel trim with reference to Section 27.

12 Unscrew the bolts securing the anchor rail to the sill, and slide the rail from the end of the seat belt **(see illustration)**.

13 On models without rear seat belt tensioners, unscrew the mounting bolt and withdraw the inertia reels.

14 On models with rear seat belt tensioners, disconnect the battery negative lead (refer to *'Disconnecting the battery'* in the *Reference* Chapter at the end of this manual), then unscrew the inertia reel mounting bolt,

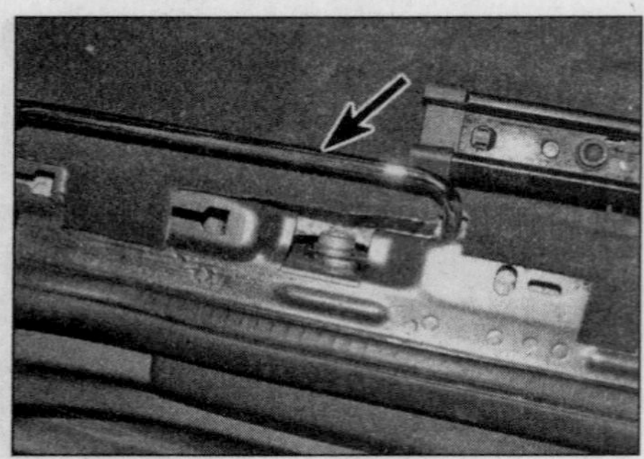
26.12 Front seat belt anchor rail on the sill

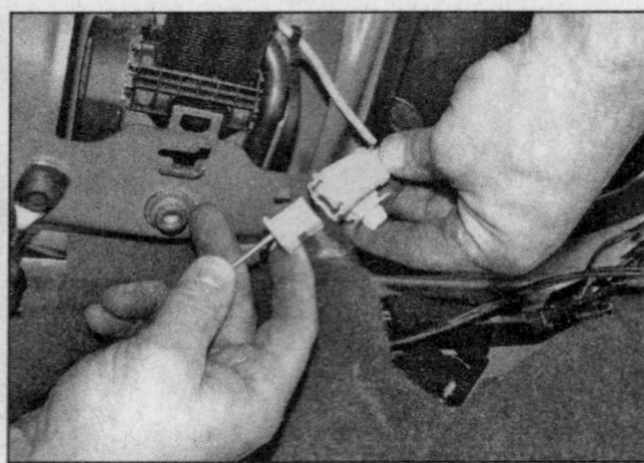
26.14a Disconnecting the wiring

26.14b Front seat belt inertia reel

26.16 Front seat belt upper anchor

withdraw the reel and disconnect the wiring **(see illustrations)**.

Warning: As a precaution against unintentional electrostatic discharge, briefly touch part of the vehicle body before disconnecting the wiring.

15 Undo the screws and remove the belt guide from the B-pillar.

16 Unscrew and remove the bolt securing the seat belt upper anchor to the height adjuster on the B-pillar **(see illustration)**.

17 Remove the seat belt assembly from the vehicle.

18 To remove the belt height adjustment, remove the securing bolt and lift upwards from the pillar.

Front seat belt stalk removal

19 Remove the front seat assembly as described in Section 24.

20 Unscrew and remove the bolt securing the stalk to the seat, and remove the stalk. On 3-door models, the stalk must be turned through 90° in order to remove it. Note that the bolt is micro-encapsulated and must be heated with a hot air blower before being loosened. Protect the seat belt with a dampened cloth while heating the bolt. Discard the bolt and obtain a new one. Also, note that the threads of the corresponding nut must be cleaned with a tap before fitting the new bolt.

Rear seat side belt removal

4- and 5-door models (except Estate)

21 Remove the rear seat cushion as described in Section 24.

22 Remove the side panel trim. **Note:** *Refer to Chapter 12 on models with rear side airbags.*

23 Remove the luggage compartment cover side support.

24 Remove the roof frame trim.

25 Remove the trim from the C-pillar.

26 Unbolt the belt from the floor anchorage.

27 On models without rear seat belt tensioners, unscrew the mounting bolt and withdraw the inertia reel **(see illustration)**.

28 On models with rear seat belt tensioners, disconnect the battery negative lead (refer to *'Disconnecting the battery'* in the *'Reference'* Chapter at the end of this manual), then unscrew the inertia reel mounting bolt, withdraw the reel and disconnect the wiring.

Warning: As a precaution against unintentional electrostatic discharge, briefly touch part of the vehicle body before disconnecting the wiring.

3-door models

29 Remove the upper trim from the B-pillar with reference to Section 27 **(see illustrations)**.

30 Remove the rear seat cushion and backrest as described in Section 24.

31 Remove the sill inner trim panel with reference to Section 27 **(see illustration)**.

32 Pull the lock carrier cover from its mountings, then undo the screws and remove the support. Disconnect the wiring from the support **(see illustration)**.

33 Remove the luggage compartment side trim, the roof frame trim and the C-pillar trim with reference to Section 27 **(see illustrations)**.

34 Unscrew the bolt and remove the belt anchor from the floor **(see illustration)**.

26.27 Rear side seat belt inertia reel mounting bolt

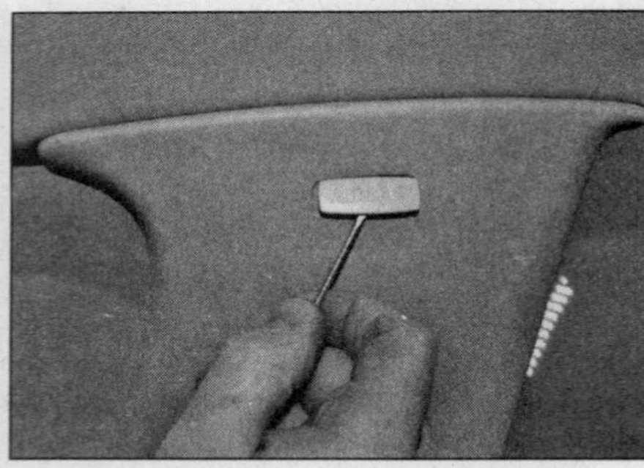
26.29a Prise out the cover...

26.29b ...undo the screw...

26.29c ...then unclip the upper trim from the B-pillar

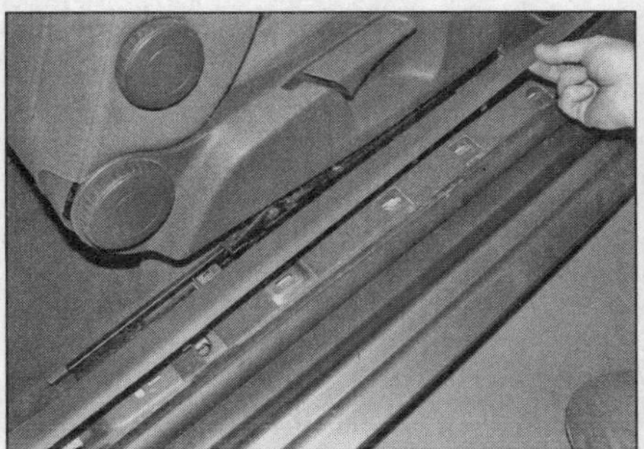

26.31 Remove the sill inner trim panel

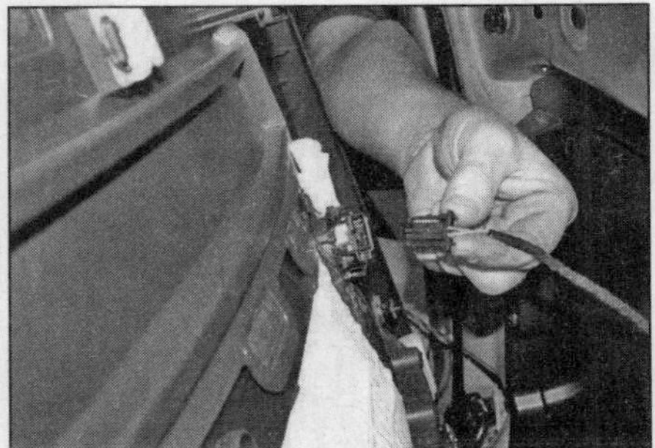

26.32 Disconnecting the wiring from the support

26.33a Remove the side trim...

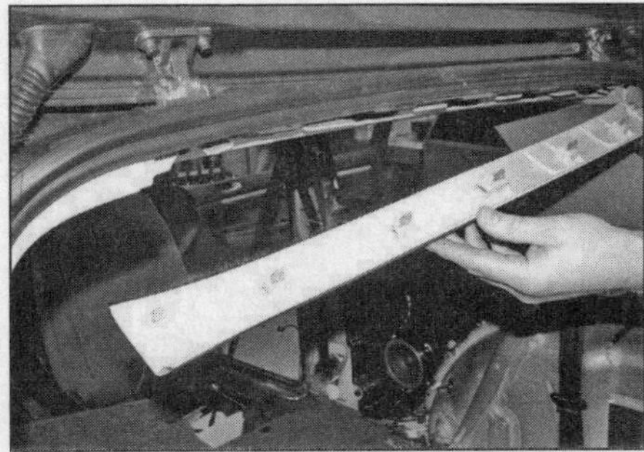

26.33b ...the roof frame trim...

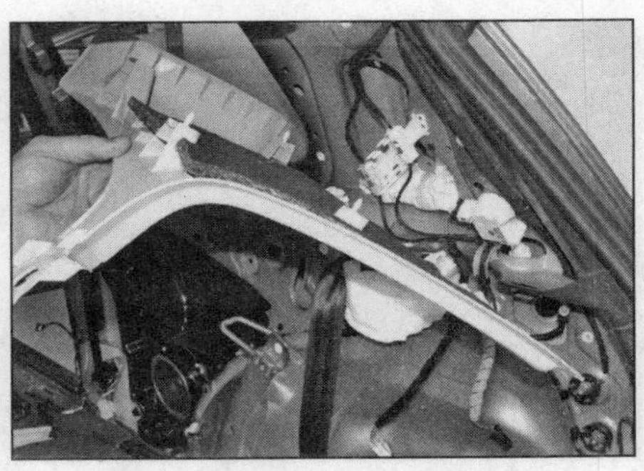

26.33c ...and the C-pillar trim

26.34 Unbolt the belt anchor from the floor

35 On models without rear seat belt tensioners, unscrew the mounting bolt and withdraw the inertia reel **(see illustration)**.

36 On models with rear seat belt tensioners, disconnect the battery negative lead (refer to *'Disconnecting the battery'* in the *'Reference'* Chapter at the end of this manual), then disconnect the wiring from the reel.

Warning: As a precaution against unintentional electrostatic discharge, briefly touch part of the vehicle body before disconnecting the wiring.

Estate models

37 On models with side airbags, disconnect the battery negative lead (refer to *'Disconnecting the battery'* in the *'Reference'* Chapter at the end of this manual.

38 Remove the rear seat backrest.

39 Prise out the cap and undo the screw at the upper side of the side trim padding – models with side airbags only.

40 Undo the nut at the base of the side padding, then pull the padding upwards from its mountings **(see illustrations)**.

41 Lift the luggage compartment floor, undo the 4 bolts and manoeuvre it from place **(see illustration)**.

42 Open the floor storage compartment, and undo the support strap lower bolt **(see illustration)**.

43 Lift up the 3 plastic covers at the front

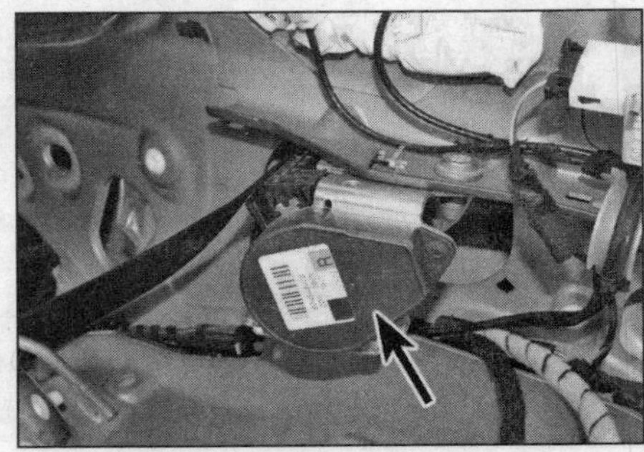

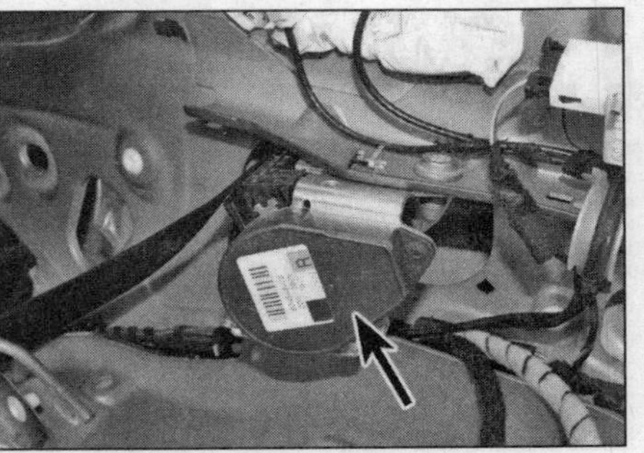

26.35 Rear seat side belt inertia reel

26.40a Undo the nut at the base of the side padding

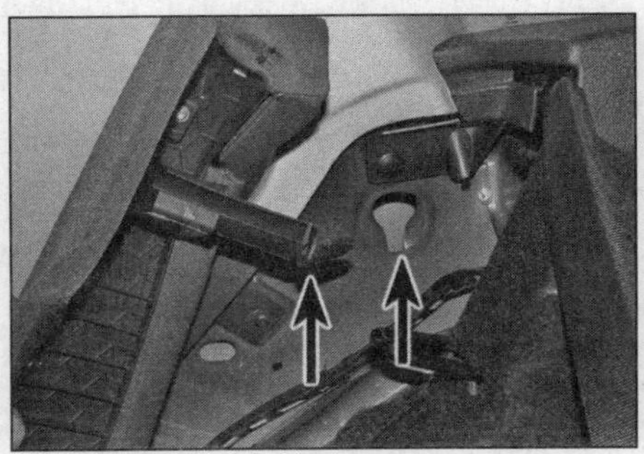

26.40b Note how the fitting at the top of the side padding engages...

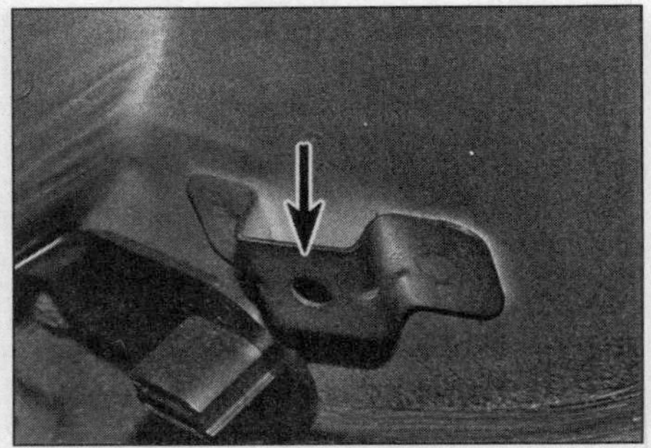

26.40c ...and at the base

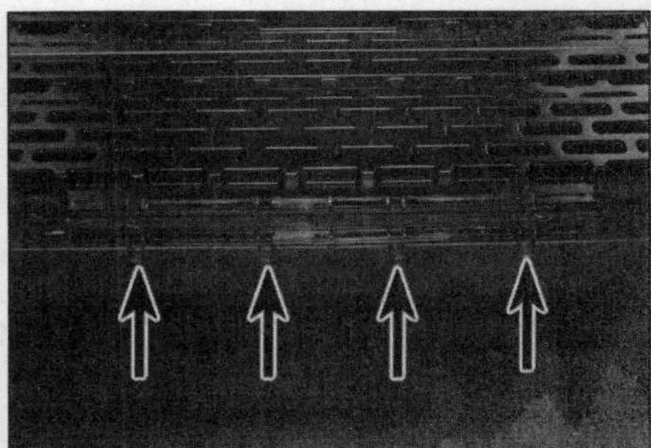

26.41 Luggage compartment floor retaining bolts

26.42 Undo the screw securing the strap

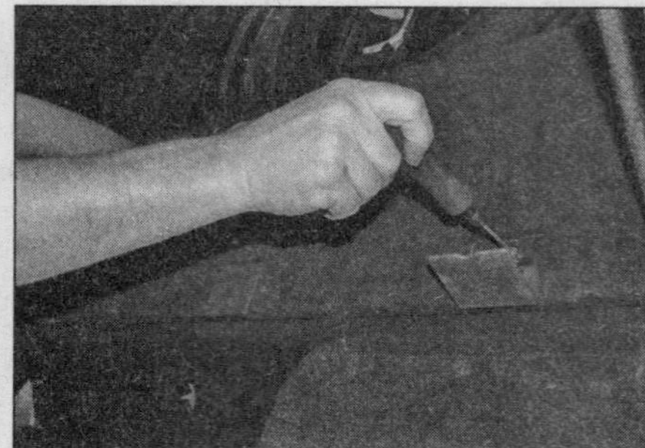
26.43 Lift up the covers, and undo the screws

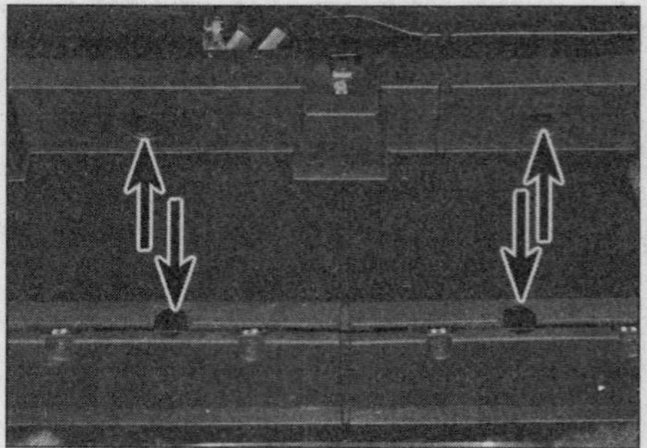
26.45a Undo the screws and nuts...

26.45b ...then slide the floor lining assembly upwards and forwards

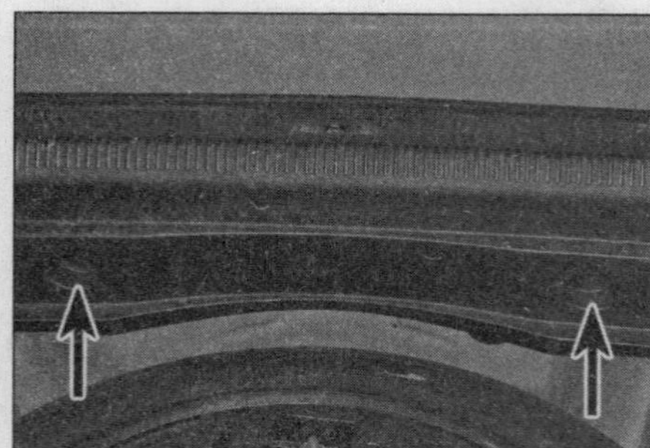
26.46a Unscrew the plastic nuts...

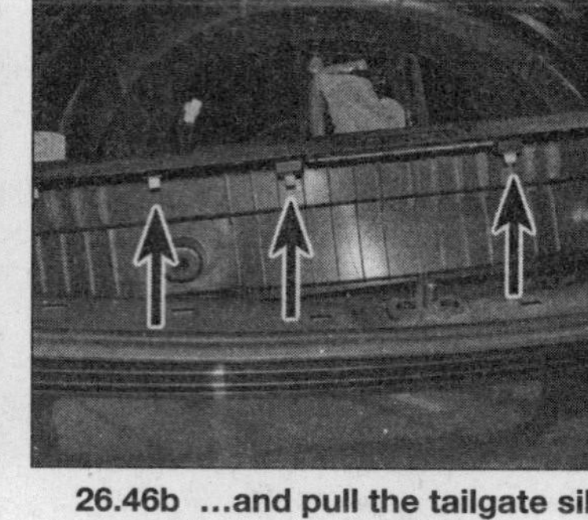
26.46b ...and pull the tailgate sill trim panel upwards to release the clips

edge, undo the retaining bolts and manoeuvre the storage compartment from place **(see illustration)**.

44 Remove the cover from over the spare wheel.

45 Undo the 2 nuts, and 2 bolts, the pull up the front edge of the floor lining assembly, then slide it forwards and remove it **(see illustrations)**.

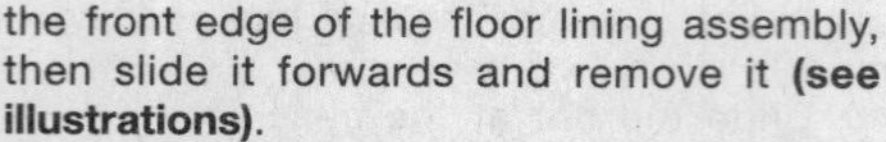

46 Undo the 2 plastic nuts and pull the tailgate sill trim panel upwards from the retaining clips **(see illustrations)**.

47 Undo the retaining bolts and remove the luggage anchorages **(see illustrations)**.

48 Remove the plastic 'scrivet' at the front, upper edge, then pull the luggage compartment side panel inwards to release the retaining clips **(see illustration)**. Take care when unclipping the panel from the D-pillar trim panel. Where applicable, disconnect the power outlet socket wiring plug as the panel is withdrawn.

49 Undo the seat belt lower anchorage bolt.

50 If required, undo the bolts securing the seat belt guide **(see illustration)**.

51 Lift up the rubber cover, remove the seat belt inertia reel retaining bolt, and manoeuvre the assembly from the vehicle. Disconnect any wiring plugs as the reel is withdrawn **(see illustration)**.

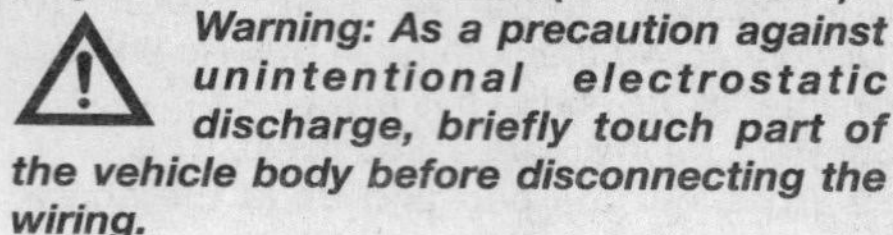

Warning: As a precaution against unintentional electrostatic discharge, briefly touch part of the vehicle body before disconnecting the wiring.

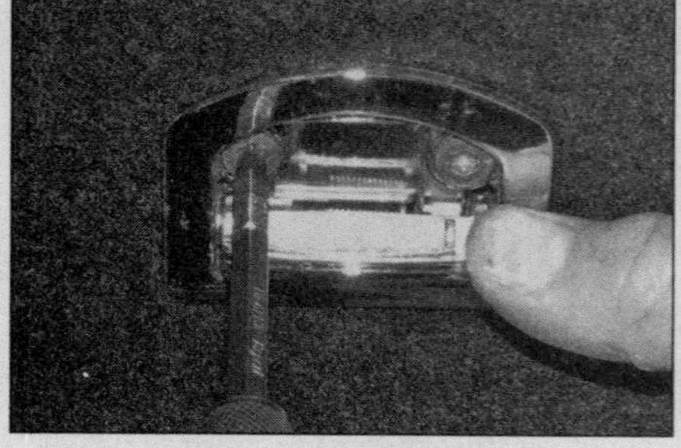
26.47a Undo the 2 bolts securing the luggage anchor...

26.47b ...and the single bolt securing the hook

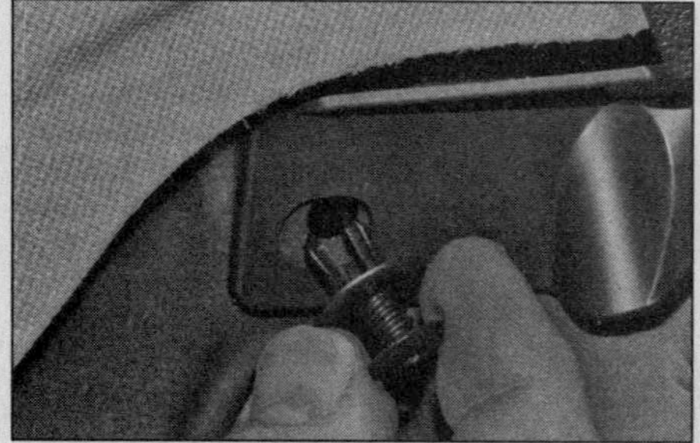
26.48 Undo the central screw, and pull out the 'scrivet' at the front, upper corner of the side panel

26.50 Seat belt guide bolts

26.51 Inertia reel retaining bolt

26.53 Rear seat belt centre buckle

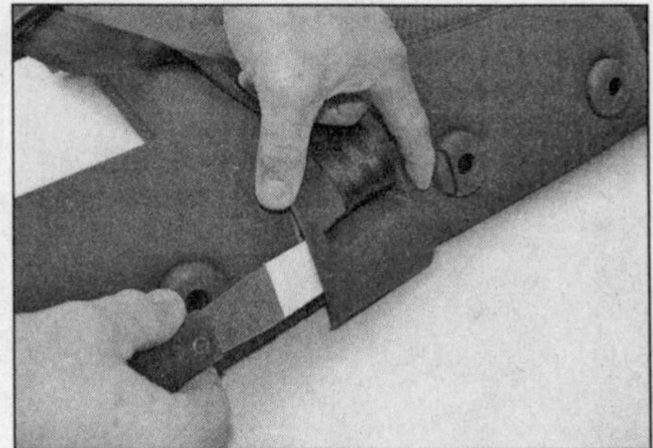
26.54a Prise out...

26.54b ...and remove the belt guide

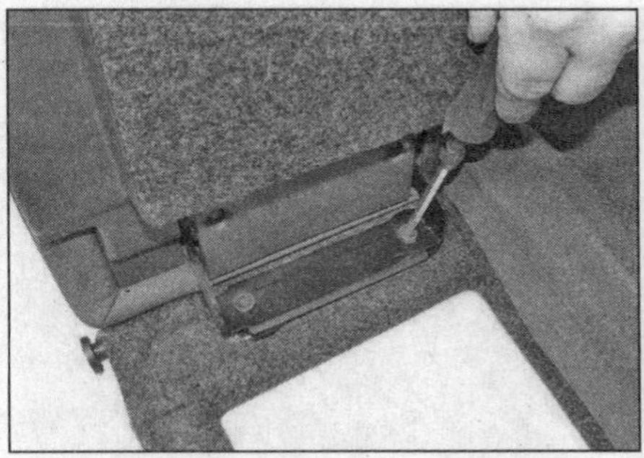
26.55 Removing the hinge screws

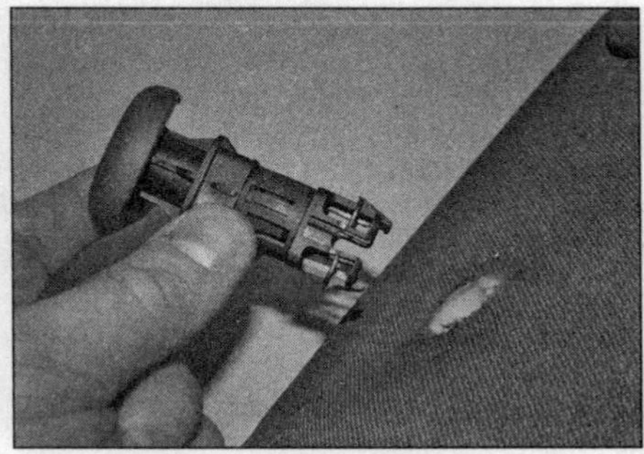
26.56 Removing the headrest guides

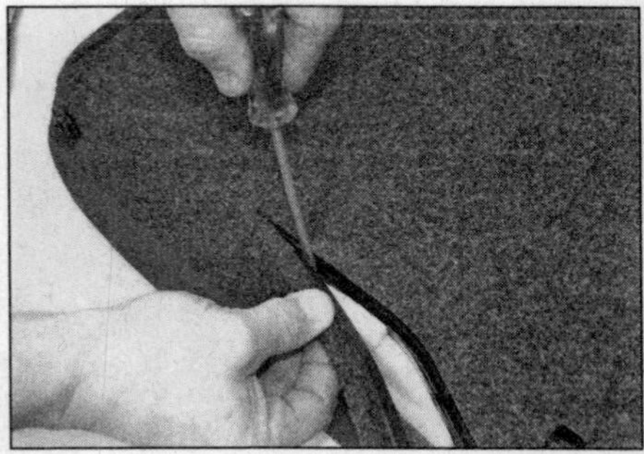
26.57 Prise out the moulding

Rear seat centre belt and buckle removal

52 Remove the rear seat cushion and backrest as described in Section 25.

53 Unscrew and remove the bolt securing the centre belt and/or buckle assembly to the floor, and remove it from the vehicle **(see illustration)**.

54 To remove the inertia reel, first prise the belt guide from the top of the backrest **(see illustrations)**.

55 Undo the screws and remove the hinge **(see illustration)**.

56 Press down the padding around the headrest guides, then use a screwdriver to release the locking lugs and pull out the headrest guides **(see illustration)**.

57 Carefully prise the moulding from the edge of the backrest **(see illustration)**.

58 Unbolt and remove the inertia reel **(see illustration)**.

26.58 Inertia reel retaining bolt

Refitting

59 Refitting is a reversal of the removal procedure, ensuring that all the seat belt units are located correctly and mounting bolts are securely tightened to their specified torque. Check all the trim panels are securely retained by all the relevant retaining clips. When refitting the upper trim panels, ensure that the height adjustment levers engage correctly with the seat belt upper mounting bolt head.

27 Interior trim – removal and refitting

Interior trim panels

1 The interior trim panels are secured using either screws or various types of trim fasteners, usually studs or clips **(see illustration)**.

2 Check that there are no other panels overlapping the one to be removed; usually there is a sequence that has to be followed, and this will only become obvious on close inspection.

3 Remove all obvious fasteners, such as screws. If the panel will not come free, it is held by hidden clips or fasteners. These are usually situated around the edge of the panel and can be prised up to release them; note, however, that they can break quite easily so new ones should be available. The best way of releasing such clips, without the correct type of tool, is to use a large flat-bladed screwdriver. Note in many cases that the adjacent sealing strip must be prised back to release a panel.

4 When removing a panel, **never** use excessive force or the panel may be damaged; always check carefully that all fasteners or other relevant components have been removed or released before attempting to withdraw a panel.

5 Refitting is the reverse of the removal procedure; secure the fasteners by pressing them firmly into place and ensure that all disturbed components are correctly secured to prevent rattles.

Glovebox

6 Switch off the ignition.

7 Using a screwdriver, lever out the facia end panel on the passenger side.

8 Remove the sill inner trim and the A-pillar lower trim.

9 Lever out the centre trim from under the facia.

10 Open up the glovebox lid then unscrew

27.1 The rear parcel shelf support is secured with screws on 5-door models

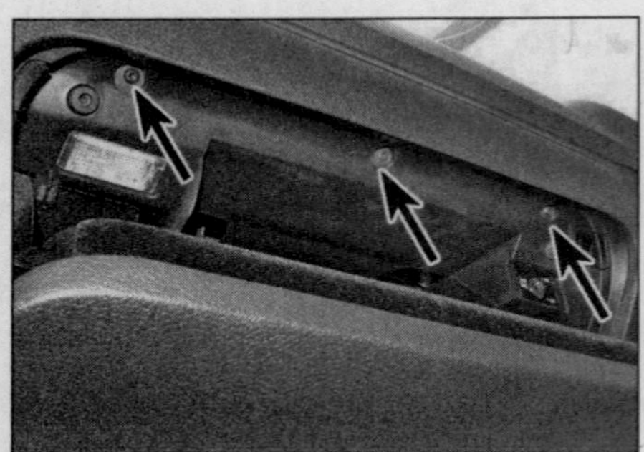
27.10a Glovebox upper...

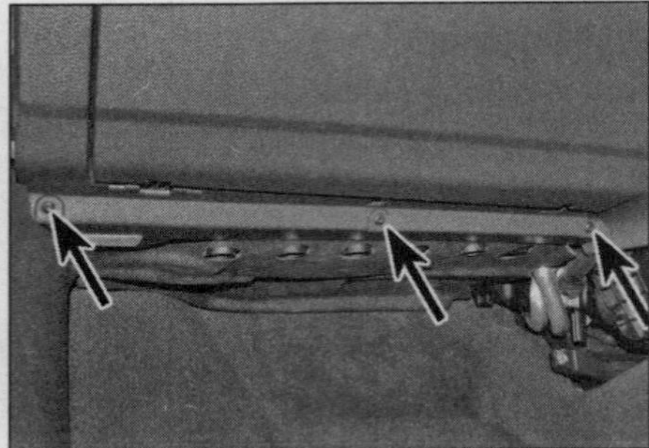
27.10b ...and lower securing screws

27.10c Disconnect the wiring from the illumination light...

27.10d ...and passenger airbag isolation switch...

27.10e ...then withdraw the glovebox...

27.10f ...and disconnect the hose for the air conditioning cooling

and remove the seven retaining screws. Slide the glovebox out of position, disconnecting the wiring connector from the glovebox illumination light as it becomes accessible. Where fitted, also disconnect the wiring from the passenger airbag isolation switch, and disconnect the air conditioning cooling hose **(see illustrations)**.

11 Refitting is the reverse of removal.

Carpets

12 The passenger compartment floor carpet is in one piece and is secured at its edges by screws or clips, usually the same fasteners used to secure the various adjoining trim panels.

13 Carpet removal and refitting is reasonably straightforward but very time-consuming because all adjoining trim panels must be removed first, as must components such as the seats, the centre console and seat belt lower anchorages.

Headlining

14 The headlining is clipped to the roof and can be withdrawn only once all fittings such as the grab handles, sun visors, sunroof (if fitted), and related upper trim panels have been removed and the door, tailgate and sunroof aperture sealing strips have been prised clear. To remove the sun visors and grab handles the plastic covers have to be unclipped first, to gain access to the securing screws.

15 Note that headlining removal requires considerable skill and experience if it is to be carried out without damage and is therefore best entrusted to an expert.

Interior mirror

16 To remove the interior mirror, turn the mirror arm anti-clockwise by 90° to release it from the baseplate. When refitting, place the mirror at 90° to the mounted position, then turn until the locking clip locks into place to secure the mirror. On models fitted with rain sensor, unclip the trim around the stem of the mirror and disconnect the wiring connector, then slide the mirror first along and then downwards from the mounting. Note that the base is attached to the windscreen with glass-metal adhesive.

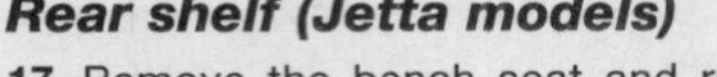

Rear shelf (Jetta models)

17 Remove the bench seat and rear side padding on both sides.

18 Remove the C-pillar trim on both sides.

19 Unclip the seat belt trim from the shelf.

20 Remove the seat belt anchor on both sides. Also, where applicable, remove the child seat anchors.

21 Release the retaining clips by lifting the front of the shelf upwards, then pull the shelf forwards to unhook the guide pins.

22 Remove the rear shelf while releasing the trim at the same time.

23 Refitting is a reversal of removal.

28.2a Release the gaiter from the centre console...

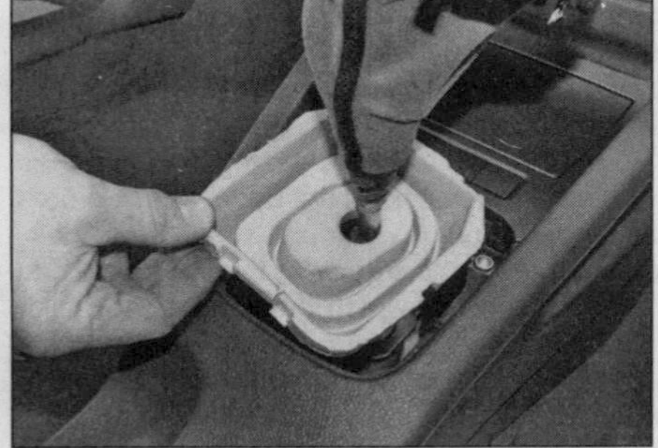
28.2b ...and remove the insulation pad...

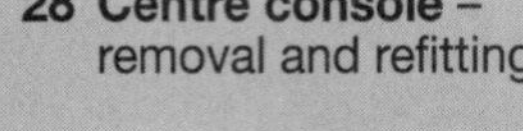

28 Centre console – removal and refitting

Removal

Low specification models

1 Switch off the ignition.

2 Release the gear/selector lever gaiter from the centre console (see Chapter 7A or 7B). Also, release the insulation pad from the lever **(see illustrations)**.

3 Pull the trim forwards off the handbrake lever.

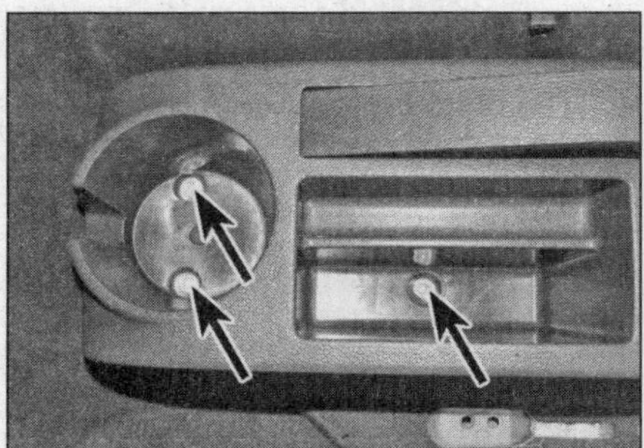
28.4 ...then undo the screws...

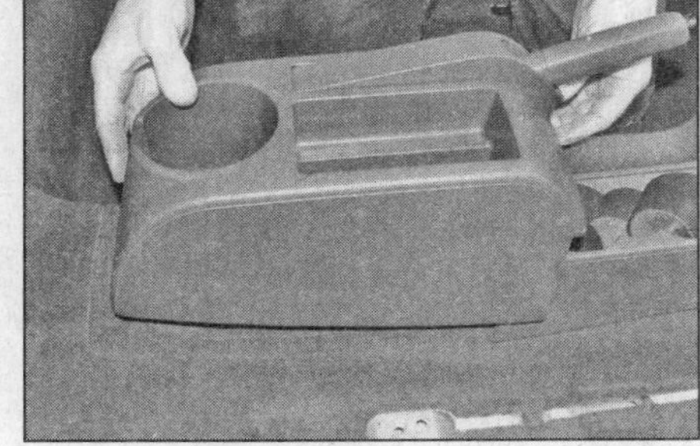
28.5 ...then withdraw the rear console forwards over the handbrake lever

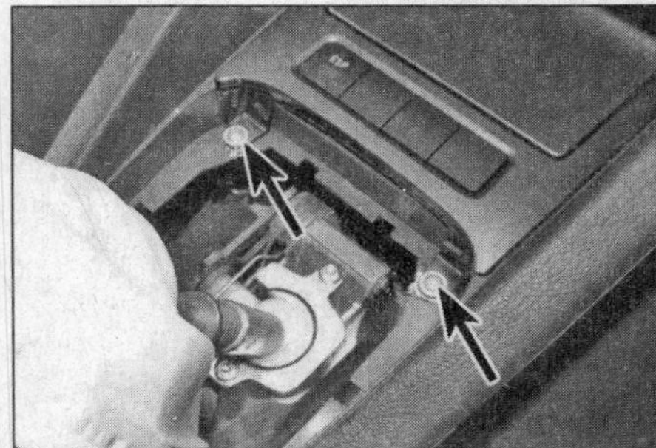
28.6a Undo the screws...

4 Remove the lining mats from the rear console oddments recesses, then undo the screws now visible **(see illustration)**.

5 Lift the rear console and withdraw it forwards over the handbrake lever **(see illustration)**. Disconnect the wiring as applicable.

6 Undo the screws and remove the front storage compartment or ashtray as applicable, then remove the switch panel **(see illustrations)**. Disconnect the wiring as applicable.

7 Prise out the covers and undo the lower side cover retaining screws. Unclip the lower covers from the centre console and remove **(see illustrations)**.

8 Prise out the small upper side covers from each side **(see illustration)**.

9 Undo the mounting screws and withdraw the centre console from inside the vehicle **(see illustrations)**.

28.6b ...and remove the ashtray...

28.6c ...then remove the switch panel

High specification models

10 Switch off the ignition.

11 Release the gear/selector lever gaiter from the centre console (see Chapter 7A or 7B). Also, release the insulation pad from the lever.

12 Pull the trim forwards off the handbrake lever.

13 On models with a CD changer, remove it as described in Chapter 12, then lift out the lining mat and undo the screw now visible.

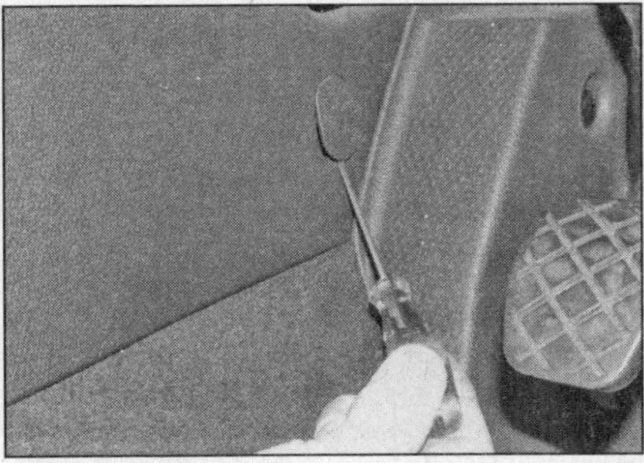
28.7a Prise out the covers and undo the lower side screws...

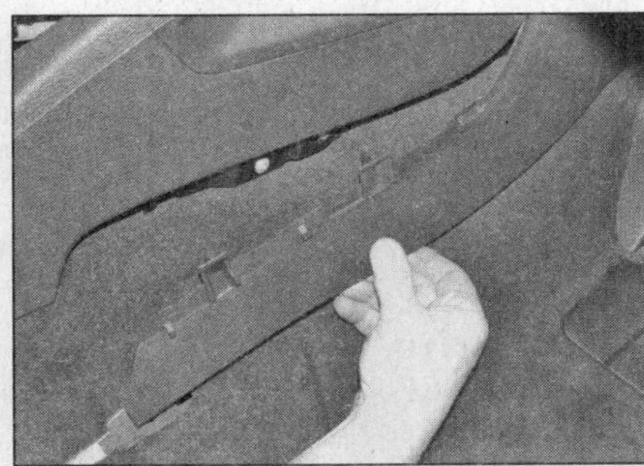
28.7b ...then unclip the lower covers

28.8 Prise out the side covers...

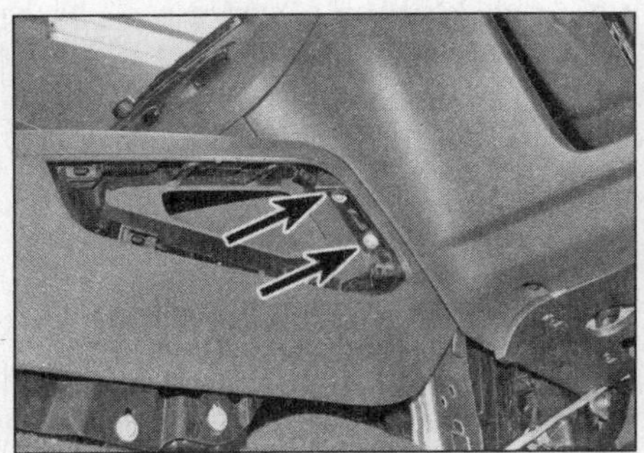
28.9a ...undo the front screws...

28.9b ...and rear screw...

28.9c ...and withdraw the centre console

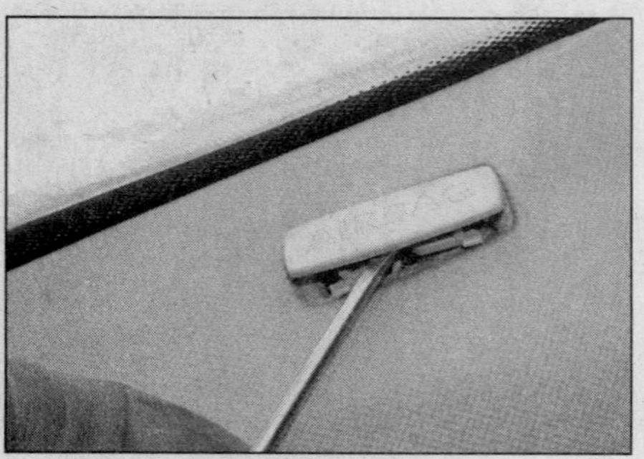

29.4a Prise out the covers...

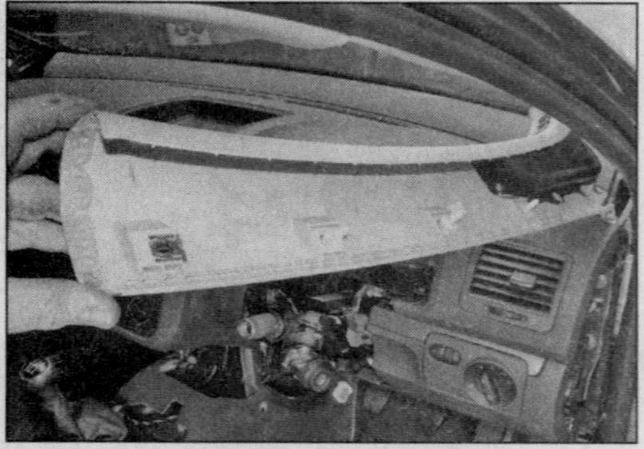

29.4c ...then unclip the A-pillar upper trim

14 On models with a cooled storage compartment, remove the lining mat, pull out the cover, and undo the screw now visible.

15 Open the drinks holder, undo the screws and remove the drinks holder from the rear of the centre console.

29.8a Lift out the lining mat and undo the screws...

29.8c Remove the centre vent panel...

29.4b ...undo the screws...

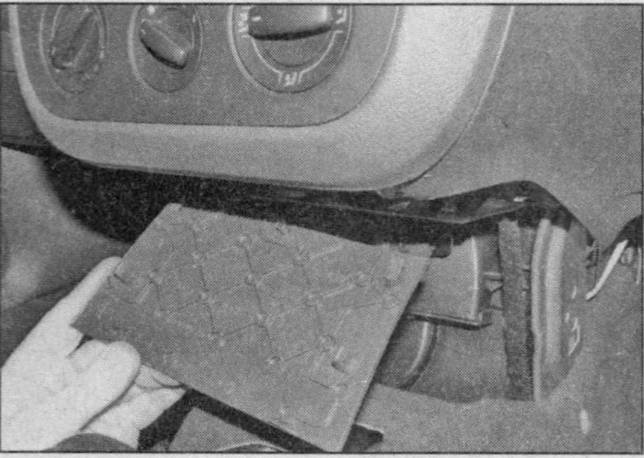

29.5 Remove the centre cover under the facia

16 Remove the rear cover from the centre console, by pulling out the lower edge, then unclipping the upper edge.

17 Undo the screws and unclip the rear console.

18 Undo the screws and remove the front storage compartment or ashtray as applicable. Disconnect the wiring as applicable.

29.8b ...then remove the storage compartment

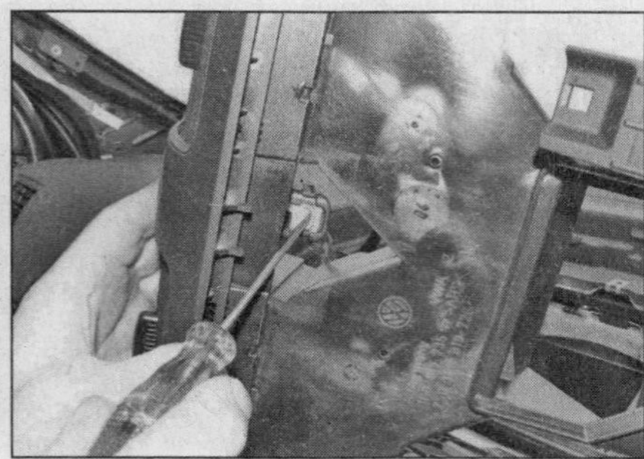

29.8d ...and disconnect the wiring

19 Prise out the covers and undo the lower side cover retaining screws. Unclip the lower covers from the centre console and remove.

20 Prise out the small upper side covers from each side.

21 Remove the lining mat from the storage compartment, then undo the mounting screws and withdraw the centre console from inside the vehicle.

Refitting

22 Refitting is a reversal of removal, but tighten the screws securing the centre console to the facia first, before tightening the rest.

29 Facia panel assembly – removal and refitting

Note: *Refer to the warnings in Chapter 12 for airbags. Before disconnecting the battery, refer to 'Disconnecting the battery' at the rear of this manual.*

Label each wiring connector as it is disconnected from its component. The labels will prove useful on refitting, when routing the wiring and feeding the wiring through the facia apertures.

Removal

1 Disconnect the battery negative lead (refer to *Disconnecting the battery* in the *Reference* Chapter at the end of this manual).

2 Remove the steering wheel as described in Chapter 10.

3 Prise out the trim panels from each end of the facia.

4 Prise out the covers, then undo the screws and remove the A-pillar upper trim **(see illustrations)**.

5 Prise out the centre cover from under the facia **(see illustration)**.

6 Remove the glovebox as described in Section 27.

7 Remove the centre console as described in Section 28.

8 Remove the facia centre vent panel as follows:

a) *On models without Climatronic, lift out the lining mat from the storage compartment on the top of the facia, then undo the screws now visible. Remove the storage compartment **(see illustrations)**.*

b) *On models with Climatronic, prise out the sunlight sensor, disconnect the wiring, and undo the screw now visible. Using a screwdriver at the front of the panel, push the panel rearwards and lift it from the vent panel.*

c) *On all models, undo the screws (where fitted) and slightly lift the front of the centre vent panel, then use a screwdriver to prise the centre vent panel from the facia. Disconnect the wiring **(see illustrations)**.*

29.9a Undo the screws...

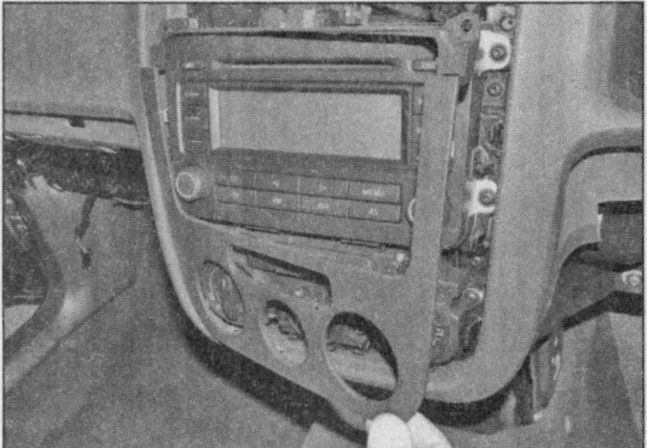

29.9b ...then prise the centre trim from the facia

29.12a Undo the screws...

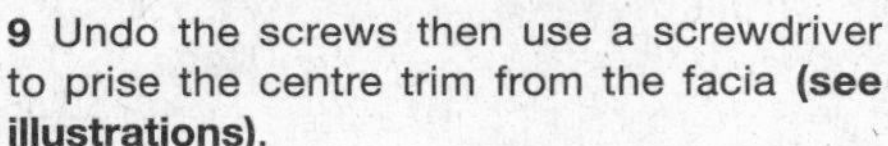

29.12b ...then remove the heater controls and disconnect the wiring

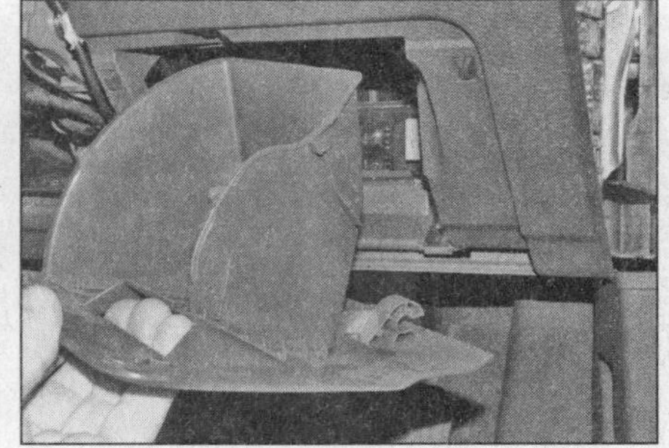

29.18a Open and remove the storage compartment...

29.18b ...then undo the screws, remove the facia trim panel, and disconnect the wiring

9 Undo the screws then use a screwdriver to prise the centre trim from the facia **(see illustrations)**.

10 Remove the radio or navigation unit as described in Chapter 12.

11 On models with Climatronic, remove the display and operating unit.

12 On models with the standard heating unit, remove the heater controls **(see illustrations)**.

13 Remove the steering column shrouds as follows:

a) *Undo the screws and remove the column height and reach adjustment handle.*

b) *Undo the two upper screws and single lower screw and remove the lower shroud from the steering column. As the shroud is being removed, release it from the height and reach adjustment handle.*

c) *Carefully prise out the gap cover, then remove the upper shroud from the steering column.*

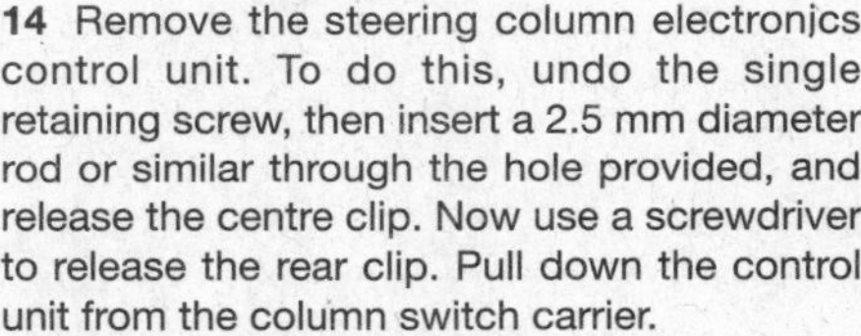

14 Remove the steering column electronics control unit. To do this, undo the single retaining screw, then insert a 2.5 mm diameter rod or similar through the hole provided, and release the centre clip. Now use a screwdriver to release the rear clip. Pull down the control unit from the column switch carrier.

15 The airbag clock spring/slip-ring must be held in its centre position while it is removed, to ensure correct refitting. Unclip the airbag clock spring/slip-ring from the combination switch carrier by lifting the retaining hooks.

16 On models with ESP, pull the steering angle sensor directly away from the combination switch carrier.

17 Remove the windscreen wiper and indicator switches by inserting a 1.0 mm feeler gauge through the slot provided to release the switch from the carrier.

18 Remove the facia trim panel located on the outside of the steering column as follows:

a) *Depress the light switch and turn it clockwise until vertical, then remove it and disconnect the wiring.*

b) *Open and remove the storage compartment* ***(see illustration)****.*

c) *Undo the retaining screws, then withdraw the facia trim panel and disconnect the wiring from the headlight range control regulator* ***(see illustration)****.*

19 Undo the retaining screws, then remove the facia trim panel located on the inside of the steering column **(see illustration)**.

20 Undo the two lower retaining screws and carefully pull the instrument panel from the facia. The electrical contacts will separate automatically from the rear of the panel.

21 Remove the lower facia trim from the driver's side by unscrewing the two upper screws, then release the diagnostic socket by depressing the lock tabs **(see illustrations)**.

29.19 Removing the trim panel from the inside of the steering column

29.21a Remove the lower facia trim...

29.21b ...then depress the lock tabs...

29.21c ...and remove the diagnostic socket

29.23 Unbolt the fusebox and place to one side

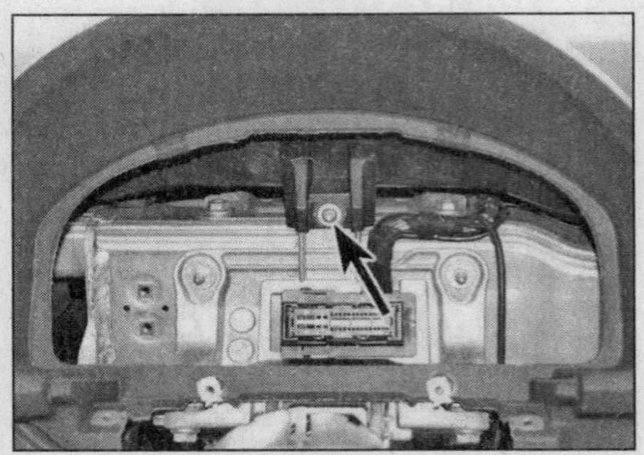

29.24 Facia mounting bolt located through the instrument panel location aperture

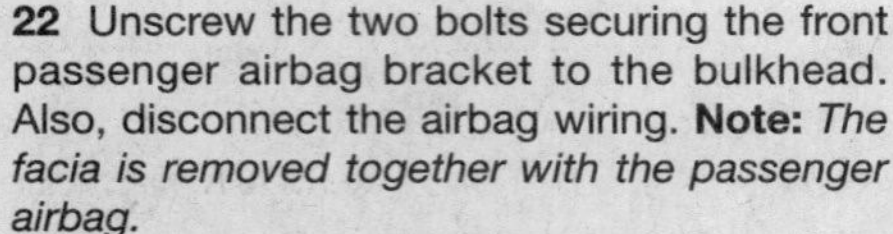

22 Unscrew the two bolts securing the front passenger airbag bracket to the bulkhead. Also, disconnect the airbag wiring. **Note:** *The facia is removed together with the passenger airbag.*

23 Unbolt the fusebox from the driver's side of the facia, and place to one side **(see illustration)**.

24 Unscrew the retaining bolts from the facia assembly, then, with the help of an assistant, pull out from the bulkhead clips and remove from the vehicle **(see illustration)**. As the facia is being removed, disconnect any remaining wiring according to model, and note its routing to aid refitting.

Refitting

25 Refitting is a reversal of the removal procedure, noting the following points:

a) *Ensure the facia guides engage correctly with the clips on the bulkhead. As the facia is being fitted, check that all wiring is routed as noted during removal.*

b) *Insert all of the retaining screws hand-tight, then close both front doors and check that the facia is positioned centrally between the door trims. If it needs to be moved one way or another, place a wad of cloth between the facia and door trim, then close the door. This should move the facia as required. When central, fully tighten the securing screws.*

c) *On completion, reconnect the battery and check that all the electrical components and switches function correctly.*

Chapter 12
Body electrical system

Contents

Degrees of difficulty

Easy, suitable for novice with little experience 	**Fairly easy,** suitable for beginner with some experience	**Fairly difficult,** suitable for competent DIY mechanic	**Difficult,** suitable for experienced DIY mechanic	**Very difficult,** suitable for expert DIY or professional 

Specifications

System type .... 12 volt negative earth

Fuses .... See *Wiring diagrams* on page 12•21

Bulbs	**Wattage**	**Type**
Direction indicators	21	Bayonet
Front foglight	55	H11
Glovebox light	5	Wedge
Headlight:		
Halogen:		
Main beam	55	H7U
Dipped beam	55	H7
Gas discharge:		
Main beam	55	H1
Dipped beam	35	DS2 (80-117 volt)
Interior light	10	Festoon
Sidelight	5	Wedge

Torque wrench setting	**Nm**	**lbf ft**
Passenger airbag and brackets	9	7

1 General information and precautions

Warning: *Before carrying out any work on the electrical system, read through the` precautions given in 'Safety first!' at the beginning of this manual, and in Chapter 5A.*

The electrical system is of 12 volt negative earth type. Power for the lights and all electrical accessories is supplied by a lead-acid type battery, which is charged by the alternator.

This Chapter covers repair and service procedures for the various electrical components not associated with the engine. Information on the battery, alternator and starter motor can be found in Chapter 5A.

It should be noted that prior to working on any component in the electrical system, the ignition and all electrical consumers must be switched off. Additionally, where stated, the battery negative lead must be disconnected, however, note the information given in *Disconnecting the battery* in the *Reference* chapter at the end of this manual, as special procedures have to be carried out when reconnecting the battery.

Some models are fitted with gas discharge headlight systems, which include automatic range control to reduce the possibility of dazzling oncoming drivers. Note the special precautions which apply to these systems as given in Section 5.

2 Electrical fault finding – general information

Note: *Refer to the precautions given in ëSafety first!í and in Chapter 5A before starting work. The following tests relate to testing of the main electrical circuits, and should not be used to test delicate electronic circuits (such as anti-lock braking systems), particularly where an electronic control module is used.*

General

1 A typical electrical circuit consists of an electrical component, any switches, relays, motors, fuses, fusible links or circuit breakers related to that component, and the wiring and connectors which link the component to both the battery and the chassis. To help to pin-point a problem in an electrical circuit, wiring diagrams are included at the end of this Chapter. **Note:** *Many of the circuits are controlled by computerised systems (for instance, the windscreen wipers will only operate with the bonnet closed), so before assuming there are faults, it is worthwhile checking if specific conditions apply.*

2 Before attempting to diagnose an electrical fault, first study the appropriate wiring diagram to obtain a complete understanding of the components included in the particular circuit concerned. The possible sources of a fault can be narrowed down by noting if other components related to the circuit are operating properly. If several components or circuits fail at one time, the problem is likely to be related to a shared fuse or earth connection.

3 Electrical problems usually stem from simple causes, such as loose or corroded connections, a faulty earth connection, a blown fuse, a melted fusible link, or a faulty relay (refer to Section 3 for details of testing relays). Visually inspect the condition of all fuses, wires and connections in a problem circuit before testing the components. Use the wiring diagrams to determine which terminal connections will need to be checked in order to pin-point the trouble spot.

4 The basic tools required for electrical fault finding include a circuit tester or voltmeter (a 12 volt bulb with a set of test leads can also be used for certain tests); a self-powered test light (sometimes known as a continuity tester); an ohmmeter (to measure resistance); a battery and set of test leads; and a jumper wire, preferably with a circuit breaker or fuse incorporated, which can be used to bypass suspect wires or electrical components. Before attempting to locate a problem with test instruments, use the wiring diagram to determine where to make the connections.

5 To find the source of an intermittent wiring fault (usually due to a poor or dirty connection, or damaged wiring insulation), a wiggle test can be performed on the wiring. This involves wiggling the wiring by hand to see if the fault occurs as the wiring is moved. It should be possible to narrow down the source of the fault to a particular section of wiring. This method of testing can be used in conjunction with any of the tests described in the following sub-Sections.

6 Apart from problems due to poor connections, two basic types of fault can occur in an electrical circuit – open-circuit, or short-circuit.

7 Open-circuit faults are caused by a break somewhere in the circuit, which prevents current from flowing. An open-circuit fault will prevent a component from working, but will not cause the relevant circuit fuse to blow.

8 Short-circuit faults are caused by a short somewhere in the circuit, which allows the current flowing in the circuit to escape along an alternative route, usually to earth. Short-circuit faults are normally caused by a breakdown in wiring insulation, which allows a feed wire to touch either another wire, or an earthed component such as the bodyshell. A short-circuit fault will normally cause the relevant circuit fuse to blow.

Finding an open-circuit

9 To check for an open-circuit, connect one lead of a circuit tester or voltmeter to either the negative battery terminal or a known good earth.

10 Connect the other lead to a connector in the circuit being tested, preferably nearest to the battery or fuse.

11 Switch on the circuit, bearing in mind that some circuits are live only when the ignition switch is moved to a particular position.

12 If voltage is present (indicated either by the tester bulb lighting or a voltmeter reading, as applicable), this means that the section of the circuit between the relevant connector and the battery is problem-free.

13 Continue to check the remainder of the circuit in the same fashion.

14 When a point is reached at which no voltage is present, the problem must lie between that point and the previous test point with voltage. Most problems can be traced to a broken, corroded or loose connection.

Finding a short-circuit

15 To check for a short-circuit, first disconnect the load(s) from the circuit (loads are the components which draw current from a circuit, such as bulbs, motors, heating elements, etc).

16 Remove the relevant fuse from the circuit, and connect a circuit tester or voltmeter to the fuse connections.

17 Switch on the circuit, bearing in mind that some circuits are live only when the ignition switch is moved to a particular position.

18 If voltage is present (indicated either by the tester bulb lighting or a voltmeter reading, as applicable), this means that there is a short circuit.

19 If no voltage is present, but the fuse still blows with the load(s) connected, this indicates an internal fault in the load(s).

Finding an earth fault

20 The battery negative terminal is connected to earth – the metal of the engine/transmission and the car body – and most systems are wired so that they only receive a positive feed, the current returning through the metal of the car body. This means that the component mounting and the body form part of that circuit. Loose or corroded mountings can therefore cause a range of electrical faults, ranging from total failure of a circuit, to a puzzling partial fault. In particular, lights may shine dimly (especially when another circuit sharing the same earth point is in operation), motors (eg, wiper motors or the radiator cooling fan motor) may run slowly, and the operation of one circuit may have an apparently unrelated effect on another. Note that on many vehicles, earth straps are used between certain components, such as the engine/transmission and the body, usually where there is no metal-to-metal contact between components due to flexible rubber mountings, etc.

21 To check whether a component is properly earthed, disconnect the battery (refer to the warnings given in the Reference section at the rear of the manual) and connect one lead of an ohmmeter to a known good earth point. Connect the other lead to the wire or earth connection being tested. The resistance reading should be zero; if not, check the connection as follows.

22 If an earth connection is thought to be faulty, dismantle the connection and clean back to bare metal both the bodyshell and the wire terminal or the component earth connection mating surface. Be careful to remove all traces of dirt and corrosion, then use a knife to trim away any paint, so that a clean metal-to-metal joint is made. On reassembly, tighten the joint fasteners securely; if a wire terminal is being refitted, use serrated washers between the terminal and the bodyshell to ensure a clean and secure connection. When the connection is remade, prevent the onset of corrosion in the future by applying a coat of petroleum jelly or silicone-based grease or by spraying on (at regular intervals) a proprietary ignition sealer or a water dispersant lubricant.

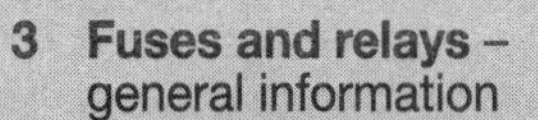

3 Fuses and relays – general information

Fuses and fusible links

1 Fuses are designed to break a circuit when a predetermined current is reached, in order to protect the components and wiring which could be damaged by excessive current flow. Any excessive current flow will be due to a fault in the circuit, usually a short-circuit (see Section 2).

2 On Golf and Jetta models, the main fuses are located in the fusebox on the driver's side of the facia; open the driver's door and unclip the fusebox cover from the end of the facia to gain access to the fuses. The fuse locations are marked onto the rear of the fusebox cover. On Golf Plus models, the main fuses are located in the fusebox below the lighting switch on the driver's side of the facia.

3 To remove a fuse, first switch off the circuit concerned (or the ignition), then pull the fuse out of its terminals **(see illustration)**.

4 The wire within the fuse should be visible; if the fuse has blown it will be broken or melted.

5 Always renew a fuse with one of the correct rating, never use a fuse with a different rating from that specified.

6 Refer to the wiring diagrams for details of the fuse ratings and the circuits protected. The fuse rating is stamped on the top of the fuse, the fuses are also colour-coded as follows.

Colour	Rating
Light brown	5A
Brown	7.5A
Red	10A
Blue	15A
Yellow	20A
White or clear	25A
Green	30A
Orange	40A

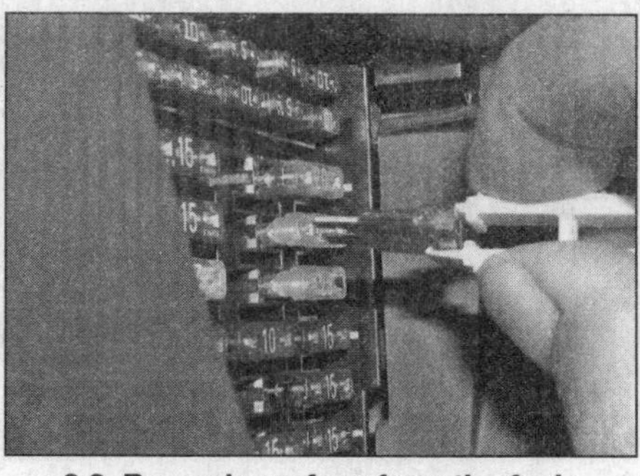

3.3 Removing a fuse from the facia fusebox

3.8 Fuse and relay box on the left-hand side of the engine compartment

7 Never renew a fuse more than once without tracing the source of the trouble. If the new fuse blows immediately, find the cause before renewing it again; a short to earth as a result of faulty insulation is most likely. Where a fuse protects more than one circuit, try to isolate the fault by switching on each circuit in turn (where possible) until the fuse blows again. Always carry a supply of spare fuses of each relevant rating on the vehicle.

8 Additional fuses and relays are located in the fusebox located on the left-hand side of the engine compartment. Unclip and open the fuse holder cover to gain access **(see illustration)**.

9 To renew a fusible link, first disconnect the battery negative terminal. Unscrew the retaining nuts then remove the blown link from the holder. Fit the new link to its terminals and reconnect the lead. Ensure the link and lead are correctly seated then refit the retaining nuts and tighten securely. Clip the cover back into position then reconnect the battery.

Relays

10 A relay is an electrically-operated switch, which is used for the following reasons:

a) *A relay can switch a heavy current remotely from the circuit in which the current is flowing, allowing the use of lighter-gauge wiring and switch contacts.*
b) *A relay can receive more than one control input, unlike a mechanical switch.*
c) *A relay can have a timer function – for example, the intermittent wiper relay.*

11 Most of the relays are located on the relay plate behind the driver's side facia, however, additional relays are located in the engine compartment fusebox **(see illustration)**.

12 Access to the relays can be obtained after removing the driver's side lower facia panel as described in Chapter 11, then removing the two relay plate retaining screws (one at either end), and lowering the plate complete with relays **(see illustration)**. Identification details of the relays are given at the start of the wiring diagrams.

13 If a circuit or system controlled by a relay develops a fault, and the relay is suspect, operate the system. If the relay is functioning, it should be possible to hear it click as it is energised. If this is the case, the fault lies with the components or wiring of the system. If the relay is not being energised, then either the relay is not receiving a main supply or a switching voltage, or the relay itself is faulty. Testing is by the substitution of a known good unit, but be careful – while some relays are identical in appearance and in operation, others look similar but perform different functions.

14 To remove a relay, first ensure that the relevant circuit is switched off. The relay can then simply be pulled out from the socket, and pushed back into position.

15 The direction indicator/hazard flasher relay is integral with the hazard warning switch. Refer to Section 4 for the switch removal procedure.

3.11 Engine compartment fusebox

3.12 Relays located behind the facia

4.13a Press the switch centre inwards and turn it slightly to the right...

4.13b ...then withdraw it...

4.14 ...and disconnect the wiring

4 Switches – removal and refitting

Ignition switch

1 Refer to Chapter 10.

Wiper and indicator/ cruise switches

2 Switch off the ignition and all electrical consumers and remove the ignition key.

3 Check that the front wheels are pointing straight-ahead and the steering wheel is in its centre position, then remove the steering wheel as described in Chapter 10.

4 Undo the screws and remove the column height and reach adjustment handle.

5 Carefully prise out the gap cover, then remove the upper shroud from the steering column.

6 Undo the two upper screws and single lower screw and remove the lower shroud.

7 Remove the steering column electronics control unit. To do this, undo the single retaining screw, then insert a 2.5 mm diameter rod or similar through the hole provided, and release the centre clip. Now use a screwdriver to release the rear clip. Pull down the control unit from the column switch carrier.

8 The airbag clock spring/slip-ring must be held in its centre position while it is removed, to ensure correct refitting. Unclip the airbag clock spring/slip-ring from the combination switch carrier by lifting the retaining hooks.

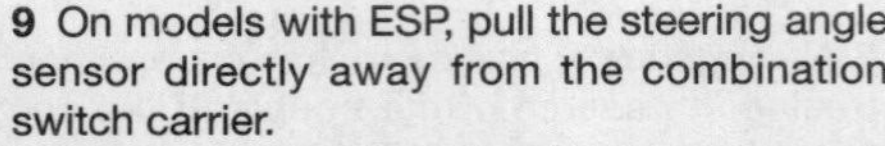

9 On models with ESP, pull the steering angle sensor directly away from the combination switch carrier.

10 Remove the relevant switch by inserting a 1.0 mm feeler gauge through the slot provided to release the switch from the carrier.

11 Refitting is a reversal of removal.

Lighting switch

12 Switch off the ignition and all electrical consumers and remove the ignition key.

13 With the light switch in position O, press the switch centre inwards and turn it slightly to the right. Hold this position and pull the switch from the dash **(see illustrations)**.

14 As the switch is withdrawn from the dash, disconnect the wiring plug **(see illustration)**.

15 To refit the switch, first reconnect the wiring plug.

16 Hold the switch and press the rotary part inwards and slightly to the right.

17 Insert the switch into the dash, turn the rotary part to position O and release. Check the switch for correct operation.

Headlamp range control and instrument illumination switch

18 Remove the lighting switch as described in paragraphs 12 to 14.

19 Remove the driver's side storage compartment.

20 Disconnect the wiring from the back of the switch.

21 Release the clips and remove the switch.

22 Refitting is a reversal of removal.

Heated seat/air conditioning/ rear window heating switches

23 Switch off the ignition and all electrical consumers and remove the ignition key.

24 Carefully prise the switch from its location in the facia panel, using a small flat-bladed screwdriver. Take care not to damage the surrounding trim.

25 Disconnect the wiring plug(s) and withdraw the switch.

26 Reconnect the switch wiring plug, and push the switch firmly into position.

Hazard warning/ESP/heated rear window switches

27 Switch off the ignition and all electrical consumers and remove the ignition key.

28 Remove the facia centre vent panel as follows:

a) *On models without Climatronic, lift out the lining mat from the storage compartment on the top of the facia, then undo the screws now visible. Remove the storage compartment.*

b) *On models with Climatronic, prise out the sunlight sensor, disconnect the wiring, and undo the screw now visible. Using a screwdriver at the front of the panel, push the panel rearwards and lift it from the vent panel.*

c) *On all models, undo the screws and slightly lift the front of the centre vent panel, then use a screwdriver to prise the centre vent panel from the facia.*

29 Disconnect the wiring then release the lugs and remove the switch from the vent panel.

Electric window switch/module

Driver's door

30 Switch off the ignition and all electrical consumers and remove the ignition key.

31 Carefully prise the control panel up from the door trim, and disconnect the wiring plug **(see illustrations)**.

32 Release the locking lugs and remove the switch module.

33 If a window switch is faulty, the complete module must be renewed.

34 Refitting is a reversal of removal.

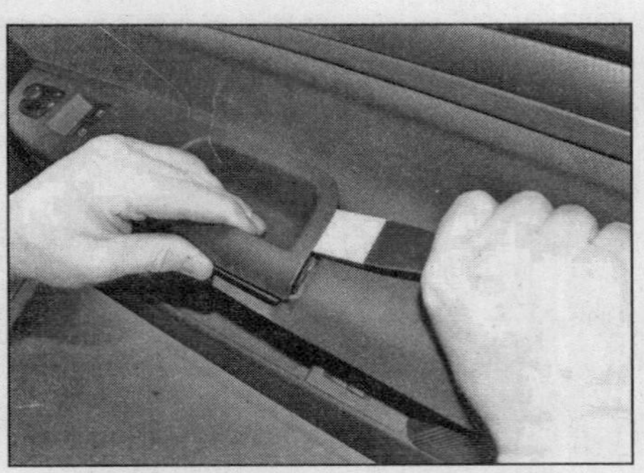

4.31a Prise out the control panel...

4.31b ...and disconnect the wiring

Passenger's door

35 Switch off the ignition and all electrical consumers and remove the ignition key.
36 Unclip the trim from the top of the interior door handle grip.
37 Disconnect the wiring.
38 Release the locking lugs and remove the switch.
39 Refitting is a reversal of removal.

Electric mirror switch

40 The procedure is the same as that described for the electric window switch/module.
41 Refitting is a reversal of removal.

Heater blower motor switch

42 The switch is integral with the heater control panel, and cannot be removed separately. Refer to Chapter 3 for details of heater control panel removal and refitting.

Handbrake 'on' warning switch

43 Refer to Chapter 9.

Brake light switch

44 Refer to Chapter 9.

Reversing light switch

45 Refer to Chapter 7A.

Courtesy light switches

46 The courtesy light switch is integrated into the door lock mechanism, and cannot be renewed independently. If the courtesy light switch is faulty, renew the door lock mechanism as described in Chapter 11.

Luggage area light switch

47 The luggage compartment light switch is integrated into the tailgate/boot lid lock mechanism, and cannot be renewed independently. If the luggage compartment light switch is faulty, renew the tailgate/boot lid lock mechanism as described in Chapter 11.

Glovebox light switch

48 Switch off the ignition and all electrical consumers and remove the ignition key.
49 Remove the glovebox as described in Chapter 11.
50 Release the lug and push out the switch from the glovebox.
51 Refitting is a reversal of removal.

Fuel filler flap release switch

52 Switch off the ignition and all electrical consumers and remove the ignition key.
53 Remove the driver's side inner door trim as described in Chapter 11. Disconnect the connector, then release the locking lugs and remove the switch from the door trim.
54 Refitting is a reversal of removal.

Interior monitoring deactivation switch

55 Switch off the ignition and all electrical consumers and remove the ignition key.
56 Carefully prise the switch from the inner sill trim, and disconnect the wiring plug.

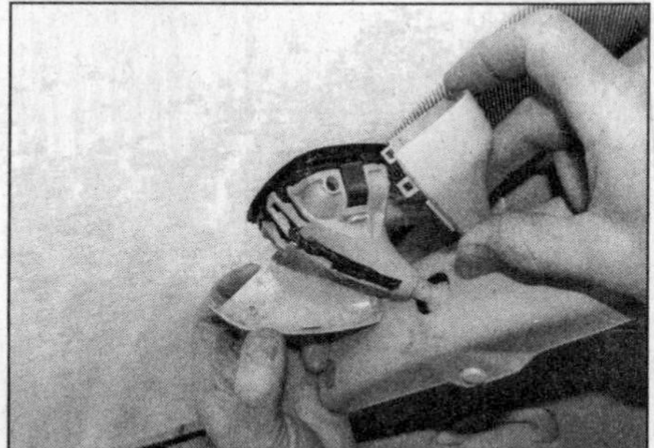

4.59a Remove the mirror base covers...

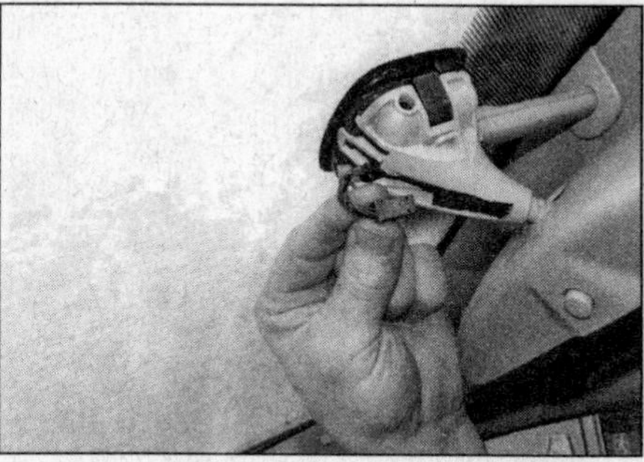

4.59b ...and disconnect the wiring plug...

57 Refitting is a reversal of removal.

Rain sensor

58 Switch off the ignition and all electrical consumers and remove the ignition key.
59 The windscreen wipers are automatically activated when droplets of water are detected by the rain sensor, located in the front of the interior mirror base. Separate the left and right mirror base covers, and disconnect the wiring plug **(see illustrations)**.
60 Pull the mirror downwards from the mirror base, remove the stay, and if necessary disconnect the wiring from the sensor **(see illustrations)**.
61 The mirror base is bonded to the windscreen. Whilst it is possible to remove the base by means of a scraper, great care must be exercised to avoid scratching the windscreen.
62 Due to the hazardous chemicals involved, it is recommended that the bonding of the mirror base to the windscreen be entrusted to a VW dealer or suitably-equipped specialist.
63 With the base in place, refit the mirror to the base.
64 Reconnect the sensor wiring plugs.
65 Refit the two halves of the mirror base covers.

Driver's door locking switch

66 Remove the door interior handle as described in Chapter 11.
67 Depress the tabs and remove the locking switch **(see illustration)**.
68 Refitting is a reversal of removal.

Garage door opener

69 The garage door opener is integrated in the driver's side sun visor. If faulty, the complete visor must be renewed.
70 Using a screwdriver, prise open the screw cover caps.

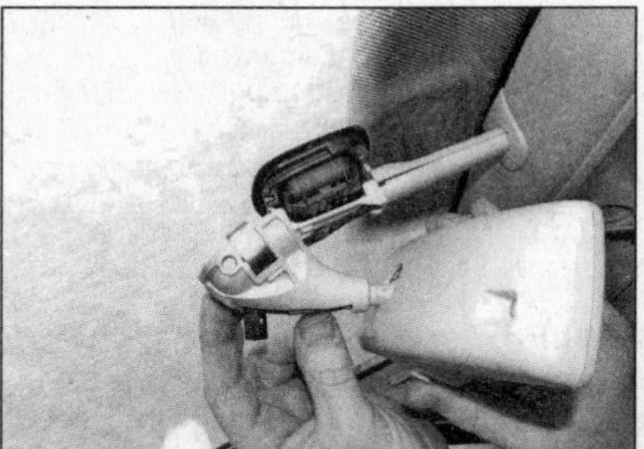

4.60a ...then pull the mirror downwards...

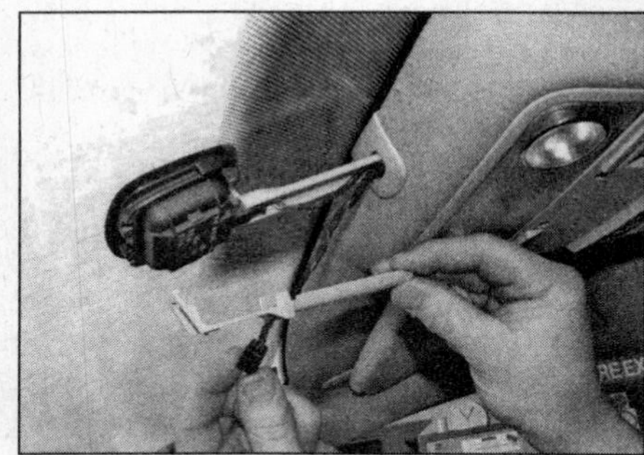

4.60b ...remove the stay...

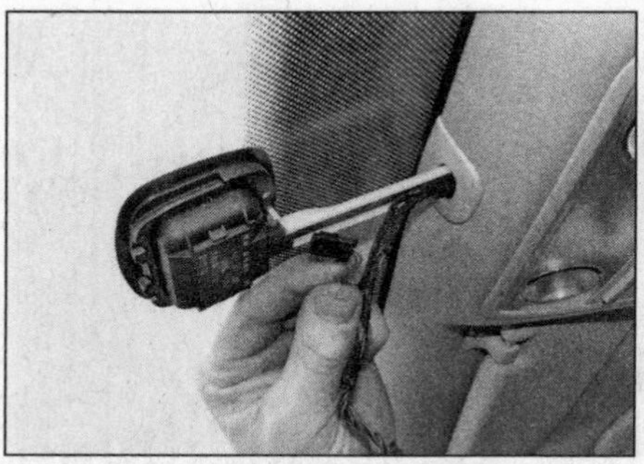

4.60c ...and if necessary, disconnect the sensor wiring

4.67 Removing the door locking switch

5.3 Remove the plastic cover...

5.4a ...disconnect the wiring...

5.4b ...unhook the clip...

5.4c ...and withdraw the bulb

71 Undo the screws and carefully pull the visor rest from the mounting. **Do not** allow the visor to hang on the wire.

72 The wiring connector must now be pulled from its retaining clip, but there is a risk of damaging the wire if it is pulled out directly. Grip the wire using the finger and thumb through the access hole, and carefully move it towards the windscreen. Once released, withdraw the wiring and release the connector.

73 Refitting is a reversal of removal.

5 Bulbs (exterior lights) – renewal

General

1 Whenever a bulb is renewed, note the following points:

a) Switch off the ignition and all electrical consumers before commencing work.

b) Remember that if the light has just been in use the bulb may be extremely hot.

c) Always check the bulb contacts and holder, ensuring that there is clean metal-to-metal contact. Clean off any corrosion or dirt before fitting a new bulb.

d) Wherever bayonet-type bulbs are fitted ensure that the spring-tensioned arms bear firmly against the bulb contacts.

e) Always ensure that the new bulb is of the correct rating and that it is thoroughly clean before fitting it.

Headlight main beam

Note: *Do not touch the glass envelope of the bulb if it is to be re-used.*

2 Switch off the ignition and all electrical consumers and remove the ignition key.

3 Working in the engine compartment, remove the plastic cover from the rear of the headlight **(see illustration)**.

4 Except on Golf Plus models, disconnect the wiring plug from the rear of the bulb, then unhook and release the ends of the bulb retaining clip from the light unit and withdraw the bulb **(see illustrations)**.

5 On Golf Plus models, turn the bulbholder anti-clockwise and remove it, then remove the bulb.

6 When handling the new bulb, use a tissue or clean cloth to avoid touching the glass with the fingers; moisture and grease from the skin can cause blackening and rapid failure of this type of bulb. If the glass is accidentally touched, wipe it clean using methylated spirit.

7 Install the new bulb, ensuring that its location tabs are correctly located in the cut-outs, and secure it in position with the retaining clip.

8 Reconnect the wiring plug, and refit the headlight cover, making sure that it is secure.

Headlight dip beam

Halogen headlights

Note: *Do not touch the glass envelope of the bulb if it is to be re-used.*

9 Switch off the ignition and all electrical consumers and remove the ignition key.

10 Working in the engine compartment, remove the outermost plastic cover from the rear of the headlight by turning it anti-clockwise **(see illustration)**.

11 Turn the bulbholder anti-clockwise and remove it from the headlight complete with bulb **(see illustration)**.

12 Pull the bulb from the bulbholder **(see illustration)**.

13 When handling the new bulb, use a tissue or clean cloth to avoid touching the glass with the fingers; moisture and grease from the skin can cause blackening and rapid failure of this type of bulb. If the glass is accidentally touched, wipe it clean using methylated spirit.

14 Fit the new bulb to the bulbholder, ensuring that the location lug is aligned with the special recess.

15 Fit the bulbholder to the headlight and turn clockwise to secure.

16 Refit the small plastic cover

5.10 Remove the plastic cover ...

5.11 ...then turn the bulbholder anti-clockwise and remove it...

5.12 ...and pull the dipped beam bulb from the bulbholder

Gas discharge headlights

Warning: The headlight bulb contains gas at very high pressure, and it is recommended that gloves and eye protection are worn to prevent potential personal injury.

Note: *Do not touch the glass envelope of the bulb if it is to be re-used.*

17 Remove the headlight as described in Section 7.

18 Remove the innermost small plastic cover from the rear of the headlight by turning it anti-clockwise.

19 Turn the starter unit anti-clockwise (OPEN) as far as possible (this will disconnect the wiring), and remove it from the headlight.

20 Turn the bulbholder anti-clockwise and remove it from the headlight complete with bulb.

21 Pull the bulb from the bulbholder.

22 When handling the new bulb, use a tissue or clean cloth to avoid touching the glass with the fingers; moisture and grease from the skin can cause blackening and rapid failure of this type of bulb. If the glass is accidentally touched, wipe it clean using methylated spirit.

23 Fit the new bulb to the bulbholder, ensuring that the location lug is aligned with the special recess.

24 Fit the bulbholder to the headlight and turn clockwise to secure.

25 Refit the small plastic cover.

Caution: After refitting a gas discharge headlamp, the basic setting of the Automatic Range Control system should be checked. Because of the requirement for specialised equipment, this can only be carried out by a VW dealer or suitably-equipped specialist.

Front sidelight

26 Switch off the ignition and all electrical consumers and remove the ignition key.

27 Working in the engine compartment, remove the innermost small plastic cover from the rear of the headlight.

28 Carefully pull the sidelight bulbholder from the headlight unit. The bulb is a push-fit in the holder and can be removed by grasping the end of the bulb and pulling it out.

29 Refitting is a reversal of removal, making sure that the headlight cover is securely refitted.

Front direction indicator

Note: *Do not touch the glass envelope of the bulb if it is to be re-used.*

30 Switch off the ignition and all electrical consumers and remove the ignition key.

31 Working in the engine compartment, remove the innermost small plastic cover from the rear of the headlight by turning it anti-clockwise.

32 Turn the bulbholder anti-clockwise and remove it from the headlight complete with bulb.

33 On halogen headlight models, pull the bulb from the bulbholder. On gas discharge headlight models, the bulb has a bayonet fitting; depress and twist the bulb to remove it.

34 When handling the new bulb, use a tissue or clean cloth to avoid touching the glass with the fingers; moisture and grease from the skin can cause blackening and rapid failure of this type of bulb. If the glass is accidentally touched, wipe it clean using methylated spirit.

35 Fit the new bulb to the bulbholder. On halogen headlight models, ensure that the location lug is aligned with the special recess.

36 Fit the bulbholder to the headlight and turn clockwise to secure.

37 Refit the small plastic cover.

Front foglight

38 Switch off the ignition and all electrical consumers and remove the ignition key.

39 Undo the retaining screw, and pull the foglight and surround from the bumper.

40 Turn the bulbholder anti-clockwise and remove it complete with bulb from the rear of the foglight. **Note:** *The bulb is integral with the bulbholder.*

41 Fit the new bulb using a reversal of the removal procedure.

Direction indicator in exterior mirror

42 There are no conventional bulbs in the exterior mirror, but LEDs instead, therefore if the direction indicator is not working, the complete unit must be renewed as described in Section 7.

Door entry illumination in exterior mirror

43 Switch off the ignition and all electrical consumers and remove the ignition key.

44 Fold the exterior mirror forwards to expose the light retaining screw on the inner end of the mirror. Undo the screw then unclip the light and withdraw it as far as the wiring will allow.

45 Pull the bulbholder from the light and depress and twist the bulb to remove it.

46 Fit the new bulb using a reversal of the removal procedure.

Rear light cluster

Note: *There are no bulbs fitted on Golf Plus or Jetta models as LEDs are fitted instead; if defective, renew the complete cluster.*

Golf hatchback

47 Remove the rear light cluster as described in Section 7.

48 Release the retaining hooks and remove the bulbholder from the rear of the cluster. The bulbs are a bayonet-fit in the bulbholder – depress and twist the relevant bulb to remove it **(see illustrations)**.

49 Fit the new bulb using a reversal of the removal procedure.

Golf estate

50 Open the access cover in the side panel trim.

51 Squeeze together the retaining clips and remove the bulbholder assembly **(see illustration)**.

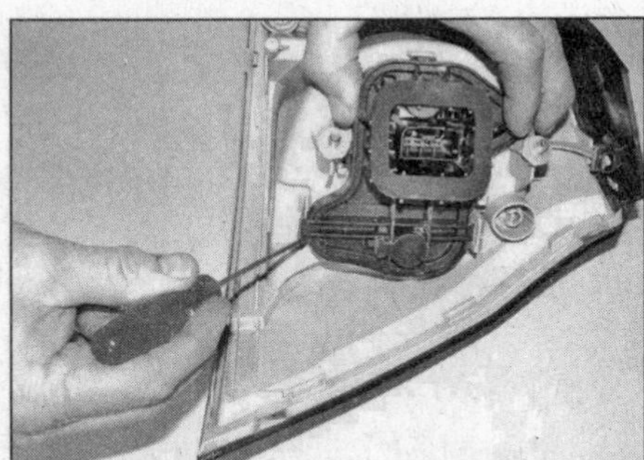

5.48a Release the retaining hooks...

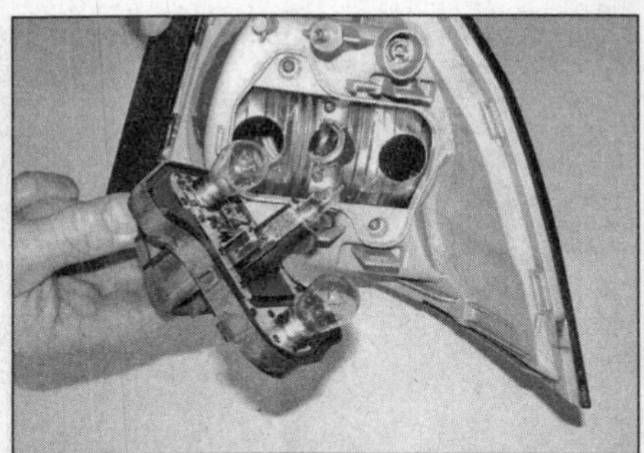

5.48b ...remove the bulbholder...

5.48c ...and remove the relevant bulb

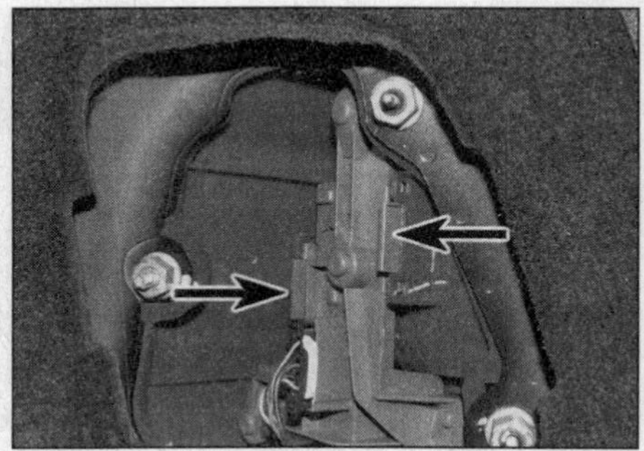

5.51 Squeeze together the retaining clips

5.52 The bulbs are a bayonet fit

5.56a Insert a wedge tool...

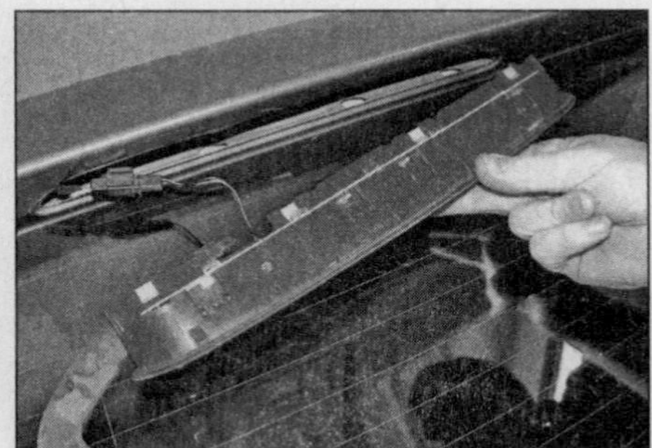
5.56b ...to remove the high-level brake light

52 The bulbs are a bayonet-fit in the bulbholder – depress and twist the relevant bulb to remove it **(see illustration)**.

53 Fit the new bulb using a reversal of the removal procedure.

High-level brake light

Golf models except GTi

Note: *The light is of LED design, therefore if faulty the complete unit must be renewed. Note that the LEDs are arranged in groups of four, and if just one group fails, the light still meets legal requirement. Failure of more than one group renders the light illegal.*

54 Switch off the ignition and all electrical consumers and remove the ignition key.

55 The high-level brake light is removed from the outside of the tailgate. First, protect the surrounding paintwork with adhesive tape.

56 Insert a wedge tool between the upper edge of the light and the tailgate, taking care not to damage the seal, then tap in the wedge to release the light unit **(see illustrations)**.

57 Disconnect the wiring and remove the light unit **(see illustration)**.

58 Fit the new light unit using a reversal of the removal procedure.

Golf GTi models

Note: *The high-level brake light is incorporated in the spoiler. Use of cutting thread is necessary to release the spoiler from the adhesive tape. Do not use cutting wire as this will damage the paintwork.*

59 Switch off the ignition and all electrical consumers and remove the ignition key.

60 Use the cutting thread on each end of the spoiler to cut through the adhesive tape.

61 Carefully prise the spoiler from the tailgate retaining clips, and disconnect the wiring.

62 Undo the screws and remove the light unit from the spoiler.

63 Refitting is a reversal of removal.

Jetta models

64 On early models where the light is located at the bottom of the rear window, disconnect the wiring then remove the parcel shelf.

65 On late models where the high-level light is located at the top of the rear window, unclip the trim from the rear of the headlining, then disconnect the wiring **(see illustrations)**.

66 Unclip and remove the light unit **(see illustration)**.

67 Depress the retaining clips and separate the bulb holder from the cover.

68 As the 32 LEDs are soldered in position and covered with a plastic strip, it is not possible to renew individual LEDs. The complete bulbholder must be renewed.

69 Refitting is a reversal of removal.

Rear number plate light

70 Switch off the ignition and all electrical consumers and remove the ignition key.

5.57 Disconnecting the wiring from the high-level brake light

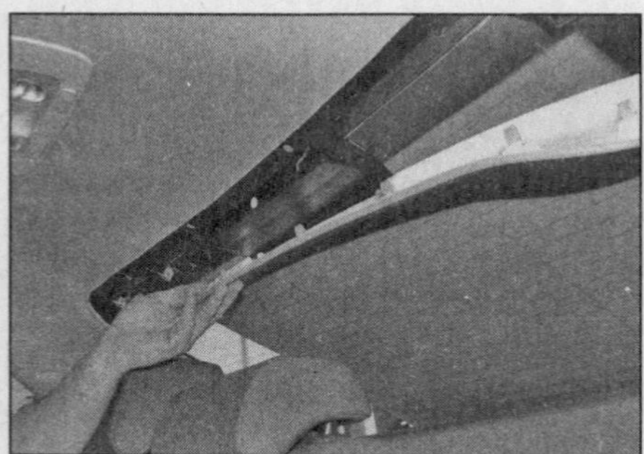
5.65a On late Jetta models, unclip the trim from the headlining...

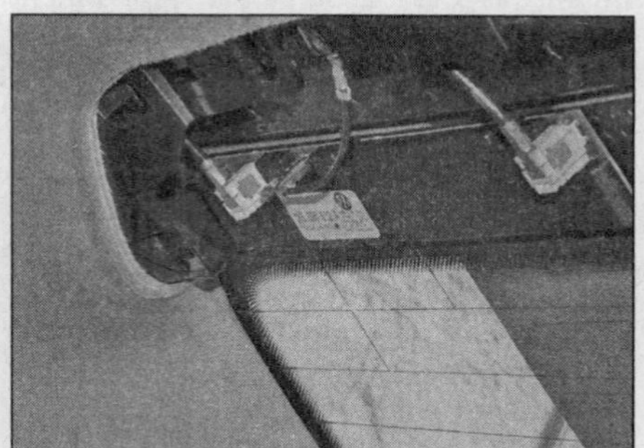
5.65b ...then disconnect the wiring...

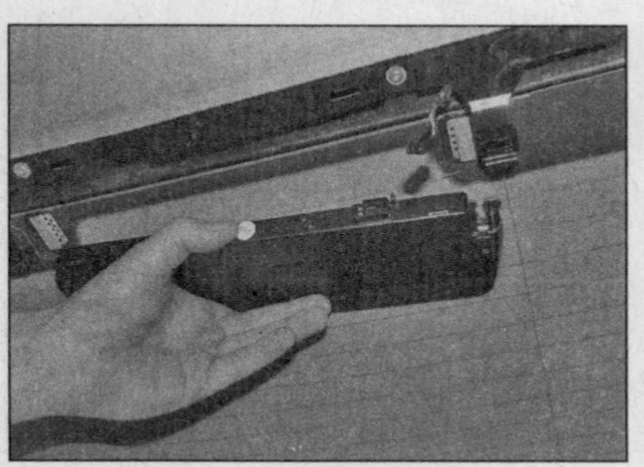
5.66 ...and unclip the high level light unit

5.71a Undo the screws...

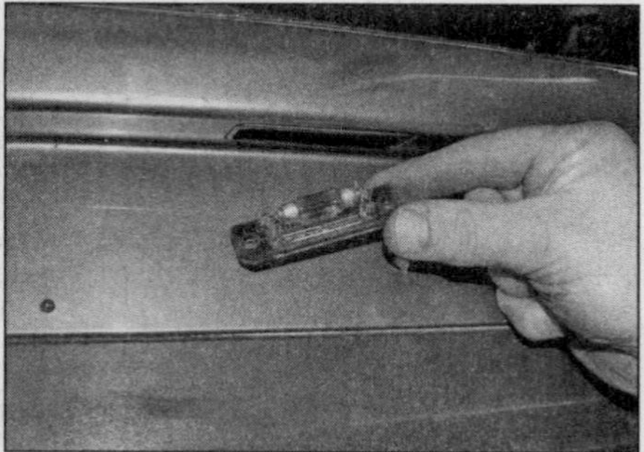
5.71b ...and remove the rear number plate light

5.75 Remove the cover...

5.76a ...turn the bulbholder anti-clockwise to remove it...

5.76b ...then remove the bulb

71 Undo the two securing screws, and withdraw the light unit from the tailgate/boot lid **(see illustrations)**.

72 Unclip the lens from the light unit. The bulb is a push-fit in the bulbholder.

73 Fit the new bulb using a reversal of the removal procedure.

Rear fog/reversing light

74 On some models, the rear fog/reversing light bulbs are located in the tailgate/boot lid; the foglight is on the left-hand side, and the reversing light is on the right-hand side on RHD models. First, switch off the ignition and all electrical consumers and remove the ignition key.

75 Open the tailgate/boot lid and use a screwdriver to prise the cover from the relevant light **(see illustration)**.

76 On Golf/Jetta models, turn the bulbholder anti-clockwise and remove it, then remove the bulb **(see illustrations)**. On Golf Plus models, unclip the bulbholder and remove it, then remove the bulb.

77 Fit the new bulb using a reversal of the removal procedure.

6 Bulbs (interior lights) – renewal

General

1 Whenever a bulb is renewed, note the following points:

a) Switch off the ignition and all electrical consumers before commencing work.

b) Remember that if the light has just been in use the bulb may be extremely hot.

c) Always check the bulb contacts and holder, ensuring that there is clean metal-to-metal contact between them. Clean off any corrosion or dirt before fitting a new bulb.

d) Wherever bayonet-type bulbs are fitted ensure that the live contact(s) bear firmly against the bulb contact.

e) Always ensure that the new bulb is of the correct rating and that it is completely clean before fitting it.

Front courtesy/reading light

2 For access to the main courtesy light bulb, carefully prise the lens from the light unit, using a small flat-bladed screwdriver. Pull the festoon-type bulb from the spring contacts **(see illustrations)**.

3 For access to the reading light bulbs, remove the light unit as follows. Unclip the covers, then undo the screws, withdraw the light from the console, and disconnect the wiring plug. Twist the bulbholder anti-clockwise to remove it, then pull out the wedge-type bulb **(see illustrations)**.

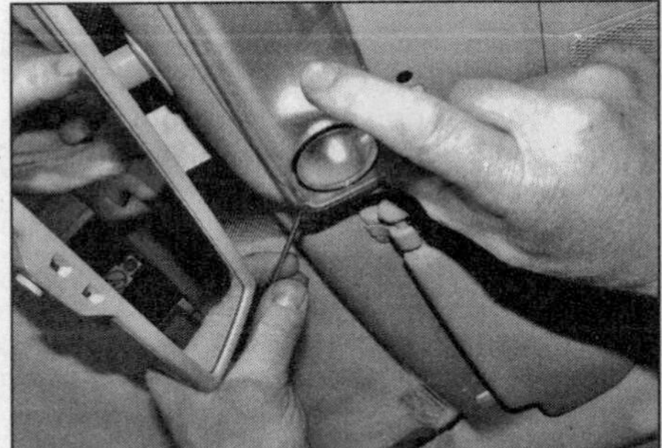

6.2a Prise off the lens...

6.2b ...then pull the festoon-type bulb from the spring contacts

6.3a Unclip the rear cover...

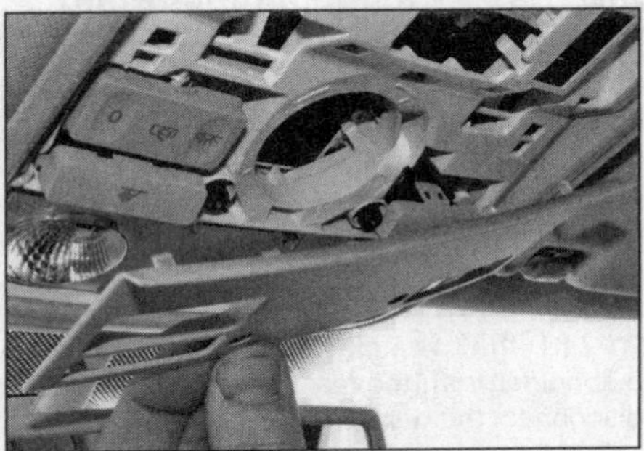

6.3b ...and front cover...

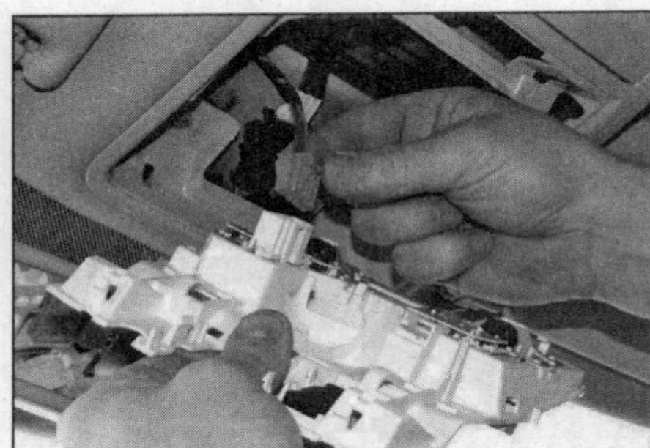

6.3c ...remove the light unit and disconnect the wiring...

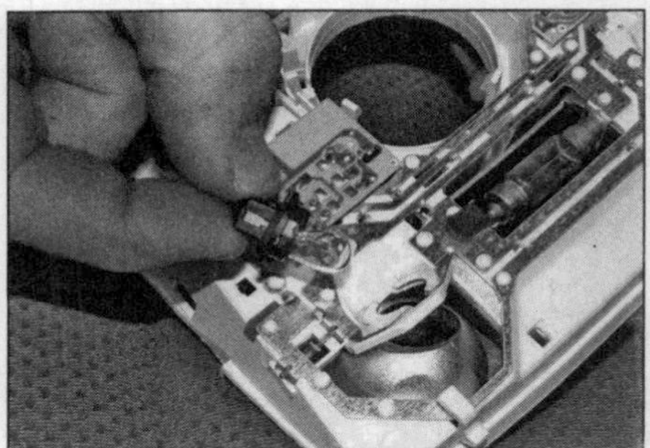

6.3d ...twist the bulbholder anti-clockwise...

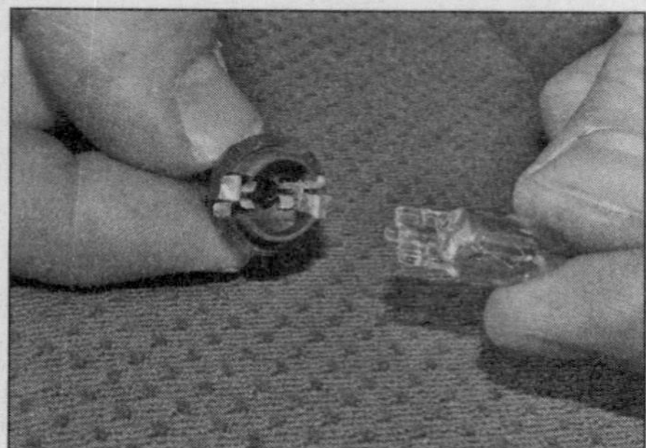

6.3e ...and pull out the wedge-type bulb

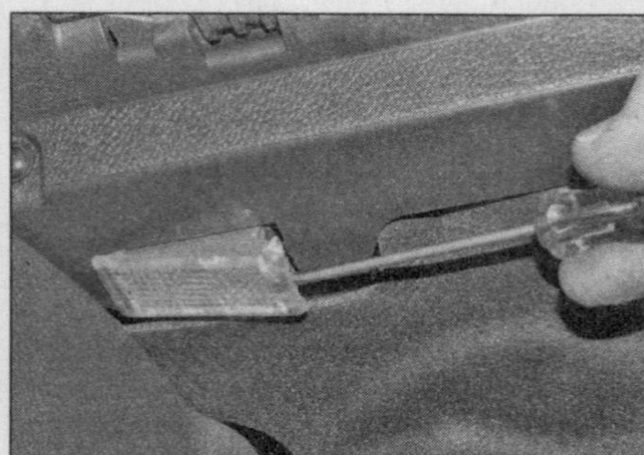

6.5a Prise out the footwell illumination light...

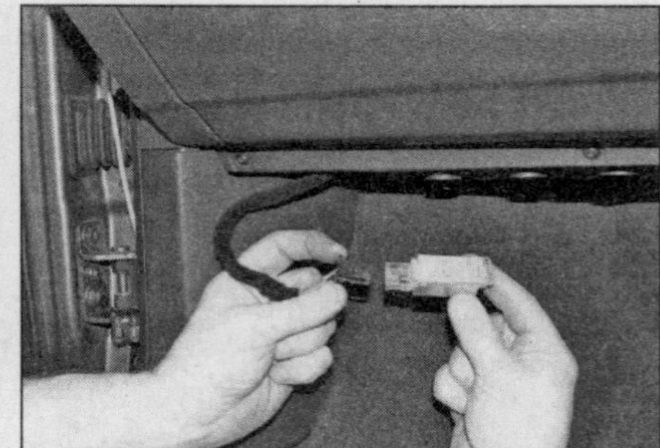

6.5b ...and disconnect the wiring...

6.6a ...prise off the lens...

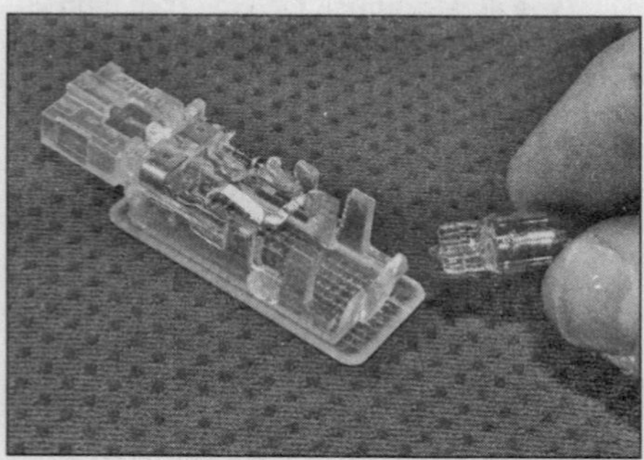

6.6b ...and pull out the wedge-type bulb

4 Fit the new bulb using a reversal of the removal procedure.

Front footwell illumination lights

5 Use a screwdriver to prise out the light, then disconnect the wiring **(see illustrations)**.

6 Prise off the lens, and pull out the wedge-type bulb **(see illustrations)**.

7 Refitting is a reverse of the removal procedure.

6.8 Remove the lens...

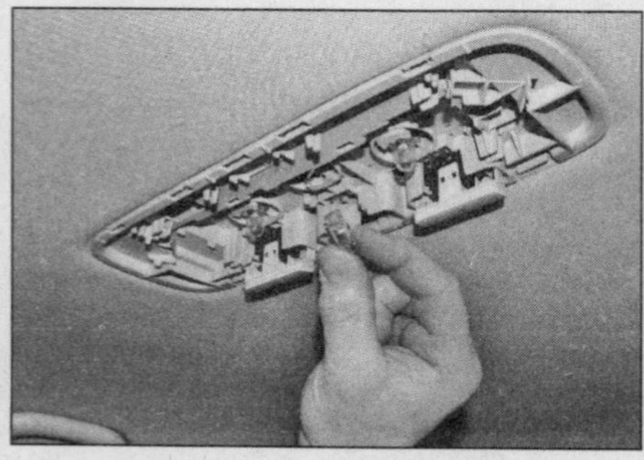

6.9 ...and pull out the wedge-type bulb

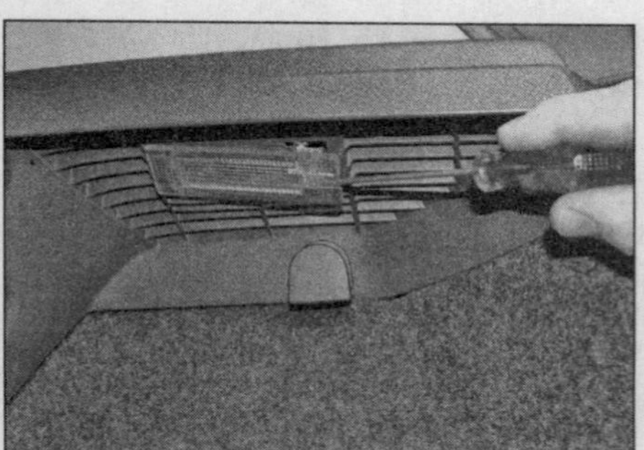

6.11a Prise out the luggage compartment light...

6.11b ...and remove the festoon-type bulb

Rear courtesy/reading lights

8 Using a screwdriver, release the locking lugs and remove the lens from the light unit **(see illustration)**.

9 Pull the wedge-type bulb from the light **(see illustration)**.

10 Fit the new bulb using a reversal of the removal procedure.

Luggage compartment light

11 Carefully prise the light unit from its location in the luggage compartment or boot lid, as applicable. The festoon-type bulb is a push-fit in the spring contacts **(see illustrations)**.

12 Fit the new bulb using a reversal of the removal procedure.

Make-up lights

13 Proceed as described previously for the luggage compartment light. The make-up light is activated by lifting the cover of the mirror built into the sun visor.

14 No renewal procedure is recommended for the microswitch in the sun visor. If the switch is faulty, the visor must be renewed.

Glovebox illumination light

15 Open the glovebox, then use a screwdriver to prise out the lens. Disconnect the wiring.

16 Remove the heat shield, then carefully lever out the wedge-type bulb.

17 Fit the new bulb using a reversal of the removal procedure.

Instrument panel illumination/ warning lights

18 The instrument panel illumination/warning lights are non-renewable LEDs.

Cigarette lighter/ ashtray illumination

19 Remove the centre console, as described in Chapter 11.

20 Lift the retaining clip, and pull the bulbholder from the rear of the assembly and disconnect the wiring plug. The bulb is integral with the bulbholder **(see illustration)**.

21 Fit the new bulb using a reversal of the removal procedure.

Heater/ventilation control panel illumination

22 The control panel is illuminated by LEDs built into the panel. Consequently, if a fault develops, renewal of the panel is necessary. However, the centre rotary control of the panel is illuminated by a bulb. Carefully pull the control from the panel, and with a length of washer tube (or similar), pull the capless bulb from the holder **(see illustration)**.

23 Fit the new bulb using a reversal of the removal procedure.

Switch illumination

24 The switch illumination bulbs are integral with the switches. If a bulb fails, the complete switch must be renewed.

Door warning lights

25 Open the relevant door, and carefully prise out the light unit.

26 Unplug the wiring connector.

27 Unclip the lens from the unit, and release the bulb from the spring contacts.

28 Refitting is a reversal of removal.

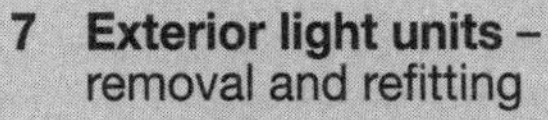

7 Exterior light units – removal and refitting

Headlight

1 Remove the front bumper cover, as described in Chapter 11.

2 Mark the position of the eccentric mountings to ensure correct alignment on refitting, then undo the mounting bolts and pull the headlight unit slightly forward **(see illustrations)**.

3 Unplug the wiring multipin connector **(see illustration)**.

4 Withdraw the headlamp forwards, while turning it as necessary to clear the front wing and plastic strip. On models with headlight washers, undo the screws and remove the plastic strip together with the washers.

5 Refitting is a reversal of removal, but on completion, check that the headlight is aligned flush with the surrounding bodywork. If not, turn the eccentric adjustment bushing near the bottom of the headlight as required. Finally, have the headlight alignment checked at the earliest opportunity.

Caution: After refitting a gas discharge headlamp, the basic setting of the Automatic Range Control system should be checked. Because of the requirement for specialised equipment, this can only be carried out by a VW dealer or suitably-equipped specialist.

Gas discharge light starter unit

Warning: The headlight bulb contains gas at very high pressure, and it is recommended that gloves and eye protection are worn to prevent potential personal injury.

6 Remove the headlight as described above.

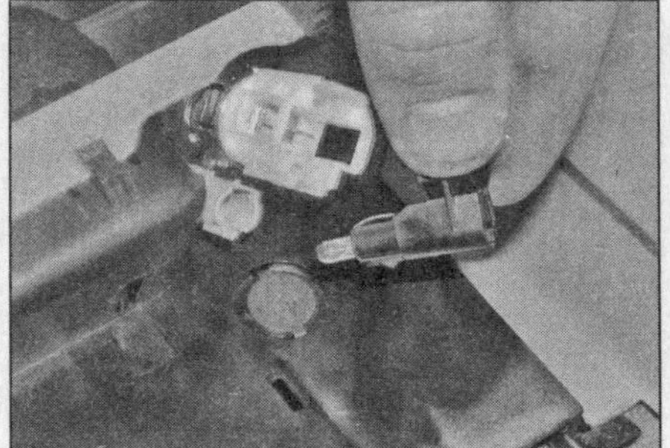

6.20 The bulb is integral with the holder

7 Remove the innermost small plastic cover from the rear of the headlight by turning it anticlockwise.

8 Turn the starter unit anticlockwise (OPEN) as far as possible (this will disconnect the wiring), and remove it from the headlight.

9 Refitting is a reversal of removal.

Gas discharge bulb control unit

10 Remove the headlight as described above.

11 Undo the retaining screws, and remove the control unit from the headlight. Note that the electrical connections are automatically separated when the unit is removed.

12 Refitting is a reversal of removal.

Direction indicator in mirror

13 Remove the exterior mirror housing as described in Chapter 11.

14 Remove the trim plate from the base of the exterior mirror by releasing the clips with a screwdriver.

15 Undo the screws and remove the indicator holder from the bottom of the mirror. Disconnect the wiring.

16 Undo the screws, and remove the indicator from the holder.

17 Refitting is a reversal of removal.

Door entry illumination in mirror

18 Fold the exterior mirror forwards to expose the light retaining screw on the inner end of the mirror. Undo the screw then unclip the light and withdraw it as far as the wiring will allow.

19 Disconnect the wiring and remove from the exterior mirror.

20 Refitting is a reversal of removal.

Rear light cluster

21 Inside the rear luggage compartment,

6.22 Use a length of washer tube to extract the bulb

7.2a Unscrew the upper...

7.2b ...and lower mounting bolts...

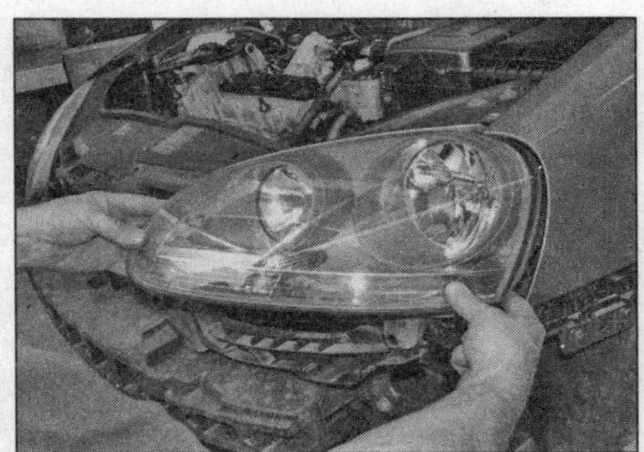

7.2c ...and pull the headlight unit slightly forward

7.3 Disconnecting the wiring

7.21 Fold back the carpet/open the access flap...

7.22a ...release the locking tab...

7.22b ...or squeeze together the clips, and disconnect the wiring plug

fold back the carpet/open the access cover to access the rear of the light cluster **(see illustration)**.

22 Disconnect the wiring plug, using a screwdriver to release the locking element **(see illustrations)**.

23 Unscrew the mounting nuts and withdraw the rear light cluster from the rear of the vehicle **(see illustrations)**.

24 Refitting is a reversal of removal.

High level brake light

25 The procedure is described as part of the bulb renewal procedure in Section 5.

Rear number plate light

26 The procedure is described as part of the rear number plate light bulb renewal procedure in Section 5.

Rear fog/reversing light

27 Remove the bulb as described in Section 5.

28 Unscrew the mounting nuts and withdraw the light from the tailgate **(see illustrations)**.

29 Refitting is a reversal of removal.

8 Headlight beam adjustment components – removal and refitting

Headlight adjustment switch

1 The switch is integral with the instrument illumination switch.

2 Removal and refitting of the switch assembly is covered in Section 4.

Headlight range adjustment motor

Halogen (Automotive Lighting)

3 Remove the headlight (see Section 7).

4 Remove the small plastic cover from the rear of the headlight by turning it anti-clockwise.

5 Access to one of the range adjustment motor mounting bolts is gained by breaking the plastic plug on the rear of the headlight. Unscrew the plastic hexagon to break the plug, then obtain a suitable plug to reseal the hole on refitting. Recover the plug from inside the headlight.

6 Unscrew the mounting bolts, then slightly lift the reflector and manoeuvre out the motor. As it is being removed, turn the ball-head to release it.

7 Disconnect the wiring and remove the motor from the headlight.

8 Refitting is a reversal of removal.

Halogen (Hella)

9 Remove the headlight (see Section 7).

10 Remove the small plastic cover from the rear of the headlight by turning it anti-clockwise.

11 Disconnect the wiring from the range control motor.

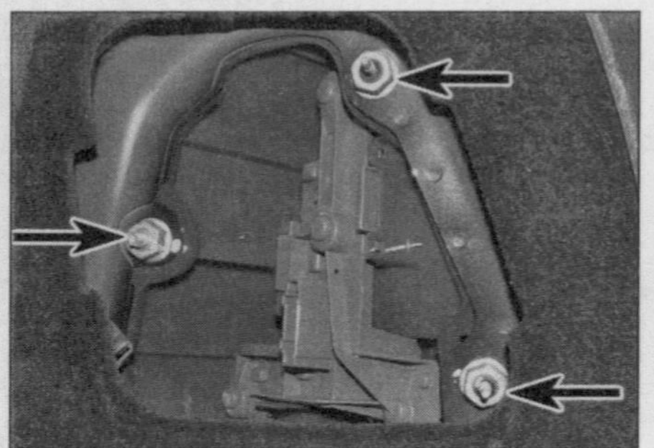
7.23a Undo the light cluster retaining nuts...

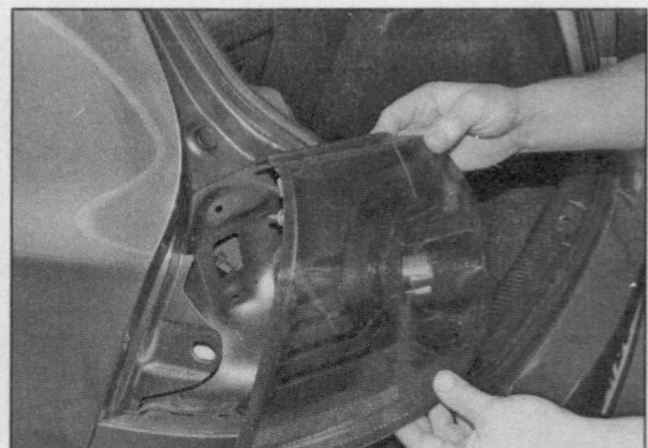
7.23b ...withdraw the rear light cluster on Golf Hatchback...

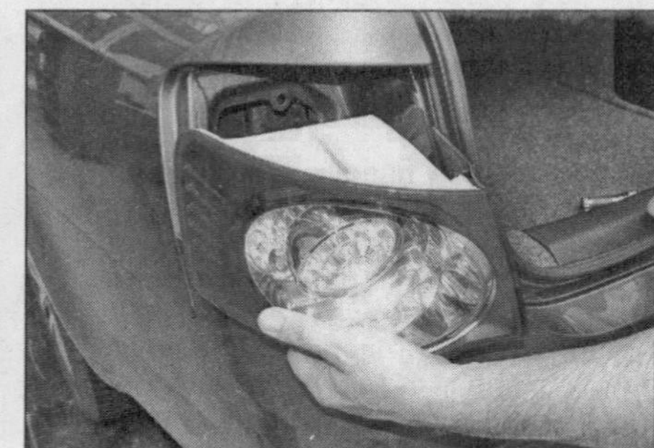
7.23c ...and Jetta models

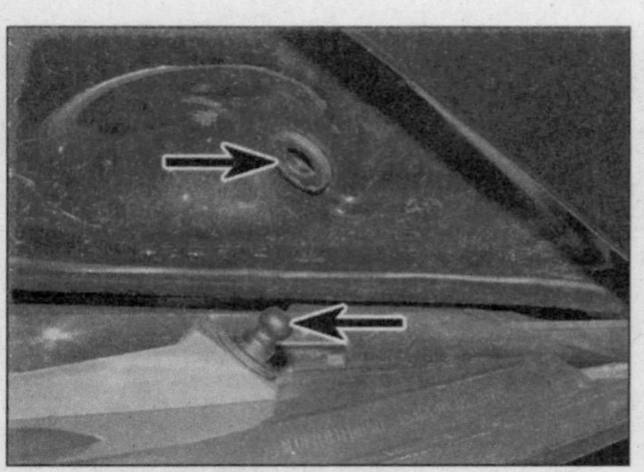
7.23d On Estate models, note the rear light locating pin and corresponding socket

7.28a Unscrew the mounting nuts...

7.28b ...and withdraw the rear fog/reversing light

12 Lift the rear of the motor and withdraw it slightly, then press the ball-head downwards out of the cup, and remove the motor.
13 Refitting is a reversal of removal.

Halogen (Visteon)

14 Remove the headlight (see Section 7).
15 Remove the small plastic cover from the rear of the headlight by turning it anti-clockwise.
16 Turn the control motor clockwise then disconnect the wiring.
17 Release the ball-head from the cup, and remove the motor.
18 Refitting is a reversal of removal.

Gas discharge

19 Remove the headlight (see Section 7).
20 Remove the small plastic cover from the rear of the headlight by turning it anti-clockwise.
21 Access to one of the range adjustment motor mounting bolts is gained by breaking the plastic plug on the rear of the headlight. Unscrew the plastic hexagon to break the plug, then obtain a suitable plug to reseal the hole on refitting. Recover the plug from inside the headlight.
22 Turn the starter unit anti-clockwise (OPEN) as far as possible (this will disconnect the wiring), and remove it from the headlight.
23 Unscrew the mounting bolts, then slightly lift the reflector and manoeuvre out the motor. As it is being removed, turn the ball-head to release it.
24 Disconnect the wiring and remove the motor from the headlight.
25 Refitting is a reversal of removal.

Automatic range control ECU

Note: *Although it is possible to remove and refit the ECU, the new unit will need to be ëcodedí before it will function correctly. This task can only be carried out by a VW dealer or suitably-equipped specialist.*
26 The ECU is located beneath the passenger end of the facia. First, prise off the end cover.
27 Release the locking bar and swivel open the wiring connector so that it can be unhooked.
28 Undo the mounting screw and withdraw the ECU from the end of the facia.
29 Refitting is a reversal of removal, but make sure the ECU is correctly located in the bracket before reconnecting the wiring.

Vehicle level sender

30 Refer to Chapter 10.

9 Headlight beam alignment – general information

1 Accurate adjustment of the headlight beam is only possible using optical beam setting equipment and this work should therefore be carried out by a VW dealer or suitably-equipped workshop.

10.3a Undo the two lower retaining screws...

10.3b ...and withdraw the instrument panel from the facia, noting that the electrical contacts will separate automatically

2 For reference, the headlights can be adjusted using the adjuster assemblies fitted to the top of each light unit. The inner adjuster alters the lateral position of the beam whilst the outer adjuster alters the height of the beam.

10 Instrument panel – removal and refitting

Removal

1 Switch off the ignition and all electrical consumers and remove the ignition key. Release the steering wheel adjustment handle, pull the wheel out as far as possible, and set it in the lowest position.
2 Carefully prise out the gap cover, then undo the screws and remove the upper shroud from the steering column.
3 Undo the two lower retaining screws and carefully pull the instrument panel from the facia. The electrical contacts will separate automatically from the rear of the panel **(see illustrations)**.

Refitting

4 Refitting is a reversal of removal.

11 Instrument panel components – removal and refitting

It is not possible to dismantle the instrument panel. If any of the gauges are faulty, the complete instrument panel must be renewed.

12 Service interval indicator – general information and resetting

1 All Golf and Jetta models are equipped with a service interval indicator. After all necessary maintenance work has been completed (see the relevant part of Chapter 1), the service interval display code must be reset. If more than one service schedule is carried out, note that the relevant display intervals must be reset individually.
2 The display is reset using the button on the left-hand side of the instrument panel (below the speedometer) and the clock setting button on the right-hand side of the panel (below the clock/tachometer). Resetting is described in the relevant part of Chapter 1.

13 Clock – removal and refitting

The clock is integral with the instrument panel, and cannot be removed separately. The instrument panel is a sealed unit, and if the clock, or any other components, are faulty, the complete instrument panel must be renewed. Refer to Section 10 to remove it.

14 Cigarette lighter – removal and refitting

Removal

1 Disconnect the battery negative lead (refer to *Disconnecting the battery* in the *Reference* Chapter at the end of this manual).
2 Remove the centre console as described in Chapter 11.
3 Remove the bulbholder as described in Section 6.
4 Push the centre element of the lighter out of the mounting.

Refitting

5 Refitting is a reversal of removal.

15 Horn – removal and refitting

Removal

1 Switch off the ignition and all electrical consumers and remove the ignition key.
2 Remove the front bumper as described in Chapter 11.
3 Disconnect the wiring, then unscrew the

15.3 Horn location (front bumper removed)

mounting bolt and withdraw the horn together with the mounting bracket **(see illustration)**.

4 Unscrew the nut and remove the horn from the bracket.

Refitting

5 Refitting is a reversal of removal.

16 Speedometer sensor – general information

All models are fitted with an electronic speedometer sensor. This device measures the rotational speed of the transmission final drive and converts the information into an electronic signal, which is then sent to the speedometer module in the instrument panel. On certain models, the signal is also used as an input by the engine management system ECU, and the trip computer.

Unlike earlier models, no electronic speedometer sensor is fitted to the models covered in this Manual. Vehicle speed is determined from the ABS wheel sensor signals, and processed by the engine management ECU.

17 Wiper arm – removal and refitting

Removal

1 Operate the wiper motor, then switch off so that the wiper arms return to the at-rest position. Alternatively, set the wiper blades to the Winter/Service (vertical) position by operating the wipers within 10 seconds of switching off the ignition. **Note:** *The wiper motor will only operate with the bonnet closed.*

2 Stick a piece of masking tape to the glass along the edge of the wiper blade to use as an alignment aid on refitting.

3 Prise off the wiper arm spindle nut cover, then slacken but do not completely remove the spindle nut. Lift the blade off the glass and pull the wiper arm until it releases from the spindle. Remove the spindle nut **(see illustrations)**. If necessary the arm can be levered off the spindle using a suitable flat-bladed screwdriver. **Note:** *If both windscreen wiper arms are to be removed at the same time mark them for identification; the arms are not interchangeable.*

Refitting

4 Ensure that the wiper arm and spindle splines are clean and dry, then refit the arm to the spindle, aligning the wiper blade with the tape fitted on removal. Refit the spindle nut, tightening it securely, and clip the nut cover back in position.

Note: *Where the wipers were set to the Winter/Service position in paragraph 1, they will only resume their normal position after actuating the wipers twice, or after starting a journey when the speed of the car is greater than 1 mph.*

18 Windscreen wiper motor and linkage – removal and refitting

Removal

1 The wiper motor control unit is integrated into the wiper motor. Note that the windscreen wiper system has an APP (alternating park position) function. Every second time the wipers are switched off, the wiper arm is moved up slightly from its lowest position in order to maintain the efficiency of the wiper blades. If the motor crank is disconnected, it must be reset by first deactivating the APP function, however, this requires the use of diagnostic equipment not available to the home mechanic. It is therefore important to accurately mark the crank in relation to the motor spindle before removing it. Reactivation of the function occurs automatically after 100 cycles of the wiper movement, and this also applies to new motors.

2 Remove the wiper arms as described in Section 17.

3 Disconnect the battery negative lead (refer to *Disconnecting the battery* in the *Reference* Chapter at the end of this manual).

4 Pull off the rubber sealing strip from the top of the bulkhead **(see illustration)**.

5 Starting on the right-hand side, carefully pull the plastic windscreen cowling from the windscreen seal **(see illustration)**.

Caution: Do not use a screwdriver lever between the cowling and windscreen as this is likely to result in the windscreen cracking.

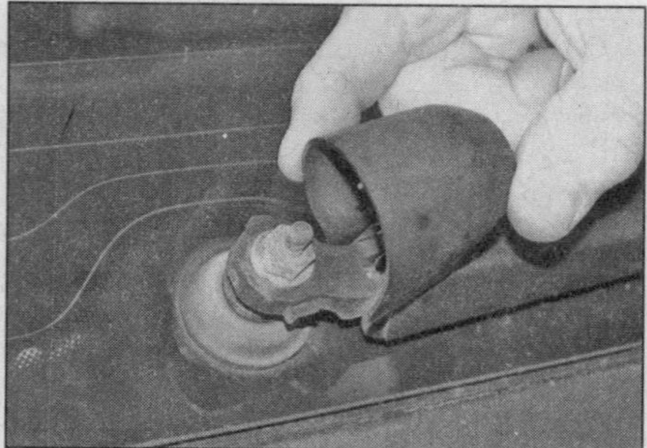

17.3a Prise up the spindle nut cover...

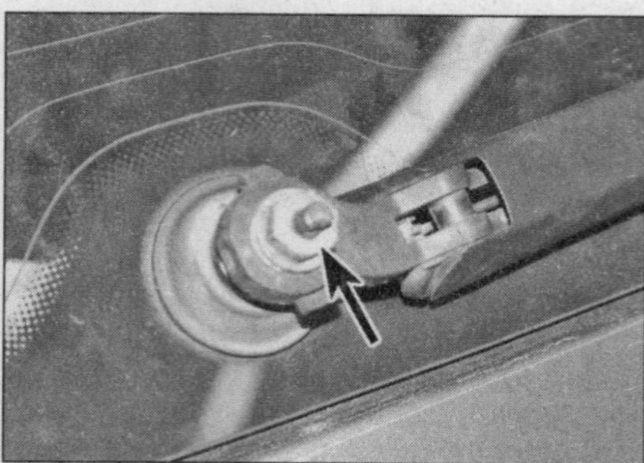

17.3b ...unscrew the spindle nut...

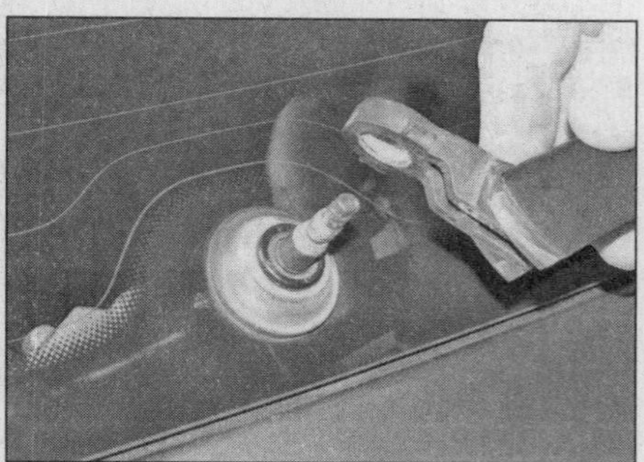

17.3c ...and remove the tailgate wiper arm

17.3d Remove the cover...

17.3e ...then unscrew the nut and remove the windscreen wiper arm

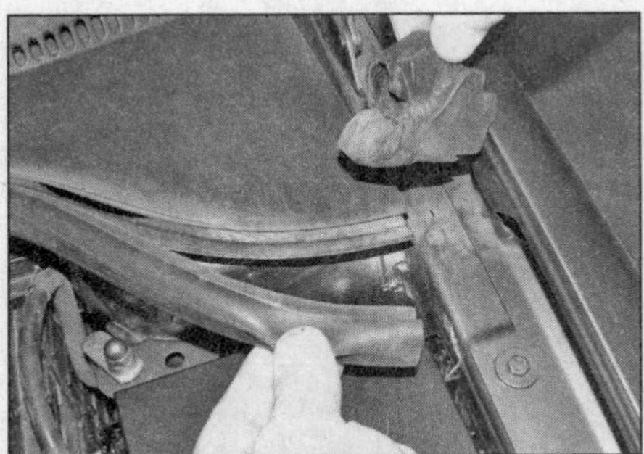
18.4 Pull off the rubber sealing strip...

18.5 ...and remove the plastic windscreen cowling

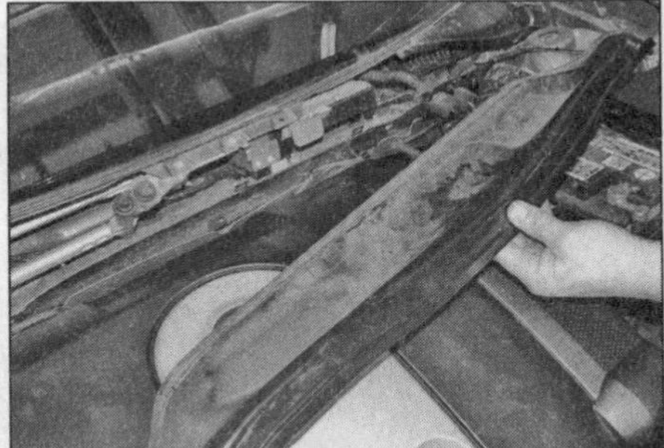
18.6 Removing the bulkhead panel

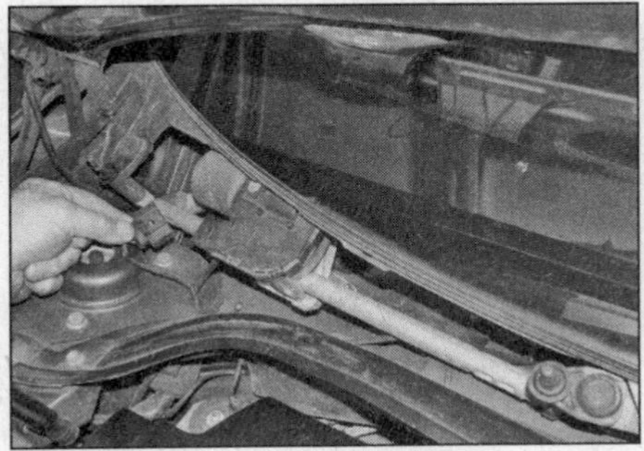
18.7 Disconnecting the wiring plug

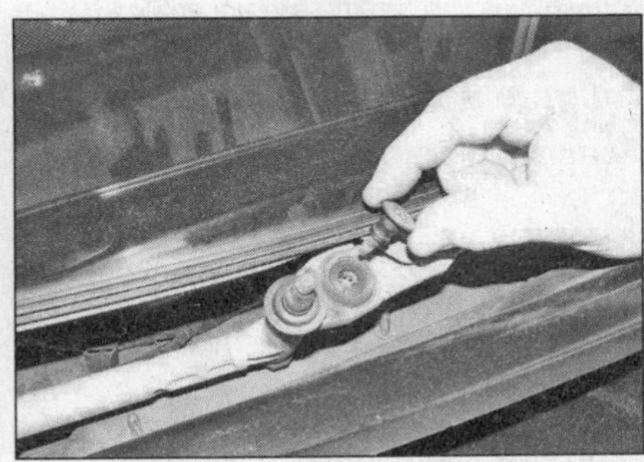
18.8a Unscrew the mounting bolts...

18.8b ...and remove the windscreen wiper motor and linkage

6 Unscrew the mounting bolt (RHS) and nut (LHS) and remove the bulkhead panel from the rear of the engine compartment **(see illustration)**.

7 Disconnect the wiring plug **(see illustration)**.

8 Unscrew the mounting bolts and manoeuvre the windscreen wiper motor and linkage out from the scuttle **(see illustrations)**.

9 Recover the washers and spacers from the motor mounting rubbers, noting their locations, then inspect the rubbers for signs of damage or deterioration, and renew if necessary.

10 To separate the motor from the linkage, proceed as follows.

a) *Make alignment marks between the motor spindle and the linkage to ensure correct alignment on refitting, and note the orientation of the linkage.*
b) *Unscrew the nut securing the linkage crank to the motor spindle.*
c) *Unscrew the three bolts securing the motor to the mounting plate, then withdraw the motor.*

Refitting

11 Refitting is a reversal of removal, bearing in mind the following points.

a) *If the motor has been separated from the linkage, ensure that the marks made on the motor spindle and linkage before removal are aligned, and ensure that the linkage is orientated as noted before removal.*
b) *Ensure that the washers and spacers are fitted to the motor mounting rubbers as noted before removal.*
c) *Lubricate the windscreen cowling mounting slots with a silicone-based spray lubricant to ease installation. Do not strike the cowling to seat it in position as this could result in the windscreen cracking.*
d) *Refit the wiper arms as described in Section 17.*

19 Rear wiper motor – removal and refitting

Removal

1 Remove the wiper arm as described in Section 17.

2 Recover the wiper motor shaft sealing ring.

3 Open the tailgate, then remove the trim panel as described in Chapter 11.

4 Unplug the wiring connector from the motor **(see illustration)**.

5 Disconnect the washer fluid hose from the washer nozzle connector on the motor assembly **(see illustration)**.

6 Unscrew the three nuts securing the motor, then withdraw the assembly. If necessary, renew the rubber grommet **(see illustrations)**.

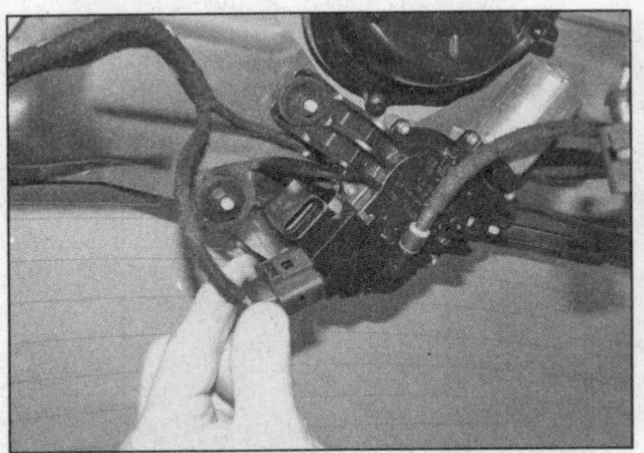
19.4 Disconnect the wiring...

19.5 ...and washer fluid hose from the tailgate wiper motor

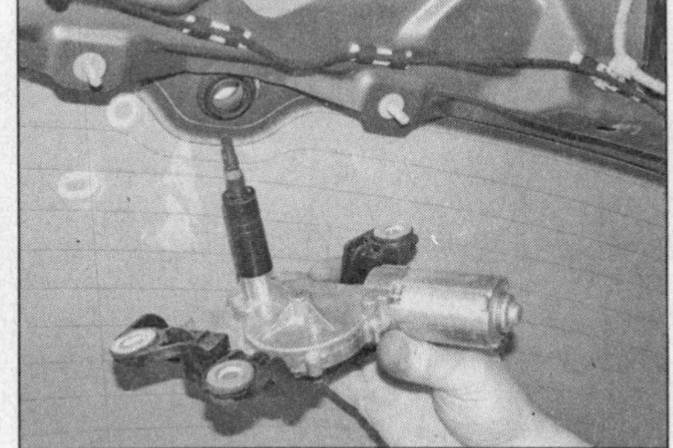
19.6a Removing the tailgate wiper motor

Refitting

7 Refitting is a reversal of removal, but ensure that the motor shaft rubber sealing ring is correctly refitted to prevent water leaks, and refit the wiper arm with reference to Section 17.

19.6b Tailgate wiper motor rubber grommet

20 Washer system components – removal and refitting

Washer fluid reservoir and pumps

Removal

1 Switch off the ignition and all electrical consumers and remove the ignition key.
2 In the engine compartment, unscrew the mounting bolt and remove the extension from the reservoir filler neck.
3 Remove the front bumper as described in Chapter 11.
4 On models with an auxiliary heater, the engine compartment front lock carrier crossmember must be positioned in its Service position as for removing the engine in Chapter 2G. The auxiliary heater intake dampers must also be removed.
5 Note that the hose connections to the reservoir are colour-coded to ensure correct fitment. Disconnect the hoses from the washer pump motors. **Note:** *Position a suitable container beneath the reservoir to catch spilt fluid.*
6 Disconnect the wiring from the fluid level sender.
7 Pull the pump motors upwards from the reservoir and disconnect the wiring **(see illustration)**.
8 Unscrew the mounting bolts and remove the reservoir from the vehicle **(see illustration)**.

Refitting

9 Refitting is a reversal of removal.

Windscreen washer jets

Removal

10 Open the bonnet, and pull the washer jet towards the front of the bonnet, and down.
11 Disconnect the washer tube and wiring, and remove the jet.

Refitting

12 Refitting is a reversal of removal. Note that the aim of the jet can be adjusted using a screwdriver and turning the eccentric shaft at the base of the washer jet.

Tailgate washer jet

Removal

13 Switch off the ignition and all electrical consumers and remove the ignition key.
14 Unclip the cover from the wiper arm spindle for access to the washer jet, and pull the jet from the centre of the spindle.

Refitting

15 On refitting, ensure that the jet is securely pushed into position. Check the operation of the jet. If necessary, adjust the nozzle, aiming the spray at a point slightly above the area of glass swept by the wiper blade.

Headlight pop-up washer jets

Removal

16 Switch off the ignition and all electrical consumers and remove the ignition key.
17 Carefully pull the washer jet out from the front bumper to its full extent, and hold it. Carefully prise the end cap from the washer jet.
18 Still holding the washer jet, lift the securing clip slightly, and pull the jet from the lift cylinder.

Refitting

19 Refitting is a reversal of removal. Operate the washers several times to bleed any trapped air.

Headlight pop-up washer jet lift cylinder

Removal

20 Remove the washer jet end cap as described in paragraphs 16 and 17.
21 Remove the front bumper as described in Chapter 11.
22 Undo the two retaining screws, and withdraw the cylinder.
23 Clamp the hose, squeeze the retaining clip, and disconnect the hose.

Refitting

24 Refitting is a reversal of removal. Operate the washers several times to bleed any trapped air.

21 Radio/CD player/changer – removal and refitting

Note: *This Section only applies to standard-fit audio equipment.*

Radio/CD player

Removal

1 The radio/CD player is equipped with an electronic anti-theft system linked to the instrument panel. If the voltage supply to the radio is temporarily disconnected, the radio will function again when the supply is reconnected, without entering the safety code number, provided the radio is located in the original vehicle. Should the radio operation be blocked, normal operation can be restored by entering the correct anti-theft code.
2 Remove any CDs which may be in the unit. Switch off the ignition and all electrical consumers, and remove the ignition key.
3 Remove the facia centre vent panel as follows:

a) *On models without Climatronic, lift out the lining mat from the storage compartment on the top of the facia, then undo the screws now visible. Remove the storage compartment.*
b) *On models with Climatronic, prise out the sunlight sensor, disconnect the wiring, and undo the screw now visible. Using a screwdriver at the front of the panel, push the panel rearwards and lift it from the vent panel.*
c) *On all models, undo the screws and slightly lift the front of the centre vent panel, then use a screwdriver to prise the centre vent panel from the facia.*

4 Undo the surround mounting screws near the top of the radio/CD player, then prise out the surround **(see illustration)**.

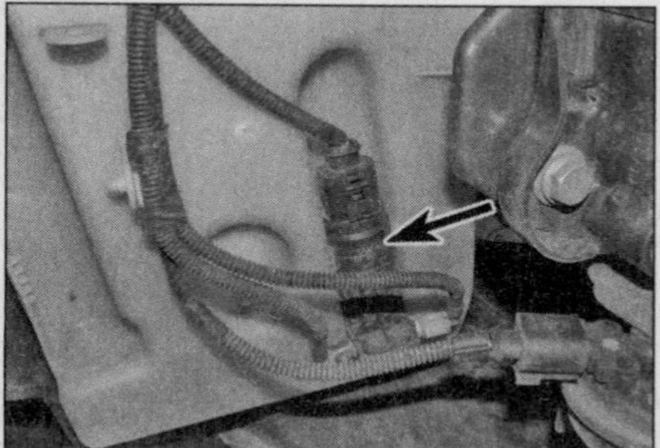

20.7 Washer fluid reservoir pump

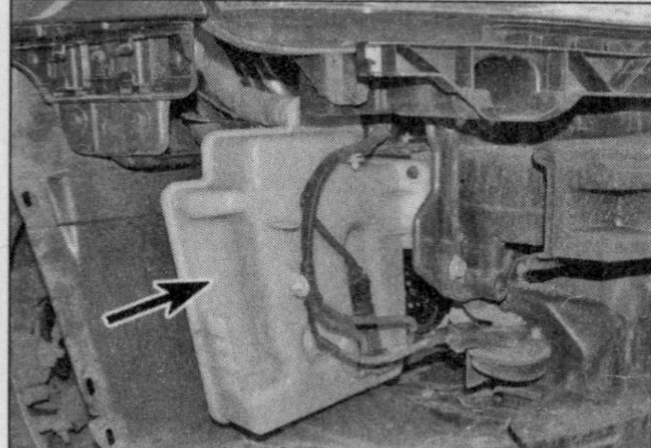

20.8 Washer fluid reservoir location

21.4 Remove the surround...

21.5a ...undo the screws...

21.5b ...then withdraw the radio/CD player from the facia...

21.5c ...and disconnect the wiring

5 Undo the radio/CD player mounting screws, and pull out the unit until the wiring plugs can be disconnected **(see illustrations)**. To do this, squeeze together the locking mechanism, swing up the locking bar, and pull off the connectors.

6 Withdraw the radio/CD player unit from the facia.

Refitting

7 Refitting is a reversal of removal.

CD changer

Removal

8 The CD changer is located in the storage compartment beneath the armrest located between the driver and passenger front seats. It is fitted with special mounting clips, requiring the use of special removal tools, which should be supplied with the vehicle, or may be obtained from an in-car entertainment specialist. Alternatively, two feeler blades can be used.

9 Switch off the ignition and all electrical consumers, and remove the ignition key.

10 Open the armrest and remove any CDs which may be in the unit.

11 Insert the tools into the slots on each side of the unit and push them until they snap into place. The CD changer can then be pulled out of the storage compartment using the tools, and the wiring connectors disconnected.

Refitting

12 Refitting is a reversal of removal.

22 Loudspeakers – removal and refitting

Front door-mounted treble

Removal

1 Switch off the ignition and all electrical consumers, and remove the ignition key.

2 Remove the door trim as described in Chapter 11.

3 Disconnect the speaker wiring plug.

4 Remove the single retaining screw, and push the mirror triangular cover upwards.

5 The loudspeaker is integral with the triangular mirror cover.

Refitting

6 Refitting is a reversal of removal.

Rear door-mounted treble

Removal

7 The loudspeaker is located on the inner trim panel. First, switch off the ignition and all electrical consumers, and remove the ignition key.

8 Remove the door trim as described in Chapter 11.

9 With the wiring disconnected from the loudspeaker, cut the trim plate clips and remove the unit from the door trim.

Refitting

10 Refitting is a reversal of removal, but use a soldering iron to 'weld' the trim plate clips in position.

Door-mounted bass

Removal

11 Switch off the ignition and all electrical consumers, and remove the ignition key.

12 Remove the door trim with reference to Chapter 11.

13 Disconnect the wiring plug from the loudspeaker.

14 Drill out the retaining rivets, and withdraw the speaker from the door **(see illustration)**. Recover the rubber sealing ring between the speaker and door trim. **Note:** *Where mid-range loudspeakers are fitted, they are secured with screws instead of rivets.*

Refitting

15 Refitting is a reversal of removal. The special-sized rivets should be available from VW dealers and in-car entertainment specialists.

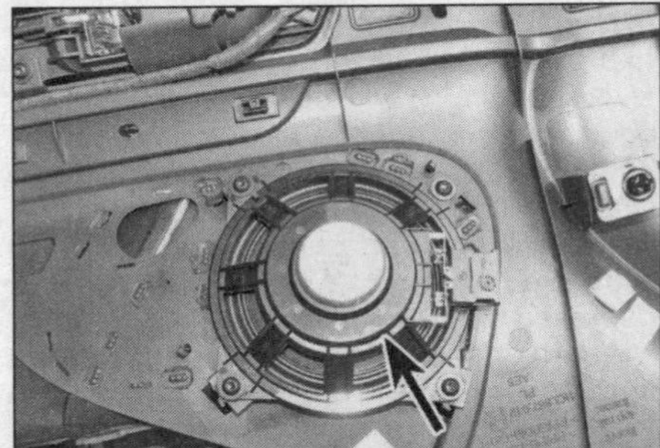
22.14 Front door-mounted bass loudspeaker

23 Radio aerials – removal and refitting

Removal

1 The radio aerial is integrated into the rear window which is bonded in position with a special adhesive. If the aerial is faulty, a new rear window must be fitted.

2 The navigation, telephone and auxiliary heater telestart aerial is fitted to the rear of the roof panel. First, remove the trim from the C-pillar.

3 Undo the screws and remove the two rear grab handles from the headlining.

4 Carefully lower the rear of the headlining and disconnect the wiring. Note the colour-coded wiring as follows:

a) Violet connector for the telephone.
b) Blue connector for the navigation system.
c) Remaining connector for the auxiliary heating remote control.

5 Unscrew the securing nut and withdraw the aerial base from the roof. Hold the aerial base as the nut is being unscrewed to prevent the base from rotating and scratching the roof panel. Recover the rubber spacer.

Refitting

6 Refitting is a reversal of removal, but make sure that the two guide lugs on the rubber spacer are correctly located in the aerial base.

24 Anti-theft alarm system and engine immobiliser – general information

Note: *This information is applicable only to the anti-theft alarm system fitted by VW as standard equipment.*

Models in the range are fitted with an anti-theft alarm system as standard equipment. The alarm has switches on all the doors (including the tailgate/boot lid), the bonnet and the ignition switch. If the tailgate/boot lid, bonnet or any of the doors

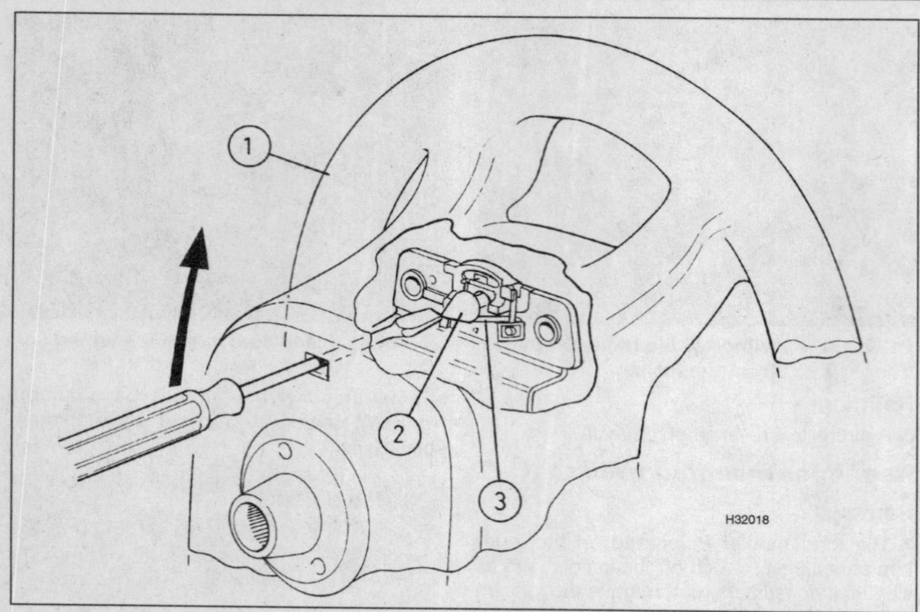

26.4a Airbag module removal

1 Steering wheel 2 Locking lug 3 Clip

are opened whilst the alarm is set, the alarm horn will sound and the hazard warning lights will flash. Some models are equipped with an internal monitoring system, which will activate the alarm system if any movement in the cabin is detected.

The alarm is set using the key in the driver's or passenger's front door lock, and tailgate/boot lid lock, or with the central locking remote control transmitter. The alarm system will then start to monitor its various switches approximately 30 seconds later.

With the alarm set, if the tailgate/boot lid is unlocked, the lock switch sensing will automatically be switched off but the door and bonnet switches will still be active. Once the tailgate/boot lid is shut and locked again, the switch sensing will be switched back on.

All models are fitted with an immobiliser system, which is activated by the ignition switch. A transponder reading coil on the ignition switch reads a code contained within the ignition key. The system sends a signal to the engine management electronic control unit (ECU) which allows the engine to start if the code is correct. If an incorrect ignition key is used, the engine will not start.

If a fault is suspected with the alarm or immobiliser systems, the vehicle should be taken to a VW dealer for examination. They will have access to a special diagnostic tester which will quickly trace any fault present in the system.

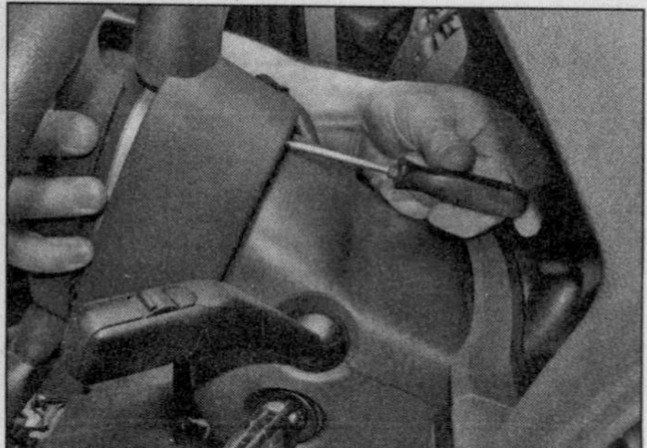

26.4b Releasing the driver's airbag retaining clips

25 Airbag system – general information and precautions

Warning: Before carrying out any operations on the airbag system, disconnect the battery negative terminal (refer to 'Disconnecting the battery' in the Reference section at the rear of this manual). When operations are complete, make sure no one is inside the vehicle when the battery is reconnected.

• Note that the airbags must not be subjected to temperatures in excess of 90°C. When the airbag is removed, ensure that it is stored the with the pad upwards to prevent possible inflation.

• Do not allow any solvents or cleaning agents to contact the airbag assemblies. They must be cleaned using only a damp cloth.

• The airbags and control unit are both sensitive to impact. If either is dropped or damaged they should be renewed.

A driver's airbag, passenger's airbag and side airbags were fitted as standard to the Golf/Jetta range. Certain models also have curtain airbags located behind the headlining on each side of the car. The airbag system consists of the airbag unit (complete with gas generator) which is fitted to the steering wheel (driver's side), facia (passenger's side), roof (where applicable) and front seats, an impact sensor, the control unit and a warning light in the instrument panel.

The airbag system is triggered in the event of a heavy frontal or side impact above a predetermined force; depending on the point of impact. The airbag is inflated within milliseconds and forms a safety cushion between the driver and the steering wheel, the passenger and the facia, and in the case of side impact, between front seat occupants and the sides of the cabin. This prevents contact between the upper body and cabin interior, and therefore greatly reduces the risk of injury. The airbag then deflates almost immediately.

Every time the ignition is switched on, the airbag control unit performs a self-test. The self-test takes approximately 3 seconds and during this time the airbag warning light on the facia is illuminated. After the self-test has been completed the warning light should go out. If the warning light fails to come on, remains illuminated after the initial 3 second period or comes on at any time when the vehicle is being driven, there is a fault in the airbag system. The vehicle should then be taken to a VW dealer for examination at the earliest possible opportunity.

26 Airbag system components – removal and refitting

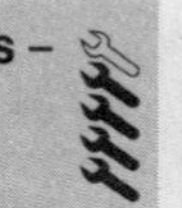

Note: *Refer to the warnings in Section 25 before carrying out the following operations.*

1 Disconnect the battery negative lead (refer to *Disconnecting the battery* in the *Reference* Chapter at the end of this manual), then continue as described under the relevant heading.

Driver's airbag

Removal

2 Set the front wheels to the straight-ahead position, and release the steering lock by inserting the ignition key.

3 Adjust the steering column to its highest position by releasing the adjustment handle, then extend the steering wheel as far as possible. Lock the column in this position.

4 With the spokes in the vertical position, insert a screwdriver approximately 8 mm into the hole in the upper rear of the steering wheel hub, then move it up to release the clip and free the airbag locking lug **(see illustrations)**. Now turn the steering wheel through 180° and release the remaining airbag locking lug.

5 Turn the steering wheel to its central, straight-ahead position.

6 Carefully withdraw the airbag module and disconnect the wiring. If necessary, use a piece of bent wire to carefully release the wiring **(see illustrations)**.

Caution: To prevent any discharge of static electricity into the airbag circuit, temporarily touch the vehicle bodywork before disconnecting the wiring.

Warning: Position the airbag in a safe and secure place, away from the work area.

Refitting

7 With the steering wheel in the straight-ahead position, locate the airbag module in position and reconnect the wiring. Carefully press in the module until both locking lugs are heard to engage. Reconnect the battery negative lead, ensuring that no-one is inside the vehicle as the lead is connected.

Passenger's airbag

Removal

8 Remove the passenger side glovebox with reference to Chapter 11.

9 Disconnect the wiring from the passenger's airbag **(see illustration)**.

Caution: To prevent any discharge of static electricity into the airbag circuit, temporarily touch the vehicle bodywork before disconnecting the wiring.

10 Unscrew the mounting bolts and remove the airbag and brackets **(see illustration)**, then unbolt the brackets.

Warning: Position the airbag in a safe and secure place, away from the work area.

Refitting

11 Refitting is a reversal of removal, but tighten the mounting bolts to the specified torque. Reconnect the battery negative lead, ensuring that no-one is inside the vehicle as the lead is connected.

Front seat side impact airbags

12 The side impact air bags are integral with the seats. As seat upholstery removal requires considerable skill and experience, if it is to be carried out without damage, it is best entrusted to an expert.

Roof curtain airbags

13 This work involves removing the headlining and major dismantling of interior trim panels, and is best entrusted to a VW dealer.

Rear side airbags

14 On saloon models, remove the rear seat cushion as described in Chapter 11. On estate models, fold the rear seat cushion forwards.

15 Undo the nut at the base of the side cushion, then prise out the cap and undo the bolt, and pull the side cushion/airbag upwards from place.

16 Disconnect the airbag wiring plug.

17 Refitting is a reversal of removal, but tighten the mounting bolts to the specified torque. Reconnect the battery negative lead, ensuring that no-one is inside the vehicle as the lead is connected.

26.6a Withdraw the driver's airbag...

26.6b ...then use a piece of bent wire to carefully release the wiring

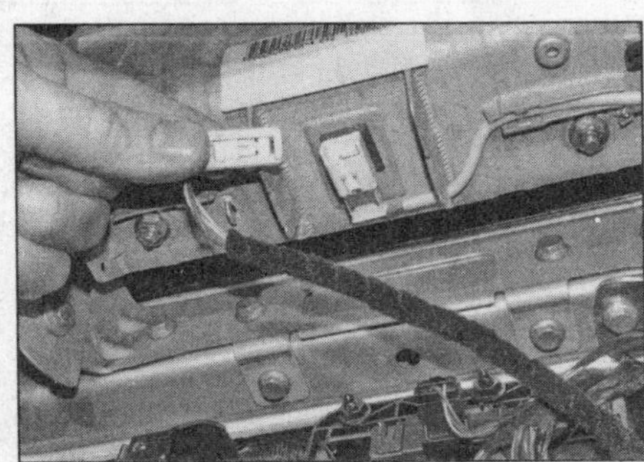

26.9 Disconnect the wiring...

26.10 ...then unscrew the mounting bolts from the passenger airbag

Airbag control unit

Removal

18 The airbag control unit is located beneath the centre of the facia, just in front of the gearchange assembly **(see illustration)**.

19 Remove the trim from each side of the centre console with reference to Chapter 11.

20 Release the locking lever and disconnect the wiring from the control unit.

21 Unscrew the nuts and remove the control unit from the vehicle.

Refitting

22 Refitting is the reverse of removal making sure the wiring connector is securely reconnected. Reconnect the battery negative lead, ensuring that no-one is inside the vehicle as the lead is connected.

Airbag wiring contact unit

Removal

23 Check that the front wheels are pointing straight-ahead and the steering wheel is in its centre position, then remove the steering wheel as described in Chapter 10.

24 Undo the screws and remove the column height and reach adjustment handle.

25 Carefully prise out the gap cover, then remove the upper shroud from the steering column.

26 Undo the two upper screws and single lower screw and remove the lower shroud.

27 The airbag clock spring/slip-ring must be held in its central position while it is removed, to ensure correct refitting. Unclip the airbag clock spring/slip-ring from the combination switch carrier by lifting the retaining hooks.

Refitting

28 Before refitting the airbag clock spring/slip-ring, check that it is in its central position as follows. There are two types fitted according to manufacturer as shown **(see illustrations)**. With the first type, the black rectangles must be visible in the window. With the second type, the yellow strip must be visible as shown.

29 The remaining procedure is a reversal of removal. Reconnect the battery negative lead, ensuring that no-one is inside the vehicle as the lead is connected.

Passenger airbag isolation switch

Removal

30 The switch is located inside the glovebox. To remove it, open the glovebox then use

26.18 Airbag control unit located beneath the centre of the facia

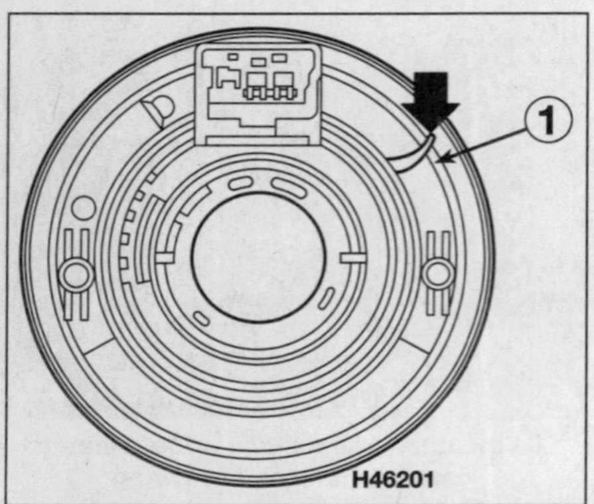

26.28a Airbag wiring contact unit centre setting – type 1

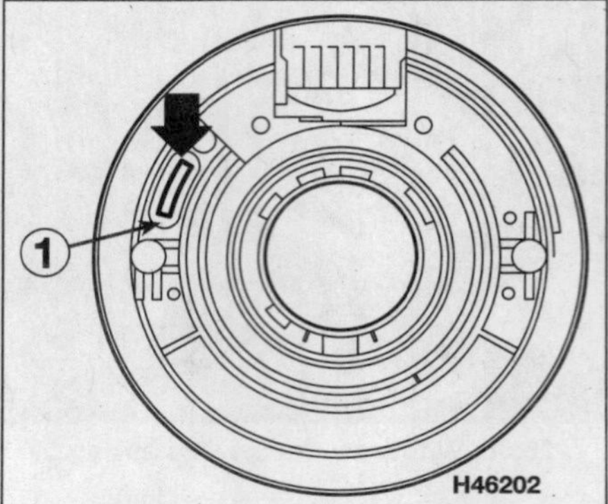

26.28b Airbag wiring contact unit centre setting – type 2

a screwdriver to prise out the switch **(see illustration)**. Disconnect the wiring.

Refitting

31 Refitting is a reversal of removal.

Front door crash sensor

Removal

32 Disconnect the battery.

33 Remove the door outer skin as described in Chapter 11.

34 Disconnect the wiring from the crash sensor **(see illustration)**.

35 Undo the mounting screws and remove the sensor.

Refitting

36 Refitting is a reversal of removal. Make sure that nobody is inside the vehicle when first switching on the ignition.

Rear wheel housing crash sensor

Removal

37 Disconnect the battery.

38 Remove the bench seat as described in Chapter 11.

39 Remove the side padding and the wheel arch liner.

40 Disconnect the wiring from the crash sensor **(see illustration)**. To do this, press the clip to the rear while pulling on the connector.

41 Undo the mounting screws and remove the sensor.

Refitting

42 Refitting is a reversal of removal. Make sure that nobody is inside the vehicle when first switching on the ignition.

27 Parking aid components – general information, removal and refitting

General information

1 The parking aid system is available as a standard fitment on highline models, and optional on other models. Four ultrasound sensors located in the rear bumper measure the distance to the closest object behind the car, and inform the driver using acoustic signals from a buzzer located under the rear luggage compartment trim. The nearer the object, the more frequent the acoustic signals.

2 The system includes a control unit and self-diagnosis program, and therefore, in the event of a fault, the vehicle should be taken to a VW dealer.

Control unit

3 The parking aid control unit is located in the luggage compartment behind the right-hand trim panel. Switch off the ignition and all electrical consumers, and remove the ignition key, then remove the right-hand trim with reference to Chapter 11.

4 Depress the locking lugs and disconnect the wiring plugs from the control unit.

5 Unclip the unit from the mounting bracket.

6 Refitting is a reversal of removal.

Range/distance sensor

7 Remove the rear bumper as described in Chapter 11.

8 Disconnect the wiring from the sensor.

9 Release the lugs and pull the sensor from the bumper.

10 Refitting is a reversal of removal. Press the sensor firmly into position until the retaining clips engage.

Warning buzzer

11 The warning buzzer is located in the luggage compartment behind the right-hand trim panel. Switch off the ignition and all electrical consumers and remove the ignition key, then remove the right-hand trim with reference to Chapter 11.

12 Disconnect the wiring, then release the clips and remove the buzzer from the mounting bracket.

13 Refitting is a reversal of removal.

26.30 Removing the passenger's airbag isolation switch from inside the glovebox

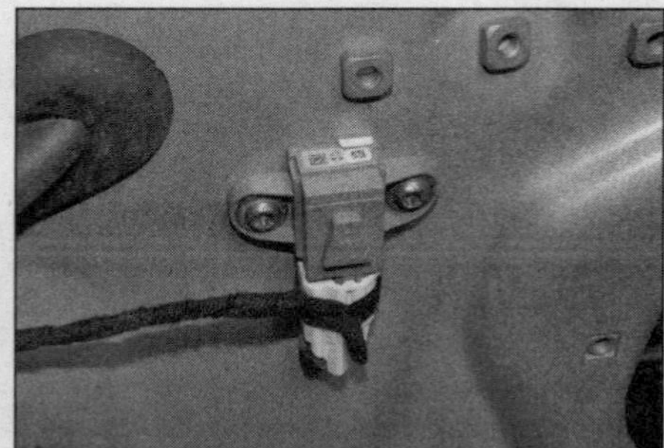

26.34 Front door crash sensor

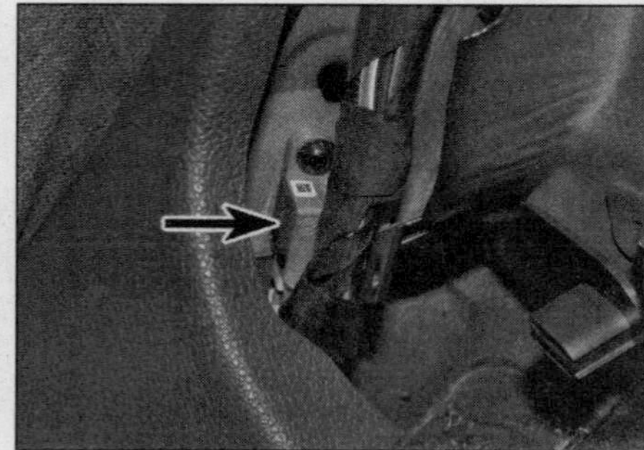

26.40 Rear side crash sensor

Volkswagen Golf & Jetta wiring diagrams — Diagram 1

Key to symbols

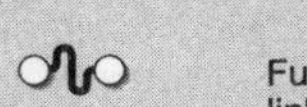

Fusible link, link number and rating

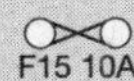

Fuse, fuse number and rating

Bulb

Heating element with indicated current rating

Electric motor

Dotted outline indicates the item (bulb) is part of a larger assembly

Solid outline and drop shadow indicates the item (bulb) is an individual part and not part of a larger assembly

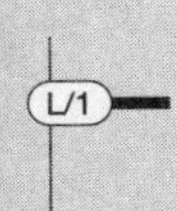

Interface connector pins

Letter indicates connector
Number indicates pin number

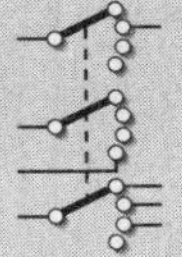

Ganged switch with multiple contacts

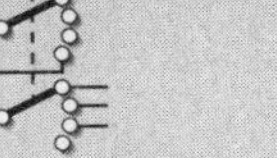

Single switch with multiple contacts

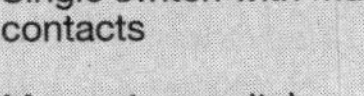

Momentary switch

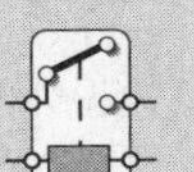

Relay

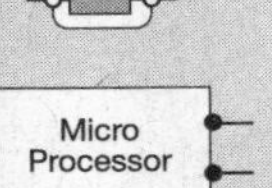

Graphical representation of a component for which no additional detail is provided

Link to another circuit; where appropriate the interfacing pin numbers are shown

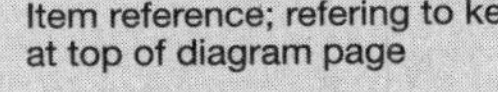

Item reference; refering to key at top of diagram page

Connecting wires

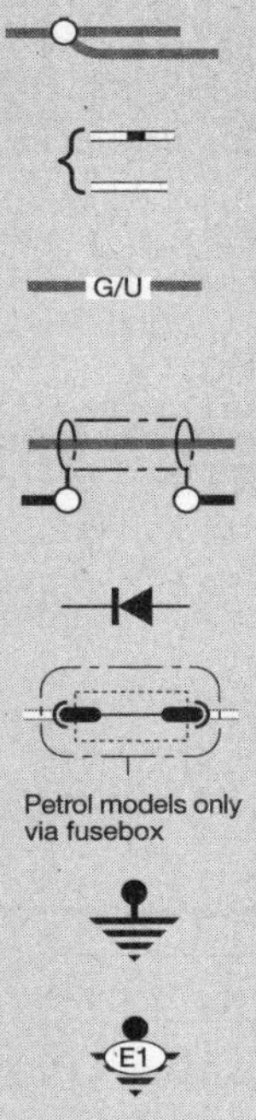

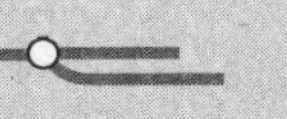

Wire splice or soldered joint

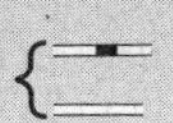

Alternative layout depending on model / year

G/U

Wire colour (Green with blue tracer)

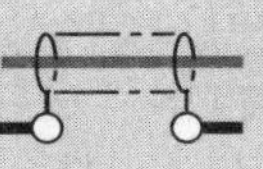

Wire enclosed in a screen (bonded both ends)

Diode

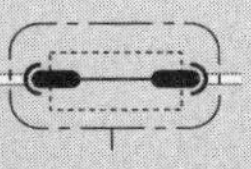

Petrol models only via fusebox

Chain dashed box indicates item specific to a paricular variant

Earth point

Earth point with reference (see earth locations on this page)

Key to circuits

Diagram 1	Information on wiring diagrams.
Diagram 2	Typical starting and charging, ignition switch.
Diagram 3	Radiator fan, horn, headlights (halogen)
Diagram 4	Directional indicators, brake / rear side lights, front side light number plate light.
Diagram 5	Fog lights, reversing lights, switch illumination, headlight levelling (halogen).
Diagram 6	Gas discharge headlights.
Diagram 7	Front / rear windscreen wipers and washers, headlight washers, hazard warning switch, cigar lighters.
Diagram 8	Central locking system.
Diagram 9	Motorised door mirrors, electric window lifts
Diagram 10	Interior lighting system, motorised sunroof.
Diagram 11	Anti-lock brake system, heated rear screen, heater blower.
Diagram 12	Seat heaters, CAN bus and diagnostic connector.
Diagram 13	Audio system.
Diagram 14	Instruments.
Diagram 15	Engine and passenger fusebox details.

Earth locations

E1	Left headlight
E2	Bottom of left A post (75mm up from to of door sill)
E3	Top of steering column
E4	Bottom of left B post
E5	Rear left side panel
E6	Right headlight
E7	Behind centre of dash
E8	Bottom of right A post, (75mm up from top of door sill)
E9	Right front floor pan, adjacent to bottom front of door opening
E10	Bottom of right B post
E11	Rear right side panel

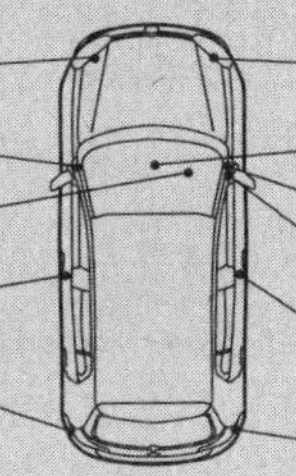

H33591

Diagram 2

Wire colours

B	Black	P	Purple
G	Green	R	Red
K	Pink	S	Grey
Lg	Light green	U	Blue
N	Brown	W	White
O	Orange	Y	Yellow

Key to items

1. Battery
2. Starter motor
3. Onboard supply control unit
   a terminal 15 supply relay (J681)
4. Ignition switch
   a key lock solenoid
5. Terminal 50 supply relay (J682)
6. Fusebox A (engine compartment)
7. Fusebox B (engine compartment)
   a = terminal 15 supply relay (J329)
   b = terminal 50 supply relay (J682)
8. Alternator
9. Engine control unit
10. Steering column control unit

H33592

Typical starting and charging system (petrol)

convenience system CAN bus

to fuse box C terminal 50 supply, see other sheets

till Oct 05
Nov 05 on

Note 1
90-120A alternator, fuse = 150A
140A alternator, fuse = 200A

Typical starting and charging system (diesel)

convenience system CAN bus

Note 1
90-120A alternator, fuse = 150A
140A alternator, fuse = 200A

Ignition switch

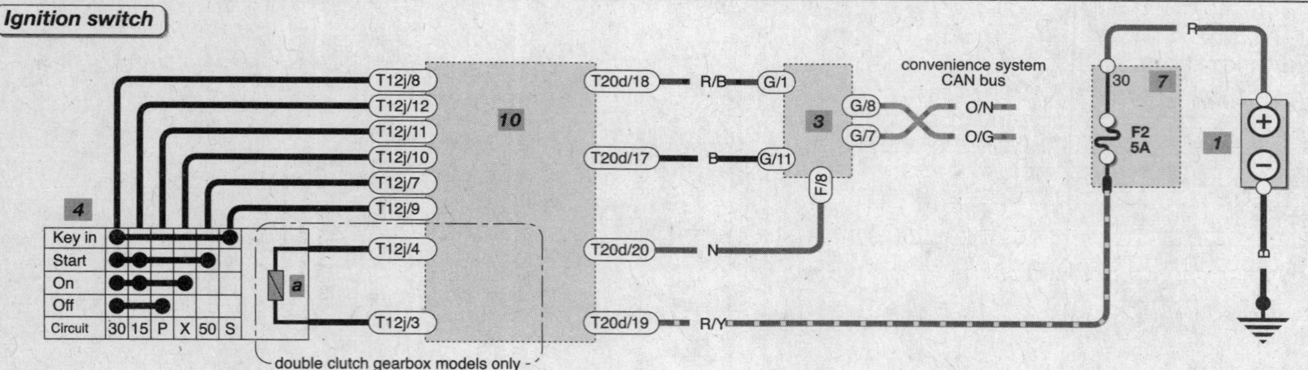

Diagram 3

Wire colours

B	Black	**P**	Purple
G	Green	**R**	Red
K	Pink	**S**	Grey
Lg	Light green	**U**	Blue
N	Brown	**W**	White
O	Orange	**Y**	Yellow

Key to items

1 Battery
3 Onboard supply control unit
b = relief relay J59
c = horn relay J413 or dual tone horn relay J4
6 Fusebox A (engine compartment)
7 Fusebox B (engine compartment)
c = petrol engine control unit supply relay J271 or terminal 30 supply relay J317 (diesel)
10 Steering column control unit
11 Radiator fan control unit / motor
12 Horn switch
13 Rotary joint
14 Horn (base)
15 Horn (treble)
16 Lighting switch
a = auto head lights, side, head lights
d = switch illumination
18 Fusebox C (passenger compartment)
19 Lefthand column switch
a = dip / flash
20 Lefthand headlight
a main beam
b dip beam
21 Righthand headlight
a main beam
b dip beam
22 Rain / light sensor

H33593

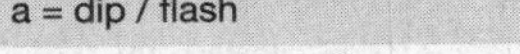

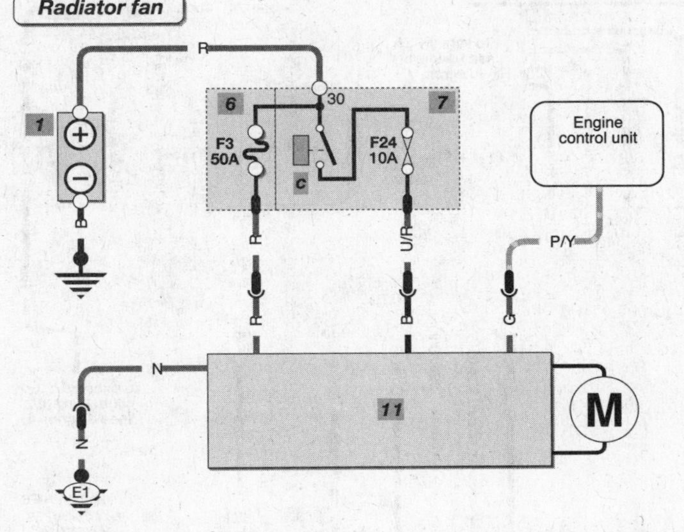

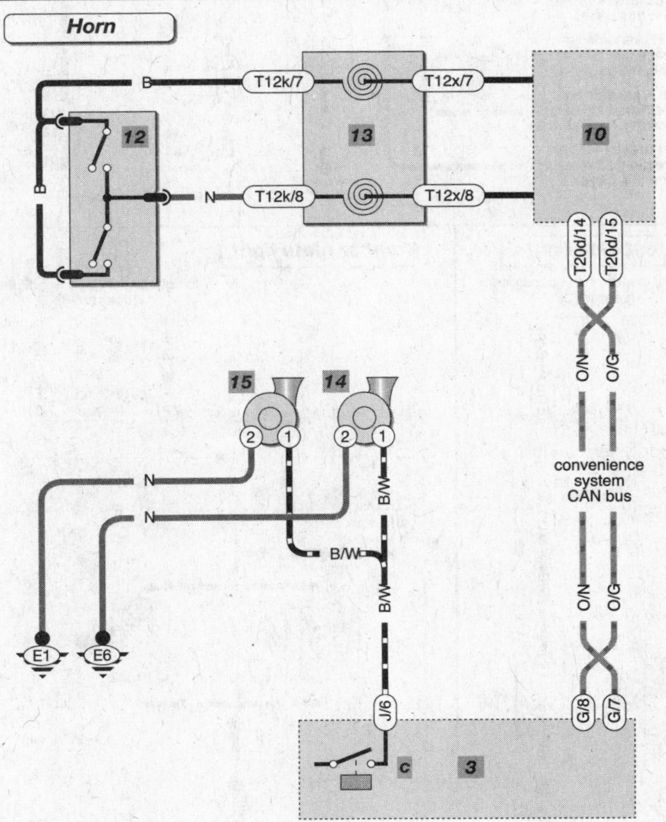

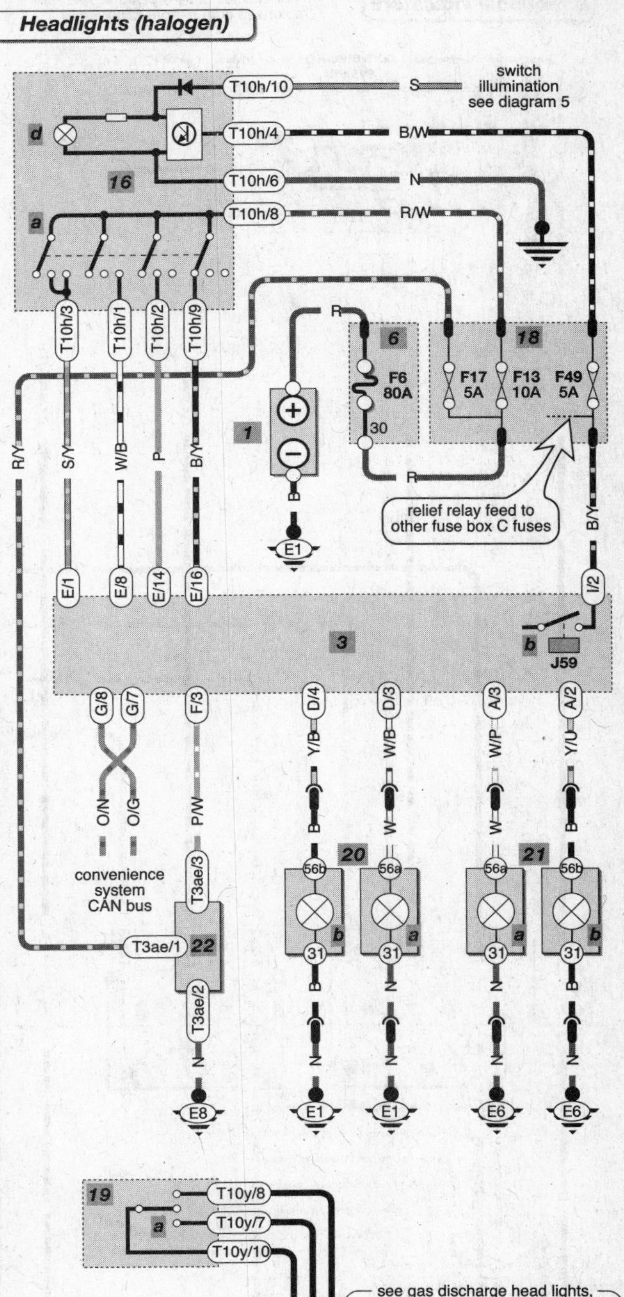

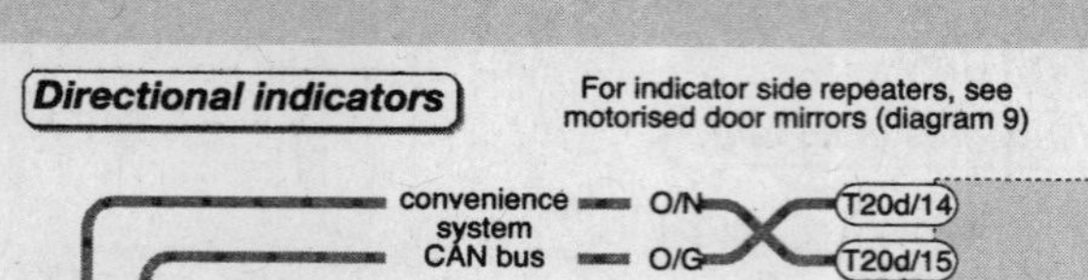

Wire colours

B	Black	**P**	Purple
G	Green	**R**	Red
K	Pink	**S**	Grey
Lg	Light green	**U**	Blue
N	Brown	**W**	White
O	Orange	**Y**	Yellow

Key to items

3 Onboard supply control unit
10 Steering column control unit
18 Fusebox C (passenger compartment
19 LH column switch
  b = indicator switch
23 Directional indicator front LH
24 Directional indicator front RH
25 Rear light cluster LH
  a= indicator
  b=tail light
  c=brake and tail light
26 Rear light cluster RH
  a=indicator
  b=tail light
  c=brake and tail light
31 Brake pedal switch
32 Brake switch
33 High level brake light
34 Sidelight front LH
35 Sidelight front RH
36 Number plate light

Diagram 4

H33594

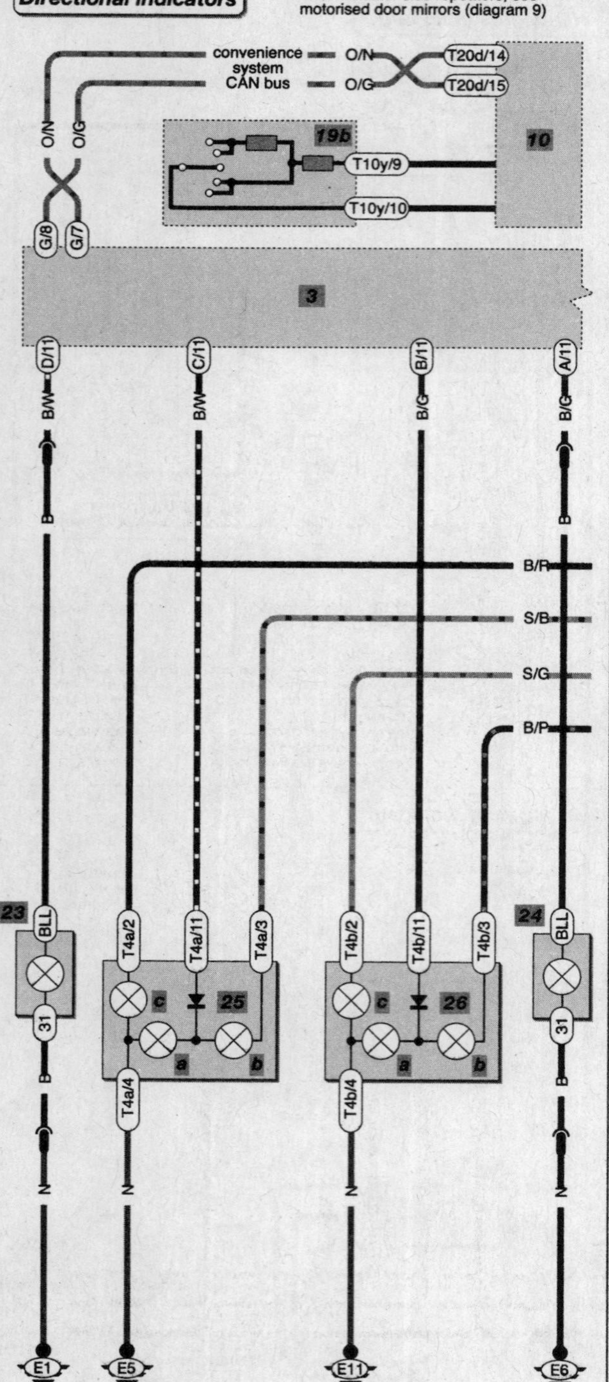

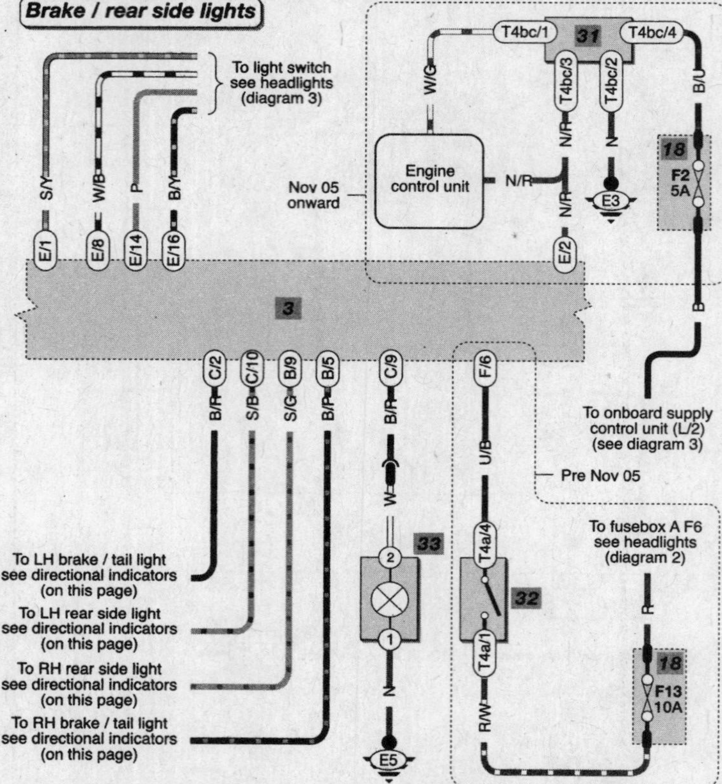

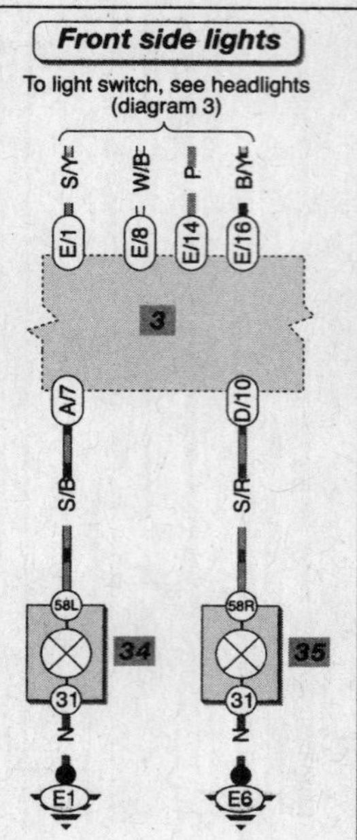

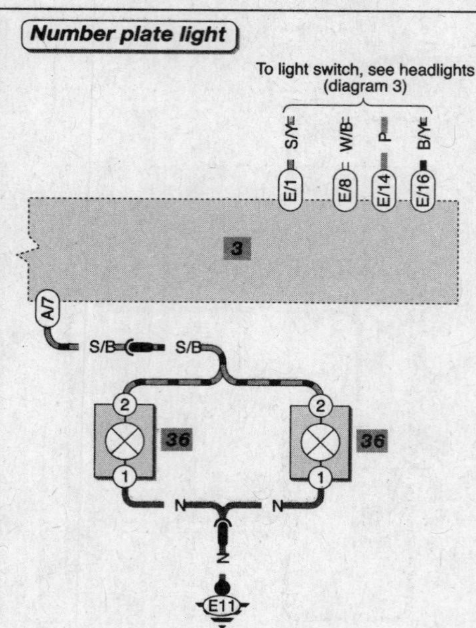

Diagram 5

Wire colours

B	Black	**P**	Purple
G	Green	**R**	Red
K	Pink	**S**	Grey
Lg	Light green	**U**	Blue
N	Brown	**W**	White
O	Orange	**Y**	Yellow

Key to items

3 Onboard supply control unit
16 Light switch
  b = front fog light switch
  c = rear fog light switch
18 Fusebox C (passenger compartment)
37 Fog light, front left
38 Fog light, front right
39 Fog light, rear
40 Reversing light
41 Reversing light switch
42 Dimmer / headlight levelling controls
  a = dimmer control
  b = switch illumination
  c = headlight levelling control
43 Headlight levelling motor, left hand
44 Headlight levelling motor, right hand

H33595

Fog lights

convenience system CAN bus
G/8 G/7
3
E/13 E/6 D/2 LHD B/4 C/3 RHD A/4
B/W Y/W Y/W B/W W
39 37 38 E1 16
T10h/5 T10h/4 B/W
to F49 fusebox C see headlights (diagram 3)

Switch illumination

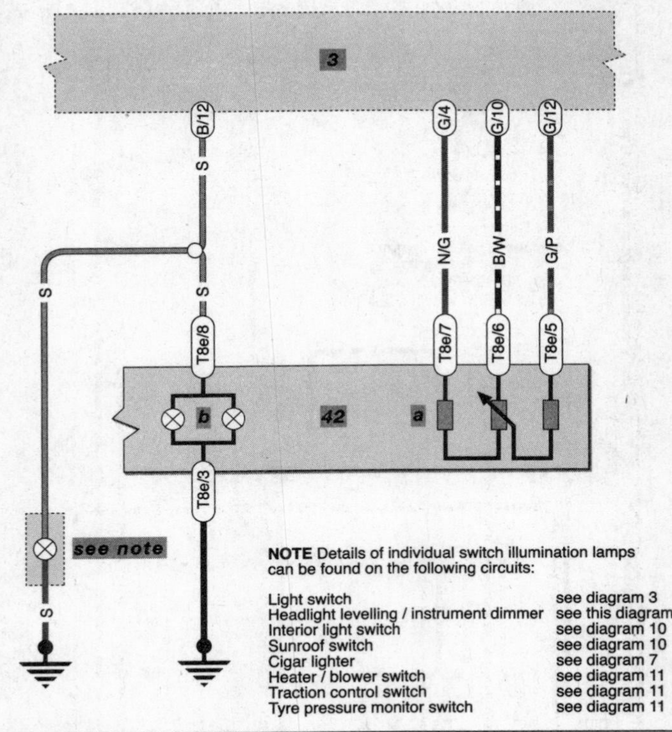

Reversing lights

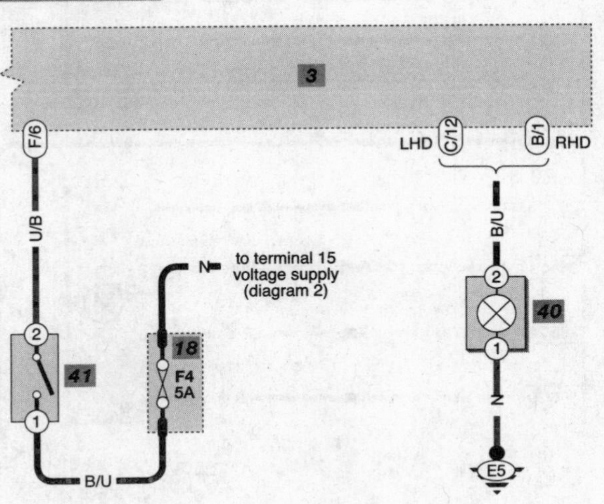

Headlight levelling (halogen)

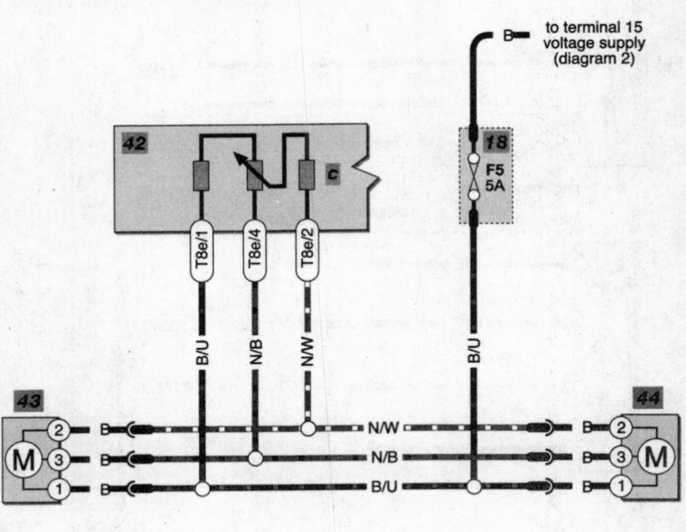

Diagram 6

Wire colours

B	Black	P	Purple
G	Green	R	Red
K	Pink	S	Grey
Lg	Light green	U	Blue
N	Brown	W	White
O	Orange	Y	Yellow

Key to items

3 Onboard supply control unit
18 Fusebox C (passenger compartment)
45 Gas discharge control unit, LHS
46 Gas discharge control unit, RHS
47 Gas discharge headlight, LHS
48 Gas discharge headlight, RHS
49 Dip beam screen motor, LHS
50 Dip beam screen motor, RHS
51 Headlight range control unit
52 Vehicle level sensor, left rear
53 Vehicle level sensor, left, front
54 Range control motor, LHS
55 Range control motor, RHS

H33596

Gas discharge head lights

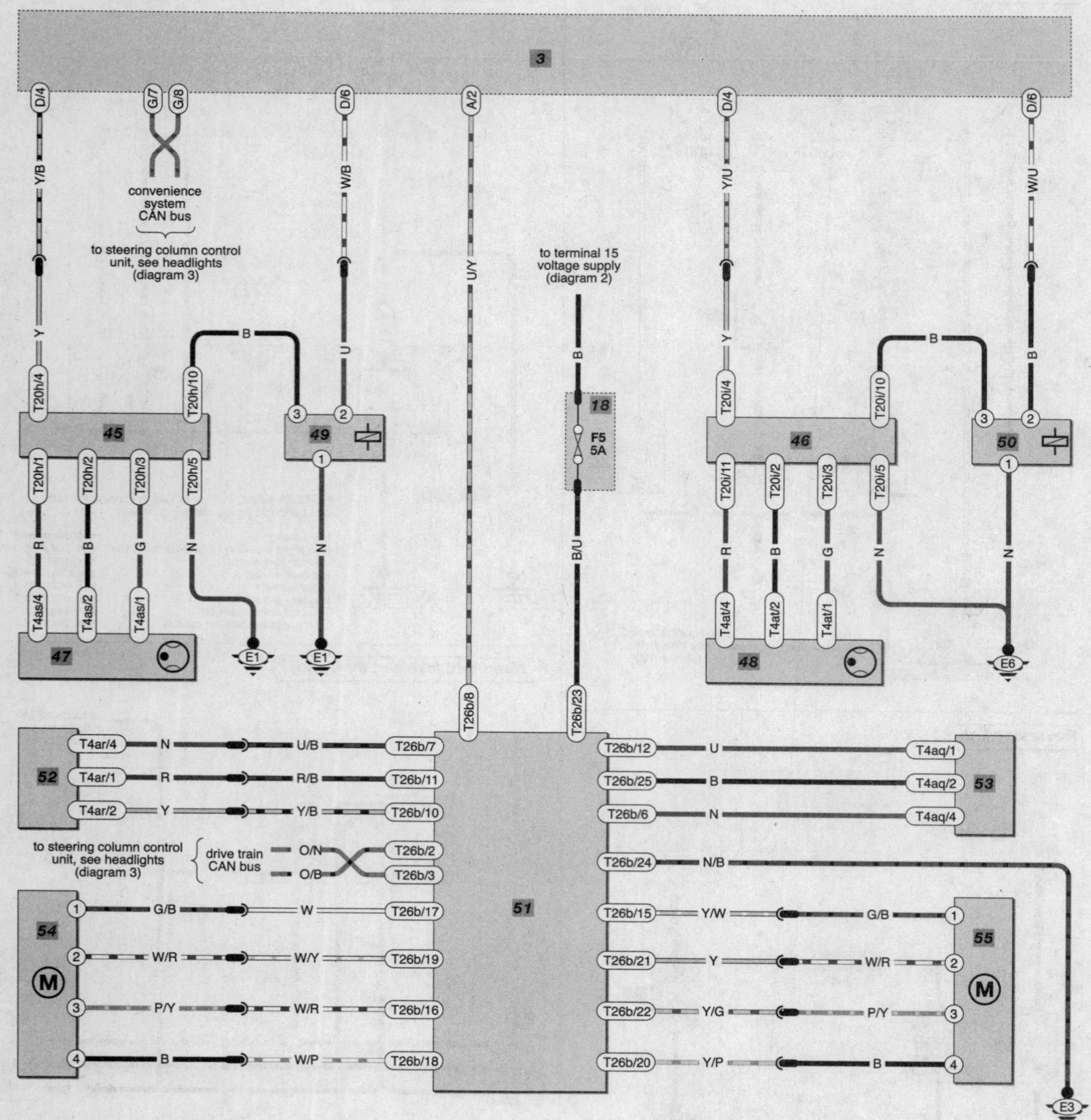

Wire colours

B	Black	**P**	Purple
G	Green	**R**	Red
K	Pink	**S**	Grey
Lg	Light green	**U**	Blue
N	Brown	**W**	White
O	Orange	**Y**	Yellow

Key to items

1 Battery
3 Onboard supply control unit
6 Fusebox A
7 Fusebox B
10 Steering column control unit
18 Fusebox C (passenger compartment)
56 Right hand column swich
 a = washer pump + rear wipe wash switch
 b = wiper switch
 c = intermittent wiper interval switch
57 Wiper motor control unit + motor
58 Rear wiper motor
59 Washer pump
60 Heated washer nozzle (RH)
61 Heated washer nozzle (LH)
62 Headlight washer relay (J39)
63 Headlight washer pump
64 Hazard warning switch
 a = hazard warning switch
 b = warning lights
65 Cigar lighter, front
66 Cigar lighter, rear

Diagram 7

H33597

Screen wipers and washer system

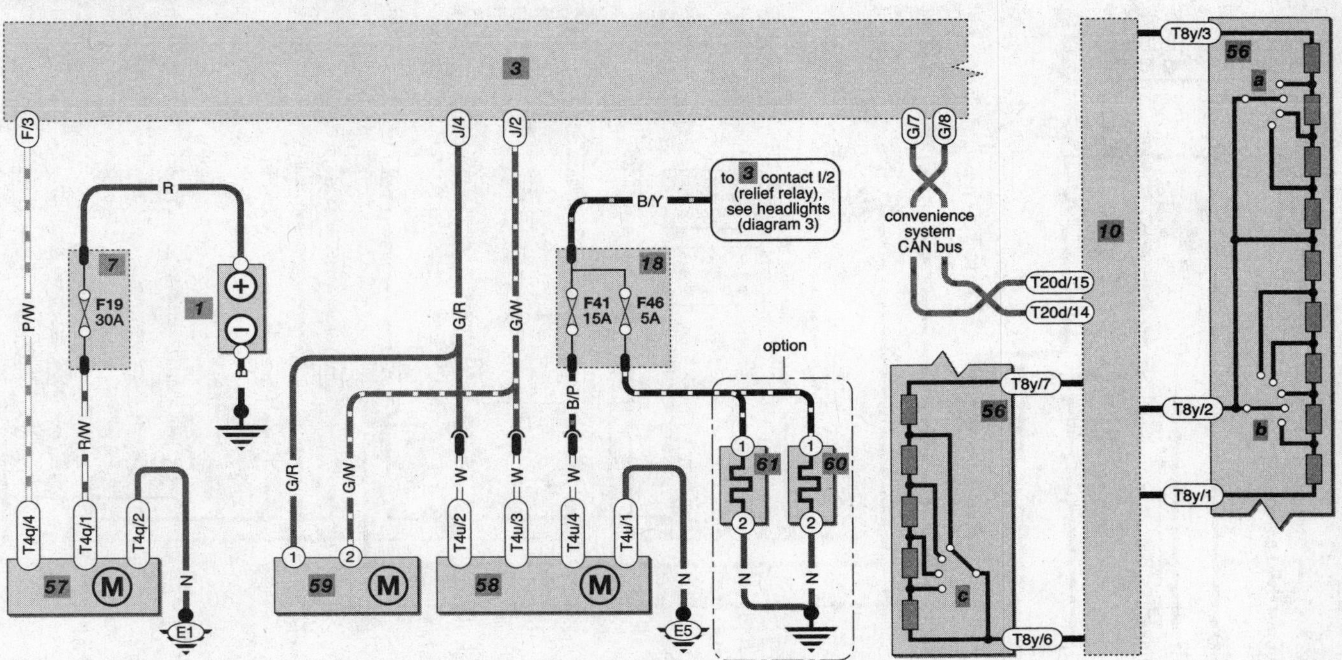

Headlight washers

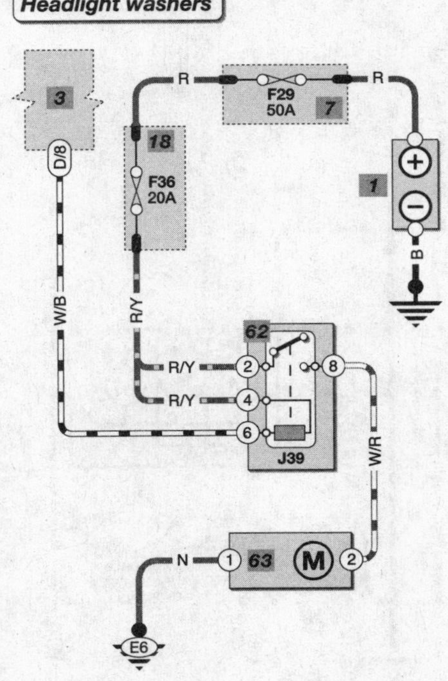

Hazard warning switch

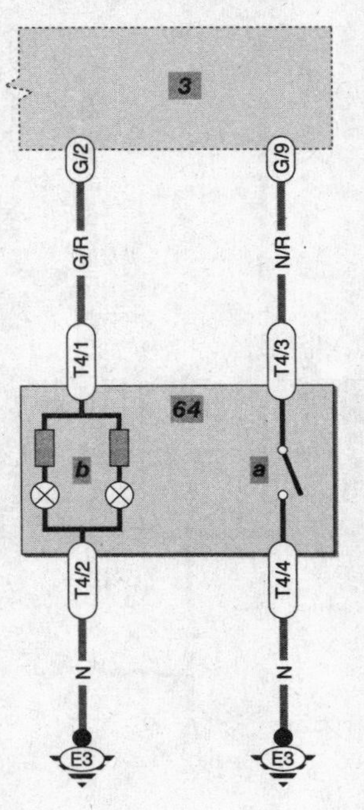

Cigar lighters

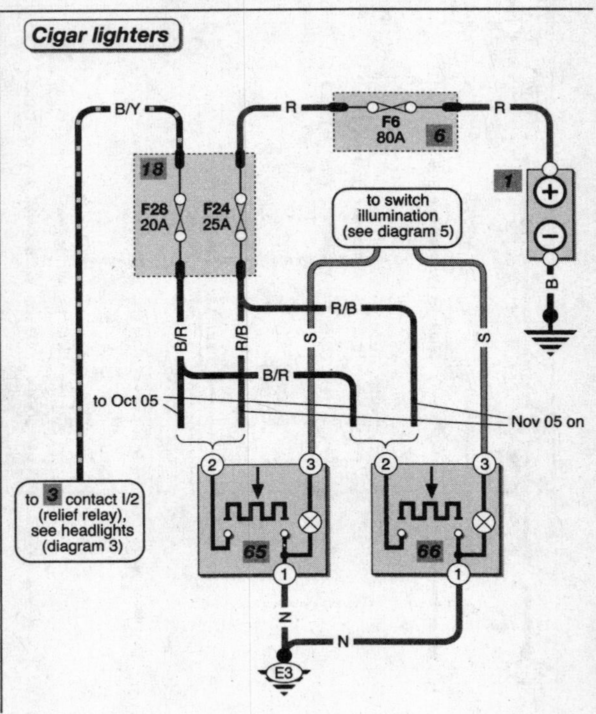

Wire colours

B	Black	P	Purple
G	Green	R	Red
K	Pink	S	Grey
Lg	Light green	U	Blue
N	Brown	W	White
O	Orange	Y	Yellow

Key to items

Diagram 8

1 Battery
3 Onboard supply control unit
6 Fusebox A
7 Fusebox B
18 Fusebox C (passenger compartment)
67 Drivers door control unit
68 Passenger door control unit
69 Convenience system central control unit
70 Drivers door
 a = dead lock motor
 b = central locking motor
 c = central locking unit
 d = door contact
71 Drivers door switch console
 a = interior locking switch
 b = interior locking warning light
 c = switch illumination
72 Deadlock warning light
73 Passenger door
 a = dead lock motor
 b = central locking motor
 c = door contact
74 Rear left central locking unit
 a = dead locking motor
 b = central locking motor
 c = door contact
75 Rear right central locking unit
 a = dead locking motor
 b = central locking motor
 c = door contact
76 Boot lid lock unit
77 Boot lid switch
78 Boot compartment light
79 Fuel flap lock motor
80 Remote control antenna
81 Fuel flap release switch
 a = switch illumination

H33598

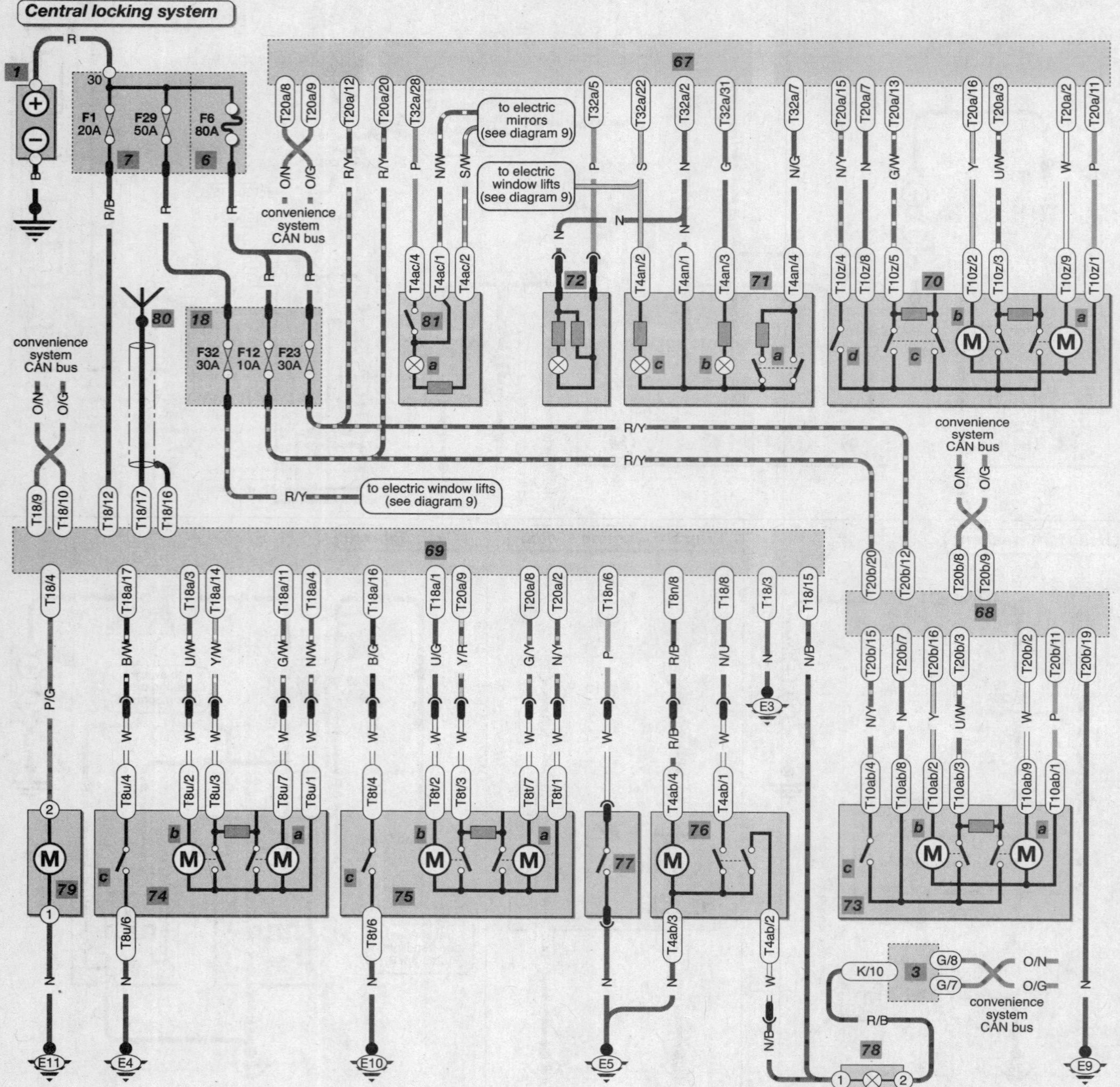

Wire colours

B	Black	**P**	Purple
G	Green	**R**	Red
K	Pink	**S**	Grey
Lg	Light green	**U**	Blue
N	Brown	**W**	White
O	Orange	**Y**	Yellow

Key to items

67 Drivers door control unit
a = window lift motor
68 Passenger door control unit
a = window lift motor
82 Drivers door mirror switch console
a = position adjustment switch
b = mirror heater switch
c = mirror change over switch
d = mirror fold switch
e = switch illumination
83 Drivers door mirror
a = position adjustment motor 1
b = position adjustment motor 2
c = folding motor
d = mirror heater

83 continued
e = indicator repeater
f = door entry light
84 Passenger door mirror
(data as per 83 above)
85 Drivers door window switch console
a = front RH window switch
b = front LH window switch
c = rear RH window switch
d = rear LH window switch
e = switch illumination
f = window disable switch (child lock)
g = child lock warning light

86 Rear left door control unit
a = window lift motor
87 Rear right door control unit
a = window lift motor
88 Passenger door window switch
a = window raise/lower switch
b = switch illumination
89 Rear left door window switch
a = window raise/lower switch
b = switch illumination
90 Rear right door window switch
a = window raise/lower switch
b = switch illumination

Diagram 9

H33599

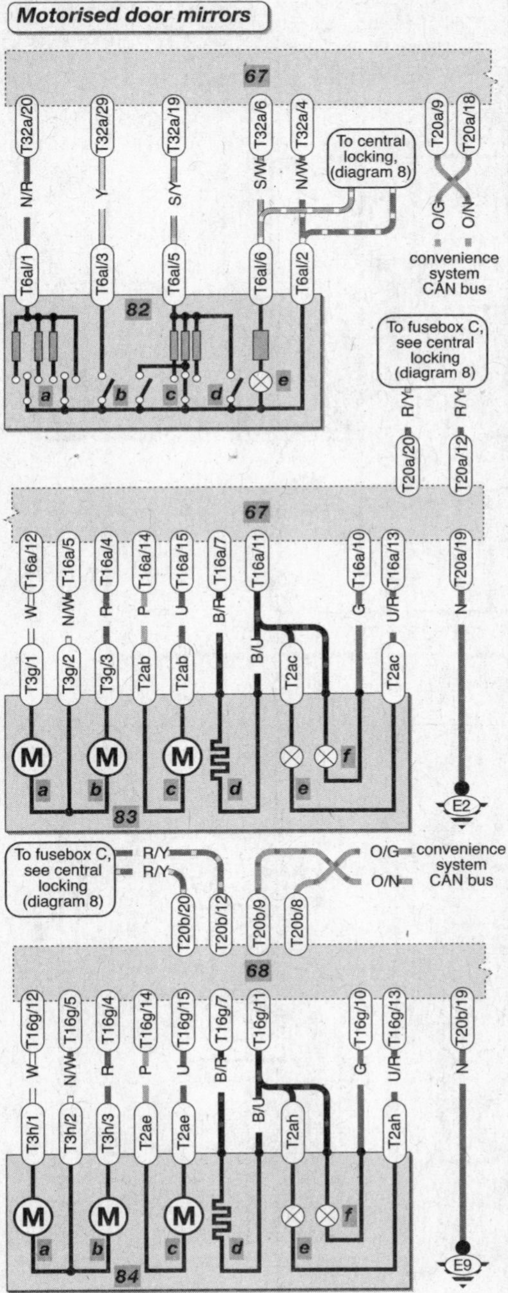

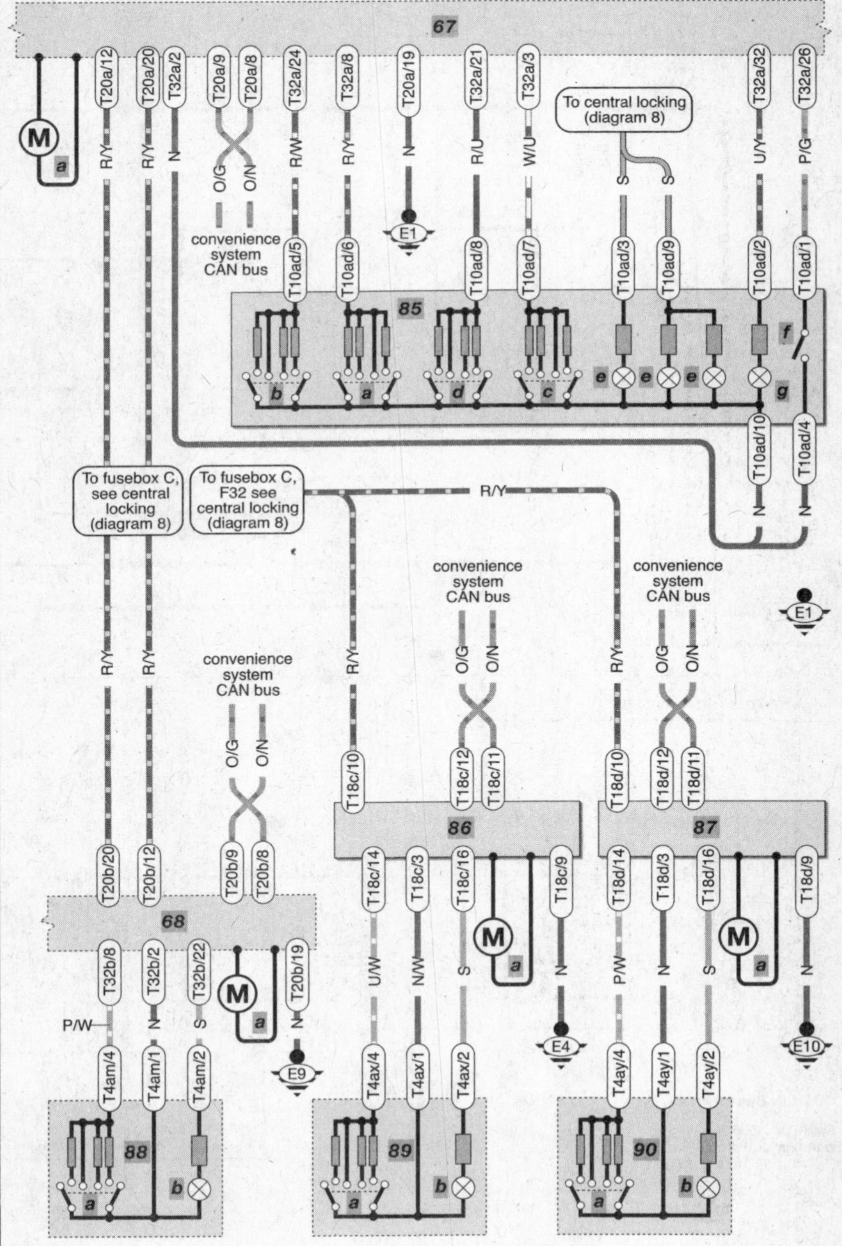

Wire colours

B	Black	P	Purple
G	Green	R	Red
K	Pink	S	Grey
Lg	Light green	U	Blue
N	Brown	W	White
O	Orange	Y	Yellow

Key to items

1 Battery
3 Onboard supply control unit
7 Fusebox B
18 Fusebox C (passenger compartment)
69 Convenience system central control unit
91 Front lighting console
 a = drivers reading light switch
 b = drivers reading light
 c = interior light switch
 d = interior light
 e = passenger reading light switch
 f = passenger reading light
 g = switch illumination
92 Rear lighting console
 a = LH reading light switch
 b = LH reading light
 c = interior light switch
 d = interior light
 e = RH reading light switch
 f = RH reading light
93 Drivers side vanity mirror light
94 Drivers side vanity mirror light switch
95 Passenger side vanity mirror light
96 Passenger side vanity mirror light switch
97 Left footwell light
98 Right footwell light
99 Glove box light switch
100 Glove box light
101 Luggage compartment light
102 Sunroof control unit
 a = sunroof motor
103 Sunroof switch console
 a = sunroof switch
 b = adjustment control
 c = switch illumination

Diagram 10

H33600

Interior lighting system

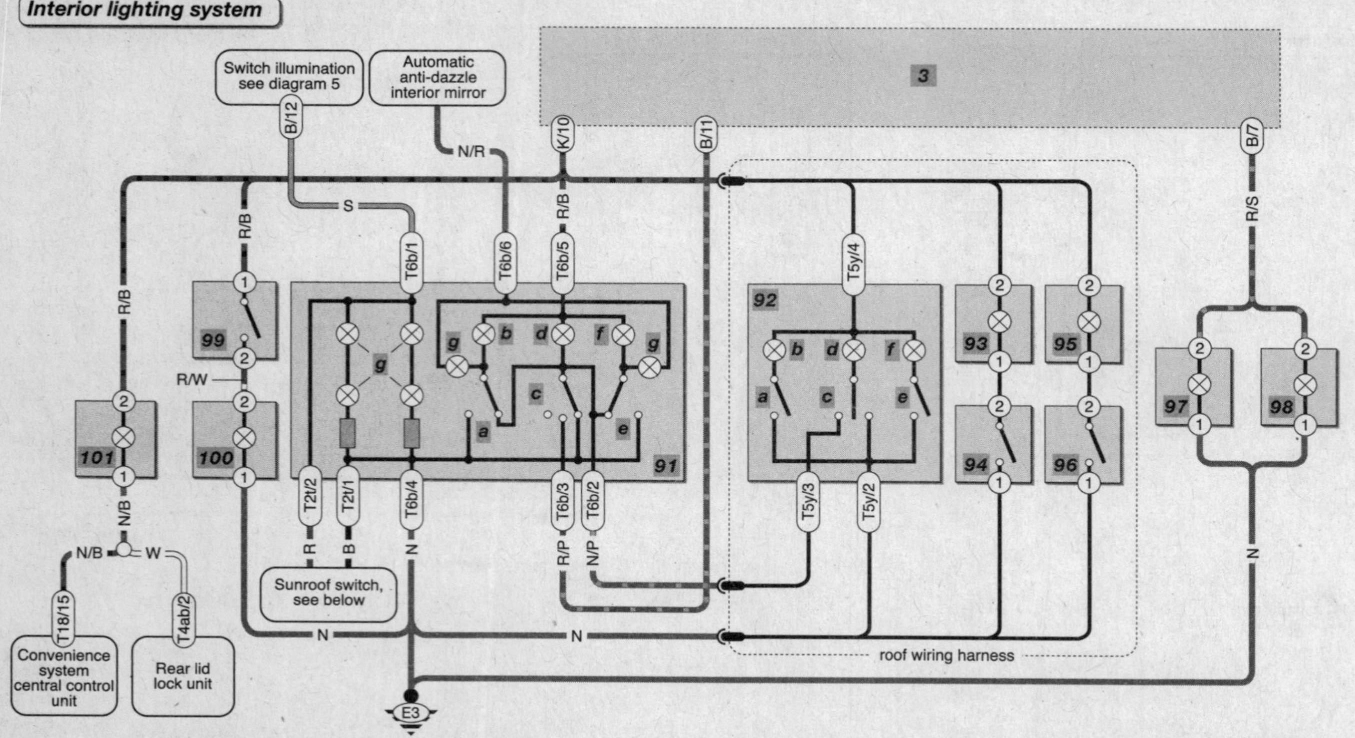

Motorised sunroof

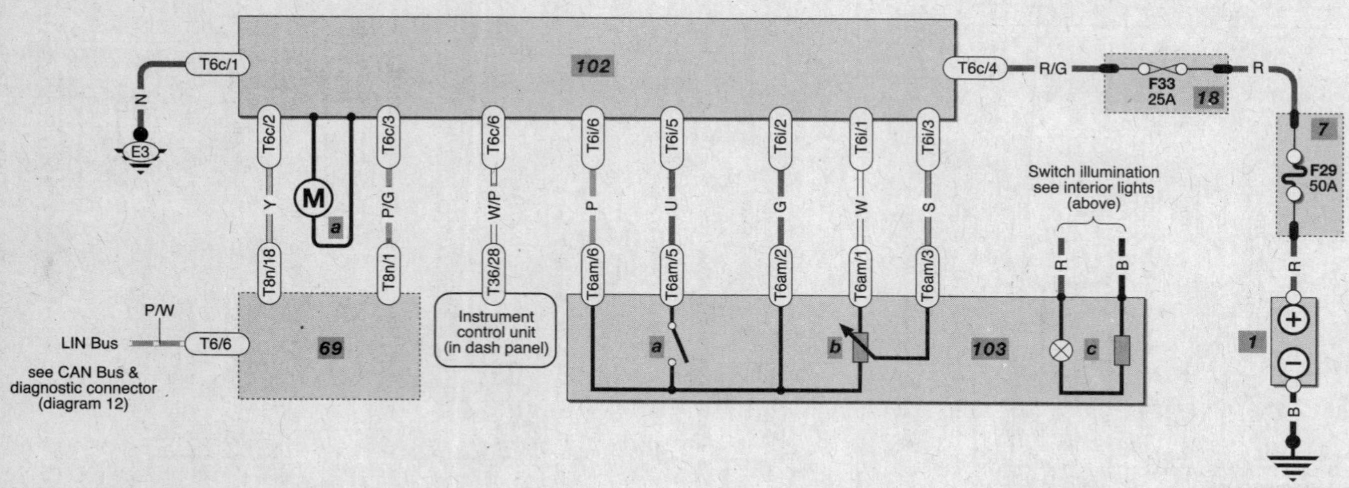

Wire colours

B	Black	**P**	Purple
G	Green	**R**	Red
K	Pink	**S**	Grey
Lg	Light green	**U**	Blue
N	Brown	**W**	White
O	Orange	**Y**	Yellow

Key to items

Diagram 11

1 Battery
3 Onboard supply control unit
6 Fusebox A
7 Fusebox B
18 Fusebox C (passenger compartment)
104 ABS contol unit
105 Tyre pressure monitor display switch
106 Traction control switch
a = switch
b = ESP/TCS warning light
c = switch illumination
107 Speed sender front left
108 Speed sensor front right
109 Speed sensor rear left
110 Speed sensor rear right
111 Rear screen heater
112 Heater switch
a = heated rear scren warning light
b = heated rear screen switch
c = air recirculation warning light
d = air recirculation flap switch
e = blower regulator
113 Blower motor
114 Recirculation flap motor
115 Resistor pack
a = thermo-fuse

H33601

Anti-lock brake system

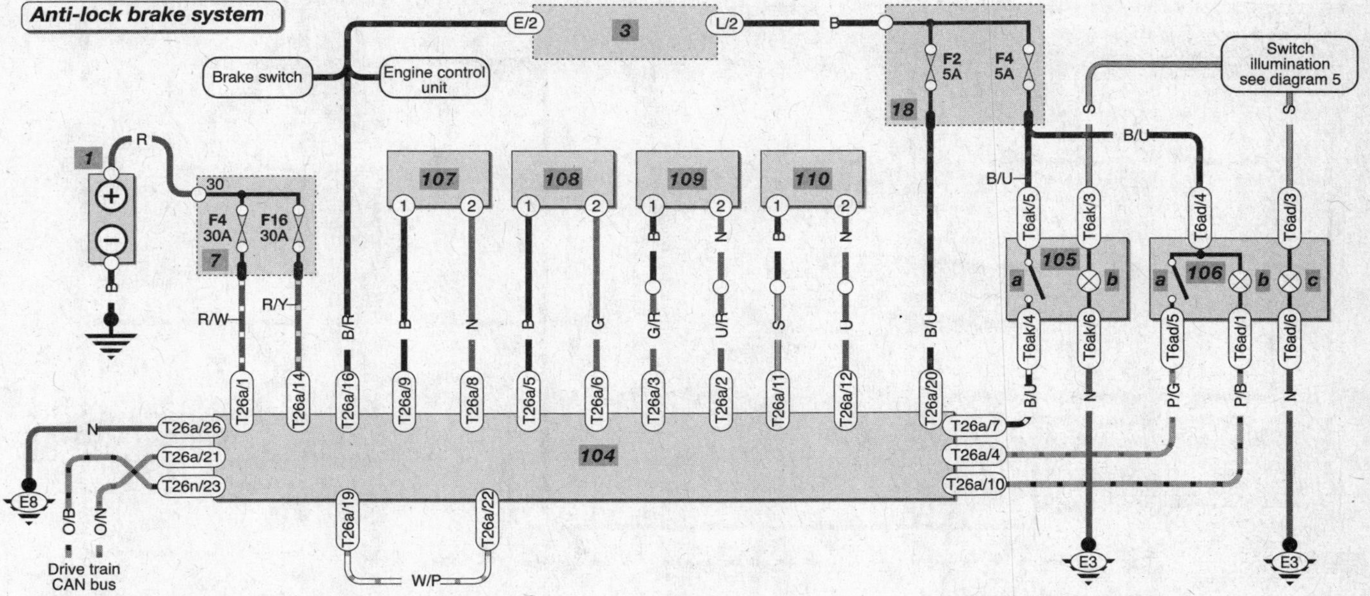

Heated rear screen

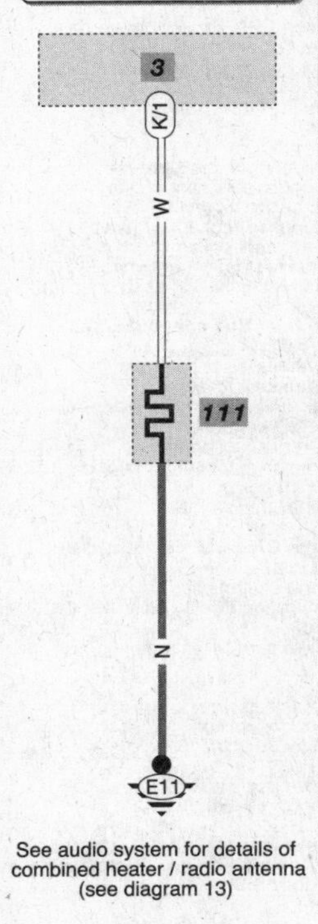

3
K/1
W
111
N
E11

See audio system for details of combined heater / radio antenna (see diagram 13)

Heater blower

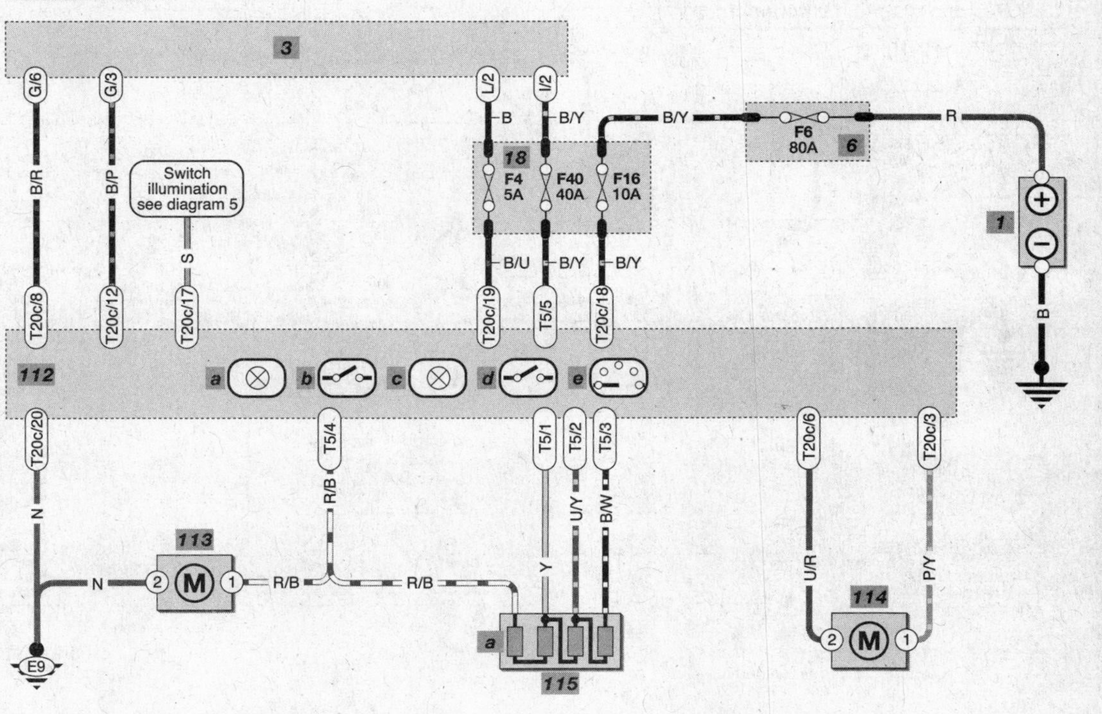

3
G/6
G/3
L/2
I/2
B
B/Y
R
F6 80A
6
18
F4 5A
F40 40A
F16 10A
B/R
B/P
Switch illumination see diagram 5
S
B/U
B/Y
T20c/8
T20c/12
T20c/17
T20c/19
T5/5
T20c/18
1
112
a b c d e
T20c/20
T5/4
T5/1
T5/2
T5/3
T20c/6
T20c/3
N
R/B
Y
U/Y
B/W
U/R
P/Y
113
M
114
a
115
E9

Wire colours

B	Black	P	Purple
G	Green	R	Red
K	Pink	S	Grey
Lg	Light green	U	Blue
N	Brown	W	White
O	Orange	Y	Yellow

Key to items

Diagram 12

1 Battery
3 Onboard supply control unit
6 Fusebox A
7 Fusebox B
18 Fusebox C (passenger compartment)
112 Heater switch
f = drivers seat temperature regulator
g = passenger seat temperature regulator
116 Heated front seats control unit
117 Drivers seat cushion heater and temp. sensor
118 Drivers seat lateral support heater 1
119 Drivers seat lateral support heater 2
120 Drivers seat back rest heater
121 Passengers seat cushion heater and temp. sensor
122 Passenger seat lateral support heater 1
123 Passenger seat lateral support heater 2
124 Passenger seat back rest heater
125 Diagnostic connector
126 Diagnostic control unit

H33602

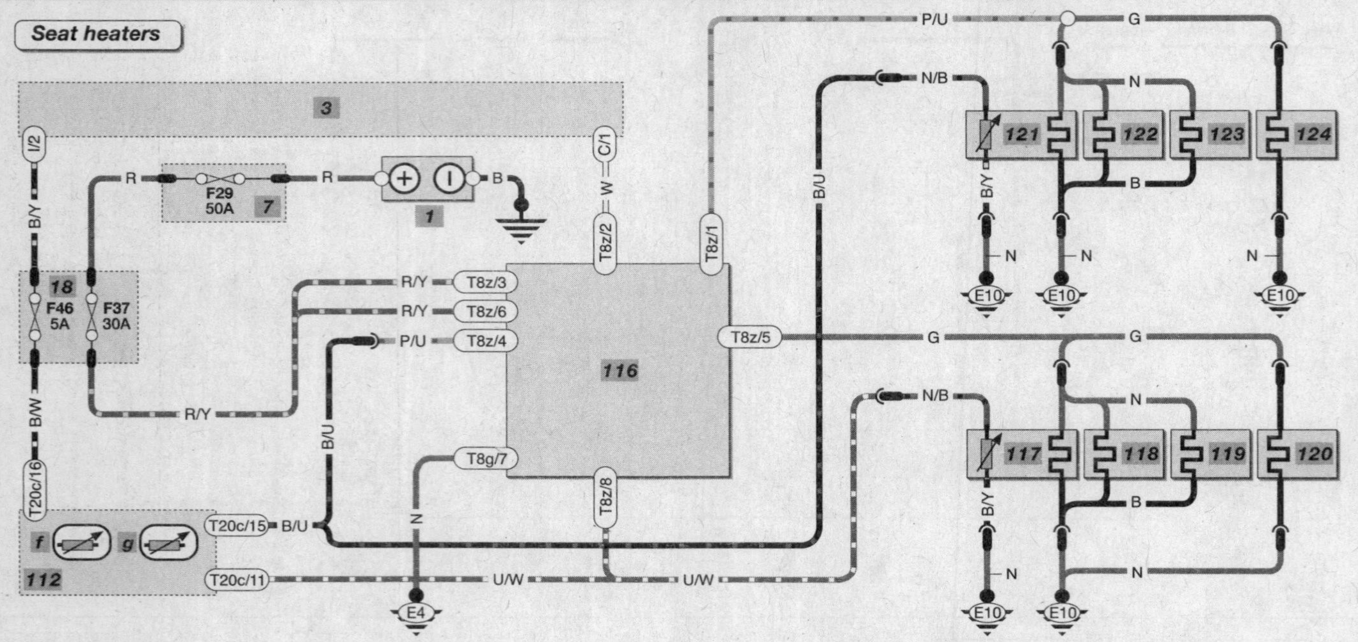

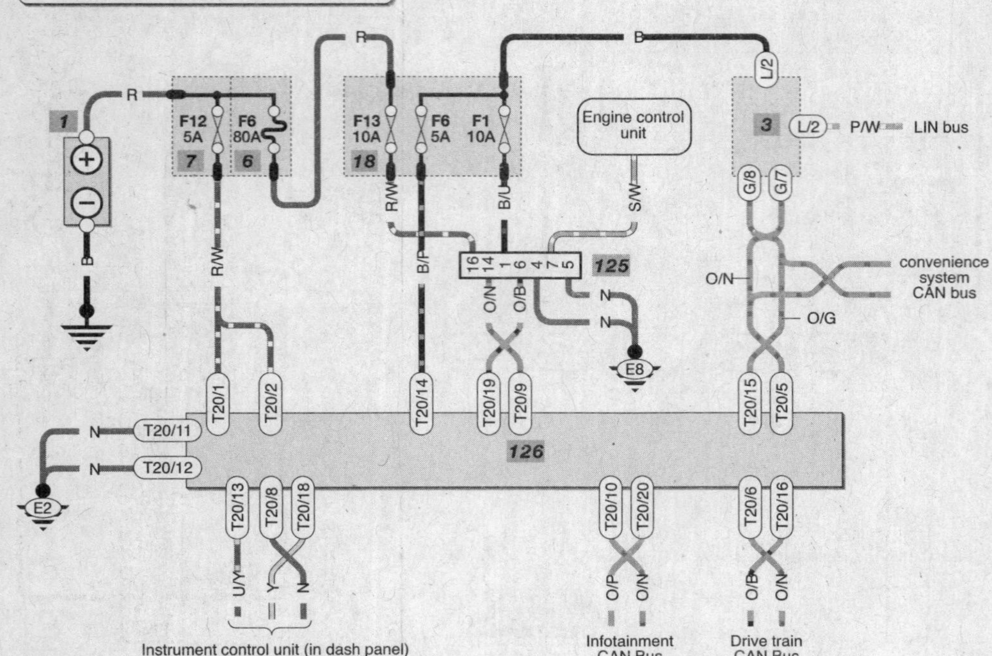

Convenience CAN Bus connected to:
Trailer detection unit
Steering column control unit (J527)
Parking aid control unit
Air conditioning control unit
Climatronic
Special vehicle control unit
Drivers door control unit (J386)
Front passenger door control unit (J387)
Rear left door control unit (J388)
Rear right door control unit (J389)
Aux air heater control unit
Convenience system control unit (J393)
Control unit with display in dash panel (J285)

Drive train CAN Bus connected to:
Airbag control unit
Anti-lock brake system control unit
Engine control unit
Mechatronic unit (direct shift gear box)
Power steering control unit
Selector lever sensor control unit
Steering column electronic control unit (J527)
Automatic gearbox control unit
4 wheel drive control unit

Infotainment CAN Bus connected to:
Aux heater control unit
Mobile phone control unit
Radio / Navigation display control unit
Satellite radio
Magnetic field sender for compass
Amplifier

LIN Bus connected to:
Wiper motor control unit
Rain and light detector sensor
Alarm horn
Vehicle inclination sensor } See note
Interior monitor sensor

NOTE: These items via LIN bus attached to convenience system control unit (see diagram 10)

Diagram 13

Wire colours

B	Black	**P**	Purple
G	Green	**R**	Red
K	Pink	**S**	Grey
Lg	Light green	**U**	Blue
N	Brown	**W**	White
O	Orange	**Y**	Yellow

Key to items

1 Battery
3 Onboard supply control unit
6 Fusebox A
7 Fusebox B
18 Fusebox C (passenger compartment)
111 Rear screen heater
127 LH aerial module
128 RH aerial module
129 FM filter
130 AM filter
131 Aerial selection unit
132 Combined Radio/Nav/Control unit with display
133 CD changer
134 Rear RH bass driver
135 Rear RH trebble driver
136 Rear LH bass driver
137 Rear LH trebble driver
138 Front RH bass driver
139 Front RH mid-range driver
140 Front RH trebble driver
141 Front LH bass driver
142 Front LH mid-range driver
143 Front LH trebble driver
144 Crossover unit
145 GPS NAV antenna
146 Radio antenna, LH
147 Radio antenna, RH

H33603

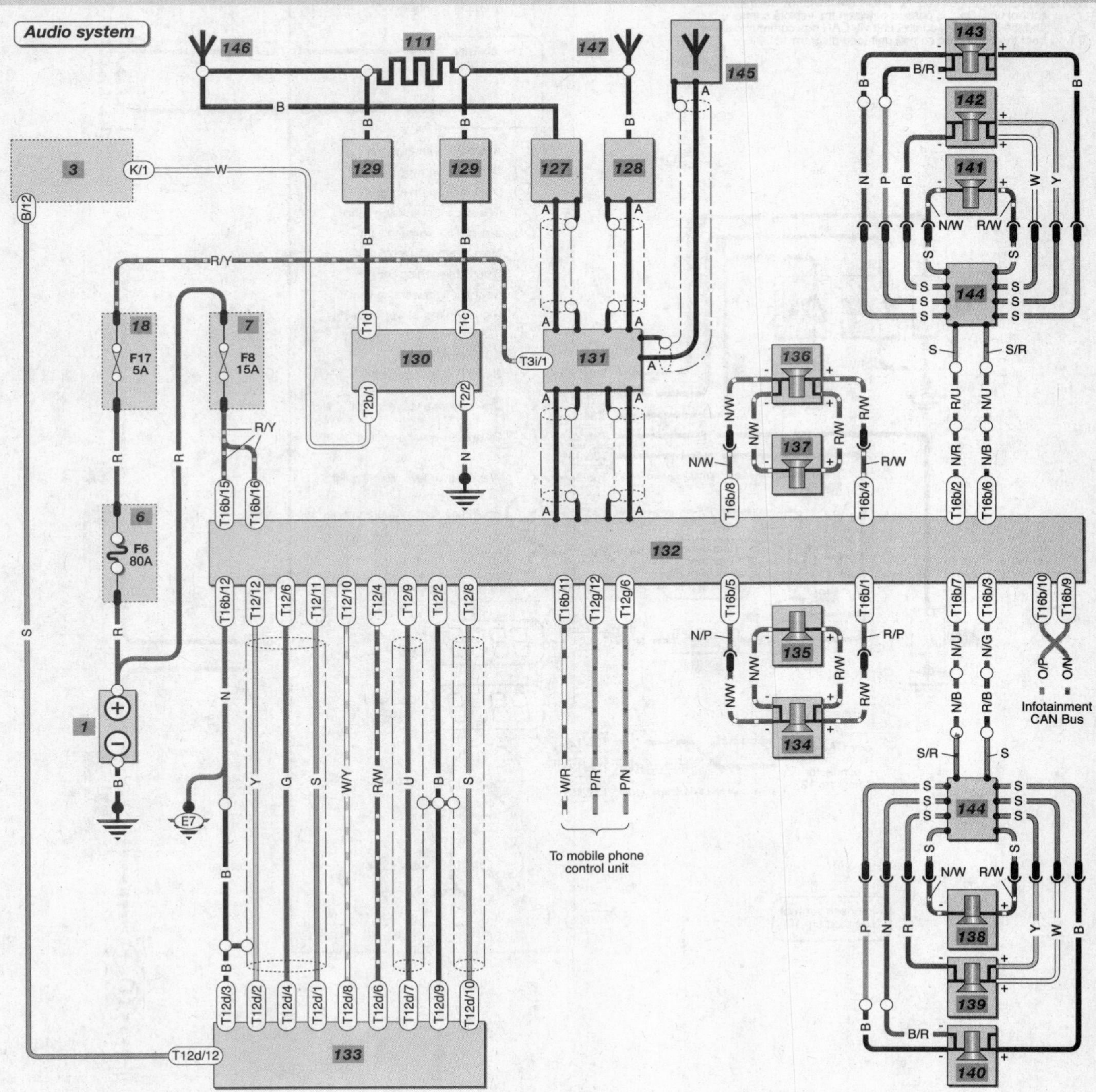

Wire colours

B	Black	P	Purple
G	Green	R	Red
K	Pink	S	Grey
Lg	Light green	U	Blue
N	Brown	W	White
O	Orange	Y	Yellow

Key to items

1 Battery
3 Onboard supply control unit
7 Fusebox B
18 Fusebox C (passenger compartment)
148 Instrument control unit (in dash panel)
149 Immobilisier coil
150 Brake wear sender
151 Brake fluid level switch
152 Handbrake switch
153 Oil pressure switch
154 Washer fluid level sensor
155 Coolant level sensor
156 Ambient temperature sensor

Diagram 14

H33613

Instruments

NOTE: Orphaned gauges and indicators are driven by the instrument control unit. Data is passed between the vehicle control units and the instrument control unit via CAN bus communications from the diagnostic control unit (see diagram 12).

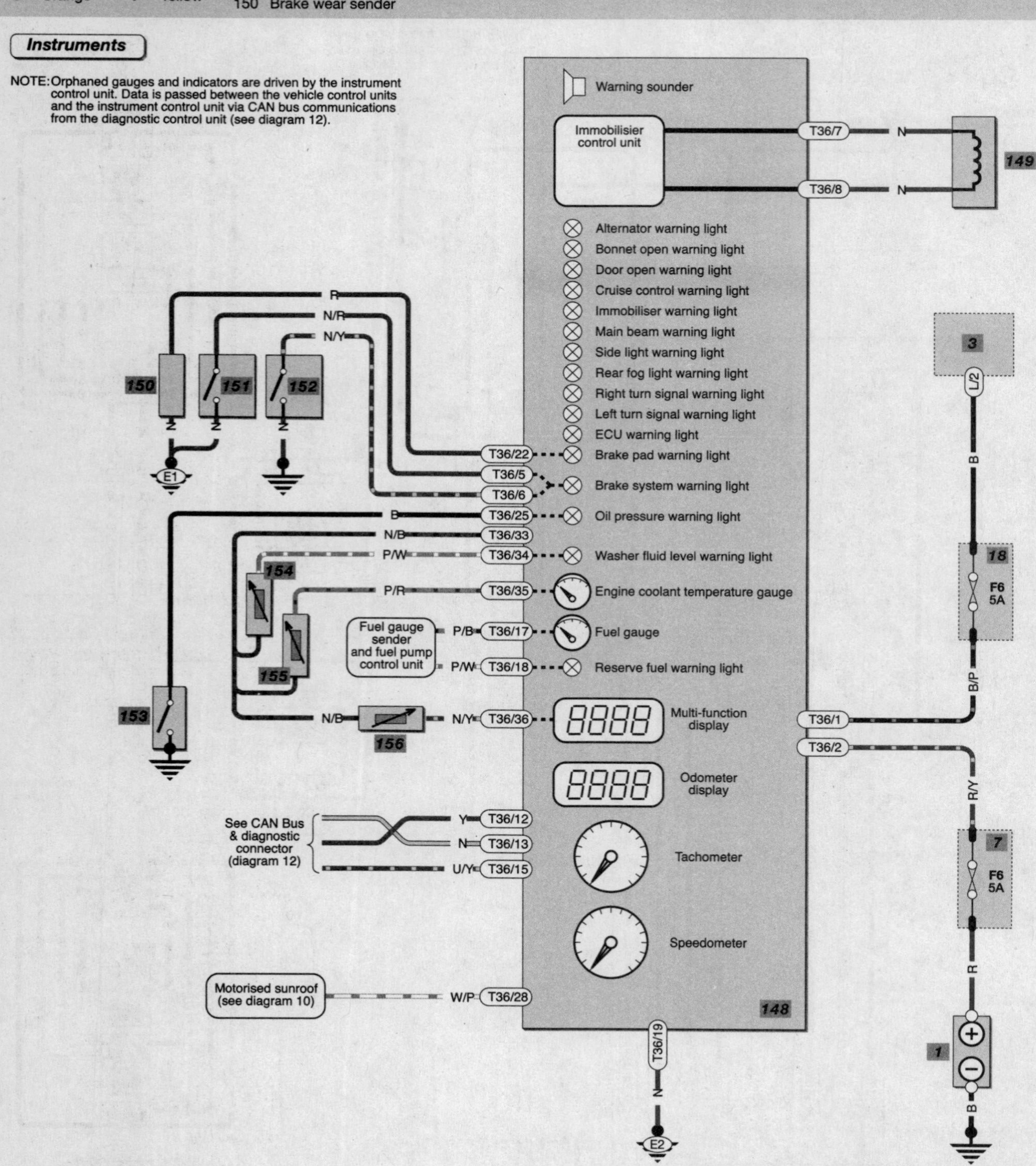

Typical fuse data based on BLF and BRU engines (may 05)

Diagram 15

Passenger compartment fuse box (Box C) 18

Fuse	Rating	Function
F1	10A	Diagnostic connector, fuel pump, ECU
F2	5A	Brake pedal switch, ABS control unit
F3	5A	Instrument control unit
F4	5A	Reversing light switch, oil level / temp. sensor, tyre pressure monitor switch, traction control switch
F5	5A	Headlamp levelling (halogen), Headlamp range control unit (gas discharge)
F6	5A	Diagnostic control unit, power steering, tiptronic switch, instruments
F7	5A	Anti dazzle interior mirror
F8	5A	Four wheel drive control unit, trailer detector control unit
F9	-	-
F10	-	-
F11	-	-
F12	10A	Drivers door / passenger door control unit
F13	10A	Light switch, brake switch, diagnostic connector
F14	5A	Auto six speed gear box
F15	7.5A	Onboard supply control unit
F16	10A	Heater switch
F17	5A	Rain / light sensor, aerial selection unit (radio)
F18	5A	Double clutch gearbox, selector lever sensors control box Tiptronic switch (six speed gear box)
F19	-	-
F20	5A	ABS control unit
F21	-	-
F22	-	-
F23	30A	Drivers door / passenger door control unit
F24	25A	Cigar lighter (Nov 05 on)
F25	25A	Fresh air blower relay
F26	20A	12v socket (luggage compartment)
F27	15A	Fuel pump control unit
F28	20A	Cigar lighter (to Oct 05)
F29	10A	Crank breather heater, air mass meter
F30	-	-
F31	20A	Brake vacuum pump
F32	30A	Electric window lifts, rear door control unit
F33	25A	Sun roof control unit
F34	-	-
F35	5A	Alarm horn, vehicle inclination sensor, interior monitor sensor
F36	20A	Headlight washer
F37	30A	Heated front seats control unit
F38	-	-
F39	20A	Auto six speed gear box control unit
F40	40A	Heater switch
F41	15A	Rear wiper motor
F42	15A	Onboard supply control unit
F43	15A	Trailer detector control unit
F44	20A	Trailer detector control unit
F45	15A	Trailer detector control unit
F46	5A	Heated washer jets (optional), heater switch
F47	5A	Aux heater relay
F48	-	-
F49	5A	Light switch

Engine compartment fuse box (Box A) 6

Fuse	Rating	Function
F1	150A/200A	Alternator
F2	80A	Power steering
F3	50A	Rad fan control unit
F4	40A	Optional equipment
F5	-	-
F6	80A	Supply distribution (to box C)
F7	-	-

Engine compartment fuse box (Box B) 7

Fuse	Rating	Function
F1	20A	Convenience system control unit
F2	5A	Steering column control unit
F3	5A	Onboard supply control unit
F4	30A	ABS control unit
F5	15A	Mechatronic unt (double clutch)
F6	5A	Onboard supply control unit
F7	-	-
F8	15A	Radio
F9	5A	Phone control unit
F10	10A	ECU (petrol)
	5A	Terminal 30 supply relay drive (diesel)
F11	20A	Aux heater control unit
F12	5A	Diagnostic control unit
F13	25A	ECU (petrol)
	30A	ECU (diesel)
F14	20A	Ignition coil
F15	40A	Starter relay (diesel)
F16	30A	ABS control unit
F17	15A	Onboard supply control unit
F18	30A	Sound system
F19	30A	Wiper motor control unit
F20	-	-
F21	15A	Lambda probe
F22	5A	Clutch position sensor
F23	15A	Fuel regulator valve
	10A	Exhaust gas recirculation cooler changeover valve, Charge pressure control solenoid valve
F24	10A	Intake manifold flap valve, charcoal filter solenoid valve, inlet camshaft control valve
F25	40A	Onboard supply control unit
F26	40A	Onboard supply control unit
F27	50A	Glow plugs control unit
F28	40A	Term 15 supply
F29	50A	Distribution to fuse box C
F30	40A	Onboard supply control unit

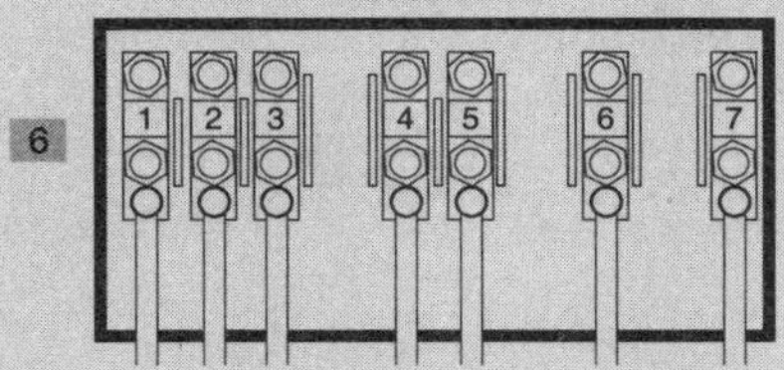

Location: Side of fusebox B inside engine bay LHS

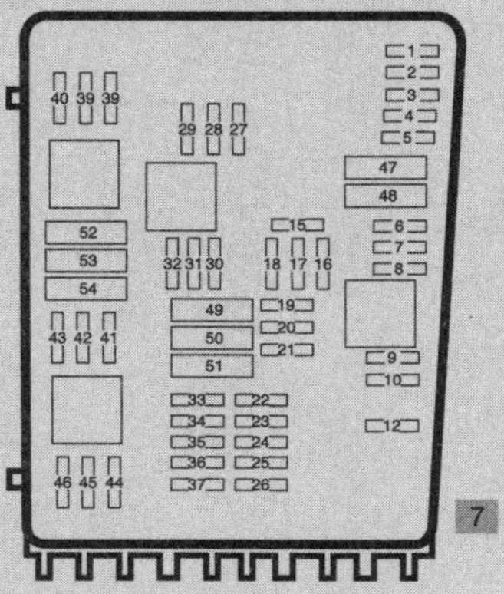

Location: Engine bay LHS

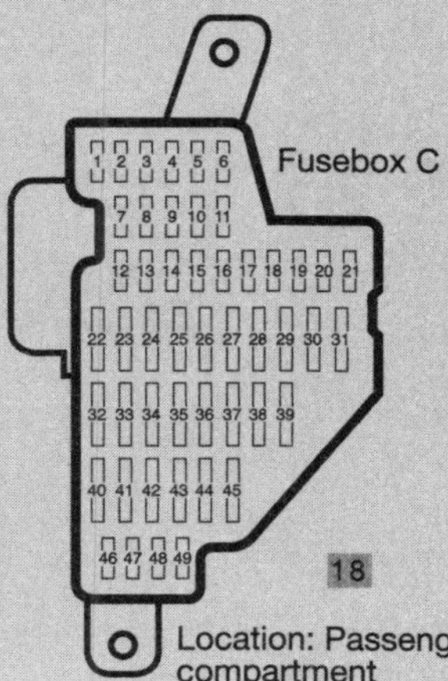

Location: Passenger compartment

H33614

Dimensions and weights

Note: *All figures and dimensions are approximate and may vary according to model. Refer to manufacturerís data for exact figures.*

Overall length

Golf models	4204 mm
Golf GTi models	4216 mm
Golf Plus models	4206 mm
Jetta models	4554 mm
Estate models	4397 mm

Overall width

All models	1781 mm

Overall height (unladen)

Golf models	1513 mm
Golf Plus models	1580 mm
Jetta models	1459 mm

Wheelbase

All models	2578 mm

Turning circle

All models	10.9 m

Weights

Kerb weight		
Golf models	1154 to 1521 kg	
Jetta models	1165 to 1303 kg	
Maximum gross vehicle weight		
Golf models	1740 to 1940 kg	
Jetta models	1710 to 1840 kg	
Maximum roof rack load		
All models	75 kg	
Maximum towing weights	**Unbraked trailer**	**Braked trailer**
Petrol engines	610 to 670 kg	1000 to 1700 kg
Diesel engines	640 to 690 kg	1000 to 1700 kg

Conversion factors

Length (distance)

Inches (in)	x 25.4	= Millimetres (mm)	x 0.0394	= Inches (in)
Feet (ft)	x 0.305	= Metres (m)	x 3.281	= Feet (ft)
Miles	x 1.609	= Kilometres (km)	x 0.621	= Miles

Volume (capacity)

Cubic inches (cu in; in^3)	x 16.387	= Cubic centimetres (cc; cm^3)	x 0.061	= Cubic inches (cu in; in^3)
Imperial pints (Imp pt)	x 0.568	= Litres (l)	x 1.76	= Imperial pints (Imp pt)
Imperial quarts (Imp qt)	x 1.137	= Litres (l)	x 0.88	= Imperial quarts (Imp qt)
Imperial quarts (Imp qt)	x 1.201	= US quarts (US qt)	x 0.833	= Imperial quarts (Imp qt)
US quarts (US qt)	x 0.946	= Litres (l)	x 1.057	= US quarts (US qt)
Imperial gallons (Imp gal)	x 4.546	= Litres (l)	x 0.22	= Imperial gallons (Imp gal)
Imperial gallons (Imp gal)	x 1.201	= US gallons (US gal)	x 0.833	= Imperial gallons (Imp gal)
US gallons (US gal)	x 3.785	= Litres (l)	x 0.264	= US gallons (US gal)

Mass (weight)

Ounces (oz)	x 28.35	= Grams (g)	x 0.035	= Ounces (oz)
Pounds (lb)	x 0.454	= Kilograms (kg)	x 2.205	= Pounds (lb)

Force

Ounces-force (ozf; oz)	x 0.278	= Newtons (N)	x 3.6	= Ounces-force (ozf; oz)
Pounds-force (lbf; lb)	x 4.448	= Newtons (N)	x 0.225	= Pounds-force (lbf; lb)
Newtons (N)	x 0.1	= Kilograms-force (kgf; kg)	x 9.81	= Newtons (N)

Pressure

Pounds-force per square inch (psi; lbf/in^2; lb/in^2)	x 0.070	= Kilograms-force per square centimetre (kgf/cm^2; kg/cm^2)	x 14.223	= Pounds-force per square inch (psi; lbf/in^2; lb/in^2)
Pounds-force per square inch (psi; lbf/in^2; lb/in^2)	x 0.068	= Atmospheres (atm)	x 14.696	= Pounds-force per square inch (psi; lbf/in^2; lb/in^2)
Pounds-force per square inch (psi; lbf/in^2; lb/in^2)	x 0.069	= Bars	x 14.5	= Pounds-force per square inch (psi; lbf/in^2; lb/in^2)
Pounds-force per square inch (psi; lbf/in^2; lb/in^2)	x 6.895	= Kilopascals (kPa)	x 0.145	= Pounds-force per square inch (psi; lbf/in^2; lb/in^2)
Kilopascals (kPa)	x 0.01	= Kilograms-force per square centimetre (kgf/cm^2; kg/cm^2)	x 98.1	= Kilopascals (kPa)
Millibar (mbar)	x 100	= Pascals (Pa)	x 0.01	= Millibar (mbar)
Millibar (mbar)	x 0.0145	= Pounds-force per square inch (psi; lbf/in^2; lb/in^2)	x 68.947	= Millibar (mbar)
Millibar (mbar)	x 0.75	= Millimetres of mercury (mmHg)	x 1.333	= Millibar (mbar)
Millibar (mbar)	x 0.401	= Inches of water (inH_2O)	x 2.491	= Millibar (mbar)
Millimetres of mercury (mmHg)	x 0.535	= Inches of water (inH_2O)	x 1.868	= Millimetres of mercury (mmHg)
Inches of water (inH_2O)	x 0.036	= Pounds-force per square inch (psi; lbf/in^2; lb/in^2)	x 27.68	= Inches of water (inH_2O)

Torque (moment of force)

Pounds-force inches (lbf in; lb in)	x 1.152	= Kilograms-force centimetre (kgf cm; kg cm)	x 0.868	= Pounds-force inches (lbf in; lb in)
Pounds-force inches (lbf in; lb in)	x 0.113	= Newton metres (Nm)	x 8.85	= Pounds-force inches (lbf in; lb in)
Pounds-force inches (lbf in; lb in)	x 0.083	= Pounds-force feet (lbf ft; lb ft)	x 12	= Pounds-force inches (lbf in; lb in)
Pounds-force feet (lbf ft; lb ft)	x 0.138	= Kilograms-force metres (kgf m; kg m)	x 7.233	= Pounds-force feet (lbf ft; lb ft)
Pounds-force feet (lbf ft; lb ft)	x 1.356	= Newton metres (Nm)	x 0.738	= Pounds-force feet (lbf ft; lb ft)
Newton metres (Nm)	x 0.102	= Kilograms-force metres (kgf m; kg m)	x 9.804	= Newton metres (Nm)

Power

Horsepower (hp)	x 745.7	= Watts (W)	x 0.0013	= Horsepower (hp)

Velocity (speed)

Miles per hour (miles/hr; mph)	x 1.609	= Kilometres per hour (km/hr; kph)	x 0.621	= Miles per hour (miles/hr; mph)

Fuel consumption*

Miles per gallon, Imperial (mpg)	x 0.354	= Kilometres per litre (km/l)	x 2.825	= Miles per gallon, Imperial (mpg)
Miles per gallon, US (mpg)	x 0.425	= Kilometres per litre (km/l)	x 2.352	= Miles per gallon, US (mpg)

Temperature

Degrees Fahrenheit = (°C x 1.8) + 32

Degrees Celsius (Degrees Centigrade; °C) = (°F - 32) x 0.56

** It is common practice to convert from miles per gallon (mpg) to litres/100 kilometres (l/100km), where mpg x l/100 km = 282*

Spare parts are available from many sources, including maker's appointed garages, accessory shops, and motor factors. To be sure of obtaining the correct parts, it will sometimes be necessary to quote the vehicle identification number. If possible, it can also be useful to take the old parts along for positive identification. Items such as starter motors and alternators may be available under a service exchange scheme – any parts returned should be clean.

Our advice regarding spare parts is as follows.

Officially appointed garages

This is the best source of parts which are peculiar to your car, and which are not otherwise generally available (eg, badges, interior trim, certain body panels, etc). It is also the only place at which you should buy parts if the car is still under warranty.

Accessory shops

These are very good places to buy materials and components needed for the maintenance of your car (oil, air and fuel filters, light bulbs, drivebelts, greases, brake pads, touch-up paint, etc). Components of this nature sold by a reputable shop are usually of the same standard as those used by the car manufacturer.

Besides components, these shops also sell tools and general accessories, usually have convenient opening hours, charge lower prices, and can often be found close to home. Some accessory shops have parts counters where components needed for almost any repair job can be purchased or ordered.

Motor factors

Good factors will stock all the more important components which wear out comparatively quickly, and can sometimes supply individual components needed for the overhaul of a larger assembly (eg, brake seals and hydraulic parts, bearing shells, pistons, valves). They may also handle work such as cylinder block reboring, crankshaft regrinding, etc.

Engine reconditioners

These specialise in engine overhaul and can also supply components. It is recommended that the establishment is a member of the Federation of Engine Re-Manufacturers, or a similar society.

Tyre and exhaust specialists

These outlets may be independent, or members of a local or national chain. They frequently offer competitive prices when compared with a main dealer or local garage, but it will pay to obtain several quotes before making a decision. When researching prices, also ask what extras may be added – for instance fitting a new valve, balancing the wheel and tyre disposal all both commonly charged on top of the price of a new tyre.

Other sources

Beware of parts or materials obtained from market stalls, car boot sales, on-line auctions or similar outlets. Such items are not invariably sub-standard, but there is little chance of compensation if they do prove unsatisfactory. In the case of safety-critical components such as brake pads, there is the risk not only of financial loss, but also of an accident causing injury or death.

Second-hand components or assemblies obtained from a car breaker can be a good buy in some circumstances, but this sort of purchase is best made by the experienced DIY mechanic.

Whenever servicing, repair or overhaul work is carried out on the car or its components, observe the following procedures and instructions. This will assist in carrying out the operation efficiently and to a professional standard of workmanship.

Joint mating faces and gaskets

When separating components at their mating faces, never insert screwdrivers or similar implements into the joint between the faces in order to prise them apart. This can cause severe damage which results in oil leaks, coolant leaks, etc upon reassembly. Separation is usually achieved by tapping along the joint with a soft-faced hammer in order to break the seal. However, note that this method may not be suitable where dowels are used for component location.

Where a gasket is used between the mating faces of two components, a new one must be fitted on reassembly; fit it dry unless otherwise stated in the repair procedure. Make sure that the mating faces are clean and dry, with all traces of old gasket removed. When cleaning a joint face, use a tool which is unlikely to score or damage the face, and remove any burrs or nicks with an oilstone or fine file.

Make sure that tapped holes are cleaned with a pipe cleaner, and keep them free of jointing compound, if this is being used, unless specifically instructed otherwise.

Ensure that all orifices, channels or pipes are clear, and blow through them, preferably using compressed air.

Oil seals

Oil seals can be removed by levering them out with a wide flat-bladed screwdriver or similar implement. Alternatively, a number of self-tapping screws may be screwed into the seal, and these used as a purchase for pliers or some similar device in order to pull the seal free.

Whenever an oil seal is removed from its working location, either individually or as part of an assembly, it should be renewed.

The very fine sealing lip of the seal is easily damaged, and will not seal if the surface it contacts is not completely clean and free from scratches, nicks or grooves. If the original sealing surface of the component cannot be restored, and the manufacturer has not made provision for slight relocation of the seal relative to the sealing surface, the component should be renewed.

Protect the lips of the seal from any surface which may damage them in the course of fitting. Use tape or a conical sleeve where possible. Where indicated, lubricate the seal lips with oil before fitting and, on dual-lipped seals, fill the space between the lips with grease.

Unless otherwise stated, oil seals must be fitted with their sealing lips toward the lubricant to be sealed.

Use a tubular drift or block of wood of the appropriate size to install the seal and, if the seal housing is shouldered, drive the seal down to the shoulder. If the seal housing is unshouldered, the seal should be fitted with its face flush with the housing top face (unless otherwise instructed).

Screw threads and fastenings

Seized nuts, bolts and screws are quite a common occurrence where corrosion has set in, and the use of penetrating oil or releasing fluid will often overcome this problem if the offending item is soaked for a while before attempting to release it. The use of an impact driver may also provide a means of releasing such stubborn fastening devices, when used in conjunction with the appropriate screwdriver bit or socket. If none of these methods works, it may be necessary to resort to the careful application of heat, or the use of a hacksaw or nut splitter device. Before resorting to extreme methods, check that you are not dealing with a left-hand thread!

Studs are usually removed by locking two nuts together on the threaded part, and then using a spanner on the lower nut to unscrew the stud. Studs or bolts which have broken off below the surface of the component in which they are mounted can sometimes be removed using a stud extractor.

Always ensure that a blind tapped hole is completely free from oil, grease, water or other fluid before installing the bolt or stud. Failure to do this could cause the housing to crack due to the hydraulic action of the bolt or stud as it is screwed in.

For some screw fastenings, notably cylinder head bolts or nuts, torque wrench settings are no longer specified for the latter stages of tightening, "angle-tightening" being called up instead. Typically, a fairly low torque wrench setting will be applied to the bolts/nuts in the correct sequence, followed by one or more stages of tightening through specified angles.

When checking or retightening a nut or bolt to a specified torque setting, slacken the nut or bolt by a quarter of a turn, and then retighten to the specified setting. However, this should not be attempted where angular tightening has been used.

Locknuts, locktabs and washers

Any fastening which will rotate against a component or housing during tightening should always have a washer between it and the relevant component or housing.

Spring or split washers should always be renewed when they are used to lock a critical component such as a big-end bearing retaining bolt or nut. Locktabs which are folded over to retain a nut or bolt should always be renewed.

Self-locking nuts can be re-used in non-critical areas, providing resistance can be felt when the locking portion passes over the bolt or stud thread. However, it should be noted that self-locking stiffnuts tend to lose their effectiveness after long periods of use, and should then be renewed as a matter of course.

Split pins must always be replaced with new ones of the correct size for the hole.

When thread-locking compound is found on the threads of a fastener which is to be re-used, it should be cleaned off with a wire brush and solvent, and fresh compound applied on reassembly.

Special tools

Some repair procedures in this manual entail the use of special tools such as a press, two or three-legged pullers, spring compressors, etc. Wherever possible, suitable readily-available alternatives to the manufacturer's special tools are described, and are shown in use. In some instances, where no alternative is possible, it has been necessary to resort to the use of a manufacturer's tool, and this has been done for reasons of safety as well as the efficient completion of the repair operation. Unless you are highly-skilled and have a thorough understanding of the procedures described, never attempt to bypass the use of any special tool when the procedure described specifies its use. Not only is there a very great risk of personal injury, but expensive damage could be caused to the components involved.

Environmental considerations

When disposing of used engine oil, brake fluid, antifreeze, etc, give due consideration to any detrimental environmental effects. Do not, for instance, pour any of the above liquids down drains into the general sewage system, or onto the ground to soak away. Many local council refuse tips provide a facility for waste oil disposal, as do some garages. You can find your nearest disposal point by calling the Environment Agency on 08708 506 506 or by visiting www.oilbankline.org.uk.

***Note:** It is illegal and anti-social to dump oil down the drain. To find the location of your local oil recycling bank, call 08708 506 506 or visit www.oilbankline.org.uk.*

Modifications are a continuing and unpublicised process in vehicle manufacture, quite apart from major model changes. Spare parts manuals and lists are compiled upon a numerical basis, the individual vehicle identification numbers being essential to correct identification of the component concerned.

When ordering spare parts, always give as much information as possible. Quote the car model, year of manufacture and registration, chassis and engine numbers as appropriate.

The *Vehicle Identification Number (VIN) plate* is visible from the outside of the vehicle, through the left-hand lower corner of the windscreen, and is also stamped on the top of the right-hand inner wing in the engine compartment **(see illustrations)**.

The *Vehicle Data Sticker* is located in the spare wheel well accessed through the luggage compartment **(see illustration)**. It contains the VIN, vehicle type, engine power, transmission type, engine and transmission codes, paint number, interior equipment, optional extras, and PR numbers (for maintenance schedule).

The *Type plate and factory plate* is located at the bottom of the front , left-hand door A-pillar, and is visible with the door open. It contains the gross vehicle weight, front axle weight and rear axle weight.

The Engine Number is stamped into the left-hand end of the cylinder block and on the right-hand end of the cylinder head on petrol engines. On diesel engines it is stamped into the front of the cylinder block, next to the engine-to-transmission joint. A barcode identification sticker is located on the top of the timing cover or on the right-hand end of the cylinder head **(see illustrations)**.

Engine codes

1.4 litre	
Indirect injection petrol engine	*BCA and BUD*
Direct injection petrol engine (FSi)	*BKG and BLN*
Direct injection petrol turbocharged engine (TSi)	*CAXA*
1.6 litre	
SOHC petrol engine	*BGU, BSE and BSF*
DOHC direct injection petrol engine (FSi)	*BAG, BLP and BLF*
2.0 litre petrol engine	
Non-turbo	*AXW, BLX, BLY, BLR, BVX, BVY and BVZ*
Turbo	*AXX, BPY and BWA*
Diesel engine	
1.9 litre, 8-valve, turbo, SOHC	*BJB, BKC, BRU, BLS, BXE and BXF*
2.0 litre PD injection:	
8-valve, non-turbo, SOHC	*BDK*
8-valve, turbo, SOHC	*BMM*
16-valve, turbo, DOHC	*AZV, BKD and BMN*
2.0 litre common rail injection	*CBDA and CBDB*

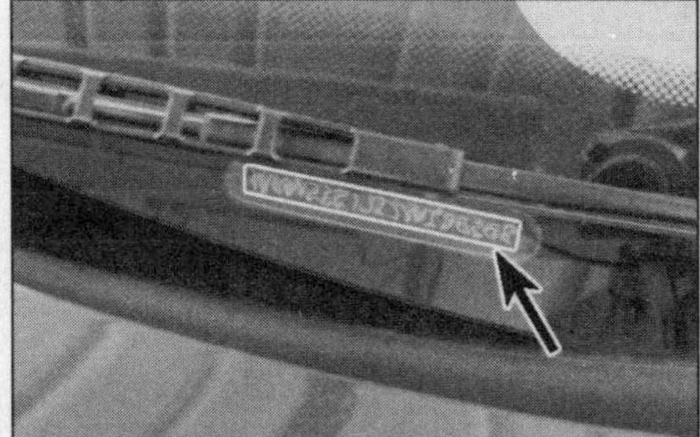

Vehicle Identification Number (VIN) located on the left-hand front edge of the windscreen

Vehicle Identification Number (VIN) located on the top of the right-hand inner wing

Vehicle Data Sticker located in the spare wheel well

Engine number located on the left-hand end of the block

Engine code sticker on the right-hand end of the cylinder head on petrol engines

Engine code sticker on the top of the timing cover on diesel engines

Jacking and vehicle support

The jack supplied with the vehicle tool kit should only be used for changing the roadwheels – see *Wheel changing* at the front of this book. When carrying out any other kind of work, raise the vehicle using a hydraulic (or 'trolley') jack, and always supplement the jack with axle stands positioned under the vehicle jacking points.

When using a hydraulic jack or axle stands, always position the jack head or axle stand head under one of the relevant jacking points.

To raise the front and/or rear of the vehicle, use the jacking/support points at the front and rear ends of the door sills, indicated by the triangular depressions in the sill panel **(see illustration)**. Position a block of wood with a groove cut in it on the jack head to prevent the vehicle weight resting on the sill edge; align the sill edge with the groove in the wood so that the vehicle weight is spread evenly over the surface of the block. Supplement the jack with axle stands (also with slotted blocks of wood) positioned as close as possible to the jacking points **(see illustrations)**.

Do not jack the vehicle under any other part of the sill, sump, floor pan, or any of the steering or suspension components. With the vehicle raised, an axle stand should be positioned beneath the vehicle jack location point on the sill.

Warning: Never work under, around, or near a raised car, unless it is supported in at least two places.

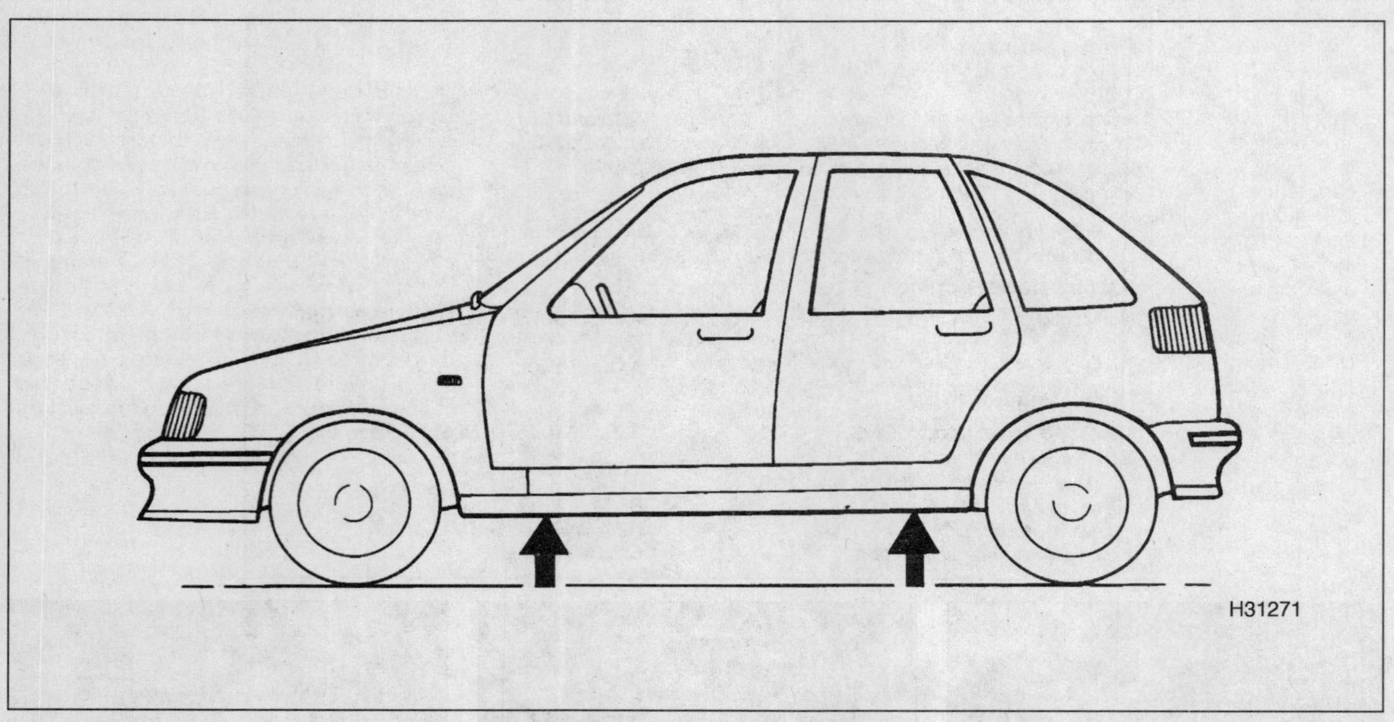

Front and rear jacking points (arrowed)

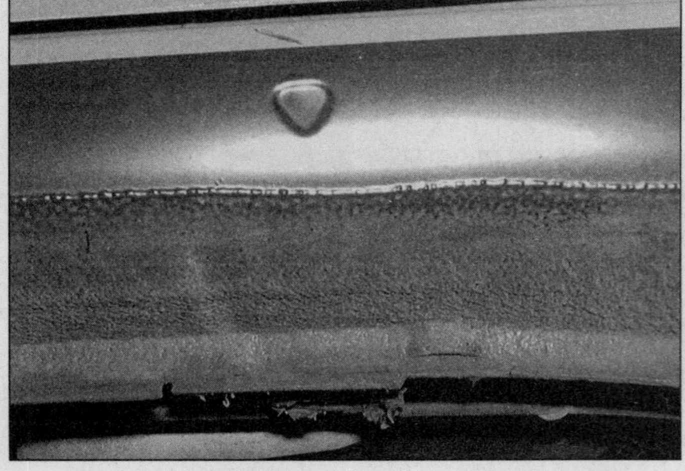

The jacking points are indicated by an arrow on the sill

Use an axle stand with a suitable block of wood

Caution: After reconnecting the battery, the safety function of the electric windows will not be re-instated until the windows have been reprogrammed. This could potentially cause severe pinching injuries.

Several of the systems require battery power to be available at all times (permanent live). This is either to ensure their continued operation (such as the clock), or to maintain electronic memory settings which would otherwise be erased. Whenever the battery is to be disconnected, first note the following points, to ensure there are no unforeseen consequences:

a) *Firstly, on any vehicle with central door locking, it is a wise precaution to remove the key from the ignition, and to keep it with you. This avoids the possibility of the key being locked inside the car, should the central locking engage when the battery is reconnected.*

b) *If a security-coded audio unit is fitted, and the unit and/or the battery is disconnected, the unit will not function until the correct security code has been entered. Therefore, if you do not know the correct security code for the radio/CD unit,* ***do not*** *disconnect either of the battery terminals, or remove the radio/CD unit from the vehicle. The code appears on a code card supplied with the car when new. Details for entering the code appear in the vehicle handbook. Should the code have been misplaced or forgotten, on production of proof of ownership, a VW dealer or in-car entertainment specialist may be able to help.*

c) *The engine management system ECU is of the 'self-learning' type, meaning that, as it operates, it adapts to changes in operating conditions, and stores the optimum settings found (this is especially true for idle speed settings). When the battery is disconnected, these 'learned' settings are lost, and the ECU reverts to the base factory settings. When the engine is restarted, it may idle and run roughly until the ECU has 'relearned' the best settings. To further this 'learning' process, take the car for a road test of at least 15 minutes' duration, covering as many engine speeds and loads as possible, and concentrating on the 2000 to 4000 rpm range. On completion, let the engine idle for at least 10 minutes, turning the steering wheel occasionally and switching on high-current-draw equipment such as the heater fan or heated rear window. If the engine does not regain its normal performance, have the system checked for faults by a VW dealer.*

d) *On vehicles equipped with an original equipment anti-theft alarm system, before disconnecting the battery, de-activate the alarm system, otherwise the alarm will be triggered.*

e) *After the battery has been reconnected, the warning lights for the ESP and electro-mechanical steering will light up and stay on. They will extinguish if you drive briefly in a straight line at a speed of 9 to 13 mph.*

Devices known as 'memory-savers' or 'code-savers' can be used to avoid some of the above problems. Precise details of use vary according to the device used. Typically, it is plugged into the cigarette lighter socket, and is connected by its own wiring to a spare battery; the vehicle battery is then disconnected from the electrical system, leaving the memory-saver to pass sufficient current to maintain audio unit security codes, and other memory values, and also to run permanently-live circuits such as the clock.

Warning: Some of these devices allow a considerable amount of current to pass, which can mean that many of the vehicle's systems are still operational when the main battery is disconnected. If a memory-saver is used, ensure that the circuit concerned is actually 'dead' before carrying out any work on it.

Introduction

A selection of good tools is a fundamental requirement for anyone contemplating the maintenance and repair of a motor vehicle. For the owner who does not possess any, their purchase will prove a considerable expense, offsetting some of the savings made by doing-it-yourself. However, provided that the tools purchased meet the relevant national safety standards and are of good quality, they will last for many years and prove an extremely worthwhile investment.

To help the average owner to decide which tools are needed to carry out the various tasks detailed in this manual, we have compiled three lists of tools under the following headings: *Maintenance and minor repair*, *Repair and overhaul*, and *Special*. Newcomers to practical mechanics should start off with the *Maintenance and minor repair* tool kit, and confine themselves to the simpler jobs around the vehicle. Then, as confidence and experience grow, more difficult tasks can be undertaken, with extra tools being purchased as, and when, they are needed. In this way, a *Maintenance and minor repair* tool kit can be built up into a *Repair and overhaul* tool kit over a considerable period of time, without any major cash outlays. The experienced do-it-yourselfer will have a tool kit good enough for most repair and overhaul procedures, and will add tools from the *Special* category when it is felt that the expense is justified by the amount of use to which these tools will be put.

Maintenance and minor repair tool kit

The tools given in this list should be considered as a minimum requirement if routine maintenance, servicing and minor repair operations are to be undertaken. We recommend the purchase of combination spanners (ring one end, open-ended the other); although more expensive than open-ended ones, they do give the advantages of both types of spanner.

- ☐ *Combination spanners:*
  Metric - 8 to 19 mm inclusive
- ☐ *Adjustable spanner - 35 mm jaw (approx.)*
- ☐ *Spark plug spanner (with rubber insert) - petrol models*
- ☐ *Spark plug gap adjustment tool - petrol models*
- ☐ *Set of feeler gauges*
- ☐ *Brake bleed nipple spanner*
- ☐ *Screwdrivers:*
  Flat blade - 100 mm long x 6 mm dia
  Cross blade - 100 mm long x 6 mm dia
  Torx - various sizes (not all vehicles)
- ☐ *Combination pliers*
- ☐ *Hacksaw (junior)*
- ☐ *Tyre pump*
- ☐ *Tyre pressure gauge*
- ☐ *Oil can*
- ☐ *Oil filter removal tool (if applicable)*
- ☐ *Fine emery cloth*
- ☐ *Wire brush (small)*
- ☐ *Funnel (medium size)*
- ☐ *Sump drain plug key (not all vehicles)*

Repair and overhaul tool kit

These tools are virtually essential for anyone undertaking any major repairs to a motor vehicle, and are additional to those given in the *Maintenance and minor repair* list. Included in this list is a comprehensive set of sockets. Although these are expensive, they will be found invaluable as they are so versatile - particularly if various drives are included in the set. We recommend the half-inch square-drive type, as this can be used with most proprietary torque wrenches.

The tools in this list will sometimes need to be supplemented by tools from the *Special* list:

- ☐ *Sockets to cover range in previous list (including Torx sockets)*
- ☐ *Reversible ratchet drive (for use with sockets)*
- ☐ *Extension piece, 250 mm (for use with sockets)*
- ☐ *Universal joint (for use with sockets)*
- ☐ *Flexible handle or sliding T "breaker bar" (for use with sockets)*
- ☐ *Torque wrench (for use with sockets)*
- ☐ *Self-locking grips*
- ☐ *Ball pein hammer*
- ☐ *Soft-faced mallet (plastic or rubber)*
- ☐ *Screwdrivers:*
  Flat blade - long & sturdy, short (chubby), and narrow (electrician's) types
  Cross blade – long & sturdy, and short (chubby) types
- ☐ *Pliers:*
  Long-nosed
  Side cutters (electrician's)
  Circlip (internal and external)
- ☐ *Cold chisel - 25 mm*
- ☐ *Scriber*
- ☐ *Scraper*
- ☐ *Centre-punch*
- ☐ *Pin punch*
- ☐ *Hacksaw*
- ☐ *Brake hose clamp*
- ☐ *Brake/clutch bleeding kit*
- ☐ *Selection of twist drills*
- ☐ *Steel rule/straight-edge*
- ☐ *Allen keys (inc. splined/Torx type)*
- ☐ *Selection of files*
- ☐ *Wire brush*
- ☐ *Axle stands*
- ☐ *Jack (strong trolley or hydraulic type)*
- ☐ *Light with extension lead*
- ☐ *Universal electrical multi-meter*

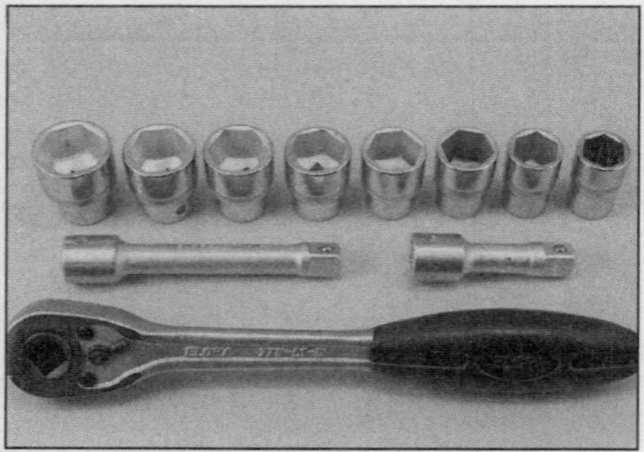
Sockets and reversible ratchet drive

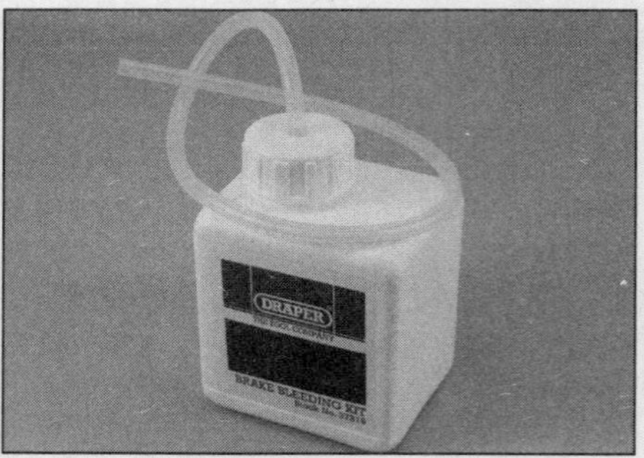

Brake bleeding kit

Torx key, socket and bit

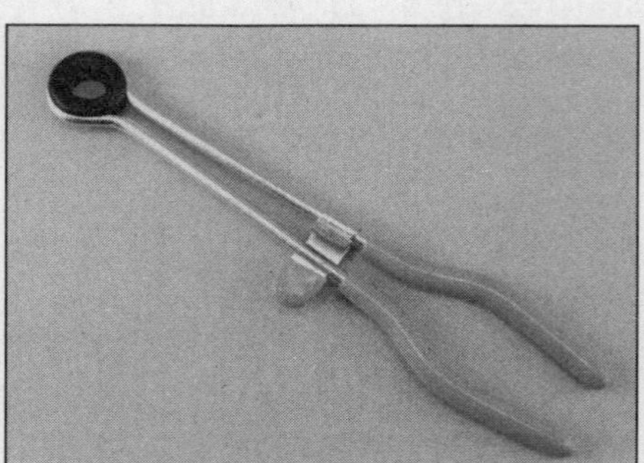
Hose clamp

Angular-tightening gauge

Special tools

The tools in this list are those which are not used regularly, are expensive to buy, or which need to be used in accordance with their manufacturers' instructions. Unless relatively difficult mechanical jobs are undertaken frequently, it will not be economic to buy many of these tools. Where this is the case, you could consider clubbing together with friends (or joining a motorists' club) to make a joint purchase, or borrowing the tools against a deposit from a local garage or tool hire specialist.

The following list contains only those tools and instruments freely available to the public, and not those special tools produced by the vehicle manufacturer specifically for its dealer network. You will find occasional references to these manufacturers' special tools in the text of this manual. Generally, an alternative method of doing the job without the vehicle manufacturers' special tool is given. However, sometimes there is no alternative to using them. Where this is the case and the relevant tool cannot be bought or borrowed, you will have to entrust the work to a dealer.

- ☐ *Angular-tightening gauge*
- ☐ *Valve spring compressor*
- ☐ *Valve grinding tool*
- ☐ *Piston ring compressor*
- ☐ *Piston ring removal/installation tool*
- ☐ *Cylinder bore hone*
- ☐ *Balljoint separator*
- ☐ *Coil spring compressors (where applicable)*
- ☐ *Two/three-legged hub and bearing puller*
- ☐ *Impact screwdriver*
- ☐ *Micrometer and/or vernier calipers*
- ☐ *Dial gauge*
- ☐ *Tachometer*
- ☐ *Fault code reader*
- ☐ *Cylinder compression gauge*
- ☐ *Hand-operated vacuum pump and gauge*
- ☐ *Clutch plate alignment set*
- ☐ *Brake shoe steady spring cup removal tool*
- ☐ *Bush and bearing removal/installation set*
- ☐ *Stud extractors*
- ☐ *Tap and die set*
- ☐ *Lifting tackle*

Buying tools

Reputable motor accessory shops and superstores often offer excellent quality tools at discount prices, so it pays to shop around.

Remember, you don't have to buy the most expensive items on the shelf, but it is always advisable to steer clear of the very cheap tools. Beware of 'bargains' offered on market stalls, on-line or at car boot sales. There are plenty of good tools around at reasonable prices, but always aim to purchase items which meet the relevant national safety standards. If in doubt, ask the proprietor or manager of the shop for advice before making a purchase.

Care and maintenance of tools

Having purchased a reasonable tool kit, it is necessary to keep the tools in a clean and serviceable condition. After use, always wipe off any dirt, grease and metal particles using a clean, dry cloth, before putting the tools away. Never leave them lying around after they have been used. A simple tool rack on the garage or workshop wall for items such as screwdrivers and pliers is a good idea. Store all normal spanners and sockets in a metal box. Any measuring instruments, gauges, meters, etc, must be carefully stored where they cannot be damaged or become rusty.

Take a little care when tools are used. Hammer heads inevitably become marked, and screwdrivers lose the keen edge on their blades from time to time. A little timely attention with emery cloth or a file will soon restore items like this to a good finish.

Working facilities

Not to be forgotten when discussing tools is the workshop itself. If anything more than routine maintenance is to be carried out, a suitable working area becomes essential.

It is appreciated that many an owner-mechanic is forced by circumstances to remove an engine or similar item without the benefit of a garage or workshop. Having done this, any repairs should always be done under the cover of a roof.

Wherever possible, any dismantling should be done on a clean, flat workbench or table at a suitable working height.

Any workbench needs a vice; one with a jaw opening of 100 mm is suitable for most jobs. As mentioned previously, some clean dry storage space is also required for tools, as well as for any lubricants, cleaning fluids, touch-up paints etc, which become necessary.

Another item which may be required, and which has a much more general usage, is an electric drill with a chuck capacity of at least 8 mm. This, together with a good range of twist drills, is virtually essential for fitting accessories.

Last, but not least, always keep a supply of old newspapers and clean, lint-free rags available, and try to keep any working area as clean as possible.

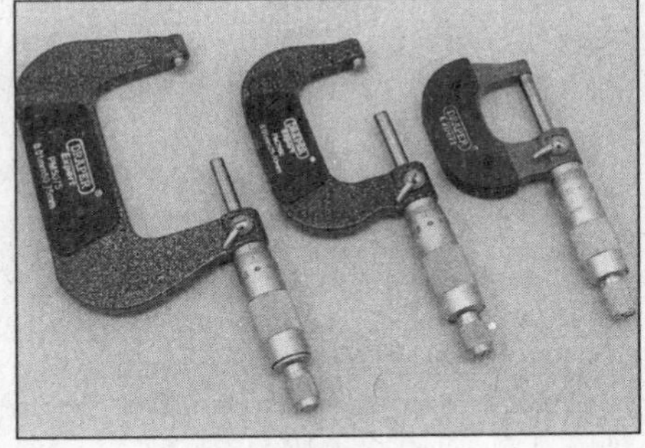

Micrometers

Dial test indicator ("dial gauge")

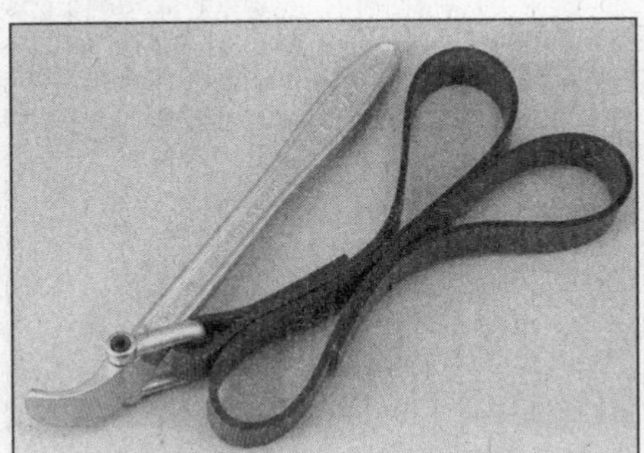

Oil filter removal tool (strap wrench type)

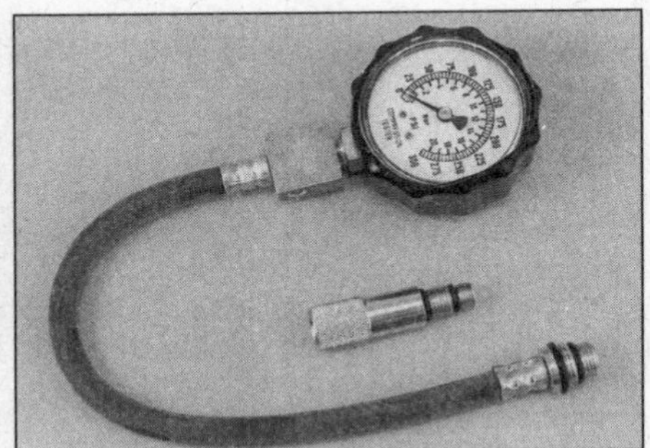

Compression tester

Bearing puller

MOT test checks

This is a guide to getting your vehicle through the MOT test. Obviously it will not be possible to examine the vehicle to the same standard as the professional MOT tester. However, working through the following checks will enable you to identify any problem areas before submitting the vehicle for the test.

It has only been possible to summarise the test requirements here, based on the regulations in force at the time of printing. Test standards are becoming increasingly stringent, although there are some exemptions for older vehicles.

An assistant will be needed to help carry out some of these checks.

The checks have been sub-divided into four categories, as follows:

1 Checks carried out **FROM THE DRIVER'S SEAT**

2 Checks carried out **WITH THE VEHICLE ON THE GROUND**

3 Checks carried out **WITH THE VEHICLE RAISED AND THE WHEELS FREE TO TURN**

4 Checks carried out on **YOUR VEHICLE'S EXHAUST EMISSION SYSTEM**

1 Checks carried out FROM THE DRIVER'S SEAT

Handbrake (parking brake)

☐ Test the operation of the handbrake. Excessive travel (too many clicks) indicates incorrect brake or cable adjustment.

☐ Check that the handbrake cannot be released by tapping the lever sideways. Check the security of the lever mountings.

☐ If the parking brake is foot-operated, check that the pedal is secure and without excessive travel, and that the release mechanism operates correctly.

☐ Where applicable, test the operation of the electronic handbrake. The brake should engage and disengage without excessive delay. If the warning light does not extinguish when the brake is disengaged, this could indicate a fault which will need further investigation.

Footbrake

☐ Depress the brake pedal and check that it does not creep down to the floor, indicating a master cylinder fault. Release the pedal, wait a few seconds, then depress it again. If the pedal travels nearly to the floor before firm resistance is felt, brake adjustment or repair is necessary. If the pedal feels spongy, there is air in the hydraulic system which must be removed by bleeding.

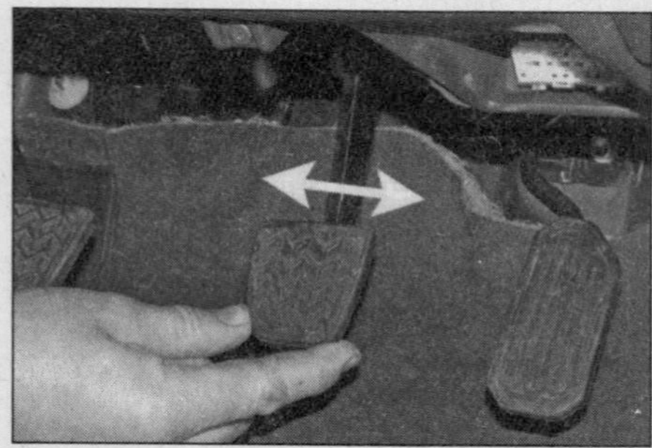

☐ Check that the brake pedal is secure and in good condition. Check also for signs of fluid leaks on the pedal, floor or carpets, which would indicate failed seals in the brake master cylinder.

☐ Check the servo unit (when applicable) by operating the brake pedal several times, then keeping the pedal depressed and starting the engine. As the engine starts, the pedal will move down slightly. If not, the vacuum hose or the servo itself may be faulty.

Steering wheel and column

☐ Examine the steering wheel for fractures or looseness of the hub, spokes or rim.

☐ Move the steering wheel from side to side and then up and down. Check that the steering wheel is not loose on the column, indicating wear or a loose retaining nut. Continue moving the steering wheel as before, but also turn it slightly from left to right.

☐ Check that the steering wheel is not loose on the column, and that there is no abnormal movement of the steering wheel, indicating wear in the column support bearings or couplings.

☐ Check that the ignition lock (where fitted) engages and disengages correctly.

☐ Steering column adjustment mechanisms (where fitted) must be able to lock the column securely in place with no play evident.

Windscreen, mirrors and sunvisor

☐ The windscreen must be free of cracks or other significant damage within the driver's field of view. (Small stone chips are acceptable.) Rear view mirrors must be secure, intact, and capable of being adjusted.

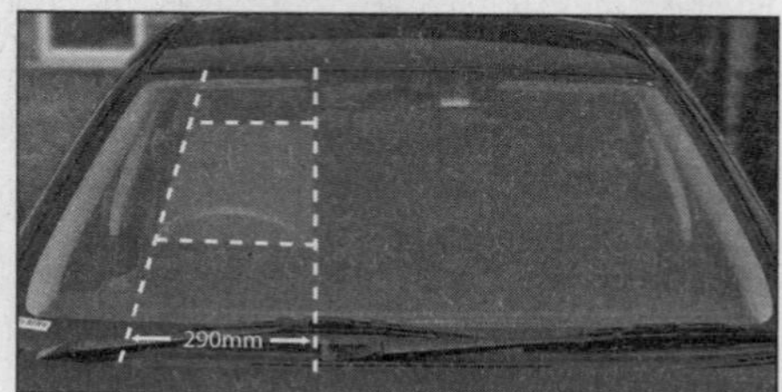

☐ The driver's sunvisor must be capable of being stored in the "up" position.

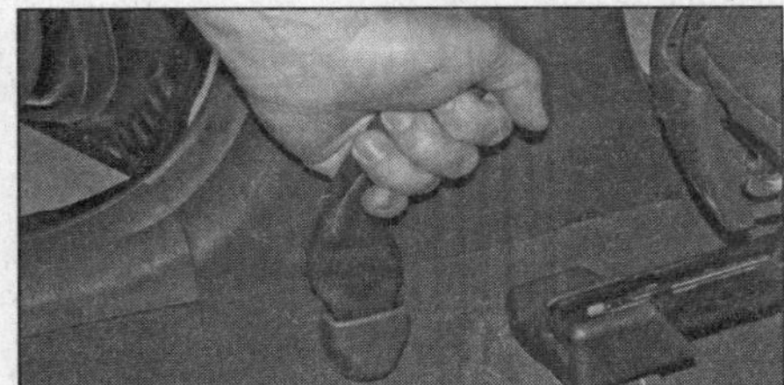

Seat belts and seats

Note: *The following checks are applicable to all seat belts, front and rear.*

☐ Examine the webbing of all the belts (including rear belts if fitted) for cuts, serious fraying or deterioration. Fasten and unfasten each belt to check the buckles. If applicable, check the retracting mechanism. Check the security of all seat belt mountings accessible from inside the vehicle, ensuring any height adjustable mountings lock securely in place.

☐ Seat belts with pre-tensioners, once activated, have a "flag" or similar showing on the seat belt stalk. This, in itself, is not a reason for test failure.

☐ The front seats themselves must be securely attached and the backrests must lock in the upright position.

Doors

☐ Both front doors must be able to be opened and closed from outside and inside, and must latch securely when closed.

Bonnet and boot/tailgate

☐ The bonnet and boot/tailgate must latch securely when closed.

2 Checks carried out WITH THE VEHICLE ON THE GROUND

Vehicle identification

☐ Number plates must be in good condition, secure and legible, with letters and numbers correctly spaced – spacing at (A) should be 33 mm and at (B) 11 mm. At the front, digits must be black on a white background and at the rear black on a yellow background. Other background designs (such as honeycomb) are not permitted.

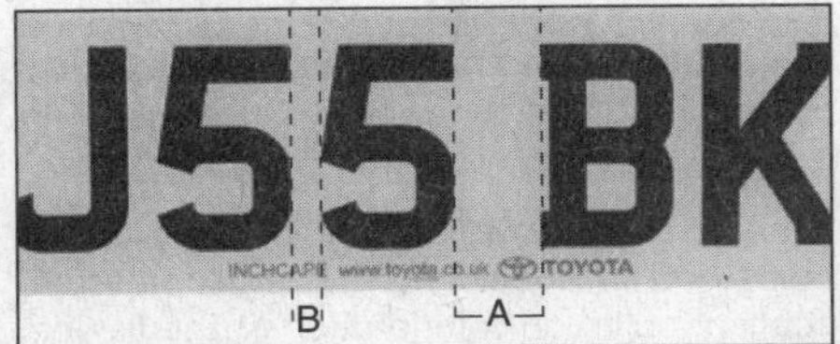

☐ The VIN plate and/or homologation plate must be permanently displayed and legible.

Electrical equipment

☐ Switch on the ignition and check the operation of the horn.

☐ Check the windscreen washers and wipers, examining the wiper blades; renew damaged or perished blades. Also check the operation of the stop-lights.

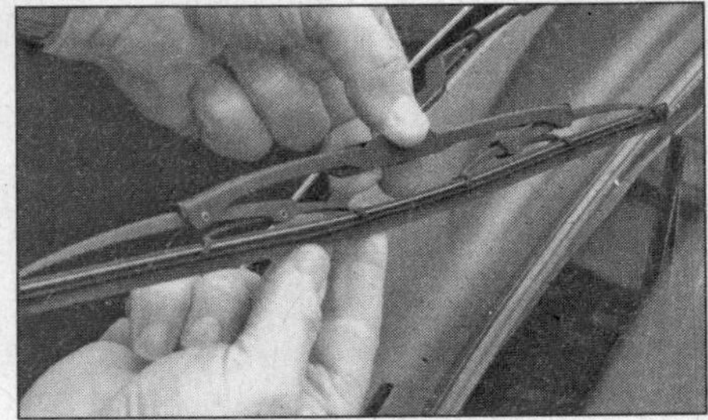

☐ Check the operation of the sidelights and number plate lights. The lenses and reflectors must be secure, clean and undamaged.

☐ Check the operation and alignment of the headlights. The headlight reflectors must not be tarnished and the lenses must be undamaged.

☐ Switch on the ignition and check the operation of the direction indicators (including the instrument panel tell-tale) and the hazard warning lights. Operation of the sidelights and stop-lights must not affect the indicators - if it does, the cause is usually a bad earth at the rear light cluster. Indicators should flash at a rate of between 60 and 120 times per minute – faster or slower than this could indicate a fault with the flasher unit or a bad earth at one of the light units.

☐ Check the operation of the rear foglight(s), including the warning light on the instrument panel or in the switch.

☐ The ABS warning light must illuminate in accordance with the manufacturers' design. For most vehicles, the ABS warning light should illuminate when the ignition is switched on, and (if the system is operating properly) extinguish after a few seconds. Refer to the owner's handbook.

Footbrake

☐ Examine the master cylinder, brake pipes and servo unit for leaks, loose mountings, corrosion or other damage. If ABS is fitted, this unit should also be examined for signs of leaks or corrosion.

☐ The fluid reservoir must be secure and the fluid level must be between the upper (**A**) and lower (**B**) markings.

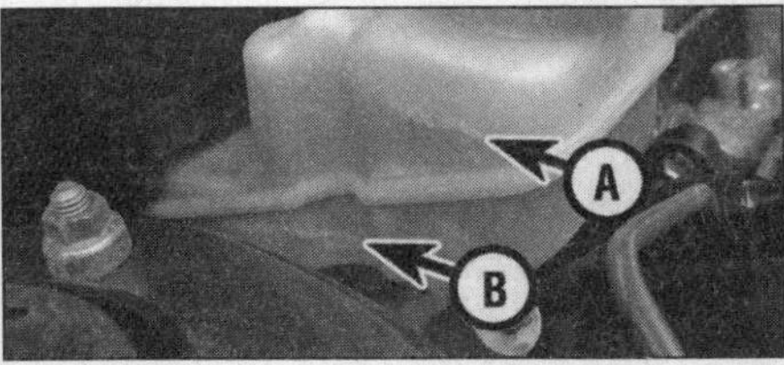

☐ Inspect both front brake flexible hoses for cracks or deterioration of the rubber. Turn the steering from lock to lock, and ensure that the hoses do not contact the wheel, tyre, or any part of the steering or suspension mechanism. With the brake pedal firmly depressed, check the hoses for bulges or leaks under pressure.

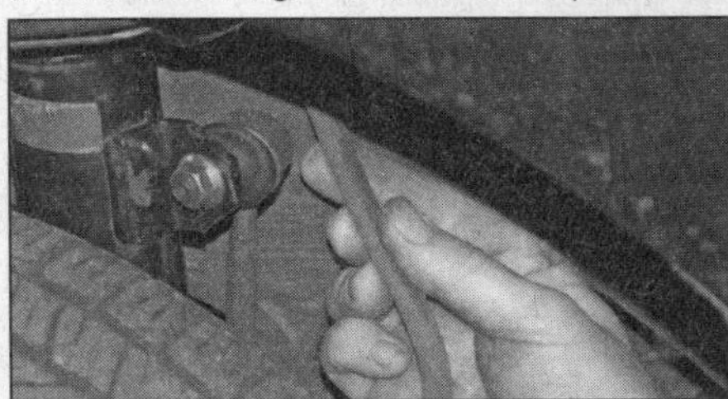

Steering and suspension

☐ Have your assistant turn the steering wheel from side to side slightly, up to the point where the steering gear just begins to transmit this movement to the roadwheels. Check for excessive free play between the steering wheel and the steering gear, indicating wear or insecurity of the steering column joints, the column-to-steering gear coupling, or the steering gear itself.

☐ Have your assistant turn the steering wheel more vigorously in each direction, so that the roadwheels just begin to turn. As this is done, examine all the steering joints, linkages, fittings and attachments. Renew any component that shows signs of wear or damage. On vehicles with power steering, check the security and condition of the steering pump, drivebelt and hoses.

☐ Check that the vehicle is standing level, and at approximately the correct ride height.

Shock absorbers

☐ Depress each corner of the vehicle in turn, then release it. The vehicle should rise and then settle in its normal position. If the vehicle continues to rise and fall, the shock absorber is defective. A shock absorber which has seized will also cause the vehicle to fail.

Exhaust system

☐ Start the engine. With your assistant holding a rag over the tailpipe, check the entire system for leaks. Repair or renew leaking sections.

3 Checks carried out WITH THE VEHICLE RAISED AND THE WHEELS FREE TO TURN

Jack up the front and rear of the vehicle, and securely support it on axle stands. Position the stands clear of the suspension assemblies. Ensure that the wheels are clear of the ground and that the steering can be turned from lock to lock.

Steering mechanism

☐ Have your assistant turn the steering from lock to lock. Check that the steering turns smoothly, and that no part of the steering mechanism, including a wheel or tyre, fouls any brake hose or pipe or any part of the body structure.

☐ Examine the steering rack rubber gaiters for damage or insecurity of the retaining clips. If power steering is fitted, check for signs of damage or leakage of the fluid hoses, pipes or connections. Also check for excessive stiffness or binding of the steering, a missing split pin or locking device, or severe corrosion of the body structure within 30 cm of any steering component attachment point.

Front and rear suspension and wheel bearings

☐ Starting at the front right-hand side, grasp the roadwheel at the 3 o'clock and 9 o'clock positions and rock gently but firmly. Check for free play or insecurity at the wheel bearings, suspension balljoints, or suspension mount-ings, pivots and attachments.

☐ Now grasp the wheel at the 12 o'clock and 6 o'clock positions and repeat the previous inspection. Spin the wheel, and check for roughness or tightness of the front wheel bearing.

☐ If excess free play is suspected at a component pivot point, this can be confirmed by using a large screwdriver or similar tool and levering between the mounting and the component attachment. This will confirm whether the wear is in the pivot bush, its retaining bolt, or in the mounting itself (the bolt holes can often become elongated).

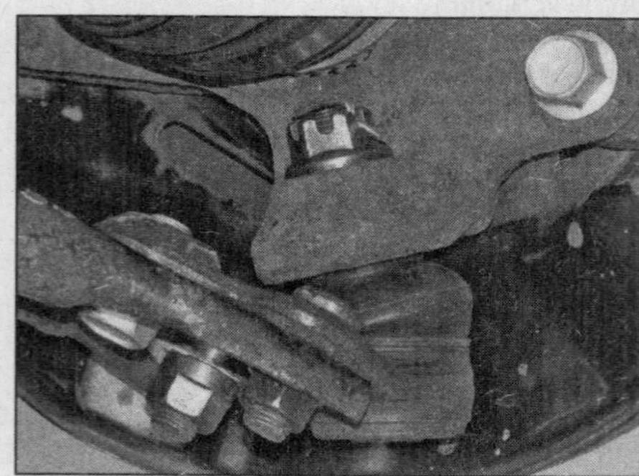

☐ Carry out all the above checks at the other front wheel, and then at both rear wheels.

Springs and shock absorbers

☐ Examine the suspension struts (when applicable) for serious fluid leakage, corrosion, or damage to the casing. Also check the security of the mounting points.

☐ If coil springs are fitted, check that the spring ends locate in their seats, and that the spring is not corroded, cracked or broken.

☐ If leaf springs are fitted, check that all leaves are intact, that the axle is securely attached to each spring, and that there is no deterioration of the spring eye mountings, bushes, and shackles.

☐ The same general checks apply to vehicles fitted with other suspension types, such as torsion bars, hydraulic displacer units, etc. Ensure that all mountings and attachments are secure, that there are no signs of excessive wear, corrosion or damage, and (on hydraulic types) that there are no fluid leaks or damaged pipes.

☐ Inspect the shock absorbers for signs of serious fluid leakage. Check for wear of the mounting bushes or attachments, or damage to the body of the unit.

Driveshafts (fwd vehicles only)

☐ Rotate each front wheel in turn and inspect the constant velocity joint gaiters for splits or damage. Also check that each driveshaft is straight and undamaged.

Braking system

☐ If possible without dismantling, check brake pad wear and disc condition. Ensure that the friction lining material has not worn excessively, (A) and that the discs are not fractured, pitted, scored or badly worn (B).

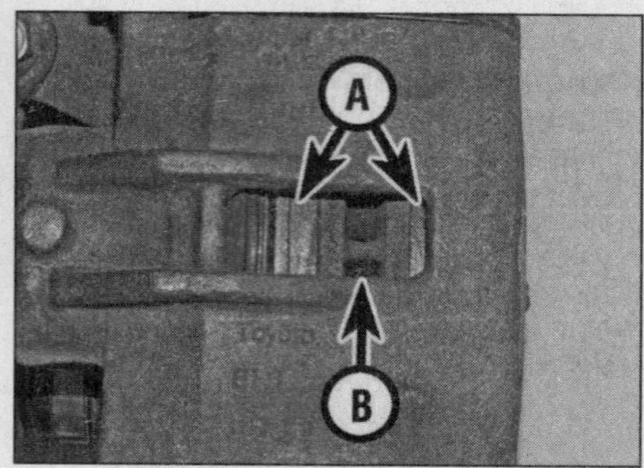

☐ Examine all the rigid brake pipes underneath the vehicle, and the flexible hose(s) at the rear. Look for corrosion, chafing or insecurity of the pipes, and for signs of bulging under pressure, chafing, splits or deterioration of the flexible hoses.

☐ Look for signs of fluid leaks at the brake calipers or on the brake backplates. Repair or renew leaking components.

☐ Slowly spin each wheel, while your assistant depresses and releases the footbrake. Ensure that each brake is operating and does not bind when the pedal is released.

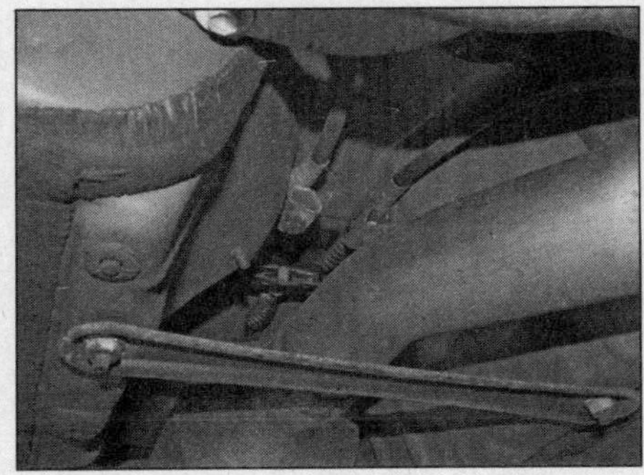

☐Examine the handbrake mechanism, checking for frayed or broken cables, excessive corrosion, or wear or insecurity of the linkage. Check that the mechanism works on each relevant wheel, and releases fully, without binding.

☐It is not possible to test brake efficiency without special equipment, but a road test can be carried out later to check that the vehicle pulls up in a straight line.

Fuel and exhaust systems

☐Inspect the fuel tank (including the filler cap), fuel pipes, hoses and unions. All components must be secure and free from leaks. Locking fuel caps must lock securely and the key must be provided for the MOT test.

☐Examine the exhaust system over its entire length, checking for any damaged, broken or missing mountings, security of the retaining clamps and rust or corrosion.

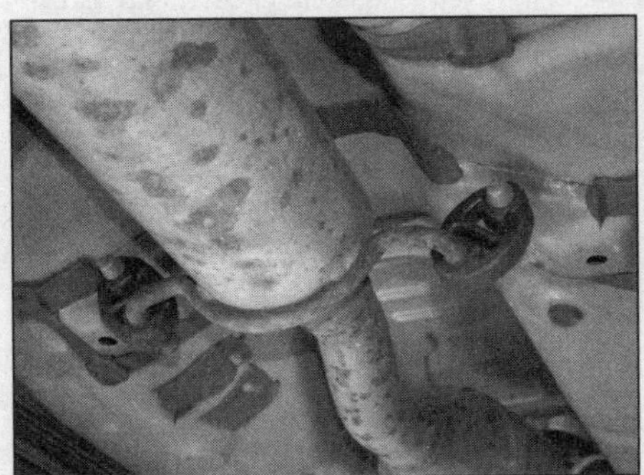

Wheels and tyres

☐Examine the sidewalls and tread area of each tyre in turn. Check for cuts, tears, lumps, bulges, separation of the tread, and exposure of the ply or cord due to wear or damage. Check that the tyre bead is correctly seated on the wheel rim, that the valve is sound and properly seated, and that the wheel is not distorted or damaged.

☐Check that the tyres are of the correct size for the vehicle, that they are of the same size and type on each axle, and that the pressures are correct.

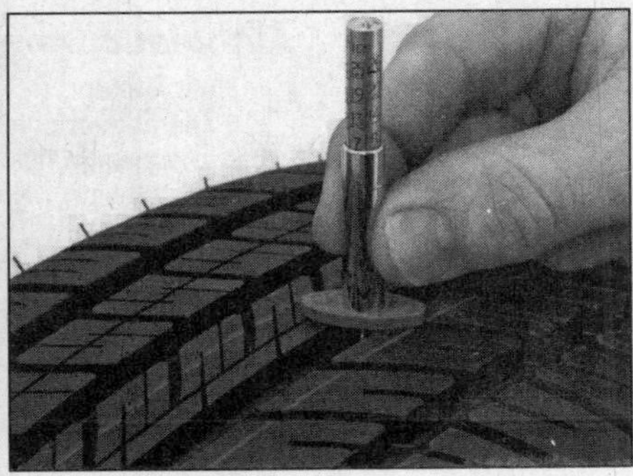

☐Check the tyre tread depth. The legal minimum at the time of writing is 1.6 mm over the central three-quarters of the tread width. Abnormal tread wear may indicate incorrect front wheel alignment or wear in steering or suspension components.

☐If the spare wheel is fitted externally or in a separate carrier beneath the vehicle, check that mountings are secure and free of excessive corrosion.

Body corrosion

☐Check the condition of the entire vehicle structure for signs of corrosion in load-bearing areas. (These include chassis box sections, side sills, cross-members, pillars, and all suspension, steering, braking system and seat belt mountings and anchorages.) Any corrosion which has seriously reduced the thickness of a load-bearing area (or is within 30 cm of safety-related components such as steering or suspension) is likely to cause the vehicle to fail. In this case professional repairs are likely to be needed.

☐Damage or corrosion which causes sharp or otherwise dangerous edges to be exposed will also cause the vehicle to fail.

Towbars

☐Check the condition of mounting points (both beneath the vehicle and within boot/hatchback areas) for signs of corrosion, ensuring that all fixings are secure and not worn or damaged. There must be no excessive play in detachable tow ball arms or quick-release mechanisms.

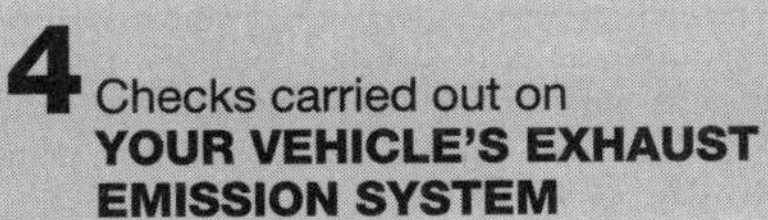

4 Checks carried out on **YOUR VEHICLE'S EXHAUST EMISSION SYSTEM**

Petrol models

☐The engine should be warmed up, and running well (ignition system in good order, air filter element clean, etc).

☐Before testing, run the engine at around 2500 rpm for 20 seconds. Let the engine drop to idle, and watch for smoke from the exhaust. If the idle speed is too high, or if dense blue or black smoke emerges for more than 5 seconds, the vehicle will fail. Typically, blue smoke signifies oil burning (engine wear); black smoke means unburnt fuel (dirty air cleaner element, or other fuel system fault).

☐An exhaust gas analyser for measuring carbon monoxide (CO) and hydrocarbons (HC) is now needed. If one cannot be hired or borrowed, have a local garage perform the check.

CO emissions (mixture)

☐The MOT tester has access to the CO limits for all vehicles. The CO level is measured at idle speed, and at 'fast idle' (2500 to 3000 rpm). The following limits are given as a general guide:

At idle speed – Less than 0.5% CO
At 'fast idle' – Less than 0.3% CO
Lambda reading – 0.97 to 1.03

☐If the CO level is too high, this may point to poor maintenance, a fuel injection system problem, faulty lambda (oxygen) sensor or catalytic converter. Try an injector cleaning treatment, and check the vehicle's ECU for fault codes.

HC emissions

☐The MOT tester has access to HC limits for all vehicles. The HC level is measured at 'fast idle' (2500 to 3000 rpm). The following limits are given as a general guide:

At 'fast idle' – Less then 200 ppm

☐Excessive HC emissions are typically caused by oil being burnt (worn engine), or by a blocked crankcase ventilation system ('breather'). If the engine oil is old and thin, an oil change may help. If the engine is running badly, check the vehicle's ECU for fault codes.

Diesel models

☐The only emission test for diesel engines is measuring exhaust smoke density, using a calibrated smoke meter. The test involves accelerating the engine at least 3 times to its maximum unloaded speed.

Note: *On engines with a timing belt, it is VITAL that the belt is in good condition before the test is carried out.*

☐With the engine warmed up, it is first purged by running at around 2500 rpm for 20 seconds. A governor check is then carried out, by slowly accelerating the engine to its maximum speed. After this, the smoke meter is connected, and the engine is accelerated quickly to maximum speed three times. If the smoke density is less than the limits given below, the vehicle will pass:

Non-turbo vehicles: 2.5m-1
Turbocharged vehicles: 3.0m-1

☐If excess smoke is produced, try fitting a new air cleaner element, or using an injector cleaning treatment. If the engine is running badly, where applicable, check the vehicle's ECU for fault codes. Also check the vehicle's EGR system, where applicable. At high mileages, the injectors may require professional attention.

Engine

- Engine fails to rotate when attempting to start
- Engine rotates, but will not start
- Engine difficult to start when cold
- Engine difficult to start when hot
- Starter motor noisy or excessively-rough in engagement
- Engine starts, but stops immediately
- Engine idles erratically
- Engine misfires at idle speed
- Engine misfires throughout the driving speed range
- Engine hesitates on acceleration
- Engine stalls
- Engine lacks power
- Engine backfires
- Oil pressure warning light illuminated with engine running
- Engine runs-on after switching off
- Engine noises

Cooling system

- Overheating
- Overcooling
- External coolant leakage
- Internal coolant leakage
- Corrosion

Fuel and exhaust systems

- Excessive fuel consumption
- Fuel leakage and/or fuel odour

Clutch

- Pedal travels to floor – no pressure or very little resistance
- Clutch fails to disengage (unable to select gears).
- Clutch slips (engine speed increases, with no increase in vehicle speed).
- Judder as clutch is engaged
- Noise when depressing or releasing clutch pedal

Manual transmission

- Noisy in neutral with engine running
- Noisy in one particular gear
- Difficulty engaging gears
- Vibration
- Jumps out of gear
- Lubricant leaks

Automatic transmission

- Fluid leakage
- General gear selection problems
- Transmission fluid brown, or has burned smell
- Transmission will not downshift (kickdown) with accelerator fully depressed
- Engine will not start in any gear, or starts in gears other than Park or Neutral
- Transmission slips, shifts roughly, is noisy, or has no drive in forward or reverse gears

Braking system

- Vehicle pulls to one side under braking
- Noise (grinding or high-pitched squeal) when brakes applied
- Brakes binding
- Excessive brake pedal travel
- Brake pedal feels spongy when depressed
- Excessive brake pedal effort required to stop vehicle
- Judder felt through brake pedal or steering wheel when braking
- Rear wheels locking under normal braking

Driveshafts

- Clicking or knocking noise on turns (at slow speed on full-lock)

Suspension and steering

- Vehicle pulls to one side
- Excessive pitching and/or rolling around corners, or during braking
- Lack of power assistance
- Wandering or general instability
- Excessively-stiff steering
- Excessive play in steering
- Wheel wobble and vibration
- Tyre wear excessive

Electrical system

- Battery will not hold a charge for more than a few days
- Ignition/no-charge warning light remains illuminated with engine running
- Ignition/no-charge warning light fails to come on
- Lights inoperative
- Instrument readings inaccurate or erratic
- Horn inoperative, or unsatisfactory in operation
- Windscreen wipers inoperative, or unsatisfactory in operation
- Windscreen washers inoperative, or unsatisfactory in operation
- Electric windows inoperative, or unsatisfactory in operation
- Central locking system inoperative, or unsatisfactory in operation

Introduction

The vehicle owner who does his or her own maintenance according to the recommended service schedules should not have to use this section of the manual very often. Modern component reliability is such that, provided those items subject to wear or deterioration are inspected or renewed at the specified intervals, sudden failure is comparatively rare. Faults do not usually just happen as a result of sudden failure, but develop over a period of time. Major mechanical failures in particular are usually preceded by characteristic symptoms over hundreds or even thousands of miles. Those components that do occasionally fail without warning are often small and easily carried in the vehicle.

With any fault-finding, the first step is to decide where to begin investigations. Sometimes this is obvious, but on other occasions, a little detective work will be necessary. The owner who makes half a dozen haphazard adjustments or component renewals may be successful in curing a fault (or its symptoms). However, will be none the wiser if the fault recurs, and ultimately may have spent more time and money than was necessary. A calm and logical approach will be found to be more satisfactory in the long run. Always take into account any warning signs or abnormalities that may have been noticed in the period preceding the fault – power loss, high or low gauge readings, unusual smells, etc – and remember that failure of components such as fuses or spark plugs may only be pointers to some underlying fault.

The pages which follow provide an easy-reference guide to the more common problems which may occur during the operation of the vehicle. These problems and their possible causes are grouped under headings denoting various components or systems, such as Engine, Cooling system, etc. The general Chapter which deals with the problem is also shown in brackets; refer to the relevant part of that Chapter for system-specific information. Whatever the fault, certain basic principles apply. These are as follows:

Verify the fault. This is simply a matter of

being sure that you know what the symptoms are before starting work. This is particularly important if you are investigating a fault for someone else, who may not have described it very accurately.

Do not overlook the obvious. For example, if the vehicle will not start, is there petrol in the tank? (Do not take anyone else's word on this particular point, and do not trust the fuel gauge either!) If an electrical fault is indicated, look for loose or broken wires before digging out the test gear.

Cure the disease, not the symptom. Substituting a flat battery with a fully-charged one will get you off the hard shoulder, but if the underlying cause is not attended to, the new battery will go the same way. Similarly, changing oil-fouled spark plugs for a new set will get you moving again, but remember that the reason for the fouling (if it was not simply an incorrect grade of plug) will have to be established and corrected.

Do not take anything for granted. Particularly, do not forget that a new component may itself be defective (especially if it's been rattling around in the boot for months). Also do not leave components out of a fault diagnosis sequence just because they are new or recently fitted. When you do finally diagnose a difficult fault, you will probably realise that all the evidence was there from the start.

Diesel fault diagnosis

The majority of starting problems on small diesel engines are electrical in origin. The mechanic who is familiar with petrol engines but less so with diesel may be inclined to view the diesel's injectors and pump in the same light as the spark plugs and distributor, but this is generally a mistake.

When investigating complaints of difficult starting for someone else, make sure that the correct starting procedure is understood and is being followed. Some drivers are unaware of the significance of the preheating warning light – many modern engines are sufficiently forgiving for this not to matter in mild weather, but with the onset of winter, problems begin.

As a rule of thumb, if the engine is difficult to start but runs well when it has finally got going, the problem is electrical (battery, starter motor or preheating system). If poor performance is combined with difficult starting, the problem is likely to be in the fuel system. The low-pressure (supply) side of the fuel system should be checked before suspecting the injectors and high-pressure pump. The most common fuel supply problem is air getting into the system, and any pipe from the fuel tank forwards must be scrutinised if air leakage is suspected. Normally the pump is the last item to suspect, since unless it has been tampered with, there is no reason for it to be at fault.

Engine

Engine fails to rotate when attempting to start

- ☐ Battery terminal connections loose or corroded (*Weekly checks*).
- ☐ Battery discharged or faulty (Chapter 5A).
- ☐ Broken, loose or disconnected wiring in the starting circuit (Chapter 5A).
- ☐ Defective starter solenoid or switch (Chapter 5A).
- ☐ Defective starter motor (Chapter 5A).
- ☐ Starter pinion or flywheel ring gear teeth loose or broken (Chapters 2A, 2B, 2C, 2D, 2E, 2F and 5A).
- ☐ Engine earth strap broken or disconnected (Chapter 5A).

Engine rotates, but will not start

- ☐ Fuel tank empty.
- ☐ Battery discharged (engine rotates slowly) (Chapter 5A).
- ☐ Battery terminal connections loose or corroded (*Weekly checks*).
- ☐ Ignition components damp or damaged – petrol models (Chapters 1A and 5B).
- ☐ Broken, loose or disconnected wiring in the ignition circuit – petrol models (Chapters 1A and 5B).
- ☐ Worn, faulty or incorrectly gapped spark plugs – petrol models (Chapter 1A).
- ☐ Fuel injection system fault (Chapter 4A and 4B).
- ☐ Air in fuel system – diesel models (Chapter 4B).
- ☐ Major mechanical failure (eg, timing belt) (Chapter 2A, 2B, 2C, 2D, 2E or 2F).

Engine difficult to start when cold

- ☐ Battery discharged (Chapter 5A).
- ☐ Battery terminal connections loose or corroded (*Weekly checks*).
- ☐ Worn, faulty or incorrectly gapped spark plugs – petrol models (Chapter 1A).
- ☐ Fuel injection system fault (Chapter 4A and 4B).
- ☐ Other ignition system fault – petrol models (Chapters 1A and 5B).
- ☐ Preheating system fault – diesel models (Chapter 5C).
- ☐ Low cylinder compressions (Chapter 2A, 2B, 2C, 2D, 2E or 2F).

Engine difficult to start when hot

- ☐ Air filter element dirty or clogged (Chapter 1A or 1B).
- ☐ Fuel injection system fault (Chapter 4A and 4B).
- ☐ Low cylinder compressions (Chapter 2A, 2B, 2C, 2D, 2E or 2F).

Starter motor noisy or excessively rough in engagement

- ☐ Starter pinion or flywheel ring gear teeth loose or broken (Chapters 2A, 2B, 2C, 2D, 2E, 2F and 5A).
- ☐ Starter motor mounting bolts loose or missing (Chapter 5A).
- ☐ Starter motor internal components worn or damaged (Chapter 5A).

Engine starts, but stops immediately

- ☐ Loose or faulty electrical connections in the ignition circuit – petrol models (Chapters 1A and 5B).
- ☐ Vacuum leak at the throttle body or inlet manifold – petrol models (Chapter 4A).
- ☐ Blocked injector/fuel injection system fault (Chapter 4A or 4B).
- ☐ Faulty injector(s) – diesel models (Chapter 4B).
- ☐ Air in fuel system – diesel models (Chapter 4B).

Engine idles erratically

- ☐ Air filter element clogged (Chapter 1A or 1B).
- ☐ Vacuum leak at the throttle body, inlet manifold or associated hoses – petrol models (Chapter 4A).
- ☐ Worn, faulty or incorrectly gapped spark plugs – petrol models (Chapter 1A).
- ☐ Uneven or low cylinder compressions (Chapter 2A, 2B, 2C, 2D, 2E or 2F).
- ☐ Camshaft lobes worn (Chapter 2A, 2B, 2C, 2D, 2E or 2F).
- ☐ Timing belt incorrectly tensioned (Chapter 2A, 2B, 2D, 2E or 2F).
- ☐ Blocked injector/fuel injection system fault (Chapter 4A or 4B).
- ☐ Faulty injector(s) – diesel models (Chapter 4B).

Engine misfires at idle speed

- ☐ Worn, faulty or incorrectly gapped spark plugs – petrol models (Chapter 1A).
- ☐ Faulty spark plug HT leads – petrol models (Chapter 5B).
- ☐ Vacuum leak at the throttle body, inlet manifold or associated hoses (Chapter 4A or 4B).
- ☐ Blocked injector/fuel injection system fault (Chapter 4A and 4B).
- ☐ Faulty injector(s) – diesel models (Chapter 4B).
- ☐ Uneven or low cylinder compressions (Chapter 2A, 2B, 2C, 2D, 2E or 2F).
- ☐ Disconnected, leaking, or perished crankcase ventilation hoses (Chapter 4C and 4D).

Engine (continued)

Engine misfires throughout the driving speed range

- ☐ Fuel filter choked (Chapter 1A or 1B).
- ☐ Fuel pump faulty, or delivery pressure low (Chapter 4A or 4B).
- ☐ Fuel tank vent blocked, or fuel pipes restricted (Chapter 4A or 4B).
- ☐ Vacuum leak at the throttle body, inlet manifold or associated hoses – petrol models (Chapter 4A).
- ☐ Worn, faulty or incorrectly gapped spark plugs – petrol models (Chapter 1A).
- ☐ Faulty spark plug HT leads (Chapter 5B).
- ☐ Faulty injector(s) – diesel models (Chapter 4B).
- ☐ Faulty ignition coil – petrol models (Chapter 5B).
- ☐ Uneven or low cylinder compressions (Chapter 2A, 2B, 2C, 2D, 2E or 2F).
- ☐ Blocked injector/fuel injection system fault (Chapter 4A or 4B).

Engine hesitates on acceleration

- ☐ Worn, faulty or incorrectly gapped spark plugs – petrol models (Chapter 1A).
- ☐ Vacuum leak at the throttle body, inlet manifold or associated hoses – petrol models (Chapter 4A).
- ☐ Blocked injector/fuel injection system fault (Chapter 4A or 4B).
- ☐ Faulty injector(s) – diesel models (Chapter 4B).
- ☐ Incorrect injection pump timing – diesel models (Chapter 4B).

Engine stalls

- ☐ Vacuum leak at the throttle body, inlet manifold or associated hoses – petrol models (Chapter 4A).
- ☐ Fuel filter choked (Chapter 1A or 1B).
- ☐ Fuel pump faulty, or delivery pressure low – petrol models (Chapter 4A).
- ☐ Fuel tank vent blocked, or fuel pipes restricted (Chapter 4A or 4B).
- ☐ Blocked injector/fuel injection system fault (Chapter 4A or 4B).
- ☐ Faulty injector(s) – diesel models (Chapter 4B).
- ☐ Air in fuel system – diesel models (Chapter 4B).

Engine lacks power

- ☐ Timing belt incorrectly fitted or tensioned (Chapter 2A, 2B, 2D, 2E or 2F).
- ☐ Fuel filter choked (Chapter 1A or 1B).
- ☐ Fuel pump faulty, or delivery pressure low – petrol models (Chapter 4A).
- ☐ Uneven or low cylinder compressions (Chapter 2A, 2B, 2C, 2D, 2E or 2F).
- ☐ Worn, faulty or incorrectly gapped spark plugs – petrol models (Chapter 1A).
- ☐ Vacuum leak at the throttle body, inlet manifold or associated hoses – petrol models (Chapter 4A).
- ☐ Blocked injector/fuel injection system fault (Chapter 4A or 4B).
- ☐ Turbocharger fault (Chapter 4A or 4B).
- ☐ Brakes binding (Chapters 1A or 1B and 9).
- ☐ Clutch slipping (Chapter 6).

Engine backfires

- ☐ Timing belt incorrectly fitted or tensioned (Chapter 2A, 2B, 2D, 2E or 2F).
- ☐ Vacuum leak at the throttle body, inlet manifold or associated hoses – petrol models (Chapter 4A).
- ☐ Blocked injector/fuel injection system fault (Chapter 4A or 4B).

Oil pressure warning light illuminated with engine running

- ☐ Low oil level, or incorrect oil grade (*Weekly checks*).
- ☐ Faulty oil pressure warning light switch (Chapter 2A, 2B, 2C, 2D, 2E or 2F).
- ☐ Worn engine bearings and/or oil pump (Chapter 2A, 2B, 2C, 2D, 2E or 2F).
- ☐ High engine operating temperature (Chapter 3).
- ☐ Oil pressure relief valve defective (Chapter 2A, 2B, 2C, 2D, 2E or 2F).
- ☐ Oil pick-up strainer clogged (Chapter 2A, 2B, 2C, 2D, 2E or 2F).

Engine runs-on after switching off

- ☐ Excessive carbon build-up in engine (Chapter 2A, 2B, 2C, 2D, 2E or 2F).
- ☐ High engine operating temperature (Chapter 3).
- ☐ Fuel injection system fault – petrol models (Chapter 4A).
- ☐ Faulty stop solenoid – diesel models (Chapter 4B).

Engine noises

Pre-ignition (pinking) or knocking during acceleration or under load

- ☐ Ignition system fault – petrol models (Chapters 1A and 5B).
- ☐ Incorrect grade of spark plug – petrol models (Chapter 1A).
- ☐ Incorrect grade of fuel (Chapter 4A).
- ☐ Vacuum leak at the throttle body, inlet manifold or associated hoses – petrol models (Chapter 4A).
- ☐ Excessive carbon build-up in engine (Chapter 2A, 2B, 2C, 2D, 2E or 2F).
- ☐ Blocked injector/fuel injection system fault – petrol models (Chapter 4A).

Whistling or wheezing noises

- ☐ Leaking inlet manifold or throttle body gasket – petrol models (Chapter 4A).
- ☐ Leaking exhaust manifold gasket or pipe-to-manifold joint (Chapter 4C or 4D).
- ☐ Leaking turbocharger air ducts (Chapter 4A or 4B).
- ☐ Leaking vacuum hose (Chapters 4A, 4B, 4C, 4D and 9).
- ☐ Blowing cylinder head gasket (Chapter 2A, 2B, 2C, 2D, 2E or 2F).

Tapping or rattling noises

- ☐ Worn valve gear or camshaft (Chapter 2A, 2B, 2C, 2D, 2E or 2F).
- ☐ Ancillary component fault (coolant pump, alternator, etc) (Chapters 3, 5A, etc).

Knocking or thumping noises

- ☐ Worn big-end bearings (regular heavy knocking, perhaps worsening under load) (Chapter 2G).
- ☐ Worn main bearings (rumbling and knocking, perhaps less under load) (Chapter 2G).
- ☐ Piston slap (most noticeable when cold) (Chapter 2G).
- ☐ Ancillary component fault (coolant pump, alternator, etc) (Chapters 3, 5A, etc).

Cooling system

Overheating

- ☐ Insufficient coolant in system (*Weekly checks*).
- ☐ Thermostat faulty (Chapter 3).
- ☐ Radiator core blocked, or grille restricted (Chapter 3).
- ☐ Electric cooling fan or thermoswitch faulty (Chapter 3).
- ☐ Pressure cap faulty (Chapter 3).
- ☐ Ignition system fault – petrol engines (Chapters 1A and 5B).
- ☐ Inaccurate temperature gauge sender unit (Chapter 3).
- ☐ Airlock in cooling system.

Overcooling

- ☐ Thermostat faulty (Chapter 3).
- ☐ Inaccurate temperature gauge sender unit (Chapter 3).

External coolant leakage

- ☐ Deteriorated or damaged hoses or hose clips (Chapter 1A or 1B).
- ☐ Radiator core or heater matrix leaking (Chapter 3).
- ☐ Pressure cap faulty (Chapter 3).
- ☐ Water pump seal leaking (Chapter 3).
- ☐ Boiling due to overheating (Chapter 3).
- ☐ Core plug leaking (Chapter 2D).

Internal coolant leakage

- ☐ Leaking cylinder head gasket (Chapter 2A, 2B, 2C, 2D, 2E or 2F).
- ☐ Cracked cylinder head or cylinder bore (Chapter 2G).

Corrosion

- ☐ Infrequent draining and flushing (Chapter 1A or 1B).
- ☐ Incorrect coolant mixture or inappropriate coolant type (Chapter 1A or 1B).

Fuel and exhaust systems

Excessive fuel consumption

- ☐ Air filter element dirty or clogged (Chapter 1A or 1B).
- ☐ Fuel injection system fault (Chapter 4A or 4B).
- ☐ Ignition system fault – petrol models (Chapters 1A and 5B).
- ☐ Faulty injector(s) – diesel models (Chapter 4B).
- ☐ Tyres under-inflated (*Weekly checks*).

Fuel leakage and/or fuel odour

- ☐ Damaged or corroded fuel tank, pipes or connections (Chapter 4A or 4B).
- ☐ Excessive noise or fumes from exhaust system (Chapters 4C or 4D)
- ☐ Leaking exhaust system or manifold joints (Chapters 1A, 1B, 4C or 4D).
- ☐ Leaking, corroded or damaged silencers or pipe (Chapters 1A, 1B, 4C or 4D).
- ☐ Broken mountings causing body or suspension contact (Chapter 1A or 1B).

Clutch

Pedal travels to floor – no pressure or very little resistance

- ☐ Hydraulic fluid level low/air in hydraulic system (Chapter 6).
- ☐ Broken clutch release bearing or fork (Chapter 6).
- ☐ Broken diaphragm spring in clutch pressure plate (Chapter 6).

Clutch fails to disengage (unable to select gears)

- ☐ Clutch disc sticking on transmission input shaft splines (Chapter 6).
- ☐ Clutch disc sticking to flywheel or pressure plate (Chapter 6).
- ☐ Faulty pressure plate assembly (Chapter 6).
- ☐ Clutch release mechanism worn or incorrectly assembled (Chapter 6).

Clutch slips (engine speed increases, with no increase in vehicle speed)

- ☐ Clutch disc linings excessively worn (Chapter 6).
- ☐ Clutch disc linings contaminated with oil or grease (Chapter 6).
- ☐ Faulty pressure plate or weak diaphragm spring (Chapter 6).

Judder as clutch is engaged

- ☐ Clutch disc linings contaminated with oil or grease (Chapter 6).
- ☐ Clutch disc linings excessively worn (Chapter 6).
- ☐ Faulty or distorted pressure plate or diaphragm spring (Chapter 6).
- ☐ Worn or loose engine or transmission mountings (Chapter 2A, 2B, 2C, 2D or 2E).
- ☐ Clutch disc hub or transmission input shaft splines worn (Chapter 6).

Noise when depressing or releasing clutch pedal

- ☐ Worn clutch release bearing (Chapter 6).
- ☐ Worn or dry clutch pedal bushes (Chapter 6).
- ☐ Faulty pressure plate assembly (Chapter 6).
- ☐ Pressure plate diaphragm spring broken (Chapter 6).
- ☐ Broken clutch disc cushioning springs (Chapter 6).

Manual transmission

Noisy in neutral with engine running

- ☐ Input shaft bearings worn (noise apparent with clutch pedal released, but not when depressed) (Chapter 7A).*
- ☐ Clutch release bearing worn (noise apparent with clutch pedal depressed, possibly less when released) (Chapter 6).

Noisy in one particular gear

- ☐ Worn, damaged or chipped gear teeth (Chapter 7A).*

Difficulty engaging gears

- ☐ Clutch fault (Chapter 6).
- ☐ Worn or damaged gear linkage (Chapter 7A).
- ☐ Incorrectly adjusted gear linkage (Chapter 7A).
- ☐ Worn synchroniser units (Chapter 7A).*

Vibration

- ☐ Lack of oil (Chapter 1A or 1B).
- ☐ Worn bearings (Chapter 7A).*

Jumps out of gear

- ☐ Worn or damaged gear linkage (Chapter 7A).
- ☐ Incorrectly adjusted gear linkage (Chapter 7A).
- ☐ Worn synchroniser units (Chapter 7A).*
- ☐ Worn selector forks (Chapter 7A).*

Lubricant leaks

- ☐ Leaking differential output oil seal (Chapter 7A).
- ☐ Leaking housing joint (Chapter 7A).*
- ☐ Leaking input shaft oil seal (Chapter 7A).*

** Although the corrective action necessary to remedy the symptoms described is beyond the scope of the home mechanic, the above information should be helpful in isolating the cause of the condition. This should enable the owner can communicate clearly with a professional mechanic.*

Automatic/DSG transmissions

Note: *Due to the complexity of the automatic/DSG transmissions, it is difficult for the home mechanic to properly diagnose and service this unit. For problems other than the following, the vehicle should be taken to a dealer service department or automatic transmission specialist. Do not be too hasty in removing the transmission if a fault is suspected, as most of the testing is carried out with the unit still fitted.*

Fluid leakage

- ☐ Automatic transmission fluid is usually dark in colour. Fluid leaks should not be confused with engine oil, which can easily be blown onto the transmission by airflow.
- ☐ To determine the source of a leak, first remove all built-up dirt and grime from the transmission housing and surrounding areas using a degreasing agent, or by steam-cleaning. Drive the vehicle at low speed, so airflow will not blow the leak far from its source. Raise and support the vehicle, and determine where the leak is coming from.

General gear selection problems

- ☐ Chapter 7B or 7C deals with checking and adjusting the selector cable on automatic transmissions. The following are common problems which may be caused by a poorly-adjusted cable:
  - a) *Engine starting in gears other than Park or Neutral.*
  - b) *Indicator panel indicating a gear other than the one actually being used.*
  - c) *Vehicle moves when in Park or Neutral.*
  - d) *Poor gear shift quality or erratic gearchanges.*

Transmission fluid brown, or has burned smell

- ☐ Transmission fluid level low (Chapter 1A or 1B). If the fluid appears to have deteriorated badly it is recommended that it is renewed.

Transmission will not downshift (kickdown) with accelerator pedal fully depressed

- ☐ Low transmission fluid level (Chapter 1A or 1B).
- ☐ Incorrect selector cable adjustment (Chapter 7B or 7C).

Engine will not start in any gear, or starts in gears other than Park or Neutral

- ☐ Incorrect selector cable adjustment (Chapter 7B or 7C).

Transmission slips, shifts roughly, is noisy, or has no drive in forward or reverse gears

- ☐ There are many probable causes for the above problems, but unless there is a very obvious reason (such as a loose or corroded wiring plug connection on or near the transmission), the car should be taken to a franchise dealer for the fault to be diagnosed. The transmission control unit incorporates a self-diagnosis facility, and any fault codes can quickly be read and interpreted by a dealer with the proper diagnostic equipment.

Braking system

Note: *Before assuming that a brake problem exists, make sure that the tyres are in good condition and correctly inflated, that the front wheel alignment is correct, and that the vehicle is not loaded with weight in an unequal manner. Apart from checking the condition of all pipe and hose connections, any faults occurring on the anti-lock braking system should be referred to a VW dealer for diagnosis.*

Vehicle pulls to one side under braking

- ☐ Worn, defective, damaged or contaminated brake pads on one side (Chapters 1A or 1B and 9).
- ☐ Seized or partially seized brake caliper piston (Chapters 1A or 1B and 9).
- ☐ A mixture of brake pad lining materials fitted between sides (Chapters 1A or 1B and 9).
- ☐ Brake caliper mounting bolts loose (Chapter 9).
- ☐ Worn or damaged steering or suspension components (Chapters 1A or 1B and 10).

Noise (grinding or high-pitched squeal) when brakes applied)

- ☐ Brake pad friction lining material worn down to metal backing (Chapters 1A or 1B and 9).
- ☐ Excessive corrosion of brake disc. This may be apparent after the vehicle has been standing for some time (Chapters 1A or 1B and 9).
- ☐ Foreign object (stone chipping, etc.) trapped between brake disc and shield (Chapters 1A or 1B and 9).

Brakes binding

- ☐ Seized brake caliper piston(s) (Chapter 9).
- ☐ Incorrectly adjusted handbrake mechanism (Chapter 9).
- ☐ Faulty master cylinder (Chapter 9).

Excessive brake pedal travel

- ☐ Faulty master cylinder (Chapter 9).
- ☐ Air in hydraulic system (Chapters 1A or 1B and 9).
- ☐ Faulty vacuum servo unit (Chapter 9).

Brake pedal feels spongy when depressed

- ☐ Air in hydraulic system (Chapters 1A or 1B and 9).
- ☐ Deteriorated flexible rubber brake hoses (Chapters 1A or 1B and 9).
- ☐ Master cylinder mounting nuts loose (Chapter 9).
- ☐ Faulty master cylinder (Chapter 9).

Excessive brake pedal effort required to stop vehicle

- ☐ Faulty vacuum servo unit (Chapter 9).
- ☐ Faulty brake vacuum pump – diesel models (Chapter 9).
- ☐ Disconnected, damaged or insecure brake servo vacuum hose (Chapter 9).
- ☐ Primary or secondary hydraulic circuit failure (Chapter 9).
- ☐ Seized brake caliper piston(s) (Chapter 9).
- ☐ Brake pads incorrectly fitted (Chapters 1A or 1B and 9).
- ☐ Incorrect grade of brake pads fitted (Chapters 1A or 1B and 9).
- ☐ Brake pads contaminated (Chapters 1A or 1B and 9).

Judder felt through brake pedal or steering wheel when braking

- ☐ Excessive run-out or distortion of discs (Chapters 1A or 1B and 9).
- ☐ Brake pad worn (Chapters 1A or 1B and 9).
- ☐ Brake caliper mounting bolts loose (Chapter 9).
- ☐ Wear in suspension or steering components or mountings (Chapters 1A or 1B and 10).

Rear wheels locking under normal braking

- ☐ Rear brake pads contaminated (Chapters 1A or 1B and 9).
- ☐ ABS system fault (Chapter 9).

Driveshafts

Clicking or knocking noise on turns (at slow speed on full-lock)

- ☐ Lack of constant velocity joint lubricant, possibly due to damaged gaiter (Chapter 8).
- ☐ Worn outer constant velocity joint (Chapter 8).

Vibration when accelerating or decelerating

- ☐ Worn inner constant velocity joint (Chapter 8).
- ☐ Bent or distorted driveshaft (Chapter 8).

Suspension and steering

Note: *Before diagnosing suspension or steering faults, be sure that the trouble is not due to incorrect tyre pressures, mixtures of tyre types, or binding brakes.*

Vehicle pulls to one side

- ☐ Defective tyre (*Weekly checks*).
- ☐ Excessive wear in suspension or steering components (Chapters 1A or 1B and 10).
- ☐ Incorrect front wheel alignment (Chapter 10).
- ☐ Accident damage to steering or suspension components (Chapter 1A or 1B and 10).

Excessive pitching and/or rolling around corners, or during braking

- ☐ Defective shock absorbers (Chapters 1A or 1B and 10).
- ☐ Broken or weak spring and/or suspension component (Chapters 1A or 1B and 10).
- ☐ Worn or damaged anti-roll bar or mountings – where applicable (Chapter 10).

Lack of power assistance

- ☐ Faulty rack-and-pinion steering gear (Chapter 10).

Wandering or general instability

- ☐ Incorrect front wheel alignment (Chapter 10).
- ☐ Worn steering or suspension joints, bushes or components (Chapters 1A or 1B and 10).
- ☐ Roadwheels out of balance (Chapters 1A or 1B and 10).
- ☐ Faulty or damaged tyre (*Weekly checks*).
- ☐ Wheel bolts loose (refer to Chapters 1A or 1B and 10 for correct torque).
- ☐ Defective shock absorbers (Chapters 1A or 1B and 10).

Excessively stiff steering

- ☐ Lack of steering gear lubricant (Chapter 10).
- ☐ Seized track rod end balljoint or suspension balljoint Chapters 1A or 1B and 10).
- ☐ Incorrect front wheel alignment (Chapter 10).
- ☐ Steering rack or column bent or damaged (Chapter 10).

Excessive play in steering

- ☐ Worn steering column intermediate shaft universal joint (Chapter 10).
- ☐ Worn steering track rod end balljoints (Chapters 1A or 1B and 10).
- ☐ Worn rack-and-pinion steering gear (Chapter 10).
- ☐ Worn steering or suspension joints, bushes or components (Chapters 1A or 1B and 10).

Wheel wobble and vibration

- ☐ Front roadwheels out of balance (vibration felt mainly through the steering wheel) (Chapters 1A or 1B and 10).
- ☐ Rear roadwheels out of balance (vibration felt throughout the vehicle) (Chapters 1A or 1B and 10).
- ☐ Roadwheels damaged or distorted (Chapters 1A or 1B and 10).
- ☐ Faulty or damaged tyre (*Weekly checks*).
- ☐ Worn steering or suspension joints, bushes or components (Chapters 1A or 1B and 10).
- ☐ Wheel bolts loose (Chapter 10).

Tyre wear excessive

Tyres worn on inside or outside edges

- ☐ Tyres under-inflated (wear on both edges) (*Weekly checks*).
- ☐ Incorrect camber or castor angles (wear on one edge only) (Chapter 10).
- ☐ Worn steering or suspension joints, bushes or components (Chapters 1A or 1B and 10).
- ☐ Excessively hard cornering.
- ☐ Accident damage.

Tyre treads exhibit feathered edges

- ☐ Incorrect toe setting (Chapter 10).

Tyres worn in centre of tread

- ☐ Tyres over-inflated (*Weekly checks*).

Tyres worn on inside and outside edges

- ☐ Tyres under-inflated (*Weekly checks*).

Tyres worn unevenly

- ☐ Tyres/wheels out of balance (Chapter 1A, 1B or 10).
- ☐ Excessive wheel or tyre run-out (Chapter 1A, 1B or 10).
- ☐ Worn shock absorbers (Chapters 1A or 1B and 10).
- ☐ Faulty tyre (*Weekly checks*).

Electrical system

Note: *For problems associated with the starting system, refer to the faults listed under 'Engine' earlier in this Section.*

Battery will not hold a charge for more than a few days

- ☐ Battery defective internally (Chapter 5A).
- ☐ Battery terminal connections loose or corroded (*Weekly checks*).
- ☐ Auxiliary drivebelt worn or incorrectly adjusted (Chapter 1A or 1B).
- ☐ Alternator not charging at correct output (Chapter 5A).
- ☐ Alternator or voltage regulator faulty (Chapter 5A).
- ☐ Short-circuit causing continual battery drain (Chapters 5A and 12).

Ignition/no-charge warning light remains illuminated with engine running

- ☐ Auxiliary drivebelt broken, worn, or incorrectly adjusted (Chapter 1A or 1B).
- ☐ Alternator brushes worn, sticking, or dirty (Chapter 5A).
- ☐ Alternator brush springs weak or broken (Chapter 5A).
- ☐ Internal fault in alternator or voltage regulator (Chapter 5A).
- ☐ Broken, disconnected, or loose wiring in charging circuit (Chapter 5A).

Electrical system (continued)

Ignition/no-charge warning light fails to come on

- ☐ Warning light LED defective (Chapter 12).
- ☐ Broken, disconnected, or loose wiring in warning light circuit (Chapter 12).
- ☐ Alternator faulty (Chapter 5A).

Lights inoperative

- ☐ Bulb blown or LED unit faulty (Chapter 12).
- ☐ Corrosion of bulb or bulbholder contacts (Chapter 12).
- ☐ Blown fuse (Chapter 12).
- ☐ Faulty relay (Chapter 12).
- ☐ Broken, loose, or disconnected wiring (Chapter 12).
- ☐ Faulty switch (Chapter 12).

Instrument readings inaccurate or erratic

Fuel or temperature gauges give no reading

- ☐ Faulty gauge sender unit (Chapters 3, 4A or 4B).
- ☐ Wiring open-circuit (Chapter 12).
- ☐ Faulty gauge (Chapter 12).

Fuel or temperature gauges give continuous maximum reading

- ☐ Faulty gauge sender unit (Chapters 3, 4A or 4B).
- ☐ Wiring short-circuit (Chapter 12).
- ☐ Faulty gauge (Chapter 12).

Horn inoperative, or unsatisfactory in operation

Horn operates all the time

- ☐ Horn push either earthed or stuck down (Chapter 12).
- ☐ Horn cable-to-horn push earthed (Chapter 12).

Horn fails to operate

- ☐ Blown fuse (Chapter 12).
- ☐ Cable or cable connections loose, broken or disconnected (Chapter 12).
- ☐ Faulty horn (Chapter 12).

Horn emits intermittent or unsatisfactory sound

- ☐ Cable connections loose (Chapter 12).
- ☐ Horn mountings loose (Chapter 12).
- ☐ Faulty horn (Chapter 12).

Windscreen/tailgate wipers inoperative, or unsatisfactory in operation

Wipers fail to operate, or operate very slowly

- ☐ Bonnet not closed (built-into the electronic control system) (Chapter 12).
- ☐ Wiper blades stuck to screen, or linkage seized or binding (*Weekly checks* and Chapter 12).
- ☐ Blown fuse (Chapter 12).
- ☐ Cable or cable connections loose, broken or disconnected (Chapter 12).
- ☐ Faulty relay (Chapter 12).
- ☐ Faulty wiper motor (Chapter 12).

Wiper blades sweep over too large or too small an area of the glass

- ☐ Wiper arms incorrectly positioned on spindles (Chapter 12).
- ☐ Excessive wear of wiper linkage (Chapter 12).
- ☐ Wiper motor or linkage mountings loose or insecure (Chapter 12).

Wiper blades fail to clean the glass effectively

- ☐ Wiper blade rubbers worn or perished (*Weekly checks*).
- ☐ Wiper arm tension springs broken, or arm pivots seized (Chapter 12).
- ☐ Insufficient windscreen washer additive to adequately remove road film (*Weekly checks*).

Windscreen/tailgate washers inoperative, or unsatisfactory in operation

One or more washer jets inoperative

- ☐ Blocked washer jet (Chapter 1A or 1B).
- ☐ Disconnected, kinked or restricted fluid hose (Chapter 12).
- ☐ Insufficient fluid in washer reservoir (Chapter 1A or 1B).

Washer pump fails to operate

- ☐ Broken or disconnected wiring or connections (Chapter 12).
- ☐ Blown fuse (Chapter 12).
- ☐ Faulty washer switch (Chapter 12).
- ☐ Faulty washer pump (Chapter 12).

Electric windows inoperative, or unsatisfactory in operation

Window glass will only move in one direction

- ☐ Faulty switch (Chapter 12).

Window glass slow to move

- ☐ Regulator seized or damaged, or in need of lubrication (Chapter 11).
- ☐ Door internal components or trim fouling regulator (Chapter 11).
- ☐ Faulty motor (Chapter 11).

Window glass fails to move

- ☐ Blown fuse (Chapter 12).
- ☐ Faulty relay (Chapter 12).
- ☐ Broken or disconnected wiring or connections (Chapter 12).
- ☐ Faulty motor (Chapter 11).

Central locking system inoperative, or unsatisfactory in operation

Complete system failure

- ☐ Blown fuse (Chapter 12).
- ☐ Faulty relay (Chapter 12).
- ☐ Broken or disconnected wiring or connections (Chapter 12).
- ☐ Faulty control unit (Chapter 11).

Latch locks but will not unlock, or unlocks but will not lock

- ☐ Faulty control unit (Chapter 11).
- ☐ Broken or disconnected latch operating rods or levers (Chapter 11).
- ☐ Faulty relay (Chapter 12).

One actuator fails to operate

- ☐ Broken or disconnected wiring or connections (Chapter 12).
- ☐ Faulty actuator (Chapter 11).
- ☐ Broken, binding or disconnected latch operating rods or levers (Chapter 11).
- ☐ Fault in door lock (Chapter 11).

A

ABS (Anti-lock brake system) A system, usually electronically controlled, that senses incipient wheel lockup during braking and relieves hydraulic pressure at wheels that are about to skid.

Air bag An inflatable bag hidden in the steering wheel (driver's side) or the dash or glovebox (passenger side). In a head-on collision, the bags inflate, preventing the driver and front passenger from being thrown forward into the steering wheel or windscreen.

Air cleaner A metal or plastic housing, containing a filter element, which removes dust and dirt from the air being drawn into the engine.

Air filter element The actual filter in an air cleaner system, usually manufactured from pleated paper and requiring renewal at regular intervals.

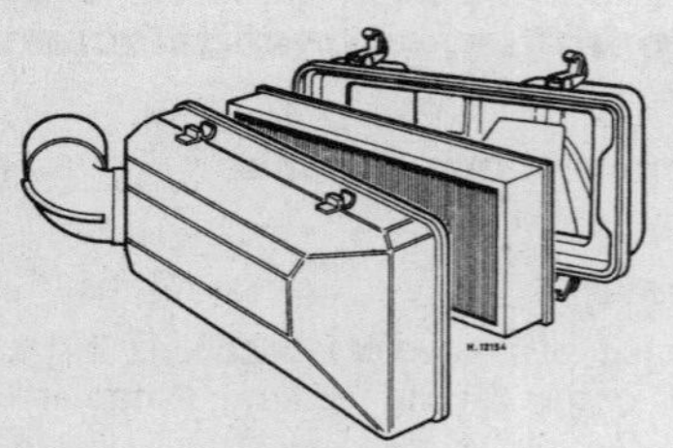

Air filter

Allen key A hexagonal wrench which fits into a recessed hexagonal hole.

Alligator clip A long-nosed spring-loaded metal clip with meshing teeth. Used to make temporary electrical connections.

Alternator A component in the electrical system which converts mechanical energy from a drivebelt into electrical energy to charge the battery and to operate the starting system, ignition system and electrical accessories.

Alternator (exploded view)

Ampere (amp) A unit of measurement for the flow of electric current. One amp is the amount of current produced by one volt acting through a resistance of one ohm.

Anaerobic sealer A substance used to prevent bolts and screws from loosening. Anaerobic means that it does not require oxygen for activation. The Loctite brand is widely used.

Antifreeze A substance (usually ethylene glycol) mixed with water, and added to a vehicle's cooling system, to prevent freezing of the coolant in winter. Antifreeze also contains chemicals to inhibit corrosion and the formation of rust and other deposits that would tend to clog the radiator and coolant passages and reduce cooling efficiency.

Anti-seize compound A coating that reduces the risk of seizing on fasteners that are subjected to high temperatures, such as exhaust manifold bolts and nuts.

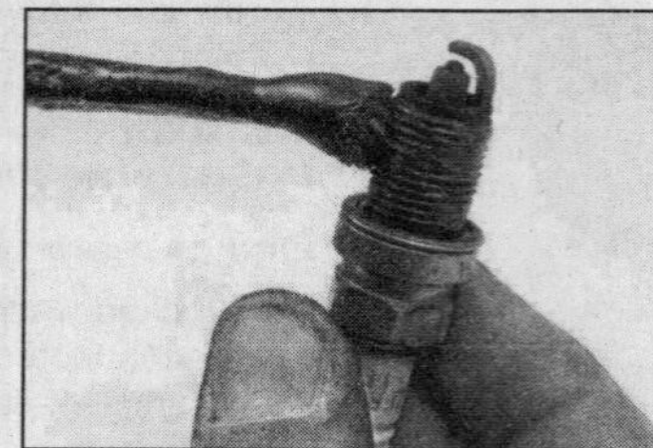

Anti-seize compound

Asbestos A natural fibrous mineral with great heat resistance, commonly used in the composition of brake friction materials. Asbestos is a health hazard and the dust created by brake systems should never be inhaled or ingested.

Axle A shaft on which a wheel revolves, or which revolves with a wheel. Also, a solid beam that connects the two wheels at one end of the vehicle. An axle which also transmits power to the wheels is known as a live axle.

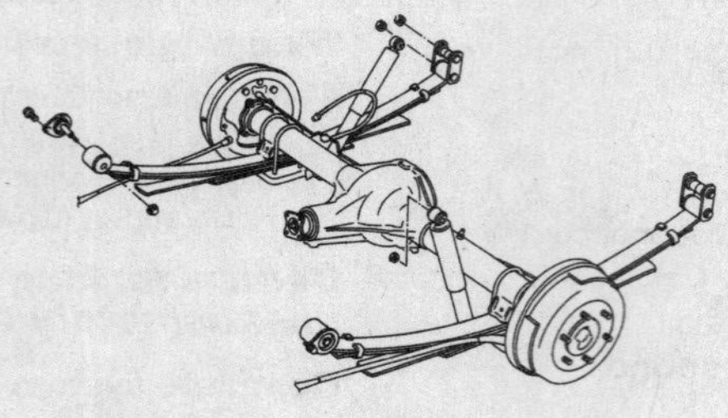

Axle assembly

Axleshaft A single rotating shaft, on either side of the differential, which delivers power from the final drive assembly to the drive wheels. Also called a driveshaft or a halfshaft.

B

Ball bearing An anti-friction bearing consisting of a hardened inner and outer race with hardened steel balls between two races.

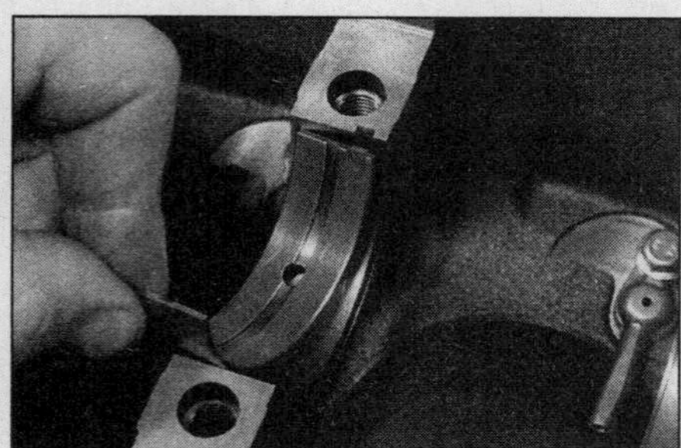

Bearing

Bearing The curved surface on a shaft or in a bore, or the part assembled into either, that permits relative motion between them with minimum wear and friction.

Big-end bearing The bearing in the end of the connecting rod that's attached to the crankshaft.

Bleed nipple A valve on a brake wheel cylinder, caliper or other hydraulic component that is opened to purge the hydraulic system of air. Also called a bleed screw.

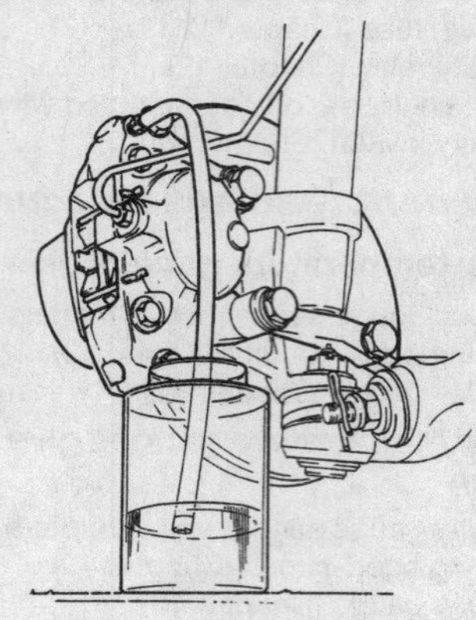

Brake bleeding

Brake bleeding Procedure for removing air from lines of a hydraulic brake system.

Brake disc The component of a disc brake that rotates with the wheels.

Brake drum The component of a drum brake that rotates with the wheels.

Brake linings The friction material which contacts the brake disc or drum to retard the vehicle's speed. The linings are bonded or riveted to the brake pads or shoes.

Brake pads The replaceable friction pads that pinch the brake disc when the brakes are applied. Brake pads consist of a friction material bonded or riveted to a rigid backing plate.

Brake shoe The crescent-shaped carrier to which the brake linings are mounted and which forces the lining against the rotating drum during braking.

Braking systems For more information on braking systems, consult the *Haynes Automotive Brake Manual*.

Breaker bar A long socket wrench handle providing greater leverage.

Bulkhead The insulated partition between the engine and the passenger compartment.

C

Caliper The non-rotating part of a disc-brake assembly that straddles the disc and carries the brake pads. The caliper also contains the hydraulic components that cause the pads to pinch the disc when the brakes are applied. A caliper is also a measuring tool that can be set to measure inside or outside dimensions of an object.

Camshaft A rotating shaft on which a series of cam lobes operate the valve mechanisms. The camshaft may be driven by gears, by sprockets and chain or by sprockets and a belt.

Canister A container in an evaporative emission control system; contains activated charcoal granules to trap vapours from the fuel system.

Canister

Carburettor A device which mixes fuel with air in the proper proportions to provide a desired power output from a spark ignition internal combustion engine.

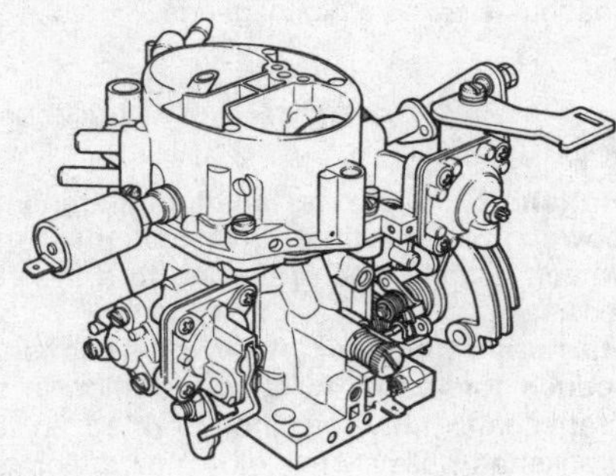

Carburettor

Castellated Resembling the parapets along the top of a castle wall. For example, a castellated balljoint stud nut.

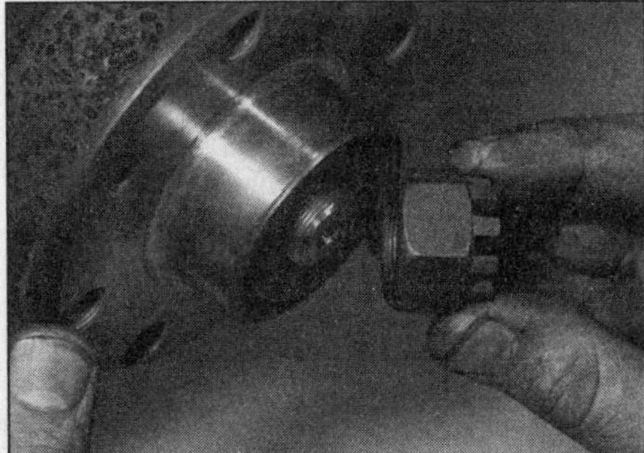

Castellated nut

Castor In wheel alignment, the backward or forward tilt of the steering axis. Castor is positive when the steering axis is inclined rearward at the top.

Catalytic converter A silencer-like device in the exhaust system which converts certain pollutants in the exhaust gases into less harmful substances.

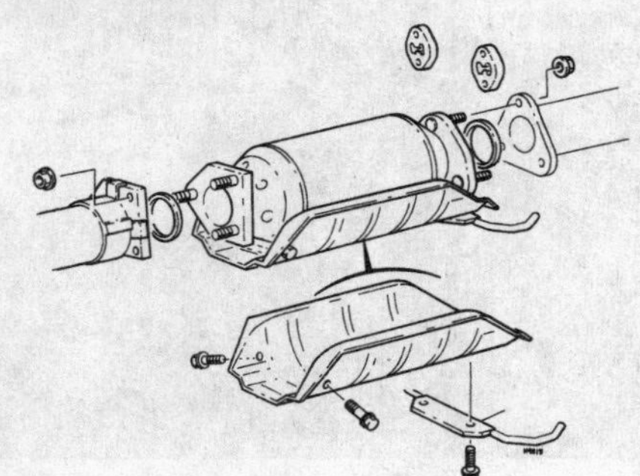

Catalytic converter

Circlip A ring-shaped clip used to prevent endwise movement of cylindrical parts and shafts. An internal circlip is installed in a groove in a housing; an external circlip fits into a groove on the outside of a cylindrical piece such as a shaft.

Clearance The amount of space between two parts. For example, between a piston and a cylinder, between a bearing and a journal, etc.

Coil spring A spiral of elastic steel found in various sizes throughout a vehicle, for example as a springing medium in the suspension and in the valve train.

Compression Reduction in volume, and increase in pressure and temperature, of a gas, caused by squeezing it into a smaller space.

Compression ratio The relationship between cylinder volume when the piston is at top dead centre and cylinder volume when the piston is at bottom dead centre.

Constant velocity (CV) joint A type of universal joint that cancels out vibrations caused by driving power being transmitted through an angle.

Core plug A disc or cup-shaped metal device inserted in a hole in a casting through which core was removed when the casting was formed. Also known as a freeze plug or expansion plug.

Crankcase The lower part of the engine block in which the crankshaft rotates.

Crankshaft The main rotating member, or shaft, running the length of the crankcase, with offset "throws" to which the connecting rods are attached.

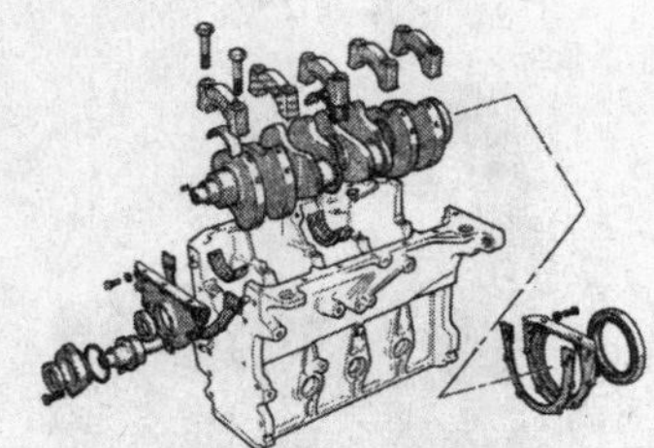

Crankshaft assembly

Crocodile clip See Alligator clip

D

Diagnostic code Code numbers obtained by accessing the diagnostic mode of an engine management computer. This code can be used to determine the area in the system where a malfunction may be located.

Disc brake A brake design incorporating a rotating disc onto which brake pads are squeezed. The resulting friction converts the energy of a moving vehicle into heat.

Double-overhead cam (DOHC) An engine that uses two overhead camshafts, usually one for the intake valves and one for the exhaust valves.

Drivebelt(s) The belt(s) used to drive accessories such as the alternator, water pump, power steering pump, air conditioning compressor, etc. off the crankshaft pulley.

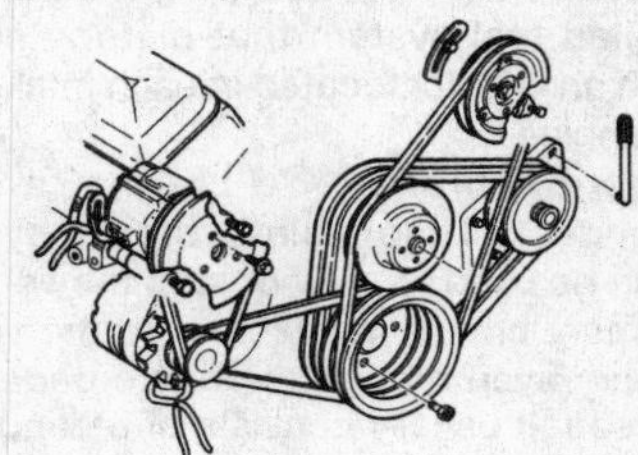

Accessory drivebelts

Driveshaft Any shaft used to transmit motion. Commonly used when referring to the axleshafts on a front wheel drive vehicle.

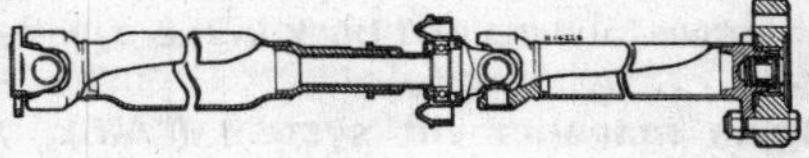

Driveshaft

Drum brake A type of brake using a drum-shaped metal cylinder attached to the inner surface of the wheel. When the brake pedal is pressed, curved brake shoes with friction linings press against the inside of the drum to slow or stop the vehicle.

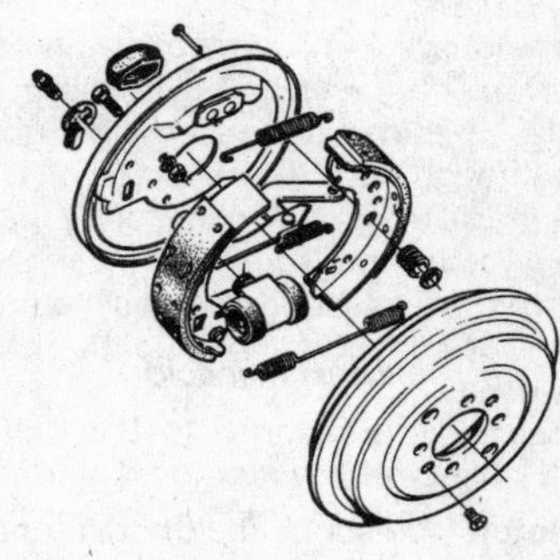

Drum brake assembly

E

EGR valve A valve used to introduce exhaust gases into the intake air stream.

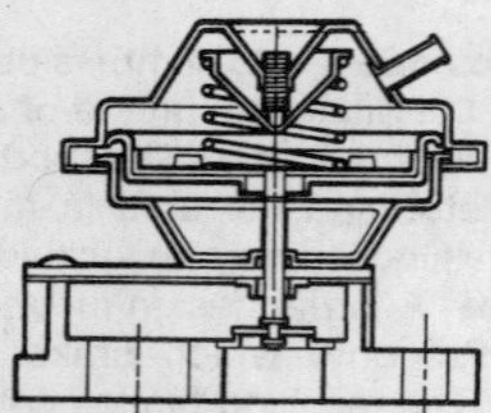
EGR valve

Electronic control unit (ECU) A computer which controls (for instance) ignition and fuel injection systems, or an anti-lock braking system. For more information refer to the *Haynes Automotive Electrical and Electronic Systems Manual.*

Electronic Fuel Injection (EFI) A computer controlled fuel system that distributes fuel through an injector located in each intake port of the engine.

Emergency brake A braking system, independent of the main hydraulic system, that can be used to slow or stop the vehicle if the primary brakes fail, or to hold the vehicle stationary even though the brake pedal isn't depressed. It usually consists of a hand lever that actuates either front or rear brakes mechanically through a series of cables and linkages. Also known as a handbrake or parking brake.

Endfloat The amount of lengthwise movement between two parts. As applied to a crankshaft, the distance that the crankshaft can move forward and back in the cylinder block.

Engine management system (EMS) A computer controlled system which manages the fuel injection and the ignition systems in an integrated fashion.

Exhaust manifold A part with several passages through which exhaust gases leave the engine combustion chambers and enter the exhaust pipe.

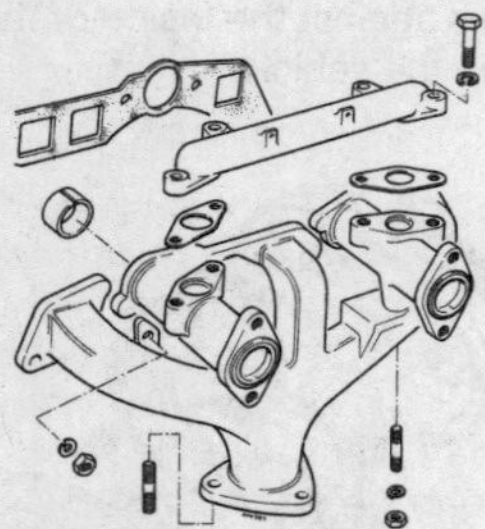
Exhaust manifold

F

Fan clutch A viscous (fluid) drive coupling device which permits variable engine fan speeds in relation to engine speeds.

Feeler blade A thin strip or blade of hardened steel, ground to an exact thickness, used to check or measure clearances between parts.

Feeler blade

Firing order The order in which the engine cylinders fire, or deliver their power strokes, beginning with the number one cylinder.

Flywheel A heavy spinning wheel in which energy is absorbed and stored by means of momentum. On cars, the flywheel is attached to the crankshaft to smooth out firing impulses.

Free play The amount of travel before any action takes place. The "looseness" in a linkage, or an assembly of parts, between the initial application of force and actual movement. For example, the distance the brake pedal moves before the pistons in the master cylinder are actuated.

Fuse An electrical device which protects a circuit against accidental overload. The typical fuse contains a soft piece of metal which is calibrated to melt at a predetermined current flow (expressed as amps) and break the circuit.

Fusible link A circuit protection device consisting of a conductor surrounded by heat-resistant insulation. The conductor is smaller than the wire it protects, so it acts as the weakest link in the circuit. Unlike a blown fuse, a failed fusible link must frequently be cut from the wire for replacement.

G

Gap The distance the spark must travel in jumping from the centre electrode to the side electrode in a spark plug. Also refers to the spacing between the points in a contact breaker assembly in a conventional points-type ignition, or to the distance between the reluctor or rotor and the pickup coil in an electronic ignition.

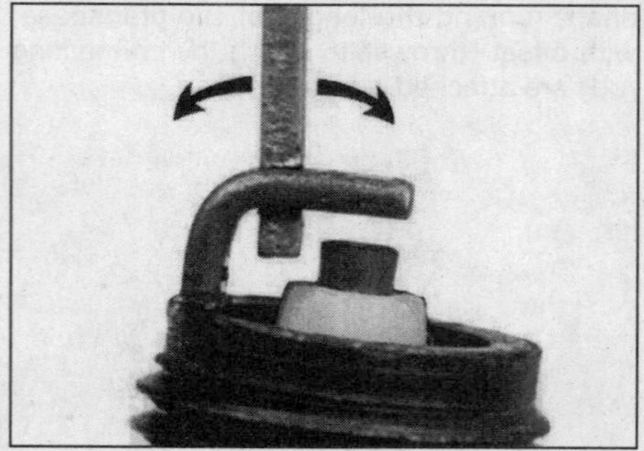
Adjusting spark plug gap

Gasket Any thin, soft material - usually cork, cardboard, asbestos or soft metal - installed between two metal surfaces to ensure a good seal. For instance, the cylinder head gasket seals the joint between the block and the cylinder head.

Gasket

Gauge An instrument panel display used to monitor engine conditions. A gauge with a movable pointer on a dial or a fixed scale is an analogue gauge. A gauge with a numerical readout is called a digital gauge.

H

Halfshaft A rotating shaft that transmits power from the final drive unit to a drive wheel, usually when referring to a live rear axle.

Harmonic balancer A device designed to reduce torsion or twisting vibration in the crankshaft. May be incorporated in the crankshaft pulley. Also known as a vibration damper.

Hone An abrasive tool for correcting small irregularities or differences in diameter in an engine cylinder, brake cylinder, etc.

Hydraulic tappet A tappet that utilises hydraulic pressure from the engine's lubrication system to maintain zero clearance (constant contact with both camshaft and valve stem). Automatically adjusts to variation in valve stem length. Hydraulic tappets also reduce valve noise.

I

Ignition timing The moment at which the spark plug fires, usually expressed in the number of crankshaft degrees before the piston reaches the top of its stroke.

Inlet manifold A tube or housing with passages through which flows the air-fuel mixture (carburettor vehicles and vehicles with throttle body injection) or air only (port fuel-injected vehicles) to the port openings in the cylinder head.

J

Jump start Starting the engine of a vehicle with a discharged or weak battery by attaching jump leads from the weak battery to a charged or helper battery.

L

Load Sensing Proportioning Valve (LSPV) A brake hydraulic system control valve that works like a proportioning valve, but also takes into consideration the amount of weight carried by the rear axle.
Locknut A nut used to lock an adjustment nut, or other threaded component, in place. For example, a locknut is employed to keep the adjusting nut on the rocker arm in position.
Lockwasher A form of washer designed to prevent an attaching nut from working loose.

M

MacPherson strut A type of front suspension system devised by Earle MacPherson at Ford of England. In its original form, a simple lateral link with the anti-roll bar creates the lower control arm. A long strut - an integral coil spring and shock absorber - is mounted between the body and the steering knuckle. Many modern so-called MacPherson strut systems use a conventional lower A-arm and don't rely on the anti-roll bar for location.
Multimeter An electrical test instrument with the capability to measure voltage, current and resistance.

N

NOx Oxides of Nitrogen. A common toxic pollutant emitted by petrol and diesel engines at higher temperatures.

O

Ohm The unit of electrical resistance. One volt applied to a resistance of one ohm will produce a current of one amp.
Ohmmeter An instrument for measuring electrical resistance.
O-ring A type of sealing ring made of a special rubber-like material; in use, the O-ring is compressed into a groove to provide the sealing action.

O-ring

Overhead cam (ohc) engine An engine with the camshaft(s) located on top of the cylinder head(s).
Overhead valve (ohv) engine An engine with the valves located in the cylinder head, but with the camshaft located in the engine block.
Oxygen sensor A device installed in the engine exhaust manifold, which senses the oxygen content in the exhaust and converts this information into an electric current. Also called a Lambda sensor.

P

Phillips screw A type of screw head having a cross instead of a slot for a corresponding type of screwdriver.
Plastigage A thin strip of plastic thread, available in different sizes, used for measuring clearances. For example, a strip of Plastigage is laid across a bearing journal. The parts are assembled and dismantled; the width of the crushed strip indicates the clearance between journal and bearing.

Plastigage

Propeller shaft The long hollow tube with universal joints at both ends that carries power from the transmission to the differential on front-engined rear wheel drive vehicles.
Proportioning valve A hydraulic control valve which limits the amount of pressure to the rear brakes during panic stops to prevent wheel lock-up.

R

Rack-and-pinion steering A steering system with a pinion gear on the end of the steering shaft that mates with a rack (think of a geared wheel opened up and laid flat). When the steering wheel is turned, the pinion turns, moving the rack to the left or right. This movement is transmitted through the track rods to the steering arms at the wheels.
Radiator A liquid-to-air heat transfer device designed to reduce the temperature of the coolant in an internal combustion engine cooling system.
Refrigerant Any substance used as a heat transfer agent in an air-conditioning system. R-12 has been the principle refrigerant for many years; recently, however, manufacturers have begun using R-134a, a non-CFC substance that is considered less harmful to the ozone in the upper atmosphere.
Rocker arm A lever arm that rocks on a shaft or pivots on a stud. In an overhead valve engine, the rocker arm converts the upward movement of the pushrod into a downward movement to open a valve.
Rotor In a distributor, the rotating device inside the cap that connects the centre electrode and the outer terminals as it turns, distributing the high voltage from the coil secondary winding to the proper spark plug. Also, that part of an alternator which rotates inside the stator. Also, the rotating assembly of a turbocharger, including the compressor wheel, shaft and turbine wheel.
Runout The amount of wobble (in-and-out movement) of a gear or wheel as it's rotated. The amount a shaft rotates "out-of-true." The out-of-round condition of a rotating part.

S

Sealant A liquid or paste used to prevent leakage at a joint. Sometimes used in conjunction with a gasket.
Sealed beam lamp An older headlight design which integrates the reflector, lens and filaments into a hermetically-sealed one-piece unit. When a filament burns out or the lens cracks, the entire unit is simply replaced.
Serpentine drivebelt A single, long, wide accessory drivebelt that's used on some newer vehicles to drive all the accessories, instead of a series of smaller, shorter belts. Serpentine drivebelts are usually tensioned by an automatic tensioner.

Serpentine drivebelt

Shim Thin spacer, commonly used to adjust the clearance or relative positions between two parts. For example, shims inserted into or under bucket tappets control valve clearances. Clearance is adjusted by changing the thickness of the shim.
Slide hammer A special puller that screws into or hooks onto a component such as a shaft or bearing; a heavy sliding handle on the shaft bottoms against the end of the shaft to knock the component free.
Sprocket A tooth or projection on the periphery of a wheel, shaped to engage with a chain or drivebelt. Commonly used to refer to the sprocket wheel itself.

Starter inhibitor switch On vehicles with an automatic transmission, a switch that prevents starting if the vehicle is not in Neutral or Park.
Strut See MacPherson strut.

T

Tappet A cylindrical component which transmits motion from the cam to the valve stem, either directly or via a pushrod and rocker arm. Also called a cam follower.
Thermostat A heat-controlled valve that regulates the flow of coolant between the cylinder block and the radiator, so maintaining optimum engine operating temperature. A thermostat is also used in some air cleaners in which the temperature is regulated.
Thrust bearing The bearing in the clutch assembly that is moved in to the release levers by clutch pedal action to disengage the clutch. Also referred to as a release bearing.
Timing belt A toothed belt which drives the camshaft. Serious engine damage may result if it breaks in service.
Timing chain A chain which drives the camshaft.
Toe-in The amount the front wheels are closer together at the front than at the rear. On rear wheel drive vehicles, a slight amount of toe-in is usually specified to keep the front wheels running parallel on the road by offsetting other forces that tend to spread the wheels apart.
Toe-out The amount the front wheels are closer together at the rear than at the front. On front wheel drive vehicles, a slight amount of toe-out is usually specified.
Tools For full information on choosing and using tools, refer to the *Haynes Automotive Tools Manual.*
Tracer A stripe of a second colour applied to a wire insulator to distinguish that wire from another one with the same colour insulator.
Tune-up A process of accurate and careful adjustments and parts replacement to obtain the best possible engine performance.
Turbocharger A centrifugal device, driven by exhaust gases, that pressurises the intake air. Normally used to increase the power output from a given engine displacement, but can also be used primarily to reduce exhaust emissions (as on VW's "Umwelt" Diesel engine).

U

Universal joint or U-joint A double-pivoted connection for transmitting power from a driving to a driven shaft through an angle. A U-joint consists of two Y-shaped yokes and a cross-shaped member called the spider.

V

Valve A device through which the flow of liquid, gas, vacuum, or loose material in bulk may be started, stopped, or regulated by a movable part that opens, shuts, or partially obstructs one or more ports or passageways. A valve is also the movable part of such a device.
Valve clearance The clearance between the valve tip (the end of the valve stem) and the rocker arm or tappet. The valve clearance is measured when the valve is closed.
Vernier caliper A precision measuring instrument that measures inside and outside dimensions. Not quite as accurate as a micrometer, but more convenient.
Viscosity The thickness of a liquid or its resistance to flow.
Volt A unit for expressing electrical "pressure" in a circuit. One volt that will produce a current of one ampere through a resistance of one ohm.

W

Welding Various processes used to join metal items by heating the areas to be joined to a molten state and fusing them together. For more information refer to the *Haynes Automotive Welding Manual.*
Wiring diagram A drawing portraying the components and wires in a vehicle's electrical system, using standardised symbols. For more information refer to the *Haynes Automotive Electrical and Electronic Systems Manual.*

Note: *References throughout this index are in the form* **"Chapter number" • "Page number"**. *So, for example, 2C•15 refers to page 15 of Chapter 2C.*

Note: *References throughout this index are in the form* **"Chapter number" • "Page number"**. *So, for example, 2C•15 refers to page 15 of Chapter 2C.*

Note: *References throughout this index are in the form* **"Chapter number" • "Page number"**. *So, for example, 2C•15 refers to page 15 of Chapter 2C.*

Note: *References throughout this index are in the form* **"Chapter number" • "Page number"**. *So, for example, 2C•15 refers to page 15 of Chapter 2C.*

Note: *References throughout this index are in the form* "**Chapter number**" • "**Page number**". *So, for example, 2C•15 refers to page 15 of Chapter 2C.*

Haynes Manuals – The Complete **UK Car** List

Title	Book No.
ALFA ROMEO Alfasud/Sprint (74 - 88) up to F *	0292
Alfa Romeo Alfetta (73 – 87) up to E *	0531
AUDI 80, 90 & Coupe Petrol (79 – Nov 88) up to F	0605
Audi 80, 90 & Coupe Petrol (Oct 86 – 90) D to H	1491
Audi 100 & A6 Petrol & Diesel (May 91 – May 97) H to P	3504
Audi A3 Petrol & Diesel (96 – May 03) P to 03	4253
Audi A3 Petrol & Diesel (June 03 – Mar 08) 03 to 08	4884
Audi A4 Petrol & Diesel (95 – 00) M to X	3575
Audi A4 Petrol & Diesel (01 – 04) X to 54	4609
Audi A4 Petrol & Diesel (Jan 05 – Feb 08) 54 to 57	4885
AUSTIN A35 & A40 (56 – 67) up to F *	0118
Mini (59 – 69) up to H *	0527
Mini (69 – 01) up to X	0646
Austin Healey 100/6 & 3000 (56 – 68) up to G *	0049
BEDFORD/Vauxhall Rascal & Suzuki Supercarry (86 – Oct 94) C to M	3015
BMW 1-Series 4-cyl Petrol & Diesel (04 – Aug 11) 54 to 11	4918
BMW 316, 320 & 320i (4-cyl)(75 – Feb 83) up to Y *	0276
BMW 3- & 5- Series Petrol (81 – 91) up to J	1948
BMW 3-Series Petrol (Apr 91 – 99) H to V	3210
BMW 3-Series Petrol (Sept 98 – 06) S to 56	4067
BMW 3-Series Petrol & Diesel (05 – Sept 08) 54 to 58	4782
BMW 5-Series 6-cyl Petrol (April 96 – Aug 03) N to 03	4151
BMW 5-Series Diesel (Sept 03 – 10) 53 to 10	4901
BMW 1500, 1502, 1600, 1602, 2000 & 2002 (59 – 77) up to S *	0240
CHRYSLER PT Cruiser Petrol (00-09) W to 09	4058
CITROEN 2CV, Ami & Dyane (67 – 90) up to H	0196
Citroen AX Petrol & Diesel (87- 97) D to P	3014
Citroen Berlingo & Peugeot Partner Petrol & Diesel (96 – 10) P to 60	4281
Citroen C1 Petrol (05 – 11) 05 to 11	4922
Citroen C2 Petrol & Diesel (03 – 10) 53 to 60	5635
Citroen C3 Petrol & Diesel (02 – 09) 51 to 59	4890
Citroen C4 Petrol & Diesel (04 – 10) 54 to 60	5576
Citroen C5 Petrol & Diesel (01 – 08) Y to 08	4745
Citroen C15 Van Petrol & Diesel (89 – Oct 98) F to S	3509
Citroen CX Petrol (75 – 88) up to F	0528
Citroen Saxo Petrol & Diesel (96 – 04) N to 54	3506
Citroen Xantia Petrol & Diesel (93 – 01) K to Y	3082
Citroen XM Petrol & Diesel (89 – 00) G to X	3451
Citroen Xsara Petrol & Diesel (97 – Sept 00) R to W	3751
Citroen Xsara Picasso Petrol & Diesel (00 – 02) W to 52	3944
Citroen Xsara Picasso (Mar 04 – 08) 04 to 58	4784
Citroen ZX Diesel (91 – 98) J to S	1922
Citroen ZX Petrol (91 – 98) H to S	1881
FIAT 126 (73 – 87) up to E *	0305
Fiat 500 (57 – 73) up to M *	0090
Fiat 500 & Panda (04 – 12) 53 to 61	5558
Fiat Bravo & Brava Petrol (95 – 00) N to W	3572
Fiat Cinquecento (93 – 98) K to R	3501
Fiat Grande Punto, Punto Evo & Punto Petrol (06 – 15) 55 to 15	5956
Fiat Panda (81 – 95) up to M	0793
Fiat Punto Petrol & Diesel (94 – Oct 99) L to V	3251
Fiat Punto Petrol (Oct 99 – July 03) V to 03	4066
Fiat Punto Petrol (03 – 07) 03 to 07	4746
Fiat Punto Petrol (Oct 99 – 07) V to 07	5634
Fiat X1/9 (74 – 89) up to G *	0273
FORD Anglia (59 – 68) up to G *	0001
Ford Capri II (& III) 1.6 & 2.0 (74 – 87) up to E *	0283
Ford Capri II (& III) 2.8 & 3.0 V6 (74 – 87) up to E	1309
Ford C-Max Petrol & Diesel (03 – 10) 53 to 60	4900
Ford Escort Mk I 1100 & 1300 (68 – 74) up to N *	0171
Ford Escort Mk I Mexico, RS 1600 & RS 2000 (70 – 74) up to N *	0139
Ford Escort Mk II Mexico, RS 1800 & RS 2000 (75 – 80) up to W *	0735
Ford Escort (75 – Aug 80) up to V *	0280
Ford Escort Petrol (Sept 80 – Sept 90) up to H	0686
Ford Escort & Orion Petrol (Sept 90 – 00) H to X	1737
Ford Escort & Orion Diesel (Sept 90 – 00) H to X	4081
Ford Fiesta Petrol (Feb 89 – Oct 95) F to N	1595
Ford Fiesta Petrol & Diesel (Oct 95 – Mar 02) N to 02	3397
Ford Fiesta Petrol & Diesel (Apr 02 – 08) 02 to 58	4170
Ford Fiesta Petrol & Diesel (08 – 11) 58 to 11	4907
Ford Focus Petrol & Diesel (98 – 01) S to Y	3759
Ford Focus Petrol & Diesel (Oct 01 – 05) 51 to 05	4167
Ford Focus Petrol (05 – 11) 54 to 61	4785
Ford Focus Diesel (05 – 11) 54 to 61	4807
Ford Focus Petrol & Diesel (11 – 14) 60 to 14	5632
Ford Fusion Petrol & Diesel (02 – 11) 02 to 61	5566
Ford Galaxy Petrol & Diesel (95 – Aug 00) M to W	3984
Ford Galaxy Petrol & Diesel (00 – 06) X to 06	5556
Ford Granada Petrol (Sept 77 – Feb 85) up to B *	0481
Ford Ka (96 – 08) P to 58	5567
Ford Ka Petrol (09 – 14) 58 to 14	5637
Ford Mondeo Petrol (93 – Sept 00) K to X	1923
Ford Mondeo Petrol & Diesel (Oct 00 – Jul 03) X to 03	3990
Ford Mondeo Petrol & Diesel (July 03 – 07) 03 to 56	4619
Ford Mondeo Petrol & Diesel (Apr 07 – 12) 07 to 61	5548
Ford Mondeo Diesel (93 – Sept 00) L to X	3465
Ford Transit Connect Diesel (02 – 11) 02 to 11	4903
Ford Transit Diesel (Feb 86 – 99) C to T	3019
Ford Transit Diesel (00 – Oct 06) X to 56	4775
Ford Transit Diesel (Nov 06 – 13) 56 to 63	5629
Ford 1.6 & 1.8 litre Diesel Engine (84 – 96) A to N	1172
HILLMAN Imp (63 – 76) up to R *	0022
HONDA Civic (Feb 84 – Oct 87) A to E	1226
Honda Civic (Nov 91 – 96) J to N	3199
Honda Civic Petrol (Mar 95 – 00) M to X	4050
Honda Civic Petrol & Diesel (01 – 05) X to 55	4611
Honda CR-V Petrol & Diesel (02 – 06) 51 to 56	4747
Honda Jazz (02 to 08) 51 to 58	4735
JAGUAR E-Type (61 – 72) up to L *	0140
Jaguar Mk I & II, 240 & 340 (55 – 69) up to H *	0098
Jaguar XJ6, XJ & Sovereign, Daimler Sovereign (68 – Oct 86) up to D	0242
Jaguar XJ6 & Sovereign (Oct 86 – Sept 94) D to M	3261
Jaguar XJ12, XJS & Sovereign, Daimler Double Six (72 – 88) up to F	0478
Jaguar X Type Petrol & Diesel (01 – 10) V to 60	5631
JEEP Cherokee Petrol (93 – 96) K to N	1943
LAND ROVER 90, 110 & Defender Diesel (83 – 07) up to 56	3017
Land Rover Discovery Petrol & Diesel (89 – 98) G to S	3016
Land Rover Discovery Diesel (Nov 98 – Jul 04) S to 04	4606
Land Rover Discovery Diesel (Aug 04 – Apr 09) 04 to 09	5562
Land Rover Freelander Petrol & Diesel (97 – Sept 03) R to 53	3929
Land Rover Freelander (97 – Oct 06) R to 56	5571
Land Rover Freelander Diesel (Nov 06 – 14) 56 to 64	5636
Land Rover Series II, IIA & III 4-cyl Petrol (58 – 85) up to C	0314
Land Rover Series II, IIA & III Petrol & Diesel (58 – 85) up to C	5568
MAZDA 323 (Mar 81 – Oct 89) up to G	1608
Mazda 323 (Oct 89 – 98) G to R	3455
Mazda B1600, B1800 & B2000 Pick-up Petrol (72 – 88) up to F	0267
Mazda MX-5 (89 – 05) G to 05	5565
Mazda RX-7 (79 – 85) up to C *	0460
MERCEDES-BENZ 190, 190E & 190D Petrol & Diesel (83 – 93) A to L	3450
Mercedes-Benz 200D, 240D, 240TD, 300D & 300TD 123 Series Diesel (Oct 76 – 85) up to C	1114
Mercedes-Benz 250 & 280 (68 – 72) up to L *	0346
Mercedes-Benz 250 & 280 123 Series Petrol (Oct 76 – 84) up to B *	0677
Mercedes-Benz 124 Series Petrol & Diesel (85 – Aug 93) C to K	3253
Mercedes-Benz A-Class Petrol & Diesel (98 – 04) S to 54	4748
Mercedes-Benz C-Class Petrol & Diesel (93 – Aug 00) L to W	3511
Mercedes-Benz C-Class (00 – 07) X to 07	4780
Mercedes-Benz E-Class Diesel (Jun 02 – Feb 10) 02 to 59	5710
Mercedes-Benz Sprinter Diesel (95 – Apr 06) M to 06	4902
MGA (55 – 62)	0475
MGB (62 – 80) up to W	0111
MGB 1962 to 1980 (special edition) *	4894
MG Midget & Austin-Healey Sprite (58 – 80) up to W *	0265
MINI Petrol (July 01 – 06) Y to 56	4273
MINI Petrol & Diesel (Nov 06 – 13) 56 to 13	4904
MITSUBISHI Shogun & L200 Pick-ups Petrol (83 – 94) up to M	1944
MORRIS Minor 1000 (56 – 71) up to K	0024
NISSAN Almera Petrol (95 – Feb 00) N to V	4053
Nissan Almera & Tino Petrol (Feb 00 – 07) V to 56	4612
Nissan Micra (83 – Jan 93) up to K	0931
Nissan Micra (93 – 02) K to 52	3254
Nissan Micra Petrol (03 – Oct 10) 52 to 60	4734
Nissan Primera Petrol (90 - Aug 99) H to T	1851
Nissan Qashqai Petrol & Diesel (07 – 12) 56 to 62	5610
OPEL Ascona & Manta (B-Series) (Sept 75 – 88) up to F *	0316
Opel Ascona Petrol (81 – 88)	3215
Opel Ascona Petrol (Oct 91 – Feb 98)	3156
Opel Corsa Petrol (83 – Mar 93)	3160
Opel Corsa Petrol (Mar 93 – 97)	3159
Opel Kadett Petrol (Oct 84 – Oct 91)	3196
Opel Omega & Senator Petrol (Nov 86 – 94)	3157
Opel Vectra Petrol (Oct 88 – Oct 95)	3158
PEUGEOT 106 Petrol & Diesel (91 – 04) J to 53)	1882
Peugeot 107 Petrol (05 – 11) 05 to 11)	4923
Peugeot 205 Petrol (83 – 97) A to P	0932

* Classic reprint